SOTHEBY'S
INTERNATIONAL PRICE GUIDE

1987-88 EDITION

(including 1986 prices)

General Editor: John L. Marion

THE VENDOME PRESS
NEW YORK : PARIS

Produced and designed by Philip Wilson Publishers Ltd
26 Litchfield Street, London WC2 9NJ

Designers: John Garrad and Christopher Matthews

House editor: Vanessa Brett
Assistant house editor (New York): Elizabeth White
Administrator: Pauline Somerville
Laurel Colvin (New York)
Captions: Caroline Behr

First published in Great Britain by Penguin Books Ltd
Harmondsworth, Middlesex

First published in the United States of America by
The Vendome Press, 515 Madison Avenue, N.Y., N.Y. 10022
Distributed in the United States of America by
Rizzoli International Publications, 597 Fifth Avenue, N.Y., 10017
Distributed in Canada by Methuen Publications

Library of Congress Cataloging-in-Publication Data
Main entry under title:
Sotheby's international price guide.
1. Sotheby's (Firm)—Prices. 2. Antiques—
Prices. I. Marion, John. II. Sotheby's (Firm)
NK1133.S68 1985 707'.5 8515730

Printed and bound in France
Aubin and A.G.M. (Forges-les-Eaux)
Paper: Calypso, Arjomari-Prioux

ISBN 0-86565-087-X
ISBN 0-86565-086-1 (pbk.)

Contents

Bold headings indicate main sections; inset headings indicate articles within these sections.

SOTHEBY'S EXPERT DEPARTMENTS

AMERICAN INDIAN ART
Ellen Napiura (Consultant, New York)

ANTIQUITIES
Felicity Nicholson (London)
Richard Keresey (New York)

ARMS AND ARMOUR
Michael Baldwin (London)
Florian Eitle (New York)

ASIAN WORKS OF ART
Brendan Lynch (London)

CHINESE WORKS OF ART
Colin Mackay (London)
Carol Conover (New York)
Mee Seen Loong (New York)

CLOCKS AND WATCHES
Tina Millar (Watches, London)
Michael Turner (Clocks, London)
Kevin Tierney (New York)
Daryn Schnipper (New York)

COINS AND BANKNOTES, MEDALS AND DECORATIONS
James Morton (London)
Mish Tworkowski (New York)

DECORATIVE ARTS FROM 1880
Philippe Garner (London)
Barbara Deisroth (New York)

EUROPEAN CERAMICS
Letitia Roberts (New York)
Peter Arney (European, London)
Peter Williams (English, London)

EUROPEAN WORKS OF ART
Elizabeth Wilson (London)
Florian Eitle (New York)
George Hughes-Hartman (Tapestries, London)

FOLK ART
Hilary Kay (London)
Nancy Druckman (New York)

FURNITURE AND DECORATIONS
Leslie Keno (American, New York)
Graham Child (English, London)
George Read (English, New York)
Thierry Millerand (French, New York)
Jonathan Bourne (Continental, London)
Elaine Whitmire (19th century, New York)
Christopher Payne (19th century, London)

GLASS AND PAPERWEIGHTS
Perran Wood (London)
Lauren Tarshis (New York)

ISLAMIC WORKS OF ART
Richard Keresey (New York)
Stephen Wolff (London)

JAPANESE WORKS OF ART
Neil Davey (London)
Jane Oliver (New York)

JEWELLERY
David Bennett (London)
Jacqueline Fay (New York)

JUDAICA
Jay Weinstein (New York)
Camilla Privaté (London)

MUSICAL INSTRUMENTS
Graham Wells (London)
Charles Rudig (New York)

OBJECTS OF VERTU
Julia Clarke (London)
Gerard Hill (New York)

PORTRAIT MINIATURES
Haydn Williams (London)

PRE-COLUMBIAN ART
Stacy Goodman (New York)
Fatma Turkkan-Wille (Consultant, New York)

RUGS AND CARPETS
William Ruprecht (New York)
Victoria Mather (London)

RUSSIAN WORKS OF ART
Heinrich Graf von Spreti (London)
Gerard Hill (New York)

19TH AND 20TH CENTURY SCULPTURE
Elaine Whitmire (New York)
Robert Bowman (London)

SILVER
Kevin Tierney (New York)
Peter Waldron (English, London)
Harry Charteris (Continental, London)

SPORTS & PASTIMES/COLLECTORS
Hilary Kay (London)
Dana Hawkes (New York)
Malcolm Barber (Cars, London)
James Booth (Sporting Guns, Sussex)

TOYS AND DOLLS
Bunny Campione (London)
Dana Hawkes (New York)

TRIBAL ART
Ellen Napiura (Consultant, New York)
Robert Fainello (London)

WINE
David Molyneux-Berry (London)

Departments not included in this guide can be found listed in catalogues

SOTHEBY'S PRINCIPAL AUCTION LOCATIONS

UNITED KINGDOM
34-35 New Bond Street,
London W1A 2AA.
Telephone (01) 493 8080.

Booth Mansion,
28 Watergate Street,
Chester,
Cheshire CH1 2NA.
Telephone (0244) 315531.

Summers Place,
Billingshurst,
Sussex RH14 9AD.
Telephone (040 381) 3933

UNITED STATES
1334 York Avenue,
New York, N.Y. 10021.
Telephone (212) 606 7000.

HOLLAND
102 Rokin,
1012 KZ Amsterdam.
Telephone (20) 246 215.

HONG KONG
PO Box 83,
705 Lane Crawford House,
64-70 Queen's Road Central,
Hong Kong.
Telephone (5) 248 121

ITALY
Palazzo Capponi,
Via Gino Capponi 26,
50121 Florence.
Telephone (55) 2479021.

MONACO
Le Sporting d'Hiver,
Place du Casino,
MC 98001 Monaco Cedex.
Telephone (93) 30 88 80.

SPAIN
Plaza de la Independencia 8,
Madrid 28001.
Telephone (1) 232 6488 & 6572.

SWITZERLAND
24 Rue de la Cité.
CH 1204 Geneva.
Telephone (22) 21 3377.

20 Bleicherweg, CH-8022,
Zurich.
Telephone (1) 202 0011.

Offices and representatives worldwide are listed in catalogues

Abbreviations of sale locations used in the captions

A	Amsterdam	**F**	Florence	**HK**	Hong Kong	**Mel**	Melbourne	**St.M**	St. Moritz
C	Chester	**G**	Geneva	**HS**	House Sale	**Mil**	Milan	**T**	Tokyo
Ct	Capetown	**Glas**	Glasgow	**JHB**	Johannesburg	**NY**	New York	**Tor**	Toronto
CS	Car Sales (various locations)	**Glen**	Gleneagles	**L**	London	**S**	Sussex	**Z**	Zurich
		HH	Hopetoun House	**M**	Monaco	**Syd**	Sydney		

Preface

It is a particular pleasure to present this edition of *Sotheby's International Price Guide* because it reflects the events of the most successful year in our firm's history. A lively market during the first part of 1986 became exceptionally strong in the fall, and by the end of the year our sales worldwide totalled nearly $900 million. This unprecedented activity was due both to the exceptional quality of the works of art offered and a dramatic expansion in the participation of collectors, particularly from the United States and Japan.

As the market grows and becomes increasingly complex, Sotheby's continues to broaden its services to collectors and to provide resources for exploring and understanding its development. The publication of *Sotheby's International Price Guide* is one example of this effort. Now in its third edition, the Guide is recognized as a comprehensive and authoritative record of international auction results in the decorative arts. More than 8,000 objects are illustrated and completely described with medium and dimensions as well as sale date and price. Most of the pieces were selected because they are representative of the various types of objects handled by each department at Sotheby's and because they are accessible to most collectors. Generally these works of art were in good condition and realized a price close to our pre-sale estimate.

Complementing the wealth of illustrations is a selection of articles written by our experts in London and New York. Many of the topics reflect special events in the art world in 1986. "Wiener Werkstätte Furniture", for example, relates directly to the major exhibition *Vienna 1900* in Vienna, Paris, and New York. Others, such as "French Ormolu" and "Reign Marks on Chinese Porcelain" are specific resources for collectors.

Sotheby's experts worldwide have worked with me to compile a guide that is truly international in scope, and I hope that it will become a valuable reference in collecting libraries.

JOHN L. MARION
Chairman
Sotheby's North America

Opportunities for Collectors

Even a cursory review of this year's *Price Guide* will alert the reader that 1986 was not an ordinary season in the auction business. A number of factors came into play last year to expand the price structures for most categories of collecting interest. From Chippendale chairs to rock and roll memorabilia, this new edition of the *Price Guide* reflects the vigor of the art market.

In many ways, the condition of the collecting market is determined by the strength of the general economy. By all standards, 1986 was nothing short of a boom year for Wall Street and most foreign financial investors. These good times have generated enormous amounts of discretionary income, some of which is finding its way into the art galleries, antique shops and auction rooms of America. Although some purchasers are buying for 'investment' purposes (as some always have), many active bidders at Sotheby's New York are private collectors, buying for their own pleasure. This is certainly not a new phenomenon, but this large group of relatively new buyers has certainly had an impact on recent price levels.

Another force of considerable importance was the extensive participation of European and Japanese bidders in New York. Healthy economies and favorable exchange rates against the Dollar reversed the circumstances of 1985, when Americans were very active in London, bidding with Dollars that came close to parity with the Pound.

High prices, of course, result from the offering of wonderful objects. In 1986, Sotheby's salerooms were brimming with extraordinary collections and individual works. From the January sale of Jerome Neuhoff's collection of English furniture to the auction of the Atwood collection of watches in December, the pattern was clear. Pieces of great quality and merit brought very strong prices. This trend has certainly continued into 1987 and, at this writing, shows absolutely no indication of slowing down.

The question then becomes whether there is still room in this expensive market for the average buyer. And the answer is a resounding 'yes', unless one has a taste for Impressionist pictures or large gem stones. Georgian silver and ceramics come to mind immediately as areas where fine collections can still be built for relatively moderate amounts of money. De Lamerie and Storr are two silversmiths whose work will always fetch a premium, but look to the less well-known makers for a bargain. 19th century American silver has only recently begun to attract broad interest and there are many wonderful examples of early Gorham, Tiffany and Kirk designs available for reasonable amounts. In the furniture area, look for under-valued neoclassical Italian and French pieces. While the great examples will bring a high price, they do not even approach the levels of their English and American counterparts.

The one constant in this ever-changing market is the indisputable verity of the often-quoted guidelines for collecting: buy what you like and buy the best examples your budget will allow. Whether your taste runs to Staffordshire pot lids or American Indian textiles, a good piece will always be a good piece and may even appreciate, if you buy wisely within an established area of collecting interest. Do not be lured into purchases of dubious quality or limited appeal. While new areas of collecting are constantly evolving (rock and roll, for example), the most enduring enjoyment and eventual financial reward will probably be found in the traditional categories.

Some people are born with an acquisitive nature and others come to collecting when time and financial situations allow for the pursuit of beautiful objects. Whether one decides to buy within a very specialized area or pursues a broad range of objects, it is important to decide on a course for collecting and to learn as much as possible about the works of art and the market before taking the plunge. Many of us have come to regret some of our earlier purchases because we paid too much or thought the object was more interesting than it turned out to be. Though you may be eager to begin collecting actively, the best advice is to take your time, speak to experts in the field and read every word written on the subject.

Sotheby's International Price Guide is an excellent tool for the novice or experienced collector. The sheer volume of objects passing through our rooms around the world can provide an accurate index for levels of value in many areas of collecting. Do not, however, rely solely on this volume for the valuation of specific pieces. No book or photograph can substitute for the experience of standing before a piece, running your eyes and fingers across its surface and filing those impressions away for use in the future. The *Guide* is aptly titled, for it can provide the ranges within which a certain example should sell. Remember, however, that the smallest bit of carving on a piece of furniture or the smallest repair on a tea cup can alter its value drastically at auction.

Get to know dealers, auctioneers and other collectors who can guide you and perhaps prevent the purchase of a mistake. Knowledgeable collecting results from a wide exposure to the market, so wander into every shop you pass and visit every auction preview you can. Any individual honestly interested in acquiring works of art can develop a good working knowledge of that field in a relatively short period of time. The most difficult task can sometimes be to admit that one doesn't know something. But when this occurs, it is a sure sign of a mature collector, pursuing his passion with reason and ability.

Richard S. Wolf
Sotheby's New York
May 1987

An Economic Review of the Art Market

The fall of 1986 was a period of unprecedented activity in the international art market, with sales of $470 million of the annual total of nearly $900 million. Any review of these exceptional results should take into account the underlying economic factors that have contributed to the fall performance.

During this period, there was an abundant flow of high quality material coming onto the market covering the full range of collecting fields. The precise motivation for selling differed between vendors. Some were undoubtedly prompted by the high prices seen last season; other property was consigned by executors of estates. Cash-flow problems contributed to the sale of at least one major collection, while some collectors simply decided, for whatever reason, that the time was right to sell. By a fortunate combination of circumstances, all these factors came together with particular strength at the same time. In addition, the revisions in American taxation which came into effect in 1987 prompted a wave of selling ahead of this change.

As for demand, the flow of property was matched by a continuing rise in the number of buyers showing a heightened interest and increasingly willing and able to pay outstandingly large sums for works of art. Many of these buyers were not new to the art market, but were active at auction for the first time. Another ongoing feature was the global spread of buying, underscoring the international nature of the art market. A further indication of the high level of confidence was the very low overall percentage of works remaining unsold. The volume of major works consigned for sale is another barometer of confidence levels and the large number offered at the fall sales bears out the current confidence of vendors.

Demand was also stimulated by exchange rate movements and the continuing strength of certain currencies proved an incentive. While the Sterling/Dollar rate changed little, the major European currencies and the Yen were appreciably stronger against both the Pound and the Dollar in the fall of 1986 than they were in 1985. For example, the Yen increased by about 33 per cent against both currencies, the Deutschmark and the Swiss Franc each rose by around 29 per cent, the Lira by approximately 27 per cent and the French Franc by some 21 per cent. As a result, currency strength clearly boosted European and Japanese buying power. However, American buying was not inhibited, as might have been expected given the realignment of the Dollar, as this was offset by the strength of domestic financial markets. During the first quarter of 1987 the Yen continued to strengthen, prompting even greater activity among Japanese buyers.

An analysis of the art market's performance over the last four months of 1986 as measured by Sotheby's Art Index (which concentrates on the middle and upper range of the market, excluding the very top limits) shows that the Aggregate Index increased by 17 per cent from 344 at the beginning of the season, to 403 at the end of December, taking it through the 400 mark for the first time. This rise is the largest ever recorded over a fall period and indicates that the good, broad-range bedrock of the market also shows an underlying firmness, a particularly healthy signal for the longer-term stability of the market.

During the fall virtually every sector experienced extremely high levels of activity. English, French and Continental furniture sales produced good results against a background of already strong competition and prices. Major events in London saw strong American bidding for English furniture added to already firm domestic demand. Many top lots went to Americans who also underbid strongly on a number of other items. Important sales of French and Continental furniture were held in Monaco, London and New York and strong international interest was shown throughout. In London, private buyers were especially determined and in common with last season's trend, in both London and New York, demand was especially firm across-the-board for unusual, decorative or attractive pieces.

In Chinese ceramics, the supply was boosted by single-owner collections. The sale in Hong Kong of the first half of T.Y. Chao's collection of ceramics and jade achieved HK$84.9 million ($7.7 million), a record for a sale of this type and almost as much as had been anticipated for the entire collection. Japanese buyers, who had not been active in this market for several years, were out in force, attracted by the prestige of the sale and greatly helped by the strength of the Yen. Hong Kong buyers, many of whom were relatively new to this market, were also active, paying much higher prices than hitherto. At other sales in London, New York and Monaco, results indicated that this market is making steady progress. Strong sales of English silver in London revealed that competition remains keen. The Geneva sales of Continental silver showed the sector making slow progress after a long period of relatively quiet activity.

During the first months of 1987, the market has remained buoyant, with an abundance of fine material offered in many fields. Particular strength has been evident in American decorative arts where a Chippendale wing armchair, from the famous suite of 'hairy paw foot' furniture commissioned by General John Cadwalader, brought $2.75 million, a world record price for a piece of furniture at auction.

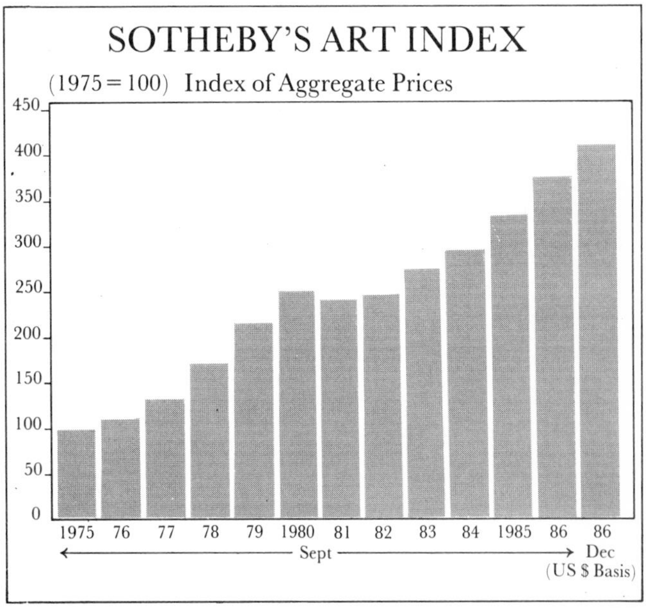

The objects in this edition were sold in 1986.

The condition of an object is crucial to its value. Although condition is mentioned in some sections of this guide, the description may not be detailed. Many entries give no indication of condition, but in the majority of cases it can be assumed that the entry is in reasonably good condition, bearing in mind the date of the piece and the nature of its material. Readers are asked to remember this when comparing similar pieces and to take into consideration fluctuations in the market and differences in the quality of objects.

English Monarchs

1558 Elizabeth I
1603 James I
1625 Charles I
1649 (Commonwealth)
1660 Charles II
1685 James II
1689 William and Mary
1694 William III
1702 Anne
1714 George I
1727 George II
1760 George III
1811 (Prince of Wales Regent)
1820 George IV
1830 William IV
1837 Victoria
1901 Edward VII
1910 George V
1936 Edward VIII
1936 George VI
1952 Elizabeth II

French Monarchs and Periods

1589	Henri IV	
1610	Louis XIII	
1643	Louis XIV	
1715	Louis XV	
1774	Louis XVI	
1792	The Republic	Directoire
1795	Directory	Directoire
1799	Consulate	Directoire
1804	Empire	
1814	Louis XVIII	Restauration
1824	Charles X	Restauration
1830	Louis Phillipe	Restauration
1848	Second Republic	
1852	Napoleon III	
1870	Third Republic	

American Furniture Periods

1620-90	Jacobean or 'Pilgrim century'
1690-1725	William and Mary
1725-60	Queen Anne
1750-80	Chippendale
1780-1810	Federal
1820-45	Classical

Furniture and Decorations

1
A Victorian mahogany secretaire bookcase,
c.1860, the secretaire drawer enclosing small pigeon holes and drawers, 243.5cm (8ft) high, *C 13 Mar,*
£1,100 ($1,661)

2
A George III mahogany secretaire bookcase,
c.1780, 216cm (7ft 1in) high, *L 2 May,*
£2,310 ($3,673)

1

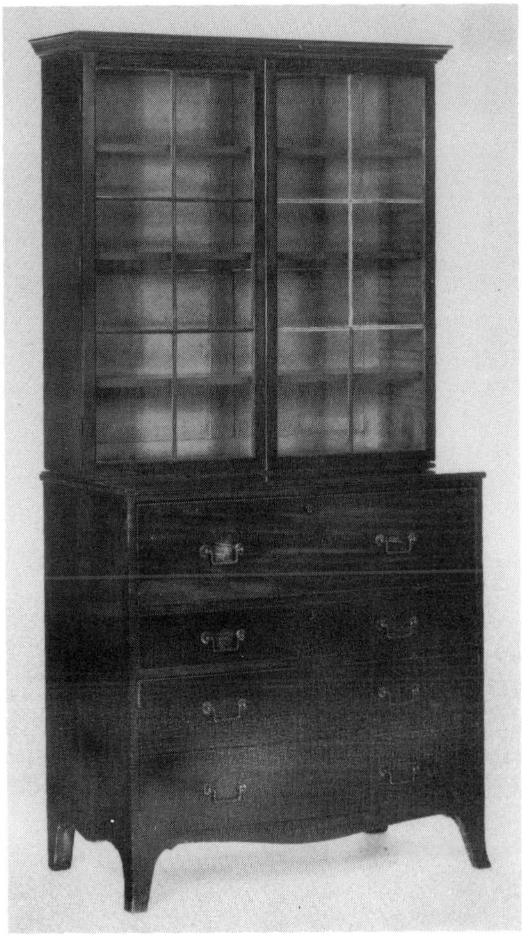
2

1

2

3

4

5

6

7

8

9

10

11

12

13

14

1
A George I burr walnut secretaire tallboy, c.1720, 179cm (70½in) high, *L 14 Nov,*
£9,020 ($12,899)

2
A George II mahogany secretaire tallboy, c.1760, the lower part with a slide above a fitted secretaire drawer, 197cm (6ft 5½in) high, *L 18 July,*
£2,090 ($3,323)

3
A George III mahogany secretaire bookcase, c.1775, the upper part with pierced swan-neck pediment, 249cm (8ft 2in) high, *L 11 July,*
£6,050 ($9,620)

4
A George III mahogany bureau bookcase, c.1770, the fall revealing a shaped and fitted interior, 225cm (7ft 4½in) high, *S 17 June,*
£1,870 ($2,954)

5
A George III inlaid mahogany secretaire cabinet, c.1790, 198cm (6ft 6in) high, *NY 18 Oct,*
$11,550 (£8,021)

6
A George III mahogany secretaire press, c.1780, the pair of panelled doors enclosing trays, 213cm (7ft) high, *C 9 July,*
£1,408 ($2,267)

7
A George III mahogany secretaire cabinet, c.1780, the drawer fitted with pigeon holes, 224cm (7ft 4in), *NY 7 June,*
$6,875 (£4,614)

8
A George III inlaid mahogany slant-front bureau bookcase, late 18th century, 205.5cm (6ft 9½in) high, *NY 14 Oct,*
$5,500 (£3,819)

9
A Regency inlaid mahogany secretaire bookcase, c.1815, 210.5cm (6ft 11in), *NY 14 Oct,*
$4,675 (£3,247)

10
A Regency inlaid mahogany secretaire cabinet, c.1815, 253cm (8ft 3½in), *NY 7 June,*
$12,100 (£8,120)

11
An Edwardian mahogany bureau bookcase, c.1910, the fall-front enclosing pigeon holes and small drawers, 213cm (7ft) high, *C 7 Aug,*
£858 ($1,330)

12
An Edwardian satinwood bureau cabinet, c.1910, decorated throughout with painted flowers, leaves, scrolls and putti, 241cm (7ft 11in) high, *L 6 Oct,*
£6,050 ($8,470)

13
A George III-style rosewood and satinwood inlaid mahogany roll-top secretaire bookcase, 19th century, the lower part with a tambour roll-top opening to a satinwood fitted interior, 203cm (6ft 8in) high, *NY 10 June,*
$5,170 (£3,293)

14
A walnut bureau cabinet, c.1700, the door frames inlaid with stylised flowers and with inlaid spandrels, 229cm (7ft 6in) high, *L 14 Nov,*
£8,250 ($11,798)

1
An English walnut-veneered kneehole writing desk, early 18th century, on bracket feet, extensively altered, 80cm (31½in), *L 2 May,*
£1,760 ($2,798)

2
A William and Mary walnut-veneered bureau, c.1695, on bun feet, 105cm (41½in) high, *L 25 Apr,*
£8,250 ($13,200)

3
A Queen Anne walnut-veneered bureau, c.1710, on bun feet, 99cm (39in) wide, *L 11 July,*
£3,740 ($5,947)

4
A George II walnut bureau, c.1730, on bracket feet, 202cm (40in) high, *L 21 Nov,*
£2,640 ($3,696)

5
A Queen Anne walnut bureau, c.1710, on bracket feet, 103cm (40½in) wide, *L 11 July,*
£10,120 ($16,091)

6
A George III mahogany bureau, c.1780, on bracket feet, 122cm (48in) wide, *C 27 Feb,*
£550 ($825)

7
A George III mahogany bureau, c.1760, on ogee bracket feet, 108cm (42½in) high, *NY 10 June,*
$2,475 (£1,576)

8
A George III mahogany tambour writing desk, c.1790, 115cm (45½in) wide, *L 11 July,*
£7,920 ($12,593)

9
A George III mahogany tambour desk, c.1780, 98cm (38½in) high, *S 11 Nov,*
£2,420 ($3,388)

10
A George III rosewood cylinder bureau, c.1800, with satinwood banding and stringing, pierced brass gallery, restored, 99cm (39in) high, *S 18 Mar,*
£2,860 ($4,376)

1

2

3

4

5

6

7

8

9

10

1

2

3

4

5

6

7

8

9

10

11

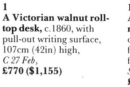

1
A Victorian walnut roll-top desk, c.1860, with pull-out writing surface, 107cm (42in) high, *C 27 Feb,*
£770 ($1,155)

2
A Victorian light oak pedestal desk, 139cm (54¾in) wide, *S 4 Mar,*
£572 ($858)

3
An oak roll-top pedestal desk, early 20th century, with panelled sides, 126cm (49½in) wide, *S 14 Jan,*
£490 ($735)

4
A late Victorian walnut partner's desk, the pedestals with panelled doors to the rear, 152cm (59¾in) wide, *S 14 Jan,*
£1,450 ($2,175)

5
A Victorian walnut pedestal desk, 137cm (54in) wide, *S 2 Sept,*
£2,090 ($3,240)

6
A mahogany writing desk, c.1900, the superstructure with a pen and letter rack flanked by two small drawers, 121cm (47½in), *C 10 Sept,*
£748 ($1,122)

7
A George III-style inlaid satinwood partner's desk, third quarter 19th century, in the manner of John Linnell, inlaid with neoclassical urns and floral strands, 157.5cm (62in) wide, *NY 14 Oct,*
$4,400 (£3,056)

8
A Victorian mahogany cylinder bureau, 152cm (59¾in) wide, *S 1 July,*
£1,100 ($1,782)

9
A George III mahogany partner's desk, early 19th century, 194cm (6ft 4½in) wide, *NY 7 June,*
$11,550 (£7,751)

10
A mahogany pedestal desk, 19th century, 133.5cm (52½in) wide, *C 7 Aug,*
£517 ($801)

11
A George III-style carved mahogany partner's desk, c.1920, of serpentine form, on ogee bracket feet, 190cm (6ft 3in) wide, *S 11 Nov,*
£10,340 ($14,476)

See also:
Library and desk furnishings *p* 100

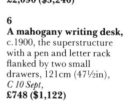

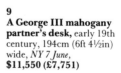

1
An Edwardian mahogany writing table, c.1910, the mirrored superstructure with a gallery with two stationery compartments, 137cm (54in) wide, *L 7 Apr,*
£825 ($1,254)

2
A Victorian rosewood bureau on stand, c.1840, with maple-veneered interior, 84cm (33in) high, *C 29 May,*
£352 ($556)

3
A Victorian walnut serpentine-fronted Davenport, c.1855, inlaid with satinwood arabesques and stringing, *S 18 Mar,*
£968 ($1,481)

4
A George III-style mahogany desk, c.1910, 130cm (51in) wide, *C 29 May,*
£572 ($904)

5
A George IV rosewood Davenport, c.1830, 86.5cm (34in) high, *C 14 May,*
£825 ($1,328)

6
A William IV walnut Davenport, c.1835, 51cm (20in) wide, *L 18 July,*
£1,925 ($3,061)

7
A Victorian walnut writing desk, c.1865, 132cm (52in) wide, *C 16 Jan,*
£1,100 ($1,650)

8
A George III-style inlaid satinwood Carlton House desk, late 19th century, the superstructure with a pierced brass gallery, 127cm (50in) wide, *NY 14 Oct,*
$5,225 (£3,628)

9
A late Victorian mahogany writing table, inlaid with stringing, 99cm (39in) wide, *S 10 June,*
£495 ($767)

10
A Victorian kingwood-veneered bonheur du jour, c.1860, stamped Edwards & Roberts, the upper part with a pair of doors each with a flower-painted Sèvres-type plaque within an ormolu border, 138cm (54½in) high, *L 21 Mar,*
£1,650 ($2,574)

11
A Victorian rosewood bonheur du jour, c.1900, inlaid with satinwood stringing and arabesques, on brass cappings and castors, 69cm (27in) wide, *S 21 Jan,*
£825 ($1,238)

12
An Edwardian rosewood bonheur du jour, c.1910, inlaid with scrolls, 104cm (41in) wide, *C 24 Sept,*
£770 ($1,178)

13
A George III-style mahogany cylinder bureau, c.1900, stamped James Shoolbred, inlaid with satinwood banding, 112cm (44in) high, *S 15 July,*
£2,530 ($3,972)

14
A rosewood and marquetry cylinder bureau bookcase, c.1880, gilt metal mounts, 155cm (61in) high, *C 16 Jan,*
£1,540 ($2,310)

See also:
English writing tables *p* 62

1

2

3

4

5

6

7

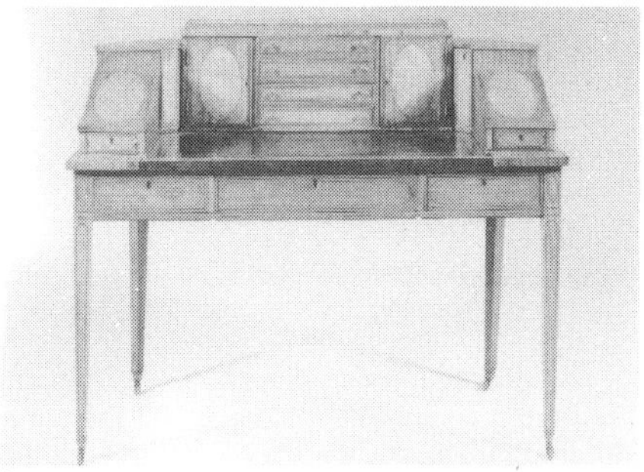
8

9

10

11

12

13

14

1

2

3

4

5

6

7

8

1
A Louis XVI cylinder bureau, stamped *Leleu,* 115cm (45¼in) high, *M 30 Nov,*
FF 198,000 (£21,522; $30,130)

2
An ormolu-mounted sycamore marquetry cylinder bureau, late 19th century, in the style of J. H. Riesener, inset with gilt-bronze panels of cherubs, 109cm (43in) high, *L 21 Mar,*
£4,400 ($6,864)

3
A Louis XVI-style kingwood and rosewood crossbanded marquetry cylinder bureau, c.1910, with gilt-metal mounts, 112cm (44in) high, *S 18 Feb,*
£2,420 ($3,678)

4
A Louis XV-style gilt-bronze-mounted kingwood lady's writing desk, late 19th century, in the manner of Cressent, kidney shaped, green gilt-tooled writing surface, 114cm (45in) high, *NY 26 Apr,*
$8,250 (£5,357)

5
A Louis XV parquetry and marquetry cylinder bureau, c.1765, stamped *I. Bircklé,* 98cm (38½in) wide, *L 12 Dec,*
£16,500 ($23,100)

6
A mahogany bonheur du jour, late 18th century, with marble top, 112cm (44in) high, *M 22 June,*
FF 32,190 (£2,872; $4,480)

7
A Régence rosewood-veneered bureau, 101cm (39¾in) high, *M 22 June,*
FF 72,150 (£6,436; $10,040)

8
A Louis XVI ormolu-mounted mahogany cylinder bureau, late 18th century, white mottled marble top, 126cm (49½in) high, *NY 4 Oct,*
$5,225 (£3,628)

1
A Louis-Philippe mahogany bureau à abattant, c.1835, green marble top, 162cm (63¼in), *M 1 Dec,*
FF 9,350 (£1,010; $1,444)

2
A French mahogany secrétaire à abattant, c.1830, 147.5cm (58in) high, *C 14 May,*
£638 ($1,027)

3
A French kingwood secrétaire semainier, c.1870, with gilt-metal mounts, the fall simulating three drawers, 125cm (49in) high, *S 11 Nov,*
£1,210 ($1,694)

4
A Louis XV provincial kingwood bureau c.1760, 98cm (38½in) high, *L 28 Nov,*
£3,740 ($5,236)

5
A Louis XV kingwood secrétaire en pente, mid 18th century, stamped Landrin, with gilt-metal sabots, 87cm (34in), *L 20 June,*
£7,700 ($12,166)

6
A Louis-Philippe porcelain-mounted kingwood bonheur du jour, c.1840, with Sèvres-type plaques within *blue-du-ciel* borders, ormolu mounts, 89cm (35in) high, *L 7 Nov,*
£7,150 ($10,010)

7
A gilt-metal-mounted ebony bonheur du jour, c.1870, inset with neoclassical medallions, bearing a label *Warn, Bruxelles,* 153cm (60in), *L 7 Nov,*
£1,320 ($1,848)

8
A Louis XV secrétaire en pente, gilt-bronze handles, stamped probably *E. Doirat,* 95.5cm (37½in) high, *M 23 Feb,*
FF 44,400 (£4,294; $6,441)

9
A Louis XV tulipwood parquetry bonheur du jour, mid 18th century, leather-lined writing surface, with later ormolu chutes, sabots and keyhole escutcheons, 103cm (40½in) high, *NY 4 Oct,*
$3,300 (£2,291)

10
A Louis XV ormolu-mounted lacquer bureau en pente, mid 18th century, leather-lined writing surface, false drawer, japanned in brown and gilt on a red ground, 92cm (36in) high, *NY 4 Oct,*
$6,325 (£4,392)

11
A rosewood and kingwood marquetry bureau de dame, c.1880, with gilt-metal mounts, 92cm (36in) high, *L 7 Nov,*
£1,760 ($2,464)

See also:
French writing tables
pp 68-69

1

2

3

4

5

6

7

8

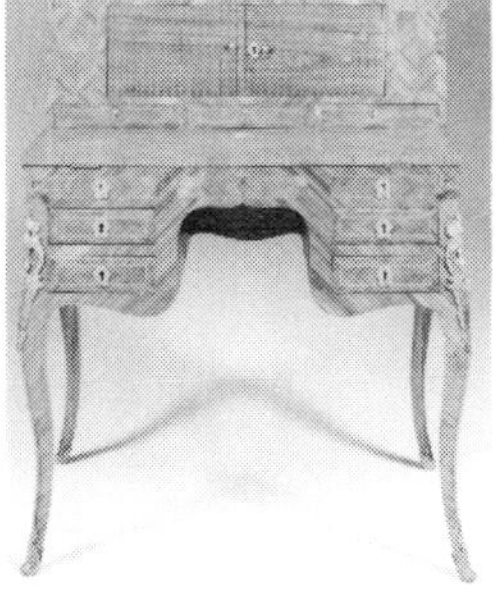
9

10

11

1

2

3

4

5

6

7

8

9

1
An Empire ormolu-mounted mahogany secrétaire à abattant, c.1800, Belgian marble top, 145cm (57in) high, *NY 4 Oct,*
$3,575 (£2,482)

2
A Louis XVI ormolu-mounted mahogany secrétaire à abattant, c.1790, signed *Delorme,* outlined with brass, 145cm (57½in) high, *NY 3 May,*
$4,400 (£2,895)

3
A Louis XVI brass-mounted mahogany secrétaire à abattant, c.1790, white mottled marble top, outlined in brass, 145cm (57in) high, *NY 4 Oct,*
$6,600 (£4,583)

4
A Louis XVI mahogany secrétaire à abattant, c.1790, grey and white marble top, 137cm (54in) high, *L 28 Nov,*
£2,090 ($2,926)

5
A Louis XVI ormolu-mounted kingwood, tulipwood and fruitwood marquetry secrétaire à abattant, signed *J.P. Letellier, JME,* grey mottled marble top, 146cm (57½in) high, *NY 17 Dec,*
$7,700 (£5,500)

6
A Transitional Louis XV/Louis XVI secretaire, c.1775, stamped *Galet,* 133cm (52½in) high, *M 22 June,*
FF 38,850 (£3,466; $5,406)

7
A secrétaire à abattant, 19th century, gilt-bronze mounts, black marble top, 148cm (58¼in) high, *M 24 Feb,*
FF 14,430 (£1,396; $2,093)

8
A Louis XVI secrétaire à abattant, stamp of Schlichtig, 139cm (54¾in) high, *M 23 Feb,*
FF 49,950 (£4,831; $7,246)

9
A secrétaire à abattant, c.1800, in light and dark woods, 148cm (58¼in) high, *M 25 Feb,*
FF 13,320 (£1,288; $1,932)

1
A Dutch marquetry secretaire, c.1700, inlaid on a walnut ground, 166cm (65½in) high, *L 28 Nov,*
£4,620 ($6,468)

2
A North Italian burr walnut, kingwood and fruitwood marquetry bureau bookcase, early 18th century, with mirrored doors, 213cm (7ft) high, *NY 22 Mar,*
$22,000 (£14,570)

3
A Dutch walnut bureau cabinet, c.1750, mirrored doors, 221cm (7ft 3in) high, *A 6 May,*
Dfl 31,050 (£9,409; $14,960)

4
A Dutch fruitwood and walnut marquetry bureau bookcase, mid 18th century, inlaid with flowering vines and urns, 202cm (6ft 6in) high, *NY 22 Mar,*
$4,950 (£3,278)

5
A Venetian burr walnut bureau bookcase, mid 18th century, mirrored doors, 144cm (8ft) high, *NY 4 Oct,*
$14,300 (£9,930)

6
A Danish oak bureau cabinet, mid 18th century, inlaid with initials *MG,* fitted interior, 221cm (7ft 3in) high, *L 28 Nov,*
£4,400 ($6,160)

7
A South German walnut and crossbanded bureau bookcase, c.1720, bevelled mirror doors, 229cm (7ft 6in) high, *S 11 Nov,*
£5,500 ($7,700)

8
A German walnut bureau cabinet, c.1740, doors altered, 229cm (7ft 6in) high, *L 23 May,*
£8,250 ($13,035)

9
A South German walnut and burr walnut bureau cabinet, c.1740, 189cm (6ft 2½in) high, *L 23 May,*
£4,400 ($6,952)

1

2

3

4

5

6

7

8

9

1

2

3

4

5

6

7

8

1
A South German bronze-mounted walnut parquetry secretaire cabinet, first half 18th century, in three parts, 280cm (6ft 10in), *NY 25 Nov,*
$9,350 (£6,679)

2
A South German walnut parquetry bureau cabinet, c.1740, 117cm (69½in), *L 23 May,*
£7,150 ($11,297)

3
A Dutch marquetry secretaire, late 18th century, the fall-front with fitted interior, 151cm (59½in), *L 28 Nov,*
£3,080 ($4,312)

4
A Swedish kingwood, tulipwood and fruitwood marquetry fall-front secretaire, last quarter 18th century, with grey marble top, ormolu mounts, 160cm (62¾in), *NY 17 Dec,*
$16,500 (£11,785)

5
An ormolu-mounted mahogany roll-top desk, late 18th century, probably Russian, in two parts, 120cm (47in), *NY 22 Mar,*
$3,850 (£2,550)

6
A Biedermeier satinwood secrétaire à abattant, c.1840, with fitted interior, 170cm (67in), *Ct 27 Oct,*
R 7,920 (£2,475; $3,465)

7
A Biedermeier birch and ebonised drop-front secretaire, first quarter 19th century, in two parts, 185cm (6ft ¾in), *NY 22 Mar,*
$5,500 (£3,642)

8
A German mahogany secrétaire à abattant, c.1840, 182cm (71½in), *Ct 27 Oct,*
R 3,850 (£1,203; $1,684)

1
A South German walnut parquetry slant-front bureau, 18th century, in three parts, 176cm (69½in), *NY 25 Nov,*
$5,500 (£3,929)

2
A South German burr walnut secretaire, c.1760, in three parts, with ormolu mounts, 178cm (6ft 2in), *NY 4 Oct,*
$12,100 (£8,402)

3
A North Italian burr walnut bureau cabinet, Piedmont, 18th century, constructed using panels from an earlier piece of furniture or panelling, 215cm (7ft ½in), *L 23 May,*
£4,620 ($7,299)

4
A South German walnut parquetry secretaire cabinet, first half 18th century, in two parts, with gilt-metal mounts, 190cm (6ft 3in), *NY 22 Mar,*
$13,750 (£9,106)

5
A South German cabinet, 18th century, in two parts, 194cm (6ft 4in), *M 25 Feb,*
FF 83,250 (£8,051; $12,077)

6
A Dutch roll-top secretaire, last quarter 18th century, in three parts, with ormolu mounts, 250cm (8ft 2in), *NY 22 Mar,*
$7,150 (£4,735)

7
A Swedish mahogany, sycamore and fruitwood drop-front secretaire, c.1800, with alabaster supports and ormolu mounts, 211cm (6ft 11in), *NY 4 Oct,*
$8,800 (£6,111)

8
A Biedermeier walnut drop-front secretaire, second quarter 19th century, 168cm (66in), *NY 4 Oct,*
$7,150 (£4,965)

9
A German mahogany drop-front secretaire, first quarter 19th century, probably Berlin, with marble columns and brass mounts, 209cm (6ft 10in), *NY 17 Dec,*
$5,500 (£3,928)

1

2

3

4

5

6

7

8

9

1

2

3

4

5

6

7

8

9

10

11

12

13

1
A South German fruitwood and walnut parquetry slant-front bureau, early 18th century, veneered with interlaced strapwork, sides veneered wth diamonds, later feet, 108cm (42½in) high, *NY 25 Nov,*
$8,250 (£5,893)

2
A South German walnut slant-front bureau, c.1740, 104cm (41in) high, *NY 25 Nov,*
$8,250 (£5,893)

3
A German brass-mounted burr walnut slant-front desk, c.1760, later brass keyhole escutcheons and handles, 108cm (42½in) high, *NY 22 Mar,*
$5,225 (£3,460)

4
A walnut marquetry slant-front desk, probably German, mid 18th century, 102cm (40in) high, *M 25 Feb,*
FF 28,860 (£2,791; $4,187)

5
A South German tulipwood and burr walnut bureau en pente, c.1760, crossbanded, 100cm (39¼in) high, *NY 17 Dec,*
$4,125 (£2,946)

6
A Dutch walnut marquetry bureau, c.1740, 106.5cm (42in) high, *L 30 May,*
£3,080 ($4,866)

7
A Cape teak bureau, late 18th century, brass handles and escutcheons, 120cm (47¼in) high, *JHB 27 Feb,*
R 2,750 (£859; $1,332)

8
A North Italian walnut bureau, mid 18th century, inlaid with trellis banding, fitted interior with secret drawers, 109cm (43in) high, *L 23 May,*
£7,150 ($11,297)

9
An Italian burr walnut slant-front desk, mid 18th century, probably Genoa, bombé body, bronze escutcheons, 99cm (39in) high, *NY 22 Mar,*
$4,400 (£2,914)

10
A Northern Italian marquetry writing desk, c.1740, 106cm (41¾in) high, *M 1 Dec,*
FF 19,800 (£2,138; $3,058)

11
A Venetian elmwood and fruitwood writing desk, third quarter 18th century, 62cm (24½in) high, *F 14 Apr,*
L 10,000,000 (£4,095; $6,347)

12
A Roman rosewood marquetry chest-of-drawers, first half 18th century, inlaid in light wood, 117cm (46in) high, *F 30 Sept,*
L 15,400,000 (£7,673; $10,742)

13
An Italian walnut writing desk, Monferrato, c.1750, 107cm (42in) high, *F 14 Apr,*
L 17,000,000 (£6,962; $10,790)

1
A North Italian walnut-veneered writing desk, mid 18th century, 106cm (41¾in), *F 30 Sept,*
L 15,400,000 (£7,673; $10,742)

2
A Central Italian walnut writing desk, second half 18th century, 124cm (48¾in), *F 19 May,*
L 3,800,000 (£1,577; $2,523)

3
A South Italian inlaid writing desk, late 18th century, the top inlaid with a trophy with musical instruments, 107cm (42in), *F 30 Sept,*
L 15,400,000 (£7,673; $10,742)

4
A Cape stinkwood and yellow-wood marquetry bureau, late 18th century, inlaid with symbols of the arts, silver escutcheons, 118cm (46½in) high, *Ct 27 Oct,*
R 39,600 (£12,375; $17,325)

5
A Venetian writing desk, late 18th century, in George II-style, 107cm (42in), *F 14 Apr,*
L 5,000,000 (£2,048; $3,174)

6
A South German inlaid walnut writing desk, c.1780, 107cm (42in) high, *M 23 June,*
FF 46,620 (£4,159; $6,488)

7
A North Italian mahogany lady's writing desk, probably Piedmont, c.1800, 140cm (55in), *F 14 Apr,*
L 3,500,000 (£1,433; $2,222)

8
A German fruitwood bureau, late 18th century, with galleried top, 119cm (46¾in) high, *L 30 May,*
£1,430 ($2,259)

9
A South German fruitwood and marquetry writing desk, late 18th century, 128cm (50¼in) high, *M 23 June,*
FF 33,300 (£2,971; $4,634)

1

2

3

4

5

6

7

8

9

1

2

3

4

5

6

7

8

9

10

11

12

1
A painted satinwood table, c.1900, the drum top with recesses for books painted with baskets of ribbon-tied flowers, 86m (34in) high, *L 12 May,*
£638 ($1,027)

2
A George III satinwood book carrier on stand, late 18th century, the carrier removable, decorated with black foliate scrolls and garlands of bellflowers, 112cm (44in) high, *NY 18 Oct,*
$2,860 (£1,986)

3
A Victorian walnut and inlaid reading table, c.1855, with gilt-metal mounts, the upper tier with a revolving candle sconce, 79cm (31in), *S 17 June,*
£286 ($452)

4
A late George III-style mahogany revolving bookstand, 19th century, the four revolving tiers each divided by book-spines, 140cm (55in), *L 28 Feb,*
£5,720 ($8,866)

5
A George III mahogany cabinet bookcase, c.1800, the moulded cornice above a pair of reeded astragal doors, on plinth base, 216cm (7ft 1in) high, *S 17 June,*
£660 ($1,043)

6
A George III mahogany cabinet bookcase, c.1770, with a dentil-moulded and fret-carved broken pediment, on plinth base, 255cm (8ft 4in) high, *NY 7 June,*
$12,100 (£8,120)

7
A George III mahogany bookcase, c.1790, on bracket feet, 214cm (7ft) high, *C 16 Jan,*
£2,750 ($4,125)

8
A Victorian maple cabinet bookcase, c.1870, with ebonised mouldings and fluted pilaster terminals, the panelled doors with shield medallions, 201cm (6ft 7in) high, *S 11 Nov,*
£1,760 ($2,464)

9
A Victorian mahogany cabinet bookcase, c.1840, mirror doors enclosing adjustable shelves, 185cm (6ft 1in) high, *S 11 Nov,*
£528 ($739)

10
An early Victorian mahogany bookcase, c.1840, 226cm (7ft 5in) high, *C 5 Nov,*
£572 ($806)

11
An Edwardian mahogany bookcase, c.1900, on plinth base, 218cm (7ft 2½in) high, *C 24 Sept,*
£1,210 ($1,851)

12
A mahogany bookcase, 19th century, with an architectural pediment above a blind fret-carved frieze and two astragal doors, on plinth base, 264cm (8ft 8in), *L 28 Feb,*
£8,360 ($12,958)

See also:
Cabinets *p* 34
English desks *pp* 11 & 12
Library and desk furnishings *p* 100

1
A William IV mahogany breakfront library bookcase, on a plinth base, 214cm (7ft) high, *C 17 Apr,* **£2,420 ($3,751)**

2
A satinwood breakfront bookcase in George III style, c.1900, 238cm (7ft 9½in) high, *L 14 Mar,* **£7,480 ($11,594)**

3
A Regency mahogany bookcase, c.1820, the corbelled cornice above two pairs of doors with brass wire grilles, on a plinth, 216cm (7ft 1in) high, *L 14 Mar,* **£4,180 ($6,479)**

4
A George III mahogany breakfront bookcase, c.1805, with four pairs of glazed doors with moulded 'hour-glass' astragals, 267cm (8ft 9in) high, *L 11 July,* **£16,500 ($26,235)**

5
A William IV mahogany breakfront bookcase, c.1830, the lower section with three inset doors, each flanked by Ionic columns, on plinth, 212cm (7ft 11in) high, *NY 14 Oct,* **$6,875 (£4,774)**

6
A Regency Irish mahogany breakfront bookcase, c.1825, with four astragal doors above, below four panelled doors with fluted spandrels, on turned feet, 256cm (8ft 5in) high, *S 17 June,* **£7,150 ($11,297)**

7
A George IV Gothic Revival library bookcase, c.1825, the upper part with a pierced Gothic cresting, the projecting lower part with frieze above four Tudor arches divided by pillars, 286cm (9ft 4½in) high, *L 2 May,* **£3,190 ($5,072)**

1

2

3

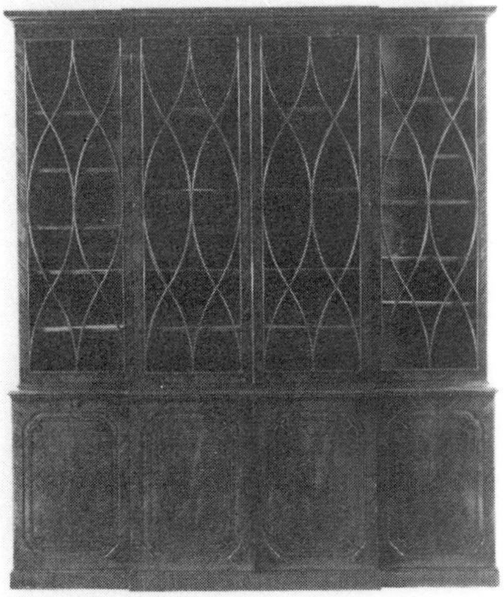
4

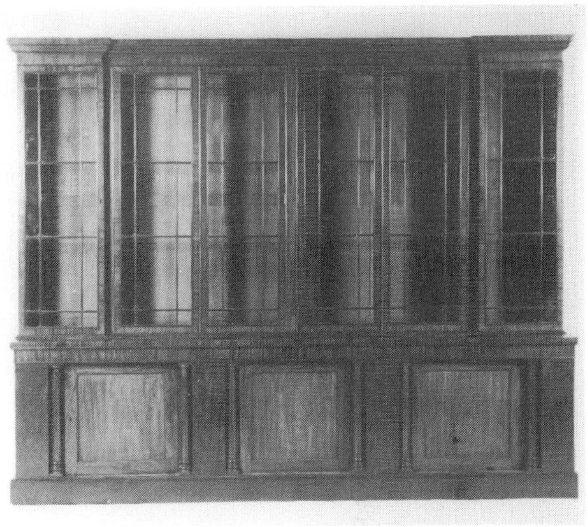
5

6

7

1

2

3

4

5

6

7

8

9

10

11

1
A pair of mahogany and marquetry book cabinets, *(one illustrated)*, late 18th century, bow-fronted and with modern *verde antico* marble tops, 94cm (37in) wide, *L 2 May,*
£2,035 ($3,236)

2
A Regency mahogany book cabinet, c.1815, in the manner of Gillows, the brass-bound top above a drawer, 99cm (39in) high, *L 24 Oct,*
£5,500 ($7,700)

3
A pair of George III satinwood standing book-shelves, *(one illustrated)*, early 19th century, with later splayed bracket feet, 105cm (41in) high, *L 21 Nov,*
£4,950 ($6,930)

4
A George IV simulated rosewood open bookcase, c.1825, the four graduated tiers above two apron drawers, 137cm (54in) high, *S 17 June,*
£1,045 ($1,651)

5
A tulipwood-veneered standing open bookshelf, c.1870, with four adjustable shelves flanked by quarter-veneered pilasters applied with gilt-bronze mounts, 215cm (7ft ½in), *L 21 Mar,*
£2,200 ($3,432)

6
A Victorian walnut break-front bookcase, 99cm (39in), *L 14 July,*
£1,210 ($1,888)

7
A Louis XVI brass-mounted mahogany bibliothèque, last quarter 18th century, the brass-galleried white marble top over a frieze drawer, 125cm (57in), *NY 22 Mar,*
$4,950 (£3,278)

8
A Louis XV ormolu-mounted tulipwood parquetry bibliothèque, mid 18th century, signed Migeon, with a brown and grey veined marble top, 163cm (64in), *NY 31 Oct,*
$17,600 (£12,482)

9
A Louis XVI brass-mounted mahogany bibliothèque, last quarter 18th century, 122cm (7ft 3in), *NY 4 Oct,*
$4,180 (£2,902)

10
A Biedermeier ormolu-mounted fruitwood bibliothèque, c.1820, 176cm (69¼in), *NY 22 Mar,*
$3,575 (£2,368)

11
A Louis XVI brass-mounted mahogany bibliothèque, last quarter 18th century, the central door with a glazed panel, the flanking doors with wire mesh inset panels, 170cm (67in), *NY 22 Mar,*
$7,975 (£5,281)

1
A Charles X maple and amaranth marquetry cheval mirror, second quarter 19th century, 180cm (72in) high, *NY 22 Mar,*
$2,750 (£1,821)

2
A pair of Charles X fruitwood tables de nuit, *(one illustrated)*, second quarter 19th century, each with a black marble top, 86cm (34in) high, *NY 22 Mar,*
$3,960 (£2,623)

3
A pair of Charles X ormolu-mounted maple tables de nuit, *(one illustrated)*, second quarter 19th century, each with mottled brown *faux marbre* top, 77cm (30½in) high, *NY 22 Mar,*
$5,500 (£3,642)

4
A Charles X maple and amaranth marquetry library cabinet, second quarter 19th century, 200cm (6ft 6½in) wide, *NY 22 Mar,*
$5,775 (£3,825)

5
A Charles X ash, maple and amaranth marquetry lit d'alcove, second quarter 19th century, 221cm (7ft 3in) long, *NY 22 Mar,*
$4,125 (£2,732)

6
A Charles X walnut secrétaire à abattant, second quarter 19th century, with marble top 155cm (61in) high, *C 24 Sept,*
£330 ($505)

7
A Charles X amaranth and ash marquetry bibliothèque, second quarter 19th century, 164cm (64½in) high, *NY 24 June,*
$3,850 (£2,468)

8
A Charles X fruitwood secrétaire à abattant, second quarter 19th century, with rectangular grey marble top, with leather inset writing surface, 144.5cm (57in) high, *NY 24 June,*
$2,090 (£1,340)

1

2

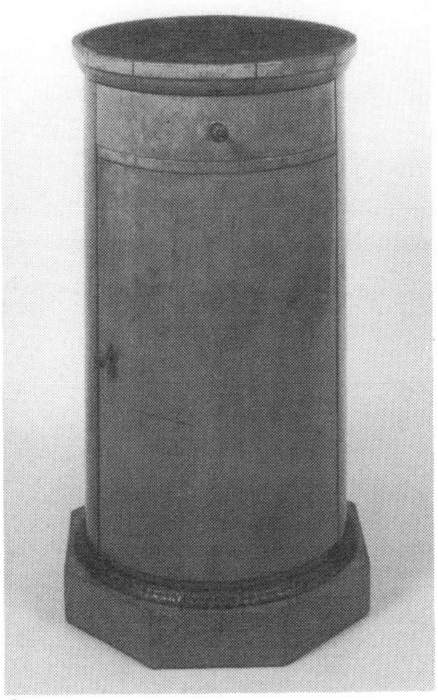
3

4

5

6

7

8

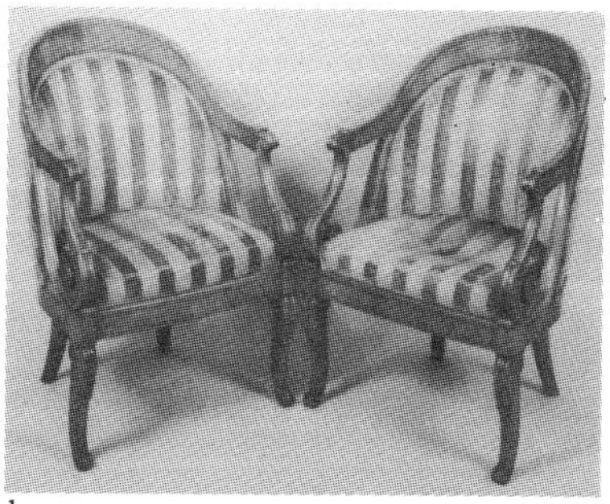
1

2

3

4

5

6

7

8

9

10

11

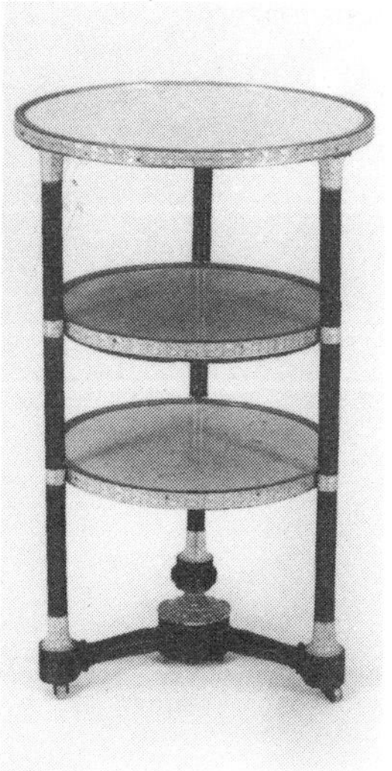
12

1
A pair of Charles X maple fauteuils en cabriolet, second quarter 19th century, *NY 22 Mar,* **$5,225 (£3,460)**

2
A pair of Charles X maple and amaranth marquetry fauteuils en cabriolet, second quarter 19th century, *NY 22 Mar,* **$11,000 (£7,285)**

3
A Charles X fruitwood bergère, c.1820, *NY 24 June,* **$1,100 (£705)**

4
A Charles X fruitwood bergère, c.1820, *NY 4 Oct,* **$3,960 (£2,750)**

5
A pair of Charles X mahogany armchairs, *(one illustrated),* c.1825, *L 23 May,* **£1,320 ($2,085)**

6
A pair of Charles X parcel-gilt mahogany fauteuils, *(one illustrated),* c.1820, *L 30 May,* **£1,320 ($2,086)**

7
A Charles X mahogany suite, *(part illustrated),* c.1825, *L 23 May,* **£3,960 ($6,257)**

8
A set of Charles X maple chairs, *(one illustrated),* second quarter 19th century, the backs inlaid in walnut, *F 30 Sept,* **L 2,200,000 (£10,962; $15,346)**

9
A Charles X mahogany marquise, c.1820, 110cm (43in) long, *NY 24 June,* **$1,430 (£917)**

10
A pair of Charles X mahogany tabourets, *(one illustrated),* second quarter 19th century, *NY 3 May,* **$11,550 (£7,599)**

11
A Charles X ormolu and enamelled steel gueridon, second quarter 19th century, with mottled peach marble top, blue enamelled frieze, 76cm (30in) high, *NY 17 Dec,* **$16,500 (£11,785)**

12
A Charles X gilt-bronze gueridon, c.1820, white marble top, 74cm (29in) high, *M 1 Dec,* **FF 104,500 (£11,285; $16,138)**

1
A Charles X mahogany and parcel-gilt centre table, second quarter 19th century, with grey and white veined marble top, 72cm (28½in), *NY 4 Oct,*
$5,225 (£3,628)

2
A Charles X maple, elm and fruitwood centre table, second quarter 19th century, the top with radiating panels of alternating woods, 79cm (31in) high, *NY 22 Mar,*
$8,250 (£5,464)

3
A Charles X mahogany and parcel-gilt centre table, second quarter 19th century, with black and ochre marble top, 73cm (28¼in) high, *NY 22 Mar,*
$12,100 (£8,013)

4
A pair of Charles X ormolu and fruitwood gueridons, *(one illustrated),* each with breccia marble top, 71cm (28in) high, *NY 22 Mar,*
$6,600 (£4,371)

5
A Charles X console side table, stamped *Kolping,* with white marble top, 126cm (49½in) wide, *M 23 June,*
FF 26,640 (£2,376; $3,707)

6
A Charles X giltwood console table, c.1825, with grey veined marble top, 124cm (49in) wide, *NY 22 Mar,*
$15,400 (£10,199)

7
A Charles X maple and amaranth marquetry gueridon, second quarter 19th century, 72cm (28½in) high, *NY 22 Mar,*
$17,600 (£11,656)

8
A Charles X brass-mounted maple and ebonised étagère, second quarter 19th century, 71cm (28in) high, *NY 22 Mar,*
$4,125 (£2,732)

9
A Charles X mahogany commode, with grey marble top, 127cm (50in) wide, *M 1 Dec,*
FF 16,500 (£1,782; $2,548)

1

2

3

4

5

6

7

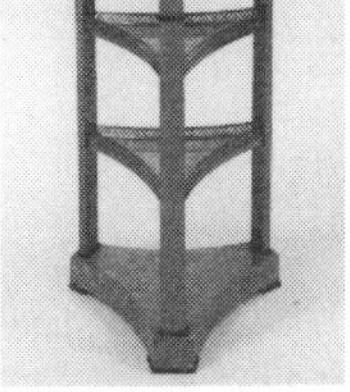
8

9

1

2

3

4

5

6

7

8

9

10

1
A Willian IV pollard elm side cabinet, c.1830, 94cm (37in) high, *NY 7 June,*
$15,400 (£10,335)

2
A Regency brass inlaid rosewood side cabinet, c.1810, attributed to Gillows, on a later plinth, 123cm (48½in) high, *NY 7 June,*
$9,900 (£6,644)

3
A George III mahogany cabinet, 122cm (48in) high, *NY 18 Oct,*
$1,430 (£993)

4
A George IV rosewood-veneered side cabinet, c.1820, with crossbanded top, gilt-wire trellis, 84cm (33in) high, *L 28 Feb,*
£2,860 ($4,433)

5
An Italian satinwood side cabinet, early 19th century, moulded black marble top, five giltwood stars, grill-inset doors, 93cm (36½in) high, *NY 4 Oct,*
$7,150 (£4,965)

6
A Regency mahogany breakfront side cabinet, c.1820, applied with pleated silk-lined brass trellis, 91cm (36in) high, *L 14 Mar,*
£1,870 ($2,898)

7
A George III-style mahogany and inlaid demi-lune cabinet, c.1890, by Edwards & Roberts, satinwood banding and rosewood crossbanding, drawer stamped, 97cm (38in) high, *S 18 Feb,*
£1,925 ($2,926)

8
A Regency mahogany small side cabinet, c.1810, cleated top with reeded edge, 86cm (34in) high, *L 14 Mar,*
£660 ($1,023)

9
A walnut and marquetry side cabinet, c.1860, with inset brass half-galleried white marble top, ormolu borders, 119cm (47in) high, *L 21 Mar,*
£2,310 ($3,604)

10
A Regency rosewood breakfront cabinet, c.1815, with marble top, doors with silk-lined brass grill panels, 97cm (38in) high, *S 17 June,*
£2,090 ($3,302)

See also:
Chiffoniers *p* 102

1
A Victorian burr walnut and gilt-metal mounted cabinet, c.1855, with amboyna banding, satin-wood stringing and arabesque inlay, 165cm (65in) wide, *S 17 June,*
£1,540 ($2,433)

2
A Victorian walnut side cabinet, c.1860, with an oval Sèvres-style plaque, 151cm (59in) wide, *L 6 Oct,*
£880 ($1,232)

3
A Victorian walnut and marquetry serpentine side cabinet, c.1860, 183cm (72in) wide, *L 24 Oct,*
£2,750 ($3,850)

4
A Victorian ebony and amboyna credenza, c.1865, with gilt-bronze mouldings and ivorene stringing, 159cm (62½in), *C 17 Apr,*
£770 ($1,194)

5
A Victorian walnut credenza, c.1860, *C 9 July,*
£1,870 ($3,011)

6
A Victorian walnut side cabinet, with marble top, mirror panel doors and mirror back, 182cm (71½in), *S 4 Mar,*
£990 ($1,485)

7
A Victorian ebonised and thuyawood banded cabinet, c.1860, with a Sèvres-style porcelain plaque, 158cm (62in) wide, *S 22 Apr,*
£418 ($656)

8
A French boulle and ebonised meuble d'appui, c.1860, with gilt-metal mounts, mirror back, 168cm (66in) wide, *S 15 July,*
£1,155 ($1,813)

9
A Victorian walnut credenza, c.1860, applied throughout with gilt-metal mouldings, 186cm (6ft 1in) wide, *C 8 Oct,*
£2,090 ($2,926)

1

2

3

4

5

6

7

8

9

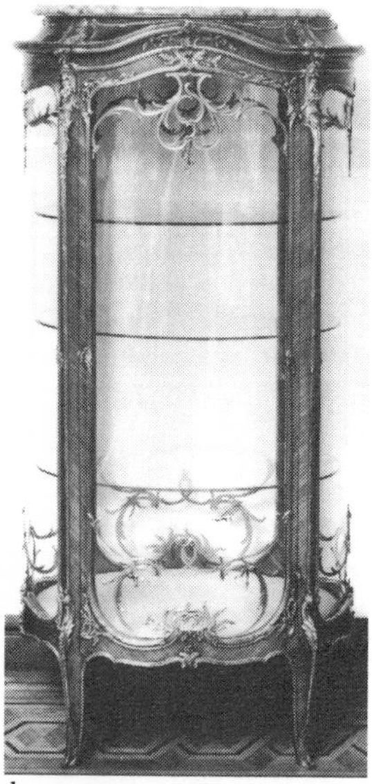
1

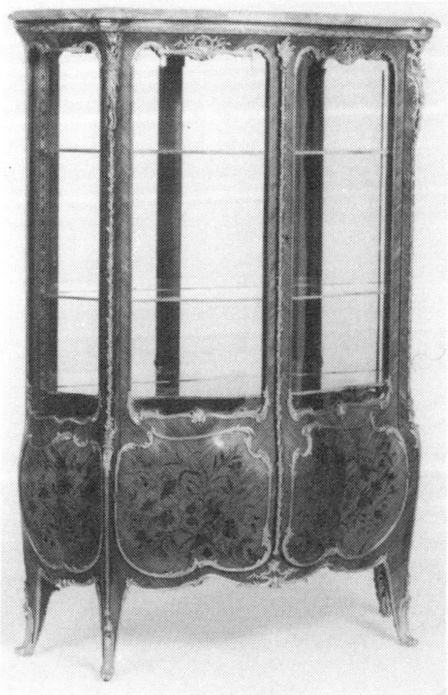
2

3

4

5

6

7

8

9

1
A gilt-bronze and tulipwood four-glass serpentine vitrine, c.1885, signed *F. Linke,* 171cm (67½in), *L 13 June,*
£13,750 ($22,000)

2
A gilt-bronze and end-cut marquetry vitrine, c.1890, with mutton-fat marble top, 199cm (6ft 6½in), *L 7 Nov,*
£5,500 ($7,700)

3
A bronze-mounted kingwood-veneered vitrine, c.1890, with mottled peach and rust marble top, 178cm (70in) high, *L 7 Nov,*
£2,860 ($4,004)

4
A French kingwood and gilt-metal mounted vitrine, c.1900, 176cm (69in) high, *S 15 July,*
£1,100 ($1,727)

5
A rosewood and Vernis Martin vitrine, c.1900, the four lower panels painted with Romantic landscapes, with gilt-bronze mounts, 188cm (6ft 2in) high, *L 13 June,*
£1,980 ($3,168)

6
A late Victorian rosewood and inlaid side cabinet, with mirror-panelled back, 229cm (7ft 5in) high, *S 6 May,*
£748 ($1,189)

7
An Edwardian mahogany display cabinet on stand, c.1900, 202cm (6ft 7½in) high, *C 16 Jan,*
£594 ($891)

8
An Edwardian satinwood display cabinet, c.1910, with two painted medallions of Roman figures, 188cm (6ft 2in), *C 8 Oct,*
£1,760 ($2,464)

9
A Vernis Martin and kingwood vitrine, c.1900, with painted panels of garden scenes, 196cm (6ft 5in) high, *L 21 Mar,*
£3,850 ($6,006)

1
An Edwardian mahogany standing corner étagère, with latticed canopy above mirrors, 239cm (94in) high, *C 25 June,*
£1,045 ($1,630)

2
A Victorian satinwood-veneered display cabinet, c.1870, with purple heart bandings, concave shelf and mirrored back, 168cm (66in) high, *L 2 May,*
£1,595 ($2,536)

3
A brass-framed vitrine, c.1900, 173cm (68in) high, *C 9 July,*
£682 ($1,098)

4
A Louis XVI-style mahogany and gilt-bronze mounted display cabinet, c.1900, 144cm (57in) high, *L 13 June,*
£935 ($1,496)

5
A walnut specimen table, c.1910, with glazed top and sides, 74cm (29in) high, *C 29 May,*
£242 ($382)

6
A kingwood and gilt-metal mounted vitrine, c.1870, top with bevelled glass panel, 86cm (33¾in) high, *L 7 Nov,*
£1,760 ($2,464)

7
A Capetown colonial rosewood flat-top-buffet, third quarter 18th century, serpentine front, 90.5cm (35½in) high, *A 14 Oct,*
Dfl 14,375 (£4,492; $6,738)

8
A boulle side cabinet, c.1860, with black marble top, set with gilt-metal mounts, 117cm (46in) high, *L 7 Nov,*
£1,595 ($2,233)

9
A pair of kingwood and rosewood painted side cabinets, *(one illustrated),* c.1860, later wooden tops, doors set with 'Sèvres' panels with gilt-metal frames, 112cm (44in) high, *L 7 Nov,*
£2,200 ($3,080)

10
A pair of William IV rosewood side cabinets, *(one illustrated),* c.1835, 83.5cm (33in) high, *L 28 Feb,*
£3,300 ($5,115)

11
A Victorian oak display cabinet, c.1890, 185.5cm (73in), *C 25 June,*
£550 ($858)

1

2

3

4

5

6

7

8

9

10

11

1

2

3

4

5

6

7

8

9

10

1
A Dutch walnut and marquetry corner display cabinet, mid 18th century, with 19th century inlay, 236cm (7ft 9in) high, *L 30 May,*
£2,970 ($4,692)

2
A quarter-veneered king-wood vitrine, c.1880, with gilt-bronze mounts of Empire influence, 170cm (67in) high, *L 7 Nov,*
£3,300 ($4,620)

3
An English pine standing corner cupboard, 19th century, 206cm (6ft 9in), *C 17 Apr,*
£1,155 ($1,790)

4
A George III mahogany standing corner display cabinet, c.1770, with later moulded cornice, 215cm (7ft ½in), *S 17 June,*
£1,265 ($1,999)

5
An Edwardian satinwood standing corner cup-board, c.1900, the base painted with an oval depicting a pastoral scene after Morland, 239cm (7ft 10in), *C 17 Apr,*
£7,700 ($11,935)

6
A pair of Biedermeier ash and ebonised vitrines, *(one illustrated),* second quarter 19th century, 158cm (62in), *NY 22 Mar,*
$4,675 (£3,096)

7
A Louis XVI display cabinet, marked *Ellaume,* the top in red Languedoc marble, 138cm (54in), *M 23 Feb,*
FF27,750 (£2,684; $4,026)

8
A George III mahogany display cabinet, c.1770, 214cm (7ft ½in), *L 21 Nov,*
£12,650 ($17,710)

9
A Louis XV provincial display cabinet, 240cm (7ft 8in), *M 25 Feb,*
FF 24,420 (£2,362; $3,543)

10
A walnut and marquetry display cabinet, c.1740, Dutch, the lower part inlaid with marquetry, 175cm (69in), *C 8 Oct,*
£3,520 ($4,928)

French cabinet makers
m.= made Master

Henri Amand m.1749
Jean Avisse m.1745
Jacques Bircklé m.1864
Leonard Boudin m.1761
Jean-Baptiste Boulard m.1755
François-Barthelemy Crespi, called Crepi, m.1778
Jean-Baptiste Cresson m.1755
Roger van der Cruse m.1755
Jean-Louis Faizelot Delorme m.1763
Jean-Baptiste Demay m.1784
Jean Demoulin m.1745
Etienne Doirat fl. c.1700-32
Adrien-Pierre Dupain m.1772
Pierre Dupré m.1766
Jean-Charles Ellaume m.1754
Jean-Gottlieb Frost m.1785
Antoine Gailliard m.1781
Jean-Baptiste Galet m.1754
Pierre Garnier m.1742
Joseph Gengenbach called Canabas m.1776
P. Gillier m.1747
Jean-Baptiste Gourdin m.1748

See also:
Bookcases *p* 24
Corner cupboards *p* 37
Whatnots and étagères *p* 104

1
A Queen Anne walnut-veneered cabinet on stand, c.1710, 159cm (62½in) high, *L 11 July,*
£6,600 ($10,494)

2
A pair of japanned cabinets on stands, *(one illustrated)*, possibly from the workshops of Martin Schnell, Dresden, c.1710, 91.5cm (36in) wide, *L 23 May,*
£29,700 ($46,926)

3
A pair of late Victorian mahogany and inlaid cabinets, c.1900, 130cm (51in) high, *S 15 July,*
£1,870 ($2,936)

4
A Flemish tortoiseshell and ebony cabinet on stand, mid 17th century, 147cm (58in) high, *L 23 May,*
£6,050 ($9,559)

5
A pair of George III-style mahogany hanging corner cupboards, *(one illustrated)*, c.1900, 122cm (48in) high, *C 27 Mar,*
£902 ($1,380)

6
A German burr walnut cabinet on stand, Frankfurt, c.1700, 210cm (6ft 9in) high, *NY 25 Nov,*
$17,600 (£12,571)

7
A William III walnut cabinet on stand, c.1700, with fitted interior, 150cm (59in) high, *L 21 Nov,*
£2,860 ($4,004)

8
A George III hanging mahogany corner cupboard, c.1790, 107cm (42in) high, *C 13 Feb,*
£660 ($977)

9
A Dutch walnut press cupboard-on-chest, c.1750, 240cm (7ft 10in), *S 9 Dec,*
£2,420 ($3,388)

10
A Louis XVI-style gilt-bronze-mounted lacquer cabinet on stand, c.1880, Millet, Paris, in the manner of Weisweiller, 175cm (68¾in) high, *NY 26 Apr,*
$16,500 (£10,714)

Jean-Baptiste Hedouin m.1738
Nicolas Heurtaut m.1755
Georges Jacob m.1765
Othon Kolping 1775-1853
Charles Krier m.1774
Germain Landrin m.1738
Jean-François Leleu m.1764
Jacques-Pierre Letellier m.1747
Jean-Pierre Louis m.1787
Pierre Migeon II m.1738
Louis Moreau m.1764
Martin Ohneberg m.1773
Nicholas Petit m.1765
Pierre Plée m.1767
C. Ronsaint (unrecorded)
Pierre Roussel m.1745
Jean-Georges Schlichtig m.1765
Joseph Schmitz m.1761
Charles Topino m.1773
Jean-Baptiste Vassou m.1767

1

2

3

4

5

6

7

8

9

10

1

2

3

4

5

6

7

8

1
A Bavarian painted schrank, dated 1849, monogrammed *MBAB*, painted with flowers on a blue ground, 132cm (52in) wide, *NY 24 June*,
$1,980 (£1,269)

2
A Biedermeier birch and ebonised armoire, second quarter 19th century, 226cm (7ft 5in) high, *NY 4 Oct*,
$3,850 (£2,673)

3
A South German walnut parquetry wardrobe, early 18th century, 162cm (64in) high, *NY 25 Nov*,
$4,125 (£5,775)

4
A German walnut armoire, c.1700, with satinwood banding and floral vase inlay, cornice inlaid with ivory, 229cm (7ft 6in) high, *S 20 May*,
£1,540 ($2,464)

5
A German fruitwood schrank, mid 18th century, with stamped brass keyhole escutcheons, later bun feet, 173cm (68in) high, *NY 25 Nov*,
$2,200 (£1,571)

6
A South German or Austrian armoire, c.1740, possibly Salzburg, with crossbanded frieze and quarter-veneered doors, 210cm (6ft 11in) high, *L 23 May*,
£13,750 ($21,725)

7
A German walnut armoire, late 17th century, 222cm (7ft 3in), *L 12 May*,
£1,430 ($2,302)

8
A North German fruitwood veneered armoire, early 18th century, Hamburg, with quarter-veneered ogee panel doors and ebonised columns, 224cm (7ft 4in), *L 30 May*,
£5,500 ($8,690)

1
An Italian painted armoire, late 18th century, 219cm (7ft 2in) high, *NY 4 Oct,*
$6,875 (£4,774)

2
A Louis XV provincial oak armoire, c.1750, 250cm (8ft 2½in) high, *S 21 Jan,*
£660 ($990)

3
A Cape yellow-wood and stinkwood cupboard, early 19th century, 219cm (7ft 2in), *Ct 27 Oct,*
R 3,740 (£1,169; $1,636)

4
A Cape stinkwood and yellow-wood armoire, late 18th century, 246cm (8ft) high, *Ct 27 Oct,*
R 4,950 (£1,547; $2,165)

5
A Victorian oak standing corner cupboard, 19th century, in two parts, 214cm (7ft), *C 9 July,*
£935 ($1,505)

6
A George III mahogany standing corner cupboard, c.1790, 231cm (7ft 7in) high, *C 17 Apr,*
£3,410 ($5,286)

7
A Louis XVI walnut marriage armoire, 290cm (9ft 5in) high, *M 25 Feb,*
FF 18,315 (£1,771; $2,657)

8
A George II mahogany blanket chest, c.1750, 112cm (44in) wide, *HS 24 Sept,*
IR£2,200 (£2,000; $2,900)

9
An oak Normandy armoire, c.1780, 292cm (9ft 5in) wide, *C 17 Apr,*
£1,650 ($2,558)

10
A George II child's oak mule chest, c.1740, 70cm (27½in) wide, *S 21 Jan,*
£638 ($957)

See also:
Corner cupboards and cabinets *pp* 34-35

1

2

3

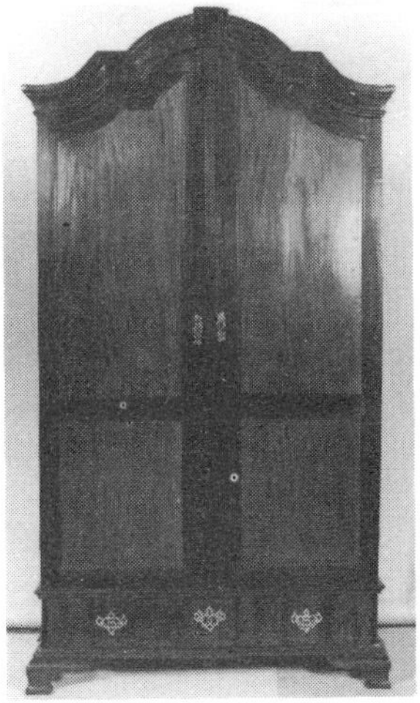
4

5

6

7

8

9

10

1

2

3

4

5

6

7

8

1
A William IV mahogany gentleman's wardrobe, c.1830, 201cm (6ft 7in) high, *C 11 June,*
£374 ($587)

2
A George III mahogany linen press, c.1770, 198cm (6ft 6in) high, *S 11 Nov,*
£1,320 ($1,848)

3
A George III inlaid mahogany linen press, last quarter 18th century, cornice later, cockbeaded drawers, 132cm (52in) wide, *NY 10 June,*
$3,850 (£2,452)

4
A George III mahogany linen press, c.1800, with inlaid ovals enclosing crossbanded drawers, 244cm (8ft) high, *C 17 Apr,*
£1,188 ($1,841)

5
A Victorian walnut and floral marquetry three-door breakfront wardrobe, 240cm (7ft 9½in) wide, *S 1 July,*
£1,100 ($1,782)

6
A Cape yellow-wood and stinkwood country wardrobe, c.1870, 209cm (6ft 10½in) high, *JHB 29 Sept,*
R 4,200 (£1,325; $1,855)

7
A William IV mahogany linen press, c.1835, 155cm (61in) wide, *NY 14 Oct,*
$1,980 (£1,375)

8
A George III mahogany linen press, c.1780, with satinwood strung borders, 216cm (7ft 1in) high, *S 9 Dec,*
£858 ($1,201)

See also:
Bedroom furnishings *pp* 98-99
Dressing tables *p* 65

1
A George II mahogany blanket chest, mid 18th century, 184cm (72½in) wide, *NY 7 June,*
$10,450 (£7,013)

2
A William and Mary walnut-veneered chest-on-stand, c.1690, 169cm (66½in) high, *L 24 Oct,*
£1,595 ($2,233)

3
A George III mahogany chest-on-chest, c.1780, 147cm (58in) high, *C 17 Apr,*
£792 ($1,228)

4
A George III mahogany chest-on-chest, 186cm (73in) high, *C 8 Oct,*
£1,870 ($2,618)

5
A Queen Anne walnut chest-on-stand, c.1715, later cabriole legs, 164cm (64½in) high, *L 21 Nov,*
£3,960 ($5,544)

6
A George III mahogany tall chest, c.1760, in the manner of Thomas Chippendale, 142cm (56in) high, *S 17 June,*
£7,700 ($12,166)

7
A George III mahogany chest-on-chest, c.1760, 188cm (6ft 2in) high, *NY 10 June,*
$4,840 (£3,083)

8
A Victorian walnut Wellington chest, 56cm (22in) wide, *S 2 Sept,*
£792 ($1,228)

1

2

3

4

5

6

7

8

1

2

3

4

5

6

7

8

9

10

11

12

13

1
A walnut chest, c.1700, with restorations, 94cm (37in) high, *C 11 June,*
£462 ($725)

2
A William and Mary walnut and crossbanded chest, c.1700, 91.5cm (36in) high, *S 18 Mar,*
£1,100 ($1,683)

3
A Queen Anne walnut bachelor's chest, c.1710, 79cm (31in) high, *L 7 July,*
£14,300 ($23,166)

4
A George II walnut chest, c.1725, 72cm (28½in), *L 18 July,*
£2,420 ($3,848)

5
A George I walnut-veneered chest, c.1720, in burr-wood with narrow chevron bandings, 77cm (30½in) high, *L 11 July,*
£28,600 ($45,474)

6
A George III mahogany chest, 105cm (41in) wide, *S 14 Jan,*
£200 ($300)

7
A George III mahogany chest, c.1780, 81cm (32in) high, *C 17 Apr,*
£935 ($1,449)

8
A George III mahogany commode, c.1780, inlaid with boxwood and ebony lines, 90cm (35½in) high, *C 16 Jan,*
£2,750 ($4,125)

9
A George III mahogany chest, c.1760, the moulded top above a brushing slide, 89cm (35in) high, *C 17 Apr,*
£2,310 ($3,581)

10
A George III mahogany bachelor's chest, last quarter 18th century, 81cm (32in) high, *NY 10 June,*
$3,960 (£2,522)

11
A George III mahogany chest, c.1755, with moulded flush top over a brushing slide, 79cm (31in) high, *L 25 Apr,*
£3,080 ($4,928)

12
A George III mahogany serpentine-fronted chest-of-drawers, last quarter 18th century, 82cm (32½in) high, *NY 7 June,*
$5,500 (£3,691)

13
A George II mahogany tall chest, c.1755, in the manner of Thomas Chippendale, 122.5cm (48¼in) high, *L 25 Apr,*
£5,060 ($8,096)

1
An early George III serpentine mahogany chest, c.1760, 110cm (45in) wide, *L 25 Apr,*
£6,600 ($10,560)

2
A George III mahogany and crossbanded serpentine-fronted commode, c.1780, with a writing drawer, 85cm (33½in) high, *S 18 Feb,*
£8,800 ($13,376)

3
A George III marquetry bombé commode, c.1775, in the French style, attributed to John Cobb, 105cm (45in) wide, *L 11 July,*
£55,000 ($87,450)

4
A George III mahogany chest-of-drawers, early 19th century, 93cm (36½in) high, *JHB 1 Dec,*
R 1,900 (£613; $850)

5
A George III mahogany chest, c.1800, in the manner of Gillows of Lancaster, 80cm (29½in) wide, *L 14 Mar,*
£990 ($1,534)

6
A George III mahogany chest, c.1790, strung in boxwood, 81cm (32in) high, *C 17 Apr,*
£880 ($1,364)

7
A late George III mahogany bow-fronted chest-of-drawers, c.1825, 91cm (36in), *NY 13 Dec,*
$2,200 (£1,571)

8
A George III inlaid mahogany serpentine-fronted chest-of-drawers, 94cm (37in) high, *NY 10 June,*
$3,850 (£2,452)

9
A George III bow-fronted satinwood-veneered chest, c.1790, 91cm (36in) high, *L 14 Nov,*
£13,200 ($18,876)

10
An early Victorian teak and brass-bound military chest, in two parts, 99cm (39in) wide, *S 9 Sept,*
£495 ($767)

11
A Victorian walnut and teak brass-bound military chest, in two parts, 99cm (39in) wide, *S 4 Feb,*
£968 ($1,355)

12
A late George III mahogany serpentine commode, c.1800, in the manner of Gillows, 102cm (40in) high, *L 25 Apr,*
£4,180 ($6,688)

13
A George III chest of drawers, c.1800, attributed to Gillows of Lancaster, 94cm (37in) high, *L 25 Apr,*
£11,000 ($17,760)

1

2

3

4

5

6

7

8

9

10

11

12

13

1

2

3

4

5

6

7

8

9

10

11

12

1
A Régence bow-front kingwood-veneered commode, c.1725, with mottled russet-grey marble top, gilt-bronze mounts, 97cm (38in) wide, *L 23 May,*
£3,080 ($4,866)

2
An early Louis XV kingwood commode, c.1730, with mottled serpentine marble top and leaf-cast gilt-metal mounts, 119cm (47in) wide, *L 28 Nov,*
£3,520 ($4,928)

3
An early Louis XV Lyonnais walnut commode, c.1740, 132cm (52in) wide, *L 28 Nov,*
£2,640 ($3,696)

4
A late Louis XIV violetwood-veneered commode, early 18th century, with red-white marble top and copper mounts, 129cm (50¾in) wide, *M 22 June,*
FF 77,700 (£6,931; $10,813)

5
A Louis XV provincial walnut commode, mid 18th century, with serpentine moulded top, ormolu mounts and escutcheons cast with Chinese figures and cornucopia, 117cm (46in) wide, *NY 24 June,*
$4,950 (£3,173)

6
A Louis XV/XVI Transitional kingwood commode, c.1765, stamped *Pierre Roussel,* of *arc-en-arballette* form, with moulded brown and white marble top, the sides and drawers inlaid with geometric stringing, 110cm (43in) wide, *L 23 May,*
£5,060 ($7,995)

7
A Louis XV provincial oak buffet, mid 18th century, with mottled red serpentine-front marble top, 135cm (53in) wide, *NY 24 June,*
$4,950 (£3,173)

8
A French provincial elm side cabinet, with brass mounts, the top possibly replaced, 122cm (48in) wide, *L 12 May,*
£572 ($921)

9
A Louis XV kingwood and fruitwood petit commode, mid 18th century, signed *L. Boudin,* with serpentine-fronted liver mottled marble top and ormolu mounts, 82cm (32½in) high, *NY 22 Mar,*
$4,950 (£3,278)

10
A Louis XV/XVI tulipwood marquetry commode, third quarter 18th century, with moulded *breche d'Alep* marble top and ormolu mounts, 73cm (29in) high, *NY 3 May,*
$10,450 (£6,875)

11
A Louis XV provincial oak buffet, third quarter 18th century, with floral carved panel-inset doors, 128cm (50½in) wide, *NY 10 June,*
$2,970 (£1,892)

12
A Louis XV/XVI kingwood parquetry commode, third quarter 18th century, with a grey *Ste. Anne* marble top and ormolu mounts, 131cm (51¾in) wide, *NY 3 May,*
$6,875 (£4,523)

1
A French provincial inlaid small cherrywood commode, 18th century, 79cm (31in), *M 30 Nov,*
FF 8,800 (£956; $1,368)

2
A Régence rosewood marquetry commode, c.1740, stamped *Hedouin,* with bronze mounts, the top of red Languedoc marble, 77cm (30in) wide, *M 30 Nov,*
FF 52,800 (£5,739; $8,207)

3
A small Louis XV violetwood marquetry commode, stamped *Migeon,* with bronze mounts, 95cm (37in) wide, *M 23 Feb,*
FF 88,800 (£8,588; $12,882)

4
A Louis XV kingwood and marquetry commode, c.1740, with 19th century mounts, 132cm (52in) wide, *L 20 June,*
£4,620 ($7,300)

5
A Louis XV ormolu-mounted kingwood parquetry commode, mid 18th century, signed *Garnier, JME,* 130cm (51in) wide, *NY 3 May,*
$27,500 (£18,092)

6
A Louis XV provincial walnut commode, mid 18th century, with gilt-brass mounts, 131cm (51in) wide, *M 1 Dec,*
FF 49,500 (£5,346; $7,644)

7
A Louis XV kingwood and tulipwood parquetry commode, mid 18th century, with a *brocatelle d'Espagne* marble top of serpentine outline, ormolu mounts, 135cm (53in) wide, *NY 22 Mar,*
$7,700 (£5,099)

8
A Louis XV kingwood commode, c.1745, the grey and *rouge Royale* marble top of serpentine outline, gilt-bronze mounts, 130cm (51in) wide, *L 12 Dec,*
£12,100 ($16,940)

9
A Louis XV/XVI kingwood commode, signed *N. Petit JME,* with brown and white marble top of breakfront outline, ormolu mounts, 98cm (38½in) wide, *NY 4 Oct,*
$5,225 (£3,628)

10
A Louis XV kingwood and rosewood small commode, c.1750, with russet marble top of serpentine outline, gilt-bronze mounts, 82cm (32in) wide, *L 12 Dec,*
£5,500 ($7,700)

11
A Louis XV/XVI tulipwood and kingwood parquetry commode, third quarter 18th century, the *breche d'Alep* marble top of breakfront outline, ormolu mounts, 93cm (37in) wide, *NY 24 June,*
$3,300 (£2,115)

12
A Louis XV/XVI Transitional small rosewood-veneered commode, stamped *C. Krier,* with marble top and gilt-bronze mounts, 63cm (24in), *M 1 Dec,*
FF 22,000 (£2,376; $3,397)

1

2

3

4

5

6

7

8

9

10

11

12

1

2

3

4

5

6

7

8

9

10

11

12

13

1
A Louis XVI mahogany meuble à portes, late 18th century, stamped *J.F. Leleu*, with copper handles, 67cm (26in) wide, *M 23 Feb,*
FF 46,620 (£4,509; $6,763)

2
A Louis XVI mahogany-veneered cabinet de curiosités, 81cm (31½in) wide, *M 23 Feb,*
FF 72,150 (£6,978; $10,467)

3
A Louis XVI satinwood-veneered commode à vantaux, c.1765, stamped *RVLC* and the mark of Jurande, with a large drawer containing a leather-covered writing flap, with red and grey marble top and gilt-bronze and copper mounts, *M 22 June,*
FF 610,500 (£54,460; $84,958)

4
A Louis XV/XVI ormolu-mounted mahogany and fruitwood parquetry commode, third quarter 18th century, signed *Schlichtig, JME,* with *breche d'Alep* marble top of breakfront outline, 130cm (51in) wide, *NY 4 Oct,*
$14,300 (£9,930)

5
A Louis XVI ormolu-mounted mahogany demi-lune commode, last quarter 18th century, signed *Vassou,* with white marble top, 127cm (50in) wide, *NY 4 Oct,*
$9,350 (£6,493)

6
A Louis XVI fruitwood and walnut parquetry commode, last quarter 18th century, with grey and white marble top, 99cm (39in) wide, *NY 24 June,*
$3,080 (£1,974)

7
An early Louis XVI kingwood commode, c.1780, the grey marble top of breakfront outline, inlaid with geometric stringing, 130cm (51in) wide, *L 28 Nov,*
£1,870 ($2,618)

8
A Louis XVI ormolu-mounted kingwood and fruitwood marquetry commode, *(illustrated),* last quarter 18th century, with a grey and beige mottled marble top, inlaid with a panel of musical instruments; sold with a later copy, 127cm (50in) wide, *NY 22 Mar,*
$8,800 (£5,828)

9
A Louis XVI brass-mounted mahogany commode, last quarter 18th century, with a grey and white mottled marble top, 128cm (50½in) wide, *NY 17 Dec,*
$3,575 (£2,553)

10
A Restauration mahogany-veneered semainier, c.1825, with grey marble top and gilt-bronze mounts, 154cm (60½in) high, *M 23 June,*
FF 12,210 (£1,089; $1,699)

11
A Directoire mahogany miniature commode, late 18th century, with white marble top, 30cm (11½in) wide, *M 24 Feb,*
FF 8,880 (£859; $1,288)

12
An Empire mahogany small chest, early 19th century, with mottled grey marble top of inverted breakfront form, gilt-bronze mounts, 84cm (33in) wide, *L 30 May,*
£1,485 ($2,346)

13
An Empire mahogany chest, c.1810, with marble top and gilt-metal mounts, 84cm (33in) wide, *L 30 May,*
£660 ($1,043)

1
An Empire ormolu-mounted mahogany commode, c.1800, with St. Anne marble top above a frieze drawer with ormolu mounts depicting Spring, 127cm (50in) wide, *NY 24 June,*
$5,775 (£3,702)

2
An Empire ormolu-mounted fruitwood commode, early 19th century, 131cm (51½in) wide, *NY 22 Mar,*
$4,400 (£2,914)

3
An Empire ormolu-mounted mahogany commode, early 19th century, the brown speckled marble top over three drawers flanked by pilasters headed by Egyptian masks, the sides with ormolu lions' masks, 128cm (50½in) wide, *NY 22 Mar,*
$4,400 (£2,914)

4
A silver chest, by Paul Sormani, c.1860, inlaid in amboyna, ebony and various exotic woods, gilt-bronze mounts, 78cm (30½in) wide, *M 24 Feb,*
FF 21,090 (£2,040; $3,059)

5
A Napoleon III kingwood and porcelain mounted small commode, c.1865, with *breche violette* marble top, the sides with oval portrait medallions, gilt-bronze mounts, 87cm (35in) high, *L 13 June,*
£825 ($1,320)

6
A Louis XV/XVI Transitional-style commode, late 19th century, the top painted to resemble marble, the drawers and sides with a parquetry trellis pattern, gilt-bronze mounts, 106cm (42in) wide, *L 21 Mar,*
£1,265 ($1,973)

7
A Louis XV-style marquetry commode, c.1880, in the manner of Riesener, with shaped Carrara marble top, decorated with gilt-metal mouldings, 173cm (68in) wide, *L 13 June,*
£5,500 ($8,802)

8
A Louis XV-style gilt-bronze-mounted parquetry and marquetry tulipwood and mahogany small commode, c.1880, G. Durand, Paris, 85cm (33½in) high, *NY 13 Sept,*
$4,675 (£3,180)

9
A Louis XV/XVI Transitional-style kingwood commode, late 19th century, with ormolu mounts, 117cm (46in) wide, *L 13 June,*
£2,035 ($3,256)

10
A Louis XV-style kingwood-veneered commode, c.1900, of serpentine form, with grey and white marble top and gilt-metal mounts, 123cm (48in) wide, *L 7 Nov,*
£1,595 ($2,233)

11
A Louis XV-style kingwood commode, c.1900, with *fleur de peche* marble top and gilt-metal mounts, 117cm (46in) wide, *L 7 Nov,*
£3,190 ($4,466)

12
A Louis XVI-style tulipwood and mahogany commode, early 20th century, by Paul Sormani, with a marble top and gilt-bronze mounts, 145cm (57in) wide, *NY 26 Apr,*
$3,300 (£2,143)

1

2

3

4

5

6

7

8

9

10

11

12

1

2

3

4

5

6

7

8

9

10

11

12

13

1
A North Italian inlaid chest-of-drawers, Lombardy, c.1700, the drawers decorated with panels of playing figures, birds and masks, ebonised sides and top, 101cm (39½in) wide, *F 30 Sept,*
L 9,350,000 (£4,659; $6,522)

2
A North Italian walnut chest-of-drawers, late 17th century, inlaid in ivory, 138cm (53¼in) wide, *F 30 Sept,*
L 5,500,000 (£2,740; $3,837)

3
A North Italian walnut-veneered parquetry commode, c.1740, 144cm (57in) wide, *L 23 May,*
£9,900 ($15,642)

4
A South German pewter-inlaid walnut commode, c.1750, 130cm (51in) wide, *L 12 Dec,*
£8,800 ($12,320)

5
A South German fruit-wood inlaid walnut chest-of-drawers, mid 18th century, 81.5cm (32in) high, *NY 25 Nov,*
$3,850 (£2,750)

6
A Dutch inlaid walnut commode, 18th century, 117cm (46in) wide, *A 14 Mar,*
Dfl 14,375 (£4,356; $6,708)

7
A pair of Swedish serpentine-fronted parquetry side cabinets *(one illustrated)* mid 18th century, 84cm (33in) high, *L 23 May,*
£6,600 ($10,428)

8
A Venetian walnut serpentine-fronted commode, mid 18th century, 79cm (31in) high, *F 14 Apr,*
L4,200,000 (£1,720; $2,666)

9
A pair of Italian walnut cabinets, *(one illustrated),* c.1750, 74cm (29in) high, *S 11 Nov,*
£2,640 ($3,696)

10
An Italian brass-mounted walnut and kingwood chest-of-drawers, mid 18th century, with grey and white marbled top, 140cm (55in) wide, *NY 4 Oct,*
$5,775 (£4,010)

11
An Italian kingwood bombé commode, c.1770, with green marble top, 147cm (58in) wide, *S 15 July,*
£2,750 ($4,318)

12
An Italian walnut commode, c.1760, the top inlaid with panels of burr elm, 147cm (57¾in) wide, *HS 24 Sept,*
IR£5,500 (£5,000; $7,250)

13
A Dutch mahogany bombé commode, c.1780, 86cm (34in) wide, *S 18 Feb,*
£2,420 ($3,678)

1
A Dutch walnut chest, c.1770, 91cm (36in) wide, *L 30 May,*
£1,265 ($1,999)

2
A Venetian painted and parcel-gilt commode, mid 18th century, with later top, 145cm (57in) wide, *L 12 Dec,*
£44,000 ($61,600)

3
A South German walnut parquetry bombé chest-of-drawers, mid 18th century, with liver and grey mottled marble top, ormolu mounts, 146cm (57½in) wide, *NY 22 Mar,*
$6,050 (£4,007)

4
A pair of marquetry commodes, *(one illustrated),* c.1760, possibly Neuwied, with *breche d'Alep* marble tops, 93cm (36½in) wide, *L 23 May,*
£22,000 ($34,760)

5
A pair of North Italian walnut, fruitwood, marquetry and parcel-gilt small commodes *(one illustrated),* last quarter 18th century, with ochre mottled marble tops, ormolu mounts, 85cm (33¾in) high, *NY 22 Mar,*
$4,950 (£3,278)

6
A Dutch mahogany buffet, c.1790, with pewter well and basin, 98.5cm (38½in) high, *A 6 May,*
Dfl 3,680 (£1,115; $1,773)

7
An Italian inlaid chest-of-drawers, Tuscany, c.1780, with marble top, 126cm (49½in) wide, *F 30 Sept,*
L 3,740,000 (£1,863; $2,609)

8
A pair of Russian mahogany and brass-inlaid demi-lune commodes *(one illustrated),* c.1795, 88cm (34½in) wide, *L 23 May,*
£30,800 ($48,664)

9
A Dutch marquetry and mahogany cabinet, c.1810, 92cm (36in) wide, *S 22 Apr,*
£990 ($1,554)

10
A Dutch marquetry and mahogany chest, c.1810, 99cm (39in) wide, *S 18 Mar,*
£1,100 ($1,683)

11
A Biedermeier fruitwood and birch small chest-of-drawers, first quarter 19th century, 82cm (32½in) high, *NY 4 Oct,*
$2,090 (£1,451)

12
A pair of German small bombé marquetry commodes, *(one illustrated),* late 19th century, each with pink marble top, 107cm (42in) wide, *L 13 June,*
£3,520 ($5,632)

1

2

3

4

5

6

7

8

9

10

11

12

1

2

3

4

5

6

7

8

1
A Venetian bronze-mounted walnut parquetry chest-of-drawers, mid 18th century, 124cm (49in) wide, *NY 25 Nov,* **$5,775 (£4,125)**

2
A Venetian bronze-mounted walnut parquetry chest-of-drawers, mid 18th century, 126cm (49½in) wide, *NY 25 Nov,* **$11,000 (£7,857)**

3
A Lombard marquetry commode, c.1790, the top banded in tulipwood, 119cm (47in) wide, *L 23 May,* **£5,280 ($8,342)**

4
An Italian brass-mounted fruitwood and walnut parquetry chest-of-drawers, late 18th century, 124.5cm (49in) wide, *NY 4 Oct,* **$5,775 (£4,010)**

5
A North Italian parcel-gilt, walnut and fruitwood marquetry commode, late 18th century, attributed to Giuseppe Maggiolini, with *bleu turquin* marble top, 122cm (48¼in) wide, *NY 22 Mar,* **$31,900 (£21,126)**

6
A pair of Italian painted chests-of-drawers, *(one illustrated),* late 18th century, the tops painted to simulate marble, 95cm (37½in) high, *NY 22 Mar,* **$12,100 (£8,013)**

7
A pair of Italian walnut and fruitwood marquetry chests-of-drawers, *(one illustrated),* late 18th century, in the manner of Maggiolini, ormolu mounts, 128cm (50½in) wide, *NY 22 Mar,* **$7,700 (£5,099)**

8
A Biedermeier bronze-mounted part-ebonised fruitwood chest-of-drawers, second quarter 19th century, 127cm (50in) wide, *NY 24 June,* **$2,090 (£1,340)**

1
A George III oak dresser, c.1775, with projecting lower section, 206cm (6ft 9½in) high, *NY 7 June,*
$4,400 (£2,953)

2
A George III pine plate rack, c.1800, 170cm (67in) long, *C 29 May,*
£330 ($521)

3
An oak breakfront dresser, c.1800, 214cm (7ft) wide, *C 9 July,*
£1,815 ($2,992)

4
An oak dresser, mid 18th century, the lower part with five drawers above an arcade and pot board, 208cm (6ft 10in) high, *C 9 July,*
£1,760 ($2,834)

5
An oak and elm dresser, c.1750, the upper part with an initialled frieze above three plate rails, 201cm (6ft 7in) high, *C 17 Apr,*
£4,180 ($6,479)

6
A George III oak dresser, 175cm (69in) wide, *C 14 May,*
£968 ($1,558)

7
A pine dresser, c.1830, with a shaped gallery above an arrangement of seven drawers, on turned feet, 216cm (6ft 8in), *C 5 Nov,*
£418 ($589)

8
An oak dresser base, mid 18th century, joined by a pot board, restorations, 196cm (6ft 5in) wide, *C 17 Apr,*
£1,540 ($2,387)

9
A George III oak dresser, c.1760, the upper part with an overhanging cornice above a shaped apron with central panelled cupboard and drawer, restorations, *C 17 Apr,*
£6,160 ($9,548)

1

2

3

4

5

6

7

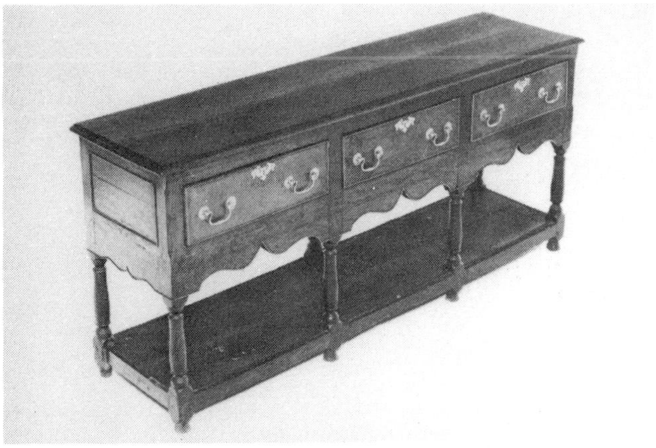
8

9

English Early Oak Furniture

VICTOR CHINNERY

In years past it was always true to say that different periods and styles of furnishings came and went in long cycles of popularity. This was certainly true of early oak furniture, which had been very popular during parts of the 19th century and between the two World Wars, but which was decidedly unfashionable in Edwardian times and in the years after the last war.

In times of approval oak was seen romantically to embody the true spirit of Olde England, and to represent all those qualities of sturdiness and steadfast dependability which the English have always perceived as the most admirable facets of their national character. In the collective imagination, the oak tree stood alongside the lion of the jungle and the eagle of the air, as ruler of its own domain. In a less popular phase, oak furniture was seen merely as rather dark and depressing; a heavy and clumsy drag on the ambience of an otherwise happy home. Fortunately, such emotional responses are now largely a thing of the past.

Thanks to modern research, and a more enlightened and positive view of our heritage generally, we are able to look objectively at early oak furniture as the product of specific technological and historical circumstances. We are able to understand more clearly how and why certain things were produced, the influences which shaped their form and decoration, and thus to enjoy each piece on its merits. Much of the pleasure (and all of the challenge) of early furniture lies in the uniqueness of each item. Every piece represents a new problem of identification and assessment, where considerations of quality and

1

2

3

4

1
A late Elizabethan court cupboard, c.1600, bottom shelf restored, 107cm (42in), *L 10 Oct,*
£7,150 ($10,010)

2
A Charles I oak centre standing chest-of-drawers, c.1640, with panelled sides and back, 122cm (48in) wide, *L 10 Oct,*
£8,800 ($12,320)

authenticity are paramount.

The old cycles of rejection and demand are almost extinct now, largely because of an increased appreciation of the subject and a very marked decrease in the supply of good quality items onto the market. There is fierce competition for fine pieces, though the field is still remarkably under-valued in comparison with some areas of collecting interest. It is still possible to buy some of the best and rarest pieces in existence for under £30,000 ($48,000), whilst the majority of collectable items upwards of three hundred years old are available at prices from £1,000 to £10,000 ($1,600 to $16,000).

The market will always pay the best prices for the rarest items, especially when these are of good design and in fine original condition, preferably with a complete lack of alteration or restoration; this was true of fig.2. The court cupboard in fig.1, however, had lost its bottom shelf, which had later been replaced. Such differences of quality can lead to enormous discrepancies in price, even in pairs of superficially similar items. A number of these have been assembled to illustrate the point (figs 3-8).

The first of these (fig.3) is an early 16th century chest in almost totally original condition, retaining the full height to its feet as well as the original spandrels to the front. The condition is remarkably untouched, with extensive traces of old red paint and with deeply-carved decoration. This carving is far better than that on fig.4, the patina is well-matured and there is an interesting provenance. Fig.4 is lacking in all these desirable qualities, resulting in a sale figure of only £275 ($432), against the £6,160 ($9,856) achieved by the better chest.

Fig.6 is a conventional late 17th century chest-of-drawers, similar to many of its kind, with geometrical mitred mouldings to the drawer-fronts and of a rather uninspired format. Fig.5, on the other hand, is quite unusual in having a restrained carving of tulips set into the drawers, deeper cushioned mouldings which add life to the articulated architectural character of the facade, and with the additional benefit of the original wrought iron handles. Fig.5 brought £3,850 ($6,237), whilst fig.6 only £825 ($1,337).

The stools in figs 7 & 8 are both of conventional type, but here the condition and character of fig.7 has given it a convincing lead over the other. The carving of the frieze is an important element, but more important are the fine, glossy patina and the original and unrestored condition. Though retaining its original turned

3
A Henry VIII boarded oak coffer, c.1540, with traces of old red paint, 111cm (43½in), *S 20 May,*
£6,160 ($9,856)

4
An oak boarded chest, early 17th century, 92cm (36in) long, *L 22 July,*
£275 ($432)

5
An oak chest-of-drawers, c.1680, the drawers with pierced fretwork panels of stylised tulips, 92cm (36in) wide, *L 4 July,*
£3,850 ($6,237)

6
An oak chest-of-drawers, late 17th century, on bun feet, 94cm (37in) wide, *L 4 July,*
£825 ($1,337)

7
A Charles I oak joint stool, c.1640, 53cm (21in) high, *L 10 Oct,*
£1,980 ($2,772)

8
An oak joint stool, partly 17th century, with replaced top, *C 24 July,*
£165 ($259)

9
An oak joint stool, late 17th century, 55.5cm (22in), *C 24 July,*
£220 ($345)

10
A harlequin set of eight Derbyshire oak chairs, including a pair dated 1660, *L 10 Oct,*
£6,050 ($8,470)

11
A pair of oak side chairs, c.1700, *L 10 Oct,*
£858 ($1,201)

5

6

7

8

9

10

11

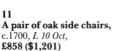

12

13

14

15

16

12
A dining table, second quarter 17th century, with three-plank cleated top, 355cm (11ft 7½in), *S 20 May,*
£7,700 ($12,320)

13
A Charles II gateleg table, c.1660, the frieze fitted with a single drawer, 122cm (48in) wide, *L 10 Oct,*
£2,090 ($2,926)

14
A Dorset coffer, dated 1653, with traces of original painted decoration, 98cm (38½in), *L 10 Oct,*
£990 ($1,386)

15
A 17th century chest, 66cm (26in) wide, *L 10 Oct,*
£1,760 ($2,464)

16
A William and Mary dresser, c.1700, 191cm (6ft 3in) high, *S 20 May,*
£5,060 ($8,096)

17

17
A George III dresser, c.1760, 205cm (7ft 9in), *L 2 May,*
£1,760 ($2,798)

feet, fig.8 has a replaced top, the frieze is plain and the colour is distinctly lack-lustre. A good natural surface is an important asset to the value of oak furniture in the market.

The remaining illustrations have been singled out to demonstrate the broad range of pieces which make up the bulk of the market in collectable oak furniture, and especially those practical items which are always in demand for furnishing period homes and for daily use. Serious collectors (who, incidentally, are surprisingly few in number), will always seek out the most unusual, and often the most impractical pieces; but the majority of buyers are looking for strong and serviceable chairs, tables, chests and dressers for everyday use. These pieces are highly appropriate in period houses and even for more modern settings, where they command an interest and vitality all their own. Carefully selected, early oak furniture will provide a lifetime of service and has over the last ten to fifteen years proved a very valuable and productive form of investment.

17th century oak furniture is not always versatile and practical enough to provide all the necessary comfort and convenience for modern life, especially in the areas of soft seating and display, and so it is particularly appropriate to supplement the earlier chests and tables with the later dressers and bureaux, which add greater flexibility to schemes of furnishing. These 18th century forms (figs 17-20 & 27-31), were made in country districts, but using the same materials and techniques as their predecessors, so that they will blend together without dissent for modern usage.

For those seeking a cheaper alternative, a large variety of Victorian copies are still available, more or less loosely based on Elizabethan and Jacobean models. The table in fig.21 is a case in point. This 19th century adaptation of earlier design elements is, in fact, completely spurious in every aspect. The design is quite impossible for an Elizabethan original, since trestle-base draw-leaf tables were never made until the 19th century, and this concoction is purely a product of Victorian imagination. Nevertheless, at £880 ($1,320) it represents extremely good value, and there are very good reasons for preserving and collecting such monuments to the antiquarian tastes inspired by early Romantic collectors such as Horace Walpole and Sir Walter Scott.

With the increasing scarcity of good furniture on the everyday market, it is only natural that the dispersal of a good collection should be the occasion of great excitement, both for the sense of occasion and the chance to acquire something of real interest.

18

19

18
A George II oak and pine dresser, c.1750, 180cm (71in) high, *S 18 Mar,*
£1,760 ($2,693)

19
A Charles II small centre table, c.1680, 66cm (26in) high, *L 10 Oct,*
£1,980 ($2,772)

1986 was unusual in seeing the dispersal of two major private collections of oak furniture, both assembled over many years and with rare discrimination. Up until the 1970s the collector of the old school was able to indulge his tastes fairly freely, and both collections represented an age of more ample expectations.

Tom Burn was only comfortably well off when he started to fill his house at Rous Lench Court in 1928, but in 1946 his father died leaving him a fortune of £90,000 ($362,700) and a thriving chain of tailoring shops. From this time on he spent most of his energy and money on a ceaseless quest for the finest pottery, porcelain, clocks and furniture he could find. Tom Burn died in 1985 at the age of 77, after a life of devotion to his acquisitions and of kindness to all those visitors who beat a path to the door of his fascinating home. The collection was sold in London in July 1986 and pieces from it appear throughout this edition of the Guide.

The second collection, sold in October 1986, came from Cold Overton Manor in the old county of Rutland, and was dispersed with less sadness than was the case with Rous Lench. The owner, Ken Binns, is still very much alive. After many pleasant years of collecting oak furniture, he decided to sell part of his collection because the house was bursting at the seams. Whereas Rous Lench had seen a broad range of furniture, clocks, sculpture and ceramics, dating from the Middle Ages into the 18th century, Cold Overton presented a more closely defined interest in post-mediaeval English oak furniture, almost entirely confined to the period from 1540 to 1700.

These two sales did much to stir up interest in oak furniture. For me, the great note of optimism is that all those pieces have been returned to circulation, so that many others may enjoy them in their turn.

Further reading:

Victor Chinnery, *Oak Furniture - The British Tradition*, 1979
Eric Mercer, *Furniture 700-1700*, 1969
Percy Macquoid & Ralph Edwards, *Dictionary of English Furniture*, 3 vols, 1924-27, revised 1954, re-published 1983 & 1986

20

21

22

23

24

20
A George I bureau, c.1720, the fall revealing a stepped and fitted interior, 98cm (38½in), *S 20 May,* **£902 ($1,443)**

21
An Elizabethan-style draw-leaf dining table, 363cm (11ft 9in), *S 11 Mar,* **£880 ($1,320)**

25

26

22
An oak panel back armchair, c.1680, Yorkshire Dales, *L 4 July,*
£1,078 ($1,746)

23
A pair of Charles II oak side chairs, *(one illustrated),* Lancashire, c.1680, *L 10 Oct,*
£1,100 ($1,540)

24
A late 17th century press, the cornice initialled RW and MW and dated 1694, 168cm (66in), *L 10 Oct,*
£1,705 ($2,387)

25
A panel back armchair, c.1680, South Lancashire/ Cheshire, stretchers replaced, *L 4 July,*
£726 ($1,176)

26
A William and Mary side table, c.1690, 67cm (26½in), *C 16 Jan,*
£2,035 ($3,053)

27
A Queen Anne oval gateleg table, c.1710, 102cm (40in) open, *L 14 July,*
£352 ($549)

28
A George I gateleg table, c.1720, on eight ring-turned supports, 175cm (69in) extended, *C 9 July,*
£1,848 ($2,975)

28

29

27

29
A Queen Anne side table, c.1710, 86cm (34in), *S 18 Mar,*
£638 ($976)

30
A cupboard on stand, c.1740, 183cm (54½in), *L 4 July,*
£2,090 ($3,386)

30

31

31
A George II low dresser, Yorkshire, now raised on ball feet, 140cm (55in), *L 10 Oct,*
£1,210 ($1,694)

1

2

3

4

5

6

7

8

9

1
A Regency mahogany octagonal library table, c.1810, with green leather-lined top and alternating real and dummy drawers, 111cm (43½in) wide, *L 28 Feb,*
£3,960 ($6,138)

2
A Regency mahogany drum table, c.1820, with alternate real and dummy drawers, 136cm (53½in) wide, *L 11 July,*
£3,080 ($4,897)

3
A George IV parcel-gilt and rosewood library drum table, c.1825, with gilt tooled leather inset top, 147cm (58in), *NY 10 June,*
$11,000 (£7,006)

4
A Victorian mahogany circular dining table, c.1880, in the manner of Jupe, with segmented top, extending to 208cm (6ft 10in), *L 14 Nov,*
£10,560 ($15,101)

5
A George IV Regency mahogany three-pedestal dining table, c.1825, 475cm (15ft) extended, *NY 10 June,*
$17,700 (£11,274)

6
A George IV circular extending dining table, c.1830, with four clip-on leaves, 210cm (6ft 11in) extended, *L 25 Apr,*
£7,480 ($11,968)

7
A walnut rectangular extending dining table, early 20th century, 241cm (7ft 9in), *S 14 Jan,*
£780 ($1,170)

8
An early Victorian extending dining table, c.1840, 561cm (18ft 5in), *C 16 Jan,*
£2,420 ($3,630)

9
A George IV mahogany D-end dining table, c.1820, 330cm (10ft 5in), *C 17 Apr,*
£2,420 ($3,751)

1
A William IV rosewood drum-top table, c.1830, with alternate real and dummy drawers, 110cm (43½in) diam., *S 17 June*, **£935 ($1,477)**

2
A George III mahogany three-pedestal dining table, c.1790, with two extra leaves, 264cm (8ft 8in), *NY 13 Dec*, **$48,400 (£34,571)**

3
A George IV mahogany dining table, c.1825, 183cm (72in) long, *C 16 Jan*, **£1,815 ($2,723)**

4
A George III mahogany D-end dining table, c.1790, with gateleg action, 238cm (7ft 9in), *S 9 Dec*, **£1,430 ($2,002)**

5
A William IV mahogany extending dining table, c.1830, extending to accept three extra leaves, 283cm (9ft 3in) fully extended, *L 18 July*, **£1,375 ($2,186)**

6
A late George III three-pedestal mahogany dining table, c.1810, 230cm (7ft 6in), *NY 7 June*, **$11,000 (£7,382)**

7
A Jupes patent mahogany capstan table, c.1830, the circular top with eight segments stamped *Jupes Patent*, 174cm (68in) diam., *L 28 Feb*, **£16,500 ($25,575)**

8
A George III mahogany extending campaign dining table, including four leaves, 277cm (9ft), *C 8 Oct*, **£5,720 ($8,008)**

See also:
Dining room furnishings *pp* 101-102

1

2

3

4

5

6

7

8

1

2

3

4

5

6

7

8

9

10

1
A William IV mahogany pedestal table, c.1835, with beaded mouldings, 130cm (51in), *S 18 Mar,*
£748 ($1,144)

2
A Victorian ebonised and amboyna octagonal table, c.1880, 98cm (38½in) wide, *L 12 May,*
£418 ($673)

3
A circular mahogany dining table, modern, by William Tillman, 160cm (63in), *L 3 Mar,*
£2,090 ($3,135)

4
An early Victorian mahogany breakfast table, c.1850, 78.5cm (31in) high, *C 1 May,*
£268 ($463)

5
A George III mahogany oval breakfast table, c.1800, the top with a wide satinwood banding, 178cm (70in), *L 11 July,*
£11,550 ($18,365)

6
A George III mahogany oval breakfast table, c.1800, the top with reeded edge, 180.5cm (71in), *L 14 Nov,*
£6,050 ($8,652)

7
A Victorian marquetry breakfast table, c.1850, the circular hinged top inlaid with reserves of summer flowers and insects, 148cm (58in), *L 7 Nov,*
£3,190 ($4,466)

8
A Victorian rosewood pedestal table, 137cm (54in), *S 7 Oct,*
£935 ($1,309)

9
A George IV brass-mounted rosewood centre table, c.1825, with brass inlaid top, 129.5cm (51in), *NY 10 June,*
$7,700 (£4,904)

10
A George III mahogany breakfast table, c.1790, 84cm (33in), *C 17 Apr,*
£902 ($1,398)

1
A George III mahogany tripod table, c.1770, the dished top tilting above a fluted turned standard, 70cm (27½in) high, *NY 7 June,*
$3,575 (£2,399)

2
A pair of walnut and satinwood tripod tables, *(one illustrated),* c.1920, in Regency style, the cross-banded tops with a moulded border and inlaid with cube parquetry, 74cm (29in) high, *L 18 July,*
£2,035 ($3,236)

3
A Regency brass-mounted and parcel-gilt mahogany centre table, early 19th century, the associated square top inlaid with foliage, raised on winged paw feet, 72cm (28½in), *NY 13 Dec,*
$4,400 (£3,143)

4
A George II mahogany tripod table, mid 18th century, with slightly-dished serpentine top, 71cm (28in) high, *NY 25 Jan,*
$7,150 (£5,144)

5
A George II mahogany tilt-top tripod table, mid 18th century, the circular top with a baluster gallery, 74cm (29in) high, *NY 25 Jan,*
$9,350 (£6,727)

6
A William IV rosewood and satinwood tripod stand, c.1835, raised on bun feet, 75cm (29½in) high, *NY 14 Oct,*
$1,100 (£764)

7
A nest of Edwardian satinwood quartetto tables, c.1910, the tops inlaid with a diamond trellis, largest 51cm (20in) wide, *L 2 May,*
£1,485 ($2,361)

8
A nest of Victorian inlaid padouk tables, c.1830, largest 46cm (18¼in) wide, *NY 13 Dec,*
$4,950 (£3,536)

9
A set of three William IV rosewood quartetto tables, c.1830, largest 49cm (19½in) wide, *L 14 Mar,*
£1,430 ($2,216)

10
A George III inlaid satinwood marquetry demi-lune console table, c.1770, the crossbanded top inlaid with a band of vines, the rim with geometric banding above a moulded frieze, 125cm (49in) wide, *NY 7 June,*
$5,500 (£3,691)

11
A quartetto of mahogany George III-style tables, c.1910, each with a cross-banded top veneered with an oval, on simulated bamboo supports, largest 65cm (25½in) high, *C 7 Aug,*
£572 ($887)

1

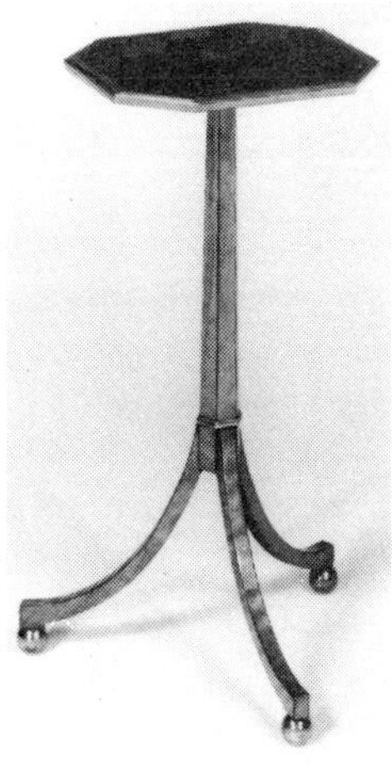
2

3

4

5

6

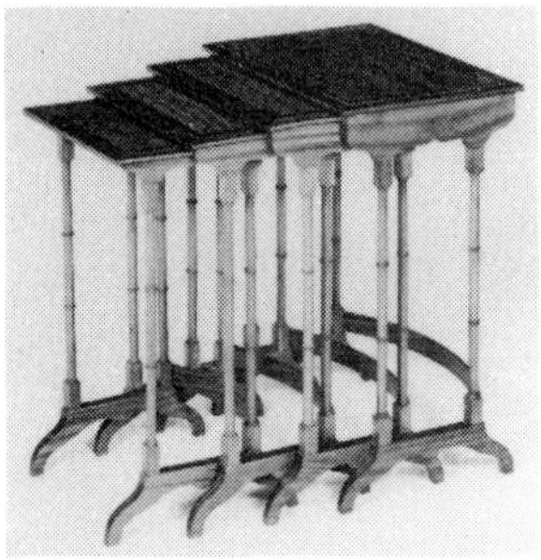
7

8

9

10

11

1

2

3

4

5

6

7

8

9

10

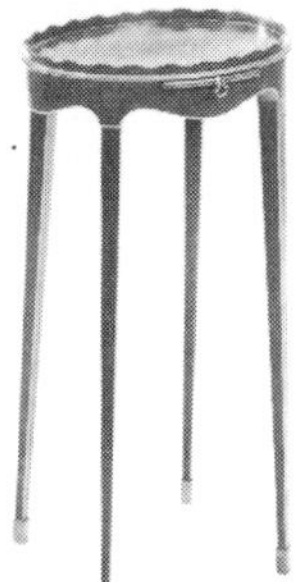

11

1
A Victorian parquetry and marquetry mahogany drop-leap table, c.1870, the top decorated in tulipwood parquetry centred by inlaid musical instruments, gilt-bronze mounts, 72.5cm (28½in) wide, *NY 26 Nov,*
$2,310 (£1,650)

2
A George II mahogany drop-leaf table, the oval top above a plain frieze, 127cm (50in) wide, *NY 10 June,*
$4,125 (£2,627)

3
A Victorian figured walnut oval Sutherland table, 68cm (26¾in) wide, *S 3 June,*
£462 ($716)

4
An ebonised walnut and marquetry centre table, c.1860, the top centred by a trophy within scrolling bands, the sides with flaps above a frieze drawer, gilt-metal mounts, *C 17 Apr,*
£638 ($989)

5
A George II mahogany 'spider-leg' gateleg table, c.1750, 75cm (29½in) wide, *L 24 Oct,*
£2,145 ($3,003)

6
A George III satinwood-veneered oval table, c.1775, in the French style, the top with four mahogany panels of crossbanding divided by paterae, the cabriole legs outlined with purpleheart, 70cm (27½in) high, *L 28 Feb,*
£3,960 ($6,138)

7
A George II mahogany oval drop-leaf table, c.1750, with a drawer, with square and fluted columnar legs, 163cm (64in) wide extended, *S 18 Feb,*
£7,480 ($11,370)

8
A George II mahogany oval drop-leaf table, c.1750, the arched apron above cabriole legs, 127cm (50in) extended, *S 15 July,*
£550 ($864)

9
A walnut gateleg table, late 17th century, the oval moulded and crossbanded top supported on turned baluster gateleg frame, 71cm (28in) high, *L 4 July,*
£2,860 ($4,633)

10
A William IV Derbyshire specimen marble centre table, c.1830, the top with a geometric veneer and conforming border on a black marble ground, on a black marble column, 92cm (36¼in) diam., *L 14 Nov,*
£5,060 ($7,236)

11
A George III mahogany oval urn table, c.1780, with satinwood strung borders, with a waved gallery and a slide, 69cm (27in) high, *S 17 June,*
£1,155 ($1,825)

1
A William IV rosewood card table, c.1835, with scarlet baize lining, 92cm (36in) wide, *S 11 Nov,*
£528 ($739)

2
A pair of Victorian walnut serpentine card tables (*one illustrated*), c.1860, 97cm (38in) wide, *S 15 July,*
£2,970 ($4,663)

3
A Victorian rosewood tea table, c.1850, 92cm (36in), *C 29 May,*
£550 ($869)

4
A Regency rosewood card table, c.1815, 91.5cm (36in) wide, *L 14 Mar,*
£1,870 ($2,898)

5
A pair of Regency brass-inlaid calamanderwood card tables, (*one illustrated*), c.1820, 92cm (36in) wide, *L 28 Feb,*
£3,300 ($5,115)

6
A Regency rosewood and crossbanded card table, c.1810, inlaid with stringing, 90cm (35½in) wide, *S 8 July,*
£418 ($677)

7
A George III inlaid crossbanded satinwood demi-lune games table, c.1790, 96.5cm (38in) wide, *NY 10 June,*
$1,650 (£1,051)

8
A pair of George III satinwood-inlaid mahogany demi-lune games tables, (*one illustrated*), last quarter 18th century, opening to a baize-lined interior, 92cm (36in), *NY 7 June,*
$8,250 (£5,536)

9
A George III mahogany games table, c.1775, 93cm (36½in) wide, *C 16 Jan,*
£660 ($990)

10
A George II mahogany tea table, c.1740, 91cm (36in) wide, *NY 13 Dec,*
$3,025 (£2,161)

11
A George II walnut tea table, c.1740, 72cm (28½in), *C 8 Oct,*
£1,265 ($1,771)

12
A pair of George III satinwood card tables (*one illustrated*), c.1790, 94cm (37in) wide, *L 25 Apr,*
£16,500 ($26,400)

13
A George III inlaid partridge wood games table, c.1790, 55cm (21¾in) wide, *NY 7 June,*
$3,575 (£2,399)

1

2

3

4

5

6

7

8

9

10

11

12

13

1

2

3

4

5

6

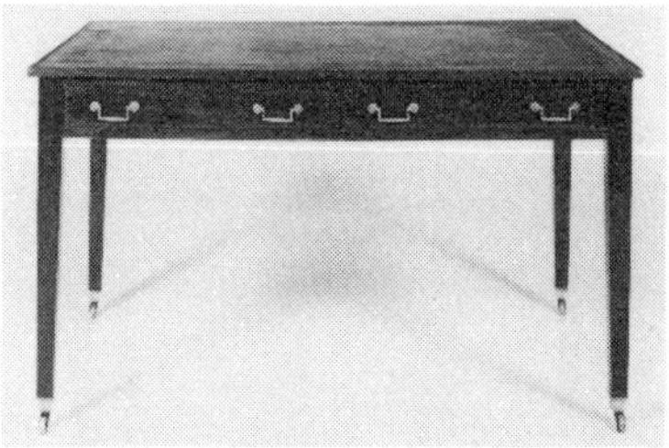
7

8

9

1
An Edwardian mahogany writing table, c.1900, the hinged top enclosing a mechanical fitted interior, 78.5cm (31in) high, *C 10 Sept,*
£528 ($792)

2
A William IV mahogany writing table, c.1830, with tooled leather inset top, 166cm (65½in) wide, *NY 10 June*
$7,700 (£4,904)

3
A William IV rosewood writing table, c.1830, *L 21 Nov,*
£2,090 ($2,926)

4
A George III mahogany writing desk or dressing table c.1780, the hinged crossbanded top enclosing a fitted interior with pigeon holes and drawers, 89cm (35in) wide, *C 17 Apr*
£440 ($682)

5
A Victorian maple library table, c.1870, 122cm (48in) wide, *C 30 Jan,*
£572 ($841)

6
A Regency mahogany writing table, c.1810, with tooled leather inset top, 139cm (54¾in) wide, *S 17 June,*
£9,900 ($15,642)

7
A George III mahogany partner's writing table, c.1800, with tooled leather inset top, 137cm (54in) wide, *NY 7 June,*
$8,800 (£5,906)

8
A Regency mahogany writing table, c.1810, 97cm (38in) wide, *L 11 July,*
£4,180 ($6,646)

9
A George III mahogany writing table, c.1815, attributed to Gillow of Lancaster, 90cm (35½in) wide, *L 11 July,*
£1,595 ($2,536)

See also:
English desks *pp* 13-15

1
A Regency calamander sewing table, c.1815, bearing a label *Manufactured by J. Flood, Cabinet, Chair, Sofa, and Dining Table Maker, No.11 Charles St. Middlesex Hospital, London,* 74cm (29in) high, *NY 7 June,*
$2,475 (£1,661)

2
A George III Irish satinwood oval work table, c.1800, inscribed *F.Davis, Nassau St., 1802,* 63cm (25in) wide, *S 11 Nov,*
£1,925 ($2,695)

3
A William IV rosewood combined work and card table, c.1830, the frieze with one real and one dummy drawer, 47cm (29in), *S 7 Oct,*
£495 ($693)

4
A George III mahogany architect's table, c.1770, 91.5cm (36in) wide, *S 18 Feb,*
£1,870 ($2,842)

5
A Louis XVI architect's table, c.1790, 84cm (33in) wide, *M 30 Nov,*
FF 104,500 (£11,359; $15,902)

6
A Victorian burr walnut combined games and work table, c.1860, inlaid with amboyna banding and boxwood ringing, the top revealing back-gammon, chess and cribbage playing surfaces, 70cm (27½in) wide, *S 11 Nov,*
£1,045 ($1,463)

7
A George IV rosewood combined writing and work table, c.1830, with leather-lined top, 74cm (29in) wide, *L 3 Feb,*
£1,155 ($1,686)

8
A Regency inlaid satinwood sofa table, c.1815, 140cm (55in) wide, *NY 7 June,*
$11,550 (£7,751)

9
An early Victorian mahogany architect's desk, c.1840, 91.5cm (36in) wide, *NY 14 Oct,*
$1,540 (£1,069)

10
A George III mahogany writing slope on stand, c.1780, with tooled leather-inset top, 61cm (24in) wide, *NY 18 Oct,*
$1,210 (£840)

11
A George III mahogany and rosewood cross-banded work table, c.1800, inlaid with satinwood stringing, with simulated drawers, 51cm (20in) wide, *S 17 June,*
£990 ($1,564)

12
A late George III inlaid mahogany sofa table, c.1810, 152.5cm (60in) wide, *NY 10 June,*
$5,225 (£3,328)

13
A Regency rosewood sofa table, c.1810, with brass inlaid top, 89cm (35in) wide, *L 21 Nov,*
£3,520 ($4,928)

14
A Regency rosewood sofa table, c.1815, 153cm (60in) wide, *L 14 Mar,*
£2,420 ($3,751)

1

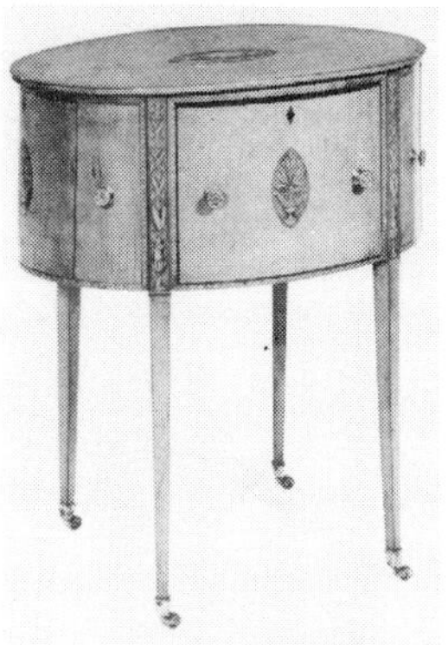
2

3

4

5

6

7

8

9

10

11

12

13

14

1

2

3

4

5

6

7

8

9

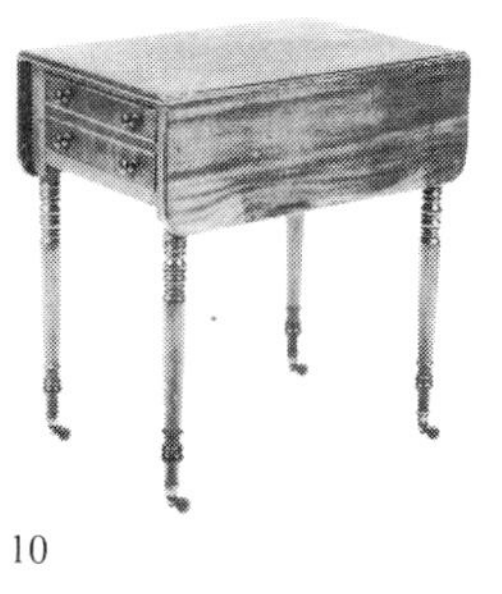
10

1
A George II walnut side table, c.1740, 113cm (44½in) wide, *C 24 Sept,*
£352 ($538)

2
A pair of George IV mahogany side tables, *(one illustrated),* c.1825, each of bowed breakfront form, 125 and 122cm (49¼ and 48in) wide, *L 28 Feb,*
£6,600 ($10,230)

3
A George III mahogany side table, c.1800, in the manner of Gillows, the top with rounded corners and reeded border, above three frieze drawers banded and edged in boxwood, 112cm (42in) wide, *L 14 Mar,*
£990 ($1,534)

4
A George III mahogany side table, c.1770, the serpentine front with a slide and two drawers, 94cm (37in) wide, *L 24 Oct,*
£1,705 ($2,387)

5
A William and Mary seaweed marquetry side table, c.1690, the moulded and crossbanded top inlaid with panels of marquetry foliage on a burr-walnut ground, 72.5cm (28½in) wide, *L 2 May,*
£1,375 ($2,186)

6
A George II mahogany side table, c.1730, the moulded top with inset corners above a single cockbeaded frieze drawer, 76cm (30in) wide, *NY 7 June,*
$3,025 (£2,030)

7
A George IV mahogany Pembroke table, with real and opposing dummy frieze drawers, 90cm (35½in) wide extended, *S 14 Jan,*
£380 ($570)

8
A George III mahogany Pembroke table, c.1780, the 'butterfly' top above a frieze drawer, 96.5cm (38in) wide, *C 25 June,*
£264 ($412)

9
A George III mahogany oval Pembroke table, with real and opposing dummy frieze drawers, 96cm (37¾in) wide extended, *S 13 May,*
£418 ($665)

10
A George III inlaid satinwood and mahogany oval Pembroke table, late 18th century, the crossbanded top above a convex frieze containing a drawer at one end, *NY 13 Dec,*
$7,425 (£5,303)

1
A George III provincial oak dressing table, late 18th century, decorated with crossbanding, 82.5cm (32½in) wide, *NY 14 Oct,*
$1,980 (£1,375)

2
A Queen Anne walnut side table, c.1710, with crossbanding and feather-banding, 76cm (30in) wide, *S 22 Apr,*
£1,155 ($1,813)

3
A Victorian mahogany wash stand, 112cm (44in) wide, *C 25 June,*
£176 ($265)

4
A George III mahogany dressing table, of bow-front outline, with satin-wood strung borders, 99cm (39in), *S 17 June,*
£990 ($1,564)

5
A George I walnut lowboy, c.1720, with moulded quarter-veneered crossbanded top, 79cm (31in) wide, *L 21 Nov,*
£3,520 ($4,928)

6
A George II mahogany dressing table, c.1750, with a later three-quarter gallery and central recessed cupboard, 77cm (30in) wide, *S 9 Dec,*
£1,320 ($1,848)

7
A George III inlaid mahogany gentleman's dressing stand, c.1780, of serpentine outline, the divided top opening to an interior fitted with an adjustable mirror flanked by compartments with ivory-handled covers, 86cm (34in) high, *NY 25 Jan,*
$2,860 (£2,057)

8
A George III mahogany Pembroke table, c.1780, the top with conforming drop leaves above an arrangement of three frieze drawers, 95cm (37¼in) wide, *NY 7 June,*
$4,000 (£2,684)

9
A George III mahogany oval Pembroke table, c.1790, with rosewood crossbanding and a bow-fronted frieze drawer, 86cm (34in) wide, *S 22 Apr,*
£990 ($1,554)

10
A late George II mahogany Pembroke table, c.1755, 93cm (36½in) wide, *L 18 July,*
£3,630 ($5,772)

See also:
Bedroom furnishings
pp 98-99

1

2

3

4

5

6

7

8

9

10

1

2

3

4

5

6

7

8

9

10

1
An Italian Renaissance walnut centre table, mid 16th century, probably Florence, 82.5cm (32½in) high, *NY 25 Nov,*
$12,100 (£8,643)

2
A Dutch rosewood and marquetry centre table, late 17th century, 71cm (28in) high, *L 30 May,*
£2,035 ($3,215)

3
An Italian walnut table, c.1600, Tuscan, with detachable top, 85cm (33¼in) high, *F 30 Sept,*
L 39,600,000 (£19,731; $27,623)

4
A Roman giltwood side table, c.1740, with verde antico marble top, 89cm (35in) high, *L 23 May,*
£2,200 ($3,476)

5
A Venetian walnut table, mid 18th century, the apron with rococo motifs, 82cm (32in) high, *F 30 Sept,*
L 13,200,000 (£6,577; $9,208

6
A Cape stinkwood and yellow-wood side table, 18th century, 70cm (27¼in) high, *Ct 27 Oct,*
R 1,980 (£619; $866)

7
A Cape Robben Island slate-topped side table, late 18th century, 70cm (27¼in) high, *JHB 27 Feb,*
R 1,650 (£516; $799)

8
An Italian marquetry table, late 18th century, with oval top, inlaid with light and exotic woods, 70cm (27¼in) high, *M 1 Dec,*
FF 19,800 (£2,138; $3,057)

9
An Italian giltwood console table, late 18th century, with peach mottled marble top, 91cm (35¾in) high, *NY 4 Oct,*
$6,875 (£4,774)

10
An Italian walnut and fruitwood marquetry games table, the inlaid top opening to an inlaid playing surface, 78cm (30½in) high, *NY 22 Mar,*
$3,850 (£2,550)

1
A North Italian marquetry walnut side table, c.1790, with internal compartment, 89cm (35½in) wide, *F 14 Apr,*
L 3,500,000 (£1,433; $2,222)

2
An Italian ormolu-mounted mahogany gueridon, early 19th century, with scagliola top, 81cm (32in) high, *NY 22 Mar,*
$1,430 (£947)

3
An Italian marquetry table, early 19th century, the top inlaid with a chessboard, the legs with marine monster supports, 75cm (29¼in) diam., *F 30 Sept,*
L 7,700,000 (£3,837; $5,371)

4
A pair of Baltic mahogany pier tables, *(one illustrated)*, c.1820, 86.5cm (34in) wide, *L 28 Nov,*
£2,860 ($4,004)

5
A German ormolu-mounted and ebonised mahogany centre table, second quarter 19th century, with giltwood base, 79cm (31in) high, *NY 17 Dec,*
$4,950 (£3,535)

6
A North Italian Empire walnut centre table, c.1815, the top with circular marble section, gilt-bronze mounts, 77cm (30in) diam., *F 14 Apr,*
L 5,000,000 (£2,048; $3,174)

7
A Russian birch centre table, early 19th century, with quarter-veneered chevron pattern inlay, 80cm (31½ in) high, *NY 22 Mar,*
$1,650 (£1,093)

8
A Biedermeier walnut centre table, early 19th century, with veneered top, 108cm (36½in) high, *L 28 Nov,*
£1,650 ($2,310)

9
A Biedermeier fruitwood occasional table, c.1820, 74cm (29in) high, *NY 4 Oct,*
$2,530 (£1,756)

10
A Beidermeier fruitwood and ebonised centre table, c.1820, 75cm (29½in) high, *NY 4 Oct,*
$1,760 (£1,222)

11
An Italian ebonised marquetry centre table, c.1870, inlaid with ivory panels of scrollwork and mythological figures, 81cm (31½in) long, *F 14 Apr,*
L 4,200,000 (£1,720; $2,666)

12
A Viennese ash circular centre table, c.1830, with rosewood banding, on ebonised feet, 101cm (39½in) diam., *L 23 May,*
£3,520 ($5,561)

13
A Dutch purplewood, satinwood and tulipwood parquetry work table, with ormolu sabots, 80.5cm (31½in) high, *NY 24 June,*
$1,100 (£705)

14
A Dutch mahogany sewing table, c.1850, 77.5cm (30½in) high, *A 14 Oct,*
Dfl 3,220 (£1,006; $1,509)

1

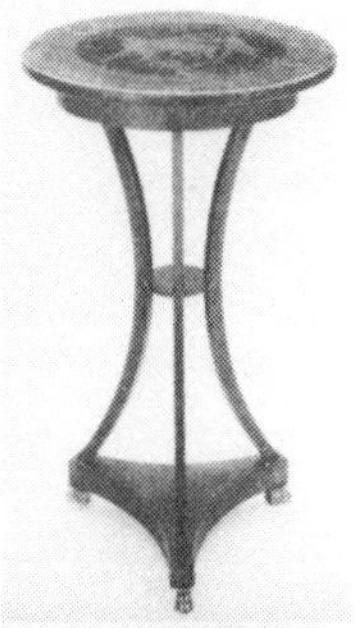
2

3

4

5

6

7

8

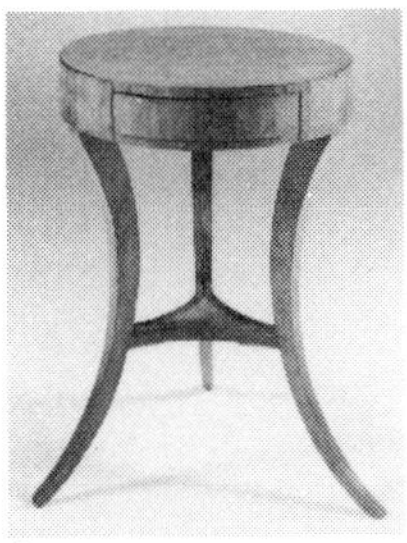
9

10

11

12

13

14

1

A Louis XV ormolu-mounted kingwood bureau plat, mid 18th century, 149cm (58in) wide, *NY 22 Mar,*
$8,800 (£5,828)

2

A Louis XVI brass-mounted mahogany bureau plat, late 18th century, 110cm (45in) wide, *NY 4 Oct,*
$4,400 (£3,055)

3

A Louis XVI rosewood marquetry bureau plat, stamped Plée, 163cm (64in) wide, *M 30 Nov,*
FF154,000 (£16,739; $23,435)

4

A Louis XVI ormolu-mounted kingwood and tulipwood bureau plat, late 18th century, with leather inset top, 194cm (6ft 4½in) wide, *NY 3 May,*
$16,500 (£10,855)

5

A Louis XVI ormolu-mounted kingwood and tulipwood parquetry bureau plat, last quarter 18th century, with leather lined top, 98cm (38¾in) wide, *NY 22 Mar,*
$5,775 (£3,825)

6

An Empire ormolu-mounted mahogany bureau plat, first quarter 19th century, with leather inset top, 149cm (58½in) wide, *NY 22 Mar,*
$4,675 (£3,096)

7

A Louis XVI ormolu-mounted mahogany tric trac table, last quarter 18th century, opening to an inlaid backgammon board, 127cm (43in) wide, *NY 22 Mar,*
$2,530 (£1,675)

8

A Louis XV-style gilt-bronze-mounted tulipwood bureau plat, with leather writing surface, 136cm (53½in) wide, *NY 26 Nov,*
$1,980 (£1,414)

9

A gilt-bronze-mounted kingwood bureau plat, early 20th century, the frieze inlaid with cube marquetry, 163cm (64in) wide, *L 21 Mar,*
£3,960 ($6,178)

10

A Louis XV-style kingwood-veneered kidney-shaped writing table, c.1910, stamped *Krieger*, 115cm (45in) wide, *L 7 Nov,*
£1,595 ($2,233)

11

A Louis XV-style gilt-bronze-mounted tulipwood parquetry bureau plat, late 19th century, with leather writing surface, 145cm (57in) wide, *NY 26 Apr,*
$3,520 (£2,286)

12

A Louis XIV-style ormolu- mounted palissander bureau plat, c.1860, 168cm (66in) wide, *L 7 Nov,*
£6,600 ($9,240)

13

A Louis XVI-style rosewood writing table, c.1900, 99cm (39in) wide, *C 27 Mar,*
£484 ($741)

See also:
French desks *pp* 16-18

1
A Louis XVI writing table, stamped *Dupré*, with white marble top, 72cm (28in) high, *M 23 Feb,*
FF 35,520 (£3,435; $5,153)

2
A Louis XV writing table, with white marble top, in satinwood marquetry, 73cm (28½in) high, *M 1 Dec,*
FF 20,900 (£2,257; $3,228)

3
A Louis XVI beechwood writing table, last quarter 18th century, with peach and grey mottled marble top, 72cm (28¼in) high, *NY 3 May,*
$2,200 (£1,447)

4
A Louis XVI writing table, c.1775, with leather-lined top, 74cm (29in) high, *L 28 Nov,*
£2,090 ($2,926)

5
A Louis XVI marquetry small writing table, stamped *J.F. Leleu Jme*, c.1775, with leather-lined writing surface and wells for writing implements, 74cm (29in) high, *L 20 June,*
£33,000 ($52,140)

6
A Louis XVI ormolu-mounted mahogany games table, late 18th century, 76cm (30in) high, *NY 22 Mar,*
$2,750 (£1,821)

7
A Louis XV kingwood parquetry small writing table, c.1760, 69cm (27in) high, *L 30 May,*
£1,760 ($2,781)

8
A kingwood and marquetry writing table, c.1860, stamped *G. Durand*, 64cm (25in) high, *L 7 Nov,*
£2,420 ($3,388)

9
A boulle small writing table, second quarter 19th century, the top inset with a velvet panel, with panels of red tortoiseshell and engraved brass, 86cm (34in), *L 13 June,*
£825 ($1,320)

10
A Louis XVI brass-mounted mahogany bouillotte table, last quarter 18th century, with white mottled marble top, 74cm (29in) high, *NY 4 Oct,*
$4,675 (£3,246)

11
A Louis XVI brass-mounted mahogany games table, last quarter 18th century, with a baize interior, 76cm (29¾in) high, *NY 4 Oct,*
$1,650 (£1,145)

12
A pair of premier and contre partie boulle and tortoiseshell card tables, *(one illustrated)*, c.1850, 85cm (33½in) wide, *L 7 Nov,*
£8,140 ($11,396)

13
A Louis XVI mahogany tric trac table, last quarter 18th century, the inside forming a backgammon surface, 115cm (45½in) wide, *NY 3 May,*
$7,150 (£4,704)

14
A Louis XVI brass-mounted mahogany and fruitwood parquetry tric trac table, last quarter 18th century, the top with inlaid chessboard, the interior fitted for backgammon, 104cm (44¾in) wide, *NY 3 May,*
$8,250 (£5,428)

1

2

3

4

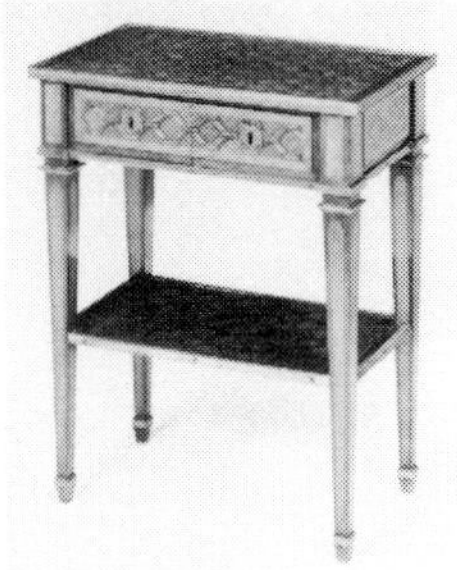
5

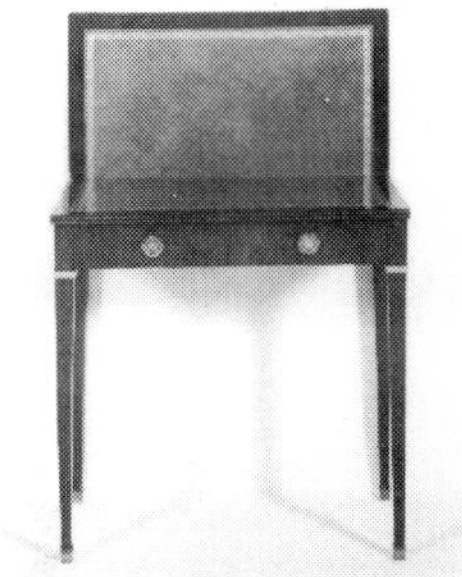
6

7

8

9

10

11

12

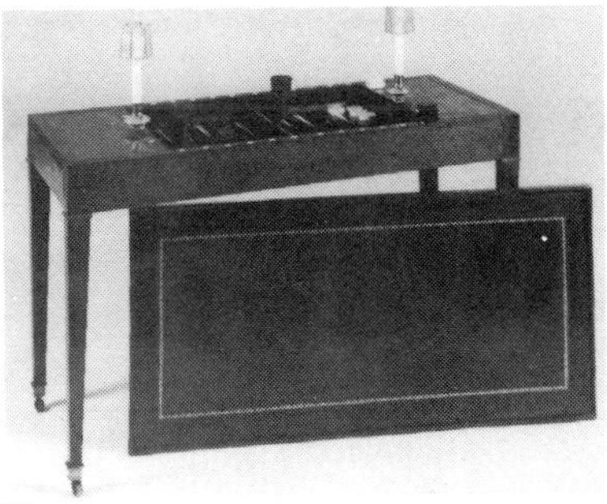
13

14

1

2

3

4

5

6

7

8

9

10

11

12

1
A Louis XV giltwood console table, c.1745, with *breche violette* marble top, 80cm (31½in) high, *L 20 June,*
£7,150 ($11,297)

2
An early Louis XV painted console table, c.1730, with mottled grey and rust marble top, 89cm (35in) high, *L 12 Dec,*
£16,500 ($23,100)

3
A Louis XVI ormolu-mounted mahogany console desserte, last quarter 18th century, 95cm (37½in), *NY 4 Oct,*
$1,540 (£1,069)

4
A Louis XVI console, in mahogany with a white marble top, 115cm (45in) high, *M 30 Nov,*
FF 46,200 (£5,022; $7,030)

5
A Louis XVI mahogany console desserte, stamped *JG Frost*, 94cm (37in) high, *M 23 Feb,*
FF 72,150 (£6,978; $10,467)

6
A pair of French Empire mahogany side tables, *(one illustrated)*, c.1820, with engine-turned mounts, 75cm (29½in) high, *S 9 Dec,*
£2,860 ($4,004)

7
An Empire mahogany pier-table, c.1815, with white marble top and mirror back, 94cm (37in) high, *L 30 May,*
£1,210 ($1,912)

8
A Directoire brass-mounted mahogany console desserte, late 18th century, 90cm (35½in) high, *NY 4 Oct,*
$11,000 (£7,638)

9
A Directoire ebonised mahogany extension dining table, late 18th century, with two later leaves, 102cm (40in) wide, *NY 22 Mar,*
$7,150 (£4,735)

10
A Louis XVI ormolu-mounted mahogany dining table, late 18th century, with two later leaves, 74cm (29¼in) high, *NY 3 May,*
$11,000 (£7,237)

11
A late Louis XVI brass-mounted mahogany extension dining table, late 18th century, the top with double brass banding, 75cm (29½in) high, *NY 22 Mar,*
$18,700 (£12,384)

12
A Louis XVI ormolu-mounted mahogany dining table, late 18th century, the top with six later leaves, 71cm (28¾in) high, *NY 22 Mar,*
$12,100 (£8,066)

1
A Transitional Louis XV/XVI marquetry drum table, c.1775, 76cm (30in) high, *M 30 Nov,*
FF 143,000 (£15,543; $21,761)

2
A Louis XV ormolu-mounted tulipwood and purplewood marquetry work table, mid 18th century, attributed to Bernard van Risamburgh, bearing a stamp *B.V.R.B.*, 67cm (26½in) high, *NY 1 Nov,*
$44,000 (£31,206)

3
A Louis XV kingwood and fruitwood marquetry table en chiffonnière, mid 18th century, signed *P. Roussel*, 69cm (27¼in) high, *NY 3 May,*
$13,200 (£8,684)

4
A Louis XV/XVI ormolu-mounted tulipwood and sycamore table de toilette, c.1775, signed *C. Topino JME*, 71cm (28in) high, *NY 1 Nov,*
$19,800 (£14,042)

5
A Louis XVI brass-mounted mahogany and kingwood parquetry table en chiffonnière, last quarter 18th century, with grey and white marbled top, 71cm (28in) high, *NY 4 Oct,*
$3,080 (£2,138)

6
A Louis XVI kingwood and marquetry table en chiffonnière, c.1775, with leather-lined top, 73cm (28½in) high, *L 12 Dec,*
£7,700 ($10,780)

7
An Empire ormolu-mounted thuyawood and mahogany table de toilette, early 19th century, attributed to Jacob Desmalter, with Chateau de St Cloud inventory marks, 127cm (50in) wide, *NY 31 Oct,*
$71,500 (£50,709)

8
A Louis XV kingwood and parquetry coiffeuse, c.1760, 78cm (30¾in) wide, *L 12 Dec,*
£4,950 ($6,930)

9
A Louis XV marquetry and satinwood coiffeuse, stamped Demoulin, 87cm (34in) wide, *M 23 Feb,*
FF 34,410 (£3,328; $4,992)

10
A Louis XV tulipwood and kingwood parquetry table de toilette, mid 18th century, the top opening to reveal mirror and wells, 79cm (31in) wide, *NY 3 May,*
$4,125 (£2,714)

11
An Empire ormolu-mounted mahogany dressing table, first quarter 19th century, later mirror plate, 142cm (56in) high, *NY 22 Mar,*
$1,760 (£1,166)

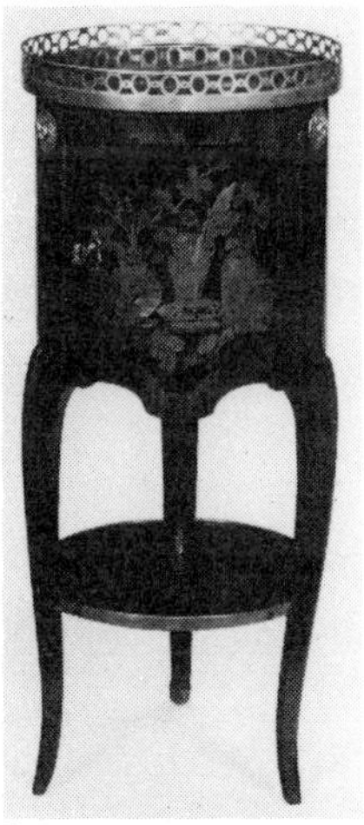
1

2

3

4

5

6

7

8

9

10

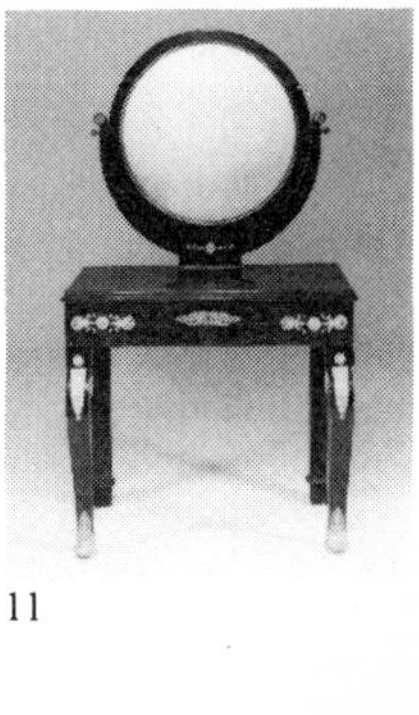
11

1

2

3

4

5

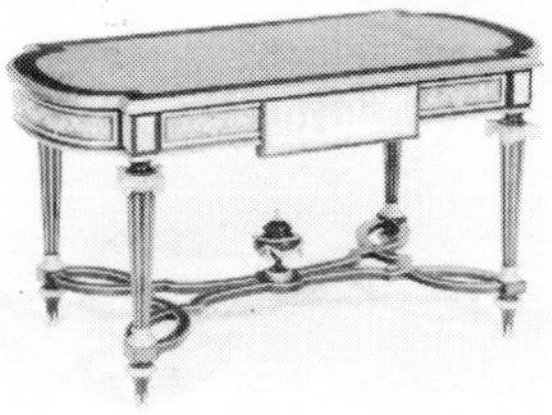
6

7

8

9

10

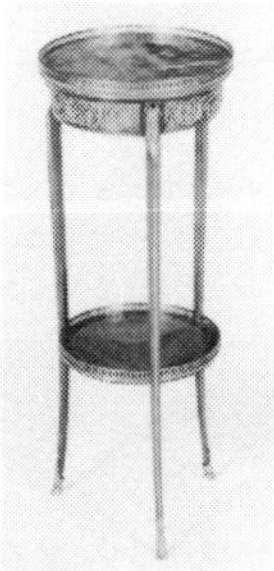
11

12

13

14

1
A pair of occasional tables, *(one illustrated)*, c.1870, with gilt-bronze mounts, 76cm (30in) high, *L 21 Mar,*
£2,640 ($4,118)

2
A Louis XVI-style mahogany and gilt-bronze-mounted occasional table, c.1880, 79cm (31in) high, *L 7 Nov,*
£1,540 ($2,156)

3
A Louis XVI-style mahogany and gilt-bronze-mounted occasional table, c.1880, 79cm (31in) high, *L 7 Nov,*
£682 ($955)

4
A Napoleon III marquetry centre table, c.1860, gilt-bronze border, inlaid on a burr walnut ground, with rosewood reserves, 75cm (29½in) high, *L 13 June,*
£2,200 ($3,520)

5
A pair of Louis XVI-style gilt-bronze and porphyry centre tables, *(one illustrated)*, c.1880, stamped *A. Beurdeley, Paris*, 87.5cm (34½in) high, *NY 13 Sept,*
$159,500 (£108,503)

6
A gilt-bronze-mounted centre table, c.1870, by Winckelsen, of Louis XVI inspiration, tooled leather top, blue ground Wedgwood plaque, 74cm (29in) high, *L 7 Nov,*
£11,550 ($16,170)

7
A Napoleon III gilt-bronze-mounted 'Boulle' marquetry centre table, c.1870, inlaid in brass marquetry, 74cm (29¼in) high, *NY 26 Nov,*
$2,475 (£1,768)

8
An Empire-style gilt-bronze-mounted mahogany centre table, c.1890, top inset with green onyx, 74cm (29¼in) high, *NY 26 Apr,*
$1,870 (£1,214)

9
A walnut calamander and marquetry centre table, mid 19th century, cross-banded top, applied with gilt-bronze mounts and sabots, 75cm (29¼in) high, *C 16 Jan,*
£1,430 ($2,145)

10
A Louis XVI-style mahogany and parquetry and gilt-bronze centre table, 20th century, 75cm (29¼in) high, *C 16 Jan,*
£968 ($1,452)

11
A Louis XVI-style gueridon, c.1900, by Paul Sormani, 79cm (31in) high, *L 13 June,*
£968 ($1,548)

12
A satinwood parquetry table, c.1900, with a diamond trellis within purpleheart banding, gilt-bronze mouldings, 75cm (29¼in) high, *L 21 Mar,*
£3,960 ($6,178)

13
A Napoleon III gilt-bronze and Sèvres porcelain circular table, the *bleu-de-ciel* dish painted with Louis XV, 75cm (29¼in) high, *L 13 June,*
£1,980 ($3,168)

14
A Louis XVI-style marquetry games table, 76cm (30in) high, *M 25 Feb,*
FF 4,440 (£429; $644)

1
An early Louis XV provincial oak centre table, c.1730, with mottled rust-coloured marble top, 94cm (37in) high, *L 28 Nov,*
£2,750 ($3,850)

2
A Louis XV kingwood-veneered small table, c.1760, the frieze with a leather-lined slide and drawer at one side, 71cm (28in) high, *L 20 June,*
£3,300 ($5,214)

3
A Louis XV kingwood table, indistinctly stamped, probably *Schmitz,* mid 18th century, with gilt-bronze mounts, 71cm (28in) high, *L 12 Dec,*
£6,050 ($8,470)

4
A Louis XVI mahogany gueridon, with marble inlaid top tier, 74cm (29in) high, *M 24 Feb,*
FF16,650 (£1,610; $2,415)

5
A Louis XVI ormolu-mounted mahogany gueridon, late 18th century, signed *L. Moreau,* with marble tiers, 99cm (38¾in), *NY 31 Oct,*
$17,050 (£12,092)

6
A Louis XVI oval parquetry table, c.1780, the top inlaid with flower-heads on a trellis ground, 76cm (30in) high, *L 20 June,*
£9,900 ($15,642)

7
A Louis XVI marquetry table, 75cm (29½in) high, *M 30 Nov,*
FF 33,000 (£3,587; $5,022)

8
An Empire mahogany gueridon, c.1810, 160cm (63in) wide, *M 23 Feb,*
FF 88,800 (£8,588; $12,882)

9
A mahogany and gilt-bronze Restauration table, 69cm (27in) high, *M 24 Feb,*
FF 8,325 (£805; $1,208)

10
A gueridon, early 19th century, with white marble top, 75cm (29½in) high, *M 23 Feb,*
FF 38,850 (£3,757; $5,636)

11
A Louis XVI ormolu-mounted mahogany gueridon porte-lumière, late 18th century, signed *J. Canabas, JME,* 74.5cm (29½in) high, *NY 3 May,*
$6,875 (£4,523)

12
An Empire ormolu-mounted mahogany centre table, early 19th century, with a marble top, 75cm (29½in) high, *NY 22 Mar,*
$5,225 (£3,460)

13
A porcelain-mounted kingwood centre table, c.1860, the top set with Sèvres-style lobed dish, 74cm (29in) high, *L 21 Mar,*
£2,035 ($3,175)

1

2

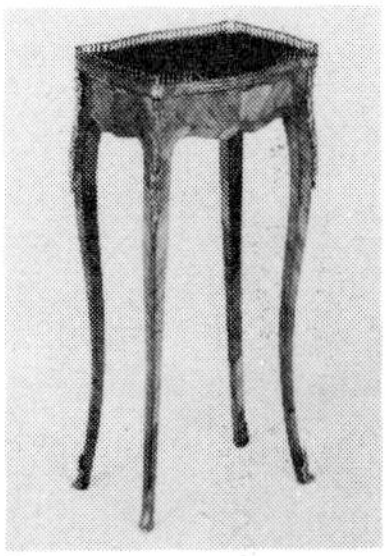
3

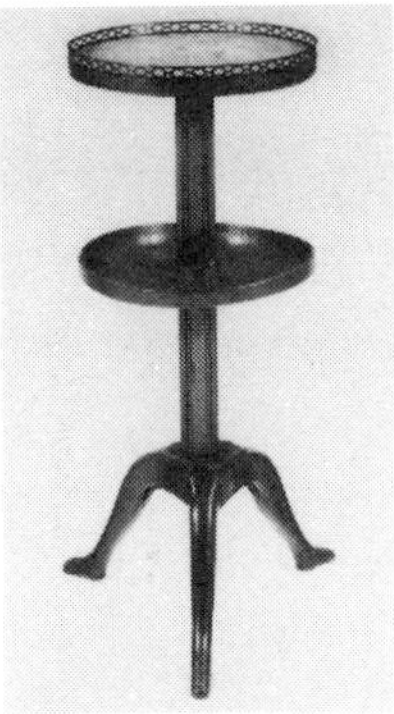
4

5

6

7

8

9

10

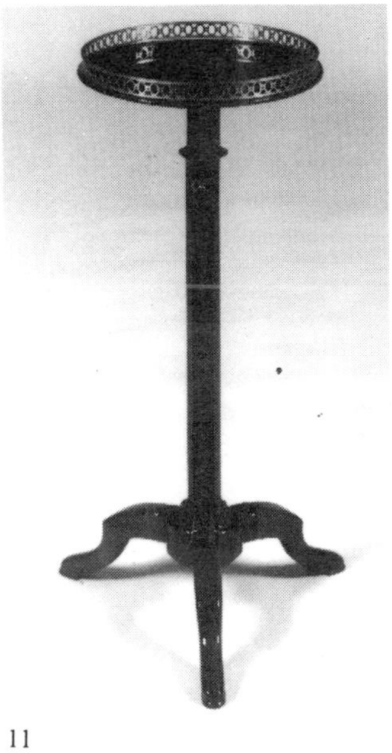
11

12

13

1

2

3

4

5

6

7

8

9

10

11

12

13

14

15

16

17

18

1
A set of three William and Mary walnut highback chairs, *(one illustrated)*, c.1690, in the style of Daniel Marot, *L 4 July*,
£3,300 ($5,346)

2
A pair of William and Mary beechwood side chairs, *(one illustrated)*, c.1690, *L 10 Oct*,
£902 ($1,263)

3
A George I walnut side chair, c.1725, *NY 25 Jan*,
$2,530 (£1,820)

4
A pair of Queen Anne walnut side chairs, *(one illustrated)*, c.1710, with later tapestry seats, *C 8 Oct*,
£1,100 ($1,540)

5
A pair of George I walnut side chairs, *(one illustrated)*, c.1725, *NY 7 June*,
$3,850 (£2,583)

6
A set of five George II provincial mahogany chairs, *(one illustrated)*, c.1755, *L 21 Nov*,
£3,080 ($4,312)

7
A George II mahogany armchair, second quarter 18th century, *NY 25 Jan*,
$4,400 (£3,165)

8
A pair of George II mahogany side chairs, *(one illustrated)*, c.1725, *L 28 Feb*,
£1,650 ($2,557)

9
A pair of George III mahogany side chairs, last quarter 18th century, *NY 25 Jan*,
$2,530 (£1,820)

10
A George III mahogany side chair, c.1770, *C 16 Jan*,
£396 ($594)

11
A George III mahogany side chair, third quarter 18th century, *NY 7 June*,
$2,310 (£1,550)

12
A set of four George III mahogany side chairs, *(one illustrated)*, c.1790, *C 29 May*,
£484 ($765)

13
A set of six George III mahogany chairs, *(one illustrated)*, c.1760, *S 18 Mar*,
£1,925 ($2,945)

14
A set of six early George III mahogany chairs, *(one illustrated)*, c.1760, *L 24 Oct*,
£5,720 ($8,008)

15
A set of six George III mahogany chairs, *(one illustrated)*, c.1780, *S 9 Dec*,
£1,925 ($2,695)

16
A set of eight George III mahogany dining chairs, *(one illustrated)*, c.1780, *L 14 Mar*,
£3,190 ($4,944)

17
A set of eight George III mahogany dining chairs, *(two illustrated)*, last quarter 18th century, *NY 7 June*,
$7,700 (£5,167)

18
A George III mahogany cockpen side chair, c.1770, *NY 7 June*,
$1,100 (£774)

1
A George III mahogany armchair, c.1785,
L 14 Mar,
£2,970 ($4,603)

2
A George III padouk armchair, probably by Gillows of Lancaster, late 18th century, *NY 25 Jan,*
$11,000 (£7,914)

3
A pair of George III mahogany side chairs, *(one illustrated)*, c.1780,
C 29 May,
£374 ($591)

4
A set of eight Regency caned oak chairs, *(one illustrated)*, c.1810, with partly ebonised turned toprails, *L 21 Nov,*
£3,740 ($5,236)

5
A set of six Regency satinwood armchairs, *(one illustrated)*, c.1810, with later floral painting,
L 21 Nov,
£6,160 ($8,624)

6
A set of six George III mahogany chairs, *(one illustrated)*, c.1775, *L 28 Feb,*
£4,180 ($6,479)

7
A set of four oak dining chairs, *(one illustrated)*, c.1800, *C 30 Jan,*
£187 ($275)

8
A set of three George III mahogany dining chairs, *(one illustrated)*, c.1800,
C 30 Jan,
£242 ($356)

9
A set of six late George III provincial mahogany dining chairs, *(one illustrated)*, *S 11 Feb,*
£440 ($616)

10
A set of seven George III mahogany dining chairs, *(one illustrated)*, c.1800,
C 16 Jan,
£1,485 ($2,228)

11
A set of six Regency mahogany rail-back chairs, *(one illustrated)*, c.1810, *S 11 Nov,*
£2,420 ($3,388)

12
A set of six William IV mahogany dining chairs, *(one illustrated)*, c.1835,
C 16 Jan,
£715 ($1,073)

13
A set of twelve Regency mahogany chairs, *(one illustrated)*, c.1810,
L 11 July,
£6,820 ($10,844)

14
A set of eight George III mahogany chairs, *(one illustrated)*, c.1800, *S 18 Feb,*
£4,620 ($7,022)

15
A set of twelve Regency mahogany dining chairs, *(one illustrated)*, c.1805,
L 25 Apr,
£11,000 ($17,600)

16
A set of six early Victorian rosewood chairs, *(one illustrated)*, c.1840, *L 24 Oct,*
£1,980 ($2,772)

17
A pair of late Georgian mahogany open armchairs, *(one illustrated)*, c.1830, *C 25 June,*
£495 ($772)

18
A set of six George IV mahogany dining chairs, *(one illustrated)*, c.1820,
C 16 Jan,
£2,200 ($3,300)

19
A set of six George IV mahogany dining chairs, *(one illustrated)*, c.1820,
C 16 Jan,
£935 ($1,403)

20
A set of six Victorian rosewood spoon-back chairs, *(one illustrated)*, c.1850, *S 22 Apr,*
£770 ($1,209)

1

2

3

4

5

6

7

8

9

10

11

12

13

14

15

16

17

18

19

20

1

2

3

4

5

6

7

8

9

10

11

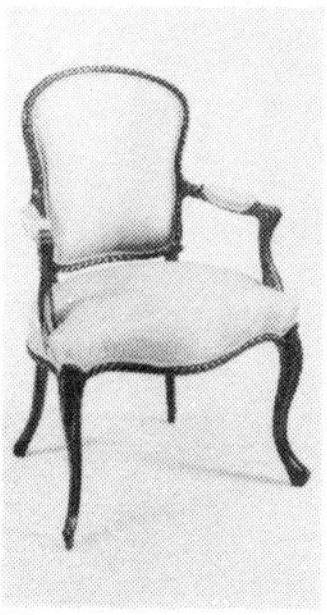
12

13

14

15

16

17

18

1
A set of six early Victorian rosewood chairs, *(one illustrated)*, c.1840, *L 2 June,*
£1,320 ($2,033)

2
A set of eight William IV mahogany rail-back chairs, *(one illustrated)*, c.1835, the stuffed seats covered in leathercloth, *S 15 July,*
£1,760 ($2,763)

3
A set of twelve mahogany dining chairs, *(one illustrated)*, c.1845, *C 17 Apr,*
£2,970 ($4,604)

4
A set of six George IV-style mahogany dining chairs, *(one illustrated)*, c.1920, *C 24 July,*
£220 ($345)

5
A set of eight Regency mahogany dining chairs, *(one illustrated)*, c.1815, including a pair of armchairs, *L 11 July,*
£2,860 ($4,547)

6
A set of six George III-style mahogany dining chairs, *(one illustrated)*, 20th century, *C 16 Jan,*
£1,155 ($1,733)

7
A set of George III-style mahogany chairs, *(one illustrated)*, c.1910, bearing trade label of Graham and Banks, 445 Oxford Street, London, *S 21 Jan,*
£1,485 ($2,228)

8
A set of fourteen George III-style mahogany dining chairs, *(one illustrated)*, modern, *L 18 July,*
£2,090 ($3,323)

9
A set of ten reproduction William IV mahogany dining chairs, *(one illustrated)*, modern, *L 12 May,*
£770 ($1,240)

10
A set of eight George II-style carved mahogany dining chairs, *(one illustrated)*, mid 19th century, *NY 14 Oct,*
$15,400 (£10,694)

11
A pair of George III painted armchairs, *(one illustrated)*, c.1780, painted in green and white, *L 11 July,*
£4,620 ($7,346)

12
A George III mahogany open armchair, third quarter 18th century, *NY 13 Dec,*
$4,125 (£2,946)

13
A George III stained beechwood bergère, c.1780, with loose squab cushion, *L 25 Apr,*
£3,960 ($6,336)

14
A George III mahogany and upholstered armchair, c.1790, covered in blue brocade, *S 17 June,*
£825 ($1,303)

15
A suite of George III painted and parcel-gilt seat furniture, *(part illustrated)*, last quarter 18th century, comprising two armchairs and four side chairs, *NY 7 June,*
$7,975 (£5,352)

16
A pair of George III giltwood armchairs, *(one illustrated)*, c.1775, *L 14 Nov,*
£4,950 ($7,079)

17
A pair of George III carved and polychrome-decorated open armchairs, *(one illustrated)*, c.1790, *NY 7 June,*
$4,400 (£2,953)

18
A set of six Louis XVI-style giltwood armchairs, *(one illustrated)*, 20th century, *L 2 June,*
£1,155 ($1,694)

1
A set of seven Regency elmwood rush-seated chairs, *(one illustrated)*, early 19th century, *L 3 Mar,*
£825 ($1,238)

2
A set of eight fruitwood country chairs, *(one illustrated)*, 19th century, *C 1 May,*
£462 ($748)

3
A matched set of six George III-style oak and elm ladderback chairs, *(one illustrated)*, 19th century, *S 20 May,*
£572 ($915)

4
A set of eight George III-style ash and elm ladder-back chairs, *(one illustrated)*, c.1900, *S 15 July,*
£1,485 ($2,331)

5
An elm and oak armchair, English, early 18th century, 111cm (43½in) high, *L 22 July,*
£220 ($345)

6
A yew-wood and elm Windsor chair, 19th century, *C 29 May,*
£330 ($521)

7
A George III yew-wood and elm Windsor arm-chair, *S 8 July,*
£1,375 ($2,228)

8
A set of nine fruit and ash wheel-back Windsor chairs, *(one illustrated)*, late 19th century, *C 14 May,*
£451 ($726)

9
A matched set of three George IV yew-wood and elm Windsor armchairs, *(one illustrated)*, c.1825, *S 20 May,*
£1,320 ($2,112)

10
A matched set of eight ash and elm Windsor arm-chairs, *(one illustrated)*, 19th century, *S 17 June,*
£1,870 ($2,954)

11
A set of eight reproduction ash and elm and beech wheel-back Windsor chairs, *(one illustrated)*, 20th century, *C 5 Nov,*
£770 ($1,086)

12
A pair of George IV mahogany hall chairs, *(one illustrated)*, c.1830, the backs with painted arms above mantling, *C 14 May,*
£176 ($283)

13
A set of six William IV mahogany hall chairs, *(one illustrated)*, *C 22 Oct,*
£902 ($1,262)

14
A George II walnut corner armchair, c.1730, with *point d'Hongrie* slip-in seat, *L 7 July,*
£9,900 ($16,038)

15
A George IV mahogany lady's bergère, c.1830, *C 29 May,*
£484 ($765)

16
A George IV mahogany library bergère, c.1820, *L 18 July,*
£990 ($1,574)

17
A Regency mahogany and button upholstered occasional chair, c.1810, *S 17 June,*
£352 ($556)

18
A George IV mahogany library bergere, c.1820, *L 28 Feb,*
£2,420 ($3,751)

1

2

3

4

5

6

7

8

9

10

11

12

13

14

15

16

17

18

1

2

3

4

5

6

7

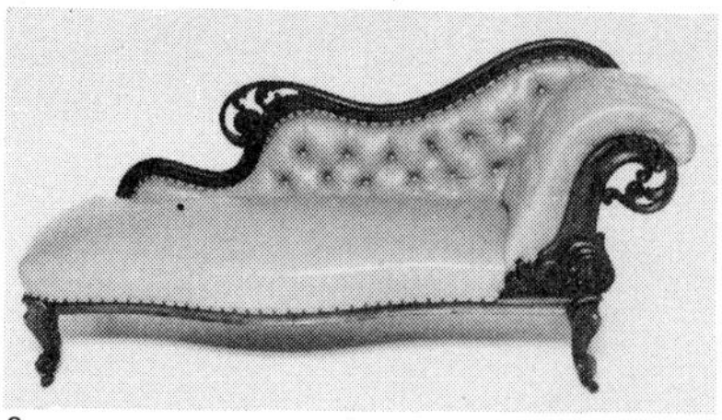
8

9

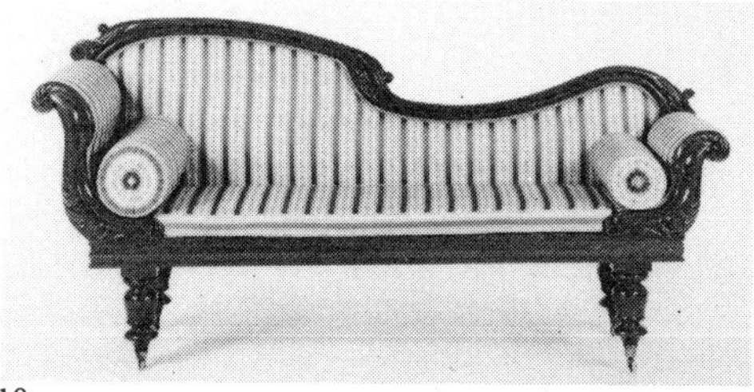
10

11

12

13

14

15

16

1
A George I walnut wing armchair, c.1715, *L 25 Apr,*
£3,850 ($6,160)

2
A George III carved mahogany library armchair, c.1760 upholstered in 19th century floral needlework, *NY 14 Oct,*
$2,970 (£2,063)

3
An early George III mahogany library armchair, c.1760, legs and arms carved with a chinoiserie blind fret, *L 14 Mar,*
£1,650 ($2,557)

4
A set of six early George III mahogany library chairs, *(one illustrated),* c.1760, covered in white horsehair, *L 25 Apr,*
£2,200 ($3,520)

5
A late Regency faded rosewood open armchair, c.1825, *C 17 Apr,*
£935 ($1,454)

6
A George III mahogany settee, c.1810, 187cm (6ft 1in) long, *C 8 Oct,*
£462 ($647)

7
A Victorian rosewood settee, c.1850, 190.5cm (6ft 3in) long, *C 11 June,*
£396 ($622)

8
A Victorian walnut chaise longue, c.1860, 203cm (6ft 6in), *C 30 Jan,*
£528 ($776)

9
A Victorian walnut settee, c.1850, 170cm (67in) long, *C 8 Oct,*
£880 ($1,232)

10
An early Victorian mahogany chaise longue, c.1850, 206cm (6ft 9in) long, *L 4 Aug,*
£1,815 ($2,813)

11
A Victorian conversation chair, c.1860, with gilded and ebonised supports, *C 6 Aug,*
£550 ($853)

12
A mid Victorian carved walnut armchair, c.1860, *L 12 May,*
£572 ($921)

13
A Victorian walnut armchair, c.1860, *L 6 Oct,*
£770 ($1,078)

14
A Victorian walnut drawing room suite, *(part illustrated),* c.1860, including six salon chairs and a lady's chair, *C 8 Oct,*
£1,375 ($1,925)

15
A nine-piece Victorian mahogany drawing room suite, *(part illustrated),* including a settee, pair of armchairs, four side chairs and two nursing chairs, *C 24 July,*
£770 ($1,209)

16
A carved walnut bergère suite, *(part illustrated),* c.1910, including a three-seater settee and a pair of armchairs, *C 29 May,*
£1,115 ($1,762)

1
A Charles II yew-wood joint stool, c.1680, 46cm (18in) wide, *L 4 July,*
£1,760 ($2,851)

2
A yew-wood joint stool, c.1640, 48cm (19in) wide, *L 4 July,*
£6,160 ($9,979)

3
A pair of Italian giltwood pliants, mid 18th century, 65cm (25½in) wide, *NY 1 Nov,*
$30,800 (£21,844)

4
A pair of Restauration giltwood stools, stamped *J. Louis,* c.1825, with inventory numbers and label for the Tuileries, *L 12 Dec,*
£6,600 ($9,240)

5
A Regency black and gilt-decorated window seat, c.1810, 96cm (38in) wide, *L 15 Jan,*
£1,045 ($1,568)

6
A Louis XIV giltwood tabouret, c.1690, *NY 3 May,*
$8,250 (£5,428)

7
A Queen Anne walnut stool, c.1710, with a square slip-in needlework seat, on pad feet, 43cm (17in) wide, *S 18 Feb,*
£990 ($1,505)

8
A George I walnut stool, c.1720, with drop-in seat and shell-carved cabriole legs and claw and ball feet, 56cm (22in), wide, *L 14 Nov,*
£5,720 ($8,180)

9
A George I carved walnut oval stool, c.1725, the overstuffed seat covered in needlepoint, *NY 25 Jan,*
$23,100 (£16,619)

10
A George III mahogany stool, c.1760, *C 9 July,*
£748 ($1,204)

11
A Louis XV beechwood tabouret, mid 18th century, the knees carved with acanthus, 53cm (21in) wide, *NY 4 Oct,*
$2,750 (£1,909)

12
An early Victorian rosewood stool, c.1840, with a padded top on 'X' scroll supports, 43cm (17in) wide, *C 1 May,*
£396 ($642)

13
A pair of Regency beechwood stools (*one illustrated*), c.1820, each with oval leather padded seat, *C 13 Mar,*
£176 ($266)

14
A pair of walnut stools (*one illustrated*), c.1840, the upholstered tops covered in early 18th century needlework, 51cm (20in) wide, *L 2 May,*
£2,860 ($4,547)

15
A Directoire mahogany and parcel-gilt tabouret, late 18th/early 19th century, 52cm (20½in) wide, *NY 3 May,*
$5,500 (£3,618)

16
A Regency carved and gilt-painted rectangular stool, c.1810, 86cm (34in) wide, *S 18 Feb,*
£1,980 ($3,010)

17
A pair of German mahogany window seats, *(one illustrated)*, c.1815, on sabre legs, 79cm (31in) wide, *L 30 May,*
£3,520 ($5,561)

1

2

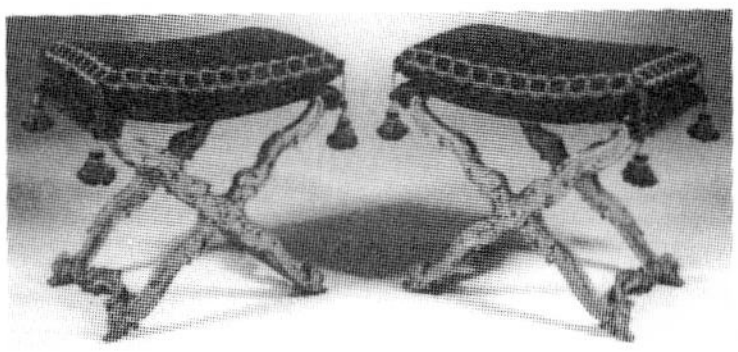
3

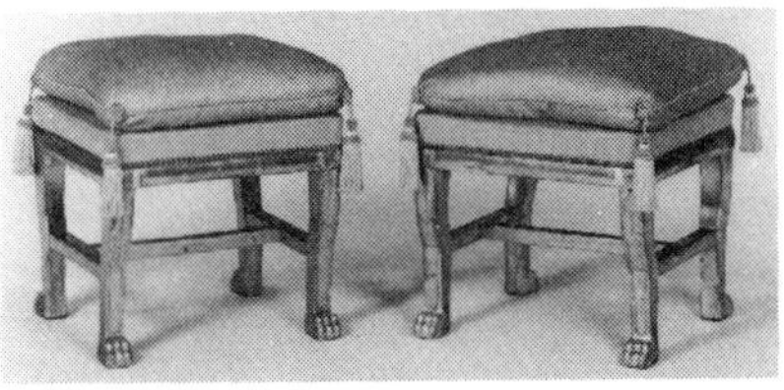
4

5

6

7

8

9

10

11

12

13

14

15

16

17

1

2

3

4

5

6

7

8

9

10

11

12

13

14

15

16

17

18

1
A Régence fauteuil, c.1720, in natural wood, upholstered in red leather, *M 22 June,*
FF 33,300 (£2,971; $4,634)

2
A Régence walnut fauteuil à la reine, c.1720, upholstered in contemporary tapestry, *NY 3 May,*
$3,300 (£2,171)

3
A Louis XV walnut fauteuil de bureau, mid 18th century, with caned seat and back, *L 20 June,*
£6,600 ($10,428)

4
A Louis XV beechwood fauteuil de cabinet, mid 18th century, signed *I.B. Cresson,* with caned seat and back, *NY 4 Oct,*
$4,125 (£2,864)

5
A pair of early Louis XV walnut fauteuils à la reine, *(one illustrated),* second quarter 18th century, upholstered in needlepoint, *NY 24 June,*
$9,350 (£5,994)

6
A Louis XV giltwood sofa, mid 18th century, attributed to Nicolas Heurtaut, 98cm (38½in) long, *NY 1 Nov,*
$16,500 (£11,702)

7
A Louis XV walnut fauteuil de malade, mid 18th century, *M 24 Feb,*
FF 15,540 (£1,503; $2,254)

8
A Louis XV beechwood fauteuil en cabriolet, mid 18th century, signed *Hamand, JME, NY 22 Mar,*
$1,980 (£1,311)

9
A Louis XV beechwood fauteuil à la reine, mid 18th century, with caned back and seat, *NY 4 Oct,*
$2,420 (£1,680)

10
A pair of Louis XV beechwood fauteuils, *(one illustrated),* mid 18th century, stamped C. Ronsaint, upholstered in tapestry, *L 20 June,*
£2,090 ($3,302)

11
A pair of Louis XV beechwood fauteuils, *(one illustrated),* mid 18th century, stamped I. Gourdin, *L 20 June,*
£4,180 ($6,604)

12
A Louis XV beechwood fauteuil en cabriolet, mid 18th century, upholstered in floral brocade, *NY 22 Mar,*
$5,775 (£3,825)

13
A Louis XV beechwood fauteuil à la reine, mid 18th century, signed *Avisse,* upholstered in contemporary needlepoint, *NY 31 Oct,*
$9,900 (£7,021)

14
A Louis XV painted bergère, mid 18th century, in the manner of Tilliard, *NY 4 Oct,*
$4,950 (£3,437)

15
A Louis XV beechwood bergère, mid 18th century, *L 20 June,*
£2,200 ($3,476)

16
A pair of Louis XV chaises en cabriolet, *(one illustrated),* mid 18th century, *NY 4 Oct,*
$4,950 (£3,437)

17
A pair of Louis XV giltwood chairs, *(one illustrated),* mid 18th century, upholstered in green velvet, *M 22 June,*
FF 94,350 (£8,417; $13,130)

18
A set of four Louis XV beechwood chaises en cabriolet, *(one illustrated),* mid 18th century, two signed *Nogaret à Lyon, NY 22 Mar,*
$8,525 (£5,646)

1
A set of six Louis XV caned beechwood chaises à la reine, *(one illustrated)*, mid 18th century, sold with a set of four later copies, *NY 3 May*,
$9,075 (£5,970)

2
A Louis XVI giltwood fauteuil, late 18th century, *M 30 Nov*,
FF 66,000 (£7,174; $10,043)

3
A suite of Louis XVI seat furniture, *(part illustrated)*, c.1780, comprising a sofa and five armchairs, upholstered in tapestry, *L 23 May*,
£3,520 ($5,561)

4
A suite of Louis XVI seat furniture, *(part illustrated)*, late 18th century, comprising a sofa and a pair of armchairs, two pieces signed *I. Gourdin*, painted off-white, sofa 201cm (6ft 5in), *NY 31 Oct*,
$13,200 (£9,362)

5
A Louis XVI giltwood marquise, late 18th century, Georges Jacob, upholstered in blue-ground silk, *M 30 Nov*,
FF 41,800 (£4,543; $6,497)

6
A set of six Louis XVI dining chairs, *(part illustrated)*, late 18th century, comprising two arm and four side chairs, *NY 22 Mar*,
$7,150 (£4,735)

7
A Louis XVI parcel-gilt bergère, c.1780, stamped A. Dupain, with associated Aubusson tapestry back and seat, *L 20 June*,
£4,950 ($7,821)

8
A pair of Louis XVI parcel-gilt chaises à la reine, *(one illustrated)*, late 18th century, *NY 4 Oct*,
$1,980 (£1,375)

9
A set of six Louis XVI mahogany chairs, *(one illustrated)*, late 18th century, stamped Demay, *M 23 Feb*,
FF 133,200 (£12,882; $19,323)

10
A pair of Louis XV/XVI fauteuils en cabriolet, *(one illustrated)*, c.1775, now painted white, *NY 4 Oct*,
$2,750 (£1,909)

11
A pair of Louis XV/XVI beechwood chaises à la reine, *(one illustrated)*, c.1775, signed *P. Gillier*, *NY 22 Mar*,
$2,090 (£1,384)

12
A set of six Louis XV beechwood chairs, *(one illustrated)*, c.1750, including an armchair, *L 30 May*,
£2,200 ($3,476)

13
A Louis XVI beechwood fauteuil de bureau, late 18th century, upholstered in brown leather, *NY 4 Oct*,
$6,050 (£4,201)

14
A Louis XVI fauteuil en cabriolet, late 18th century, the armrests on guilloché carved supports, *NY 22 Mar*,
$1,650 (£1,093)

15
A Louis XVI giltwood fauteuil, late 18th century, upholstered in blue velvet, *M 23 June*,
FF 14,430 (£1,287; $2,008)

16
A pair of Louis XVI fauteuils, *(one illustrated)*, late 18th century, stamped J. B. Boulard and with the mark of the royal château of Fontainebleau, *M 30 Nov*,
FF 110,000 (£11,957; $16,739)

17
A Louis XVI fauteuil à la reine, late 18th century, with guilloché carved borders and apron, painted grey, *NY 3 May*,
$8,800 (£5,789)

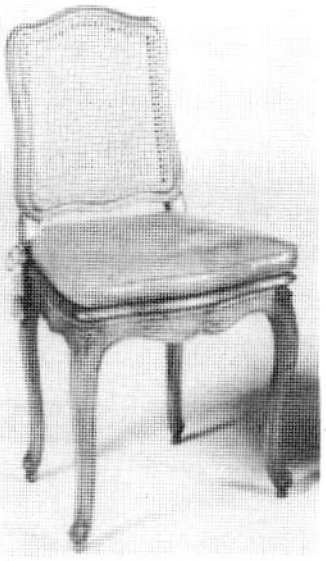
1

2

3

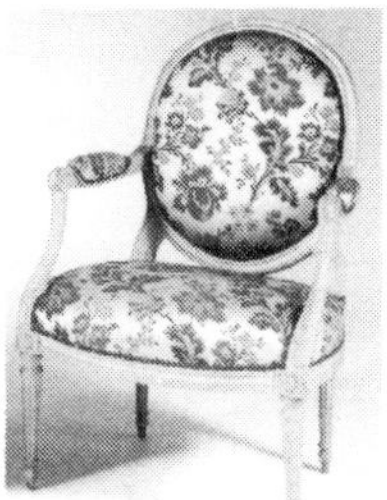
4

5

6

7

8

9

10

11

12

13

14

15

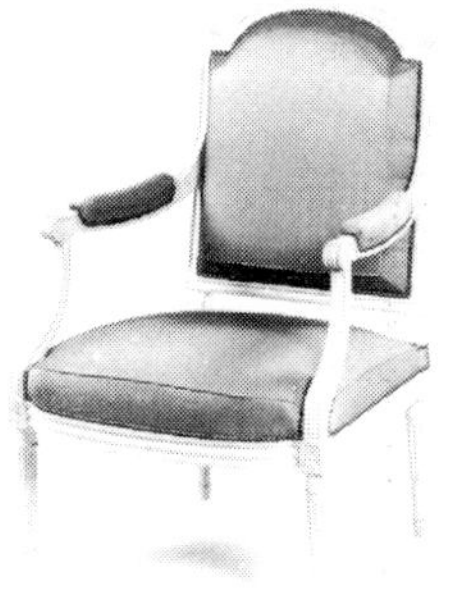
16

17

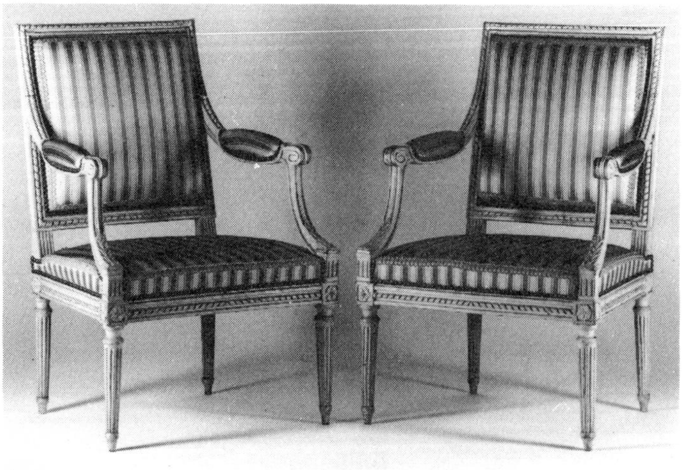
1

2

3

4

5

6

7

8

9

1
A pair of Louis XVI white-lacquered armchairs, c.1780, signed *Georges Jacob, M 23 Feb,* **FF 72,150 (£6,978; $10,467)**

2
A pair of Empire mahogany armchairs, *(one illustrated)*, c.1810, the arms in the form of carved dolphins, *L 30 May,* **£2,035 ($3,215)**

3
A pair of Empire mahogany chairs, *(one illustrated)*, stamped *J.D.* for François-Honoré-Georges Jacob called Jacob Desmalfer, *M 30 Nov,* **FF 49,500 (£5,380; $7,533)**

4
A pair of Empire mahogany and parcel-gilt fauteuils à la reine, early 19th century, the arms in the form of dolphins, *NY 4 Oct,* **$6,600 (£4,583)**

5
A set of six Empire mahogany chaises en gondole, *(one illustrated)*, *L 30 May,* **£2,420 ($3,824)**

6
An Empire mahogany suite, *(part illustrated)*, early 19th century, comprising a sofa, four armchairs and two bergères, upholstered in tapestry, sofa 164cm (60½in) long, *M 22 June,* **FF 111,000 (£9,813; $15,308)**

7
A set of six Empire mahogany dining chairs, *(one illustrated)*, early 19th century, *NY 3 May,* **$11,550 (£7,599)**

8
A Directoire mahogany suite en gondole, *(part illustrated)*, comprising a sofa and four bergères, two signed *Dohet*, sofa 132cm (52in), *M 30 Nov,* **FF 253,000 (£27,500; $38,500)**

9
A Directoire mahogany Duchesse Brisée, 18th/19th century, upholstered in blue silk, 152cm (60in) long, *NY 17 Dec,* **$2,530 (£1,807)**

1
A set of seven Directoire mahogany dining chairs *(part illustrated)*, late 18th century, signed *G. Jacob*, sold with a later copy of a pair of armchairs and six side chairs, *NY 4 Oct,*
$16,500 (£11,458)

2
A set of four Directoire painted chairs, *(part illustrated)*, late 18th century, now painted pale blue, *NY 4 Oct,*
$1,980 (£1,375)

3
A pair of Directoire fauteuils, *(one illustrated)*, late 18th century, in carved and lacquered wood, *M 24 Feb,*
FF 9,102 (£880; $1,320)

4
A set of six Restauration mahogany chairs, *(one illustrated)*, c.1820, the arms terminating in swans' heads, *M 23 June,*
FF 24,420 (£2,178; $3,398)

5
A Napoleon III-style carved giltwood conversation settee, upholstered in floral needlework, *NY 26 Apr,*
$4,400 (£2,857)

6
A Louis XVI-style giltwood salon suite, *(part illustrated)*, 19th century, comprising a sofa and four armchairs, sofa 123cm (48¼in), *M 23 June,*
FF 24,420 (£2,178; $3,398)

7
A Louis XVI-style giltwood suite, *(part illustrated)*, comprising a settee, two side and two armchairs, *NY 26 Apr,*
$3,575 (£2,321)

8
A Louis Philippe walnut salon chair, c.1850, *C 24 July,*
£110 ($173)

9
A pair of Charles X-style mahogany fauteuils, *(one illustrated)*, c.1825, *NY 10 June,*
$3,850 (£2,452)

10
A set of four Louis XV-style giltwood fauteuils, *(one illustrated)*, late 19th century, two without upholstered backs, *L 21 Mar,*
£2,970 ($4,633)

11
A Louis XV-style giltwood suite, *(part illustrated)*, c.1860, comprising a sofa, two armchairs, two side chairs and a stool, *NY 13 Sept,*
$8,250 (£5,612)

12
A Louis XVI-style nine-piece suite, *(one piece illustrated)*, c.1900, comprising two armchairs, six chairs and a sofa, the sofa 160cm (63in), *L 21 Mar,*
£1,485 ($2,317)

See also:
Charles X furniture *p* 28

1

2

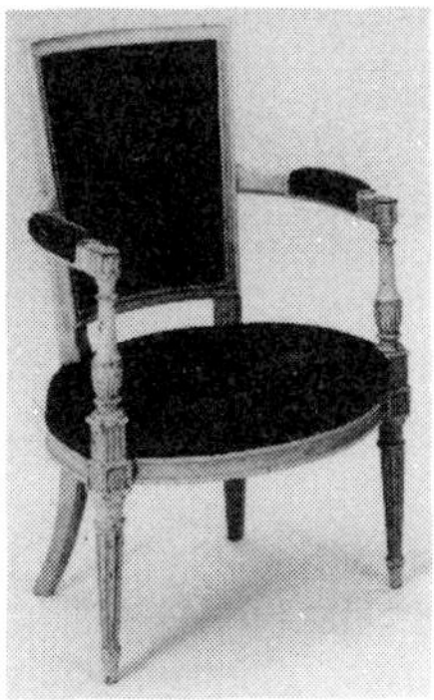
3

4

5

6

7

10

8

9

11

12

1

2

3

4

5

6

7

8

9

10

11

12

13

14

15

16

17

18

19

1
A Tuscan walnut sgabello, 16th century, *NY 25 Nov,*
$2,750 (£1,964)

2
Two Lombardy inlaid chairs, *(one illustrated),* late 17th/early 18th century, *F 14 Apr,*
L 2,600,000 (£1,065; $1,650)

3
A Flemish walnut upholstered armchair, c.1670, with gros-point needlework upholstery, *L 4 July,*
£1,650 ($3,673)

4
A pair of Venetian walnut armchairs, *(one illustrated),* 17th century, *NY 25 Nov,*
$5,775 (£4,125)

5
A pair of Dutch blue and gold lacquered chairs, *(one illustrated),* early 18th century, *M 30 Nov,*
FF 20,900 (£2,272; $3,249)

6
A pair of Italian walnut armchairs, Genoa, c.1700, *F 14 Apr,*
L 7,500,000 (£3,071; $4,760)

7
A pair of North Italian walnut armchairs, *(one illustrated),* first half 18th century, *L 23 May,*
£4,400 ($6,952)

8
A set of four Lombard bone-inlaid walnut chairs, *(one illustrated),* c.1740, inlaid in Renaissance style, *L 23 May,*
£3,520 ($5,562)

9
A Venetian giltwood armchair, mid 18th century, *NY 24 June,*
$2,090 (£1,340)

10
A pair of North Italian side chairs, *(one illustrated),* mid 18th century, *F 19 May,*
L 1,050,000 (£436; $697)

11
A pair of Venetian walnut armchairs, *(one illustrated),* c.1760, *F 14 Apr,*
L 6,000,000 (£2,457; $3,808)

12
A pair of Italian giltwood armchairs, *(one illustrated),* Rome, mid 18th century, *F 30 Sept,*
L 7,150,000 (£3,563; $4,988)

13
A set of six Italian chairs, *(one illustrated),* Piedmont, second half 18th century, *F 30 Sept,*
L 14,850,000 (£7,399; $10,359)

14
A set of seven Italian chairs, *(one illustrated),* probably Genoese, c.1750, *M 23 June,*
FF 111,000 (£9,902; $15,447)

15
A set of eight Italian walnut chairs, *(one illustrated),* Lombardy, mid 18th century, *F 14 Apr,*
L 13,000,000 (£5,324; $8,251)

16
A pair of Venetian painted armchairs, *(one illustrated),* mid 18th century, *L 23 May,*
£3,300 ($5,214)

17
A set of six Italian caned painted side chairs, *(one illustrated),* mid 18th century, *NY 17 Dec,*
$4,400 (£3,142)

18
A set of five Venetian walnut chairs, *(one illustrated),* mid 18th century, *F 30 Sept,*
L 8,800,000 (£4,385; $6,139)

19
A pair of Italian painted hall chairs, *(one illustrated),* second half 18th century, *NY 4 Oct,*
$3,575 (£2,482)

1
A pair of Dutch walnut marquetry chairs, *(one illustrated)*, late 18th century, *M 25 Feb*,
FF 11,100 (£1,074; $1,610)

2
A set of six Dutch brass-inlaid elm dining chairs, *(one illustrated)*, c.1790, *L 30 May*,
£1,375 ($2,172)

3
A set of six Cape stinkwood dining chairs, *(one illustrated)*, late 18th century, *JHB 29 Sept*,
R 3,200 (£1,009; $1,413)

4
A Dutch mahogany armchair *(illustrated)*, **and four side chairs,** 19th century, *A 31 Jan*,
Dfl 1,265 (£383; $563)

5
A set of three Neapolitan armchairs, *(one illustrated)*, c.1780, *F 30 Sept*,
L3,960,000 (£1,973; $2,762)

6
A set of six Italian neoclassical walnut side chairs, *(one illustrated)*, last quarter 18th century, *NY 17 Dec*,
$6,600 (£4,714)

7
A set of three Italian armchairs, *(one illustrated)*, c.1800, the wood lacquered in yellow and red, *M 25 Feb*,
FF 32,190 (£3,113; $4,670)

8
A pair of North Italian armchairs, *(one illustrated)*, late 18th century, with gilt decoration, *F 19 May*,
L3,800,000 (£1,577; $2,523)

9
A set of eight Russian neoclassical mahogany dining chairs, *(one illustrated)*, c.1815, comprising six side chairs and a pair of armchairs, *NY 31 Oct*,
$11,000 (£7,801)

10
A pair of Swedish neoclassical small armchairs, c.1810, now painted in cream, *NY 17 Dec*,
$9,350 (£6,678)

11
A set of six Biedermeier mahogany dining chairs, *(one illustrated)*, with embossed leather drop-in seat, *C 8 Oct*,
£528 ($739)

12
A set of four Biedermeier fruitwood and ebonised side chairs, *(one illustrated)*, c.1820, *NY 22 Mar*,
$3,300 (£2,185)

13
A set of four Biedermeier chairs, *(one illustrated)*, c.1820, of mahogany and fruitwood, *M 30 Nov*,
FF 66,000 (£7,174; $10,043)

14
A set of six Biedermeier walnut dining chairs, *(one illustrated)*, c.1830, *L 28 Nov*,
£3,190 ($4,466)

15
A set of three Dutch fruitwood and marquetry side chairs, *(one illustrated)*, c.1850, *C 17 Apr*,
£528 ($880)

16
A pair of Biedermeier fruitwood and ebonised armchairs, *(one illustrated)*, c.1820, *NY 22 Mar*,
$8,250 (£5,464)

17
An Italian walnut armchair, c.1840, *F 19 May*,
L 700,000 (£290; $465)

18
A late 19th century Italian walnut rocking chair, c.1860, the scrolled arms with masks and flowers supported by winged beasts, the rockers with seahorse heads, *L 13 June*,
£1,320 ($2,112)

1

2

3

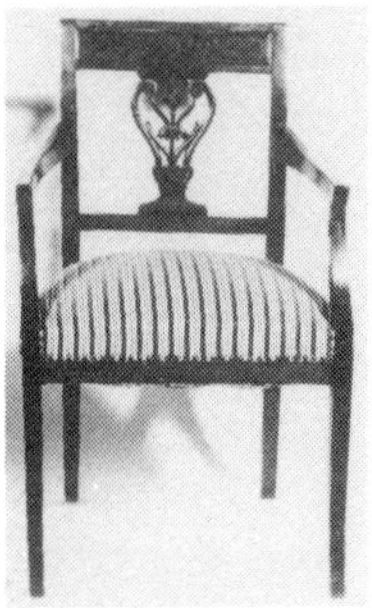
4

5

6

7

8

9

10

11

12

13

14

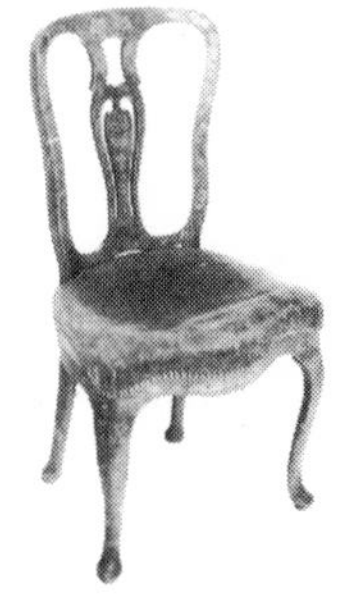
15

16

17

18

1

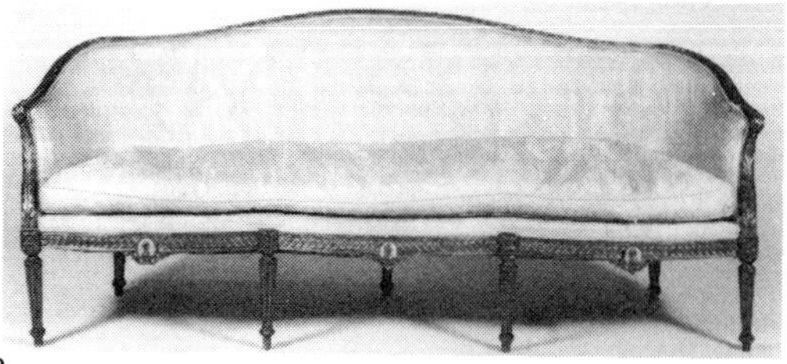
2

3

4

5

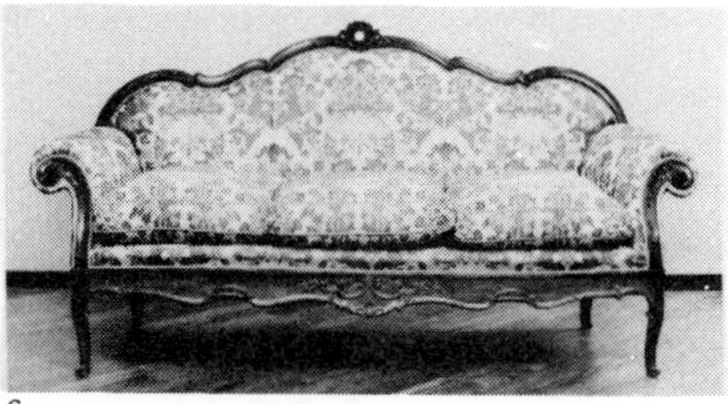
6

7

8

9

10

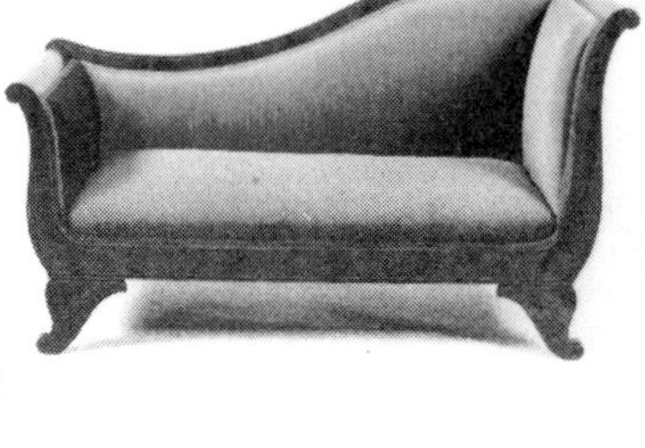
11

1
An Italian giltwood and painted hall seat, Venetian, early 20th century, the back panel painted in the manner of Hondecoeter, 150cm (59in) wide, *C 17 Apr,*
£1,045 ($1,620)

2
An Italian giltwood settee, last quarter 18th century, 226cm (7ft 5in), *NY 17 Dec,*
$4,950 (£3,535)

3
A pair of North Italian settees, *(one illustrated),* c.1760, in engraved and lacquered wood, 210cm (6ft 10in), *F 19 May,*
L 2,400,000 (£996; $1,593)

4
A satinwood settee, German or Dutch, early 19th century, with ebony stringing, 182cm (72in), *C 17 Apr,*
£715 ($1,108)

5
A pair of Italian walnut settees (*one illustrated),* Venetian, mid 18th century, 140cm (55in), *F 14 Apr,*
L 17,000,000 (£6,962; $10,790)

6
A North Italian walnut settee, mid 18th century, 240cm (7ft 10½in), *F 14 Apr,*
L5,000,000 (£2,048; $3,174)

7
A Dutch marquetry and mahogany scroll-end sofa, c.1830, 224cm (7ft 2in), *S 11 Nov,*
£1,430 ($2,002)

8
A Louis XVI beechwood sofa, last quarter 18th century, 152cm (60in), *NY 4 Oct,*
$4,400 (£3,055)

9
A Biedermeier ebonised birch settee, first quarter 19th century, 193cm (6ft 4in), *NY 4 Oct,*
$4,950 (£3,437)

10
A German limewood settle, c.1850, probably Black Forest, 140cm (55in), *C 8 Oct,*
£1,155 ($1,617)

11
An inlaid mahogany settee, Continental, second quarter 19th century, 157.5cm (62in), *NY 24 June,*
$1,760 (£1,128)

1
An oyster-veneered cushion framed wall mirror, late 17th century, 76cm (30in), *C 9 July,*
£1,012 ($1,629)

2
A Queen Anne pier glass, c.1710, 155cm (61in), *L 25 Apr,*
£5,280 ($8,448)

3
A George II gilt-gesso wall mirror, c.1730, 185.5cm (6ft 1in), *L 14 Nov,*
£10,120 ($14,472)

4
A Louis XV giltwood wall mirror, c.1750, 168cm (66in) high, *NY 3 May,*
$11,000 (£7,237)

5
A George II giltwood wall mirror, c.1740, 129cm (51in), *L 14 Mar,*
£2,530 ($3,921)

6
A mid Georgian mahogany wall mirror, the cresting pierced with a *ho-o,* 94cm (37in) high, *C 25 June,*
£308 ($480)

7
A George I carved giltwood wall mirror, c.1725, 88cm (34½in), *C 9 July,*
£3,300 ($5,313)

8
A late George II oval giltwood wall mirror, c.1755, 106cm (42in) high, *L 2 May,*
£3,190 ($5,072)

9
A George II oval giltwood wall mirror, c.1750, *L 28 Feb,*
£1,540 ($2,387)

10
An Italian carved giltwood oval wall mirror, mid 18th century, 140cm (55in) high, *L 23 May,*
£1,320 ($2,086)

11
A pair of Italian rococo giltwood mirrors, *(one illustrated),* mid 18th century, 115.5cm (45½in) high, *NY 4 Oct,*
$2,090 (£1,451)

12
A set of four Venetian girandole mirrors, *(one illustrated),* mid 18th century, each shaped plate engraved with a mythological figure standing on a bracket, 73cm (28½in) high, *L 12 Dec,*
£5,500 ($7,700)

13
A late George II giltwood oval wall mirror, c.1755, 140cm (55in) high, *L 25 Apr,*
£8,800 ($14,080)

1

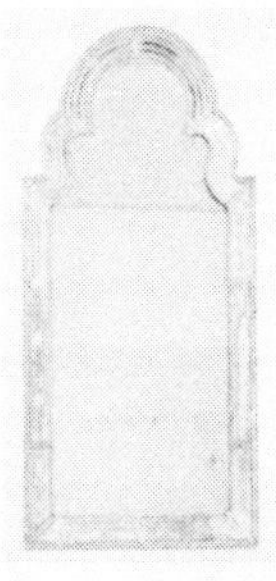
2

3

4

5

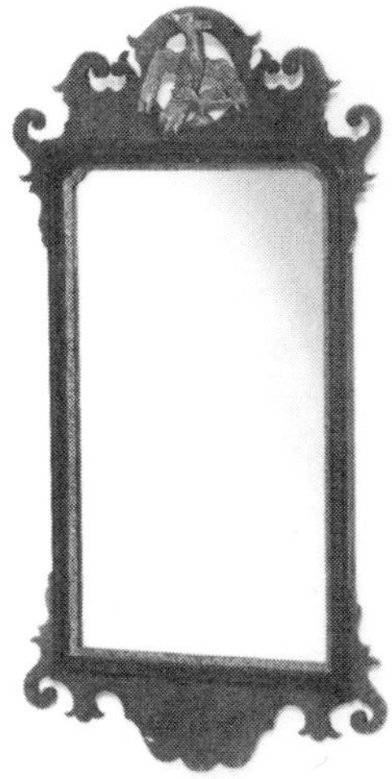
6

7

8

9

10

11

12

13

1

2

3

4

5

6

7

8

9

10

11
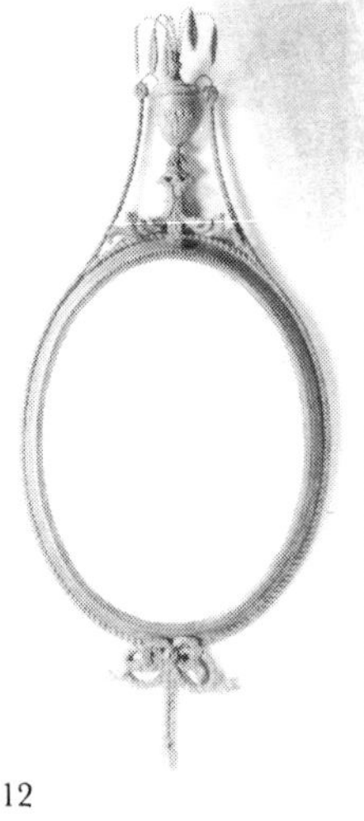
12
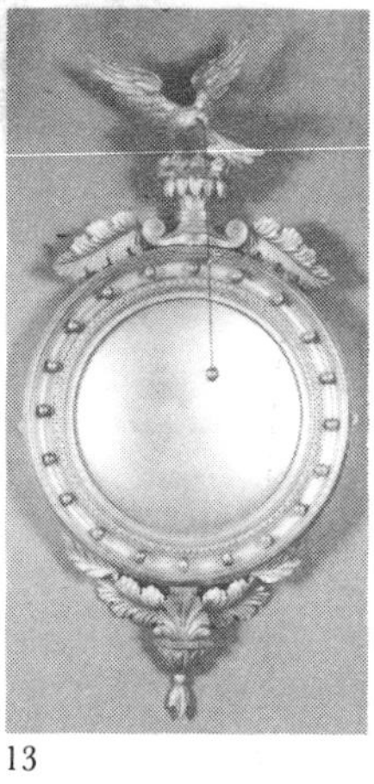
13

1
A George III giltwood mirror, c.1775, 128cm (50in), *NY 7 June,*
$6,325 (£4,244)

2
An Italian giltwood mirror, c.1800, 182cm (71½in), *F 14 Apr,*
L 4,500,000 (£1,843; $2,856)

3
An Italian giltwood mirror, Piedmont, third quarter 18th century, 235cm (7ft 7in) high, *F 30 Sept,*
L 7,700,000 (£3,837; $5,371)

4
A Régence giltwood mirror, c.1720, 227cm (7ft 4in) high, *M 23 Feb,*
FF 88,800 (£8,588; $12,882)

5
An Italian fruitwood, painted and parcel-gilt mirror, early 19th century, 135cm (53½in), *NY 22 Mar,*
$3,960 (£2,623)

6
An Italian painted and parcel-gilt mirror, c.1775, 168cm (66in) high, *NY 22 Mar,*
$3,575 (£2,368)

7
A Regency giltwood mirror, c.1805, the frieze panel with silver *verre eglomisé* trellis, 98cm (38½in), *L 2 May,*
£1,078 ($1,714)

8
An Italian painted and parcel-gilt mirror, c.1790, now painted white, 114cm (45in) high, *NY 24 June,*
$990 (£635)

9
A Regency carved giltwood convex mirror, c.1810, 99cm (39in), *NY 14 Oct,*
$1,980 (£1,375)

10
A Regency giltwood girandole, c.1810, 158cm (62in), *L 11 July,*
£6,050 ($9,620)

11
A Regency giltwood pier mirror, c.1810, 225cm (7ft 4½in) high, *L 14 Nov,*
£5,940 ($8,494)

12
A George III oval giltwood wall mirror, c.1770, 124cm (49in), *L 14 Mar,*
£2,860 ($4,433)

13
A Regency giltwood convex mirror, c.1810, 117cm (46in) high, *NY 25 Jan,*
$3,850 (£2,770)

1
A pair of ivory and bone mirrors, *(one illustrated)*, c.1880, fitted with bone heraldic motifs, putti, a lyre and shields, 82.5cm (32½in) high, *NY 26 Nov,*
$4,950 (£3,536)

2
A Victorian carved giltwood wall mirror, c.1900, in the Chinese Chippendale manner, 165cm (65in) high, *S 11 Nov,*
£2,860 ($4,004)

3
A Biedermeier fruitwood dressing mirror, c.1830, 62cm (24¼in) high, *NY 17 Dec,*
$1,045 (£746)

4
A Napoleon III gilt-bronze-mounted ebonised wood mirror, c.1870, 102cm (44in) high, *NY 13 Sept,*
$2,530 (£1,721)

5
An overmantel mirror, c.1860, with panels of enamel decoration over a red background, 104cm (41in), *Mel 24 June,*
Aus$3,300 (£1,435; $2,238)

6
A Venetian carved pinewood wall mirror, c.1880, 230cm (7ft 6½in) high, *L 13 June,*
£4,950 ($7,920)

7
A Queen Anne walnut toilet mirror, c.1710, 38cm (15in) wide, *S 11 Nov,*
£825 ($1,155)

8
A George III mahogany toilet mirror, c.1790, 61cm (24in) high, *C 16 Jan,*
£319 ($479)

9
An etched and cut glass wall mirror, late 19th century, 98cm (38½in) high, *C 17 Apr,*
£374 ($580)

10
A pair of Italian giltwood girandoles, *(one illustrated)*, 19th century, with a candle arm below, 104cm (41in) high, *L 3 Feb,*
£715 ($1,044)

11
A Queen Anne walnut toilet mirror, c.1720, the box base with two drawers, 79cm (31¼in) high, *C 16 Jan,*
£418 ($627)

12
A Regency mahogany cheval dressing mirror, c.1810, 192cm (6ft 3½in) high, *S 18 Feb,*
£660 ($1,003)

13
A Victorian mahogany cheval mirror, mid 19th century, 132cm (52in) high, *C 25 June,*
£253 ($395)

14
An Empire ormolu-mounted mahogany cheval mirror, c.1810, 194cm (6ft 4½in) high, *NY 17 Dec,*
$3,300 (£2,357)

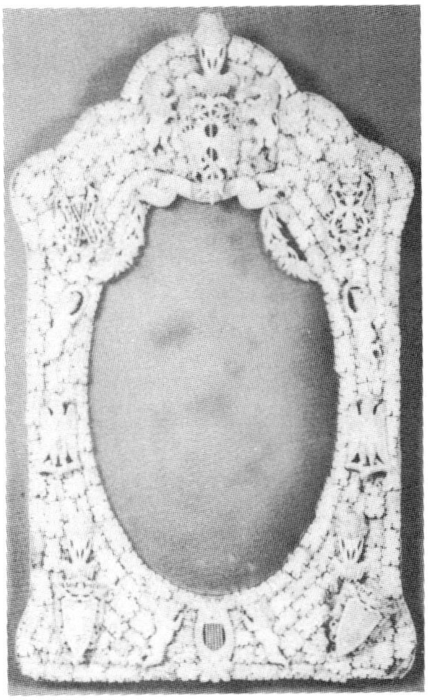
1

2

3

4

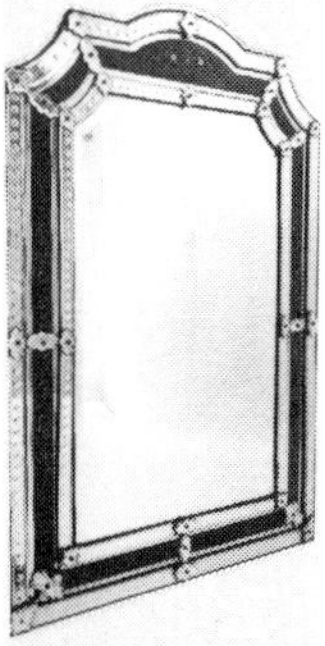
5

6

7

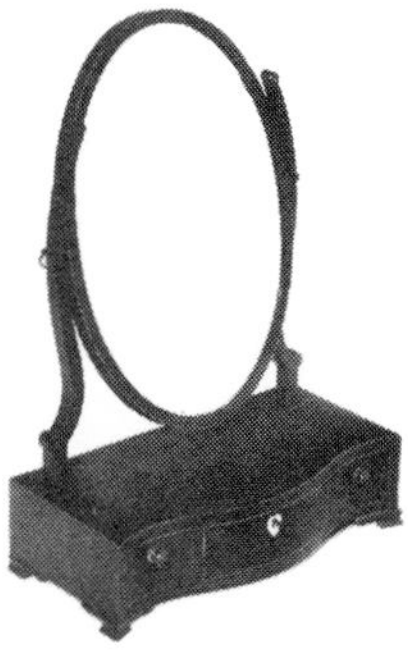
8

9

10

11

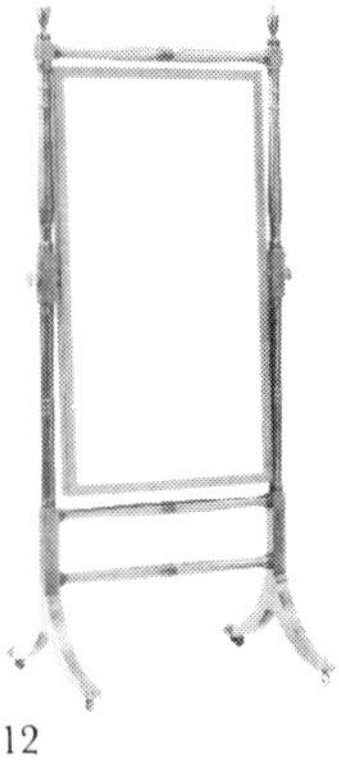
12

13

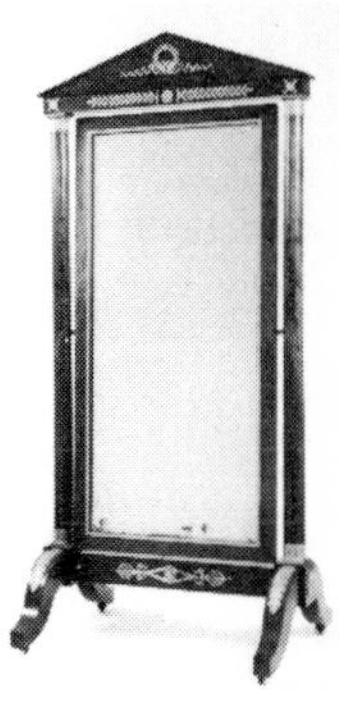
14

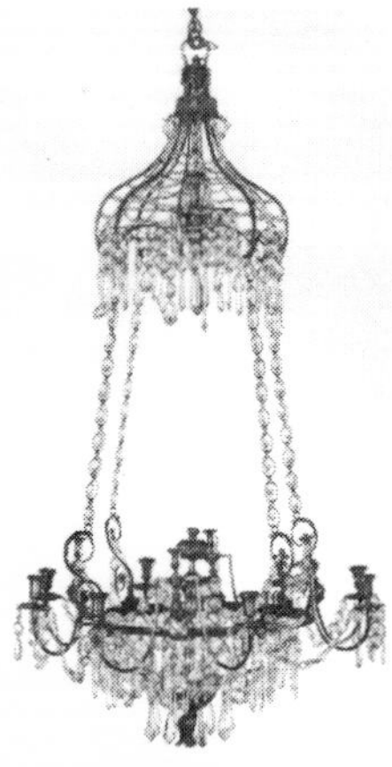
1

2

3

4

5

6

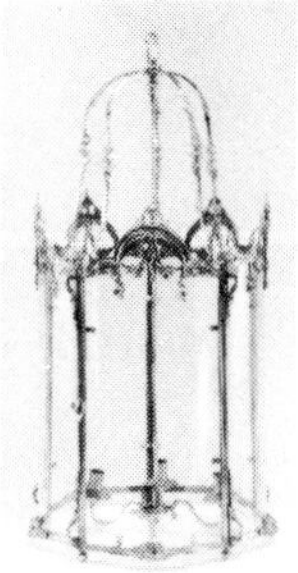
7

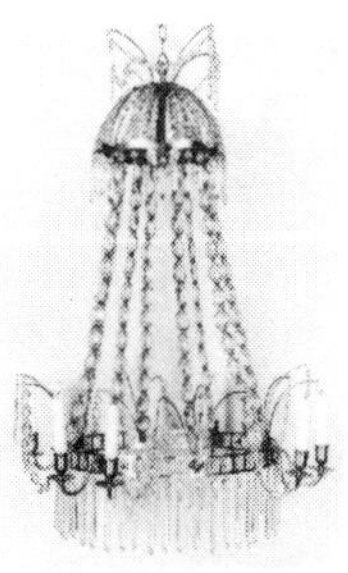
8

9

10

11

12

1
A Baltic gilt-bronze and cut glass chandelier, c.1800, of twelve lights, 104cm (41in) high, *L 23 May,*
£5,500 ($8,690)

2
A Louis XV-style gilt-bronze and cut glass chandelier, of nine lights, 125cm (49¼in) high, *M 22 June,*
FF 27,750 (£2,581; $4,027)

3
A gilt-bronze chandelier, c.1870, in Transitional style, with six scrolling candle-arms, 92cm (36¼in) high, *L 13 June,*
£1,430 ($2,288)

4
A gilt-bronze and cut glass chandelier, c.1870, of fourteen lights, the central glass baluster continuing to a gilt-bronze foliate spray and trumpet-form glass vase, damages, 117cm (46in) high, *NY 13 Sept,*
$14,850 (£10,102)

5
A gilt-bronze chandelier, c.1880, of sixteen lights, with two tiers of 'S' scroll arms, the stem case with leaves, fluting, masks and horses, 80cm (32in) high, *L 7 Nov,*
£2,035 ($2,849)

6
A brass adjustable pendant ceiling lamp, c.1860, fitted with an oil burner with opalene glass shade, contained by three pairs of candle-arms, 140cm (55in) high, *C 17 Apr,*
£880 ($1,364)

7
A pair of Louis XV ormolu lanterns, *(one illustrated)*, mid 18th century, the ormolu borders decorated with floral garlands and covered urns, the upper part supporting four candle-arms, 78cm (31½in) high, *NY 3 May,*
$9,900 (£6,513)

8
A Swedish brass and cut glass chandelier, c.1800, with umbrella corona and with eight scroll candle-arms, *L 30 May,*
£1,265 ($1,999)

9
A Continental brass and cut glass chandelier, late 18th century, probably Swedish, of cage form, with six lights, 97cm (38in) high, *NY 4 Oct,*
$5,225 (£3,628)

10
A Louis XV-style gilt-bronze and cut glass chandelier, early 20th century, of fifteen lights, the crown hung with amethyst glass drops, the whole hung with glass flowerheads, drops and pendants, electrified, 152cm (60in) high, *NY 26 Apr,*
$2,200 (£1,429)

11
A pair of Murano glass chandeliers, *(one illustrated)*, 1910, each of eighteen lights, decorated with clear and polychrome flowers and leaves, 92cm (36in) diam., *L 7 Nov,*
£3,300 ($4,620)

12
A George IV gilt-bronze Colza oil hanging light, c.1820, the square body applied with cast scroll-work and with four projecting arms, 84cm (33in) high, *L 18 July,*
£2,090 ($3,323)

1
A Viennese gilt-bronze candelabrum, late 18th/early 19th century, with central flambeau urn on a fluted column supporting three scroll candle-branches, 53cm (21in) high, *L 23 May,*
£3,300 ($5,214)

2
A George IV gilt-brass hall lantern, decorated with flower- and leaf-cast scrollwork, 64cm (25in) high, *L 18 July,*
£1,870 ($2,973)

3
A pair of glass and Wedgwood-type candlesticks, 19th century, each with thistle-shaped nozzle, the gilt-metal drum with white-on-blue jasperware decoration, 29cm (11¾in) high, *L 18 July,*
£715 ($1,137)

4
A pair of George III parcel-gilt mahogany candlesticks, late 18th century, each with cast brass nozzle and leaf-cast drip-pan, 94cm (37in) high, *L 11 July,*
£2,530 ($4,023)

5
A pair of English parcel-gilt bronze candelabra, *(one illustrated)*, c.1835, each of two lights with floral cast detachable nozzles, the central ring-turned column with leaf finial, 24cm (9½in) high, *C 17 Apr,*
£550 ($853)

6
A pair of George III gilt-brass, cut glass and jasperware two-light candelabra, late 18th century, each with four scrolled candle-arms and jasperware base, 69cm (27in) high, *NY 25 Jan,*
$5,775 (£4,155)

7
A pair of Regency bronze, gilt-bronze and cut glass candelebra, c.1820, each with two candle-branches and drop-hung, rose-cast coronas, 37cm (14½in) high, *L 2 May,*
£8,800 ($13,992)

8
A pair of gilt and patinated bronze candelabra, *(one illustrated)*, c.1830, each with a whippet lying on a marble plinth, detachable nozzles, 27cm (10in) high, *C 17 Apr,*
£880 ($1,364)

9
A bronze figural lamp, c.1870, with a winged female figure supporting two extended candle-arms, stepped marble base, 98.5cm (38¾in) high, *NY 26 Nov,*
$2,750 (£1,964)

10
A gilt-brass ceiling lantern, c.1880, the frame surmounted by a band of cast neoclassical urns, the centre section with four electric lights, 81cm (32in) high, *C 16 Jan,*
£880 ($1,320)

11
A brass telescopic standard oil lamp, c.1890, the reservoir clasped in four scrolls, the retracting support in a Corinthian column, electrified, 165cm (65in) high, *C 27 Feb,*
£330 ($495)

See also:
Ormolu *pp* 93-97

1

2

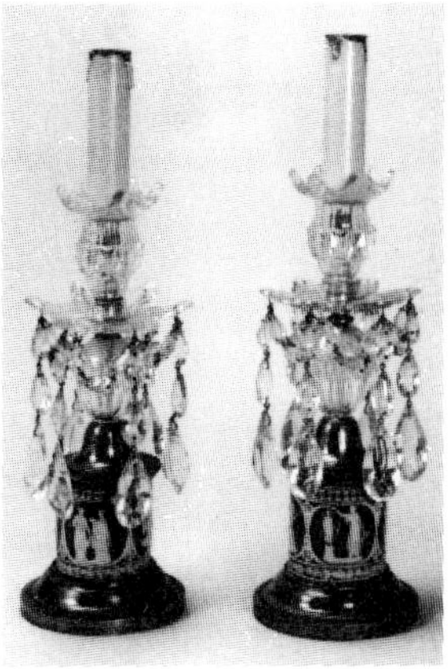
3

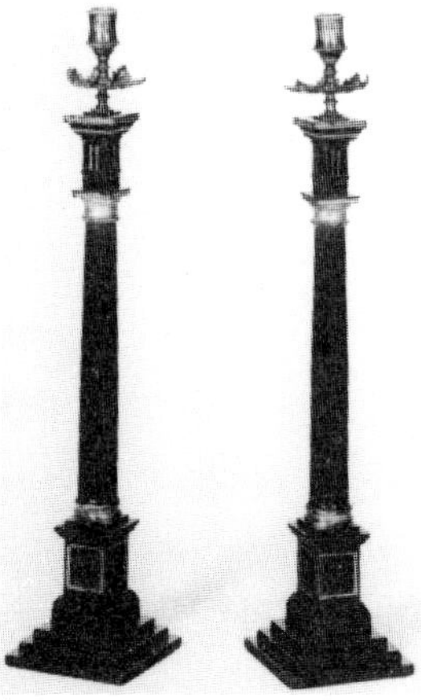
4

5

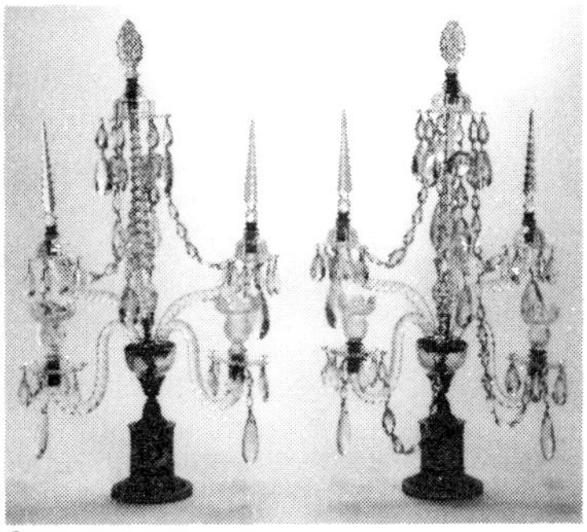
6

7

8

9

10

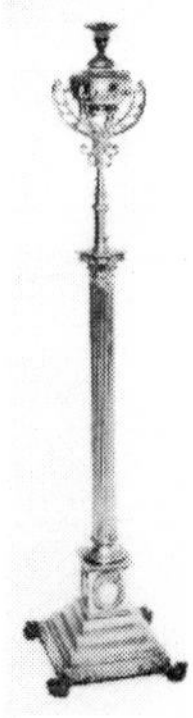
11

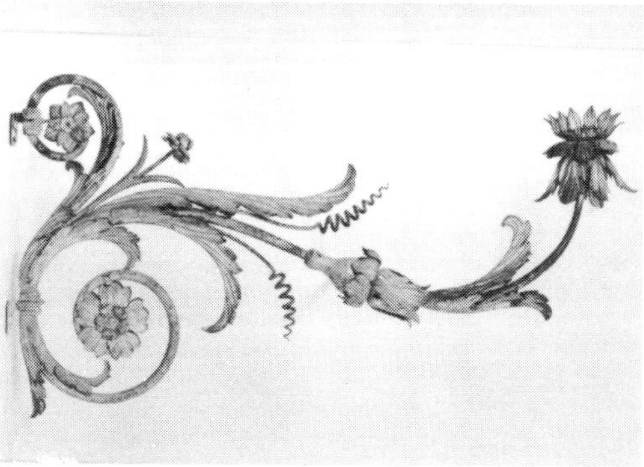
1

2

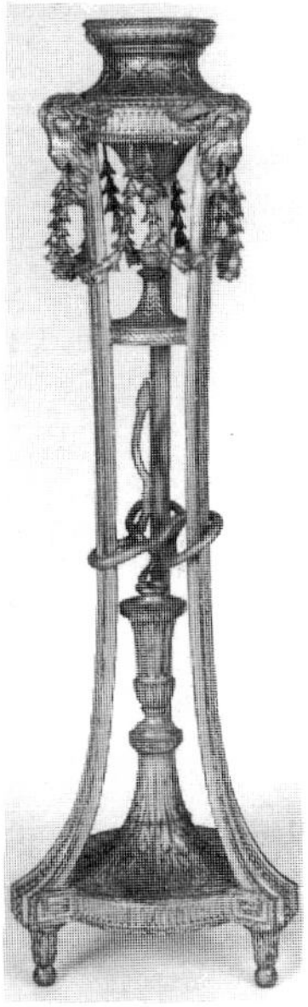
3

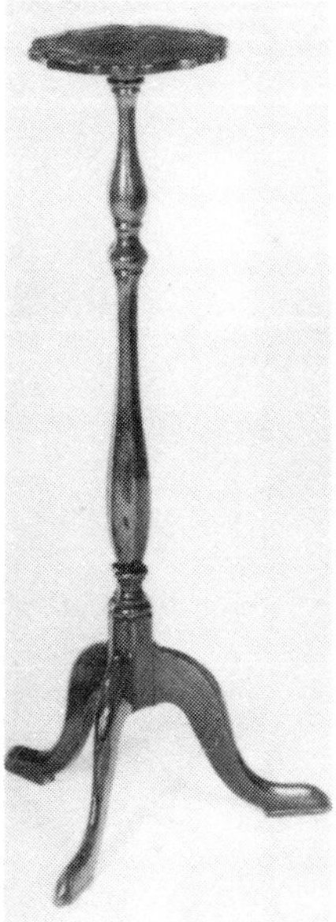
4

5

6

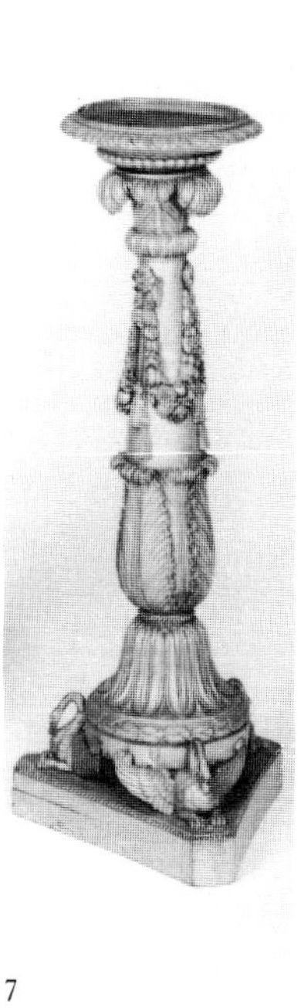
7

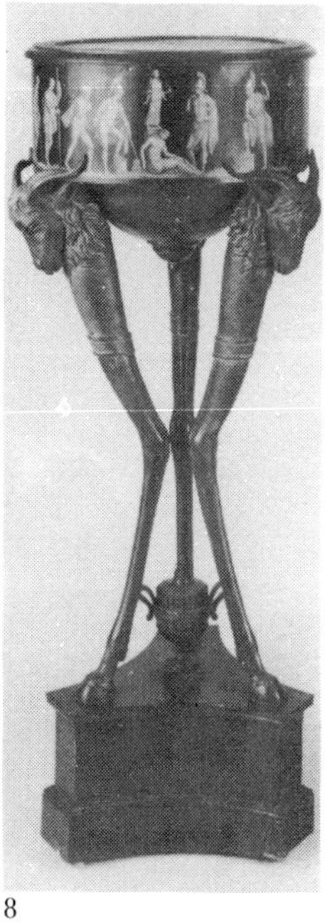
8

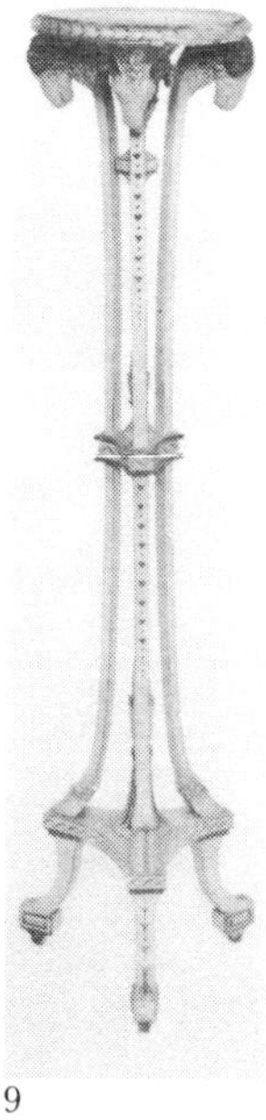
9

1
A pair of Venetian gilt-bronze wall-lights, *(one illustrated)*, 18th century, 110cm (43¼in), *M 1 Dec,* **FF 38,500 (£4,158; $5,945)**

2
A pair of Regency gilt-bronze candlesticks, *(one illustrated)*, c.1800, each nozzle in the form of an antique oil lamp, the base with three griffins, 16cm (6½in), *L 11 July,* **£3,080 ($4,897)**

3
A pair of George III giltwood torchères, *(one illustrated)*, c.1775, the circular tops decorated with acanthus leaves and flowerheads, 155cm (61in), *HS 24 Sept,* **IR£18,700 (£17,000; $24,650)**

4
A pair of George II mahogany tripod torchères, *(one illustrated)*, c.1750, 94cm (37in), *L 24 Oct,* **£1,705 ($2,387)**

5
A pair of Italian figures of blackamoors, mid 18th century, each with later stand, *NY 4 Oct,* **$6,875 (£4,774)**

6
A Venetian gesso and wood blackamoor figure, 20th century, painted in various colours, 182cm (71½in), *C 16 Jan,* **£1,265 ($1,898)**

7
A pair of Empire giltwood torchères, *(one illustrated)*, c.1810, the leaf-carved stems supported on swan feet, 112cm (44in), *L 20 June,* **£7,150 ($11,297)**

8
A pair of Italian painted torchères, *(one illustrated)*, late 18th century, each with a circular white marble top above a frieze painted *en grisaille* with classical figures, the supports painted to simulate bronze, 158cm (62¼in), *NY 22 Mar,* **$14,300 (£9,470)**

9
A pair of Adam Revival torchères, *(one illustrated)*, c.1850, each circular dished top above composition ram's masks, painted cream and green, 140cm (55in), *C 9 July,* **£1,078 ($1,736)**

French Ormolu

GILLIAN ARTHUR

With steady progression from the latter part of the 17th century and for the following one hundred years, there evolved in France an unprecedented outpouring of creativity in interior design and furnishings which is as yet unequalled. Broadly speaking, baroque, rococo and neoclassical designs are representative of this period, and keeping step with these divergent trends was the phenomenally diverse use and application of objects and mounts created from ormolu.

The word ormolu, in use since the early 1760s, is an English derivation of the French term *bronze dore d'or moulu*. Ormolu, *bronze dore* and gilt-bronze all refer to the same material, which was used to make mounts and objects of all kinds. The process for the production of ormolu is an ancient one, described by Pliny, by medieval craftsmen and at length by Cellini. During the 18th century the demand for gold decoration coupled with the loss of precious metals to finance the wars of Louis XIV and Louis XV, gave rise to the refinement and diverse use of this ancient technique. Though not a French, or even an 18th century innovation, ormolu was used in France at that time to a previously unparalleled extent.

During this period, the production of a piece of furniture was the result of a collaboration among members of a number of strictly legislated medieval craft guilds: *La Corporation des Menuisiers* (or *Menuisiers-Ebenistes* as it became when the technique of veneering was recognised in the revised guild statutes of 1744-51); *La Corporation des Fondeurs-Ciseleurs* who contributed the mounts, from the simplest drawer handle to the most elaborate ornament; and *La Corporation des Ciseleurs-Doreurs*, who carried out any chasing

1
A pair of Régence ormolu two-light bras de lumière, *(one illustrated)*, first quarter 18th century, pierced for wiring, 23.5cm (9¼in), *NY 1 Nov,*
$6,050 (£4,291)

2
A pair of Louis XIV gilt-bronze candlesticks, early 18th century, 40cm (15½in), *L 20 June,*
£46,200 ($72,996)

3
A pair of Louis XV gilt-bronze wall-lights, *(one illustrated)*, mid 18th century, 43cm (17in), *L 12 Dec,*
£3,080 ($4,312)

4
A pair of Louis XV gilt-bronze chenets, mid 18th century, 41cm (16in), *L 20 June,*
£3,080 ($4,866)

1

2

3

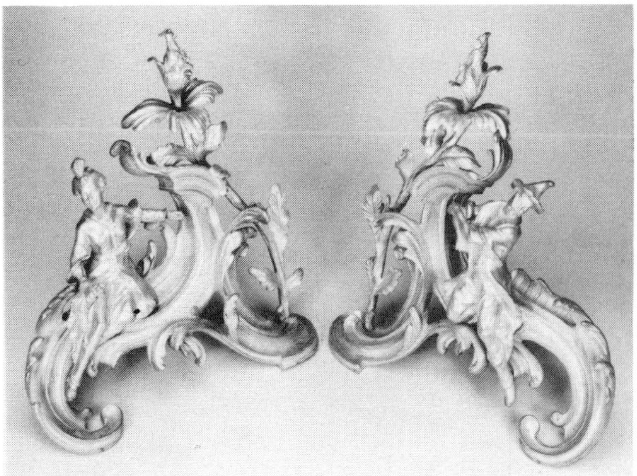
4

or gilding required.

With the exception of a few craftsmen under the protection of the Court, crafts could be practised only by guild members. No member of a guild was permitted to engage in a craft that was the prerogative of another without facing severe penalties, ranging from heavy fines to the possible destruction of the pieces involved. Thus Charles Cressent and Jean-Pierre Latz, both members of the guild of *menuisiers-ébénistes*, were prosecuted on more than one occasion by the *Corporation des Fondeurs-Ciseleurs* for making the mounts for their own furniture. The destruction of Cressent's work was prevented only by the intervention of his patron the Duc d'Orleans. In fact, a *maître-ébéniste* was not even permitted to go and fetch the completed mounts he had ordered: these had to be carried to his *atelier* by a member of the *ciseleurs-doreurs*, in spite of the fact that most *ébénistes* habitually used the same *ciseleur-doreur* who was probably a close neighbour. As Sir Francis Watson has pointed out, it is almost surprising that the *ébéniste* was permitted to affix the mounts to the piece of furniture himself!

In addition to mounts for furniture, which initially probably served a purely functional purpose to protect vulnerable parts of the case, such diverse articles as lighting devices of every

5

6

5
A pair of rare Louis XV ormolu three-light chimney-piece appliques, mid 18th century, bearing the crowned C mark, originally intended for the corners of a large chimney-piece, 132cm (51¾in) high, *NY 1 Nov,*
$363,000 (£257,447)

6
A pair of Louis XV ormolu and cut glass seven-light girandoles, mid 18th century, the whole hung with cut glass beads, prisms and pendants, formerly fitted for electricity, 81cm (32in) high, *NY 3 May,*
$20,900 (£13,750)

7
A pair of Louis XV gilt-bronze candelabra, mid 18th century, on domed bases cast with coats of arms, 37cm (14¼in) high, *L 23 May,*
£3,300 ($5,214)

8
A pair of Louis XVI gilt-bronze-mounted blue glass vases, c.1785, 21cm (8½in), *L 23 May,*
£880 ($1,390)

9
A Louis XV gilt-bronze and porcelain ornament, second quarter 18th century, in the form of an Arita pot flanked by two swans, 17.5cm (7in) high, *L 23 May,*
£1,320 ($2,085)

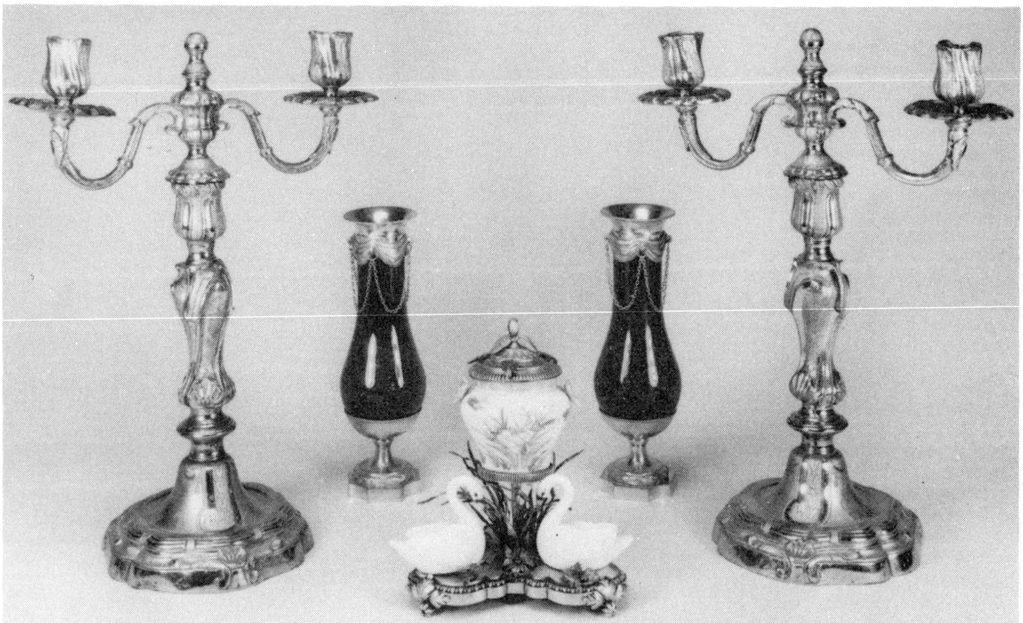

7 8 9 8 7

conceivable type, clock cases, hearth equipment, door fittings, mounts for porcelain as well as small decorative sculptures, were manufactured in ormolu.

The first step in the manufacture of any of these articles was the sculpting of a model in either wood or wax. This work was sometimes undertaken by distinguished sculptors. With the 'Avignon' clock, presented to the Governor of Avignon in 1771 and now in the Wallace Collection in London, the model was sculpted by Louis-Simon Boizot. The model was then cast in bronze by a *fondeur*, usually by the *cire-perdue* (lost wax) process, but sometimes from a mould of clay or sand. The *cire-perdue* process produced a finer finish but only one cast. The wax model enclosed within the mould reproducing its surface was melted away before the molten metal could be poured in. As a result, when the *cire-perdue* process was used, a wooden model was kept to provide further wax models. The finishing process could be undertaken by the *fondeur*, the *ciseleur* (chaser) or the *doreur* (gilder) and was often carried to an extraordinary degree of refinement using an array of instruments of ever-increasing precision. Not all bronzes were gilded; some were simply cleaned in acid and then lacquered. This does not imply that they were in any way inferior, indeed a great number of the mounts on furniture belonging to Mme de Pompadour were treated in this way, and entries in Lazare-Duvaux's *Livre-Journal* show that she sent such mounts to be re-dipped and re-lacquered (*resaucés*) to maintain their lustre.

Only the finest bronzes were gilded, probably because it was an enormously expensive process. In mercury gilding, the process most often used, finely divided particles of gold were dissolved in heated mercury to form an amalgam that coated bronze. The bronze was then heated to drive off the mercury, which vaporises at a relatively moderate temperature. This is an extremely hazardous process since mercury vapours are exceedingly noxious. As a result, the life of the 18th century gilder could be rather short, but the payment he received was extremely high. The 'Avignon' clock was delivered for a cost of 11,414.15 Livres; of this 9,200 Livres was paid to Pierre Gouthiere who had cast the bronze, finished and gilded it. Gouthiere was the leading exponent of his craft, however Louis-Simon Boizot, who was

10
A pair of Louis XVI ormolu candlesticks, *(one illustrated)*, last quarter 18th century, each with indistinct ink signature under base, 30cm (12in), *NY 4 Oct,*
$1,870 (£1,298)

11
A pair of Louis XVI ormolu candlesticks, *(one illustrated)*, attributed to Dugourc, 33cm (13in), *M 30 Nov,*
FF 71,500 (£7,772; $10,880)

12
A pair of Louis XVI ormolu candlesticks, 28cm (11in), *M 23 Feb,*
FF 38,350 (£3,757; $5,636)

13
An early Louis XVI gilt-bronze inkstand, c.1775, 20cm (8in) wide, *L 12 Dec,*
£2,420 ($3,388)

14
A pair of Louis XVI wall-lights, *(one illustrated)*, pierced for electricity, 50cm (19½in), *M 22 June,*
FF 44,400 (£3,961; $6,179)

10

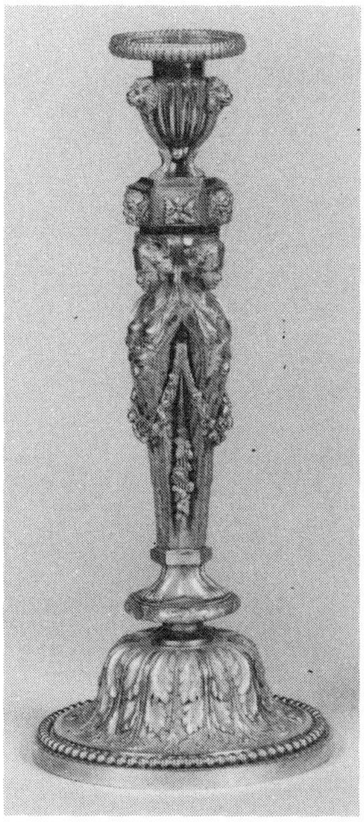

11

12

13

14

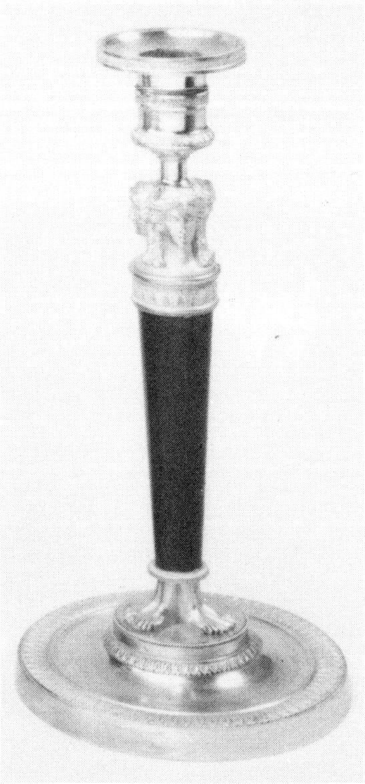
15

16

17

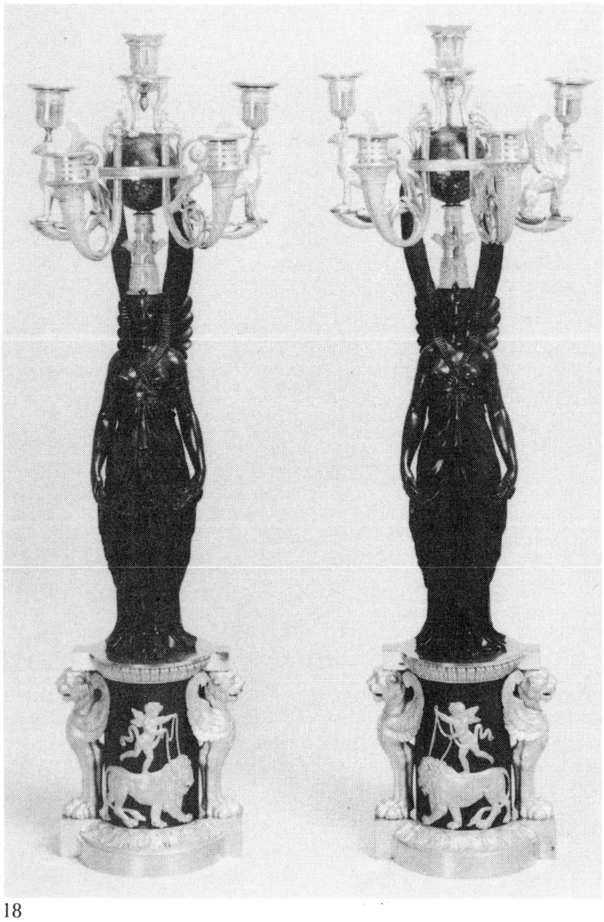
18

19

15
A pair of Directoire bronze and gilt-bronze candlesticks, *(one illustrated)*, c.1795, with three adorsed neoclassical female heads, *L 20 June*,
£1,375 ($2,172)

16
A pair of Directoire bronze, gilt-bronze and marble tapersticks, *(one illustrated)*, late 18th century, in the form of a pot of tulips, 18.5cm (7½in), *L 12 Dec*,
£2,200 ($3,080)

17
A pair of Empire ormolu candlesticks, *(one illustrated)*, early 19th century, bases drilled, 29cm (11½in), *NY 4 Oct*,
$1,540 (£1,069)

18
A pair of Empire bronze and gilt-bronze candelabra, early 19th century, in the manner of Pierre-Philippe Thomire, in the form of a female Egyptian figure, 78.5cm (31in), *L 20 June*,
£16,500 ($26,070)

19
A pair of Louis XVI ormolu six-light candelabra, *(one illustrated)*, last quarter 18th century, 58cm (23in), *NY 3 May*,
$6,875 (£4,523)

hardly less celebrated, received only 1,500 Livres for executing the model; Delunesy was paid 360 Livres for providing the clock's movement — barely more than the 354.14 Livres for packing and transportation to Avignon.

Many pieces of ormolu are marked with the 'Crowned C', a response to a royal edict of 4 February 1749, imposing a duty on metals having copper as a base (see below *Further reading*). Amongst other metal articles, this edict applied to all mounts and ormolu objects and covered not only articles manufactured during the span of the edict, but also those items made at an earlier date and currently available for sale. The mounts were struck with the mark as proof that the duty had been paid. Contrary to popular belief, the 'Crowned C' is not a symbol of quality, nor should it be perceived today as an enhancement of the value of any object on which it might be found.

Ormolu objects and mounts are as highly prized today as they were in the 18th century, and judging their authenticity presents the modern cataloguer and collector with the greatest challenge. There are no easy formulae to follow, and experience is the only teacher. One must weigh stylistic criteria, the assembly of components, quality and, when possible, compare the object at hand with other recorded examples. Once satisfied that the object is of 18th century manufacture, one cannot assume that the gilding is original, especially as we know that both lacquered and gilded bronzes were frequently sent to be restored in the 18th century. Collectors then, much like their 20th century descendants, wanted their metalwork bright and shiny, and we should assume that 19th century owners were no less fastidious. With experience, one learns to recognise that some gilding is quite obviously not original. The colour just will not look 'right': it might be too orange, too yellow or just too bright. It might also have been applied so thickly that the original chasing is barely discernible.

It is the existence of all these questions and the absence of any hard-and-fast proof (for ormolu objects were only very rarely signed and then by only a handful of craftsmen) that makes the study of 18th century ormolu such a challenging field: we must always try to keep an open mind. We must also recall that any ormolu object represents a cultivated way of life and an era unsurpassed in the history of metalworking.

Further reading:

Geoffrey de Bellaigue, *The James A. de Rothschild Collection at Waddesdon Manor*, vol.I, 1974. (See pp.31-35 for a discussion of the 'Crowned C' mark.)
F.J.B. Watson, *Wallace Collection Catalogues, Furniture*, 1956
F.J.B. Watson, *The Wrightsman Collection*, vol.I, 1966
Pierre Verlet, *Les Bronzes Dorés du XVIIIe Siècle*, 1987

20
A Louis XV ormolu-mounted tulipwood, kingwood and purple-wood marquetry jewel casket, mid 18th century, attributed to Bernard van Risamburgh, the top fitted with a mirror, lined with blue silk, fitted with drawers, 100cm (39¼in) high, *NY 1 Nov*,
$38,500 (£27,305)

21
A Régence kingwood-veneered serpentine commode, c.1720, stamped F.F., with mottled grey marble top and gilt-bronze escutcheons and handles, the corners with mask and scroll mounts, 86cm (34in) high, *L 12 Dec*,
£6,050 ($8,470)

22
A Louis XVI ormolu-mounted mahogany bureau plat, last quarter 18th century, signed Crepi, top inset with green leather, 81cm (31¾in) high, *NY 31 Oct*,
$62,700 (£44,468)

20

21

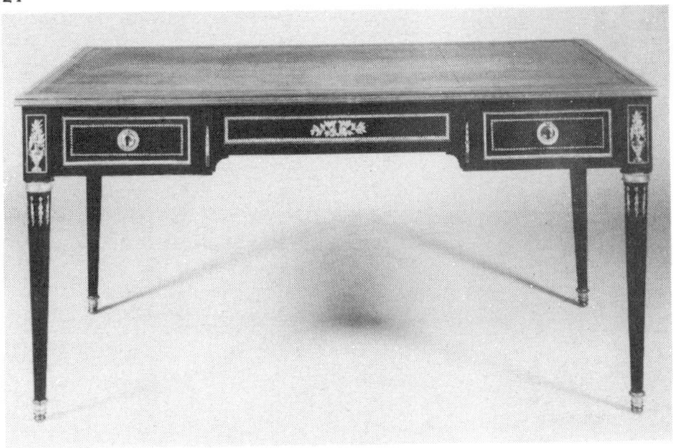

22

1

2

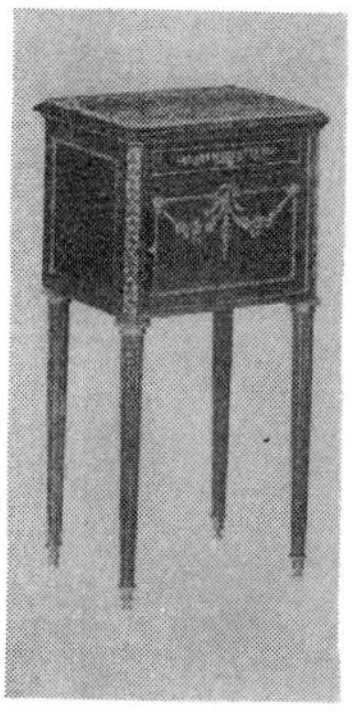

3

4

5

6

7

8

9

10

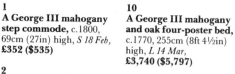

1
A George III mahogany step commode, c.1800, 69cm (27in) high, *S 18 Feb,*
£352 ($535)

2
A set of George IV mahogany bedsteps, c.1820, the three leather-lined treads hinged to reveal a commode, 74cm (29in) long, *L 2 May,*
£1,870 ($2,973)

3
A Linke mahogany and gilt-bronze bedroom suite, c.1930, comprising an armoire, a double bed, bedside table *(illustrated),* and a commode, *L 13 June,*
£5,060 ($8,096)

4
A Louis XVI painted 'lit à Polonaise', last quarter 18th century, now painted grey and highlighted with blue, 206cm (6ft 9in) long, *NY 4 Oct,*
$3,300 (£2,291)

5
A blue lacquer bedroom suite, early 20th century, including a gentleman's wardrobe, a lady's wardrobe, a bedside cupboard *(illustrated),* and a kidney-shaped dressing table, *C 8 Oct,*
£2,035 ($2,849)

6
A William IV mahogany gentleman's dressing cabinet, c.1830, the interior fitted with mirror and compartments above two drawers, 89cm (35in) high, *NY 18 Oct,*
$770 (£535)

7
A pair of steel beds, *(one illustrated),* early 19th century, 195cm (6ft 4in), *M 24 Feb,*
FF 31,080, (£3,006; $4,509)

8
A George III inlaid mahogany dressing stand, c.1780, 71cm (28in) high, *NY 25 Jan,*
$3,190 (£2,295)

9
An early Victorian four-poster bed, c.1840, with a box sprung and hair mattress, 251cm (8ft 3in) high, *L 18 July,*
£2,090 ($3,323)

10
A George III mahogany and oak four-poster bed, c.1770, 255cm (8ft 4½in) high, *L 14 Mar,*
£3,740 ($5,797)

See also:
English tables *p* 65
French tables *p* 71
Mirrors *p* 89
Wardrobes and armoires *pp* 36-38

1
A George IV rosewood and brass-bound travelling toilet box, hallmarked London 1829/30, the fitted interior including jars and boxes each with a silver cover, 31cm (12in) wide, *C 9 July,*
£330 ($531)

2
An early Victorian calamander and brass inlaid toilet box, c.1845, the jar covers hallmarked London 1845, 33cm (13in) wide, *C 9 July,*
£825 ($1,328)

3
A pair of George III satinwood bowfront bedside cupboards, *(one illustrated)*, c.1790, the tambour cupboard with spines in satinwood and purpleheart, 82cm (32in) high, *L 14 Nov,*
£5,720 ($8,180)

4
A George III inlaid mahogany tambour-fronted cabinet, c.1790, 83cm (33½in), *NY 25 Jan,*
$3,300 (£2,374)

5
A George III mahogany corner washstand, c.1810, 83cm (33in) high, *C 27 Feb,*
£352 ($528)

6
A George III mahogany tray top commode, c.1760, 81cm (32in) high, *C 9 July,*
£396 ($638)

7
A pair of George III mahogany bedside cupboards *(one illustrated)*, c.1765, 52cm (20½in) wide, *L 11 July,*
£6,050 ($9,620)

8
A George III mahogany and harewood marquetry bedside commode, inlay later, 48cm (18½in) wide, *S 8 July,*
£495 ($802)

9
A pair of North Italian walnut bedside tables, *(one illustrated)*, c.1760, probably Veneto, 76cm (30in) high, *L 23 May,*
£4,840 ($7,647)

10
A pair of late George III mahogany bedside cabinets, *(one illustrated)*, in the manner of Thomas Hope, each with a rectangular St. Anne marble top, 84cm (33in) high, *L 2 May,*
£1,650 ($2,623)

11
An early Victorian mahogany flush commode, c.1840, the lid enclosing a blue and white porcelain pan, 53cm (21in) wide, *C 27 Feb,*
£198 ($297)

12
A George III satinwood quadrant-shaped corner wash stand, late 18th/early 19th century, with two small glass bowls, 97cm (38in) high, *L 25 Apr,*
£1,650 ($2,640)

13
A George III fret-carved mahogany basin stand, c.1770, 84cm (33in) high, *NY 25 Jan,*
$4,950 (£3,561)

14
A pair of Regency mahogany wash stands *(one illustrated)*, c.1810, in the manner of Gillow, 77cm (30½in) wide, *S 11 Nov,*
£1,705 ($2,387)

15
A George III mahogany commode, c.1800, attributed to Gillows of Lancaster, the front formed of two dummy drawers, oval panels crossbanded in rosewood, 70cm (30in) high, *L 25 Apr,*
£7,480 ($11,968)

16
A George III mahogany basin stand, c.1760, 77cm (30½in) high, *C 16 Jan,*
£297 ($446)

1

2

3

4

5

6

7

8

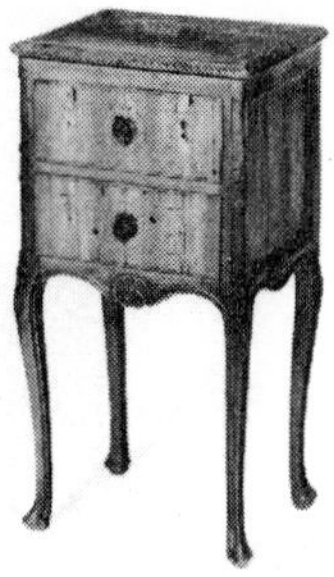
9

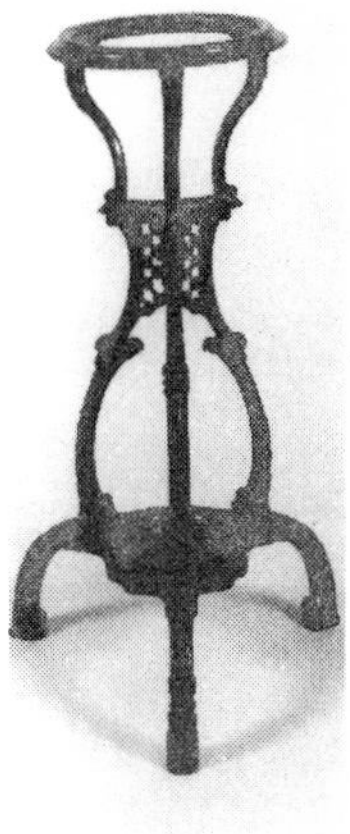
13

10

11

12

14

15

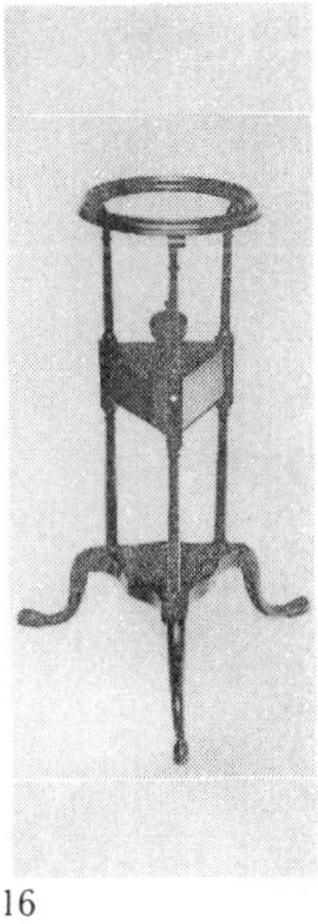
16

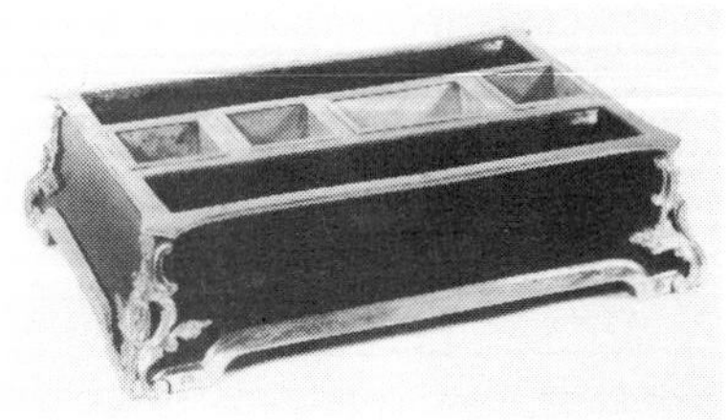
1

2

3

4

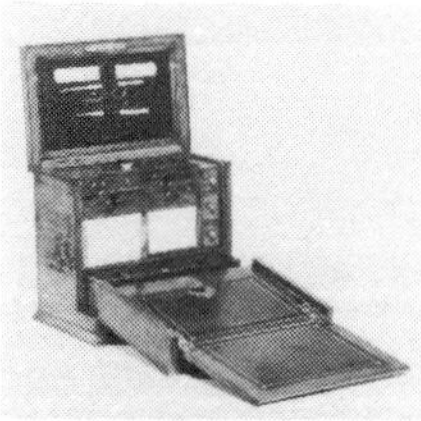
5

6

7

8

9

10

11

12

13

1
A Louis XVI inkstand, in ebonised wood with gilt-bronze decoration, 39cm (15in) wide, *M 23 Feb,*
FF 11,100 (£1,073; $1,610)

2
A Louis XVI inkstand, with gilt-bronze mounts and lacquer panels, 29cm (11½in), wide, *M 30 Nov,*
FF 47,300 (£5,141; $7,198)

3
A Regency brass-inlaid ebony inkstand, c.1815, 34cm (13½in), *NY 7 June,*
$1,100 (£738)

4
A Charles X ormolu-mounted verde antico standish, c.1825, 36.5cm (14½in), *NY 24 June,*
$450 (£288)

5
An oak combination writing and stationery box, early 20th century, applied with a presentation plaque, 32cm (12¾in), *C 14 May,*
£264 ($425)

6
A Victorian coromandel and cut-brass inlaid writing box, c.1870, by Pearce of London, 40cm (15½in) wide, *S 15 July,*
£396 ($622)

7
A French amboyna and ebonised writing box, c.1870, inlaid throughout with cut brass and mother-of-pearl, 36cm (14in) wide, *S 9 Dec,*
£506 ($708)

8
A George IV rosewood and brass-mounted writing box, c.1825, the base with a drawer, 51cm (20in) wide, *S 18 Feb,*
£660 ($1,003)

9
An Anglo-Indian engraved ivory and sandalwood desk box, c.1850, the back with detachable stationery compartment, 41cm (16in) wide, *S 11 Nov,*
£902 ($1,263)

10
A Regency rosewood table book-shelf, c.1815, 41cm (16in) wide, *S 17 June,*
£990 ($1,564)

11
A George IV rosewood table book-shelf, c.1825, 40cm (15½in), *L 21 Nov,*
£825 ($1,155)

12
A set of Victorian oak library steps, c.1870, 258cm (8ft 5½in), *L 14 Nov,*
£3,190 ($4,562)

13
A set of English oak library steps, 19th century, 182cm (5ft 11½in) high, *L 18 July,*
£1,650 ($2,624)

See also:
Bookcases *pp* 24-26
Canterburys *p* 105
Desks *pp* 11-23
Writing tables *pp* 62, 68-69

1
A Regency sarcophagus-shaped mahogany cellaret, c.1810, the body enclosing a zinc-lined well, 76cm (30in) wide, *L 2 May,*
£858 ($1,364)

2
A William IV mahogany cellaret, c.1835, the lid revealing a lead-lined interior, 120cm (47¼in) wide, *S 22 Apr,*
£715 ($1,122)

3
A George IV mahogany cellarette, c.1825, 60cm (23½in), *C 17 Apr,*
£495 ($767)

4
A George III mahogany decanter box, late 18th/early 19th century, containing four soda metal decanters, 31cm (12¼in) high, *C 9 July,*
£220 ($354)

5
A George III mahogany wine cooler on a stand, c.1780, 72cm (28½in) high, *C 16 Jan,*
£1,122 ($1,683)

6
A George III mahogany cellarette, c.1800, strung in boxwood, 63.5cm (25in) high, *C 17 Apr,*
£1,078 ($1,671)

7
An early Victorian mahogany adjustable dumb waiter, with telescopic action, 114cm (44½in), *S 4 Mar,*
£572 ($858)

8
A George III mahogany cellarette, c.1800, enclosing an iron fuel container, *C 9 July,*
£682 ($1,098)

9
A George III mahogany cellarette, late 18th century, the top with inlaid paterae decoration, with lion's head and ring handles, 66cm (26in), *NY 14 Oct,*
$2,310 (£1,604)

10
A George II mahogany dumb waiter, c.1750, 112cm (44in) high, *C 8 Oct,*
£638 ($893)

11
A William IV mahogany dumb waiter, c.1835, the tiers supported by fluted brass pilasters, 100cm (39in) high, *L 21 Nov,*
£1,078 ($1,509)

See also:
English tables *pp* 56-57
French tables *p* 70

1

2

3

4

5

6

7

8

9

10

11

1

2

3

4

5

6

7

8

9

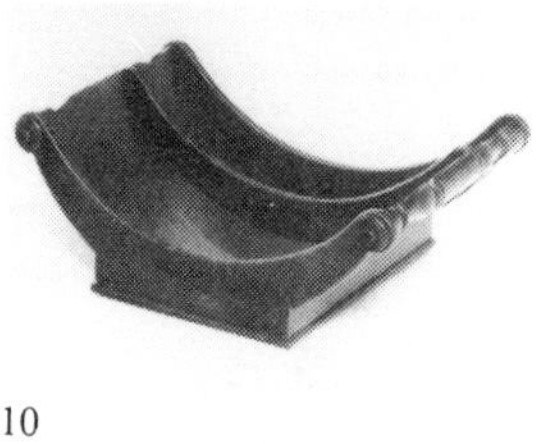
10

11

12

13

14

15

16

1
An Edwardian mahogany tantalus, c.1900, the case with inlaid satinwood shell decoration, the interior fitted with a cribbage scorer and a spring release drawer for gaming pieces, 38cm (15in) high, *Ct 27 Oct,*
R1,540 (£481; $674)

2
A French ebonised wood decanter box, c.1870, inlaid with brass, tortoise-shell and mother-of-pearl, 27cm (10½in), *S 16 Sept,*
£418 ($585)

3
A George III mahogany four-bottle port porter, early 19th century, the decanters with later stoppers, 37cm (14½in), *C 17 Apr,*
£726 ($1,125)

4
A pair of George III silver-mounted inlaid mahogany cutlery boxes, c.1790, raised on silver claw and ball feet, 36cm (14in) high, *NY 25 Jan,*
$9,350 (£6,727)

5
A George III mahogany and painted knife box, c.1780, with kingwood banding and chevron stringing, 69cm (27in) high, *S 11 Nov,*
£1,870 ($2,618)

6
A pair of George III mahogany cutlery urns, c.1800, 74cm (29in) high, *L 21 Nov,*
£2,530 ($3,542)

7
A pair of Regency mahogany knife boxes, c.1810, 61cm (24in), *L 7 July,*
£3,520 ($5,702)

8
A George III brass-mounted mahogany plate bucket, last quarter 18th century, now fitted with a brass liner, 30cm (11¾in), *NY 25 Jan,*
$3,850 (£2,770)

9
A walnut port porter, c.1750, pierced with fifteen decanter apertures, 46cm (18in) diam., *C 9 July,*
£352 ($567)

10
A William IV mahogany cheese coaster, 34cm (13½in) wide, *C 8 Oct,*
£220 ($308)

11
A George III mahogany butler's tray on stand, early 19th century, 91cm (36in) high, *C 16 Jan,*
£528 ($792)

12
A George III-style yew-wood plate and cutlery stand, c.1900, 67.5cm (27in), *C 3 Dec,*
£385 ($539)

13
A Regency brass-mounted satinwood side cabinet, c.1820, 128.5cm (50½in) high, *NY 14 Oct,*
$2,090 (£1,451)

14
A George IV mahogany chiffonier, c.1820, with a hinged mirror-back shelf, 124cm (49in) high, *L 4 Aug,*
£715 ($1,108)

15
A Victorian mahogany chiffonier, c.1850, 157.5cm (62in) high, *C 24 Sept,*
£286 ($437)

16
A Regency rosewood chiffonier, c.1810, with brass grille doors, stamped *A. Solomon, 59 Great Queen Street,* 117cm (46in) high, *S 11 Nov,*
£1,650 ($2,310)

See also:
Side cabinets *pp* 30-31

1
A George III mahogany sideboard, c.1800, of breakfront outline, 198cm (6ft 6in) wide, *C 16 Jan,*
£1,540 ($2,310)

2
A George III inlaid mahogany sideboard, c.1790, 230cm (7ft 6½in) wide, *NY 10 June,*
$6,050 (£3,854)

3
A George IV mahogany sideboard, c.1820, on plinth base, 168cm (66in) wide, *C 8 Oct,*
£1,265 ($1,771)

4
A George III mahogany and crossbanded bow-front sideboard, c.1790, inlaid with satinwood stringing and fan medallions, with raised rear brass gallery, 152cm (60in) wide, *S 17 June,*
£3,960 ($6,257)

5
A Regency mahogany sideboard, c.1820, in the manner of Thomas Sheraton, with brass gallery above a panelled breakfront frieze drawer, 207cm (6ft 9½in) wide, *L 14 Nov,*
£7,150 ($10,225)

6
An early Victorian mahogany sideboard, of breakfront outline, 183cm (6ft) wide, *S 13 May,*
£330 ($525)

7
A George III mahogany serpentine sideboard, c.1780, inlaid with boxwood stringing, 198.5cm (6ft 6¼in), *L 2 May,*
£4,400 ($6,996)

8
A late Victorian mahogany and inlaid pedestal sideboard, c.1900, by Edwards & Roberts, of inverted breakfront form, with satinwood banding and urn and arabesque inlay, 229cm (7ft 6in), *S 11 Nov,*
£1,430 ($2,002)

1

2

3

4

5

6

7

8

1

2

3

4

5

6

7

8

9

10

11

12

1
A George III mahogany whatnot, c.1800, 124.5cm (49in), *C 9 July,*
£902 ($1,452)

2
A Victorian mahogany whatnot, c.1840, 140cm (55in), *NY 18 Oct,*
$1,650 (£1,146)

3
A Victorian rosewood whatnot, c.1840, 120cm (47in), *S 17 June,*
£902 ($1,425)

4
A Regency mahogany hanging shelf, c.1815, 83.5 cm (33in), *NY 10 June,*
$1,650 (£1,051)

5
A Victorian walnut whatnot, c.1860, each tier inlaid with boxwood, 106cm (41½in), *C 9 July,*
£484 ($779)

6
A Regency rosewood whatnot, c.1820, 85cm (33½in), *C 17 Apr,*
£528 ($818)

7
A Victorian gilt-bronze and walnut whatnot, c.1840, 100cm (39½in), *L 2 May,*
£3,080 ($4,897)

8
A George IV japanned set of hanging shelves, c.1820, *C 8 Oct,*
£858 ($1,201)

9
A Victorian walnut corner whatnot, c.1870, 135cm (53in), *JHB 1 Dec,*
R 2,200 (£710; $994)

10
A pair of Italian lacquered corner cupboards, *(one illustrated),* Piedmont, mid 18th century, 103cm (40½in), *F 14 Apr,*
L6,500,000 (£2,662; $4,126)

11
A Louis XVI ormolu-mounted mahogany étagère, c.1790, 130cm (51¼in) high, *NY 3 May,*
$8,800 (£5,789)

12
A George IV rosewood étagère, c.1825, 170cm (67in), *NY 10 June,*
$3,575 (£2,277)

See also:
Cabinets and vitrines *pp* 32-34

1
A Regency mahogany canterbury, c.1810, 51cm (20in) wide, *L 2 May,*
£1,870 ($2,973)

2
A George IV boat-shaped mahogany canterbury, c.1825, 58cm (23in) wide, *L 11 July,*
£3,850 ($6,122)

3
A Victorian rosewood canterbury, c.1840, 51cm (20in) wide, *S 15 July,*
£528 ($829)

4
A Victorian rosewood canterbury, c.1850, 54cm (21in) high, *C 9 July,*
£1,540 ($2,479)

5
A Victorian walnut canterbury, c.1860, 89cm (35in) high, *C 25 June,*
£352 ($549)

6
A Victorian rosewood canterbury, c.1870, in the manner of Edwards & Roberts, the recess with mirror back, 97cm (38in) high, *S 21 Jan,*
£484 ($726)

7
A George III mahogany music stand, c.1770, 37cm (14½in) wide, *S 17 June,*
£1,155 ($1,825)

8
A William IV rosewood music stand, c.1835, 122cm (48in) high, *S 18 Mar,*
£990 ($1,515)

9
A George IV mahogany folio stand, c.1830, 114cm (45in), *C 8 Oct,*
£935 ($1,309)

10
A mahogany duet stand, c.1840, 106cm (42in) high, *L 2 May,*
£1,980 ($3,148)

11
A mahogany gilt-metal mounted music stand, c.1880, 81cm (32in) high, *L 7 Nov,*
£990 ($1,386)

12
A Belgian mahogany quartet stand, early 19th century, *L 28 Nov,*
£2,420 ($3,388)

13
A Victorian wrought-iron and brass music stand, *C 11 June,*
£220 ($345)

14
A Victorian walnut and inlaid music canterbury, 65cm (25½in) wide, *S 6 May,*
£528 ($840)

1

2

3

4

5

6

7

8

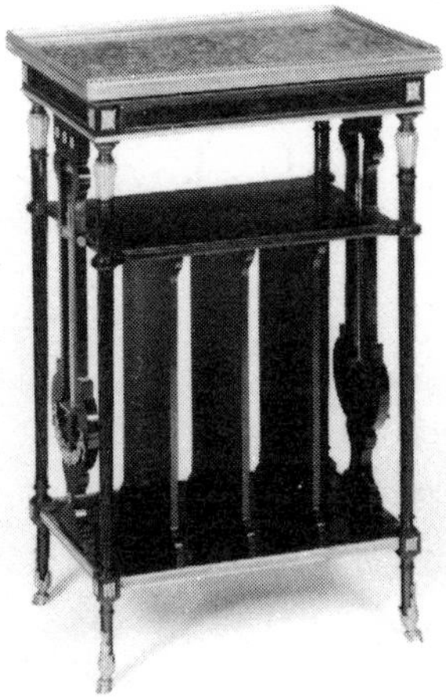
11

9

10

12

13

14

1

2

3

4

5

6

7

8

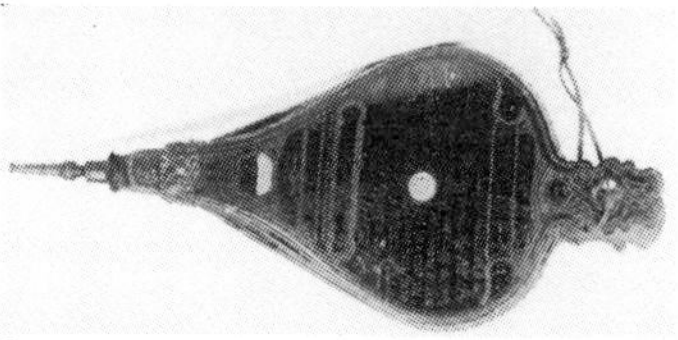

9

10

11

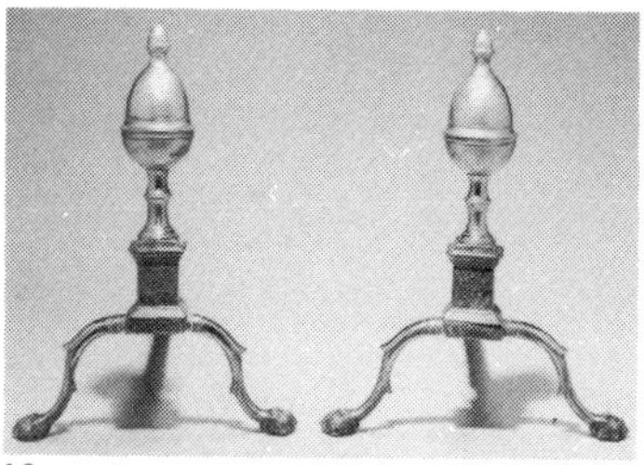

12

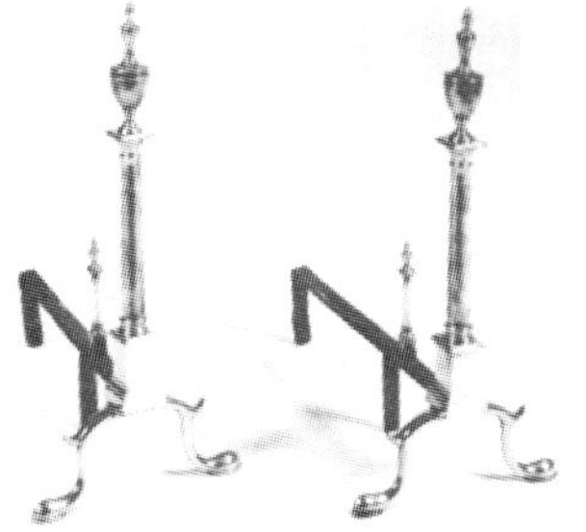

13

14

15

16

1
A punched and painted toleware fire screen, possibly American, late 19th century, with green aspidistra on a rust coloured ground, 60cm (23½in) high, *L 22 July,*
£440 ($691)

2
A copper log tub, 19th century, applied with lion ring handles, 45cm (18in) high, *C 22 Oct,*
£352 ($493)

3
A Victorian black Japanned coal scuttle, c.1860, the hinged lid painted with a Lakeland scene, complete with shovel, 43cm (17in), *C 22 Oct,*
£242 ($339)

4
A pair of brass-bound mahogany navette-form peat buckets, *(one illustrated)*, early 19th century, 33cm (13in), *NY 17 Oct,*
$2,090 (£1,451)

5
A George III brass-mounted navette-form peat bucket, late 18th century, fitted with a later brass liner, 38cm (15in), *NY 7 June,*
$3,575 (£2,399)

6
An early George III circular mahogany pail, c.1760, with brass liner, 33cm (13in) high, *L 15 Jan,*
£2,310 ($3,465)

7
A George II mahogany bucket, c.1755, with brass liner, 38cm (15in), *L 24 Oct,*
£1,320 ($1,848)

8
A pair of walnut and silver-mounted fire bellows, c.1850, with a 17th century petit point panel, *C 9 July,*
£506 ($815)

9
A pair of mahogany bellows, early 18th century, decorated with the Lord's prayer in piqué, inscribed *...Maker, Birmingham,* 78cm (30½in), *L 7 July,*
£1,485 ($2,406)

10
A bronze and ormolu fender, of Louis XVI design, late 19th century, 130cm (51in), *S 11 Nov,*
£792 ($1,109)

11
A pierced brass fender, English or Dutch, 18th century, 160cm (63in), *S 20 May,*
£715 ($1,144)

12
A pair of American engraved brass and wrought-iron andirons, c.1800, together with fireplace fender and two fireplace tools, *NY 26 June,*
$2,530 (£1,675)

13
A pair of Federal brass andirons, Rhode Island, early 19th century, together with a brass and wrought-iron fireplace shovel and tongs, *NY 1 Feb,*
$3,575 (£2,535)

14
A steel fire grate with matching fender and fire-iron set, c.1900, the fender 193cm (76in) wide, *S 11 Nov,*
£660 ($924)

15
A brass fire grate, of Adam design, with cast-iron fireback, 103cm (40½in) wide, *S 11 Nov,*
£1,650 ($2,310)

16
A set of George III engraved steel fireplace tools and fire fender, late 18th century, *NY 25 Jan,*
$7,700 (£5,540)

1
A carved pine fire surround, 19th century, 212cm (6ft 11½in), *S 28 May,*
£385 ($608)

2
A George III marble fireplace surround, late 18th century, 142cm (56in), *NY 13 Dec,*
$7,150 (£5,107)

3
A Victorian carved white marble chimney surround, c.1850, 163cm (64in) wide, *S 28 May,*
£10,450 ($16,511)

4
A painted carved pine fire surround, together with beaded and veined marble and black slate inset, 231cm (7ft 7in) wide, *S 28 May,*
£3,300 ($5,214)

5
A cast-iron cinder guard in the form of a cottage, late 19th century, by Chas. Ezard, No.58, with a registration mark 1880, 26.5cm (10½in) high, *C 19 Nov,*
£176 ($246)

6
A Regency steel and brass fender, early 19th century, 100cm (39in), *JHB 29 Sept,*
R 5,200 (£1,640; $2,296)

7
A Berlin woolworked screen, 193cm (6ft 4in), *C 1 May,*
£748 ($1,212)

8
A Victorian walnut fire-screen, c.1860, now with glazed sliding panels enclosing woolworked picture, 106cm (42in) high, *C 7 Aug,*
£176 ($273)

9
A late George II mahogany pole screen, c.1755, 176cm (69½in) high, *L 11 July,*
£2,750 ($4,373)

10
A George IV rosewood framed pole screen, c.1825, with watercolour panel, 145cm (57in), *S 22 Apr,*
£308 ($483)

11
An early Victorian pollard oak fire-screen, c.1840, with a wool-worked panel, 132cm (52in), *C 14 May,*
£220 ($354)

1

2

3

4

5

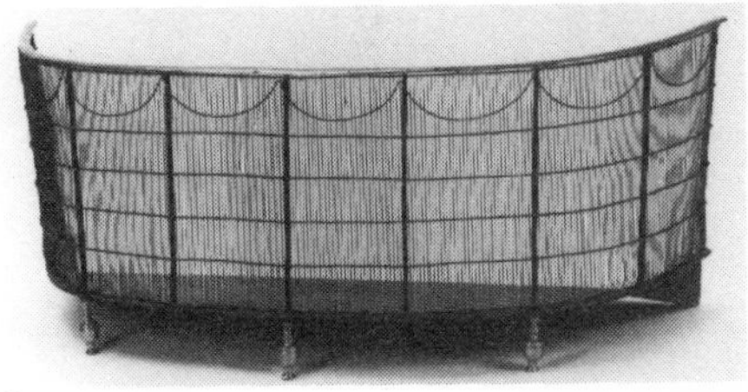
6

7

9

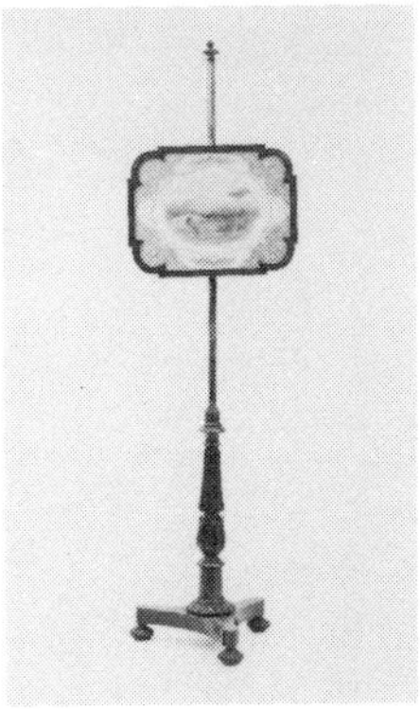
10

8

11

1

2

3

4

5

6

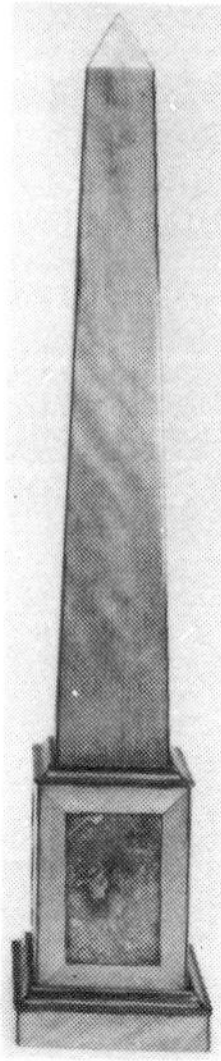
7

8

9

10

11

12

13

14

1
A mahogany tray, mid 18th century, with a ply gallery and shell moulded handles, 70cm (27½in), *C 9 July,*
£440 ($708)

2
An Edwardian inlaid satinwood tray, with scrollwork and brass gallery, 63cm (25in), *L 3 Mar,*
£352 ($528)

3
A French kingwood jardinière, c.1870, with pierced gallery and removable metal liner, the sides quarter-veneered, with carrying handles, 36cm (14in) wide, *S 17 June,*
£385 ($608)

4
A carved pine hall stand, c.1880, German or Austrian, in the form of a bear holding a branch in his hands with two small bears climbing up, 210cm (6ft 10½in) high, *L 7 Nov,*
£3,080 ($4,312)

5
A carved and stained wood umbrella stand, c.1870, in the form of a puppy holding a brass whip in its paws, 78cm (31in) high, *L 13 June,*
£1,760 ($2,816)

6
A Louis XVI ebony obelisk, late 18th century, with an ivory portrait medallion depicting Louis XIV, on later ebonised base, 65.5cm (25¾in), *NY 3 May,*
$3,300 (£2,171)

7
A pair of satinwood-veneered obelisks, *(one illustrated),* early 19th century, each base set with a mottled marble panel, 61cm (24in), *L 28 Feb,*
£2,530 ($3,921)

8
An early George III mahogany urn, c.1760, carved with satyr masks and hung with oak leaf swags, 35cm (13¾in) high, *L 21 Nov,*
£1,540 ($2,156)

9
A pair of Italian rosewood-veneered stands, *(one illustrated),* c.1830, Lombardy, inlaid in light wood with floral motifs, 25cm (9¾in), *F 14 Apr,*
L 500,000 (£205; $317)

10
A French mahogany jardinière, early 19th century, with ormolu mounts and feet, raised on curved brass supports, 83cm (32¾in) high, *NY 17 Dec,*
$2,200 (£1,571)

11
A George II oak napkin press, c.1750, with adjustable platform, 55cm (21½in) wide, *S 20 May,*
£231 ($370)

12
A Tunbridgeware and rosewood coin cabinet, mid 19th century, the hinged cover inlaid with Battle Abbey, inner trays possibly later, 23cm (9in) high, *C 22 Oct,*
£165 ($231)

13
An early Victorian mahogany boot jack, c.1840, with turned uprights, 74cm (29in) high, *C 25 June,*
£143 ($223)

14
A French walnut spinning wheel, 18th century, with turned and carved frame, 80cm (31½in), *L 15 Jan,*
£462 ($693)

1
A Victorian four-fold rosewood and papier-mâché screen, second half 19th century, decorated on both sides, 183cm (72in) high, *NY 13 Dec,*
$3,300 (£2,357)

2
A brass and tulipwood inlaid walnut easel, c.1885, 193cm (6ft 4in) high, *NY 26 Nov,*
$2,310 (£1,650)

3
A Louis XVI beechwood and mahogany needlework frame, late 18th century, signed *M. Ohneberg,* 100cm (39½in), *NY 3 May,*
$3,300 (£2,171)

4
A German limewood umbrella stand, c.1850, 96cm (38in), *C 8 Oct,*
£770 ($1,078)

5
A German pine bear umbrella stand, c.1900, 102cm (40in), *S 18 Mar,*
£462 ($707)

6
A George IV oak spinning wheel, 79cm (31in) wide, *S 20 May,*
£220 ($352)

7
A bentwood and walnut hat and coat stand, c.1900, 210.5cm (6ft 11in), *C 27 Mar,*
£187 ($286)

8
A Continental five-fold needlepoint screen, worked in green, brown and iron-red on a beige ground, 182cm (71½in) high, *NY 4 Oct,*
$2,420 (£1,680)

9
An Anglo-Indian ivory two-compartment work box, 19th century, made for the Persian market, 30.5cm (12in) long, *NY 10 June,*
$220 (£140)

10
An Anglo-Indian ivory, ebony and sadeli combination jewellery/work box, painted with scenes of the Taj Mahal and the Golden Temple at Amritsar, 39.5cm (15½in), *C 8 Oct,*
£968 ($1,355)

11
A Victorian mahogany hall stand, c.1860, with a marble top over a frieze door, 228cm (7ft 5in), *C 25 June,*
£484 ($755)

12
A wood and iron lacemaker's table, 18th century, 67cm (26½in), *L 22 July,*
£550 ($864)

1

2

3

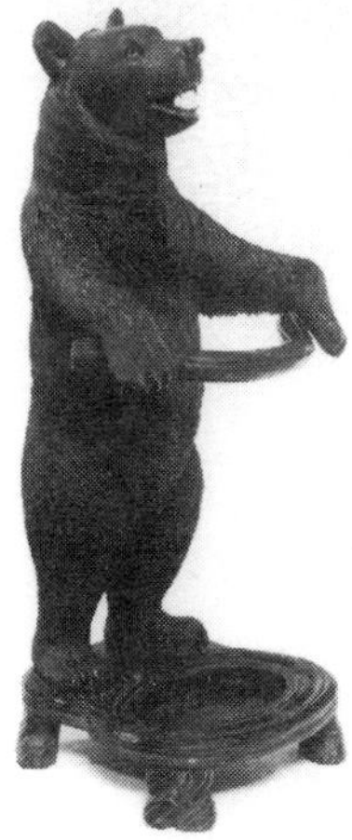
4

5

6

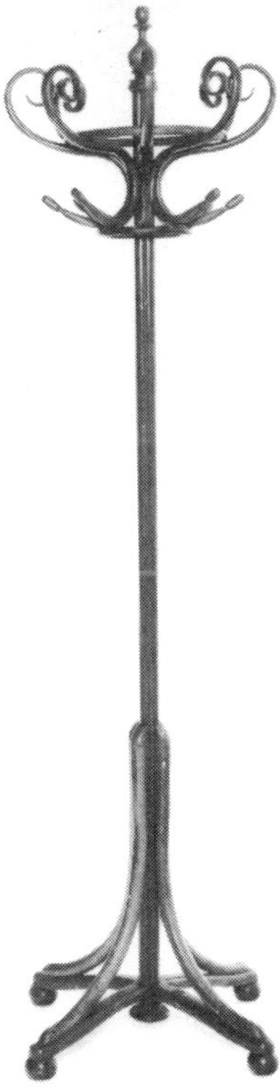
7

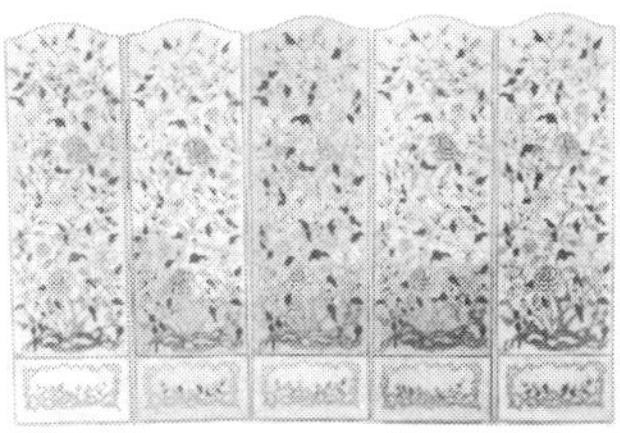
8

9

10

11

12

1

2

3

4

5

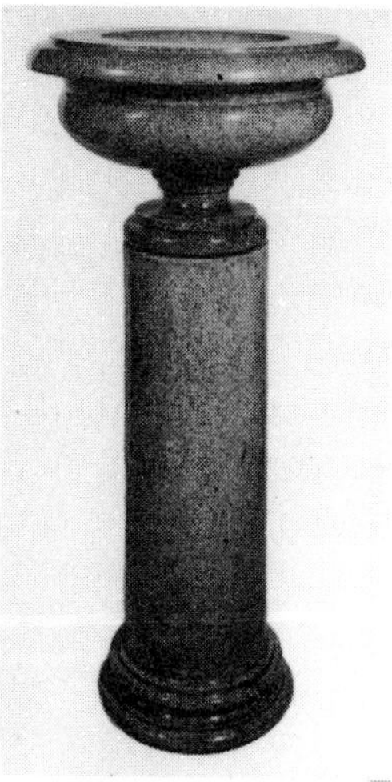
6

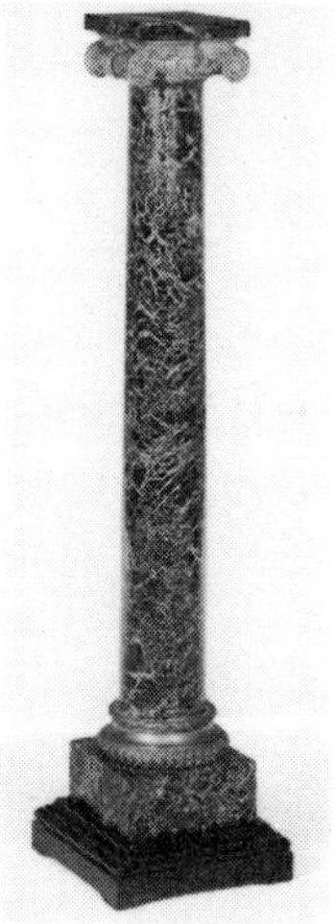
7

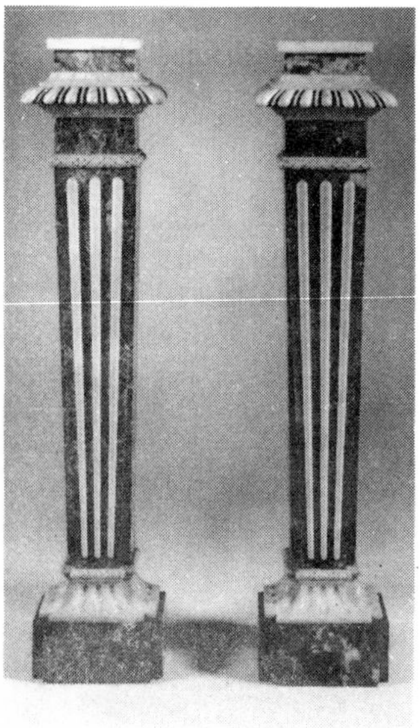
8

9

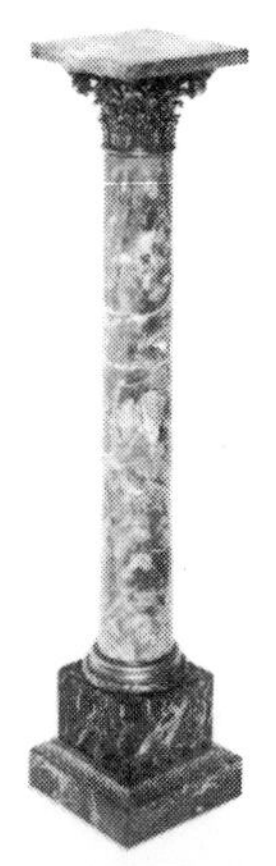
10

1
A George IV blue-john urn, c.1825, with amethyst and violet markings, black marble base, 21cm (8¼in), *L 14 Mar,*
£660 ($1,023)

2
A pair of George III Derbyshire spar urns, early 19th century, restorations, 24cm (9½in) high, *NY 7 June,*
$6,600 (£4,429)

3
A suite of three blue-john urns, 19th century, on square slate plinths, the largest 26cm (10in), *C 16 Jan,*
£825 ($1,238)

4
A pair of Cornish hardstone candlesticks, late 19th century, 28.5cm (11¼in) high, *NY 10 June,*
$1,540 (£981)

5
A red serpentine marble urn, c.1900, applied with ram's heads handles, with liner, 53cm (21in), *L 21 Mar,*
£1,100 ($1,716)

6
A grey granite urn on a column, c.1860, 110cm (43¼in) high, *M 23 Feb,*
FF 166,500 (£16,102; $24,153)

7
A pair of verde antico marble columns, *(one illustrated),* c.1860, with leaf cast gilt-metal capitals, guilloché collars, 130cm (51in) high, *L 13 June,*
£1,815 ($2,904)

8
A pair of George II inlaid marble pedestals, second quarter 18th century, 135cm (54in) high, *NY 25 Jan,*
$9,900 (£7,122)

9
A pair of breche violette marble columns, c.1900, square revolving tops with gilt-bronze capitals, 130cm (51in), *L 7 Nov,*
£7,700 ($10,780)

10
A marble and gilt-bronze column, c.1900, cast gilt-bronze capital, 125cm (49in), *C 16 Jan,*
£990 ($1,485)

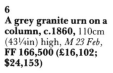

1
A Regency rectangular papier-mâché tray, c.1820, the centre painted with gilt flowers on a scarlet ground, 89cm (35in), *S 17 June,*
£1,705 ($2,693)

2
A Regency graduated set of three papier-mâché tea trays, c.1810, with green gilt border over black ground, some damage, the largest 76cm (30in) the smallest 47cm (18½in), *C 17 Apr,*
£396 ($614)

3
A scallop-shaped papier-mâché tray, English, c.1830, with inlaid mother-of-pearl, 69cm (27in), *S 16 Sept,*
£902 ($1,263)

4
A Victorian tôle peinte oval tray, late 19th century, 66cm (26in), *NY 10 June,*
$605 (£385)

5
A George III oval painted tin tray, c.1790, decorated with the *Return from School* after William Redmore Bigg, 76cm (30in), *L 11 July,*
£3,960 ($6,296)

6
A Victorian oval papier-mâché tray, c.1850, the centre inlaid with mother-of-pearl, 78cm (31in), *S 17 June,*
£550 ($869)

7
A George III rolled paper-work reticule, c.1785, with an ivory silk bag and pale blue ribbons, 31cm (12in), *L 28 Feb,*
£550 ($852)

8
A pair of green-painted and gilt-decorated tôle tea canisters, 45cm (17½in), *NY 17 Oct,*
$990 (£688)

9
A pair of yellow-painted and gilt-decorated tôle tea canisters, 37cm (14½in), *NY 17 Oct,*
$1,045 (£1,505)

10
A sarcophagus-shaped papier-mâché jewel casket, Jennens and Bettridge, early 19th century, inlaid with mother-of-pearl, 29cm (11½in), *C 9 July,*
£143 ($230)

11
A pair of Victorian japanned papier-mâché wine coasters, c.1840, one centre slightly damaged, 18.5cm (7¼in), *C 9 July,*
£264 ($425)

12
A pair of Victorian tole peinte urns, *(one illustrated)* 24cm (9½in), *NY 10 June,*
$467 (£298)

13
A pair of Victorian papier-mâché chairs *(one illustrated)*, c.1860, *S 21 Jan,*
£418 ($627)

14
A nest of four Victorian papier-mâché tables, c.1840, the largest painted with a farmyard scene after Herring, one inlaid for draughts, the other two with scenes with horses, 75cm (29½in), *C 16 Jan,*
£1,210 ($1,815)

15
An early Victorian papier-mâché workbox, c.1840, stamped Jennens & Bettridge, with a scene of Warwick Castle, 23.5cm (9½in), *L 3 Mar,*
£528 ($792)

16
A George III rolled paper-work and mica tea caddy, c.1790, 18cm (7in), *L 25 Apr,*
£2,860 ($4,576)

1

2

3

4

5

6

7

8

9

11 10

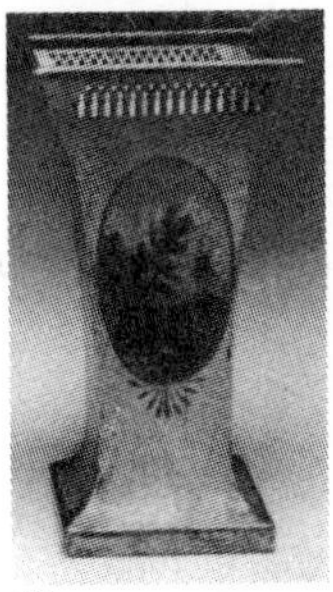
12

13

14

15

16

1

2

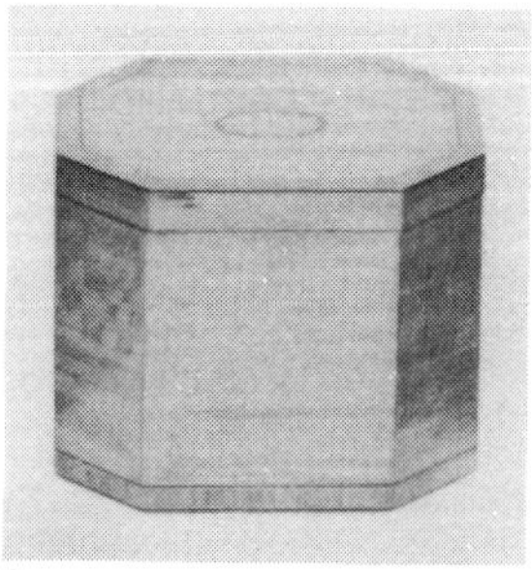
3

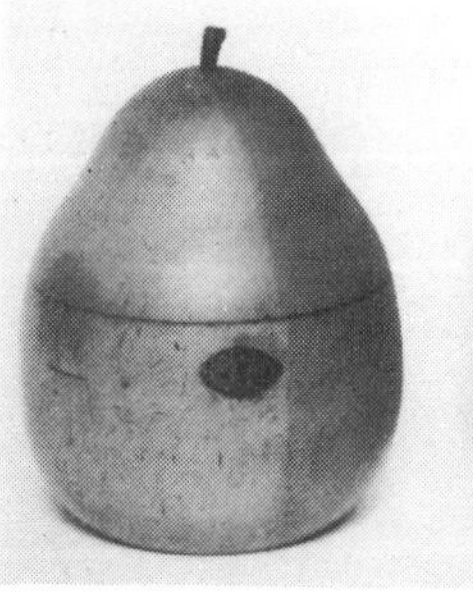
4

5

6

7

8

9

10

11

12

13

1
A George III satinwood and tulipwood banded hexagonal tea caddy, c.1770, with foil-lined interior, 13cm (5¼in), *C 17 Apr,*
£352 ($546)

2
A George III satinwood tea caddy, c.1780, banded in boxwood, 12cm (4¾in), *C 16 Jan,*
£242 ($363)

3
A George III satinwood tea caddy, c.1790, with kingwood banding and stringing, 15cm (6in), *S 21 Jan,*
£165 ($248)

4
A fruitwood tea caddy, third quarter 18th century, in the form of a pear, 15cm (6in), *C 16 Jan,*
£1,210 ($1,815)

5
A fruitwood tea caddy, third quarter 18th century, in the form of an apple, foil-lined interior, 11cm (4½in), *C 16 Jan,*
£715 ($1,073)

6
A George III tortoiseshell veneered tea caddy, c.1800, with lidded divisions, 18cm (7in), *S 18 Feb,*
£231 ($351)

7
A George III satinwood tea caddy, c.1800, with ebonised lines and brass handle, the interior fitted with Bristol blue glass mixing-bowl flanked by two lidded compartments, 30.5cm (12in), *JHB 1 Dec,*
R 420 (£135; $189)

8
A Regency cut-brass and rosewood teapoy, c.1810, of sarcophagus form, with four lidded canisters, 41cm (16in) wide, *S 18 Feb,*
£990 ($1,505)

9
A George III ivory and tortoiseshell tea caddy, c.1800. silver-coloured heraldic shield, one division, 11cm (4½in), *S 11 Nov,*
£825 ($1,155)

10
A Charles X porcelain and gilt-bronze mounted amboyna wood tea caddy, c.1820, the plaque painted in a design after Monoyer, with a pair of cut glass bottles with silver engraved tops, 16cm (6¼in) high, *NY 7 June,*
$990 (£664)

11
A Regency inlaid satinwood tea caddy, first quarter 19th century, decorated with geometric motifs and feather banding, interior fitted with three lidded compartments, 17cm (6¾in), *NY 7 June,*
$1,650 (£1,107)

12
A George IV mahogany and parquetry tea caddy, c.1825, veneered with lattice panels on embossed metal feet, 20cm (8in) high, *C 13 Feb,*
£264 ($391)

13
A William IV rosewood drum-top teapoy, on a chamfered and carved stem, 40cm (15¾in) diam., *S 10 June,*
£418 ($648)

1
A painted pine longcase clock, Johannes Spitler, Shenandoah County, Virginia, 1801, 217cm (7ft 1½in) high, *NY 25 Oct,* **$203,500 (£144,326)**

2
An American painted Windsor fan-back side chair, c.1810, with yellow and red highlights on a black ground, *NY 25 Oct,* **$2,310 (£1,638)**

3
A painted pine hanging corner cupboard, Lancaster County, Pennsylvania, early 19th century, 88cm (34½in) high, *NY 25 Oct,* **$20,900 (£14,823)**

4
A miniature painted pine chest-of-drawers, possibly New England, c.1840, painted in yellow, green and red, 32cm (8¾in) wide, *NY 25 Oct,* **$9,075 (£6,436)**

5
A painted pine chest-of-drawers, New England, c.1830, painted in ochre on a green ground, 119cm (47in) high, *NY 25 Oct,* **$8,525 (£6,046)**

6
A painted maple and pine stand, New England or Midwest, c.1830, each side with a different design, 78cm (30¾in) high, *NY 25 Oct,* **$8,800 (£6,241)**

7
A painted pine blanket chest, the decoration attributed to the 'Flat Tulip' artist (Daniel Otto), Centre County, Pennsylvania, c.1820, 122cm (48in) wide, *NY 25 Oct,* **$27,500 (£19,504)**

8
A painted maple and pine cupboard, Pennsylvania, c.1830, 198cm (6ft 5½in) high, *NY 25 Oct,* **$115,500 (£81,915)**

9
A painted pine blanket chest, probably New York State, early 19th century, 109cm (43in) wide, *NY 25 Oct,* **$2,310 (£1,638)**

See also:
Folk art *pp* 154-160

1

2

3

4

5

6

7

8

9

1

2

3

4

5

6

7

8

9

1
A Queen Anne curly maple flat-top highboy, New England, c.1765, in two sections, 189cm (6ft 2½in) high, *NY 1 Feb,*
$13,200 (£9,362)

2
A Queen Anne cherry-wood slant-front desk on frame, Connecticut, c.1775, in two sections, 89cm (35in) wide, *NY 26 June,*
$18,700 (£12,384)

3
A Queen Anne carved and figured maple flat-top highboy, Massachusetts, c.1750, in two sections, 226cm (7ft 5in) high, *NY 26 June,*
$5,775 (£3,825)

4
A Queen Anne walnut flat-top highboy, Pennsylvania or New Jersey, c.1760, in two sections, 192cm (6ft 3½in) high, *NY 26 June,*
$23,100 (£15,298)

5
A Chippendale mahogany oxbow slant-front desk, Massachusetts, c.1780, 105cm (41½in) wide, *NY 1 Feb,*
$5,500 (£3,901)

6
A William and Mary burl-walnut veneered flat-top highboy, Massachusetts, c.1730, in two sections, 159cm (62½in) high, *NY 25 Oct,*
$5,775 (£4,095)

7
A Queen Anne cherry-wood bonnet-top highboy, New England, c.1765, in two sections, 224cm (7ft 4in) high, *NY 1 Feb,*
$10,450 (£7,411)

8
A Chippendale walnut oxbow slant-front desk, Massachusetts, c.1775, 105cm (41½in) wide, *NY 1 Feb,*
$20,900 (£14,823)

9
A Federal satinwood-inlaid mahogany secretary bookcase, North Shore, Massachusetts, c.1810, 203cm (6ft 6in) high, *NY 26 June,*
$9,075 (£6,010)

1
A Chippendale mahogany music and candlestand, Newport, Rhode Island, c.1770, having a rod standard with ring and vase-turned base supporting a ratcheted adjustable music rest, 137.5cm (54in) high, *NY 25 Oct,*
$23,100 (£16,382)

2
A Federal inlaid cherrywood bow-front chest-of-drawers, New England, c.1800, flaring bracket feet, 100cm (39½in) high, *NY 25 Oct,*
$6,875 (£4,875)

3
A Queen Anne cherrywood chest-of-drawers, probably Stratford area, Connecticut, of serpentine form, stylised trifid feet, 100cm (39½in) wide, *NY 25 Oct,*
$25,300 (£17,943)

4
A Federal curly maple-inlaid mahogany lady's writing desk, Eastern Massachusetts, c.1810, in two sections, the upper with lid opening to a baize-lined writing surface and various short drawers, the lower with two inlaid long drawers, 121cm (47¾in) high, *NY 1 Feb,*
$2,750 (£1,950)

5
A Federal inlaid mahogany lady's writing desk, Eastern New England, c.1810, 132cm (52in) high, *NY 26 June,*
$5,225 (£3,460)

6
A Chippendale cherrywood oxbow-front chest-of-drawers, New England, probably Connecticut, c.1785, ogee bracket feet, 105cm (40½in) wide, *NY 26 June,*
$12,100 (£8,013)

7
A Queen Anne mahogany and cherrywood lowboy, possibly New York, c.1750, 83cm (32¾in) wide, *NY 1 Feb,*
$5,225 (£3,706)

8
A Federal inlaid mahogany bow-front chest-of-drawers, Middle Atlantic States, c.1805, bracket feet, 97cm (38in) high, *NY 26 June,*
$3,520 (£2,331)

9
A Chippendale cherrywood chest-of-drawers, probably Connecticut, c.1800, on ogee bracket feet (replaced), 103cm (40¾in), *NY 26 June,*
$3,575 (£2,368)

10
A Chippendale maple slant-front desk, New England, c.1785, on ogee bracket feet, 102cm (40in) high, *NY 25 Oct,*
$2,200 (£1,560)

11
A Queen Anne walnut lowboy, Pennsylvania, c.1760, on stocking trifid feet, 95cm (37½in) wide, *NY 1 Feb,*
$30,800 (£21,844)

12
A Chippendale cherrywood oxbow-front chest-of-drawers, Connecticut, c.1780, the top with serpentine front, 103cm (40½in) wide, *NY 26 June,*
$52,250 (£34,603)

1

2

3

4

5

6

7

8

9

10

11

12

1

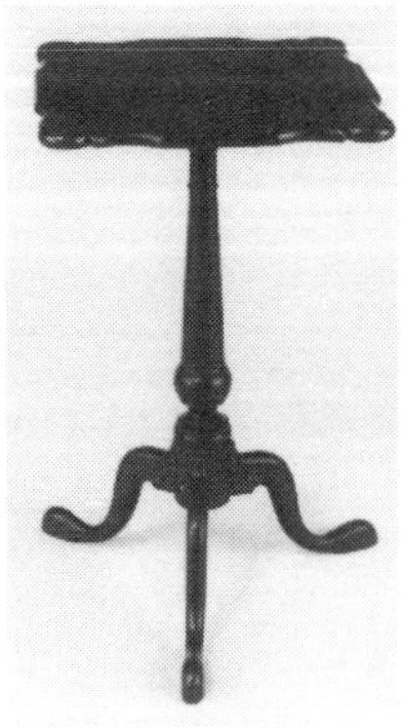
2

3

4

5

6

7

8

9

10

1
A Chippendale walnut tilt-top tea table, Pennsylvania, c.1780, the circular top tilting and revolving above a bird-cage support, 81cm (32in) diam., *NY 25 Oct,*
$2,860 (£2,028)

2
A Chippendale cherry-wood candlestand, attributed to the Chapin family, Hartford County, Connecticut, c.1790, with a label on the underside inscribed *This stand belonged to my grandmother Thankful Chapin and is probably over one hundred years old. May22d, 1899 Lucy A. Stark,* 70cm (27½in) high, *NY 1 Feb,*
$14,850 (£10,532)

3
A Federal inlaid mahogany dressing table, probably Salem, Massachusetts, c.1800, in two sections, the upper with mirror swivelling on a shaped support, the case with serpentine inlaid drawer, the lower section conformingly shaped, 137cm (54in) high, *NY 26 June,*
$3,850 (£2,550)

4
A curly maple and pine tavern table, probably Pennsylvania, 1740-70, the top above a single drawer, 109cm (43in) wide, *NY 1 Feb,*
$3,300 (£2,340)

5
A Federal mahogany side table, New York, c.1810, 76cm (30in) high, *NY 25 Oct,*
$4,675 (£3,315)

6
A Federal inlaid mahogany writing table, Boston, Massachusetts, c.1800, the top hinged and adjustable, 74cm (29in) high, *NY 1 Feb,*
$10,450 (£7,411)

7
A Federal mahogany lady's writing table, New York, c.1810, the hinged top opening to a baize-lined writing surface, 76cm (30in) high, *NY 26 June,*
$3,410 (£2,258)

8
A Federal satinwood inlaid mahogany sewing table, Eastern New England, c.1805, with concave front, 76cm (30in) high, *NY 1 Feb,*
$6,600 (£4,681)

9
A Queen Anne burl-walnut veneered side table, possibly Eastern Massachusetts, c.1740, 80cm (31½in) wide, *NY 26 June,*
$4,400 (£2,914)

10
A Federal inlaid mahogany marble-top side table, Eastern New England, c.1820, the beige marble top probably of later date, 97cm (38in) wide, *NY 1 Feb,*
$3,300 (£2,340)

American furniture periods

1620-90 Jacobean or 'Pilgrim century'

1690-1725 William and Mary

1725-60 Queen Anne

1750-80 Chippendale

1780-1810 Federal

1820-45 Classical

1
A Federal brass-inlaid mahogany library table, New York, c.1815, width extended 114cm (45in), *NY 1 Feb,*
$2,970 (£2,106)

2
A Classical giltwood rosewood marble-top centre table, New York City, c.1815, stencilled with foliate motifs and eagle heads, veined black marble top probably replaced, 91.5cm (36in) diam., *NY 26 June,*
$20,900 (£13,841)

3
A Chippendale walnut Pembroke table, Pennsylvania, c.1780, width extended 98cm (38¾in), *NY 26 June,*
$9,350 (£6,192)

4
A Federal mahogany card table, Salem, Massachusetts, c.1805, the carving attributed to Samuel McIntire, carved with a frieze centring a basket of fruit, 92cm (36in) wide, *NY 1 Feb,*
$8,250 (£5,851)

5
A Federal inlaid mahogany and maple card table, Boston area, Massachusetts, c.1810, the oblong top with hinged leaf, 91cm (35¾in) wide, *NY 26 June,*
$4,950 (£3,278)

6
A Chippendale walnut tilt-top candlestand, Philadelphia, c.1770, 53cm (21in) diam., *NY 26 June,*
$11,000 (£7,285)

7
A Federal satinwood-inlaid mahogany card table, New York, c.1795, the oblong top with line-inlaid edge and radiating satinwood fan, 91cm (35¾in) wide, *NY 25 Oct,*
$14,300 (£10,141)

8
A Federal satinwood-inlaid mahogany Pembroke table, Newport, Rhode Island, c.1800, width extended 96cm (38in), *NY 1 Feb,*
$20,900 (£14,823)

9
A Queen Anne walnut concertina-action card table, Boston, Massachusetts, c.1735, the oblong top opening to form a green baize-lined playing surface fitted with candle supports and wells for counters, the rear legs fitted with an accordion mechanism, 85cm (33½in) wide, *NY 1 Feb,*
$29,700 (£21,064)

10
A Federal inlaid mahogany Pembroke table, c.1805, width extended 96cm (38in), *NY 1 Feb,*
$4,840 (£3,433)

11
A Federal mahogany card table, New York, c.1820, the top with hinged leaf swivelling above a well, on an acanthus and plume-carved standard, carved animal paw feet, 91cm (35¼in) wide, *NY 26 June,*
$1,760 (£1,166)

12
A Classical marble-top console table, New York, c.1825, the white marble top above a plain frieze and marble columns, a mirror behind, gilt-metal mounts, on animal paw feet, 107cm (42in) wide, *NY 26 June,*
$5,225 (£3,460)

13
A Classical mahogany and rosewood marble-top pier table, c.1810, the veined black marble top above a frieze and veined black marble columns, a mirror behind, gilt-metal mounts, 107cm (42in) wide, *NY 1 Feb,*
$13,750 (£9,752)

1

2

3

4

5

6

7

8

9

10

11

12

13

1

2

3

4

5

6

7

8

9

1
A Federal inlaid mahogany sideboard, probably Connecticut, c.1800, all inlaid with pattern stringing and icicle inlaid dyes continuing to bellflower-inlaid tapering legs, 181cm (71in) wide, *NY 25 Oct,*
$26,400 (£18,723)

2
A William and Mary walnut gateleg dining table, American, c.1720, 145cm (57in) width extended, *NY 1 Feb,*
$20,900 (£14,823)

3
A Federal mahogany three-part dining table, New York, c.1805, 272cm (8ft 11in) length extended, *NY 1 Feb,*
$11,550 (£8,191)

4
A Chippendale walnut six-leg drop-leaf dining table, New York, c.1770, 122cm (48in), *NY 26 June,*
$5,775 (£3,825)

5
A Queen Anne maple small dining table, New England, c.1765, 103cm (40½in) width extended, *NY 1 Feb,*
$9,350 (£6,631)

6
A Federal inlaid mahogany sideboard, Massachusetts, c.1805, 185cm (6ft 1in), *NY 26 June,*
$11,000 (£7,285)

7
A Queen Anne maple drop-leaf breakfast table, 90cm (35½in) width extended, *NY 26 June,*
$2,200 (£1,457)

8
A Federal satinwood-inlaid mahogany sideboard, New York, c.1795, the top with a superstructure centring an inlaid oval satinwood reserve, 166cm (65½in) wide, *NY 26 June,*
$4,400 (£2,914)

9
A Federal mahogany drop-leaf dining table, probably Boston, Massachusetts, c.1820, on hinged mechanical stretchers, 150cm (59in) width extended, *NY 1 Feb,*
$4,675 (£3,316)

1
A set of four Federal inlaid mahogany side chairs, *(two illustrated)*, Boston area, Massachusetts, c.1805, *NY 25 Oct,*
$7,975 (£5,656)

2
A set of six Queen Anne maple side chairs, *(two illustrated)*, Philadelphia, c.1760, with wicker seats, *NY 1 Feb,*
$99,000 (£70,213)

3
A Queen Anne walnut side chair, Newport, Rhode Island, c.1760, *NY 26 June,*
$11,000 (£7,285)

4
A pair of curly maple side chairs, *(one illustrated)*, New England, 1740-60, with turned legs and rush seats, *NY 26 June,*
$12,650 (£8,377)

5
A set of eight painted side chairs, *(one illustrated)*, probably New England, c.1840, each painted and stencilled in yellow and black on a brown ground, with rush seats, *NY 25 Oct,*
$6,875 (£4,875)

6
A Chippendale walnut side chair, Philadelphia, c.1765, *NY 25 Oct,*
$12,650 (£8,971)

7
A Classical mahogany armchair, Boston, c.1830, *NY 26 June,*
$2,200 (£1,457)

8
A pair of Federal mahogany side chairs, *(one illustrated)*, Haines-Connelly School, Philadelphia, Pennsylvania, c.1810, *NY 1 Feb,*
$1,980 (£1,404)

9
A pair of Windsor brace-back bow-back side chairs, *(one illustrated)*, c.1800, later painted, *NY 1 Feb,*
$2,640 (£1,872)

10
A Chippendale mahogany open armchair, New York, c.1775, *NY 1 Feb,*
$3,850 (£2,730)

11
A Queen Anne maple armchair, New England, 1740-60, with wicker seat, *NY 1 Feb,*
$5,500 (£3,901)

12
A pair of American rosewood side chairs, *(one illustrated)*, New York, c.1855, attributed to John Henry Belter, sold with a rosewood armchair by John and Joseph Meeks, *NY 26 Apr,*
$4,950 (£3,214)

13
A set of twelve Classical style mahogany dining chairs, *(one illustrated)*, probably New York, second half 19th century, comprising two armchairs and ten side chairs, *NY 26 June,*
$6,875 (£4,553)

14
A set of seven Federal mahogany dining chairs, *(one illustrated)*, New York, c.1805, comprising six side chairs and one armchair, sold with a similar armchair of later date, *NY 1 Feb,*
$9,900 (£7,021)

15
A Federal mahogany sofa, c.1815, the carving possibly by Whitman, Boston, Massachusetts, with removable upholstered seat, 177cm (69½in), *NY 1 Feb,*
$3,300 (£2,340)

16
A Windsor writing armchair, c.1825, painted and decorated, with shaped writing surface, *NY 25 Oct,*
$4,070 (£2,886)

1

2

3

4

5

6

7

8

9

10

11

12

13

14

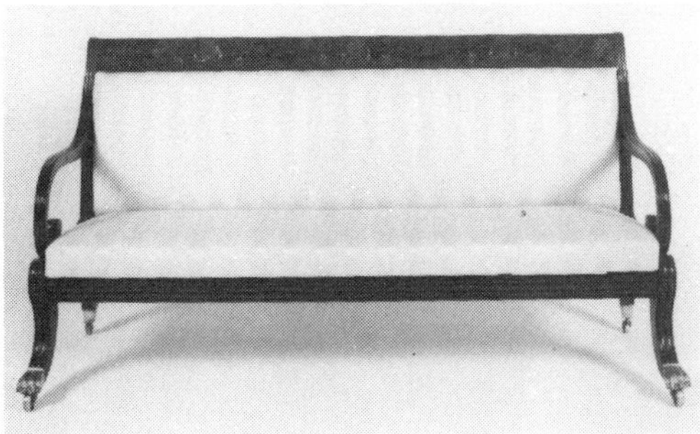
15

16

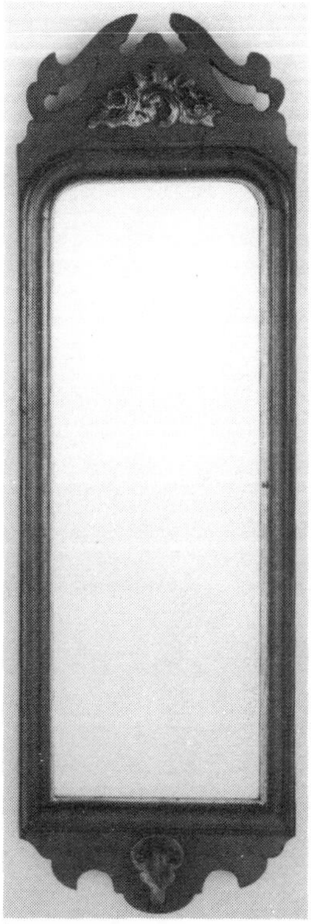
1

2

3

4

5

6

7

8

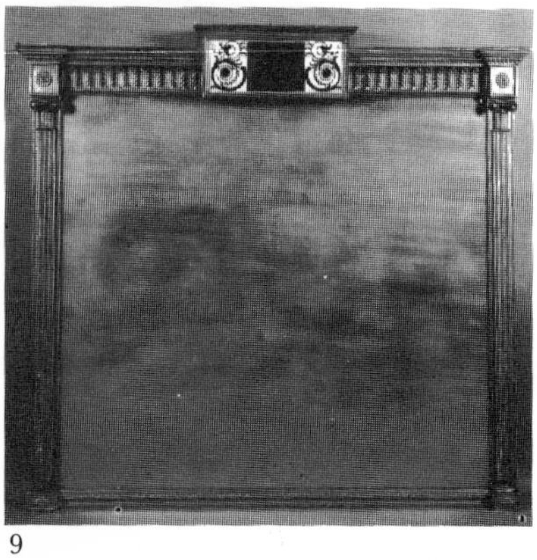
9

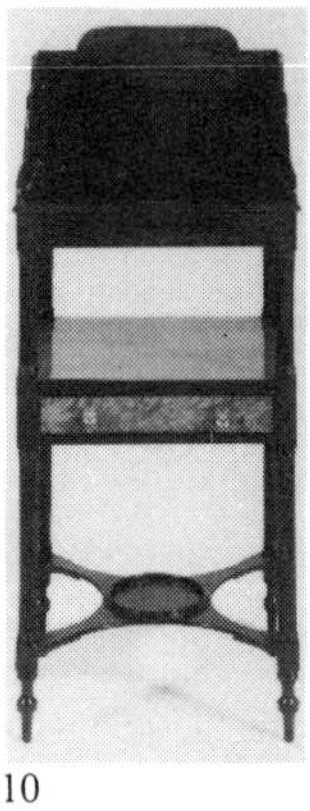
10

11

1
A Queen Anne walnut and giltwood wall mirror/ sconce, 18th century, lacking candle-arm, 76cm (30in) high, *NY 1 Feb,* **$3,410 (£2,418)**

2
A Chippendale mahogany wall mirror, 18th century, 97cm (38in), *NY 26 June,* **$2,530 (£1,675)**

3
A Federal inlaid mahogany and giltwood wall mirror, c.1795, the gilt swan's neck cresting ending in gilt flowerheads and centring an urn with spray of wheat, 114cm (55½in) high, *NY 26 June,* **$5,500 (£3,642)**

4
A pair of Federal inlaid mahogany knife boxes, c.1795, each with an interior pierced for cutlery, 37cm (14½in) high, *NY 25 Oct,* **$2,420 (£1,716)**

5
A Classical giltwood convex wall mirror, second quarter 19th century, surmounted by a wing-spread eagle with chains of spherules hung from its beak, 137cm (54in) high, *NY 26 June,* **$4,675 (£3,096)**

6
A Federal giltwood and eglomisé wall mirror, c.1810, the projecting cornice hung with spherules above a polychrome *eglomisé* panel depicting a house in a landscape, 119cm (46¾in) high, *NY 1 Feb,* **$2,200 (£1,560)**

7
A Federal mahogany corner basin stand, Eastern New England, c.1810, with a surface pierced for receptacles, 97cm (38in), *NY 25 Oct,* **$1,760 (£1,248)**

8
A Federal carved mahogany basin stand, Salem, Massachusetts, c.1810, the top pierced with three circular cut-outs below a shaped splashback, 102cm (40in) high, *NY 1 Feb,* **$4,675 (£3,316)**

9
A Classical giltwood and eglomisé overmantel mirror, c.1820, the moulded cornice with a reserve depicting a seated woman crowning a cherub in *verre eglomisé,* 169cm (66½in) wide, *NY 1 Feb,* **$19,800 (£14,043)**

10
A Federal flamed-birch inlaid mahogany basin stand, Massachusetts, c.1810, the top pierced with three circular cut-outs below a shaped splashback, 100cm (39¼in), *NY 1 Feb,* **$9,900 (£7,021)**

11
A Federal inlaid walnut cellarette, Upper Valley Region, Virginia, c.1800, in two sections, the upper with hinged lid opening to a divided well, the lower with line-inlaid drawer, 94cm (37in), *NY 25 Oct,* **$11,000 (£7,801)**

1
A Queen Anne inlaid walnut tall chest-of-drawers, Pennsylvania, c.1765, the upper long drawer bearing the initials *RM*, 146cm (57½in), *NY 1 Feb,*
$12,100 (£8,582)

2
An American Eastlake maple bedroom suite, c.1880, comprising a bedstead *(illustrated)*, dressing bureau, sewing table and three chairs, *NY 26 Nov,*
$5,775 (£4,125)

3
A Chippendale carved maple tall chest-of-drawers, New England, c.1785, 145cm (57½in) high, *NY 25 Oct,*
$6,050 (£4,290)

4
A Classical carved mahogany wardrobe, New York, c.1825, 219cm (7ft 2in), *NY 26 June,*
$4,400 (£2,914)

5
A carved pine and cherrywood corner cupboard, probably Pennsylvania, c.1800, in two parts, 211cm (6ft 11in), *NY 25 Oct,*
$2,310 (£1,638)

6
A Chippendale carved and inlaid walnut schrank, Pennsylvania, dated 1780, lacks ball feet, 204cm (6ft 8½in) high, *NY 1 Feb,*
$9,075 (£6,436)

7
A Federal carved mahogany four-poster bedstead, probably Pennsylvania, c.1780, 235cm (7ft 8½in) high, *NY 1 Feb,*
$9,900 (£7,021)

8
A Federal carved mahogany four-poster bedstead, American, first half 19th century, 218cm (7ft 2in) high, *NY 1 Feb,*
$5,775 (£4,096)

1

2

3

4

5

6

7

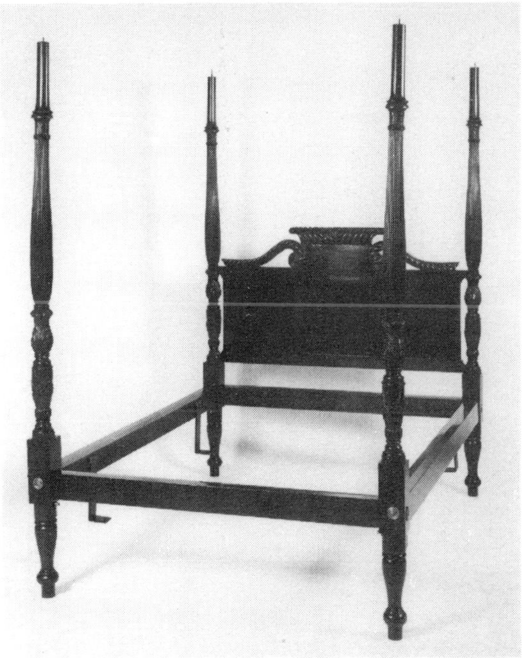
8

Clocks and Watches

1

2

3

4

5

6

7

8

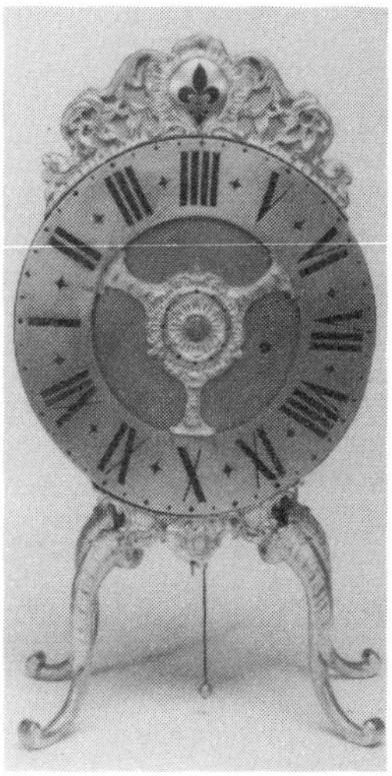
9

10

1
A German gilt-metal quarter-striking alarum table clock, c.1600, unconverted, bells lacking, 32.5cm (12¾in), *L 7 July,*
£6,380 ($10,336)

2
A lantern clock, the dial signed *Will Fox of Meltonmobray,* top finial reduced, 38cm (15in), *L 7 July,*
£2,530 ($4,099)

3
A quarter-striking lantern clock, the dial signed *Michael Bird Oxon,* later anchor escapement, alarum work lacking, 46cm (18in), *L 24 July,*
£4,950 ($7,772)

4
An 18th century lantern clock, c.1760, the dial signed *John Porthouse Penrith,* 16cm (6¼in) high excluding later bell, *L 1 May,*
£1,540 ($2,495)

5
A Victorian brass mantel timepiece, with an oval silvered dial, 11cm (4¼in), *L 20 Feb,*
£275 ($418)

6
A French alarum lantern clock, 18th century, signed *Grandjean A Paris,* the movement with verge escapement and outside count wheel, the alarum work behind, 39cm (15½in), *L 20 Feb,*
£1,320 ($2,006)

7
A French alarum lantern clock, early 18th century, a gilt-bronze fret depicting astronomy above the dial, side frets and doors later, 54cm (21¼in), *L 20 Feb,*
£2,090 ($3,177)

8
An alarum capucine, early 19th century, 28cm (11in), *L 20 Feb,*
£1,210 ($1,839)

9
An alarum night clock, 18th century, the square-plated repeating movement signed *R.L. Cresp Amsterdam,* 35.5cm (14in), *L 20 Feb,*
£3,080 ($4,682)

10
A German spring-driven Telleruhr, mostly 18th century, in a limewood case, 42cm (16½in), *A 6 May,*
Dfl 4,370 (£1,324; $2,106)

1
An Austrian Grande Sonnerie and alarum Pendule d'officier, early 19th century, the case with a carrying handle and shell supports, 16cm (6¼in), *G 11 Nov,*
SF 1,980 (£825; $1,155)

2
A solar-powered mantel timepiece, 20th century, Patek Philippe, Geneva, the rotating domed top with circular light sensory panel, 23cm (9in), *S 19 June,*
£715 ($1,129)

3
A gilt-metal travelling timepiece, c.1848, attributed to Thomas Cole, the engraved silver dial signed for Hunt and Roskell, 12cm (4¾in), *L 16 Oct,*
£935 ($1,309)

4
A tortoiseshell-veneered desk timepiece, 19th century, with associated French timepiece movement, incorporating a barometer, a hand-set calendar and Réaumur and Centigrade thermometers (one broken), 26cm (10¼in), *L 16 Oct,*
£550 ($770)

5
A French desk clock with calendar, c.1930, Cartier, Paris, strut support, 11cm (4½in), *NY 29 Oct,*
$3,410 (£2,418)

6
An agate and gold desk clock, Cartier, diamond-set hands, 6.3cm (2½in), *St.M 20 Feb,*
SF 11,000 (£3,754; $5,706)

7
A gilt-metal strut timepiece, c.1854, attributed to Thomas Cole, the circular 8-day lever movement signed ... *London,* 11cm (4¼in), *L 16 Oct,*
£715 ($1,001)

8
A silver and silver-gilt table clock, Cartier, 11.5cm (4½in), *St.M 20 Feb,*
SF 9,900 (£3,378; $5,135)

9
A silver desk timepiece, signed for Tonnel Paris, with a compass, barometer, two thermometers and a hand-set calendar, thermometer tubes lacking, 6cm (2¼in), *L 24 July,*
£1,100 ($1,727)

10
An eight-day metal and brass small lighthouse clock, c.1880, probably French, wind vane finial damaged, 24cm (9½in), *Mel 24 June,*
Aus$1,320 (£574; $895)

11
A painted copper automaton figure of a Turk, 18th century, bearing a dial on the stomach, moving eyes and articulated jaw, 36.5cm (14¼in), *L 20 Feb,*
£4,180 ($6,354)

12
A German polychrome wood automaton, last quarter 18th century, with white enamel dial, *A 14 Oct,*
Dfl 7,360 (£2,300; $3,450)

13
A clock picture of a country landscape, 19th century, painted on copper, later timepiece movement, windmill sails lacking, 82cm (32½in) wide, *L 24 July,*
£935 ($1,468)

14
A clock picture, the oil painting in the manner of Verwee, the two train movement striking on a gong, 56cm (22in) wide, *C 9 Oct,*
£770 ($1,078)

1

2

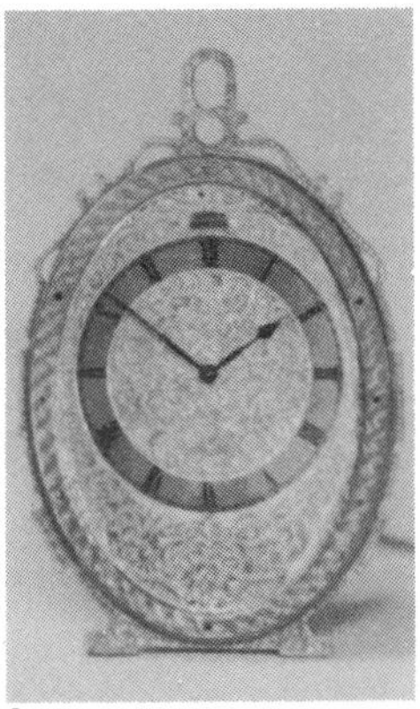
3

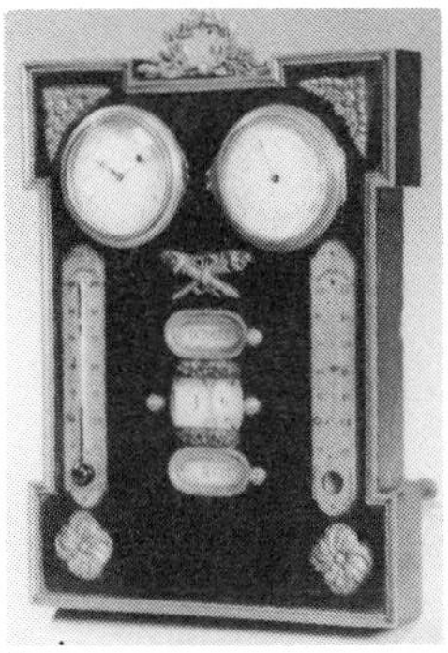
4

5

6

7

8

9

10

11

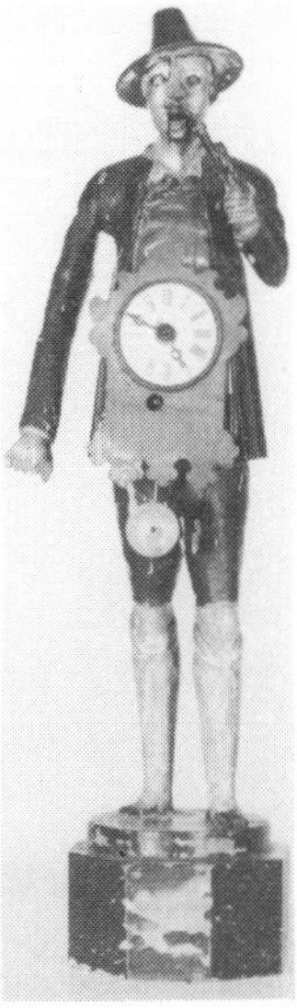
12

13

14

1

2

3

4

5

6

7

8

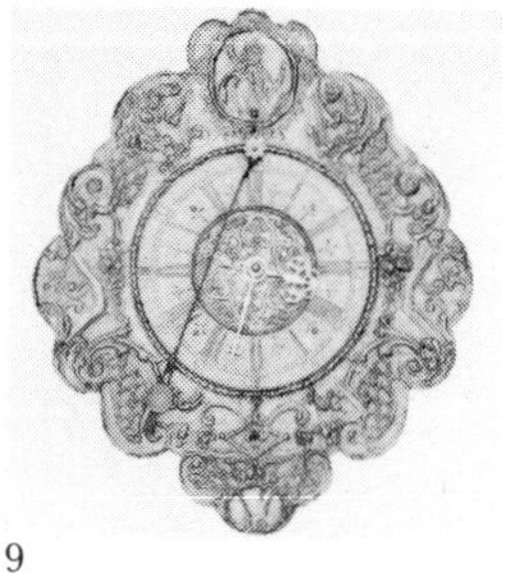
9

10

11

12

1
A Louis XV ormolu cartel clock, mid 18th century, signed on the dial *Pierre Le Roy De La Société des Arts à Paris*, 104cm (41in), *NY 1 Nov*,
$40,700 (£28,865)

2
A Louis XVI cartel clock, signed *Regnault à Paris*, surmounted by a cherub holding an effigy of Henry IV, 100cm (39½in), *M 22 June*,
FF 79,920 (£7,129; $11,122)

3
A Louis XV cartel clock, signed *Gudin à Paris*, 47cm (18½in), *M 22 June*,
FF 38,850 (£3,466; $5,406)

4
A gilt-bronze cartel clock, c.1890, enamel dial signed *Mougin Paris*, 66cm (26in), *L 21 March*,
£550 ($858)

5
A gilt-bronze cartel clock, c.1900, 61cm (24in), *L 21 Mar*,
£1,078 ($1,682)

6
A stoelklok, signed *Goslinck Ruempol, Laren 1739*, 69cm (27in), *A 14 Oct*,
Dfl 9,775 (£3,055; $4,582)

7
A Friesland stoelklok, 18th century, the dial painted with a townscape, 76cm (30in), *L 18 Dec*,
£1,980 ($2,772)

8
An oak staartklok, 19th century, the arch painted with a Dutch landscape, flanked by ebonised pilasters, 163cm (64in), *L 24 July*,
£550 ($864)

9
A German weight-driven quarter-striking wall clock, dial and movement 18th century, 47cm (18½in), *L 1 May*,
£1,650 ($2,673)

10
An eight-day Black Forest wall clock, c.1840, dial signed for *Bouloy à Ladon*, some wear, 31cm (12¼in), *L 1 May*,
£220 ($356)

11
A Black Forest quarter-striking automaton wall clock, c.1840, 44cm (17½in), *L 20 Feb*,
£2,420 ($3,678)

12
A Black Forest wall cuckoo clock, c.1890, the back with the label of Camerer Cuss & Co., 63cm (25in), *L 18 Dec*,
£528 ($739)

Clock in general (see watch), any timekeeper not designed to be carried in the pocket or worn; in particular (see timepiece), a clock that strikes the hours every hour.

Watch a timekeeper with a balance, and designed to be carried in the pocket or worn.

Timepiece a timepiece that does NOT strike regularly, but may repeat.

Clockwatch a watch that strikes the hours regularly.

Regulator a clock (usually a timepiece) designed for precision timekeeping.

1
A George III black-japanned tavern clock, signed *Dwerrihouse, Berkeley Square,* the minute hand inscribed *Browning, Bury,* 125cm (49¼in), *L 16 Oct,*
£3,300 ($4,620)

2
A George III black-japanned wall timepiece, the case signed *Tho. Fordham,* 116cm (45½in), *L 24 July,*
£5,280 ($8,290)

3
A mahogany wall clock, early 19th century, dial signed *Lacey Bristol,* 143cm (56in), *L 24 July,*
£1,540 ($2,418)

4
A green-japanned dial clock, 19th century, brass dial signed *Tompion, Londini, 1795,* 155cm (61in), *C 16 Jan,*
£858 ($1,287)

5
A George III mahogany wall timepiece, silvered dial signed *Jno. Lloyd, Minories, London,* 36.5cm (14¼in), *L 24 July,*
£858 ($1,347)

6
A walnut wall clock, late 19th century, English-style fusee movement by Winterhalder & Hofmeier, 106cm (41¾in), *L 14 July,*
£550 ($858)

7
A walnut year-going Vienna regulator, c.1880, the two-piece enamel dial signed *Schonberger, Vienna,* bezel replaced, 120cm (47¼in), *L 20 Feb,*
£1,540 ($2,341)

8
A walnut and ebonised Vienna regulator timepiece, c.1870, 122cm (48in), *C 16 Jan,*
£440 ($660)

9
A Vienna style walnut cased wall clock, with Lenzkirch movement, 58.5cm (23in), *C 10 July,*
£396 ($638)

10
A mahogany Vienna regulator, c.1840, the enamel dial signed *Josef Lorenz in Wien,* 100cm (39½in), *L 16 Oct,*
£3,080 ($4,312)

11
A German walnut wall regulator, c.1900, 173cm (68in), *JHB 25 Mar,*
R3,000 (£937; $1,462)

12
A Victorian mahogany wall clock, mid 19th century, 179cm (70½in), *C 9 Oct,*
£352 ($493)

Automaton a timekeeper with animated figure(s) actuated by the movement.

Cartel clock a type of decorative spring-driven wall clock, usually metal-cased and very often French; 18th century or later.

Lantern clock a particularly early (c.1600-1750) type of metal-cased weight-driven wall clock; also used of later spring-driven copies.

Musical a musical clock or watch plays a tune (or tunes) on bells, gongs, pipes or a steel comb.

Mystery, Mysterieuse timekeeper in which the means of maintaining motion are not obvious. In one type there is no visible connection between the hands and the movement.

Pendule D'Officier a type of metal-cased French travelling clock, usually late 18th or early 19th century.

1

2

3

4

5

6

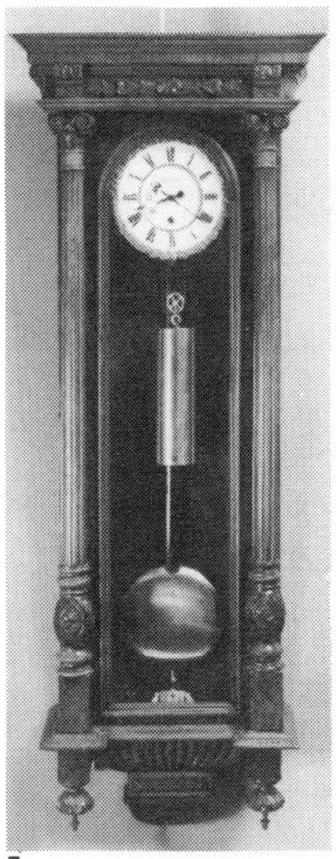
7

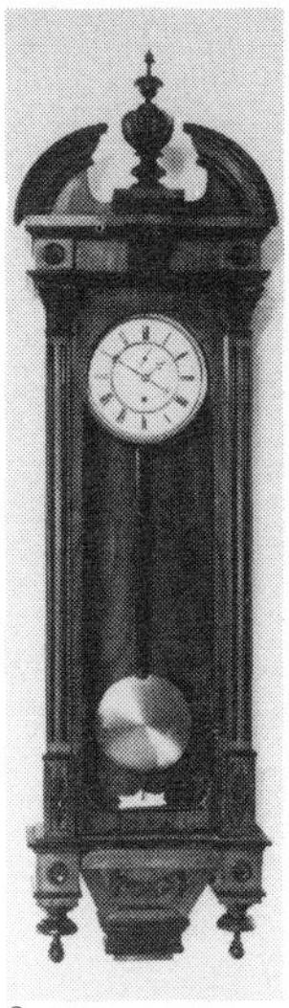
8

9

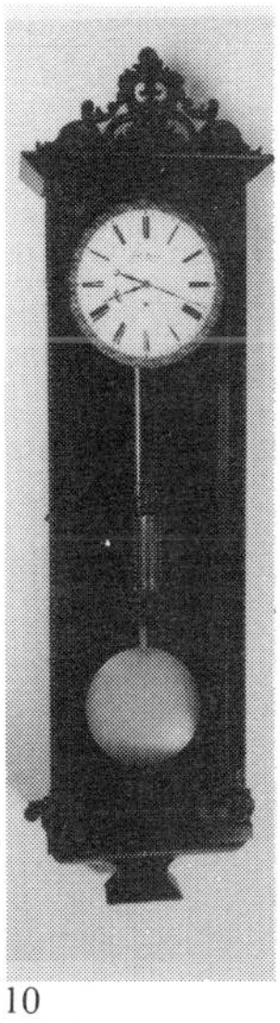
10

11

12

1
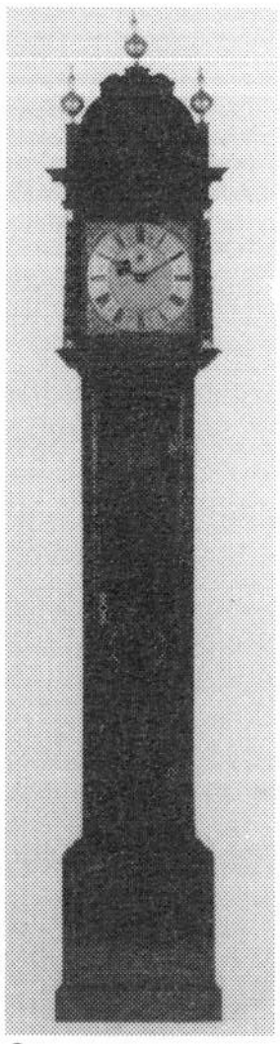
2
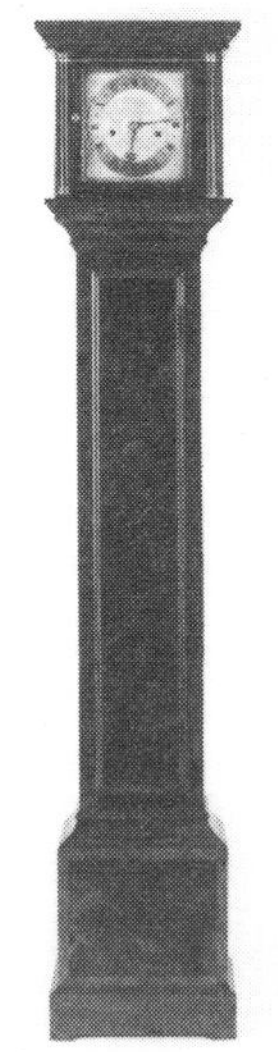
3
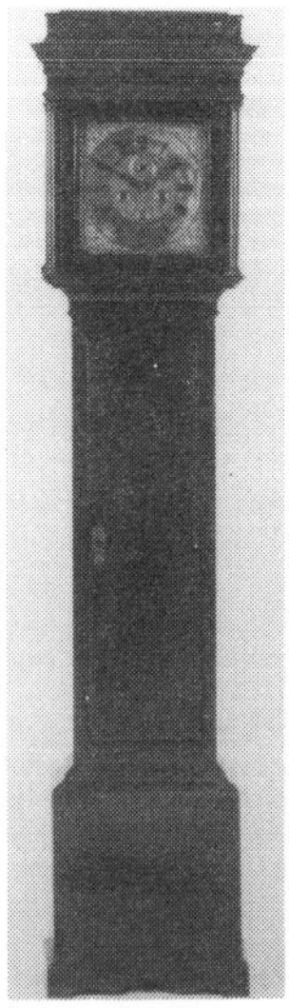
4
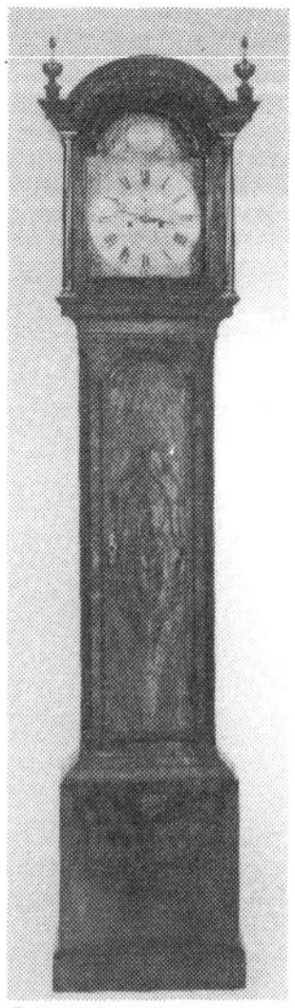
5
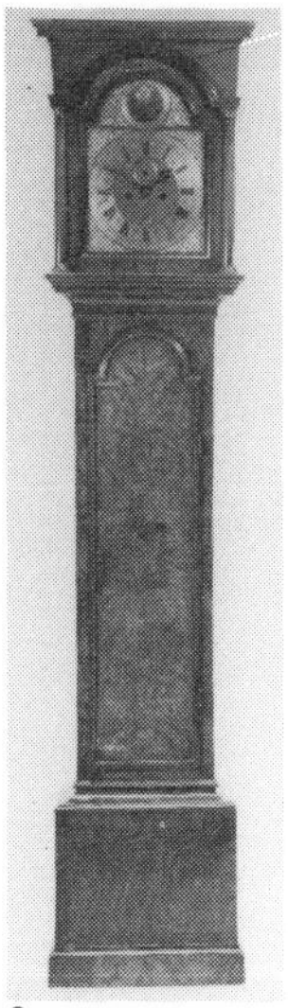
6
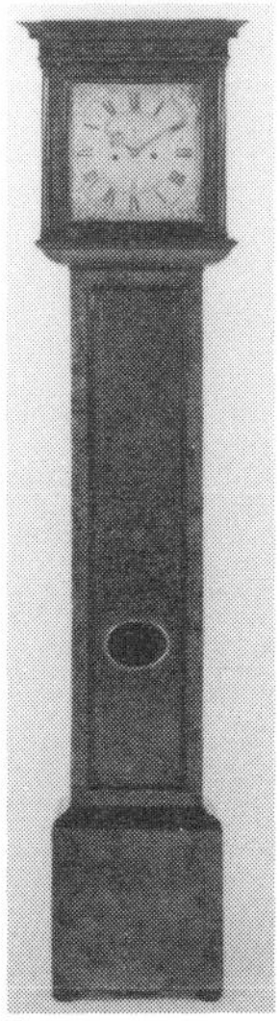
7
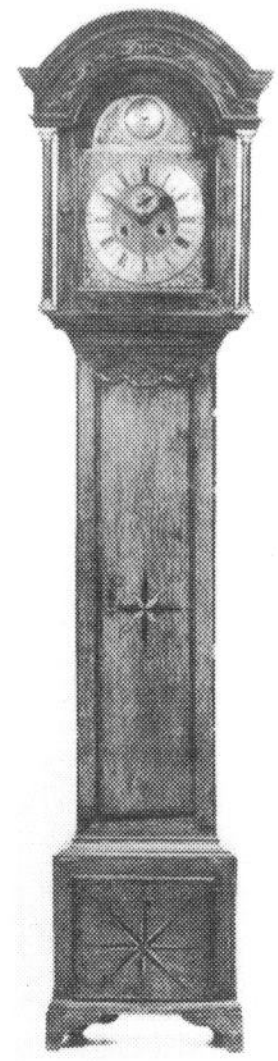
8
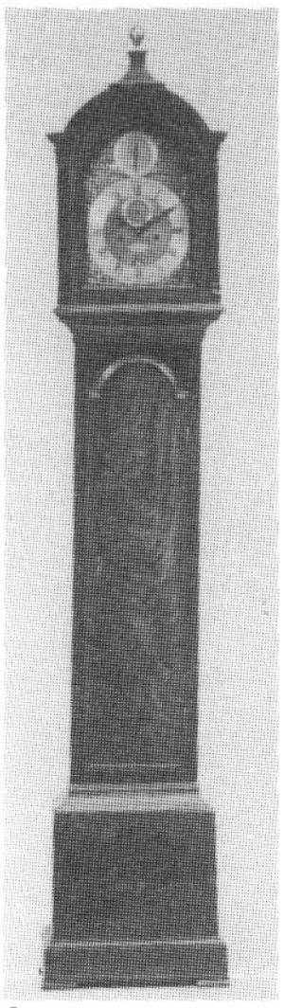
9

10
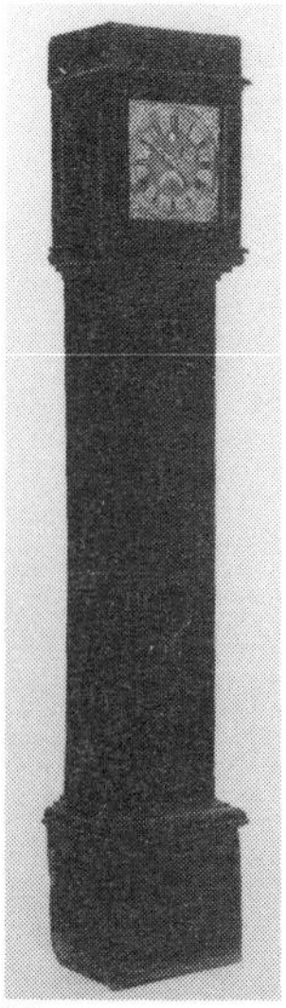
11
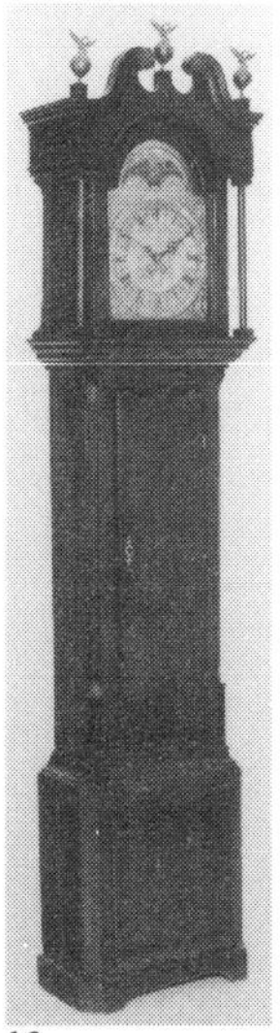
12
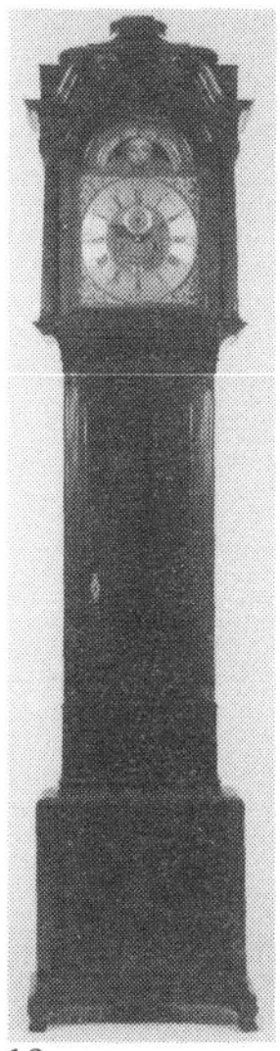
13
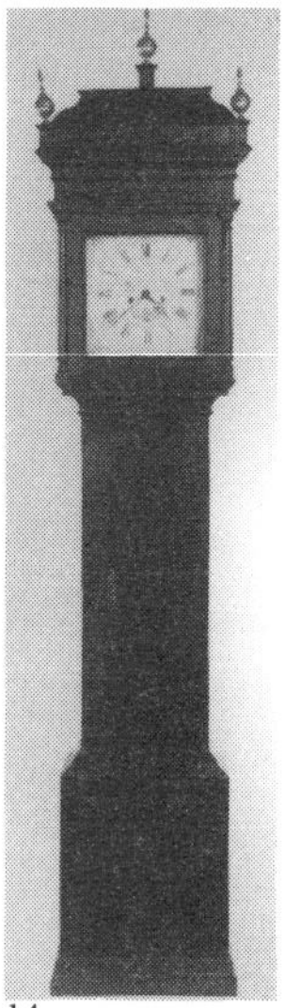
14

15

1
A walnut marquetry long-case clock, the dial signed *Charles Gretton in Fleete Streete,* with cherub and leaf spandrels, hood and plinth with alteration, 229cm (7ft 6in), *L 18 Dec,*
£7,920 ($11,088)

2
A walnut longcase clock, late 17th century, the dial signed *John Barnett Londini fecit,* with cherub and leaf spandrels, retaining its original surface and with early metal bosses, 242cm (7ft 11in), *L 16 Oct,*
£9,350 ($13,090)

3
A George I burr walnut longcase clock, first quarter 18th century, signed *Peter Wise, London,* 183cm (6ft), *NY 25 Jan,*
$4,675 (£3,363)

4
A George II red walnut longcase clock, the dial signed *Henry Swaine, Hill-parton,* cherub and crown spandrels, one pillar lacking, 223.5cm (7ft 4in), *L 16 Oct,*
£2,420 ($3,388)

5
A George II walnut long-case clock, Thomas Haley, North Waltham, mid 18th century, later urn finials, 234cm (7ft 8in), *NY 13 Dec,*
$7,700 (£5,500)

6
A walnut longcase clock, early 18th century, 228cm (7ft 6in), *S 18 Sept,*
£4,400 ($6,160)

7
A 'Mulberrywood' month longcase clock, the dial signed *Henry Jones in the Temple,* cherub and leaf spandrels, 204cm (6ft 10in), *L 16 Oct,*
£7,150 ($10,010)

8
An oak longcase clock, c.1740, the brass dial inscribed *Richd. Midgeter, Halifax* and *Dum Spectas fugio* ('Whilst you look I am flying'), 223cm (7ft 4in), *S 21 Feb,*
£880 ($1,338)

9
A mahogany longcase clock, the dial signed *John Holmes London,* 219cm (7ft 2in), *L 20 Feb,*
£5,280 ($8,026)

10
A George III provincial mahogany longcase clock, the dial indistinctly signed ... *Moore Warminster,* with spandrels of the Seasons and a damaged moon disc, 237cm (7ft 9in), *L 24 July,*
£2,200 ($3,454)

11
A Welsh oak longcase clock, the brass dial signed *Hampson, Wrexham,* the case with an unusual pull-out hood, 214cm (7ft), *C 5 Nov,*
£330 ($465)

12
An oak longcase clock, the brass dial signed *Joseph Batty, Halifax,* and dated 1770, the lunar arch inscribed *James Butler,* 231cm (7ft 7in), *C 18 Apr,*
£440 ($682)

13
A George III mahogany longcase clock, last quarter 18th century, 244cm (8ft), *NY 25 Jan,*
$2,750 (£1,978)

14
A George III provincial mahogany longcase clock, the enamel dial decorated with puce rococo scroll-work, 247cm (8ft 1in), *L 7 July,*
£1,760 ($2,851)

15
A George III mahogany longcase clock, signed *Ja (James) Causon, Liverpool,* 242cm (7ft 11in), *NY 10 June,*
$5,500 (£3,503)

1
An oak longcase clock, c.1800, signed *Alex Fergurson, Cupar, Fife,* 215cm (7ft 1in), *C 9 Oct,*
£825 ($1,155)

2
A pollard oak longcase clock, the brass dial signed *Saml. Whalley, Manchester,* the boss inscribed *Tempus Fugit,* 224cm (7ft 4in), *C 9 Oct,*
£1,210 ($1,694)

3
An oak longcase clock, late 18th century, the restored enamel dial signed *Wm. Steppney,* the dial plate cast *Osborne,* 218cm (7ft 2in), *C 9 Oct,*
£396 ($554)

4
A George III oak and mahogany longcase clock, the brass dial signed *William Bull, Leicester,* with gilt-bronze capitals, 231cm (7ft 7in), *C 18 Apr,*
£748 ($1,159)

5
An oak and mahogany longcase clock, early 19th century, the enamel dial signed *Griffiths & Son, Denbigh,* 238cm (7ft 10in), *C 1 May,*
£506 ($820)

6
A mahogany longcase clock, the enamel dial signed *Jano Shafton, Newcastle,* the spandrels painted with the four continents, 216cm (7ft 1in), *C 10 July,*
£440 ($708)

7
A George III mahogany longcase clock, the brass dial signed *Robert Wood, London,* 244cm (8ft), *L 24 July,*
£1,870 ($2,936)

8
A mahogany longcase clock, the enamel dial signed *Robt. Jones Liverpool,* 233cm (7ft 8in), *C 1 May,*
£506 ($820)

9
A mahogany longcase clock, c.1800, the painted dial inscribed *Thos. Baker, Devizes,* 221cm (7ft 3in), *S 19 June,*
£935 ($1,477)

10
A mahogany longcase clock, c.1770, the brass dial with gilt spandrels and inscribed *Allam & Clements, London,* 244cm (8ft), *S 24 Apr,*
£3,190 ($5,008)

11
A mahogany longcase clock, early 19th century, the enamel dial signed *Jas. Joyce and Son, Ruthin,* the spandrels allegorical of the four continents, 238cm (7ft 10in), *C 6 Aug,*
£374 ($580)

12
A mahogany longcase clock, early 19th century, the painted dial indistinctly inscribed, the spandrels with figures representing the Seasons, 226cm (7ft 2in), *S 18 Sept,*
£858 ($1,201)

13
A George III mahogany chiming longcase clock, the dial signed *Jno. Flook London,* 239cm (7ft 10in), *L 18 Dec,*
£2,860 ($4,004)

14
A George III mahogany longcase clock, the dial signed *John Monkhouse, London,* 259cm (8ft 6in), *C 16 Jan,*
£2,255 ($3,383)

15
A George III mahogany longcase clock, the dial signed *Joseph Stephens London,* 262cm (8ft 7in), *L 16 Oct,*
£3,080 ($4,312)

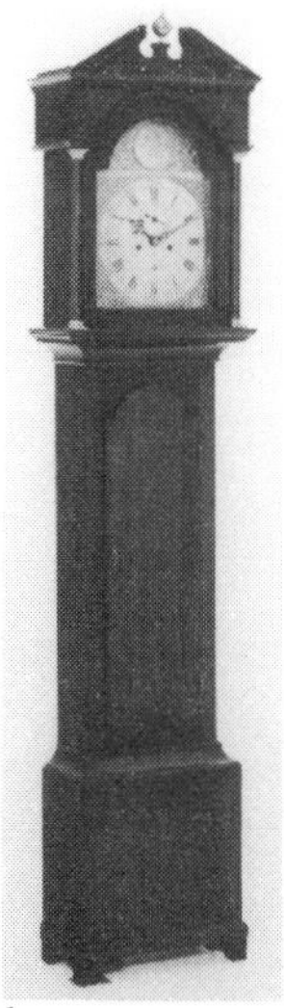
1

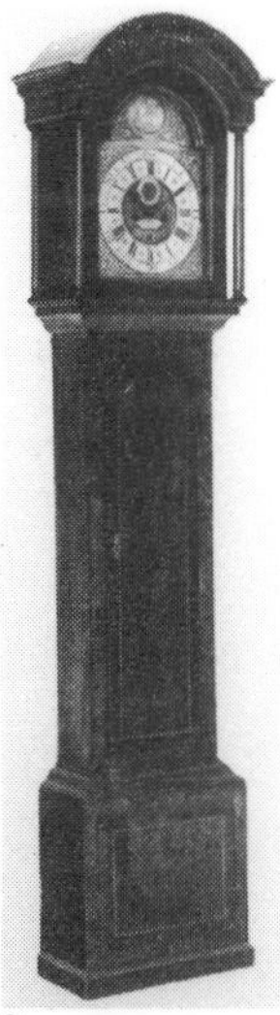
2

3

4

5

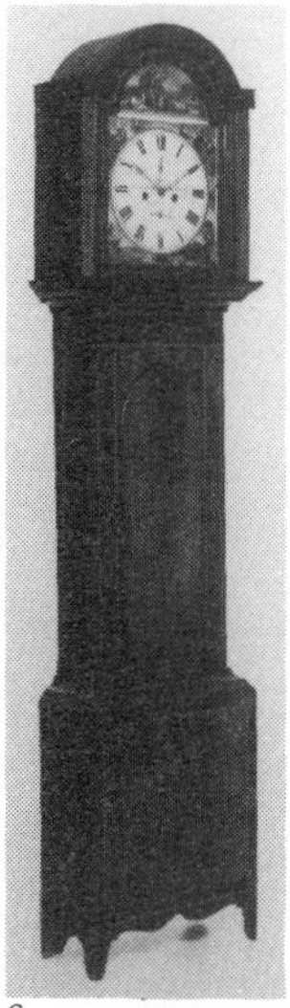
6

7

8

9

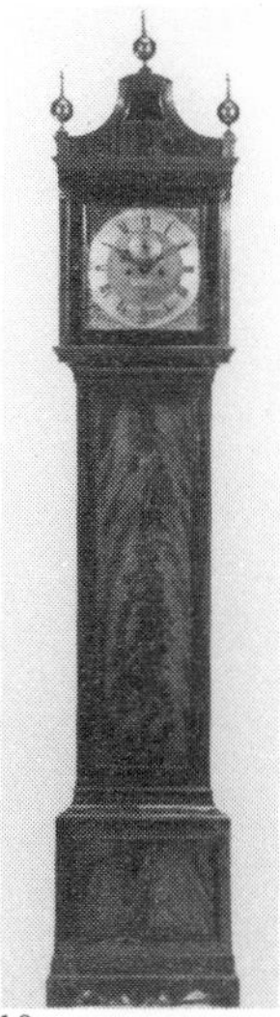
10

11

12

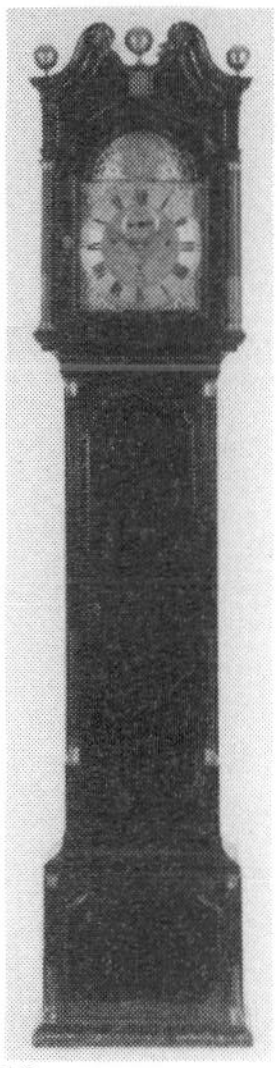
13

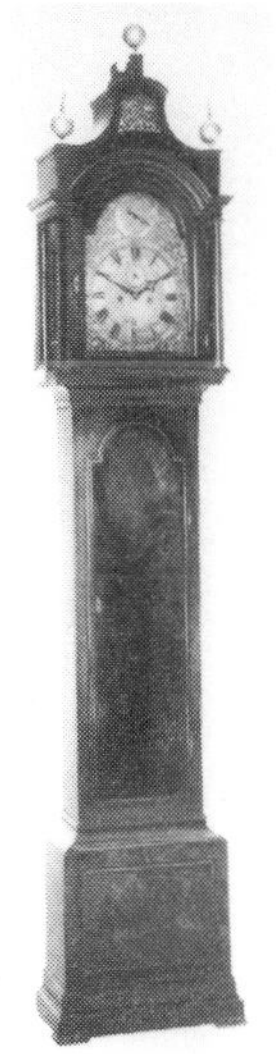
14

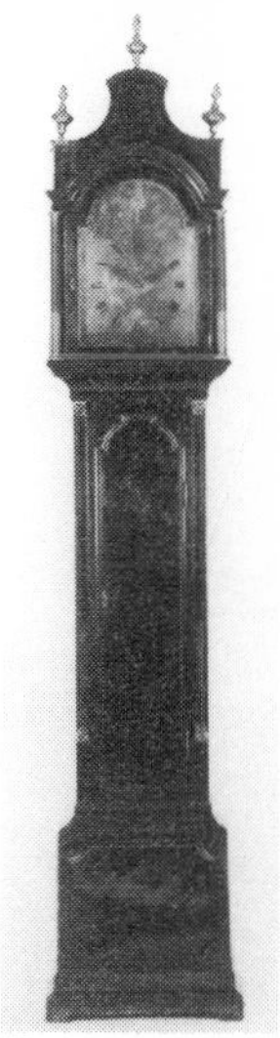
15

1

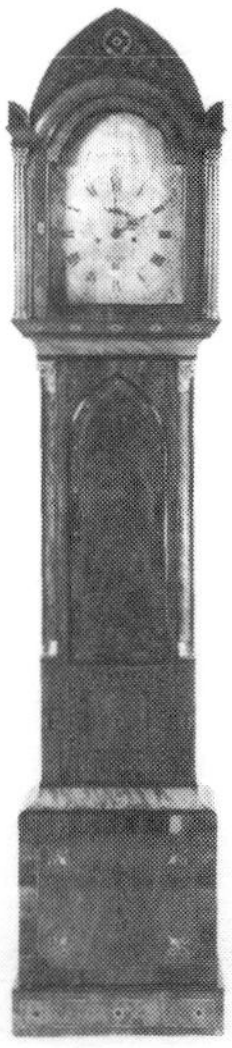
2

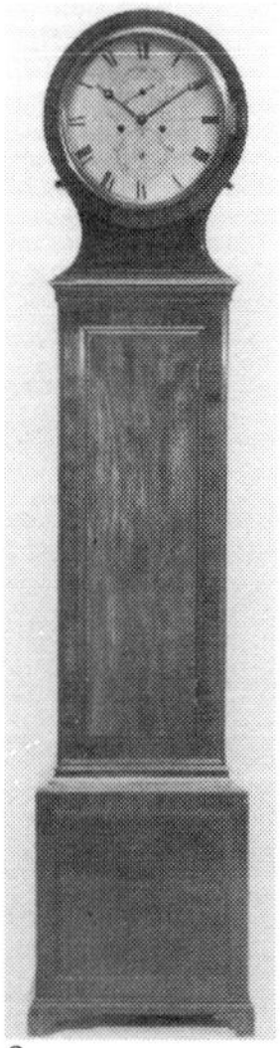
3

4

5

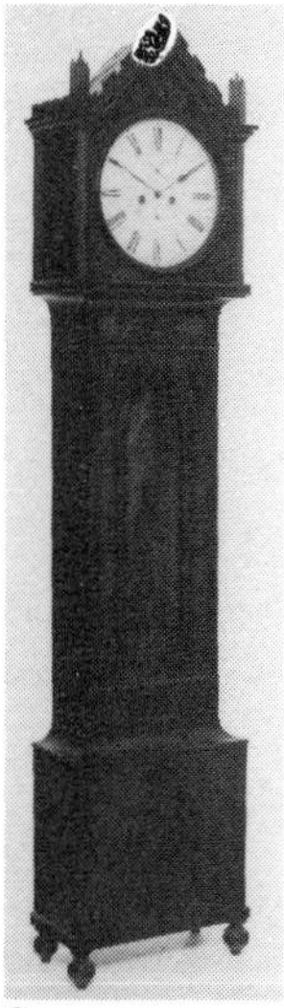
6

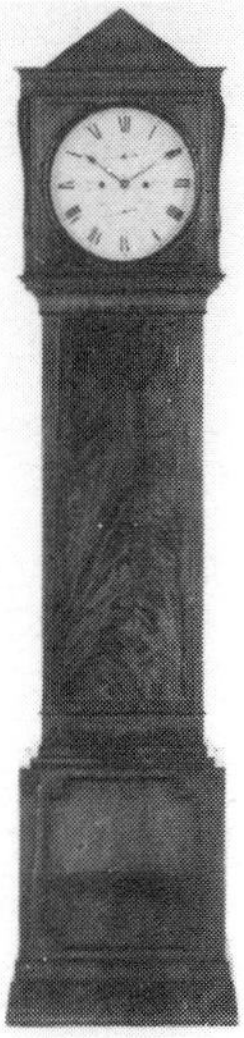
7

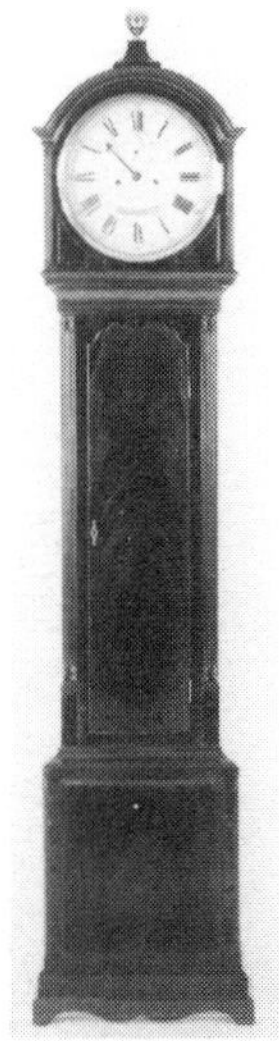
8

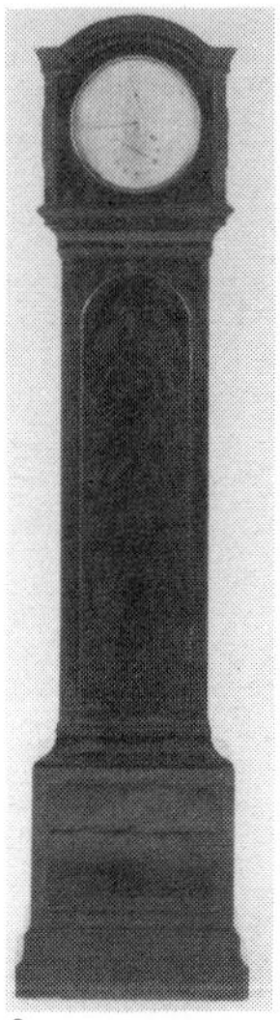
9

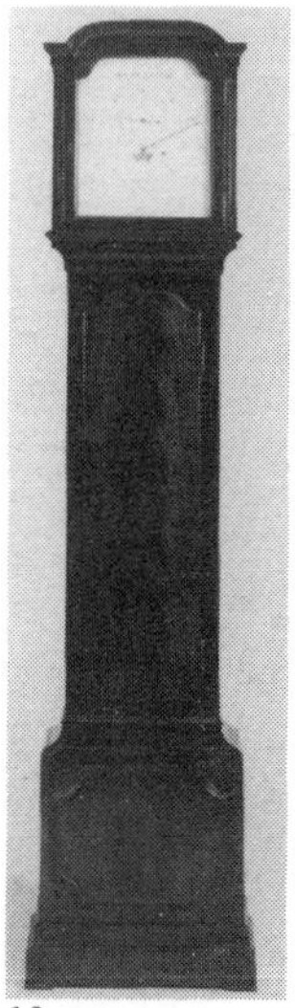
10

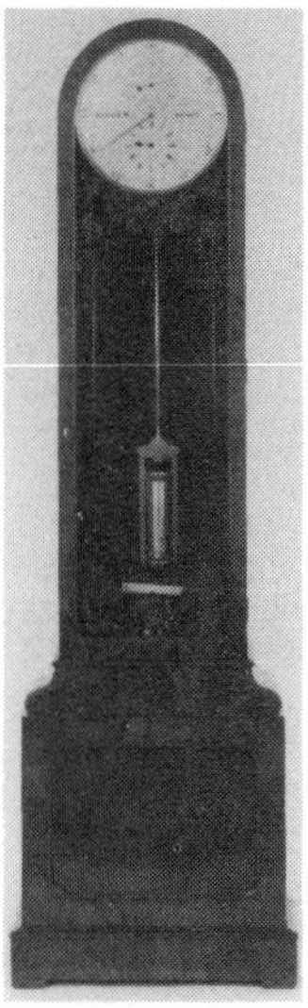
11

12

13

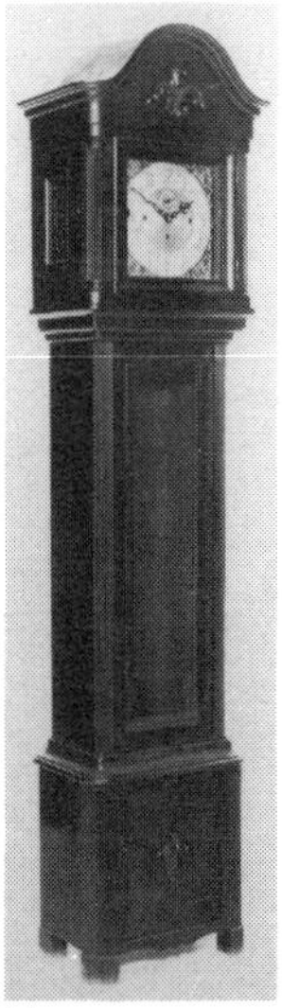
14

15

1
A mahogany longcase clock, c.1830, the dial indistinctly signed *Shaw Liverpool*, 251cm (8ft 3in), *C 13 Mar,*
£440 ($664)

2
A Regency brass-mounted mahogany long-case clock, first quarter 19th century, by Smith, Canterbury, 224cm (7ft 4in), *NY 13 Dec,*
$7,425 (£5,303)

3
A mahogany longcase clock, c.1800, the dial inscribed *Alex & Phillip, Edinburgh*, 206cm (6ft 9in), *S 19 June,*
£462 ($729)

4
A Scottish mahogany longcase clock, c.1830, the circular painted dial signed *Liddall & Sons, Edinburgh*, 207cm (6ft 10in), *L 12 May,*
£1,430 ($2,302)

5
A mahogany longcase clock, c.1840, the dial signed *Jas. Cassels, Lanark*, 206cm (6ft 9in), *C 9 Oct,*
£550 ($770)

6
A mahogany longcase clock, second quarter 19th century, 215cm (7ft), *C 9 Oct,*
£594 ($832)

7
A Scottish mahogany longcase clock, early 19th century, the painted dial signed *John Todd Glasgow*, 203cm (6ft 8in), *L 20 Feb,*
£1,650 ($2,508)

8
A mahogany calendar longcase clock, early 19th century, the repainted dial signed *Richard Ganthony London,* minute hand lacking, 224cm (7ft 4in), *L 1 May,*
£1,760 ($2,851)

9
A George IV mahogany regulator, the dial signed *Binns, No.137 Strand, London,* 191cm (6ft 3in), *L 16 Oct,*
£4,180 ($5,852)

10
A Regency mahogany regulator, first quarter 19th century, by *Jas. Attenborough, 32 Strand,* 190cm (6ft 3in), *NY 17 Oct,*
$4,950 (£3,438)

11
A Victorian mahogany regulator, the silvered dial signed *Benzie, Cowes,* 206cm (6ft 11in), *L 16 Oct,*
£4,950 ($6,930)

12
An Edwardian mahogany chiming longcase clock, c.1906, the dial inscribed *Howell & James Ltd., Regent St. London,* Whittington/ Westminster dials in the arch, 261cm (7ft 11in), *S 21 Feb,*
£2,750 ($4,180)

13
A chiming mahogany longcase clock, late 19th/early 20th century, Whittington/Westminster dial in the arch, 225cm (7ft 4in), *C 18 Apr,*
£1,320 ($2,046)

14
An Edwardian mahogany chiming longcase clock, 239cm (7ft 10in), *C 16 Jan,*
£550 ($825)

15
An Edwardian inlaid mahogany chiming longcase clock, early 20th century, Whittington/ Westminster chimes, 246cm (8ft 1in), *S 18 Sept,*
£2,310 ($3,234)

1
An American mahogany longcase clock, c.1765, the brass dial inscribed *James Wady, Newport,* 230cm (7ft 6½in), *NY 26 June,*
$9,075 (£6,010)

2
An American mahogany longcase clock, c.1790, the painted dial signed *David Williams, Newport,* 224cm (7ft 4in), *L 16 Oct,*
£5,500 ($7,700)

3
An American mahogany longcase clock, William Stanton, Providence, Rhode Island, c.1800, minor repairs, 233cm (7ft 7¾in), *NY 25 Oct,*
$19,800 (£14,042)

4
An American mahogany longcase clock, Nathaniel Munroe, Concord, Massachusetts, c.1810, feet and crest restored, 224cm (7ft 4in), *NY 25 Oct,*
$10,450 (£7,411)

5
An American mahogany longcase clock, New Jersey, c.1800, repair, 246cm (8ft ¾in), *NY 26 June,*
$11,550 (£7,649)

6
An American mahogany longcase clock, Isaac Brokaw, Bridgetown, New Jersey, c.1810, some restoration and repair, 243cm (7ft 11½in), *NY 26 June,*
$4,125 (£2,732)

7
An Italian inlaid longcase clock, Emilia, second half 18th century, the face (not belonging to the mechanism) signed *François Barbier,* 305cm (10ft ¼in), *F 14 Apr,*
L 3,000,000 (£1,229; $1,904)

8
A German inlaid mahogany chiming longcase clock, the dial with a plaque inscribed *Tempus Fugit* and the backplate stamped *HWN Pendellge,* 214cm (7ft), *L 6 Oct,*
£770 ($1,078)

9
A Louis XV provincial oak and marquetry longcase clock, 243cm (7ft 11½in), *M 24 Feb,*
FF 6,660 (£644; $966)

10
A Dutch fruitwood marquetry longcase clock, third quarter 18th century, the subsidiary dial inscribed *Roger Dunster,* 280cm (8ft 4in), *NY 4 Oct,*
$5,225 (£3,628)

11
A Dutch mahogany longcase clock, mid 18th century, the face with a painted automaton scene depicting a fisherman by a church and a windmill, 265.5cm (8ft 8½in), *L 18 Dec,*
£4,400 ($6,160)

12
A Dutch inlaid burr walnut musical longcase clock, 18th century, the dial signed *Jan Hermelink Amsterdam,* and with four tune selection, 264cm (8ft 10in), *L 18 Dec,*
£7,700 ($10,780)

13
A Dutch walnut longcase clock, Jacob Oosterwijck, Amsterdam, first half 18th century, 226cm (7ft 5in), *A 14 Oct,*
Dfl 31,050 (£9,703; $14,554)

14
An ormolu-mounted mahogany month regulator, the enamel dial signed *Lepaute A Paris* and *Dubuisson,* 214cm (7ft), *L 16 Oct,*
£4,950 ($6,930)

15
An onyx, marble and champlevé enamel longcase clock, c.1890, the gong striking GLT movement, (Thieble of Paris), with a Brocot escapement, 127cm (50in), *L 7 Nov,*
£4,620 ($6,468)

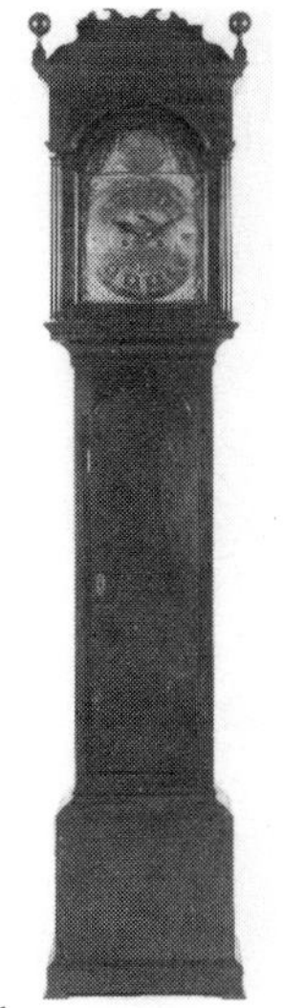
1
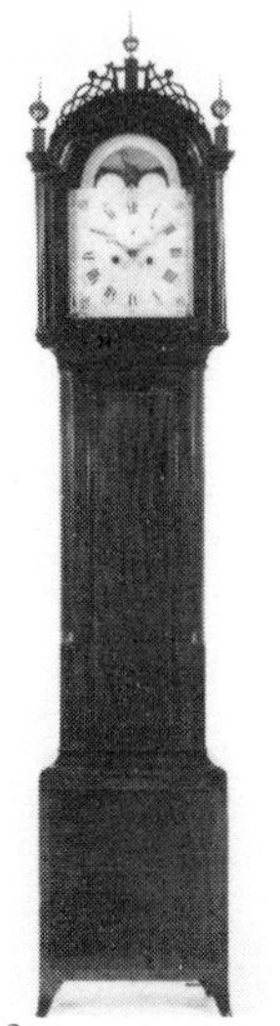
2

3
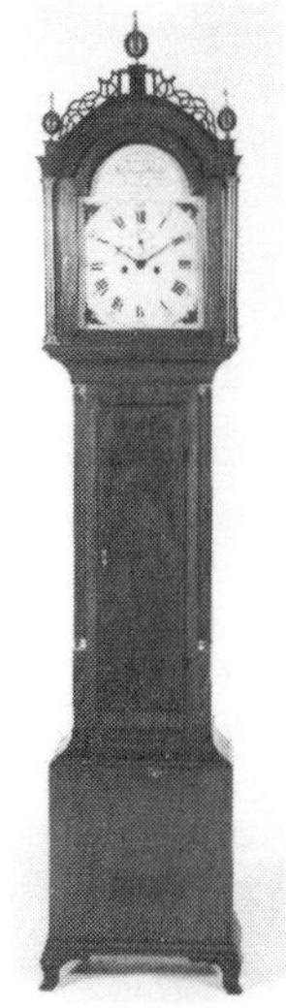
4
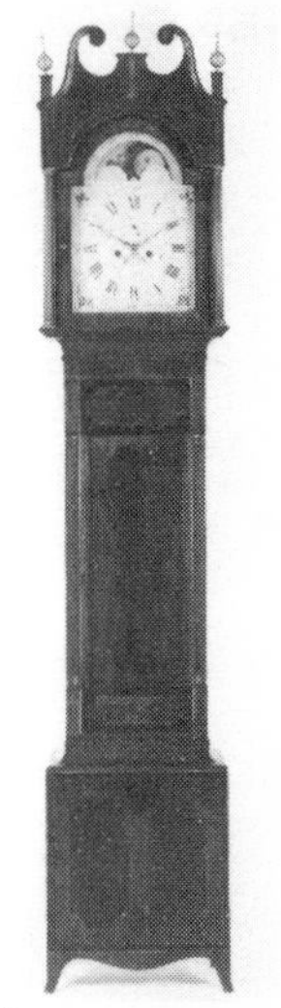
5
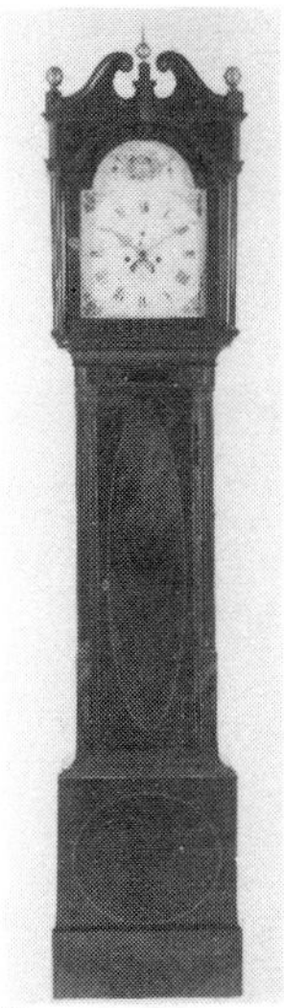
6
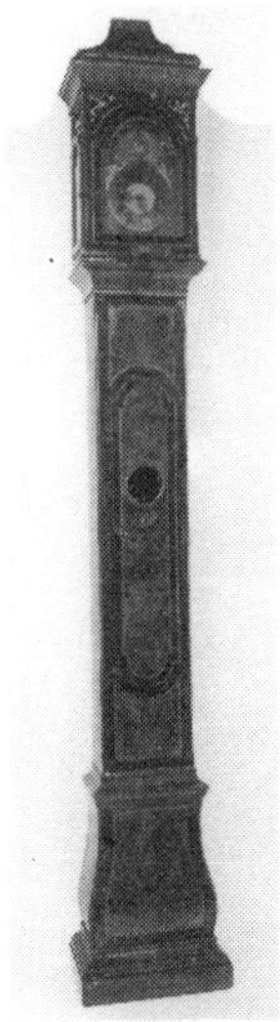
7
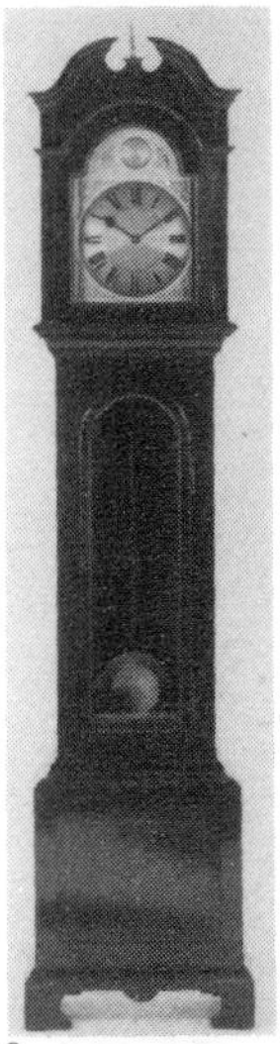
8
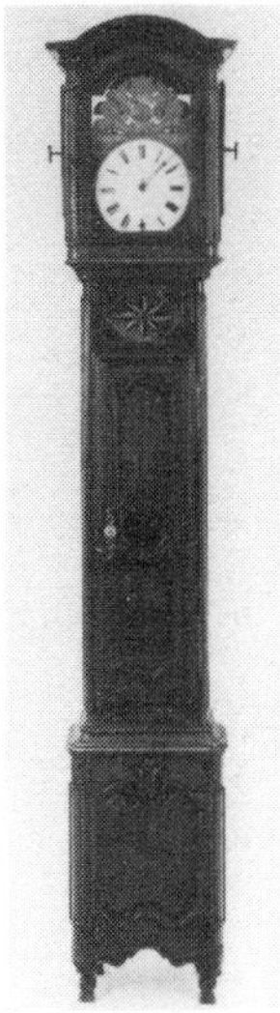
9

10

11

12
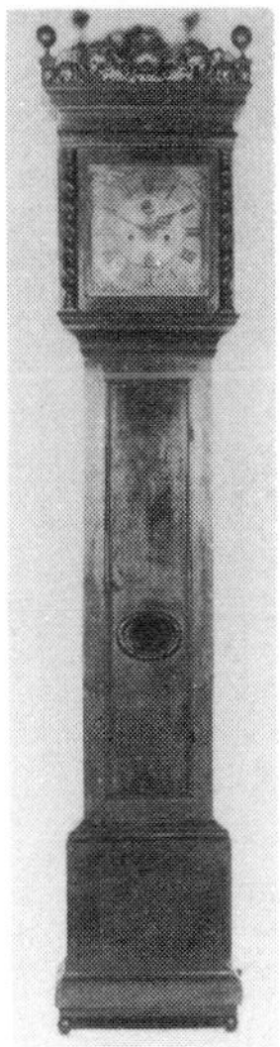
13
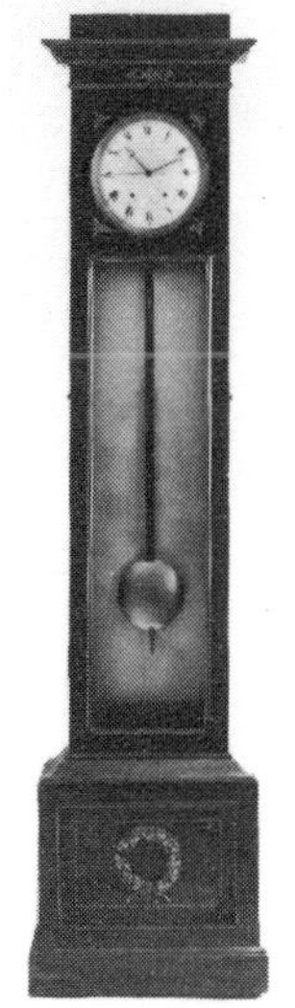
14

15

1

2

3

4

5

6

7

8

9

10

11

12

13

14

1
A brass repeating carriage clock, late 19th century, with a leather travelling case, 14cm (5½in), *C 9 Oct,*
£286 ($400)

2
A quarter-striking carriage clock, the enamel dial signed *Klaftenberger,* 13.5cm (5¼in), *G 11 Nov,*
SF 1,320 (£550; $770)

3
A quarter-striking carriage clock, the silvered platform stamped *JS No.81,* 14cm (5½in), *G 11 Nov,*
SF 2,200 (£917; $1,283)

4
A brass repeating alarm carriage clock, late 19th century, the ivorine chapter ring signed *A La Montre De Geneve, E Sauvage, Quimper,* 14cm (5½in), *C 10 July,*
£330 ($531)

5
A repeating carriage clock with alarm, the dial inscribed *Chas. Frodsham & Co., à Paris,* with travelling case, 17cm (6½in), *S 18 Sept,*
£836 ($1,170)

6
A gilt bronze Grande Sonnerie repeating alarm carriage clock, c.1890, inscribed *Le Roy & Fils,* with a red morocco travelling case, 20cm (8in),*C 18 Apr,*
£1,705 ($2,643)

7
An alarm carriage clock, the enamel dial signed *Leroy & Fils Hers. Palais Royal 13 & 15 Paris,* between calendar and alarum dials, 13cm (5in), *L 20 Feb,*
£1,045 ($1,588)

8
An alarm carriage clock, the enamel dial signed *Dent A Paris,* 14.5cm (5¾in), *L 1 May,*
£880 ($1,426)

9
A Viennese Grande Sonnerie carriage clock, the enamel dial signed *Marenzeller,* with single wheel duplex escapement, 14cm (5½in), *L 20 Feb,*
£990 ($1,505)

10
A champlevé enamel repeating and alarm carriage clock, with a later lever escapement, decorated with polychrome enamel, 18cm (7in), *L 16 Oct,*
£3,300 ($4,620)

11
A silvered and brass Petite Sonnerie carriage clock with alarm, the foliate engraved dial inscribed *Breguet,* 17cm (6½in), *S 13 Nov,*
£770 ($1,078)

12
An enamel-mounted carriage clock, the repeating lever movement with the stamp of Maurice et Cie, 18cm (7in), *L 20 Feb,*
£2,090 ($3,177)

13
A porcelain-mounted repeating carriage clock, decorated with polychrome enamelled birds, the gong-striking Achille Brocot movement with a lever escapement, 15.5cm (6in), *L 18 Dec,*
£1,430 ($2,002)

14
A mahogany and brass bound sedan timepiece, early 19th century, the verge movement signed *Bishop, Portland Street,* 16.5cm (6½in), *C 9 Oct,*
£253 ($354)

Chiming sounding every quarter on four or more bells or gongs.

Petite Sonnerie sounding every quarter (but the hours only at the hour). Usually synonymous with quarter-striking.

Grande Sonnerie sounding the quarters AND the last hour every quarter.

Striking in particular, sounding the hours regularly (almost always on one bell or gong); more generally, of a timekeeper with any type of striking or chiming mechanism.

Quarter-striking sounding every quarter on up to three bells or gongs.

1
A miniature carriage timepiece, the movement with a lever escapement, minute hand lacking, 7.5cm (3in), *L 24 July,*
£462 ($725)

2
A miniature enamel-mounted carriage timepiece, the dial surround painted with birds and sprays of flowers, with a travelling case, 6cm (2¼in), *L 24 July,*
£1,155 ($1,813)

3
A Margaine Mignonnette No.2 carriage timepiece, maker's stamp on backplate, in a lacquered brass obis case, 10cm (4in), *S 21 Feb,*
£297 ($451)

4
A Drocourt Mignonnette No.2 carriage timepiece, the backplate with maker's stamp, the porcelain dial painted with peasant figures in a rustic setting, 10cm (4in), *S 21 Feb,*
£1,100 ($1,672)

5
A porcelain-mounted carriage timepiece, in the Japanese taste, with a leather travelling case, 9cm (3½in), *L 20 Feb,*
£1,870 ($2,842)

6
A carriage timepiece with alarm, the dial inscribed *Langree, Lorient,* 11cm (4½in), *S 21 Feb,*
£363 ($552)

7
A brass and champlevé enamel carriage timepiece, c.1920, 12cm (4¾in), *C 1 May,*
£154 ($249)

8
A French porcelain-mounted carriage clock, the dial signed *Boxell Brighton,* the sides painted with children and flowers, turquoise and 'pearl' borders, 14cm (5½in), *L 20 Feb,*
£2,200 ($3,344)

9
A French carriage timepiece, c.1890, in a glazed brass Doucine case, 13cm (5¼in), *L 3 Mar,*
£198 ($297)

10
A repeating carriage clock with alarm, 18cm (7in), *S 24 Apr,*
£616 ($967)

11
An English Grande Sonnerie carriage clock, mid 19th century, the dial inscribed *Upjohn Bright & Wood, 15 King William Strt., Strand,* with a baize-lined mahogany carrying case, 33cm (13in), *S 18 Sept,*
£3,410 ($4,774)

12
An English carriage timepiece, the silvered dial signed *Hunt & Roskell 25 Old Bond St. London,* 21.5cm (8½in), *L 1 May,*
£1,430 ($2,317)

13
A brass carriage clock, c.1880, with engraved gilt dial, 19cm (7½in), *C 18 Apr,*
£495 ($767)

14
An English carriage clock, the silvered dial signed *John Moore & Sons, Clerkenwell, London,* with a leather travelling case, 21cm (8¼in), *L 20 Feb,*
£2,640 ($4,013)

Repeating in particular, of a timekeeper that can repeat the hours only; more generally, of any timekeeper with more elaborate repeating work. Many timekeepers repeat but do not strike.

Quarter-repeating repeating the hours and quarters.

Minute-repeating repeating the hours, quarters and minutes (up to 14) within each quarter, usually on two bells or gongs.

1

2

3

4

5

6

7

8

9

10

11

12

13

14

Mystery Clocks

MICHAEL TURNER

For centuries the mechanical clock has accompanied man measuring his time on earth, and maybe because of this it has been regarded by some as having mysterious or even supernatural qualities. Every mechanical clock made before the machine age is individual; its unique voice in the form of its tick and strike adds considerably to the view that a clock has a distinct personality. Few people understand what keeps a clock going, apart from knowing that it has to be wound regularly.

Throughout the whole period of mechanical clocks horologists strove to produce clocks that were more than just timekeepers and, encouraged by wealthy patrons, they incorporated complicated automata and musical mechanisms into their clocks. Many of these clocks were hailed as great masterpieces and were certainly regarded as having mysterious qualities. But it was not until the 19th century, when there was an even greater demand for unusual novelty clocks, that the first true mystery clocks appeared in any number.

By studying a clock mechanism even a completely non-horological person will be able to see that it is basically a simple train of wheels which is forced to revolve by the action of a spring or a weight and which is prevented from running down at high speed by a device called an escapement. The pendulum or balance wheel is attached to the escapement and determines how frequently it operates. A true mystery clock, though, incorporates at least one secret device to prevent the interaction of the driving force through the wheels, to the escapement, being apparent.

Mystery clocks originated in France; they are quite distinctive as they have glass or opaque dials and although the hands indicate the time, as in any other clock, there is no visible connection between them and the movement. The earliest form of mystery clock, thought to have been invented by Robert Houdin, had one hand and a circular dial (see fig.1). The illusion is created by the

1
A French mystery clock, c.1850, the two-train bell-striking movement with Garnier's two-plane escapement, stamped *Brevet D'Invention*, 34.5cm (13½in) high, *L 16 Oct*,
£2,640 ($3,696)

2
A French mystery timepiece, c.1910, the lever movement inscribed *A.C. Paris*, on a mahogany base, the hands revolving without apparent connection to the movement, 37cm (14½in) high, *L 24 July*,
£2,530 ($3,972)

3
A coral and rock crystal mystery clock, by Cartier, c.1928, the case applied with a mother-of-pearl chapter ring with an inner rose diamond border, underside engraved *made by European Watch & Clock Co. France for Cartier, Paris*, 13cm (5in), *StM 21-23 Feb 1985*,
SF 176,000 (£53,172; $68,060)

3

dial being made of three pieces of glass, the central one (to which the hand is attached) having a toothed rim concealed by the bezel and being driven by a small gear wheel hidden within the decorative support and connected to the movement in the base. The popularity of this type of clock endured for many years and it was produced in a variety of forms until at least the 1930s.

The later models had two hands and some were even more mysterious as they had square or shaped dials which could not conceal a toothed glass wheel (fig.2). The ingenious makers devised a way of moving the central panel of glass in such a way as to impart circular motion to the hands. An electric mystery clock with a square glass dial was made by Smiths in the 1930s and now is popular amongst collectors. Perhaps the most sought-after mystery clock, of this type, was made by Cartier (fig.3). A number of models were produced with circular or square dials and were cased in precious metals decorated with jewels and rare polished stone. These clocks only appear on the open market very occasionally and consequently sell for many thousands of pounds.

The type of mystery clock most commonly encountered was also made in France, but for a much shorter period, between 1870 and 1890. These clocks usually take the form of a marble mantel clock surmounted by a classically dressed female figure holding aloft the pendulum in her outstretched hand. The mysterious feature is that the pendulum oscillates enthusiastically to and fro although it is quite impossible to determine what is keeping it in motion. The secret lies in the fact that the figure is supported on a massive steel shaft pivoted within the clock case and moved imperceptibly by the clock movement (figs 4 & 5). They have a most unusual escapement mounted on the front plate of the movement. Although not originally visible, some of these clocks have now been fitted with a glass dial to reveal the escapement. Their maker is also something of a mystery: all known examples have been stamped G.L.T. This is thought to refer to A.R. Guilmet who invented a mystery clock in 1872. However G.L.T. is also registered as the mark of the 19th century maker Thieble of Paris, who is recorded as producing mystery clocks (an example of his work, though not a mystery clock, is shown on page 129 fig.15). It is hoped that further investigation will shed more light on this particular mystery before long.

Another frequently found clock was first produced in France during the 1880s. Here the clock movement is concealed within the actual pendulum which, once again, is held aloft by a figure and oscillates without apparent impulse. The trick is brought about by a small secondary pendulum concealed within the movement which acts as a counter-balance to the main pendulum and keeps it going. Two examples are illustrated as figs 6 and 7. This type of clock was made a short time later, in a denigrated

4
A French mystery clock, c.1880, with slate dial, bell movement stamped *G.L.T. Breveté*, surmounted by a bronzed spelter figure holding the pendulum, 64cm (25¼in) high, *L 1 May*, **£2,640 ($4,277)**

4

5
A French mystery clock, c.1880, with an enamel dial, the bell-striking G.L.T. movement contained in a polished Belgian slate plinth case, surmounted by a bronzed spelter figure, 59cm (23¼in), *L 16 Oct*, **£2,200 ($3,080)**

5

6
A French bronzed spelter mystery clock, c.1900, with 8-day movement, the red marble plinth entitled *Chasse par Math. Moreau (Hors Concours)*, 54cm (21¼in), *L 18 Dec*, **£990 ($1,386)**

6

7
A bronzed spelter mystery timepiece, c.1880, the French movement with a Brocot escapement, inscribed *'Le Temps des Roses' par Aug. Moreau*, 117cm (46in), *L 24 July*, **£2,200 ($3,454)**

7

form, in German and American factories. They were quick to realise that these clocks, with their simple counter-balance mechanism and cheaply cast spelter figures, could easily be produced at a relatively low cost by machine. The result was that a large number of mystery clocks of this type were produced from the 1890s until the 1920s. Many were regarded as amusing novelties and were discarded after a relatively short time. However there are still a good number of clocks available to the present-day collector and the amount which he or she will have to pay will depend on the overall condition and the rarity of the figure supporting the clock. The most usually encountered model is that of a young girl dressed in the Art Nouveau style; it should be possible to buy one of these for less than £200 ($320). The rarer models, such as the kangaroo, the elephant or the child with a bat (figs 8-10), inevitably cost considerably more.

For the enthusiast wishing to form an unusual collection of clocks there are still many fascinating avenues to be explored. Apart from the clocks mentioned above the collector might do well to consider a swinging cherub clock (fig.12), incorporating Farcot's variation of Peter Debaufre's two-wheel escapement, enabling the 'pendulum' to swing from front to back. There was an earlier form of this clock with a conventional escapement but the amplitude of the swing was less and therefore not so eye-catching (fig.11).

A 'night clock' would also be an interesting addition to a collection. They were made in many forms but usually the movement was concealed, as in a mystery clock, and the time indicated by a glass globe, painted with the numerals, which revolved against a fixed pointer; at night a candle or a night-light was placed inside the globe. An example is illustrated as fig.13.

For many years horological collectors concentrated on examples made by the eminent makers of the 17th and 18th centuries, but now that clocks from that period are becoming scarce and expensive, many aspiring collectors are turning their attention to the more unusual and highly inventive products of the 19th century. Besides the clocks already referred to, many other firms, particularly in France and Germany, produced a number of fascinating and well made novelty clocks which would enhance any collection. Whether you have one clock or several, your friends and relatives will probably be far more intrigued by the mystery clock than the early 18th century bracket clock, though you may tire of explaining how it works!

8

9

10

11

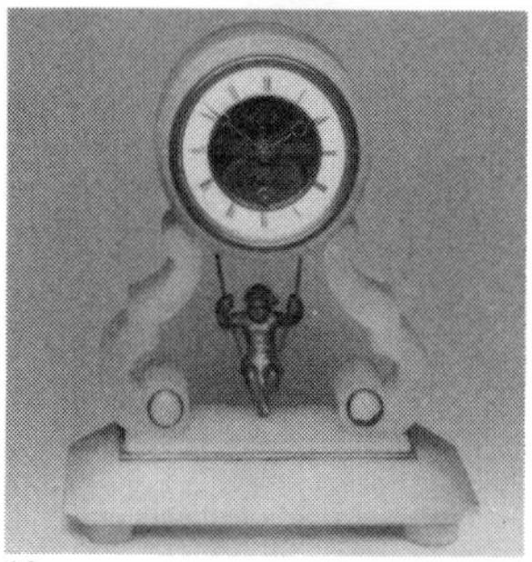

12

13

8
A bronzed spelter kangaroo mystery timepiece, c.1900, with enamel dial and Junghans movement, 26.5cm (10½in), *L 20 Feb,*
£462 ($702)

9
A bronzed spelter mystery timepiece, c.1900, the movement with an enamel dial, the timepiece oscillating without apparent impulse, 44cm (17½in), *L 16 Oct,*
£374 ($524)

10
A bronzed spelter elephant mystery timepiece, c.1900, with enamel dial, 28.5cm (11¼in), *L 16 Oct,*
£308 ($431)

11
An ebonised 'swinging cherub' portico clock, c.1850, with bell-striking Raingo Frères movement, 44cm (17¼in), *L 8 Oct 1985,*
£748 ($1,107)

12
An alabaster 'swinging cherub' mantel timepiece, c.1870, with skeletonised movement, 24cm (9½in), *L 24 July,*
£330 ($518)

13
A French night timepiece, c.1865, the movement with a tic-tac escapement, 27.5cm (10½in), *L 25 Apr 1985,*
£572 ($875)

1
A walnut barometer, early 18th century, the plate signed *Jno.Hallifax Barnsley Invt. & Fecit 1710,* the recording dial in the trunk, hands missing, 125cm (49in), *L 7 July,*
£40,700 ($65,934)

2
A mahogany barometer, mid 18th century, with paper scales inscribed *John Noseda fecit,* 94cm (37in), *S 19 June,*
£484 ($765)

3
A George III mahogany stick barometer, c.1780, the silvered register applied with a thermometer, signed *Roncheti & Gatty,* 97cm (38¼in), *C 16 Jan,*
£528 ($792)

4
A mahogany stick barometer, c.1800, the silvered scales inscribed *Dollond, London,* base missing, 98cm (38½in), *S 21 Feb,*
£3,850 ($5,852)

5
A George III mahogany cistern barometer, mid 18th century, 111cm (43¾in), *NY 25 Jan,*
$8,800 (£6,331)

6
A mahogany stick barometer, late 18th century, signed *G. Gobbo, York,* with restorations, 97cm (38in), *C 18 Apr,*
£385 ($597)

7
A George IV mahogany wheel barometer, early 19th century, signed *J. Comoli, Warrented,* 98cm (38½in), *C 10 July,*
£330 ($531)

8
A walnut pillar barometer, in the manner of Daniel Quare, 99cm (39in), *L 1 May,*
£1,760 ($2,851)

9
A George III mahogany wheel barometer, signed *Ant. Gatty, Glasgow,* 89cm (39in), *C 18 Apr,*
£616 ($955)

10
A Victorian walnut stick barometer, c.1855, the ivory register signed *E. Cetti, 11 Brook Str., London,* 99cm (39in), *C 10 July,*
£385 ($620)

11
A Victorian ebony-inlaid mahogany cistern barometer and thermometer, mid 19th century, Andrew Ross, London, 100cm (39½in), *NY 25 Jan,*
$1,650 (£1,187)

12
A Victorian ivory and brass-mounted mahogany ship's barometer, mid 19th century, Jas. Bassnett, Liverpool, 97cm (38in), *NY 25 Jan,*
$6,600 (£4,748)

13
A rosewood stick barometer, mid 19th century, the ivory register signed *Chadburn Bros, Opticians,* 91cm (36in), *C 9 Oct,*
£352 ($493)

14
A walnut marine barometer, the etched ivory register inscribed *J. Bassnett, Liverpool,* 97cm (38in), *C 18 Apr,*
£1,320 ($2,046)

15
A brass marine barometer, late 19th century, the case inscribed *Negretti & Zambra,* 94cm (37in), *S 18 Sept,*
£297 ($416)

16
A rosewood and cut mother-of-pearl wheel barometer, c.1850, 97cm (38in), *C 18 Apr,*
£209 ($324)

17
A rosewood and mother-of-pearl inlaid wheel barometer, the dial signed *W. Desilva,* 104cm (41in), *C 9 Oct,*
£165 ($231)

18
An oak stick barometer, c.1870, the ivorine register signed *J.B. Dancer, Manchester,* 109cm (43in), *C 10 July,*
£440 ($708)

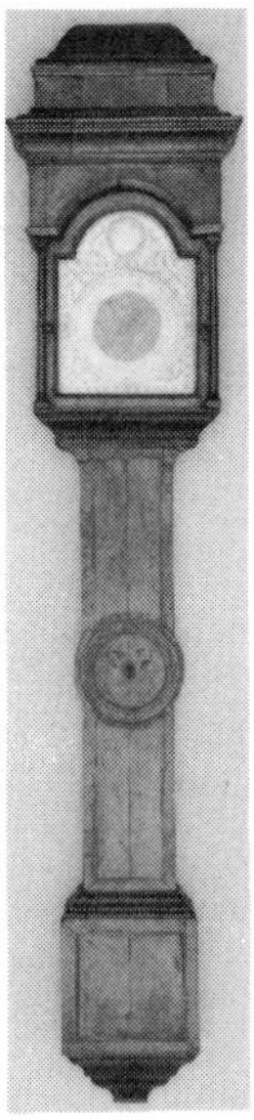
1

2

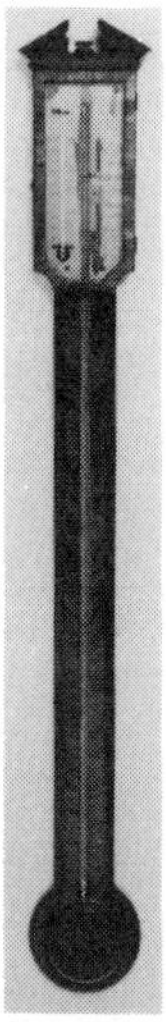
3

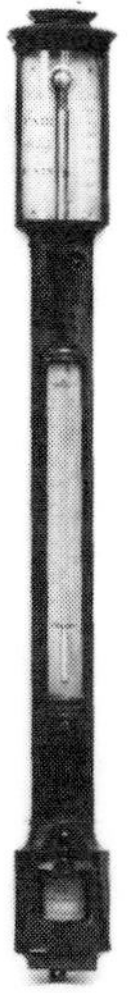
4

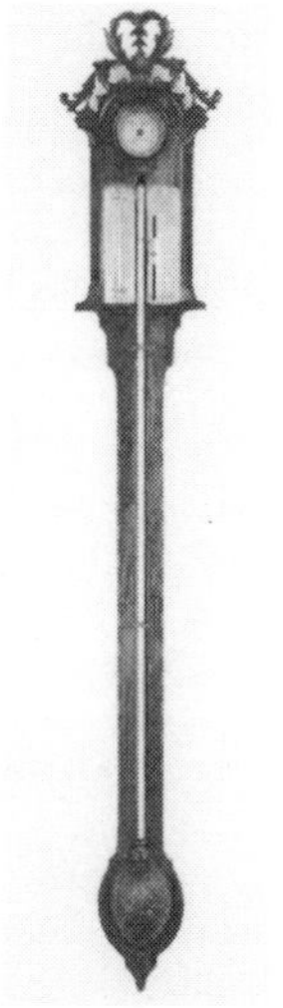
5

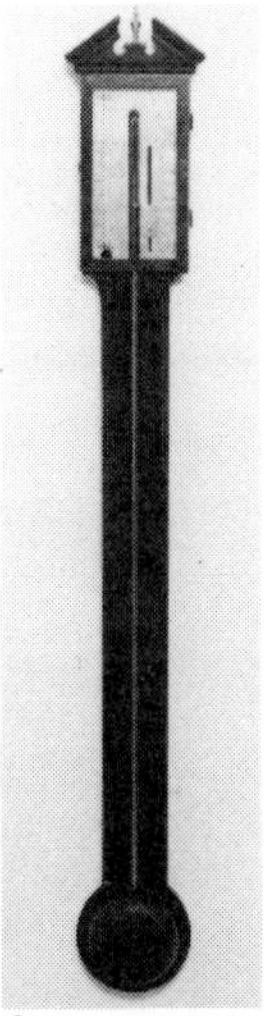
6

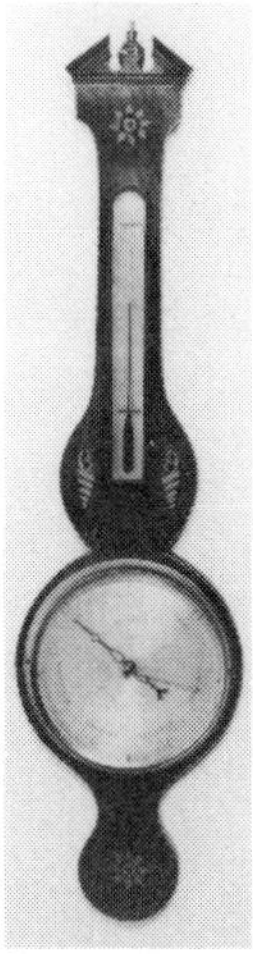
7

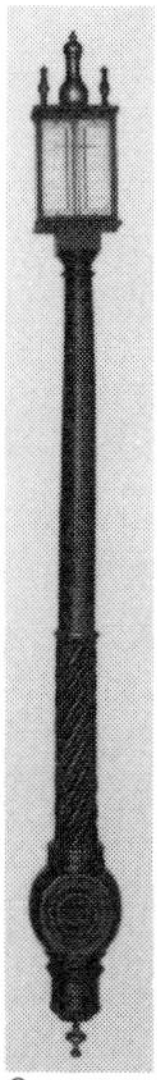
8

9

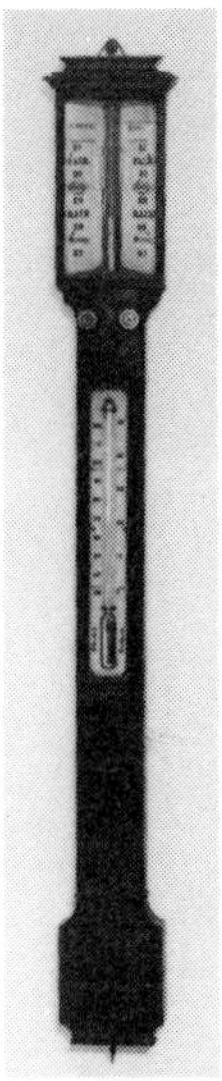
10

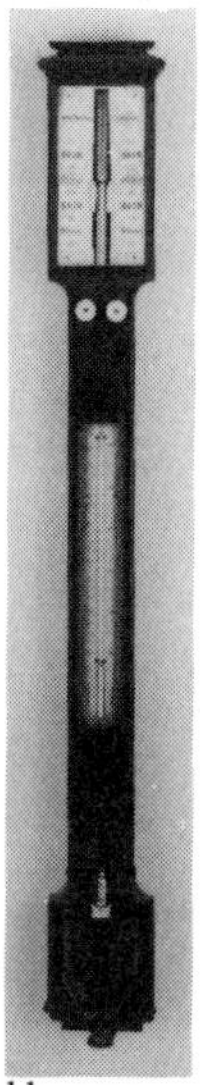
11

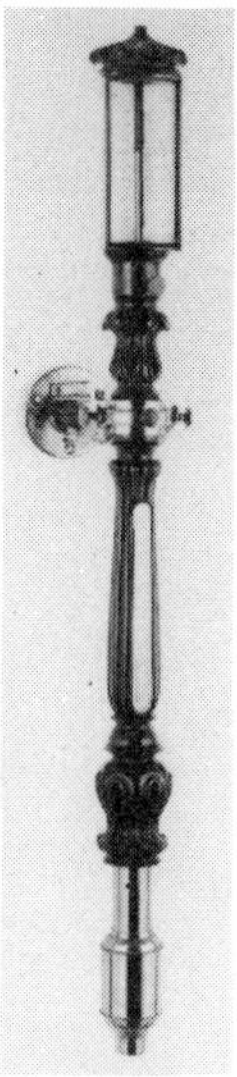
12

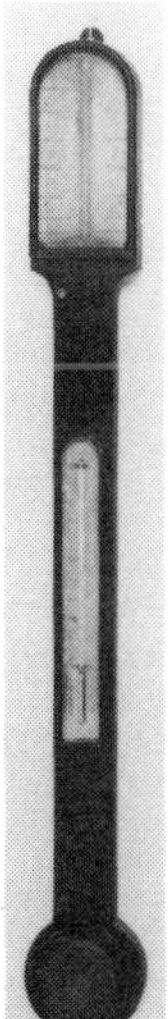
13

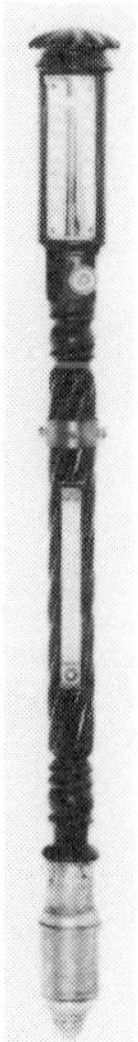
14

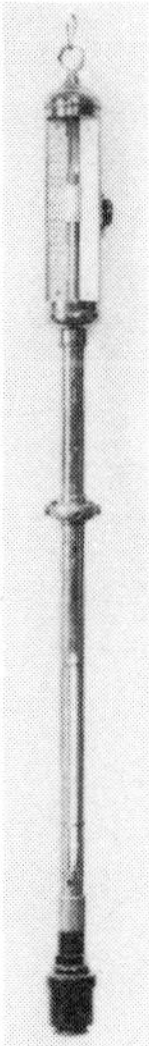
15

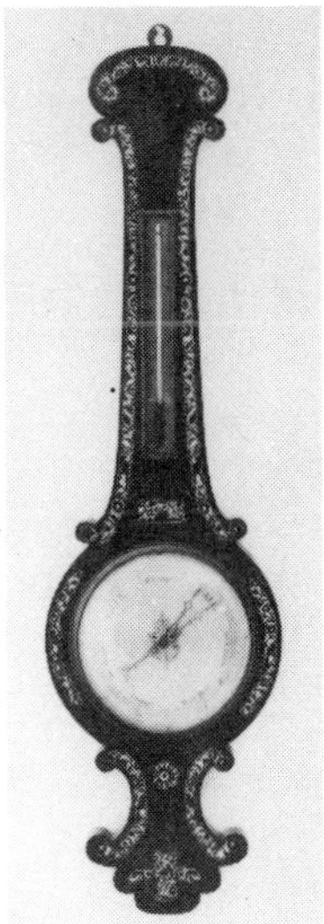
16

17

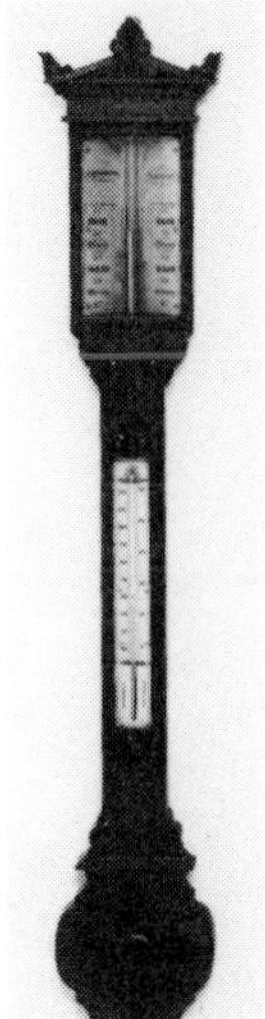
18

1

2

3

4

5

6

7

8

9

10

11

12

13

14

15

1
An ebonised basket-top bracket clock, backplate signed *Henry Younge in the Strand,* with altered verge escapement, later scroll feet, repeating work removed, 33cm (13in), *L 16 Oct,*
£2,090 ($2,926)

2
An ebony-veneered quarter-repeating bracket clock, late 17th century, the dial signed *S. De Charmes London,* minute hand replaced, some mouldings detached, 35.5cm (14in), *L 24 July,*
£3,300 ($5,181)

3
An ebonised quarter-repeating basket-top bracket clock, late 17th-early 18th century, the dial signed *Nicholas Paris at Warwick,* 38cm (15in), *L 16 Oct,*
£4,620 ($6,468)

4
A George I ebonised quarter-repeating bracket clock, the dial signed *Vick London,* 34cm (13½in), *L 24 July,*
£1,870 ($2,936)

5
An ebonised bracket clock, the dial signed *Marmd. Storr London,* the repeating five pillar movement with later anchor escapement, the case inscribed *Joseph Bell 1760,* 46cm (18in), *L 16 Oct,*
£1,320 ($1,848)

6
A George II ebonised quarter-repeating bracket clock, the dial signed *Jasper Taylor Holborn London,* 46cm (18in), *L 16 Oct,*
£2,860 ($4,004)

7
An ebony-veneered quarter-repeating alarum bracket clock, the dial signed *Du Hamel London,* 42cm (16½in), *L 18 Dec,*
£3,630 ($5,082)

8
A mahogany bracket clock, 1727-33, the dial and backplate signed *Delander London,* the movement with later anchor escapement, 41cm (16in), *L 1 May,*
£6,050 ($9,801)

9
A George III brass-inlaid ebonised quarter-repeating bracket clock, the dial signed *Jno. Fladgate London,* unusual bracket feet, 38cm (15in), *L 18 Dec,*
£5,280 ($7,392)

10
A George III mahogany bracket clock, the dial signed *Thos. Smoult Newcastle,* 49.5cm (19½in), *L 1 May,*
£1,320 ($2,138)

11
A mahogany bracket timepiece, c.1790, the silvered dial signed *Daniel Dickerson, Framlingham,* 29cm (11½in), *L 1 May,*
£605 ($980)

12
A brass-inlaid ebony chiming bracket clock, third quarter 18th century, the chipped enamel dial signed *Webster London,* 46cm (18in), *L 20 Feb,*
£2,640 ($4,013)

13
A George III mahogany bracket clock, the enamel dial signed *J & T Farr, Bristol,* 40cm (16in), *L 18 Dec,*
£1,375 ($1,925)

14
A rosewood bracket clock, c.1840, the dial signed *Grohe, Wigmore Str. London,* the case with brass stringing and side frets, 35cm (13¾in), *L 16 Oct,*
£968 ($1,355)

15
A George III mahogany bracket clock, mid 18th century, by Joseph Flickman, London, 48.5cm (19in), *NY 14 Oct,*
$3,850 (£2,674)

1
A walnut and oak mantel clock, early 19th century, the arched silvered dial signed *James Tupman Gt. Russell Street Bloomsbury,* 35.5cm (13in), *L 16 Oct,*
£770 ($1,078)

2
A bronze mantel clock, early 19th century, the dial signed *James McCabe Royal Exchange London,* the case with anthemion and leaf frets, 23cm (9in), *L 24 July,*
£990 ($1,554)

3
A mahogany and brass inlaid mantel clock, c.1830, the chipped enamel dial signed *John Webb, London,* 42cm (16½in), *C 9 Oct,*
£484 ($678)

4
An ebonised bracket timepiece, c.1840, the dial signed *Edkins, High St. Kensington,* 36cm (14¼in), *L 1 May,*
£550 ($891)

5
A William IV rosewood 'Gothic' bracket clock, the dial signed *Roskell & Sons, Liverpool,* on a rosewood bracket, 99cm (39in), *C 10 July,*
£770 ($1,240)

6
A mahogany cased mantel timepiece, mid 19th century, the dial signed *Clerke, I Royal Exchange, London,* in a balloon case with brass finial and feet, 62cm (24½in), *C 9 Oct,*
£330 ($462)

7
A walnut quarter-chiming mantel clock, mid 19th century, the dial signed *J.W. Bell, Leeds,* the case carved with grape laden vines, 49.5cm (19½in), *C 9 Oct,*
£352 ($493)

8
A mantel clock, mid 19th century, the dial signed *Vulliamy London,* the case flanked by fluted pilasters, 26cm (10¼in), *L 16 Oct,*
£1,980 ($2,772)

9
A George III-style mahogany bracket clock, c.1900, the convex painted dial signed *Maple & Co. Ltd., London,* 40cm (15¾in), *L 6 Oct,*
£462 ($647)

10
A mahogany cased repeating chiming mantel clock, late 19th century, the case with satinwood inlay, repeat pull, 44cm (17½in), *C 6 Aug,*
£154 ($239)

11
A brass-inlaid ebonised chiming bracket clock, c.1870, the two train back-wound fusee and chain movement signed *John Moore & Sons, Clerkenwell, London,* 61cm (24in), *L 1 May,*
£1,760 ($2,851)

12
A Victorian ebonised chiming bracket clock, the dial signed *Thompson & Vine, Aldersgate, London,* the case with gilt-bronze mouldings and side frets, 66cm (26in), *L 1 May,*
£935 ($1,515)

13
A Victorian ebonised chiming bracket clock, the dial signed *Barrie Edinburgh,* with subsidiary dials for regulator and chime selection, 57cm (22½in), *L 16 Oct,*
£990 ($1,386)

14
An Edwardian mahogany chiming bracket clock, c.1900, 62cm (24½in), *S 21 Feb,*
£682 ($1,037)

15
A rosewood chiming bracket clock, c.1880, with foliate engraved brass dial, originally silvered, 56cm (22in), *S 21 Feb,*
£396 ($602)

16
A George III-style satinwood and kingwood crossbanded veneered bracket clock, late 19th century, 64cm (25in), *S 19 June,*
£1,760 ($2,780)

1

2

3

4

5

6

7

8

9

10

11

12

13

14

15

16

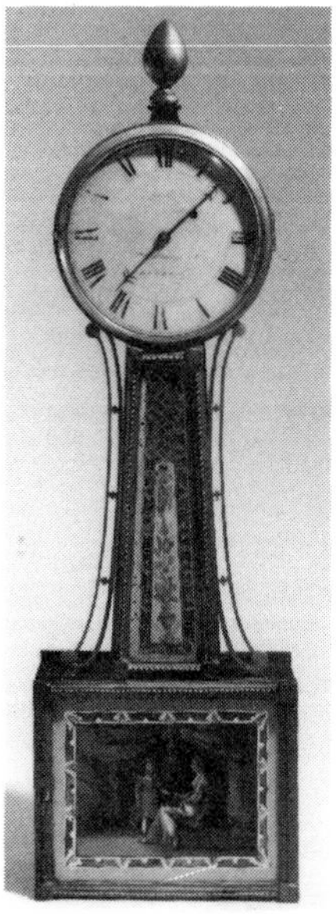
1

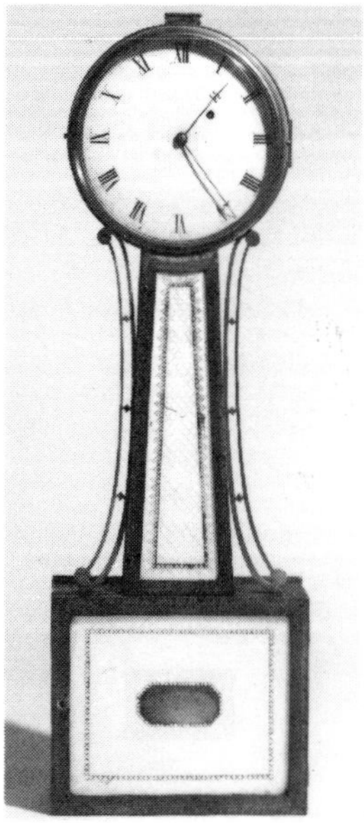
2

3

6

4

5

7

8

9

10

11

1
An American mahogany and eglomisé banjo clock, c.1825, Aaron Willard, Jr., Boston, Massachusetts, 83cm (32¾in), *NY 25 Oct,*
$18,700 (£13,262)

2
An American cross-banded mahogany and eglomisé banjo clock, c.1825, Simon Willard's Patent, Massachusetts, lacks baseboard, 74cm (29¼in), *NY 25 Oct,*
$19,800 (£14,042)

3
An American stencilled and eglomisé bride's shelf clock, c.1820, Daniel Hubbard, Medfield, Massachusetts, parts painted black over the original white, 82cm (32½in), *NY 1 Feb,*
$19,800 (£14,043)

4
An Italian quarter-striking double-dialled bracket clock, c.1690, the backplate signed *Ludovico Lanscron*, 41cm (16in), *G 11 Nov,*
SF 15,400 (£6,417; $8,983)

5
A Dutch ormolu-mounted burl walnut musical bracket clock, c.1765, Wilhelm Koster, Amsterdam, 91cm (36in), *NY 13 Dec,*
$13,200 (£9,428)

6
A Swiss ormolu-mounted painted musical bracket clock, mid 18th century, decorated in polychrome with floral motifs on a dark green ground, 130cm (51in), *NY 22 Mar,*
$5,500 (£3,642)

7
A German walnut quarter-striking bracket clock, late 18th century, the gilt plate signed *Ignati Mogele Augsburg*, 42cm (16½in), *G 11 Nov,*
SF 2,300 (£958; $1,342)

8
A South German oak quarter-striking alarum bracket clock, 18th century, the backplate engraved with leafy scrolls and a flowerhead, 43cm (17in), *G 11 Nov,*
SF 1,320 (£550; $770)

9
An American alarum mantel clock, by Welch, c.1870, the unusual carved case surmounted by three circular bevelled mirrors and flanked by removable boxes, 76cm (30in), *C 13 Feb,*
£187 ($277)

10
A Viennese gilt-copper, rosewood and ebony mantel clock, first half 19th century, the dial chipped, 60cm (23½in), *A 14 Oct,*
Dfl 3,220 (£1,006; $1,509)

11
A German walnut figural clock, c.1870, the case depicting rocks, trees and leafage, surmounted and flanked on one side by St. Bernard dogs, the dial of later date, 59cm (23¼in), *NY 13 Sept,*
$2,475 (£1,684)

1
A Régence boulle bracket clock and bracket, c.1720, the movement signed *André Bory A Paris,* the case veneered with brown shell inlaid with engraved brass and with gilt-bronze mounts, 98cm (38½in) high overall, *L 28 Nov,*
£2,200 ($3,080)

2
A Louis XV green shell-veneered bracket clock and bracket, the dial signed *Lepaute à Paris,* the case and bracket with rococo gilt-bronze mounts, 125cm (4ft 1½in), *L 20 June,*
£4,620 ($7,300)

3
A Louis XV boulle marquetry cartel clock, mid 18th century, the case signed *B. Lieutaud,* the dial inscribed *Viger a Paris,* the whole with scrolling ormolu borders, red tortoiseshell ground, 99cm (39in), *NY 3 May,*
$8,250 (£5,428)

4
A Louis XV red-shell and copper marquetry cartel clock, the dial signed *Fil Hausburg à Paris,* later movement, 42cm (16½in), *M 23 June,*
FF 15,540 (£1,386; $2,163)

5
An ormolu and bronze mantel clock, early 19th century, the bell striking movement stamped AG and with a later spring suspension, 31.5cm (12¼in), *L 24 July,*
£748 ($1,174)

6
A Louis XVI vase-shaped clock, the dial signed *Causard, Horloger du Roy suivant la Court,* decorated with satyrs' heads and with serpent handles, 44cm (17¼in), *M 30 Nov,*
FF 72,600 (£7,891; $11,048)

Compare with fig.13 p.141.

7
A Louis XVI ormolu and marble mantel clock, last quarter 18th century, Jean-Antoine Lépine, the case surmounted by a bacchante and resting on a stretcher born by cherubs astride goats, 48cm (19in), *NY 31 Oct,*
$17,600 (£12,482)

8
An ormolu and marble mantel clock, late 18th century, the enamel dial inscribed *Boundieu,* the movement converted to steel suspension, with oval base on adjustable feet, 60cm (24in), *S 13 Nov,*
£1,870 ($2,618)

9
A Louis XVI ormolu-mounted marble mantel clock, in the form of a pagoda, the dial inscribed *Mignolet a Paris,* 61cm (24in), *NY 31 Oct,*
$6,600 (£4,681)

10
A Louis XVI ormolu and patinated bronze mantel clock, late 18th century, surmounted by the figures of art and music represented as children at play, with grey and brown mottled stepped socle, 66cm (26in), *NY 4 Oct,*
$1,760 (£1,222)

11
A French skeleton clock, late 18th century, the dial signed *Serton à Paris,* on black marble plinth, dial cracked and chipped, 51cm (20in), *L 24 July,*
£2,200 ($3,454)

1

2

3

4

5

6

7

8

9

10

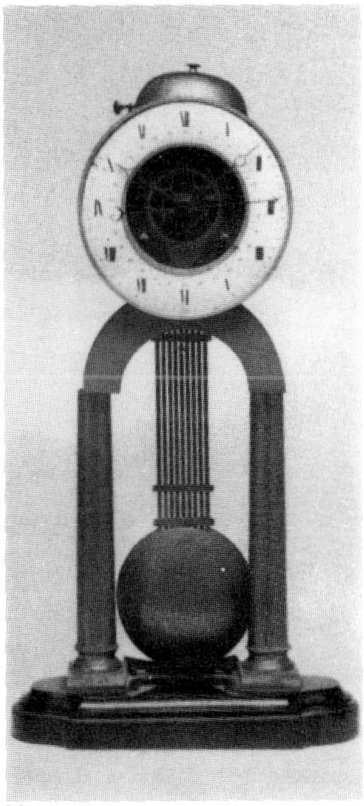
11

1

2

3

4

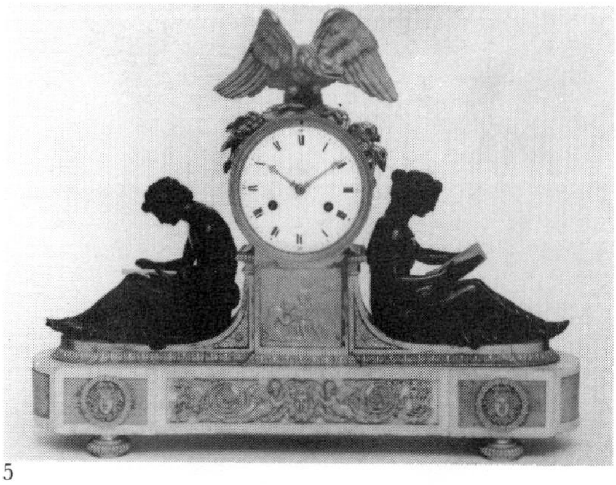
5

6

7

8

9

10

11

1
A Directoire ormolu and patinated bronze mantel clock, 18th century, the case depicting Diana spearing the serpent, 47.5cm (18¾in), *NY 3 May,*
$10,450 (£6,875)

2
A Directoire gilt-bronze clock, the dial signed *Charles Roland à Marseille,* 50cm (19¾in), *M 23 June,*
FF 17,760 (£1,984; $2,472)

3
An Empire desk regulator, with gilt-bronze case, the movement signed *Mugnier Horloger de l'Empereur et Roi,* 42cm (16½in), *M 22 June,*
FF 133,200 (£11,882; $18,536)

4
An Empire gilt-bronze mantel clock, c.1815, on verde antico base, 34cm (13½in), *L 20 June,*
£2,420 ($3,824)

5
A Directoire gilt-bronze, marble and bronze mantel clock, c.1790, the dial signed *A Paris,* the movement signed *Pignot,* 52.5cm (20¾in), *L 28 Nov,*
£2,750 ($3,850)

6
A Directoire porcelain mantel clock, the movement replaced, 63cm (24¾in), *M 22 June,*
FF 33,300 (£2,971;$4,634)

7
An Empire patinated bronze and gilt-bronze mantel clock, depicting a woman at her toilette, 42cm (16½in), *M 30 Nov,*
FF 22,000 (£2,391; $3,348)

8
A marble, gilt and patinated bronze mantel clock, early 19th century, the dial signed *Lignereux A Paris,* the winged figure of Cupid standing to the side, 82cm (32½in), *L 12 Dec,*
£4,620 ($6,468)

9
A Restauration ormolu mantel clock, the suspension movement contained in the well-modelled body of a dolphin surmounted by Apollo, 50cm (19¾in), *L 1 May,*
£550 ($891)

10
A Restauration bronze and rouge royale marble clock and pair of candelabra, *(clock illustrated),* c.1820, the clock attributed to Pierre-Philippe Thomire, 100cm (39½in), *L 12 Dec,*
£11,000 ($15,400)

11
A Charles X ormolu mantel clock, second quarter 19th century, with later movement, 51cm (16in), *NY 4 Oct,*
$825 (£572)

1
An ormolu and silvered bronze mantel clock, c.1830, signed *Le Roy & Fils Hgers. du Roi A Paris,* 54cm (21¼in), *L 7 Nov,*
£1,100 ($1,540)

2
An ormolu mantel clock, c.1830, movement by Pons, 40cm (15¾in), *L 12 May,*
£528 ($850)

3
A walnut temple clock, c.1830, white enamel dial signed *Gros a Paris, C 18 Apr,*
£440 ($682)

4
An ebony and carved ivory mantel clock, c.1850, bell striking Pons movement signed for *Brunel A Dieppe,* surmounted by an ivory figure of St. Joan, brass inlaid ebonised stand, 59cm (23¼in), *L 7 Nov,*
£1,925 ($2,695)

5
A French gilt bronze mantel timepiece, c.1840, the movement with anchor escapement, 35.5cm (14in), *C 18 Apr,*
£330 ($512)

6
A pietra dura French mantel clock, c.1850, enamel dial and ormolu laurel leaf bezel, movement signed *Vallois A Paris,* dial chipped, hour hand lacking, 44.5cm (17½in), *L 21 Mar,*
£902 ($1,407)

7
An ormolu and porcelain mantel clock, c.1865, dial signed *Howell James & Co. to the Queen,* Japy Frères movement, decorated in black and gilt against a *bleu céleste* ground, 43cm (17in), *L 21 Mar,*
£550 ($858)

8
A perpetual calendar mantel regulator, late 19th century, in gilt brass case, silvered dial, Brocot-type calendar work, 51.5cm (19in), *L 24 July,*
£3,300 ($5,181)

9
A four glass brass mantel clock, late 19th century, Achille Brocot escapement, Marti movement, 33cm (13in), *C 9 Oct,*
£440 ($616)

10
A French table regulator, c.1870, jewelled Brocot escapement, signed for *Allan & Hayes Calcutta,* Ellicott pendulum stamped *JBD,* 51cm (20in), *L 24 July,*
£2,090 ($3,281)

11
A French year-going mantel regulator, c.1880, visible Brocot escapement, Ellicott pendulum, brass case, 35cm (13¾in), *L 18 Dec,*
£1,320 ($1,848)

12
A French spelter and porcelain mantel clock, c.1880, Japy Frères movement, 38cm (15in), *C 1 May,*
£209 ($339)

13
An ormolu and marble mantel clock, mid 19th century, dial inscribed *Vitoz à Paris,* base with presention plaque, 47cm (18½in), *S 19 June,*
£660 ($1,042)

Compare with fig.6 p.139.

1

2

3

4

5

6

7

8

9

10

11

12

13

1

2

3

4

5

6

7

8

9

10

11

12

1
A champlevé enamel mantel clock, c.1885, with a gilt dial signed for Howell & James Ltd., the case decorated with polychrome enamel, 42.5cm (16¾in), *L 7 Nov,*
£858 ($1,201)

2
A gilt bronze and marble mantel clock, late 19th century, with Vincenti movement, 34.5cm (13½in), *C 29 May,*
£308 ($487)

3
A French marble and ormolu lyre clock, c.1880, the dial inscribed *Causard Hger.du Roy, Paris,* on oval base, 46cm (18in), *S 18 Sept,*
£1,155 ($1,617)

4
A gilt-bronze mantel clock, c.1860, the case flanked by two cherubs holding a bird and a nest, 67cm (26¼in), *L 13 June,*
£2,200 ($3,520)

5
A French perpetual calendar mantel clock, c.1870, the dial signed *Le Roy & Fils, Regent Street, London,* and with Brocot escapement, the Belgian slate case inset with panels of red marble, 43cm (17in), *L 20 Feb,*
£605 ($920)

6
A Louis XVI-style gilt-bronze mantel clock, third quarter 19th century, inscribed *Ernest Royer,* 70.5cm (27¾in), *NY 26 Apr,*
$2,310 (£1,500)

7
A 'Sèvres'-mounted gilt-bronze figural mantel clock, c.1890, the dial inscribed *Leroy/Paris,* on the back of a porcelain elephant and surmounted by a gilt-bronze basket holding porcelain flowers, losses, 45cm (17¾in), *NY 13 Sept,*
$1,870 (£1,272)

8
An ormolu, bronze and marble mantel clock, c.1870, with a figure of Cupid unveiling the dial signed *Martinot A Paris,* 58.5cm (23in), *L 7 Nov,*
£1,870 ($2,618).

9
An ormolu and boulle mantel clock, late 19th century, the case with scrolling foliate mounts, 53cm (21in), *S 24 Apr,*
£506 ($794)

10
A Louis XV-style gilt-bronze mantel clock, late 19th century, retailed by Tiffany & Co., the dial inscribed, 64.5cm (25¼in), *NY 26 Apr,*
$2,530 (£1,643)

11
A white marble and gilt-bronze lyre clock, c.1900, the case flanked with cornucopias and with an Apollo cresting, 60cm (23½in), *L 16 Oct,*
£572 ($801)

12
A brass and champlevé enamel four glass mantel clock, early 20th century, with Japy Frères movement, 30.5cm (12in), *C 9 Oct,*
£638 ($893)

1
A porcelain mounted ormolu clock garniture, c.1885, the Brocot escapement signed *Roblin & Fils Frères à Paris,* the ten porcelain panels painted with flowers and insects against a blue ground, 42cm (16½in), with two conforming four-light candelabra, 46cm (18¼in), *L 7 Nov,*
£3,410 ($4,774)

2
An onyx and ormolu clock garniture, c.1880, the dial with Brocot escapement signed *Augte. Lemaire, Paris,* surmounted by a gilt-bronze group of a woman dancing with two children, signed A. Carrier, 92cm (34¼in), with two conforming eight-light foliate cast candelabra, 87cm (34¼in), *L 7 Nov,*
£5,500 ($7,700)

3
A gilt-bronze and white marble lyre clock garniture, c.1890, the dial decorated with garlands of flowers and lyre hands, 35.5cm (13¼in), with two conforming three-light rose-bush form candelabra, 29cm (11½in), *L 13 June,*
£1,485 ($2,376)

4
A bronze, ormolu and salmon pink marble clock garniture, c.1890, the enamel dial decorated with garlands of flowers, the case flanked by two cherubs, 30.5cm (12in), with two two-branch candelabra, the lights supported by cherubs, 32cm (12½in), *L 21 Mar,*
£1,705 ($2,660)

5
A gilt and patinated bronze clock garniture, Christofle & Cie, c.1880, the case in Japanese style, 52cm (20½in), with two conforming vases, 29cm (11¼in), *L 21 Mar,*
£2,640 ($4,118)

6
A marble and bronze Egyptian-style clock garniture, c.1880, surmounted by a parcel-gilt bronze of Cleopatra seated on a sphinx, 64.5cm (25½in), with two similar bronze and marble urns, 52.5cm (20¾in), *L 7 Nov,*
£2,090 ($2,926)

7
A rouge antico marble and slate clock garniture, c. 1870, the dial signed *Boxell, Brighton,* Japy Frères movement, the architectural case engraved with trailing vines, 21cm (8¼in), with two covered urns, 45.5cm (18in), *C 6 Aug,*
£209 ($324)

8
An ormolu and porcelain garniture, c.1870, on giltwood plinths, 29 and 18cm (11½ and 7in), *S 19 June,*
£495 ($742)

9
An ormolu mounted mahogany lyre clock garniture, c.1900, the enamel dial signed *Kinable à Paris,* 46cm (18in), with two conforming four-light rosebush-form candelabra, 39.5cm (15½in), *L 7 Nov,*
£2,090 ($2,926)

10
A gilt-bronze and champlevé clock garniture, c.1900, Japy Frères movement, 39cm (15½in), with two conforming urns, 30cm (11¾in), *C 18 Apr,*
£1,100 ($1,705)

1

2

3

4

5

6

7

8

9

10

Electric Clocks

MICHAEL TURNER

For many years electric clocks were not regarded by serious horological collectors as being worthy of consideration. As the concept of forming a collection of electric clocks is quite new there are still wonderful opportunities for the collector of modest means to form a fascinating collection and one that will undoubtedly be an investment.

It is generally thought that electric clocks made their appearance in the 1930s and were little more than electric motors; the truth, however, is far more interesting. The idea of combining electricity and horology was conceived almost a hundred years earlier. It seems likely that, as larger offices and factories were built in the 19th century, a need arose for a clock system which could be relied upon to record exactly the same time in every part of the building; no group of mechanical clocks could be expected to keep exactly in step. Eventually the master clock driving a number of slaves was evolved.

The greatest difficulty facing the early electrical horologists was to find a constant source of power. The principle of electromagnetism had been known for many years and it was discovered that this could be used to keep a pendulum oscillating, but the early batteries were so expensive and unreliable that it was not possible to produce an electric clock that could be marketed commercially. However in 1842 a Scotsman, Alexander Bain (1810-77), who was a pioneer of electrical horology, devised a simple earth battery consisting of a zinc plate and a copper plate buried about one foot apart in moist soil. It was found that this battery provided a relatively constant voltage and was ideal for driving Bain's pendulum clocks. He successfully patented his device and was able to produce a number of clocks commercially. Many of these clocks have been discarded or seriously altered over the last century, but now that electrical horology is recognised as an important subject in its own right, Alexander Bain has been accorded his rightful position as the most influential horologist in this field. His surviving clocks, which are much sought after, have mostly found their way into museums and so are unlikely to appear on the open market.

The collector need not be discouraged, however: a great many other interesting electric clocks were produced during the three-quarters of a century following Bain's invention. Generally speaking the most collectable items were made from 1900 to

1
An electrically rewound skeleton timepiece, c.1900, 34.5cm (13½in) high, *L 18 Dec,*
£2,640 ($3,696)

2
An electric timepiece, by Bulle, the silvered dial inscribed *Modele XA,* 24cm (9½in), *L 16 Oct,*
£286 ($400)

3
An electric mantel timepiece, by Bulle, with a cut glass dome, 34cm (13½in), *L 16 Oct,*
£396 ($554)

1930. By this time many of the problems encountered by the early makers had been overcome and it was possible to produce certain types of clocks by factory methods. The present-day buyer is thus ensured of a relatively large number of models from which to form a collection.

The introduction of the National Grid in Great Britain in 1927 (it was already in use in North America), which standardised the alternating current electricity supply, opened the way for the synchronous motor clock and although some interesting battery clocks were made after this date, it was the mains driven clock that was the leader in the field until the relatively recent appearance of quartz battery clocks. Before the synchronous motor clocks appeared, there were two distinct types of electric clock. The first, perhaps the rarer of the two, is basically a mechanical clock driven by a weight or a spring which is electrically re-wound and is therefore only indirectly driven by electricity, (a skeletonised example is shown in fig.1). The second type is where the pendulum or the balance is directly impulsed by an electrical device. These were produced in a variety of forms by several different companies and the price which would have to be paid for one today depends almost entirely on the rarity of the particular model.

The most commonly found clock is that invented by M.T. Favre-Bulle in 1920. It was manufactured in France and first patented in England in 1922. The small table models covered by a glass dome and standing on a circular wooden plinth are worth collecting and can be found in working condition for less than £200 ($320). Examples of the same model made after 1930, which have a bakelite base, are good starting points for a collection as they can be purchased for less than £100 ($160). Two unusual Bulle clocks are shown as figs 2 and 3.

Another collectable French clock, which first appeared about ten years before the Bulle, was that invented by the Brillié brothers. The most commonly seen model is mounted as a wall clock on a marble plinth and covered by a glazed wood case. The clocks have a distinctive spherical brass pendulum bob and usually an attractive enamel dial. A number of models sold at auction in December 1986 for prices ranging from £150 ($240) to £350 ($560).

Perhaps the most visually appealing clock is that known as the 'Eureka'. The Eureka Clock Company manufactured a number of different models between 1909 and 1914; all were well made and incorporated a large balance wheel which was usually visible (figs 4-6). Generally the desirability, and therefore the value, is greater if the movement is fully exposed, as in a four-glass clock or under a dome.

A much rarer electric clock is shown in fig.7. This incorporated a large horizontal balance which was given a rather fierce clout every few seconds by a lever attached to an electric magnet. The same principle was applied to a number of the pendulum master clocks made by the Synchronome Company of England, and others. As the amplitude of the pendulum or balance decreased, a

4

4
An electric timepiece, with enamel dial signed *Eureka Clock Co. Ltd. London,* battery concealed in the base, 34cm (13½in), *L 1 May,*
£660 ($1,069)

5
An electric mantel timepiece, by Eureka, dial signed *Eureka Clock Co. Ltd., London,* 23.5cm (9¼in), *L 16 Oct,*
£286 ($400)

6
An electric timepiece, by Eureka, 26cm (10¼in), *C 9 Oct,*
£231 ($323)

5

6

switch is triggered which energises an electro-magnet causing an impulse to be given to the pendulum or balance.

Another interesting clock is fig.9, known as the 'Ever Ready' clock. It was one of the earliest examples of an English electric clock made for domestic use and was first patented in 1902 by Herbert Scott, a Yorkshireman. He had some difficulty finding a financial backer for his invention but eventually managed to interest the Ever Ready Electric Company and that is how the clock acquired its name. These clocks are quite rare as they were made for a period of less than ten years and only two models were produced. Their characteristic feature is that the pendulum swings, unusually, from front to back. This, combined with the mirrored back fitted to the later models, presents a fascinating appearance when seen working.

One of the rarest clocks to appear in the saleroom was an electric longcase clock patented by Percival Bentley in 1910 (fig.8). Rather surprisingly the Bentley clocks have many similarities to those produced by Alexander Bain over half a century earlier, including the fact that they were designed to run on an earth battery. The Bentley clocks were extremely well made and usually fitted into handsome glazed cases displaying the pendulum and quite often the movement. Although a successful venture for the Bentley Manufacturing Company, production of clocks was halted on the outbreak of war in 1914 and never restarted. The total number of clocks produced by the firm is thought to have been no more than seventy, thus causing those that do occasionally appear on the market to be very sought after.

Apart from the clocks mentioned above, many other electric clocks were produced in all parts of the world and several of them incorporate most unusual mechanisms. In this area there are still discoveries to be made and a collector will find it rewarding to study auction room catalogues, visit street markets and peruse junk shops. Even the early synchronous motor clocks made in the 1930s were sometimes fitted with extraordinary subsidiary mechanisms and other curious features and so are worth considering too. They can only increase in value as we get further from the time they were made. For the novice collector the best advice is to read as much as possible about the subject and buy unusual items whenever the opportunity presents itself— even if you don't understand what you have bought!

Further reading:

Frank Hope-Jones, *Electrical Timekeeping*, 1949
Science Museum Catalogue, *Electrifying Time*, 1976
Charles K. Aked, *Conspectus of Electrical Timekeeping*, 1976
H.L. Belmont, *La Bulle Clock; Horlogerie Electrique*, 1975

7

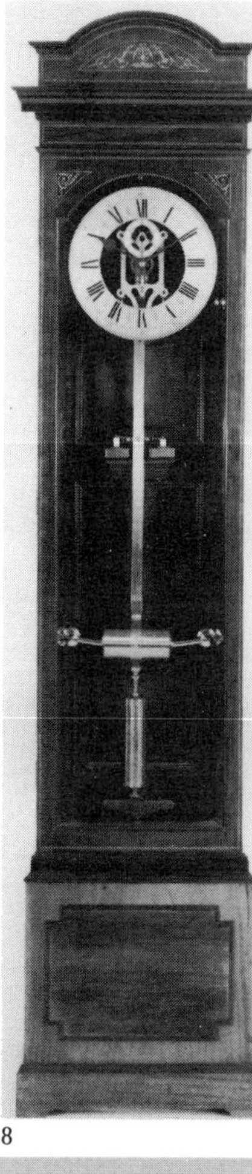
8

9

7
An electric timepiece, inscribed *Electric Clock made by The Reason Mfg. Co. Ltd. Brighton Murday's Patent,* 32cm (12½in), *L 18 Dec,* **£2,530 ($3,542)**

8
A mahogany Bentley's patent electrical longcase timepiece, inscribed *Earth Driven Electrical Clock No. 202,* 225cm (7ft 3in), *L 18 Dec,* **£6,600 ($9,240)**

9
An electric mantel timepiece, by 'Ever Ready', c.1905, 36.5cm (14½in), *L 20 Feb,* **£935 ($1,421)**

1
A platinum openface centre seconds watch, Cartier, European Watch & Clock Co., c.1925, 5cm (2in), *NY 15 Feb,*
$2,200 (£1,517)

2
An 18-carat gold openface watch, Rolex Imperial, c.1940, 4.5cm (1¾in), *NY 16 June,*
$1,540 (£1,027)

3
An 18-carat gold dress watch, Audemars Piguet, 4cm (1½in), *L 24 July,*
£880 ($1,382)

4
A silver eight-day time-piece, 1935, retailed by Cartier, the movement by Jaeger le Coultre, case hallmarked 1935, 8cm (3in), *L 16 Oct,*
£638 ($893)

5
A silver combined eight-day watch and lighter, the dial signed Dunhill, 10cm (4in), *L 16 Oct,*
£660 ($924)

6
A silver combined watch and lighter, Dunhill, 1927, 4.5cm (1¾in), *L 16 Oct,*
£462 ($647)

7
An 18-carat vari-coloured gold ball-form watch, Patek Philippe & Co., Geneva, c.1925, 2.5cm (1in), *NY 16 June,*
$3,575 (£2,383)

8
A gold pocket watch and fob, Lêpine, 19th century, 3.5cm (1¼in), *M 24 Feb,*
FF 6,660 (£644; $966)

9
A collection of nine agate set watch keys, *L 16 Oct,*
£440 ($616)

10
An enamelled gold cockle shell-form watch, signed *Caillot à Paris,* c.1800, 4cm (1½in), *NY 11 Dec,*
$3,025 (£1,008)

11
A collection of thirteen gold and rolled gold watch keys, *L 16 Oct,*
£374 ($524)

12
A gilt-metal and horn mandolin-form watch, probably Austrian, late 19th century, 9cm (3½in), *NY 11 Dec,*
$495 (£353)

13
An 18-carat gold self-winding wristwatch, Patek Philippe & Co., Geneva, c.1960, 3.5cm (1¼in), *NY 29 Oct,*
$1,650 (£1,170)

14
An 18-carat gold wrist-watch with black dial, Patek Philippe & Co., Geneva, c.1955, 3.5cm (1¼in), *NY 16 June,*
$1,540 (£1,027)

Chronograph or Stopwatch a watch with a seconds hand that can be started, stopped and returned to zero at will.

Chronometer a precision timekeeper (usually a watch) with a detent escapement. Now also used (especially on the Continent) of watches tested to a certain standard of precision.

Multi-calibrated chronograph one which combines more than one calibrated scale, such as telemeter, pulsemeter etc.

Perpetual chronograph a watch which has both perpetual calendar and chronograph work.

Calibrated scale a scale with graduated measurement found in chronograph such as telemeter or tachometer.

Tonneau a case style usually looking, more or less, like a shaped rectangle.

Register a subsidiary dial which records lapsed time.

Sweep seconds the seconds hand is mounted to the centre wheel as opposed to a watch with subsidiary seconds.

1

2

3

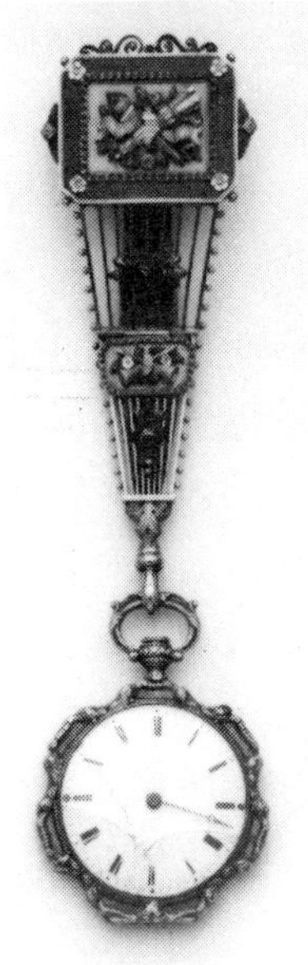
8

5

4

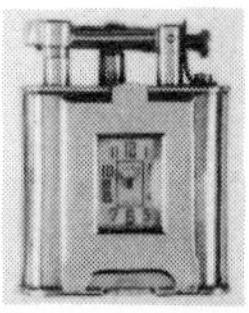
6

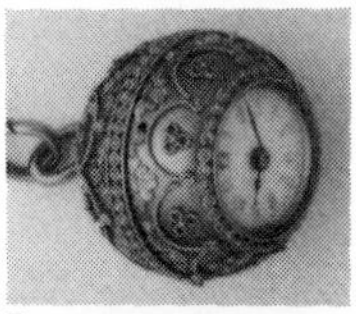
7

9

10

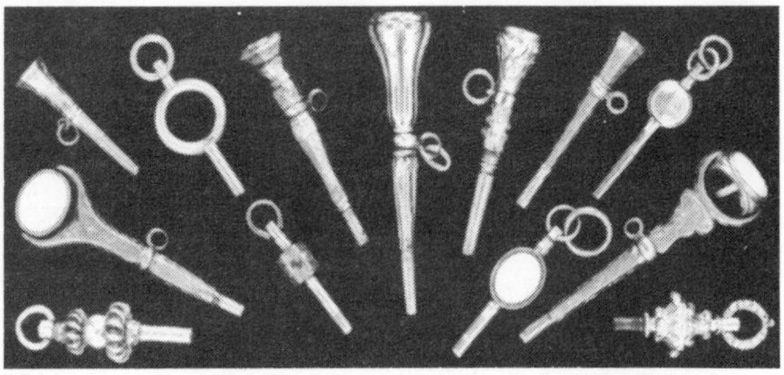
11

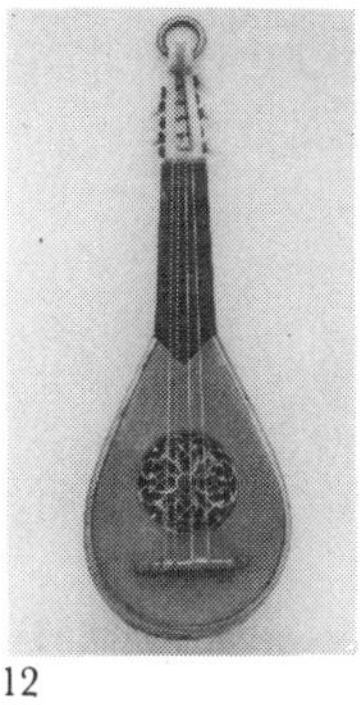
12

13

14

1

2

3

4

5

6

7

8

9

10

11

12

13

14

15

16

1
A platinum tonneau wristwatch, Patek Philippe & Co., Geneva, c.1915, 3cm (1¼in), *NY 15 Feb,*
$3,190 (£2,200)

2
An 18-carat gold and enamel cushion-form wristwatch, Patek Philippe & Co., Geneva, c.1920, retailed by Shreve & Co., San Francisco, 3cm (1¼in), *NY 16 June,*
$2,090 (£1,393)

3
A two-tone 18-carat gold square wristwatch, Patek Philippe & Co., Geneva, c.1940, retailed by Walserwald, 2.5cm (1in), *NY 15 Feb,*
$2,090 (£1,441)

4
An 18-carat gold square wristwatch with gold bracelet, Patek Philippe & Co., Geneva, c.1960, 2.5cm (1in), *NY 15 Feb,*
$2,530 (£1,745)

5
An 18-carat gold square wristwatch, Patek Philippe & Co., c.1955, 3cm (1¼in), *NY 16 June,*
$1,650 (£1,100)

6
A stainless steel chronograph with tachometer and register, Patek Philippe & Co., Geneva, 3.5cm (1¼in), *NY 29 Oct,*
$6,325 (£4,486)

7
A stainless steel self-winding wristwatch, Patek Philippe & Co., Geneva, Nautilus retailed by Gübelin, with date and matching bracelet, 4cm (1½in), *NY 15 Feb,*
$1,760 (£1,214)

8
A 9-carat pink gold octagonal wristwatch, Rolex Oyster, 1928, 3cm (1¼in), *NY 16 June,*
$1,430 (£953)

9
A 9-carat gold watch, Rolex, 1930, 4cm (1½in), *L 20 Feb,*
£495 ($752)

10
An 18-carat two-colour gold wristwatch, Rolex Prince, 4cm (1½in), *L 24 July,*
£3,080 ($4,836)

11
A 9-carat gold wristwatch, Rolex Prince, 1934, 4cm (1½in), *L 16 Oct,*
£2,200 ($3,080)

12
A lady's 18-carat gold wristwatch, Rolex Oyster, with matching gold bracelet, 2cm (¾in), *NY 29 Oct,*
$1,540 (£1,092)

13
A 14-carat pink gold Rolex chronometer wristwatch, c.1950, case, dial and movement signed, 3.5cm (1¾in), *NY 16 June,*
$2,420 (£1,613)

14
A gilt metal and steel wristwatch, Rolex Prince, 4.5cm (1¾in), *L 18 Dec,*
£825 ($1,155)

15
A 9-carat gold centre seconds wristwatch, Rolex Oyster, dial restored, 3cm (1¼in), *L 16 Oct,*
£572 ($801)

16
An 18-carat gold date perpetual wristwatch, Rolex Oyster, with original jubilee bracelet, 3.5cm (1¼in), *L 16 Oct,*
£2,200 ($3,080)

1
An 18-carat gold wrist-watch, Bailey, Banks & Biddle of Philadelphia, movement signed and numbered, 3.5cm (1¼in), *L 20 Feb,*
£550 ($836)

2
An 18-carat gold cushion wristwatch with enamel dial, Ulysse Nardin, Locle, c.1925, 3cm (1¼in), *NY 29 Oct,*
$1,210 (£858)

3
A steel-cased Reverso wristwatch, Jaeger Le Coultre, 4cm (1½in), *L 18 Dec,*
£770 ($1,078)

4
A 9-carat gold wristwatch, Waltham, 1930, Dennison cushion-form case, with Birmingham hallmark for 1930, 3cm (1¼in), *L 24 July,*
£418 ($656)

5
An 18-carat gold chrono-graph wristwatch, Ulysse Nardin, Locle, c.1945, 3.5cm (1¼in), *NY 16 June,*
$1,320 (£880)

6
An 18-carat gold chrono-graph wristwatch, with moon phases, calendar and tachometer, Universal Genève, c.1960, 4cm (1½in), *NY 16 June,*
$2,200 (£1,467)

7
An 18-carat gold lady's wristwatch with gold bracelet, Audemars Piguet, Geneva, 2.5cm (1in), *NY 16 June,*
$1,980 (£1,320)

8
An 18-carat gold skeletonised self-winding wristwatch, Audemars Piguet, Geneva, c.1970, 4cm (1½in), *NY 29 Oct,*
$9,900 (£7,021)

9
An 18-carat gold auto-matic wristwatch, Baume & Mercier, 1971, 3.5cm (1¼in), *L 20 Feb,*
£990 ($1,505)

10
An 18-carat white gold rectangular wristwatch, Movado, retailed by J. W. Benson, 4.5cm (1¾in), *L 20 Feb,*
£1,320 ($2,006)

11
A 14-carat gold centre seconds wristwatch, Longines, 3cm (1¼in), *L 24 July,*
£242 ($380)

12
An 18-carat gold self-winding wristwatch, Cartier, with 18-carat buckle, 3.5cm (1¼in), *NY 16 June,*
$1,430 (£953)

13
An 18-carat gold wrist-watch with gold bracelet, Cartier, 3cm (1¼in), *NY 16 June,*
$2,530 (£1,687)

14
An 18-carat gold self-winding tank wristwatch, Cartier, Paris, 3.5cm (1¼in), *NY 15 Feb,*
$1,870 (£1,290)

15
An 18-carat gold wristwatch, Breguet, 3cm (1¼in), *L 16 Oct,*
£1,980 ($2,772)

16
A silver wristwatch, with signed Swiss lever move-ment, 5cm (2in), *L 24 July,*
£572 ($898)

1

2

3

4

5

6

7

8

9

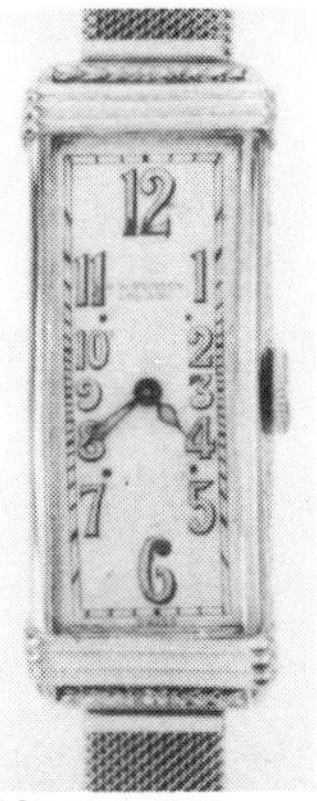
10

11

12

13

14

15

16

1

2

3

4

5

6

7

8

9

10

11

12

13

14

15

1
A silver astronomical watch, C. Cameel, Strasbourg, c.1670, the case with a classical scene, 7cm (2¾in), *NY 11 Dec,*
$12,100 (£8,643)

2
A gold pair case quarter-repeating watch, Daniel Quare, London, c.1700, the case with a classical betrothal scene, monogrammed *EA* for Ernest Augustus, father of George I, 5.5cm (2¼in), *NY 11 Dec,*
$12,100 (£8,643)

3
A silver pair case quarter-repeating and striking coach watch with calendar and alarm, Sebastian Bauman, c.1750, the case with a classical scene, signed *FCL* for Friederich Christian Langpaur, 11cm (4¼in), *NY 11 Dec,*
$26,400 (£18,857)

4
A multi-coloured gold dumb quarter-repeating verge watch and chatelaine, Gudin, Paris, c.1780, 4cm (1½in), *L 1 May,*
£3,080 ($4,990)

5
A silver alarum verge oignon, Etienne Lenoir, Paris, early 18th century, 6cm (2½in), *L 18 Dec,*
£1,540 ($2,156)

6
A gold quarter-repeating musical cylinder watch, c.1820, signed on the gilt cuvette *Du Bois & Fils,* 5.5cm (2¼in), *L 20 Feb,*
£2,530 ($3,846)

7
A gold cased open-faced pocket watch, London, 1727, signed *Oba Gardner, S 18 Sept,*
£770 ($1,078)

8
A silver verge watch with world time dial, c.1820, plain silver cases with traces of gilding, with four concentric chapter rings labelled Paris, Le Caire, Cayaine, Pekin, 5cm (2in), *NY 11 Dec,*
$1,320 (£943)

9
A gold quarter-repeating automaton watch, signed on the gilt cuvette *Leroi à Paris,* slightly rubbed, 5.5cm (2¼in), *G 11 Nov,*
SF 7,700 (£3,208; $4,492)

10
A gilt metal open-faced virgule watch, by Antonio Gayon, Padova, dial, pendant and bow of later date, 4.5cm (1¾in), *C 9 Oct,*
£308 ($431)

11
A gold quarter-repeating automaton watch, c.1820, Louis Duchene et Fils, 5.5cm (2¼in), *L 16 Oct,*
£2,420 ($3,388)

12
A silver double-dial world time watch, c.1900, centred by a revolving dial painted with names of world cities, 6cm (2½in), *NY 11 Dec,*
$1,980 (£1,414)

13
An 18-carat gold hunting case chronograph with special setting feature, A. Huguenin & Sons, Locle, c.1865, 5cm (2in), *NY 16 June,*
$1,320 (£880)

14
A silver pocket chronometer, Edward Baker 1824, silver case hallmarked 1824, 5.5cm (2¼in), *L 16 Oct,*
£770 ($1,078)

15
An 18-carat gold open-faced split second chronograph with register, Patek Philippe & Co., Geneva, retailed by Spaulding & Co., c.1920, 4.5cm (1¾in), *NY 15 Feb,*
$3,190 (£2,200)

Oignon the popular name given to the large and rather bulbous French watches of the late 17th and early 18th centuries.

Bras-en-l'air a watch in which, when the pendant is depressed, the time is shown by a figure with two arms pointing to the hours and minutes.

1
A Swiss gold minute repeating keyless lever calendar chronograph, 6cm (2½in), *L 1 May,*
£3,740 ($6,059)

2
A gold hunting cased minute repeating perpetual calendar keyless lever watch, 6cm (2½in), *L 20 Feb,*
£8,250 ($12,540)

3
A gold hunting cased keyless lever minute repeating clockwatch, Zenith, engine-turned covers, 6cm (2½in), *L 24 July,*
£4,620 ($7,253)

4
A gold open-faced keyless five minute repeating watch, Jules Jurgensen, c.1880, 18-carat plain case signed and numbered, 5cm (2in), *NY 11 Dec,*
$4,950 (£3,536)

5
A gold open-faced keyless lever perpetual calendar watch, the case stamped Ekegren, 5cm (2in), *L 18 Dec,*
£3,300 ($4,620)

6
A gold half-hunting case minute repeating keyless lever watch, Charles Frodsham, 1896, the dial signed Willis, 5cm (2in), *NY 11 Dec,*
$4,125 (£2,946)

7
An 18-carat gold hunting cased keyless lever watch, A. Lange & Sohne, 5cm (2in), *L 1 May,*
£2,750 ($4,455)

8
An 18-carat gold gentleman's hunting cased quarter-repeating pocket watch, London, 1877, the backplate signed *Geo. Hooper, S 13 Nov,*
£935 ($1,309)

9
A 14-carat gold hunting case double dial calendar watch with moon phases, monogrammed case, 5cm (2in), *NY 16 June,*
$1,540 (£1,027)

10
An 18-carat gold half-hunting cased keyless fusee lever watch, Charles Frodsham, 1862, case maker's mark J.W.S., *S 24 April,*
£407 ($639)

11
An 18-carat gold gentleman's keyless-wind open-faced pocket watch, London, 1875, the dial and backplate signed, *S 18 Sept,*
£440 ($616)

12
A gentleman's keyless-wind quarter-repeating open-faced pocket watch, in a Swiss case, *S 13 Nov,*
£330 ($462)

13
An 18-carat gold hunting cased keyless lever watch, the Rockford Watch Co., Illinois, 1892, broken mainspring, 5.5cm (2¼in), *L 20 Feb,*
£1,122 ($1,705)

14
A gun metal cased quarter-repeating open-faced keyless lever watch, the movement signed *Brevet,* 5cm (2in), *C 9 Oct,*
£220 ($308)

15
An 18-carat gold open-faced minute repeating watch, Ulysse Nardin, Locle, c.1900, case, dial and movement signed, 5cm (2in), *NY 15 Feb,*
$2,530 (£1,745)

Hunting cased a watch with front and back cover.

Half-hunter, half-hunting cased the front cover with a small aperture showing the hands and dial centre beneath.

Open-faced with a glass over the dial, but no further cover.

Pair cased two cases for one watch. The inner case containing the movement, removed from the outer for winding. Almost universal in English watches from about 1650 to 1800, but less common on the Continent.

1

2

3

4

5

6

7

8

9

10

11

12

13

14

15

1

2

3

4

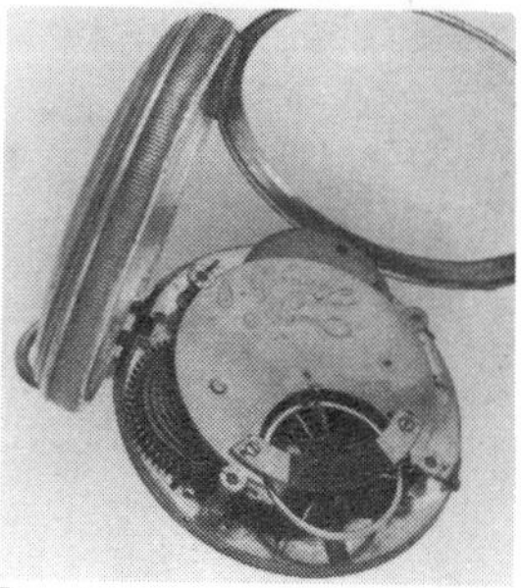
5

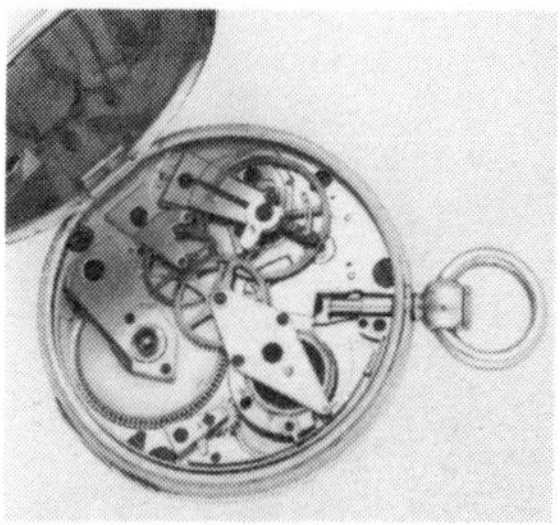
6

7

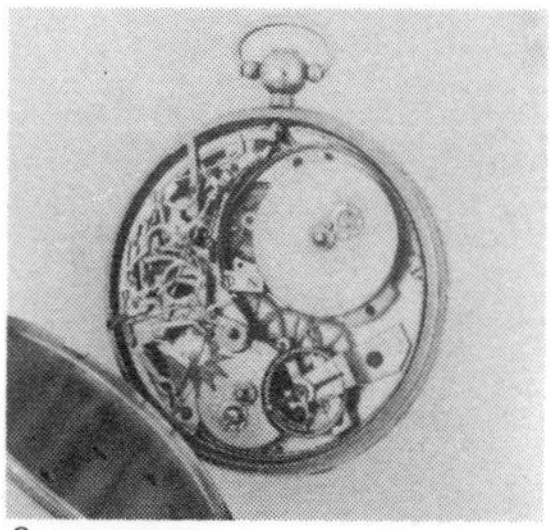
8

9

10

11

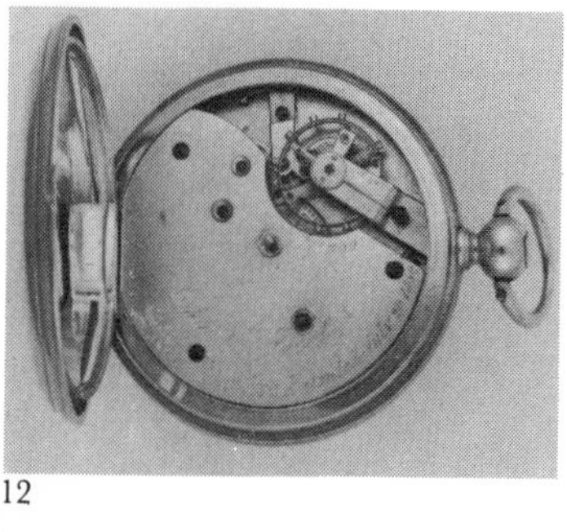
12

13

1
An Italian silver quarter-repeating, striking and alarm carriage watch, Mauro Pastorino, c.1750, 7cm (2¾in), *NY 16 June,*
$7,425 (£4,950)

2
A two-colour gold quarter-repeating cylinder watch, Robin à Paris, c.1784, bezel signed, case with Paris gold marks for 1784, 5.5cm (2¼in), *NY 11 Dec,*
$1,760 (£1,257)

3
A gold skeletonised watch, c.1780, 4cm (1½in), *NY 29 Oct,*
$1,100 (£780)

4
A gold perpetuelle calendar watch, c.1790, sweep seconds, subsidiary dial for date, 6cm (2½in), *NY 11 Dec,*
$4,400 (£3,143)

5
A silver watch with double virgule escapement, J. Girardoni, Vienna, c.1800, the case of slightly later date, 6cm (2½in), *NY 11 Dec,*
$2,420 (£1,729)

6
A platinum half-quarter ruby cylinder watch, Breguet, 1810, with engine-turned case, 5.5cm (2¼in), *NY 11 Dec,*
$19,250 (£13,750)

7
A gold half-quarter-repeating duplex watch, Vulliamy, London, c.1815, case by Louis Comtesse, 5.5cm (2¼in), *NY 11 Dec,*
$19,800 (£14,143)

8
A gold quarter-repeating and quarter-striking clockwatch, Gutkäs, Dresden, 1820, with levers for strike/silent and grande and petite sonnerie, 6cm (2½in), *NY 11 Dec,*
$19,800 (£14,143)

9
A silver and mother-of-pearl watch, c.1830, Johan Viderberg, Kisa & GodSilinder, with decorative backplate, 6cm (2½in), *NY 11 Dec,*
$1,870 (£1,336)

10
A gold quarter-repeating keyless cylinder watch, Le Fevre, Paris, c. 1830, 6cm (2½in), *NY 11 Dec,*
$1,430 (£1,021)

11
A gold hunting cased one-minute tourbillon, Swiss, c.1858, the movement probably La Chaux-de-Fonds, 5.5cm (2¼in), *NY 11 Dec,*
$34,100 (£24,357)

12
A gold hunting cased watch, with patented star duplex movement, Charles E. Jacot, c.1855, 5.5cm (2¼in), *NY 11 Dec,*
$3,410 (£2,436)

13
A gold hunting cased simple chronograph, A. Lange & Sohne, c.1910, the case 14-carat, 5.5cm (2¼in), *NY 11 Dec,*
$9,900 (£7,071)

Verge escapement a recoil escapement, and the first escapement applied to mechanical timekeepers. In use continuously from 1300 to 1900.

Cylinder escapement an escapement invented by George Graham in 1726. A cylinder, with a segment cut away, forms part of the balance staff. Early examples had steel cylinders and brass escape wheels. From about 1760 some high-grade watches had ruby cylinders and steel escape wheels, to reduce wear.

Lever escapement a type of precision escapement invented in the 18th century and employed in the great majority of pocket and wrist-watches of the late 19th and 20th century.

Detent Escapement a type of precision escapement invented in the 18th century and employed in the great majority of marine and pocket chronometers. At first the detent was pivoted, but the spring detent is now almost universal.

1
A silver-gilt pearl and enamel openface watch, with jump seconds, for the Chinese market, c.1840, 6cm (2¼in), *NY 16 June,*
$3,025 (£2,017)

2
An 18-carat gold and enamel lapel watch, Patek Philippe & Co., Geneva, c.1905, retailed by Spaulding & Co., Chicago, 3cm (1¼in), *NY 16 June,*
$3,575 (£2,383)

3
A two-colour gold and pearl-set daisy-form watch, Swiss, c.1890, 4.5cm (1¾in), *NY 11 Dec,*
$2,310 (£1,650)

4
A silver sector watch with flyback hands, Record Watch Co., Tramelan, c.1900, 6cm (2½in), *NY 11 Dec,*
$1,430 (£1,021)

5
A 14-carat triple-colour gold hunting cased keyless lever watch, the American Waltham Watch Co., 5cm (2in), *L 24 July,*
£770 ($1,209)

6
An enamelled gold cylinder watch, Thuny, Geneva, c.1830, 4cm (1½in), *NY 11 Dec,*
$2,200 (£1,571)

7
A two-day marine chronometer, the Barraud movement with Earnshaw spring detent escapement, bezel 11cm (4¼in), *L 16 Oct,*
£2,420 ($3,388)

8
A North German two-day marine chronometer, Krille Kessels Nachfolger Altona, c.1860, 15cm (6in), *NY 16 June,*
$2,750 (£1,833)

9
A two-day marine chronometer, Ulysse Nardin, Locle, 20th century, signed on dial, 19cm (7½in), *NY 16 June,*
$1,760 (£1,173)

10
An eight-day marine chronometer, Barwise, the movement with Earnshaw spring detent escapement, bezel 14.5cm (5¾in), *L 1 May,*
£3,960 ($6,415)

11
An eight-day mantel chronometer, Hamilton & Inches, 29cm (11¼in), *L 20 Feb,*
£2,200 ($3,344)

12
A two-day marine chronometer, Eiffe, the movement with Earnshaw spring detent escapement, bezel 11cm (4¼in), *L 18 Dec,*
£1,540 ($2,156)

Duplex escapement the escapement in its widely used form was invented by Thomas Tyrer in 1782. It was popular during the first half of the 19th century.

Tourbillon a type of revolving carriage carrying the escapement of a watch. As it turns through 300° the effects of errors are neutralised. Invented by A L Breguet and patented in 1801.

Free-sprung of a watch which can only be regulated by adjusting the screws on the balance, and lacking a regulation pointer. Chronometers and many high-grade watches are free-sprung.

Keyless of a watch that is wound from the crown and does not have a separate key.

Jump hour an hour hand which does not advance steadily, but jumps forward an hour at a time.

Karrusel a type of revolving carriage patented in 1894 by Bahne Bonniksen, in which (unlike the tourbillon) the carriage and escape wheel are driven separately.

1

2

3

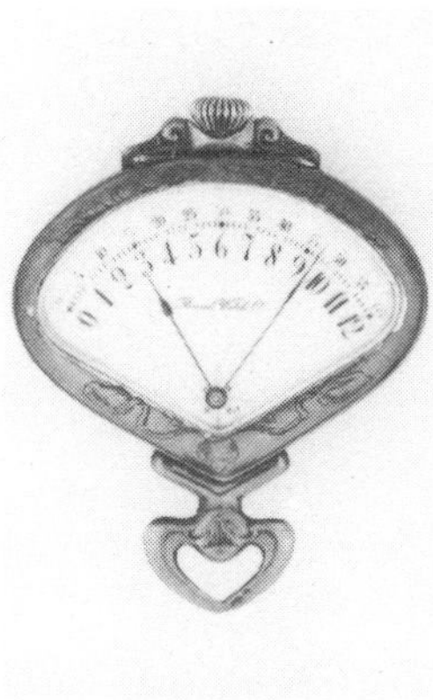
4

5

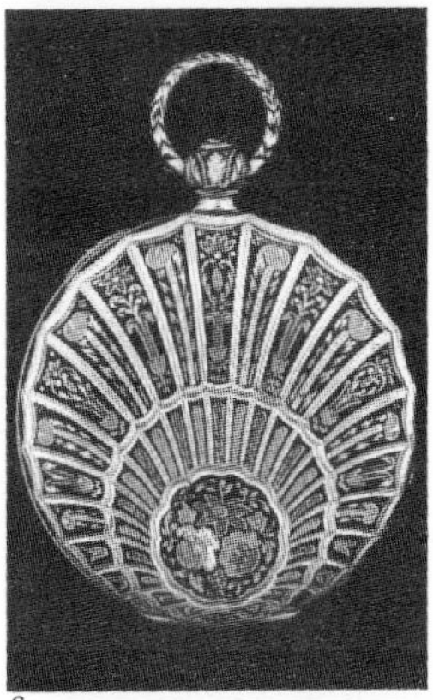
6

7

8

9

10

11

12

Folk Art

1 2 3 4

5

6

7

8

9

10

11

12

See also:
Colour illustrations *p* 482
American furniture *p* 113
Textiles *pp* 176, 178, 181-183, 188

1
A woven splint oval basket, American, 19th century, painted red, stationary ash handles, 29.5cm (11½in) long, *NY 25 Oct,*
$1,100 (£780)

2
A woven splint basket, American, 19th century, painted blue, with swing handle, 23cm (9in) high, *NY 25 Oct,*
$1,320 (£936)

3
A woven splint basket, American, 19th century, painted blue, 23.5cm (9¼in) diam., *NY 25 Oct,*
$605 (£429)

4
An Indian-made woven splint basket, early 19th century, alternating yellow and red splints with potato stamp decoration, 25.5cm (10in) long, *NY 25 Oct,*
$522 (£370)

5
A wooden pantry box, American Midwest, 19th century, painted overall with yellow and pink vinegar graining, cracked, 33cm (13in) high, *NY 25 Oct,*
$770 (£546)

6
A miniature trunk, Maine, mid 19th century, the interior lined with a Maine newspaper, the *Eastern Argus* dated May 13, 1823, the ground grain-painted in red and brown, and with yellow grapes and foliage, 61cm (24in) long, *NY 1 Feb,*
$1,540 (£1,092)

7
A small box, Lancaster County, Pennsylvania, first half 19th century, with compass-drawn decoration and white and red foliage on a slate-blue ground, 18cm (7in) long, *NY 25 Oct,*
$3,850 (£2,730)

8
A wooden bonnet box, Pennsylvania, late 18th century, decorated in the manner of a dower chest in red, yellow, black and white, and with green leafage and vines, on a green ground, some wear, 53cm (21in) long, *NY 25 Oct,*
$5,775 (£4,096)

9
A pine box, probably New York, c.1830, decorated in red and yellow vinegar graining, and inscribed *Capt. GF Kitts, Rochester, NY, by RR.*, 77cm (30¼in) long, *NY 25 Oct,*
$2,200 (£1,560)

10
A miniature chest, Shenandoah County, Virginia, c.1850, painted with circle and dot decoration in dark green and red on a mustard yellow ground, 22cm (8¾in) long, *NY 25 Oct,*
$9,075 (£6,436)

11
A pantry box, New England, c.1830, painted overall with vinegar graining to resemble bird's-eye maple, with yellow-brown dots on a pink ground, 21cm (8¼in) diam., *NY 25 Oct,*
$1,760 (£1,248)

12
A pine box, probably New England, c.1830, painted with leafage and blossoms in green, yellow, blue and red within green borders, light yellow ground, 29cm (11¼in) long, *NY 25 Oct,*
$1,980 (£1,404)

1
A glazed redware bowl, American, early 19th century, decorated with brown streaks on a brown-green ground, 13cm (5¼in) diam., *NY 25 Oct,*
$1,760 (£1,248)

2
A glazed redware pot, attributed to Peter Clark, Braintree, Massachusetts, or Lyndeboro, New Hampshire, c.1770, decorated with brown on a yellow-green ground, chips, 17.5cm (7in) high, *NY 25 Oct,*
$3,080 (£2,184)

3
A glazed redware miniature pot, New England, c.1825, with cover and applied with ribbing handle, decorated with brown on a yellow-green ground, chips, 11.5cm (4½in), *NY 25 Oct,*
$1,100 (£780)

4
A stoneware 'Acrobats' jug, Fulper Brothers, Flemington, New Jersey, c.1890, decorated in cobalt-blue with a gentleman with a top hat and a lady performing a handstand, 42cm (16½in) high, *NY 25 Oct,*
$28,600 (£20,284)

5
A salt-glazed stoneware 'Farmer' crock, William A. Macquoid & Co., New York, c.1860, decorated in cobalt-blue with a farmer holding a rake and sickle, 25.5cm (10in) high, *NY 25 Oct,*
$7,150 (£5,071)

6
A glazed redware jar, American, c.1860, decorated with brown patches on a light-green ground, chip, 17cm (7in), *NY 25 Oct,*
$990 (£702)

7
A glazed redware jar, New England, probably New Bedford, Massachusetts, early 19th century, with cover and decorated with brown streaks on a green-yellow ground, slight glaze flake, 21cm (8½in) high, *NY 25 Oct,*
$2,860 (£2,028)

8
A salt-glazed stoneware 'Pointing Hand' jug, American, c.1880, decorated in cobalt-blue, crack, 48cm (19in) high, *NY 25 Oct,*
$2,750 (£1,950)

9
An unglazed pottery face vessel, Ohio, second half 19th century, chips, 19cm (7¾in) high, *NY 25 Oct,*
$2,530 (£1,794)

10
A glazed redware pot, attributed to Kain Pottery, eastern Tennessee, mid 19th century, decorated with black patches on an orange ground, chips, 39cm (15½in), *NY 25 Oct,*
$4,400 (£3,120)

11
A salt-glazed stoneware pig flask, Midwestern, c.1860, with the inscription *Fine Old Bourbon, in a Hogs...Cairo Mounds, Chicago, St. Louis, Cincinnati,* with cobalt-blue highlighted eyes, 18cm (7in) long, *NY 25 Oct,*
$1,320 (£936)

12
A glazed redware figure of a rooster, Pennsylvania, late 19th century, decorated in an orange-brown glaze with dark brown markings, 35cm (14½in) high, *NY 25 Oct,*
$1,760 (£1,248)

1

2

3

4

5

6

7

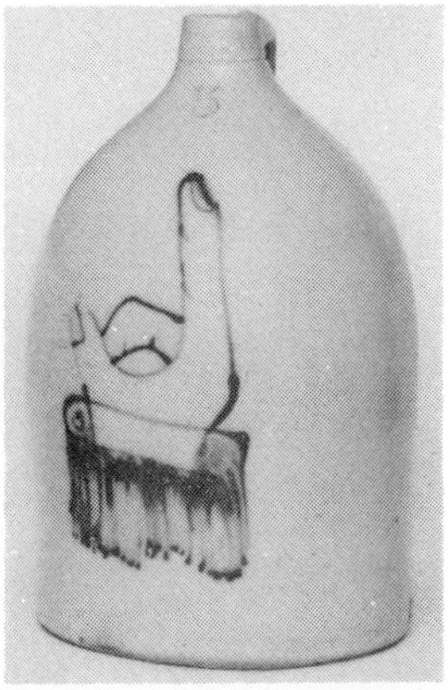
8

9

10

11

12

1

2

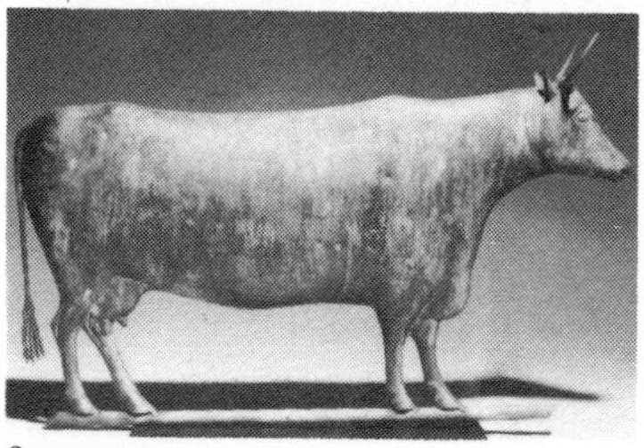
3

4

5

6 7 8

9

10

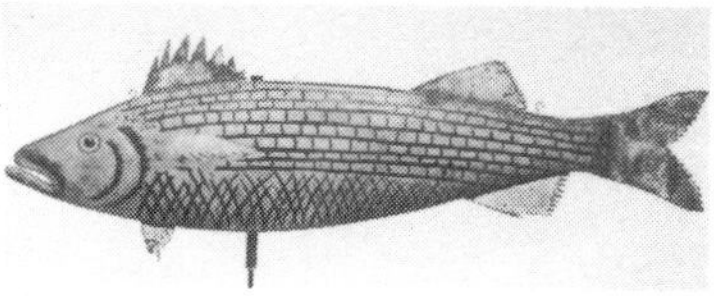
11

1
A wooden swordsman whirligig, probably Newport, New Hampshire, c.1835, painted in black, blue, red, gold and buff, the arms fitted with sword blades, 57cm (22½in), *NY 25 Oct,*
$42,900 (£30,426)

2
A copper cockerel weathervane, probably English, early 19th century, with green patination and traces of original gilt finish, some shotgun damage, 48cm (19in), *L 22 July,*
£825 ($1,295)

3
A copper and zinc cow weathervane, L. W. Cushing & Sons, Waltham, Massachusetts, third quarter 19th century, the copper body with applied cast zinc antlers, 70cm (27½in) long, *NY 25 Oct,*
$4,180 (£2,965)

4
A metal blacksmith's sign, French, 19th century, depicting two blacksmiths working over an anvil, 72cm (28½in) high, *L 22 Apr,*
£330 ($518)

5
A sheet-tin horse and rider weathervane, American, 19th century, painted in black, green and white, the figure mounted on a mobile arrow with wind wheel, on rod standard, 250cm (8ft 2in) high, *NY 1 Feb,*
$3,850 (£2,730)

6
A tin ship weathervane, mid 19th century, mounted above cardinal points, some wear, 121cm (47½in), *L 22 July,*
£605 ($950)

7
A tin cockerel weathervane, English, 19th century, 56cm (22in), *L 22 July,*
£55 ($86)

8
A copper cupid weathervane, English, late 18th century, repaired, 57cm (23½in), *L 22 July,*
£385 ($604)

9
A copper and zinc horse weathervane, American, c.1875, the head of cast zinc, 87cm (34¼in) long, *NY 1 Feb,*
$4,400 (£3,120)

10
A copper and zinc plough weathervane, American, 19th century, 106cm (41½in), *NY 25 Oct,*
$7,425 (£5,266)

11
A wooden fish weathervane trade sign, American, 19th century, the body gilded, its scales painted in black and with inset copper fins, later stand, 85cm (33½in) long, *NY 25 Oct,*
$7,150 (£5,071)

1
An iron and metal cigarstore Indian, Wm. Demuth & Co., New York, 1875, painted in bright colours (some restoration), 198cm (78in), *NY 1 Feb,*
$11,000 (£7,801)

2
A wooden barber's sign: Dapper Dan, Philadelphia or Washington, c.1880, painted in blue, red and white, on later pedestal, 196cm (77¼in), *NY 25 Oct,*
$258,000 (£183,333)

3
A cast-lead Indian Princess, American or Canadian, third quarter 19th century, 69cm (27in), *NY 26 June,*
$4,290 (£2,841)

4
A wooden cigarstore Indian, American, 19th century, 198cm (6ft 6in), *NY 1 Feb,*
$6,050 (£4,291)

5
A wooden tavern sign, William Follett, Western Massachusetts, c.1830, 127cm (50in) high, *NY 25 Oct,*
$25,300 (£17,943)

6
A painted iron shop sign, French, 18th century, 148cm (58in) high, *L 22 July,*
£1,320 ($2,072)

7
An iron and sheet steel locksmith shop sign, probably French, 18th century, 142cm (56in) high, *L 22 July,*
£660 ($1,036)

8
A wooden horse's head, 19th century, with traces of the original paint, 55cm (21½in) high, *NY 26 June,*
$1,320 (£874)

9
A wooden tavern sign, W. Bursley, Barnstable, Massachusetts, mid 19th century, 97cm (38½in) wide, *NY 25 Oct,*
$7,425 (£5,266)

10
A wooden butcher's shop pig, English, from Boston, Lincs, late 19th or early 20th century, 47cm (16½in), *L 22 July,*
£1,155 ($1,813)

1

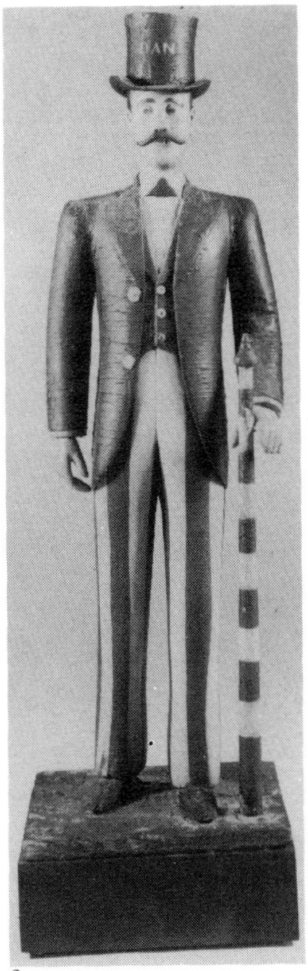
2

3

4

5

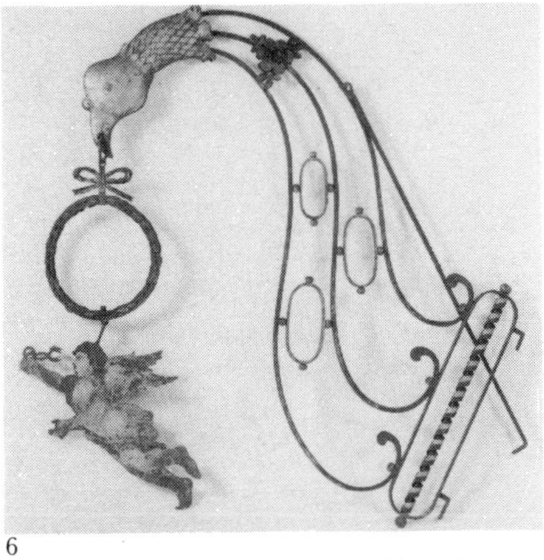
6

7

8

9

10

1

2

3

4

5

6 7 8

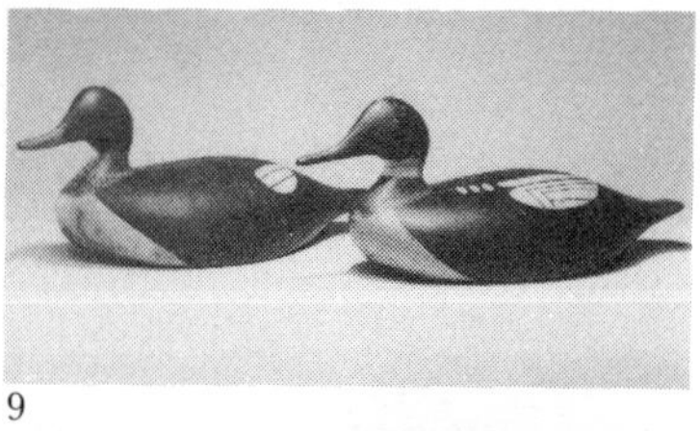
9

10 11 10

1
A wooden draughts (checkers)/parcheesi board, American, c.1870, painted in yellow, red, green, brown and black, within a moulded border, 53.5 x 52.5cm (21 x 20¾in), *NY 25 Oct,*
$4,400 (£3,121)

2
A wooden parcheesi board, American, c.1870, painted in red, green, black and orange, within a moulded border, 41cm (16in) square, *NY 25 Oct,*
$3,190 (£2,262)

3
A canvasback decoy, Wisconsin, late 19th century, in the original paint, *NY 25 Oct,*
$4,070 (£2,887)

4
A wooden fairground-organ figure, possibly Dutch, late 19th century, with bandleader uniform and one articulated arm and head, re-painted, 87.5cm (34½in) high, *L 22 July,*
£385 ($604)

5
A pair of black wooden heads, probably South Carolina, 20th century, perhaps from a carnival ball-toss game, 36cm (14¼in) high, *NY 1 Feb,*
$1,870 (£1,326)

6
A wooden decoy of a Canadian black duck, Ontario, Canada, c.1900, in original paint, 42cm (16½in) long, *L 22 July,*
£352 ($553)

7
A wooden decoy of a Red Head drake, American, modern, from the Eastern shore of Maryland, carved by the Elliott Brothers (who were once market hunters) in original paint, 39cm (15¼in) long, *L 22 July,*
£154 ($242)

8
A wooden decoy duck, Reno, Nevada, early 20th century, in original paint, 34cm (13½in) long, *L 22 July,*
£198 ($311)

9
A pair of mergansers, Willie Ross, Chebeague Island, Maine, c.1920, the male with replaced bill. Willie Ross made his living as a clam basket maker in the 1930s and 1940s. *NY 25 Oct,*
$4,125 (£2,926)

10
A pair of birds, Pennsylvania, 19th century, painted in red, black and yellow, with wire legs on later gilded acorn bases, repaired bills, 29cm (11½in) high, *NY 25 Oct,*
$5,060 (£3,589)

11
A wooden bird tree, Pennsylvania, c.1870, comprising nine finely carved figures of birds with yellow bodies and green-black wings and tails, the top bird suspended from a wire hanger, the middle group swivelling on a cross bar, the lower group suspended from the cross bar on wire rings, 23cm (9in) high, *NY 25 Oct,*
$5,500 (£3,901)

1
A pair of shell-mounted mirrors, English, early 19th century, the shells applied to a cardboard mount, mahogany frame, 58cm (22in) long, *L 22 July,*
£660 ($1,036)

2
A prisoner-of-war work straw picture, probably c.1810, depicting an ostrich chick flanked by bullrushes, giltwood frame, 56.5cm (22½in) wide, *C 17 Apr,*
£484 ($750)

3
A tinsel picture, English, c.1840, depicting Mrs Egerton as Helen McGregor, rosewood frame, 25cm (9¾in) high, *L 22 July,*
£176 ($276)

4
A woolwork picture, English, mid 19th century, depicting a steam and sailing ship, maple frame, 54cm (21¼in) wide, *L 3 June,*
£495 ($767)

5
A sailor's Valentine shell picture, Jamaican, late 19th century, 23cm (9in) diam., *L 3 June,*
£550 ($852)

6
A woolwork picture, English, mid 19th century, stitched to portray a ship-of-the-line within a border of flags of all nations, a wreath and drapes, 56cm (22in) wide, *L 3 June,*
£528 ($818)

7
A toleware tray, Pennsylvania, c.1830, painted in black, white and grey with yellow, on a red ground, 23cm (9in) wide, *NY 25 Oct,*
$5,500 (£3,900)

8
A 'horn' book, English, late 18th century, the shaped bone pallet decorated with a hand-painted alphabet in black and scarlet, 9.5cm (3¾in) long, *L 22 July,*
£308 ($484)

9
A carved mahogany cake board, attributed to J. Conger, Massachusetts, c.1800, carved with the figure of Columbia carrying the American standard, on the right an angel holding the United States shield, in the centre the American eagle above the scales of Justice, 68cm (26¾in) wide, *NY 25 Oct,*
$11,000 (£7,801)

10
A tin wrigglework coffee pot, Pennsylvania, early 19th century, the body with an American eagle and floral decoration, some wear, 22cm (12½in) high, *NY 25 Oct,*
$3,080 (£2,184)

11
A birch washing bat, Scandinavian, early 19th century, 35cm (13¾in), *S 12 Feb,*
£330 ($462)

12
A cedarwood mangling board, English North Country, 18th century, carved with scrolling strapwork, 50cm (19¾in), *S 12 Feb,*
£308 ($431)

13
A birch mangling board, Scandinavian, early 19th century, with traces of original painted decoration, horse handle, 74cm (29in) long, *S 12 Feb,*
£308 ($431)

14
A beechwood mangling board, Scandinavia or Friesland, 17th century, with horse handle, 64cm (25in), *S 12 Feb,*
£275 ($385)

15
A painted beechwood mangling board, Scandinavian, with horse handle and naive depiction of a vase of flowers, 61cm (24in), *S 12 May,*
£198 ($277)

16
A wooden mangling board, dated 1717, 78cm (30¾in), *A 24 Apr,*
Dfl 1,840 (£557; $874)

17
A wooden mangling board, Scottish, 1752, 85cm (33½in), *L 22 July,*
£550 ($864)

1

2

3

4

5

6

7

8

9

10

11 12 13 14 15

16

17

1

2

3

4

5

6

7

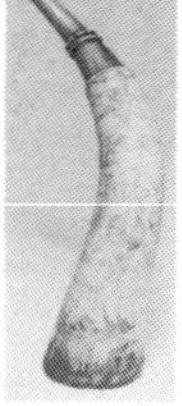
8

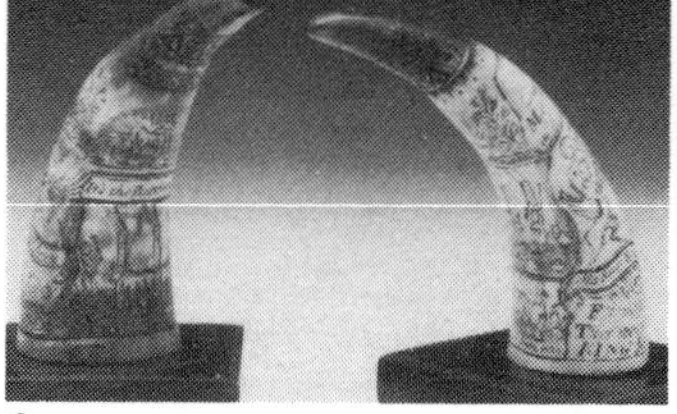
9

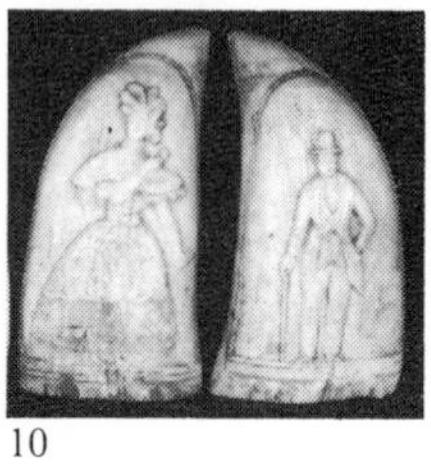
10

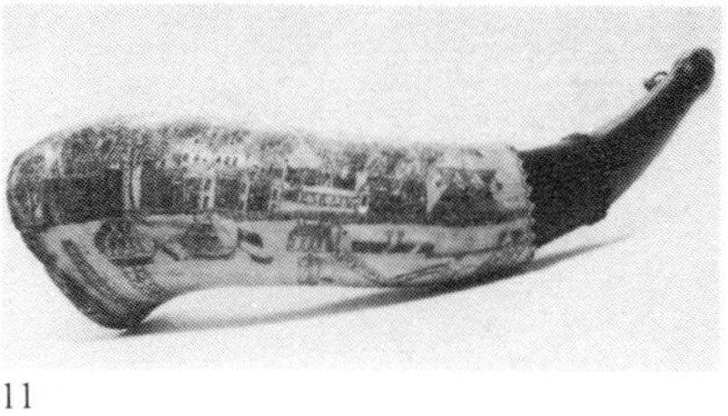
11

12

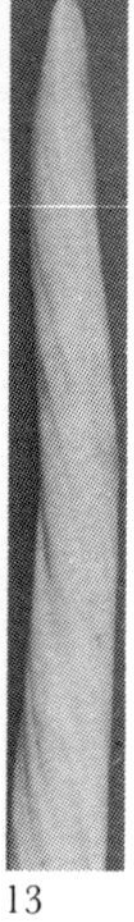
13

1
A prisoner-of-war bone model of a 120-gun ship-of-the-line, French, early 19th century, rigging restored, 48 x 65cm (19 x 25½in), *L 3 June,*
£8,800 ($13,640)

2
A prisoner-of-war bone Spinning Jenny, French, early 19th century, the naively carved spinner with poke bonnet, skirt painted in brilliant colours, hand crank to the front causing the figure to move, 156cm (61½in) high, *L 3 June,*
£440 ($682)

3
A prisoner-of-war bone games box, French, c.1810, the sliding cover flanked by a cribbage board and opening to a set of dominoes, *L 3 June,*
£352 ($545)

4
A prisoner-of-war bone Spinning Jenny, French, c.1810, the seated Breton lady spinning at her wheel with small windmill adjacent, replaced ivory base, 13cm (5in) high, *L 3 June,*
£418 ($648)

5
Two whalebone models of a triple block, 20th century, each with three pulley wheels and copper nails, 10.5cm (4in) long, *L 3 June,*
£198 ($306)

6
A scrimshawed dolphin's jawbone, English, mid 19th century, decorated on either side with a portrait of a merchant ship and a bouquet of roses and thistles, 53cm (21in), *L 3 June,*
£858 ($1,330)

7
An engraved horn beaker, English, c.1830, decorated with a coach-and-four passing two country houses, 12cm (4¾in) high, *L 22 July,*
£143 ($225)

8
A powder horn, mid 18th century, engraved with a war map of New York State and the British coat of arms, lacking base and lobe, 33cm (13in), *NY 1 Feb,*
$2,420 (£1,716)

9
A pair of decorated butcher's horns, English, c.1830, each decorated with the arms of the Worshipful Company of Butchers, mahogany bases, 13cm (5in) high, *L 22 July,*
£572 ($898)

10
A pair of scrimshawed whale's teeth, English, c.1835, one carved with a lady in a crinoline and feathered bonnet and the other with a gentleman in tail coat and top hat, 14.5cm (5¾in) high, *L 3 June,*
£440 ($682)

11
A scrimshawed powder horn, possibly American, early 19th century, inscribed with Indians, a sword fight and a harbour scene, lacking base panel, 28cm (11in) long, *L 22 July,*
£440 ($691)

12
A scrimshawed whale-bone busk, English, mid 19th century, engraved with three landscape vignettes, 37cm (14½in) long, *L 28 Oct,*
£330 ($462)

13
An ivory narwhal tusk, 19th century, with a fine patina, 168cm (66in), *NY 26 June,*
$2,200 (£1,457)

1
A William and Mary floral marquetry cabinet on stand, c.1690, the legs later, 121cm (48in) wide, *L 28 Feb,*
£11,000 ($17,050)

2
A Régence walnut armchair, c.1730, covered in floral tapestry, *L 20 June,*
£3,300 ($5,214)

3
A George II serpentine console table, c.1740, in the manner of William Jones, with wooden top, 183cm (6ft) wide, *L 11 July,*
£28,600 ($45,474)

4
A Régence satinwood and burr walnut commode, first quarter 18th century, the drawer fronts and sides with geometric parquetry, with ormolu figural drawer handles, 122cm (48in) wide, *NY 4 Oct,*
$14,300 (£9,930)

1

2

3

4

1

2

3

1
A North Italian parcel-gilt walnut side table, c.1740, with serpentine top and frieze, decorated in penwork technique on a gilt ground with figures amongst scrollwork and flowers, 132cm (52in) wide, *L 12 Dec,*
£11,550 ($16,170)

2
A George II oval drop-leaf table, c.1750, with 'French' scroll feet, 133cm (52½in) wide, *L 28 Feb,*
£4,400 ($6,820)

3
A George II kneehole mahogany dressing table, mid 18th century, 107cm (42in) wide, *NY 25 Jan,*
$13,200 (£9,496)

1
A George III oval mahogany Pembroke table, c.1770, cross-banded in satinwood and tulipwood, 106cm (41½in) open, *L 11 July,* **£5,500 ($8,745)**

2
A George III satinwood demi-lune small side cabinet, c.1775, in the manner of the Linnells, the convex door inlaid with two figures in Near Eastern costume, 86cm (34in) high, *L 28 Feb,* **£17,600 ($27,280)**

3
A Louis XVI kingwood parquetry, bonheur du jour, stamped *D. Deloose, JME,* c.1775, the upper part with white marble top, the lower with hinged leather-lined writing surface, gilt-bronze mounts, the legs inlaid to simulate fluting, 105cm (41½in) high, *L 20 June,* **£9,900 ($15,642)**

4
A Regency brass-inlaid rosewood side cabinet, c.1810, pleated silk panelled doors, 135cm (53in) high, *L 25 April,* **£8,250 ($13,200)**

1

2

3

4

1

2

1
A George I inlaid faded walnut bureau, c.1720, the slant-front opening to a fitted interior, on shaped bracket feet, 109cm (43in) high, *NY 7 June,*
$12,100 (£8,120)

2
A German walnut parquetry bureau cabinet, c.1740, the upper part with a broken cornice above a pair of doors, the lower part with a sloping front enclosing a fitted interior, 244cm (7ft 4½in) high, *L 23 May,*
£5,280 ($8,342)

3
A George III mahogany serpentine chest, c.1770, the top with a moulded border, and with moulded chamfered corners and bracket feet, 133cm (52½in) wide, *L 28 Feb,*
£6,600 ($10,230)

4
A George III mahogany secretaire bookcase, c.1790, the dentil-moulded cornice above a pair of moulded glazed doors, the lower part with fitted secretaire drawer veneered in satinwood, on bracket feet, 244cm (8ft) high, *HS 24 Sept,*
IR£4,950 (£4,500; $6,525)

3

4

1
A set of eight George III mahogany dining chairs, *(one illustrated)*, including a pair of armchairs differing in minor detail, upholstered in leather, *L 25 Apr*, **£7,700 ($12,320)**

2
A set of six Louis XVI mahogany fauteuils, *(one illustrated)*, late 18th century, probably made in 1778 by Garnier for the Marquis de Marigny, with caned backs, *M 23 Feb*, **FF 560,550 (£54,212; $81,318)**

3
A pair of Louis XVI mahogany jardinières, *(one illustrated)*, late 18th century, the tops surrounded by a pierced brass gallery and fitted with a metal liner and grey marble top, the legs ending in brass *sabots*, 91cm (36in) high, *NY 31 Oct*, **$28,600 (£20,284)**

4
A Louis XVI fruitwood and mahogany table à écrire, late 18th century, attributed to David Roentgen, the top of oval form, the frieze containing one drawer fitted with a leather-lined writing slide opening to reveal a well and two small drawers, ormolu mounts, 72.5cm (28½in) wide, *NY 3 May*, **$19,800 (£13,026)**

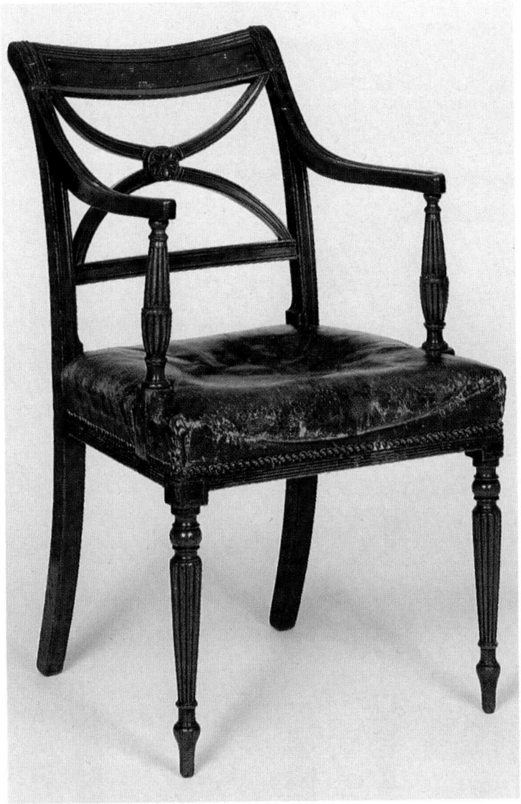
1

2

3

4

1

2

top row: 3,4,5 *bottom row:* 6,7,8,7,9

1
A George IV mahogany extending three-pedestal dining table, c.1820, 360cm (11ft 10in) extended, *L 11 July,*
£16,500 ($26,235)

2
A George IV mahogany extending dining table, c.1820, 374cm (12ft 3½in) extended, *L 11 July,*
£9,680 ($15,391)

3
A George III silver-mounted inlaid satinwood tea caddy, late 18th century, the front with a view of the Alien Priory at Wenlock, 13cm (5¼in) high, *NY 25 Jan,*
$4,950 (£3,561)

4
A George III inlaid yew-wood lap desk, late 18th century, 34cm (13½in) wide, *NY 25 Jan,*
$1,430 (£1,028)

5
A George III inlaid satinwood and mahogany tea caddy, late 18th century, with painted panels of the English countryside, 15cm (5in) high, *NY 25 Jan,*
$1,650 (£1,187)

6
A George III silver-mounted tortoiseshell and ivory tea caddy, late 18th century, 13.5cm (5¼in) high, *NY 25 Jan,*
$1,760 (£1,266)

7
A George III oval inlaid harewood tea caddy and an inlaid mahogany tea caddy, both late 18th century, 12cm (4½in), *NY 25 Jan,*
$660 (£475)

8
A George III brass-mounted carved padouk jewellery casket, late 18th century, with later Brahmah lock, 17cm (6½in), *NY 25 Jan,*
$6,050 (£4,353)

9
A George III satinwood and mahogany parquetry tea caddy, last quarter 18th century, interior with three tole boxes with engraved brass tops, 13cm (5in), *NY 25 Jan,*
$2,200 (£1,583)

1
A North German ormolu-mounted walnut secretaire, last quarter 18th century, probably Oldenburg, the upper part with stepped galleried superstructure, the middle with leather-lined surface, and the lower part with slide writing surface, 179cm (70½in) high, *NY 22 Mar,*
$11,000 (£7,285)

2
A Restauration mahogany étagère, c.1825, with mirror back, and guilloché mounts, 164cm (64½in) high, *L 20 June,*
£15,400 ($24,332)

3
An Empire ormolu-mounted mahogany centre table, early 19th century, with grey marble top, the columnar supports joined by scrolled stretchers centred by a brass roundel, 73cm (28¾in) high, *NY 31 Oct,*
$11,000 (£7,801)

4
A Biedermeier fruitwood ebonised and parcel-gilt centre table, c.1820, the columnar supports with gilt corinthian capitols and terminals, 75cm (29½in) high, *NY 4 Oct,*
$8,525 (£5,920)

1

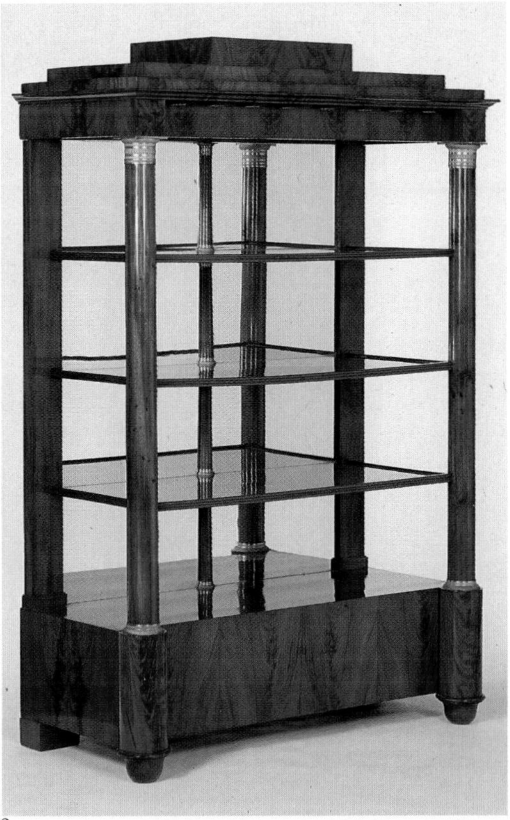
2

3

4

1

2

4

3

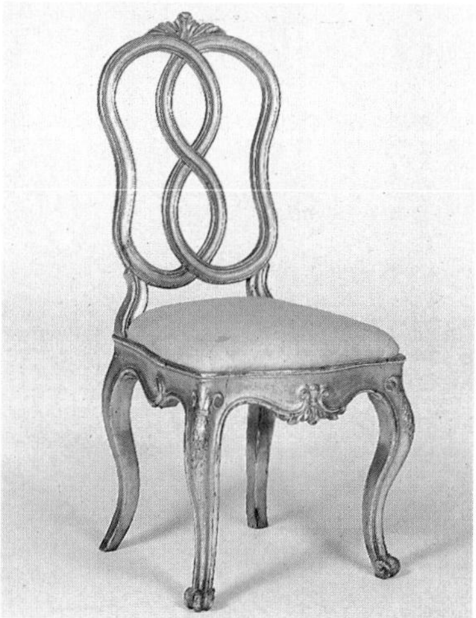
5

1
A set of six Louis XVI beechwood chairs *(one illustrated)*, late 18th century, the seats covered in Aubusson tapestry depicting the Fables of la Fontaine, *L 20 June*,
£11,000 ($17,380)

2
A set of six Louis XVI painted fauteuils à la Reine *(two illustrated)*, last quarter 18th century, signed *A. Gailliard*, *NY 3 May*,
$25,300 (£16,645)

3
A pair of George III painted armchairs *(one illustrated)*, c.1775, *L 25 Apr*,
£6,600 ($10,560)

4
A pair of Louis XV giltwood fauteuils *(one illustrated)*, c.1750, *L 12 Dec*,
£3,520 ($4,928)

5
A set of six North Italian giltwood chairs, *(one illustrated)*, c. 1760, probably Venetian, the seats inscribed *Galleria* and each with a different number, *L 23 May*,
£5,280 ($8,342)

1
A Continental glass and mosaic mirror, mid 19th century, with glass tiles on a gold foil ground, 145cm (57½in) high, *NY 13 Sept,*
$31,900 (£21,701)

2
A gilt-bronze-mounted mahogany small writing table, c.1860, stamped *Durand*, with leather inset top, the frieze with three drawers, centred by a plaque of cherubs, 99cm (39in) wide, *L 7 Nov,*
£8,800 ($12,320)

3
A Napoleon III 'Sèvres' porcelain-mounted dressing table, c.1870, the cresting with a flower-cast plaque of Louis XVI, the legs jointed by a gilt-bronze hour-glass stretcher, 152cm (60in) high, *L 13 June,*
£7,480 ($11,968)

4
A Victorian walnut break-front cabinet, c.1870, with gilt-metal mounts, amboyna banding and satinwood inlay, 104cm (41in) high, *S 17 June,*
£2,860 ($4,518)

5
A gilt-bronze-mounted bow-ended satinwood and marquetry side cabinet, by Dasson, with inset Spanish brocatelle top, 107cm (42in) high, *L 21 Mar,*
£17,050 ($26,598)

1

2

3

4

5

1

2

1
A Chippendale carved mahogany flat-top chest-on-chest, New York, c.1770, in two parts, 198cm (6ft ¼in), *NY 25 Oct,* **$17,600 (£12,482)**

2
A Classical inlaid and carved mahogany wardrobe, New York, c.1815, 241cm (7ft 11in), *NY 25 Oct,* **$18,150 (£12,872)**

3
A bone and tulipwood inlaid ebonised rosewood side table, c.1880, Herter Brothers, New York, 122cm (48in) wide, *NY 13 Sept,* **$40,700 (£27,687)**

3

1
A Queen Anne carved walnut small drop-leaf breakfast table, Massachusetts, c.1750, 71cm (28in) high, *NY 25 Oct,* **$22,000 (£15,602)**

2
A Federal inlaid walnut serpentine-front chest-of-drawers, Maryland or Virginia, c.1800, 92cm (36in) high, *NY 1 Feb,* **$25,300 (£17,943)**

3
A Federal inlaid mahogany lolling chair, signed John Wells, Hartford, Connecticut, c.1800, bears brand of maker, *NY 1 Feb,* **$26,400 (£18,723)**

4
A Classical brass-mounted crossbanded mahogany card table, labelled *Duncan Phyfe, New York,* c.1820, the hinged top swivelling to reveal a marbelised paper interior and maker's mark, 80cm (31½in) high, *NY 25 Oct,* **$11,000 (£7,801)**

1

2

3

4

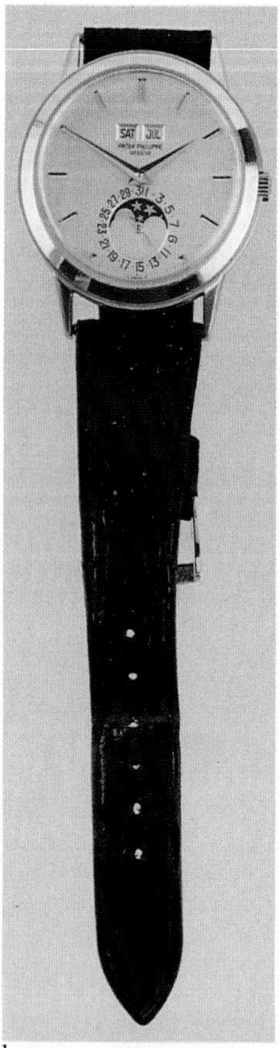

1

2

3

4

1
An 18-carat gold perpetual calendar automatic wristwatch, Patek Philippe, 1964-70, the case with London import mark for 1971, 4cm (1½in), *L 16 Oct,*
£8,800 ($12,320)

2
A Directoire patinated bronze and gilt-bronze chased negro porter clock, 36cm (14in), *M 22 June,*
FF 83,250 (£7,426; $11,585)

3
An ormolu and marble urn clock, third quarter 19th century, the movement by A. D. Mougin, signed *Maline Horloger,* the time indicated by a bullrush, 72.5cm (28½in), *L 21 Mar,*
£18,150 ($28,314)

4
A gilt and painted bronze chinoiserie mantel clock, c.1830, the enamel dial signed *Monbro Ainé A Paris, Jacquier Her.,* decorated with oriental figures, their costumes in shades of red, gilt and black, 59cm (23¼in), *L 13 June,*
£8,580 ($13,728)

1
A gold and enamel watch, J. H. Kuhn, Amsterdam, c.1790, with white enamel dial of Roman numerals, the decorated case showing Liberty sitting on a lion, 4.5cm (1¾in), *NY 16 June,*
$3,025 (£2,017)

2
A porcelain-mounted alarum carriage clock, the engraved case decorated with young musicians in a garden, within pink and gilt borders, 14cm (5½in), *L 20 Feb,*
£2,090 ($3,177)

3
A George I walnut bracket clock, Dav. Hubert, London, c.1720, the spandrels mounted with gilt-brass ornaments, 33cm (13in), *NY 25 Jan,*
$9,900 (£7,122)

4
A gold fusee keyless lever tourbillon, Charles Frodsham, the signature and number repeated and inscribed *AD Fmsz,* the back hallmarked 1912, and also engraved with the coat of arms of the Smith family of Woodhall Park, 6cm (2¼in), *L 20 Feb,*
£23,100 ($35,112)

5
An 18-carat gold chronograph wristwatch with tachometer, telemeter and registers, Rolex, retailed by Milan T. Stefanovich, Belgrade, c.1945, the dial bearing the crest of the Yugoslavian Royal family, 3.5cm (1¼in), *NY 16 June,*
$14,300 (£9,533)

6
An 18-carat gold wristwatch, Patek Philippe c.1925, the movement with wolf's tooth winding, London import mark for 1925, the case signed and numbered, 4cm (1½in), *G 11 Nov,*
SF 11,550 (£4,813; $6,738)

1

2

3

4

5 *(enlarged)*

6

1

2

1
A French gentleman's court coat and breeches, c.1790, of ribbed lilac-grey silk, *L 5 Feb,*
£2,200 ($3,168)

2
A French needlepoint carpet, late 19th century, 396 x 310cm (13ft x 10ft 2in), *NY 31 Oct,*
$23,100 (£16,383)

3
A European needlework carpet, 273 x 216cm (9ft x 7ft 1in), *L 16 Apr,*
£2,860 ($4,433)

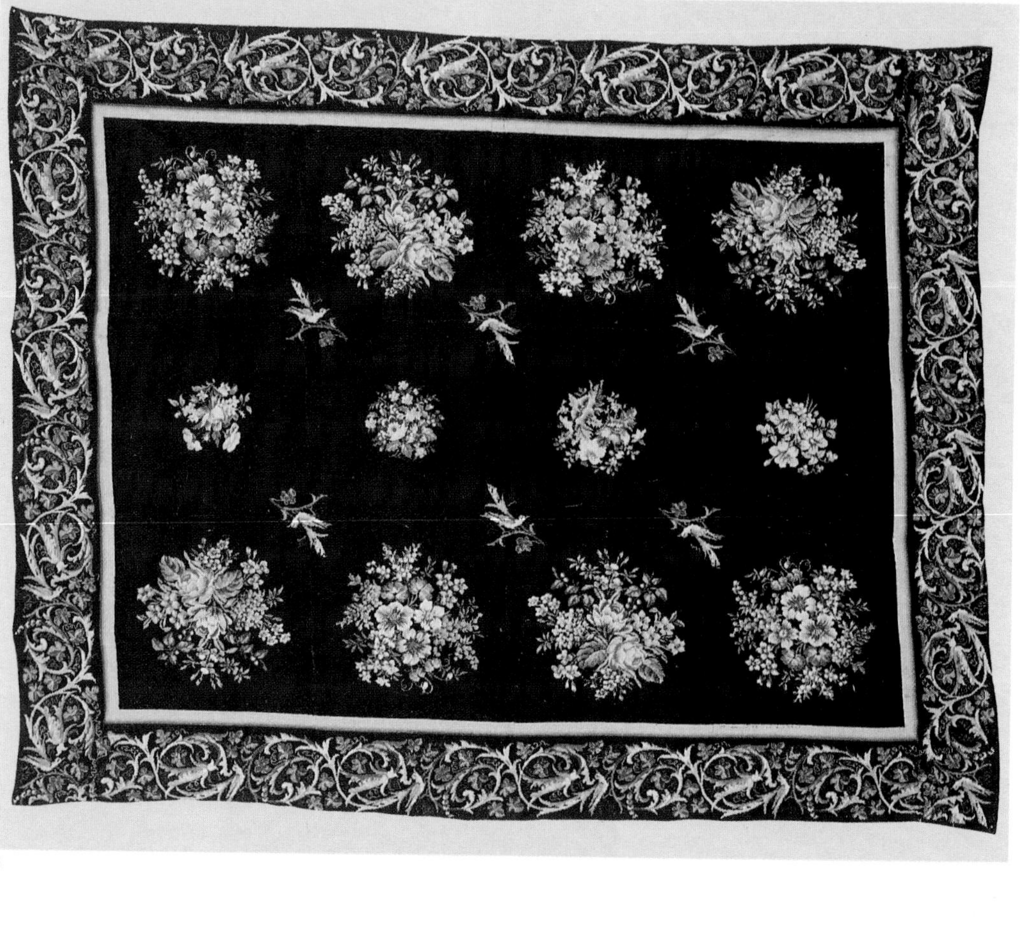

3

1
A Charles II beadwork picture, c.1660, on ivory satin ground, tortoiseshell frame, slight wear, 34 x 44.5cm (13½ x 17½in), *L 20 May,*
£2,420 ($3,872)

2
A Charles II stumpwork picture, c.1660, in a late 17th century carved wood and parcel-gilt frame, 20 x 30cm (8 x 11¾in), *L 4 July,*
£5,500 ($8,855)

3
A Charles II silk embroidered and stump-work casket, in original oyster veneered olive-wood casket, c.1660, initialled in pearls, *MG,* worked on an ivory satin ground with allegorical figures of Justice, Faith, Hope and Charity, the front panels depicting King Solomon and the Queen of Sheba, the casket containing mirror, glass bottles, inkwell, sifter and numerous hidden compartments, 42cm (16½in) high, *L 4 July,*
£41,800 ($67,298)

4
A George III embroidered linen sampler, c.1800, *worked by Sarah Baker, aged 11,* excellent condition, 50 x 41cm (19¾ x 16in), *L 22 July,*
£1,980 ($3,109)

1

2

3

4

1
A pieced calico and cotton Mennonite quilt, c.1920, Pennsylvania, the patches arranged in a variation of the Mariner's Compass pattern, 193 x 203cm (76 x 80in),
NY 25 Oct,
$4,125 (£2,925)

2
A pieced Mennonite all-wool crib quilt, Pennsylvania, late 19th century, the patches arranged in a Windmill-Blades pattern, 127 x 127cm (50 x 50in),
NY 25 Oct,
$4,125 (£2,925)

3
An American pictorial dalmatian hooked rug, Waldoboro, Maine, 1865-75, some minor fraying, 79 x 138cm (31 x 54½in),
NY 1 Feb,
$4,400 (£3,120)

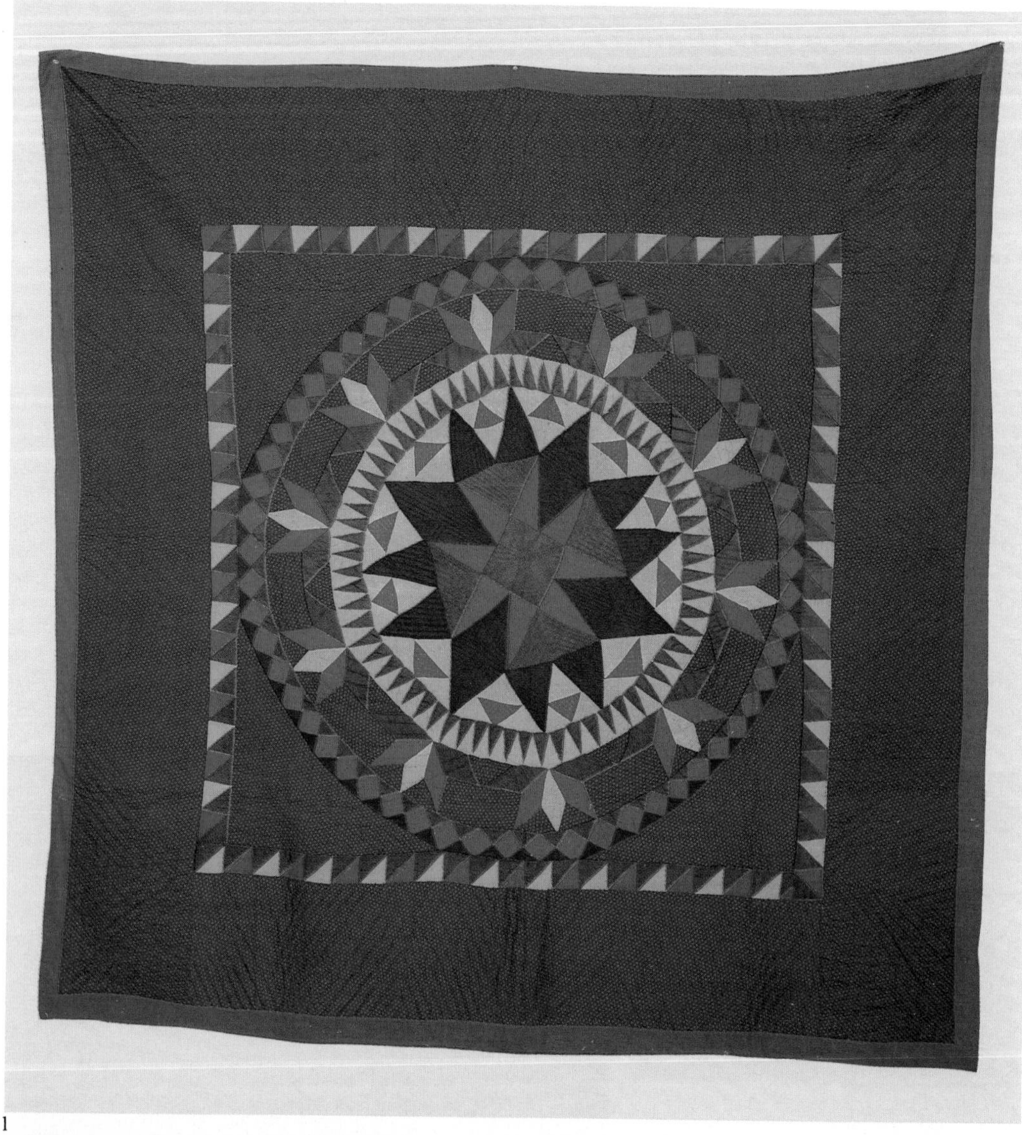

1

2

3

Textiles

Article:
American samplers *pp* 181-183
See also:
Colour illustrations *pp* 174-176
Chinese works of art *p* 689
Islamic works of art *p* 631
Oriental rugs and carpets *pp* 632-651
Main sub-sections:
American quilts *p* 188
Costume *pp* 184-185
English samplers *p* 180
European rugs and carpets *pp* 186-187

1
A Charles I silk embroidered picture, c.1640-50, within a moulded frame, 16 x 26.5cm (6¼ x 10½in), *L 22 July,*
£858 ($1,347)

2
A pair of English silk embroidered pictures of 'Christ and Woman of Sumaria' and 'Rebecca Offering Water to Abraham's Servant', (*one illustrated*), c.1700-30, several pin-sized holes, 21.5 x 24cm (8½ x 9½in), *L 23 Sept,*
£770 ($1,078)

3
A Charles I embroidered portrait of Queen Henrietta Maria, second half 17th century, two minute holes in satin ground, 18.5 x 22.5cm (7¼x 9in), *L 23 Sept,*
£1,980 ($2,772)

4
A Charles II circular beadwork panel, dated 1667, some beads detached along one border, 23.5cm (9¼in), *L 22 July,*
£770 ($1,209)

5
A Charles II beadwork basket, dated 1663, loose beads in several areas, padding revealed on leopard and lion, 61.5cm (24¼in), *L 4 July,*
£9,900 ($15,939)

6
A Charles I embroidered silk and silver thread tent-stitched picture, dated 1648, signed and dated in the top border *Alice Carter 1648,* 29 x 36cm (11¾ x 14¼in), *L 4 July,*
£1,100 ($1,771)

7
A Charles II silk embroidered picture, c.1660, on ivory satin ground, some splits, 23 x 35.5cm (9 x 14in), *L 4 July,*
£715 ($1,151)

8
A Charles II embroidered stumpwork mirror surround, c.1660, on ivory satin ground, mirror and carved wood mirror surround probably early 19th century, repairs, 42 x 36cm (16½ x 14in), *L 23 Sept,*
£2,860 ($4,004)

9
An English embroidered stumpwork picture, mid 17th century, crease and split to lower left-hand corner, 30.5 x 43cm (12 x 16¾in), *L 22 July,*
£2,200 ($3,454)

10
A Commonwealth tent-stitched picture, mid 17th century, depicting the expulsion of Hagar and Ishmael, tortoiseshell frame, 24 x 32cm (9½ x 12½in), *L 4 July,*
£2,640 ($4,250)

11
An English beadwork picture, 17th century, within marble and mother-of-pearl inlaid Renaissance frame, 25.5 x 14cm (10 x 5½in), *NY 25 Nov,*
$1,650 (£1,179)

12
A Charles I embroidered Bible cover, mid 17th century, depicting the Virgin and Child and the temptation of Eve, 16.5 x 26cm (6½ x 10¼in), *L 23 Sept,*
£3,080 ($4,312)

1

2

3

4

5

6

7

8

9

10

11

12

1

2

3

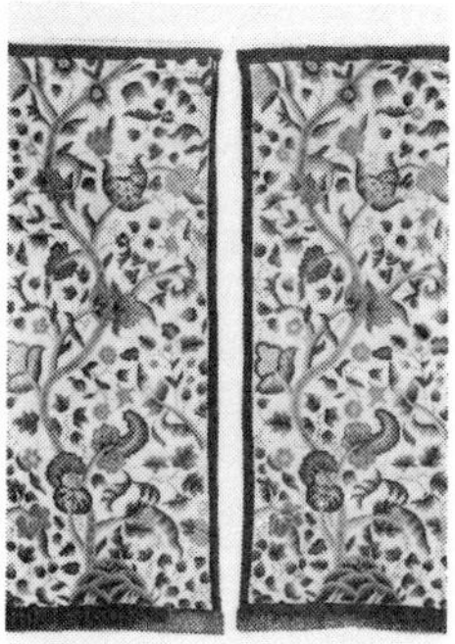
4

5

6

7

8

9

10

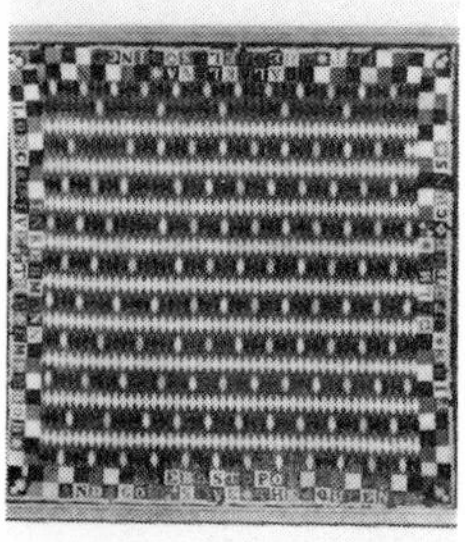
11

12

1
An Italian petit-point embroidery of a hunter in 16th century dress, 19th century, 18 x 13cm (7¼ x 5¼in), *S 21 Jan,*
£462 ($693)

2
An English needlework panel, 17th century, depicting the sacrifice of Isaac, 35 x 43cm (13¾ x 17in), *NY 25 Nov,*
$1,760 (£1,257)

3
A pair of crewelworked curtains, (*part illustrated*), 18th century, the linen ground worn and re-paired in several places, the whole re-mounted onto sturdy linen coloured lining, 230 x 173cm, 224 x 173cm (90½ x 68in, 88 x 68in), *L 22 July,*
£2,860 ($4,490)

4
A pair of English embroidered curtains, late 17th-early 18th century, some damage to backing, colours excellent, 204 x 81cm (80 x 32in), *S 27 May,*
£935 ($1,496)

5
An Italian embroidered silk four-fold screen, *(part illustrated)*, late 18th century, *L 20 May,*
£440 ($704)

6
An applique-work coverlet, *(part illustrated)*, late 18th century, probably Portuguese, some splits, 244 x 262cm (94 x 103in), *L 5 Feb,*
£330 ($475)

7
A pair of crewelwork cushions, probably early 20th century, 56 x 56cm (22 x 22in), *C 9 July,*
£418 ($673)

8
An American floral hooked rug, c.1885, New England, some small repairs to the edges, 211 x 364cm (8ft 3in x 10ft 2in), *NY 26 June,*
$2,200 (£1,457)

9
An American wool embroidered panel, datec 1876, Reading, Pennsylvania, initialled *MED*, some repairs and imperfections, 59 x 68.5cm (23¼ x 27in), *NY 26 June,*
$2,090 (£1,384)

10
An American yarn sewn hearth rug, dated 1824, initialled *P.S.*, Vermont, some minor repair, 54 x 188cm (21¼ x 74¼in), *NY 25 Oct,*
$25,300 (£17,943)

11
An English Crimean War patchwork horse blanket, mid 19th century, composed of black, gold and scarlet wool patches from soldiers' uniforms, 142 x 142cm (56 x 56in), *L 22 July,*
£880 ($1,382)

12
A North Italian purple silk altar frontal, first half 18th century, probably Venetian, 97 x 208cm (38 x 82in), *NY 25 Nov,*
$1,650 (£1,179)

1
An American silk embroidered picture, c.1800, Sally Phelps, (b.1787) Litchfield, Connecticut, in an oval black glass mat and original frame, small crack, 58.5 x 49cm (23 x 19¼in), *NY 26 June,*
$9,900 (£6,556)

2
A George I embroidered picture, dated 1728, Anne Henchman, annotated 'Proud Jezebel doth fall to dogs for taking Naboth's guiltless life away', 19 x 18cm (7½ x 7in), *L 5 Feb,*
£1,430 ($2,059)

3
An English silk embroidered picture of a shepherd and shepherdess, first half 18th century, walnut frame, 22 x 35cm (8¾ x 13¾in), *L 23 Sept,*
£1,045 ($1,463)

4
A set of twelve embroidered drawer fronts, (*two illustrated*), early 18th century, probably Dutch or Flemish, ten 11.5 x 35cm (4¼ x 13¾in); two 12 x 37.5cm (4¾ x 14¾in), *L 4 July,*
£1,980 ($3,188)

5
A pair of George Smart collage pictures, c.1830, English, comprising the Postman of Frant and the Goose Woman, some moth damage, satinwood frames, 27 x 21.5cm (10¾ x 8½in), *L 22 July,*
£1,650 ($2,590)

6
A lace tablecover and twelve napkins, *(part illustrated)*, probably early 20th century, Continental, 239 x 165cm (94 x 61in), *NY 25 Nov,*
$2,750 (£1,964)

7
A silk and coarse linen picture, late 18th century, 22.5 x 18cm (8¾ x 7in), *C 17 Apr,*
£83 ($128)

8
A George III silkworked picture, c.1815, 36.5 x 36.5cm (14¼ x 14¼in), *C 17 Apr,*
£330 ($512)

9
A patchwork cover, *(part illustrated)*, late 19th century, unbacked, in excellent condition, 170 x 194cm (67 x 76in), *C 14 Feb,*
£286 ($423)

10
An Irish patchwork quilt, late 19th century, 208 x 230cm (82 x 90½in), *L 20 May,*
£352 ($563)

1

2

3

4

5

6

7

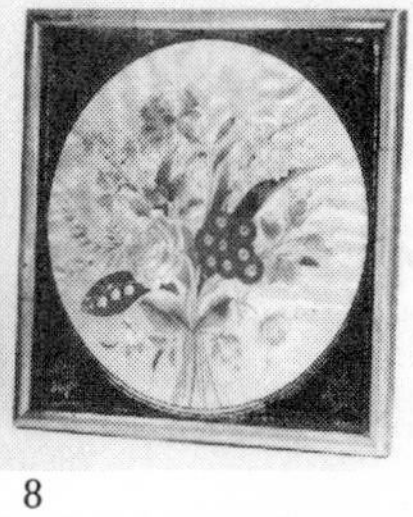
8

9

10

1

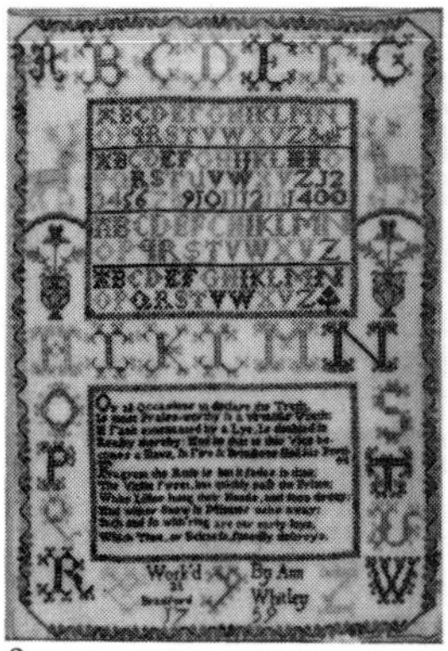
2

3

4

5

6

7

8

9

10

11

1
A linen worked sampler, English, 1828, by Anne Milne, with a country house in a park and a verse, 42 x 33cm (16½ x 13in), *C 17 Apr,*
£858 ($1,330)

2
An embroidered linen sampler, English, 1759, by Ann Whitley, brightly worked in silks with alphabet and numeral tests, 31 x 22cm (12 x 8¾in), *L 20 May,*
£770 ($1,232)

3
An embroidered sampler, English, 1813, by Sarah Titchmarsh *in the ninth year of her age*, worked with nativity motifs and an extract of *When Shepherds Watched Their Flocks By Night*, glue stains, 48.5 x 33cm (19¼ x 13in), *S 9 Dec,*
£528 ($739)

4
An embroidered sampler, English, 1801, by Elizabeth Harry, worked with stag hunt and forest scenes, some wear, 54 x 43cm (21½ x 17½in), *S 9 Dec,*
£286 ($400)

5
A long embroidered sampler, English, 1710, initialled *E.G.*, worked in multi-coloured silks with flowers and religious text, very good condition, *S 9 Dec,*
£1,705 ($2,387)

6
An embroidered sampler, English, 1822, by Lisa Prentice, worked with a house and a parrot surrounded by animals and flowering plants, 37 x 30cm (14½ x 11¾in), *S 9 Dec,*
£550 ($770)

7
An embroidered cross-stitch sampler, English, 1798, by Jean Ormant, worked in muted pink, green and yellow with part of the alphabet, houses, trees and a verse, worn, 33 x 30cm (13 x 11¾in), *JHB 1 Dec,*
R 1,200 (£387; $542)

8
An embroidered linen sampler, English, 1711, by Grace Fowle, worked in blue, green, cream and red with alphabet and numeral tests, 'boxers' and border tests, 47 x 21cm (18½ x 8¼in), *L 22 July,*
£935 ($1,468)

9
An embroidered sampler English, 1793, by Salley Willett, aged 9, worked with text flanked by animal and flower designs above a basket of flowers, small holes, 35 x 33cm (13¾ x 13in), *S 9 Dec,*
£704 ($985)

10
An embroidered linen sampler, English, mid 19th century, worked with a brown woollen house bordered by birds and blooms and a religious verse, and annotated with the names of the Bell family, 43cm (17in) square, *L 22 July,*
£550 ($864)

11
An embroidered sampler English, 1838, by Caroline Mulcock, age 11, worked in 18th century style with a stag, birds, butterflies and two verses, 41.5 x 32cm (16¼ x 12½in), *L 22 July,*
£440 ($691)

American Samplers

NANCY DRUCKMAN

'May spotless innocence and truth,
My every action guide,
And guard my unexperienced youth,
From arrogance and pride.'

The pious and modest sentiment expressed in this verse, which the eleven-year old Eliza Waterman of Providence, Rhode Island stitched on her sampler in 1788 seems very much at odds with the fevered contest that its sale ignited in January 1987, when it established a new world record for an American sampler of $192,000 (£120,000). This high price reflects levels achieved by first-quality works, where prices in the six-figure level are now routine. Despite the sampler's small scale, relative perishability and child-like execution, there are few other categories of American folk art that command the same sort of prices. However it is a field in which the scale of values is very wide. The finest examples may only be accessible to a few wealthy buyers, but there are many samplers of great charm which are still available for the collector of more modest means.

During the late 17th, 18th and 19th centuries, samplers were made by young girls attending schools which offered a curriculum of a variety of the usual subjects — reading, writing, languages, deportment, music and dancing, as well as intensive instruction in needlework. Proficiency in needlework was not only a necessity but an important mark of social accomplishment and artistic expression. The young student worked her sampler under the watchful eye and strict supervision of her instructress. The sampler was so named because it was an 'exemplar' of the repertoire of stitches and embroideries that the child was learning to master. Once having achieved skill in the execution of the sampler, the young girl would go on to more elaborate pictorial works made from more costly silks and satins. The compositions of the samplers were almost invariably to a formula developed by the teacher. The individuality and spontanaiety that exist in the works result from the varying degree of talent, technical mastery and inspiration of the particular student.

While samplers are unique artefacts usually signed and dated by their makers, often stating their place of origin, or readily attributable to that place by the repetition of identifiable regional characteristics linking various schools to a given place, it is primarily the look and charm of these pieces that makes one more desirable and highly sought after than another. As in most categories of American folk art, (a field that encompasses such diverse objects as paintings, quilts, weathervanes, duck decoys and scrimshaw — see pp.154-160), it is the strength of the design, the vibrancy of the colours, the vitality of the patterns, the impact and visual appeal, which is of over-riding importance to the collector today. These qualities are affected by the age, condition, rarity, historical significance and provenance of the sampler, which in turn influence their value.

The initiation of samplers into the ranks of the most desirable categories of American folk art began in January 1974 with the first of eight sales offering the folk art collection of Colonel Edgar William and Bernice Chrysler Garbisch. At that time the collection contained in excess of 3,500 objects and the Garbisches decided to concentrate their energies on naive painting and to sell

1

2

1
A needlework sampler, Mary Hofecers, Pennsylvania, dated 1798, in green, blue, red, yellow, pink and white silk on a linen ground, 53 × 51cm (21 × 20in), *NY 26 June,* **$2,530 (£1,675)**

2
A needlework sampler, Abigail H. Cook, aged 11, Newburyport, November 1827, executed in blue, green, pink and yellow silk on a linen ground, 44.5 × 42cm (17½ × 16½in), *NY 25 Oct,* **$4,180 (£2,965)**

the folk art at auction. The excellence, rarity, variety and superb condition of most of the pieces, enhanced by the Garbisch name, ensured resoundingly successful sales. The knowledge that most pieces of similar quality had long-since disappeared from the market-place served to focus collectors' attention on folk art and establish it as an important collecting category. In that first sale, a world record was established for an 18th century sampler stitched in Boston with the figures of Adam and Eve and the serpent, which fetched $3,250 (£1,354). In successive Garbisch sales, from 1975 to 1980, samplers and other needlework and textiles continued to bring the highest prices.

It was, however, the sale of the collection of American samplers belonging to the Philadelphia businessman, the late Theodore H. Kapnek Snr, in January 1981, that really laid the groundwork for the explosion of interest in this field. The highest price in the sale was for an 1830 sampler of a twelve-year old Berks County girl, Matilda Filbert, which brought an astounding $41,000 (£19,806). The composition, based on Edward Savage's well-known engraving of *The Goddess of Liberty offering sustenance to the Bald Eagle*, was given an unmistakable dose of Pennsylvania charm in the painted cut-out paper face, the out-size figure of the girl towering above the rooftop and trees and the large baskets of fruits and flowers in the upper corners. Other, more modestly priced, samplers from this sale are illustrated as figs 6-10.

The years since the the Kapnek sale have seen the most extraordinary appreciation in prices for samplers. Fig.3 illustrates an exquisite silk embroidered pictorial sampler of a townscene in New England. According to the family in which the piece had descended the piece was made by a nine-year old girl living in Newburyport, Massachusetts during the first decades of the 19th century. Originally estimated at $20,000 to $30,000, it brought $101,750 (£72,163) in January 1986. The following October, a

3

4

3
A needlework pictorial sampler, probably Newburyport, Massachusetts, late 18th/early 19th century, in green, blue, white, pink, yellow and brown silk on a linen ground, 41 x 44.5cm, (16¼ x 17½in), *NY 30 Jan/1 Feb,* **$101,750 (£72,163)**

4
A needlework sampler, Sarah Otilla Ann Carver, Pennsylvania, dated 1833, '...wrought in the 9th year of her age', in green, blue, yellow, rose and brown silk on a linen ground, 46 × 47.5cm (18 × 18¾in), *NY 25 Oct,* **$3,410 (£2,418)**

5

6

5
A 'black-background' needlework sampler, signed Mary Russell, Bristol, Rhode Island or Marblehead, Massachusetts, date 1791, worked with long silk stitches on a linen ground, *NY 25 Oct,* **$121,000 (£85,816)**

6
A needlework sampler, Catherine Heister (born 1772), Reading, Berks County, Pennsylvania, dated 1786, in pink, green, white and yellow silk on a linen ground, 55 × 43cm (21¾ × 17in), *NY 31 Jan 1981,* **$4,400 (£2,125)**

rare, black-background pictorial sampler from either Bristol, Rhode Island or Marblehead, Massachusetts, stitched by the thirteen-year old Mary Russell in the year 1791, brought $121,000 (£85,816), (fig.5).

The enormous popularity of samplers today is the result of their charm, the visual appeal of the pieces themselves and the fact that, unlike most other antique objects, they are social, educational and historical documents. Additionally, through the unflagging work and dedication of scholars in the field, there have been numerous books, journal and magazine articles and museum exhibitions, which have helped enormously in increasing knowledge and interest in these pieces.

Further reading:

Glee Krueger, *A Gallery of American Samplers, The Theodore H. Kapnek Collection*, 1978
Betty Ring, *Let Virtue Be a Guide to Thee: Needlework in the Education of Rhode Island Women, 1730-1830*, 1983
Betty Ring, 'Needlework, An Historical Survey', *The Magazine Antiques*, 1975
Ethel Stanwood Bolton and Eva Johnston Coe, *American Samplers*, 1921

7
A needlework sampler, Mary H. Garrett, Willistown, Chester County, Pennsylvania, dated 1820, in blue, green, white and brown silk on gauze, 55.5 × 70cm (21¾ × 27½in), *NY 31 Jan 1981*, **$2,750 (£1,328)**

8
A needlework sampler, Ann H. Vodges (born 1808), Chester County, Pennsylvania, dated 1823, in green, blue, yellow, brown and white silk on a linen ground, 64 × 58.5cm (25 × 23in), *NY 31 Jan 1981*, **$3,630 (£1,753)**

9
A needlework sampler, Sarah Harding, Philadelphia, dated 1741, in red, green, yellow and blue silk on a linen ground, 46 × 26cm (18 × 10¼in), *NY 31 Jan 1981*, **$8,525 (£4,118)**

10
A needlework sampler, Ann Amelia Matilda Borden (born 1825), probably New England, dated 1839, in red, green, orange, blue, gold and white silk and wool on a linen ground, 42 × 41.5cm (16½ × 16¼in), *NY 31 Jan 1981*, **$4,400 (£2,125)**

7

8

9

10

1

2

3

4

5

6

7

8

9

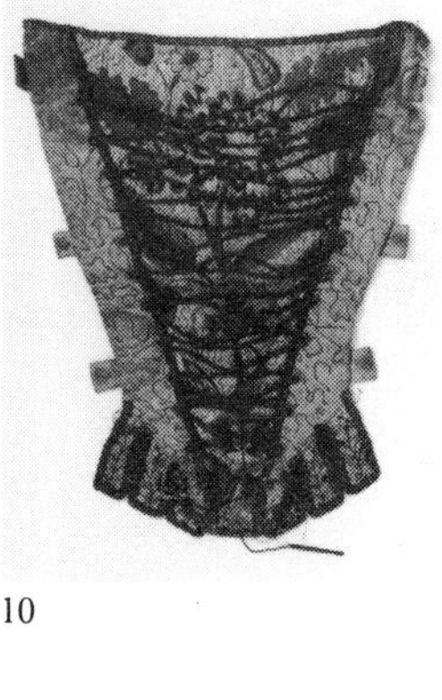
10

1
A bronze silk day dress, c.1835, repair and minor stains, *L 23 Sept,*
£935 ($1,309)

2
A striped woven silk day gown, c.1820, sleeves holed in several places, *L 23 Sept,*
£880 ($1,232)

3
A brown silk lady's pelisse, late 1820s, English, silk lining perished, otherwise good condition, *L 5 Feb,*
£605 ($871)

4
A white lawn morning dress, c.1820-25, with white cotton petticoat trimmed with cutwork, *L 20 May,*
£605 ($968)

5
A printed muslin gown, late 1790s, probably English, numerous holes, printed gauze trim added probably in the 1820s, *L 20 May,*
£550 ($880)

6
A gentleman's waistcoat, c.1740-60, applied with 19th century polished cotton sleeves and lace cuffs, two patches to one rear panel, *L 5 Feb,*
£935 ($1,346)

7
A pair of lady's brocaded silk shoes, c.1720s, silk split in several places, *L 5 Feb,*
£880 ($1,267)

8
A gentleman's undress embroidered velvet cap, early 18th century, probably English, *L 5 Feb,*
£1,760 ($2,534)

9
A pair of turquoise leather lady's shoes, late 1790s, slight damage, *L 23 Sept,*
£286 ($400)

10
An embroidered stomacher, c.1710-20, gold braid criss-cross stringing overlay, 26cm (10¼in) long, *L 23 Sept,*
£528 ($739)

1
A Handley-Seymour beaded evening gown, c.1930, English, labelled *Handley-Seymour, 47-48 New Bond St. London, L 23 Sept,*
£440 ($616)

2
A Jeanne Lanvin pale green and silver sequinned full-length evening gown, 1934-35, French, labelled *Jeanne Lanvin, Paris,* slight seam pull to centre back of bodice and halter strap, *L 20 May,*
£1,430 ($2,288)

3
A Jean Patou beaded crêpe-de-chine cocktail dress, c.1928, French, labelled *Jean Patou, 2 rue St. Florentin, Paris,* slight stains to under-arms, *L 20 May,*
£4,620 ($7,392)

4
A peach chiffon beaded cocktail dress, late 1920s, French, possibly by Patou, some splits to scallop hemline, *L 20 May,*
£2,200 ($3,520)

5
A Beer blue sequinned evening gown, c.1928, French, labelled *Beer, 7 Place Vendome,* petticoat silk frail, *L 20 May,*
£1,760 ($2,816)

6
A beige chiffon cocktail dress, late 1920s, French, slight pull to one shoulder seam, a few rust marks, *L 20 May,*
£990 ($1,584)

7
A cream silk and black chantilly lace two piece gown, late 1890s, English, by W. Jones & Co., Bridgnorth, together with a cream silk burnouse cape edged with black chantilly, and a black chantilly lace canopied carriage parasol, *L 5 Feb,*
£418 ($602)

8
A striped taffeta day dress and accessories, c.1845, *L 20 May,*
£528 ($845)

9
A Worth et Cie brocaded satin and velvet evening gown, c.1895, English, the skirt altered, *L 23 Sept,*
£770 ($1,078)

10
A linen day dress, c.1910, Irish, *L 23 Sept,*
£550 ($770)

11
A Fortuny Renaissance-style silk and velvet gown, Italian, c.1920, several beads missing, slight wear, *L 5 Feb,*
£2,860 ($4,118)

12
A black and white striped silk day dress, c.1865, one buttonhole worn, otherwise good condition, *L 20 May,*
£330 ($528)

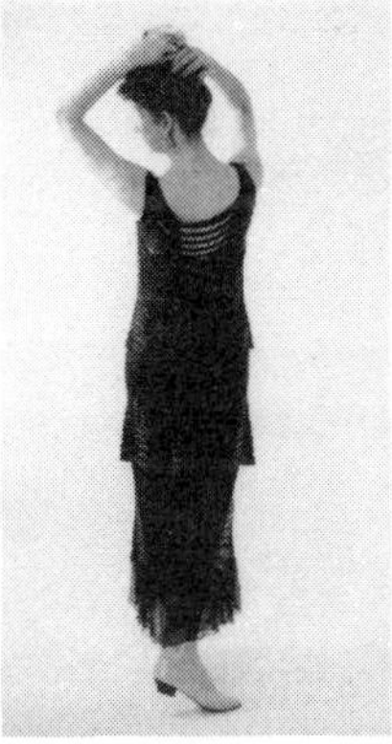
1

2

3 *(left)* 4 *(right)*

5

6

7

8

9

10

11

12

1

2

3

4

5

6

1
An Aubusson carpet, third quarter 19th century, minor stains, 685 x 401cm (22ft 3in x 13ft 2in), *NY 31 Oct,*
$17,600 (£12,482)

2
An Aubusson carpet, 556 x 456cm (18ft 3in x 15ft), *L 16 Apr,*
£7,920 ($12,276)

3
A silk Aubusson rug, c.1875, 224 x 180cm (7ft 4in x 5ft 11in), *NY 31 May,*
$4,400 (£2,993)

4
A Louis XV1-style Savonnerie carpet, 506 x 400cm (16ft 5in x 13ft 1in), *M 22 June,*
FF 188,700 (£16,833; $26,260)

5
An Aubusson carpet, 18th century, 394 x 333cm (12ft 11in x 10ft 11in), *L 15 Oct,*
£7,260 ($10,164)

6
An Aubusson carpet, last quarter 19th century, 589 x 290cm (19ft 4in x 9ft 6in), *NY 31 May,*
$9,900 (£6,735)

1
A Bessarabian rug, mid 19th century, signed lower left with altered date, reweaves, 196 x 180cm (6ft 5in x 5ft 11in), *NY 31 May,*
$5,060 (£3,442)

2
A Rya rug, c.1800, 205 x 150cm (6ft 9in x 4ft 11in), *L 12 Feb,*
£2,640 ($3,934)

3
A Bessarabian carpet, last quarter 19th century, restorations and rewoven areas, 572 x 450cm (18ft 9in x 14ft 9in), *NY 31 May,*
$41,250 (£28,061)

4
An English needlepoint rug, third quarter 19th century, 315 x 201cm (10ft 4in x 6ft 7in), *NY 7 June,*
$6,600 (£4,430)

5
A needlepoint carpet, 200 x 150cm (6ft 6½ x 4ft 11in), *M 25 Feb,*
FF 13,320 (£1,288; $1,932)

6
An English needlepoint rug, c.1875, minor repairs, 173 x 117cm (5ft 8in x 3ft 10in), *NY 7 June,*
$1,650 (£1,107)

7
An English needlepoint rug, late 19th century, 282 x 175cm (9ft 3in x 6ft 9in), *NY 7 June,*
$17,600 (£11,812)

8
An English needlepoint carpet, c.1875, 724 x 472cm (23ft 9in x 15ft 6in), *NY 7 June,*
$46,200 (£31,007)

1

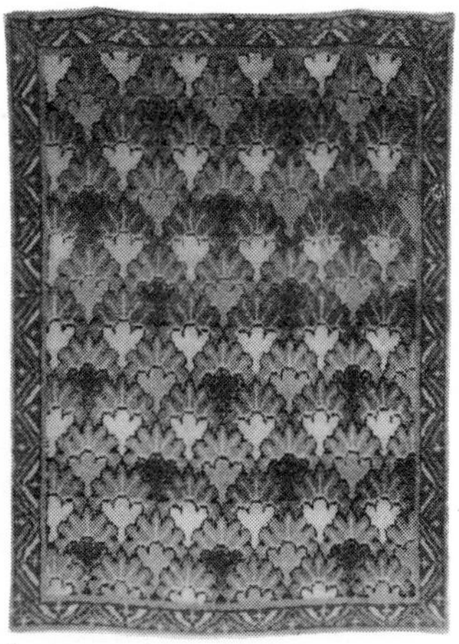
2

3

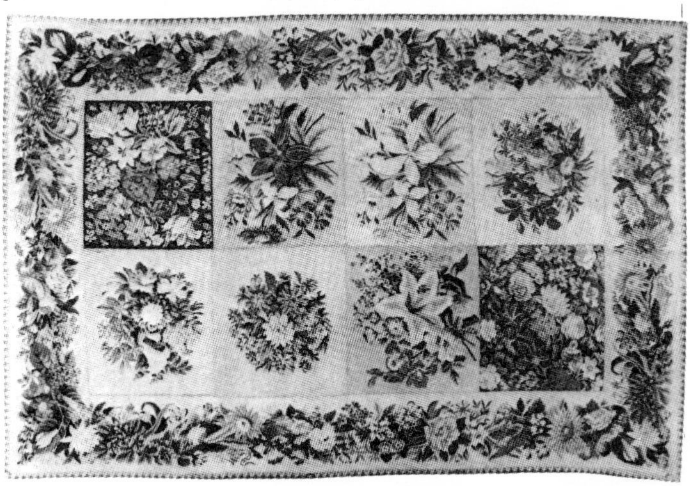
4

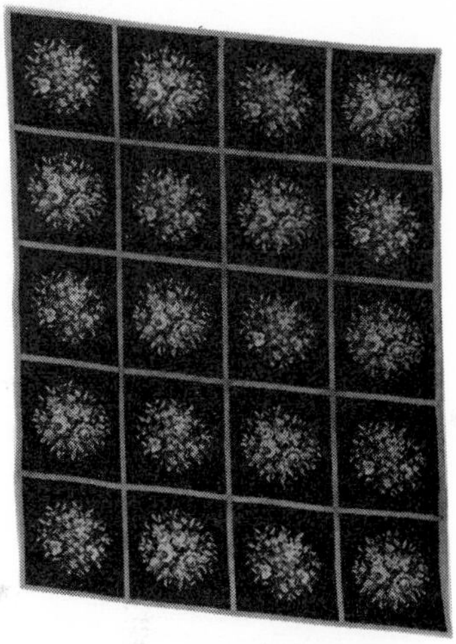
5

6

7

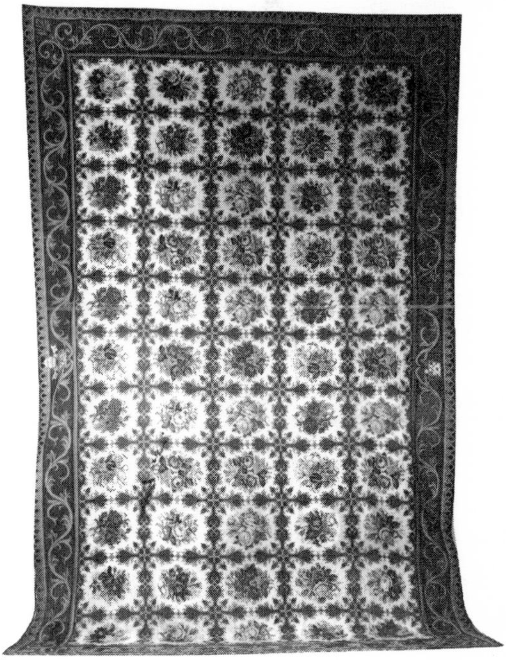
8

1

2

3

4

5

6

7

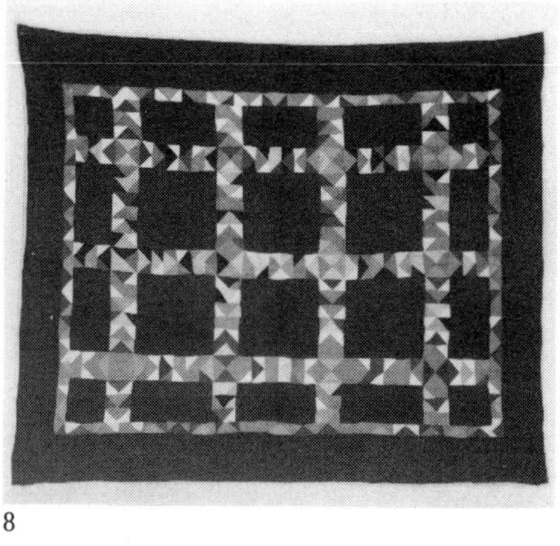
8

1
A President's Wreath pattern appliqued friendship quilt, dated 1859, American, some staining, approximately 264 x 259cm (102 x 104in), *L 22 July,*
£2,200 ($3,454)

2
A pieced and appliqued calico quilt, dated 1855, the upper border signed in embroidery *Martha Hewitt, Age 56, Michigan, 1855,* some fabric loss and stain, approximately 183 x 203cm (72 x 80in), *NY 1 Feb,*
$29,700 (£21,064)

3
A pieced and appliqued friendship quilt, c.1860, American, two joined hands inscribed *MD Coleman,* some stain and fabric loss, 173 x 175cm (68 x 69in), *NY 1 Feb,*
$2,970 (£2,106)

4
A pieced cotton and wool flannel Amish quilt, c.1925, Lagrange County, Indiana, arranged in a bowtie pattern, small hole, 183 x 203cm (72 x 80in), *NY 25 Oct,*
$4,125 (£2,926)

5
A pieced cotton Amish quilt, c.1920, Ohio, a variation of the oceanic waves pattern, some minor fading, 183 x 183cm (72 x 72in), *NY 25 Oct,*
$4,620 (£3,277)

6
A pieced calico and cotton sunburst quilt, dated 1860, signed *S.T. By Her Mother,* probably Pennsylvania, some minor fading, 206 x 206cm (81 x 81in), *NY 26 June,*
$1,320 (£874)

7
An appliqued calico and cotton crib quilt, dated 1860, probably Pennsylvania, with the inscription *Presented to J. Miller Merritt,* 91 x 89cm (30 x 35in), *NY 26 June,*
$1,430 (£947)

8
A pieced cotton Amish quilt, c.1920, Indiana, 142 x 193cm (56 x 76in), *NY 25 Oct,*
$4,070 (£2,887)

European Ceramics

Articles:

See also:

Main sub-sections:

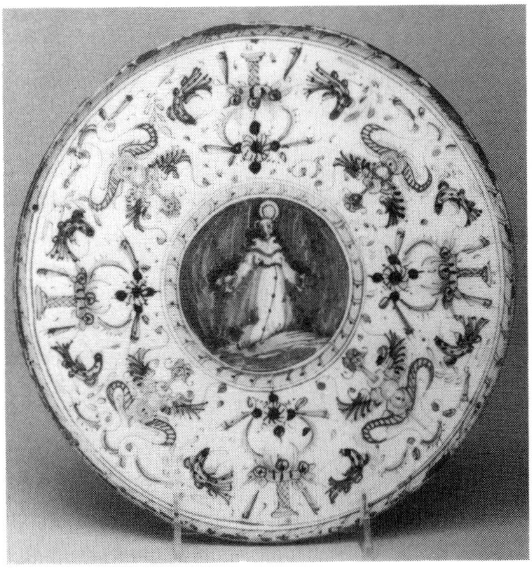
1

2

3

4

5

6

7

8

9

1
An Italian maiolica dish, first third 17th century, possibly Deruta, the central medallion painted with St. Francis kneeling, 25cm (9¾in), *NY 25 Nov,*
$880 (£629)

2
An Italian Deruta faience footed dish, c.1660, painted in yellow on brown, 24.5cm (9½in), *M 25 Feb,*
FF 4,400 (£429; $644)

3
A faenza crespina, mid 16th century, painted in green, blue, ochre and yellow, hair cracks, 28cm (11in), *L 4 Mar,*
£990 ($1,485)

4
An Urbino Istoriato plate, dated 1545, painted in the Fontana workshop, depicting the sirens luring Ulysses' men to their death, small cracks, 26cm (10¼in), *L 4 Mar,*
£5,720 ($8,580)

5
A pair of Castelli maiolica plates, *(one illustrated)*, early 18th century, 18.5cm (7¼in), *L 7 Oct,*
£2,310 ($3,234)

6
A sgraffiato dish, late 15th/early 16th century, probably Venetian, the decoration picked out in green and ochre, minor chips, 44.5cm (17½in), *L 17 June,*
£1,485 ($2,346)

7
A Venice Istoriato deep dish, c.1560, possibly the workshop of Domenico da Venezia, cracked, minor chips, 30.5cm (12in), *L 17 June,*
£2,750 ($4,345)

8
An Urbino Istoriato dish, second half 16th century, depicting Judith with Holofernes' head, restored, 25.5cm (10in), *L 4 Mar,*
£1,012 ($1,518)

9
An Italian maiolica plate, Casteldurante, first half 16th century, restored, 24cm (9½in), *F 14 Apr,*
L 3,800,000 (£1,556; $2,412)

1

2

3

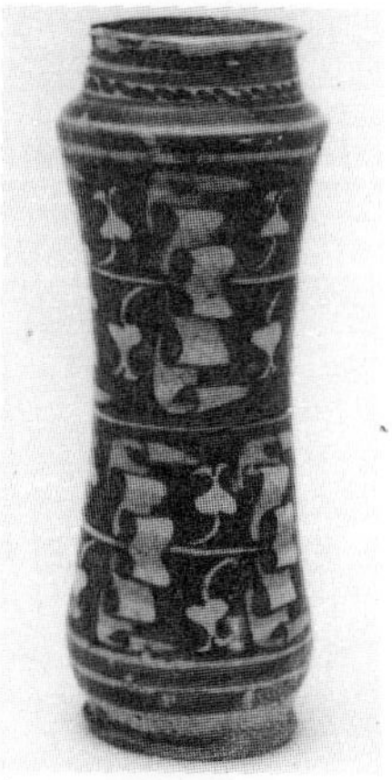
4

5

6

7

8

9

10

11

12

13

14

15

1
A Montelupo maiolica dish, early 17th century, painted in ochre, yellow, green and manganese, hair crack, 30.5cm (12in), *L 17 June,*
£880 ($1,390)

2
A Castilian maiolica dish, 17th century, Talavera or Puente del Arzobispo, with the addition of yellow and green to the usual palette, chipped, 34.5cm (13½in), *L 7 Oct,*
£2,090 ($2,926)

3
A Castilian maiolica dish, 17th century, Talavera or Puente del Arzobispo, outlined in manganese, chipped, 35cm (13¾in), *L 7 Oct,*
£1,760 ($2,464)

4
A pair of Trapani albarelli, *(one illustrated),* predominantly painted in cobalt blue, slightly chipped and cracked, 30.5cm (12in), *L 17 June,*
£1,045 ($1,651)

5
A Talavera jug, 17th century, in green, manganese, yellow and blue, chipped, 38cm (15in), *L 4 Mar,*
£605 ($907)

6
A Spanish lustre ware albarello, late 15th century, Manises, blue and gold on cream ground, 29cm (11½in), *NY 31 May,*
$13,200 (£8,979)

7
A Montelupo maiolica albarello, late 16th century, 21cm (8¼in), *F 30 Sept,*
L 19,800,000 (£9,865; $13,812)

8
A South Italian albarello, first half 17th century, painted in Venetian style, cracked, minor restoration to rim, 24cm (9½in), *L 4 Mar,*
£440 ($660)

9
A pair of Venice albarelli, *(one illustrated),* late 16th century, inscribed with the name of the drug, small chips, 22cm (8¾in), *L 7 Oct,*
£2,310 ($3,234)

10
A Faenza drug bottle, c.1725, with pharmacy mark, 25.5cm (10in), *L 7 Oct,*
£2,750 ($3,850)

11
A North Italian sgraffiato bottle, 17th century, Ferrara or Bologna, with roundels enclosing a bull (St. Luke) and a lion (St. Mark), chips and flakes, 20.5cm (8in), *L 7 Oct,*
£770 ($1,078)

12
A pair of South Italian maiolica albarelli, *(one illustrated),* inscribed in manganese with the name of the drug, 14.5cm (5½in), *L 7 Oct,*
£682 ($955)

13
A Venice maiolica jar, c.1530-40, cracked and repaired, 22cm (8½in), *L 17 June,*
£6,050 ($9,559)

14
A Venice maiolica drug jar, c.1570, cracked and chipped, some damage, 27cm (10¾in), *L 17 June,*
£990 ($1,564)

15
A Sicilian maiolica jar, dated 1617, the lip chipped, 31.5cm (12½in), *NY 31 May,*
$2,860 (£1,945)

1
A Creussen enamelled stoneware apostle tankard, second half 17th century, each of the 13 figures applied in relief, the colours in tones of blue, yellow, white, black, green and rust over brown, pewter foot, later rim and cover; sold with an imitation of another apostle tankard, 16.5cm (6in), *NY 25 Nov,*
$9,350 (£6,679)

2
A Westerwald stoneware tankard, c.1700, the sides moulded with a pattern of a vase and flowers, incised with hearts below, pewter lid, chips, 17cm (6¾in), *NY 31 May,*
$550 (£374)

3
A Frechen stoneware jug, c.1600, covered in a ferruginous 'tiger skin' glaze with blue splashes, with roundels bearing the coat of arms of Bavaria and the Pfalz, the neck with a medallion stamped with the arms of Jülich-Kleve-Berg, slight restoration, 44cm (17¼in), *L 17 June,*
£6,050 ($9,559)

4
An Austrian pewter-mounted jug, 18th century, probably Salzburg, decorated in blue with stylised flowers, minor chips, 21cm (8¼in), *L 7 Oct,*
£1,430 ($2,002)

5
A Freiberg pewter-mounted stoneware 'humpen', dated 1650, decorated with *Kerbschnitt* above a frieze of florets, an inscription on the rim, 19cm (7½in), *L 7 Oct,*
£3,960 ($5,544)

6
A Muskau 'tüllenkanne', second half 18th century, detailed in a brown-black glaze, contemporary pewter mounts, 14.5cm (5½in), *L 17 June,*
£660 ($1,043)

7
A Thüringian 'walzenkrug', second half 18th century, BPF, decorated with polychrome stylised flowers, pewter mounts, 26.5cm (10½in), *A 11 June,*
Dfl 2,300 (£689; $1,102)

8
A German pewter-mounted tankard with cover, 18th century, with green glazing, marked IR, 21cm (8½in), *A 11 June,*
Dfl 2,300 (£689; $1,102)

9
A stoneware bellarmine, 17th century, covered in a lustrous salt glaze and moulded with a bearded mask above a sunburst medallion, chip, 22cm (8¾in), *S 19 Mar,*
£187 ($286)

10
A Westerwald grey stoneware jug, c.1700, with the royal initials GR beneath crown, decorated in blue, the neck in manganese, 20.5cm (8¼in), *NY 31 May,*
$440 (£299)

11
A Raeren stoneware jug, c.1600, the brown-glazed body carved with a *Kerbschnitt* pattern, cracked, 18cm (7in), *L 17 June,*
£880 ($1,390)

12
A Waldenburg stoneware pewter-mounted 'schneppkanne', second quarter 17th century, applied with panels bearing the symbols of charity and the initials GK, the coat of arms of Meissen and another, 26.5cm (10½in), *L 7 Oct,*
£1,375 ($1,925)

13
A Rhenish stoneware jug, dated 1602, sprigged with seven coats of arms beneath titled torsos of their bearers, some wear, 27.5cm (10¾in), *S 16 July,*
£275 ($432)

14
A stoneware bellarmine, 17th century, covered in a brown salt glaze and moulded with a bearded mask above a medallion containing a coat of arms and two smaller whorled medallions, cracks, 38cm (15in), *S 19 Mar,*
£330 ($505)

1

2

3

4

5

6

7

8

11

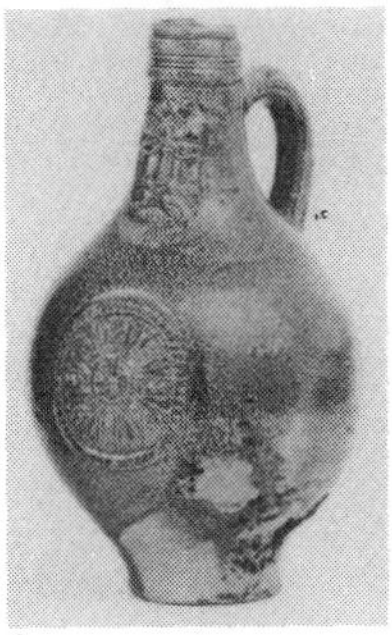
9

10

12

13

14

1

2

3

4

5

6

7

8

9

10

11

12

13

14

1
A Dutch Delft plate, 18th century, decorated in green, yellow and manganese on a turquoise ground, some flaking, 16.5cm (6½in), *A 14 Oct,*
Dfl 2,415 (£755; $1,132)

2
A Dutch Delft blue and white plate from the 'Herring Fishing' series, 't Fortuyn, c.1775, chips, mark in blue for Johan Herman Frerkingh, 23cm (9in), *NY 28 Jan,*
$1,100 (£785)

3
A Dutch Delft dish, c.1700, enamelled and gilt with the coat of arms of the 2nd or 3rd Earl of Burlington, cracks and chips, APK in iron-red for the Adriaen Pynacker factory, 21.5cm (8½in), *L 4 Mar,*
£990 ($1,485)

4
Nine Dutch Delft tiles, *(one illustrated)*, 18th century, decorated in blue on a light manganese ground with figures in a landscape, *A 23 Apr,*
Dfl 1,207 (£366; $574)

5
A Dutch Delft plaque, possibly c.1760, painted in blue with a fashionable couple strolling in an Italianate garden, the frame in polychrome enamel, WRC in manganese, 24.5cm (9¾in), *NY 28 Jan,*
$2,200 (£1,571)

6
A Dutch Delft tile, c.1700, decorated in manganese with a horseman, *A 23 Apr,*
Dfl 368 (£111; $174)

7
A Dutch Delft dish, c.1700, decorated with chinoiserie flowers, 35.5cm (14in), *A 14 Oct,*
Dfl 805 (£251; $377)

8
A Dutch Delft plaque, c.1760, painted in high temperature colours with a chinoiserie scene, minor chips, 38cm (15in), *L 17 June,*
£2,970 ($4,693)

9
A Dutch Delft tobacco jar, second quarter 18th century, painted in tones of blue with the arms of Amsterdam surrounded by parcels and jars of tea, tobacco and other India trade commodities, three bells mark in blue, 26.5cm (10¼in), *S 16 July,*
£770 ($1,209)

10
A pair of Dutch Delft blue and white vases and covers, *(one illustrated)*, c.1710, with ribbed octagonal bodies, some wear and chips, numeral 18 marks in blue, 42.5cm (16¾in), *NY 28 Jan,*
$2,310 (£1,650)

11
A pair of Dutch Delft figures of a lady and gentleman, probably De 3 Vergulde Astonnekens, c.1760, decorated in polychrome enamels, repairs and chip, 26 and 26.5cm (10¼ and 10½in), *NY 28 Jan,*
$1,980 (£1,414)

12
A Dutch Delft six-tile picture, 19th century, depicting a yellow canary in a blue birdcage, chips, 40.5cm (16in), *NY 28 Jan,*
$1,100 (£785)

13
A Dutch Delft bust of a classical maiden, 18th century, possibly allegorical of one of the Four Continents, decorated in polychrome enamels, repairs, 20cm (8in), *NY 28 Jan,*
$330 (£235)

14
A Dutch Delft six-tile picture, possibly Friesian, 19th century, decorated in manganese, blue, yellow and green, repairs, 40cm (15¾in), *NY 28 Jan,*
$3,740 (£2,671)

1
A Dutch Delft cruet set, late 18th century, decorated with chinoiserie scenes, 19cm (7½in), *A 14 Oct,*
Dfl 3,910 (£1,222; $1,833)

2
A Dutch Delft teakettle on stand, dated 1762, decorated with foliage, 23.5cm (9¼in), *A 14 Oct,*
Dfl 4,370 (£1,366; $2,048)

3
A pair of Dutch Delft tulip vases, 18th century, Roos factory, each in the shape of a pyramid constructed in three sections, each with four flower-spouts, decorated in blue, 42cm (16½in), *A 6 May,*
Dfl 16,675 (£5,053; $8,034)

4
A Dutch Delft pewter-mounted 'Enghalskrug', late 17th century, painted in 'trekked' cobalt blue in Chinese Transitional style, 26.5cm (10¼in), *L 7 Oct,*
£880 ($1,232)

5
A pair of Dutch Delft figures of seated hounds, *(one illustrated),* 18th century, decorated in yellow, green and black, the features in blue and red, chips, 12cm (4¾in), *L 7 Oct,*
£528 ($739)

6
A Dutch Delft blue and white tulip vase, De Grieksche A, c.1700, chips and repairs, AK monogram and numeral 12 in blue for Adriaen Kocks, 27cm (10½in), *NY 28 Jan,*
$2,090 (£1,492)

7
A Dutch Delft blue and white flower brick, c.1750, painted with chinoiserie scenes, 17cm (6¾in), *S 19 Mar,*
£440 ($673)

8
A Dutch Delft chamber pot, De Metalen Pot, 1700-20, painted in blue, green and iron-red, cracks, VE and other monogram marks, 21cm (8½in), *NY 28 Jan,*
$825 (£589)

9
A Dutch Delft condiment box, late 17th century, painted with chinoiserie scenes of flowers and birds, marked Adriaen Kocks (De Grieksche A), 30.5cm (12in), *A 14 Oct,*
Dfl 6,440 (£2,012; $3,018)

10
A Dutch Delft teapot and cover, c.1725, decorated in iron-red, green, manganese and yellow on a pale blue ground, 11.5cm (4½in), *NY 28 Jan,*
$825 (£589)

11
A Dutch Delft butter dish and cover, De Witte Starre, c.1764, the cover modelled as a yellow doe, ears restored, AK mark, 12.5cm (5in), *NY 28 Jan,*
$1,210 (£864)

12
A Dutch Delft Doré butter dish and cover, c.1740, painted in Kakiemon palette with chinoiserie scenes, numerals in iron-red, 12.5cm (5in), *NY 28 Jan,*
$1,760 (£1,257)

13
A Dutch Delft blue and white Royal portrait dish, c.1689, painted with half-length portraits of King William III and Queen Mary, minor cracks and chip, 33.5cm (13¼in), *NY 28 Jan,*
$2,970 (£2,121)

14
A Dutch Delft cuspidor, 18th century, decorated with figures in a landscape, flaking, 11cm (4¼in), *A 14 Oct,*
Dfl 2,185 (£683; $1,024)

15
A Dutch Delft blue and white dish, De 3 Vergulde Astonnekens, 1680-1700, painted in blue edged in black with a chinoiserie scene, GK monogram mark for Gerrit Pietersz Kam, 34.5cm (13½in), *NY 28 Jan,*
$275 (£196)

1

2

3

4

5

6

7

8

9

10

11

12

13

14

15

1

2

3

4

5

6

7

8

9

10

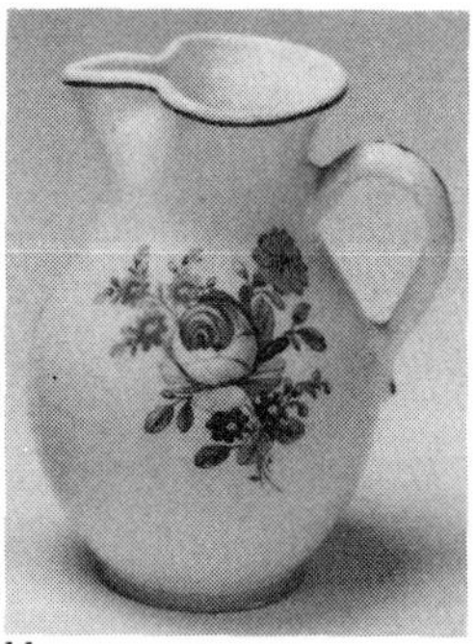
11

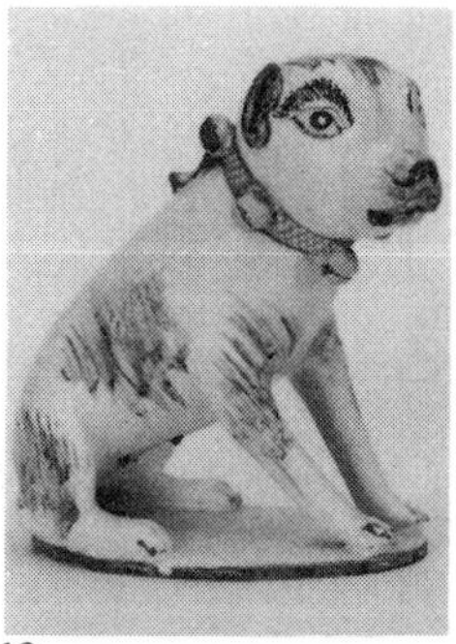
12

13

14

15

16

1
An Austro-Hungarian footed dish, 1675, painted in tones of yellow, green, blue and manganese, 20cm (8in), *L 7 Oct,*
£660 ($924)

2
A Frankfurt faience 'Fächerplatte', c.1700, painted in cobalt-blue with a chinoiserie scene, cracked, 41cm (16in), *L 4 Mar,*
£330 ($495)

3
A Hanau faience dish, early 18th century, painted in manganese and yellow with a chinoiserie roundel, painter's letter b (?) mark, cracks, 35.5cm (14in), *NY 9 Dec,*
$330 (£232)

4
A Nuremberg faience dish, c.1720, decorated in blue with a chinoiserie scene, crack and small restorations, 39.5cm (15½in), *L 4 Mar,*
£1,100 ($1,650)

5
A green glazed earthenware tile, possibly Austrian, third quarter 16th century, centred by a female profile bust, 25cm (10in), *NY 31 May,*
$1,320 (£898)

6
A Proskau faience bowl, c.1765, painted in high temperature colours, black rim, minor restoration, P in purple and black, 34cm (13¼in), *L 17 June,*
£1,210 ($1,912)

7
A Bayreuth faience 'Kinderhumpen', mid 18th century, painted in yellow, manganese, blue and green with a peacock among trees, chips, 8cm (3in), *L 17 June,*
£550 ($869)

8
An Erfurt faience pewter-mounted tankard, mid 18th century, decorated with two oriental figures conversing in a Chinese garden, K mark in manganese, minor crack, 21.5cm (8½in), *L 17 June,*
£495 ($782)

9
A South German faience tankard, mid 18th century, probably Künersberg, painted in blue, green and manganese, 07 in manganese, restored crack and flakes, 17cm (6¾in), *L 7 Oct,*
£1,375 ($1,925)

10
A Höchst faience tea caddy and a cover, c.1750, moulded in shallow relief with flowering stems in the manner of contemporary oriental textiles, painter's mark R, slight wear, 12cm (4½in), *L 17 June,*
£1,320 ($2,086)

11
A Holitsch faience jug, late 18th century, painted in colours, the spout and handle decorated in iron-red, H in black, 21.5cm (8½in), *L 7 Oct,*
£660 ($924)

12
A pair of South German faience figures of dogs, *(one illustrated),* second half 18th century, probably Offenbach, decorated in blue, yellow and manganese, minor chips, 14cm (5½in), *L 4 Mar,*
£2,640 ($3,960)

13
A South German blue and white 'Helmkanne', 1710-20, probably Ansbach, painted on either side in Chinese Transitional style, the foot bound in pewter, chipped, 19cm (7½in), *L 17 June,*
£3,135 ($4,953)

14
A Frankfurt faience jar, c.1700, painted in Chinese Transitional style, 33cm (13in), *S 19 Mar,*
£682 ($1,043)

15
A Crailsheim faience tureen and cover, c.1755, modelled after a Höchst original, painted in colours, minor crack, 33cm (13in), *L 4 Mar,*
£1,100 ($1,650)

16
An Ansbach faience five-finger vase, second quarter 18th century, painted in blue, the foot bound in pewter, minor chips, 21.5cm (8½in), *L 17 June,*
£1,078 ($1,703)

1
A Moustiers faience platter, d'Olérys workshop, 18th century, decorated in yellow, 38cm (15in), *M 25 Feb,*
FF 5,328 (£515; $773)

2
A Moustiers faience teapot, d'Olérys workshop, 18th century, decorated in green with grotesque figures and flowers, some restoration, 13.5cm (5¼in), *M 25 Feb,*
FF 11,100 (£1,074; $1,610)

3
A Strasbourg faience dish, c.1765, decorated in *petit-feu* enamels, brown-edged rim, slight chips, numerals in blue and brown, 30cm (11¾in), *L 17 June,*
£1,650 ($2,607)

4
A Lyon faience dish, 18th century, decorated in polychrome in the style of the d'Olérys workshop at Moustiers, 25.5cm (10in), *M 25 Feb,*
FF 8,880 (£859; $1,288)

5
Four Marseille faience plates, *(two illustrated),* Gaspar Joseph Robert workshop, 18th century, decorated in polychrome, 25cm (9¾in), *M 25 Feb,*
FF 17,760 (£1,718; $2,576)

6
Two Strasbourg faience plates, *(one illustrated),* c.1765, painted in *petit-feu* enamels, the rims edged in brown, slight chip, numerals in blue and brown, 24.5cm (9½in), *L 17 June,*
£1,650 ($2,607)

7
A Niderviller faience tureen and cover, c.1765, painted in pink, bue, yellow and green, the rims edged in iron-red, the knop formed of two peaches, wear and repairs, 25.5cm (10in), *NY 9 Dec,*
$990 (£697)

8
A Moustiers faience fountain and cover, Clérissy workshop, late 17th century, decorated in blue, restorations, 60cm (23½in), *M 25 Feb,*
FF 55,500 (£5,368; $8,051)

9
A Strasbourg faience lettuce tureen and cover, Paul Hannong, c.1755, with green leaves ribbed and veined in yellow, some wear, 36cm (14in), *NY 9 Dec,*
$41,800 (£29,437)

10
A Mettlach vase, 1885, decorated with two panels of amorous cherubs against a brown ground, 49cm (19¼in), *L 20 Mar,*
£605 ($950)

11
A Mettlach stoneware tankard, inscribed to the body with figures at revelry, between inscriptions, metal mounts, 20cm (8in), *C 2 Dec,*
£264 ($370)

12
A Mettlach stoneware ewer, 1884, decorated in a subdued palette, central frieze of grotesques, 43cm (17in), *L 20 Mar,*
£418 ($656)

13
A French faience model of a seated bulldog, c.1900, minor chips, 33cm (13in), *S 16 July,*
£374 ($587)

14
A French jardinière and stand, Clement Massier, c.1890, decorated overall with a petrol-green glaze, repairs, impressed mark, 120.5cm (47½in), *L 20 Mar,*
£550 ($863)

15
A pair of Mettlach stoneware vases, *(one illustrated),* late 19th century, incised with panels of cherubs, 36cm (14in), *C 15 Jan,*
£275 ($413)

1

2

3

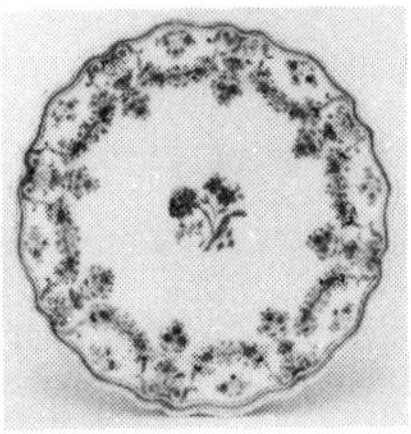
4

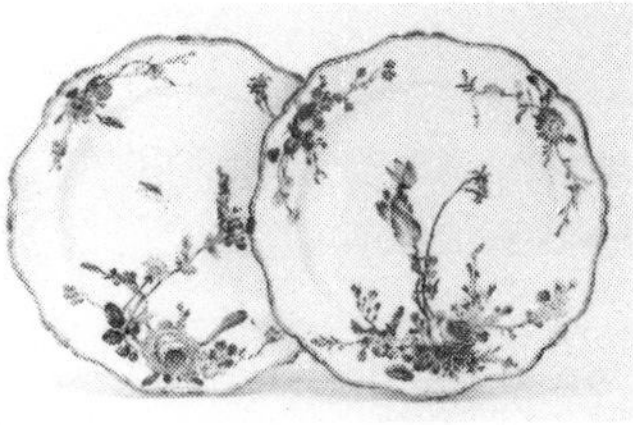
5

6

7

8

9

10

11

12

13

14

15

1

2

3

4

5

6

7

8

9

1
A set of six Meissen plates, *(one illustrated),* c.1735-40, painted in Kakiemon style with the 'Fliegender Hund' pattern, crossed swords in underglaze-blue, impressed E, some wear, 23cm (9in), *L 4 Mar,*
£2,310 ($3,465)

2
A Meissen armorial teabowl and saucer, c.1735, painted with the coat of arms of Mauro d'Avero of Naples, gilding rubbed, crossed swords in underglaze-blue, 13cm (5in), *L 4 Mar,*
£2,750 ($4,125)

3
A pair of Meissen soup plates, c.1740, gilt-edged rims, gilding rubbed, crossed swords in underglaze-blue, impressed numerals, 22cm (8½in), *L 4 Mar,*
£1,265 ($1,897)

4
A Böttger tankard, 1715-20, early 19th century silver mounts, the silver cover Vienna 1732, 17cm (8½in), *NY 9 Dec,*
$3,025 (£2,127)

5
A Meissen ornithological plate, c.1750, the gilt edge worn, crossed swords mark in underglaze-blue, impressed numeral and the former's mark for Muller, 24cm (9½in), *NY 9 Dec,*
$550 (£387)

6
A Meissen coffee pot and cover, c.1750, crossed swords mark in underglaze-blue and incised N or Z, minor chips, 23.5cm (9¼in), *NY 9 Dec,*
$1,210 (£852)

7
A Meissen 'Hausmaler' bowl, c.1755, painted by F. Mayer von Pressnitz, in *Schwarzlot,* iron-red and yellow within gilt *Bandelwerk* border, crossed swords in underglaze-blue, impressed 6, *L 4 Mar,*
£1,100 ($1,650)

8
A Meissen 'Hausmaler' slopbowl, c.1765, painted by F.J. Ferner, crossed swords and dot in underglaze-blue, impressed 3, 17cm (6¾in), *L 4 Mar,*
£1,650 ($2,475)

9
A Meissen tureen and cover, c.1765, crossed swords and dot in underglaze-blue, 38.5cm (15in), *L 4 Mar,*
£2,090 ($3,135)

1
A Meissen ewer and basin, c.1730, enamelled in Kakiemon palette, in the manner of Kangxi export ware, restoration to ewer, crossed swords in underglaze-blue, 28cm (11in), *L 17 June,*
£2,530 ($3,997)

2
A Meissen plate, 1736-40, from the Swan service by J.J. Kändler and C.F. Eberlein, with the coat of arms of Graf Heinrich v. Brühl, crossed swords in underglaze-blue, incised marks, 30.5cm (12in), *L 17 June,*
£11,000 ($17,380)

3
A Böttger Augsburg-decorated saucer, c.1730, probably from the Aufenwerth workshop, painted in purple *camaieu* within a gilt *Laub- und Bandelwerk* framework, flaked, incised mark, *L 17 June,*
£385 ($608)

4
A Meissen chinoiserie teabowl and saucer, 1740-45, colourfully painted with a gilt border, crossed swords in underglaze-blue, cup 8cm (3in) diam., *NY 9 Dec,*
$2,200 (£1,549)

5
A Meissen turquoise-ground cream pot and cover, c.1735, heightened with gilding, some wear and touching up, crossed swords in underglaze-blue, gilder's mark Z, 11.5cm (4½in), *NY 9 Dec,*
$2,310 (£1,627)

6
A Meissen yellow-ground hot water jug and cover, 1735-40, painted in puce *camaieu* with shipping scenes, crossed swords in underglaze-blue, painter's mark IZ, former's mark for Rehschuck, 18cm (7in), *L 17 June,*
£1,540 ($2,433)

7
A Meissen spoontray, c.1740, probably painted by Ch. F. Herold, crossed swords in underglaze-blue and numerals, 15.5cm (6in), *L 17 June,*
£770 ($1,217)

8
A Meissen 'chocolatière', c.1740, probably painted by Ch. F. Herold, crossed swords in underglaze-blue, 16.5cm (6½in), *L 17 June,*
£2,200 ($3,476)

9
A Meissen rectangular tea caddy and cover, c.1740, painted in shades of iron-red, puce, brown, green, yellow and blue, within gilt-banded edges, crossed swords in underglaze-blue and numerals, 12.5cm (5in), *NY 9 Dec,*
$2,530 (£1,782)

10
A Meissen part tea and coffee service, 1740-45, comprising 12 pieces *(part illustrated)*, probably painted after engravings by Georg Philipp Rugendas, some restoration, crossed swords in underglaze-blue, gilder's mark 66, impressed and incised marks, *L 17 June,*
£4,950 ($7,821)

11
A Meissen 'Hausmaler' hot milk jug and cover, mid 18th century, in the manner of F. J. Ferner, chipped, crossed swords and Q in underglaze-blue, 16.5cm (6½in), *L 7 Oct,*
£902 ($1,263)

12
A Meissen 'Hausmaler' sugar bowl and cover, mid 18th century, from the Ferner workshop, iron-red trellis and gilt borders, crossed swords and W in underglaze-blue, 13cm (5in), *L 7 Oct,*
£968 ($1,355)

13
A Marcolini Meissen caddy and cover, late 18th/early 19th century, painted with a German town scene, blue and gilt trellis rim, cover restored, crossed swords and star in underglaze-blue, 13cm (5in), *S 16 July,*
£418 ($656)

14
A Marcolini Meissen covered cup, c.1800, crossed swords and star mark in underglaze-blue, 17cm (6¾in), *Mel 24 June,*
Aus$440 (£191; $298)

1

2

3

4 5

6

7 8

9

10

11

12

13

14

1

2

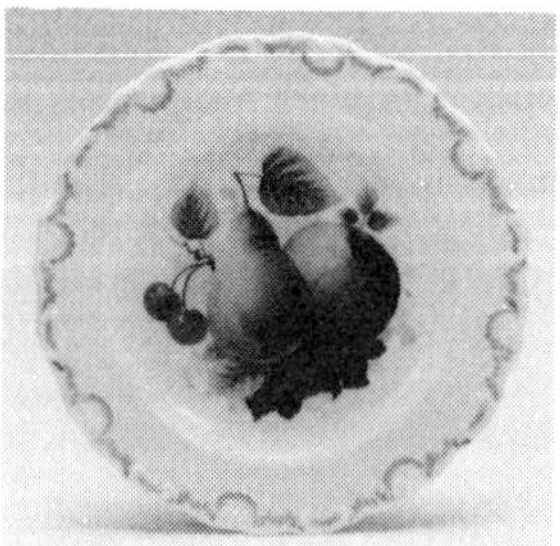
3

4

5

6

7

8

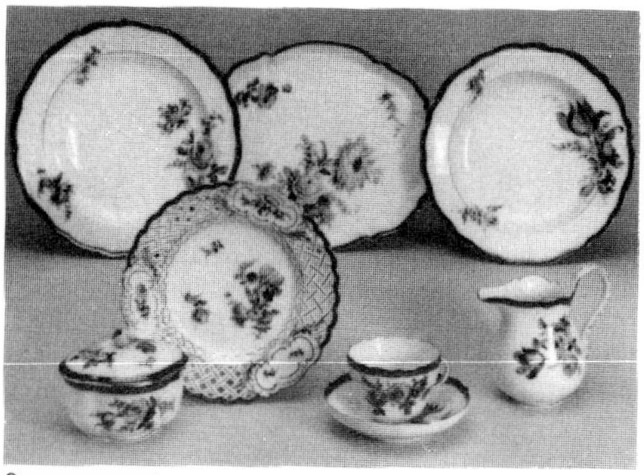
9

10

11

12

1
A Meissen part table service, *(one illustrated)*, modelled by Altbrandenstein, comprising 37 pieces, crossed swords in blue, impressed and incised marks, *M 1 Dec,*
FF 7,700 (£837; $1,197)

2
A Meissen vase and cover, third quarter 19th century, minor chips, crossed swords in underglaze-blue, 28cm (11in), *L 6 Nov,*
£968 ($1,374)

3
A set of ten Meissen dessert plates, *(one illustrated)*, mid 19th century, heightened in blue with gilt details, slight wear, hair cracks, crossed swords in underglaze-blue, 21.5cm (8½in), *L 6 Nov,*
£1,320 ($1,874)

4
A Meissen 'Schneeballen' vase and cover, mid 19th century, chips and cracks, crossed swords in underglaze blue, incised 2773, 84cm (33in), *L 6 Nov,*
£3,850 ($5,467)

5
A Meissen ewer, late 19th century, some damage and pieces missing, crossed swords in blue, 66cm (26in), *C 9 July,*
£990 ($1,544)

6
A pair of Meissen 'Blue Onion' pattern four-light candelabra, late 19th century, crossed sword marks in underglaze-blue, incised 2618, 42cm (16½in), *NY 13 Sept,*
$990 (£673)

7
A pair of Meissen centrepieces, second half 19th century, crossed swords in underglaze-blue, impressed and incised numerals, 30.5cm (12in), *S 10 Dec,*
£1,595 ($2,233)

8
A Meissen tureen and cover, mid 19th century, after an original model by J.J. Kändler, richly gilt, knop detached, crossed swords in underglaze-blue, 18cm (7in), *L 12 June,*
£2,640 ($4,224)

9
A Meissen dinner servic
(part illustrated), c.1880, comprising 138 pieces, crossed swords in underglaze-blue, impressed numerals, *L 6 Nov,*
£9,020 ($12,808)

10
A Meissen 'named view' bowl and cover, third quarter 19th century, painted with two views of Dresden, crossed swords in underglaze-blue, painted titles, 11.5cm (4½in), *L 6 Nov,*
£902 ($1,280)

11
A Meissen 'onion' patter service, *(part illustrated)*, third quarter 19th century, comprising 62 pieces, chips, crossed swords in underglaze-blue, 25cm (9¾in), *L 6 Nov*
£2,860 ($4,061)

12
A Meissen clock case, third quarter 19th century, crossed swords in underglaze-blue, incised M68, 39cm (15¼in), *L 20 Mar,*
£1,540 ($2,418)

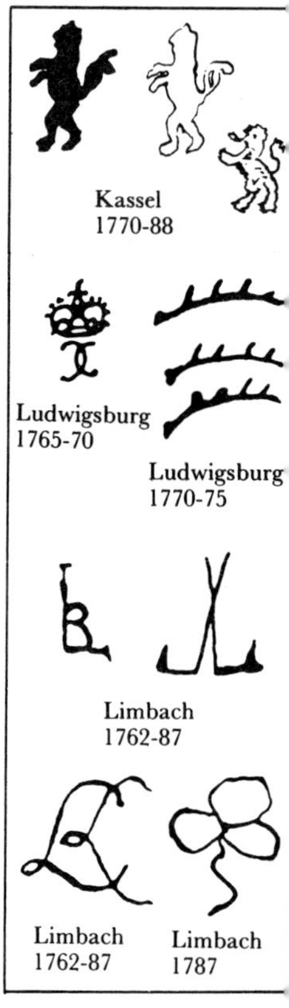

Berlin Porcelain

ANGELA GRÄFIN VON WALLWITZ

For a long time Berlin porcelain was bought only by a small, specialised group of collectors. Even the antique trade did not begin to take an interest in the figures and wares of this factory until towards the end of the 19th century, by which time all the other German factories had enjoyed keen demand amongst collectors for many years. By 1945 only two or three important collections of Berlin porcelain were in private hands. A new market for this factory was established when a small private collection was sold in a German saleroom in June 1975; since then prices have doubled. Part of one of the best-known Berlin collections was sold by Sotheby's on 7 October 1986. It was the largest group of antique Berlin porcelain to come on the market so far this century and it revolutionised the appreciation of the factory. Prices have risen steadily but moderately since the War but the factory has not been the subject of speculative interest. It is therefore a field in which the young collector as well as the established connoisseur has more opportunities than in other more fashionable areas.

As early as 1713 unsuccessful attempts to produce 'real' (hard paste) porcelain were made in Berlin. But it was only at the beginning of Frederick the Great's reign in Prussia in 1740 that these efforts were developed through the offer of a wool

1
A group of Berlin porcelain figures, c.1769-75, *L 7 Oct,*

2
A Berlin centrepiece, comprising a central fruit-stand and two stands each supporting four covered pots, c.1763-64, made for Frederick the Great, sceptre mark and letter G in blue, 46cm (18in) high, *M 1 Dec,*
FF 440,000
(£47,826; $68,391)

3
A pair of Wegely figures of a lion and lioness, *(one illustrated)*, c.1752-57, on later ormolu bases, 15cm (5¾in), *L 30 June 1981,*
£4,620 ($9,563)

4
A Wegely vase and cover, marked W in underglaze-blue, incised numerals, cracked, 54cm (21in), *L 21 Oct 1980,*
£2,860 ($5,920)

1

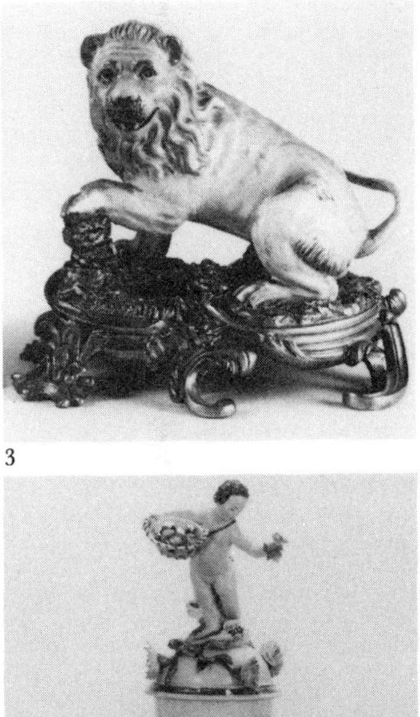

3

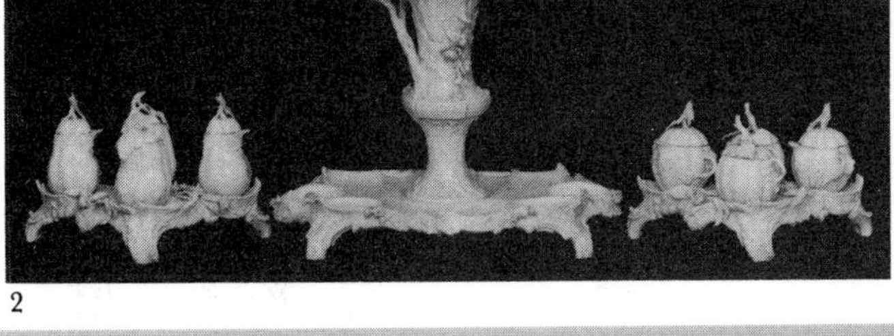

2

4

facturer, Wilhelm Caspar Wegely, to start a Prussian porcelain factory. With the help of the arcanist Johann Benckgraff, the Meissen modeller Ernst Heinrich Reichard (who was made artistic director) and the Meissen painter Isaac Jacques Clauce, a variety of figures and wares were produced which were strongly influenced by the Meissen factory. The famous Italian Comedy figures and a pair of lion and lioness are the best known copies; (see pp 208-9 for Meissen figures). Until the closure of the Wegely factory in 1756 the emphasis of its production lay in figures, with 140 different models known. Most typical are the various figures of children, putti in disguise and the famous vases, which were decorated with birds perched on flowering branches spirally applied around the body.

Wegely figures and wares are often marked with a combination of incised numerals, W in underglaze blue or impressed. Sometimes both the incised numerals and the W marks can be found on one piece (fig.A).

Johann Ernst Gotskowsky, also a clothing manufacturer, started the second porcelain factory in Berlin in 1761 at a time when the Seven Years War still lingered on. He was able to persuade several good artists from Meissen to join him and so produced objects of a high level in terms of quality and design from the beginning. The brothers Friedrich Elias and Wilhelm Christian Meyer, who had been highly respected modellers at Meissen, were almost solely responsible for the Berlin porcelain figures in rococo and neoclassical styles, some of them based on Mannerist originals (fig.1). The new, more subtle use of colours enhanced the shapes and forms of these figures. Gotskowsky was enthusiastically supported by Frederick the Great whose wish had always been to surpass the quality and fame of the Saxon porcelain factory. But even large and frequent orders from the King, through which he hoped to stimulate the artistic inspirations of artists in porcelain, couldn't stop the decay of the early Prussian rococo style, the famous complexity and homogeneity of which he had earlier been able to influence so heavily. By 1763 Johann Ernst Gotskowsky found himself in such serious financial difficulties that he had to sell the undertaking, including a large stock of unglazed and undecorated wares, to the King. Frederick named it

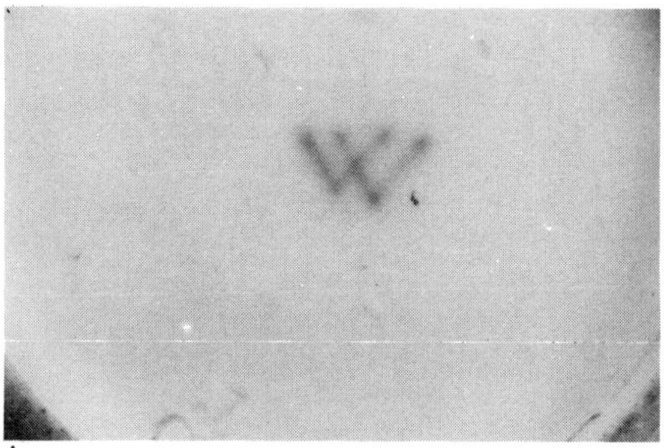
A

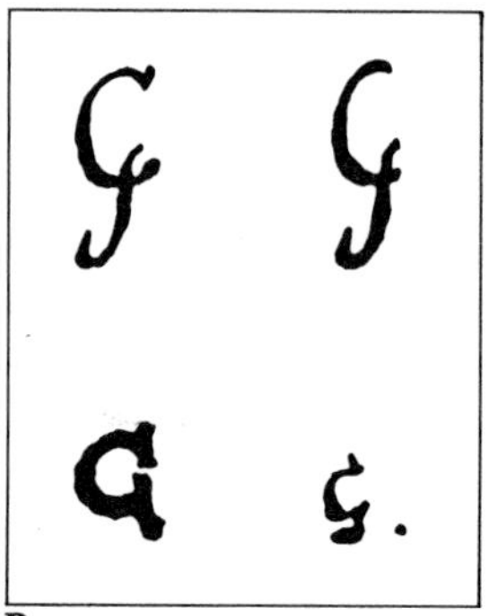
B

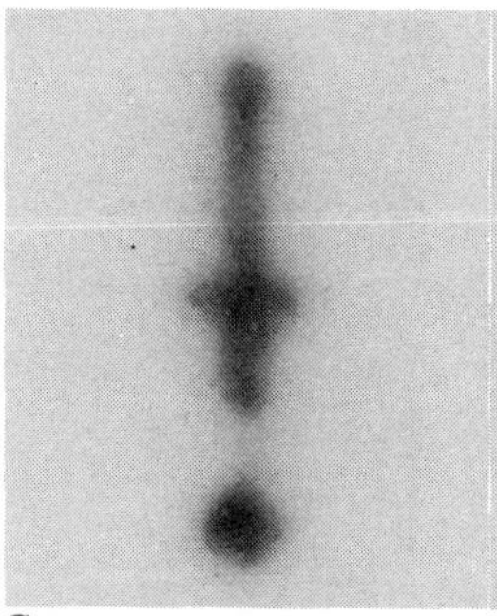
C

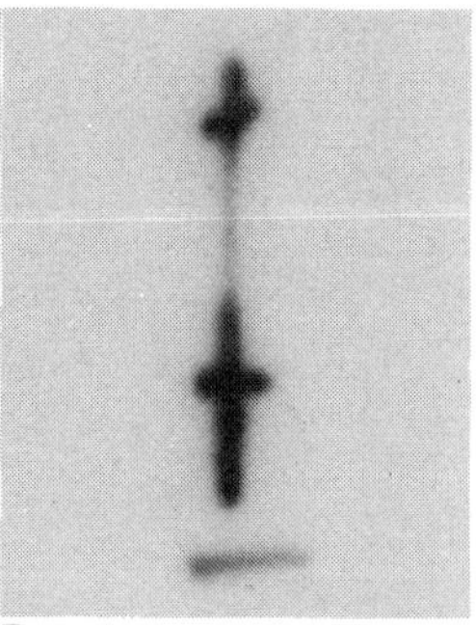
D

E

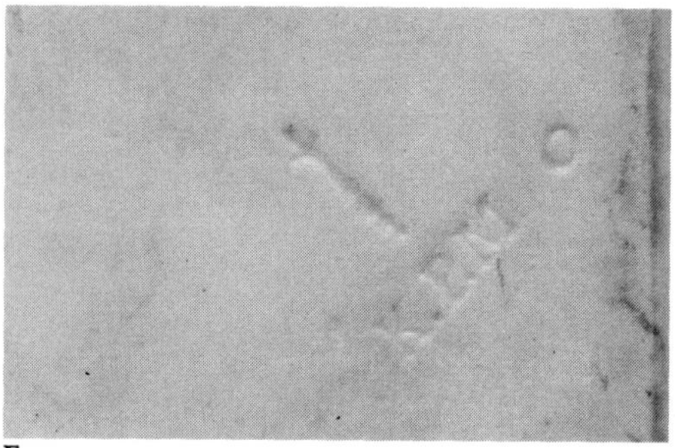
F

G

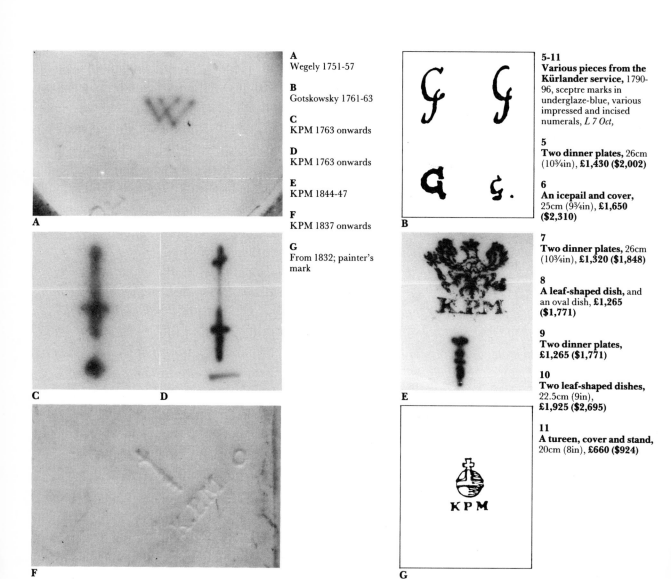

A
Wegely 1751-57

B
Gotskowsky 1761-63

C
KPM 1763 onwards

D
KPM 1763 onwards

E
KPM 1844-47

F
KPM 1837 onwards

G
From 1832; painter's mark

5-11
Various pieces from the Kürlander service, 1790-96, sceptre marks in underglaze-blue, various impressed and incised numerals, *L 7 Oct,*

5
Two dinner plates, 26cm (10¾in), **£1,430 ($2,002)**

6
An icepail and cover, 25cm (9¾in), **£1,650 ($2,310)**

7
Two dinner plates, 26cm (10¾in), **£1,320 ($1,848)**

8
A leaf-shaped dish, and an oval dish, **£1,265 ($1,771)**

9
Two dinner plates, £1,265 ($1,771)

10
Two leaf-shaped dishes, 22.5cm (9in), **£1,925 ($2,695)**

11
A tureen, cover and stand, 20cm (8in), **£660 ($924)**

12
A Berlin porcelain teacup and saucer, c.1775, of 'Reliefzierrat' form, painted with Watteau scenes, sceptre marks in underglaze-blue, impressed *30, L 7 Oct,*
£1,760 ($2,464)

13
A Berlin porcelain teacup and saucer, c.1775, sceptre marks in underglaze-blue, impressed *30, L 7 Oct,*
£1,650 ($2,310)

14
A Berlin porcelain tray, (Anbietplatte), c.1760, repair to one handle, chips to footrim, sceptre mark in underglaze-blue, 35.5cm (14in), *L 7 Oct,*
£880 ($1,232)

15
A Berlin porcelain miniature teapot and cover, c.1775, painted in iron-red *camaieu* with two Watteau scenes, sceptre mark in underglaze-blue, *L 7 Oct,*
£1,760 ($2,464)

16
A Berlin porcelain cup, cover and saucer, c.1777, of 'Neuglatt' form, portrait medallion *en grisaille* of King Frederick the Great, the saucer decorated with an eagle, lyre and palm branch, hair cracks, sceptre marks in underglaze-blue, *9.* in iron-red, *L 7 Oct,*
£858 ($1,201)

17
A Berlin porcelain commemorative cup and saucer, c.1810-20, with a portrait of Louise, Queen of Prussia, sceptre mark in underglaze-blue, painter's mark, incised marks and numerals, *L 24 Feb,*
£418 ($865)

18
A Berlin porcelain candle-snuffer (Löschhütchen), c.1770, of conical form, details in green and puce, sceptre mark in underglaze-blue, 7.5cm (3in), *L 7 Oct,*
£825 ($1,155)

19
A Berlin porcelain eye-bath, 1767-75, sceptre mark in underglaze-blue, 4.5cm (1¾in), *L 7 Oct,*
£605 ($847)

20
A Berlin porcelain Easter egg, c.1725, painted with a view of Schloss Sanssouci, minor wear to gilding, 6.5cm (2½in), *L 7 Oct,*
£3,190 ($4,466)

21
A Berlin porcelain Easter egg, 1825-35, painted with a view of Schloss Babelsberg, gilt-metal mounts, 6.5cm (2½in), *L 7 Oct,*
£2,035 ($2,849)

22
A Berlin porcelain Easter egg, 1825-35, painted with a view of Palais d. Kronprinzen in Berlin, gilt-metal mounts, 6.5cm (2½in), *L 7 Oct,*
£3,740 ($5,236)

5-11

12-15

16

17

20 18 21 19 22

a Royal factory, by decree, and it has remained Prussian state property ever since, called KPM (Königliche Porzellan Manufaktur).

The G mark in underglaze-blue, very rarely found in gilt or brown, was applied on many, but by no means all, Gotskowsky porcelains (fig.B). During Wegely's and Gotskowsky's times the paste never reached the desirable 'cool' whiteness which had made the Meissen factory so famous. It was creamy and 'soft' looking, as the kaolin from Bavaria (the most important ingredient for hard paste porcelain) had different qualities from the kaolin found in Saxony (fig.2). Early in 1771 kaolin was found in Prussia and the porcelain changed into a hard, almost bluish-looking white paste.

The KPM factory became most famous for its tablewares and vases. The first pattern for services in relief was the 'Neuzierrat' pattern with a relatively simple scrollwork border around the rims. The most famous pattern was the 'Mosaic' or scale pattern which was used together with the 'Spalier' or radiating trellis ribs in the so-called 'first Potsdam Service' made for Frederick the Great for his Neue Palais residence in 1765. It became one of the most famous services in continental porcelain and was copied, only differing in colour, in 1766 for King Frederick's brother-in-law the Margrave of Ansbach. Replacements for this service made in the Ansbach factory (in South Germany) provide the opportunity to compare the style of painting in a royal and a more provincial porcelain factory. The painting of the tablewares in the period of Frederick the Great was technically of a very high standard with the use of brilliant enamels, but generally the painting lacked individuality and was often over-carefully executed. In particular, the combination of two shades of green in the beautiful flower painting proves to be a very useful indicator when trying to identify Berlin porcelain. The crimson colour, the almost fiery orange-red, grey or black, are the most typical colours often used in monochromes.

Towards 1780 the style of production changed to the more fashionable neoclassical taste. The relationship of porcelain to its user changed fundamentally during this period. The forms are reduced to pure, almost geometrically defined shapes which speak more through proportion than through imagination. The

23

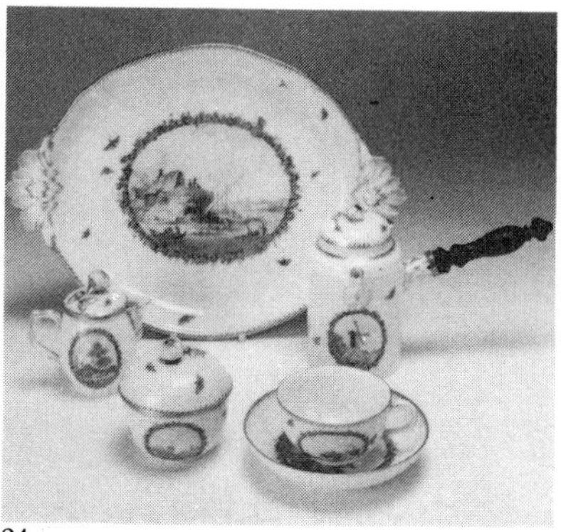
24

25

23
A Berlin cup, cover and saucer, c.1785, with a black portrait medallion of a man and the initial B on the saucer in gilding, chip to cup, sceptre marks and incised numerals, *L 7 Oct,*
£935 ($1,309)

24
A Berlin porcelain 'solitaire', c.1770, each piece decorated in purple *camaieu*, sceptre marks, impressed and incised numerals, 31cm (12¼in), *L 7 Oct,*
£5,500 ($7,700)

25
A Berlin cabinet cup and saucer, 1815-20, with a view of the ruins of Santa Francesca Romana and the Basilica of Constantine, sceptre mark in underglaze-blue, painter's mark and impressed numerals, *L 17 June,*
£1,540 ($2,433)

26
A Berlin porcelain cup, cover and saucer, c.1777, of 'Neuglatt' form, the initials 'FvW' on the saucer, hair crack to cup, sceptre marks in underglaze-blue, incised numerals, *L 7 Oct,*
£715 ($1,001)

27
A Berlin porcelain cup and saucer, c.1800, ground painted to simulate porphyry, sceptre marks in underglaze-blue, – in blue enamel, incised numerals and marks, *L 7 Oct,*
£1,430 ($2,002)

28
A Berlin porcelain cup and saucer, c.1800, restored, sceptre marks in underglaze-blue, – in blue enamel, *L 7 Oct,*
£495 ($693)

29
A Berlin topographical vase, c.1858 painted with two scenes of Potsdam, small chip to one handle, slight rubbing to gilding, sceptre and circular mark in underglaze-blue, inscribed *No.1 1858*, 67.5cm (27in), *L 6 Nov,*
£6,050 ($8,591)

30
A Berlin Royal presentation vase, 1832, painted with a distant view of Berlin, sceptre mark in underglaze-blue, KPM and eagle mark printed in manganese, 63cm (25in), *L 17 Mar 1987,*
£24,200 ($38,720)

31
A Berlin porcelain vase, c.1800, of scutiform and in two sections, sceptre mark in underglaze-blue, painter's mark and incised numerals, 48.5cm (19in), *L 7 Oct,*
£9,900 ($13,860)

32
Three Berlin topographical plates, c.1840, painted with views of Berlin and Schloss Stolzenfels, gilding slightly worn, sceptre and KPM or eagle in underglaze-blue, 26cm (9¾in), *L 17 June,*
£2,750 ($4,345)

employment of Johann Gottfried Schadow, the son of a tailor, accelerated this development. Schadow started work in the factory in 1783 as a very talented artist and was made, at only twenty-four years old, director of all sculptures. By 1800 unglazed biscuit and glazed porcelain sculptures dominated the production of the Royal Prussian factory. The biscuit body was preferred because of its similarity to marble, the most favoured material in neoclassical times. Johann G. Schadow's best known porcelain model is the 'Princess' group. Princess Louise von Mecklenburg-Strelitz, wife of the Prussian Crown Prince, and her sister Friederike, who was married to the Crown Prince's brother, were shown standing arm-in-arm wearing thin loose dresses. A life-size model in plaster was made first in 1794 and the biscuit porcelain group (54cm (21in) high) was made two years later.

The custom of depicting the much admired or beloved on drinking vessels became very fashionable in aristocratic and scholarly circles towards the middle of the 17th century. After the discovery of hard paste porcelain in Europe in the early 18th century, this custom was continued on representational pieces made out of the 'white gold'. The increasing popularity of King Frederick the Great after the successful ending of the Seven Years War in 1763 initiated the production of cabinet cups painted with his portrait or at least bearing the Royal initials, which were cheap enough to be bought by the middle classes (figs 16 & 26). The idea of showing love or respect by ordering a piece of porcelain with the portrait of a friend or colleague became so fashionable after 1800 that the Berlin factory could hardly cope with the demand (figs 23, 27-28).

During the reign of Frederick the Great's son, Friedrich Wilhelm III, (1786-1840), many different shapes of large presentation vases were created. During the brief period between 1829 and 1849 the King and his successor Friedrich Wilhelm IV presented eighty-nine vases of one shape only. Institutions, companies and societies started to use these large, richly and most superbly decorated vases as commemorative presents (figs 29-31).

From about 1840 onwards the old models were reproduced and only a very small part of the porcelain production of the Berlin factory was devoted to the creation of new styles (figs 39-

26

27

29

30

31

28

32

44). The famous Berlin plaques, which copied well-known Old Master paintings, show Pre-Raphaelite scenes, religious subjects and portraits of well-known people. These pictures on porcelain were very well painted and enjoyed a very high demand (figs 36-38). They were subsequently copied by the lesser factories in the bordering principalities of Thuringia and Silesia.

The famous sceptre mark which was painted on all figures and wares in underglaze-blue, varies considerably between 1763 and the present day (figs C & D). From the second quarter of the 19th century 'KPM' and other printed marks were used in addition to the sceptre (fig.E). On plaques an impressed sceptre mark is mostly used (fig.F).

When starting to buy porcelain, the collector should make a conscious decision whether to collect out of interest and love for the subject or to buy predominantly for investment, in which case only pieces of the very best quality and historic importance, in perfect condition, should be acquired. If buying in the first category, a new collector should not be afraid to collect to his or her very own taste. Condition always affects the market price of an object, but a chip or crack should never deter from a very rare or particularly well-painted piece. Slowly with increasing knowledge of the chosen field a collector's taste will probably change, and through buying and selling, raising the level of quality and inevitably making mistakes, the collection will come alive and be a reflection of the collector's personality.

Further reading:

G. Zick, *Berliner Porzellan der Manufaktur von Wilhelm Caspar Wegely 1751-1757,* 1978
W. Baer, *Von Gotzkowsky zur KPM,* 1986
E. Köllmann, *Berliner Porzellan,* vols.1 & 2, 1966

33 34 35 33

33
A Berlin cup and saucer, c.1830, in Empire style, blue sceptre and red-brown eagle marks, and another cup and saucer, c.1835, with blue sceptre and red-brown orb marks, *L 4 Mar,*
£682 ($1,023)

34
A Berlin oval basket, c.1820-30, with pierced pale-green and gilt lattice sides, sceptre mark in blue, 37cm (14¾in), *L 4 Mar,*
£1,650 ($2,475)

35
A Berlin yellow-ground coffee can and saucer, c.1780, sceptre in underglaze-blue, painter's mark *56* in iron red, incised numerals and marks, *L 4 Mar,*
£858 ($1,287)

36
A Berlin plaque, late 19th century, painted and signed by R. Dittrich, with Ruth in a cornfield, impressed KPM and sceptre mark, 28cm (18¾in), *C 16 Apr,*
£1,540 ($2,387)

37
A Berlin plaque, third quarter 19th century, painted by F. Böhm, impressed KPM and sceptre, 28cm (11in), *L 20 Mar,*
£2,750 ($4,317)

38
A Berlin oval plaque
'Gitana', late 19th century, painted after Asti by Wagner, impressed KPM and sceptre marks, 27cm (10¼in), *NY 13 Sept*,
$4,400 (£2,993)

39
Five Berlin figures, *(three illustrated)*, late 19th century, from a set of Months of the Year, chips, sceptre in underglaze-blue, 10cm (4in), *L 20 Mar*,
£308 ($483)

40
A Berlin teapot, late 19th century, gilt details and polychrome flower painting, sceptre in underglaze-blue, 11cm (4¼in), *JHB 1 Dec*,
R680 (£212; $296)

36

37

38

39

40

41
A pair of Berlin vases and covers, *(one illustrated)*, late 19th century, each painted with classical figures, sceptre marks in underglaze-blue, 34.5cm (13¾in), *C 16 Apr*,
£792 ($1,228)

42
A pair of Berlin desk ornaments, *(one illustrated)*, third quarter 19th century, each modelled as a terrestrial or celestial globe, one as a pounce pot and cover, the other as a pin box and cover, sceptre in underglaze-blue, 7.5cm (3in), *L 6 Nov*,
£605 ($859)

43
A Berlin clock garniture, *(part illustrated)*, c.1890, painted in pastel colours, knop chipped, one sconce restored, sceptre in underglaze-blue, printed orb and KPM in red, 38 and 29cm (15 and 11½in), *L 6 Nov*,
£1,650 ($2,343)

44
A pair of Berlin vases, *(one illustrated)*, with gilt-bronze decoration, late 19th century, 51cm (20in), *M 23 June*,
FF 9,990 (£891; $1,390)

1

2

3

4

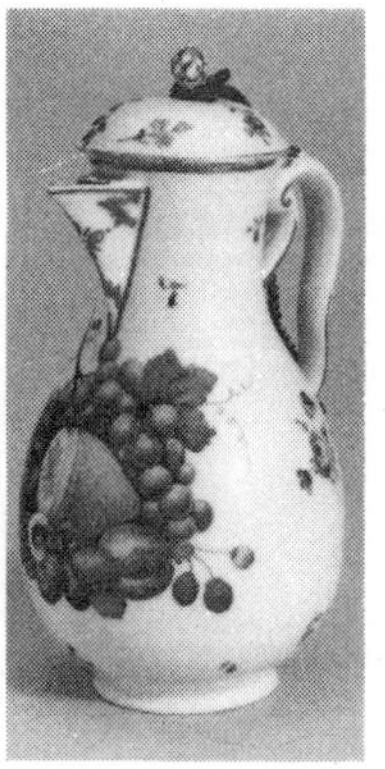
5

6

7

8

9

10

11

12 13

14

15

16

1
An Ansbach coffee pot and cover, c.1775, impressed and incised marks, minor damage, some restoration, 24cm (9½in), *L 4 Mar,*
£550 ($825)

2
An Ansbach cup and saucer, c.1775, in underglaze-blue, impressed and painter's marks, 13cm (5in), *L 4 Mar,*
£550 ($825)

3
A set of six Frankenthal custard cups and covers, *(one illustrated),* c.1760, CT and crown in underglaze-blue, 8cm (3¼in), *L 17 June,*
£2,310 ($3,650)

4
A Fürstenberg blue and white coffee pot and cover, c.1780, turned wood handle, impressed mark, 12.5cm (4¾in), *NY 9 Dec,*
$495 (£349)

5
A Frankenthal milk jug and cover, c.1780, CT beneath crown in underglaze-blue, incised H2, minor chip, 17cm (6¾in), *L 4 Mar,*
£858 ($1,287)

6
A pair of Frankenthal flower bowls and covers, *(one illustrated),* 1786 and 1788, gilding slightly rubbed, crowned CT, 86 and 88 in underglaze-blue, 29cm (11½in), *L 4 Mar,*
£2,640 ($3,960)

7
A Frankenthal cream jug, c.1770, crown, letters and numbers in underglaze-blue, 7.5cm (3in), *L 7 Oct,*
£495 ($693)

8
A Frankenthal trembleuse cup, cover and stand, c.1780, restored, crown, monogram and underlined triangle in underglaze-blue, *S 10 Dec,*
£572 ($801)

9
A Frankenthal tea caddy and cover, c.1765, marks, crown and monogram in underglaze-blue, some restoration, 15cm (6in), *L 7 Oct,*
£1,100 ($1,540)

10
A Höchst cylindrical tea caddy and cover, c.1775, probably painted by Johann Heinrich Usinger, the cover probably married, crowned wheel mark in underglaze-blue and incised NI mark, 13.5cm (5¼in), *NY 9 Dec,*
$3,300 (£2,324)

11
A Höchst potpourri vase and cover, c.1765, small chips, crowned wheel mark in underglaze-blue and incised NI mark, 15.5cm (6in), *NY 9 Dec,*
$990 (£697)

12
A set of four Höchst dessert plates, *(one illustrated),* 1765-70, wheel mark in underglaze-blue and incised IN mark, minor chips, 24cm (9½in), *L 4 Mar,*
£715 ($1,072)

13
A Höchst candlestick, 1775-80, wheel mark in underglaze-blue, minor chip, 18cm (7in), *L 4 Mar,*
£550 ($825)

14
A Höchst cream jug, c.1760, moulded in Sèvres style, 10cm (3¾in), *L 7 Oct,*
£418 ($585)

15
A Ludwigsburg tea caddy and cover, 1765-70, impressed 2 KM, 13.5cm (5¼in), *L 17 June,*
£440 ($695)

16
A Kassel bowl and cover, c.1770, lion rampant mark in underglaze-blue, 9cm (3½in), *L 7 Oct,*
£3,630 ($5,082)

Nymphenburg
1890-98

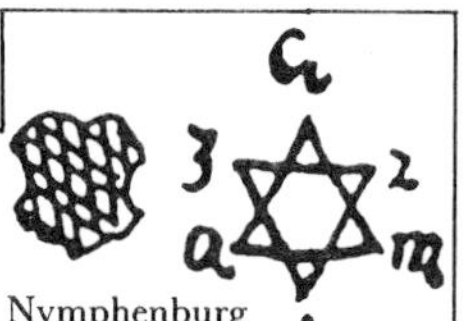
Nymphenburg
18th century

1
A Thuringian tankard, c.1793, possibly Ilmenau, enamelled in iron-red *camaieu,* slight enamel flaking, 16cm (6¼in), *L 17 June,*
£1,078 ($1,703)

2
A pair of German covered compotes, late 19th century, pseudo crossed swords marks in underglaze-blue, 122cm (48in), *NY 13 Sept,*
$8,800 (£5,986)

3
A pair of Dresden 'Schneeballen' vases, *(one illustrated),* late 19th century, pseudo crossed swords marks in underglaze-blue, 51.5cm (20¼in), *NY 26 Nov,*
$1,870 (£1,307)

4
A pair of Dresden candelabra, *(one illustrated),* 43cm (17in), *C 22 July,*
£264 ($414)

5
A Dresden centrepiece, modelled with two cherubs seated before a flower-encrusted column, 43cm (17in), *C 5 Aug,*
£286 ($443)

6
A pair of Potschappel potpourri vases and covers, late 19th century, each painted with mythological scenes, cross and T in underglaze-blue, cracks and chips, 37.5cm (14¾in), *L 12 June,*
£462 ($739)

7
A Dresden mirror frame, late 19th century, moulded with pink and turquoise scrolls and applied with cherubs and birds amongst trails of flowers and foliage, some damage, 95.5cm (37½in), *L 6 Nov,*
£2,860 ($4,061)

8
A Potschappel vase, cover and stand, late 19th century, cross and T in underglaze-blue, chips, 85cm (33½in), *L 20 Mar,*
£1,870 ($2,936)

9
A pair of Helena Wolfsohn vases and covers, *(one illustrated),* late 19th century, AR monogram in underglaze-blue, one cover and neck restored, 50.5cm (19¾in), *L 12 June,*
£682 ($1,091)

Potschappel

Closter Veilsdorf
1760-97

Wallendorf
1763-87

Capodimonte
1743-59

Doccia
1737-1850

Doccia
2nd half 19th century

Nove
1752-1832

1

2

3

4

5

6

7

8

9

1

2

3

4

5

6

7

8

9

10

11

12

1
A Meissen figure of a musician, c.1750-60, modelled by J.J. Kändler, in yellow jacket and green breeches, both hands restored, crossed swords in underglaze-blue, 27.5cm (10¾in), *L 4 Mar,*
£715 ($1,072)

2
A pair of Meissen figures of gardeners, *(one illustrated),* c.1760, probably modelled by J.J.Kändler and P. Reinicke, watering cans picked out in oxidized silver, chips, crossed swords in underglaze-blue, incised marks and numerals, 12cm (4¾in), *L 7 Oct,*
£1,320 ($1,848)

3
A Meissen figure of a coppersmith, c.1750, probably modelled by J.J. Kändler, slight restoration to the hammer, crossed swords in underglaze-blue, 19cm (7½in), *L 4 Mar,*
£3,520 ($5,280)

4
A Meissen figure of a carpenter, c.1750, probably modelled by J.J. Kändler, slight repair to the saw, crossed swords in underglaze-blue, 22cm (8¾in), *L 4 Mar,*
£3,740 ($5,610)

5
A Meissen figure of a publican, mid 18th century, minor damage, crossed swords in blue, 13.5cm (5½in), *S 19 Mar,*
£1,760 ($2,693)

6
A Meissen figure of a shepherd, c.1750-60, modelled by J.J. Kändler, left hand restored, crossed swords in underglaze-blue, 25cm (9¾in), *L 4 Mar,*
£825 ($1,237)

7
A Meissen group of dancing peasants, c.1750, probably modelled by Peter Reinicke, some restoration, crossed swords in underglaze-blue, 14cm (5½in), *L 17 June,*
£572 ($904)

8
A pair of Meissen allegorical sweetmeat figures *(one illustrated),* c.1755, representing Spring and Autumn, minute chips, crossed swords in underglaze-blue, 14cm (5½in), *L 7 Oct,*
£1,980 ($2,772)

9
A pair of Meissen figures of children, mid 18th century, both dancing, some damage and restoration, crossed swords in underglaze-blue, impressed marks, 13cm (5in), *L 7 Oct,*
£660 ($924)

10
A Meissen group of a shepherd and a shepherdess, third quarter 19th century, coloured in a pastel palette, some restoration, crossed swords in underglaze-blue, incised 1290, 25cm (9¾in), *L 20 Mar,*
£528 ($829)

11
A pair of Meissen allegorical figures of Spring and Summer, *(one illustrated),* c.1760, modelled by Elias Meyer, draped in puce lined robes, chipped, crossed swords in underglaze-blue, 23cm (9in), *L 17 June,*
£715 ($1,130)

12
A Meissen group of Spring, late 19th century, crossed swords in blue, incised numerals, 17cm (6¾in), *C 8 Oct,*
£550 ($770)

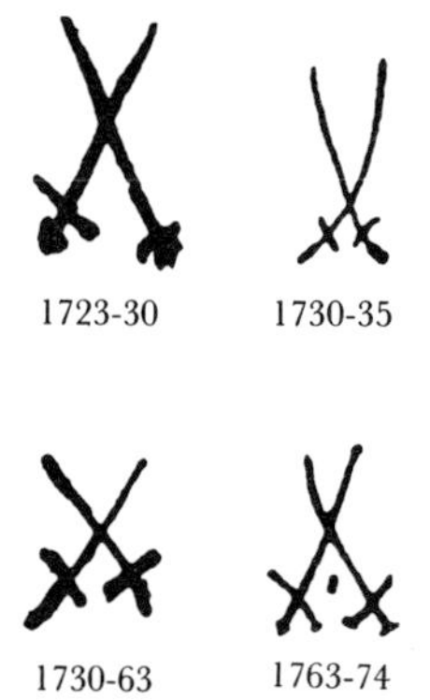

Meissen

pair of Meissen groups f Sight and Smell, *(one 'ustrated)*, second half)th century, modelled as 3th century women, res- ration, crossed swords underglaze-blue, 1.5cm (6in), *S 4 Sept,* **748 ($1,159)**

Meissen figure of pollo, third quarter 18th entury, restoration to ngers and pipe, flowers hipped, crossed swords underglaze-blue, 0.5cm (4in), *L 7 Oct,* **275 ($385)**

Meissen figure of Columbine playing a urdy gurdy, c.1745, nodelled by Johann oachim Kändler, in a gilt dged hat and bodice, ight ankle repaired, faint rossed swords in nderglaze-blue, 13cm 5¼in), *NY 9 Dec,* **$770 (£542)**

A Meissen sweetmeat igure of a blackamoor, .1745, crossed swords in blue, incised 37, 19.5cm 7½in), *L 17 June,* **£1,650 ($2,607)**

5
A Meissen 'crinoline' group, third quarter 19th century, after a model by Kändler, said to be Augus- tus III and Queen Maria Josepha von Habsburg, chips, crossed swords in underglaze-blue, im- pressed numerals, 21cm (8¼in), *L 20 Mar,* **£660 ($1,036)**

6
A Meissen group of lovers, third quarter 19th century, minor chips, crossed swords in underglaze-blue, incised 551, 18cm (7in), *L 12 June,* **£440 ($704)**

7
A Meissen group of lovers, c.1880, coloured in a pastel palette, minor chips, crossed swords in underglaze-blue, incised Y34, 12.5cm (5in), *L 20 Mar,* **£572 ($898)**

8
A pair of Meissen sweet- meat figures, second half 19th century, modelled as an 18th century gallant and companion, minor chips, crossed swords in underglaze-blue, impressed and incised numerals, 20cm (8in), *S 16 July,* **£495 ($777)**

9
A Meissen figure of a lady playing cards, late 19th century, base with gilt border, some lace trim- mings missing, crossed swords in underglaze- blue, incised F83, 16cm (6¼in), *L 6 Nov,* **£715 ($1,015)**

10
A Meissen group of lovers, c.1880, base with gilt border, chips, crossed swords in underglaze- blue, incised numerals F83, 20.5cm (8in), *L 12 June,* **£638 ($1,020)**

11
Two Meissen groups of Mars and Minerva, third quarter 19th century, bases edged with gilt scrolls, some damage, crossed swords in under- glaze-blue, incised numerals D1 and D2, 21.5cm (8½in), *L 20 Mar,* **£462 ($725)**

12
A Meissen group of water nymphs, third quarter 19th century, minor damage, crossed swords in underglaze-blue, incised C35, 32.5cm (12¾in), *L 20 Mar,* **£880 ($1,382)**

13
Two Meissen figures of cherubs, late 19th century, bases edged with gilt scrolls, minor chips, crossed swords in underglaze-blue, 12cm (4¾in), *L 20 Mar,* **£572 ($898)**

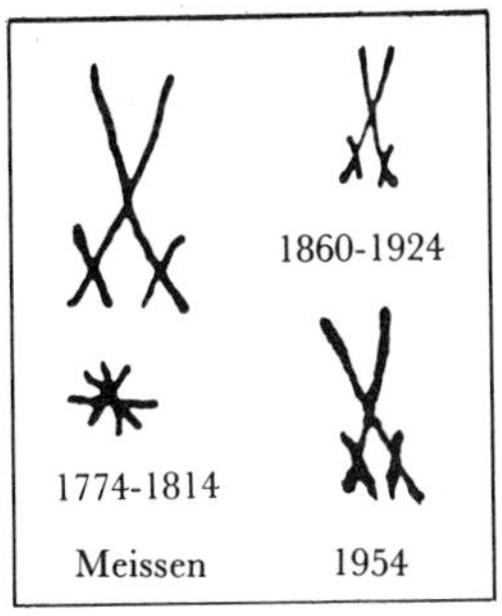

1

2

3

4

5

6

7

8

9

10

11

12

13

1

2

3

4

5

6

7

8

9

10

11

12

13

14

15

16

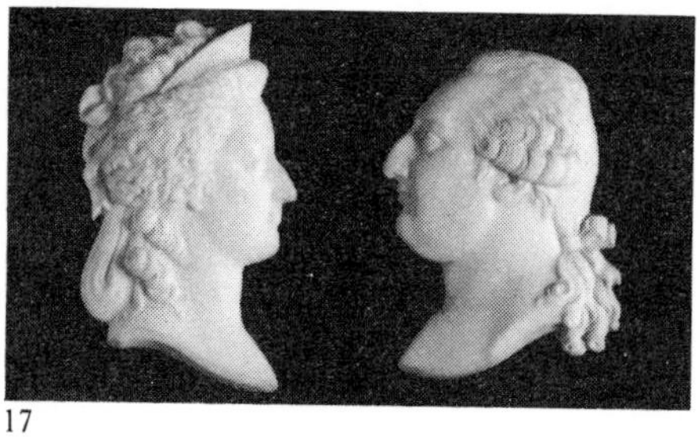
17

1
A French porcelain group, late 19th century, in Meissen style, some damage, pseudo sword mark in underglaze-blue, 41.5cm (16¼in), *C 8 Oct,*
£495 ($693)

2
A pair of French huntsman vases, *(one illustrated),* late 19th century, in Meissen style, pseudo sword marks in underglaze-blue, 38.5cm (15¼in), *C 8 Oct,*
£440 ($616)

3
A Frankenthal group of putti, c.1770, modelled by J.W. Lanz, some damage, CT, crown and B in underglaze-blue, 23.5cm (9¼in), *L 4 Mar,*
£715 ($1,072)

4
A Frankenthal figure, 1756-59, modelled by J.W. Lanz, slight damage, lion mark in underglaze-blue, 14.5cm (5¾in), *C 9 July,*
£605 ($944)

5
A Fulda figure of a musician, c.1781-88, some restoration, crowned FF in underglaze-blue, 14.5cm (5¾in), *L 4 Mar,*
£2,090 ($3,135)

6
A Fürstenberg group of two children with a goat, c.1760, modelled by Simon Feilner, small restorations, incised 58, 13cm (5in), *L 4 Mar,*
£770 ($1,155)

7
A Höchst allegorical group of Love, c.1775, modelled by J.P. Melchior, mark in underglaze-blue, 15cm (6in), *L 4 Mar,*
£990 ($1,485)

8
A Höchst porcelain figure of a young boy, c.1770, modelled by J.P. Melchior, some restoration, wheel in underglaze-blue, 17cm (6½in), *L 17 June,*
£990 ($1,564)

9
A Höchst figure of a boy, c.1770, modelled by J.P. Melchior, some restoration, wheel in underglaze-blue, incised N56E1/9, 17cm (6½in), *L 17 June,*
£715 ($1,130)

10
A pair of Ludwigsburg figures of children, c.1760, chips, interlaced C's in underglaze-blue, impressd C3 and incised marks, 11cm (4¼in), *L 7 Oct,*
£880 ($1,232)

11
A Höchst figure of a gardener, c.1760, chips, incised wheel mark and I, 12cm (4¾in), *L 7 Oct,*
£550 ($770)

12
A Ludwigsburg figure of a boy, c.1770, one hand restored, interlaced C's in underglaze-blue, incised I, 11cm (4¼in), *L 7 Oct,*
£484 ($678)

13
A Ludwigsburg group of dancers, 1760-65, modelled by Joseph Nees, some repairs, crowned interlaced C's mark in underglaze-blue, incised and impressed marks, 15.5cm (6in), *NY 9 Dec,*
$1,760 (£1,239)

14
A pair of Vienna figures of dancers, 1760-65, some restoration and damage, impressed P, incised 4, 21cm (8¼in), *L 4 Mar,*
£1,100 ($1,650)

15
A Ludwigsburg figure of a peasant, c.1765, possibly modelled by J. Chr. Haselmeyer, minor chip, interlaced C's beneath crown, 14cm (5½in), *L 4 Mar,*
£1,210 ($1,815)

16
A Doccia pastoral group, c.1780, slight damage, 23cm (9in), *L 7 Oct,*
£1,078 ($1,509)

17
Ten Sèvres hard-paste biscuit silhouette portraits, *(two illustrated),* 1815-25, modelled by A. Brachard jeune, showing members of the French royal family, one damaged, three signed *Prachard f,* impressed *Sèvres,* 7cm (2¾in), *L 17 June,*
£440 ($695)

1
A Sèvres white biscuit group of 'La Mangeuse de Gimblettes', c.1757, modelled by Etienne-Maurice Falconet, probably after Boucher, boy's neck repaired, 16cm (6¼in), *NY 9 Dec,*
$1,320 (£930)

2
A pair of Sèvres white biscuit figures of 'La Jardinière au Vase', and 'Le Jardinier au Plantoire', c.1755, modelled by Claude Suzanne after Boucher, some repair and damage, incised F under her base, *NY 9 Dec,*
$1,540 (£1,085)

3
A Sèvres white biscuit group, 1755-65, by Etienne-Maurice Falconet from a drawing by Boucher, chipped, firing cracks, incised letter B, 17.5cm (7in), *NY 9 Dec,*
$1,320 (£930)

4
A pair of Sèvres biscuit groups, *(one illustrated),* 19th century, 30.5cm (12in), *M 1 Dec,*
FF 9,900 (£1,069; $1,529)

5
A Sèvres biscuit group of 'Diane Au Bain', 19th century, impressed mark, 41cm (16in), *Mel 24 June,*
Aus$660 (£287; $448)

6
A pair of French coloured biscuit figures of Morning and Evening, third quarter 19th century, some restoration, applied blue tablet mark inscribed VB, 46cm (18in), *L 12 June,*
£440 ($704)

7
A French coloured biscuit group, late 19th century, modelled as a naked Pan and Cupid in pastel tones, impressed numerals, 47cm (18½in), *L 12 June,*
£352 ($563)

8
A Gille Jeune coloured biscuit figure of a maiden teased by a cupid, mid 19th century, chips and cracks, applied blue tablet mark, 61cm (24in), *L 20 Mar,*
£660 ($1,036)

9
A pair of Royal Dux figures, c.1920, picked out in pink, green and gold, goat's ear missing, applied triangle mark, 64cm (25¼in), *C 16 Apr,*
£440 ($682)

10
A Royal Dux group, 1920s, base cracked, printed *Made in Czechoslovakia* in green, 51.5cm (20¼in), *C 16 Apr,*
£418 ($648)

11
A pair of French porcelain scent bottles, *(one illustrated),* 19th century, in gilt and white, some chips, 33cm (13in), *C 16 Apr,*
£286 ($443)

12
A pair of Royal Dux Eastern figures, *(one illustrated),* slight damage, applied pink triangle marks, 64cm (25in), *C 9 July,*
£550 ($858)

13
A Royal Dux portrait of a young girl, 51cm (20in), *C 25 Feb,*
£286 ($429)

Copenhagen
1760-66

1775-1801

1897 1923
Copenhagen

Vienna 1770-1820
Vienna since 1922

Zurich 1765-90

1

2

3

4

5

6 7 6
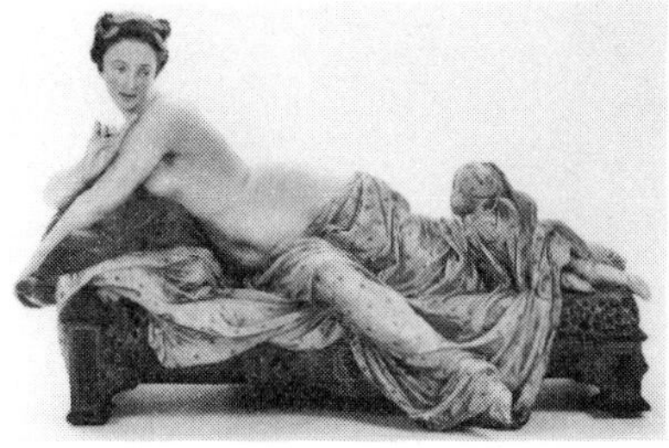
8

9 10 9

11

12
13

1

2

3

4

5

6

7

8 9

10

11

12

13

14

15

1
An Ellwangen snuff box, 1758-69, painted in colours by Joh A. Bechdolff, the inside showing a portrait of the Fürstprobst Anton Ignaz Josef Graf von Fugger, gilt metal mounts, 7.5cm (3in), *L 17 June,*
£25,300 ($39,974)

2
A Capodimonte silver-mounted snuff box, 1750-55, modelled by G. Gricci with shells and corals in shades of green, blue, purple, iron-red, yellow and black, inside cover painted after P. Longhi, the mounts with marks of J.L. Leferre, Paris 1798-1809, 8cm (3in), *L 17 June,*
£12,650 ($19,987)

3
A Fürstenberg silver-gilt mounted snuff box, c.1760, the bombé-shaped body moulded with floral scroll-edged cartouches, the cover inside painted by Joh. H. Eisenträger after J. E. Nilson, 7cm (2¾in), *L 17 June,*
£2,200 ($3,476)

4
A Fulda porcelain snuff box, 1770-75, the finely painted figures in landscapes in 'Watteau' style, gilt-metal mounts, 8cm (3in), *L 17 June,*
£5,500 ($8,690)

5
A German porcelain silver-gilt mounted snuff box, 1765-70, probably Berlin, with a portrait of Prince Heinrich of Prussia after Anton Graff, minor wear, 6.5cm (2½in), *L 17 June,*
£7,920 ($12,514)

6
An Ansbach porcelain snuff box, 1760-65, minor wear, 7cm (2¾in), *L 17 June,*
£4,950 ($7,821)

7
A Meissen snuff box, 1735-40, inset with a biscuit portrait depicting Augustus III of Saxony, 8cm (3in), *L 17 June,*
£4,620 ($7,299)

8
A Meissen gold-mounte rectangular snuff box an cover, c.1755, unidentified maker's mark and Paris discharge mark, an eagle's head struck twice, 9cm (3½in), *NY 9 Dec,*
$5,500 (£3,873)

9
A Meissen gold-mounte rectangular snuff box an cover, c.1755, the rims with a later hinged mount, crack and chip, 9cm (3½in), *NY 9 Dec,*
$2,090 (£1,472)

10
A Meissen metal-mount snuff box, c.1760, decorated in colours, 7cm (2¾in), *L 4 Mar,*
£990 ($1,485)

11
An Ansbach porcelain snuff box, 1765-70, painted in purple *camaieu,* gilt-metal mounts, 6.5cm (2½in), *L 17 June,*
£6,050 ($9,560)

12
A Meissen silver-mounted snuff box, 1760-70, painted with scenes of Don Quixote, cartouches in puce, orange and yellow, 8cm (3¼in), *L 17 June,*
£1,210 ($1,912)

13
A Fürstenberg snuff box, 1760-65, painted in purple with seascapes, the interior with a lady, after J. E. Nilson, gilt-metal mounts, 7.5cm (3in), *L 17 June,*
£1,650 ($2,607)

14
A Frankenthal silver-gilt mounted snuff box, 1759, the cover's interior painted by A. Ph. Oettner, 8cm (3in), *L 17 June,*
£5,720 ($9,038)

15
A Meissen gold-mounted snuff box, c.1740, the cover with a portrait of Augustus the Strong, gilt line borders, 6cm (2¼in), *L 17 June,*
£6,600 ($10,428)

1
A Vienna teapot and cover, 1750-60, finely painted with figures in *grisaille* landscapes, shield in underglaze-blue, incised marks, 10.5cm (4in), *L 7 Oct,*
£330 ($462)

2
A Vienna basket and stand, c.1812,, shield marks in underglaze-blue, impressed *812* and *Q* painter's mark, 30.5cm (12in); sold with a set of four similar Vienna pierced baskets and stands, c.1805, 31cm (12¼in), *L 7 Oct,*
£990 ($1,386)

3
A Nove bowl and cover with stand, c. 1780, the stand 21cm (8¼in), *F 30 Sept,*
L 4,180,000 (£2,083; $2,916)

4
A Du Paquier beaker and saucer, 1725-35, painted in iron-red with chinoiseries on a dark blue ground and overpainted with foliate scrolls in silver, incised mark, *L 17 June,*
£1,925 ($3,042)

5
A Zurich milk jug and cover, 1765-70, chipped spout and rim, Z and three dots in underglaze-blue, 13.5cm (5¼in), *L 17 June,*
£495 ($782)

6
A Vienna Du Paquier mug, c.1740, decorated in *Schwarzlot* and gilt, with a chinaman with long beard sitting in a garden, 9.5cm (3¾in), *L 4 Mar,*
£1,430 ($2,145)

7
A Du Paquier sauce boat, c.1735, finely decorated with large sprays of flowers, crack to one handle, 25.5cm (10in), *L 4 Mar,*
£880 ($1,320)

8
A Doccia teabowl and saucer, c.1770, decorated *alla Sassonia* with chinoiserie scenes within blue-panelled gilt scrollwork borders enriched in iron-red, gilt rims, *L 17 June,*
£770 ($1,217)

9
A Vienna ewer-on-stand, painted by Wagner, signed, painted on a ground of pale yellow, claret, pink, blue and apricot heightened in gilding, pseudo shield mark in underglaze-blue, 42cm (16½in), *NY 26 Nov,*
$1,100 (£769)

10
A Vienna vase, c.1900, painted by Wagner, signed, with Amphitrite attended by cupids, on a lustrous brown ground, marks obscured by a gilt decorator's rose, number 38887 in iron-red enamel, 31cm (12¼in), *NY 26 Nov,*
$2,640 (£1,846)

11
A Vienna charger, c.1900, the centre painted by Wipp, signed, showing Venus, Jupiter and Aeneas, mark in underglaze-blue, title in black, 63cm (24¾in), *S 16 July,*
£1,815 ($2,850)

12
A Vienna wall plaque, late 19th century, painted by A. Beer, signed, showing Christ and the woman from Canaan after Titian, on a ruby-red and lilac ground, shield in underglaze-blue, painted title, impressed numerals, 60.5cm (23¾in), *L 20 Mar,*
£2,090 ($3,281)

13
A pair of Vienna porcelain vases and covers, 19th century, 53cm (21in), *F 14 Apr,*
L 5,000,000 (£2,048; $3,174)

14
A Royal Copenhagen vase, c.1850, painted by A. Juuel, signed, with the City and Castle of Elsinore, slight wear to the gilding, three lines in underglaze-blue, 52cm (20½in), *L 6 Nov,*
£1,595 ($2,265)

1 2

3

4

5

6

7

8

9

10

11

12

13

14

1

2

3

4 5

6

7

8

9

10

11

1
A Vincennes cup and saucer, c.1750, *bleu-du-roi* ground, tooled and burnished gilding, interlaced L's, in underglaze-blue, incised marks, 18.5cm (7¼in), *L 7 Oct,*
£6,050 ($8,470)

2
A Vincennes mustard pot, cover and stand, c.1753, *bleu lapis* ground, gilt dentil rims, interlaced L's in blue enclosing date letter, 17cm (6¾in), *L 7 Oct,*
£1,980 ($2,772)

3
A Sèvres écuelle, cover and stand, c.1770, colourfully painted, gilt-dashed blue band border, within a gilt dentil edge, interlaced L's and painter's mark for Vincent Taillandier in blue enamel, 19.5cm (7½in), *NY 9 Dec,*
$660 (£465)

4
A Sèvres ewer, 1764, gilt edged, interlaced L's and date letter in blue, 20.5cm (8in), *NY 9 Dec,*
$330 (£232)

5
A Sèvres helmet-shaped milk jug, 1791, colourfully painted, gilt-edged, on blue ground, interlaced L's, date letter and painter's mark for Nicquet in blue enamel, incised 43, 14.5cm (5¾in), *NY 9 Dec,*
$1,650 (£1,162)

6
A Sèvres water jug and cover, c.1765, blue line and gilt dentil borders, contemporary metal gilt mounts, interlaced L's, date letter and painter's mark T, 16cm (6¼in), *L 7 Oct,*
£858 ($1,201)

7
A Sèvres jug and a basin, c.1753, *feuille-de-choux* pattern, outlined in blue, interlaced L's, dots and date letter, 18cm (7in), *L 17 June,*
£1,760 ($2,781)

8
A Sèvres cup and stand, 1816, painted with a portrait medallion probably of Empress Louise, blue line borders and matt gold bands, printed interlaced L, fleur-de-lis Sèvres, incised repairer's marks MC, *S 16 July,*
£2,145 ($3,368)

9
A Sèvres cabinet cup and saucer, c.1826, palmettes and interior of cup gilt, interlaced L's and date in blue, *L 7 Oct,*
£605 ($847)

10
Two Sèvres plates, *(one illustrated),* 1813, probably by D.D. Riocreux, encircled by a gilt gothic ornamental frieze, dark green ground, minor chips, factory marks in red, painter's marks RX and S, date letters and incised marks, 24cm (9½in), *L 7 Oct,*
£770 ($1,078)

11
A Sèvres bleu-céleste ground seaux à bouteille, c.1770, *ciselé* gilt borders, interlaced L's in blue, painter's mark, 19cm (7½in), *L 17 June,*
£1,155 ($1,825)

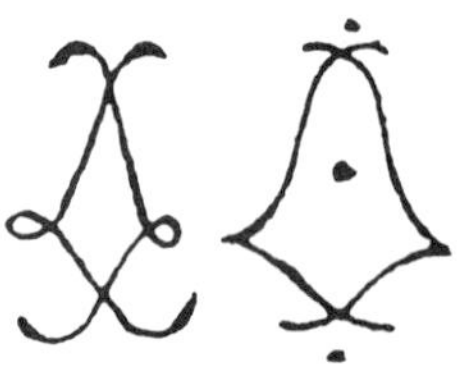
Vincennes
1740-52

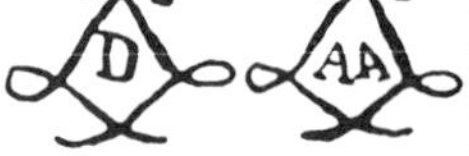

Sèvres
1756-93

Sèvres
1769-93

1
A pair of Tournai soft paste plates, *(one illustrated)*, 18th century, gold mark, 24cm (9½in), *M 23 June,*
FF 5,550 (£495; $772)

2
A Rue de Bondy, Paris, 'Duc D'Angouleme' coffee can and stand, late 1780s, deep-blue ground lavishly gilt, chipped, stencilled marks in iron-red, gilder's mark F,
S 10 Dec,
£264 ($370)

3
A Mennecy silver-mounted 'bonbonnière', 1750-60, in the form of a swan, 6cm (2½in), *L 4 Mar,*
£495 ($742)

4
A pair of Marseille faience 'bouquetiers', c.1770, in manganese, yellow and green, one restored, 28cm (11in),
L 17 June,
£1,760 ($2,781)

5
A Vieux Paris cylindrical jar and cover, 1780-90, Locré Factory at La Courtille, painted with a portrait of Benjamin Franklin, crossed swords mark in underglaze-blue, 40cm (15¾in), *NY 24 Oct,*
$2,750 (£1,950)

6
A Chantilly soft paste cup and cover, mid 18th century, decorated in blue, yellow and pink, red horn mark, 14.5cm (5¾in), *M 25 Feb,*
FF 12,765 (£1,235; $1,852)

7
A Tournai ornithological seau à bouteille, 1785-95, in shades of brown, black, grey, green and yellow, inscribed in gilding, chipped, inscribed 4 and j, 12cm (4½in), *NY 9 Dec,*
$1,870 (£1,317)

8
A Mennecy silver-mounted 'bonbonnière', 1750-60, in yellow, puce, brown, blue and iron-red, 5.5cm (2¼in), *L 4 Mar,*
£660 ($990)

9
A Mennecy soft paste coffee cup and saucer, 18th century, polychrome decoration with red border, marked D.V., 6cm (2½in), *M 23 June,*
FF 2,220 (£198; $308)

10
A trembleuse cup and saucer, c.1785, probably from the Bourdon Factory, Orleans, B in underglaze-blue, incised C, 9.5cm (3¾in), *L 7 Oct,*
£715 ($1,001)

11
A Mennecy soft paste sugar bowl and tray, mid 18th century, marked D.V., 24cm (9½in),
M 25 Feb,
FF 15,540 (£1,503; $2,254)

12
A Mennecy soft paste sugar bowl, mid 18th century, crimson border, marked D.V., 15cm (6in),
M 25 Feb,
FF 6,660 (£644; $966)

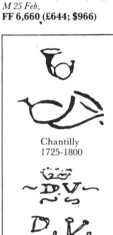

Chantilly
1725-1800

Mennecy
1738-73

St. Cloud
1677-1722

St. Cloud
1722-66

Tournai
1756-1800

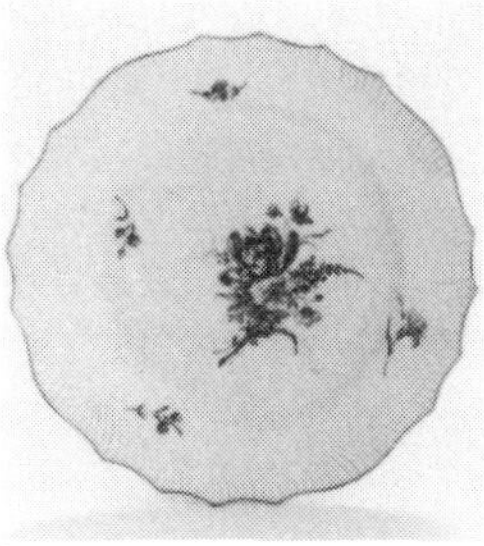
1

2

3

4

5

6

7

8

9

10

11

12

1

2

3

4

5

6

7

8

9

10

1
A French cup and plate, c.1810, painted with a design of playing cards on a green ground, gilt borders, *F 30 Sept,*
L 1,210,000 (£603; $844)

2
An F. D. Honoré & Cie, Boulevard Poissonnière, Paris tea and coffee service, *(coffee pot illustrated),* c.1815, comprising 32 pieces, decorated in purple on a peach-coloured ground, gilt borders, stencilled mark, 26cm (10¼in), *L 4 Mar,*
£1,210 ($1,815)

3
A Paris vase, c.1800, painted after H. Salembier with arabesques and masks enclosing musical trophies, all above a turquoise band, 9cm (3½in), *L 17 June,*
£330 ($521)

4
A pair of Darte Frères vases, early 19th century, each painted in tones of brown, one with a maiden feeding grapes to a cherub, the other with a bacchic youth by a basket of fruits, gilt borders, slight wear, 68.5cm (27in), *L 12 June,*
£6,380 ($10,208)

5
A Paris inkwell, Jacob Petit (1830-66), depicting a dog lying on a cushion with polychrome flowers on a blue ground, slight faults, 35cm (13¾in), *M 1 Dec,*
FF 11,000 (£1,196; $1,710)

6
A French clockcase, c.1850, depicting a highwayman seated on a grass mound, the dial signed *Leroy à Paris*, some wear, 45cm (17¾in), *C 16 Apr,*
£495 ($767)

7
A French clock garniture, Jacob Petit, c.1830, comprising 11 pieces, each applied in relief with sprays of colourful flowers, chips, JP in underglaze-blue, retailer's mark for Marc Schoelcher, 39cm (15¼in), *L 12 June,*
£1,045 ($1,672)

8
A Paris vase-on-stand, third quarter 19th century, the ovoid vessel painted on either side with flower panels, gilt borders, 40cm (15¾in), *NY 26 Nov,*
$1,430 (£1,000)

9
A centrepiece, c.1830, the base modelled with three ram heads and stylised palm leaves, decorated overall in burnished gilding, 33.5cm (13in), *L 17 June,*
£792 ($1,251)

10
A pair of French vases, *(one illustrated),* each painted with a shooting scene, dog mask handles, *C 22 July,*
£297 ($466)

Paris
1774-1800

Paris
1774-1850

Paris
1790-late 19th century

Edmé Samson

1
A set of 24 'Sèvres' plates, *(one illustrated)*, 1851-52, painted in polychrome decoration, *M 23 June*,
FF 19,980 (£1,782; $2,780)

2
Two 'Sèvres' jewelled cabinet plates, *(one illustrated)*, mid 19th century, each with a portrait of Mme de Montespan or Mme de Fontanges, heightened with red, white and blue enamels, slight wear, interlaced L's, 25cm (10in), *L 20 Mar*,
£968 ($1,520)

3
A pair of 'Sèvres' double-handled vases and covers, 19th century, on a gilt enriched and jewelled deep-blue ground, some damage, interlaced L's and F, 31cm (12in), *S 16 July*,
£528 ($829)

4
A pair of 'Sèvres' gilt-bronze-mounted vases, *(one illustrated)*, late 19th century, each painted by Bertren, 93.5cm (36¾in), *NY 13 Sept*,
$9,900 (£6,735)

5
A 'Sèvres' biscuit jardinière, third quarter 19th century, painted interlaced L's, 49cm (19¼in), *L 6 Nov*,
£3,520 ($4,998)

6
A 'Sèvres' gilt-bronze-mounted covered vase, c.1900, painted by F. Bellanger, signed, cover secured, base repaired, 82cm (32¼in), *NY 26 Nov*,
$1,430 (£1,000)

7
A 'Sèvres' gilt-bronze-mounted vase, late 19th century, incribed *D.P. Fragonard*, handles re-gilt, painted interlaced L's, 76.5cm (30in), *L 12 June*,
£770 ($1,232)

8
A 'Sèvres' gilt-bronze-mounted ewer and a cover, late 19th century, *bleu-du-roi* glaze, with *M.Imp le de Sevres* mark in iron-red enamel, 65cm (25½in), *NY 26 Nov*,
$2,475 (£1,731)

9
A 'Sèvres' vase and cover, mid 19th century, with gilt and jewelled borders, on a *bleu céleste* ground, 65cm (25½in), *Syd 12 Nov*,
Aus$2,200 (£1,000; $1,400)

10
A 'Sèvres' gilt-bronze-mounted vase, late 19th century, painted by L. Moreau, signed, depicting ladies in 18th century costume, on a *bleu-du-roi* ground, 95.5cm (37½in), *NY 26 Nov*,
$3,300 (£2,307)

11
A set of six 'Sèvres' Napoleonic plates, c.1900, painted by Guillou, signed, *bleu-du-roi* border gilded, with an N between laurel branches, *M.Imp le de Sevres* marks in iron-red enamel. 24cm (9½in), *NY 13 Sept*,
$1,760 (£1,197)

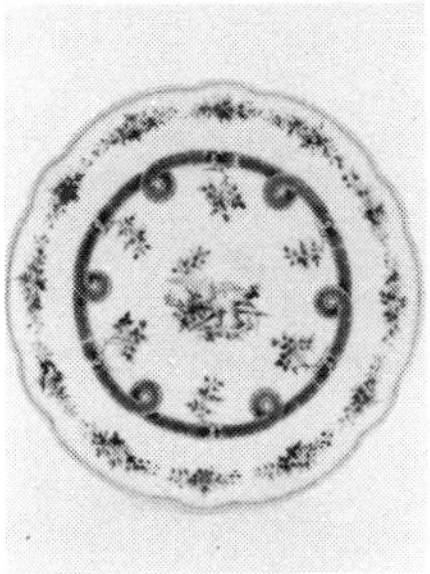
1

2

3

4

5

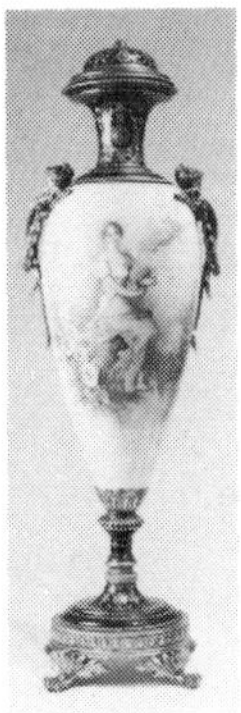
6

7

8

9

10

11

1

2

3

4

5

6

7

8

9

10

11

1
A 'Sèvres' oval dish, c.1880, painted with the death of Gaston de Foix on a *gros-bleu* ground, slight wear, painted interlaced L's and titles in blue, 35cm (13¾in), *L 20 Mar,*
£550 ($863)

2
A Sèvres-style ormolu mounted vase and cover, 19th century, painted with gilt-lined jewelled panels on a dark blue ground, 25.5cm (10in), *C 9 July,*
£209 ($326)

3
A pair of 'Sèvres' gilt-bronze-mounted candlesticks, *(one illustrated),* late 19th century, pseudo interlaced L's and numeral 3 in blue enamel, 30.5cm (12in), *NY 26 Nov,*
$1,430 (£1,000)

4
A 'Sèvres' gilt-bronze-mounted clock garniture, mid 19th century, signed *Bourdin à Paris,* the plaques with painted instructions for the mounting, minor chips, 57 and 58.5cm ((22½ and 23in), *L 20 Mar,*
£4,400 ($6,908)

5
A 'Sèvres' gilt-bronze-mounted centre bowl, third quarter 19th century, with *bleu céleste* ground, painted interlaced L's, 44.5cm (17½in), *L 6 Nov,*
£935 ($1,328)

6
A 'Sèvres' centrepiece, late 19th century, 41cm (16in), *L 12 June,*
£1,100 ($1,760)

7
A 'Sèvres' ormolu-mounted centrepiece, 19th century, with a *bleu céleste* ground, *S 16 July,*
£1,320 ($2,072)

8
A pair of 'Sèvres' jewelled vases and covers, mid 19th century, the enamel jewelling motifs against a *gros bleu* ground, minor restoration and cracks, some wear, painted interlaced L's, 71cm (28in), *L 20 Mar,*
£7,700 ($12,089)

9
A pair of 'Sèvres' gilt-bronze-mounted and jewelled vases and covers, mid 19th century, with a *gros bleu* ground and red and blue enamel jewelling, slight wear, painted interlaced L's, 47.5cm (18¾in), *L 20 Mar,*
£4,180 ($6,563)

10
A pair of 'Sèvres' gilt-bronze-mounted pot-pourri vases and covers, mid 19th century, with colourful enamel jewelling and reserved on a *bleu céleste* type ground, some wear, 30.5cm (12in), *L 6 Nov,*
£1,430 ($2,031)

11
A 'Sèvres' gilt-bronze-mounted centrepiece, 19th century, painted by Lebere, 54cm (21¼in), *A 6 May,*
Dfl 4,600 (£1,394; $2,216)

English Salt-glazed Stoneware

PETER ARNEY

English pottery of the 17th and 18th centuries, though always very collectable, has undergone a remarkable revaluation in the past three or four years, largely due to greatly increased interest in the United States. The traditionally more desirable English white porcelain has been left far behind (and is an increasingly good bet for a similar review by collectors in the near future). Among the most keenly sought-after types of pottery is the uniquely English salt-glazed stoneware of the middle years of the 18th century.

Stoneware is nowadays principally known for its use in drain-pipes and other industrial ceramics, thanks to its great strength and its cheapness of materials and manufacture. The widely available earthenware clays used in the manufacture of stoneware today need only a simple glazing in vaporised salt during a single firing, compared with the previously required second firing covered in a lead-based glaze. However, stoneware's noble pedigree is derived from qualities better understood in the 18th century than now; principally the fact that the strong and dense body can be potted very thinly to achieve an elegance rivalling the much rarer and more expensive porcelain bodies.

From the 15th to the late 17th centuries, there existed a near-monopoly and vast export market for the highly productive stoneware potters of Cologne, Frechen and other centres in Germany, making stoutly-potted jugs, tankards and wine bottles

1

2

3

4

5

1
A German stoneware jug, c.1600, with the arms of Elizabeth I of England *(author's collection)*.

2
A Dwight saltglaze bulbous mug, late 17th century, mounted in silver, small star crack, 9.5cm (3¾in), *L 1 July*,
£4,400 ($7,040)

3
A Nottingham saltglaze brown stoneware carved jug, c.1705, rim chips, 11.5cm (4½in), *L 27 May*,
£1,045 ($1,641)

(Captions to 4 and 5 on p.220.)

including the well-known 'Bellarmine' jugs (illustrated on page 191). The secrets of stoneware manufacture still being unknown in England, even pieces with the English Royal arms (fig.1) had to be imported from Cologne. In a patriotic age, there naturally grew up a strong public desire to replace this lucrative foreign trade with a home-grown product.

After several abortive (or at least short-lived) ventures in London, which produced robustly-potted jugs almost indistinguishable from the German, the production of stoneware in England got under way in the late 17th century, at first in Fulham and then in Nottingham. English potters, with the advantage of a pure white clay more refined than the grey or buff bodies typical of the German potteries, began to exploit the elegance of which stoneware was capable, creating a unique English contribution to ceramics. So fine were the results that inroads were even made into the porcelain market, hitherto a monopoly of the Chinese. In Fulham, John Dwight produced fine work, most typically small mugs, thinly-potted and light, undecorated apart from reeding at the neck, often with a silver-mounted rim (fig.2). The Nottingham potters, most notably John Morley, made equally fine pieces in a brown-washed body often, as seen in fig.3, potted with a double wall, the outer surface pierced with flowers and incised with foliage.

The idea was soon taken up in Staffordshire, the centre of the English ceramic industry. By the second quarter of the 18th century, salt-glazed stoneware provided the cheapest (and indeed for a while the only) English answer to the craze for porcelain which was sweeping Europe. The whiteness and delicacy of the body now came into its own, with the production of pieces in direct imitation of Meissen and other fashionable European porcelain, such as the simple but refined rosewater bottle (fig.4) and the very rare figure of a wild boar (fig.5).

Alongside this new fashion, the Staffordshire potters also continued to make pieces in the purely English rustic tradition, still most elegantly potted but imbued with the English sense of humour and intended simply for fun. With its great charm and its strong flavour of 'folk art' this type is now the most desirable of English salt-glazed stoneware. Indeed, the world record for any piece of English ceramics is currently held by the important 'pew group' (fig.6) from the Rous Lench collection. From the same

6

7

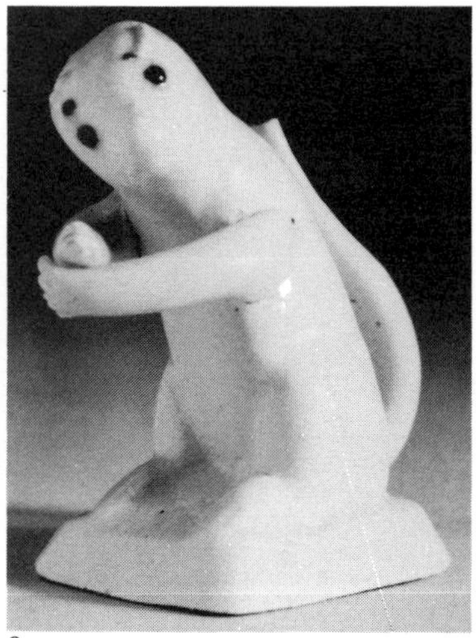
8

9

10

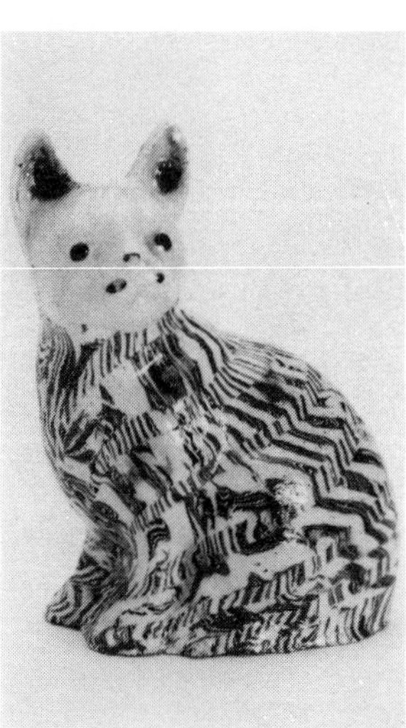
11

4 *(illustrated on p219)*
A saltglaze rosewater bottle, c.1735, foot chips, 22.5cm (8¾in), *L 1 July,*
£935 ($1,496)

5 *(illustrated on p219)*
A saltglaze freestanding figure of a boar, c.1750, after a Meissen original, tail and leg restored, 12.5cm (5in), *L 1 July,*
£2,640 ($4,224)

6
A very rare saltglaze pew group, c.1745, said to have been modelled by Aaron Wood, some areas of restoration, 16.5cm (6½in), *L 1 July,*
£112,200 ($179,520)

7
A saltglaze crinoline figure of a lady, c.1740, modelled as a table bell, minor restoration to bodice, 11cm (4½in), *L 1 July,*
£52,800 ($84,480)

8
A saltglaze figure of a squirrel, c.1750, the eyes and brows picked out in brown, tip of tail missing, 6cm (2¼in), *L 21 Oct,*
£1,485 ($2,079)

9
A saltglaze figure of a cat, c.1750, eyes touched in brown, base chip, 9cm (3½in), *L 21 Oct,*
£1,265 ($1,771)

tradition comes the even more charming table bell modelled as a finely-dressed lady (fig.7). Amusing pieces of the same type may be had for less exceptional prices, among them many simply-modelled figures of birds and animals (figs 8 & 9).

Very often a piece was left undecorated or simply picked out in a blue or brown wash, but other techniques soon came into use, among the first being the combination of two differently-coloured clays to create a randomly-marbled effect known as 'solid-agate' (figs 10 and 11). Enamelling in the porcelain manner was also popular, though the necessity for repeated firings of the enamels would have cut down considerably on the cost advantages of stoneware. The enamels used were typically of a strong, clear palette which lends a particular distinction to the type (figs 12-17).

Around the middle of the 18th century the development of moulding techniques such as slip-casting and block-moulding led to increasingly elaborate and indeed fantastic pieces, from the silver-derived shapes such as the double-handled sauce boat (fig.18) to the extraordinary series of teapots and coffee pots in the form of shells, houses, animals (fig.23) and other outlandish creations.

Throughout the period under review, it is extremely uncommon to find a marked or dated piece of English stoneware, which makes a refreshing change from the obsessions of collectors of other types of ceramics who sometimes become over-concerned with marks. The lack of marks on stoneware leads to a concern with the intrinsic qualities of each piece rather than to collecting fashions for particular factories, but it is of course frustrating that we know so little of the detailed history of most of the pieces we come across. Very seldom can we safely attribute an object to a single potter, unless it be taken from a known mould. All the more reason, then, to value the occasionally-found documentary piece. Even such a simple object as the inkwell (fig.27) is highly valued for its incised date. A piece such as the rather crude tea cannister (fig.30), with the name of its owner, its maker and even the day of its manufacture incised into its body, is a rarity indeed.

Typically, the supplanting of one type of ceramic body by another takes place because of the invention of new and more serviceable types (either a more expensive improvement or a cheaper but acceptable alternative), and follows a decline in quality of the older type. Neither could really be said to be true of salt-glazed stoneware. Production more or less ceased by the end

10
A saltglaze 'solid-agate' figure of a seated pug, c.1745, 7cm (2¾in), *L 1 July,*
£4,180 ($6,688)

11
A saltglaze 'solid-agate' figure of a seated cat, c.1745, details picked out in brown and blue, 13cm (5in), *L 1 July,*
£1,430 ($2,288)

12
A saltglaze basket-moulded plate, c.1760, brightly painted, the rim edged in purple, 24.5cm (9¾in), *L 1 July,*
£1,540 ($2,464)

13
A saltglaze rose-ground cream jug, c. 1770, minor hair cracks, 9cm (3½in), *L 1 July,*
£935 ($1,496)

14
A Staffordshire saltglaze enamelled plate, c.1760, painted with a variation of the 'Parrot and fruit' pattern after Robert Hancock, 23.5cm (9¼in), *NY 9 Dec,*
$3,300 (£2,324)

12

13

14

15
A saltglaze bell-shaped mug, c.1760, brightly enamelled, the interior with a chevron and flowerhead border, cracked, 9cm (3¼in), *L 1 July,*
£825 ($1,320)

16
A saltglaze sucrier, c.1760, on three lion-mask and paw feet, rim restored, *L 1 July,*
£605 ($968)

17
A Staffordshire saltglaze teapot and cover, c.1750, cracks and some restoration, 8cm (3¼in), *L 25 Feb,*
£825 ($1,237)

15

16

17

of the 18th century, but there had been no falling-off of standards and the reason for the decline of stoneware is not certain. The newer creamware body had charms of its own but was little cheaper to produce and certainly less strong. It may be that by this time porcelain had become less of an exciting and expensive novelty; smaller porcelain factories were coming into being, and moving down-market by producing cheaper ranges of simply-enamelled wares which perhaps came too close to the price of creamwares and pearlwares (see pages 228-229) to leave room in the market for stoneware.

The rougher brown types of stoneware in the earlier style, which had never ceased production, continued to be made throughout the 19th century culminating in a brief but important late flowering at the Doulton factory from the 1870s (see page 290). Since then, most stonewares (including much of the excellent studio pottery produced today by artist-potters — see page 295) have built on the robust and massive traditions of European and Chinese stoneware, while the other possibilities of the body have been largely forgotten.

Further reading:

Arnold Mountford, *Staffordshire Salt-Glazed Stoneware,* 1971
Robin Hildyard, *Browne Muggs,* Victoria & Albert Museum, 1985
Adrian Oswald, *English Brown Stoneware,* 1982
Sally Mount, *The Price Guide to 18th Century English Pottery,* 1979

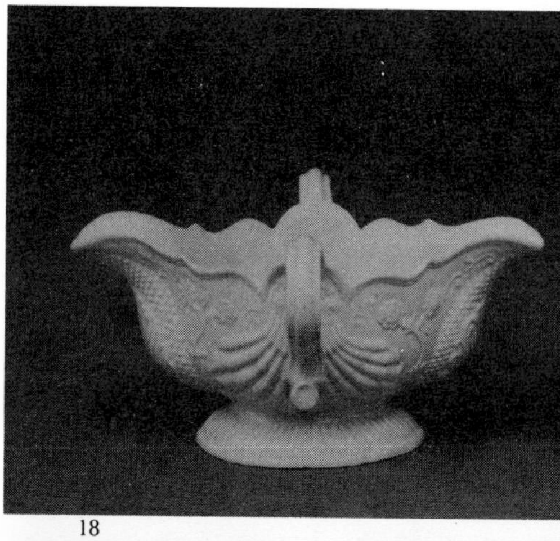
18

19

20

21

22

8
Staffordshire saltglaze wo-handled sauce boat, .1750, two small hair racks, 17cm (6¾in), *IY 9 Dec,* **2,090 (£1,472)**

9
Staffordshire saltglaze ug, c.1745, footrim with mall chip, 12.5cm (5in), *VY 9 Dec,* **4,675 (£3,292)**

0
Staffordshire saltglaze sauce boat, William Greatbatch, c.1764, hair rack, 17.5cm (7in), *VY 9 Dec,* **$1,540 (£1,085)**

21
A saltglaze double-handled sauce boat, c.1760, hair crack, 16cm (6¼in), *L 21 Oct,* **£1,650 ($2,310)**

22
A saltglaze piggin or cream stoup, c.1750 modelled as a miniature bucket, minute hair crack, 8cm (3¼in), *L 1 July,* **£528 ($845)**

23
A saltglaze squirrel teapot and cover, c.1745, the handle in the form of a lamprey, hair cracks, 15cm (6in), *L 1 July,* **£8,250 ($13,200)**

24
A Staffordshire saltglaze, teapot and cover, 1750s, with bird's head spout, chipped, 12cm (4¾in), *C 15 Jan,* **£462 ($693)**

25
A saltglaze hexagonal vase, c.1760, of baluster form, minor chips, 12cm (4¾in), *L 1 July,* **£572 ($915)**

26
A saltglaze fish jelly mould, c.1755, 16.5cm (6½in), *L 1 July,* **£308 ($493)**

27
A dated saltglaze inkwell, c.1761, of capstan form, inscribed in scratch-blue *W.M. 1761,* chips, 8cm (3½in), *L 1 July,* **£1,100 ($1,760)**

23

24

25

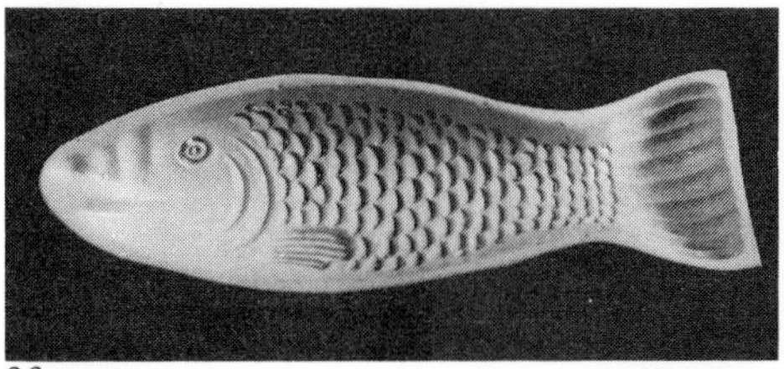
26

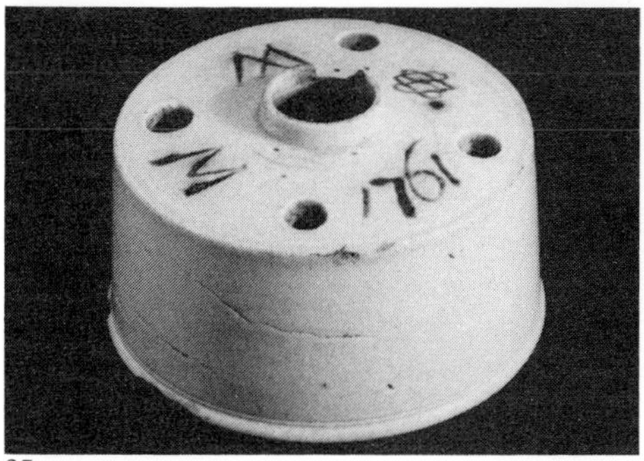
27

28

29

30

31

28
A Staffordshire saltglaze 'Admiral Vernon' commemorative teapot and cover, c.1740, with the inscriptions *by ad Vernon fort. chagre* and *Porto bello taken,* small chips and hair cracks, 14cm (5½in), *NY 9 Dec,* **$10,450 (£7,359)**

29
A documentary Suffolk stoneware cylindrical jug, c.1756, incised *Joseph Griffin Dishturner in Bury St. Edmunds, January y First 1756,* rim chips, 20.5cm (8in), *L 1 July,* **£1,100 ($1,760)**

30
A documentary saltglaze square tea canister, c.1767, the top incised *Mary Coall, 1767,* the base *Made by Tho:s Prouse, September ye 26th 1767,* chips discoloured, 12cm (4¾in), *L 1 July,* **£1,760 ($2,816)**

31
A pair of saltglaze stoneware figures of spaniels, mid 19th century, chips, 29.5cm (11¾in), *L 25 Feb,* **£440 ($660)**

1

2

3

4

5

6

7

8

9

10

11

1
A Lambeth Delft plate, 1756-63, painted in blue with a portrait bust of Frederick the Great, King of Prussia, minor chips, 22cm (8¾in), *L 1 July,*
£1,485 ($2,376)

2
A Delftware 'blue dash' tulip charger, c.1700, with everted rim, painted in turquoise, yellow, blue and brown, chip and flakes, 35cm (13¾in), *L 27 May,*
£1,265 ($1,986)

3
A Delftware charger, c.1700, painted in manganese, green and yellow with a portrait of a monarch, probably intended as William III, flakes, 36cm (14in), *L 25 Feb,*
£935 ($1,402)

4
A Delftware Apothecaries' Company pill slab, 18th century, 30cm (11¾in), *S 19 Mar,*
£1,870 ($2,861)

5
A Liverpool Delft puzzle jug, third quarter 18th century, painted in blue with a wager, cracked, 19cm (7½in), *C 16 Apr,*
£220 ($341)

6
A Liverpool Delft flower brick, c.1750, the blue-washed top pierced with holes, each side painted with stylised plants, 16cm (6¼in), *L 1 July,*
£440 ($704)

7
A Lambeth Delft globular mug, c.1690, inscribed in blue *GOD:BLES:KING: WILIAM:&:Q:MAR,* glaze flaking restored, 11cm (4¼in), *L 1 July,*
£8,250 ($13,200)

8
An inscribed and dated Delftware mug, 1720, painted *To the Pious Memory of Queen Anne 1720* between ribbed and lined bands, repair, flakes and chips, 16cm (6¼in), *L 27 May,*
£4,070 ($6,390)

9
A Liverpool Delft vase, c.1760, painted in blue with figures among classical ruins, minor chips, 19cm (7½in), *L 21 Oct,*
£550 ($770)

10
A Liverpool Delftware double-lipped sauceboa c.1760, with twin fox handles and fluted spouts, painted in blue with chinoiserie flowering plants, flaking, 21.5cm (8½in), *S 10 Dec,*
£286 ($400)

11
A Lambeth Delft bowl, c.1756-63, the interior inscribed *Success To The British Arms,* the exterior painted in blue, yellow and manganese with figures on chinoiserie islands, crack and chips, 27cm (10½in), *L 1 July,*
£396 ($634)

1
A Lambeth Delft ballooning plate, c.1785, painted in blue, green and manganese, minor chips and flaking, 22.5cm (8¾in), *L 21 Oct,*
£1,265 ($1,771)

2
A Bristol Delft tulip charger, 1720-40, brightly painted in blue, yellow dark green and touches of red, minor flaking, 35.5cm (14in), *L 1 July,*
£1,320 ($2,112)

3
A Bristol Delft blue and white scalloped plate, c.1760, painted with a river scene, 20cm (8in), *NY 9 Dec,*
$440 (£310)

4
A pair of London Delft blue and white plates, *(one illustrated)*, painted with a shepherd and his sweetheart before an Italianate ruin, 23cm (9in), *NY 9 Dec,*
$440 (£310)

5
A Lambeth Delftware dish, c.1750, painted in blue, iron-red, yellow and green with a Chinaman in a garden, hills beyond, rim chips, 33.5cm (13in), *L 27 May,*
£330 ($518)

6
A Bristol or Liverpool Delft bourdaloue, c.1740, painted in blue with two scenes of a chinoiserie couple in a landscape, 23cm (9in), *L 1 July,*
£5,720 ($9,152)

7
A pair of Bristol Delftware flowerbricks, *(one illustrated)*, c.1740, each pierced on the top with a square aperture and smaller holes, minor chips and cracks, 14 and 14.5cm (5½ and 5¾in), *L 27 May,*
£440 ($691)

8
A Bristol Delft sucrier and cover, c.1720, brightly painted with stylised flowers, cracks and minor chips, 11cm (4¼in), *L 1 July,*
£682 ($1,091)

9
A Lambeth Delft pill jar, early 18th century, inscribed in manganese on a blue tasselled cherub-and-shell label, minor rim chip, 9cm (3½in), *L 1 July,*
£418 ($669)

10
A Lambeth Delft bottle vase, c.1740, painted in blue, 14cm (5½in), *L 1 July,*
£330 ($528)

11
A Bristol Delft blue and white urn, c.1760, painted in the so-called 'Bowen' style, cracks and minor chips, 23.5cm (9¼in), *L 1 July,*
£935 ($1,496)

12
A Lambeth Delft drug jar, c.1670, chips and crack, 19.5cm (7¾in), *L 1 July,*
£1,210 ($1,936)

1

2

3 4

5

6

7

10

8

9

11

12

1

2

3

4

5

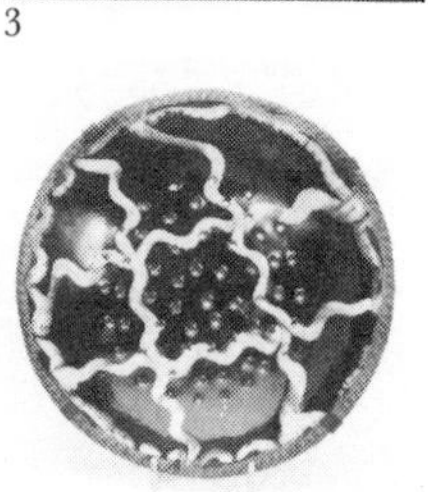
6

7 8

9 10 11 12

13

14

15

16

17

1
A Staffordshire slipware posset pot, c.1680, cracks and chips, 10.5cm (4in), *L 1 July,*
£1,210 ($1,936)

2
A Staffordshire slipware posset pot, inscribed *RICHARD MARE 1690,* minor chips, 11cm (4¼in), *L 1 July,*
£6,820 ($10,912)

3
A Staffordshire slipware jug, dated 1704, slip-trailed in dark brown and dotted in cream with a central stylised tulip flanked by birds on branches, 23cm (9in), *L 1 July,*
£55,000 ($88,000)

4
A Staffordshire slipware bleeding bowl, c.1693, with the inscription *IOSEPH 1693,* cracks, 11.5cm (4½in), *L 1 July,*
£5,280 ($8,448)

5
A slipware deep dish, c.1680, the cream ground trailed in tones of brown and washed in blueish-green with cross-hatched fruit and foliage, cracks and flaking, 41.5cm (16¼in), *L 1 July,*
£12,100 ($19,360)

6
A Staffordshire slipware strainer, mid to late 18th century, pierced with numerous holes, lead glaze, 34cm (13¼in), *L 25 Feb,*
£495 ($742)

7
An Elers redware mug, c.1690, stamped in relief with a prunus spray, cracks and repairs, 9cm (3½in), *L 27 May,*
£1,210 ($1,900)

8
A treacle-glazed miniature mug, c.1690, minor chips, 6.5cm (2½in), *L 27 May,*
£528 ($829)

9
An Elers redware hexagonal teapot and cover, c.1690, inset with reserves moulded in low relief with exotic birds and plants, minor chips, 9.5cm (3¾in), *L 27 May,*
£1,155 ($1,813)

10
A Whieldon redware cream jug, c.1760, moulded in relief with a naked Chinese boy among foliage, repair, 8cm (3in), *L 27 May,*
£902 ($1,416)

11
An Elers redware tankard, c.1690, with panels of applied decoration including a wyvern and a 'Merry Andrew', cracks, 17.5cm (6¾in), *L 27 May,*
£1,595 ($2,504)

12
An Elers redware milk jug, c.1690, applied with a wyvern and a 'Merry Andrew', minor chips, 11cm (4½in), *L 27 May,*
£1,155 ($1,813)

13
A Staffordshire solid agate-ware pecten-shell-moulded teapot and cover, c.1755, veined in tones of blue, brown, cream and ochre, restored, 13.5cm (5¼in), *L 25 Feb,*
£1,320 ($1,980)

14
A Staffordshire solid agate-ware cream jug and a stand, c.1740, of silver shape, veined in blue, cream and brown, lead-glazed, repairs, jug 9cm (3½in), *S 19 Mar,*
£1,100 ($1,683)

15
A Staffordshire solid agate-ware cream jug, 1740-45, of silver shape, veined in blue, cream and brown, 8cm (3¼in), *NY 9 Dec,*
$4,400 (£3,099)

16
A Staffordshire solid agate-ware cream jug, c.1740, of silver shape, veined in blue, cream and brown with touches of yellow, tiny chip, 9cm (3½in), *L 1 July,*
£1,540 ($2,464)

17
A Staffordshire solid agate-ware teapot and cover, possibly Whieldon, 1740-45, veined in blue, cream and brown, repairs, lion knop, 12cm (4¾in), *NY 9 Dec,*
$2,090 (£1,472)

1
A Whieldon 'house' tea cannister, c.1760, the body moulded as a three-storey house below a frieze of oak leaves and grotesque masks, uneven treacle glaze, 12.5cm (5in), *L 21 Oct,*
£1,540 ($2,156)

2
A Whieldon sugar bowl and cover, c.1760, applied with trailing branches of fruit and flowers, bird knop, traces of gilding, cover repaired, 10cm (4in), *L 1 July,*
£605 ($968)

3
A Whieldon child's mug, c.1760, splashed in manganese, minor chips, 7.5cm (3in), *L 21 Oct,*
£1,155 ($1,617)

4
A Whieldon-type toy jug and two toy teabowls, c.1770, all sponged in a manganese 'tortoiseshell' glaze, handle glued, 6cm (2¼in), *S 10 Dec,*
£440 ($616)

5
A Whieldon-type covered melon sauce tureen on attached stand, c.1770, the whole covered in yellow and green glazes, some discolouration, 19.5cm (7¾in), *NY 9 Dec,*
$8,800 (£6,197)

6
A chocolate-brown stoneware teapot and cover, c.1730, applied with prunus sprays, chips, 11cm (4¼in), *L 27 May,*
£440 ($691)

7
A Wedgwood/Whieldon 'cauliflower' teapot and cover, c.1765, cover possibly married, with white florettes above green-glazed leaves, spout tip mounted in silver, 12.5cm (5in), *NY 9 Dec,*
$495 (£349)

8
A Wedgwood/Whieldon 'cauliflower' milk jug and a cover, c.1765, cover possibly married, with white florettes above green-glazed leaves, 15.5cm (6in), *NY 9 Dec,*
$385 (£271)

9
A 'Jackfield' teapot and cover, c.1760, decorated in relief with trails of flowering and fruiting vine, bird knop, glazed overall in black, traces of gilding, 14.5cm (5¾in), *L 25 Feb,*
£715 ($1,072)

10
A glazed Redware teapot and cover, c.1765-70, decorated with engine-turned bands, chips, impressed pseudo seal mark, 8.5cm (3¼in), *L 25 Feb,*
£308 ($462)

11
A 'Jackfield' jug, c.1760, decorated in relief with a trail of vines picked out in gilding, glazed overall in black, gilding rubbed, minor chips, 14cm (5½in), *L 27 May,*
£253 ($397)

1

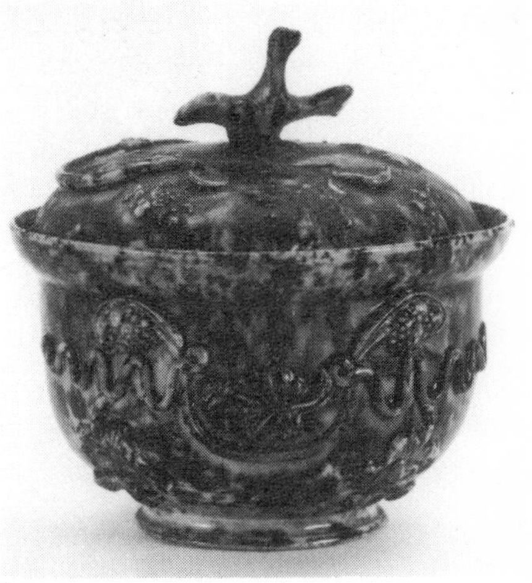
2

3

4

5

6

7 8

9 10

11

1

2

3

4

5

6

7

8

9

10

11

12

13

14

1
A creamware teapot and cover, 1770s, with entwined strap handle and reeded spout, spout lip repaired, 11.5cm (4½in), *C 8 Oct,*
£242 ($339)

2
A Cockpit Hill teapot and cover, c.1770, painted probably by a Derby porcelain artist, cover repaired, 9.5cm (3¾in), *L 21 Oct,*
£682 ($955)

3
A Wedgwood creamware teapot and cover, 1770s, impressed *Wedgwood*, 13cm (5½in), *C 8 Oct,*
£1,045 ($1,463)

4
A Wedgwood armorial creamware part tea and coffee service, (*part illustrated*), late 18th century, comprising 26 pieces, chip to one plate, impressed marks, *S 16 July,*
£825 ($1,295)

5
A creamware commemorative jug, c.1786, painted with farming implements and inscribed *God Speed the Plough* and *Success to the Grain Returned,* slight chip, 22cm (8¾in), *C 8 Oct,*
£462 ($647)

6
A pair of Wedgwood creamware plates, (*one illustrated*), c.1800, impressed marks, 24cm (9½in), *C 4 Nov,*
£176 ($248)

7
A Wedgwood creamware dessert service,(*part illustrated*), early 19th century, comprising 26 pieces, one damaged, slight wear, painted pattern no.1141, *L 25 Feb,*
£1,430 ($2,145)

8
A Melbourne octagonal sauce tureen and cover, c.1770, transfer-printed in black with exotic bird vignettes and Arcadian scenes of dancers, small chip to cover, 18cm (7in), *L 21 Oct,*
£352 ($493)

9
A polychrome enamelled Leeds creamware teapot and cover, c.1770, cover cracked, 14cm (5¾in), *S 10 Dec,*
£1,430 ($2,002)

10
A creamware teapot and cover, c.1790, with a cold gilded inscription *Eliz. Mulley, Little Cornard*, cracks to cover and handle, 13.5cm (5¼in), *S 10 Dec,*
£264 ($370)

11
A Leeds baluster coffee pot and cover, c.1770, cover damaged, handle with firing fault, 20cm (8in), *L 21 Oct,*
£330 ($462)

12
A Wedgwood creamware tea caddy, c.1770, some chips, impressed *Wedgwood*, 10cm (4in), *S 10 Dec,*
£165 ($231)

13
A Bristol pottery barrel, c.1820, painted in a Pratt-type palette of oxides, one end initialled J.C., 11cm (4½in), *S 10 Dec,*
£264 ($370)

14
A puzzle jug, early 19th century, of Pratt type, rim chip repaired, 29cm (11½in), *L 27 May,*
£506 ($794)

1
An inscribed pearlware bowl, late 18th/early 19th century, enamelled with a farm scene, inscribed *Isaac and Elizth. Gouldsack/ Success to the Farmer/ And God speed the Plough,* 23.5cm (9¼in), *S 19 Mar,*
£462 ($707)

2
A commemorative pearlware coffee pot and cover, 1788, the body inscribed *Elizabeth Beet, 1788,* restored spout lip, 26.5cm (10½in), *C 16 Apr,*
£363 ($523)

3
A Sunderland pearlware enamelled punch bowl, Phillips & Co., 1810-15, transfer-printed with a scene of a sailing vessel, a view of the cast-iron bridge over the River Wear at Sunderland, and with a portrait of Sir Francis Burdett (made after the latter's release from the Tower of London in 1810), crack, 41cm (16in), *NY 9 Dec,*
$1,100 (£775)

4
A creamware transfer-printed and enamelled jug, c.1815, printed in sepia with a strolling couple on one side and on the reverse with a British ship, heightened in colours, 22cm (8½in), *NY 9 Dec,*
$550 (£387)

5
A pearlware mug, painted in green, yellow, brown and blue enamels with a boat, sailor and anchors, inscribed, 14cm (5½in), *C 4 Nov,*
£77 ($108)

6
A Staffordshire 'coaching' jug, c.1830, some wear, 16cm (6¼in), *L 27 May,*
£352 ($553)

7
A pottery jug, c.1830, printed in brown with two scenes of rural life and inscription, 26cm (10¼in), *S 19 Mar,*
£462 ($707)

8
An enamelled earthenware jug, dated 1813, possibly Don Factory, painted with a scene of a butcher and a shield bearing his tools, inscribed *Thomas Jones/Butcher/1813,* repair and crack, 19.5cm (7¾in), *S 10 Dec,*
£1,210 ($1,694)

9
A J. Harley (Lane End) pearlware jug, early 19th century, commemorating the campaign against or the capture of Napoleon, with a satirical scene entitled *John Bull Showing the Corsican Monkey,* crack, printed marks, 15.5cm (6in), *S 10 Dec,*
£418 ($585)

10
A pearlware blue and white jug, 1809, printed with oriental figures in a rocky river landscape, with a heart inscribed *Joseph & Elizabeth Clegg 1809,* 30.5cm (12in), *C 21 Oct,*
£429 ($600)

11
A pearlware blue and white jug, 1797, inscribed *Ralph and Bettey Pots Didsbury 1797,* 16cm (6¼in), *C 9 July,*
£176 ($275)

12
A Liverpool creamware 'Nelson' jug, c.1805-10, transfer-printed with a scene entitled *Britannia weeping over the Ashes of her Matchless Hero, Lord Nelson,* 18cm (7in), *L 25 Feb,*
£418 ($627)

13
A Liverpool creamware jug, 1797, printed in colours on one side with a view of Liverpool lighthouse on Bidston Hill and on the other with a house with figures inscribed *Bowness 1797,* chip and rubbing, 21cm (8½in), *C 9 July,*
£462 ($721)

1

2

3 4

5

6

7

8

9

10

11

12

13

1 2

3

4

5 6

7

8

9

10 11

12

13

14

1
A Neale variegated vase, 1776-78, the blue and brown speckled ground decorated in relief with a portrait medallion on the front and a patera on the reverse, highlighted with gilding, black basaltes base, impressed mark, 21cm (8¼in), *NY 9 Dec,*
$770 (£542)

2
A Palmer variegated vase and a cover, c.1775, the solid agate body veined in brown, black, blue, white, mauve and grey, applied with a portrait medallion one side and a patera on the other, crest repaired and both handles removed, black basaltes base, impressed mark, 19.5cm (7¾in), *NY 9 Dec,*
$825 (£581)

3
A Turner smear-glazed stoneware part tea service, c.1810, each piece decorated in relief with figural vignettes flanked by lilies on a brown ground, each with impressed mark, teapot 16cm (6¼in), *NY 9 Dec,*
$1,430 (£1,007)

4
A Turner caneware part tea service, c.1790, each piece decorated with engine-turned bamboo and enriched with blue enamel line borders, marked, teapot 11cm (4½in), *NY 9 Dec,*
$1,100 (£775)

5
A Turner smear-glazed jug, c.1790, moulded with angels between leaves and vines, brown glazed neck and plated mounts, 25.5cm (10in), *C 10 June,*
£187 ($294)

6
A Turner smear-glazed water jug and cover, c.1790, moulded with bacchanalian figures and cherubs, 18cm (7in), *C 10 June,*
£187 ($294)

7
A Wedgwood black basaltes bust of Cicero, 19th century, minor chips, impressed mark and title, 29cm (11¼in), *L 27 May,*
£352 ($553)

8
A Wedgwood black basaltes bust of Mercury, c.1891-1900, impressed mark, 43cm (17in), *Syd 12 Nov,*
Aus$693 (£315; $441)

9
A 'three-colour' Wedgwood vase and cover, 19th century, applied with two medallions, the signs of the Zodiac above, crack, 24cm (9½in), *C 16 Apr,*
£297 ($460)

10
A pair of Wedgwood black basaltes vases and covers, *(one illustrated),* c.1800, each body sprigged with the 'dancing hours', impressed marks, 23cm (9in), *S 16 July,*
£572 ($898)

11
A Wedgwood cassolette vase, 1805, on tripod support, chip, lacking cover, impressed mark and date, 17cm (6¾in), *S 16 July,*
£440 ($691)

12
A Wedgwood black basaltes plaque of 'Lioness and Cupids', late 18th/early 19th century, impressed mark, 28cm (11in), *L 27 May,*
£605 ($950)

13
A pair of Wedgwood 'three-colour' covered vases, *(one illustrated),* 19th century, each with a black ground decorated in white with figures from 'Domestic Employment', repairs, impressed mark, 23cm (9in), *NY 9 Dec,*
$1,430 (£1,007)

14
A pair of Wedgwood vases and covers, *(one illustrated),* 1879, each sprigged with white reliefs of classical vignettes on a brown ground, chips and repairs, impressed mark and date code, 24cm (9½in), *L 25 Feb,*
£528 ($792)

1
A Wedgwood & Bentley black basaltes vase and cover, 1769-80, decorated in relief, minor chips, impressed mark, 19.5cm (7¾in), *NY 9 Dec,*
$1,430 (£1,007)

2
A Wedgwood & Bentley black basaltes vase and a cover, 1769-80, decorated in relief, impressed mark, 22cm (8¾in), *NY 9 Dec,*
$605 (£426)

3
A pair of Wedgwood black basaltes triton candlesticks, *(one illustrated),* 19th century, each modelled as a merman on a rockwork base, chip and repairs, impressed mark, 27.5 and 28cm (10¾ and 11in), *NY 9 Dec,*
$935 (£658)

4
A Wedgwood rosso antico pyrophorus vase, c.1815, the central inkwell with detachable cone and matching inner pot, minor chip, impressed mark, 9.5cm (4in), *S 10 Dec,*
£418 ($585)

5
A pair of Wedgwood & Bentley black basaltes vases, *(one illustrated),* c.1775, replacement wood covers, chips, moulded circular mark, 23cm (9in), *L 21 Oct,*
£792 ($1,109)

6
A Wedgwood rosso antico amphora, c.1805, decorated in black relief, lacking cover, impressed mark, 21.5cm (8½in), *NY 9 Dec,*
$990 (£697)

7
A Wedgwood rosso antico covered canopic urn, c.1805, decorated in black relief, the interior with a sunk box, small chips, impressed mark, 26.5cm (10½in), *NY 9 Dec,*
$4,125 (£2,905)

8
A Wedgwood blue and white jasper scent bottle, late 18th century, decorated in white relief with Venus and Cupid, with contemporary gilt-metal mounts, 12.5cm (5in), *NY 19 Sept,*
$715 (£483)

9
A Wedgwood blue jasper portrait medallion, 19th century, of Richard Howe, First Earl, impressed mark, incised title, 11cm (4¼in), *C 15 Jan,*
£110 ($165)

10
A garniture of three Adams blue and white jasper covered vases, *(part illustrated),* each decorated in white relief with Venus and Cupid, repair and crack, impressed mark, largest 28.5cm (11¼in), *NY 9 Dec,*
$1,430 (£1,007)

11
A Wedgwood 'Lahore' pattern lustre bowl, 1920-29, printed urn mark, 25cm (9¾in), *L 25 Feb,*
£1,540 ($2,310)

12
A Wedgwood flame fairy-land lustre vase, 1920s, decorated with the 'Imps on a Bridge and Tree House' design, initials S.M-J., printed urn mark, 29.5cm (11½in), *L 27 May,*
£1,430 ($2,245)

13
A Wedgwood fairyland lustre vase, 1920s, decorated with the 'Butterfly Women' design, printed urn mark, 20cm (8in), *L 27 May,*
£572 ($898)

14
A Wedgwood flame fairy-land lustre bowl, 1920s, the exterior with the 'Poplar Trees' pattern, printed urn mark, 23cm (9in), *L 27 May,*
£748 ($1,174)

15
A Wedgwood fairyland lustre bowl, 1920s, the interior decorated with the 'Woodland Elves' design, the exterior with 'Castle on a Road' panels, gilding rubbed, printed urn mark, 24cm (9½in), *L 21 Oct,*
£682 ($955)

WEDGWOOD
Wedgwood
from c.1900

1 2

3

4

5

6

7

8

9

10

11

14

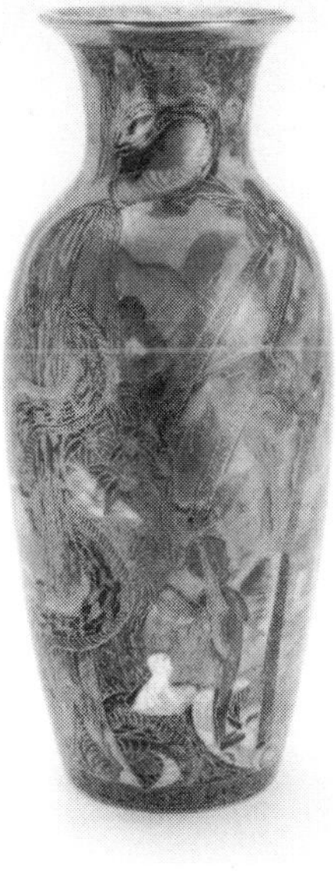
12

13

15

1

2

3

4

5

6

7

8

9

10

11

12

13

1
A Ralph Hall earthenware meat dish, c.1830, 43cm (17in), *Syd 12 Nov,*
Aus$187 (£85; $119)

2
A pair of Rogers blue and white meat dishes, *(one illustrated)*, depicting the North East view of Lancaster, 53.5cm (21in), *C 4 Nov,*
£341 ($481)

3
A pair of Staffordshire blue and white meat dishes, (*one illustrated*), early 19th century, 53.5cm (21in), *C 16 Dec,*
£352 ($493)

4
A Mason's Ironstone sauce tureen, cover and stand, 1815-20, in the so-called 'Mogul' pattern, some enamel flaking, 19cm (7½in), *C 8 Oct,*
£231 ($323)

5
A Spode Ironstone breakfast service, (*part illustrated*), comprising 82 pieces, each painted in underglaze-blue and famille-rose enamels, printed marks in underglaze-blue and pattern no.2061 in iron-red, some damage, *C 9 July,*
£1,320 ($2,059)

6
A Mason's Ironstone part dinner service, (*part illustrated*), early 19th century, comprising 40 pieces, printed marks in sepia, some damage, *C 9 July,*
£1,012 ($1,579)

7
A Mason's Ironstone 'Old Japan' dinner service, (*part illustrated*), 1815-20, comprising 59 pieces, some damage, impressed circular marks, *S 19 Mar,*
£4,180 ($6,395)

8
A harlequin set of twelve Mason's Ironstone china jugs, (*one illustrated*), late 19th century, painted with red, blue and green Imari-style decoration, glaze chips and kiln cracks, 24 to 7.5cm (9½ to 3in), *JHB 29 Sept,*
R 2,800 (£883; $1,236)

9
A blue and white meat dish, S. Keeling & Co., of Hanley, c.1840-50, in the Abbey pattern, 54cm (21¼in), *Syd 12 Nov,*
Aus$330 (£150; $210)

10
An Ashworth Bros. Iron stone part dinner servic *(part illustrated)*, late 19th century, comprising 49 pieces, some damage, impressed and printed marks, *L 27 May,*
£770 ($1,209)

11
A Mason's Ironstone baluster vase, c.1845, 51cm (20in), *NY 10 June,*
$605 (£385)

12
A Staffordshire Ironston Imari vase and cover, 1830-40, minor restoration and cracks, 79.5cm (31¼in), *NY 9 Dec,*
$1,650 (£1,162)

13
A Mason's patent Ironstone 'Japan' pattern par dinner service, (*part illustrated*), 1815-20, comprising 69 pieces, some damage, *NY 9 Dec,*
$2,530 (£1,782)

Hicks & Meigh
c.1806-22

Mason's Ironstone China
c.1820 onwards

See also *Sotheby's Guide* vol.II p.277.

‹ Wood group of St. ›eorge and the Dragon, 770-90, minor resto- ations, 29cm (11½in), . *21 Oct,*
990 ($1,386)

‹ Wood equestrian group ›f St. George and the ›ragon, 1770-80, the ›rown horse with tail ›estored, the spear a metal ›eplacement, minor ›epairs, 27.5cm (11in), *›Y 9 Dec,*
›1,925 (£1,356)

›
‹ Wood group of Cupid ›n a lioness, c.1770, ›estorations, impressed ›umeral 46, 21.5cm 8¾in), *NY 25 Jan,*
›2,640 (£1,899)

›
‹ Wood figure of a ›himneysweep's lad, ›.1780, wearing a brown ›vaistcoat and yellow ›reeches, 24cm (9½in), *› 16 July,*
›1,045 ($1,641)

›
A Wood group of Venus ›nd Cupid, c.1780, ›upid's wing restored, ›6.5cm (10½in), *L 25 Feb,*
›682 ($1,023)

›
A Walton group of ›Songsters', c.1810, the ›ase titled between blue ›scrolls, some restoration, ›mpressed mark, 20cm ›8in), *L 25 Feb,*
£286 ($429)

7
A pearlware figure of Venus, late 18th century, on a square base lined in brown, 21cm (8¼in), *S 19 Mar,*
£209 ($320)

8
A pearlware mask jug, depicting Admiral Howe, c.1800, cracked and chipped, 16cm (6½in), *C 8 Oct,*
£330 ($462)

9
A pearlware model of a horse, c.1800, ears damaged, 14cm (7½in), *S 16 July,*
£1,485 ($2,331)

10
A Leeds-type pearlware figure of a horse, 1810-20, on an olive green base edged with a border of cobalt-blue moulded leafage, chip and hair cracks, 30cm (12in), *NY 19 Sept,*
$9,075 (£6,132)

11
A pair of Prattware figures of a sportsman and companion, *(one illustrated)*, c.1790, 20cm (8in), *NY 9 Dec,*
$2,200 (£1,549)

12
A pair of Prattware figures of Elijah and the Widow of Zarephath, c.1790, minor repairs, 25 and 25.5cm (9¾ and 10in), *NY 9 Dec,*
$880 (£620)

13
A Pratt-type cradle model, c.1800, chipped, 12cm (4¾in), *S 19 Mar,*
£594 ($909)

14
A pearlware bust of the young Napoleon, early 19th century, wearing the uniform of the first Consul, flaking, impressed *Bonaparte*, 24cm (9½in), *S 4 Sept,*
£242 ($375)

1

2

3

4

5

6

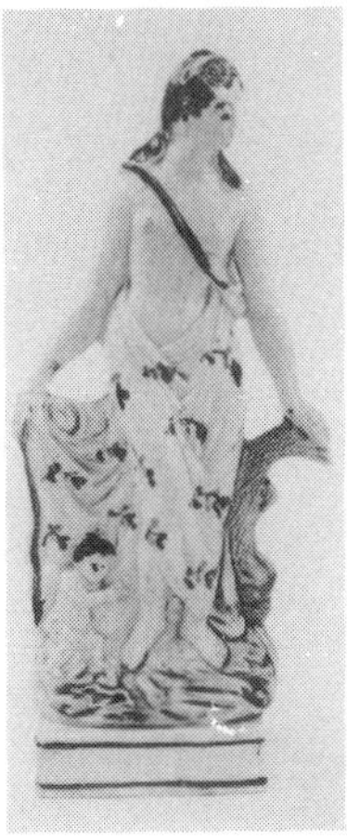
7

8

9

10

11

12

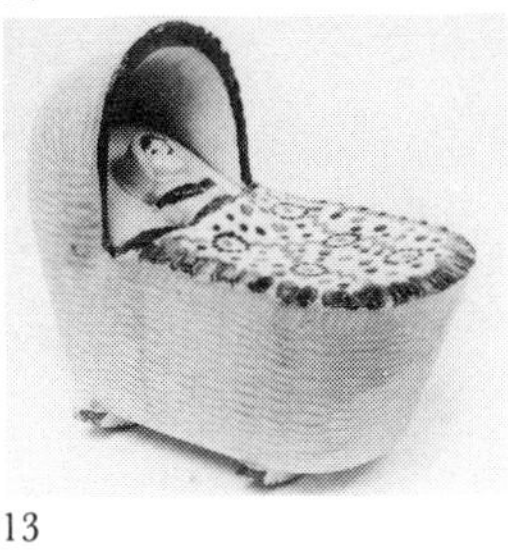
13

14

1

2

3

4

5

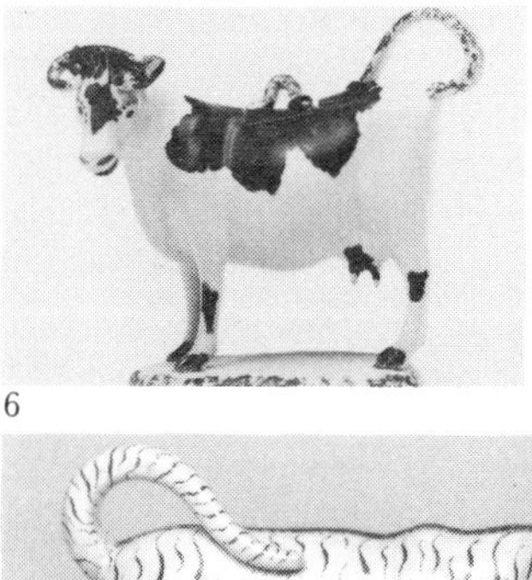
6

7

8

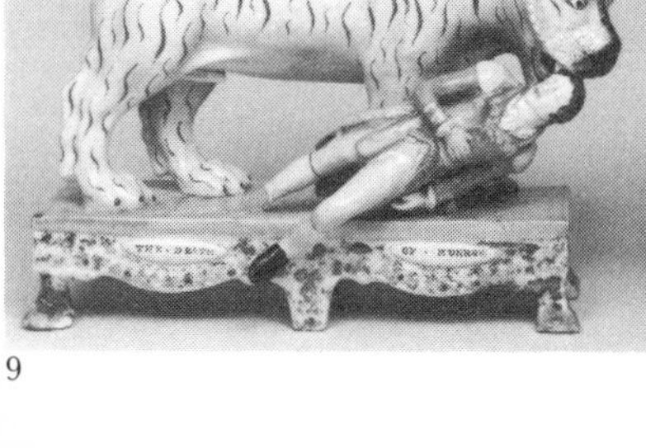
9

10

1
A Leeds pottery model of a stallion, c.1800, wearing a yellow bridle, on a green sponged plinth, one ear missing, some cracking to two legs, 43cm (17in), *C 15 Jan,*
£5,500 ($8,250)

2
A Yorkshire pottery horse, 18th/19th century, manganese dappled, wearing a blue saddle, ears chipped, tail repaired, 16.5cm (6½in), *C 15 Jan,*
£1,430 ($2,145)

3
A pair of Yorkshire cow groups (*one illustrated*), c.1800, some chips and cracks, 15.5cm (6¼in), *C 16 Apr,*
£2,035 ($3,154)

4
A Yorkshire cow group, c.1790, on a base sponged in green, blue, black and ochre, ear chipped, horn repaired, 14cm (5½in), *L 25 Feb,*
£935 ($1,402)

5
A creamware cow creamer and cover, late 18th/19th century, probably Leeds, restoration to tail and horns, 15.5cm (6in), *L 25 Feb,*
£1,155 ($1,732)

6
A Yorkshire cow creamer and cover, c.1800, on an oval base sponged in puce, green and black, chipped ears, 15.5cm (6¼in), *C 15 Jan,*
£528 ($792)

7
An Obadiah Sherratt group of 'The Widow of Zarephath', c.1830, inscribed 'Widow', small repairs to tree, 29cm (11¼in), *NY 25 Jan,*
$385 (£277)

8
An Obadiah Sherratt bust of Maria Foote, 1820-30, repaired at join to bust, inscribed on the front *Miss Foot,* 29cm (11¼in), *NY 9 Dec,*
$2,090 (£1,472)

9
An Obadiah Sherratt group of 'The Death of Monrow', c.1830, Monrow's right foot missing, other repairs, 37cm (14¾in), *NY 25 Jan,*
$7,700 (£5,539)

10
An Obadiah Sherratt bull baiting group, c.1830, inscribed *Bull.beating now Captin Lad,* minor damage and repairs, 36.5cm (14¼in), *NY 25 Jan,*
$2,970 (£2,137)

1
A Staffordshire figure of 'Jenny Lind as Alice in Meyerbeer's Opera', c.1847, crack and minor glaze flakes, 33.5cm (13¼in), *L 27 May,*
£462 ($725)

2
A Staffordshire bust of John Wesley, mid 19th century, after an Enoch Wood original, 32cm (12½in), *C 25 Feb,*
£231 ($347)

3
An Enoch Wood bust of John Wesley, early 19th century, signed, 31.5cm (12¼in), *S 19 Mar,*
£462 ($707)

4
A Staffordshire figure of 'Albert in Riding Attire', c.1848, his costume picked out in bright enamels, crack, no.A35/95, 19cm (7½in), *C 16 Dec,*
£198 ($277)

5
A Staffordshire group of the Duke of Wellington, c.1852, no.B4/25, 29.5cm (11½in), *C 5 Aug,*
£286 ($443)

6
A pair of Staffordshire figures of Albert and Victoria, 1840s, nos A8/10 and 11, 27 and 28cm (10½ and 11in), *C 5 Aug,*
£275 ($426)

7
A pair of Staffordshire figures of 'Cardinal Manning' and 'His Holiness the Pope', late 19th century, Pope's hand missing, 35.5cm (14in), *S 16 July,*
£385 ($604)

8
A pair of Staffordshire dogs, *(one illustrated)*, mid to late 19th century, each smoking a pipe, 25.5cm (10in), *L 25 Feb,*
£715 ($1,072)

9
A Staffordshire pigeon tureen and cover, c.1850, picked out in iron-red, on a green and brown base, chip, 22cm (8¾in), *C 16 Dec,*
£242 ($339)

10
A pair of Staffordshire greyhounds, *(one illustrated)*, c.1860, each holding hares in their mouths, brown markings, 28cm (11in), *C 16 Dec,*
£319 ($447)

11
A Staffordshire figure of a lion, early 19th century, glaze flaking, 13.5cm (5¼in), *L 25 Feb,*
£286 ($429)

12
A pair of Staffordshire spill holders, c.1880-1900, each in the form of a stag running before a flowering tree trunk, chased by a dog, 28cm (11in), *NY 10 June,*
$880 (£560)

13
A Staffordshire pottery money box, 19th century, picked out in bright enamels, on four bun feet, chip and some wear, 19cm (7½in), *C 16 Dec,*
£242 ($339)

14
A Staffordshire model of a hall, c.1870, with figure and dog finial, picked out in colours and gilt, 24cm (9½in), *C 16 Dec,*
£242 ($339)

15
A Staffordshire pottery pastille burner, c.1850, moulded with applied blue sherds, painted in brown, yellow and green, 29.5cm (11½in), *C 29 May,*
£176 ($278)

16
A Staffordshire group of 'The Flute Player', early 19th century, after an original by Ralph Wood, the details in colourful enamels, minor damage and repairs, 24cm (9½in), *L 25 Feb,*
£385 ($577)

1

2

3

4

5 6

7

8

9

10

11

12

13

14

15

16

1

2

3

4

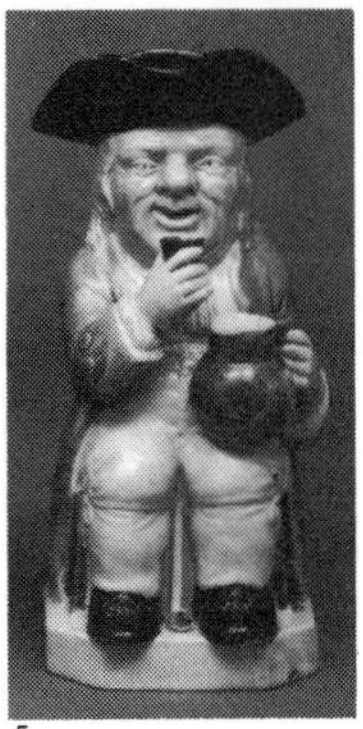
5

6

8

7

9

10

11

12

1
A Wemyssware pig, early 20th century, his coat painted with sprays of thistles, tail repaired, painted mark and the numeral 8, 43cm (17in), *L 21 Oct,*
£2,035 ($2,849)

2
A Wemyssware pig, c.1900, impressed mark, tail and rear trotter glued, 46cm (18in), *C 9 July,*
£935 ($1,459)

3
A Toby jug, late 18th century, of Wood type, wearing a blue coat with yellow waistcoat, restored, 28cm (11in), *L 21 Oct,*
£935 ($1,309)

4
A Wood Toby jug, c.1770, one finger restored, impressed *Ra. Wood Burslem* and 51, 24cm (9½in), *L 25 Feb,*
£2,860 ($4,290)

5
A Wood Toby jug, c.1770, the base chipped, impressed mould no.51, 24.5cm (9¾in), *NY 9 Dec,*
$2,640 (£1,859)

6
A creamware sailor Toby jug, late 18th century, repaired hat, 29.5cm (11½in), *S 16 July,*
£198 ($311)

7
A set of nine 'Carruthers Gould' Wilkinson Ltd, Toby jugs, each modelled as one of the First World War allied leaders, 26cm (10¼in), *S 10 Dec,*
£2,640 ($3,696)

8
A Wilkinson 'Winston Churchill' Toby jug, c.1940, designed by Clarice Cliff, modelled as a caricature of the statesman as First Lord of the Admiralty, base chipped, printed mark, facsimile signature, numbered 54, 29cm (11¾in), *L 25 Feb,*
£385 ($577)

9
A Wilkinson Ltd, 'Winston Churchill' Tob jug, c.1940, designed by Clarice Cliff, seated on a bulldog draped with the Union Jack, printed mark, facsimile signature, numbered 41, 30cm (11¾in), *L 25 Feb,*
£825 ($1,237)

10
A Wilkinson Ltd, 'Carruthers Gould' Toby jug, dated 1917, modelled as Admiral Beatty, printed marks, 25cm (10in), *S 16 July,*
£198 ($311)

11
A Goss model of 'The Priest's House, Prestbur Cheshire', c.1900, printed Goshawk in black enamel, 9cm (3½in), *C 9 July,*
£275 ($429)

12
A Goss model of the 'Abbot's Kitchen, Glastonbury', the brown building with green mossy markings and red door, 9cm (3½in), *C 2 Dec,*
£187 ($262)

R H & S

Robert Heron
(Wemyss ware)
c.1850-1929

1
A pair of Chelsea plates from the 'Duke of Cambridge' service, c.1765, each painted in iron-red, green, puce, yellow and brown, gold anchor marks, 23.5cm (9in), *NY 9 Dec,*
$2,420 (£1,704)

2
A Chelsea botanical plate, c.1755, painted with a sprig of purple blossoms with pale blue petals and green leaves, red anchor mark, 24cm (9½in), *NY 25 Jan,*
$1,760 (£1,266)

3
A Chelsea dish, c.1752-57, painted red anchor mark, 21.5cm (8½in), *Mel 24 June,*
Aus$880 (£383; $597)

4
A Chelsea botanical dish, c.1755, painted in blue, yellow, puce, brown, iron-red, black and green, cracks and chip, red anchor mark, 26.5cm (10½in), *NY 9 Dec,*
$550 (£387)

5
A Chelsea teabowl and saucer, c.1750, painted in Kakiemon style, enclosed within iron-red, blue, turquoise and yellow border, chip, *L 21 Oct,*
£660 ($924)

6
A Chelsea scolopendrium-moulded teabowl, c.1750, moulded with green leaves picked out in sepia and yellow, *L 21 Oct,*
£660 ($924)

7
A Chelsea fluted teabowl and saucer, c.1752-58, chips and hair crack, red anchor marks, *L 1 July,*
£374 ($598)

8
A Chelsea scolopendrium-moulded beaker, c.1753, minor chips, raised anchor mark, 7cm (2¾in), *L 1 July,*
£990 ($1,584)

9
A Chelsea 'cabbage leaf' bowl, 1752-56, the leaves in green and yellow with puce veins, the interior painted with a flower spray and scattered sprigs, hair crack, painted red anchor mark, 15.5cm (6in); sold with a Chelsea sunflower dish, *L 25 Feb,*
£1,045 ($1,567)

10
A Chelsea lobed beaker, c.1750, enamelled in Kakiemon style with a long-tailed bird on pierced rocks, the reverse with a phoenix in flight, 7cm (2¾in), *L 21 Oct,*
£4,510 ($6,314)

11
A Chelsea 'goat and bee' jug, c.1745-49, in the white, after a silver original, the body supported by two recumbent goats beneath a flowering branch applied with a bee, chips, incised triangle, 11cm (4¼in), *L 25 Feb,*
£3,300 ($4,950)

12
A Chelsea-Derby cup and saucer, c.1775, decorated in the atelier of James Giles, with swags of green flowers and foliage between claret-ground panels enriched in tooled gilding, saucer 12.5cm (5in), *L 27 May,*
£550 ($863)

13
A Chelsea-Derby bowl, early 1770s, with flower sprays beneath a lapis-blue band gilt with a vine, firing crack, gilt D and anchor mark, 26cm (10¼in), *S 16 July,*
£209 ($328)

14
A Chelsea lobed jug or 'cream ewer', c.1745, the body moulded with brightly coloured flowering branches, the foot applied with strawberry plants, cracks and restoration, incised triangle mark, 14cm (5½in), *L 1 July,*
£2,750 ($4,400)

Chelsea-Derby
1769-84

1

2

3

4

5 6

7

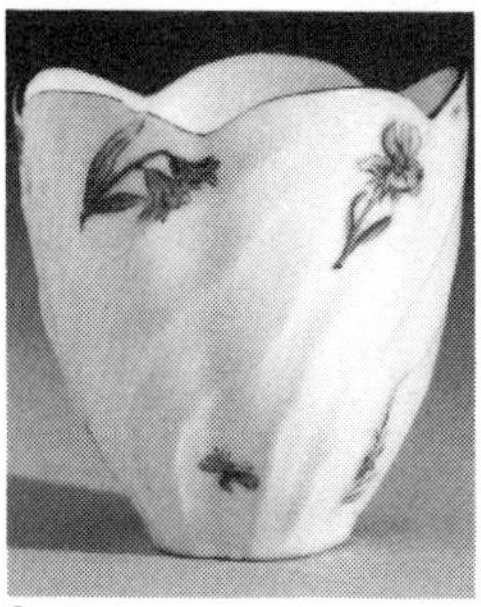
8

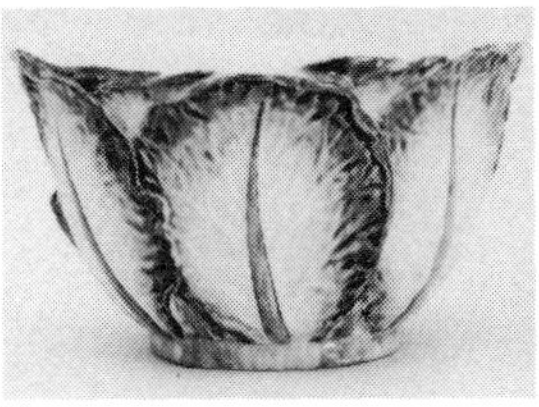
9

10

12

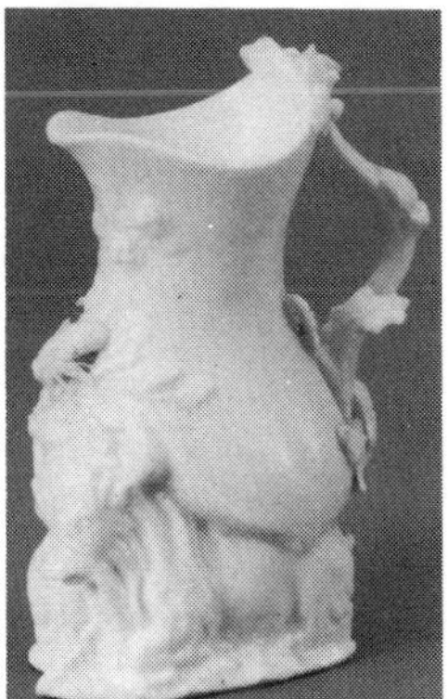
11

13

14

1

2

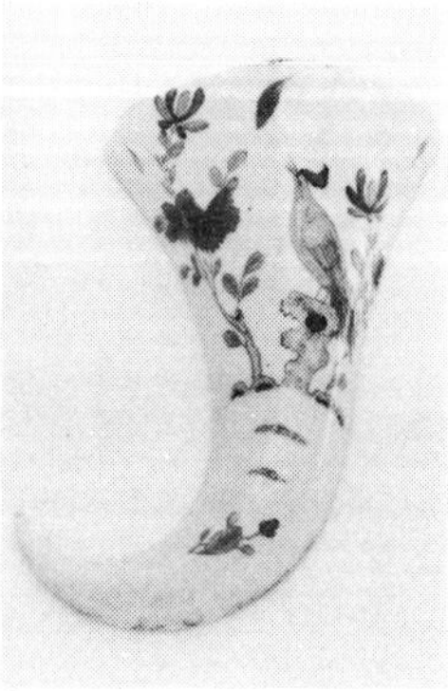
3

4

5

6

7 8 7

9

10

11

12

13

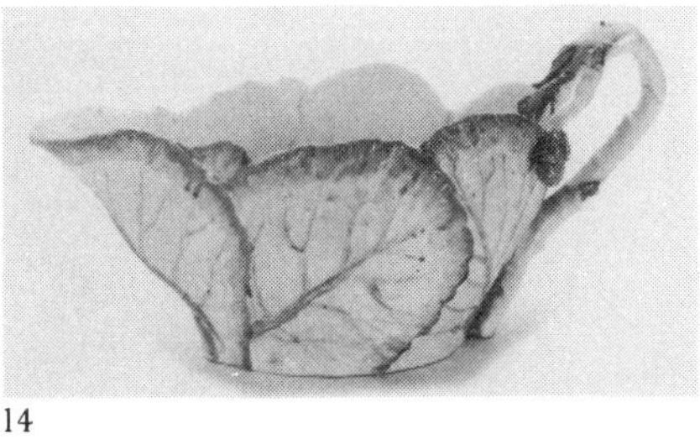
14

1
A Christian's Liverpool coffee pot and cover, c.1765, enamelled in colours with a repeated scene of orientals, 25cm (10in), *S 16 July,*
£770 ($1,209)

2
A Derby blue and white centrepiece, 1765-70, chips and hair cracks, 23cm (9in), *NY 9 Dec,*
$1,100 (£775)

3
A pair of William Ball, Liverpool, wall pockets, *(one illustrated)*, c.1755-60, brightly enamelled in 'famille-verte' style, chip, 12cm (4¾in), *L 1 July,*
£3,080 ($4,928)

4
Two Derby potpourri vases and covers, *(one illustrated)*, c.1760, each painted in a soft palette, chips, 18.5cm (7¼in), *L 25 Feb,*
£935 ($1,402)

5
A Derby coffee pot and cover, c.1760, painted in a soft palette, minor chip, 23cm (9in), *L 25 Feb,*
£2,090 ($3,135)

6
A Derby chinoiserie coffee pot and cover, c.1760, painted in iron-red, yellow, purple, blue, black, green and gold with two chinoiserie scenes, hair crack and repaired chips, 24cm (9½in), *NY 25 Jan,*
$770 (£554)

7
A pair of Derby custard cups and covers, c.1800, crowned batons and D in iron-red, 34 in black, 9cm (3½in), *S 16 July,*
£319 ($501)

8
A Derby cup and saucer, late 18th century, painted with turquoise festoons threaded through loops in a gilt dentil border, crowned batons and D in puce, gilder's numeral 2, impressed 1, *S 16 July,*
£154 ($242)

9
A Derby sugar bowl and cover, c.1800, of oval section, painted in the manner of John Brewer with two shipping scenes, painted crown, crossed batons and D in blue, 16cm (6¼in), *L 27 May,*
£605 ($950)

10
A Longton Hall scalloped plate, c.1755, painted by the 'Trembly Rose Painter' in shades of rose, purple, iron-red, green, blue and yellow, hair crack, 24.5cm (9½in), *NY 9 Dec,*
$770 (£542)

11
A Lowestoft teabowl and stand, c.1775, 'Dromedaries on Raft' pattern, *S 19 Mar,*
£209 ($320)

12
An early Longton Hall mug, c.1753, brightly enamelled in 'famille-rose' style, minor chip and hair crack, 9cm (3½in), *L 1 July,*
£704 ($1,126)

13
A Pennington's Liverpool sauce boat, c.1775-80, printed in blue with quails, floral border, stained, crack, 17.5cm (7in); sold with a Pennington's cream jug, and a Christian's Liverpool sauce boat, *C 15 Jan,*
£110 ($165)

14
A Longton Hall strawberry-leaf-moulded sauce boat, c.1755, the leaves veined in pale puce and edged in bright green, the interior with a rose spray, minor chips, 21cm (8¼in), *L 1 July,*
£1,045 ($1,672)

1
A Worcester 'King of Prussia' mask jug, first period, c.1760, transfer-printed by Robert Hancock with a portrait of Frederick, King of Prussia, and on the reverse with the angel of Fame, small chips, 15cm (6in), *NY 25 Jan,*
$550 (£396)

2
A Worcester mug, 1770-75, transfer-printed in blue with a portrait of George III, flanked by figures of Fame and Britannia, 15cm (5¾in), *L 1 July,*
£2,310 ($3,696)

3
A Worcester 'famille-verte' coffee cup, first period, 1752-53, two small chips, incised mark, 6.5cm (2½in), *NY 9 Dec,*
$1,650 (£1,162)

4
A Worcester cabbage leaf dish, first period, c.1765, moulded with veins issuing from a lavender midrib, painted in rose, iron-red, yellow, purple blue, brown and green, 21.5cm (8½in), *NY 9 Dec,*
$1,210 (£852)

5
A Worcester baluster mug, c.1765, unusually painted with a large strawberry among sprays of garden flowers, 15.5cm (6in), *L 1 July,*
£682 ($1,091)

6
A Worcester 'wet-blue'-ground dish, 1765-75, the centre painted with the 'Sir Joshua Reynolds' pattern, in Kakiemon style, fretted square mark, 22.5cm (9in), *L 21 Oct,*
£462 ($647)

7
A Worcester fluted dish, c.1765, from the 'Earl Manvers' service, 21.5cm (8½in), *L 1 July,*
£1,485 ($2,376)

8
A pair of Worcester 'Joshua Reynolds' coffee cups, *(one illustrated),* c.1760, each brilliantly enamelled with a long-tailed bird on a turquoise rock, *S 19 Mar,*
£352 ($539)

9
A Worcester finger bowl and stand, c.1761, bowl 7.5cm (3in), *L 1 July,*
£990 ($1,584)

10
A Worcester cabbage-leaf-moulded mask jug, c.1760, printed in black with a continous scene of a fox hunt, chip, 29.5cm (11¾in), *L 1 July,*
£1,430 ($2,288)

11
A Worcester teabowl and stand, c.1760, each piece enamelled with a gilt turquoise band bearing iron-red flowers about or above a medallion of flowers in the Compagnie-des-Indes style, *S 19 Mar,*
£330 ($505)

12
A Worcester trio, c.1760, each piece painted with a puce-edged rococo cartouche bearing the arms of Haywood with Parsons of Quedgley House in pretence, crossed swords and 9 mark in underglaze-blue, *L 1 July,*
£770 ($1,232)

1

2

3

4

5

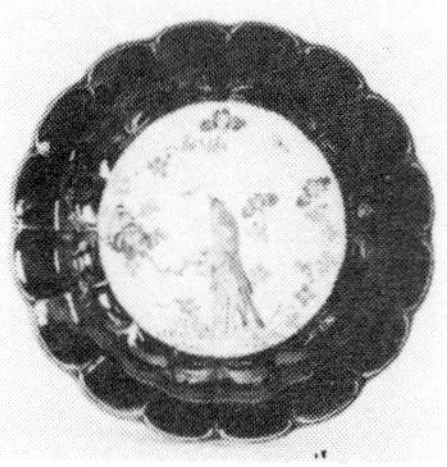
6

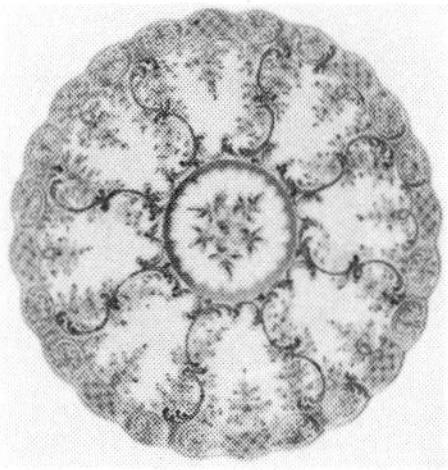
7

8

9

10

11

12

1

2

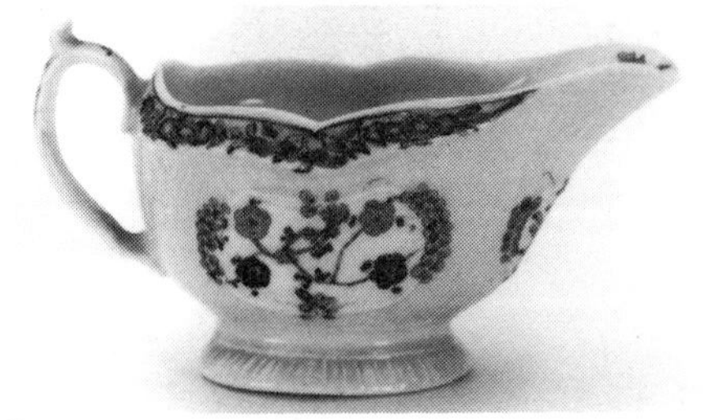
3

4

5

6

7

8

9

10

11

12

13

14

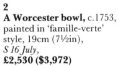

1
A Worcester yellow-ground cabbage-leaf-moulded jug, c.1765, with reserves of chinoiserie islands and flower sprays in European and Japanese styles, 29cm (12in), *L 1 July,*
£8,580 ($13,728)

2
A Worcester bowl, c.1753, painted in 'famille-verte' style, 19cm (7½in), *S 16 July,*
£2,530 ($3,972)

3
A Worcester yellow-ground sauce boat, 1765-70, with three reserves of Japanese-style flowers, 15cm (6in), *L 1 July,*
£2,530 ($4,048)

4
A Worcester sauce boat, c.1765, of silver shape, transfer-printed in black with vignettes after Hancock, the interior with the 'Piper' pattern of a girl dancing, 16cm (6¼in), *L 27 May,*
£660 ($1,036)

5
A Worcester cream jug, 1750s, with moulded cartouches enclosing polychrome floral sprays, crack, 10.5cm (4in), *S 10 Dec,*
£748 ($1,047)

6
A Worcester shell-shaped dish, 1750s, with polychrome floral spray, 8cm (3in), *S 10 Dec,*
£462 ($647)

7
A Worcester teapot and a cover, c.1760, 'pencilled' in black with the 'Red Bull' pattern of an oriental riding a buffalo in a landscape, chips, 11cm (4¼in), *L 27 May,*
£495 ($777)

8
A Worcester teapot and cover, c.1755-60, painted with a Chinese lady and boy in a garden, minute chips, painter's mark on both pieces, 9cm (3½in), *L 25 Feb,*
£1,650 ($2,475)

9
A Worcester 'scratch cross' jug, c.1755, delicately enamelled with vignettes of children and adult companions in Arcadian landscapes, 18cm (7in), *L 1 July,*
£5,060 ($8,096)

10
A Worcester mug, c.1770, painted and gilt with the arms of Miss Bland of Hurworth Manor, gilding flaked, crescent in underglaze-blue, 12cm (4¾in), *L 27 May,*
£440 ($691)

11
A Worcester teapot and cover, c.1770, painted in enamels with two exotic birds, minor cracks and chips, 13cm (5¼in), *L 21 Oct,*
£330 ($462)

12
A Worcester blue and white cream jug, c.1780, 'The Fruit Sprays', open crescent mark and scratched cross, 9cm (3½in), *S 19 Mar,*
£88 ($135)

13
A Worcester blue-scale-ground teapot and cover, c.1770, painted with panels of exotic birds, chips and crack, pseudo seal mark in underglaze-blue, 15cm (6in), *L 27 May,*
£572 ($898)

14
A Worcester apple-green-ground vase, c.1770, decorated with exotic birds, glaze flake, 18cm (7in), *L 1 July,*
£770 ($1,232)

. Worcester blue-scale-
'round vase and cover,
.1770, and a pair of
omplimentary vases *(one*
'llustrated), painted in
right enamels with panels
f exotic birds and dra-
ons amongst Japanese-
tyle flowering branches,
hip and crack, pseudo
eal mark in underglaze-
lue, 25.5cm (10in) and
8cm (7in), *L 27 May,*
,1,595 ($2,504)

. Worcester yellow-
;round plate, c.1770,
rightly painted in the
telier of James Giles,
:1cm (8½in), *L 1 July,*
:1,980 ($3,168)

. Worcester sugar bowl
nd cover, c.1770, with
ilt-edged panels of
lowers reserved on a gilt-
prigged blue ground,
ninor chips, 12.5cm (5in),
L 25 Feb,
:550 ($825)

A pair of Worcester mugs,
'one illustrated), c.1775, each
painted with a turquoise-
ground *caillouté* reserve,
below a *gros-bleu* and gilt
border, crescent mark,
3cm (3in), *L 1 July,*
£2,090 ($3,344)

5
A Worcester fluted teapot
and cover, c.1770, painted
with flower sprays below
an irregular French-
green-ground border,
12cm (4¾in), *L 1 July,*
£572 ($915)

6
A Worcester dish, c.1770,
the blue rim sprinkled
with gilt stars, slight wear,
script W mark, 26.5cm
(10½in), *L 25 Feb,*
£242 ($363)

7
A Worcester tureen and
cover, c.1770, moulded
with basket-weave and
painted by Fidelle
Duvivier with birds in a
landscape, large bud
knop, 16.5cm (6½in),
L 25 Feb,
£935 ($1,402)

8
A Worcester ovoid vase,
c.1778, painted in black
with the 'Milkmaids'
pattern, the reverse with
flower sprays, 18.5cm
(7¼in), *L 1 July,*
£330 ($528)

9
A Worcester teapot and
cover, c.1770, painted in
colourful enamels with the
'Wheatsheaf' pattern of
Japanese-style flowers and
wheat sheaves, between
blue-ground borders,
chips, pseudo seal mark in
underglaze-blue, enam-
elled crescent in iron-red,
13cm (5in), *L 27 May,*
£495 ($777)

10
A Worcester teapot and
cover, c.1770, painted
with a 'Japan' pattern of
Kakiemon-style panels
between blue-ground and
gilt borders, pseudo seal
mark in underglaze-blue,
15cm (6in), *L 25 Feb,*
£748 ($1,122)

Worcester
c.1760-90

Worcester
c.1765-75

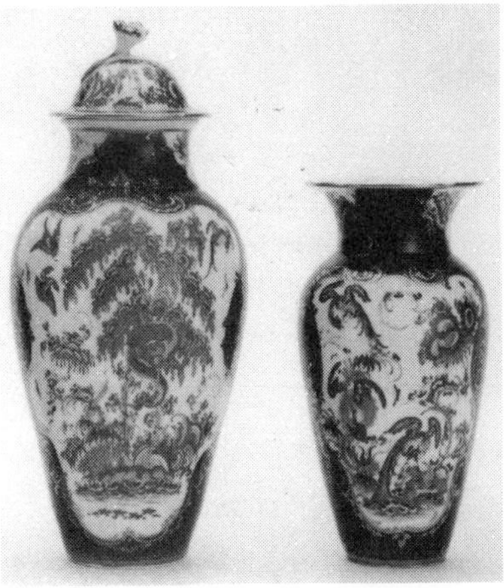

1

2

3

4

5

6

8

7

9

10

1

2

3

5

6

4

7

8

9

10

11

12

13

1
A Flight & Barr jug, dated 1802, inscribed in red *John Lord 1802*, 21.5cm (8½in), *L 27 May,*
£528 ($829)

2
A Flight, Barr & Barr honeypot and cover, c.1810, with gold and salmon-pink decoration, knop glued, painted mark including address, 12cm (4¾in), *S 19 Mar,*
£2,145 ($3,282)

3
A pair of Flight & Barr cache pots and stands, *(one illustrated)*, c.1800, painted bands of black ground set with brightly coloured garden flowers, gilding rubbed, painted mark and incised numerals, 15cm (6in), *L 27 May,*
£858 ($1,347)

4
A Barr, Flight & Barr mug, early 19th century, painted with views of Worcester, impressed BFB beneath a crown, 8.5cm (3½in), *C 8 Oct,*
£462 ($647)

5
A Flight plate from the 'Hope' service, 1790-92, made for the Duke of Clarence, centre painted *en grisaille* by Pennington, the rim in gilt on a rich blue ground, underglaze-blue *'Flight'* with a crown above and crescent below, 24.5cm (9¾in), *Mel 24 June,*
Aus$1,320 (£574; $895)

6
A Flight plate, c.1792, from the Hope service, painted *en grisaille* by Pennington, gilt rubbed, underglaze-blue crowned *'Flight'* and crescent mark, 24.5cm (9¾in), *L 21 Oct,*
£880 ($1,232)

7
A Barr, Flight & Barr bowl, c.1807, painted in the manner of Thomas Baxter, simulated grey marble ground, incised B, 16.5cm (6½in), *L 27 May,*
£1,870 ($2,936)

8
A pair of Flight, Barr & Barr topographical plat *(one illustrated)*, 1820-25, depicting the *Castle of Ler in the Gulph of Spesia* and *Waterfall and Bridge at Ryd Yorkshire*, green ground, slight surface wear, printed and impressed marks, 24.5cm (9¾in), *L 21 Oct,*
£528 ($739)

9
A pair of Flight, Barr & Barr vases, *(one illustrated* c.1810, painted with land-scape panels on a simu-lated grey marble ground, small chip, painted mark including address, 12.5cm (5in), *L 27 May,*
£1,925 ($3,022)

10
A pair of Barr, Flight & Barr sauce tureens, covers and stands, c.181 painted in puce and gilt, and a similar tureen, cove and stand, minor chips, printed and impressed marks, *S 19 Mar,*
£935 ($1,431)

11
A Flight, Barr & Barr ju c.1820, painted with a vie of Kirkstall Abbey, York-shire, on a ground enriched with pink bands and gilding, painted and impressed marks, 11.5cm (4½in), *S 16 July,*
£495 ($777)

12
A Barr, Flight & Barr dessert service, *(part illus trated)*, c.1810, comprising sixteen pieces, painted in reddish-brown, some damage and wear, im-pressed and printed marks, *L 21 Oct,*
£715 ($1,001)

13
A Flight, Barr & Barr inkstand, 1820s, depicting *Children gathering Water Cresses* with two gilt brass well covers, mark and retailer's mark, 15cm (6in), *S 10 Dec,*
£792 ($1,109)

ı pair of Flight, Barr & ßarr green-ground ›otanical vases, c.1815, ‹light damage, impressed rowned FBB marks and ıddress in script, 22.5cm 9in), *NY 19 Sept,* **ı1,100 (£743)**

:
ı Flight, Barr & Barr ırcular soup tureen, over and stand, c.1825, ach piece painted in ›urple and gold with prays of flowers and eaves, stand with mpressed crowned FBB nark, 27cm (10¾in), *VY 25 Jan,* **ß880 (£633)**

ı Chamberlain Worcester eticulated potpourri vase ınd cover, c.1870, honey-omb design, script mark n puce, 18cm (7¼in), *: 9 July,* **:770 ($1,201)**

ı Chamberlain Worcester ea and coffee set, *(part llustrated)*, c.1815, Japan ›attern 290, comprising ·1 pieces, some cracked, *; 4 Sept,* **:880 ($1,364)**

ı topographical and ›otanical mug, c.1810, ›robably Chamberlain, Vorcester, painted titles, '.5cm (3in), *L 27 May,* **:968 ($1,520)**

ı Chamberlain Worcester ›astille burner, 1820-25, aised on a green mound ›ase, cracked, painted nark, 14cm (5½in), *: 27 May,* **ı2,530 ($3,972)**

ı Worcester jug, painted *n grisaille*, the base nscribed and dated 1807, light rubbing to gilding, ‹6cm (6¼in), *L 27 May,* **:352 ($553)**

ı Chamberlain Worcester ›art dessert service, ‹790s, comprising 35 ›ieces, gilt and enamel lecoration, some pieces lamaged, script marks in ›uce or gilding, *S 19 Mar,* **:5,280 ($8,078)**

9
A pair of Swansea dessert plates, *(one illustrated)*, 1814-22, painted by Henry Morris, slight wear, 20cm (8in), *L 21 Oct,* **£770 ($1,078)**

10
A pair of Swansea plates, *(one illustrated)*, c.1817, from the service made for Lord Dynevor, each piece painted by David Evans or William Pollard, slight wear, 21.5cm (8½in), *L 21 Oct,* **£1,650 ($2,310)**

11
A Chamberlain Worcester dessert service, *(part illustrated)*, c.1850, comprising ten pieces, decorated against a grey ground, one plate cracked, impressed mark, plate 23.5cm (9¼in), *L 27 May,* **£550 ($863)**

C
Flight

Worcester,
Flight period
c.1783-92

B

Worcester (incised)
Flight & Barr period
c.1792-1804

Worcester
Barr, Flight & Barr period
c.1804-13

Worcester
Flight, Barr & Barr period
1813-40

See also *Sotheby's Guide* vol.II p.277.

1

2

3

4

5

6

7

8

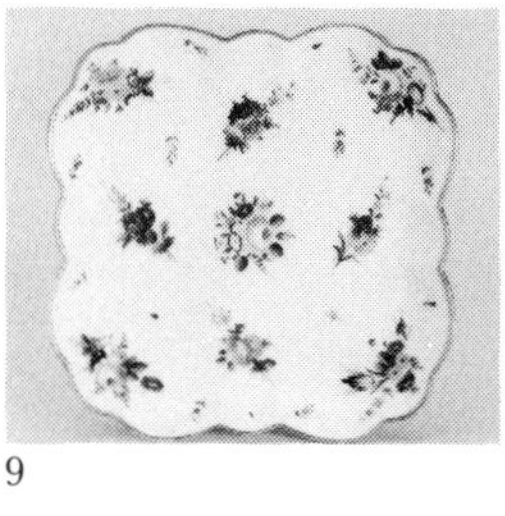
9

10

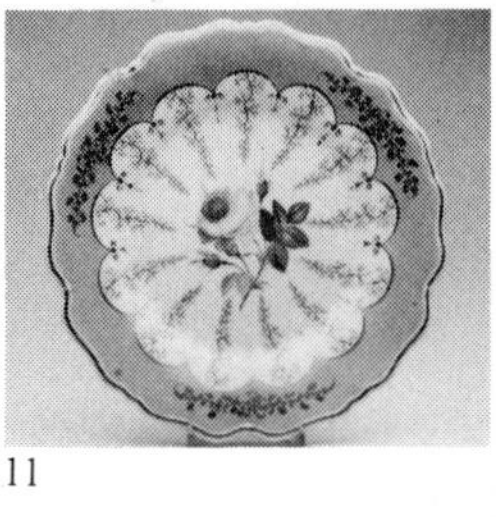
11

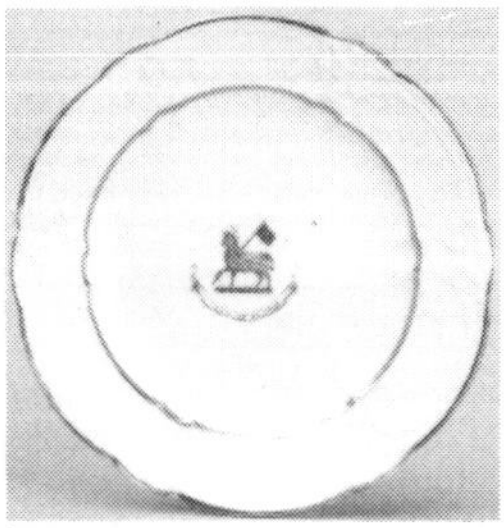
1

2

3

4

5

6

7

8

9

10

11 12 13

1
Two Swansea crested plates, *(one illustrated),* 1814-22, gilding slightly rubbed, one with impressed mark, the other with stencilled mark in red, 21.5 and 21cm (8½ and 8¼in), *L 21 Oct,*
£264 ($369)

2
A Swansea plate, 1814-22, painted with a trailing branch of pink convolvulus, gilded rim, rubbed, 23cm (9in), *L 21 Oct,*
£1,375 ($1,925)

3
A pair of Swansea dinner plates, *(one illustrated),* c.1814-22, from the Lysaght service, painted by Henry Morris, deep blue and gilt rim, slight wear, 24.5cm (9¾in), *L 25 Feb,*
£1,650 ($2,475)

4
A Swansea part tea service, *(sample illustrated),* c.1814-22, comprising fifteen pieces, painted in an Imari-style pattern on a blue ground, some damage, stencilled mark, painted pattern number, *L 27 May,*
£1,045 ($1,641)

5
A Swansea breakfast cup and saucer, c.1816, probably painted by William Billingsley in sepia, traces of stencilled mark on cup, saucer 14.5cm (5¾in), *L 21 Oct,*
£352 ($493)

6
A Staffordshire 'named view' dessert service, *(part illustrated),* late 19th century, comprising sixteen pieces, tazza cracked, *C 8 Oct,*
£330 ($462)

7
A Staffordshire dessert service, *(part illustrated),* c.1830, comprising eighteen pieces, each painted with pink and blue flowers, slight wear, some cracks and repairs, painted pattern number 212, 22.5cm (8¾in), *L 21 Oct,*
£374 ($524)

8
A Staffordshire botanica dessert service, *(part illustrated),* c.1840, comprising eleven pieces, each with a different specimen named on the reverse in iron-red script, within turquoise bands and gilt borders, *C 8 Oct,*
£275 ($385)

9
A Copeland Spode dinne service, *(part illustrated),* comprising 155 pieces, each printed and painted in green and gilt, *C 2 Dec,*
£968 ($1,355)

10
A garniture of three Copeland and Garrett vases, *(one illustrated),* 15 tc 12cm (6 to 4¾in), *C 10 June,*
£275 ($432)

11
A Spode spill vase, c.1820, the flowers painted against an underglaze-blue and gilt-scale ground, Spode 1166 mark, 10.5cm (4¼in), *L 21 Oct,*
£352 ($493)

12
A Spode gilt-ground vase,c.1820, with bands of false beading around the foot and inner rim, red enamel mark and pattern no.711, 15cm (6in), *L 21 Oct,*
£638 ($893)

13
A Spode miniature ewer and basin, c.1820, handle cracked, red enamel marks and pattern no.1166, the ewer 9cm (3½in), *L 21 Oct,*
£440 ($616)

1
A Spode chamber candle-stick, c.1830, painted mark and pattern number 1166, 10cm (4in), *L 25 Feb,*
£935 ($1,402)

2
A Spode 'Prince of Wales service' milk jug, early 19th century, decorated in gilding and sepia, pattern number 1112 in gilding, slight rubbing, 14cm (5½in), *C 16 Apr,*
£187 ($290)

3
A Spode part tea and coffee service, *(sample illustrated),* c.1815, comprising 40 pieces, each painted in iron-red and gold, Spode marks and pattern number 1970, *NY 9 Dec,*
$1,320 (£930)

4
A Rockingham miniature teapot and cover, c.1830, the body applied with branches of coloured flowers, minor chips and flaking to enamels, printed puce griffin mark, Cl.2 in red, 6.5cm (2½in), *L 21 Oct,*
£385 ($539)

5
A Minton Sèvres-style inkstand, dated 1876, in a *bleu céleste* ground edged with gilding, impressed marks and painted mark, 37.5cm (15in), *NY 25 Jan,*
$550 (£396)

6
A Minton 'Globe' pot-pourri vase and cover, c.1825, painted with a view of Warwick Castle, blue crossed swords mark, minor chips, 16.5cm (6½in), *C 15 Jan,*
£165 ($248)

7
A Minton dessert service, *(part illustrated),* dated 1869, comprising eighteen pieces, each painted with landscapes, painted pattern number G141, slight wear, 23.5cm (9¼in), *L 27 May,*
£605 ($950)

8
A Minton garniture comprising three vases, *(one illustrated),* c.1840, each painted with a rustic scene, the reverse with exotic birds, the foot and neck with blue and gilt details, chips and cracks, 28.5 and 32cm (11¼ and 12½in), *L 21 Oct,*
£495 ($693)

9
A Minton dessert service, *(part illustrated),* c.1825, comprising eleven pieces, each painted in underglaze-blue and colourful enamels with gilding, some damage, three dishes with pseudo Sèvres mark, painted pattern no.184, 20cm (8in), *L 21 Oct,*
£1,155 ($1,617)

10
A garniture of three Bloor Derby 'named view' vases, c.1825, in two sizes, each painted with a landscape panel, handles repaired, thumb printed mark, painted titles, 22.5 and 30cm (8¾ and 11¾in), *L 27 May,*
£462 ($725)

11
A pair of Derby dishes, *(one illustrated),* c.1815, probably painted by Richard Dodson with colourful birds against a duck-egg blue ground, slight wear, painted crown, crossed baton, D and 36 in red, 25.5cm (10in), *L 25 Feb,*
£440 ($660)

12
A Derby garniture of three bough pots and covers, *(one illustrated),* c.1820, with D-shaped bombé bodies, possibly painted by Richard Dodson, some damage, crowned crossed batons and D marks and painter's numeral 18 in iron-red, 22 and 19cm (8¾ and 7½in) long, *NY 9 Dec,*
$2,530 (£1,782)

1

3

2

4

5

6

7

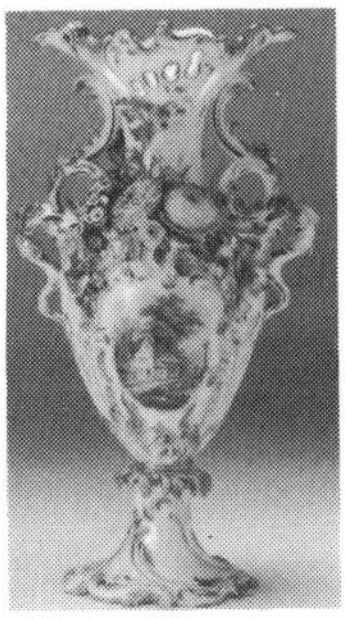
8

9

10

11

12

1

2

3

4

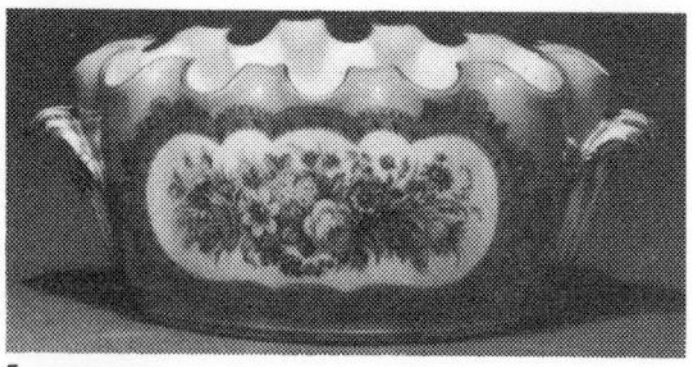
5

6

7

8

9

10

11

12

1
A Derby jug, c.1820, enriched with gilt scrollwork, iron-red mark, 11cm (4¼in), *S 19 Mar,*
£319 ($488)

2
A Derby 'Japan' pattern part dinner service, *(part illustrated)*, c.1825, comprising 59 pieces, minor damage, crowned crossed batons and D marks, various painters numerals, *NY 25 Jan,*
$4,180 (£3,007)

3
A Derby 'King's' pattern part dinner service, *(part illustrated)*, c.1825, comprising 31 pieces, each painted in underglaze-blue, iron-red and gold, crowned crossed batons and D marks, *NY 25 Jan,*
$2,310 (£1,662)

4
A Derby potpourri vase and cover, c.1820, with satyr mask handles, painted with coloured flowers on a rich blue and gilt ground, repaired finial, slight rubbing, crown crossed batons and D in iron-red, *C 16 Apr,*
£605 ($938)

5
A pair of Coalport Sèvres-style verrières, *(one illustrated)*, 1861-75, now fitted with metal liners, minor cracks, printed monogram marks in gilding, 31.5cm (12½in), *NY 26 Nov,*
$2,530 (£1,769)

6
An English armorial mug, probably Coalport decorated with playing cards centred by armorials, inscribed *David 1849 Hughes,* 12.5cm (5in) high, *NY 25 Jan,*
$440 (£316)

7
A Coalport part dessert service, *(sample illustrated)*, c.1835, comprising fifteen pieces, each painted in the centre with a pastel floral cluster within a pale peach border, *NY 19 Sept,*
$1,210 (£818)

8
A Coalport two-handled vase, painted with brightly coloured flowers against an apple green ground, 28cm (11in), *C 22 July,*
£242 ($380)

9
A 'Japan' pattern dessert service, *(part illustrated)*, c.1810, probably John Rose Coalport, comprising 54 pieces, each painted in underglaze-blue, iron-red, green bronze and gilding, some damage and repairs, *L 27 May,*
£18,700 ($29,359)

10
An Anstice, Horton & Rose, Coalport tea service, *(part illustrated)*, c.1810, comprising 32 pieces, cracks, painted pattern number 629, *L 21 Oct,*
£550 ($770)

11
A John Rose Coalport tea and coffee service, *(part illustrated)*, 1810-14, each piece painted with an Imari pattern, comprising 28 pieces, four cracked, 316 in gilding, *C 16 Apr,*
£1,430 ($2,217)

12
A yellow-ground bough pot and cover, c.1815, of Coalport type, small chips and gilding a little rubbed, 18.5cm (7¼in), *L 21 Oct,*
£1,265 ($1,771)

Derby
c.1782-1825

Derby
1861-1935

Derby Crown Porcelain
c.1878-90

Royal Crown Derby
c.1890 onwards

1
A Bow figure of Neptune, 1750s, personifying 'Water' from 'The Elements', astride a green, puce and yellow dolphin, metal trident, restored arms, 15cm (6in), *S 16 July,*
£176 ($276)

2
A Bow white figure of a sportsman, c.1756, repairs, 18.5cm (7¼in), sold with a pair of Derby figures of buntings, repairs, *NY 25 Jan,*
$1,320 (£950)

3
A Bow figure of Autumn, c.1765, modelled as a young boy in yellow spotted breeches and blue-lined puce coat, minor chips and restoration, 18cm (7in), *S 16 July,*
£605 ($950)

4
Four Bow figures of The Seasons, c.1765, each seated amongst flowering branches on a scrolled base heightened in gilding, some damage, repairs and restoration, painted dagger and anchor marks, 15 to 16cm (6 to 6¼in), *L 27 May,*
£1,265 ($1,986)

5
A Bow toy figure of a recumbent dog, 1755-60, his fur pencilled in reddish-brown with patches, minor base chips, 5cm (2in), *L 1 July,*
£1,870 ($2,992)

6
A Bow figure of a pug, c.1755, his fur detailed in brown and ochre, wearing a yellow and puce collar, chips and grazes to glaze, 6.5cm (2½in), *L 21 Oct,*
£396 ($554)

7
A Bow bocage group of a Turk and companion, c.1765, taken from the Meissen original modelled by Kändler, some losses to branches and chips, 25.5cm (10in), *NY 9 Dec,*
$2,200 (£1,549)

8
A pair of Chelsea figures of a gardener and companion, c.1765, costumes heightened in gold, imperfections and small restorations, gold anchor marks, 24cm (9½in), *NY 9 Dec,*
$1,320 (£930)

9
A Plymouth bocage group of two putti and a goat, 1769-70, small chips, 19.5cm (7¾in), *NY 9 Dec,*
$550 (£387)

10
A pair of Samson 'Chelsea' figures of musicians, c.1880, the man playing bagpipes, his companion the lute, each raised on a puce and gilt base, minor damage, gilt interlaced S's, 28 and 27cm (11 and 10½in), *L 20 Mar,*
£286 ($449)

11
A pair of Chelsea dog and fox candlesticks, *(one illustrated),* c.1765, the russet fox with tail restored, each on a gilt-edged base, gold anchor marks, 28cm (11in), *NY 25 Jan,*
$1,045 (£752)

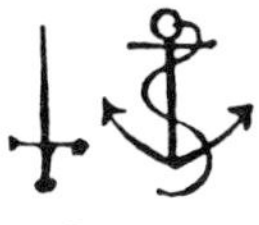
Bow
c.1760-76

Plymouth
c.1768-70

Chelsea
c.1756-69

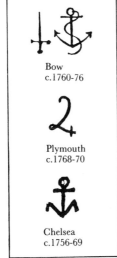

1

2

3

4

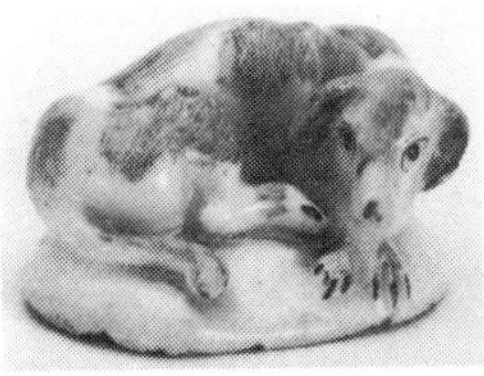
5

6

7

8

9

10

11

1

2

3

4

5 6 5

7

8

9

10

11

1
A Derby candlestick figure of 'Punch as a nightwatchman', 1756-60, wearing a gilt-trimmed brightly coloured costume, minor cracks and repairs, 24cm (9½in), *NY 9 Dec,*
$2,310 (£1,627)

2
A Derby group of John Wilkes, 1772-75, probably modelled by Pierre Stephan, holding a red-bound book titled *Lock on Govt*, small chips and repairs, 30.5cm (12in), *NY 9 Dec,*
$495 (£348)

3
A Derby group of 'The Tithe Pig', c.1775, brightly coloured, small cracks and repairs, incised no.293 G mark, 16.5cm (6½in), *NY 9 Dec,*
$550 (£387)

4
A pair of Derby figures of Milton and Shakespeare, last quarter 18th century, the former in a pink-lined robe, each on a canted rectangular base, incised N305 and no.291, 27cm (10½in), *S 19 Mar,*
£297 ($454)

5
A pair of Derby figures of a shepherd and shepherdess, 1760-65, in coloured enamels, slight damage, 22.5cm (9in), *C 15 Jan,*
£770 ($1,155)

6
An early Derby candlestick figure, c.1760, 22.5cm (9in), *C 15 Jan,*
£308 ($462)

7
A pair of Derby figures of a Jewish pedlar and companion, *(one illustrated)*, c.1770, some damage and restoration, 19cm (7½in), *S 19 Mar,*
£1,045 ($1,599)

8
A pair of Derby figures of 'The Dresden Shepherds', 1760-65, brightly coloured, on a base heightened in turquoise and gold, minor damage, 21cm (8¼in), *NY 9 Dec,*
$1,925 (£1,356)

9
A Derby mythological figure of Minerva, c.1765, small chips, 37cm (14½in), *NY 9 Dec,*
$550 (£387)

10
A Derby bocage candlestick, c.1780, the leaf-moulded candle sconce picked out in turquoise, patch marks, minor damage, 24cm (9¼in), *L 1 July,*
£264 ($422)

11
A pair of Derby figures of a stag and hind, *(one illustrated)*, c.1765, some restoration and damage, 19 and 17.5cm (7½ and 7in), *L 27 May,*
£572 ($898)

1
A Rockingham figure of a milkmaid, c.1830, yoke missing, crack and repair, impressed mark, incised no.47, 18.5cm (7¼in), *L 27 May,*
£715 ($1,122)

2
A pair of Bloor Derby groups, *(one illustrated),* c.1830, modelled as a hairdresser and a shoe fitter with companions, minor damage, incised no.18, painted crossed swords and interlaced L's in blue, *S 16 July,*
£550 ($864)

3
A Rockingham figure of a milkmaid, c.1828, damaged, printed griffin mark in red, incised no.2, 18cm (7in), *L 25 Feb,*
£770 ($1,155)

4
A pair of Bloor Derby figures, c.1830, one a gentleman in colourful costume, the other a woman holding a child, both restored, 15cm (6in), *C 15 Jan,*
£330 ($495)

5
A Derby figure of a pug, c.1800, on a green base edged with gilt, wearing a gilt collar with a flower, incised 2, 7cm (2¾in), *L 25 Feb,*
£286 ($429)

6
A Staffordshire porcelain group, c.1830, of a bitch and three puppies in a basket, in salmon-ground wicker basket, 11cm (4¼in), *L 21 Oct,*
£462 ($647)

7
A Copeland Parian bust of 'The Veiled Bride', 1861, after the original sculpture by Raphael Monti, made for the Crystal Palace Art Union, minor chips, impressed mark, moulded sculptor's name and date, impressed Art Union title, 37cm (14½in), *L 25 Feb,*
£1,045 ($1,567)

8
A pair of Copeland Parian centrepieces, *(one illustrated),* c.1860, each pierced basket supported by three maidens in classical robes, chip, one with impressed mark, 40cm (15¾in), *L 27 May,*
£682 ($1,071)

9
A Minton Parian figure of Prince Leopold, 1861, holding a net and standing on an oval base moulded with shells, impressed marks and date cypher, 40cm (15¾in), *S 19 Mar,*
£638 ($976)

10
A Parian figure of Canova, 38cm (15in), *C 11 Mar,*
£220 ($332)

11
A Robinson and Leadbeater Parian figure of Queen Victoria, marked, 37.5cm (14¾in), *C 4 Nov,*
£330 ($465)

12
A Copeland Parian bust of Clytie, 1886, after an original sculpture by C. Delpech, the goddess metamorphosing into a sunflower, impressed mark and date code, 58cm (22¾in), *L 25 Feb,*
£770 ($1,155)

13
A Parian group of a guardian angel, c.1860, after an original sculpture by John Hancock, encouraging a child to embrace a baby seated on her knee, moulded signature, 57cm (22¼in), *L 21 Oct,*
£462 ($647)

Rockingham Works Brameld

Rockingham
c.1826-30

R&L

Robinson & Leadbeater, (parian)
c.1885 onwards

1

2

3

4

5

6

7

8

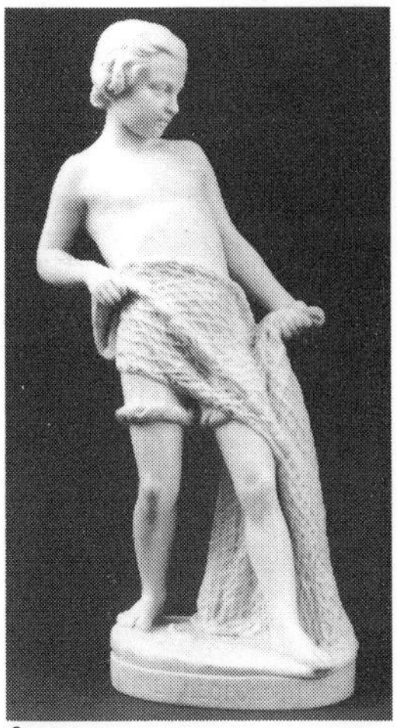
9

10

11

12

13

1

2

3

4

5

6

7 8

9

10

11

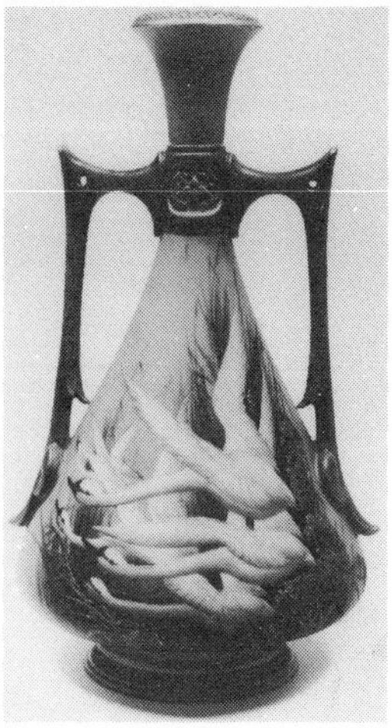
12

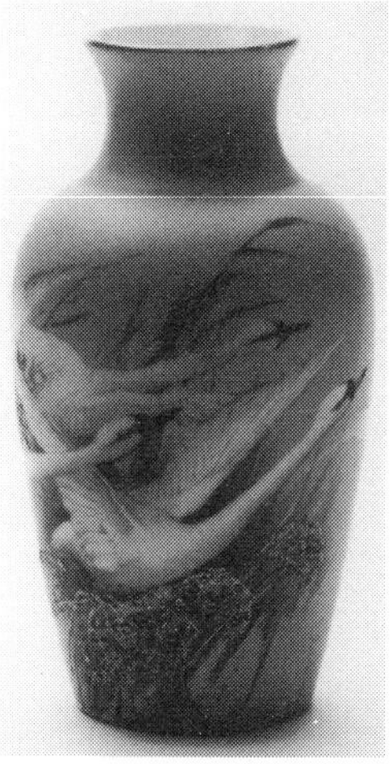
13

14

1
A set of twelve Royal Worcester game plates *(one illustrated)* **and a platter,** dated 1887, each printed and painted with a game bird, the whole enriched with gilding, crowned circle marks, date ciphers and pattern no., platter 42cm (16½in), *NY 25 Jan,*
$1,100 (£791)

2
A Royal Worcester plate, painted by R. Sebright, the centre with peaches and grapes between a gilt, blue and pink border, 23cm (9in), *C 11 Feb,*
£220 ($328)

3
A Royal Worcester game service, *(part illustrated),* 1898, comprising sixteen pieces, each printed and painted with game birds, printed crowned circle mark and date code, plate 22.5cm (8¾in), *L 25 Feb,*
£440 ($660)

4
A Royal Worcester pot-pourri vase and cover, 1909, painted and signed by J. Stinton with pheasants in a landscape, 14.5cm (5¾in), *C 16 Apr,*
£550 ($853)

5
A Royal Worcester set of six coffee cups and saucers, *(part illustrated),* 1919, painted by T. Lockyer, F. Harper and W. Hart, burnished interiors, purple printed marks and date code, *C 9 July,*
£770 ($1,201)

6
A Royal Worcester pierced and double-walled cabinet teapot and cover, 1878, by George Owen, decorated in turquoise, pink and white, crowned circle marks, impressed date code, decorator's marks, 12cm (4¾in), *L 27 May,*
£1,595 ($2,504)

7
A Royal Worcester vase, 1916, painted and signed by H. Stinton with Highland cattle in a misty landscape, gilding rubbed, printed crowned circle mark and date code, 14cm (5½in), *L 27 May,*
£330 ($518)

8
A Royal Worcester vase, 1905, painted and signed by C.H.C. Baldwyn with four great tits in bushes on a turquoise ground, printed crowned circle mark and date code, 20.5cm (8in), *L 27 May,*
£682 ($1,071)

9
A pair of Royal Worceste vases and covers, 1908, painted and signed by M. E. Eaton with sprays of pink and pale-yellow roses amongst foliage, chips, printed crowned circle mark and date code, 23.5cm (9¼in), *L 21 Oct,*
£330 ($462)

10
A Royal Worcester ewer, c.1910, by George Owen, the body reticulated with bands of honeycomb and foliate motifs, handle restored, crowned circle mark, incised signature, 16.5cm (6½in), *Syd 12 Nov,*
Aus$3,960 (£1,800; $2,520)

11
A Royal Worcester ewer, c.1905, painted and signed by C. Baldwyn with swans in flight, marks obscured by fixed wood base, 44.5cm (17½in), *L 21 Oct,*
£1,760 ($2,464)

12
A Royal Worcester double-handled vase, 1905, painted and signed by C. Baldwyn with swans and a swallow on a sky-blue ground, purple printed mark and date code, 24cm (9½in), *C 8 Oct,*
£825 ($1,155)

13
A pair of Royal Worceste vases, *(one illustrated),* 1906, each painted and signed by C. Baldwyn with swans in flight, chip, printed crowned circle mark and date code, 15cm (6in), *L 25 Feb,*
£528 ($792)

14
A Royal Worcester vase, 1921, painted and signed by R. Sebright with a basket of fruits reserved on a royal-blue ground, repair, printed crowned circle mark and date code, 50cm (19¾in), *L 25 Feb,*
£1,210 ($1,815)

1
A Doulton Burslem dessert service, *(part illustrated)*, c.1890, comprising fifteen pieces, each signed in monogram on the reverse, two fruit stands repaired, slight wear, retailer's mark for Osler, London, *L 21 Oct,*
£605 ($847)

2
A pair of Minton plates, *(one illustrated)*, 1927, in Sèvres style, painted and signed by J. Colclough, printed globe marks in gilding, *C 16 Apr,*
£880 ($1,364)

3
A Derby dessert service, *(part illustrated)*, c.1930, comprising eleven pieces, each piece signed by M.K. Clark, hair crack, impressed mark and date codes, *L 25 Feb,*
£825 ($1,237)

4
A Mintons pâte-sur-pâte pilgrim vase, c.1880, decorated in white slip enriched by gilding, printed globe mark in gilding, 25.5cm (10in), *NY 26 Nov,*
$880 (£615)

5
A George Jones pâte-sur-pâte vase, c.1880, probably decorated by George Schenck, 26.5cm (10¼in), *NY 26 Nov,*
$715 (£500)

6
A Belleek basket and cover, 1863-91, rim repaired, chips, applied label with impressed mark, 27cm (10½in), *L 21 Oct,*
£1,650 ($2,310)

7
A Royal Crown Derby Imari pattern dinner service, *(part illustrated)*, 1883, comprising 62 pieces, printed marks in underglaze-blue including date code, *C 16 Apr,*
£2,420 ($3,751)

8
A pair of Mintons pâte-sur-pâte urns and covers, 1897, each signed L. Solon, impressed and printed orb marks, incised shape no. 2708, 50.5cm (20in), *L 21 Oct,*
£11,550 ($16,170)

9
A Royal Crown Derby vase and cover, 1902, painted by A. Gregory, signed, printed mark and date code, 22cm (8½in), *L 27 May,*
£1,100 ($1,727)

10
A Royal Doulton two-handled loving cup, c.1935, commemorating the Silver Jubilee of King George V and Queen Mary, limited edition no.119 of 1000 copies, 26cm (10¼in), *Syd 12 Nov,*
Aus$660 (£300; $420)

11
A Belleek pink-ground vase and cover, c.1865, first period mark, 31cm (12¼in), *L 21 Oct,*
£748 ($1,047)

12
A set of twelve Doulton and Company game plates *(part illustrated)*, c.1893, each signed H. Mitchell, crowned Doulton and Burslem marks, 23cm (9in), *NY 26 Nov,*
$825 (£577)

13
A Doulton limited edition jug, moulded with Dickensian characters, printed marks, 27.5cm (10¾in), *C 9 Sept,*
£506 ($759)

Minton
c.1850 onwards

Minton
c.1863-72

Minton
c.1912-50

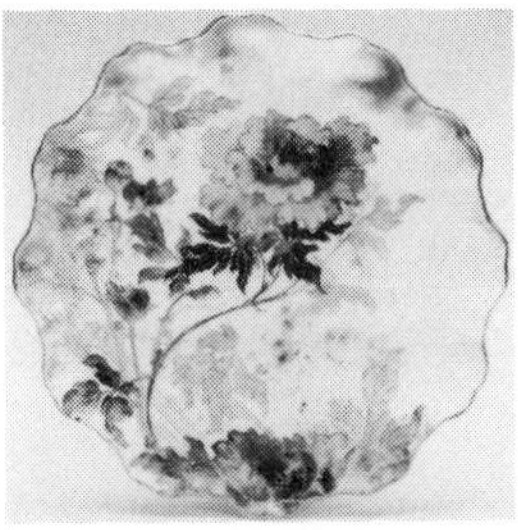
1

2

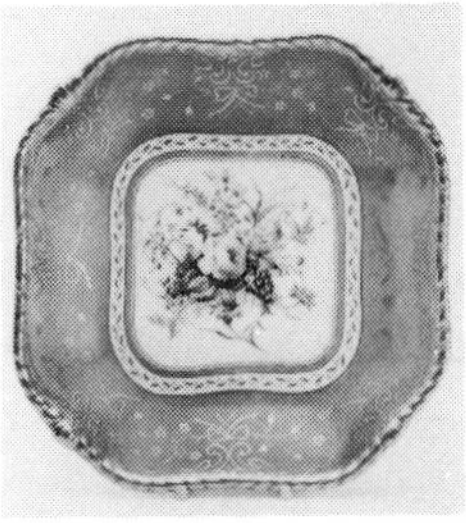
3

4 5

6

7

8

9

10

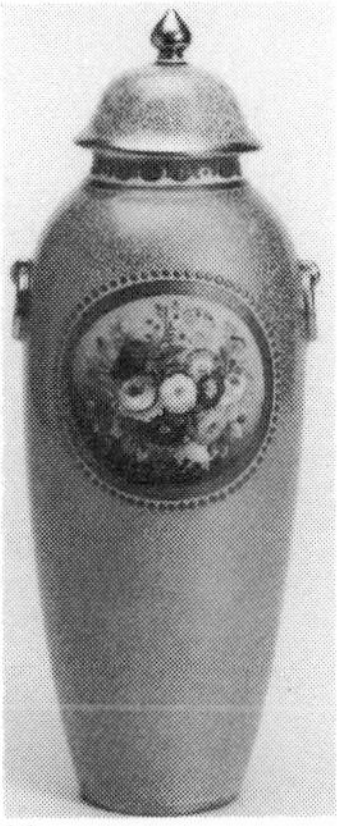
11

12

13

1

2

3

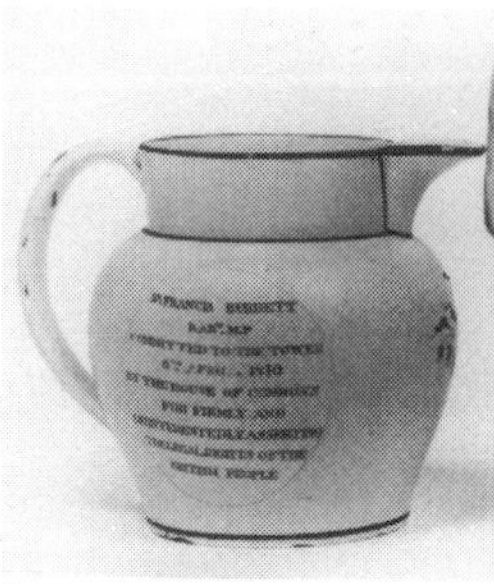
4

5

6

7

8

9

10

11

12

1
A set of Fife pottery carpet bowls, *(part illustrated),* mid 19th century, comprising fourteen balls and a jack, with designs in blue, green, mauve or pink, some wear, each 9cm (3½in) diam., *L 21 Oct,*
£572 ($801)

2
A Queen Caroline 'In Memoriam' pearlware plate, c.1821, the centre with a portrait of T. Denman, (the Queen's defence lawyer), over-printed in blue with her funeral procession, 15cm (5¾in), *S 16 July,*
£396 ($622)

3
A commemorative pottery jug, early 19th century, printed with a view of St. Luke's Church Liverpool on each side, divided by an inscribed bell, repair, 30.5cm (12in), *C 16 Apr,*
£253 ($392)

4
A yellow-ground commemorative jug, dated 1810, printed with a bust portrait of Sir Francis Burdett, the reverse with a descriptive medallion, 11.5cm (4½in), *C 25 Feb,*
£187 ($281)

See p.229, fig.3 for a Burdett bowl.

5
A commemorative silver resist jug, printed with two rustic views and the inscription *Robert Rock,* 14cm (5½in), *C 25 Feb,*
£72 ($107)

6
A Staffordshire railway jug, 19th century, printed with the Manchester and Liverpool Railway, 15cm (6in), *C 5 Aug,*
£253 ($392)

7
A Staffordshire jug, c.1815, printed with two landscape scenes of figures in a meadow, silver lustre line borders, 14cm (5½in), *L 25 Feb,*
£297 ($445)

8
A copper lustre jug, sprigged with the Royal arms and a lion and a leopard on a blue band, 15cm (6in); sold with two others, *C 25 Feb,*
£121 ($182)

9
A commemorative mug, 1829, made after the fire at York Minster, on February 2nd, 1829, transfer-printed in blue with a view of the Minster in flames, the reverse with a portrait of Jonathan Martin, the arsonist, and inscription, slight discolouration, 9cm (3½in), *L 25 Feb,*
£385 ($577)

10
Two Sunderland lustre plates, *(one illustrated),* printed with a bust of Wesley and Adam Clark between pink and copper lustre borders, 22.5cm (9in), *C 4 Nov,*
£121 ($171)

11
A yellow-ground copper lustre jug, printed with a mother and child on an Empire-style day bed, 17.5cm (7in); sold with two other jugs, *C 25 Feb,*
£154 ($231)

12
A pair of Staffordshire pearlware enamelled jugs, *(one illustrated),* c.1815, moulded on one side with a yellow eagle bearing green olive branches, and on the reverse with a yellow, iron-red and green rose sprig, 16.5cm (6½in), *NY 19 Sept,*
$825 (£557)

1
A Minton majolica jardinière vase, c.1860, glazed in typical majolica colours of ochre, green, brown, blue and lilac, stem damaged, chips, 95cm (37½in), *L 21 Oct,*
£4,620 ($6,468)

2
A majolica model of a stork, c.1880, standing on one leg beside a spill vase, minor chips, 37cm (14½in), *C 16 Apr,*
£275 ($426)

3
A Minton majolica garden seat, 1867, glazed in typical majolica colours, chips, impressed mark, shape no.589 and date code, 46cm (18in), *L 21 Oct,*
£6,820 ($9,548)

4
A George Jones majolica game pie dish, cover and liner, c.1875, liner discoloured, moulded P.O.D.R. mark, 33.5cm (13¼in), *L 21 Oct,*
£1,705 ($2,387)

5
A Minton majolica game pie dish, cover and liner, 1864, the interior turquoise, damaged liner, impressed shape no.669 and date code, 31.5cm (12½in), *C 8 Oct,*
£440 ($616)

6
A Minton majolica jardinière, 1865, painted and signed by Edouard Rischgitz, two cracks, impressed marks to base, 24cm (9½in), *C 9 July,*
£440 ($686)

7
A Minton majolica jardinière, 1871, in royal blue, the interior in lilac, impressed mark, shape number and date code, 59.5cm (23½in), *L 27 May,*
£385 ($604)

8
A majolica fish paste dish, cover and stand, 1860s, the lobster chipped, 20cm (8in), *S 16 July,*
£242 ($380)

9
A George Jones majolica stilton cheese dish and cover, c.1880, glazed overall in tones of green, brown ochre and pale pink, interior turquoise, cover cracked, base 31cm (12¼in), *L 21 Oct,*
£330 ($462)

10
A Minton majolica game pie dish, cover and liner, 1877, minor chips and repairs, impressed mark, shape no.2062, 39cm (15¼in), *L 21 Oct,*
£1,650 ($2,310)

11
A George Jones majolica punch bowl, c.1875, the figure of Mr Punch supporting the bowl, cracks, impressed JG monogram, 27.5cm (10¾in), *L 27 May,*
£1,980 ($3,109)

12
A pair of Minton majolica sweetmeat figures, *(one illustrated),* 1870, of a boy and girl, impressed factory marks and date code, the boy with incised numerals, slight chips, *C 15 Jan,*
£308 ($462)

13
A Minton majolica bonbonnière, 1859, the bowl in mottled colours, impressed date code, 30.5cm (12in), *L 27 May,*
£1,760 ($2,763)

14
A Minton majolica garden seat, 1869, minor chips, impressed mark, shape number and date code, 46.5cm (18¼in), *L 25 Feb,*
£1,155 ($1,732)

1

2

3

4

5

6

7

8

9

10

11

12

13

14

1

2

3

4

5

6

7

8

9

10

11

12

13

14

1
A Charles Vyse figure of 'The Piccadilly Rose Woman', 1923, chips, painted CV monogram, Chelsea and 1923, 21.5cm (8½in), *L 27 May,*
£440 ($691)

2
A Charles Vyse figure of a balloon seller, 1923, repair, painted CV monogram, Chelsea and 1929, *L 27 May,*
£352 ($553)

3
A Charles Vyse figure of 'In Petticoat Lane', c.1935, modelled as a Middle Eastern tie-seller with a case at his feet, incised *Vyse Chelsea*, 29.5cm (11½in), *L 27 May,*
£1,320 ($2,072)

4
A Charles Vyse figure of a clown, c.1935, incised *C. Vyse, Chelsea*, 29cm (11½in), *L 27 May,*
£1,375 ($2,159)

5
A Charles Vyse group of a Punch and Judy show, 1928, incised *C. Vyse, Chelsea, 1928*, 31cm (12¼in), *L 27 May,*
£1,485 ($2,331)

6
A Royal Doulton 'George Robey' jug and cover, 1926, modelled as a caricature of the music hall star in his stage attire, the cover with later silver mounts, printed mark, impressed date code, 25cm (9¾in), *L 27 May,*
£3,300 ($5,181)

7
A Doulton figure of 'Pussy', 1918, after a design by F. C. Stone, modelled as a girl holding a black cat on her lap, painted mark and title, printed mark, incised date code, 19cm (7½in), *L 21 Oct,*
£4,620 ($6,468)

8
A Royal Doulton figure of 'The Hunts Lady', dated 5.26, HN 1201, some damage, 21cm (8¼in), *C 9 Sept,*
£385 ($578)

9
A Royal Doulton figure of 'The Queen Mother', HN 2882, limited edition, 20cm (8in), *S 4 Sept,*
£528 ($820)

10
A Royal Doulton figure of 'Janice', HN 2022, 18.5cm (7½in), *S 4 Sept,*
£165 ($256)

11
A Royal Doulton figure of 'Elfreda', HN 2078, 19cm (7½in), *S 4 Sept,*
£308 ($477)

12
A Royal Doulton pilot figure, dated 2.5.35, depicting a lady with her hands behind her head, wearing a floral dress and pink robe, 18.5cm (7½in), *C 13 May,*
£990 ($1,594)

13
A Royal Doulton figure of 'A Lady of the Georgian Period', 1920, designed by E. W. Light, printed and painted marks, painted title and HN331, impressed date code, 25.5cm (10in), *L 27 May,*
£990 ($1,554)

14
A Royal Doulton figure of 'Sweet and Twenty', HN 809, 15cm (6in), *S 4 Sept,*
£110 ($170)

British marks are reproduced courtesy Century Hutchinson, from *Encyclopaedia of British Pottery and Porcelain Marks*, Geoffrey A. Godden, publ. Barrie & Jenkins, 1964.

1
A Royal Doulton figure of 'Rosina', 1930, wearing a fur-trimmed red cloak, printed mark, painted mark, title and HN1358, impressed date code, 14.5cm (5¾in), *L 25 Feb,*
£396 ($594)

2
A Royal Doulton 'London Cry' figure, impressed date, 17cm (6¾in), *C 28 Jan,*
£451 ($663)

3
A Royal Doulton figure of 'The Sunshine Girl', 1930, sheltering beneath a colourful parasol, small firing crack, printed and painted marks, 12.5cm (5in), *L 25 Feb,*
£1,045 ($1,567)

4
A pair of Doulton Burslem figures of Shylock and Antonio, c.1895, after original models by C. J. Noke, moulded signature, repairs and chips, printed crowned mark, 40.5 and 45cm (16 and 17¾in), *L 25 Feb,*
£462 ($693)

5
A Doulton figure of 'Pierrette', painted title, HN644, printed and impressed marks, 17.5cm (7in), *S 10 Dec,*
£330 ($462)

6
A Royal Doulton 'Hatless Drake' character jug, c.1940, the reverse with Drake's Drum, printed mark, title and Rd.No.838085, 14.5cm (5¾in), *L 27 May,*
£1,980 ($3,109)

7
A Royal Doulton figure of a jester, dated 12.23, HN55, signed *Noke*, slight damage to foot, 25cm (9¾in), *C 9 Sept,*
£1,485 ($2,228)

8
A Royal Doulton figure of 'The Bather', 1928, printed and painted marks, painted title and HN687, impressed date code, 19.5cm (7¾in), *L 25 Feb,*
£330 ($495)

9
A pair of Royal Worcester figures, *(one illustrated)*, c.1870, allegorical of Joy and Sorrow, picked out in pale colours, impressed mark, 26cm (10¼in), *C 9 July,*
£385 ($601)

10
A Royal Doulton two-faced character jug of Mephistopheles, printed marks, 14cm (5½in), *S 16 July,*
£990 ($1,554)

11
A pair of Royal Worcester Eastern water carriers, 1914, each picked out in gilding and ivory tones, purple printed marks, including date code, 24.5cm (9¾in), *C 8 Oct,*
£572 ($801)

12
A Royal Worcester group, 1884, modelled by James Hadley, facsimile signature, printed mark in green, impressed mark, 25cm (10in), *C 8 Oct,*
£638 ($893)

13
A Royal Worcester model of a swan, modelled as a vase, 19cm (7½in), *C 10 June,*
£242 ($380)

Royal Worcester
c.1876-91

Royal Worcester
from 1891

Doulton
c.1902 onwards

1

2

3

4

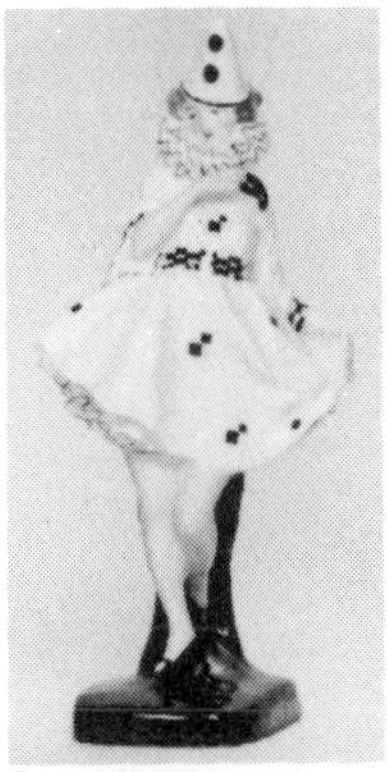
5

6

7

8

9

10

11

12

13

Glass

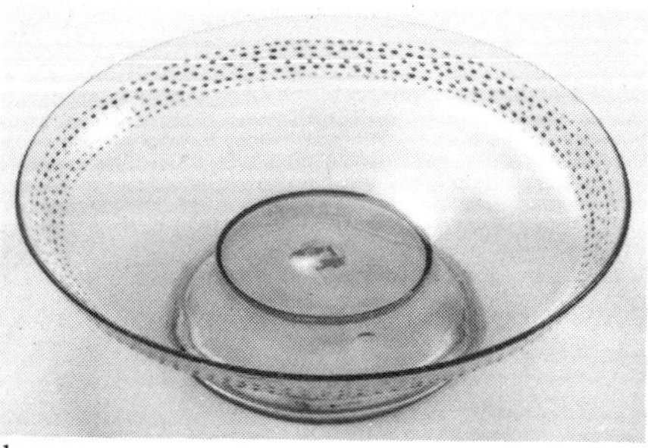

1

2

3

4

5

6

7

8

9 10 11

See also:
Colour illustrations *p* 352
Antiquities *pp* 590-591
Chinese works of art *p* 694
Decorative arts from 1880 *pp* 279-286
Islamic works of art *p* 631
Russian works of art *p* 379

Main sub-sections:
Glass *pp* 256-266
Paperweights *pp* 267-268

1
A Venetian enamelled and gilt tazza, c.1500, decorated with blue-enamel and gilt dot borders, 22cm (8¾in) diam., *L 24 Nov,*
£990 ($1,395)

2
A South German 'rubinglas' silver-gilt mounted bowl, late 17th century, the mounts by T. Baur, Augsburg, 14cm (5½in) diam., *L 24 Nov,*
£2,420 ($3,412)

3
A German 'Kuttrolf', 17th century, of amber-tinted metal, the body with mould-blown wrythen ribs below four twisted tubes ending in a spout, 23cm (9in), *L 24 Nov,*
£2,090 ($2,946)

4
A German blue-tinted mounted jug, 17th century, the handle with later pewter strap, 27cm (10½in), *L 24 Nov,*
£2,200 ($3,102)

5
A Netherlandish green-tinted serving bottle, 17th century, 21.5cm (8½in), *L 10 Feb,*
£2,530 ($3,719)

6
A Low Countries blue glass serving bottle, late 17th century, 16.5cm (6½in), *S 19 Mar,*
£825 ($1,262)

7
A Dutch blue-tinted bottle, 17th century, with metal mounts, 26cm (10½in), *L 24 Nov,*
£3,080 ($4,342)

8
A South Italian green-tinted gilt-metal mounted bowl, possibly Naples, 17th century, 14cm (5½in), *L 24 Nov,*
£1,375 ($1,938)

9
A South German 'rubinglas' silver-gilt mounted bottle and stopper, c.1700, mounts probably Augsburg, 23cm (9in), *L 24 Nov,*
£1,485 ($2,093)

10
A pair of South German 'rubinglas' engraved bottles, *(one illustrated)*, c.1720, each engraved in the manner of Johann Heel with birds perched on flowers and fruit, 23cm (9in), *L 24 Nov,*
£3,520 ($4,963)

11
A South German 'rubinglas' silver-gilt mounted cream jug, early 18th century, 10cm (4in), *L 24 Nov,*
£990 ($1,395)

1
An early sealed wine bottle, dated 1711, dark green tinted metal, inscribed *Wingerworth 1711* (for Wingerworth Hall, near Chesterfield), string ring damaged, 17cm (6¾in), *L 24 Nov,*
£792 ($1,177)

2
A Constantia wine bottle, c.1800, olive green glass, 22cm (8¾in). *Ct 27 Oct,*
R 1,320 (£413; $578)

3
A Constantia wine bottle, c.1880, brown bottle, 23cm (9in), *Ct 27 Oct,*
R 660 (£206; $289)

4
A Constantia wine bottle, mid 19th century, green glass, 22cm (8¾in), *Ct 27 Oct,*
R 935 (£292; $409)

5
A covered sweetmeat, c.1720, 25.5cm (10in), *L 10 Feb,*
£1,155 ($1,698)

6
An incised-twist sweetmeat, early 18th century, 10.5cm (4in), *L 10 Feb,*
£308 ($453)

7
An early sweetmeat or champagne, c.1700, 13cm (5in), *L 10 Feb,*
£1,650 ($2,425)

8
A stand or sweetmeat, first half 18th century, 12cm (4¾in), *L 10 Feb,*
£242 ($356)

9
The Applewhaite-Abbot colour-twist candlestick, c.1765, the central opaque core entwined with opaque-white and translucent royal-blue threads, 20.5cm (8in), *L 24 Nov,*
£13,750 ($19,387)

10
A sweetmeat or patchstand, c.1750, 9cm (3½in); sold with a two-handled loving cup, 18th century, 12.5 cm (5in), *L 10 Feb,*
£682 ($1,002)

11
A baluster candlestick, c.1740, 19cm (7½in), *L 10 Feb,*
£825 ($1,213)

12
A candlestick, c.1745, 18cm (7in), *L 10 Feb,*
£935 ($1,374)

13
A Beilby enamelled bowl, dated 1765, of ovoid form, the rim with traces of gilding above diaper work and foliate scrolls flanking the initials M.L., 7cm (2¾in) high, *L 10 Feb,*
£1,925 ($2,830)

14
An Irish blue-tinted finger bowl, c.1800, Dublin, with the mould mark *Armstrong Ormond Quay*, only the fourth piece to be recorded from this factory, 9cm (3½in), *L 10 Feb,*
£682 ($1,002)

See also p.549 for wine bottles

1

2 3 4

5

6 7

8

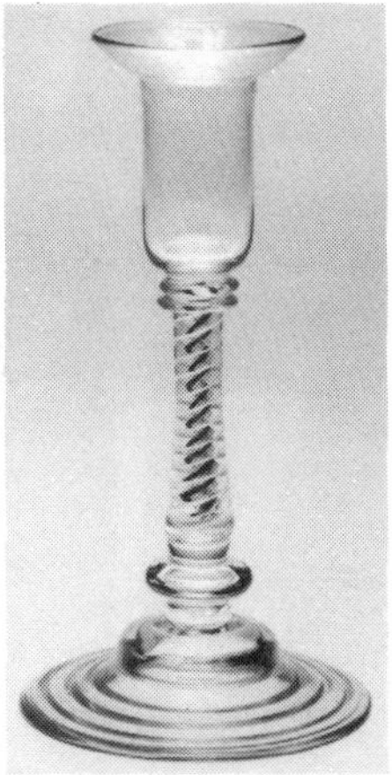
9

10

11

12

13

14

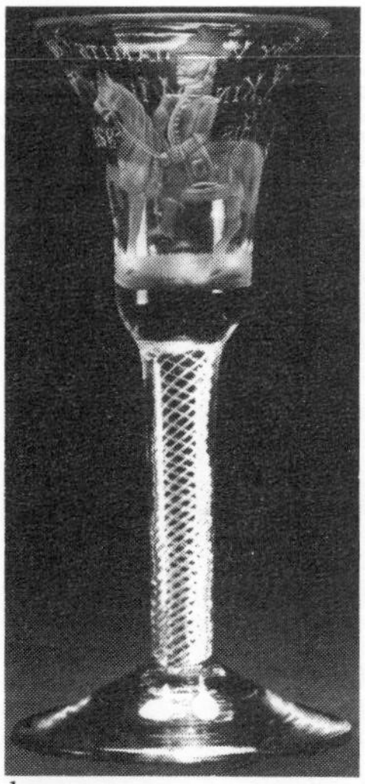

1

2

3 4

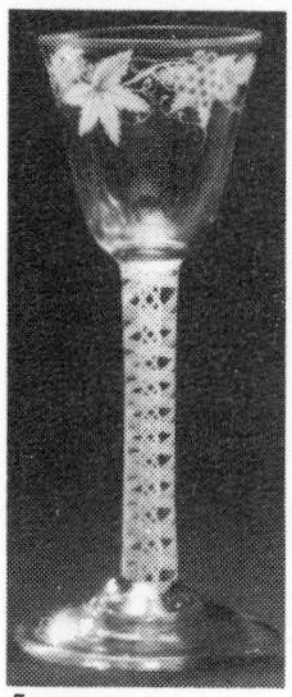

5

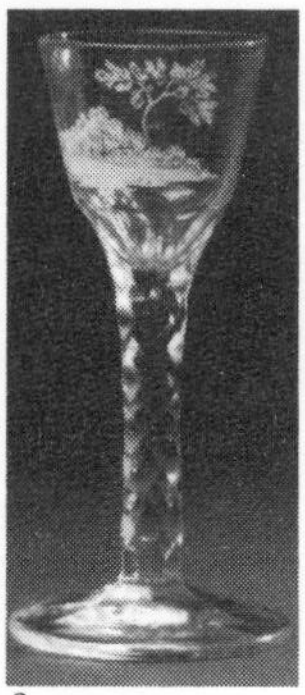

6

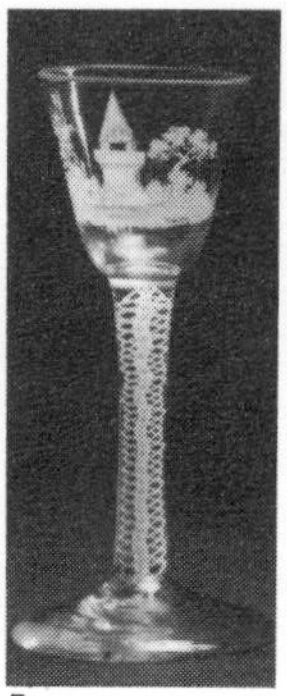

7

8

9

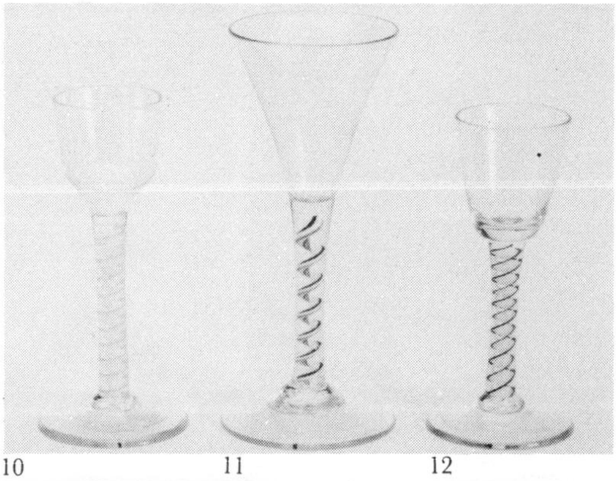

10 11 12

13

14

15

1
A Williamite engraved wine glass, second half 18th century, the bowl engraved with an equestrian portrait of King William, inscribed on the reverse *DERRY WILLIAMITE CLUB/ KING WILLIAM/ HIS GLORIOUS CAUSE,* 16cm (6½in), *L 24 Nov,*
£1,870 ($2,636)

2
A Jacobite portrait glass, c.1750, engraved with a portrait of Prince Charles Edward Stuart in Highland dress, 19cm (7½in), *L 10 Feb,*
£1,430 ($2,102)

3
A Beilby enamelled wine glass, c.1770, the rim painted in white enamel, gilt rim, multi-spiral opaque-twist stem, 17cm (6¾in), *L 24 Nov,*
£682 ($961)

4
A wine glass, c.1750, with honeycomb moulding on the lower half of the bowl, and multi-spiral air-twist stem, 16.5cm (6½in), *L 24 Nov,*
£385 ($542)

5
A Beilby enamelled wine glass, c.1770, the funnel-bowl painted in opaque white with a meander of fruiting vine, 14.5cm (5¾in), *L 10 Feb,*
£528 ($776)

6
A Beilby enamelled wine glass, c.1770, the bowl painted in greens with a bosky scene, facet-cut stem, 13.5cm (5¼in), *L 10 Feb,*
£1,320 ($1,940)

7
A Beilby enamelled wine glass, c.1770, the bowl painted in white with an obelisk flanked by foliage, double-series opaque-twist stem, 14.5cm (5¾in), *L 10 Feb,*
£2,310 ($3,396)

8
A Jacobite portrait firing glass, c.1750, engraved with a bust portrait of Prince Charles Edward in Scottish costume, 9cm (3½in), *L 10 Feb,*
£2,860 ($4,204)

9
A Beilby enamelled armorial marriage goblet, c.1765, painted on one side with the arms of Anderson of Newcastle within a puce rococo shield, the reverse with fruiting vine in white, rim gilt, opaque-twist stem, bowl damaged, 19cm (7½in), *L 24 Nov,*
£5,280 ($7,444)

10
A colour-twist wine glass, c.1770, the stem enclosing a central opaque-white corkscrew within translucent-blue and a white thread, 15cm (6in), *L 10 Feb,*
£550 ($808)

11
A colour-twist wine glass, c.1770, the stem enclosing an opaque-white ribbed corkscrew edged in brick-red, blue and green, 18cm (7in), *L 10 Feb,*
£1,320 ($1,940)

12
A colour-twist wine glass, c.1770, with a double-series opaque-twist stem incorporating brick-red and lime-green threads, 14.5cm (5¾in), *L 10 Feb,*
£858 ($1,261)

13
An engraved topographical goblet, c.1800, the bowl decorated on one side with a view of the Exchange, and on the reverse with the Sunderland Bridge, 17.5cm (7in), sold with a 19th century rummer, *L 10 Feb,*
£792 ($1,164)

14
A Sunderland goblet, 1830s, the bowl engraved with a view of Sunderland Bridge, 20.5cm (8in), *C 15 Jan,*
£297 ($446)

15
A Sunderland goblet, the bowl engraved on one side with a sailing vessel, and on the reverse with a monogram within a wreath of hops and barley, 20cm (8in), *C 21 Oct,*
£99 ($139)

1
A baluster goblet, c.1700, 24.5cm (9¾in), *L 24 Nov,*
£352 ($496)

2
A baluster goblet, c.1700, 23.5cm (9¼in), *L 24 Nov,*
£462 ($651)

3
A baluster goblet, c.1710, 20cm (8in), *L 24 Nov,*
£462 ($651)

4
A baluster goblet, c.1700, 20cm (8in), *L 10 Feb,*
£792 ($1,164)

5
A goblet, c.1720, 18cm (7in), *L 10 Feb,*
£682 ($1,002)

6
A wine glass, c.1740, 16.5cm (6½in), *L 10 Feb,*
£1,155 ($1,698)

7
A gilt wine glass, c.1760, the ogee bowl gilt with fruiting vine and flower sprigs in the manner of James Giles, opaque-twist stem, 18cm (7in), *L 24 Nov,*
£462 ($651)

8
A wine glass, c.1750, the funnel bowl honeycomb-moulded overall, 16cm (6¼in), *L 10 Feb,*
£660 ($970)

9
An armorial wine glass, c.1745, 18cm (7in), *L 10 Feb,*
£418 ($614)

10
A Jacobite wine glass, c.1750, the funnel bowl engraved with a rose and single bud, multi-spiral air-twist stem, 16.5cm (6½in), *L 10 Feb,*
£308 ($453)

11
A colour-twist wine glass, c.1770, the stem enclosing an opaque-white core edged in translucent-green and entwined with white and translucent-red threads, 17cm (7in), *L 24 Nov,*
£660 ($930)

12
A Jacobite wine glass, c.1750, the funnel bowl engraved with a rose, single bud and thistle spray and inscribed *Fiat*, multi-spiral air-twist stem, 16cm (6¼in), *L 24 Nov,*
£770 ($1,085)

13
A Jacobite goblet, c.1750, the bucket bowl engraved with a rose and single bud, the stem with air cable corkscrew, 21cm (8¼in), *L 24 Nov,*
£440 ($620)

14
A Jacobite wine glass, c.1750, the bowl engraved with a rose, two buds, oak leaf and star, multi-spiral air-twist stem, 16cm (6½in), *L 10 Feb,*
£352 ($517)

15
A large Jacobite goblet, c.1750, the bowl engraved with large rose spray with two buds and a moth, multi-spiral air-twist stem, 20.5cm (8in), *L 24 Nov,*
£440 ($620)

1 2 3

4

5

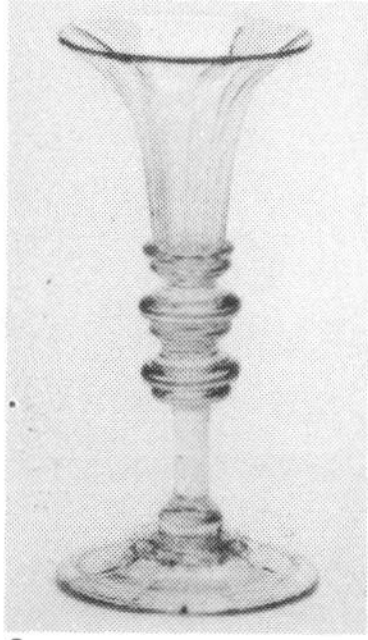
6

7

8

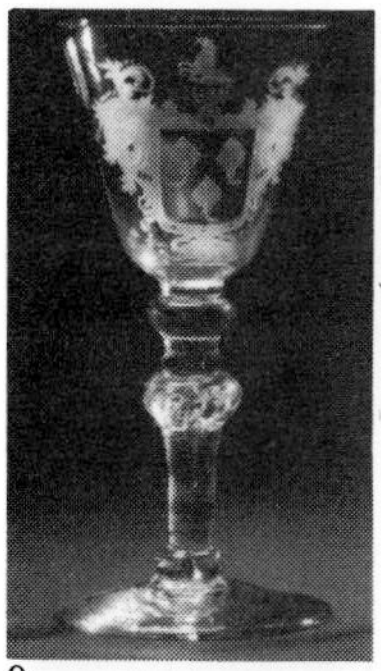
9

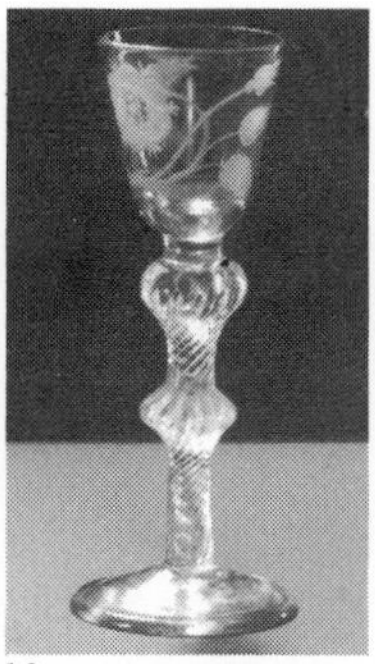
10

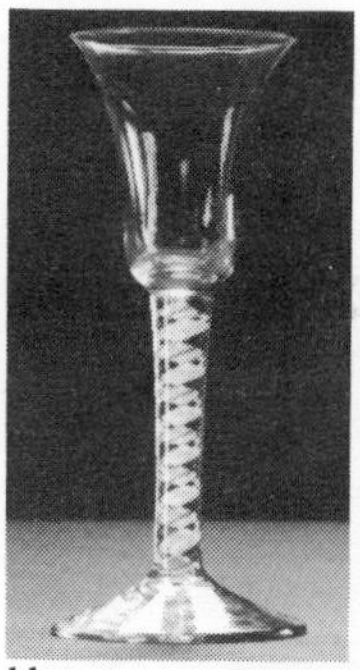
11

12

13

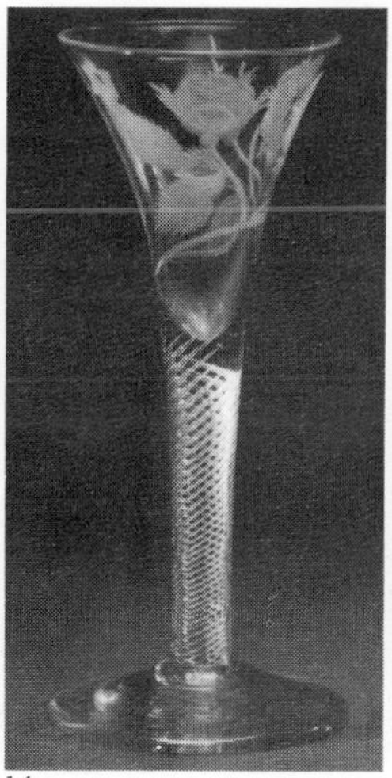
14

15

1

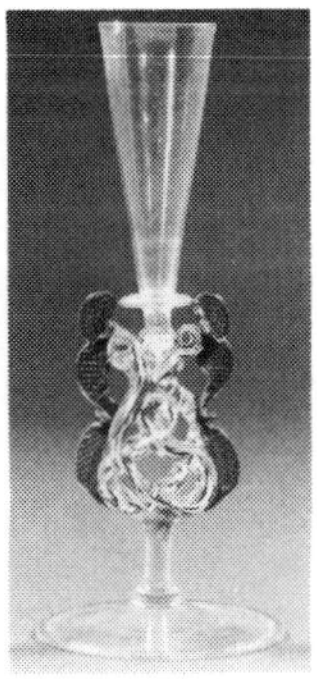
2

3

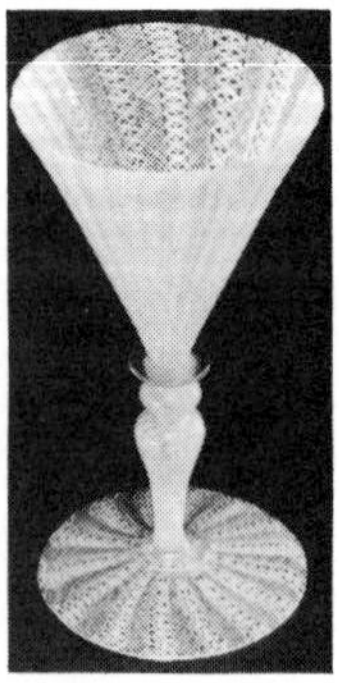
4

5 6

7

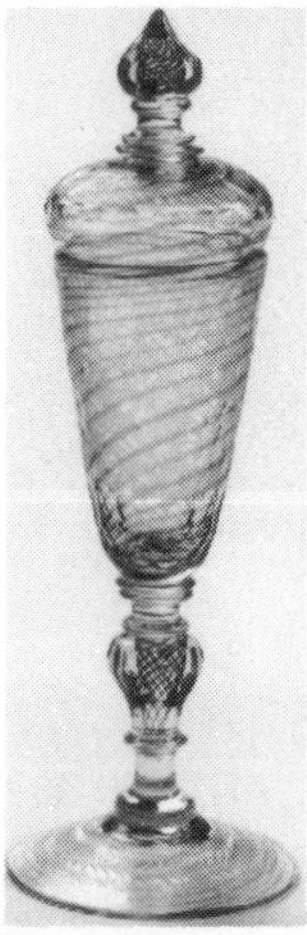
8

9

10

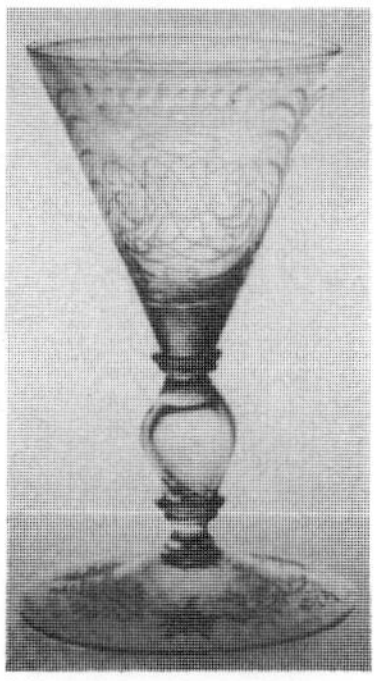
11

12

13

14 15

16

1
A façon de Venise winged stem goblet, 17th century, the bowl in 'ice glass' set on a hollow stem with yellow sea horse handles, 15.5cm (6¼in), *L 10 Feb,*
£1,100 ($1,617)

2
A façon de Venise serpent goblet, probably Southern Netherlands, 17th century, 18cm (7in), *A 6 May,*
Dfl 3,220 (£976; $1,551)

3
A façon de Venise goblet, Lowlands, second half 17th century, 18cm (7in), *L 24 Nov,*
£1,078 ($1,520)

4
A façon de Venise filigree wine glass, 17th/18th century, the funnel bowl and foot in *vetro a fili*, 17cm (6¾in), *L 24 Nov,*
£1,760 ($2,481)

5
A Netherlands diamond-engraved wine glass, second half 17th century, decorated with two bands of foliate scrolls, 15cm (6½in), *L 24 Nov,*
£1,210 ($1,706)

6
A façon de Venise double-walled glass, probably Netherlands, 17th century, the stem decorated with applied white trails, 10cm (4in), *L 24 Nov,*
£495 ($697)

7
A façon de Venise wine glass, possibly South Netherlands, 17th century, 13cm (5in), *L 24 Nov,*
£825 ($1,163)

8
An engraved and coloured Bohemian goblet and cover, c.1710, decorated with translucent-red swirling threads, 32cm (12½in), *L 24 Nov,*
£770 ($1,085)

9
A German double-bowled goblet, probably Bohemian, dated 1715, the two funnel bowls separated by a baluster knop with blue and white inclusions, the lower bowl fitted with a clapper, 21cm (8¼in), *L 10 Feb,*
£462 ($679)

10
A Bohemian 'zwischengold' goblet, c.1730, the double-walled funnel bowl decorated in gilt on one side with a mirror monogram and on the reverse with arabesques and putti, 17cm (6¾in), *L 10 Feb,*
£880 ($1,294)

11
A German wine glass, the funnel bowl engraved on one side with a crowned mirror monogram and scrolling flowers on the reverse, 18.5cm (7¼in), *C 21 Oct,*
£242 ($339)

12
An engraved goblet, Riesengebirge, c.1745, the bowl decorated with a female allegorical figure and hunting vignettes, 18cm (7in), *L 24 Nov,*
£1,870 ($2,636)

13
A Saxon engraved goblet and cover, c.1745, the funnel bowl decorated with the infant Bacchus astride a barrel, 17.5cm (7in), *L 24 Nov,*
£528 ($744)

14
A Potsdam engraved goblet and cover, c.1725, decorated in the manner of Elias Rosbach with Venus *en deshabille* with putti, 31cm (12¼in), *L 24 Nov,*
£1,650 ($2,326)

15
A large armorial goblet, possibly Braunschweig, c.1740, 25.5cm (10in), *L 24 Nov,*
£550 ($775)

16
A German goblet, third quarter 18th century, the bowl engraved with a cartouche enclosing birds and a dog, with associated domed cover, 21cm (8¼in), *NY 25 Nov,*
$825 (£589)

1
A Dutch glass, 18th century, the bowl engraved with two sailing vessels, 18cm (7in), *A 14 Oct,*
Dfl 977 (£305; $458)

2
A Dutch glass, 18th century, engraved with a man in his wine-cellar and the text *VIVAT DE WIJNKOOPEREY*, 19.5cm (7¾in), *A 14 Oct,*
Dfl 747 (£233; $350)

3
A Dutch 'Friendship' glass, c.1750, the funnel bowl engraved with clasped hands, 20cm (8in), *L 10 Feb,*
£550 ($808)

4
A Dutch armorial goblet, c.1750, the funnel bowl engraved with the arms of William IV of Orange within the ribbon of the Garter, 20.5cm (8in), *L 24 Nov,*
£660 ($930)

5
A Dutch armorial goblet, c.1745, the funnel bowl engraved with the royal arms of the House of Orange within the ribbon of the Garter, 19.5cm (7¾in), *L 24 Nov,*
£572 ($806)

6
An enamelled Dutch wine glass, c.1760, the funnel bowl painted in colours on one side with a dove in yellow within a snake, the reverse engraved with the bound arrows of the Netherlands, surmounted by a white enamelled dove, 17cm (6¾in), *L 24 Nov,*
£4,620 ($6,514)

7
A Dutch Newcastle 'Friendship' glass, the glass c.1760, engraved 1784, on composite stem and foot, 19.5cm (7¾in), *C 16 Apr,*
£418 ($648)

8
A Dutch 'Friendship' glass, 18th century, the bowl engraved with the text *EEN GLAASIE VAN VRINDSCHAP*, 17.5cm (7in), *A 14 Oct,*
Dfl 1,725 (£539; $808)

9
A Dutch commemorative glass, 18th century, diamond-point engraved, signed J. van den Blijk, the design by P. van Braam, 19cm (7¾in), *A 14 Oct,*
Dfl 5,060 (£1,581; $2,372)

10
A Dutch beaker, 18th century, engraved with a motto referring to a mother and her newborn child, 13.5cm (5in), *A 6 May,*
Dfl 1,610 (£488; $776)

11
A Dutch 'Drink uit' goblet, 18th century, the bowl engraved with a mother and child, the foot in the shape of a bell with clapper, 25cm (10in), *A 6 May,*
Dfl 7,820 (£2,370; $3,768)

12
A Dutch armorial goblet, 18th century, the bowl engraved with the arms of the city of Amsterdam, 20cm (8in), *A 6 May,*
Dfl 2,760 (£836; $1,330)

13
A Dutch glass, 18th century, the bowl engraved with an altar and two hearts, 19cm (7¾in), *A 30 Jan,*
Dfl 1,552 (£470; $691)

14
A Dutch armorial goblet, c.1750, the funnel bowl engraved with the arms of Overyssel, 25cm (10in), *L 24 Nov,*
£660 ($930)

15
A Dutch goblet, the glass c.1750, the decoration 19th century, the funnel bowl decorated in stipple engraving with a gallant serenading a lady, foot chipped, 22cm (8½in), *L 24 Nov,*
£858 ($1,209)

16
A Dutch armorial wine glass, c.1750, the bowl engraved with the arms of William IV of Orange within the ribbon of the Garter, 18cm (7in), *L 24 Nov,*
£660 ($930)

1 2 3

4 5

6

7

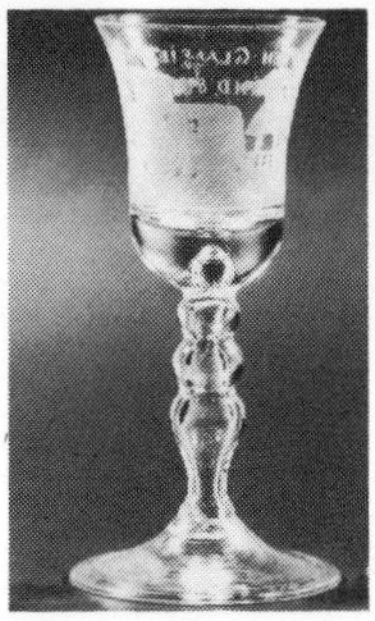
8

9

10

11

12

13

14 15 16

1

2

3

4 5 6

10

7

8

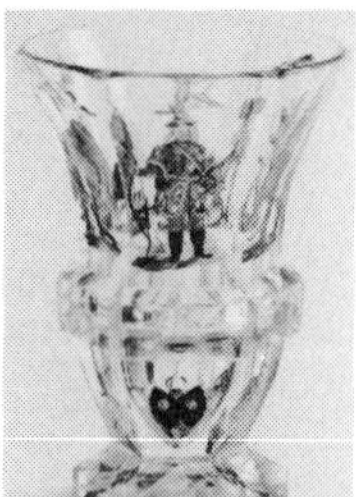
9

11

12

1
A Bohemian tumbler, c.1690-1700, the heavy sides decorated in *tiefschnitt* and *mattschnitt* with three cartouches, the first with the arms of Austria, the second with a portrait of the Emperor Leopold I and the third with his wife Charlotte, 11.5cm (4½in), *L 10 Feb,*
£1,320 ($1,940)

2
A German enamelled glass guild humpen, dated 1705, decorated in blue, grey-blue, yellow, rust and green with three shields and an inscription, 21cm (8¼in), *NY 25 Nov,*
$6,600 (£4,714)

3
A German enamelled glass guild beaker, dated 1732, decorated in rust, yellow, white, green and manganese with an armorial shield and inscription, 13cm (5¼in), *NY 25 Nov,*
$1,980 (£1,414)

4
A Central European enamelled tumbler, 18th century, painted in colours with a mounted cavalryman, 10cm (4in), *L 10 Feb,*
£253 ($372)

5
A Central European enamelled flask, 18th century, painted in colours with stylised flowers, 17cm (6¾in), *L 10 Feb,*
£220 ($323)

6
A Central European enamelled flask, 18th century, painted in colours with a vase of stylised flowers, chips, 21.5cm (8½in), *L 10 Feb,*
£330 ($485)

7
A Central European enamelled flask, 18th century, sold with a glass, 15.5cm (6¼in), *A 23 Apr,*
Dfl 862 (£261; $409)

8
A blue glass urn and cover, English or Bohemian, possibly late 18th century, decorated in gold, some abrasion, 51cm (20in), *NY 25 Nov,*
$1,760 (£1,257)

9
A Bohemian transparent-enamelled beaker, c.1830-40, the bowl cut with broad facets each painted in translucent colours in the manner of C. von Scheidt, alternately with birds and chinoiserie figures, 14cm (5½in), *L 24 Nov,*
£1,540 ($2,171)

10
A transparent-enamelled topographical beaker, Dresden or Leipzig, 1812, signed S. Mohn and dated, 10cm (4in), *L 24 Nov,*
£18,700 ($26,367)

11
A South Bohemian gilt hyalith preserve pot and cover, Buquoy Glass-house, c.1830, the black body gilt with chinoiserie vignettes, 13cm (5in), *L 24 Nov,*
£495 ($697)

12
A Bohemian transparent-enamelled footed beaker, c.1830, the bowl cut with broad facets and painted in transparent colours on one side with a scene of a returning huntsman, the reverse with lens, 13cm (5in), *L 24 Nov,*
£550 ($775)

1
A Bohemian amber-flashed engraved goblet, c.1850, engraved on one side with a horse, chip, 14cm (5½in), *L 24 Nov,*
£330 ($465)

2
A Bohemian amber-flashed engraved goblet, c.1850, engraved on one side with a mounted officer at full gallop, 17.5cm (7in), *L 24 Nov,*
£660 ($930)

3
A Bohemian amber-flashed engraved beaker, c.1850, the sides with roundels each engraved with animals and birds connected with the chase, 12.5cm (5in), *L 24 Nov,*
£330 ($465)

4
A North Bohemian transparent-enamelled beaker, late 19th century, with a panel depicting a Greek maiden at a sacrifice, 10.5cm (4in), *L 24 Nov,*
£440 ($620)

5
A transparent-enamelled beaker, late 19th century, with panels depicting artisans and tradesmen, rim bruised, 14.5cm (5¾in), *L 24 Nov,*
£264 ($372)

6
A Viennese transparent-enamelled beaker, c.1830, painted beneath the rim with a circlet of violas flanked by amber-flashed borders, 10.5cm (4in), *L 24 Nov,*
£5,720 ($8,065)

7
A North Bohemian cut and engraved beaker, possibly Franz Anton Riedel, early 19th century, 9.5cm (3¾in), *L 24 Nov,*
£605 ($853)

8
A Viennese transparent-enamelled topographical beaker, attributed to the workshop of Anton Kothgasser, c.1830, the bowl painted in transparent colours with views of the Royal Library and the Josephsplatz, 12cm (4¾in), *L 24 Nov,*
£6,050 ($8,530)

9
A Viennese rock crystal goblet with gilt and enamelled mounts, mid 19th century, the body inlaid with a satyr and a nymph, the base with enamels and precious stones, 15.5cm (6in), *F 30 Sept,*
L 4,180,000 (£2,083; $2,916)

10
A Bohemian ruby-flashed goblet, dated 1851, engraved with a picture of the Crystal Palace and inscribed *The Industrial Exhibition for 1851*, 22cm (8¾in), *S 19 Mar,*
£396 ($606)

11
A Bohemian ruby-flashed goblet, engraved with three panels of buildings, including a town hall and a coffee house, 22cm (8¾in), *C 25 Feb,*
£264 ($396)

12
A pair of French opaline glasses, *(one illustrated)*, c.1825, decorated in gold and blue, 13cm (5in), *M 1 Dec,*
FF 4,400 (£475; $679)

13
A French turquoise and gilt-bronze opaline casket, c.1825, 12cm (4¾in) high, *M 24 Feb,*
FF 33,300 (£3,221; $4,831)

14
A French opaline casket, c.1825, with gilt-bronze mounts, 13cm (5in) high, *M 24 Feb,*
FF 15,540 (£1,503; $2,254)

15
A pair of French turquoise opaline bottles *(one illustrated)*, c.1825, with gilt-bronze mounts, 18cm (7in) high, *M 24 Feb,*
FF 17,750 (£1,718; $2,576)

1 2 3

4 5

6

8

9

7

10

11

12

13

14

15

1

2

3

4

5 6 7 8 9 10

11

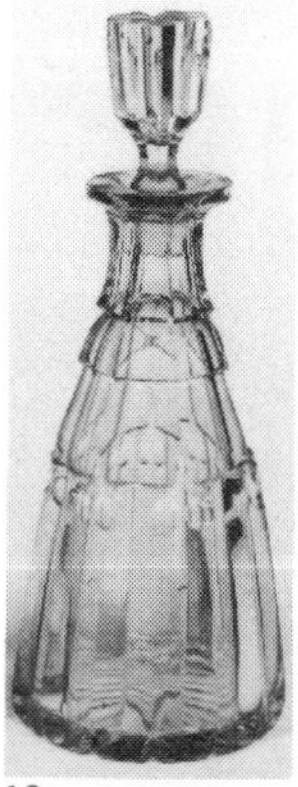
12

13 14

15

16

17

1
A Colchester volunteer decanter and stopper, dated 1797, the body with the arms of Colchester within a garter inscribed *LOYAL COLCHESTER VOLUNTEERS*, 26cm (10¼in), *L 24 Nov,*
£990 ($1,395)

2
A pair of Cork decanters and stoppers, *(one illustrated)*, c.1800, marked, 26cm (10¼in), *L 24 Nov,*
£385 ($542)

3
A pair of Cork decanters and stoppers, *(one illustrated)*, c.1800, marked, 28cm (11in), *L 24 Nov,*
£1,100 ($1,551)

4
A cut decanter and stopper, c.1820, decorated with four oval panels bearing the initials GR and a crown, the base cut with Prince-of-Wales feathers, 27cm (10½in), *L 24 Nov,*
£2,200 ($3,102)

5
A pair of cut glass decanters and stoppers, *(one illustrated)*, first quarter 19th century, minor chips, 28cm (11in), *NY 25 Jan,*
$1,760 (£1,266)

6
A pair of cut glass decanters and stoppers, *(one illustrated)*, early 19th century, 27cm (10¾in), *NY 25 Jan,*
$2,860 (£2,058)

7
Two similar cut glass decanters and stoppers, *(one illustrated)*, first quarter 19th century, 32 and 34cm (12½ and 13½in), *NY 25 Jan,*
$1,540 (£1,108)

8
A pair of cut glass decanters and stoppers, *(one illustrated)*, first quarter 19th century, 29cm (11½in), *NY 25 Jan,*
$1,760 (£1,266)

9
A pair of cut glass decanters and stoppers, *(one illustrated)*, first quarter 19th century, 30cm (11¾in), *NY 25 Jan,*
$1,760 (£1,266)

10
A pair of cut glass decanters and stoppers, *(one illustrated)*, first quarter 19th century, 29cm (11½in), *NY 25 Jan,*
$1,760 (£1,266)

11
A pair of cut glass decanters and stoppers, *(one illustrated)*, early 19th century, 23cm (9in), *NY 10 June,*
$495 (£315)

12
A pair of cut glass decanters and stoppers, *(one illustrated)*, 33.5cm (13¼in), *HS 24 Sept,*
IR£286 (£260; $377)

13
A pair of ship's decanters and stoppers, *(one illustrated)*, one damaged, 25cm (9¾in), *HS 24 Sept,*
IR£154 (£140; $203)

14
A pair of hobnail-cut claret decanters and stoppers, *(one illustrated)*, one damaged, 30.5cm (12in), *HS 24 Sept,*
IR£308 (£280; $406)

15
Four decanters and stoppers, *(one illustrated)*, one pair 25.5cm (10in), the other 22cm (8¾in), *C 25 Feb,*
£396 ($594)

16
A Scottish sulphide ship's decanter and stopper, c.1870, with a sulphide profile portrait of Robert Burns, impressed on the shoulder *J Moore*, the reverse with a profile head of Shakespeare, 29cm (11½in), *L 24 Nov,*
£2,090 ($2,946)

17
A Victorian claret jug, probably Stourbridge, c.1870, finely engraved with foliate scrolls with exotic animals and insects in intaglio, 31cm (12¼in), *L 24 Nov,*
£2,750 ($3,877)

1
A cut glass honey jar and cover, 19th century, slight chips, 22.5cm (8¾in), *C 15 Jan,*
£187 ($281)

2
A cut glass jar and cover, early 19th century, slight chips, 29.5cm (11½in), *C 15 Jan,*
£198 ($297)

3
A cut glass honey jar and cover, early 19th century, foot slightly chipped, 32.5cm (12¾in), *C 15 Jan,*
£176 ($264)

4
A pair of cut glass jars and covers *(one illustrated)*, 18th/19th century, 34.5cm (13½in), *A 14 Oct,*
Dfl 1,610 (£503; $755)

5
A pair of ginger jars and covers, 19th century, 32cm (12½in), *A 12 Mar,*
Dfl 1,150 (£348; $537)

6
A centrepiece, 1868, with silver foot, 50cm (19¾in), *A 12 Mar,*
Dfl 2,300 (£697; $1,073)

7
A pair of cut glass preserve jars and covers, 19th century, 19cm (7½in), *JHB 11 Nov,*
R 2,100 (£656; $919)

8
A cut glass preserve bowl, cover and stand, c.1820, 14.5cm (5¾in), *JHB 11 Nov,*
R 1,300 (£406; $569)

9
A pair of heavy cut glass jars, covers and stands, 18cm (7in), *HS 24 Sept,*
IR£638 (£580; $841)

10
A pedestal fruit bowl, some damage, 30.5cm (12in), *HS 24 Sept,*
IR£286 (£260; $377)

11
A cut glass Irish fruit bowl, c.1800, 30cm (11¾in) diam., *L 24 Nov,*
£748 ($1,054)

12
A Hawkes cut and polished stemware service, 20th century, comprising 140 pieces, chips, *NY 26 Apr,*
$2,970 (£1,929)

13
A cut and engraved stemware service, probably English, 20th century, comprising 131 pieces, all decorated with cornucopia, swags, foliate scrolls and some with initials, restorations, water goblet 30cm (11¾in), *NY 13 Sept,*
$4,675 (£3,180)

14
A suite of cut glass, comprising 41 drinking glasses, 2 tazzas, a vase, 3 decanters, a claret jug and 2 carafes, *C 29 May,*
£308 ($487)

15
A French cut glass and gilt-bronze mounted three-piece garniture, probably Baccarat, late 19th century, 27 and 19cm (10½ and 7½in), *NY 24 June,*
$1,500 (£961)

1 2 3

4

5 6 5

7 8 7

9 10 9

11

12

13

14

15

1

2

3

4

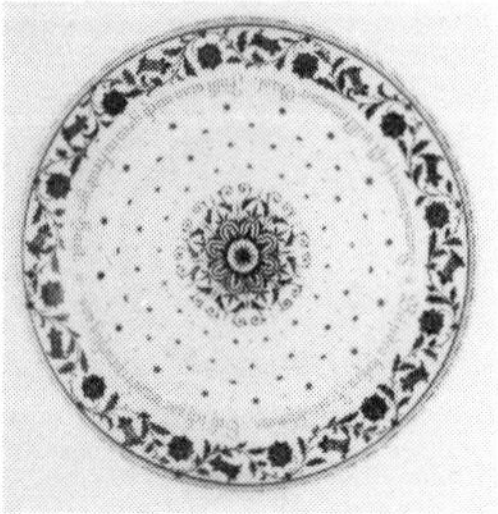

8

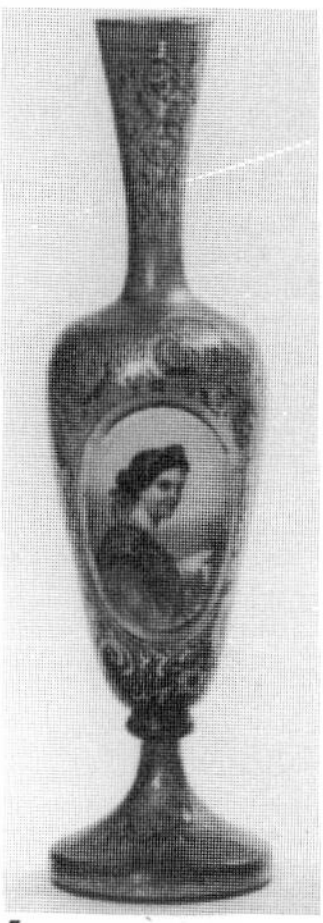

5

6

7

9

10

11

12

13 14 15 16

1
An enamelled and gilt Bohemian urn and pedestal, c.1880, 42.5cm (16¾in), *S 10 Dec,*
£594 ($832)

2
A Bohemian enamelled and gilt cranberry vase, c.1880, 33cm (13in), *S 10 Dec,*
£275 ($385)

3
A pair of Bohemian enamelled and gilt tulip vases, *(one illustrated),* c.1880, cranberry bodies overlaid in white, 34cm (13½in), *S 10 Dec,*
£506 ($708)

4
A Bohemian cameo centrepiece, late 19th century, overlaid in white on a red glass ground, 26cm (10¼in), *C 8 Oct,*
£539 ($755)

5
A pair of enamelled and gilt green vases, *(one illustrated),* Bohemian/Venetian, c.1860, repair to stem, 33cm (13in), *S 10 Dec,*
£132 ($185)

6
A pair of Bohemian cut and gilt-decorated enamel overlay vases, *(one illustrated),* c.1880, 43cm (17in), *NY 13 Sept,*
$1,650 (£1,122)

7
A pair of Bohemian enamel overlay and gilt decorated vases, *(one illustrated),* late 19th century, 45cm (17¾in), *NY 13 Sept,*
$1,650 (£1,122)

8
A Lobmeyr enamelled and inscribed charger, late 19th century, tinted olive green, with blue dots, the reverse with Lobmeyr logo in blue and white anchor painter's mark, 42cm (16½in), *L 24 Nov,*
£715 ($1,008)

9
A Lobmeyr enamelled and gilt vase, c.1880, decorated in *arabischen stil,* the base with Lobmeyr logo, 17cm (6½in), *L 24 Nov,*
£2,750 ($3,878)

10
A French enamelled tazza c.1870, decorated and signed by A. Bucan, 25cm (10in) diam., *L 24 Nov,*
£495 ($698)

11
A French enamelled tazza c.1870, decorated and signed in red by A. Bucan, 25cm (10in) diam., *L 24 Nov,*
£550 ($776)

12
A cameo biscuit barrel, c.1880, probably Webb, opaque steel-blue body overlaid in white, 19cm (7½in), *L 24 Nov,*
£792 ($1,116)

13
A cameo vase, Stevens and Williams, c.1880, translucent lime-green body overlaid in opaque white, 17cm (6½in), *L 24 Nov,*
£605 ($853)

14
A cameo vase, Stevens and Williams, c.1880, translucent steel-blue, overlaid in opaque white, 20cm (8in), *L 24 Nov,*
£1,100 ($1,551)

15
A cameo vase, Stevens and Williams, c.1880, plum-coloured overlaid in opaque white, 20cm (8in), *L 24 Nov,*
£1,210 ($1,706)

16
A cameo vase, Stevens and Williams, c.1880, deep translucent turquoise, overlaid in opaque white, 18cm (7in), *L 24 Nov*
£495 ($697)

1
A Millville pedestal ship weight, 10cm (4in) high, *NY 12 Mar,*
$1,320 (£904)

2
A Whitefriars millefiori inkwell and stopper *(illustrated)* and matching paperweight, 19.5cm (7½in), 9cm (3½in) diam., *NY 12 Mar,*
$1,100 (£753)

3
A St. Louis scent-bottle and stopper, c.1845, the paperweight base in the form of a crown, 16.5cm (6½in), *L 24 Nov,*
£2,860 ($4,033)

4
A Whitefriars oil lamp base, the clear glass base set with assorted millefiori canes, 35.5cm (14in) high, *NY 12 Mar,*
$880 (£603)

5
A Clichy millefiori newell post, 12.5cm (5in) high, *NY 12 Mar,*
$1,210 (£829)

6
A Clichy wafer stand, the base composed of a mille fiori weight, base 5cm (2in) diam., *NY 12 Mar,*
$770 (£527)

7
A Baccarat millefiori wafer dish, dated B 1848, the base composed of a close millefiori weight, 9.5cm (3¾in) high, *NY 12 Mar,*
$2,750 (£1,884)

8
A Ray and Bob Banford complex bouquet weight, signed, 8cm (3in), *NY 12 Mar,*
$880 (£603)

9
A Clichy wafer stand, mid 19th century, 9.5cm (3¾in), *L 24 Nov,*
£1,375 ($1,939)

10
A Clichy millefiori wafer stand, mid 19th century, 10cm (4in), *L 10 Feb,*
£2,750 ($4,042)

11
A New England fruit weight, set with an arrangement of apples and cherries, 7cm (2¾in), *NY 12 Mar,*
$330 (£226)

12
A Charles Kaziun pedestal rose weight, signed, 9cm (3½in), *NY 12 Mar,*
$990 (£678)

13
A Charles Kaziun faceted green double overlay weight, signed, 5.5cm (2¼in), *NY 12 Mar,*
$2,420 (£1,657)

14
A French apple weight, c.1845, 7.5cm (3in), *L 24 Nov,*
£528 ($744)

15
A Clichy two-colour swirl weight, 6.5cm (2½in), *NY 12 Mar,*
$1,320 (£904)

16
A Clichy millefiori piedouche weight, 7cm (2¾in) diam., *NY 12 Mar,*
$9,075 (£6,216)

17
A Clichy millefiori piedouche weight, 7.5cm (3in), *NY 12 Mar,*
$880 (£603)

18
A Clichy colour-ground weight, c.1845, 8cm (3in), *L 24 Nov,*
£374 ($527)

19
A Clichy millefiori colour-ground weight, 7cm (2¾in), *NY 12 Mar,*
$1,540 (£1,055)

1

2

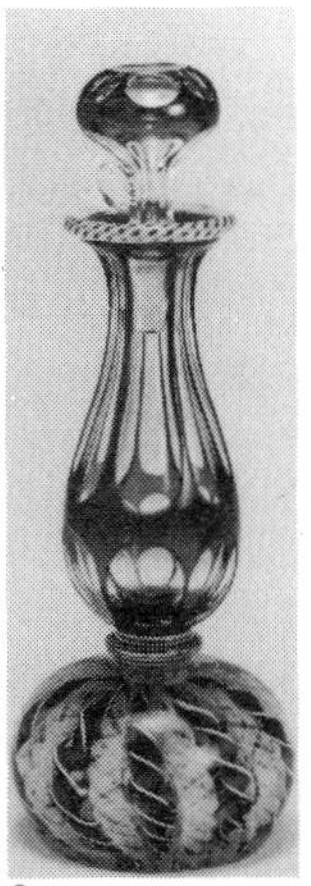
3

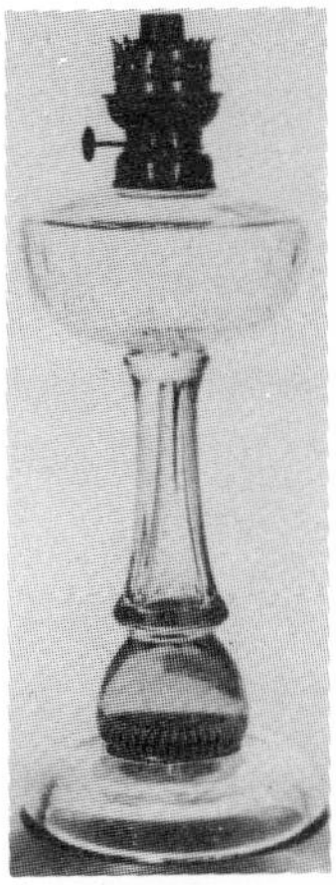
4

5 6 7

8

9

10

11

12

13

14

15

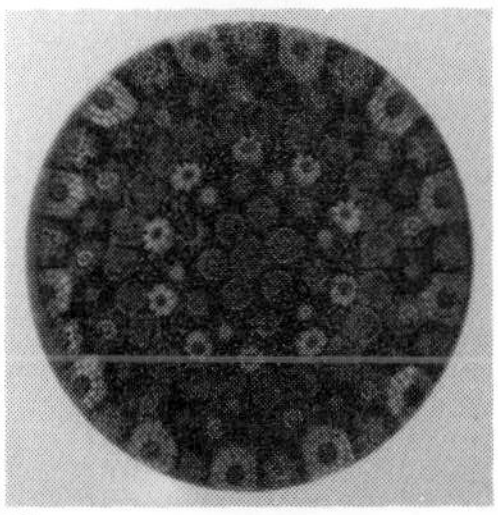
16

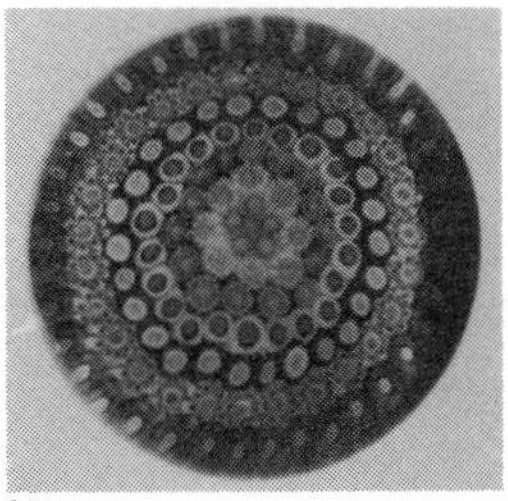
17

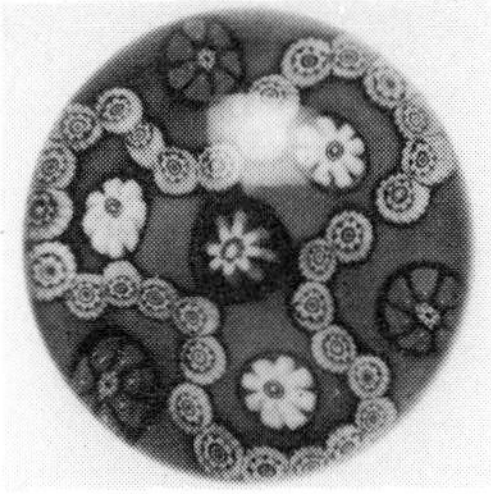
18

19

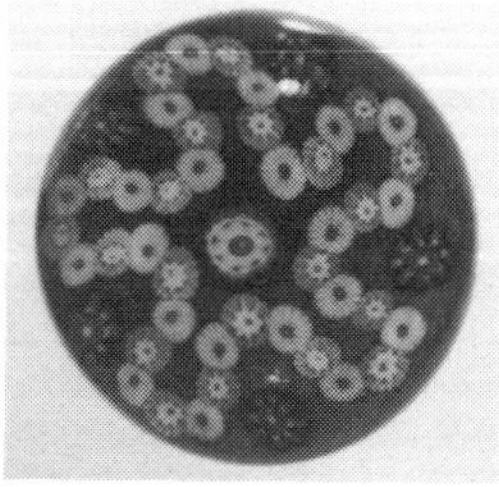
1

2

3

4

5

6

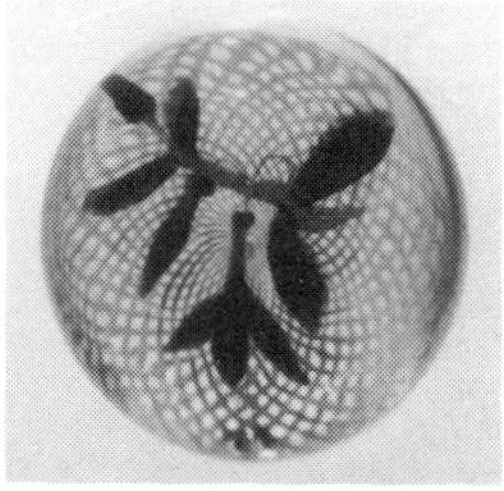
7

8

9

10

11

12

13

14

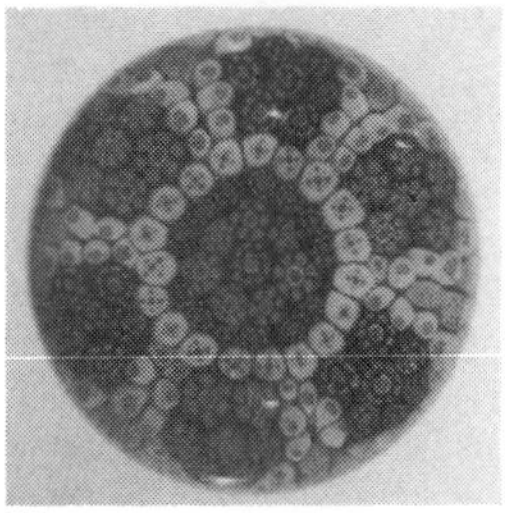
15

16

17

18

1
A Clichy millefiori colour-ground weight, 8.5cm (3¼in), *NY 12 Mar,*
$1,760 (£1,205)

2
A Clichy pansy weight, 5.5cm (2¼in), *NY 12 Mar,*
$880 (£603)

3
A Clichy patterned-millefiori weight, c.1845, 8cm (3in), *L 24 Nov,*
£990 ($1,396)

4
A Clichy swirl weight, c.1845, 7cm (2¾in), *L 24 Nov,*
£572 ($807)

5
A St. Louis miniature fruit weight, set with a pear and three cherries, 4.5cm (1¾in), *NY 12 Mar,*
$825 (£565)

6
A St. Louis pelargonium weight, 7cm (2¾in), *L 10 Feb,*
£1,210 ($1,779)

7
A St. Louis fuchsia weight, 6.5cm (2½in), *NY 12 Mar,*
$1,650 (£1,130)

8
A St. Louis signed and dated mushroom weight, 1848, 7cm (2¾in), *L 24 Nov,*
£1,078 ($1,520)

9
A St. Louis miniature three-colour crown weight, 5.5cm (2¼in), *NY 12 Mar,*
$770 (£527)

10
A St. Louis 'Marbrie' weight, c.1845, 8cm (3in), *L 24 Nov,*
£2,090 ($2,947)

11
A St. Louis millefiori mushroom weight, 7cm (2¾in), *NY 12 Mar,*
$1,540 (£1,054)

12
A Baccarat sulphide weight, c.1845, the ruby-flashed base set with a profile portrait bust of Queen Victoria, 9cm (3½in), *L 24 Nov,*
£880 ($1,241)

13
A Baccarat sulphide weight, set with the head of the Comte de Chambord, 6.5cm (2½in), *NY 12 Mar,*
$192 (£132)

14
A Baccarat garlanded butterfly weight, 8cm (3in), *NY 12 Mar,*
$2,750 (£1,883)

15
A Baccarat carpet-ground weight, 6.5cm (2½in), *NY 12 Mar,*
$3,025 (£2,072)

16
A Baccarat clematis bud weight, 8cm (3in), *NY 12 Mar,*
$1,540 (£1,055)

17
A Baccarat garlanded clematis weight, 7.5cm (3in), *NY 12 Mar,*
$1,760 (£1,205)

18
A Baccarat gentian weight, 7.5cm (3in), *NY 12 Mar,*
$8,800 (£6,027)

19th and 20th Century Sculpture

See also:
Colour illustrations *p* 483
Decorative arts from 1880 *pp* 296-297
European works of art *pp* 357-358
Garden statuary *pp* 544-545
Russian works of art *p* 377
Main sub-sections:
Animalier bronzes *pp* 277-278
Continental bronzes *pp* 273-276
English bronzes *p* 272
Marble *pp* 269-270
Spelter and cold-painted bronzes *p* 271
Terracotta *p* 270

1
Giovanni Bertoli, a marble bust of a young boy, late 19th century, 62cm (24½in), *L 20 Mar,*
£572 ($898)

2
After Etienne Falconnet, a marble figure of a bather, mid 19th century, after the original plaster model in the Hermitage Museum, Leningrad, 130cm (51in), *M 23 June,*
FF 33,300 (£2,971; $4,634)

3
George Halse, a marble figure entitled *Young England*, signed, 72.5cm (28½in), *L 1 Oct,*
£6,050 ($8,651)

4
Jean-Antoine Houdon, a marble bust of Diana, c.1870, signed, 61cm (24in), *L 20 Mar,*
£660 ($1,036)

5
Pasquale Romanelli, a Carrara marble figure of Master Tell, c.1875, the arrow having pierced an apple near his head, signed, 114cm (45in), *C 8 Oct,*
£2,860 ($4,004)

6
Alessandro Lazzerini, a pair of marble figures of dogs, third quarter 19th century, signed, *(one illustrated)*, 104 and 106.5cm (41 and 42in) wide, *L 12 June,*
£15,400 ($24,640)

7
After the Antique, a marble figure of Venus, late 19th century, 65.5cm (25¾in), *L 7 Apr,*
£418 ($635)

8
Professor A. Petrilli, a marble figure of Napoleon, late 19th/early 20th century, damages, 119.5cm (47in), *NY 13 Sept,*
$7,150 (£4,864)

9
Tito Tadolini, a marble figure of a woman, c.1863, signed, 103cm (40½in), *L 20 Mar,*
£10,450 ($16,406)

10
Flle ** Pugi, a marble bust of Beatrice, late 19th century, a scroll at the base inscribed with a verse from Dante, signed, 65cm (25½in), *L 6 Nov,*
£1,760 ($2,499)

11
Emile Wolff, a marble bust of Prince Albert, c.1842, signed, 61cm (24in), *L 6 Nov,*
£2,090 ($2,968)

12
A marble bust of a girl, Italian, c.1890s, 80cm (31½in), *S 11 Nov,*
£836 ($1,170)

1

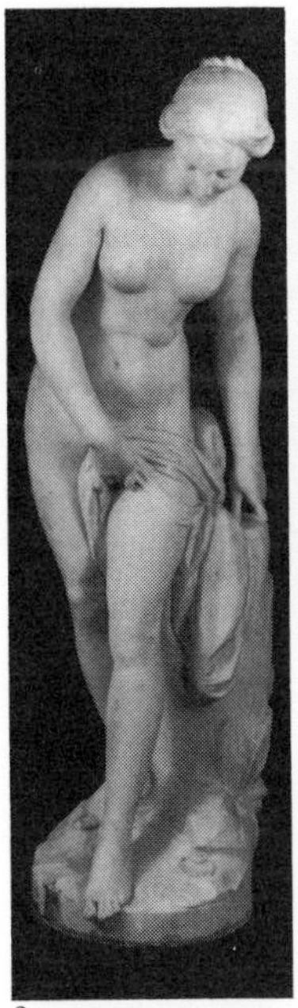
2

3

4

5

6

7

8

9

10

11

12

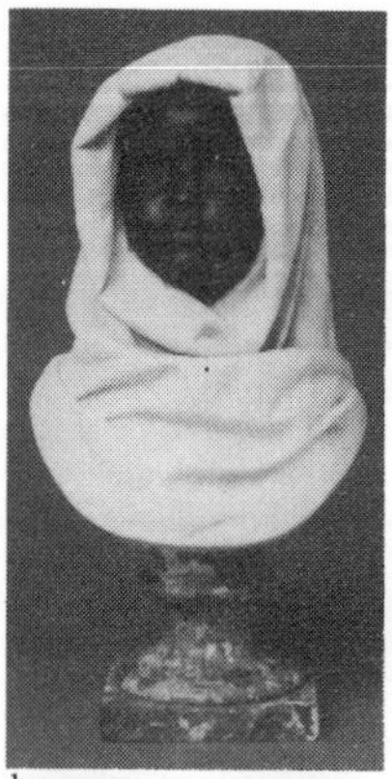
1

2

3

4

5

6

7

8

9

10

11

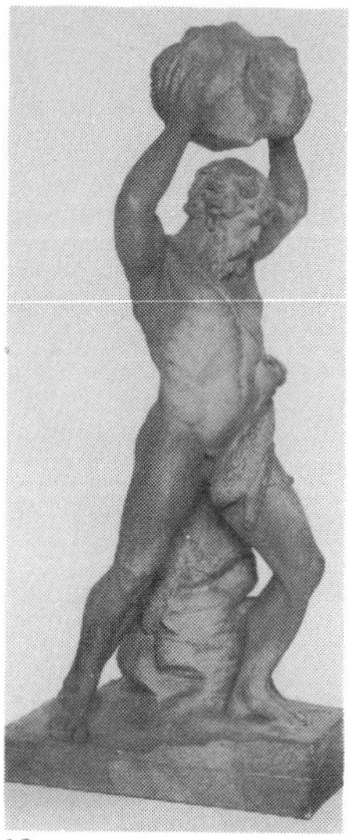
12

13

1
Raimondo Pereda, a bronze and marble bust of a negro child, c.1880, with textured white marble drapery and bronze face, 52cm (20½in), *NY 13 Sept,*
$4,675 (£3,180)

2
Dominique Alonzo, a gilt-bronze and marble bust of a young girl entitled *Arlestenne*, c.1915, the girl with a white marble face and wearing a gilt-bronze cap and garment, 56cm (22in), *NY 13 Sept,*
$1,980 (£1,347)

3
A* J* Lavergne, a pair of terracotta busts of young girls, 58cm (23in), *C 17 Apr,*
£880 ($1,364)

4
A* Gory, a gilt-bronze and marble bust of a lady, c.1900, with marble face and breast and gilt-bronze drapery, chip, 73cm (28¾in), *NY 13 Sept,*
$3,850 (£2,619)

5
Gustave Fréderic Michel, a gilt-bronze and ivory bust entitled *La Pensée* ('Thought'), c.1900, the classical man wearing a laurel leaf crown and toga, 32cm (12½in), *S 17 June,*
£880 ($1,390)

6
Jean Baptiste Carpeaux, a terracotta figure of the Prince Imperial, son of Napoleon III, c.1865, 45cm (17¾in), *A 6 May,*
Dfl 3,680 (£1,115; $1,773)

7
Jean Baptiste Carpeaux, a terracotta bust entitled *La Fiancée*, 20th century, 63.5cm (25in), *L 6 Oct,*
£880 ($1,232)

8
Christophe Fratin, a terracotta figure of a lion, eating an antilope, 42cm (16½in), *M 23 June,*
FF 14,985 (£1,337; $2,085)

9
An ivory, bronze and marble group of a seated classical lady, French, c.1910, 22cm (8¾in), *S 17 June,*
£1,375 ($2,172)

10
After Pajou, a terracotta bust of Madame du Barry, late 19th century, 55cm (21½in), *L 6 Oct,*
£440 ($616)

11
A terracotta bust of a young woman, wearing a revealing dress, 81cm (31in), *L 2 June,*
£462 ($711)

12
A terracotta figure of Polythemus, late 19th century, 47cm (18½in), *C 22 Oct,*
£198 ($277)

13
Claire Jeanne Robert Colinet, a bronze and ivory group of a Valkyrie, c.1910, the young woman mounted on a horse, mid brown and dark brown patination, 47cm (18½in), *L 6 Nov,*
£4,400 ($6,248)

1
E* Loiseau,** a pair of cold-painted spelter groups of a horse and jockey, late 19th/early 20th century, 25.5cm (10in), *L 20 Mar,*
£495 ($777)

2
N* Plaza,** a spelter figure entitled *The Last of the Mohicans,* rubbed dark brown patination, 86cm (34in), *S 16 Sept,*
£550 ($770)

3
A patinated spelter group of a horse and jockey, late 19th/early 20th century, 42cm (16½in), *L 6 Nov,*
£682 ($968)

4
A patinated spelter figure of a vestal virgin, c.1880, standing holding a torch, 201cm (79in), *C 16 Jan,*
£1,012 ($1,518)

5
A pair of patinated spelter lamps, c.1880, *(one illustrated),* each holding aloft a torch, 89cm (35in), *C 16 Jan,*
£495 ($743)

6
A pair of cold-painted spelter figures of Arab boys, c.1900, each holding a brass bowl, 42cm (16½in), *L 20 Mar,*
£572 ($898)

7
A cold-painted bronze figure of an Arab, displaying a Persian carpet, 22cm (8½in), *S 18 Feb,*
£792 ($1,204)

8
A cold-painted bronze model of a bulldog, Austrian, early 20th century, 11cm (4¼in), *S 22 Apr,*
£407 ($639)

9
A cold-painted bronze figure of an owl, Austrian, early 20th century, 25cm (9¾in), *L 12 June,*
£638 ($1,020)

10
A cold-painted bronze group of five budgerigars, Austrian, early 20th century, 25cm (9¾in), *S 16 Sept,*
£462 ($647)

11
Franz Bergman, a cold-painted bronze figure of a cookaburra, c.1900, painted in realistic colours, 17cm (6½in), *L 12 June,*
£792 ($1,267)

12
Franz Bergman, a cold-painted bronze figure of a rabbit, Austrian, c.1900, 14cm (5½in), *S 11 Nov,*
£484 ($678)

1

4

5

2

3

6

7

8

9

10

11

12

1

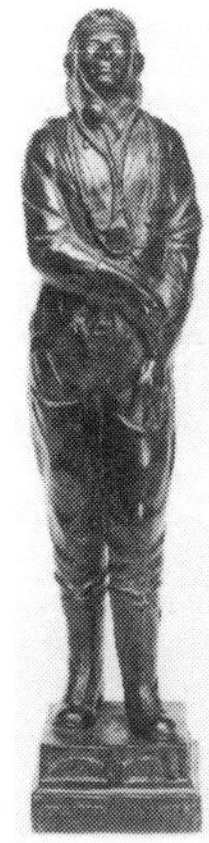
2

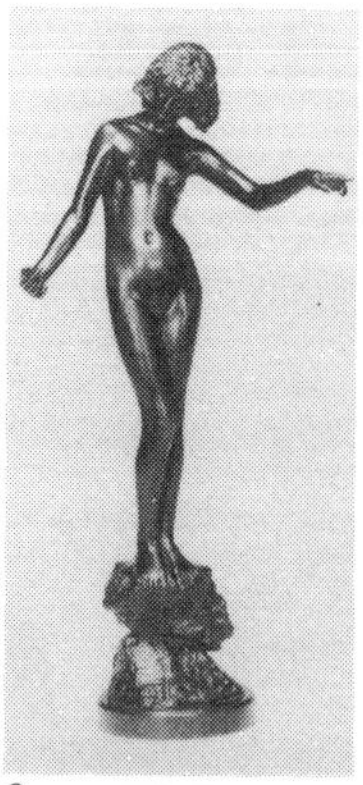
3

4

5

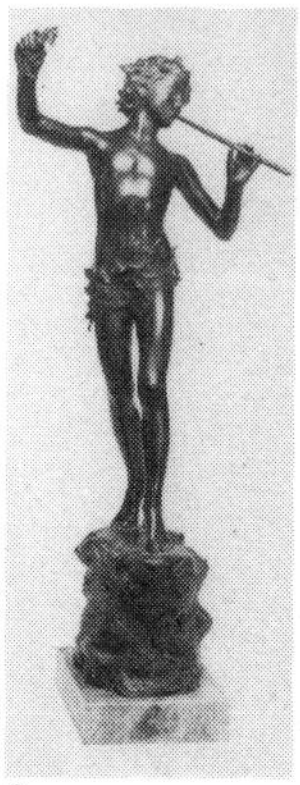
6

9

7

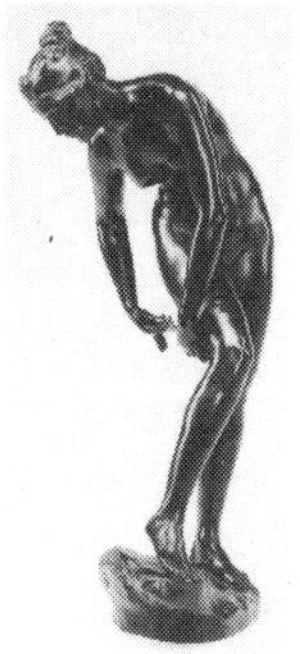
8

10

11

1
Joseph Edgar Boehm, a bronze bust of Queen Victoria, c.1887, founders *Elkington & Co.*, mid brown patination, 34cm (13¼in), *S 11 Nov,*
£660 ($924)

2
Thomas James Burns, a bronze figure of a pilot, c.1941, the plinth inscribed *Per Ardua ad Astra*, green/black patination, 52cm (20½in), *L 20 Mar,*
£1,650 ($2,590)

3
Edward Onslow Ford, a bronze figure of a young woman entitled *Folly*, dark green/black patination, 50cm (19¾in), *L 16 Apr,*
£1,540 ($2,387)

4
Sir Alfred Gilbert, a bronze figure entitled *Perseus Arming*, 31cm (14½in), *L 11 June,*
£8,250 ($12,953)

Note size when comparing prices of nos. 4 and 9.

5
William Reid Dick, a bronze bust of a boy, early 20th century, green/black patination, 28cm (11in), *S 18 Feb,*
£4,400 ($6,688)

6
Bertram Pegram, a bronze figure of Pan, brown patination, 66cm (26in), *L 11 June,*
£1,760 ($2,763)

7
Sir Alfred Gilbert, a bronze figure of Victory, brown patination, 14cm (5½in), *L 11 June,*
£715 ($1,126)

8
Bertram MacKennal, a bronze figure entitled *Diana Wounded*, rich brown patination, *E. Gruet Jeune Fondeur*, 37cm (14½in), *L 1 Oct,*
£6,820 ($9,753)

9
Sir Alfred Gilbert, a bronze figure entitled *Perseus Arming*, dark brown patination, 72.5cm (28½in), *L 26 Nov,*
£16,500 ($23,100)

10
Charles Leonard Hartwell, a bronze group of a British soldier comforting a young girl in Breton costume, green/brown rubbed patination, 30cm (12in), *S 16 Sept,*
£440 ($616)

11
Thomas Thornycroft, a bronze group of the young Queen Victoria riding side-saddle, c.1853, dark brown patination, 56cm (22in), *S 16 Sept,*
£3,300 ($4,620)

Sir Joseph Edgar Boehm, 1834-90, fl.London.

Thomas James Burns, b.1888, fl.Scotland and England.

Sir William Reid Dick, 1879-1961, fl.London.

Edward Onslow Ford, 1852-1901, fl.London.

Sir Alfred Gilbert, 1853-1934, fl.London and Bruges. Pupil of Boehm.

Charles Leonard Hartwell, 1873-1951, fl.England. Pupil of Edward Onslow Ford.

Frederic, Lord Leighton, 1830-96, fl.Brussels, Paris and London.

Sir Edgar Bertram MacKennal, 1863-1931, fl.London and Australia.

Bertram Pegram, 1873-1941, fl.England.

Thomas Thornycroft, 1815-85, fl.London.

1
Eugène-Antoine Aizelin, a bronze figure entitled *Nymphe de Diane*, c.1880, brown patination, 79cm (31in), *L 20 Mar,*
£3,960 ($6,217)

2
Henri Allouard, a bronze figure of the Marquis de Lafayette, c.1870, green/brown patination, 49cm (19in), *S 22 Apr,*
£473 ($743)

3
Antoine Boffil, a bronze figure of a boy singer, green patination, 18.5cm (7¼in), *M 24 Feb,*
FF 3,330 (£322; $483)

4
Eutrope Bouret, a bronze figure of a pierrot, late 19th century, red/brown patination, 46cm (18in), *L 20 Mar,*
£418 ($656)

5
Albert Ernest Carrier-Belleuse, a bronze and ivory figure entitled *La Liseuse*, c.1880, 61cm (24in), *L 20 Mar,*
£2,200 ($3,454)

This cast is worth more than no.6 because it is partly ivory.

6
Albert Ernest Carrier-Belleuse, a bronze figure entitled *La Liseuse*, c.1880, rich brown patination, 61.5cm (24¼in), *L 20 Mar,*
£990 ($1,554)

7
***** Duchoiselle,** a bronze figure of an Indian brave in a canoe, third quarter 19th century, dark brown patination, 102cm (40½in), *NY 26 Apr,*
$8,250 (£5,357)

8
Albert Ernest Carrier-Belleuse, a bronze figure of a royal guardsman, c.1875, dark brown patination, 77.5cm (30½in), *C 19 Nov,*
£506 ($708)

9
Alfred Boucher, a bronze figure of man digging, late 19th century, rich brown patination, *F. Barbedienne Fondeur Paris*, 68cm (26¾in), *L 20 Mar,*
£968 ($1,520)

10
After Coustou, a large pair of bronze Marly horses, *(one illustrated)*, mid 19th century, dark brown patination, 58cm (23in), *S 22 Apr,*
£660 ($1,036)

11
Camille Claudel, a bronze group entitled *La Valse*, c.1900, the dancing figures embracing, dark patination, 47cm (18½in), *A 6 May,*
Dfl 62,100 (£18,818; $29,921)

12
Etienne-Henri Dumaige, a bronze group of a woman and child, late 19th century, brown/green patination, 74.5cm (29¼in), *NY 26 Apr,*
$1,540 (£1,000)

13
Edmé Dumont, a bronze figure of the Milo of Croton, c.1870, splitting the tree stump with his bare hands, rich red/dark brown patination, 77.5cm (30½in), *L 12 June,*
£1,760 ($2,816)

Eugène-Antoine Aizelin, 1821-1902, fl.France.

Henri Allouard, 1844-1929, fl.Paris.

Louis Ernest Barrias, 1841-1905, fl.France.

Antoine Louis Barye, 1796-1875, fl.Paris.

Albert Ernest Carrier-Belleuse, 1824-87, fl.England and France.

Isidore Jules Bonheur, 1827-1901, fl.Paris.

Rosa Bonheur, 1822-99, fl.Paris. Sister of Isidore.

Alfred Boucher, 1850-1934, fl.France.

Eutrope Bouret, 1833-1906, fl.France.

Joseph Victor Chemin, 1825-1901, fl.Paris.

1

2

3

4

5

6

7

8

9

10

11

12

13

1

2

3

4

5

6

7

8

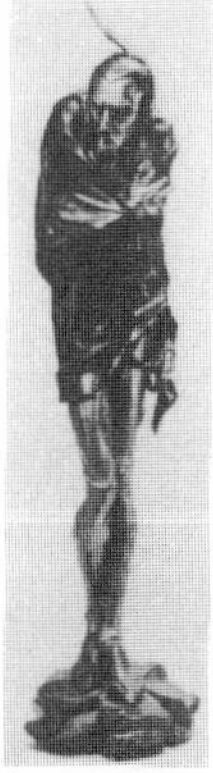
9

10

11

12

13

14

1
Edouard Drouot, a bronze group of Hercules and the Nemean Lion, c.1890, green patination, foundry seal *LNJL Paris*, 72cm (28in), *L 12 June,*
£1,100 ($1,760)

2
Jules Aimé Dalou, a bronze bust of a young boy, 1884, rich brown patination, 51cm (20in), *L 16 Apr,*
£825 ($1,279)

3
Seraphin Denécheau, a bronze figure of Diana, c.1900, curled up in a crescent moon supported by clouds, weathered patination, 99cm (39in), *NY 26 Apr,*
$9,350 (£6,071)

4
Jean Didier Début, a bronze figure of a young woman, c.1870, brown patination, 84cm (33in), *NY 13 Sept,*
$3,575 (£2,432)

5
Jean Didier Début, a bronze figure of a strolling minstrel, the young man holding a hurdy-gurdy, chocolate brown patination, 70cm (27½in), *C 16 Jan,*
£990 ($1,485)

6
Paul Dubois, a bronze figure of a Neapolitan lute player, c.1869, inscribed *F. Barbedienne Fondeur*, brown patination, 63cm (24¾in), *L 20 Mar,*
£1,430 ($2,245)

7
Paul Dubois, a bronze figure of a jester, c.1880, light brown patination, 59cm (23in), *L 6 Nov,*
£990 ($1,406)

8
Paul Dubois, a bronze figure of a jester, c.1880, light brown patination, 84cm (33in), *L 6 Nov,*
£1,650 ($2,343)

Note size when comparing prices of nos 7 and 8.

9
Jacques-Louis Gautier, a cold-painted bronze figure of Mephistopheles, late 19th/early 20th century, sword lacking, 89cm (35in), *NY 13 Sept,*
$2,090 (£1,422)

This is a late commercial casting; for example it lacks the texturing of the earlier model below.

10
Jacques-Louis Gautier, a bronze figure of Mephistopheles, c.1855, brown, green/brown and black patination, 85cm (33½in), *L 17 June,*
£3,080 ($4,866)

11
Constantin Meunier, a bronze figure of a stevedore, c.1890, rich brown patination, *V. Verbeyst Fondeur Bruxelles,* 48cm (19in), *L 6 Nov,*
£1,815 ($2,577)

12
Jean François Theodore Gechter, a bronze group of two knights fighting, c.1850, dark brown patination, 38cm (15in), *L 12 June,*
£1,210 ($1,936)

13
Louis Auguste Hiolin, a bronze group entitled *Au Loup*, c.1888, rich light brown patination, foundry seal *Pinedo Bronzes Paris*, 79cm (32in), *L 12 June,*
£5,500 ($8,800)

14
Agathon Leonard, a parcel-gilt bronze bust of young Diana, c.1880, gilt and brown patination, 52cm (20½in), *L 6 Nov,*
£1,045 ($1,484)

Joseph Cuvelier, fl.France. Exhibited 1868-78.

Jules Aimé Dalou, 1838-1902, fl.Paris and London.

Jean Didier Début, 1824-93, fl.Paris.

Seraphin Denécheau, 1831-1912, fl.Paris.

Edouard Drouot, exhibited 1892 and 1900, fl.France. Pupil of Mathurin Moreau.

1
Marius-Jean-Antonin Mercié, a parcel-gilt bronze group of Gloria Victis, late 19th century, lacking sword, brown patination, *F. Barbedienne Fondeur*, 92cm (36¼in), *NY 26 Apr*,
$4,400 (£2,857)

2
Marius-Jean-Antonin Mercié, a bronze group of Gloria Victis, c.1885, dark brown patination, 107cm (42in), *NY 13 Sept*,
$7,975 (£5,425)

Note size when comparing prices of nos 1 and 2.

3
Eugène Marioton, a bronze figure of a young woman, c.1884, playing a flute, brown patination, 100cm (39¼in), *L 20 Mar*,
£2,970 ($4,663)

4
Eugène Marioton, a bronze figure entitled *Esmeralda*, c.1880, cast with a young woman dancing with a kid at her side, brown patination, 69cm (27in), *L 6 Nov*,
£1,210 ($1,718)

5
Emile Louis Picault, a bronze figure of a blacksmith, c.1880, rich green/brown patination, 52cm (20½in), *S 16 Sept*,
£275 ($385)

6
Eugène Marioton, a bronze figure of a lion tamer, entitled *Belluaire*, c.1880, a crouching lion at his feet, stick broken, brown patination, 51cm (20in), *S 16 Sept*,
£308 ($431)

7
Auguste Moreau, a bronze figure of a girl Cupid, c.1890, light and dark brown patination, 69cm (27in), *L 6 Nov*,
£2,310 ($3,280)

8
Auguste Moreau, a bronze figure of a girl Cupid, late 19th century, coppery-brown patination, 66cm (26in), *S 17 June*,
£1,375 ($2,172)

9
Hippolyte Moreau, a bronze figure representing Sunset, late 19th century, golden brown patination, 72cm (28½in), *L 12 June*,
£1,210 ($1,936)

10
Mathurin Moreau, a bronze figure of a young woman seated on a rock listening to the sea, c.1880, on a swivelling socle, rich brown patination, 79cm (31in), *L 12 June*,
£2,420 ($3,872)

11
Marius Montagne, a bronze figure of Mercury, c.1870, rich red brown patination, 69cm (27in), *L 6 Nov*,
£1,980 ($2,812)

12
Gustave Obiols, a bronze figure of a young woman gardening, late 19th century, brown and red-brown patination, 54cm (21in), *L 12 June*,
£770 ($1,232)

13
Raphael Peyre, a gilt-bronze group of three children, late 19th century, one holding a pair of cymbals and the other two dancing, 62cm (24½in), *L 20 Mar*,
£1,980 ($3,109)

14
After Jean-Jacques Pradier, a bronze figure of a young woman representing Music, a lyre behind her, dark brown patination, 24cm (9½in), *C 9 July*,
£264 ($425)

Paul Dubois, b.1859, fl.Belgium.

Alfred Dubucand, exhibited 1867-83, fl.Paris.

Etienne Henri Dumaige, 1830-88, fl.France.

Edmé Dumont, 1722-75, fl.France.

Maximilien-Louis Fiot, exhibited 1911 and 1923, fl.France.

1

2

3

4

5

6

7

8

9

10

11

12

13

14

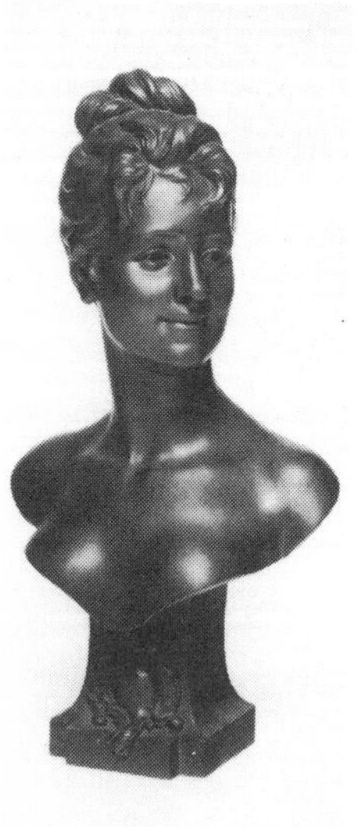
1

2

3

4

5

6

7

8

9

10

11

12

1
Emile Pinedo, a bronze bust of a young girl, c.1900, entitled *Lys*, mid brown patination, 43cm (17in), *C 8 Oct*,
£605 ($847)

2
G* Prunier,** a Goldscheider figure of an Arabian warrior, late 19th century, 81cm (32in), *L 12 June*,
£825 ($1,320)

3
Henri-Honoré Plé, a bronze group of a dancing couple, early 20th century, brown patination, 66cm (26in), *NY 26 Apr*,
$2,310 (£1,500)

4
Emile Picault, a pair of bronze figures of soldiers, *(one illustrated)*, c.1880, *Société de Fabr. des Bronzes* seal, rich brown patination, 38 and 41cm (15 and 16in), *L 20 Mar*,
£528 ($829)

5
Emile Picault, a bronze bust of Napoleon, late 19th century, rich red-brown patination, 85cm (23in), *L 3 Feb*,
£1,155 ($1,686)

6
Gaetano Russo, a bronze figure of a crab fisherman, Naples, c.1880, holding a torch in his right hand, 126cm (49½in), *F 14 Apr*,
L 11,000,000 (£4,505; $6,982)

7
Louis Rochet, a bronze figure of the young Napoleon, c.1860, a globe by his side, dark brown patination, 46cm (18in), *S 16 Sept*,
£638 ($893)

8
Edmé Augustin Jean Moreau Vauthier, a bronze figure of a woman seated on a large shell, 72cm (28in), *L 17 June*,
£2,750 ($4,345)

9
Emmanuele Villanis, a bronze figure of a dancer, c.1890, holding a tambourine, golden patination, 73cm (28½in), *L 12 June*,
£1,650 ($2,640)

10
Jean Jules Salmson, a parcel-gilt bronze group of a young man and woman, c.1880, the winged youth with bow and arrows, light brown patination, 81cm (32in), *L 20 Mar*,
£2,640 ($4,145)

11
Emmanuele Villanis, a bronze bust entitled *Dalila*, c.1900, the young woman wearing a head-dress with Arabic coins, green, brown and light brown patination, stamped *Société des Bronzes de Paris*, 42.5cm (16¾in), *L 6 Nov*,
£1,485 ($2,109)

12
Hans Schuler, a bronze figure of a young woman lying naked on a rock, late 19th century, light brown patination, founder's mark *Siot*, 36cm (14in), *L 6 Nov*,
£1,980 ($2,812)

Christophe Fratin, c.1800-64, fl.France.

Jacques Louis Gautier, exhibited 1855-68, fl.Paris.

Jean François Théodore Gechter, 1796-1844, fl.Paris.

Louis Auguste Hiolin, 1846-1910, fl.France.

Henri Alfred Marie Jacquemart, 1824-96, fl.Paris.

Prosper LeCourtier, 1855-1924, fl.Paris.

Agathon Léonard, exhibited c.1879-1900, fl.France.

Eugène Marioton, exhibited 1882-1922, fl.France.

Pierre Jules Mène, 1810-71, fl.Paris.

Marius-Jean-Antonin Mercié, 1845-1916, fl.Paris.

Constantin Meunier, 1831-1905, fl.Belgium.

ntoine Louis Barye, bronze figure of a tiger, ark green patination, 3cm (17in), *M 24 Feb,* **'F 11,100 (£1,074; 1,610)**

fter Rosa Bonheur, bronze figure of a ecumbent ewe, rich rown patination, 23cm 9in) wide, *C 17 Apr,* **396 ($614)**

ntoine Louis Barye, bronze group of a stag unt, dark brown and reen patination, 47cm 18½in) high, *L 17 June,* **4,180 ($6,604)**

ntoine Louis Barye, a ronze model of the Percheron stallion, late 9th century, green/ rown patination, 20cm 8in), *S 17 June,* **£1,925 ($3,041)**

5
sidore Bonheur, a bronze model of a jockey on horseback, c.1860s, brown patination, 36cm (14in), *S 17 June,* **£2,420 ($3,823)**

6
Antoine Louis Barye, a bronze figure of a ten point stag, c.1850, rich brown patination, 19cm (7½in), *L 20 Mar,* **£528 ($829)**

7
Joseph Cuvelier, a bronze figure of a horse, c.1880, standing in full tack, rich brown patination, 38cm (15in), *L 20 Mar,* **£880 ($1,382)**

8
Christophe Fratin, a bronze group of a mare and foal, mid 19th century, rich brown patination, 37cm (14½in), *L 20 Mar,* **£2,970 ($4,663)**

9
Joseph Victor Chemin, a bronze figure of a greyhound, c.1860, dark brown patination, 14.5cm (5¾in), *S 11 Nov,* **£572 ($801)**

10
Henri-Alfred-Marie Jacquemart, a bronze model of a heron, c.1870s, the bird with a snake in its beak, mid brown patination, 31cm (12in), *S 17 June,* **£506 ($799)**

11
Alfred Dubucand, a bronze group of a pheasant and a lizard, c.1870, the bird looking down at the lizard, slightly rubbed light and dark brown patination, 71cm (28in), *L 20 Mar,* **£1,650 ($2,590)**

12
Maximilien-Louis Fiot, a bronze figure of a stag, c.1910, green patination, 60cm (23½in), *L 12 June,* **£550 ($880)**

Jules Moigniez, 1835-94, fl.France.

Pierre Marius Montagne, 1828-79, fl.Toulon and Paris.

Auguste Moreau, exhibited 1861-1910, fl.France.

Hippolyte François Moreau, exhibited 1888-1917, fl.Paris.

Mathurin Moreau, 1822-1912, fl.Paris. Assistant to Carrier-Belleuse.

Gustave Obiols, fl.19th century, Paris.

Raphael Peyre, exhibited from c.1894, fl.Paris. Pupil of Mercié.

Emile Louis Picault, exhibited 1863-1909, fl.Paris.

Emile Pinedo, first exhibited 1870, fl.Paris.

Henri-Honoré Plé, 1853-1922, fl.Paris. Pupil of Mathurin Moreau.

Jean-Jacques Pradier, 1792-1852, fl.Paris.

1

2

3

4

5

6

7

8

9

10

11

12

1

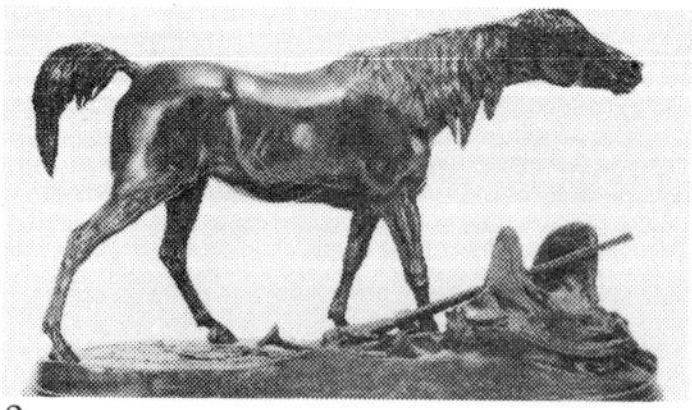
2

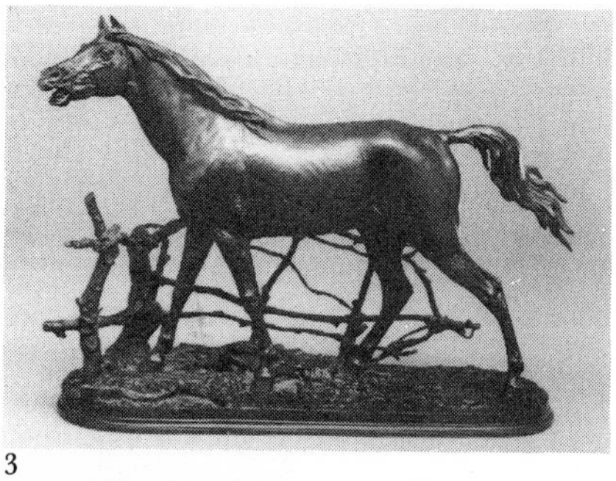
3

4

5

6

7

8

9

10

11

12

13

1
Professor Poertzel, a bronze group of two pheasants, c.1920, green patination, 36cm (14in), *L 6 Oct,*
£484 ($678)

2
Pierre Jules Mène, a bronze figure of an Arab horse with its harness, green/brown patination, 47cm (18½in) wide, *M 24 Feb,*
FF 10,545 (£1,020; $1,530)

3
Pierre Jules Mène, a bronze figure of a stallion entitled *Djinn*, third quarter 19th century, dark brown patination, 38.5cm (15in) wide, *NY 13 Sept,*
$1,980 (£1,347)

4
Jules Moigniez, a bronze figure of a stallion entitled *Chef Baron*, c.1920, light and dark brown patination, 35cm (14in), *L 6 Nov,*
£1,155 ($1,640)

5
Pierre Jules Mène, a bronze group of two whippets, c.1860, at play with a ball, brown patination, 15cm (6in), *L 20 Mar,*
£770 ($1,209)

6
Pierre Jules Mène, a bronze figure of a retriever, c.1840s, 16cm (6¼in), dark brown rubbed patination, *S 18 Feb,*
£660 ($1,003)

7
Prosper LeCourtier, a bronze group of a hound and three pups, late 19th century, black/green patination, 41cm (16¼in), *NY 26 Apr,*
$1,980 (£1,286)

8
After Bologna, a bronze figure of Mercury, third quarter 19th century, mid brown patination, 101.5cm (40in), *C 9 July,*
£396 ($638)

9
After the Antique, a bronze group entitled *The Farnese Bull*, Italian, 18th century, after the original in the Museo Nazionale, Naples, black lacquered, *A 6 May,*
Dfl 6,670 (£2,021; $3,214

10
After the Antique, a bronze figure of Narcissus, c.1870, dark green patination, 63.5cm (25in), *C 17 Apr,*
£440 ($682)

11
After the Antique, a bronze figure of an athlete, late 19th century, dark green/brown patination, 67.5cm (26½in), *C 19 Nov,*
£462 ($647)

12
After the Antique, a bronze figure entitled *Il Spinero* depicting a young man extracting a thorn from his foot, green patination, *Fonderia Sommer Napoli*, 47cm (18in), *L 6 Nov,*
£990 ($1,406)

13
After the Antique, a bronze figure of 'The Borghese Gladiator', French, 19th century, dark brown patination, 68cm (27in), *S 22 Apr,*
£1,012 ($1,589)

Louis Rochet, 1813-78, fl.Paris.

Gaetano Russo, exhibited from 1880, fl.Rome.

Jean Jules Salmson, 1832-1902, fl.Paris.

Hans Schuler, b.1874, fl.France and America.

Edmé Augustin Jean Moreau-Vauthier, 1831-93, fl.Paris.

Emmanuele Villanis, exhibited 1889, fl.Italy.

Decorative Arts from 1880

Article:
Wiener Werkstätte furniture *pp* 316-320

Featured:
Dutch decorative arts *pp* 287-289

See also:
Colour illustrations *pp* 348-351
Ceramics *pp* 189-255
Furniture *pp* 11-121
Glass *pp* 265-266
Jewellery *pp* 321-336
19th and 20th century sculpture *pp* 269-278
Silver *pp* 386-443

Main sub-sections:
Ceramics *pp* 290-294
Furniture *pp* 306-315
Glass *pp* 279-286
Jewellery *p* 298
Sculpture *pp* 296-297
Silver and metalwork *pp* 299-304
Studio pottery *p* 295

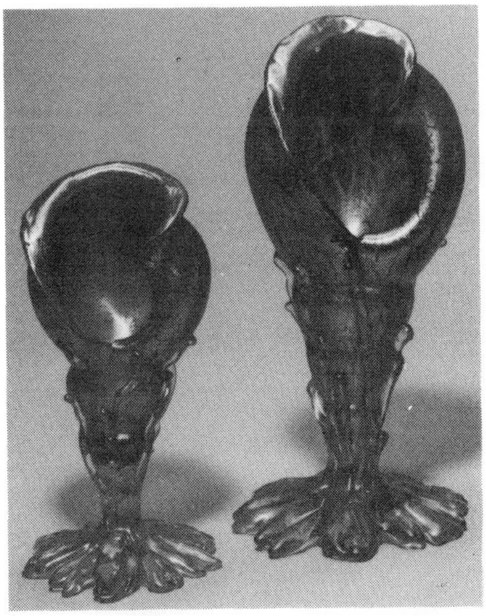
1

2

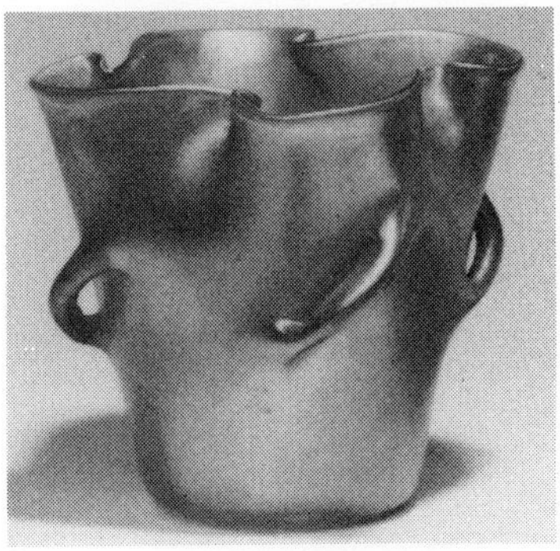
3

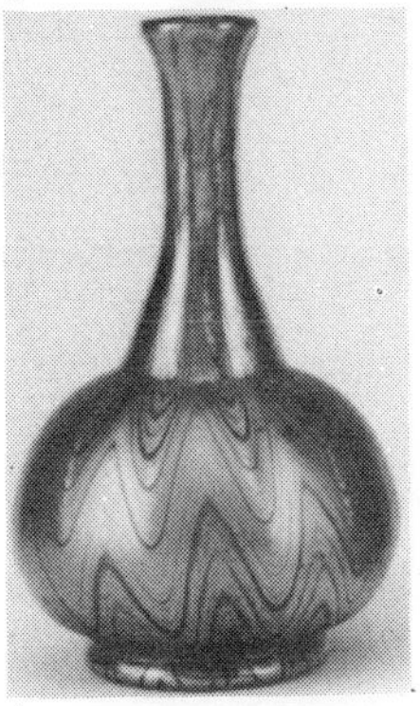
4

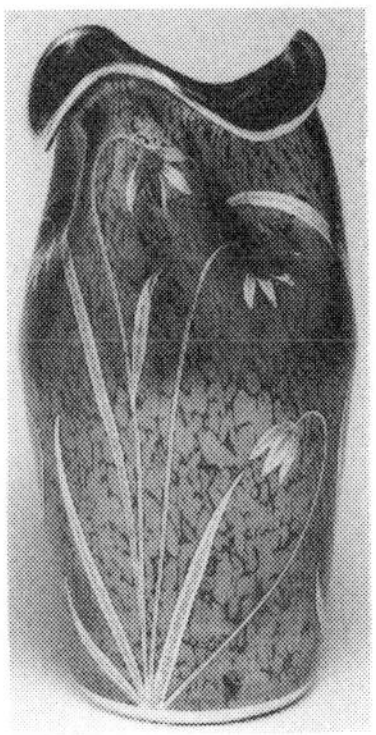
5

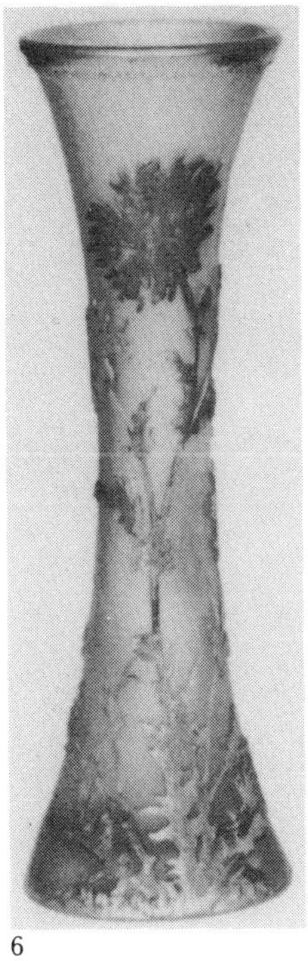
6

7

8

1
Two Loetz iridescent glass shell-form vases *(illustrated)*, c.1900, the vases decorated with silvery-blue iridescent spotting, cameo mark, sold with a Loetz cameo glass vase, largest 24cm (9½in), *NY 19 June*,
$990 (£664)

2
A Loetz iridescent glass bowl, c.1900, in amber glass with silvery-blue iridescence, unsigned, 26.5cm (10¼in) diam., *NY 11 Oct*,
$1,430 (£1,000)

3
A Loetz iridescent glass four-handled vase, c.1900, in amber and pink iridescence, unsigned, 13.5cm (5¼in), *NY 11 Oct*,
$550 (£385)

4
A Loetz opalescent glass vase, c.1900, decorated in opalescent blue-green festoons, 19cm (7½in), *M 13 Apr*,
FF 3,108 (£273; $423)

5
A Loetz overlaid iridescent glass vase, c.1900, the blue glass body decorated with peacock blue and gold lustre, overlaid with snowdrops, 24.5cm (9¾in), *L 19 Dec*,
£825 ($1,155)

6
A Daum opalescent glass vase, c.1900, decorated in relief with flowers picked out in gilding, marked *Daum Nancy*, 34cm (13½in), *M 13 Apr*,
FF 7,215 (£633; $982)

7
A Daum cameo-glass vase, c.1900, in mottled yellow glass lined in reddish brown, decorated in cameo with exotic flowers, marked *Daum Nancy*, 39.5cm (15½in), *M 13 Apr*,
FF 9,990 (£877; $1,359)

8
A Daum etched and enamelled glass vase, c.1900, in mottled grey/white glass, with streaks of purple rising from a purple foot, etched with wild pansies, marked *Daum Nancy*, 40.5cm (16in), *L 16 May*,
£2,090 ($3,323)

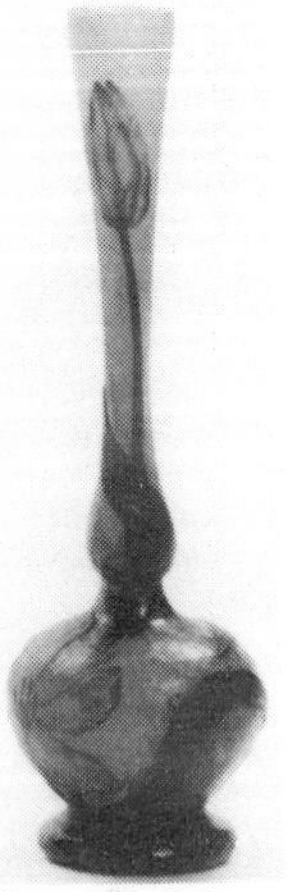
1

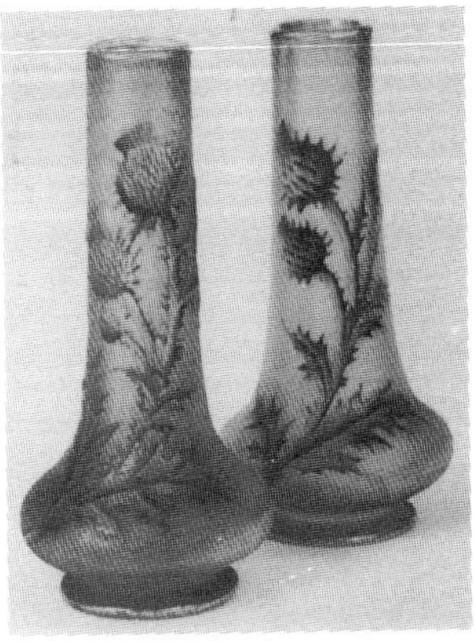
2

3

4

5

6 7 8

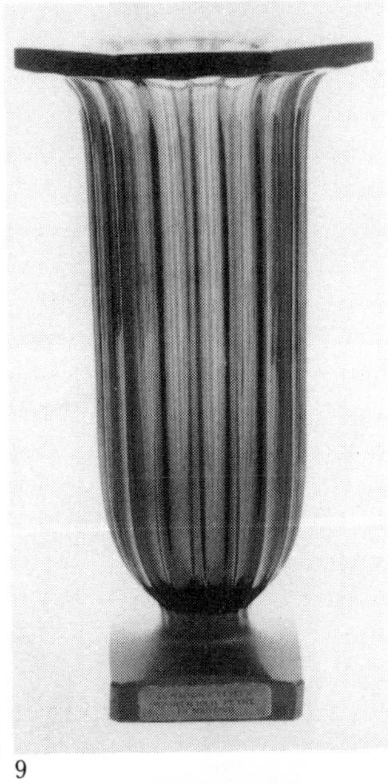
9

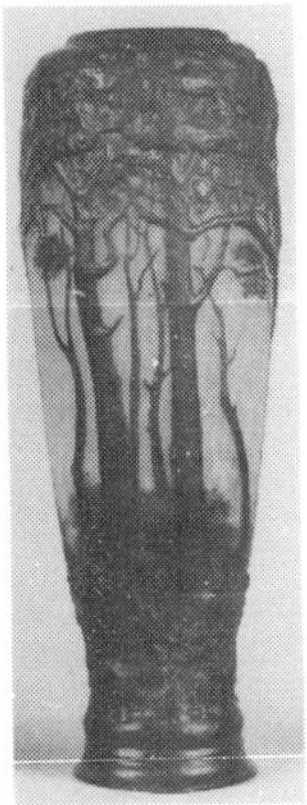
10

11

12

13

14

1
A Daum cameo glass vase, c.1900, the pink glass overlaid in opalescent blue and green, with carved cameo floral decoration, engraved mark *Daum Nancy*, 19.5cm (7¾in), *L 19 Dec,*
£3,410 ($4,774)

2
A pair of Daum glass vases, c.1900, in opalescent pale green and amber glass speckled with red, and enamelled with thistles, *Daum Nancy* mark, 11.5cm (4½in), *M 13 Apr,*
FF 6,660 (£585; $906)

3
A Daum cameo glass lamp, c.1900, in yellow glass tinted with red and etched with flowers, cameo mark, 47cm (18½in), *A 6 May,*
Dfl14,375 (£4,356; $6,926)

4
A Daum enamelled glass vase, c.1900, in grey glass speckled with blue, engraved with a landscape scene, *Daum Nancy* mark, 16cm (6¼in), *M 19 Oct,*
FF 4,440 (£477; $668)

5
A Daum cameo glass vase, c.1900, in mottled amber glass, overlaid in bright yellow and etched with sprays of mimosa, *Daum Nancy* mark, 12cm (4¾in), *L 16 May,*
£550 ($874)

6
A Daum cameo glass vase, c.1915, the yellow sides overlaid in red and cut with trumpet flower blossoms and foliage, signed *Daum Nancy France* 23.5cm (9¼in), *NY 19 June,*
$1,100 (£738)

7
A Daum cameo glass vase, c.1900, in mottled yellow glass overlaid with brown and cut with a sylvan landscape, signed *Daum Nancy*, 41cm (16in), *NY 19 June,*
$880 (£590)

8
A Daum cameo glass vase, c.1910, in mottled yellow, gold and pink glass, overlaid in brown and cut with maple branches, signed *Daum Nancy*, 30cm (11¾in), *NY 19 June,*
$660 (£443)

9
A Daum smoked glass vase, 1920s, with everted rim, engraved *Daum Nancy France*, 40cm (15¾in), *L 16 May,*
£1,980 ($3,148)

10
A Daum cameo-glass vase, c.1900, in pale blue and yellow glass lined in steel blue, decorated in cameo with trees in relief, marked *Daum Nancy*, 40cm (15¾in), *M 19 Oct,*
FF 19,980 (£2,148; $3,008)

11
A Daum glass bowl, c.1925, in pale mint-green glass, etched with radiating geometric devices, signed *Daum Nancy France*, 30.5cm (12in), *NY 19 June,*
$495 (£332)

12
A Daum cameo glass vase, c.1900, the colourless glass overlaid in orange, red and green, the ground with hammered surface, marked *Daum Nancy*, 19.5cm (7¾in), *L 19 Dec,*
£1,540 ($2,156)

13
A Daum glass vase, c.1925, of bell form, in pale blue glass engraved with frosted bands, marked *Daum Nancy*, 29.5cm (11½in), *M 19 Oct,*
FF 7,215 (£776; $1,086)

14
A Daum glass vase, c.1930, acid-etched, with internal decoration, the yellow glass walls enclosing gold-coloured foil, cut with scattered square and fan motifs, signed *Daum Nancy France*, 21cm (8¼in), *NY 6 Dec,*
$1,430 (£1,000)

1
A Daum smoked glass vase, c.1925, marked *Daum Nancy France,* 64cm (25¼in), *M 13 Apr,*
FF 9,435 (£828; $1,284)

2
A Muller Frères enamelled cameo glass vase, c.1910, in grey glass mottled with magenta and blue, the sides enamelled with a forest scene, signed *Muller Fres/Luneville,* 30.5cm (12in), *NY 19 June,*
$1,650 (£1,107)

3
A Daum glass and wrought-iron chandelier, c.1925, signed *Daum Nancy France,* 132cm (52in) high, *NY 20 June,*
$2,750 (£1,846)

4
A Handel glass and patinated-metal lamp, early 20th century, the shade with 'chipped' exterior, painted in blue, apricot and green on a black ground, inscribed *Handel 7040,* 59.5cm (23½in), *NY 19 June,*
$6,600 (£4,430)

5
A Veles cameo glass vase, c.1900, overlaid in purple on a pink ground, cameo signature, 40.5cm (16in), *S 10 Dec,*
£462 ($647)

6
A Legras enamelled glass vase, c.1900, enamelled on the pinkish white ground with a landscape scene, 36cm (14in), *M 13 Apr,*
FF 4,995 (£438; $658)

7
An Arsall cameo glass vase, c.1905, in grey glass overlaid with green and brown and etched with rose hips and leaves, 30cm (11¾in), *L 19 Dec,*
£462 ($646)

8
A Muller Frères glass vase, c.1930, the colourless glass lined in blue and sprinkled in gold, marked *Muller ...,* 27.5cm (11in), *M 13 Apr,*
FF 6,105 (£536; $831)

9
A Muller Frères cameo glass vase, c.1930, the smoked glass lined in red and decorated with flowers in cameo, marked *Muller,* 28.5cm (11½in), *M 13 Apr,*
FF 4,440 (£390; $604)

10
A Muller Frères cameo glass vase, c.1930, the pink glass lined in amber and sprinkled with gold, marked *Muller Fres Lunéville,* 23.5cm (9¼in), *M 13 Apr,*
FF 4,440 (£390; $604)

11
A wrought-iron lamp with Argy-Rousseau pâte de cristal shade, 1920s, the shade in grey glass with petal and flower motifs in red and amethyst, the shade marked *G. Argy-Rousseau,* the base marked *Van Loo,* 30cm (11¾in), *L 19 Dec,*
£2,420 ($3,388)

12
A Davesn glass vase, c.1925, the colourless glass moulded with elephants and palm leaves, heightened in blue, factory mark, 22cm (8¾in), *M 13 Apr,*
FF 4,440 (£390; $604)

13
A Schneider Le Verre Français cameo glass vase, c.1925, the grey glass mottled with lavender, overlaid in brown and orange and cut with cherries, signed *Le Verre Français,* 26cm (10¼in), *NY 19 June,*
$385 (£258)

14
A Fugère cold-painted lamp with cameo glass shade, c.1910-20, the base cast with a semi-nude woman seated by a tree with a faun, the shade in yellow glass overlaid in red, the base marked *Austria ...,* signed *H. Fugère,* 46.5cm (18¼in), *L 16 May,*
£2,200 ($3,498)

1

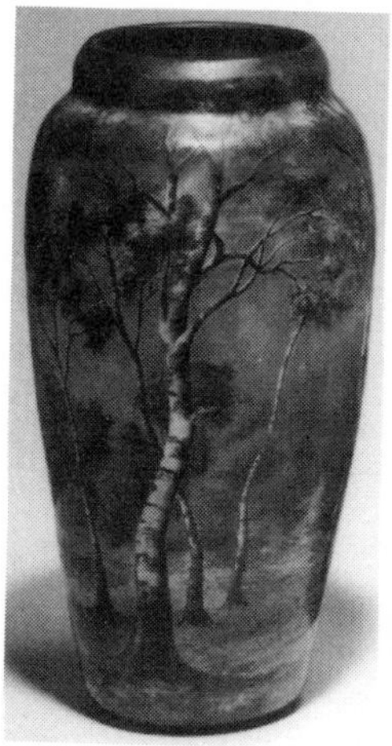
2

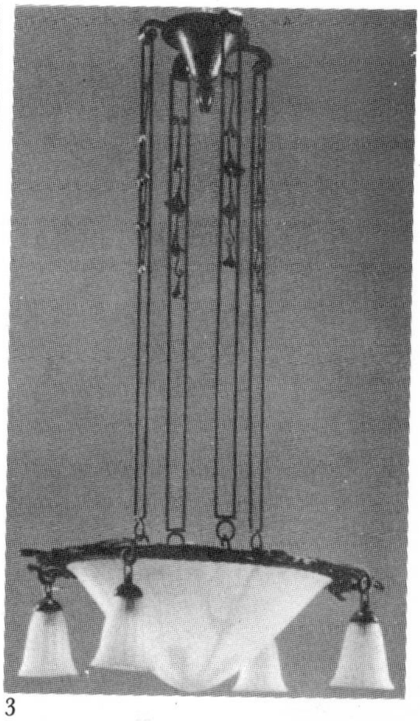
3

4

5

6

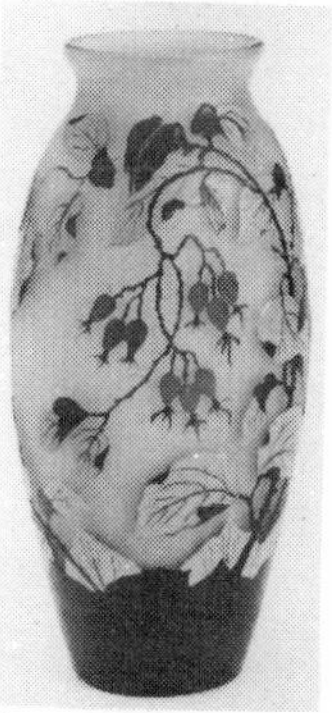
7

8 9 10

11

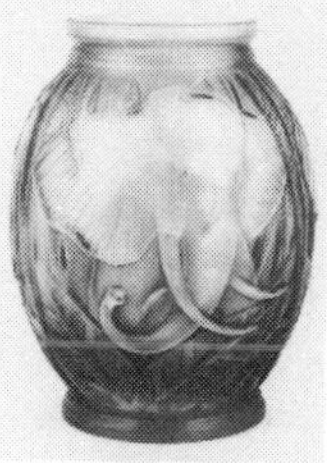
12

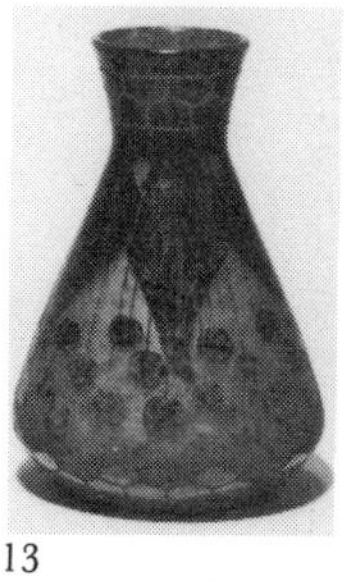
13

14

1

2

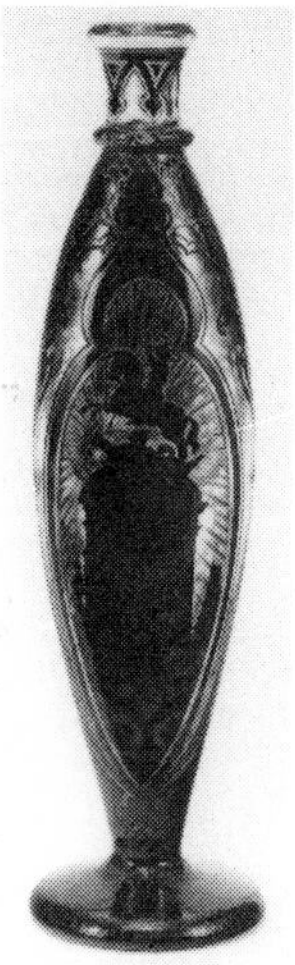
3

4

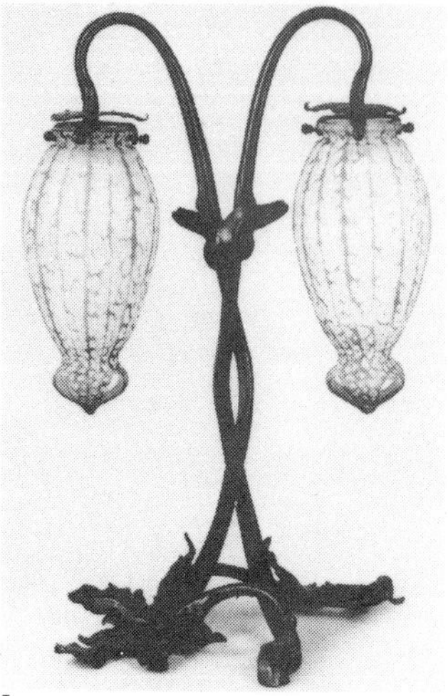
5

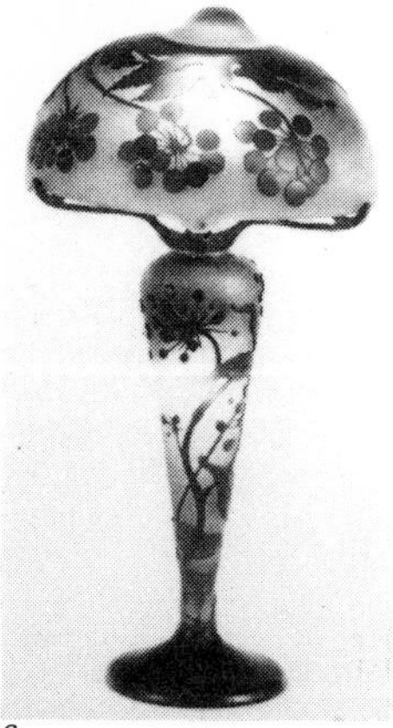
6

7

8

9

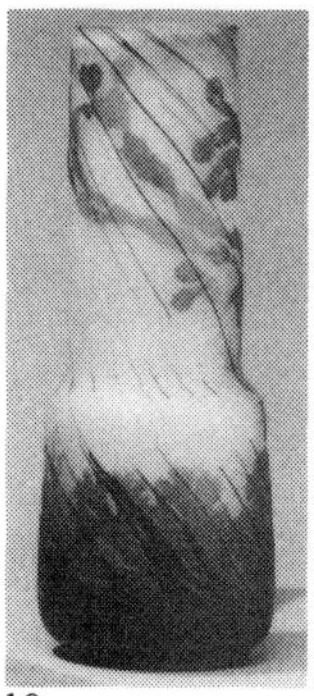
10

11

1
A Gallé enamelled glass drinking set, 1890s, comprising fifteen pieces, the colourless glass with enamelled sprays of flowers, heightened with gilding, one carafe marked *E. Gallé*, the tray *E. Gallé à Nancy*, carafe 19cm (7½in), *L 19 Dec,*
£1,870 ($2,618)

2
A Gallé enamelled glass drinking set, c.1900, comprising three pieces, in smoked glass enamelled with thistles, marked *E. Gallé Nancy*, 20cm (8in), *M 19 Oct,*
FF 6,660 (£716; $1,003)

3
A Gallé cameo glass 'Joan of Arc' vase, c.1900, the colourless glass lined in dark pink, decorated in cameo with Joan of Arc in silhouette in front of a stylised sun, also decorated with thistles, fleurs-de-lis and the cross of Lorraine, heightened in gilding, marked *Gallé*, 31cm (12in), *M 13 Apr,*
FF 68,820 (£6,042; $9,365)

4
A Gallé cameo glass lamp and base, c.1900, the pale yellow ground overlaid in purplish-brown, cameo signature, 43cm (17in), *S 10 Dec,*
£3,740 ($5,236)

5
A Gallé cameo glass and bronze lamp, c.1900, the shades in white-green glass lined in green, cameo mark, 50cm (19¾in), *M 19 Oct,*
FF 33,300 (£3,581; $5,013)

6
A Gallé cameo glass lamp, c.1900, the grey and pink glass lined in green and brown, 37cm (14½in), *M 13 Apr,*
FF 46,620 (£4,093; $6,344)

7
A Gallé cameo glass lamp, c.1900, in yellow/grey glass overlaid with orange and brown and etched with swallows in flight on the shade and a landscape on the base, cameo mark, 53.5cm (21in), *L 19 Dec,*
£11,000 ($15,400)

8
A Gallé cameo-glass lamp, c.1900, in yellow glass lined with red, decorated with branches of prunus, cameo mark, 34.5cm (13½in), *M 19 Oct,*
FF 155,400 (£16,710; $23,394)

9
A Gallé enamelled glass vase, c.1890, of 17th century form, the waist moulded with an enamel band of stylised flowers, the sides enamelled with cartouches enclosing equestrian knights, marked *E & G depose Emile Gallé à Nancy*, 14.5cm (5¾in), *NY 19 June,*
$1,540 (£1,034)

10
A Gallé cameo glass marine vase, c.1900, in grey glass streaked with pink, overlaid in ochre and cut with seaweed, shells and marine plants, cameo mark, 29.5cm (11¾in), *NY 6 Dec,*
$3,300 (£2,307)

11
A Gallé internally decorated cameo glass vase, c.1900, in pink brown glass speckled with yellow, overlaid in brown and etched with flowers, cameo mark, 42cm (16½in), *L 19 Dec,*
£3,520 ($4,928)

1
A Gallé cameo glass vase, after 1904, in salmon pink glass overlaid in lilac, white, purple and green, and etched with clematis, cameo mark, 34cm (13¼in), *L 19 Dec,*
£1,045 ($1,463)

2
A Gallé cameo glass vase, c.1900, in grey and yellow lined with blue and amethyst, decorated in cameo with a landscape, a peacock in the foreground, cameo mark, 34cm (13¼in), *M 19 Oct,*
FF 61,050 (£6,565; $9,190)

3
A Gallé cameo glass vase, c.1900, in grey glass tinted with yellow/green, overlaid with green and etched with ferns, cameo mark, 27cm (10¾in), *L 16 May,*
£605 ($962)

4
A Gallé cameo glass vase, c.1900, in orange glass overlaid with brown and etched with flowering iris, cameo mark, 20.5cm (8in), *L 16 May,*
£682 ($1,084)

5
A Gallé cameo glass vase, c.1900, in grey and yellow glass lined in mauve, cameo mark, 15.5cm (6in), *M 19 Oct,*
FF 5,106 (£549; $769)

6
A Gallé cameo glass vase, c.1900, in yellow glass lined in blue/mauve, cameo mark, 16cm (6¼in), *M 13 Apr,*
FF 6,660 (£585; $906)

7
A Gallé cameo glass vase, c.1900, in grey glass lined in green, cameo mark, 34cm (13¼in), *M 13 Apr,*
FF 6,660 (£585; $906)

8
A Gallé enamelled glass vase, c.1900, decorated with enamelled flowers, enamelled mark EG, 42.5cm (16¾in), *M 13 Apr,*
FF 11,655 (£1,023; $1,586)

9
A Gallé cameo glass vase, c.1900, in yellow opalescent glass lined in red, cameo decoration of flowers, cameo mark, 20.5cm (8in), *M 19 Oct,*
FF 15,540 (£1,671; $2,339)

10
A Gallé cameo glass vase, c.1900, in yellow and orange glass, overlaid in red and brown with plum branches, cameo mark, 33cm (13in), *NY 6 Dec,*
$11,550 (£8,077)

11
A Gallé cameo glass vase, c.1920, in grey glass shaded with beige and raised on a brown foot, overlaid in brown and cut with a river landscape, cameo mark, 36cm (14¼in), *NY 6 Dec,*
$3,850 (£2,692)

12
A Gallé marbled glass vase, in grey glass with dark grey marbling, the foot mottled with yellow, marked *Gallé*, 21cm (8¼in), *M 13 Apr,*
FF 24,420 (£2,144; $3,323)

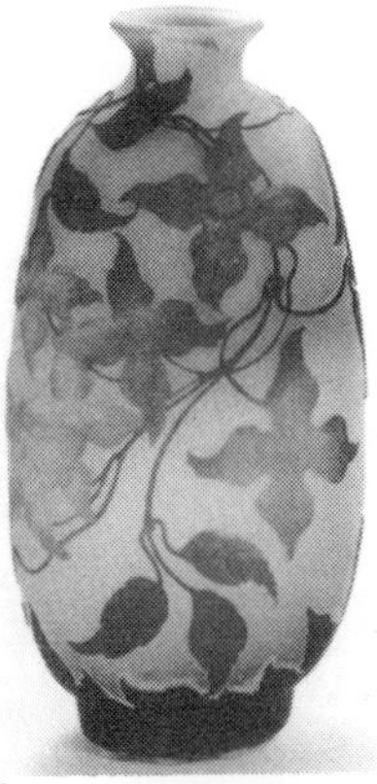
1

2

3

4

5

6

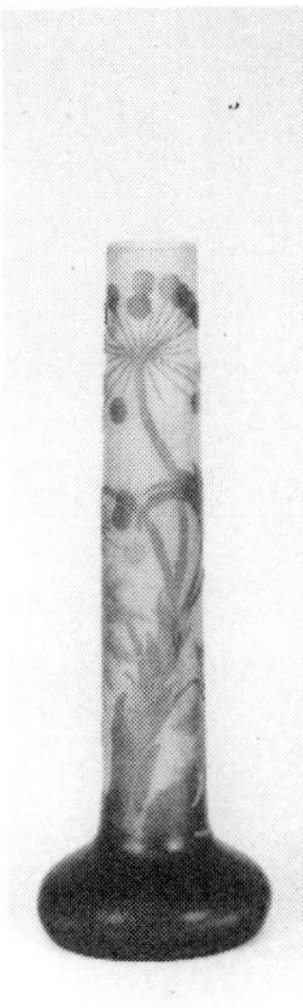
7

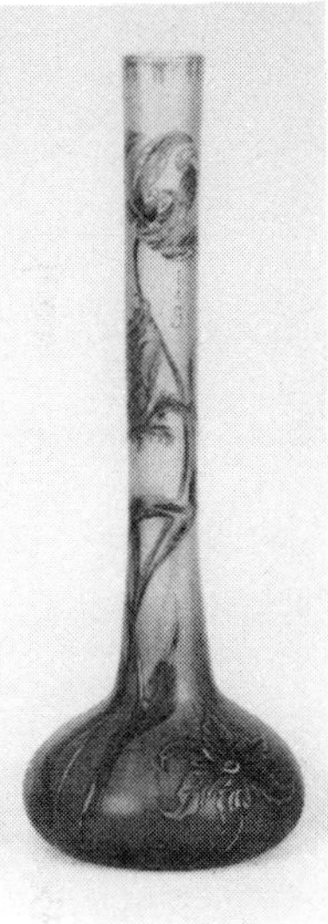
8

9

10

11

12

1

2

3

4

5

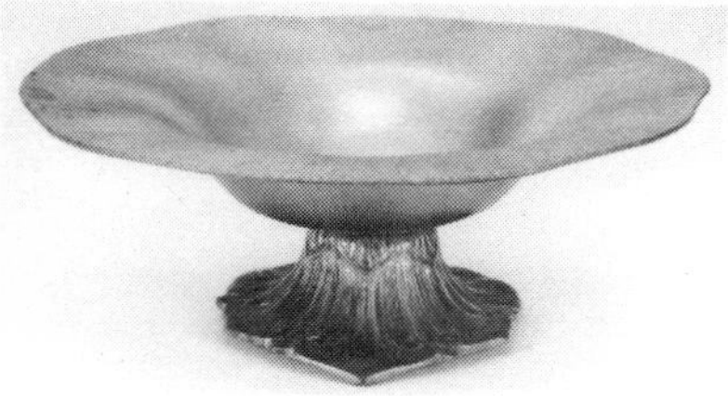
6

7

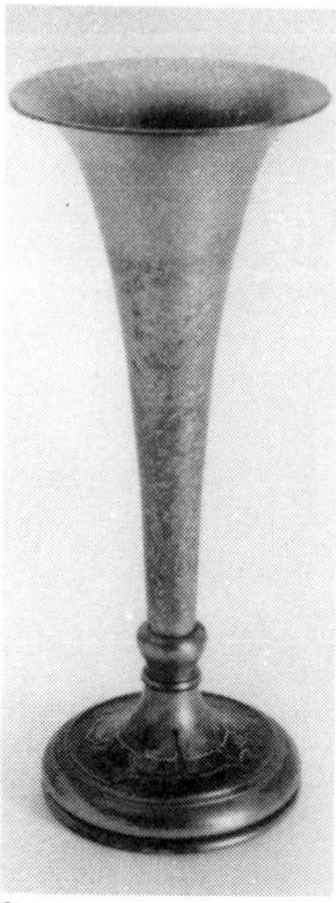
8

9

10

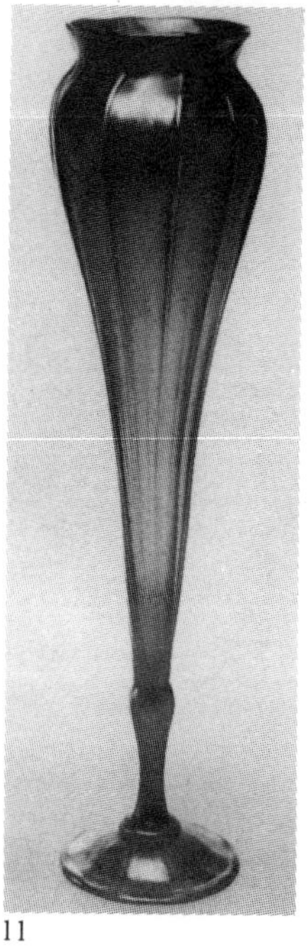
11

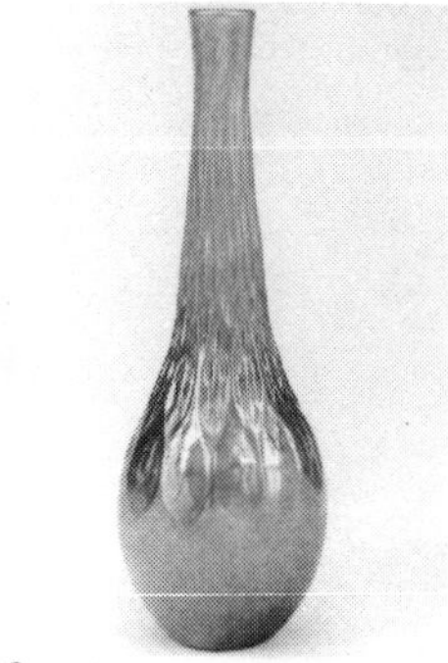
12

13 14

1
A Tiffany Studio bronze student lamp, c.1900, the shade in pink/green/gold iridescent glass, 62cm (24½in), *L 16 May,*
£2,090 ($3,323)

2
A Tiffany Studio leaded glass and bronze table lamp, c.1905, the shade with panels of mottled red glass and blue and green glass rim, marked, 63cm (24¾in), *L 19 Dec,*
£9,350 ($13,090)

3
A Tiffany Favrile glass and gilt-bronze lily lamp, 1899-1920, the ten shades in amber iridescent glass, crack, one petal lacking, marked, 53.5cm (21in), *NY 20 June,*
$9,900 (£6,644)

4
A Tiffany Favrile glass and bronze lily pad lamp, 1899-1920, the shade with emerald and blue lily pads against a blue-green ground striated with red, marked, 48.5cm (23in), *NY 20 June,*
$28,600 (£19,195)

5
A Tiffany Favrile glass and bronze lotus lamp, 1899-1920, the shade composed of opalescent green glass tiles, marked, 56cm (22in), *NY 6 Dec,*
$13,200 (£9,230)

6
A Tiffany opalescent glass and gilt-bronze bowl, c.1900, in gold and pale blue glass, the rim with 'crackled' effect, marked, 31cm (12¼in) diam., *M 13 Apr,*
FF 8,325 (£731; $1,133)

7
A Tiffany Favrile red glass cabinet vase, c.1906, the shoulder with amber iridescent striated lappets, marked, 6.5cm (2¾in), *NY 20 June,*
$3,025 (£2,030)

8
A Tiffany Favrile gilt-bronze and enamelled vase, c.1900, the base decorated with mottled green/gold enamelled and white feathered trails, marked, 33.5cm (13¼in), *L 19 Dec,*
£605 ($847)

9
A Tiffany Favrile iridescent glass vase, c.1920 the amber glass body with blue glass rim, marked, 14.5cm (6in), *C 9 Sept,*
£242 ($363)

10
A Tiffany Favrile millefiore glass vase, 1905, decorated with peacock/gold lustre, with trailing green lustre lily pads with yellow and white millefiore flowers, marked, 10cm (4in), *L 19 Dec,*
£935 ($1,309)

11
A Tiffany opalescent glass vase, 1905, in gold and peacock blue glass, marked, 48cm (19in), *M 13 Apr,*
FF 12,210 (£1,072; $1,661)

12
A Tiffany opalescent glass vase, 1900, in gold and peacock blue glass, the surface with honeycombing in light relief, marked, 35cm (13¾in), *M 13 Apr,*
FF 7,770 (£682; $1,057)

13
A Tiffany Favrile glass bud vase, c.1916, the emerald-green glass vessel decorated on the base with amber iridescent feathering, marked, 26cm (10¼in), *NY 19 June,*
$495 (£332)

14
A Tiffany Favrile glass vase, c.1917, the amber iridescent glass walls decorated with olive green leaves and tendrils, marked, 22.5cm (9in), *NY 19 June,*
$1,100 (£738)

1
A Lalique opalescent glass 'shell' plate, c.1925, 26.5cm (10½in), *Mil 12 Mar,*
L 1,320,000 (£555; $854)

2
A Lalique coloured glass perfume spray, c.1925, decorated with a frieze of female figures, 12.5cm (5in), *Mil 12 Mar,*
L 1,760,000 (£739; $1,139)

3
A Lalique smoked glass vase, 'Piriac', 1920s, with a row of fish in high relief, 18cm (7in), *L 16 May,*
£1,430 ($2,274)

4
A Lalique glass lamp, 1920s, moulded with dancing classical figures holding garlands of flowers, 25cm (10in), *L 19 Dec,*
£4,070 ($5,698)

5
A Lalique opalescent glass vase, c.1925, moulded with pairs of lovebirds, 24.5cm (9¾in), *L 16 May,*
£1,320 ($2,099)

6
A Lalique green glass vase, c.1925, moulded with bands of overlapping upright leaves, 23cm (9in), *Syd 12 Nov,*
Aus$3,850 (£1,750; $2,450)

7
A Lalique opalescent glass centrepiece, c.1925, 'Martigues', moulded on the underside with a band of swimming fish, 37cm (14½in), *NY 19 June,*
$1,540 (£1,036)

8
A Lalique grey glass vase, c.1925, moulded with stylised fish, 26cm (10½in), *M 19 Oct,*
FF 21,090 (£2,268; $3,175)

9
A pair of Lalique glass decanters, *(one illustrated),* 1930s, the flat stoppers moulded with two dancing satyrs, 26cm (10½in); sold with two Lalique frosted glass birds, *L 16 May,*
£550 ($874)

10
A Lalique glass vase, c.1925, moulded with a design of feathers, 21cm (8¼in), *L 16 May,*
£352 ($560)

11
A Lalique glass vase, 1930s, moulded to simulate a sea urchin, heightened with blue staining, 18cm (7in), *L 16 May,*
£484 ($769)

12
A Lalique glass vase, c.1925, moulded with teazles in high relief, traces of brown staining, 21cm (8in), *L 16 May,*
£528 ($839)

13
A Lalique glass service, *(part illustrated),* 1930s, comprising 34 pieces, each with stepped frosted triangular design at the base, various sizes, *L 19 Dec,*
£1,100 ($1,540)

14
A Lalique glass drinking set, *(part illustrated),* 1930s, comprising a jug and six glasses, each moulded with stylised daisies, heightened with blue, jug 19cm (7½in), *L 19 Dec,*
£550 ($770)

1

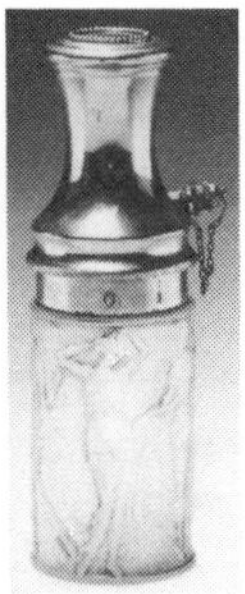
2

3

4

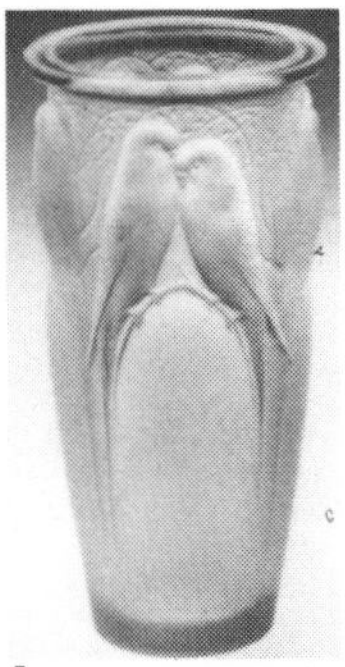
5

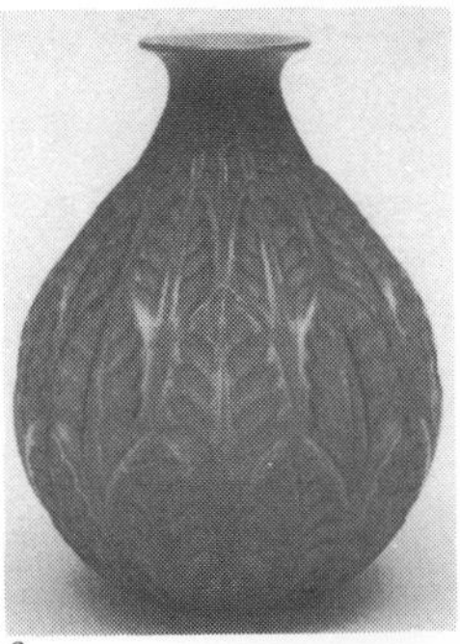
6

8

9

7

10 11 12

13 14

1

2

3

4

5

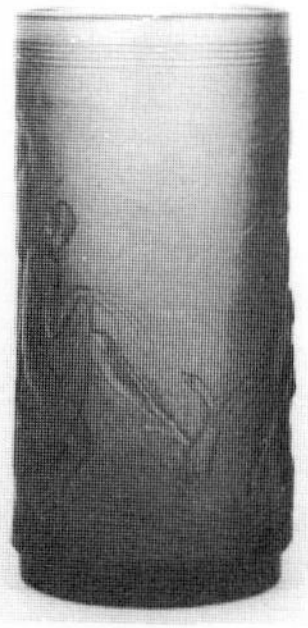
6

7

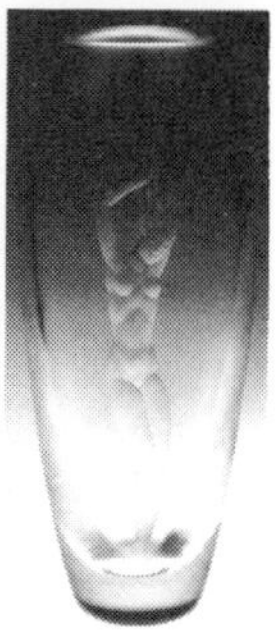
8

9

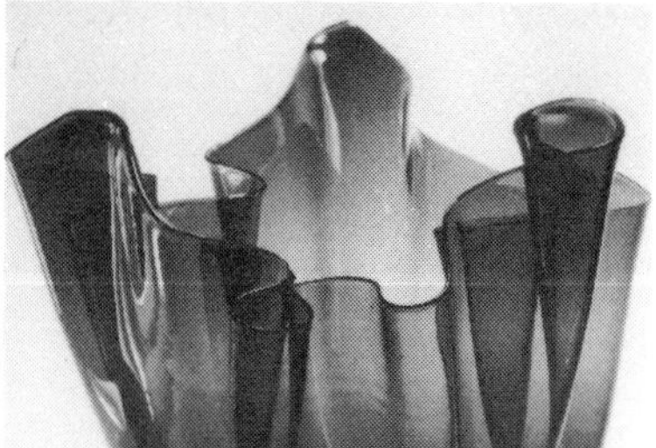
10

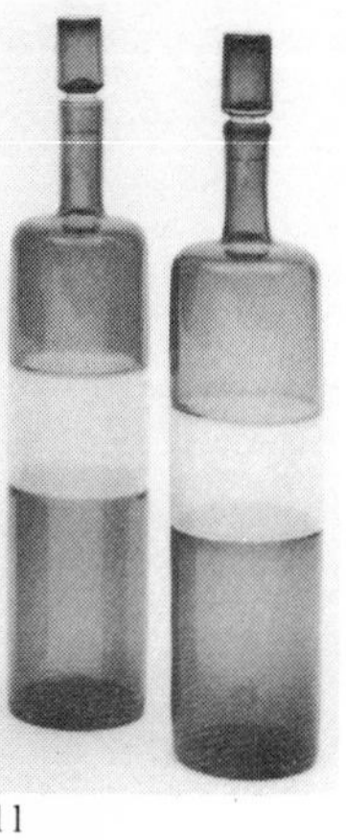
11

12

13

14

1
A uranium glass-footed centrepiece, probably designed by Josef Hoffmann, c.1920, on three scrolling feet, 31cm (12¼in), *NY 11 Oct,*
$467 (£327)

2
Three black glass perfume bottles, designed by Sue et Mare for D'Orsay, c.1925, largest 21.5cm ((8½in), *L 16 May,*
£550 ($874)

3
An enamelled white glass vase, 1920s, possibly by the Wiener Werkstätte, decorated with black and red flowers, and coloured banding, 23.5cm (9¼in), *L 19 Dec,*
£198 ($277)

4
A Knut Berqvist Orrefors Graal glass vase, 1923, in deep amethyst glass, internally decorated in 'Graal' technique, 24cm (9½in), *L 16 May,*
£1,870 ($2,973)

5
A Fains glass vase, c.1930, the colourless glass with horizontal silvered bands, 23cm (9in), *M 13 Apr,*
FF 5,550 (£487; $755)

6
A Sabino glass vase, c.1925, in smoked glass, decorated with a frieze of naked women and swans, 23.5cm (9¼in), *M 19 Oct,*
FF 4,440 (£477; $668)

7
A Lobmeyr set of iridescent glasses, *(part illustrated)*, designed by Oswald Hertl, c.1935, comprising 112 pieces, all in amber iridescence with a coat of arms, largest 22cm (8½in), *NY 11 Oct,*
$7,700 (£5,385)

8
An Orrefors glass vase, designed by Vicke Lindstrand, 1930s, engraved with a nude figure of a woman with long flowing hair, 34.5cm (13½in), *L 16 May,*
£330 ($525)

9
An Orrefors engraved glass bowl and stand, c.1930, of yellow glass, 9.5cm (3¾in) high, *NY 19 June,*
$605 (£406)

10
A Venini red glass handkerchief vase, c.1955, acid stamped *Venini/Murano/Italia*, 28.5cm (11¼in), *NY 19 June,*
$770 (£517)

11
A pair of Venini glass bottles and stoppers, 1950s, one amethyst, the other smoked, each with central band applied with fine yellow lines, each marked *Venini Murano,* 37cm (14½in), *L 19 Dec,*
£462 ($647)

12
A Steuben engraved glass vase and cover, 'Adam and Eve', c.1950, designed by Sidney Waugh, 1938, signed, 43cm (17in), *NY 19 June,*
$3,300 (£2,215)

13
A Kosta engraved glass vase, designed by Vicke Lindstrand, 1950s, with stylised cat and lattice festoons, 34cm (13½in), *L 19 Dec,*
£330 ($462)

14
A Salviati glass vase, by Livio Seguso after a design by Luciano Gaspari, c.1955, in rose/amethyst glass lined in mauve, marked *Salviati Venezia*, 26cm (10½in), *M 13 Apr,*
FF 6,105 (£536; $831)

1
A Zuid-Holland pair of vases, *(one illustrated),* c.1900, with polychrome decoration of iris, 22cm (8½in), *A 10 Mar,*
Dfl 517 (£157; $238)

2
A Brouwer jug, 1902, decorated in brown on a yellow ground, 12cm (4¾in), *A 10 Mar,*
Dfl 632 (£191; $291)

3
A Brouwer jug, dated July 1907, decorated in blue in the form of an owl, 12.5cm (5in), *A 10 Mar,*
Dfl 1,495 (£453; $689)

4
A pair of Holland vases with covers, *(one illustrated),* c.1900, with polychrome floral decoration, 14cm (5½in), *A 10 Mar,*
Dfl 1,840 (£557; $847)

5
A Haga vase, c.1904-07, with polychrome linear decoration, 16.5cm (6¾in), *A 10 Mar,*
Dfl 460 (£139; $212)

6
A Colenbrander vase with cover, Rozenburg, 1885, with polychrome floral decoration, signed *Colenbrander, Wolff von Gudenberg, Carbasius,* 40cm (15¾in). J. A. Carbasius was the financier of the Rozenburg factory, of which this vase may have come from the first oven load. It is the only known specimen to bear the signature of the designer, the director and the financier. *A 10 Mar,*
Dfl 15,525 (£4,704; $7,151)

7
A Nienhuis bowl, De Distel, c.1905, with grey, blue and ochre decoration on a matt white ground, *A 10 Mar,*
Dfl 5,060 (£1,533; $2,330)

8
A Colenbrander vase, Ram, 1920-23, with polychrome 'all-over' decorations, 26cm (10¼in), *A 10 Mar,*
Dfl 4,140 (£1,254; $1,907)

9
A Colenbrander dish, Rozenburg, 1890, with polychrome floral decoration, 15.5cm (6in) diam., *A 10 Mar,*
Dfl 1,150 (£348; $529)

10
A Colenbrander bowl, Ram, c.1925, with polychrome decoration, the outside glazed in two shades of yellow, titled *Landelijk* (rural), 12cm (4¾in) diam., *A 10 Mar,*
Dfl 977 (£296; $450)

11
A pair of Colenbrander jars and covers, *(one illustrated),* Rozenburg, c.1890, decorated in yellow, grey, brown, blue, green and black, on a white crackled ground, 46cm (18in), *M 19 Oct,*
FF 6,660 (£716; $1,003)

12
A Colenbrander vase, Ram, 1925, decorated in dark yellow and black, titled *Tweekleur* (two-coloured), 22cm (8½in), *A 10 Mar,*
Dfl 1,495 (£453; $688)

13
A Van der Hoef vase with cover, Amphora, c.1908, decorated in blue, green and yellow with stylised hearts, on a cream glazed ground, 38cm (15in), *A 10 Mar,*
Dfl 4,600 (£1,394; $2,119)

14
A Van der Hoef dish, Amstelhoek, dated 19 July 1905, with yellow inlaid decoration on a brown ground, 38.5cm (15¼in) diam., *A 10 Mar,*
Dfl 632 (£191; $291)

DESIGNERS

Berlage, H. P., 1856-1934.

Blinxma, J., 1872-1941.

Brouwer, Willem Coenraad, 1877-1933.

Colenbrander, Theodorus A. C., 1841-1930; artistic director of Rozenburg 1884-89; designed for Zuid Holland 1912-13; designs produced at Ram 1920-28.

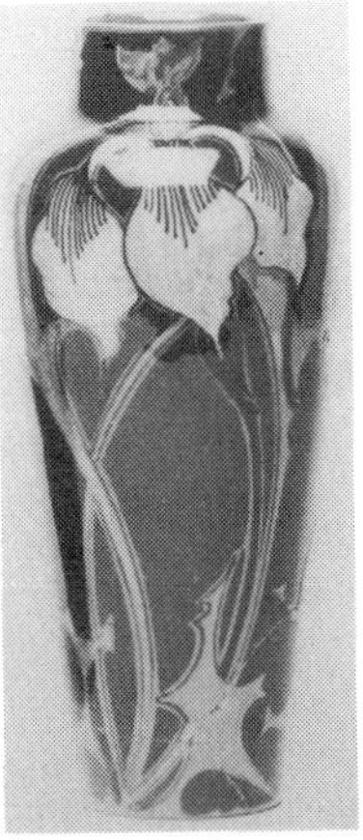
1

2

3

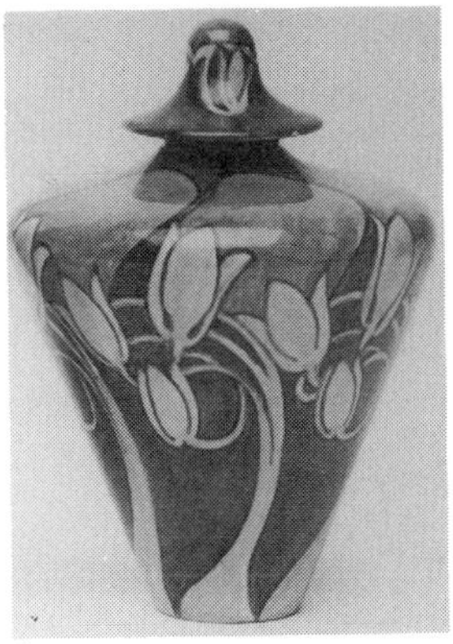
4

5

6

7

8

9

10

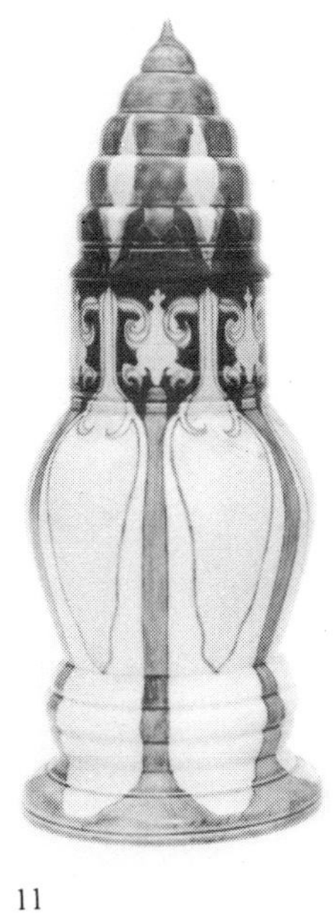
11

12

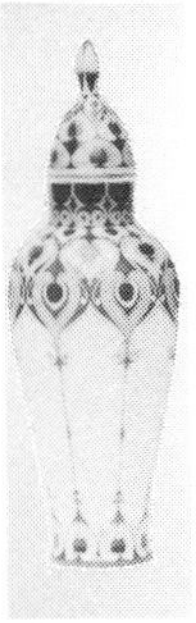
13

14

1

2

3

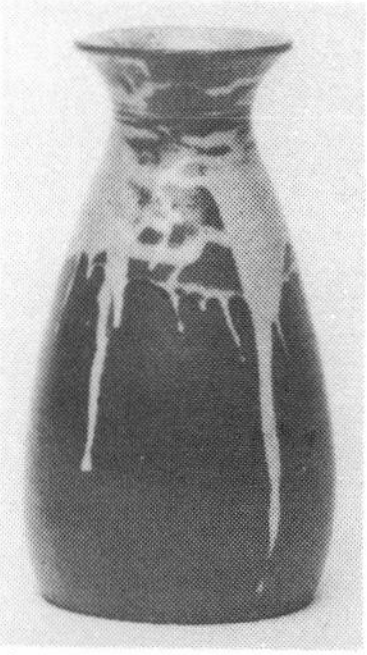
4

5

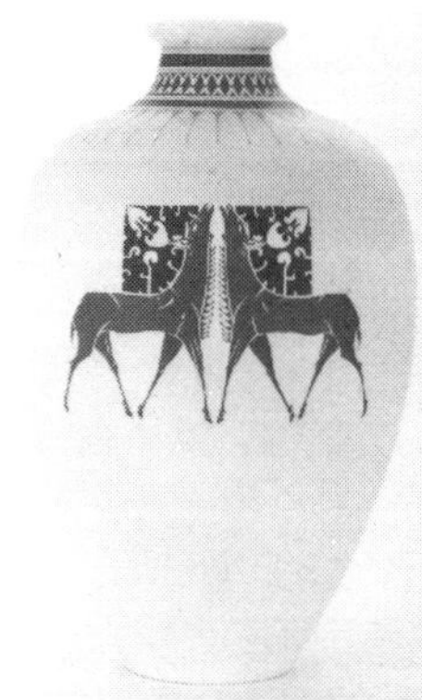
6

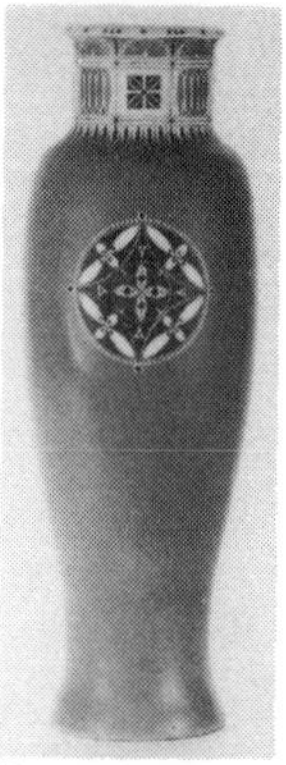
7

8

9

10

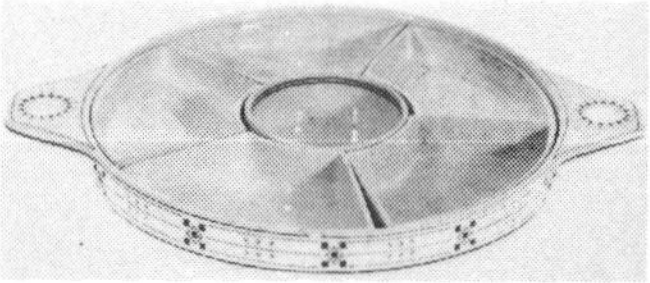
11

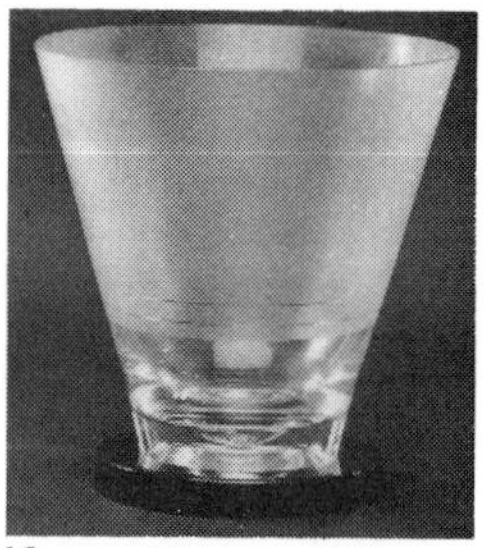
12

13

14

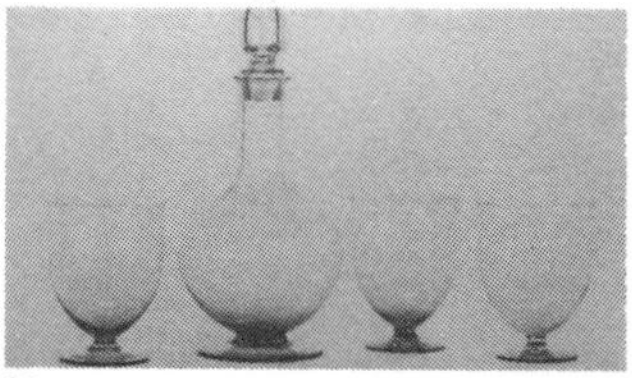
15

16

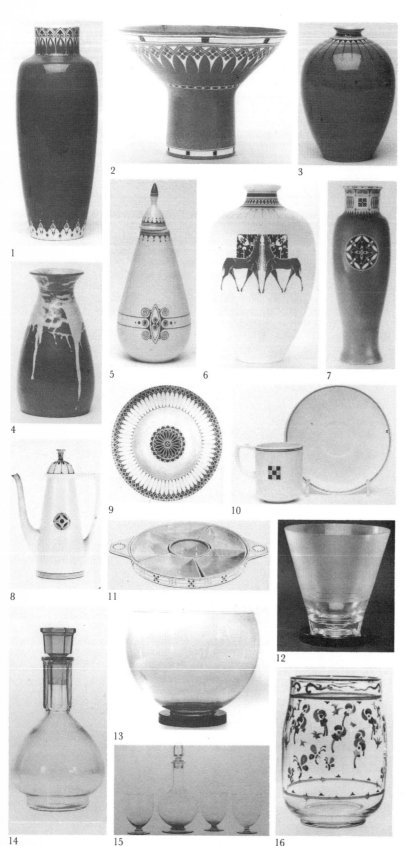

1
A Van der Hoef vase, Amphora, c.1908, decorated in yellow, green and white on a blue glazed ground, 27cm (10½in), *A 10 Mar,*
Dfl 3,450 (£1,045; $1,589)

2
A Van der Hoef bowl, Amstelhoek, dated 7 January 1905, with an inlaid white and dark brown decoration on a yellow-brown ground, 17cm (6¾in) high, *A 10 Mar,*
Dfl 3,450 (£1,045; $1,589)

3
A Van der Hoef vase, Amphora, c.1908, decorated in white, black and ochre on an ochre-yellow ground, *A 10 Mar,*
Dfl 1,035 (£313; $477)

4
A Brouwer vase, dated 1904, decorated in yellow on a brown ground, 13cm (5in), *A 10 Mar,*
Dfl 230 (£69; $106)

5
A Van der Hoef vase and cover, Amphora, c.1908, decorated with brown lines on a white glazed ground, *A 10 Mar,*
Dfl 575 (£174; $265)

6
A Van der Hoef vase, Amphora, c.1908, decorated with brown, black, green and yellow, with two deer, 38cm (15in), *A 10 Mar,*
Dfl 8,050 (£2,439; $3,708)

7
A Van der Hoef vase, Amphora, c.1908, decorated in white, green, brown and black on an ochre ground, 36.5cm (14¼in), *A 10 Mar,*
Dfl 2,530 (£767; $1,165)

8
A Van der Hoef coffee service, *(coffee pot illustrated)*, Amphora, c.1908, comprising 27 pieces, *A 10 Mar,*
Dfl 4,600 (£1,394; $2,119)

9
A Van der Hoef dish, Zuid-Holland, c.1903, decorated in brown and blue, 41.5cm (16¼in) diam., *A 10 Mar,*
Dfl 11,040 (£3,345; $5,085)

10
A Van der Hoef cup and saucer, Zuid-Holland, c.1903, decorated in green and ochre, 8cm (3in) high, *A 10 Mar,*
Dfl 391 (£118; $180)

11
An hors d'oeuvre set, Amphora, c.1905, decorated in blue and ochre on a white glazed ground, 32cm (12½in) wide, *A 10 Mar,*
Dfl 460 (£139; $212)

12
A Copier partly frosted vase, Leerdam, c.1930, on a black glass stand, 22.5cm (8¾in) high, *A 10 Mar,*
Dfl 1,006 (£305; $463)

13
A Copier glass bowl, Leerdam, c.1930, 22cm (8½in), *A 10 Mar,*
Dfl 805 (£244; $371)

14
A Copier green glass whisky decanter with stopper, Leerdam, 1927, 25cm (10¼in), *A 10 Mar,*
Dfl 632 (£191; $291)

15
A Copier green glass decanter with stopper and three glasses, Leerdam, 1928, decanter 29cm (11½in), *A 10 Mar,*
Dfl 1,725 (£523; $794)

16
A Lebeau vase, c.1927, with polychrome enamel decoration, 11.5cm (4½in), *A 10 Mar,*
Dfl 920 (£279; $424)

DESIGNERS cont'd

Copier, Andries J. D., b.1901.

Ehrlich, Christa, b.1903.

Eisenloeffel, Jan, 1876-1957.

Van der Hoef, Christian J., 1875-1957; worked for Amstelhoek 1894-1903; his designs also made at Zuid-Holland 1904, Haga 1904-07, Amphora from 1908; designed silver from 1910.

Lanooy, C. J., 1881-1947.

1
A Leerdam yellow pressed glass tea service, 1924, designed by H. P. Berlage, *A 10 Mar,*
Dfl 8,740 (£2,648; $4,026)

2
Two Eisenloeffel silver teaspoons, *(one illustrated),* c.1905, with white and blue enamel inlay, 9cm (3½in), *A 10 Mar,*
Dfl 632 (£191; $291)

3
Two Eisenloeffel silver teaspoons, *(one illustrated),* c.1900, with green enamel inlay, 12.5cm (5in), *A 10 Mar,*
Dfl 632 (£192; $291)

4
Two Eisenloeffel silver teaspoons, *(one illustrated),* c.1900, with yellow and blue enamel inlay, 12cm (4¾in), *A 10 Mar,*
Dfl 667 (£202; $307)

5
Two silver knife-rests, J.Blinxma, 6.5cm (2½in), *A 10 Mar,*
Dfl 632 (£191; $291)

6
A silver sauce boat and stand, c.1935, designed by Emmy Rooth, of oval form, with raffia handle, *A 10 Mar,*
Dfl 3,450 (£1,045; $1,589)

7
An Eisenloeffel silver napkin ring, 1916, with green, brown and blue enamel inlay, 3.5cm (1¼in) diam., *A 10 Mar,*
Dfl 2,070 (£627; $953)

8
A silver biscuit box, cover and stand, 1936, designed by Christa Ehrlich, with wooden knob, 11.5cm (4½in) high, *A 10 Mar,*
Dfl 2,530 (£766; $1,165)

9
An Eisenloeffel brass inkstand, with two inkwells, 28cm (11in) long, *A 10 Mar,*
Dfl 718 (£217; $331)

10
An Eisenloeffel copper sugar bowl and cover, the cover inlaid with polychrome enamel, 6.5cm (2½in) high, *A 10 Mar,*
Dfl 546 (£165; $251)

11
An Eisenloeffel brass cream jug, 6cm (2½in) high, *A 10 Mar,*
Dfl 276 (£84; $127)

12
An Eisenloeffel brass teapot, with wooden knob and raffia handle, 9cm (3½in) high, *A 10 Mar,*
Dfl 546 (£165; $251)

13
An Eisenloeffel brass coffee pot, with raffia handle, 22.5cm (8¾in), *A 10 Mar,*
Dfl 1,495 (£453; $688)

14
A silver tea service, designed by Christa Ehrlich, with wooden knobs and handles, *A 10 Mar,*
Dfl 6,900 (£2,091; $3,178)

FACTORIES

Amphora, Oegstgeest, near Leiden, founded 1908.

Amstelhoek, Amsterdam, founded 1894; bankrupt 1903, continued as V. H. Amstelhoek; taken over by De Distel 1910.

De Distel, Amsterdam, founded 1895; took over Amstelhoek 1910; taken over by Goedewagen, Gouda, 1923.

Haga, Purmerend, founded 1904; taken over by Amstelhoek 1907.

Holland, Utrecht, 1894-1920.

Leerdam, founded 1891.

Ram, Arnhem, founded 1920 to produce work of Colenbrander; closed 1928.

Rozenburg, The Hague, founded 1883; closed 1917.

Zuid-Holland, Gouda, 1898-1964.

1

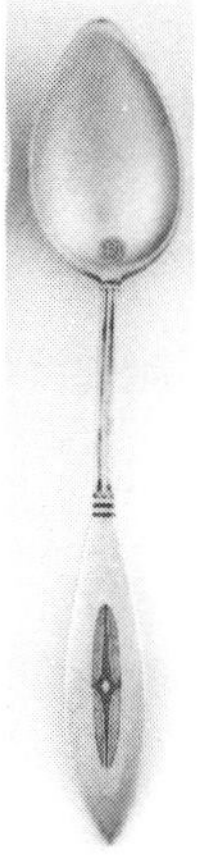
2

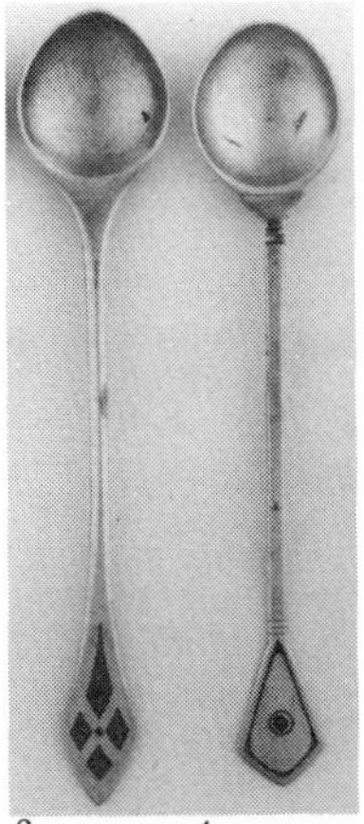
3 4

5

6

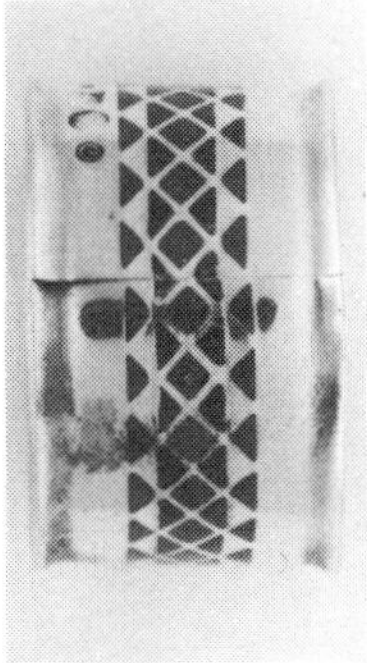
7

8

9

10

11

12

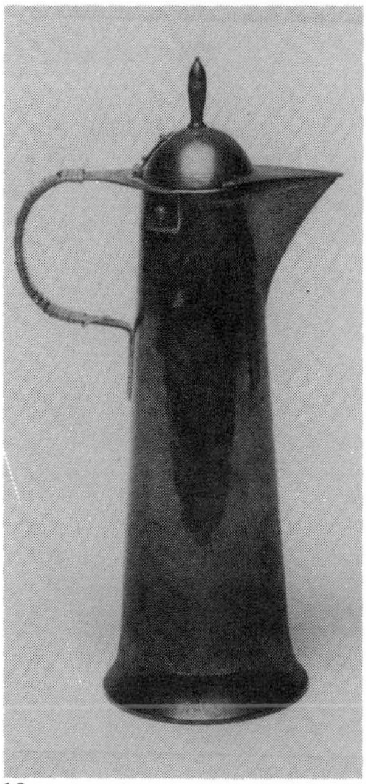
13

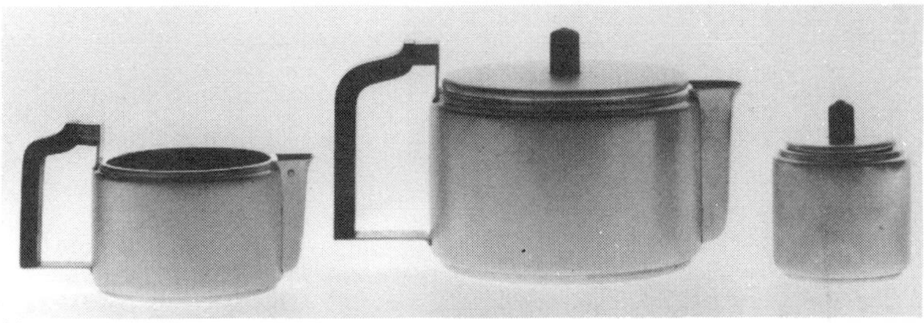
14

1

2

3

4

5

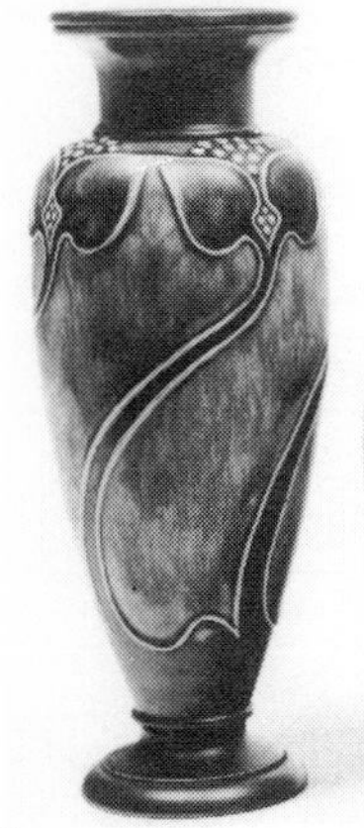
6

7

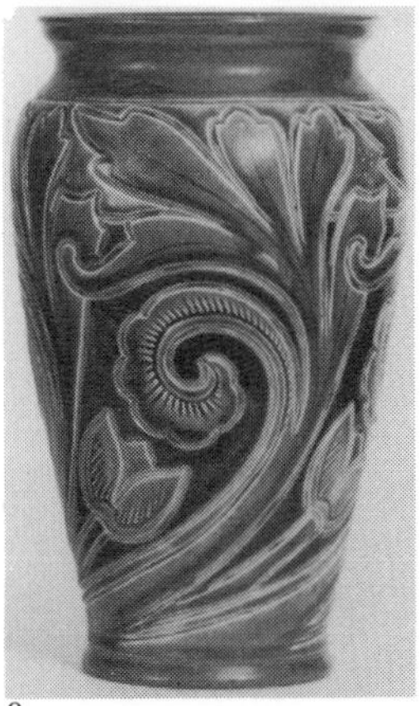
8

9

10

11

12

13

14

15

1
A Doulton stoneware mug, 1878, decorated by Hannah Barlow, silver mount by Harry Atkins, 11.5cm (4½in), *C 28 Jan,*
£209 ($307)

2
A Doulton stoneware tyg, 1885, decorated by Florence Barlow, monogrammed, impressed and incised marks, 15cm (6in), *S 10 Dec,*
£330 ($462)

3
A pair of Royal Doulton vases, *(one illustrated)*, early 1900s, decorated by Hannah Barlow, one chipped, signed, impressed and incised marks, 41cm (16in), *S 10 Dec,*
£440 ($616)

4
A Doulton stoneware jug, 1890s, decorated by Hannah Barlow, monogrammed, impressed and incised marks, 40cm (15¾in), *S 10 Dec,*
£682 ($955)

5
A pair of Doulton vases, *(one illustrated)*, 1890s, decorated by Eliza Simmance, on a mottled blue and green ground, impressed Lambeth mark, incised monogram, 42.5cm (16¾in), *C 13 May,*
£286 ($460)

6
A pair of Royal Doulton vases, *(one illustrated)*, 1903, decorated by Frank Butler, glazed in shades of green, brown and blue, impressed lion, crown and circle, date code, incised monogram, 8.5cm (11¼in), *C 13 May,*
£275 ($443)

7
A pair of Doulton Lambeth faience vases, *(one illustrated)*, 1880s, decorated by Mary Butterton, on amber and pale green ground, impressed mark, painted monogram, 24cm (9½in), *C 13 May,*
£616 ($992)

8
A Royal Doulton stoneware vase, early 20th century, decorated by Frank Butler, monogrammed, impressed and incised, 26.5cm (10½in), *S 10 Dec,*
£187 ($409)

9
A Doulton stoneware vase, 1876, by W. Baron, in blues and browns, impressed mark and incised monogram, 28cm (11in), *C 9 Sept,*
£88 ($132)

10
A Doulton stoneware jug, 1881, in blues and browns, impressed marks and incised monogram, 17cm (6¾in), *C 9 Sept,*
£110 ($165)

11
A Doulton stoneware jug, designed by Louisa E. Edwards, chipped spout, 29cm (11½in), *C 28 Jan,*
£110 ($162)

12
A Doulton Lambeth silicon jardinière, 1884, decorated by Alice Longhurst, in white and shades of blue and brown, some chips, impressed mark, monogram and date, 27cm (10¾in), *JHB 27 Feb,*
R 572 (£179; $277)

13
A pair of Doulton faience vases, *(one illustrated)*, 1890s, painted by Margaret Thompson, monogrammed, impressed, painted and printed marks, 35cm (13¾in), *S 16 July,*
£528 ($829)

14
A Doulton stoneware clockcase, 1882, decorated by Eliza Simmance, impressed marks and monogram, 30cm (12in), *C 13 May,*
£682 ($1,098)

15
A jar and cover, 1912, decorated by Harry Nixon, in underglaze-blue, painted signature and date, 23cm (9in), *L 27 May,*
£220 ($345)

1
A Charles Meigh & Son vase, c.1855, in green and yellow on rich puce ground, 87cm (43¼in), *Mel 24 June,*
Aus$2,200 (£956; ($1,492)

2
A William De Morgan ruby lustre 'rice dish', 1898-1907, late Fulham period, 41cm (16¼in), *C 9 Sept,*
£352 ($528)

3
A Martin Brothers love-bird group, 1914, mottled green glaze with specks of black, blue and brown, incised *R.W. Martin & Bro London & Southall 25.3.1914,* 14.5cm (5¾in), *L 16 May,*
£2,860 ($4,547)

4
A Martin Brothers triple bird group, 1906, mottled blue and green with specks of brown and lavender, incised *Martin Bros London and Southall, 3-1906,* 19.5cm (7¾in), *L 19 Dec,*
£7,150 ($10,010)

5
A Martin Brothers clock case, 1909, glazed in shades of grey, pale blue and olive green, incised mark *Martin Bros London and Southall, 3-1909,* 32cm (12½in), *L 19 Dec,*
£352 ($493)

6
A Martin Brothers 'gourd' vase, 1904, glazed mottled ochre with raised brown spots, detailed in green, incised mark and date, 26cm (10¼in), *L 16 May,*
£330 ($525)

7
A Martin Brothers John Barleycorn flask, 1910, incised mark and dates, 18cm (7in), *S 10 Dec,*
£1,045 ($1,463)

8
A Martin Brothers 'gourd' vase, 1900, ribs glazed green, incised mark and date, 19.5cm (7¾in), *L 16 May,*
£264 ($420)

9
A pair of Moorcroft MacIntyre 'cornflower' vases, *(one illustrated),* c.1910, in brown and green, signed *W. Moorcroft,* 25.5cm (10in), *C 9 Sept,*
£374 ($561)

10
A Maw & Co. Ltd 'diver' vase, 1890s, designed by Walter Crane, decorated in rich red, 22cm (8¾in), *C 9 Sept,*
£968 ($1,452)

11
A Moorcroft 'hazeldene' pattern vase, c.1910, painted in green and speckled turquoise on a dark blue ground, signature and impressed marks, 31cm (12¼in), *S 19 Mar,*
£1,045 ($1,599)

12
A Moorcroft MacIntyre 'Florian Ware' vase, c.1900, in shades of amber and blue, printed mark and painted *W. Moorcroft des,* 7.5cm (10¾in), *C 13 May,*
£704 ($1,133)

13
A Maw & Co. lustre vase, 1889, in red lustre, painted *Maw & Co., Feb 1899* on base, 32cm (12½in), *C 9 Sept,*
£275 ($413)

14
A pair of Leeds Art Pottery jardinières, early 20th century, on a pink and green ground, incised mark, 107cm (42in), *Ct 27 Oct,*
R 3,080 (£963; $1,348)

15
A Bretby earthenware jardinière, 1880s, the design attributed to Christopher Dresser, rich ruby red glaze with yellow interior, stamped *Bretby,* 30.5cm (12in), *L 16 May,*
£528 ($839)

16
A Frederick Passenger lustre glazed earthenware roundel, 1902, in Persian blue with grey, green and red details, reverse monogrammed *F.P. 1902,* 18cm (7in), *L 19 Dec,*
£242 ($338)

1

2

3

4

5

6

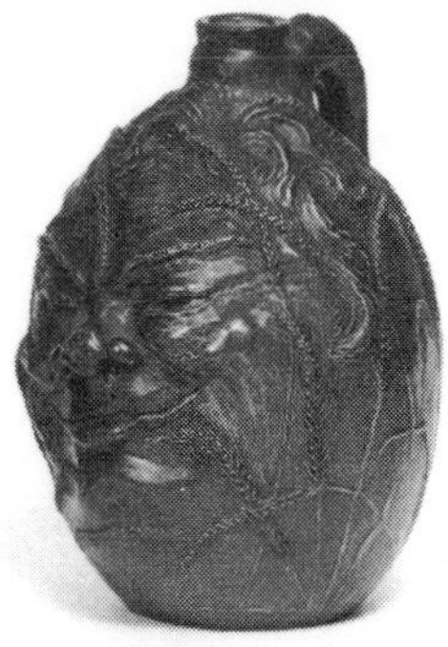
7

8

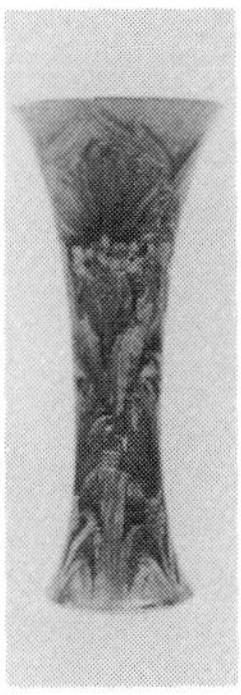
9

10

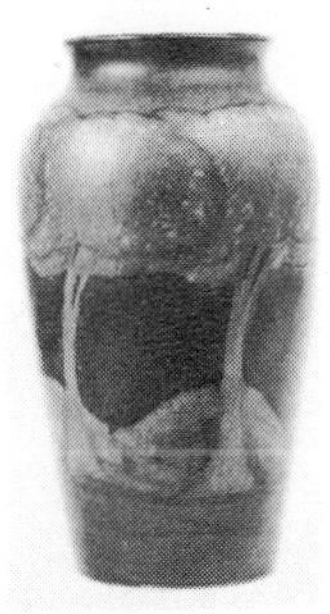
11

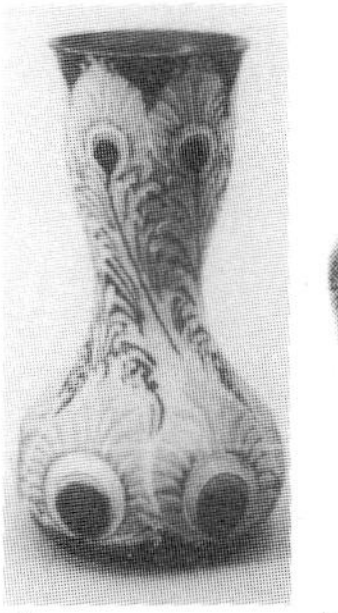
12

13

14

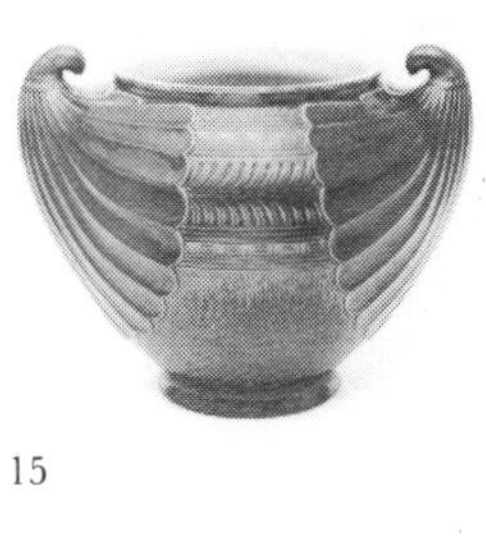
15

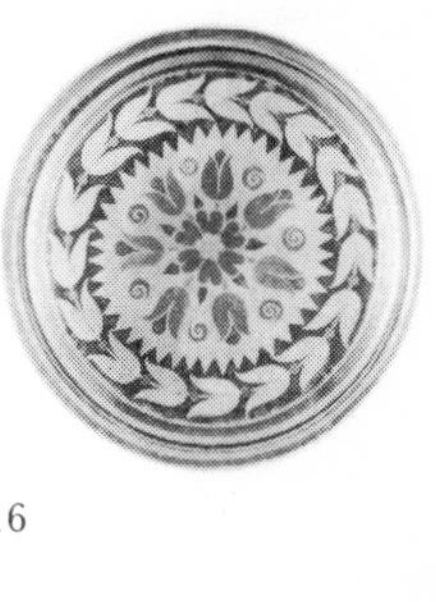
16

1

2

3
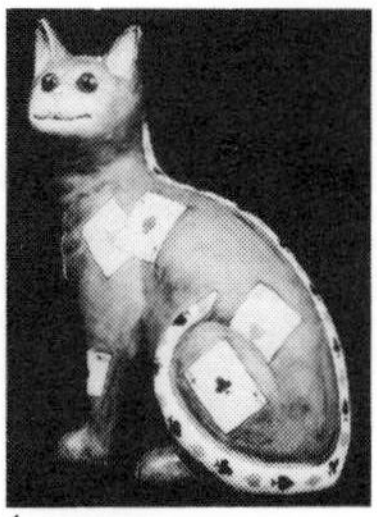
4
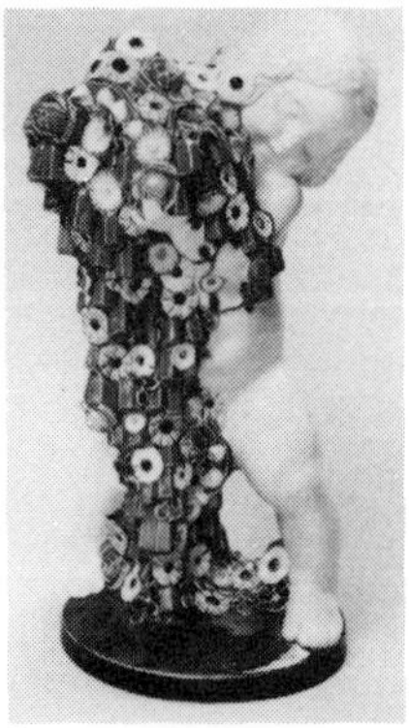
5
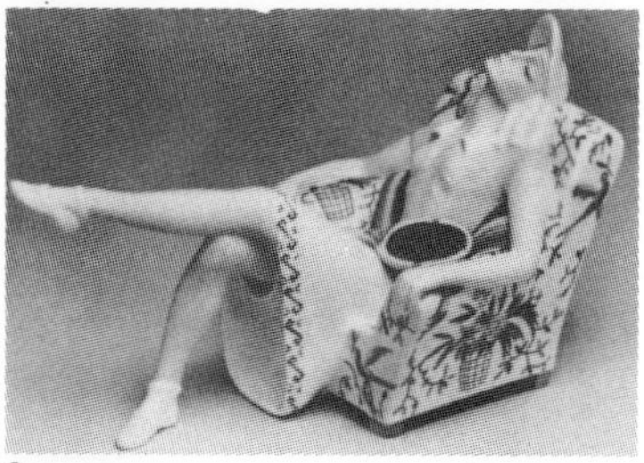
6

7

8

9
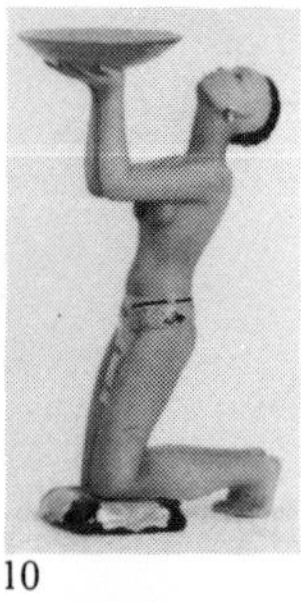
10

11

12

13
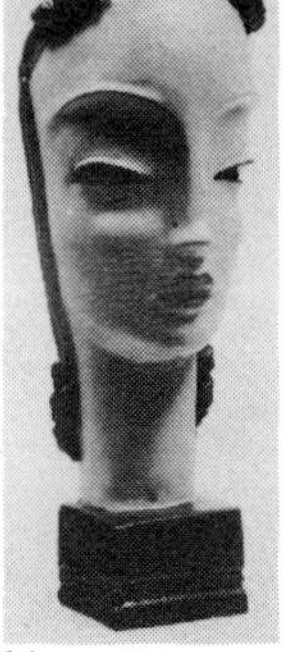
14

1
A Gallé faience inkstand, c.1880, decoration in dark blue on pale blue ground, mark *E. Gallé Nancy*, 29.5cm (11¾in), *L 16 May,* **£572 ($909)**

2
A Gallé faience service, c.1880, comprising 40 pieces, most marked *Gallé* and *E. Bourgeois, M 19 Oct,* **FF 22,200 (£2,387; $3,342)**

3
A Gallé faience clock, 1896, in blue and white, signed *E. Gallé G Depose*, 56.5cm (22¼in), *L 16 May,* **£1,870 ($2,973)**

4
A Gallé faience cat, c.1880, marked *C. Gallé Nancy*, 33cm (13in), *M 13 Apr,* **FF 22,755 (£1,998; $3,096)**

5
A polychrome ceramic sculpture, c.1910, by Michael Powolny, impressed *Wiener Keramik*, 37.5cm (14¾in), *Mil 12 Mar* **L 6,600,000 (£2,773; $4,270)**

6
A ceramic tennis player, c.1935, marked *Festy Made in Italy M. di Vacchetti*, 21.5cm (8½in), *M 13 Apr,* **FF 11,655 (£1,023; $1,586)**

7
A polychrome maiolica and lustre vase, 1914-19, by Galileo Chini, decorated in blue, green, red and yellow on a white ground, marked *Chini e Co. Mugello Italia*, 43cm (17in), *Mil 12 Mar,* **L 3,850,000 (£1,618; $2,491)**

8
A Czechoslovakian glazed earthenware group of exotic dancers, 1930s, decorated in green, red and gold, 34.5cm (13¾in), *L 19 Dec,* **£198 ($277)**

9
A Lachenal dinner service, c.1900, comprising 56 pieces, decorated in blue and white, maker's marks, *M 13 Apr,* **FF 5,550 (£487; $755)**

10
An Italian figure, 1930s, kneeling on a black cushion and holding an orange tray, 28.5cm (8¼in), *S 16 July,* **£121 ($190)**

11
A St. Leu earthenware head, 1930s, white glaze with gilding, marked *St. Leu France*, 35.5cm (13¾in), *L 16 May,* **£176 ($280)**

12
A Goldscheider earthenware wall mask, 1920s, with orange hair, holding a yellow apple, marked *Goldscheider Wien Made in Austria*, 34.5cm (13½in), *L 16 May,* **£286 ($455)**

13
A Goldscheider figure, c.1930, after a model by Lorenzl, printed factory marks, facsimile signature *Lorenzl*, 34.5cm (13½in), *Syd 12 Nov,* **Aus$1,265 (£575; $805)**

14
A Goldscheider earthenware standing face mask, c.1930, gold hair, blue eyes and orange lips, printed marks, *Goldscheider Wien, Made in Austria*, 37cm (14½in), *C 9 Sept,* **£748 ($1,122)**

1
A Goldscheider group, 1930s, the woman in green lace skirt and jacket, restored, printed mark, 32cm (12½in), *S 10 Dec,*
£143 ($200)

2
A group of five German porcelain musicians, 1920s, impressed *CW,* 7.5cm (3½in), *S 10 Dec,*
£330 ($462)

3
A Goldscheider figure, 1930s, wearing a purple lace dress, printed and impressed marks, 30.5cm (12in), *S 10 Dec,*
£286 ($400)

4
A Goldscheider figure, 1930s, in blue floral skirt, minor damage, printed and impressed marks, 38cm (15in), *S 16 July,*
£638 ($1,002)

5
A Goldscheider figure, 1930s, after a design by Lorenzl, printed and impressed marks, 44cm (17¼in), *S 16 July,*
£715 ($1,123)

6
A Goldscheider figure, 1930s, wearing a red and grey skirt, damage to one hand, impressed, painted and printed marks, 37cm (14½in), *S 16 July,*
£572 ($898)

7
A Goldscheider figure, 1930s, after Lorenzl, in a green and black dress, small chip, printed and impressed marks, 41cm (16in), *S 16 July,*
£528 ($829)

8
A Goldscheider figure, 1930s, holding a pink and yellow drape, printed and impressed marks, 40cm (15¾in), *S 16 July,*
£990 ($1,554)

9
A Katzhutte pottery model, c.1930, in a blue dress, printed marks, 51cm (20in), *C 13 May,*
£297 ($478)

10
A Katzhutte model of a girl, c.1930, wearing a blue and purple dress, printed and painted marks, 32.5cm (12¾in), *C 9 Sept,*
£110 ($165)

11
A Lenci figure, 1930s, painted marks, 38cm (15in), *S 10 Dec,*
£770 ($1,078)

12
A Lenci earthenware figure, 1929, stamped and painted *Lenci, Made in Italy,* 51.5cm (20¼in), *L 16 May,*
£825 ($1,312)

13
A Lenci pottery bowl, dated 1932, turquoise interior, painted mark, 56cm (22in), *S 10 Dec,*
£715 ($1,001)

14
An Austrian porcelain pot and cover, 1920s, decorated with gold dots, on a purple ground, marked *Fraureuta Kunstart...,* 18.5cm (7¼in), *L 16 May,*
£418 ($665)

15
A Mougin stoneware vase, c.1936, probably designed by Joseph Mougin, with umber coloured spirals against a hatched pewter ground, moulded and inscribed, 30.5cm (12in), *NY 6 Dec,*
$1,320 (£923)

16
A Lenci group, the woman wearing brown and red, marked *Lenci Made in Italy Torino,* 40cm (15¾in), *L 19 Dec,*
£1,100 ($1,540)

17
A Gray's pottery jug, c.1930, painted with golfing scenes, crack, printed marks, 19cm (7½in), *S 16 July,*
£94 ($147)

18
A Gray's pottery lamp base, c.1930, painted with golfing scenes, printed and painted marks, 15cm (6in), *S 16 July,*
£275 ($432)

1

2

3

4 5 6 7 8

9

10

11

12

13

14

15

16

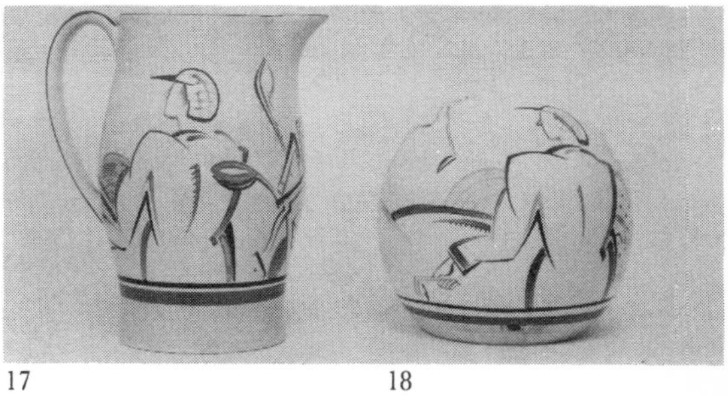
17 18

1

2

3

4

5

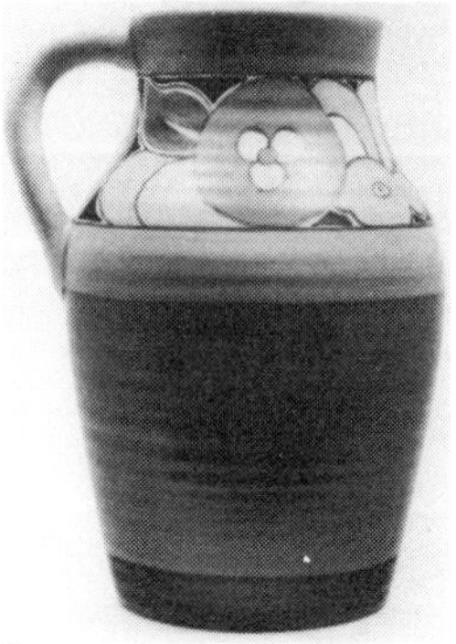
6

7

8 9 10

11

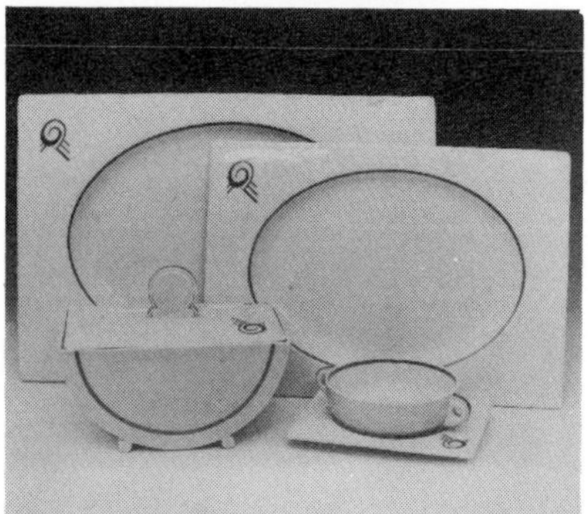
12

13

1
A Wilkinson Ltd Bizarre jug, 1930s, designed by Laura Knight, in brown and red with black and turquoise details, printed marks, 28cm (11in), *L 19 Dec,*
£440 ($616)

2
A Cowan pottery punch-bowl, c.1931, designed by Viktor Schreckengost, glazed in black over vivid turquoise, lip restored, impressed marks, 35cm (14in), *NY 20 June,*
$6,875 (£4,614)

3
A Guido Gambone earthenware pitcher, 1950s, white and brown on turquoise ground, with thick milky overglaze, marked *G. Vietri Italy,* 44cm (17¼in), *L 19 Dec,*
£308 ($431)

4
A Guido Gambone terra-cotta vase, 1930, marked *Vietri,* 28cm (11in), *Mil 12 Mar,*
L 770,000, (£324; $498)

5
A Royal Copenhagen porcelain vase, c.1936-38, designed by Thorkild Olsen, with bronze cover designed by K. Andersen, crackled salmon pink orange glaze, monogram *K.A.,* factory marks, 40.5cm (16in), *L 19 Dec,*
£1,760 ($2,464)

6
A Clarice Cliff Newport pottery jug, c.1930, in orange, yellow and black, printed marks, 30cm (11¾in), *C 13 May,*
£209 ($336)

7
A pottery tea service, c.1940, painted by Guido Andlovitz, marked *Società Ceramica Italiana di Laveno, Mil 12 Mar,*
L 770,000 (£324; $498)

8
A Clarice Cliff Wilkinson Ltd 'Fantasque' vase, 1930s, in red, blue and green, printed marks, 17.5cm (7in), *L 16 May,*
£264 ($420)

9
A Clarice Cliff Wilkinson Ltd Bizarre 'Fantasque' jar and cover, 1930s, in blue, green, yellow, purple and red, printed marks, 20cm (8in), *L 16 May,*
£825 ($1,312)

10
A Clarice Cliff Newport pottery Bizarre 'Fantasque' vase, 1930s, in red, green, and purple with touches of blue and black, printed mark, 20cm (8in), *L 16 May,*
£286 ($455)

11
A Clarice Cliff Newport pottery Bizarre 'Fantasque' landscape jug, 1930s, in bright orange, yellow and black, printed marks, 28.5cm (11¼in), *C 9 Sept,*
£935 ($1,403)

12
A Royal Staffordshire dinner service, 1930s, designed by Clarice Cliff, comprising 46 pieces, each piece with silver lustre rim, printed marks, and facsimile signature, *C 13 May,*
£352 ($567)

13
A Newport pottery plate, 1925, in green, black, yellow and orange, printed marks, 26cm (10¼in), *C 9 Sept,*
£105 ($157)

1
A Lucie Rie stoneware bowl, 1950s, speckled brown/white glaze, manganese brown at rim, impressed LR seal, 14cm (5½in), *L 16 May,*
£825 ($1,312)

2
A Lucie Rie porcelain bowl, 1950s, with dark matt manganese glaze, impressed LR seal, 11.5cm (4½in), *L 16 May,*
£990 ($1,574)

3
A Lucie Rie stoneware bowl, 1950s, glazed in brown, speckled ashen white, impressed LR seal, 8.5cm (3½in), *L 19 Dec,*
£352 ($493)

4
A Lucie Rie porcelain bowl, c.1960, ochre exterior, celadon centre and beige interior separated by brown wax resist ring, impressed LR monogram, 24cm (9½in) diam., *L 19 Dec,*
£1,045 ($1,463)

5
A Hans Coper stoneware vase, late 1960s, deep brown black glaze, impressed HC seal, 14.5cm (5¾in), *L 19 Dec,*
£5,720 ($8,008)

6
A Hans Coper stoneware vase, c.1970, brown black glaze with cream at base and rim, impressed HC seal, 16cm (6¼in), *L 19 Dec,*
£3,300 ($4,620)

7
A Ladi Kwali stoneware vase, late 1960s, pale grey glaze against mottled green ground, impressed Abuja and LK seals, 37.5cm (14¾in), *L 19 Dec,*
£1,045 ($1,463)

8
A Hamada Shoji stoneware dish, 1950s, in speckled orange/brown stripes, reverse with label *Made in Japan,* 28.5cm (11¼in) diam., *L 16 May,*
£605 ($962)

9
A Hamada Shoji stoneware vase, with wax relief designs on a metallic brown glazed ground, repaired neck, 22cm (8¾in), *C 28 Jan,*
£297 ($437)

10
A Rookwood standard glaze pottery figural jug, 1891, decorated by Kataro Shirayamadani, impressed factory mark, incised artist's signature, 11.5cm (4½in), *NY 19 June,*
$1,430 (£960)

11
A Gertrud and Otto Natzler pottery bowl, mid 20th century, glazed in chartreuse revealing reddish underbody, unglazed signature, 13.5cm (5¼in), *NY 19 June,*
$1,430 (£960)

12
A Michael Cardew Wenford Bridge stoneware jar and cover, 1970s, impressed seals, 83cm (32½in), *L 19 Dec,*
£880 ($1,232)

1

2

3

4

5

6

7

8

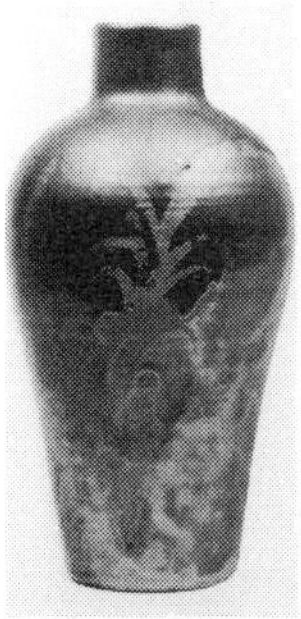
9

10

11

12

1

3

4

2

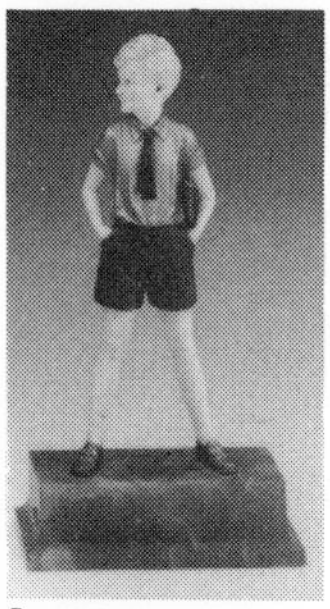
5

6 7 8

10

9

11

12

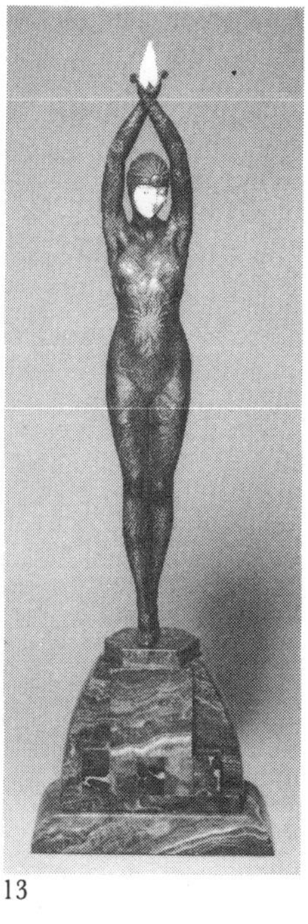
13

1
A Lorenzl bronze figure, c.1930, on a green marble plinth, composition head, marked *Lorenzl*, 26cm (10¼in), *C 9 Sept,*
£550 ($825)

2
A Preiss bronze and ivory figure of a little girl, 1930s, in silvery green bloomer suit, marked *F. Preiss*, 19.5cm (7¾in), *L 16 May,*
£2,860 ($4,547)

3
A Preiss bronze and ivory figure of a young woman, c.1930, dressed in silver and green, between pedestals of green marble, marked *F. Preiss*, foundry mark *PK*, 24.5cm (9¾in), *L 16 May,*
£2,860 ($4,547)

4
A Preiss bronze and ivory figure, 1930s, 'The Torch Dancer', engraved *F. Preiss*, 34.5cm (13½in), *L 16 May,*
£3,960 ($6,296)

5
A Preiss bronze and ivory figure of a schoolboy, 1930s, in blue and silver, marked *F. Preiss*, 21.5cm (8½in), *L 16 May,*
£1,540 ($2,449)

6
A Preiss bronze and ivory tennis player, c.1930, with silvered racquet, on green marble block, engraved *F. Preiss*, 28cm (11in), *L 19 Dec,*
£4,400 ($6,160)

7
A Preiss bronze and ivory group, 1930s, 'The Butterfly Girls', one in pink, the other green, foundry mark *PK*, 33cm (13in), *L 19 Dec,*
£6,050 ($8,470)

8
A Preiss bronze and ivory figure, 1930s, 'Con Brio', green-gold cold painted costume with pink highlights, marked *F. Preiss*, 34cm (13¼in), *L 19 Dec,*
£6,380 ($8,932)

9
A bronze and ivory figural tazza, c.1925, after Fritz Preiss, black onyx bowl, damage to one arm, 21.5cm (8½in), *NY 20 June,*
$2,750 (£1,846)

10
A Chiparus polychrome bronze and ivory figure of a dancer, c.1925, on a raised onyx base, 33.5cm (13¼in), *NY 6 Dec,*
$7,150 (£5,000)

11
A Chiparus bronze and ivory figure, 'The Squall', details picked out in gilding, 19cm (7½in), *S 10 Dec,*
£1,650 ($2,310)

12
A Reitz bronze and ivory figure of a dancing girl, 1930s, incised marks, 25.5cm (10in), *S 10 Dec,*
£770 ($1,078)

13
A Chiparus bronze and ivory figure, c.1930, 'The Starfish Girl', in metallic blue-green cold painted cat suit, with studded decoration, 74.5cm (29½in), *L 19 Dec,*
£24,200 ($33,880)

1
A Hagenauer wooden and bronze figure of a horse and jockey, c.1925, 26cm (10¼in) long, *NY 11 Oct,*
$1,760 (£1,231)

2
A Hagenauer wooden head of a negress, 1920s, with silvered metal base in the form of three necklets, 17.5cm (6¾in), *L 16 May,*
£1,650 ($2,624)

3
A Hagenauer wooden bust of a negress, 1920s, 34.5cm (13½in), *L 19 Dec,*
£1,760 ($2,464)

4
A Hagenauer wooden and copper figure of a woman, c.1920, on an oval copper base, 72.5cm (28½in), *NY 11 Oct,*
$3,850 (£2,692)

5
A pair of Giuraud Riviere silvered bronze figures, *(one illustrated),* c.1930, black wooden bases, 17cm (6¾in) high, *L 16 May,*
£528 ($839)

6
A Richard Garbe bronze plaque, 1917, depicting the goddess Diana with an antelope behind her, oxidised silver patina, 32cm (12½in) diam., *L 19 Dec,*
£440 ($616)

7
A Frederic Focht bronze figure of an athlete, c.1930, green patina, black marble base, 75cm (29½in) high, *NY 20 June,*
$4,125 (£2,768)

8
A Kaesbach bronze study of a Greek warrior, 1930s, black patinated with gilt helmet and loincloth, marble base, 43.5cm (17¼in), *L 16 May,*
£2,640 ($4,198)

9
A Hagenauer bronze and ebony oriental mask, c.1925, 19cm (7½in), *M 13 Apr,*
FF 33,300 (£2,924; $4,532)

10
A Marcel Bouraine silvered-bronze figure of a spear thrower, on marble base, 16.5cm (6½in) high, *NY 19 June,*
$1,870 (£1,255)

11
A brass figural group, 20th century, cast as two female figures in a stylised dance pose, one patinated black, onyx base, 30.5cm (12in) high, *NY 19 June,*
$1,650 (£1,107)

12
A Guy Debe spelter figure of a jaguar, c.1930, on black slate and yellow veined marble base, rich green patination, 62cm (24½in), *S 19 Mar,*
£396 ($606)

1

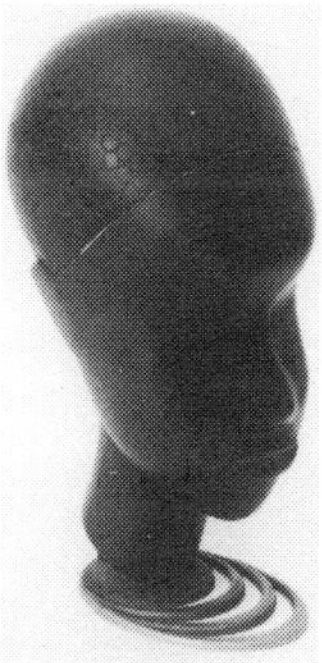
2

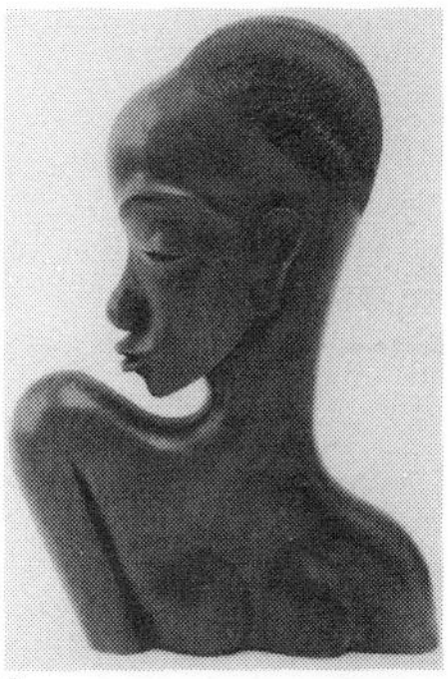
3

4

5

6

7

8

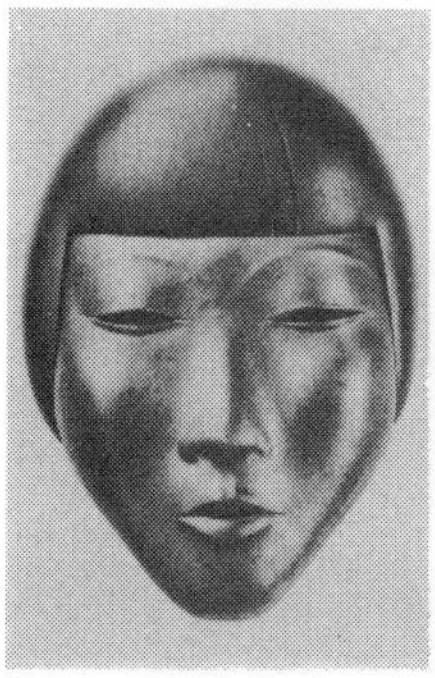
9

10

11

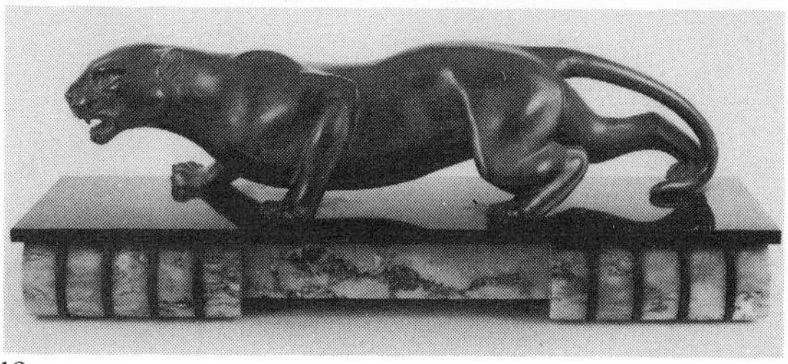
12

1

2

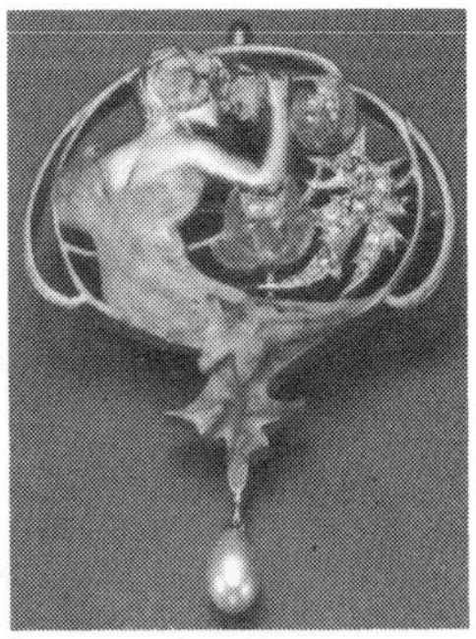
3

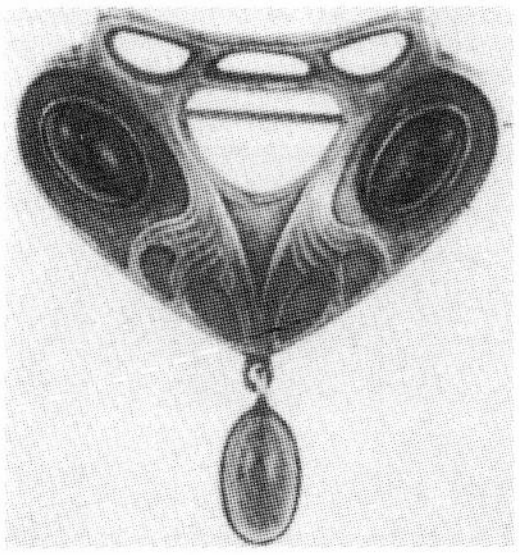
4

5

6

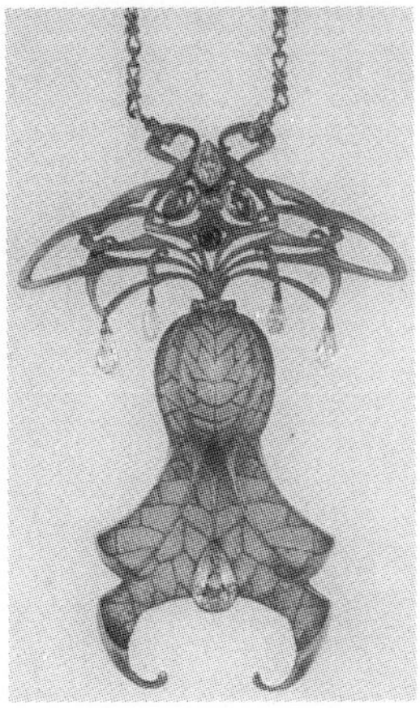
7

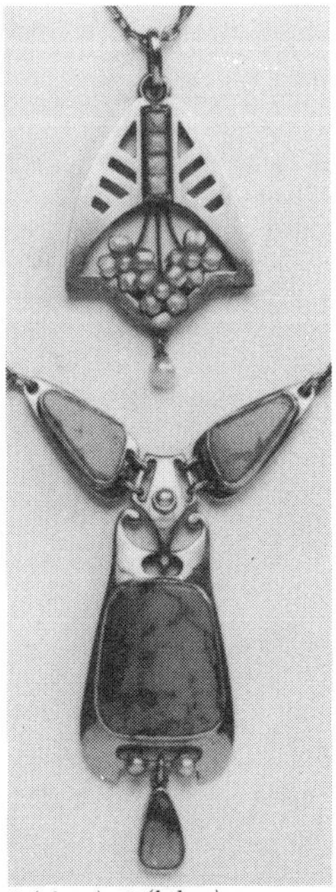
8 *(above)* 9 *(below)*

10

11

12

1
A Masriera gold, plique-à-jour enamel, sapphire and diamond pendant/brooch, surmounted by blue and green leaves, *NY 20 Oct,*
$8,800 (£6,154)

2
A Masriera & Carreras gold and plique-à-jour enamel brooch, applied with green, gold and shaded lavender enamel, *NY 20 Oct,*
$5,225 (£3,654)

3
A Masriera & Carreras gold, enamel and diamond brooch, applied with shaded blue and green enamel, completed by an oval-shaped pearl pendant, *NY 20 Oct,*
$7,975 (£5,577)

4
A silver and cornelian brooch, c.1905, design attributed to Patriz Huber, hung with a pendant drop, marked *déposé,* 3.5cm (1½in), *L 16 May,*
£132 ($210)

5
A Masriera & Carreras gold, plique-à-jour enamel and diamond brooch, with carved ivory face, ruby and diamond medallion, applied with white and blue enamel, pendant pearl, *NY 20 Oct,*
$8,250 (£5,769)

6
A Wiener Werkstätte silver-gilt, mother-of-pearl and lapis lazuli pendant, c.1915, designed by Dagobert Peche, stamped *WW,* Austrian silver standard mark, 6cm (2¼in), *NY 11 Oct,*
$11,550 (£8,077)

7
A Philippe Wolfers gold and enamel brooch/pendant, c.1900, applied with green, white and pink enamel, set with diamonds, stamped *Ex. unique* and monogrammed *P.W.,* *M 19 Oct,*
FF 266,400 (£28,645; $40,103)

8
A pearl and opal enamelled pendant, c.1905, details in pale green and pink, *L 19 Dec,*
£286 ($400)

9
A Murrle Bennett and Co. pendant, c.1905, with turquoise drop, maker's mark, *L 19 Dec,*
£352 ($493)

10
A G. Desbazeilles gold bracelet, c.1890, with allegorical cast plaques representing the four Arts, maker's mark G.D. with a star in a diamond, *L 8 May,*
£5,280 ($8,553)

11
A Phoebe Traquair gold and enamel pendant with matching earrings, 1912, detailed in rich red, blue, purple and green enamels, one earring monogrammed *PAT,* *L 19 Dec,*
£1,760 ($2,464)

12
A Georges Fouquet carved horn, opal, enamel and gold hair comb, c.1900, of Egyptian inspiration, detailed in green and black enamel, engraved mark *G. Fouquet,* *L 19 Dec,*
£5,720 ($8,008)

1
A pair of German silver vases, *(one illustrated),* c.1900, of flower form, silver coloured metal, 25.5cm (10in), *L 16 May,*
£385 ($612)

2
A German silvered metal tankard, WMF, c.1900, cast in relief with dancing maidens, cherub finial, 43cm (17in), *C 7 Oct,*
£572 ($801)

3
A German silver-plated four-piece tea and coffee service with matching tray, WMF, c.1900, embossed and chased with berried leaves, coffee pot 28cm (11in), *NY 20 June,*
$2,970 (£1,993)

4
A German silver-plated six-piece desk set, WMF, c.1900, each decorated with tendrils, gilt clover or berries, inkstand 34.5cm (13½in), *NY 20 June,*
$1,210 (£812)

5
A German pewter dish, WMF, c.1900, a female figure reclining on the pierced tray, 34.5cm (13½in), *S 16 July,*
£462 ($725)

6
A German silver-plated dish, WMF, c.1900, in the form of a fairy cradling a small bird in her hands, waterlily leaves on stalks behind, 28cm (11in) wide, *S 16 July,*
£440 ($691)

7
A German pewter ink-well, WMF, c.1900, in the form of a young girl seated reading on a tear-drop-shaped base, 19cm (7½in), *S 16 July,*
£176 ($276)

8
A German electroplated pewter mirror, WMF, c.1905, swivel mounted, the protruding front forming a shelf, 66.5cm (26¼in), *L 19 Dec,*
£1,320 ($1,848)

9
A German pewter frame, WMF, c.1900, cast with a young woman gazing at her reflection, 37.5cm (14¾in), *L 16 May,*
£605 ($962)

10
A German electroplated dish, WMF, c.1900, cast with a young woman stroking a dove, large lily pads behind, 21cm (8¼in), *L 19 Dec,*
£902 ($1,263)

11
A German pewter-mounted green glass claret jug, WMF, c.1900, 41cm (16in), *S 10 Dec,*
£374 ($534)

12
A pair of German pewter candlesticks, Kayserzinn, possibly designed by Hugo Leven, c.1900, 42.5cm (16¾in), *L 19 Dec,*
£858 ($1,201)

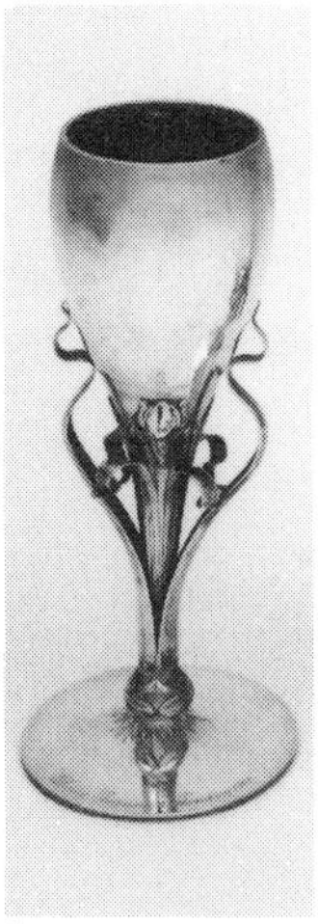
1

2

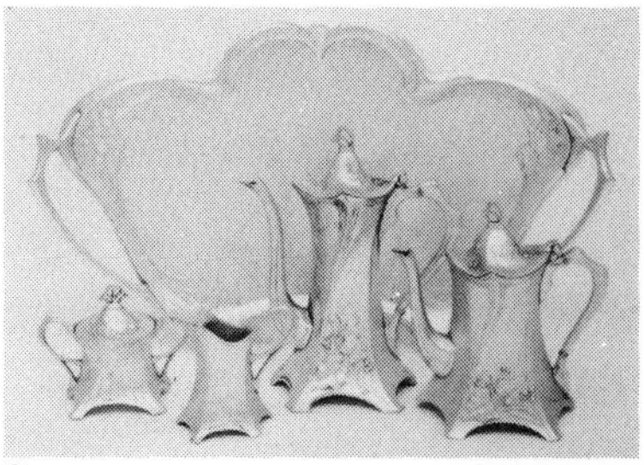
3

4

5 6 7

8

9

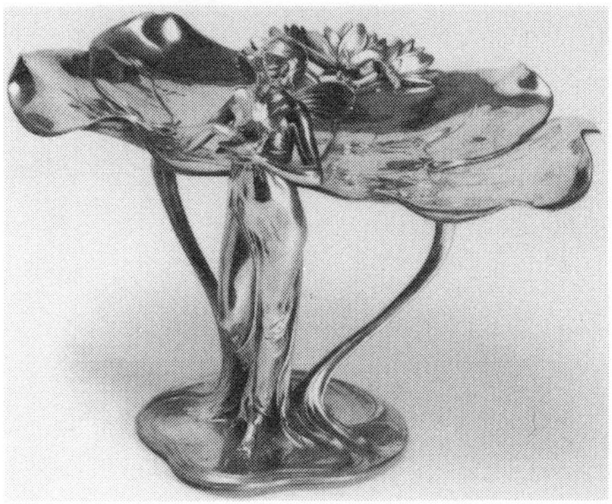
10

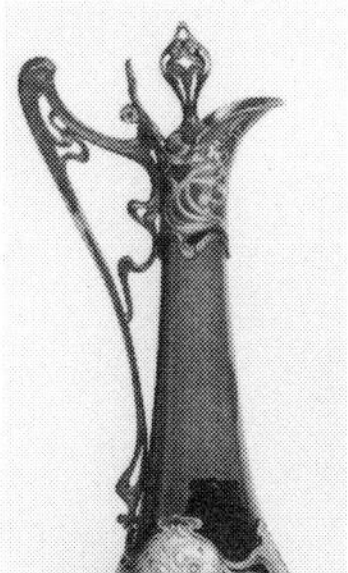
11

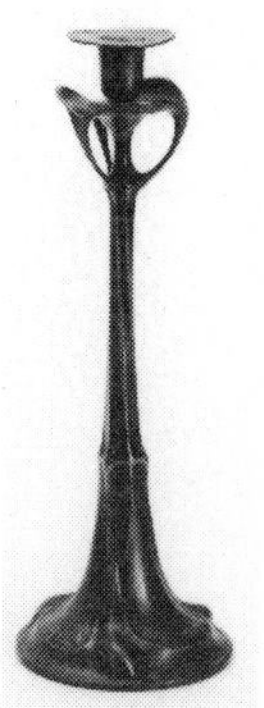
12

1

2

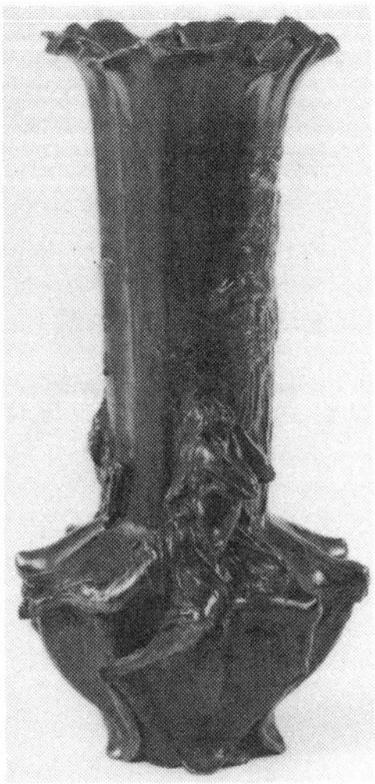
3

4

5

6

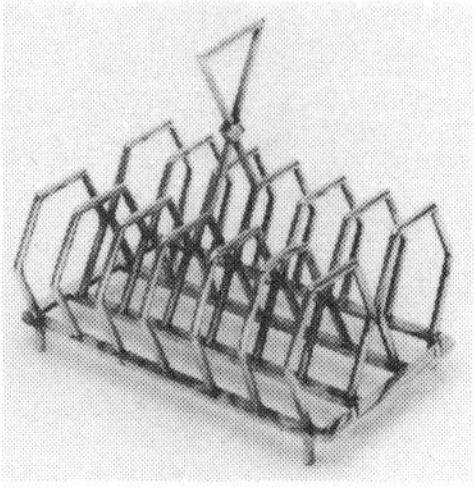
7

8

9 10 11

12

13

14

15

1
A bronze figural inkwell and lamp, Leo Laporte Blairsy, early 20th century, the base in the form of lily pads supporting a blossom-form inkwell, surmounted by a young woman leaning forward and supporting a heavy poppy blossom enclosing a light, greenish-brown patina, inkwell cover lacking, 41cm (16in), *NY 20 June,*
$3,300 (£2,215)

2
A Tiffany & Co. 'Oriental Style' silver jug, New York, c.1875, the hammered surface etched with pomegranates, 25.5cm (10in), *NY 20 June,*
$2,310 (£1,550)

3
A Raoul Larche bronze vase, c.1900, cast with male and female figures and a grotesque figure with snake neck and bat wings, 79cm (31in), *L 19 Dec,*
£3,080 ($4,312)

4
A 'Japanese Style' silver and mixed metal assembled three-piece tea service, Gorham Mfg. Co., Providence, R.I., 1883-86, 14.5cm (5¾in) max., *NY 20 June,*
$2,750 (£1,846)

5
A Tiffany & Co. silver cup and saucer, c.1880, saucer 15cm (6in) diam., *NY 6 Dec,*
$660 (£461)

6
A Hukin and Heath electroplated pot with hinged cover, designed by Christopher Dresser, 1879, chased with 'Aesthetic' cartouches of flowers and blossoms, *L 16 May,*
£990 ($1,574)

7
A James Dixon and Sons electroplated toast rack, designed by Christopher Dresser, 1880s, 16cm (6¼in), *L 19 Dec,*
£1,100 ($1,540)

8
A Hukin and Heath electroplated tureen and cover, designed by Christopher Dresser, 1880, 16cm (6¼in), sold with a soup ladle, *L 19 Dec,*
£1,430 ($2,002)

9
A silver-gilt vase, 1903, attributed to L. Movio, maker's mark of Walker & Tolhurst for Johnson, Walker & Tolhurst, London, 41.5cm (16¼in), *L 16 May,*
£1,870 ($2,973)

10
A Gilbert Marks silver dish, 1896, Britannia Standard, London, 42cm (16½in), *L 16 May,*
£2,860 ($4,547)

11
A Gilbert Marks silver bowl, 1897, London, 40.5cm (16in), *L 16 May,*
£2,640 ($4,547)

12
A Hukin and Heath electroplated egg holder, designed by Christopher Dresser, 1878, 19.5cm (7¾in), *L 16 May,*
£1,100 ($1,749)

13
A Duchess of Sutherlands Cripples Guild silver dish, 1916, Birmingham, 56cm (22in), *L 16 May,*
£1,980 ($3,148)

14
A silver-mounted photograph frame, Spurrier & Co., Birmingham, 1903, stamped with trailing lilies, 26cm (10¼in), *C 28 Jan,*
£313 ($461)

15
A silver mirror frame, 1904, Birmingham, detailed with rich blue and green enamel, 22cm (8¾in), *L 19 Dec,*
£682 ($955)

\ Liberty & Co. pewter
ınd enamel clock,
lesigned by Archibald
Knox, c.1905, the copper
ace enamelled in rich blue
ınd green, with central
notif detailed in red,
'0cm (8in), *L 19 Dec,*
,880 ($1,232)

\ pair of Liberty & Co.
ewter vases, *(one illus-*
rated), c.1900-10, each
orpedo-shaped body
lecorated with a frieze of
tylised leaves, hearts and
trapwork heightened
vith blue/green enamel
laques, 29cm (11½in),
16 July,
:319 ($501)

\ Liberty & Co. 'Cymric'
ilver, enamel, mother-of-
earl and turquoise clock,
903, Birmingham, 10cm
4in), *L 19 Dec,*
:3,740 ($5,236)

\ Liberty & Co. silver
nd ivory tea and coffee
et, 1899, Birmingham,
offee pot 19cm (7½in),
16 May,
2,420 ($3,848)

\ set of six Liberty & Co.
Cymric' silver and
namel spoons, *(three illus-*
rated), 1904, Birmingham,
he pointed finials cast
vith leaves and stems,
letailed in orange and
lue/green enamel,
1.5cm (4½in), *L 16 May,*
418 ($665)

\ pair of Liberty & Co.
ilver candlesticks,
lesigned by Rex Silver,
906, London, with four
quare section stems, base
ightly hammered, 25.5cm
10in), *L 16 May,*
7,700 ($12,243)

\ Liberty & Co. 'Cymric'
ilver frame, designed by
\rchibald Knox, 1902,
Birmingham, the edges set
vith tiny cabochon
urquoises and pearls,
9cm (7½in), *L 16 May,*
2,970 ($4,722)

8
A set of six Liberty & Co. silver and enamel coffee spoons *(three illustrated)*, **with matching sugar tongs,** 1930, Birmingham, the finials detailed in blue and green enamel, 11cm (4¼in), *L 19 Dec,*
£770 ($1,078)

9
An Omar Ramsden silver-mounted mazer, 1928, London, with raised foot, the silver rim cast with fleur-de-lis design, 21.5cm (8½in), *L 16 May,*
£1,210 ($1,924)

10
A pair of silvered-bronze candelabra, *(one illustrated)*, designed by Georges de Feure, c.1900, each with three floriform candle holders, 34cm (13½in), *NY 6 Dec,*
$4,950 (£3,461)

11
A Hugo Leven electro-plated bowl, c.1900, the bowl cast on each side with the head of a young woman with long hair, 29.5cm (11¾in), *L 16 May,*
£572 ($909)

12
A silver and tortoiseshell caviar knife, c.1900, designed by Henry van de Velde, 19cm (7½in), *M 19 Oct,*
FF 16,650 (£1,790; $2,506)

1

2

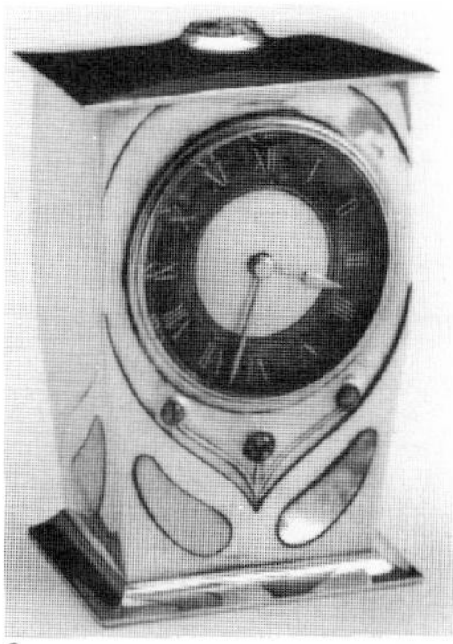
3

4

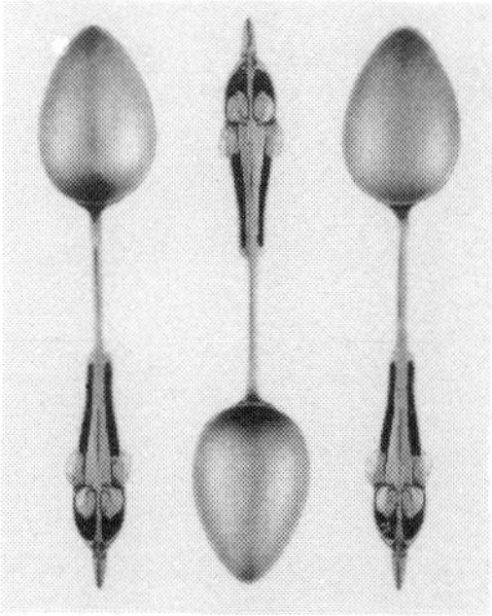
5

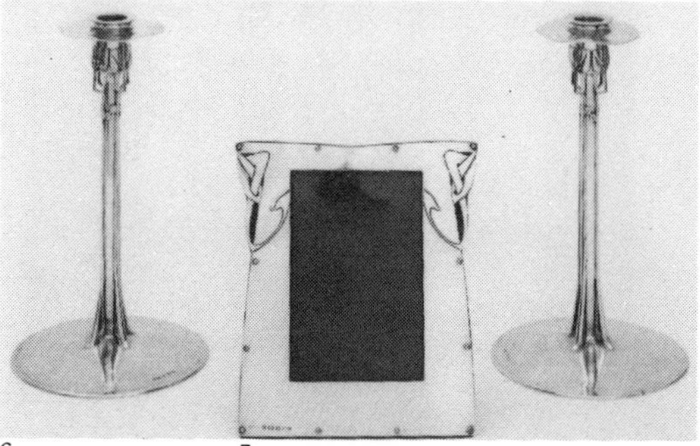
6 7

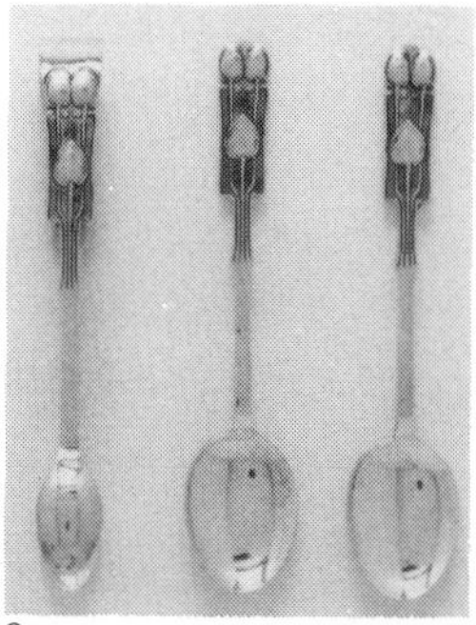
8

9

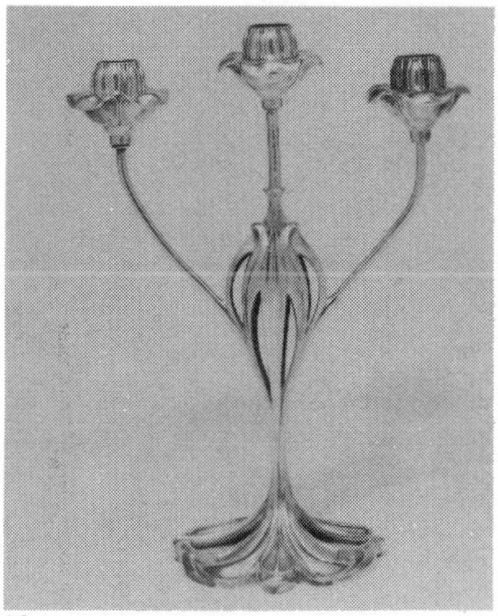
10

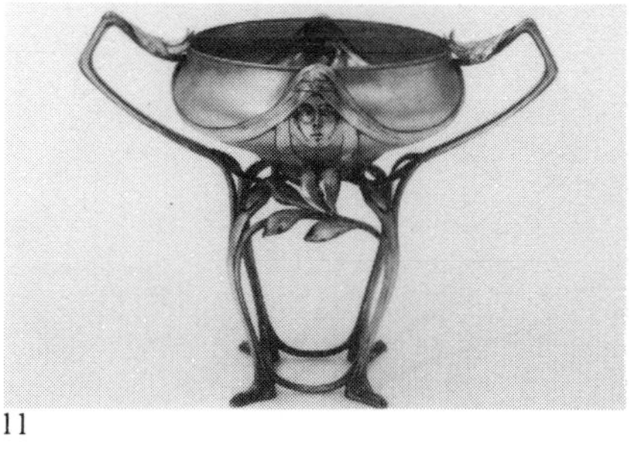
11

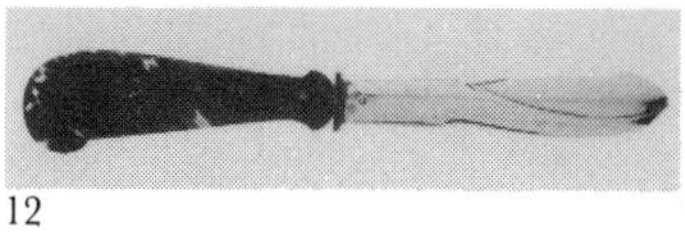
12

1

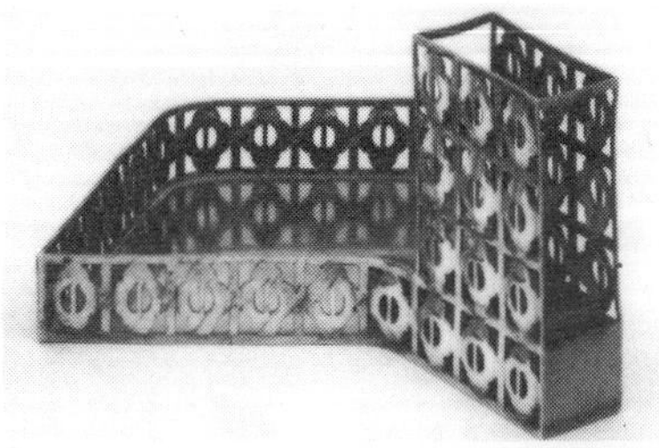
2

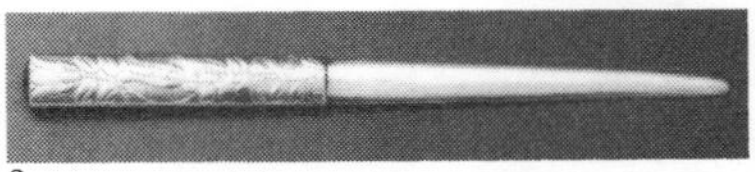
3

4

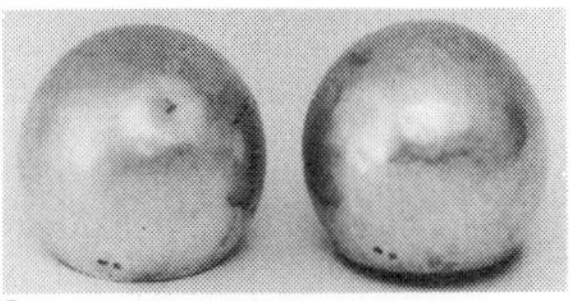
5

6

7

8

9

10

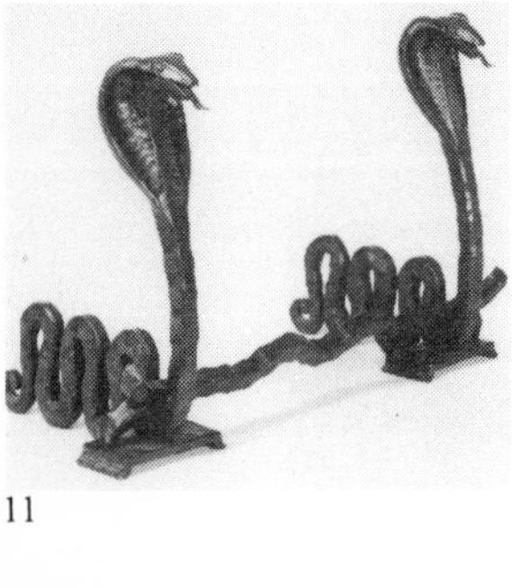
11

12

13

1
Three pieces of Wiener Werkstätte silver cutlery, designed by Josef Hoffmann, 1903-04, 24cm (9½in) max., *M 13 Apr,*
FF 94,350 (£8,283; $12,839)

2
A Wiener Werkstätte electroplated smoker's companion, designed by Josef Hoffmann, c.1905, the shallow ashtray with a matchbox holder mounted at the side, 7cm (2¾in) high, *L 16 May,*
£605 ($962)

3
A Wiener Werkstätte silver and lapis lazuli letter opener, attributed to Carl Otto Czeschka, c.1910, 18.5cm (7¼in), *NY 11 Oct,*
$2,750 (£1,923)

4
A Wiener Werkstätte silver basket, probably designed by Josef Hoffmann, c.1905, 900 standard, with original glass liner, 26.5cm (10¼in), *NY 11 Oct,*
$3,850 (£2,692)

5
Two Wiener Werkstätte bottle tops, designed by Josef Hoffmann, c.1905, each hammered spherical, one with central cork, silver coloured metal, 5cm (2in) diam., *L 19 Dec,*
£220 ($308)

6
A Wiener Werkstätte footed bowl, designed by Dagobert Peche, c.1920, 900 standard, 30.5cm (12in), *NY 20 June,*
$11,000 (£7,382)

7
A Wiener Werkstätte hammered brass vase, designed by Josef Hoffmann, c.1920, 18cm (7in), *NY 20 June,*
$1,540 (£1,033)

8
An Edgar Brandt wrought-iron fire-screen, c.1925, wrought with leafy branches and central fountain, 126cm (49½in) wide, *NY 6 Dec,*
$7,975 (£5,577)

9
An Edgar Brandt wrought-iron fire-screen c.1925, with central motif of birds within a nest, exhibited at the Paris 1925 International Exhibition, 105cm (41¼in) high, *L 19 Dec,*
£7,700 ($10,780)

10
An Edgar Brandt wrought-iron and alabaster double wall light, 1920s, the central 'basket' wrought with stylised flowers and wickerwork, 50cm (19¾in) wide, *L 16 May,*
£1,870 ($2,973)

11
A pair of Edgar Brandt wrought-iron fire-irons, in the form of cobras, c.1925, black patina, 104cm (41in) wide, *M 19 Oct,*
FF 333,000 (£35,806; $50,128)

12
An Edgar Brandt wrought-iron mirror, c.1925, decorated with Leda and the swan in light relief, 59.5cm (23½in), *M 13 Apr,*
FF 21,090 (£1,852; $2,870)

13
A Jean Dunand pewter vase, c.1910, in the form of an acorn, hammered surface, 16cm (6¼in), *M 13 Apr,*
FF 8,880 (£780; $1,208)

. Jean Dunand lacquer-n-copper vase, c.1925, acquered in rust and ubergine, 14cm (5½in), *Y 6 Dec,*
1,320 (£923)

. pair of Jean Puiforcat ilver and silver-gilt andelabra, c.1935, 14cm 5½in), *M 19 Oct,*
'F 44,400 (£4,774; 6,684)

. Jean Dunand lacquered netal covered box, .1930, decorated with ggshell lacquer triangles gainst a Chinese red round, minor losses, 7cm (6¾in) diam., *Y 6 Dec,*
3,410 (£2,384)

. Jean Puiforcat parcel-ilt bowl, c.1925, on ircular ring base with ight gilt ball supports, 2.5cm (5in) high, *'Y 6 Dec,*
2,750 (£1,923)

. Jean Puiforcat vase, .1930, with four raised ertical ribs, wooden base, lver coloured metal, naker's mark of Emile 'uiforcat, 13cm (5in), *19 Dec,*
858 ($1,201)

. Cartier silver desk set, .1935, comprising nkwell/clock, blotter, note ook and large box, all vith gold monogrammed laques, black onyx clasps, nkwell 24.5cm (9¾in), *1 13 Apr,*
'F 35,520 (£3,118; 4,834)

. Cardeilhac silver ocktail shaker, c.1930, ngraved with figures laying various sports, 1.5cm (8½in), *M 13 Apr,*
'F 11,655 (£1,023; 1,586)

. Jean Puiforcat silver overed box, c.1925, the entre applied with a rec-angular bar and half-rod ory handle, 20cm (8in) iam., *NY 20 June,*
4,675 (£3,137)

9
A Ronson metal and chrome cigarette container and lighter, c.1925, in the shape of a bar with a Caribbean bartender, 17.5cm (7in) high, *A 14 Oct,*
Dfl 1,840 (£575; $862)

10
A silver and ivory tea set, 1935, comprising four pieces, each of oval form, maker's marks *F & S,* Sheffield, water jug 20cm (8in) high, *L 16 May,*
£495 ($787)

11
A Zeppelin cocktail shaker, c.1935, comprising a bottle and cork, shaker, five mugs, corkscrew and two spoons, stamped *Germany,* 30.5cm (12in), *M 13 Apr,*
FF 8,658 (£760; $1,178)

12
A Christofle 'Como' plated tea service, designed by Lino Sabattini, 1960, water jug 21.5cm (8½in), *M 13 Apr,*
FF 44,400 (£3,898; $6,042)

1

2

3

4

5

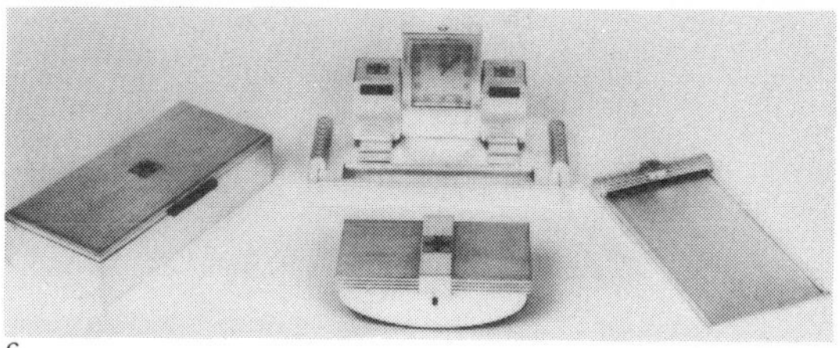
6

7

8

9

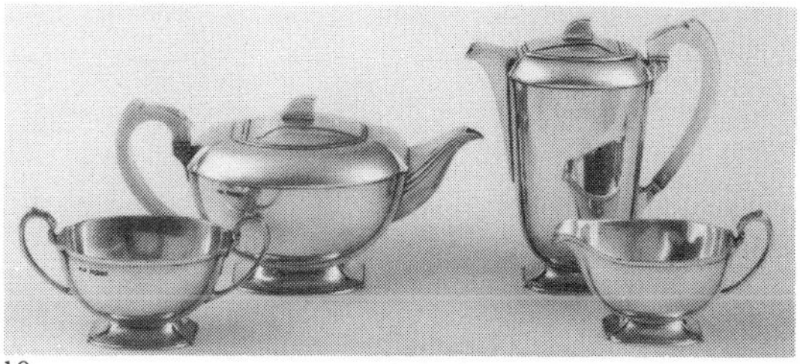
10

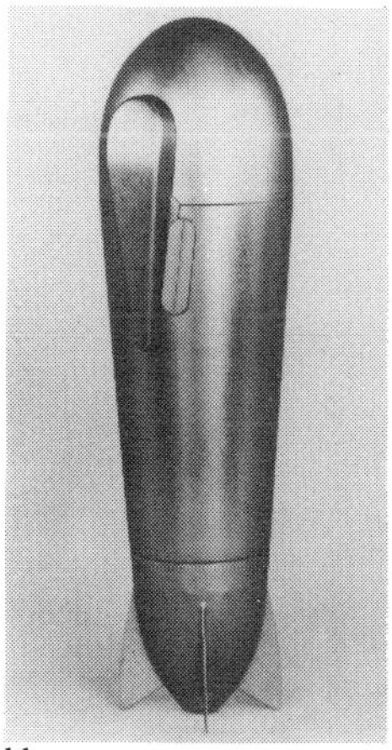
11

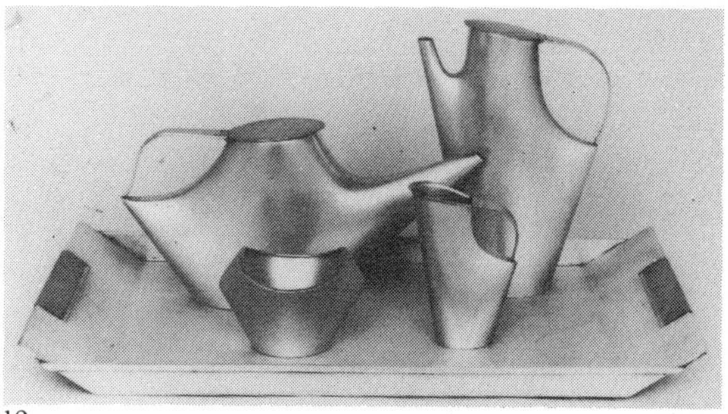
12

1

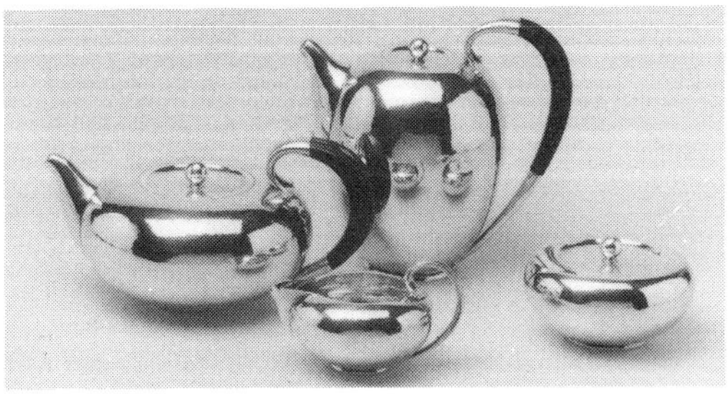
2

3

4

5

6

7

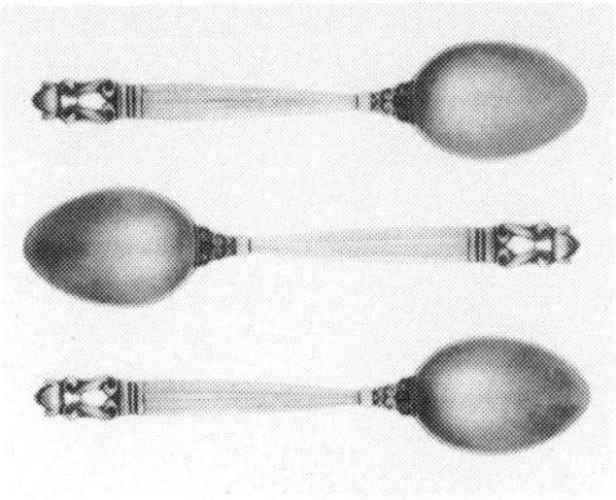
8

9

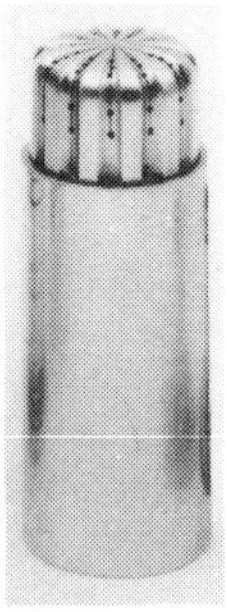
10

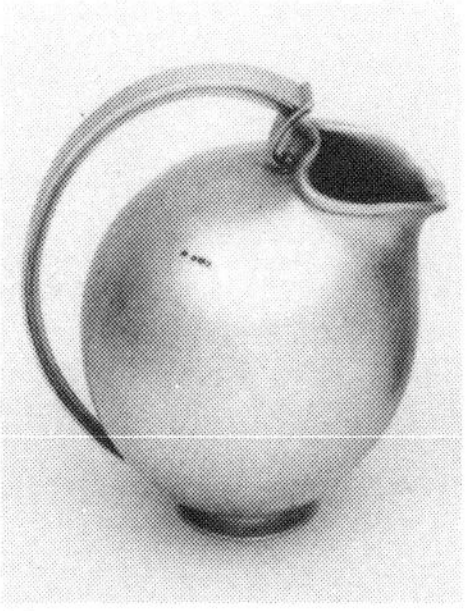
11

12

13

14

1
A Georg Jensen silver footed bowl, designed by Johan Rohde, hammered surface, 13.5cm (5½in), *NY 20 June,*
$605 (£406)

2
A Georg Jensen silver four-piece teaset, designed by Johan Rohde c.1930, post 1945, slightly hammered finish, detachable dished covers, water jug 17cm (6¾in), *JHB 22 Oct,*
R 8,000 (£2,500; $3,500)

3
A Georg Jensen silver covered tureen, c.1945-51, designed by Georg Jensen, circular, with grape bunch handles and finial, 24cm (9½in), *NY 6 Dec,*
$4,675 (£3,269)

4
A Georg Jensen silver covered tureen, designed by Georg Jensen, oval, with grape bunch handles and finial, 26.5cm (10½in), *NY 20 June,*
$3,025 (£2,030)

5
A Georg Jensen silver and ebony jug, designed by Johan Rohde, hammered surface, 22.5cm (8¾in), *NY 6 Dec,*
$1,320 (£923)

6
A Georg Jensen two-handled silver bowl, c.1930, designed by Gustav Pedersen, on ring foot, 40cm (15¾in), *NY 20 June,*
$1,320 (£886)

7
A pair of Georg Jensen two-light candelabra, *(one illustrated)*, designed by Harald Nielsen, slightly hammered surface, 15.5cm (6in), *NY 6 Dec,*
$2,200 (£1,538)

8
A set of twelve Georg Jensen silver teaspoons, *(part illustrated)*, 1938, 'Acorn' pattern, 13cm (5in), *L 16 May,*
£385 ($612)

9
A Georg Jensen silver ewer, c.1950, designed by Henning Koppel, 35cm (13¾in), *NY 20 June,*
$15,950 (£10,705)

10
A Georg Jensen sugar shaker, designed by Sigvard Bernardotte, c.1960, silver coloured metal, 12.5cm (5in), *L 19 Dec,*
£264 ($370)

11
A Georg Jensen silver ju designed by Harald Nielsen, 1930, hammered surface, 15cm (6in), *L 16 May,*
£462 ($734)

12
Georg Jensen table silve *(part illustrated)*, designed by Harald Nielsen, in the 'Pyramid' pattern, comprising 87 pieces, *NY 20 June,*
$5,500 (£3,691)

13
Georg Jensen table silve *(part illustrated)*, designed by Harald Nielsen, in the 'Pyramid' pattern, comprising 194 pieces, *NY 6 Dec,*
$12,100 (£8,461)

14
Georg Jensen table silve *(part illustrated)*, designed by Sigvard Bernadotte in 1939, 'Bernadotte' pattern, comprising 190 pieces, *M 13 Apr,*
FF 88,800 (£7,796; $12,084)

. Raniery pewter clock, .1900, signed, 57.5cm 22¾in), *L 16 May,* **374 ($595)**

. Lalique moulded char-oal glass figural clock, .1932, Le Jour et La Nuit, n a bronze truncated yramidal base, acid tched *R. Lalique*, 37.5cm 14¾in), *NY 20 June,* **12,650 (£8,490)**

black marble, brass and namel clock, c.1925, narked *La Gerbe D'Or,* 2.5cm (36in), *L 19 Dec,* **528 ($739)**

chrome mantel clock, .1930, 14cm (5½in), *9 Sept,* **176 ($264)**

n amber glass and hromium-plated mantel imepiece, c.1930, signed *Jarrard-Le Coultre,* 12cm 4¾in), *C 9 Sept,* **83 ($124)**

Boris Lacroix nickel-lated and glass lamp, .1930, 60cm (23½in) liam., *M 13 Apr,* **F 13,320 (£1,169; 1,813)**

7
German copper clock, .1900, with Arabic umerals, inscribed, 43cm 17in), *NY 6 Dec,* **$825 (£576)**

8
A Viennese inlaid-walnut wall clock, c.1900, in various woods, the dial signed *Joh. Puhm./Wien,* 85.5cm (32in), *NY 11 Oct,* **$2,530 (£1,769)**

9
A mottled glass and wrought iron lamp, 20th century, probably French, in mottled grey and orange, 44.5cm (17½in), *NY 19 June,* **$770 (£517)**

10
A Pertzel electroplated table lamp, c.1930, base with facsimile signature, 46.5cm (18¼in), *L 19 Dec,* **£825 ($1,155)**

11
A Bauhaus electroplated table lamp, 1929, designed by Christian Dell, the shade marked *Kaiser Original idell,* 43.5cm (17in), *L 19 Dec,* **£165 ($231)**

12
A carved fruitwood long-case clock, c.1900, French, incomplete works, 234cm (7ft 8in), *NY 20 June,* **$2,860 (£1,919)**

13
A nickel-plated, glass and leather lamp, c.1935, attributed to Jacques Adnet, 41cm (16in), *M 13 Apr,* **FF 4,995 (£438; $680)**

14
A Modernist carpet, c.1930, in blue, dark brown and cream, 210 x 120cm (83 x 47in), *M 19 Oct,* **FF 12,210 (£1,313; $1,838)**

1

2

3

4

5

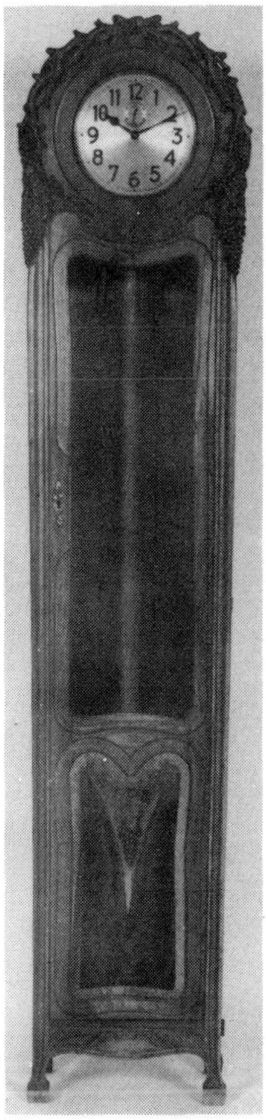

6

7

8

9

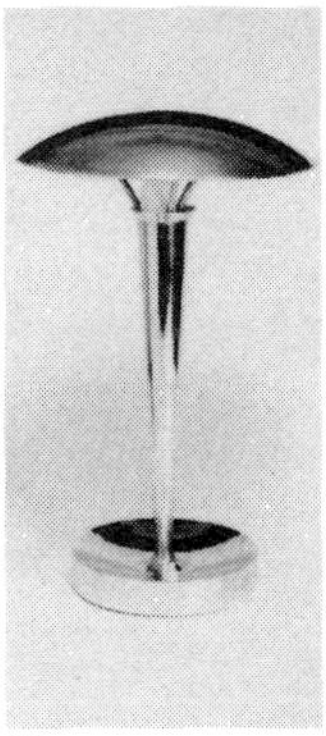
10

11

12

13

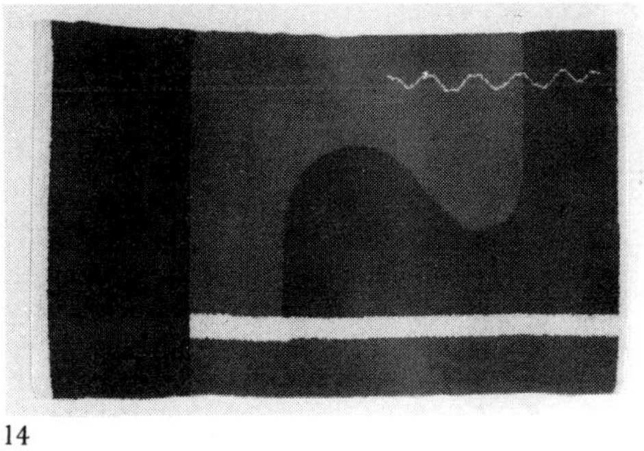
14

1

2

3

4

5

6

7

8

9

1
A Gothic octagonal table 1880s, marble top on brass-studded column, 74.5cm (29½in), *L 16 May,* **£297 ($472)**

2
A walnut sideboard, c.1905, with embossed copper mounts, 190cm (6ft 2¾in), *S 16 July,* **£418 ($656)**

3
A Gothic part bedroom suite 1880s, comprising dressing table and wardrobe, with inlaid floral panels, dressing table 157cm (61¾in) wide. *L 16 May,* **£770 ($1,224)**

4
A mahogany occasional table, c.1880, designed by E. W. Godwin, 65.5cm (25¾in), *L 16 May,* **£396 ($630)**

5
A Liberty and Co. inlaid mahogany 'Thebes' stool 1890s, leather upholstery, 43.5cm (17in), *L 16 May,* **£935 ($1,487)**

6
A painted and leaded glass screen, c.1905-10, painted in the manner of Walter Crane, 204cm (80½in), *L 19 Dec,* **£660 ($924)**

7
An Aesthetic Movement painted and leaded glass screen, c.1880, red glass edges, black painted wood surround, 86cm (34in), *L 19 Dec,* **£330 ($462)**

8
An oak and leaded glass writing cabinet, c.1903, designed by E. A. Taylor, manufactured by Wylie and Lockhead, inset with white and purple leaded glass, silvered metal handles over green leather, 47.5cm (18¾in) wide, *L 19 Dec,* **£9,130 ($12,782)**

9
An oak cabinet, dated 1905, stamped *WDML,* 107cm (42in), *S 16 July,* **£176 ($276)**

. green stained oak edroom suite, *(part illus-ated)*, c.1900, comprising dressing chest, ward-obe, lead-glazed cup-oard, pedestal cupboard nd washstand, applied nroughout with cop-ered bands, *C 9 Sept,* **352 ($528)**

display cabinet, c.1930, vith moulded cornice bove an oak frieze, 68cm (66in), *C 9 Sept,* **297 ($446)**

Robson and Sons Ltd nahogany cabinet, .1905, inlaid with various voods and mother-of-earl, applied with beaten ilvered metal strap inges, affixed label, 21cm (47¾in) high, *19 Dec,* **1,375 ($1,925)**

Guild of Handicraft Ltd ak table, c.1900, feet with ilt detailing, stamped, nonogrammed *JF*, 71cm 28in) high, *L 16 May,* **2,860 ($4,547)**

William Birch oak rmchair, c.1905, lesigned by E. G. Punnett, ush seat, 85.5cm (33¾in), *16 May,* **715 ($1,137)**

6
An oak dressing mirror, 930s, herringbone parquetry surround, 47cm 18½in), *S 19 Mar,* **£165 ($252)**

7
An Art Deco armchair, 1920s, upholstered in textured cream fabric piped with yellow, 104.5cm (41in) high, *L 16 May,* **£1,430 ($2,274)**

8
An Arts and Craft dining room suite, *(part illustrated)* c.1900, comprising table, sideboard and four chairs, inlaid ebony dots, table 76cm (30in) high, *L 19 Dec,* **£748 ($1,047)**

9
A Gustav Stickley oak settle, c.1910, re-upholstered in blue velvet, red decal mark, 73cm (28¾in) high, *NY 19 June,* **$5,500 (£3,691)**

10
A Gustav Stickley oak centre table, c.1910, top upholstered in brown with studded edges, red decal mark, 77.5cm (30½in) high, *NY 19 June,* **$7,700 (£5,168)**

11
A Hille salon suite, *(part illustrated)*, 1930s, comprising settee, two armchairs, two upright chairs and occasional table, in ebonised wood, upholstered in red brocade, table 60cm (23½in) high, *L 16 May,* **£3,410 ($5,422)**

1

2

3

4

5

6

7

8

9

10

11

1

2

3

4

5

6

7

8

1
A Heal's oak dining room suite, *(part illustrated)*, c.1930, comprising table, four chairs and fireside chair, sold with sideboard and corner cupboard, *L 19 Dec,*
£1,100 ($1,540)

2
A Heal's limed oak tub chair, 1930s, original patterned cut velvet, 76.5cm (30¼in), *S 19 Mar,*
£253 ($387)

3
A Heal's limed oak part bedroom suite, 1920s, comprising a dressing table and two wardrobes; sold with a 1930s dressing table *(illustrated)*, *L 16 May,*
£660 ($1,049)

4
A Gordon Russell bedroom suite, *(part illustrated)*, c.1935, comprising wardrobe, chest of drawers, dressing table and stool, double bed-end, in Japanese chestnut, banded with walnut inlay, wardrobe 189cm (6ft 2½in) high, *L 19 Dec,*
£462 ($647)

5
A Gordon Russell desk and chair, c.1935, in rosewood and waxed elm, banded walnut, rocking chair in tan leather, desk 74.5cm (29¼in) high, *L 19 Dec,*
£1,760 ($2,464)

6
A Hille cocktail cabinet, 1930s, ebonised panels, 152.5cm (60in), *L 16 May,*
£1,430 ($2,274)

7
A Modernist side table, 1930s, veneered in zebra wood, steel handles, 74.5cm (29¼in), *L 16 May,*
£990 ($1,574)

8
A Hille dining room suite, *(part illustrated)*, 1930s, comprising table, eight chairs, two sideboards and three cabinets, walnut and zebra wood veneer, table 103cm (40½in) wide, *L 16 May,*
£2,860 ($4,547)

1
A Bugatti chair, c.1900, vellum covered, inlaid with pewter, applied with beaten brass strips, silk fringes, 124cm (48¾in), *L 19 dec,*
£1,650 ($2,310)

2
A Bugatti stool, c.1900, applied with beaten brass strips, inlaid with pewter, red velvet, 42.5cm (16¾in), *L 16 May,*
£660 ($1,049)

3
A Bugatti side chair, c.1900, 100cm (39½in), *L 16 May,*
£2,090 ($3,323)

4
A Bugatti selette, c.1900, vellum covered, applied with strips and medallions of beaten copper, inlaid with pewter, 111cm (43¾in), *L 16 May,*
£1,870 ($2,973)

5
A set of four side chairs, *(one illustrated)*, c.1905, designed and manufactured by Vittorio Valabrega, 87cm (34¼in), *L 16 May,*
£1,430 ($2,274)

6
A two-tier table, c.1905, designed and manufactured by Vittorio Valabrega, indented oval top, 74cm (29in) high, *L 16 May,*
£1,100 ($1,749)

7
A pair of armchairs, *(one illustrated)*, designed and manufactured by Vittorio Valabrega, in sycamore, upholstered in silver/grey watered silk, 104cm (41in), *L 16 May,*
£1,760 ($2,798)

8
A white-painted and ebonised-wood bedroom suite, c.1911, designed by Robert Oerley, comprising four pieces *(three illustrated)*, dressing table 144cm (56½in), *NY 11 Oct,*
$7,700 (£5,385)

9
A white-painted and ebonised-wood flower stand, c.1905-08, designed by Robert Oerley, 79cm (31in) high, *NY 11 Oct,*
$2,310 (£1,615)

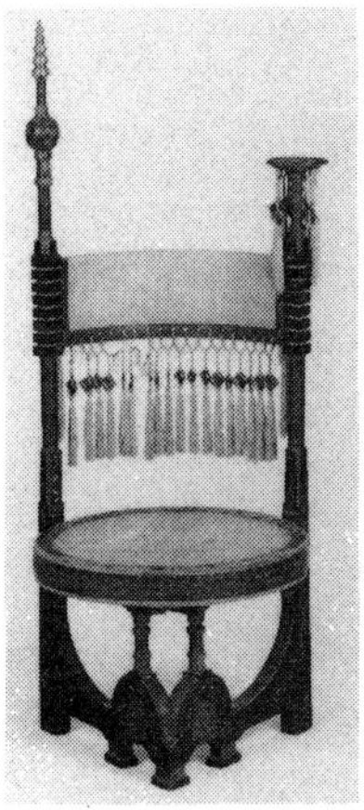
1

2

3 4

5 6 7

8

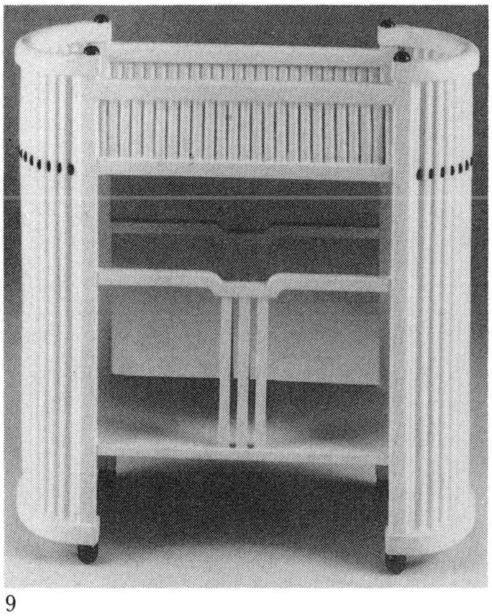
9

1

2

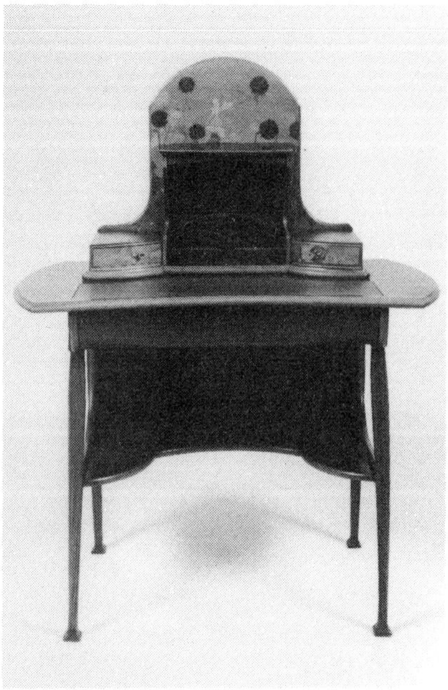
4

3

5

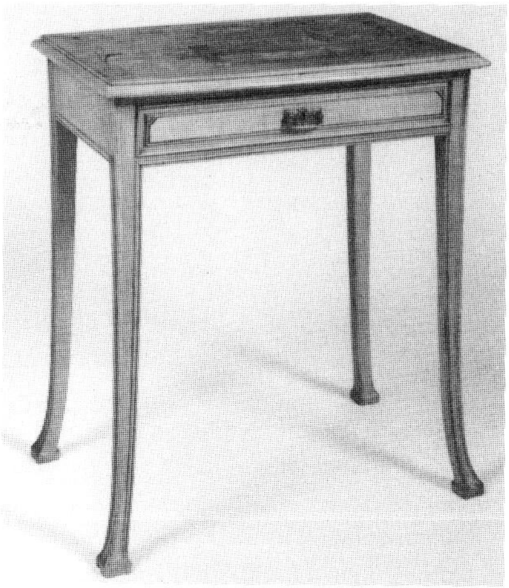
6

7

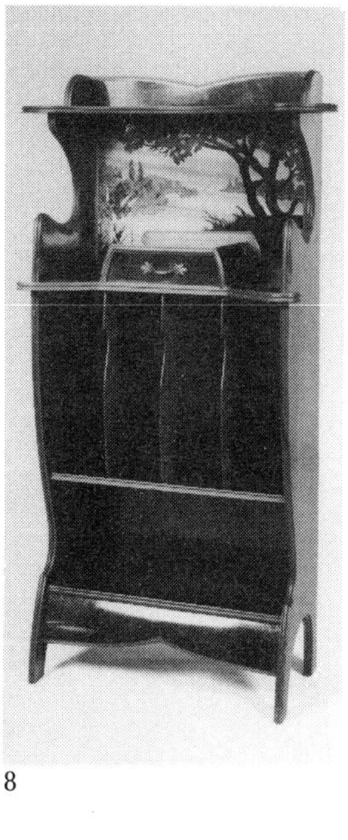
8

9

1
A Gallé fruitwood marquetry table, c.1900, 75cm (29½in) high, *NY 20 June,*
$4,125 (£2,768)

2
A Gallé fruitwood marquetry revolving library table, c.1900, 85cm (33½in) high, *M 13 Apr,*
FF 10,545 (£926; $1,435)

3
A Gallé fruitwood marquetry tray, c.1915, decorated with silhouettes of soldiers, 69cm (27in) long, *M 19 Oct,*
FF 11,100 (£1,194; $1,671)

4
A Gallé fruitwood marquetry desk, c.1900, 128cm (50¼in) high, *NY 20 June,*
$3,300 (£2,215)

5
A pair of Majorelle fruitwood night tables, *(one illustrated)*, c.1900, 115cm (45½in) high, *NY 20 June,*
$1,980 (£1,329)

6
A Majorelle fruitwood marquetry table, c.1900, the top inlaid with bunches of tulip blossoms, 77cm (30½in) high, *NY 20 June,*
$2,750 (£1,846)

7
A Majorelle mahogany and gilt-bronze chair, c.1900, the back with bronze mounts in the form of water-lily branches, flowers and leaves, the *sabot* bronze feet in the form of water-lily leaves, 93cm (36½in), *M 19 Oct,*
FF 83,250 (£8,952; $12,532)

8
A Majorelle mahogany and fruitwood marquetry music stand, c.1900, the rear panel inlaid with a view of a boat on a lake, 143cm (56¼in) high, *NY 6 Dec,*
$3,080 (£2,153)

9
A Majorelle dressing table, c.1900, 178cm (70in) high, *L 16 May,*
£2,530 ($4,023)

1
A pair of Majorelle fruit-wood side chairs, *(one illustrated)*, c.1900, the back of each carved in relief with poppy blossoms and buds, *NY 20 June*,
$1,870 (£1,255)

2
A Chareau mahogany library table, c.1925-30, with oval base, 51cm (20in) high, *M 13 Apr*,
FF 55,500 (£4,873; $7,553)

3
A nest of wooden tables, c.1930, composed of black painted X section and four fitting tables in light wood, 66cm (26in) high, *M 13 Apr*,
FF 6,105 (£536; $831)

4
A Chareau iron smoker's side table, c.1930, 64.5cm (25½in) high, *M 13 Apr*,
FF 61,050 (£5,360; $8,308)

5
A Majorelle 'Chicorée' buffet, c.1900, the upright supports carved with leaves, 240cm (7ft 10½in), *L 19 Dec*,
£4,950 ($6,930)

6
A French Modernist dressing table, c.1930, burr veneered, 136cm (53½in) high, *L 16 May*,
£715 ($1,137)

7
A pair of Leleu amboyna and marble night tables, 56cm (22in) high, *NY 6 Dec*,
$4,675 (£3,269)

8
A pair of Chareau rose-wood armchairs, pre-1928, upholstered in yellow, 79cm (31in) high, *M 19 Oct*,
FF 160,950 (£17,306; $24,229)

9
A pair of French rose-wood armchairs, *(one illustrated)*, upholstered in black brocade, *NY 19 June*,
$1,430 (£960)

1

2

3

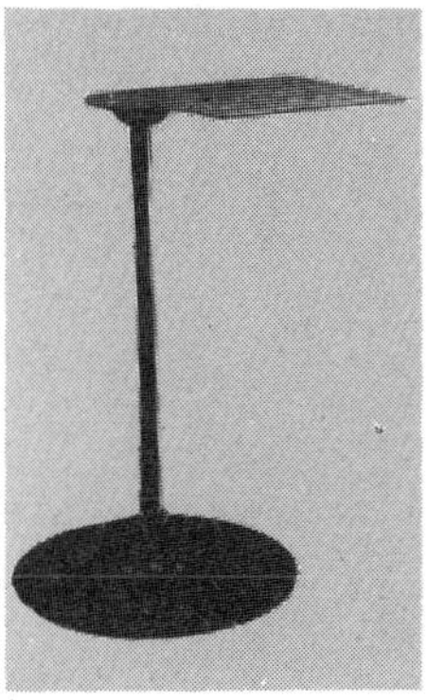
4

5

6

7

8

9

1

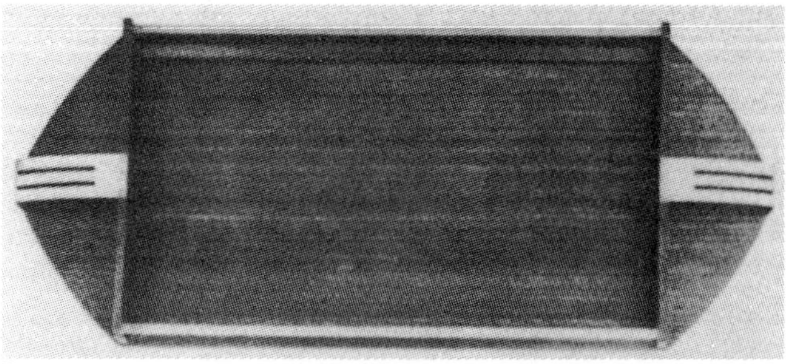
2

3

4

5

6

7

8

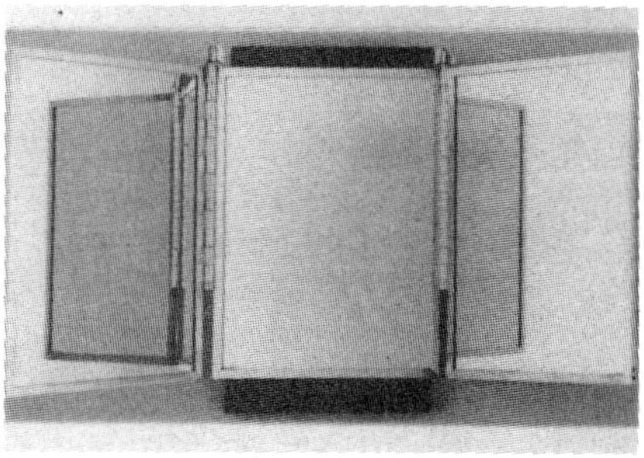
9

1
A pair of oak and copper book-ends, Serrurier-Bovy, c.1903, 54cm (21in), *M 19 Oct,*
FF 11,100 (£1,194; $1,671)

2
A wooden and copper tray, Serrurier-Bovy, c.1905, 72cm (28¼in), *M 13 Apr,*
FF 6,660 (£585; $906)

3
A rosewood and leather chair, Emile-Jacques Ruhlmann, c.1925-30, 64cm (25in), *M 19 Oct,*
FF 19,980 (£2,148; $3,008)

4
A violetwood low table, Lambiotte: designed by Emile-Jacques Ruhlmann, c.1927, the support applied on each side with ivory-edged panels, 84cm (33in) long, *NY 6 Dec,*
$23,100 (£16,153)

5
An ebony and ivory low table, Emile-Jacques Ruhlmann, c.1920-22, 80cm (31½in) diam., *M 19 Oct,*
FF 244,200 (£26,258; $36,761)

6
A rosewood low table, 'Colonette', Emile-Jacques Ruhlmann, c.1920, the top and supports inlaid with ivory, 68cm (26¾in) diam., *NY 6 Dec,*
$16,500 (£11,538)

7
A rosewood and ivory low table, in the style of Ruhlmann, c.1925, 83cm (32¾in) diam., *M 13 Apr,*
FF 32,190 (£2,826; $4,380)

8
An ebonised-wood and silvered-chrome dressing table mirror, Emile-Jacques Ruhlmann, c.1912, 34.5cm (13½in) high, *NY 6 Dec,*
$5,500 (£3,846)

9
An ebony and silvered-metal cheval-glass, Emile-Jacques Ruhlmann, c.1925-30, 79cm (31in) long, *M 13 Apr,*
FF 49,950 (£4,385; $6,797)

1
A sycamore, ebonised-wood and chrome cheval-glass, René Prou, c.1925, 140cm (55in) high, *NY 6 Dec,* **$3,025 (£2,115)**

2
A wrought-iron and marble dining table, Raymond Subes, c.1930, 194cm (6ft 4¼in) long, *NY 6 Dec,* **$9,900 (£6,923)**

3
A set of six Dominique dining chairs, *(one illustrated),* c.1930, upholstered in cream textured velvet, 85cm (33½in) high, *L 16 May,* **£1,430 ($2,274)**

4
A silvered-bronze and glass table mirror, probably French, c.1930, 51.5cm (20¼in) high, *NY 20 June,* **$8,800 (£5,906)**

5
An oak, metal and leather desk and two armchairs, *(part illustrated),* attributed to Jacques Adnet and Hermès, c.1950, desk 158cm (62in) long, *M 13 Apr,* **FF 21,090 (£1,852; $2,870)**

6
A metal and leather rocking chair, attributed to Jacques Adnet and Hermès, c.1935, 86cm (34in), *M 13 Apr,* **FF 6,660 (£585; $906)**

7
A nickelled tubular metal cheval-glass, Louis Sognot, c.1930, 180cm (71in), *M 13 Apr,* **FF 8,880 (£780; $1,208)**

8
A chrome metal and lacquered wood dressing table, attributed to Jacques Adnet, c.1930, 124cm (48¾in) high, *M 13 Apr,* **FF 6,438 (£565; $876)**

9
A lacquered table, c.1935, in red-brown lacquer with bands simulating ivory, 91cm (36in) wide, *M 13 Apr,* **FF 32,190 (£2,826; $4,380)**

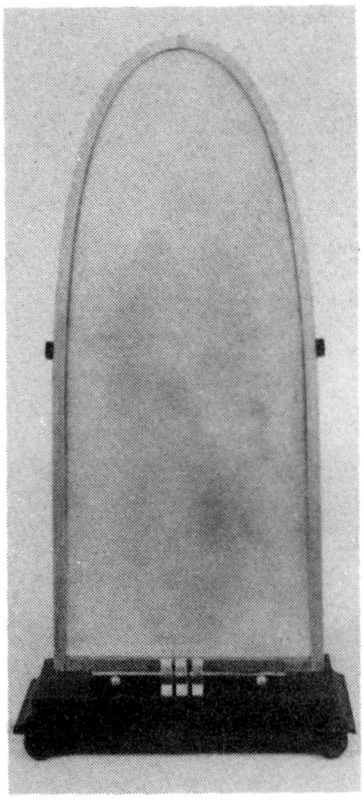
1

2

3

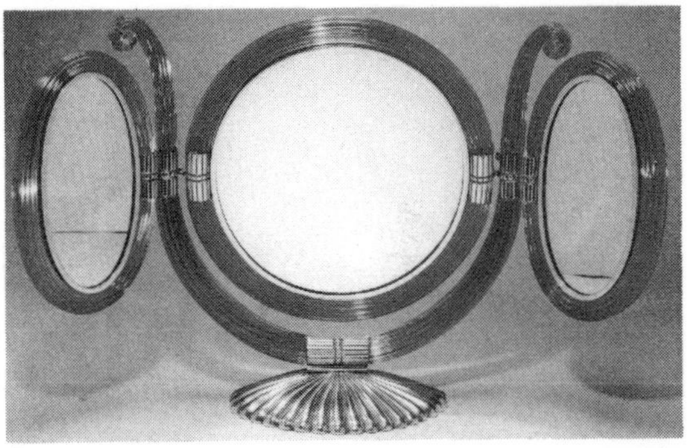
4

5

6

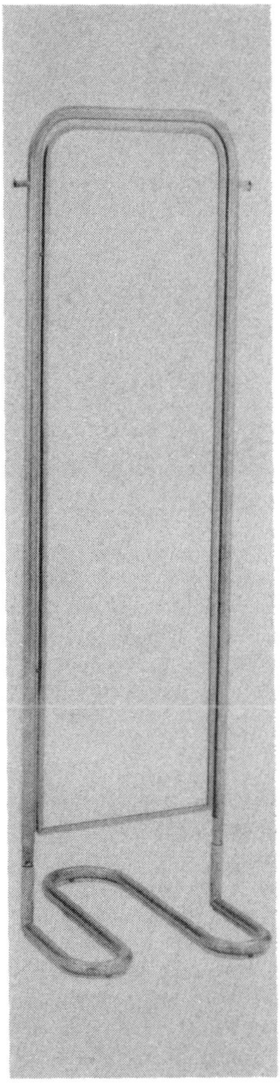
7

8

9

1

2

3

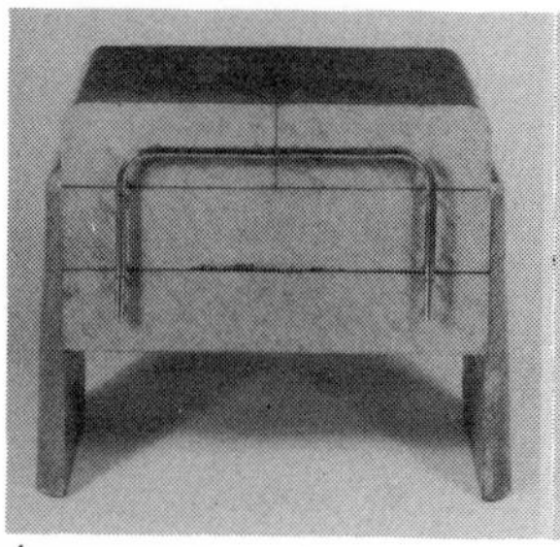

4

5

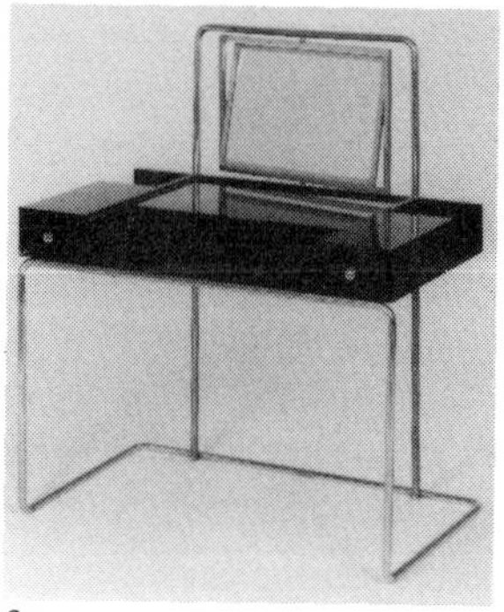
6

7

8

9

1
A leather upholstered three-piece suite, *(part illustrated)*, 1930s, comprising sofa and two matching chairs, upholstered in cream leather, 80cm (31½in) high, *L 16 May,*
£528 ($839)

2
A leather upholstered three-piece suite, comprising sofa *(illustrated)* and two matching chairs, upholstered in green leather, 83cm (32¾in), *L 19 Dec,*
£1,540 ($2,156)

3
A nest of three walnut-veneered Modernist side tables, 1930s, the tops banded in satinwood, the largest 59.5cm (23½in) high, *L 19 Dec,*
£308 ($431)

4
A Modernist bedroom suite, 1930s, comprising dressing table, chest of drawers *(illustrated)*, wardrobe and a pair of bedside cabinets, in burred blond wood with chromed tubular handles, dressing table 137cm (54in) high , *L 16 May,*
£1,650 ($2,623)

5
A 'Sureline' cocktail cabinet, 1950s, semi-circular, the top with sliding fluted doors, the lighted interior with mirror panels decorated with a cocktail theme, 140cm (55in), *S 16 July,*
£88 ($138)

6
A Modernist dressing table, 1930s, black stained wood, chromed tubular steel frame, and recessed compartment set in the top with glass sliding cover, 99.5cm (39¼in) wide, *L 16 May,*
£396 ($630)

7
A pair of Modernist side units, *(one illustrated)*, the central cupboard with steel handles, 163cm (64in) wide, *L 16 May,*
£550 ($874)

8
A Modernist desk, 1930s, in dark stained wood mounted on a large chromed tubular steel framework, 157cm (61¾in) wide, with cantilever armchair, *L 16 May,*
£990 ($1,574)

9
A cocktail cabinet, 1930s, dark veneered, with a semi-circular central shelf and fitted cabinet above to receive bottles and glasses, lower shelf-lined cabinet, 160cm (63in) high, *L 16 May,*
£605 ($962)

1
A Leleu circular coffee table, c.1930, burr veneered, glass top, 48.5cm (19in) high, *L 19 Dec,*
£1,430 ($2,002)

2
Two fruitwood armchairs, *(one illustrated),* c.1930, designed by Paul Frankl, *NY 20 June,*
$2,750 (£1,846)

3
A chest of drawers, c.1935, designed by Guglielmo Ulrich, in vellum and black lacquer, 82cm (32in), *M 13 Apr,*
FF 27,750 (£2,436; $3,776)

4
A set of four tubular metal chairs, *(one illustrated),* c.1930-35, designed by Robert Mallet-Stevens, upholstered in black leather, 82.5cm (32½in), *M 19 Oct,*
FF 12,765; (£1,373; $1,922)

5
A pair of Finmar Ltd plywood armchairs, *(one illustrated),* 1930s, designed by Alvar Aalto, pink-orange painted seats, Finmar labels, 83cm (32½in), *L 19 Dec,*
£5,720 ($8,008)

6
An Isokon laminated plywood chaise longue, 1935/6, designed by Marcel Breuer, grey wool upholstery, 80cm (31½in), *L 16 May,*
£990 ($1,574)

7
A dining table and four chairs, 1930s, designed by Alvar Aalto, table with central 'lazy Susan', table 126cm (49¾in) diam., *L 16 May,*
£1,210 ($1,924)

8
A pair of chrome and leather 'Barcelona' side chairs, *(one illustrated),* designed by Ludwig Mies van der Rohe for the 1929 Barcelona Exhibition, retailed by Knoll Associates Inc., 1967, upholstered in olive leather, *NY 19 June,*
$1,870 (£1,255)

9
A parquetry and leatherette low table, c.1941, designed by Gilbert Rohde for Herman Miller, covered in pale green synthetic leather, stamped, height 39cm (15½in), *NY 19 June,*
$880 (£591)

10
A pair of armchairs, designed by Joe Colombo for Kartell, 1963-65, *Mil 12 Mar,*
L 3,080,000 (£1,294; $1,993)

11
A plywood coffee table, c.1950, designed by Charles Eames, covered in black formica, 174cm (68¾ in), *S 19 Mar,*
£286 ($438)

1

2

3

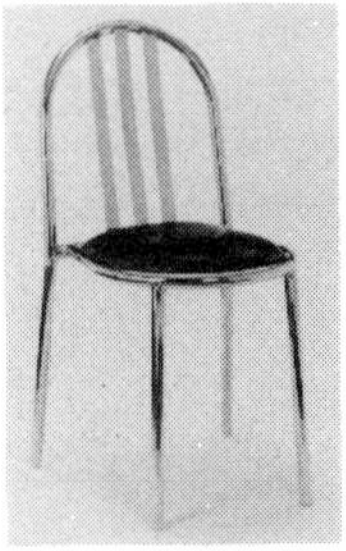
4

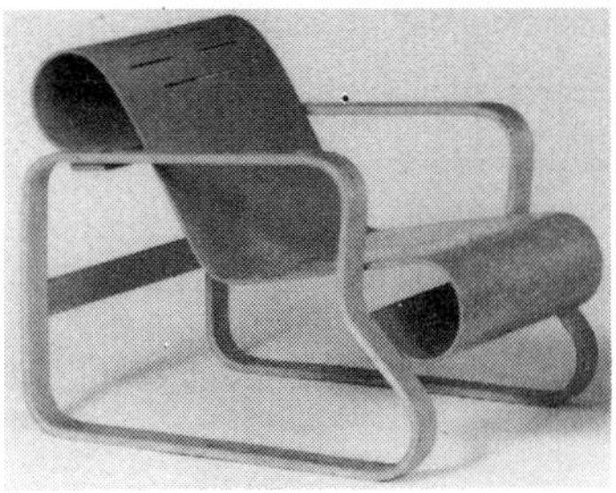
5

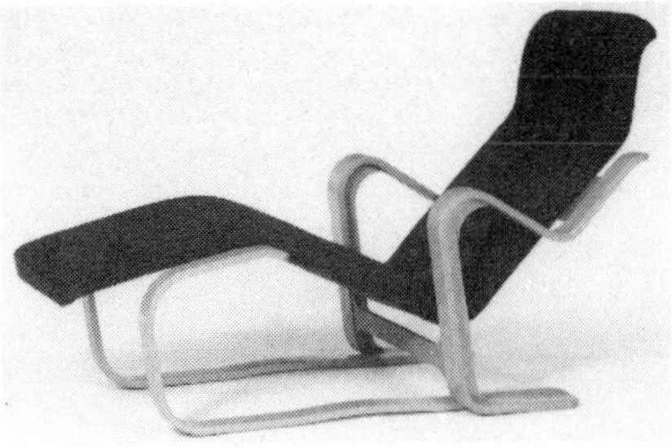
6

7

8

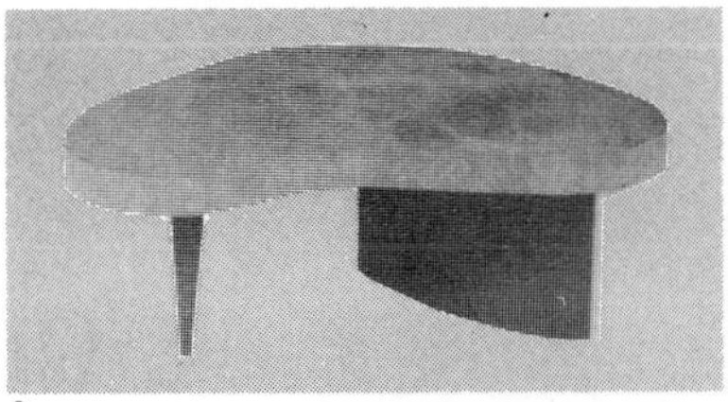
9

10

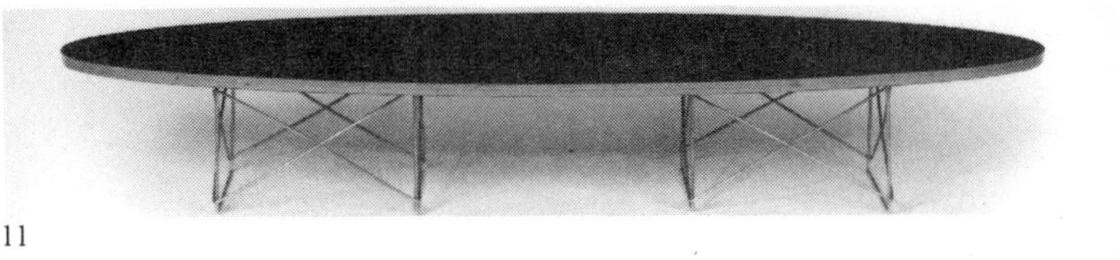
11

Wiener Werkstätte Furniture

BARBARA DEISROTH

Interest in all things Viennese dating from the turn of the century has progressed at an astonishing pace, reaching a climax in 1986 with major international exhibitions in Vienna, Paris and New York. Seemingly overnight, the names of Josef Hoffmann, Koloman Moser, Adolf Loos and Otto Wagner, among others, are on the lips of new collectors anxious to learn more about this intriguing mid-European style. Luckily for scholars and collectors alike, there is a vast amount of material available both in Europe and the United States, and many collectors and patrons of the period are still alive to share their memories of those times with new collectors.

Unlike the vogue for the styles of Art Nouveau and Art Deco, which disappeared for decades and then re-emerged in the late 1960s, interest in Viennese design of 1900 has never entirely gone underground, but has retained a steady, albeit modest, following in the salerooms and museums.

One of the leading design forces in Vienna was the Wiener Werkstätte. This design collective was founded by Josef Hoffmann and Koloman Moser in 1903 under the tenet of producing the finest quality designs in the decorative arts, elevating them to the level of fine arts and developing a new, more contemporary style suitable for modern life. 'We wish to create an inner relationship linking public, designer and worker and we want to produce good and simple articles of everyday use... Our guiding principle is function, utility our first condition, and our strength must lie in good proportions and the proper treatment of material... Handicrafts must be measured by the same standards as the work of a painter or sculptor... We cannot and will not compete with cheap work.' So stated Hoffmann and Moser in the *Work Programme of the Wiener Werkstätte.*

Influenced by the Scotsman Charles Rennie Mackintosh, who exhibited at the 1900 Secession exhibition, and by Biedermeier design dating from the early 19th century, the Wiener Werkstätte and other Viennese furniture designers borrowed the motif of small decorative squares from the Scottish Arts and Crafts movement and rectilinear simplicity from the Biedermeier, and created a design that was entirely and uniquely Viennese.

Early furniture designed by Moser and Hoffmann, some pre-dating the formation of the Wiener Werkstätte, is characterised by straight simple lines, and black, grey or white paint with an absence of superfluous ornamentation. Often their early designs are interchangeable, as their adherence and early commitment to the design tenets was so strict. Hoffmann's belief in the straight spare lines of functional furniture was stronger than that of Moser, who was known as the master of decoration. It is interesting to compare two of their early pieces. The first, a

1

1
A painted wood commode, c.1901-03, designed by Josef Hoffmann, painted white with blue base, nickel-plated handles, 68.5cm (27in) high, *M 19 Oct,* **FF 55,500 (£5,968; $8,355)**

commode by Hoffmann (fig.1), is a simple rectangle relieved by a series of drawers and cupboard doors, painted white with nickel metal pulls. Its only ornamentation, if it can be so classified, are inset panels painted blue. The other piece, by Moser (fig.2), a desk of similarly simple outline, is entirely inlaid in exotic woods with geometric patterns centring a central panel of highly stylised attenuated women. The panel is one of the few design elements seen in Viennese and Wiener Werkstätte furniture that echoes the French and Belgian Art Nouveau, but without that movement's sinuous curving lines. Furniture of this complexity and refinement was usually executed for the Wiener Werkstätte by Portois & Fix, a fine furniture company which produced more elaborate furniture than the bentwood and other simple designs discussed below.

After the Wiener Werkstätte's early years, few pieces of furniture can be attributed definitely to manufacture in their workrooms, even though we know them to have been designed by one of its members. Figs 1,3,4 and 5 are four early pieces which are universally felt to have been not only designed by Hoffmann or Moser, but also to have been manufactured in their

2
A veneered desk, in ivory and various woods, 1902, designed by Koloman Moser, for Charlottenlund, near Stockholm, 120cm (47in) wide, *M 19 Apr,*
FF 1,665,000 (£151,916; $271,930)

3
A black foxed oak side chair, c.1902, designed by Josef Hoffmann, with original geometric velvet upholstery, *NY 11 Oct,*
$3,300 (£2,308)

4
A painted wood cabinet, c.1904, designed by Kolomon Moser, painted in pale grey, polished oak interior with shelves missing, original silvered bronze key, 150cm (59in), *NY 11 Oct,*
$2,860 (£2,000)

5
A white-painted spruce dressing table, 1906, designed by Josef Hoffmann for the apartment of Hermann Wittgenstein, Salesianergasse 7, Vienna, with inset grey leather surface and brass escutcheons, 77.5cm (30½in), *NY 11 Oct,*
$5,500 (£3,846)

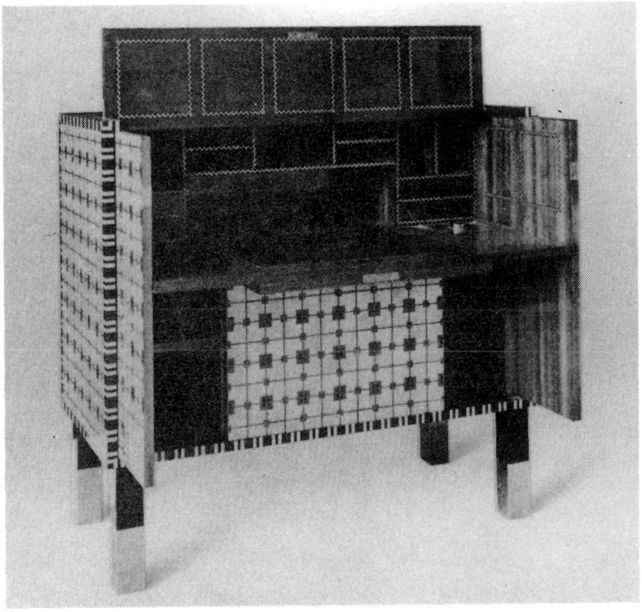
2

3

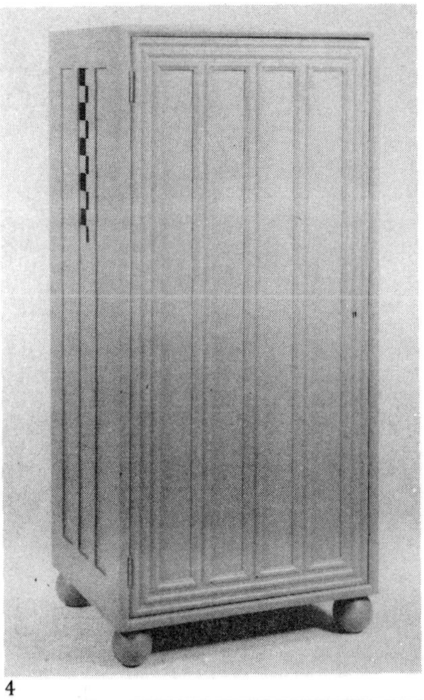
4

5

workrooms. Both founders soon recognised the need to find other manufacturers to produce their designs on a larger scale than was available to them through the capabilities of the Wiener Werkstätte. Austria, and particularly Vienna, was at that time the centre of good quality mass-produced bentwood furniture.

Michael Thonet (1796-1871) was awarded a patent in 1853 to produce bentwood furniture. His factories first produced designs in the rococo revival style so popular in Vienna in the mid 19th century, turning to simpler designs later in the century (figs 6 & 9) and to more modern designs early in the 20th century. Otto Wagner, who dominated Austrian design in the late 19th century and continued to do so through his many students (Hoffmann, Moser and Josef Maria Olbrich among them), turned to Thonet to manufacture several of his most successful and enduring designs for the Postsparkasse, the Postal Savings Bank in Vienna. This furniture (figs 7, 8 & 10), produced by Thonet in 1904-06, is characterised by the simple outline raised to a spare elegance by the early use of aluminium fittings on the feet and nail heads. The fact that these desks, stools and chairs are still in constant use today says much for their quality of design and craftsmanship.

A factory of equal importance to Thonet, which produced many Wiener Werkstätte designs, was founded by Jacob and Josef Kohn in Vienna in 1867. By 1869 Thonet no longer held an exclusive patent for the bentwood process, and this opened the way for J & J Kohn to become one of the largest and most aggressive bentwood manufacturers. Along with the designs by

6

7

8

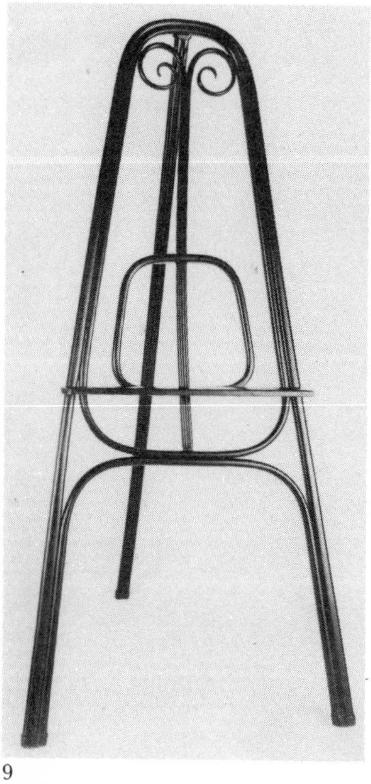
9

10

6
A nest of four bentwood tables, c.1905, by Thonet, painted black, 77.5cm (30½in) high, *M 13 Apr,*
FF 14,430 (£1,267; $1,964)

7
A stained beechwood and aluminium open armchair, 1904-06, designed by Otto Wagner for the Committee Room of the Öesterrichische Post-sparkasse, executed by Gebruder Thonet, branded Thonet and with original paper label, *NY 11 Oct,*
$20,900 (£14,615)

8
A stained beechwood and aluminium stool, 1904-06, designed by Otto Wagner for the Öesterrichische Postsparkasse, executed by Gebruder Thonet, the top pierced with a geometric pattern of holes, branded Thonet, with original Thonet label, 47cm (18¾in) high, *NY 11 Oct,*
$12,650 (£8,846)

9
A Thonet ebonised bentwood easel, 1888, with adjustable support, 213cm (7ft) high, *NY 11 Oct,*
$3,960 (£2,769)

10
A stained beechwood and aluminium writing table, 1904-06, designed by Otto Wagner for the Öesterrichische Postsparkasse, executed by Gebruder Thonet, the top with beige felt inset, the panels with aluminium studs, 110cm (43¼in) high, *NY 11 Oct,*
$46,750 (£32,692)

11
A nest of four ebonised wood tables, c.1906, designed by Josef Hoffmann for J.&J. Kohn, with original J.&J. Kohn paper label and with metal tag from Hungarian retailer, 75cm (29½in) high, *NY 11 Oct,*
$4,070 (£2,846)

12
A stained ash 'Stizmachine', c.1905, designed by Josef Hoffmann for J.&J. Kohn, *NY 11 Oct,*
$16,500 (£11,538)

13
A beechwood and maple writing table and chair, 1904-06, designed by Josef Hoffmann, executed by J.&J. Kohn, with original black leather writing surface, the chair with original Wiener Werkstätte patterned fabric, both with J.&J. Kohn paper labels, 98cm (38½in) high, *NY 11 Oct,*
$29,700 (£20,769)

14
A stained ash side chair, c.1905, designed by Josef Hoffmann for J.&J. Kohn, the laminated surround with brass studs, *NY 11 Oct,*
$4,400 (£3,077)

15
An inlaid mahogany cabinet, c.1905, designed by Koloman Moser for J.&J. Kohn, glazed door, maple inlay, remnants of label, 196cm (6ft 5½in) high, *NY 11 Oct,*
$11,000 (£7,692)

16
A stained beechwood and brass cabinet/vitrine, c.1908, designed by Josef Hoffmann for J.&J. Kohn, composed of bentwood slats, with brass mounts, original paper label, 179cm (70½in) high, *NY 11 Oct,*
$18,700 (£13,077)

17
A bentwood plant stand, c.1900, designed by Gustav Siegel for J.&J. Kohn, with original paper label, 130cm (51in), *NY 11 Oct,*
$1,100 (£769)

11

12

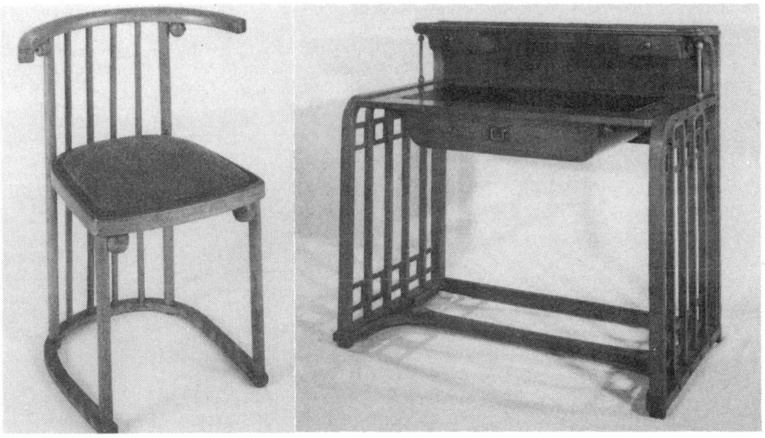

13

14

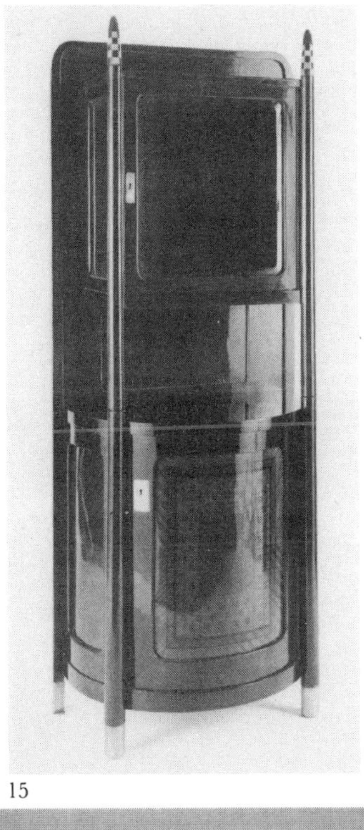

15

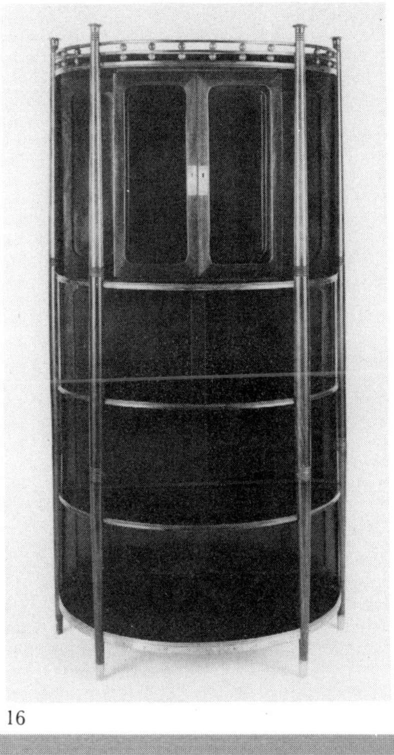

16

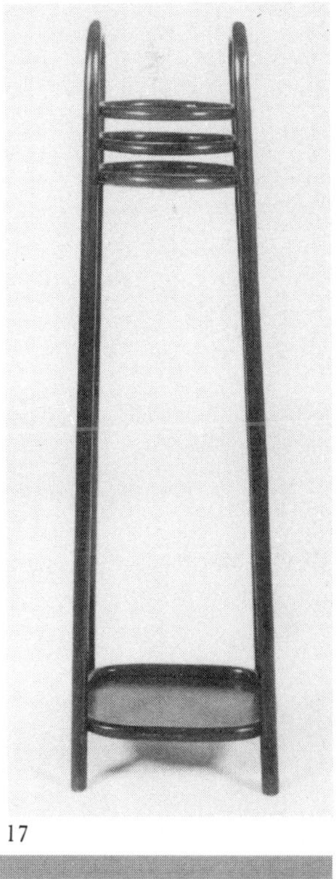

17

Hoffmann and Moser (figs 11-16), J & J Kohn produced many successful avant garde pieces by their principal designer Gustav Siegel, a former student of Hoffmann's whose many designs (figs 17 & 18) echoed his concepts and beliefs. Siegel's designs for J & J Kohn earned him and his company a Grand Prix at the Paris 1900 Exhibition. In the late 1920s Kohn merged with Thonet and while continuing to produce many earlier designs, focused primarily on the tubular steel designs emanating from the Bauhaus.

As tastes changed, so did the Wiener Werkstätte. Dagobert Peche became associated with the Wiener Werkstätte after 1915 and began a new, more highly decorative approach to their production. Fig.19 illustrates a carved and giltwood floor lamp designed by Peche and executed at the Wiener Werkstätte in 1920; it represents his early highly architectural style incorporating decorative panels of baroque inspiration. This later style of Peche and the Wiener Werkstätte is today gaining in popularity along with the more recognisable early works.

Certainly, much of the interest today in the Wiener Werkstätte is dependent upon current fashion. But these designs, which have survived political upheavals and periods of fashionable disfavour, will certainly continue to be respected and appreciated by museums and collectors and accorded a place of importance in the study of decorative arts of the 20th century.

Further reading:

Vienna: A Birthplace of 20th Century Design, Fischer Fine Art Limited, London 1981
June Kallir, *Viennese Design and Wiener Werkstätte*, 1986
Kirk Varnadoe, *Vienna 1900 — Art, Architecture and Design*, The Museum of Modern Art, New York, 1986

18

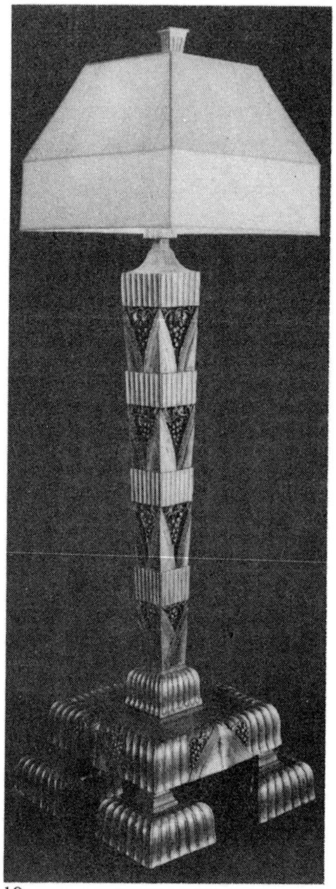

19

18
A bentwood centre table, c.1905, designed by Gustav Siegel for J.&J. Kohn, branded Teschen/Austria, with original paper label, 78cm (30¾in) high, *NY 11 Oct,* **$4,180 (£2,923)**

19
A carved and giltwood floor lamp, c.1920, designed by Dagobert Peche, silk shade and later finial, 241cm (7ft 11in) high, *NY 11 Oct,* **$34,100 (£23,846)**

Jewellery

Article:
1940s Jewellery *pp* 332-336

See also:
Colour illustrations *pp* 337-338
Antiquities *p* 591
Decorative arts from 1880 *p* 298
European works of art *p* 359

1
A gold, shell cameo and gem-set necklace, c.1820, with shell cameos depicting Greek mythological scenes alternating with turquoise and half-pearl flowerhead clusters,
L 8 May,
£2,200 ($3,564)

2
A gold, cornelian cameo habillé and pearl ring, c.1865, the cameo depicting a negress's head,
M 1 Dec,
FF 3,850 (£416; $595)

3
A gold and stained green chalcedony cameo brooch/pendant, c.1865, the cameo of Athena decorated with granulation and corded wire in archaeological style; sold with a gold and onyx cameo tiepin, *L 12 May,*
£935 ($1,514)

4
A gold, enamel, sardonyx cameo, half-pearl and diamond brooch, last quarter 19th century,
L 30 Jan,
£748 ($1,099)

5
An onyx cameo and diamond brooch, last quarter 19th century, the cameo depicting Diana,
L 30 Jan,
£770 ($1,132)

6
A sardonyx, onyx and half-pearl pendant, second half 19th century, the cameo depicting Flora; with a ruby and half-pearl necklace,
L 11 Dec,
£638 ($893)

7
A gold, pearl and hardstone cameo brooch, last quarter 19th century,
C 7 Oct,
£462 ($647)

8
A gold and onyx cameo brooch, c.1870, the cameo of Athena set within a gold border decorated with granulation and corded wire; sold with a rock-crystal reverse intaglio and diamond brooch, *L 11 Dec,*
£1,540 ($2,156)

9
A gold and onyx cameo ring, second half 19th century, *L 11 Dec,*
£264 ($370)

10
A gold, sardonyx cameo, half-pearl and rose diamond brooch/pendant, second half 19th century, the cameo depicting a maenad in profile,
L 11 Dec,
£2,420 ($3,388)

11
A hardstone cameo brooch, 19th century, of chalcedony and cornelian, depicting a bust of Jupiter, with a gold and blue enamel mount, *NY 10 Dec,*
$1,540 (£1,077)

12
An agate cameo and diamond dress set, *(part illustrated),* 19th century, comprising twelve buttons, a pair of cufflinks and a stickpin, the greyish-brown and white agate cameos carved with the heads of the twelve Apostles, angels and the head of Christ, *NY 10 June,*
$4,675 (£3,076)

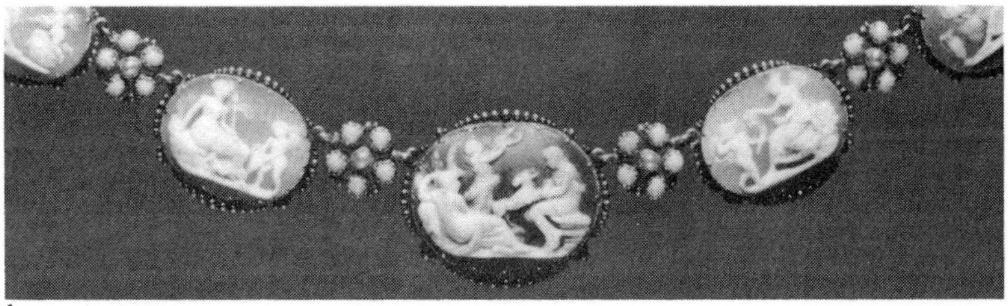
1

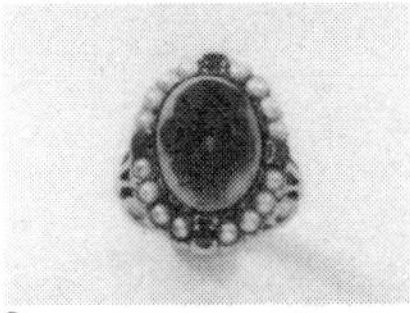
2

4

5

3

7

8

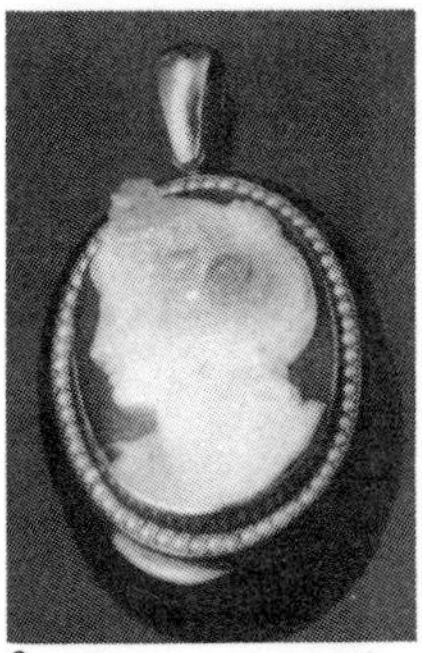
6

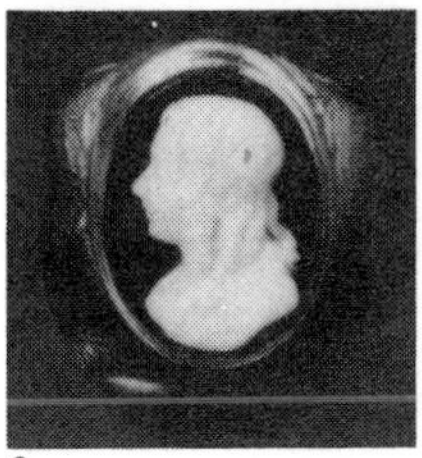
9

10

11

12

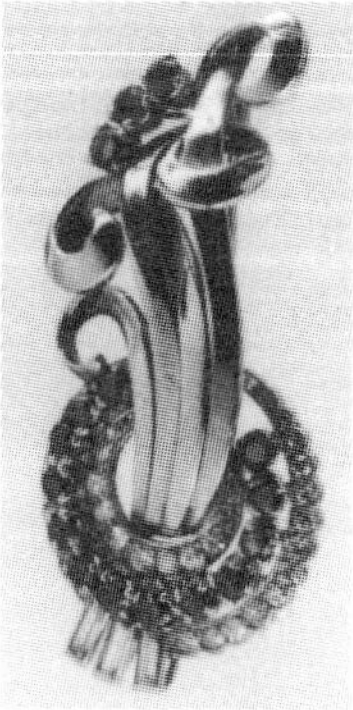
1

2

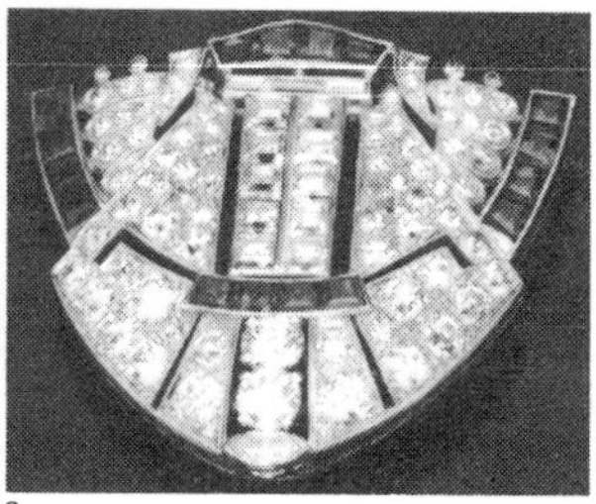
3

4

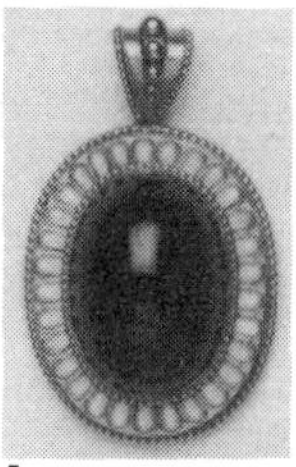
5

6

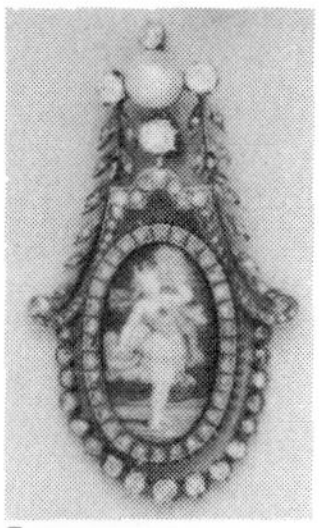
7

8

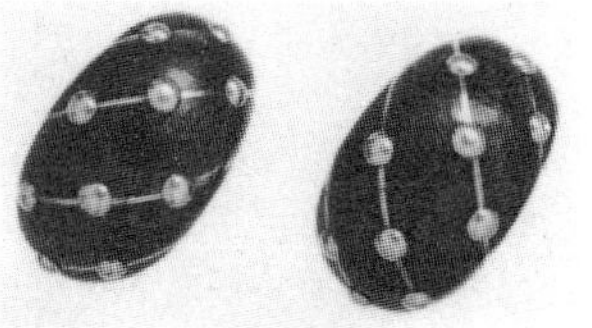
9

10

11

12

13

14

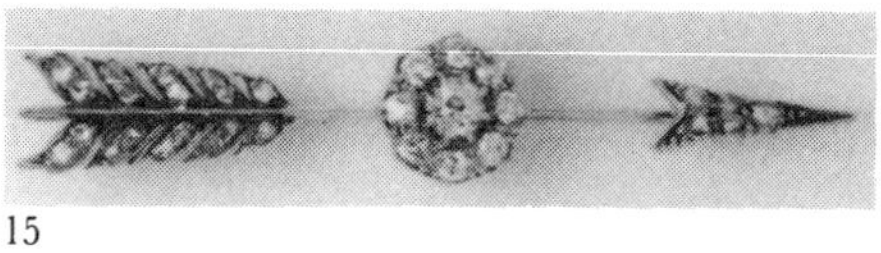
15

16

17

1
A gold, ruby and diamond brooch, c.1940, *L 10 Apr,*
£825 ($1,262)

2
A sapphire and diamond brooch, c.1935, platinum mount, *NY 10 Dec,*
$8,250 (£5,769)

3
A sapphire and diamond clip, c.1935, platinum mount, *NY 10 Dec,*
$4,950 (£3,461)

4
A gold, quartz cat's eye and diamond brooch/ pendant, c.1875, *L 11 Dec,*
£2,750 ($3,850)

5
A gold, carbuncle and enamel pendant, c.1870, *L 30 Jan,*
£770 ($1,132)

6
A sapphire and diamond flower brooch, c.1940, mounted in platinum, *NY 20 Oct,*
$7,700 (£5,385)

7
An Austrian gold, enamel, pearl and diamond pendant, c.1890, the oval plaque painted with a polychrome enamel allegory of Time, *L 8 May,*
£1,155 ($1,871)

8
A Swiss gold and enamel brooch/pendant, mid 19th century, with a landscape of the Château of Chillon, *NY 10 Dec,*
$495 (£346)

9
An 18-carat gold and blue enamel bangle bracelet with matching ear-clips, Schlumberger, *St.M 20 Feb,*
SF 8,250 (£2,815; $4,278)

10
A French four-colour gold locket, c.1830, decorated with a bouquet of forget-me-nots within a garland of roses, *L 11 Dec,*
£682 ($955)

11
A gold, enamel and gem-set Holbeinesque pendant, Carlo Giuliano, c.1870, decorated with blue, black and white piqué enamel and set with cabochon rubies and half-pearls, enamel slightly imperfect, on a chain necklet, *L 11 Dec,*
£1,980 ($2,772)

12
An Italian gold and Roman mosaic demi-parure, c.1875, comprising a brooch and a pair of pendant-earclips, the brooch with a micro-mosaic of a swimming duck, and the earclips with micro-mosaics of beetles, *NY 10 Dec,*
$2,310 (£1,615)

13
A gold, carbuncle and diamond pendant, last quarter 19th century, *C 14 Jan,*
£594 ($891)

14
A diamond and pearl brooch, last quarter 19th century, sold with a sapphire and diamond half-hoop ring, *L 5 June,*
£220 ($343)

15
A diamond brooch, last quarter 19th century, designed as an arrow with central cluster, *L 13 Nov,*
£440 ($616)

16
A diamond and pearl brooch, last quarter 19th century, *NY 10 June,*
$1,320 (£868)

17
A sapphire and diamond brooch/pendant, last quarter 19th century, lacking pendant loop, *L 19 June,*
£1,980 ($3,128)

1
A diamond brooch/ pendant, c.1890, lacking loop, one stone deficient, *L 10 Apr,*
£2,310 ($3,534)

2
A diamond brooch, last quarter 19th century, *L 8 May,*
£1,760 ($2,851)

3
A diamond and half-pearl brooch, last quarter 19th century, *L 5 June,*
£572 ($892)

4
A ruby and diamond bar brooch, last quarter 19th century, designed as a hoop of rubies between scroll shoulders set with diamonds, *Glen 25 Aug,*
£352 ($553)

5
A gold, enamel and gem-set brooch, Carlo Giuliano, c.1890, designed as a stylised dahlia, the petals decorated with pink guilloché enamel, enamel slightly imperfect, *L 11 Dec,*
£902 ($1,263)

6
An amethyst and diamond brooch, c.1900, slightly imperfect, *L 13 Nov,*
£1,045 ($1,463)

7
A sapphire and diamond brooch, *St.M 22 Feb,*
SF 8,800 (£3,003; $4,565)

8
A pearl, amethyst and diamond pendant, last quarter 19th century, *L 10 July,*
£715 ($1,151)

9
A diamond and sapphire flower basket brooch, c.1925, platinum mounting, gold brooch pin, *NY 10 June,*
$2,310 (£1,520)

10
A diamond and pearl pendant, last quarter 19th century, mounted in gold and silver, *NY 10 June,*
$1,650 (£1,085)

11
A diamond, red and white enamel brooch, the enamel on initials *CRX* (Christian of Denmark) with a diamond-set crown above, *C 8 July,*
£220 ($343)

12
A gold, opal and diamond brooch, c.1900, the central opal set within a star of diamonds, *C 8 July,*
£264 ($412)

13
A sapphire and diamond bar brooch, *L 11 Dec,*
£990 ($1,386)

14
A diamond pendant on chain, c.1905, designed as a lace-like rosette set with small diamonds, *G 14 May,*
SF 4,400 (£1,481; $2,385)

15
An onyx and diamond bar brooch, c.1910, the central diamond within a double border of calibré-cut onyx and circular-cut diamonds, *L 10 Apr,*
£770 ($1,178)

16
A diamond pendant, c.1905, designed as a foliate garland with diamond swing centre, with fine chain necklet with smaller garland motif, one diamond deficient, *L 19 June,*
£4,950 ($7,821)

17
An amethyst and diamond flower brooch/ pendant, the petals formed of four heart-shaped amethysts, *NY 16 Apr,*
$4,125 (£2,750)

18
A sapphire and diamond brooch, c.1900, *L 5 June,*
£605 ($944)

19
A sapphire and diamond brooch, c.1920, platinum mounting, *NY 20 Oct,*
$5,775 (£4,038)

20
A French diamond scroll brooch, c.1900, *G 14 May,*
SF 3,300 (£1,111; $1,789)

1

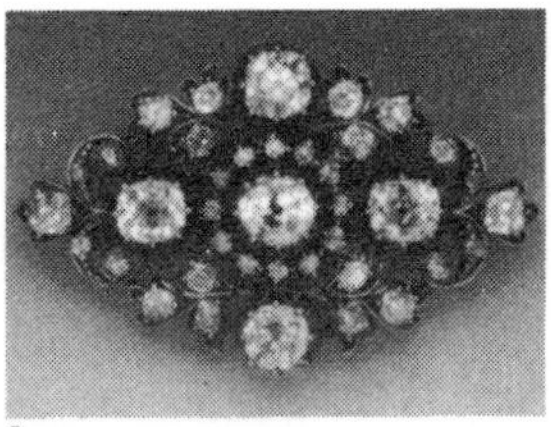
2

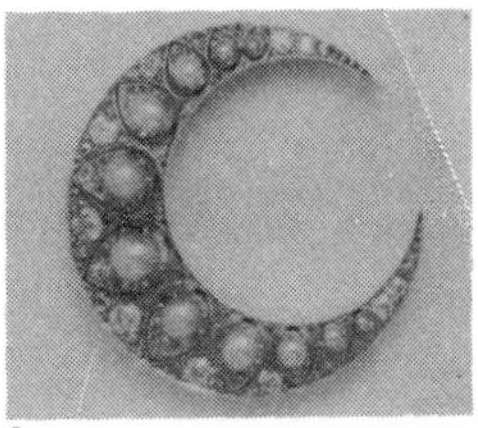
3

4

5

8

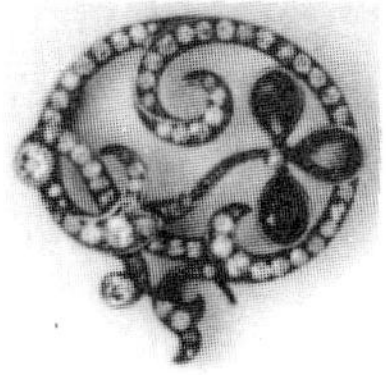
6

7

11

9

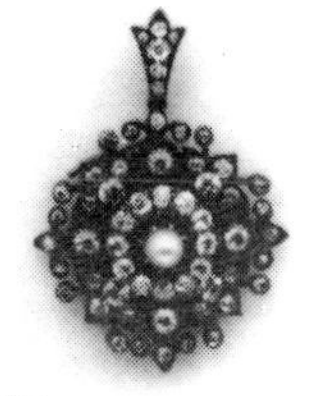
10

12

13

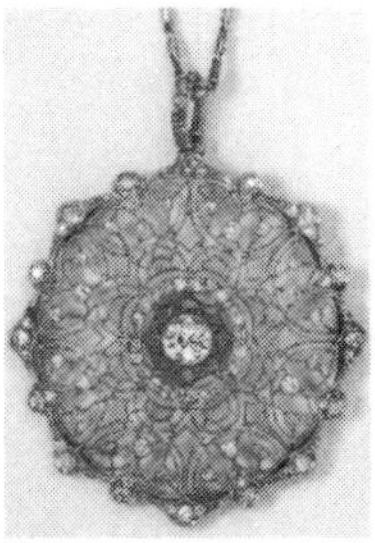
14

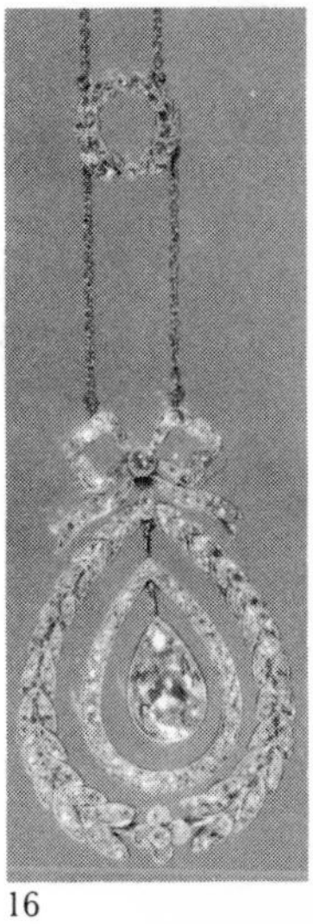
16

15

17

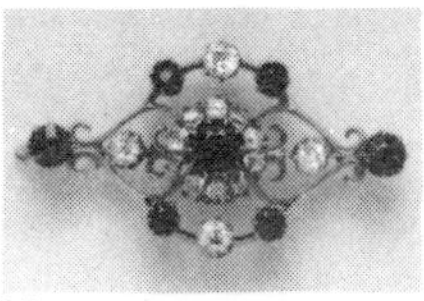
18

19

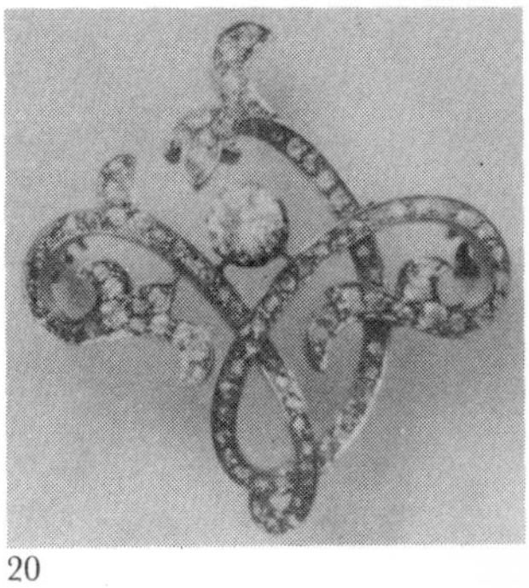
20

1

2

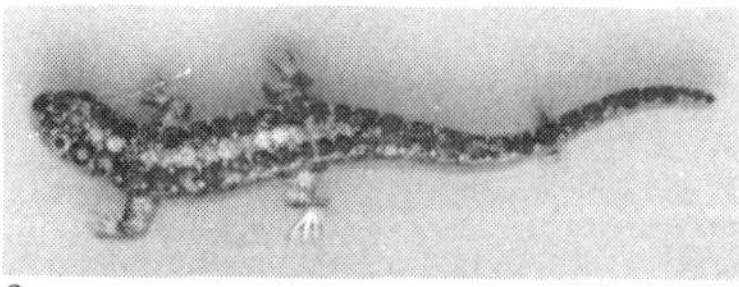

3

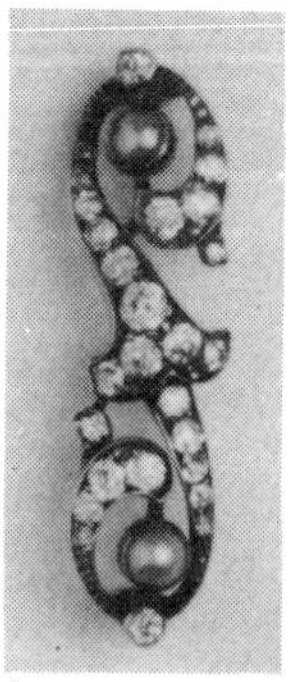

4

5

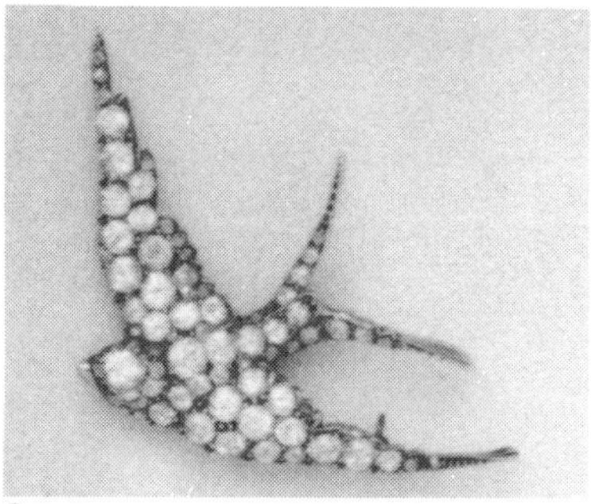

6

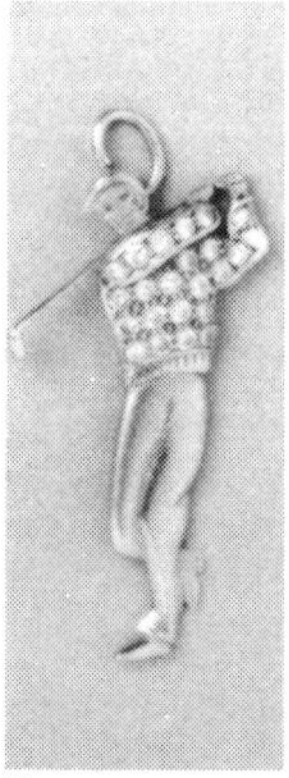

7

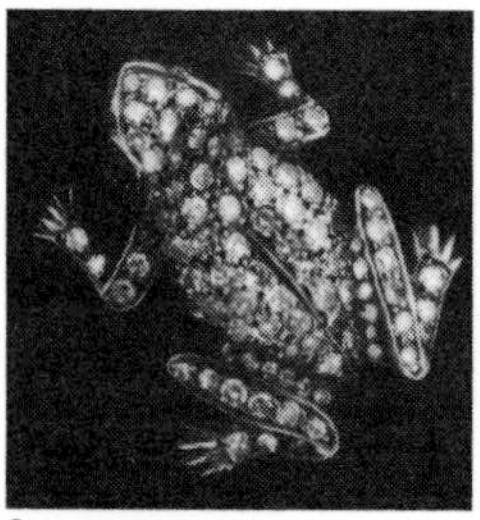

8

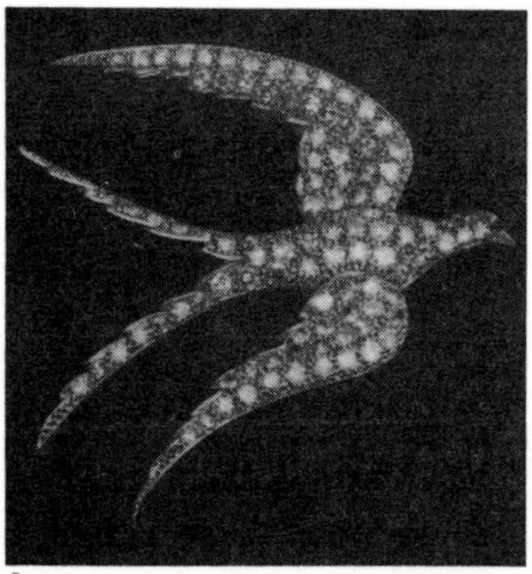

9

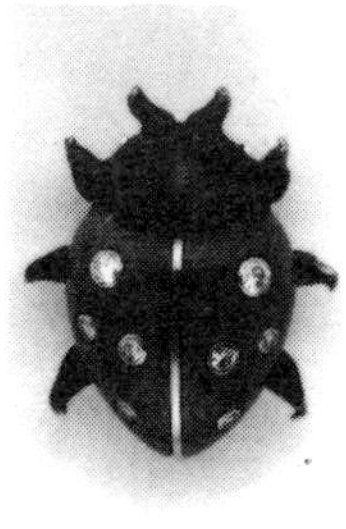

10

11

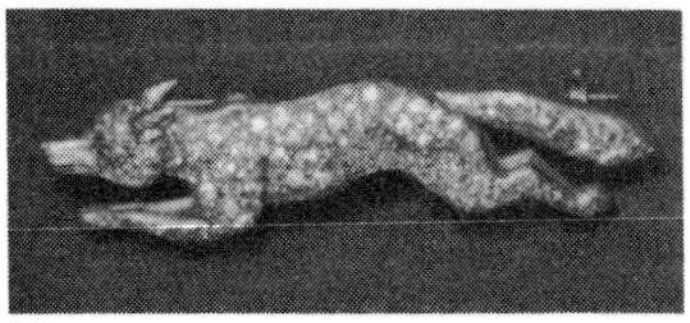

12

13

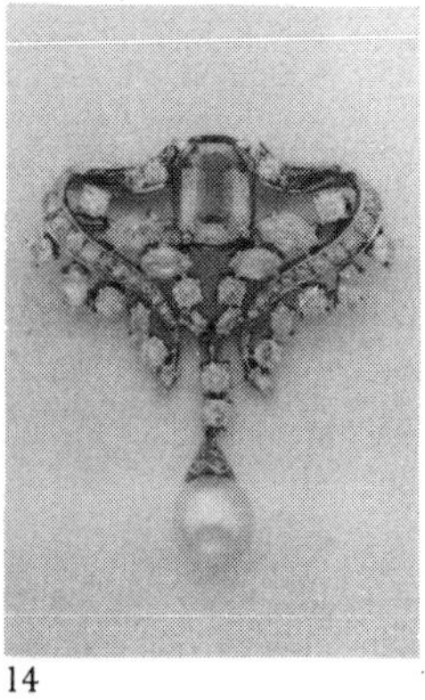

14

15

1
A gold and gem-set brooch, last quarter 19th century, designed as a butterfly set with rubies, sapphires, and diamonds, *L 9 Oct,*
£1,485 ($2,079)

2
A ruby, sapphire, opal and diamond brooch/ pendant, last quarter 19th century, designed as a butterfly, *Glen 25 Aug,*
£935 ($1,468)

3
A demantoid garnet and diamond brooch, last quarter 19th century, designed as a lizard, *L 8 May,*
£1,650 ($2,673)

4
A half-pearl and diamond brooch, last quarter 19th century, *Glas 5 Feb,*
£385 ($554)

5
A pearl, demantoid garnet and rose diamond brooch, last quarter 19th century, designed as a thistle, *L 8 May,*
£506 ($819)

6
A diamond brooch, last quarter 19th century, designed as a swallow, *L 8 May,*
£1,375 ($2,227)

7
A gold and diamond pendant, designed as a golfer in full swing, *Glen 25 Aug,*
£605 ($950)

8
A diamond and ruby frog brooch, c.1900, the gold and silver frog set with numerous single-cut diamonds, the eyes with two round rubies, *NY 16 Apr,*
$4,290 (£2,860)

9
A platinum and diamond swallow brooch, c.1900, pavé-set with single-cut diamonds, *NY 16 Apr,*
$3,300 (£2,200)

10
A white gold, coral, diamond and enamel ladybird brooch, Cartier, London, *NY 16 Apr,*
$3,080 (£2,053)

11
A gold and gem-set 'Daisy Duck' brooch, Van Cleef & Arpels, Daisy wearing a ruby-set hat and diamond-set tie, her dress a large cabochon sapphire, *St.M 21 Feb,*
SF 2,860 (£976; $1,483)

12
A diamond brooch, c.1900, designed as a running fox, *S 17 Sept,*
£715 ($1,001)

13
A gold and tinted crystal intaglio locket, c.1870, the gold locket designed as a kennel set with a tinted crystal intaglio of an old English sheepdog, *L 8 May,*
£825 ($1,336)

14
An emerald pearl and diamond brooch/pendant, c.1930, *NY 16 Apr,*
$5,363 (£3,575)

15
A diamond brooch, c.1900, designed as a horseshoe, with fox's mask at the centre and two crossed riding crops behind, *S 18 June,*
£792 ($1,251)

1
A diamond and enamel horse and jockey brooch, the diamond-set horse jumping over a whip, the jockey wearing blue and white colours, *St.M 20 Feb,*
£825 ($1,255)

2
An emerald and diamond brooch, Lacloche Frères, c.1925, with a central step-cut emerald, in platinum, *St.M 22 Feb,*
SF 26,400 (£9,010; $13,695)

3
A sapphire and diamond bar brooch, Dreicer & Co., c.1930, *NY 10 Dec,*
$3,300 (£2,308)

4
An emerald, pearl and diamond bar brooch, Koch, with a central diamond and pearl between calibré-cut emeralds, *Glen 25 Aug,*
£572 ($898)

5
A sapphire and diamond bow brooch, c.1920, the platinum bow set with a square-shaped sapphire, *NY 10 Dec,*
$4,125 (£2,885)

6
A diamond double clip brooch, c.1930, each clip set with baguette, step- and brilliant-cut diamonds, *L 11 Dec,*
£2,420 ($3,388)

7
A pair of diamond dress-clips, c.1930, each set with circular-cut and baguette diamonds, *St.M 20 Feb,*
SF 7,150 (£2,440; $3,709)

8
A diamond double clip brooch, each clip set with baguette and brilliant-cut stones, *Glen 25 Aug,*
£1,430 ($2,245)

9
A ruby and diamond clip, Cartier, London, c.1930, *NY 20 Oct,*
$9,350 (£6,538)

10
A diamond double clip brooch, each clip of stylised shell design, set throughout with circular-cut stones, *L 8 May,*
£1,980 ($3,207)

11
A platinum and diamond double clip brooch, *(one illustrated)*, c.1930, the navette-shaped brooch separating into a pair of stylised triangular clips, *NY 10 June,*
$8,800 (£5,789)

12
A diamond and ruby double clip bow brooch, c.1930, mounted in platinum, *NY 20 Oct,*
$8,800 (£6,154)

13
An 18-carat gold sapphire and diamond clip brooch, Kutchinsky, designed as a tied ribbon, *L 30 Jan,*
£1,320 ($1,940)

1

2

3

4

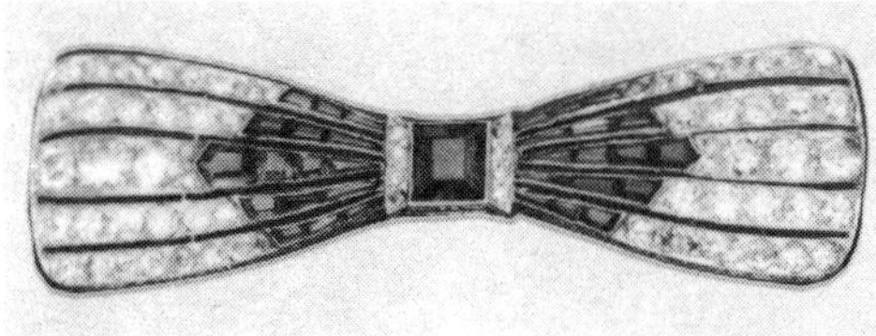
5

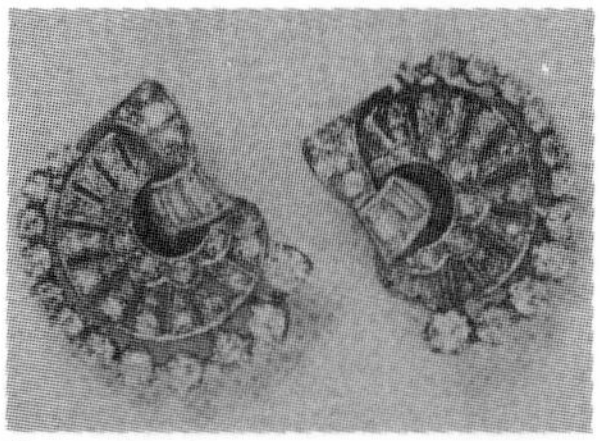
7

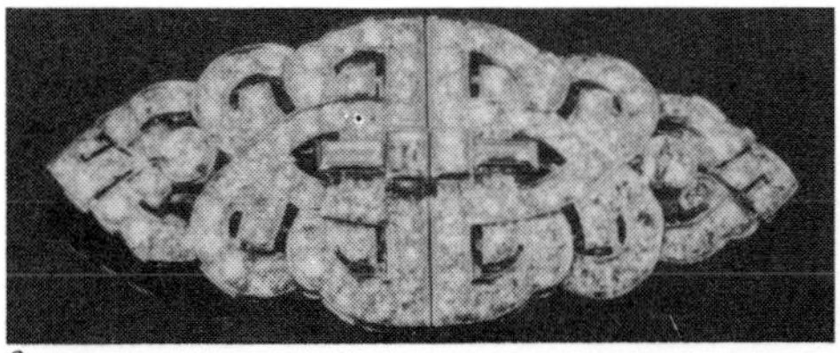
6

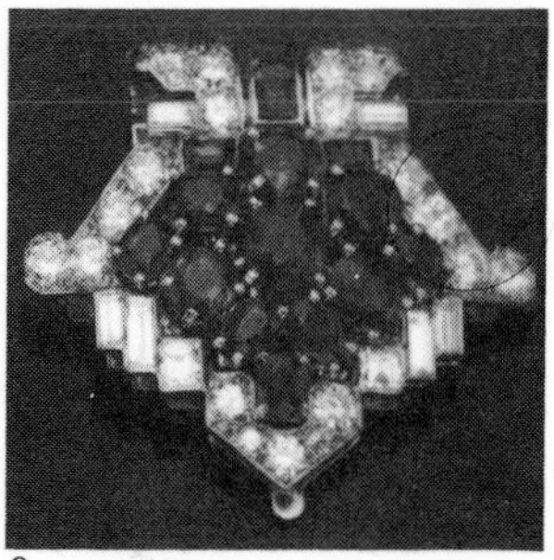
9

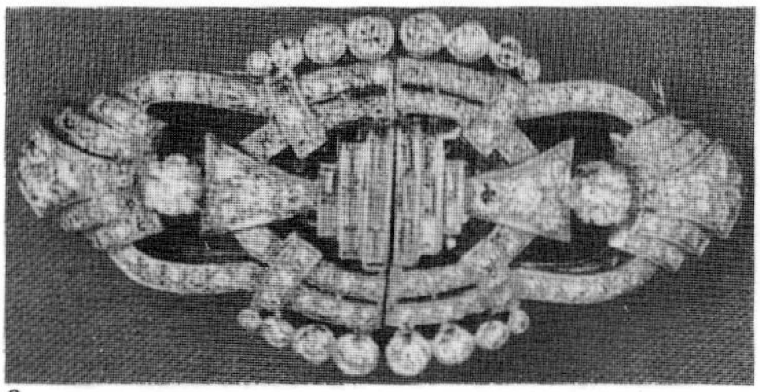
8

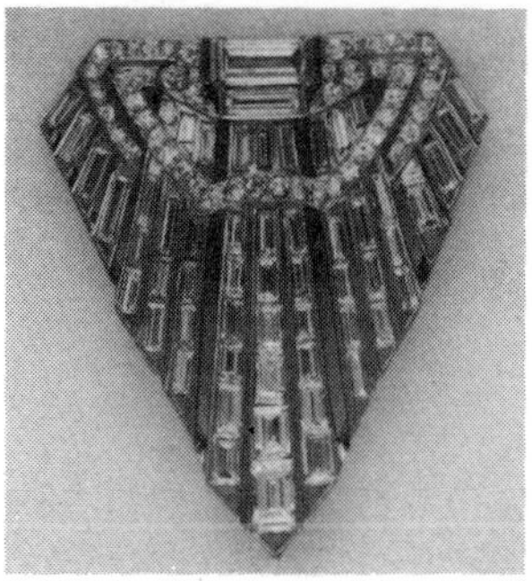
11

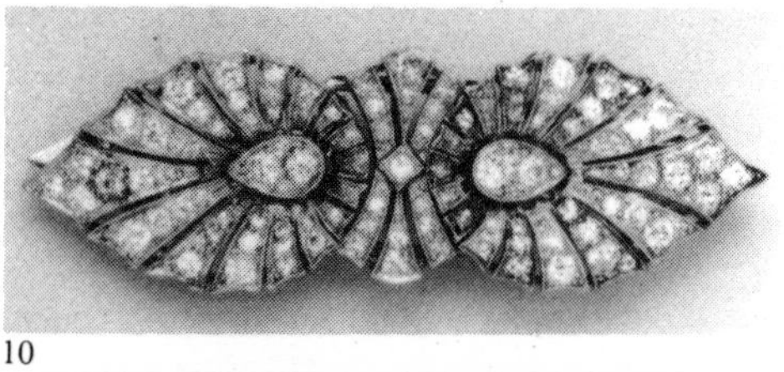
10

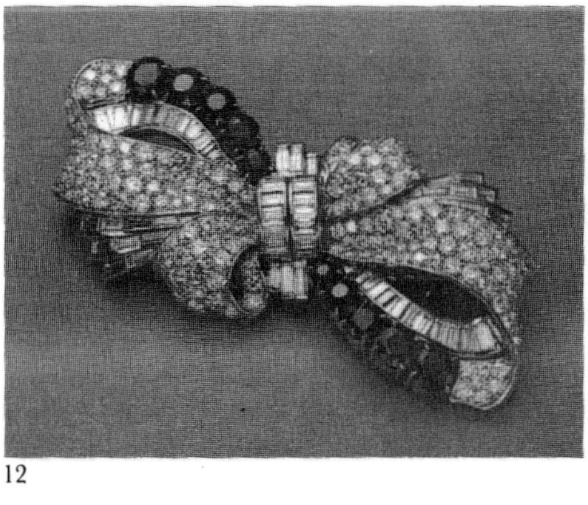
12

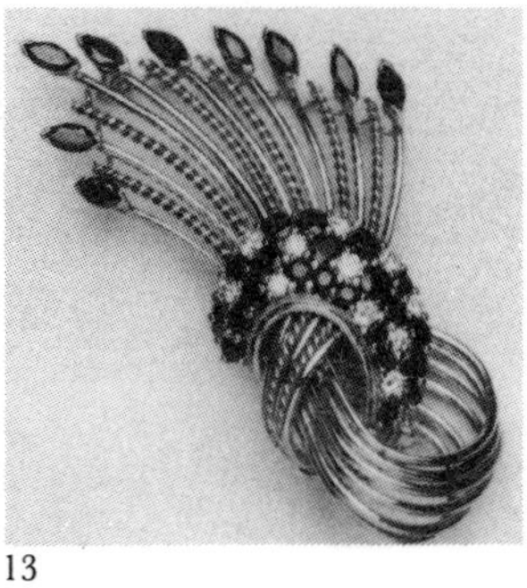
13

1

2

3

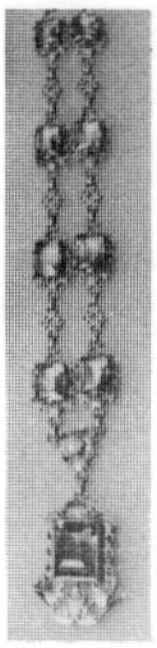
4

5

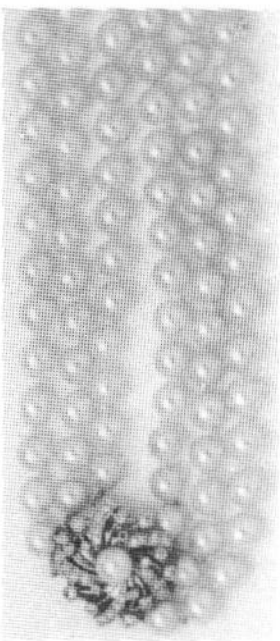
6

7

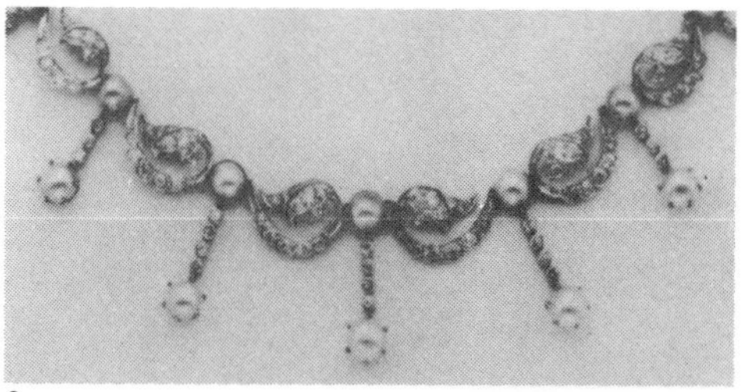
8

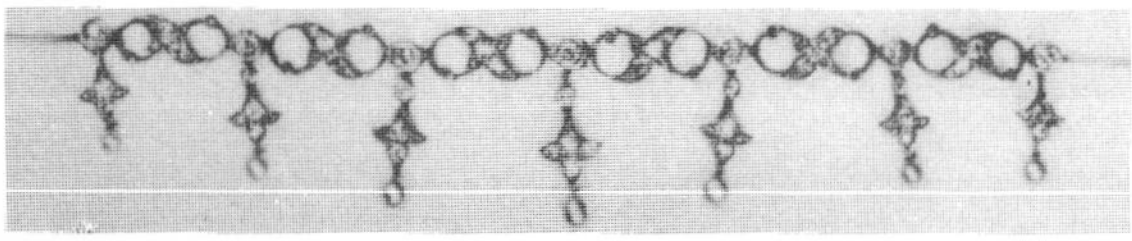
9

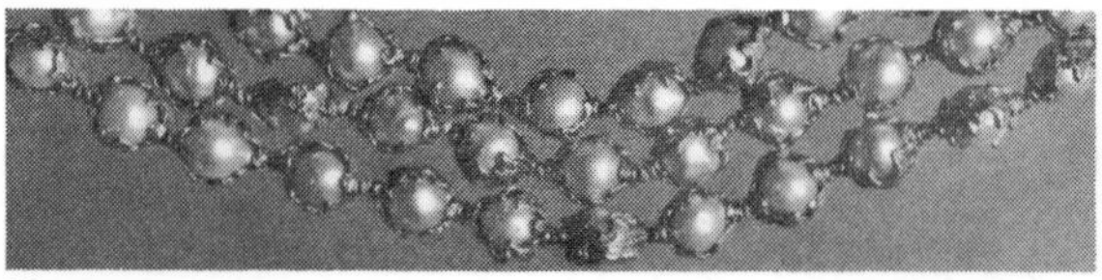
10

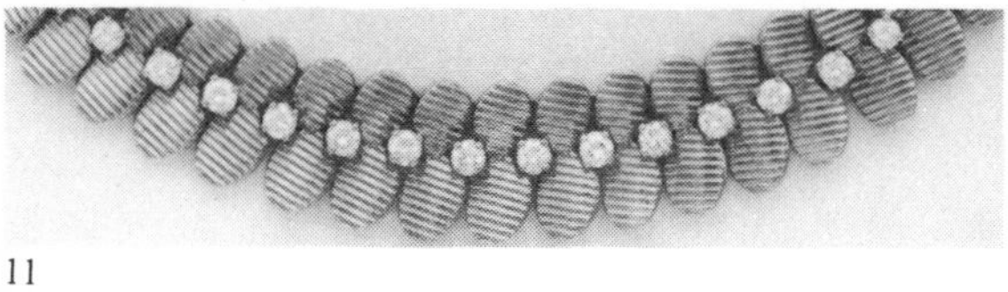
11

12

1
A turquoise and diamond necklet, c.1870, *L 9 Oct,*
£2,750 ($3,850)

2
A gold and hardstone intaglio necklace, Castellani, c.1875, in classical style, the choker set with a row of intaglios in varieties of chalcedony and quartz, spaced by gold links and bordered top and bottom by garnet beads, one broken, with a safety chain, *NY 10 June,*
$14,850 (£9,770)

3
A gold necklace and matching earrings, Robert Phillips of Cockspur St., London, c.1865, in archaeological revival style, *NY 10 Dec,*
$5,500 (£3,846)

4
A French gold and amethyst necklace, c.1880, the clasp inscribed *par Cartier,* slightly imperfect, *L 11 Dec,*
£1,595 ($2,233)

5
A jade bead necklace, Cartier, London, c.1920, the double-string jade necklace suspending a jade plaque carved on both sides with a floral spray, the platinum clasp and pendant loop decorated with diamonds and black onyx, *NY 10 Dec,*
$8,800 (£6,154)

6
A cultured pearl necklace, with a cultured pearl and diamond cluster clasp, *L 13 Nov,*
£968 ($1,355)

7
A white-gold and diamond necklace,
C 14 Jan,
£594 ($891)

8
A pearl and diamond necklace, c.1910, composed of a series of platinum and gold scroll-shaped links alternating with fringes set with split pearls in shades of pink and grey, decorated with old European-cut diamonds, platinum chain, *NY 10 June,*
$5,500 (£3,618)

9
A diamond and pearl necklace, c.1905, mounted in gold and silver, the diamond-set fleur-de-lis motifs with pearl drops spaced by diamond-set figure of eight links, collet-set back chain, *C 7 Oct,*
£1,045 ($1,463)

10
A gold and three-row baroque pearl necklace, Charles de Temple, and bracelet *en suite, L 10 July,*
£2,750 ($4,427)

11
An 18-carat gold and diamond necklace, the front studded with 26 round diamonds, approx 38cm (15in) long, *NY 20 Oct,*
$6,600 (£4,615)

12
A platinum and diamond sautoir, c.1910, the chain collet-set with 216 old European-cut diamonds, approx 127cm (50in) long, *NY 20 Oct,*
$40,700 (£28,461)

1
A woven yellow gold bracelet, the clasp of yellow gold and black enamel set with half-pearls, *M 24 Feb,*
FF 11,100 (£1,074; $1,610)

2
A two-colour gold and diamond bracelet, designed as five rows of ropetwist linking in yellow and white gold, connected at intervals by bars of brilliant-cut diamonds, *Glas 5 Feb,*
£770 ($1,108)

3
A gold and amethyst bracelet, c.1840, the clasp set with an oval-shaped amethyst framed by filigree, beadwork and small shell motifs, *NY 10 June,*
$1,430 (£941)

4
A gold, enamel and hardstone bracelet, Giacinto Melillo, c.1900, in archaeological revival style, the front decorated with a knot motif set with a hardstone intaglio of Cupid between green, white and blue enamel shoulders, the clasp similarly enamelled, imperfect, *L 11 Dec,*
£1,100 ($1,540)

5
A charm bracelet, supporting six diamond-set charms including a rabbit, a pheasant, a stalking dog, a partridge, a heron and a cat, *St.M 21 Feb,*
SF 9,900 (£3,378; $5,134)

6
A French diamond and seed pearl bracelet, c.1905, the seed pearl bracelet with a platinum panel set with diamonds, diamond-set platinum clasp, *NY 10 June,*
$2,420 (£1,592)

7
A seed pearl, sapphire and diamond bracelet, c.1920, decorated with three platinum openwork panels set with marquise-shaped and single-cut diamonds and with calibré-cut sapphires, *NY 10 Dec,*
$5,775 (£4,038)

8
A seed pearl, emerald, diamond and enamel bracelet, Cartier, c.1920, with emerald and rose-diamond clasp, *NY 10 June,*
$2,420 (£1,592)

9
An 18-carat gold bracelet, Cartier, *L 10 Apr,*
£1,265 ($1,935)

10
An onyx and diamond bracelet, designed as a row of seven onyx and diamond links alternating with calibré- and circular-cut diamond letters, reading *Dottie, L 5 June,*
£528 ($824)

11
A platinum and diamond bracelet, c.1920, composed of interlocking circular, oval and fancy-shaped links, set with 172 round diamonds, *NY 10 Dec,*
$6,325 (£4,423)

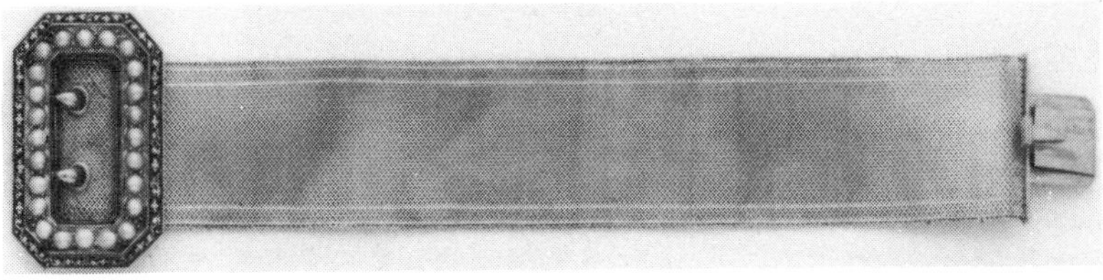
1

2

3

4

5

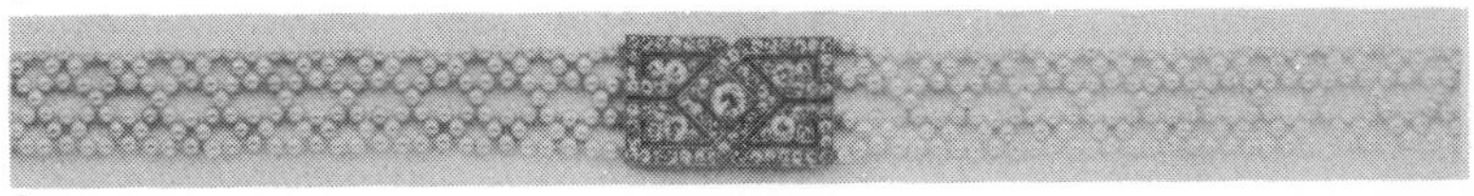
6

7

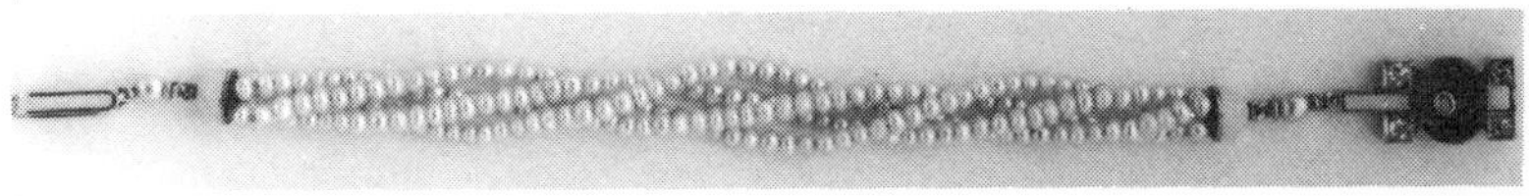
8

9

10

11

1

2

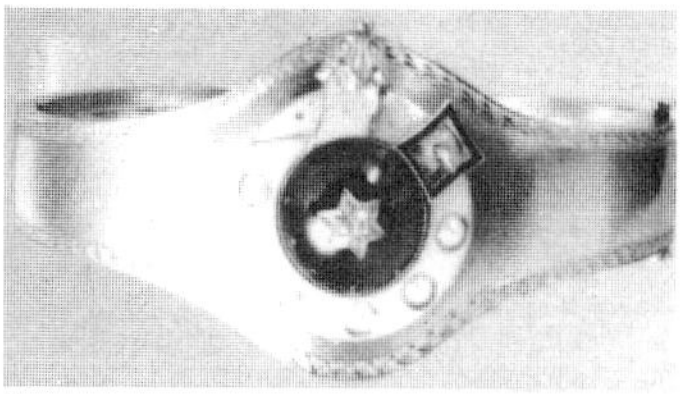
3

4

5

6

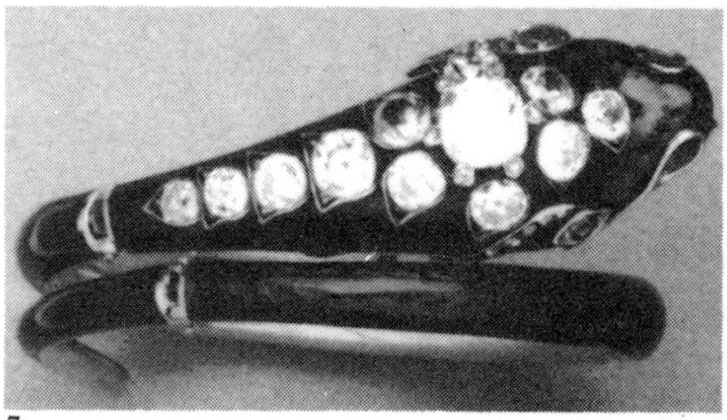
7

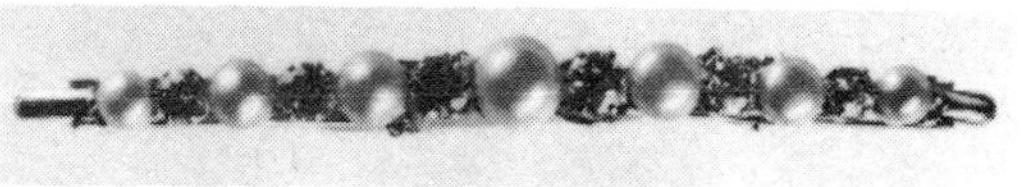
8

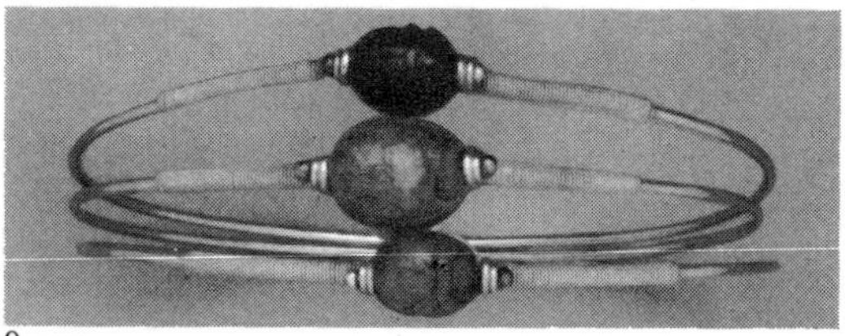
9

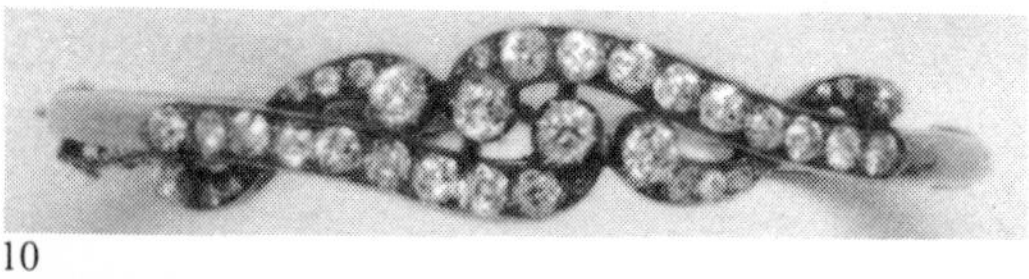
10

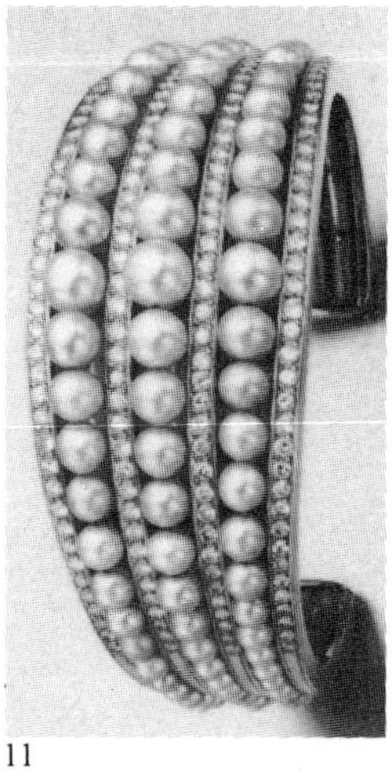
11

12

1
A gold and gem-set longchain, c.1830,
L 11 Dec,
£1,320 ($1,848)

2
A pearl and yellow gold choker necklace, last quarter 19th century, the clasp in yellow gold and decorated with a female bust, 32.5cm (12¾in),
M 24 Feb,
FF 13,320 (£1,288; $1,932)

3
A gold, enamel and gem-set bangle, c.1865, the front with a carbuncle star-set at the centre with a diamond, *L 8 May,*
£330 ($534)

4
A gold, enamel, coral and diamond hinged bangle, c.1865, the blue enamel bombé centre star-set with pink corals and rose diamonds, the shoulders similarly set; with a brooch/pendant and a brooch *en suite*, one coral deficient, *L 11 Dec,*
£1,925 ($2,695)

5
A gold and gem-set hinged bangle, c.1845, designed as two gold coiled serpents, the heads set with half-pearls and carbuncle, the eyes with onyx, *L 11 Dec,*
£1,650 ($2,310)

6
A gold, quartz cat's eye and diamond bangle, last quarter 19th century,
L 11 Dec,
£2,200 ($3,080)

7
A gold, enamel and diamond flexible bangle, c.1845, designed as a serpent, the body decorated with blue guilloché enamel, the head applied with a diamond foliate motif, the eyes set with cabochon rubies and rose diamonds, enamel slightly damaged, *L 8 May,*
£5,500 ($8,910)

8
A pearl and diamond bracelet, c.1900,
L 10 Apr,
£968 ($1,481)

9
A gold triple-hoop bangle, last quarter 19th century, the front set with three scarabs between corded wire shoulders,
L 8 May,
£935 ($1,514)

10
A gold and diamond hinged bangle, last quarter 19th century,
L 5 June,
£1,210 ($1,888)

11
A pearl and diamond bangle, c.1910, the rigid gold cuff applied with rows of pearls spaced by 120 round diamonds arranged in four rows of platinum, *NY 16 Apr,*
$6,325 (£4,217)

12
An 18-carat gold and diamond hinged bangle, the fluted band set with seven diagonal rows of pavé-set diamonds,
JHB 18 June,
R 2,310 (£722; $1,012)

1
A lady's gold, ruby and diamond cocktail watch, c.1940, slightly imperfect, *L 30 Jan,*
£462 ($679)

2
A lady's diamond wrist-watch, Baume and Mercier, Geneva, *L 10 Apr,*
£660 ($1,010)

3
A diamond and black enamel wristwatch, Black, Starr & Frost, c.1930, the movment by Audemars Piguet, set with 117 round and old European-cut diamonds, one missing, *NY 20 Oct,*
$8,250 (£5,769)

4
A lady's seed pearl and diamond wristwatch, Vulcain, 1930s, *G 14 May,*
SF 4,180 (£1,407; $2,266)

5
A lady's platinum, diamond and seed pearl wristwatch, French, c.1920, set with a total of 133 round diamonds, *NY 16 Apr,*
$3,025 (£2,017)

6
A gold, black enamel, onyx, diamond and pearl pendant/watch, Cartier, c.1915, some repair to enamel, *NY 20 Oct,*
$4,675 (£3,269)

7
A silver, gold, ruby and diamond lapel-watch, last quarter 19th century, the watch case applied with a turtle formed of round rubies, reversing to a white enamel dial, *NY 10 June,*
$2,530 (£1,664)

8
A gold, jade and diamond watch-clip, Van Cleef & Arpels, Paris, c.1935, the curved base applied with calibré-cut jades and bordered by 16 round diamonds, *NY 16 Apr,*
$2,750 (£1,833)

9
An 18-carat gold, platinum, diamond and enamel pendant/watch, Tiffany & Co., c.1910, the case applied with blue translucent enamel over a guilloché ground, the white enamel dial with subsidiary seconds dial, supported by a chain composed of alternating blue enamel links and small seed pearls, slight losses to enamel, *NY 16 Apr,*
$2,750 (£1,833)

10
Five yellow-gold watch chains, 27 to 43cm (10½ to 17in), *M 24 Feb,*
FF 6,882 (£666; $998)

11
An 18-carat gold watch chain, the oblong links connected by a rope motif, toggle and additional links, 41cm (16in), *JHB 22 Oct,*
R 2,900 (£906; $1,269)

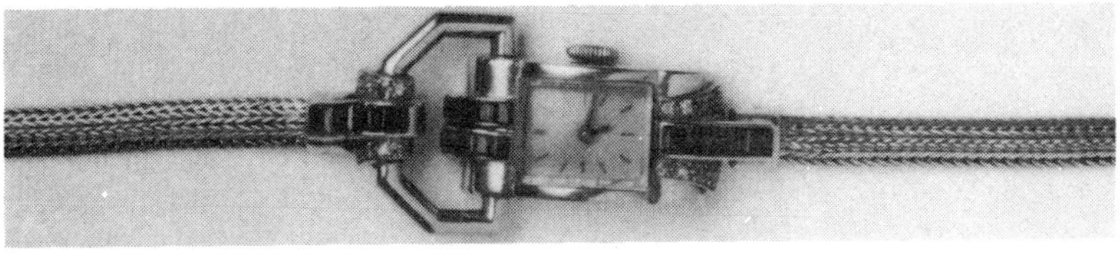
1

2

3

4

5

6

7

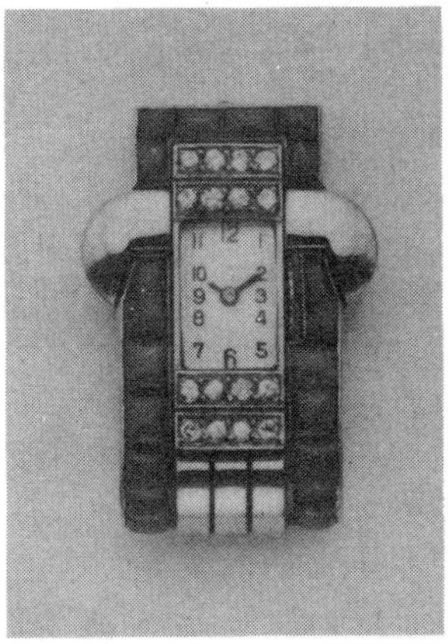
8

9

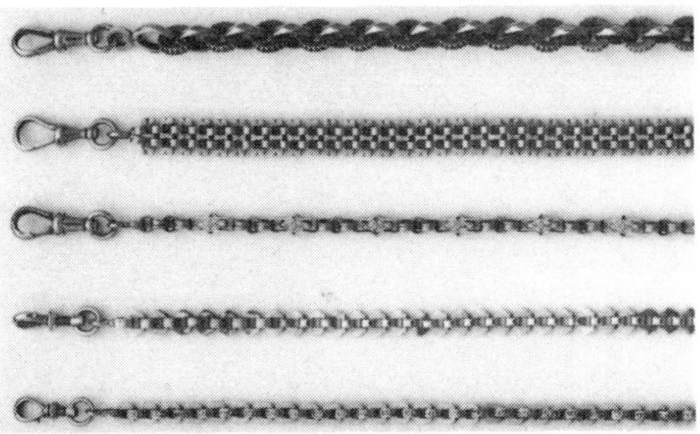
10

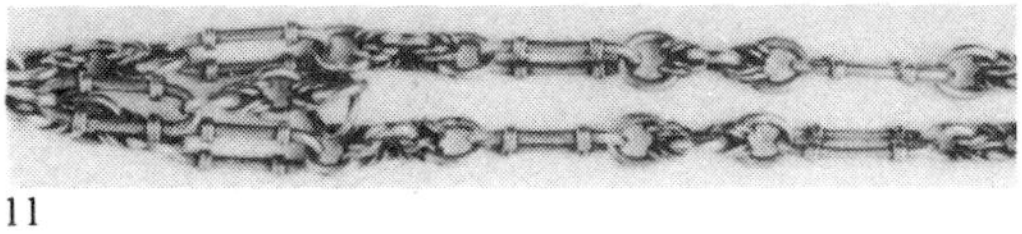
11

1

2

3

4

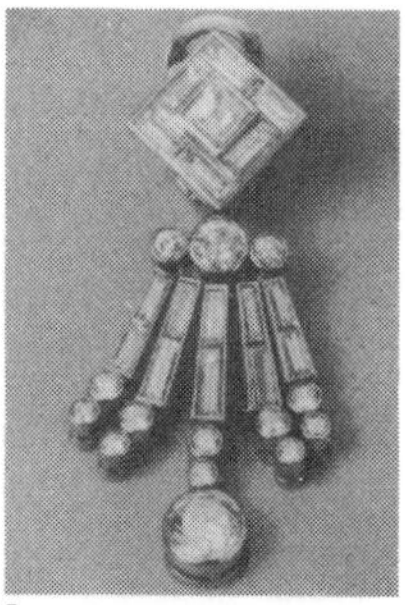
5

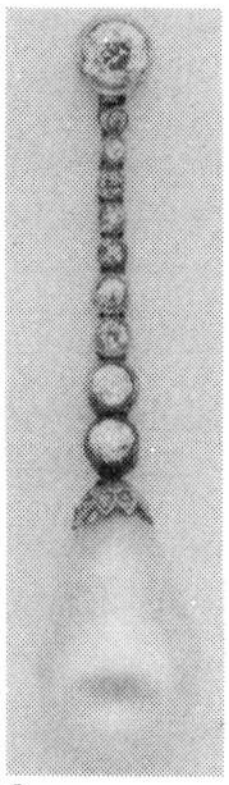
6

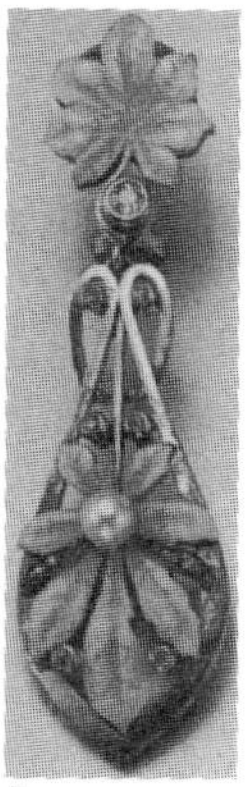
7

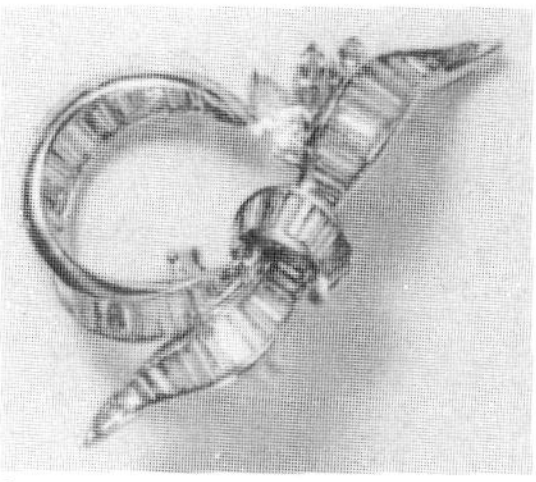
8

9

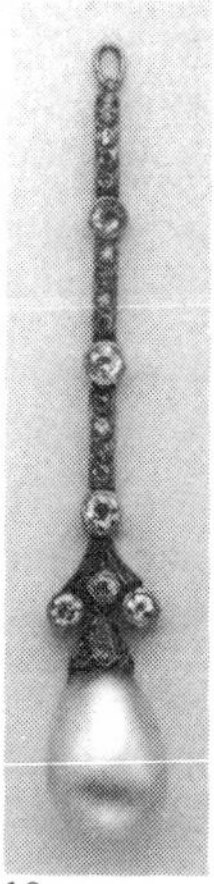
10

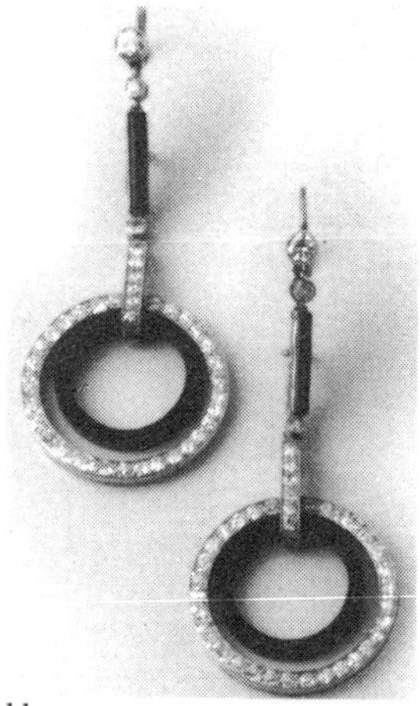
11

12

13

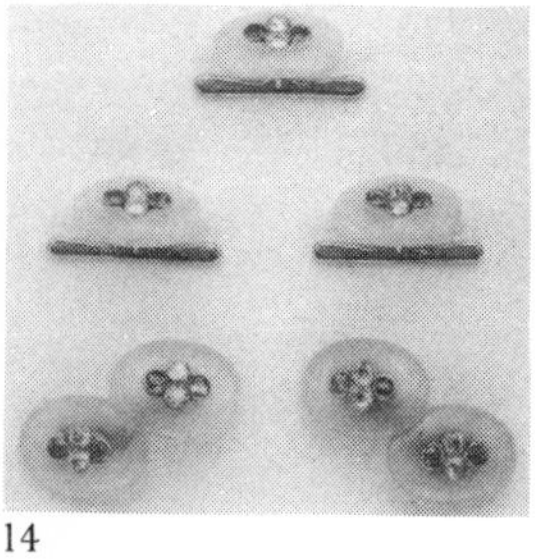
14

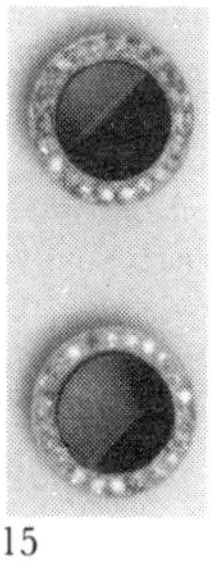
15

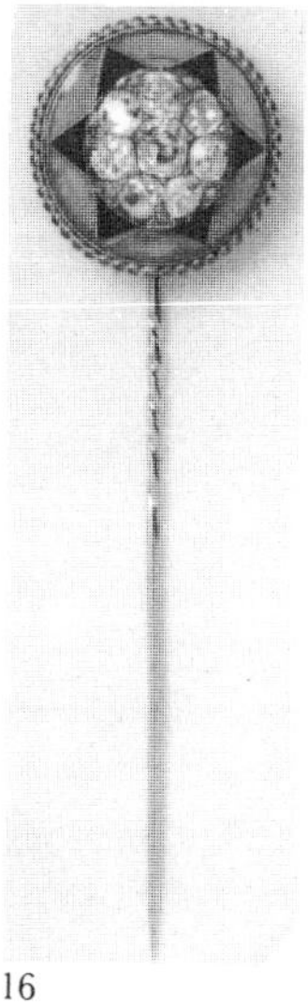
16

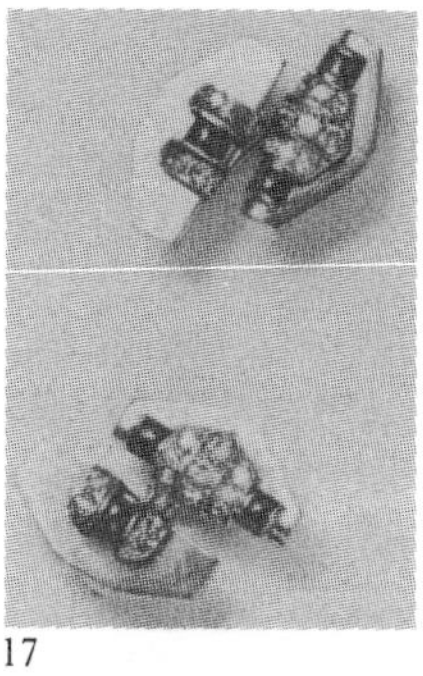
17

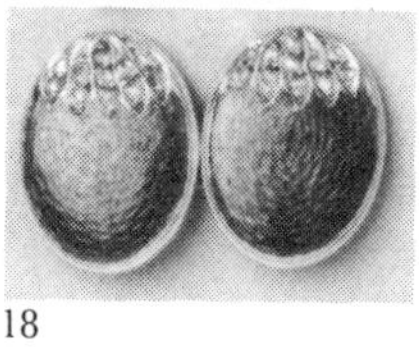
18

1
A pair of emerald and diamond pendent earrings, c.1925, one diamond deficient, later fitted case, *L 19 June,*
£3,630 ($5,735)

2
A pair of diamond ear-clips, each of flowerhead and foliate design, *L 10 July,*
£418 ($673)

3
A pair of emerald and diamond pendent earrings, *L 10 July,*
£605 ($974)

4
A pair of ruby and diamond earclips, c.1940, each of bouquet and coiled ribbon design, *L 13 Nov,*
£880 ($1,232)

5
A pair of diamond pendent earclips, *(one illustrated), L 11 Dec,*
£3,850 ($5,390)

6
A pair of natural pearl and diamond pendent earrings, *(one illustrated),* c.1920, the pendants in white gold with 20 European-cut diamonds, terminating in natural pearl drops with small rose-cut diamonds, *NY 10 Dec,*
$18,700 (£13,077)

7
A pair of gold, diamond and enamel pendent earrings, *(one illustrated),* Masriera, applied with leaf motifs shaded in green enamel, *NY 20 Oct,*
$3,575 (£2,500)

8
A pair of diamond ear-clips, *(one illustrated),* each designed as a tied ribbon set with baguette diamonds and embellished with three navette diamonds, *St.M 20 Feb,*
SF 7,150 (£2,440; $3,709)

9
A pair of pearl and diamond earrings, white gold mounts, *Tor 4 June,*
Can$962 (£476; $743)

10
A pair of natural pearl and diamond ear-pendants, *(one illustrated),* c.1920, the fringes of platinum set with old European-cut diamonds, *NY 10 Dec,*
$5,500 (£3,846)

11
A pair of onyx and diamond pendent earrings, of twin hoop design, *L 9 Oct,*
£2,970 ($4,158)

12
A pair of cultured black pearl and diamond ear-clips, *(one illustrated),* each designed as a stylised flowerhead motif, *Glen 25 Aug,*
£748 ($1,174)

13
A pair of 18-carat gold and diamond earclips, *(one illustrated),* Kutchinsky, of twisted Creole design set with brilliant-cut stones, *L 10 Apr,*
£1,100 ($1,683)

14
A chalcedony, demantoid garnet and diamond dress set, c.1915, comprising a pair of cufflinks and three studs, *NY 10 Dec,*
$3,080 (£2,154)

15
An onyx and diamond dress set, *(part illustrated),* comprising a pair of cufflinks, four buttons and two studs, *L 5 June,*
£1,760 ($2,746)

16
A gold, enamel and diamond tie pin, last quarter 19th century, *L 5 June,*
£935 ($1,459)

17
A pair of ruby and diamond cufflinks, each formed of a *bâton* set with small brilliants and cabochon rubies, *St.M 21 Feb,*
SF 3,520 (£1,201; $1,826)

18
A pair of gold, enamel and rose diamond cuff-links, *(one illustrated),* c.1910, each designed as a hazelnut, decorated with appropriately coloured enamel and set with rose diamonds, *Glen 25 Aug,*
£528 ($830)

1
A diamond ring, last quarter 19th century, set with cushion-shaped stones, *Glen 25 Aug,*
£858 ($1,347)

2
A royal blue enamel and diamond ring, c.1800, some diamonds deficient, *L 11 Dec,*
£1,430 ($2,002)

3
A three-colour gold and gem-set ring, c.1830, designed as a turquoise and ruby cluster, *L 8 May,*
£605 ($980)

4
An opal, enamel and diamond ring, c.1900, the opal chipped and cracked, *NY 16 Apr,*
$1,650 (£1,100)

5
A diamond ring, c.1905, set with rose and brilliant-cut stones, *Glas 5 Feb,*
£638 ($918)

6
An opal and diamond cluster ring, c.1900, *L 10 July,*
£638 ($1,027)

7
A jade and diamond ring, c.1925, the oval-shaped jade set between diamond shoulders, *L 11 Dec,*
£3,850 ($5,390)

8
An emerald and diamond plaque ring, *L 30 Jan,*
£1,760 ($2,587)

9
A diamond ring, designed as a stylised bow, *Glen 25 Aug,*
£550 ($864)

10
A half-pearl and diamond ring, last quarter 19th century, designed as a pair of hearts, *L 8 May,*
£682 ($1,104)

11
A pearl and diamond ring, c.1900, in the form of two entwined hearts beneath a bow, *NY 10 June,*
$3,080 (£2,026)

12
An 18-carat gold and diamond band ring, the wide band pavé-set with 192 round diamonds, *Tor 4 June,*
Can$4,400 (£2,178; $3,398)

13
A ruby and diamond 'heart' ring, Tiffany & Co., c.1910, *NY 10 Dec,*
$12,100 (£8,461)

14
A coral, black onyx and diamond ring, René Boivin, Paris, c.1935, the carved coral section studded with black onyx cabochons, centering a rock crystal disc applied with a diamond-set platinum medallion, *NY 10 June,*
$6,875 (£4,523)

15
A gold, black enamel and diamond minaudière, Cartier, c.1925, opening to reveal two compartments, a lipstick and fitted mirror, *NY 20 Oct,*
$7,150 (£5,000)

16
A silver-gilt and enamel compact, Cartier, London, 1933, with a coral bead and diamond thumbpiece, *L 19 June,*
£495 ($782)

17
A 14-carat gold and enamel necessaire with attached lipstick holder, c.1925, *St.M 20 Feb,*
SF 3,190 (£1,088; $1,654)

18
A pair of single pearl hairpins, each mounted in 18-carat gold with an oval-shaped pearl, *G 13 May,*
SF 4,400 (£1,486; $2,392)

19
A gold mesh evening bag, the hoop set with diamonds and five cabochon emeralds, French marks, 13.5cm (5¼in), *St.M 20 Feb,*
SF 8,250 (£2,815; $4,279)

20
A platinum, jade and diamond lorgnette, c.1915, the handle formed of a cylindrical jade, with a silver chain, *NY 10 Dec,*
$2,750 (£1,923)

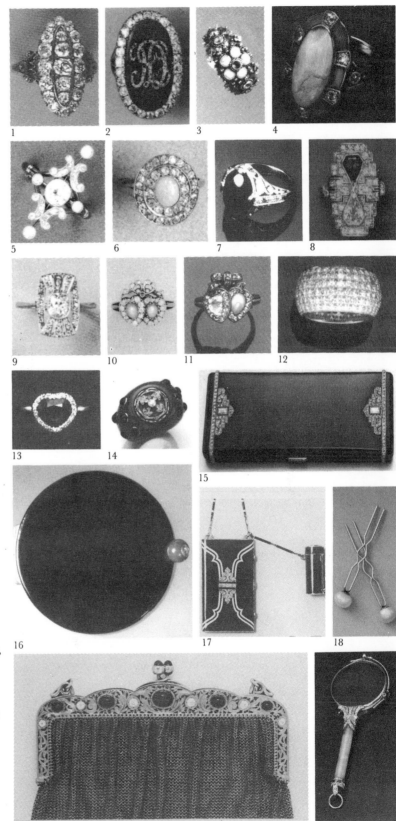

1

2

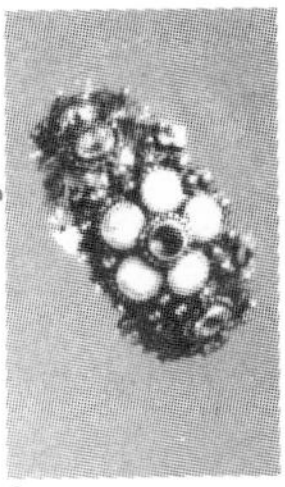
3

4

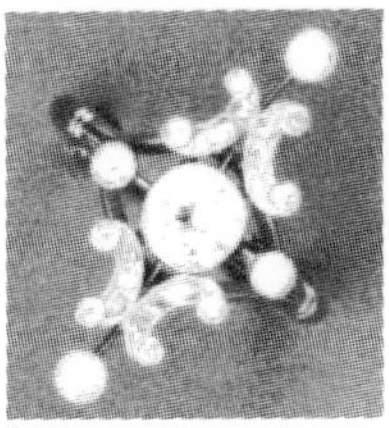
5

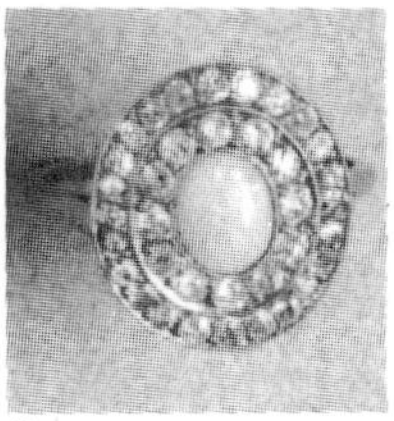
6

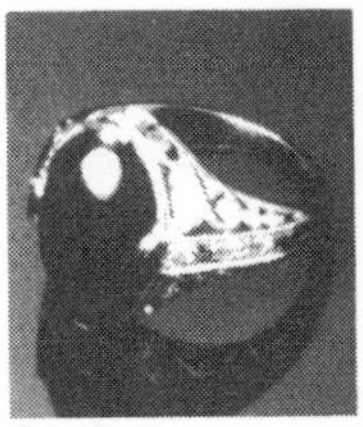
7

8

9

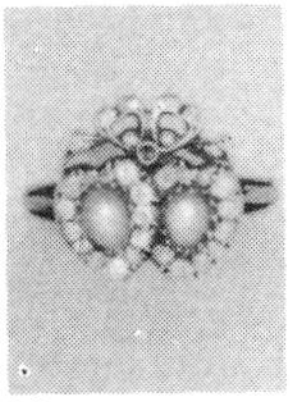
10

11

12

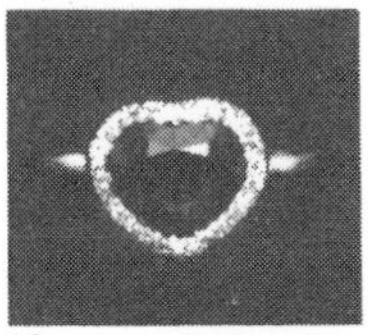
13

14

15

16

17

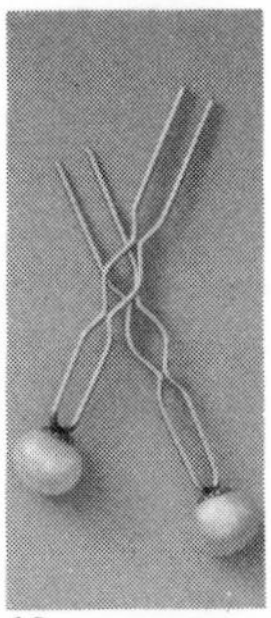
18

19

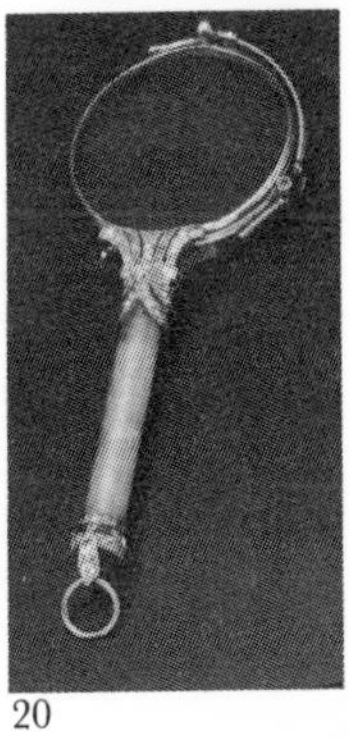
20

1940s Jewellery

JACQUELINE FAY

The decade of the 1940s conjures up the image of big gold and semi-precious stone jewellery. Platinum and diamond jewellery still existed, of course, for no style stops abruptly, but instead slides through a transition.

The preceding three decades presented white on white. At the turn of the century, gold jewellery was made with a platinum top, a novel idea to enhance the diamonds without the tarnishing greyness of silver, the white metal that preceded it (figs 1 and 2). As the decades passed, jewels were made entirely of platinum, striding towards the future, banishing the look of the 19th century entirely. Jewellers of the 1920s and 1930s took semi-precious stones from secondary jewellery and incorporated them in important new designs, accenting diamonds with pink or red coral, black onyx, turquoise, lapis and jade, cut or carved into

1

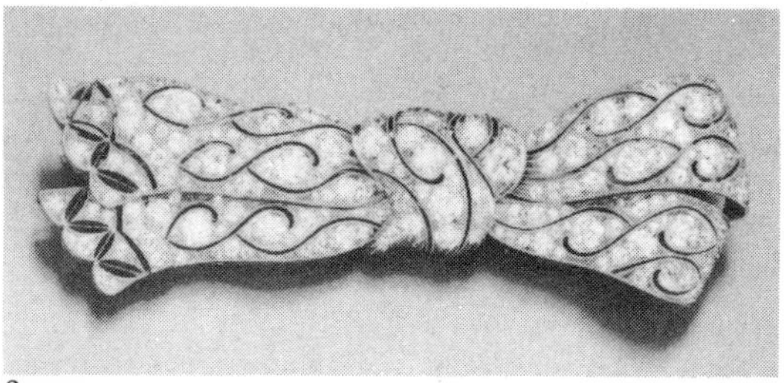

2

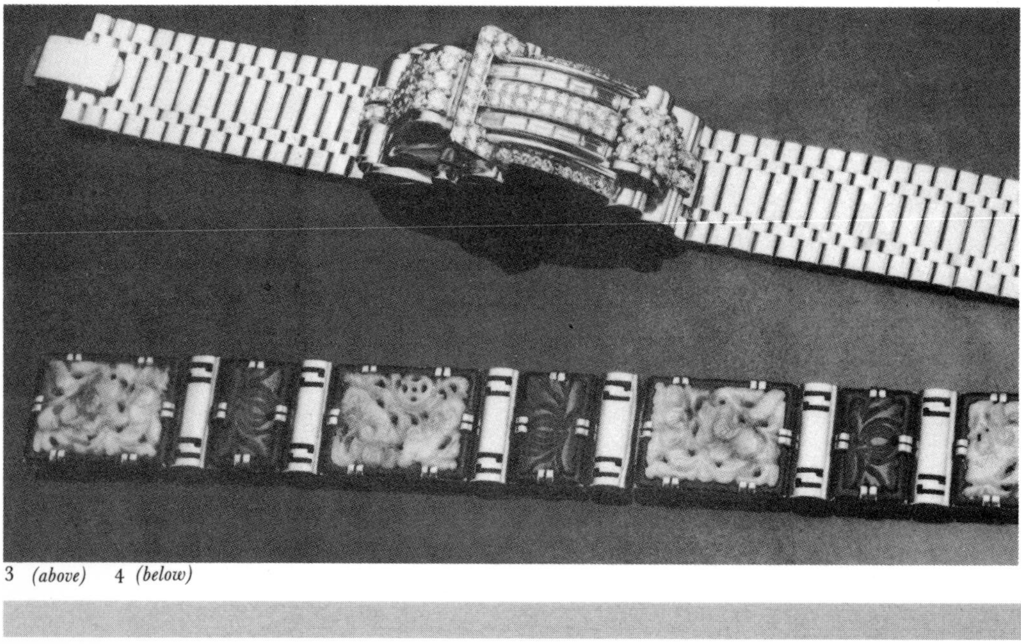

3 *(above)* 4 *(below)*

1
A diamond bracelet, c.1925, set throughout with circular cut diamonds, *L 13 Mar,*
£7,920 ($12,196)

2
A platinum and diamond bow brooch, Spaulding & Co., c.1920, *NY 10 June,*
$3,850 (£2,533)

3
A 14-carat gold and diamond bracelet-watch, c.1940, set with 10 baguette and 114 round and single-cut diamonds, opening to reveal a dial, *NY 10 June,*
$5,225 (£3,437)

4
A carved jade, coral and black enamel bracelet, Janesich, c.1930, *NY 10 June,*
$5,775 (£3,799)

shapes (fig.4). Small rubies, sapphires and emeralds received similar treatment, carved or calibré-cut to give colour or outline to all the white glitter of diamonds and platinum (figs 5 & 6).

With the Second World War, women's lives changed dramatically. Women burst into the workforce and joined the military in unprecedented numbers, donning tailored suits, wearing trousers in leisure time, showing more leg with short skirts, and adding large padded shoulders for balance. Jewellery had to change.

The military and industrial tone of the time is conveyed by the size and weight of the jewellery and by the polished gleam of metal. Patriotic jewels appeared — flags, aeroplanes and tanks (figs 7 & 8). Other designs evoked tank treads, chains of brickwork or tubular corrugated straps (figs 3, 9-10, 15). These pieces reflect the influence of Art Deco but in a heavier, bolder and more forceful style. This bravado demanded new stones. Citrus yellow to deep amber citrines, sky-blue to sea-green aquamarines, peridots and beryls in shades of green to yellow, deep royal purple amethysts (the so-called 'semi-precious' stones) could be had in giant sizes. Twenty, thirty, forty or fifty carats were used for a ring, whimsically, if not absurdly, flanked by petite two-tone gold bows. Eighty, ninety, one hundred carats were worn without a blink of the eye on the wrist in a bangle (figs 11-12 and colour illustrations p.337, figs 4 & 5). These were dramatic times and no time to be timid. Gold, with its maleability and its wonderful chameleon quality, changing from its natural yellow to pink, green or white when alloyed with copper, silver, or nickel, was ideal for these large pieces (figs 13-14, 25-26, and colour illustration p.337, fig.6). It was also used as an accent on the cheaper, and thus more readily-available, silver: for example

5

6

7

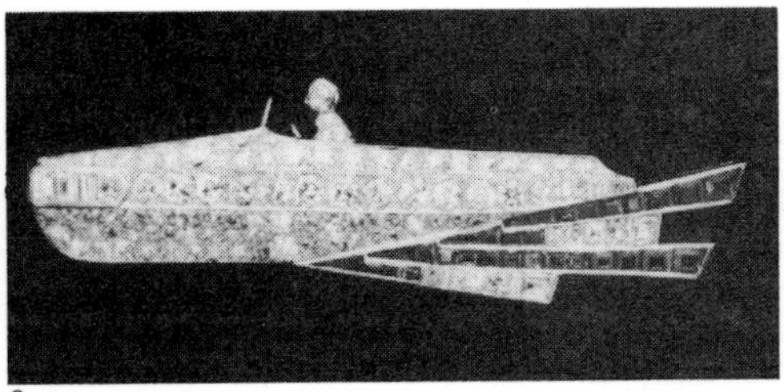

8

11

9

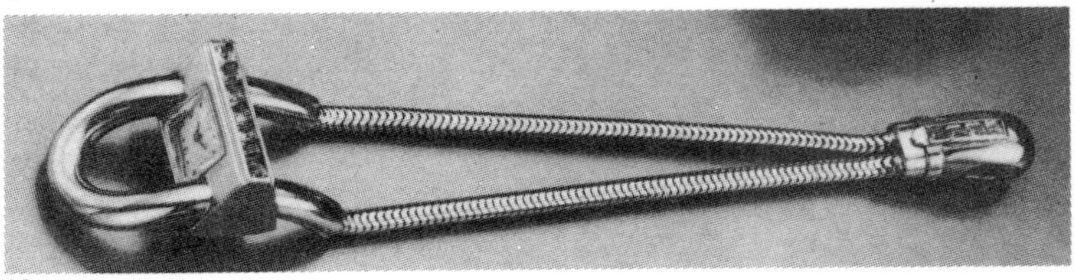

10

5
A diamond and synthetic sapphire bracelet, c.1930,
NY 10 June,
$5,225 (£3,437)

6
An emerald and diamond plaque brooch, c.1920, in fitted case, *L 19 June,*
£3,520 ($5,562)

7
A ruby, diamond and sapphire American flag brooch, Cartier, c.1930,
NY 12 June 1985,
$6,325 (£5,270)

8
A diamond and sapphire speedboat brooch, Cartier, c.1935, *NY 12 June 1985,*
$4,125 (£3,437)

9
A pink and gold and ruby wristwatch, c.1940, flanked by a stylised buckle motif,
NY 20 Oct,
$6,050 (£4,231)

10
A lady's gold and emerald wristwatch, Van Cleef & Arpels, New York, c.1940,
NY 10 June,
$7,425 (£4,885)

11
A pair of aquamarine and diamond pendent earings, c.1945, *L 30 Jan,*
£3,410 ($5,013)

for compacts and cigarette cases, badges of women's new independence.

Naturally the war affected the production of jewellery. In many countries, platinum was controlled to prevent it from falling into enemy hands. The flow of precious stones was interrupted by hostilities in the Far East and the use of synthetic rubies increased because the mines in Burma and Siam were cut off from the West. In Europe studios and workshops were destroyed, bringing ruin to some jewellers. Gold was rationed, and often the customer had to supply the gold and precious stones for new pieces.

The established jewellery houses survived and even flourished after the war. Cartier, Van Cleef & Arpels, Harry Winston and Tiffany & Co. continued to create their sumptuous feasts of diamonds, pearls and coloured stones, but also contributed to the 'New Look' (figs 16-17, 27-30).

Van Cleef & Arpels sold an exotic array of dancers (figs 18-20) designed by Maurice Duvalet and made by John Rubel's company. Ballerinas, can-can dancers and flamenco dancers, with flying legs and swirling skirts of rose-cut diamonds and bouquets of tiny coloured stones and pearls were both feminine and fun. Although John Rubel and Van Cleef & Arpels parted in 1943, they continued to produce these pieces independently until the early 1950s.

Paul Flato started his firm in the 1920s. A decade later he was famous from New York to Hollywood for his fashionable jewels and accessories, the work of designers such as Verdura, (fig.21). Fulco, Duc de Verdura, the premier designer of costume jewellery for Coco Chanel, came to New York in 1937, where he took a job as a designer for Flato. During the time he ran Flato's

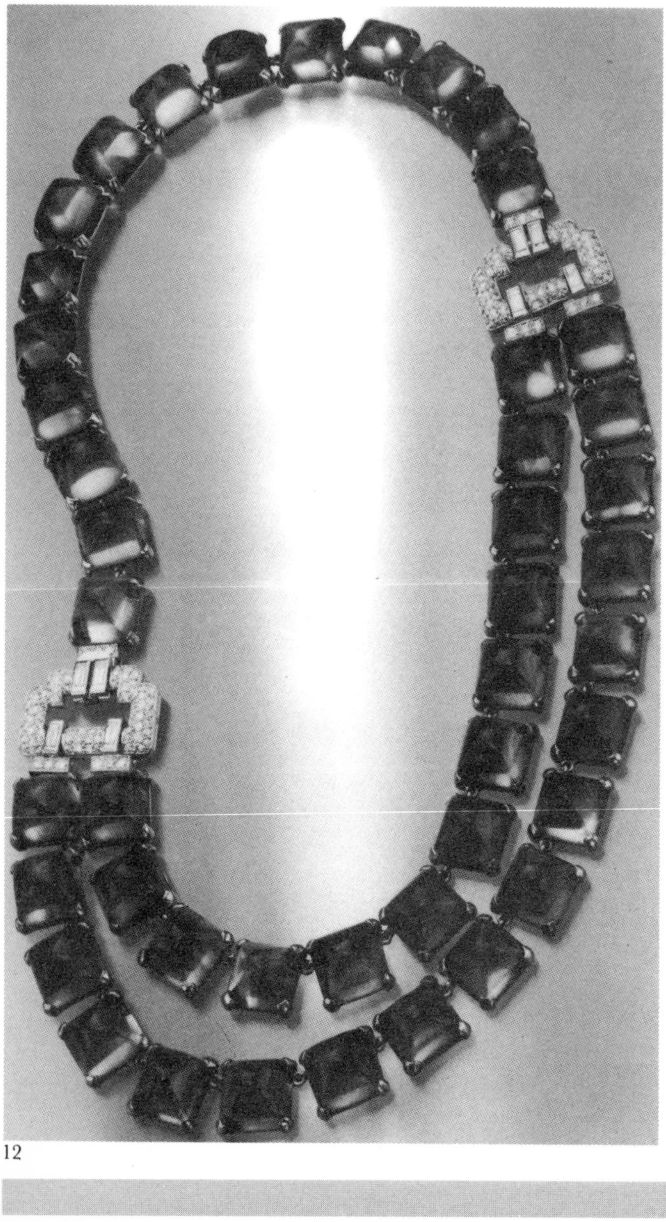

12

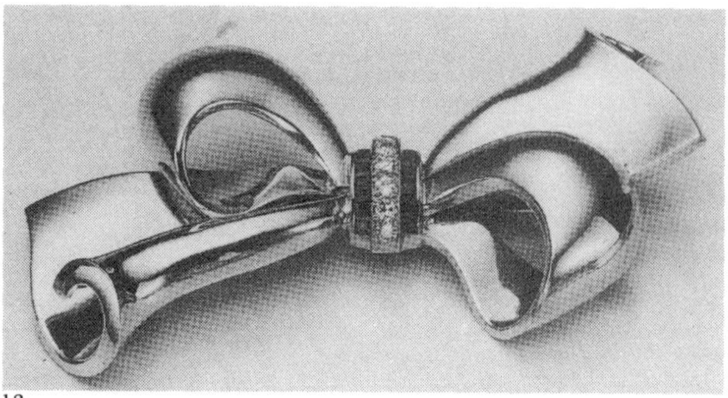

13

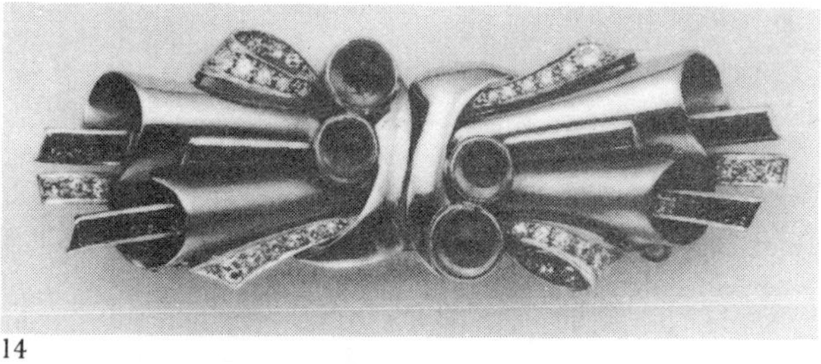

14

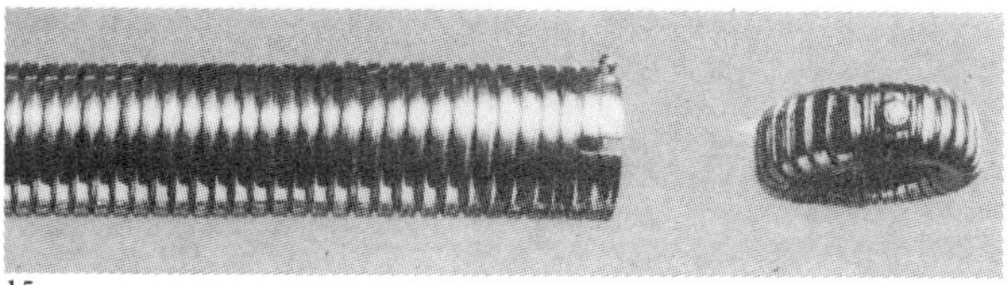

15

12
A citrine quartz and diamond necklace, Cartier, c.1940, composed of 45 square-shaped sugarloaf cabochon citrine quartz within gold prongs, *NY 20 Oct,* **$31,900 (£22,308)**

13
A gold, ruby and diamond bow brooch, c.1940, *NY 10 Dec,* **$9,350 (£6,538)**

14
A sapphire and diamond double-clip/brooch, c.1940, designed as curling drapery, *NY 10 Dec,* **$4,125 (£2,885)**

15
A gold necklace of flexible tubular linking *(not illustrated)* with a bracelet and similar gold and diamond ring, *L 10 July,* **£1,430 ($2,302)**

16
A pair of coral, amethyst and diamond earclips, Van Cleef & Arpels, *St M 20 Feb,*
SF 8,250 (£2,815; $4,280)

17
A gold and sapphire bracelet, Van Cleef & Arpels, New York, c.1940, with 196 square-shaped sapphires, *NY 16 Apr,*
$7,700 (£5,133)

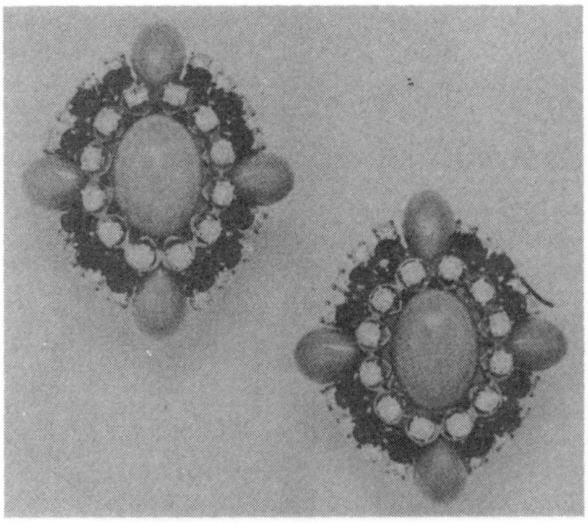

16

17

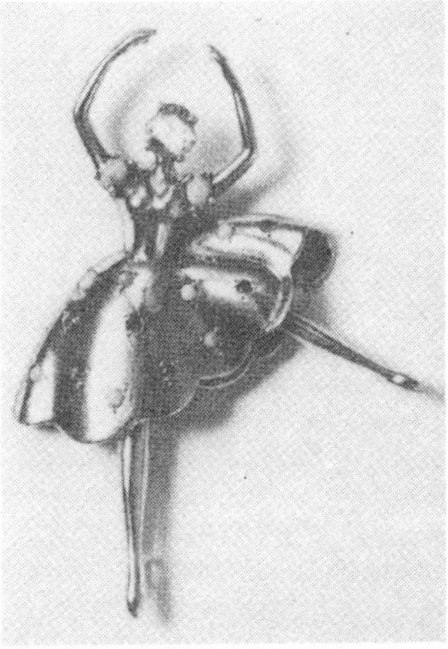

18

19

18
A gold and gem-set ballerina brooch, Van Cleef & Arpels, c.1940, her face formed of a single rose-cut diamond, *St M 20 Feb,*
SF 2,090 (£713; $1,084)

19
A diamond, ruby and emerald ballerina brooch, Van Cleef & Arpels, c.1940, *NY 10 Dec 1985,*
$41,800 (£29,857)

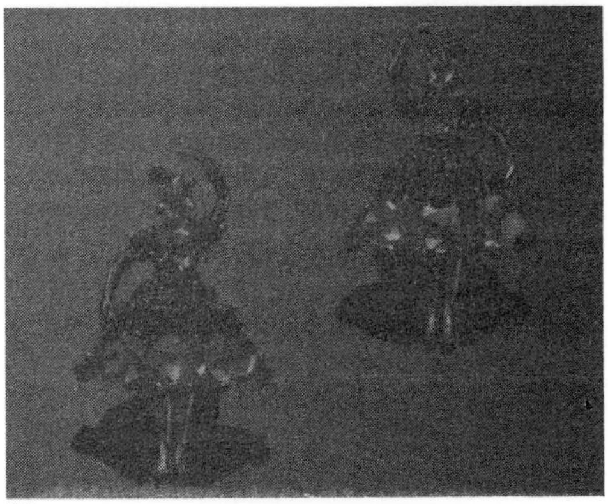

20

20
A pair of diamond, ruby and emerald ballerina earclips, Van Cleef & Arpels, c.1940, *NY 10 Dec 1985,*
$17,600 (£12,571)

21
A gold, diamond and citrine quartz brooch, Paul Flato, c.1940, *NY 22 Apr 1985,*
$3,850 (£3,208)

22
An amethyst, sapphire and diamond flower brooch, Schlumberger, c.1953, *NY 6 Dec 1984,*
$9,900 (£8,250)

23
An emerald, amethyst and diamond Pegasus clip, Schlumberger, c.1941, *NY 6 Dec 1984,*
$9,350 (£7,791)

24
An amethyst, pink tourmaline and diamond shell clip, Schlumberger, c.1951, *NY 6 Dec 1984,*
$23,100 (£19,250)

21

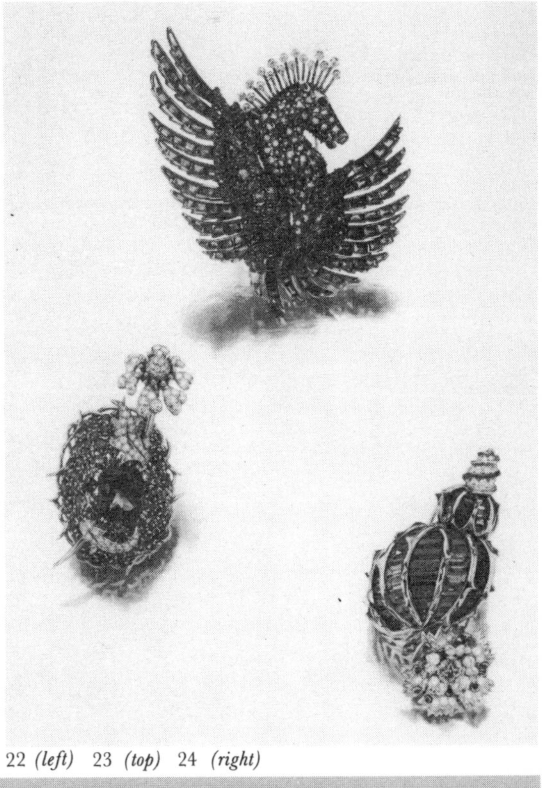

22 *(left)* 23 *(top)* 24 *(right)*

Hollywood shop on Sunset Boulevard, he designed jewellery for Katharine Hepburn to wear in the movie *Philadelphia Story*. In 1939, Verdura returned to New York to open his own shop on Fifth Avenue and his unique and idiosyncratic designs often made the covers of *Vogue* and *Harpers' Bazaar*. He opened another shop in Paris in 1947 and was popular throughout the 1950s.

Jean Schlumberger also had his roots in the world of haute couture as a costume jewellery designer for Schiaparelli (figs 22-24). His experiments with his own designs became the rage in the late Thirties and when he came to New York in 1940 to flee the Nazis, he created a jewelled suite of armour called 'Trophy' for Diana Vreeland, the 'high priestess' of fashion and editor of *Vogue*.

After the war women's lives changed again as men returned to reclaim the jobs they had temporarily filled and fashions changed too: off came military uniforms and business suits. In 1947 Christian Dior created another 'New Look', banishing shoulder pads in favour of natural, rounded shoulders and cinching in waistlines, which then burst out into long, full swirling skirts. Jewels had to change too, and the style we now think of as 'Forties' passed into oblivion. Today, however, after languishing in drawers and bank vaults for forty years, these pieces are back in vogue.

Further reading:
Sotheby's Geneva, *The Jewels of the Duchess of Windsor*, sale catalogue, 2/3 April, 1987
Melissa Gabardi, *Gioielli Anni '40, The Jewels of the 1940s in Europe*, 1982
Peter Hinks, *Twentieth Century British Jewellery, 1900 to 1980*, 1983
Sylvie Raulet, *Van Cleef & Arpels*, 1986

25
A gold, ruby and diamond brooch, c.1945, of draped ribbon design, *L 10 July*, **£715 ($1,151)**

26
A rosé-gold and diamond dress-clip, c.1940, with two cabochon sapphires, *St M 21 Feb*, **SF 4,180 (£1,426; $2,168)**

27
An emerald and diamond ring, Trabert & Hoeffer, Mauboussin, c.1940, *NY 10 Dec*, **$6,600 (£4,615)**

28
An 18-carat gold and diamond dress-clip, Gübelin, c.1940, simulating folds of lace, *St M 20 Feb*, **SF 6,050 (£2,064; $3,138)**

29
A gold and diamond brooch, Cartier, c.1940, *NY 10 Dec*, **$1,760 (£1,231)**

30
A coral, amethyst and diamond bracelet, Van Cleef & Arpels, *St M 20 Feb*, **SF 13,750 (£4,692; $7,133)**

25

26

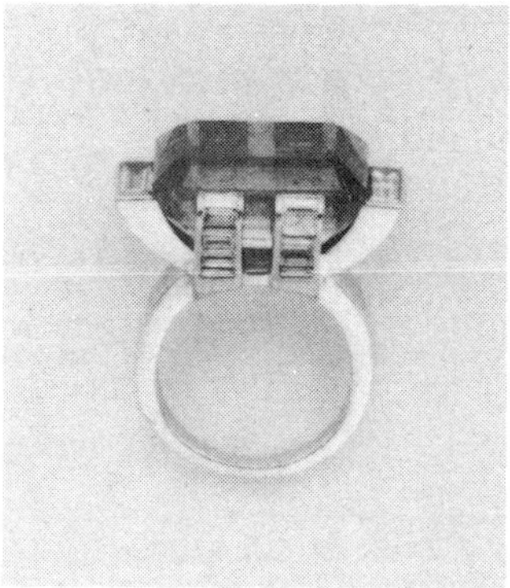
27

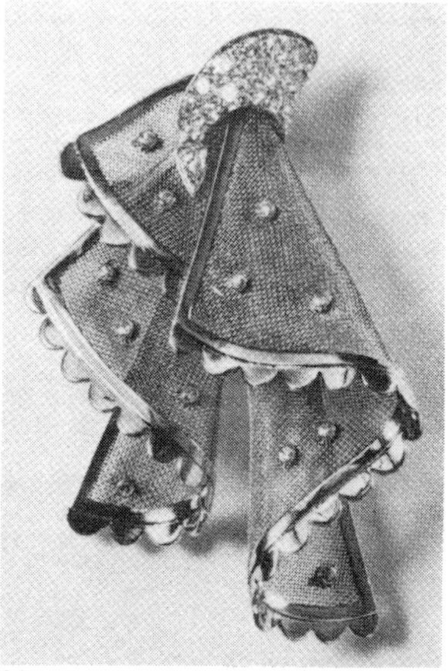
28

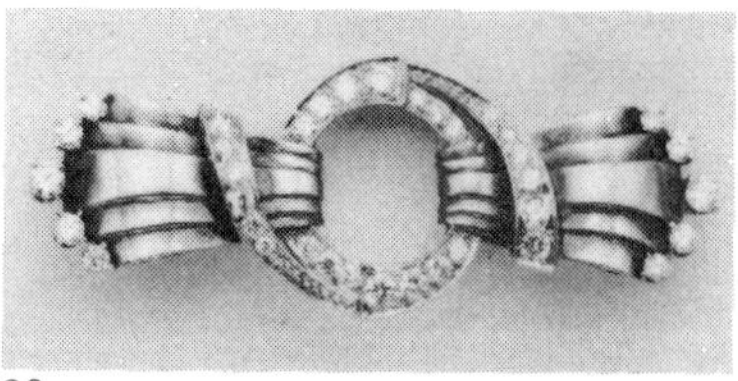
29

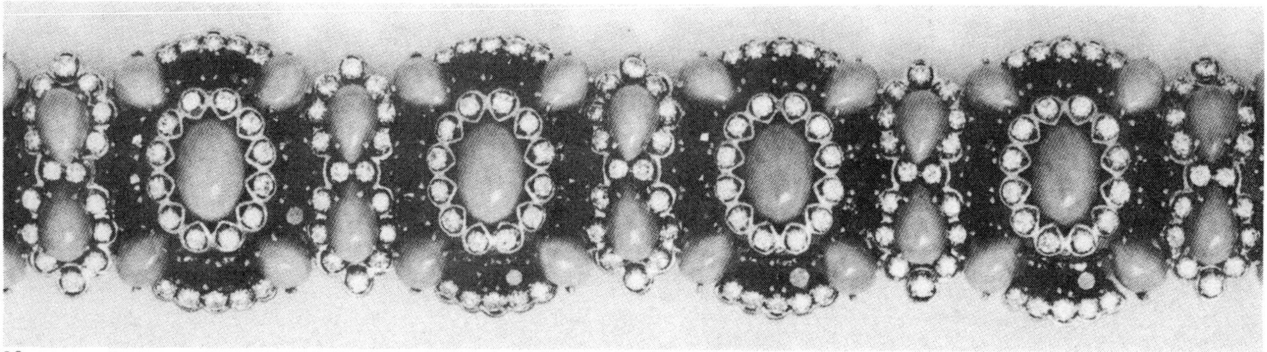
30

1
An opal and diamond brooch, c.1900, *L 30 Jan,*
£825 ($1,213)

2
A sapphire, pearl and diamond pendant, c.1910, *L 11 Dec,*
£990 ($1,386)

3
A pair of lapis lazuli and diamond ear-pendants, French, c.1920, *St.M 22 Feb,*
SF 11,000 (£3,754; $5,706)

4
A green beryl, diamond and sapphire ring, c.1940, the 18-carat pink and yellow gold mounting set with one large emerald-cut green beryl flanked by diamonds and calibré-cut sapphires, *NY 10 June,*
$9,900 (£6,513)

5
A citrine quartz and diamond brooch, Cartier, London, c.1940, *NY 10 June,*
$3,575 (£2,352)

6
A gold, ruby and diamond bangle-bracelet, c.1940, of stylised crossover design, *NY 10 June,*
$7,700 (£5,066)

7
A black enamel and diamond lorgnette and chain, Boucheron, Paris, c.1920, the chain of later date, approx 91.5cm (36in) long, *NY 10 June,*
$6,875 (£4,523)

8
A rock crystal and sapphire brooch, René Boivin, Paris, c.1935, the rock crystal ring suspended from a platinum loop set with sapphires and two shaped rock crystal sections, *NY 10 June,*
$2,750 (£1,809)

9
A sapphire and diamond pansy brooch, c.1935, unsigned but made by Oscar Heyman & Bros., *NY 10 June,*
$6,600 (£4,342)

1

2

3

4

5

6

7

8

9

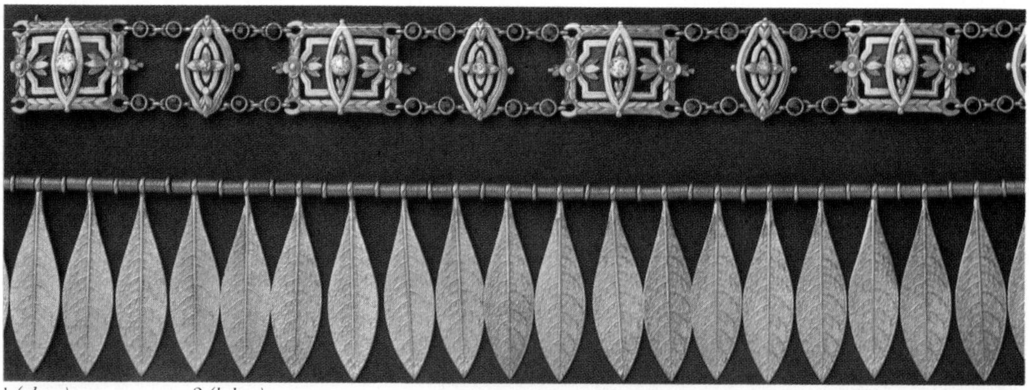

1 *(above)* 2 *(below)*

3

4

5

6

7

8

9

1
A gold, enamel, sapphire and diamond bracelet, M Gautrait for L. Gariod, last quarter 19th century, *L 8 May,*
£5,720 ($9,266)

2
A gold necklace, Phillips of Cockspur Street, London, c.1870, designed as a deep fringe of foliate motifs in Hellenistic style, slightly imperfect, and a pair of pendent earrings *en suite, L 8 May,*
£6,050 ($9,801)

3
An opal and diamond ring, *St.M 22 Feb,*
SF 18,700 (£6,382; $9,701

4
A sapphire and diamond brooch, last quarter 19th century, mounted in silver and gold, *G 14 May,*
SF 19,800 (£6,667; $10,733)

5
A pair of plique-à-jour enamel and diamond ear-pendants, *(one illustrated),* c.1900, *St.M 22 Feb,*
SF 14,300 (£4,880; $7,418

6
A gold, pearl and cameo habillé brooch, last quarter 19th century, the onyx cameo of an African girl, with necklace *en suite* and a pair of gold, enamel and gem-set earrings, each designed as a blackamoor, *L 8 May,*
£3,300 ($5,346)

7
A French gold, sapphire and diamond snake bangle-bracelet, last quarter 19th century, *NY 20 Oct,*
$4,950 (£3,461)

8
A French gold and cornelian intaglio necklace, c.1875, composed of chased gold sections depicting Medusa heads and satyrs, alternating with intaglios depicting the profiles of warriors, approx 41cm (16in), *NY 20 Oct,*
$7,700 (£5,385)

9
A diamond bracelet, designed as two elongated buckle motifs, *L 30 Jan,*
£3,740 ($5,498)

1
A German silver-gilt tea urn, burner and stand, Johann George Humbert, Berlin, 1821-37, with cast eagle finial, engraved *28M2* being a weight mark for the Royal House of Prussia, 49cm (19¼in) high, 210oz 12dwt (6551gr), *G 11 Nov,*
SF 57,200 (£23,636; $33,800)

2
A German silver-gilt travelling chocolate set, Johann Erhard Heuglin II, Augsburg, 1720-21, applied with medallions symbolising Summer, Spring, Autumn, Diana and Mars, and with Böttger porcelain cup with gilt chinoiserie decoration, 21.5cm (8½in) wide, 35oz 10dwt (1106gr), *G 11 Nov,*
SF 29,700 (£12,273; $17,550)

3
A German silver-gilt tankard, maker's mark apparently RN over I within a shield, Frankfurt, c.1600, the body and cover matted between plain bands, 15cm (6in) high, 10oz 12dwt (332gr), *G 11 Nov,*
SF 19,800 (£8,182; $11,700)

4
A German silver-gilt tankard, Hans Manhart I, Augsburg, 1590-95, with three applied ovals pierced with a cherub and his dog, within strapwork and foliage, 15.5cm (6¼in) high, 15oz 8dwt (480gr), *G 11 Nov,*
SF 57,200 (£23,636; $33,800)

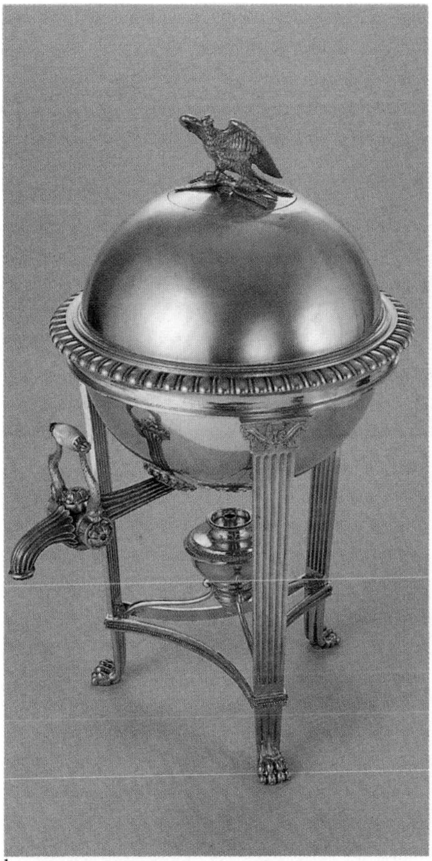
1

2

3

4

1

2

3-8

1
A pair of George III tea caddies, maker's mark T.I., London, 1771, in contemporary unmarked silver-mounted tortoise-shell-veneered casket, 10.5cm (4in) high, 20oz (622gr), *L 19 June,*
£23,100 ($36,498)

2
A pair of George III three-light candelabra, Benjamin Smith, London, 1814, 47cm (18½in), 147oz (4540gr), *L 19 June,*
£8,250 ($13,035)

3
A George III silver-gilt four-piece tea and coffee set, Edward Cornelius Farrell, London, 1817, Britannia Standard, and a tea kettle on lampstand by John Pero, London, 1737, decorated c.1817 (?by Farrell), 24.5cm (9½in), 237oz (7370gr), *NY 12 Dec,*
$11,550 (£8,250)

4
A George III silver-gilt sugar sifter and two caddy spoons, Edward Cornelius Farrell, London, 1817-18, 9oz 10dwt (295gr), *NY 12 Dec,*
$1,100 (£786)

5
A set of four George III silver-gilt salts, Edward Cornelius Farrell, London, 1818, 7cm (2¾in), 23oz 10dwt (730gr), *NY 12 Dec,*
$2,310 (£1,650)

6
Two George III silver-gilt bowls, Edward Cornelius Farrell, London, 1817, Britannia Standard, 18cm (7in) diam., 55oz (1710gr), *NY 12 Dec,*
$3,300 (£2,357)

7
Two George III silver-gilt covered bowls, Edward Cornelius Farrell, London, 1817, Britannia Standard, 18 and 14.5cm (7 and 5¾in), 67oz (2084gr), *NY 12 Dec,*
$2,860 (£2,043)

8
A George III silver-gilt tea caddy set, Edward Cornelius Farrell, London, 1817, Britannia Standard, 86oz 10dwt (2690gr), *NY 12 Dec,*
$14,300 (£10,214)

1
A French silver-gilt nécessaire, Strasbourg, c.1730-80, comprising an écuelle, cover and stand by Louis Imlin, a spice-box by Charles-Louis Emmerich, and a knife, fork and spoon, fiddle and thread pattern, by Jean-Jacques Kirstein, bowl 30.5cm (12in), 54oz 18dwt (1710gr), *M 24 June,*
FF 288,600 (£25,745; $40,162)

2
A French parcel-gilt four-piece tea and coffee set with tray, J. V. Morel & Co., Paris, c.1845, retailed by Duponchel, in fitted case with the crowned monogram of Louis Philippe, the sides formed of matted and fluted shells, coffee pot 29cm (11½in), 250oz (7775gr), *NY 8 Apr,*
$49,500 (£34,138)

3
A Victorian ivory-mounted parcel-gilt silver electrotype tankard, Elkington & Co., Birmingham, 1868, after the original designed by Auguste Adolphe Willms and chased by Léonard Morel-Ladeuil, inset with four ivory plaques depicting Comedy, Tragedy, Song and Dance, 33cm (13in), 91oz 10dwt (2845gr), *L 24 Apr,*
£4,400 ($7,040)

4
A set of two identical pairs of Georgian silver-gilt table candlesticks, after designs by William Kent, one pair by Edward Wakelin, 1757, the other by John Parker and Edward Wakelin, London, 1775, with four silver-gilt three-light branches by Paul Storr, 1810, to match, formerly in the collection of the Duke of Newcastle, sold 1921, candlesticks 30.5cm (12in), 429oz (13342gr), *NY 5 Nov,*
$110,000 (£77,465)

1

2

3

4

1

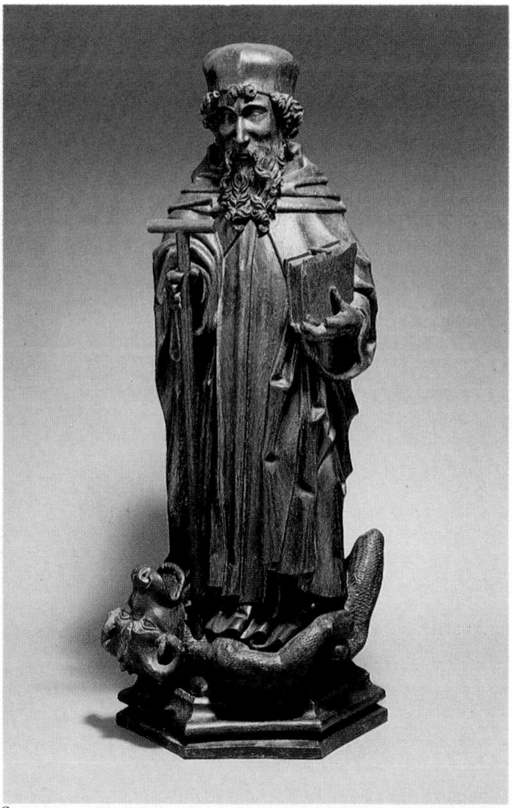
2

3

4

1
A giltwood and polychrome figure of St. George, late 15th century, probably Tyrol, in full Gothic armour, lance replaced, gilding probably original, face repainted, 95cm (37½in), *L 3 July,*
£10,450 ($16,825)

2
A North German oak figure of St. Anthony, c.1480, trampling on a devil, a book of gospels in his left hand, crutch replaced, 113cm (44½in), *L 3 July,*
£7,150 ($11,512)

3
A French bronze figure of Bacchus, early 18th century, workshops of Pierre Garnier, on gilt bronze base, 33.5cm (13½in), *L 11 Dec,*
£19,800 ($27,720)

4
A North Italian terracotta Madonna and Child, c.1447-53, from the workshops of Donatello, traces of pigmentation and gilding, some losses, including the tip of the child's nose, 70.5cm (27¾in), *NY 25 Nov,*
$41,800 (£29,857)

1
An English carved lime-wood coronation relief of Queen Anne, c.1702, workshop of Grinling Gibbons, the Queen wearing the Garter Star, carved with fruit and flowers including acorns for England, thistles for Scotland, shamrock for Ireland and marguerites for France, in beaded surround, 108cm (42½in), *L 3 July,*
£20,900 ($33,649)

2
A marble bust of Mademoiselle d'Harcourt, dated 1754, by Jean-Baptiste Pigalle, inscribed *Mademoiselle D'Harcourt, fait par J. B. Pigalle*, probably Louise-Angelique , daughter of 4th Duke of Harcourt, tip of nose replaced, 56cm (22in), *NY 25 Nov,*
$33,000 (£23,571)

3
A South German walnut and fruitwood marquetry games board, early 18th century, the exterior for chess or draughts, with raised borders,crowned by female portrait heads, 53.5m (21in), *L 3 July,*
£11,000 ($17,710)

4
A late Louis XV steel door lock and key, c.1772, key dated, with coat of arms and initials G.L., lock 39.5cm (15½in), *L 22 Apr,*
£6,380 ($10,017)

5
A heliotrope goblet, c.1600, probably from the Imperial court workshop at Prague, mount with white enamelling, enamelled gold relief of the Virgin and Child in centre, 7.5cm (3in), *L 11 Dec,*
£5,720 ($8,008)

1

2

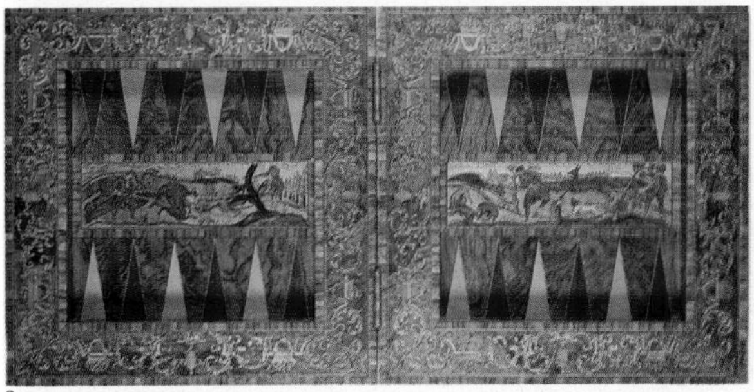
3

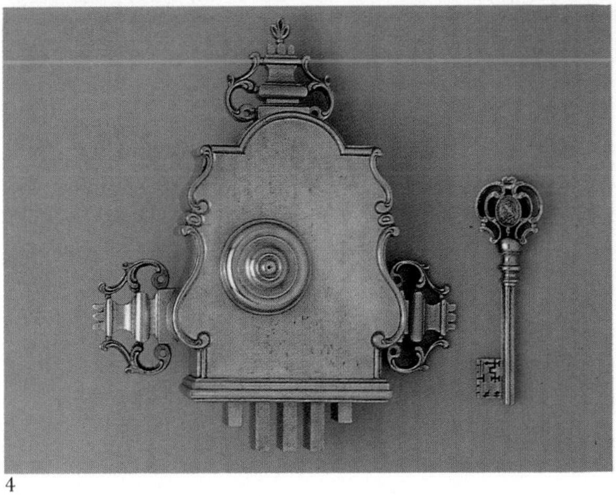
4

5

1

2

3

1
A Florentine 'oak-leaf' drug jar, second quarter 15th century, painted on each side with a pair of stylised birds among oak leaves, rim chip, glaze rubbed, the unglazed base incised *Hn*, and inscribed and dated July 1873, 15cm (6in), *L 7 Oct,*
£35,200 ($49,280)

2
A Montelupo 'oak-leaf' drug jar, second half 15th century, with a naively painted animal within a circular panel reserved on a ground of oak leaves, 15.5cm (6in), *L 7 Oct,*
£12,100 ($16,940)

3
A garniture of three Coalport 'Japan' pattern vases and covers, 1805-15, comprising a pair and one larger, each hexagonal, with dolphin's mask handles, gilt seated *kylin* knop, some cracks and repairs, 51 and 65cm (20 and 25½in), *NY 25 Jan,*
$9,350 (£6,727)

1
A Chelsea asparagus tureen and cover, 1752-58, a slender stalk caught between the ribbons forming the knop, red anchor marks and painter's numerals 66, 18cm (7in), *L 1 July,*
£12,100 ($19,360)

2
A Liverpool Delftware nautical punch bowl, c.1760, painted with a sailing ship above the inscription *Success to the Ann and Catharine*, the rim with a panelled and diaper border, the exterior with two sprays of flowers in a typical 'Fazackerly' palette, slight grazing to the rim, 26.5cm (10½in), *L 25 Feb,*
£5,500 ($8,250)

3
An Obadiah Sherratt group of Polito's menagerie, c.1810, modelled as a fairground booth, damaged, 29cm (11½in), *L 25 Feb,*
£9,900 ($14,850)

4
A Worcester plate from the Duke of Gloucester service, 1770-75, enamelled with a spray of plums, strawberries, hops and a peach encircled by moths, insects and fruiting branches, the border with reserves of insects, gilt crescent mark, 23cm (9in), *L 1 July,*
£9,350 ($14,960)

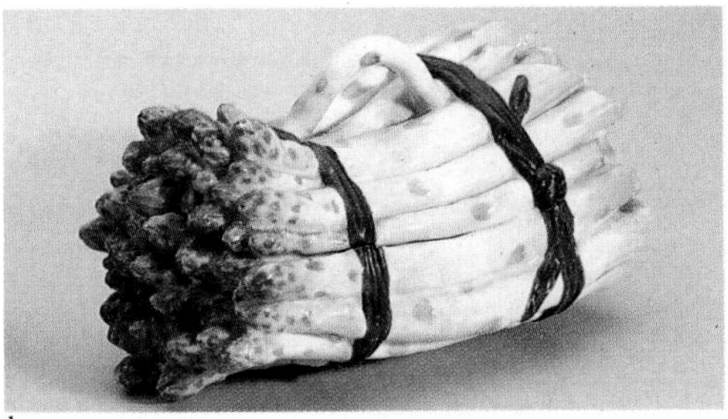
1

2

3

4

1

2

1
A Moustiers faience tureen and cover, Frères Ferrat workshop, c.1770, decorated in *petit-feu* tones with chinoiserie scenes, the knop in the form of an apple, slight restoration, 37cm (14½in), *M 25 Feb,*
FF 111,000 (£10,735; $16,103)

This very rare piece is the only known tureen of this type with chinoiserie decoration from this workshop.

2
A Meissen dinner service, *(part illustrated),* Marcolini period, early 19th century, with later decoration, comprising 116 pieces, crossed swords marks in blue with star, *M 23 June,*
FF 77,700 (£6,931; $10,813)

1
A Meissen figure of Harlequin, c.1744, from the series of the Commedia dell'Arte modelled by P. Reinicke and J. J. Kändler for the Duke of Weissenfels, in dancing pose before a tree-stump support, restored, 14cm (5½in), *L 7 Oct,*
£4,400 ($6,160)

2
A Nymphenburg figure of a fisherman, c.1760, modelled by F. A. Bustelli, holding a large carp, a fishing net lying on the ground, on rococo-shaped base outlined in gilding, one finger missing, impressed shield mark and I, painter's mark *Nis/sf* in brown, 16cm (6¼in), *L 4 Mar,*
£8,250 ($12,375)

3
A Meissen armorial tureen, cover and stand, c.1740, from the service made for Johann Christian von Hennicke, of baroque silver shape, the sides painted with *Indianische Blumen* and applied with naturalistic European flowers, the cover and stand with the coat of arms, repairs, crossed swords in blue, 41cm (16in), *L 7 Oct,*
£7,480 ($10,472)

4
An early Meissen 'Wöchnerinnen Terrine', cover and stand, c.1723, painted by J. G. Höroldt with chinoiserie scenes, one Oriental brewing tea and others at various pursuits, gilder's mark 3, 16cm (6½in), *L 4 Mar,*
£15,950 ($23,925)

1

2

3

4

1

2

1
A Gallé fruitwood and marquetry buffet, c.1900, the lower part with bronze mounts in the form of ears of wheat, the upper part with bronze mounts in the form of branches and leaves, and decorated with a marquetry panel of a stylised landscape, 191.5cm (6ft 3½in) high, *M 19 Oct,*
FF 466,200 (£50,129; $70,181)

2
A rosewood and ivory book-case, Emile-Jacques Ruhlmann, 1926, with seven movable shelves, 174cm (68½in) high, *M 19 Oct,*
FF 94,350 (£10,145; $14,203)

3
A Bugatti day bed, c.1900, inlaid with brass and pewter, the head end with traces of painted design of formalised bamboo shoots, upholstered in chamois leather, 220cm (7ft 3in) long, *L 19 Dec,*
£16,500 ($23,100)

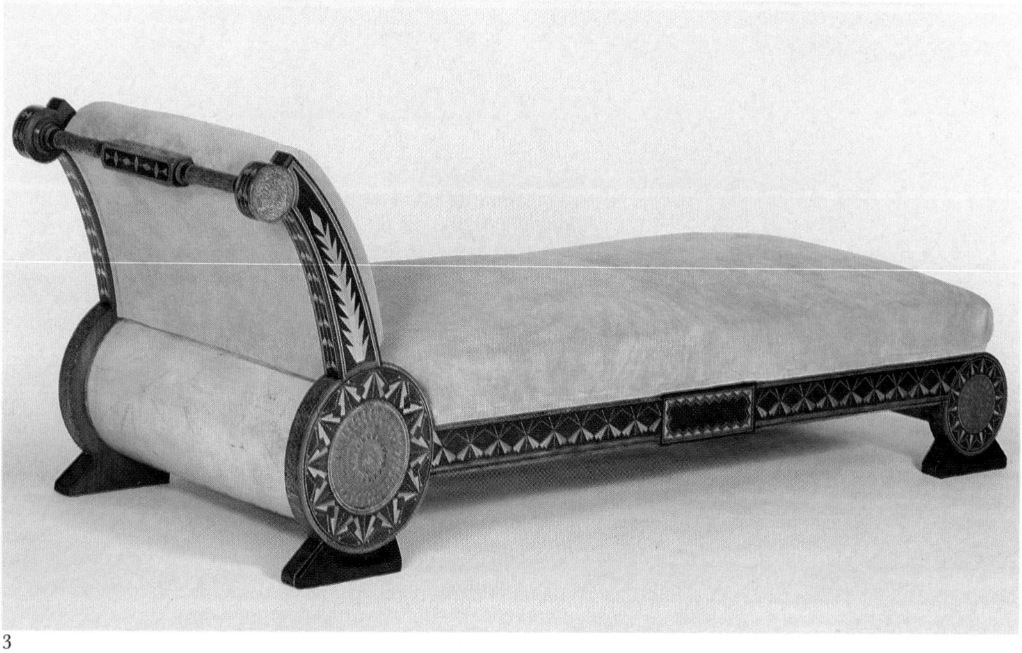

3

1
An Elizabeth Fritsch stoneware pot, c.1975, 22.5cm (8¾in), *L 16 May,*
£1,430 ($2,274)

2
A Hamada Shoji stoneware bottle vase, 1950s, brushed in resist with stylised grasses against a *kaki* ground, 23.5cm (9¼in), *L 16 May,*
£1,540 ($2,449)

3
An Elizabeth Fritsch stoneware 'Optical' pot, c.1975, 21.5cm (8¼in), *L 16 May,*
£2,420 ($3,848)

4
A Bernard Leach stoneware bottle vase, 1960s, both larger facets quartered with the 'Tree' pattern, 19.5cm (7¾in), *L 16 May,*
£1,320 ($2,099)

5
An Elizabeth Fritsch stoneware 'Spout' pot, c.1975, 22cm (8½in), *L 16 May,*
£1,210 ($1,924)

6
A Gallé 'Egyptian' vase, c.1900, decorated with a frieze of lotus flowers, 26cm (10¼in), *M 19 Oct,*
FF 49,950 (£5,371; $7,519)

7
A Gallé vase, c.1900, 40cm (15¾in) diam., *M 19 Oct,*
FF 47,730 (£5,132; $7,185)

8
A Tiffany 'Cypriote' glass vase in bronze mount, 1899, verdigris patination with acid texturing, 35.5cm (14in), *L 19 Dec,*
£6,930 ($9,702)

1 2 3 4 5

6

7

8

1

2

1
A Dunand lacquer vase, c.1925, decorated with concentric bands of rectangles, zig-zags and stripes, 19cm (7½in) high, *NY 6 Dec,*
$28,600 (£20,000)

2
A Gallé cameo glass and bronze lamp, c.1900, with floriform shade and socket, 43cm (17in) high, *NY 6 Dec,*
$14,850 (£10,384)

3
A Boucheron three-piece tea service, c.1900, each piece with finely chased and wrought leaves and rosebuds at the handles and spout, and forming the cover finials, the tea-pot with ivory insulators set into the handles, gilt interiors, silver coloured metal, teapot 18.5cm (7¼in) wide, *L 19 Dec,*
£2,420 ($3,388)

3

1
Two carved ivory and silver figural candelabra, the ivory carved by Egide Rombaux, the silver by Franz Hoosemans, c.1900, each with three candle cups cast as thistles, the oval base further cast with leafage, stepped Skryos alpha marble bases, restorations, minor losses to silver, 37cm (14½in), *NY 20 June,*
$45,100 (£30,268)

2
A Wiener Werkstätte silver four-piece tea service, Josef Hoffmann, c.1925, 900 standard, the teapot and cream jug with carved ivory handles, the tray with wood base painted black, teapot 12cm (4¾in) high, *NY 11 Oct,*
$8,800 (£6,154)

3
A painted-bronze and ivory figure of an acrobat: Flame Leaper, after Johann Philipp Ferdinand Preiss, c.1930, on black onyx base, 35cm (13¾in), *NY 6 Dec,*
$37,400 (£26,154)

1

2

3

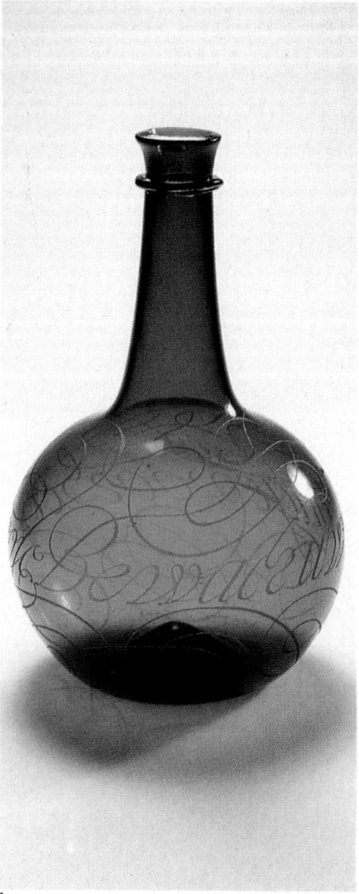

1

2

3

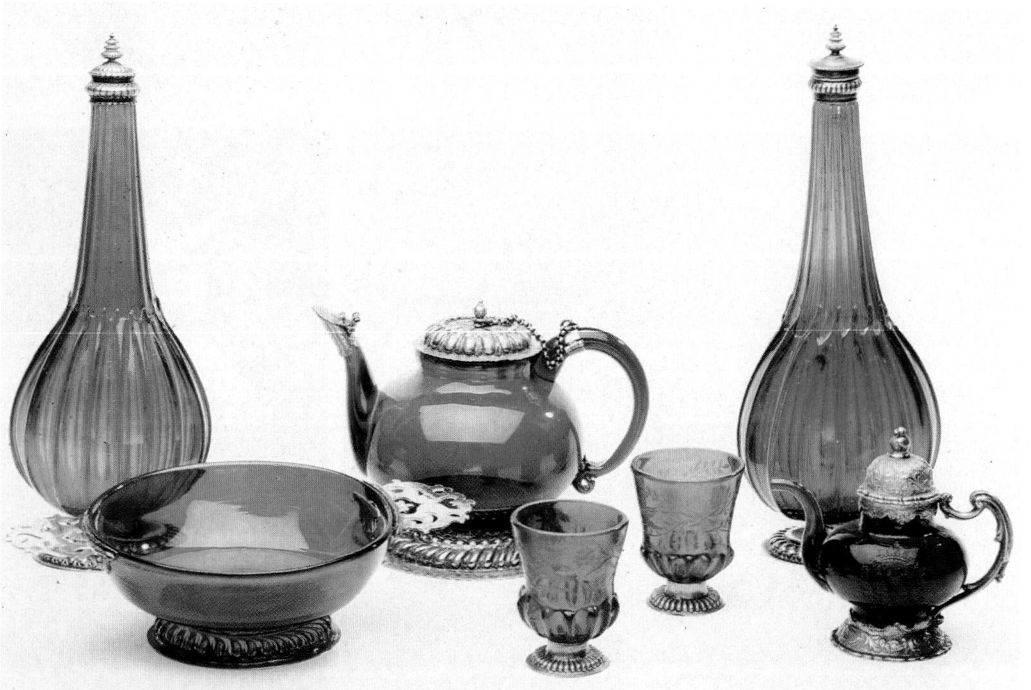

4 5 6 7 8

1
A Dutch diamond-engraved serving bottle, engraved, signed and dated by William Jacobsz van Heemskerk, Leiden 1676, the body decorated in elaborate calligraphic script with an inscription, 24cm (9¾in), *L 24 Nov,*
£35,200 ($49,632)

2
A St. Louis glass vase with crown weight base, 16cm (6¼in), *NY 12 Mar,*
$6,050 (£4,144)

3
A cameo vase, by George Woodall, c.1880, signed, carved on one side with the goddess Diana, 19.5cm (7¾in), *L 24 Nov,*
£15,400 ($21,714)

4
A pair of South German 'rubinglas' silver-gilt mounted bottles, c.1705, mounts by Tobias Baur, Augsburg, 24.5cm (9¾in), *L 10 Feb,*
£4,290 ($6,306)

5
A South German 'rubinglas' silver-gilt mounted two-handled bowl, c.1690-1700, 21cm (8½in) diam., *L 10 Feb,*
£2,530 ($3,719)

6
A South German 'rubinglas' silver-gilt mounted teapot, c.1690-95, mounts marked probably for Johann Jacob Frings I, Augsburg, 11.5cm (4½in), *L 10 Feb,*
£3,960 ($5,821)

7
A set of six 'rubinglas' engraved footed beakers, *(two illustrated)*, first quarter 18th century, engraved with flowers and birds, 6.5cm (2½in), *L 10 Feb,*
£2,530 ($3,719)

8
A Dresden silver-gilt mounted 'ruby-flashed' miniature teapot, glass probably Böttger, c.1713-18, mounts Schwerino Bergkstädt Dresden c.1758, engraved with the royal arms of Saxony and the cypher AR (for Augustus the Strong), body cracked, 10cm (4in), *L 10 Feb,*
£2,860 ($4,204)

European Works of Art

1
A North German oak figure of St. Michael, early 16th century, minor losses and repair, traces of pigment, 82.5cm (32½in), *NY 25 Nov,*
$6,600 (£4,714)

2
A South German limewood relief of St. Barbara, early 16th century, some original colour beneath later restoration, 66cm (26in), *L 11 Dec,*
£6,600 ($9,240)

3
A Florentine glazed terracotta roundel of the Virgin and Child, 16th century, in the style of Della Robbia, in a red velvet covered frame, 42cm (16½in), *L 3 July,*
£3,740 ($6,021)

4
A Franconian limewood relief of St. Anna Selbdritt, c.1510, much original paint beneath later restoration, 67cm (26¼in), *L 11 Dec,*
£7,700 ($10,780)

5
A Malines polychrome wood group of the Virgin and Child, c.1520, her robe with some original gilding, worn, some restoration, 37cm (14½in), *L 11 Dec,*
£3,080 ($4,312)

6
A French carved walnut group of the Trinity, 16th century, symbol of the Holy Ghost missing, some recarving, 75.5cm (29¾in), *L 3 July,*
£1,375 ($2,214)

7
An oak group of St. Roch, second half 16th century, Flemish, wings lacking and left arm of saint missing, 84cm (33in), *L 11 Dec,*
£1,320 ($1,848)

8
A South German painted wood figure of the mourning Virgin, 16th century, extensive traces of pigmentation, wormed and losses, 91.5cm (36in), *NY 25 Nov,*
$2,310 (£1,650)

9
A North Italian terracotta figure of the Virgin, early 16th century, 102cm (42in), *L 22 Apr,*
£3,300 ($5,181)

10
A South German wood figure of the Virgin Mary, early 16th century, later polychrome and base, the casket and left hand replaced, (the figure now appears to represent one of the Holy Women at the Entombment), 108cm (42½in), *L 3 July,*
£3,960 ($6,376)

1

2

3

6

4

5

7

8

9

10

1

2

3

4

5

6

7

8

9

10

11

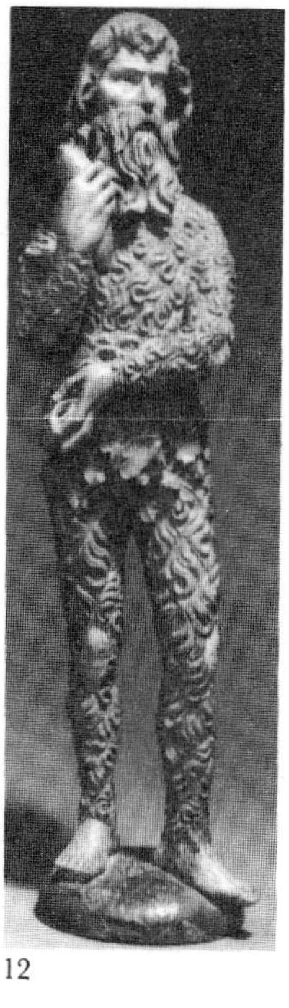
12

1
A Low Countries polychrome wood figure of a seated bishop, c.1300, some original paint, left arm missing and other losses, some recarving, 112cm (44in), *L 3 July,*
£5,060 ($8,147)

2
A French Gothic painted wood figure of St. Barbara, first half 15th century, traces of paint, worm damage, 77.5cm (33½in), *NY 31 May,*
$2,420 (£1,646)

3
A South Netherlandish painted oak group of the Presentation in the Temple, c.1490, probably Antwerp, later overpaint, but much original colour beneath, 67cm (26½in), *L 3 July,*
£17,600 ($28,336)

4
A Nottingham alabaster relief of the Crucifixion, early 15th century, repairs, 51.5 x 26cm (20¼ x 10¼in), *L 3 July,*
£5,500 ($8,855)

5
A Della Robbia workshops white-glazed terracotta figure of a kneeling angel, c.1500, some damage and repairs, 81cm (32in), *L 3 July,*
£5,280 ($8,500)

6
A Tyrol polychrome wood figure of St. George, late 15th century, traces of original colour, 99cm (39in), *L 22 Apr,*
£1,760 ($2,763)

7
A French limestone figure of St. James, late 15th century, probably Troyes, holding a staff, partly missing, 89cm (35in), *L 11 Dec,*
£8,800 ($12,320)

8
A French polychrome walnut group of St. Hubert, first quarter 16th century, some traces of original colour, stag's horns damaged and other minor losses, 60.5cm (23¾in), *L 3 July,*
£880 ($1,417)

9
A Netherlandish oak figure of the Virgin of the Annunciation, c.1480, left hand replaced and colour and gilding restored at a later date, 90cm (43in), *L 11 Dec,*
£16,500 ($23,100)

10
A Flemish oak relief of the Lamentation of the Virgin, late 15th century, on an oak stand, 27cm (10½in), *L 11 Dec,*
£3,520 ($4,928)

11
A Lower Rhenish walnut group of the Madonna and Child, second half 15th century, crown and parts of the base replaced, some worming, traces of pigment, 38.5cm (15in), *NY 25 Nov,*
$8,525 (£6,089)

12
A Swabian polychrome wood figure of St. Onuphrius, c.1470-80, from the workshops of Michel Erhart, 59.7cm (23½in), *L 11 Dec,*
£28,600 ($40,040)

1
A Venetian pearwood relief, in later brass frame, 24cm (9½in), *L 11 Dec,*
£2,200 ($3,080)

2
A South German wooden polychrome sculpture of a lantern holder, second half 17th century, some damage, 118cm (46½in), *F 30 Sept,*
L 7,700,000 (£3,837; $5,371)

3
A pair of Flemish carved wood putti, *(one illustrated)*, 18th century, 90cm (33¼in), *L 22 Apr,*
£7,920 ($12,434)

4
A stained oak figure of Charles Albert, Elector of Bavaria, c.1740-42, (crowned Emperor Charles VII 1742, died 1745), stained dark, some losses and replacements, 145cm (57in), *NY 25 Nov,*
$11,000 (£7,857)

5
An oak figure of Summer, early 18th century, Flemish, from a set of the Seasons, later base, 75cm (29½in), *L 3 July,*
£1,430 ($2,302)

6
A South German box-wood figure of Mary Magdalene, first half 17th century, her left thumb replaced, 23cm (9in), *NY 25 Nov,*
$3,850 (£2,750)

7
A South German box-wood memento mori figure, second half 17th century, 24.5cm (9½in), *L 11 Dec,*
£9,350 ($13,090)

8
An Italian terracotta bust of Raphael Maffei, first half 16th century, some restoration, on later wood base inscribed *Raphael Volaterranus*, 47.5cm (18¾in), *L 3 July,*
£6,600 ($10,626)

9
An Italian terracotta figure of a water divinity, late 17th century, the base inscribed *Emilia Panaro,* 116cm (45½in), *F 30 Sept,*
L 7,150,000 (£3,563; $4,988)

10
A terracotta figure of a Bacchante, Jean-Baptiste Cadet de Beaupre, signed *Beaupre 1791,* some damage, 44cm (17¼in), *M 22 June,*
FF 99,900 (£8,912; $13,902)

11
A pair of Italian Lava busts, *(one illustrated)*, early 19th century, after the antique, of Livia and Zingara, some minor damages, 40.5cm (16in), *L 11 Dec,*
£3,300 ($4,620)

12
A French terracotta figure of a marshall, c. 1810, minor restorations, 31cm (12¼in), *M 23 Feb,*
FF 9,435 (£912; $1,369)

13
A French terracotta bust of a nymph, signed *Joseph Marin,* 18cm (7in), *L 11 Dec,*
£4,180 ($5,852)

14
A terracotta figure of a putto and child, 18th century, restoration to one wing, 47cm (18½in), *M 1 Dec,*
FF 8,800 (£950; $1,359)

1

2

3

4

5

6

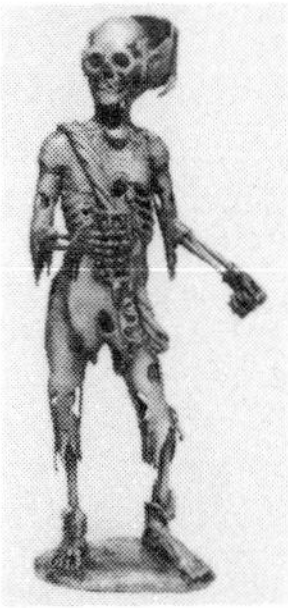
7

8

9

10

11

12

13

14

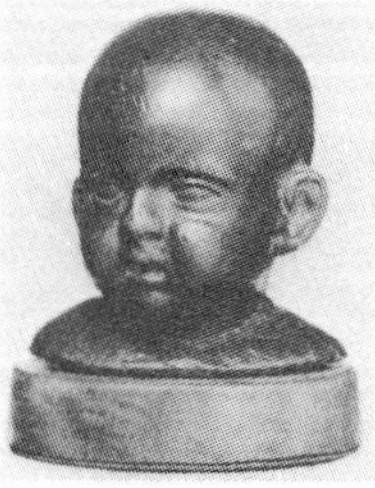
1

2

3

4

5

6

7

8

9

10

11

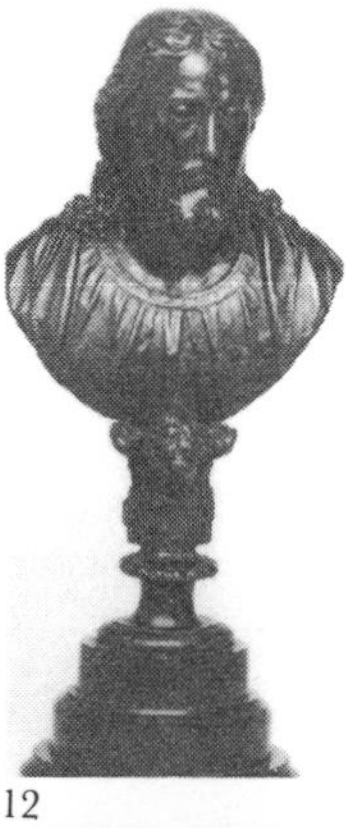
12

13

14

1
A North Italian bronze head of a boy, traces of lacquer, on wooden base, 10cm (4in), *NY 25 Nov,*
$2,090 (£1,493)

2
A bronze of a reclining dog, 16th century, possibly South German and from the workshop of Hermann Vischer, light brown patina, golden bronze, 15.5cm (6in), *NY 31 May,*
$1,870 (£1,272)

3
An Italian bronze figure of David, 16th century, standing in Michael-angesque pose, apparently unfinished, dark brown patina, 20.5cm (8in), *L 11 Dec,*
£6,380 ($8,932)

4
A North Italian bronze inkwell, late 16th/17th century, brown patina, casting flaws, 10cm (4in), *NY 31 May,*
$715 (£486)

5
A South German bronze fountain figure of Venus, South German, late 16th century, probably Nurem-berg, traces of dark brown lacquer, light brown patina, on green marble base, 18.5cm (7¼in), *NY 31 May,*
$9,625 (£6,548)

6
A Venetian gilt-bronze figure of St. John the Baptist, second half 16th century, on marble socle, 21.5cm (8½in), *L 22 Apr,*
£9,350 ($14,680)

7
An Italian bronze figure of Christ at the column, second half 16th century, the torso and legs cast separately, traces of golden brown lacquer, brown patina, 23.5cm (9¼in), *NY 25 Nov,*
$1,760 (£1,257)

8
A pair of Venetian bronze figures, *(one illustrated)*, late 16th century, from the workshop of Tiziano Aspetti, of Mars and Minerva, 38cm (15in), *L 3 July,*
£7,150 ($11,512)

9
An Italian bronze group of a toad and crab, 16th century, dark brown patina, 13.5cm (5¼in), *L 22 Apr,*
£2,310 ($3,627)

10
An Italian bronze toad, 16th century, with heavily warted skin and staring eyes, 16cm (6¼in), *L 22 Apr,*
£3,080 ($4,836)

11
An Italian bronze inkwell of two toads, 16th century, Paduan, the young toad forming the cover, some claws missing, 15cm (6in), *L 11 Dec,*
£4,950 ($6,930)

12
A Roman bronze bust of Christ, third quarter 16th century, from the work-shop of Guglielmo della Porta, the cartouche inscribed, dark brown patina, on turned ebonised wood base, 24.5cm (9½in), *NY 25 Nov,*
$51,700 (£36,929)

13
A Florentine bronze bull, early 17th century, from the Susini workshops, red gold lacquer, black marble base, 15.5cm (6in), *L 22 Apr,*
£4,950 ($7,772)

14
An Italian bronze bull, 17th century, after Giam-bologna, dark brown patina, on marble base, 18.5cm (7¼in), *NY 25 Nov,*
$8,250 (£5,729)

1
A bronze figure of a duck, early 17th century, Innsbruck, attributed to circle of Caspar Gras, 13cm (5¼in), *L 11 Dec,*
£12,100 ($16,940)

2
A Roman bronze bust of St. Susannah, second half 17th century, after Francois Duquesnoy, 17.5cm (7in), *L 11 Dec,*
£1,320 ($1,848)

3
An Italo-Flemish bronze child, 17th century, from the workshops of Francois Duquesnoy, 18.5cm (7¼in), *L 11 Dec,*
£1,320 ($1,848)

4
A bronze group of two wrestlers, c.1700, after the antique, Florence, attributed to Giovacchino Fortini (1671-1736), 41cm (16in), *M 30 Nov,*
FF 71,500 (£7,772; $10,880)

5
An Italian bronze figure of a seated baby, second half 17th century, 18cm (7in), *F 14 Apr,*
L 4,000,000 (£1,638; $2,539)

6
A bronze figure of Mars, early 17th century, possibly German, from the circle of Hans Krumper, rich brown patina, mounted on black marble base, 45cm (17¾in), *NY 31 May,*
$9,350 (£6,360)

7
A bronze equestrian statue of Louis XIV, after Martin Desjardins, early 18th century, traces of black lacquer on brown copper-coloured patina, 53.5cm (21in), *M 22 June,*
FF 244,200 (£21,784; $33,983)

8
A pair of French bronze groups, *(one illustrated),* 18th century, representing the kidnap of Proserpine, after Girardon, and of Orithyie, after Gaspard Marsy and Anselme Flamen, 52.5cm ((20¾in), *M 22 June,*
FF 355,200 (£31,686; $49,430)

9
A bronze statue of Louis XIV, early 18th century, after Guillaume de Groff, 66cm (26in), *M 23 Feb,*
FF 66,600 (£6,441; $9,661)

10
A bronze figure of the Venus Italica, c.1790, after Canova, traces of reddish brown lacquer over light brown patina, 31cm (12in), *L 11 Dec,*
£1,540 ($2,156)

11
A Florentine figure of David, 18th century, inspired by Michelangelo, black lacquer on a bronze pedestal, left leg fractured, 32cm (12½in), *L 3 July,*
£2,090 ($3,365)

12
A gilt bronze figure of the Belvedere Antinous, 18th century, after the antique, on circular bronze base, 27.5cm (10¾in), *L 22 Apr,*
£2,640 ($4,145)

13
A pair of Italian bronze figures, *(one illustrated),* Giuseppe Caputi, first half 19th century, Rome, of the crouching Venus and Ludovisi Mars, stamped *CAPUTI D,* 29 and 31.5cm (11½in and 12½in), *L 22 Apr,*
£2,420 ($3,799)

1

2

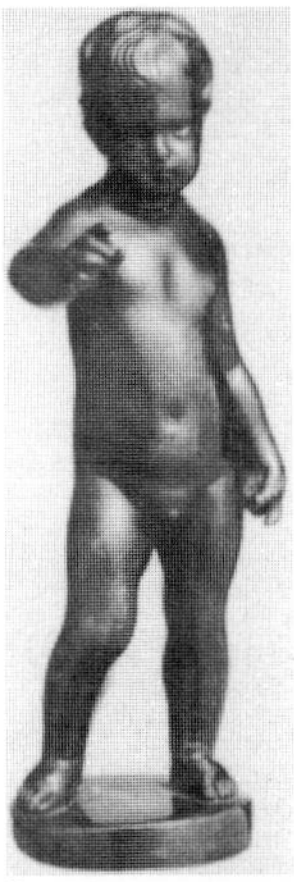
3

4

5

6

7

8

9

10

11

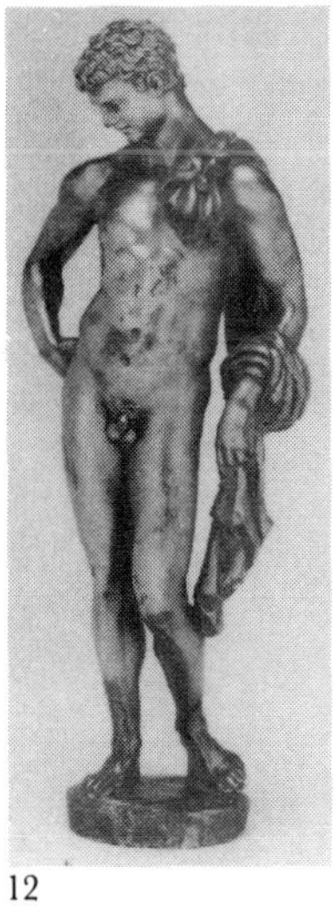
12

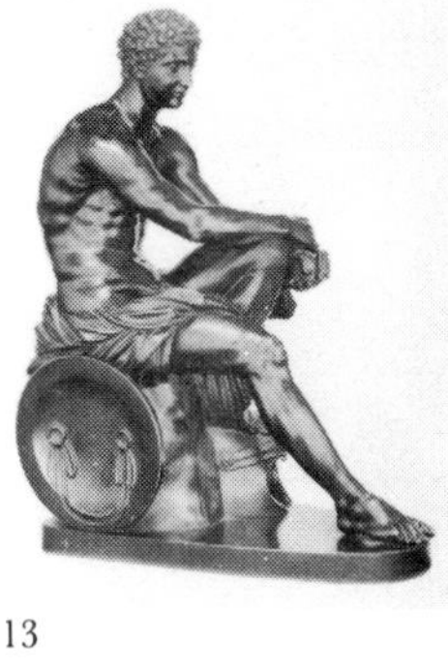
13

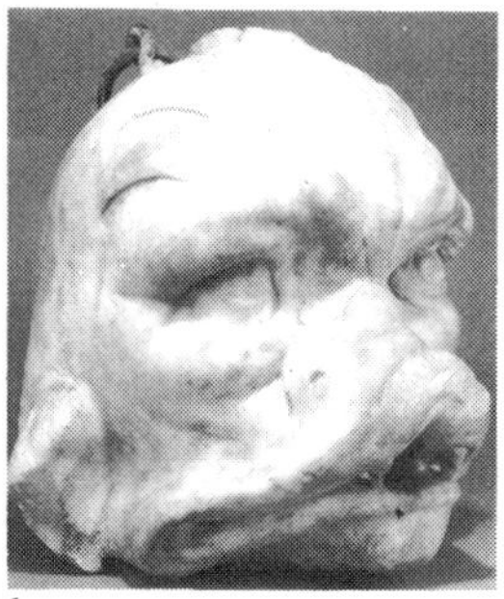
1

2

3

4

5

6

7

8

9

10

11

1
A Tuscan marble head of a dolphin, early 17th century, from the circle of Pietro Tacca, drilled to accommodate water pipe, the reverse hollowed, with iron hook for suspension, 33cm (13in) high, *NY 25 Nov,*
$5,775 (£4,125)

2
A white marble bust of King Charles I, third quarter 17th century, attributed to the circle of Francois Dieussart, 72.5cm (28in), *L 22 Apr,*
£8,800 ($13,816)

3
A white marble bust of Nicolas-Pierre Camus de Pontcarre (1667-1734), 101cm (39¾in), *M 30 Nov,*
FF 66,000 (£7,174; $10,043)

4
An Italian white marble portrait relief of Venus, c.1700, set into a verde antico mount with a sienna marble frame, 38cm (15in), *L 11 Dec,*
£6,600 ($9,240)

5
A French marble bust of Alexander the Great, probably first half 18th century, slightly weathered, 73cm (28¾in), *NY 31 May,*
$5,775 (£3,928)

6
A white marble bust of a warrior, probably Mars, by Baron Francois-Joseph Bosio (1768-1845), signed *Bosio F.*, 60cm (23½in), *M 23 Feb,*
FF 210,900 (£20,396; $30,595)

7
An Italian white marble statue, late 18th century, after the antique, 135cm (53in), *M 23 June,*
FF 72,150 (£6,436; $10,040)

8
An Italian white marble relief of Venus and Cupid, c.1820, 70cm (27½in), *L 3 July,*
£1,815 ($2,922)

9
A white marble portrait bust of a lady, by Raimondo Trentanove, dated 1819, signed *R. Trentanove Roma Fece 1819,* 61cm (24in), *L 11 Dec,*
£2,860 ($4,004)

10
A white marble portrait bust of Elisa Baciocchi, Grand Duchess of Tuscany, c.1810, from the workshops of Lorenzo Bartolini, signed *Bartolini fecit,* minor chips, 58.5cm (23in). The sitter (1777-1820) was the eldest sister of Napoleon. *L 22 Apr,*
£5,500 ($8,635)

11
A white marble statue of Love disguised as a shepherd, by John Gibson (1791-1866), one of seven known copies executed c.1830-33, 130cm (51¼in), *M 23 Feb,*
FF 55,500 (£5,367; $8,051)

1
A medieval gold ring, 13th/14th century, probably Italian, illegible inscription, *L 11 Dec,*
£4,620 ($6,468)

2
An English gold signet ring, first half 16th century, the circular bezel incised with the arms of Wilbraham of Nantwich, *L 11 Dec,*
£4,950 ($6,930)

3
A gold signet ring, 16th century, inscribed *Piere Vido,* bent, *L 11 Dec,*
£990 ($1,386)

4
A German gilt bronze signet ring, late 16th/17th century, with a shield bearing a merchant's mark and with initials *HS,*
L 11 Dec,
£440 ($616)

5
A Renaissance gold enamelled finger ring, third quarter 16th century, probably South German, some loss of enamel, 2cm (¾in), *NY 25 Nov,*
$2,750 (£1,964)

6
A gold, agate and diamond finger ring, late 18th century, possibly Austrian, the bezel inlaid in white agate with the head of an angel in high relief, 1.5cm (½in), *NY 25 Nov,*
$3,025 (£2,161)

7
An agate cameo, in classical style, 2cm (¾in), *NY 25 Nov,*
$495 (£354)

8
An Italian hardstone cameo, late 16th century, now mounted as a gold ring, mount c.1800, 2.5cm (1in), *L 22 Apr,*
£2,420 ($3,799)

9
A gilt-bronze portrait medallion of a man in bas-relief, early 19th century, signed *P. Row T. Barker,* 15cm (6in), *M 24 Feb,*
FF 2,775 (£268; $407)

10
A bronze double portrait medallion, 18th century, signed *T. Wells EK,* 18cm (7in), *M 24 Feb,*
FF 6,105 (£590; $886)

11
A silver medallion of Charles, Prince of Wales, c.1616, attributed to Simon De Passe, depicted on the obverse in quarter-length, in a later oval leather covered case, 6cm (2½in), *L 3 July,*
£1,045 ($1,682)

12
A Dutch mother-of-pearl dish, 17th century, 26cm (10¼in), *L 11 Dec,*
£2,310 ($3,234)

13
A French terracotta roundel of Marie Antoinette, Jean-Baptiste Nini, after 1774, the exergue inscribed *Maria.Antonia.ARC.AUST. GALLORUM.REGINA,* 11.5cm (4½in), *NY 31 May,*
$1,650 (£1,122)

14
An English yellow-stained glass head of an Apostle, 15th century, 23cm (9in), *L 3 July,*
£748 ($1,204)

15
Four Limoges oval enamel plaques, *(one illustrated),* second half 17th century, from the workshops of Jacques I Laudin, painted *en grisaille,* later gilt frames, 7cm (2¾in), *L 22 Apr,*
£715 ($1,123)

16
A South German engraved gilt copper portable altar, 16th century, in a contemporary *cuir-bouilli* case, 7.5cm (3in), *L 11 Dec,*
£1,650 ($2,310)

17
A Limoges grisaille enamel ewer, Pierre Reymond, 16th century, depicting the crossing of the Red Sea and the Israelites in the wilderness, after Bernard Salomon, 28cm (11in), *L 11 Dec,*
£3,080 ($4,312)

1

2

3

4

5
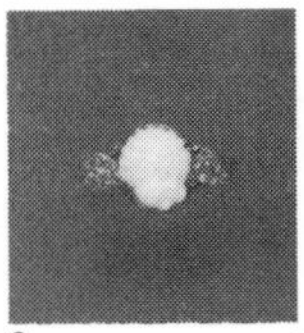
6

7

11

8

9

10

13
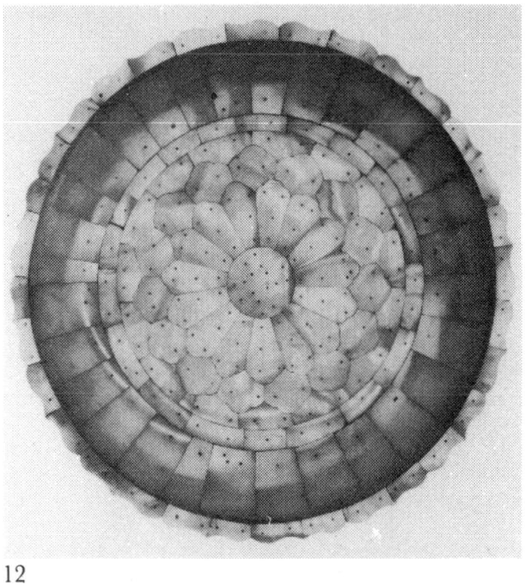
12

14

15

16
17

1

2

3

6

4

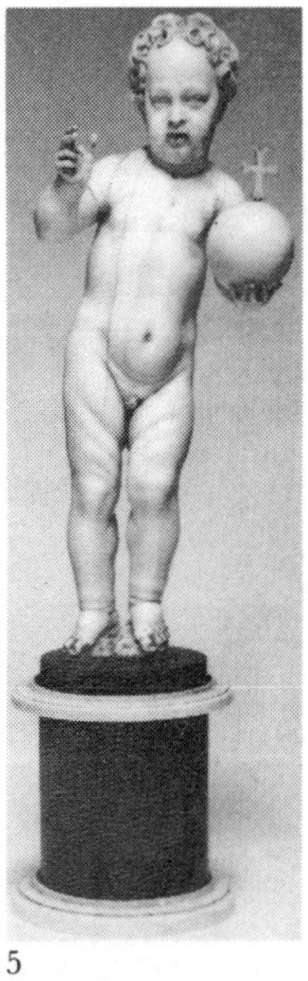
5

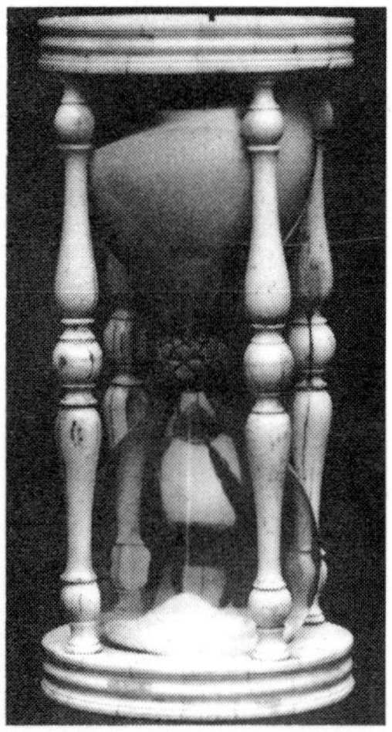
7

8

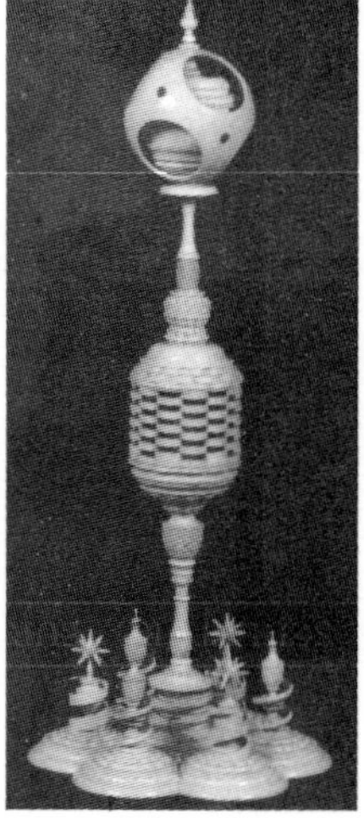
9

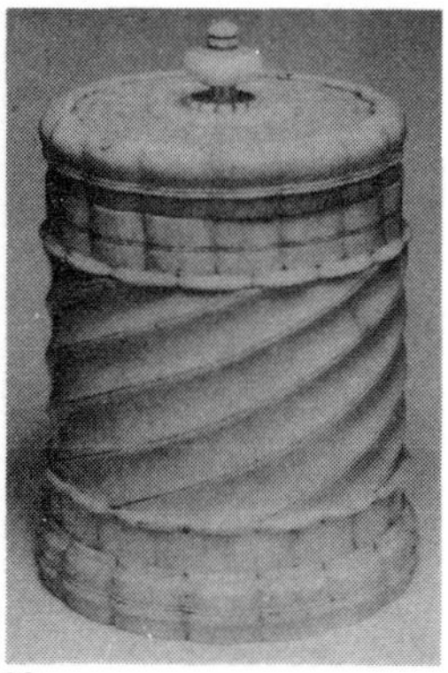
10

1
An ivory handle, 13th century, 9cm (3½in), *L 11 Dec,*
£4,840 ($6,776)

2
A French ivory relief or writing tablet, 14th century, of the Coronation of the Virgin, seated next to God the Father, the reverse with a circular recess, 9cm (3½in), *L 22 Apr,*
£1,155 ($1,813)

3
A Bavarian ivory roundel, c.1500, carved in relief with a seated jester supporting three shields of the Elector Palatine, 3.5cm (1½in), *L 22 Apr,*
£1,045 ($1,640)

4
An ivory figure of the young Christ, second half 17th century, possibly French, 16cm (6¼in), *NY 25 Nov,*
$2,750 (£1,964)

5
A South German ivory figure of the Christ Child, early 17th century, 17.5cm (7in), *L 11 Dec,*
£1,320 ($1,848)

6
A Flemish ivory rosary bead, 16th century, the reverse with a skull within ribbonwork, inscribed beneath *Cogita Mori,* gold suspension mounts, 6.5cm (2½in), *L 11 Dec,*
£2,640 ($3,696)

7
An ivory sand glass, 17th century, 19.5cm (7¾in), *A 6 May,*
Dfl 3,680 (£1,115; $1,773)

8
A Netherlandish ivory relief of Meleager and Atlanta, c.1700, 17cm (6¾in), *L 3 July,*
£1,320 ($2,125)

9
A turned ivory centrepiece, partly 17th century, the lower part 19th century, 59cm (23¼in), *M 30 Nov,*
FF 99,000 (£10,761; $15,065)

10
A North German turned ivory box, late 17th century, 14cm (5½in), *L 22 Apr,*
£2,310 ($3,627)

1
A Dutch ivory relief of the month of July, late 17th century, 11.5cm (4½in), *L 11 Dec,*
£880 ($1,232)

2
A Dutch ivory snuff rasp, early 18th century, carved in low relief with the bust of an old woman representing Avarice, 22cm (8½in), *L 3 July,*
£792 ($1,275)

3
A French ivory snuff rasp, early 18th century, carved with Venus teasing Cupid, original rasp partly missing, 21.5cm (8½in), *L 3 July,*
£1,100 ($1,771)

4
A French ivory tobacco rasp, 18th century, hinge damaged, 19cm (7½in), *L 3 July,*
£990 ($1,594)

5
A French Régence ivory box and cover, hairline cracks and restorations, 6.5cm (2½in), *M 24 Feb,*
FF 4,440 (£429; $644)

6
An ivory figure of Christ, 19th century, signed on the loincloth: *F. Dallorso,* 45cm (17¾in), *NY 25 Nov,*
$2,310 (£1,650)

7
A German ivory group of Diana and Cupid, first half 18th century, attributed to Jacob Dobbermann, 14cm (5½in), *L 3 July,*
£5,500 ($8,855)

8
A Flemish ivory memento mori figure, early 18th century, 12cm (4¾in), *L 11 Dec,*
£2,860 ($4,004)

9
An ivory bust of Menelaus, after the antique, c.1800, possibly English, on later wood column, 18cm (7in), *L 11 Dec,*
£4,180 ($5,852)

10
An Italian carved ivory figure of a blackamoor servant boy, early 18th century, carrying a parade close helmet, 24cm (9½in), *L 22 Apr,*
£6,820 ($10,707)

11
An Italian ivory figure of a nereide, 18th century, 13cm (5in), *F 14 Apr,*
L1,100,000 (£450; $698)

1

2

3

4

5

6

7

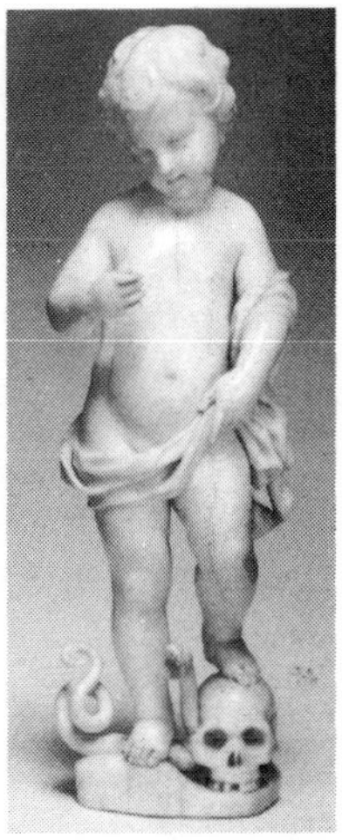
8

9

10

11

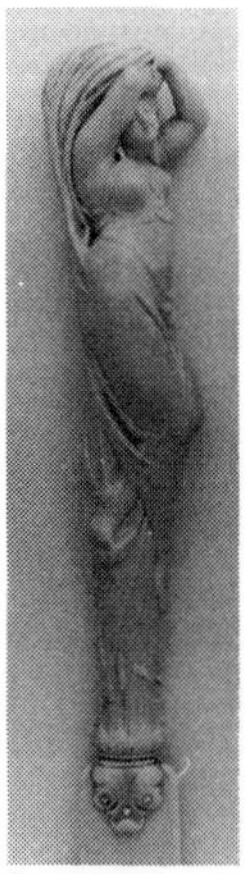
1

2

3

4

5

6

7

8

9

10

11

12

13

14

1
An ivory letter-opener, c.1860, 41cm (16in), *A 6 May,*
Dfl 1,380 (£418; $665)

2
An ivory letter-opener, c.1870, 35cm (13¼in), *A 6 May,*
Dfl 1,092 (£331; $526)

3
An ivory group of Venus and Adonis embracing, W. Schwarz, 19th century, 28.5cm (11¼in), *A 6 May,*
Dfl 4,140 (£1,255; $1,995)

4
A pair of French ivory musicians, c.1900, in the manner of Callot, each in 17th century jester's dress, 12cm (5in), *S 20 May,*
£176 ($282)

5
A pair of French ivory figures representing Dawn and Dusk, c.1900, 69 and 72cm (27 and 28¼in), *L 6 Nov,*
£23,100 ($32,802)

6
A German ivory goblet, c.1845, carved in relief with a continuous stag hunting scene, 23cm (9in), *C 15 Jan,*
£715 ($1,073)

7
A French ivory figure of a lady, early 19th century, 18cm (7in), *A 6 May,*
Dfl 2,760 (£836; $1,330)

8
A French ivory figure of Winter, late 19th century, in the form of a naked nymph loosely wrapped in fur, 20cm (8in), *L 12 June,*
£440 ($704)

9
A German ivory cup and pedestal, c.1880, decorated with satyrs and nymphs, silver oval base, 24cm (9½in), *F 14 Apr,*
L 12,500,000 (£5,119; $7,934)

10
An ivory figure of Mary Queen of Scots, late 19th century, of *vierge ouvrante* type, the interior of her skirts carved with a triptych of a marriage scene, 21.5cm (8½in), *C 15 Jan,*
£418 ($627)

11
A French ivory figure of Marie Antoinette, late 19th/early 20th century, of *vierge ouvrante* type, the interior of her skirts carved with the arrest of Louis XVI, 27.5cm (10¼in), *L 20 Mar,*
£1,012 ($1,589)

12
A silver-mounted ivory tankard, late 19th century, the body carved with a continuous Bacchanalian scene, the cover with a Bacchus infant finial, 22.5cm (8¾in), *C 15 Jan,*
£1,815 ($2,723)

13
A German silver-mounted ivory tankard, late 19th century, the body carved with a continuous battle scene, the cover with kneeling centurion finial, 44.5cm (17½in), *C 15 Jan,*
£4,620 ($6,930)

14
A French jewelled ivory figure of Joan of Arc, late 19th/early 20th century, of *vierge ouvrante* type, set with green and red pastes (some missing), the interior of her skirts carved with episodes of her martyrdom, 23cm (9in), *L 6 Nov,*
£1,265 ($1,796)

1
A set of four German silver-mounted ivory figures, *(three illustrated),* late 19th century, each on oval rock crystal bases, 26cm (10¼in), *L 6 Nov,*
£12,650 ($17,963)

2
A Hungarian enamelled and gem-set silver and hardstone standing cup and cover, late 19th century, the cage-work rock crystal applied with a pair of leaping horses restrained by a hero, with oval grey and rust agate bowl fringed with emeralds, 23cm (9in), *L 20 Mar,*
£2,530 ($3,972)

3
A pair of Viennese silver and enamel horn-form vases, Hermann Böhm, late 19th century, the bodies and bases enamelled with mythological scenes, 41.5cm (16¼in), *NY 12 June,*
$26,400 (£17,368)

4
A Viennese silver and enamel table clock, Karl Bank, late 19th century, the stem in the form of a musician, 28cm (11in), *NY 12 June,*
$2,420 (£1,592)

5
A Viennese silver-gilt and enamel goblet, Ludwig Politzer, late 19th century, the handle formed as a satyr, the body enamelled with mythological scenes, 22cm (8¾in), *NY 12 June,*
$4,675 (£3,076)

6
A Viennese enamel vase, late 19th century, the cornucopia body terminating in a dolphin's head, enamelled with mythological scenes, 20cm (8in), *NY 12 June,*
$2,200 (£1,447)

7
A Viennese silver, lapis lazuli and enamel ewer set with jewels, Herman Böhm, late 19th century, 22cm (8½in), *NY 12 June,*
$5,720 (£3,763)

8
A Viennese enamel dish, late 19th century, silver border, 31.5cm (12½in), *L 20 Mar,*
£1,540 ($2,418)

9
A Viennese enamel scent flask, Hermann Ratzersdorfer, late 19th century, painted on each side with Actaeon admiring Diana, silver-gilt mounts, 5.5cm (2¼in), *S 19 Feb,*
£253 ($385)

10
A Viennese enamel scent flask, Hermann Ratzersdorfer, late 19th century, painted with classical figures, silver-gilt mounts, 8cm (3in), *S 19 Feb,*
£330 ($502)

11
A Hungarian gem-set silver and hardstone dish, late 19th century, 18cm (9in), *L 20 Mar,*
£1,870 ($2,936)

12
A Viennese silver-gilt and enamel sedan chair, late 19th century, 10cm (4in) wide, *S 18 June,*
£990 ($1,564)

13
A jewelled silver-gilt mounted rock crystal cup, Austrian or German, late 19th century, in 16th century style, 13.5cm (5¼in), *L 12 June,*
£1,650 ($2,640)

14
A Viennese silver-mounted enamel cup and cover, Hermann Böhm, late 19th century, painted with mythological vignettes and grotesques, 16cm (6¼in), *S 18 June,*
£715 ($1,130)

15
A Viennese enamel tankard, Karl Rössler, Vienna, late 19th century, painted with beaded vignettes of Juno and other gods, 48cm (19in), *L 12 June,*
£9,900 ($15,840)

16
A Viennese engraved rock crystal ewer with enamelled silver-gilt mounts, c.1890, maker's mark *JW*, 19cm (7½in), *L 12 June,*
£4,180 ($6,688)

1

2

3

4

5

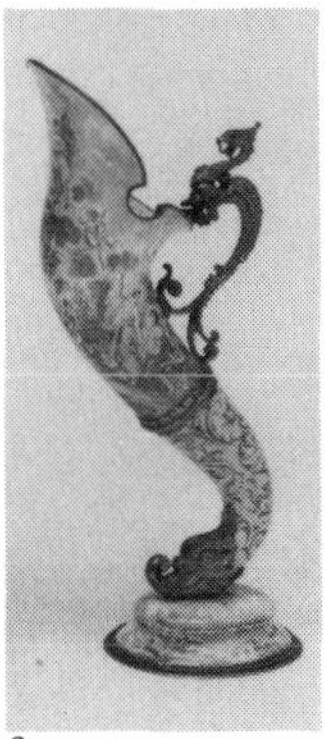
6

7

8

9

10

11

12

13

14

15

16

1

2

3

4

5

8 9 10

6 7

11 12 13

14

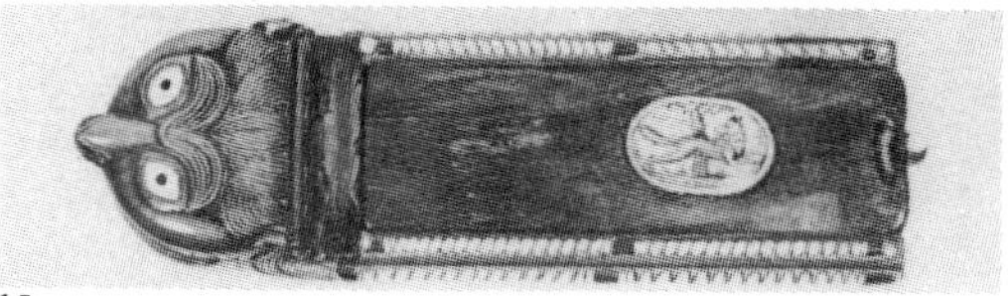
15

1
A set of twelve Elizabethan fruitwood trenchers, *(six illustrated)*, c.1600, each one painted with a contemporary homily, in a wood case with domed cover, 13cm (5¼in), *L 3 July,*
£1,925 ($3,099)

2
A pair of yew-wood candlesticks, c.1680, 64cm (25in), *L 4 July,*
£1,155 ($3,731)

3
An oak and ash adjustable candle stand, c.1700, 66 x 36cm (26 x 14in), *L 4 July,*
£2,860 ($4,633)

4
A lignum vitae wassail bowl, 17th century, English, old damages, 28cm (11in) high, *S 9 Dec,*
£605 ($847)

5
A silver-mounted lignum vitae wassail bowl, late 17th century, struck with maker's mark *T.U.* twice, legs on base struck *M*, the body with later engraved silver band, 34cm (13½in), *L 4 July,*
£3,080 ($4,990)

6
A pair of candlesticks, *(one illustrated)*, 18th century, 19cm (7½in), *S 20 May,*
£143 ($229)

7
A mahogany or red walnut spill vase, 18th century, old damages, 17cm (6½in), *S 20 May,*
£132 ($211)

8
A silver-mounted turned mulberry goblet, early 17th century, 10.5cm (4¼in), *L 22 July,*
£638 ($1,002)

9
A lidded turned lignum vitae wassail bowl, 17th century, lid broken cleanly, 30.5cm (12in), *L 22 July,*
£275 ($432)

10
A turned lignum vitae wassail bowl, 17th century, hairline crack, 16cm (6¼in) diam., *L 22 July,*
£550 ($864)

11
A pair of fruitwood spill vases, early 19th century, 12cm (5in), *S 20 May,*
£143 ($229)

12
A lignum vitae coffee grinder, 18th century, English, original mechanism and winder, 18cm (7in), *S 20 May,*
£165 ($264)

13
A lignum vitae coffee grinder, 18th century, with non-original winding key, 16cm (6½in), *S 20 May,*
£176 ($282)

14
A tobacco jar and cover, early 19th century, 23cm (9in), *S 12 Feb,*
£264 ($370)

15
A fruitwood and ivory inlaid coaster snuff rasp, early 18th century, Dutch or French, restored, 23cm (9in), *S 12 Feb,*
£638 ($893)

1
A Norwegian tankard, late 18th century, damage to base of handle, 20cm (8in), *S 20 May,*
£242 ($387)

2
A Norwegian birchwood 'lion' tankard, late 18th century, 21cm (8¼in), *S 20 May,*
£308 ($493)

3
A Norwegian burr-wood tankard, 18th century, 22cm (8½in), *S 12 Feb,*
£484 ($678)

4
A Scandinavian pine tankard, 23cm (9in), *L 4 July,*
£1,980 ($3,207)

5
A Scandinavian carved birchwood tankard, c.1683, in the manner of Samuel Halvorsen Fanden, 21.5cm (8½in), *L 22 Apr,*
£29,700 ($46,629)

6
A Scandinavian coopered wood tankard, 19th century, painted wood grain finish, 17cm (6¾in), *S 9 Dec,*
£121 ($169)

7
A Norwegian carved and polychrome wood tankard, second half 18th century, by Iver Gundersen Ovstrud (1711-75), painted primarily in red and black, spout lacking, 34cm (13½in), *L 22 Apr,*
£17,600 ($27,632)

8
A Norwegian polychrome stavework ewer, 18th century, painted all over in red, yellow and black geometric swirls, 22cm (8¾in), *L 22 Apr,*
£715 ($1,123)

9
A mahogany and ebonised shoe snuff box, the heel dated 1879, 11cm (4¼in), *S 12 Feb,*
£220 ($308)

10
A yew-wood and pewter inlaid shoe snuff box, 19th century, possibly Dutch, 11cm (4¼in), *S 12 Feb,*
£176 ($246)

11
A Norwegian painted wood ale bowl, c.1761, 26cm (10in), *S 9 Dec,*
£396 ($554)

12
A burr boxwood pounce pot, 18th century, 9cm (3½in), *S 12 Feb,*
£198 ($277)

13
Two Tyrolean fruitwood nut crackers, *(one illustrated),* 19th century, each with swivelling torsos, 20cm (8in), *S 12 Feb,*
£396 ($554)

14
A horn flask, 18th century, Dutch, 8cm (3¼in), *L 3 July,*
£440 ($708)

15
An English carved wooden crest, 19th century, of a camel's head, finished in original gold leaf, 81cm (32in), *L 22 July,*
£418 ($656)

16
A German rhinoceros horn cup, 17th century, 13cm (5in), *L 3 July,*
£660 ($1,063)

17
A set of four graduated leather blackjack toby jugs, *(one illustrated),* late 18th century, with traces of original paint decoration, 27 to 18cm (10½ to 7in), *S 20 May,*
£792 ($1,267)

1

2

3

4

5

6

7

8

9

10

11

12

13

14

15

16

17

Caskets

ELISABETH MITCHELL

The term 'casket' covers a multitude of boxes of all shapes and intended for very different purposes. From the earliest years of Christianity, their religious use included caskets for holding relics, for containing the host and holy oils, for the safekeeping of prayer books and for guarding the offertory. In secular life caskets were intended for storing valuables such as jewellery or coins and, in later years, for containing a variety of small precious objects. Security was often of paramount importance and thus the locks employed, especially from the 16th century, are extremely intricate, often with the keyhole concealed.

The collector has enormous choice when it comes to the range of materials used: wood, ivory, leather, iron and steel, brass, copper and bronze, to name but a few. The value of these materials is reflected in the prices realised today. The higher end of the market naturally includes the early medieval French and German ivory caskets, Gothic gilt metal reliquaries and those made of rock crystal, inlaid hardstone (pietra dura) (fig.1) and Limoges enamels (fig.2). Lower down the price scale the choice for the collector is still very wide. Wood was the cheapest material available and was extensively used in the production of caskets. However, it is not durable and thus very early examples are rare. It is only from the 16th and 17th centuries that wood caskets are

1

1
A Florentine pietra dura casket, from the Grand Ducal workshop, c.1700-20, inlaid with lapis, agate and marble, some losses, 53cm (20¾in) wide, *NY 25 Nov,*
\$187,000 (£133,571)

2
A Limoges champlevé enamel chasse, c.1190, engraved with God the Father in Majesty flanked by the Virgin and St. John, the lapis ground with fleurettes, some replacements, 20cm (7¾in) wide, *L 11 Dec,*
£66,000 (\$92,400)

3
A French wrought-iron jewellery casket, 17th century, with later key, 18.5cm (7¼in), *L 3 July,*
£880 (\$1,417)

4
A South German etched iron casket, probably Nuremberg, late 16th century, 15cm (6in) wide, *NY 31 May,*
\$2,200 (£1,496)

2

readily available today, often decorated with polychrome paintwork or chip carving.

Throughout Europe large numbers of iron caskets were produced principally from the mid 16th century onwards (fig.3). In Germany the locksmith and gunsmith centres of Nuremberg and Augsburg produced extremely decorative examples (fig.4). The exterior is typically found engraved or etched with attractive allegorical or biblical scenes with the figures in contemporary costume. As would be expected from gunsmith centres, steel was a popular medium, often blued or gilt for further decoration. The lock, occasionally shooting as many as eight bolts, was incorporated into the interior of the lid. The most interesting and attractive examples were those made by Michael Mann, a Nuremberg gunsmith of the late 16th/early 17th century (figs 5-7), whose work in copper and brass with blued steel locks was unusual in that it was often signed (fig.6). Further examples of his work are illustrated in Sotheby's Guide vol.1 page 403, nos 8 & 9 and vol.2 page 458 no.14. The detail of his engraving is intricate and his work is all the more appealing because of its size, ranking amongst the smallest of caskets, not more than three inches (8cm) wide. The presence of the original gilding and bluing is important and will considerably affect the price his work fetches today, which usually ranges between £2,000 ($3,200) and £3,000 ($4,800).

Another type of casket which survives in relatively large numbers is the missal box or casket, used for containing medieval prayer books and dating from the 15th and 16th centuries. Often they were made of wood with intricate iron strapwork and hasp. Owing to the vulnerability of the wood, examples that appear on the market today are normally those where the ironwork is predominant and the wood core of secondary importance. France and Spain produced a type with elaborate wrought-iron tracery, a solid construction which has withstood the ravages of time (figs 8-10). Occasionally leather, which would originally have been painted, is laid over the wood core and beneath the ironwork, for further decoration (fig.11). Leather was a popular medium in the construction of medieval and later caskets. It is comparatively easy to work and can be painted, incised and even

3

5

6

5
A South German gilt-brass and copper miniature casket, by Michael Mann, c.1600, the inside of the base engraved with a figure of Fortitude, 7.5cm (3in) wide, *L 3 July*, **£3,740 ($6,021)**

6
Detail of no. 7

7
A South German gilt-brass miniature casket, by Michael Mann, c.1600, signed on the keyhole cover, 7cm (2¾in), *L 11 Dec*, **£1,760 ($2,464)**

4

7

boiled (cuir bouilli), to produce decorative objects. From the 17th century leather was not only dyed but also stamped with gilt decoration, borders of strapwork and stylised flowers (fig.12). The construction is simpler, with less emphasis on the mounts for decoration, except those hailing from provincial areas where fashion was of less importance.

Ivory is another material which has survived, owing to its durability and treasured status. Gothic ivory carvers of France and Germany produced intricately carved examples, although, as fashion changed, these became considerably simplified in the 16th century. Ivory was often combined with wood, as in the marquetry produced by the Embriachi workshops in Italy in the 15th and 16th centuries. Since ivory was a luxury, bone was also used; it has a similar effect at far less cost. Examples can be found from well into the 18th century, such as the pierced and engraved bone caskets from Russia (fig.13).

With the expansion of European colonies in the 17th century, tortoiseshell and exotic woods such as ebony were imported into Europe and were used in the manufacture of a wide variety of social artefacts. Netherlands craftsmen combined imported ebony with native alabaster in the production of caskets. Tortoiseshell could be found not only in the workshops of the Netherlands but also in France (fig.14), Italy and Germany, and caskets were often veneered with tortoiseshell and inlaid with mother-of-pearl and other materials such as brass and silver. From the end of the 17th century and into the 19th century caskets were exported from the colonies, made and decorated to suit European taste (fig.15).

Sources of information on caskets are many and varied, as they tend to feature in the literature of numerous different fields rather than forming their own specialist subject. It is, however, this myriad variety with its wide choice of material, period, size, shape and style, which gives the collecting of caskets such appeal.

8
A missal box, c.1500, French or Spanish, the wooden core covered with wrought-iron tracery over leather, 31cm (12¼in) wide, *L 3 July,*
£2,310 ($3,719)

9
A missal box, c.1500, French or Spanish, of wrought-iron tracery over leather, four suspension rings, 26cm (10¼in), *L 3 July,*
£1,870 ($3,011)

10

10
A missal box, c.1500, French or Spanish, the wooden core with wrought-iron tracery over leather, 19.5cm (7½in), *L 3 July,*
£1,980 ($3,188)

11
A small leather-covered missal box, early 16th century, probably Flemish, the lid with riveted iron bands, 17cm (6½in), *L 3 July,*
£770 ($1,240)

11

12

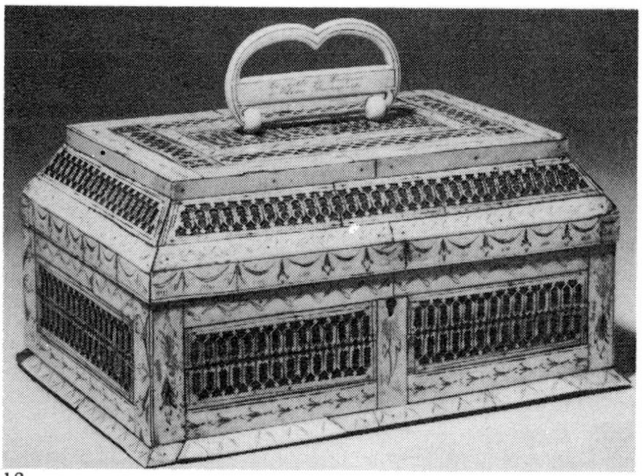
13

14

12
A French red leather-covered casket, c.1600, the side sliding to reveal a hidden drawer, gilt-brass mounts, 26cm (10¼in) wide, *L 3 July,*
£2,200 ($3,542)

13
A Russian bone casket, 18th century, stained in green and underlaid with silver foil, probably presented to Napoleon's sister when given the principality of Lucca in June 1805, inscribed *La ville de Lucques a Elisa Buonaparte,* 11cm (28in) wide, *NY 31 May,*
$2,860 (£1,945)

14
A Louis XIV boulle marquetry casket, 32cm (12½in), *M 22 June,*
FF 35,520 (£3,169; $4,943)

15
A Colonial tortoiseshell casket, late 17th century, probably Jamaican, 20.5cm (8in) wide, *L 11 Dec,*
£770 ($1,078)

15

1

2

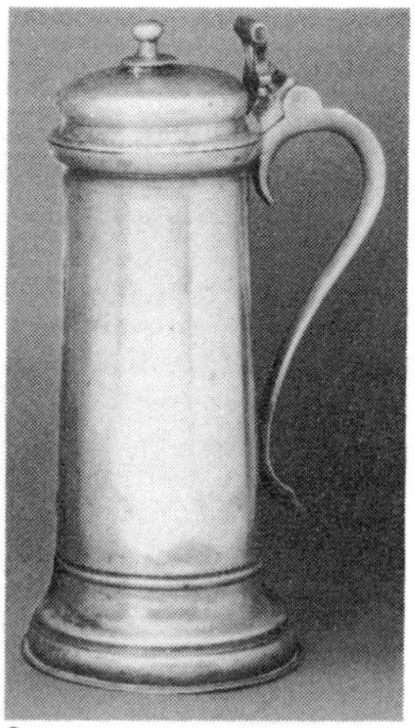
3

4

5

6

7

8

9

10 11

12 13

14

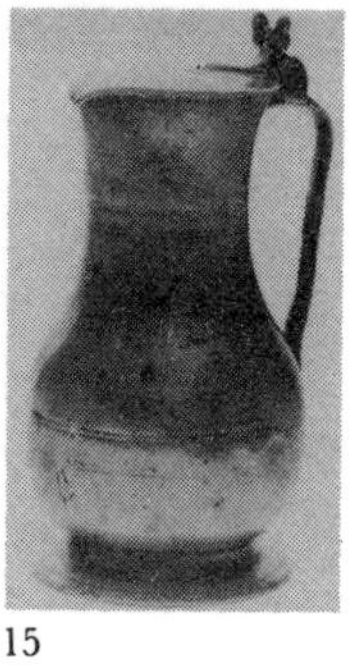
15

1
An English lidless gallon ale flagon, early 19th century, engraved *T. Baylis, Liquorpond Str,* made by *Geradin & Watson of London,* 29cm (11½in), *S 15 July,*
£396 ($622)

2
A Stuart flat-lidded flagon, by the maker WB, c.1685-90, the cover with 'heart and leaf spray' billet, 28cm (11in), *L 22 Apr,*
£2,860 ($4,490)

3
A Charles I flagon, by the maker EG, c.1635, the 'bun' cover with heart-pierced billet, 30.5cm (12in), *L 22 Apr,*
£3,520 ($5,526)

4
A South German dish, Nicolaus Horchaimer, Nuremberg, late 16th/early 17th century, repairs, 35.5cm (14in) diam., *NY 25 Nov,*
$6,875 (£4,917)

5
A pair of Continental wall sconces, early 18th century, the pricket candle arms stamped with mark of *IHP*, 42.5cm (16¾in), *L 3 July,*
£2,090 ($3,365)

6
An English 'wriggle-work' plate, Francis Kingston, c.1730, the 'well' with a goat, 21.5cm (8½in), *L 22 Apr,*
£550 ($864)

7
A Charles II 'wriggle-work' tankard, Charles Wareing, c.1675, the drum engraved with a design of three tulips, 16cm (6½in), *L 22 Apr,*
£7,920 ($12,434)

8
A Queen Anne or George I tankard, c.1710-20, 18.5cm (7¼in), *L 22 Apr,*
£550 ($864)

9
A George II Bristol tankard, Allen Bright, c.1750, with 'fishtail' thumbpiece, 19cm (7½in), *L 22 Apr,*
£385 ($604)

10
A Brussels flagon, 18th century, 27cm (10½in), *A 20 Oct,*
Dfl 977 (£301; $425)

11
A Dutch flagon, 18th century, 21.5cm (8½in), *A 20 Oct,*
Dfl 862 (£266; $375)

12
An English baluster measure, mid 18th century, with unusual flat base, 15cm (6in), *S 9 Dec,*
£143 ($200)

13
An English quart tankard, possibly Bristol, late 18th century, broken handle and some restoration, 20cm (8in), *S 9 Dec,*
£187 ($262)

14
A set of four English quart mugs, *(one illustrated),* 19th century, centred by initials, 16.5cm (6½in), *C 14 May,*
£154 ($248)

15
A Guernsey flagon, 18th century, 18cm (7in), *A 13 June,*
Dfl 1,035 (£310; $496)

1
A set of seven English measures, 19th century, 14.5cm (5¾in), *A 20 Oct,*
Dfl 747 (£230; $325)

2
A Swiss bauchkanne, 18th century, 32cm (12½in), *A 20 Oct,*
Dfl 3,680 (£1,136; $1,601)

3
A series of four English baluster-shaped wine measures, late 17th/18th century, the quart by W. Bancks, 21.5 to 11cm (8¼ to 4¼in), *L 22 Apr,*
£572 ($898)

4
A Dutch flagon, Rotterdam, c.1600, marked on the handle with the Rotterdam coat of arms and the maker's initials *PAP*, 12.5cm (5in), *A 20 Oct,*
Dfl 3,680 (£1,136; $1,601)

5
An English ale measure, late 18th century, 21cm (8¼in), *A 20 Oct,*
Dfl 2,185 (£674; $951)

6
A Swiss stegkanne, late 18th century, marked on lid, 31.5cm (12½in), *A 20 Oct,*
Dfl 2,990 (£923; $1,301)

7
A Scottish crested 'tappit-hen' measure, c. last quarter 18th century, 29cm (11½in), *L 22 Apr,*
£440 ($691)

8
A Scottish crested Chopin measure, late 18th century, of typical 'tappit-hen' shape, 24cm (9½in), *L 22 Apr,*
£880 ($1,382)

9
An English ale or cider measure, Grimes, early 19th century, engraved *Robin Hood Tavern*, 22cm (8¾in), *S 9 Dec,*
£154 ($216)

10
A Swiss prismenkanne, late 18th century, by Matheus Bauer of Chur, 29cm (11½in), *L 22 Apr,*
£825 ($1,295)

11
A Dutch flagon, early 18th century, interior marked with initials *AR*, 12.5cm (5in), *A 21 Oct,*
Dfl 2,530 (£781; $1,101)

12
A series of four Bristol conical measures, *(one illustrated)*, first half 19th century, all by Fothergills, 18 to 8cm (7 to 3¼in), *L 22 Apr,*
£396 ($622)

13
A Dutch tobacco box, 18th century, 13cm (5in), *A 20 Oct,*
Dfl 862 (£266; $375)

14
A Dutch tobacco box, 18th century, marked, 17cm (6¾in), *A 20 Oct,*
Dfl 322 (£99; $140)

15
A pair of English entrée dishes and covers, *(one illustrated)*, early 19th century, by Thomas Compton, 28cm (11in), *S 9 Dec,*
£264 ($369)

1

2

3

4

5

6

7

8

9

10

11

12

13

14

15

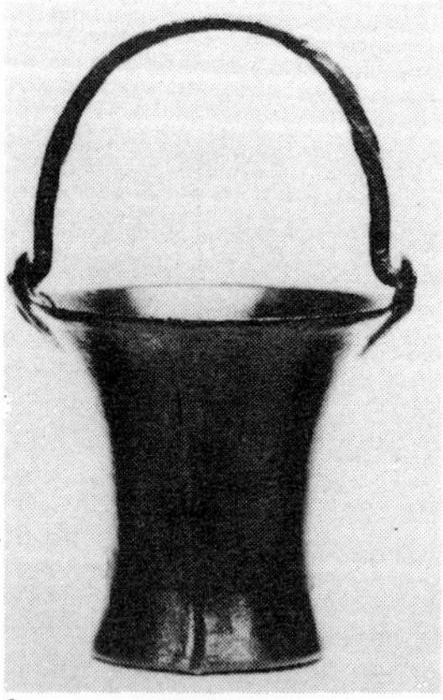
1

2 3

4

5

6

7

8

9

10

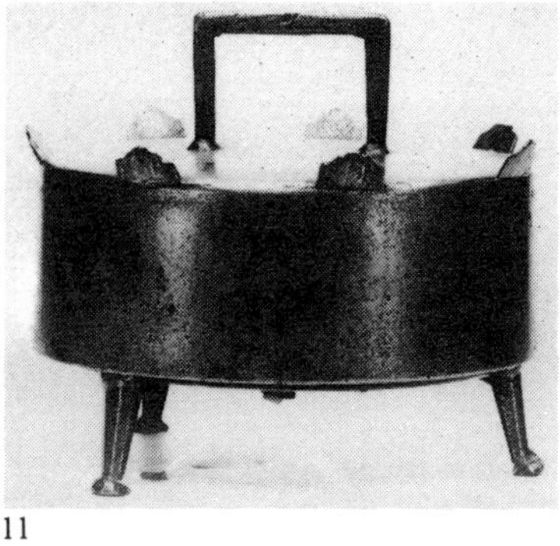
11

12

1
A bronze Gothic holy water bucket, 15th century, 19cm (7½in), *A 20 Oct,*
Dfl 1,380 (£426; $600)

2
A Dutch bronze mortar, dated 1738, 17.5cm (7in), *A 20 Oct,*
Dfl 8,740 (£2,697; $3,803)

3
A bronze mortar, Hendrick Kemper, Amsterdam, 1727, the plain body with cast inscription, 13cm (5in), *A 20 Oct,*
Dfl 2,645 (£816; $1,151)

4
An English bronze mortar, by Clement Tozier (fl c.1679-1727), Salisbury, c.1709, the body with the inscription *Clement Tosiear cast mee in/the year 1709,* 20.5cm (8in), *L 22 Apr,*
£1,210 ($1,900)

5
An etched bell metal bowl, South German or possibly Swiss, late 16th/17th century, rich brown patina, 18.5cm (7¼in), *NY 31 May,*
$1,870 (£1,272)

6
A bronze mortar, Maliens, Peter van den Ghein IV, dated 1649, the body with cast inscription *Peeter Vanden Ghein me fecit 1649,* 13cm (5in), *A 20 Oct,*
Dfl 1,725 (£532; $750)

7
A bronze long-handled pan, 17th century, the handle marked *3R,* on three small feet, 41.5cm (16¼in), *A 13 June,*
Dfl 368 (£110; $176)

8
A German bronze mortar, 16th century, with inside rim, 15cm (6in), *A 20 Oct,*
Dfl 2,070 (£639; $901)

9
A German Gothic bronze mortar, c.1400, 19.5cm (7½in), *L 3 July,*
£3,300 ($5,313)

10
A bronze mortar, probably Dutch/German border, dated 1469, with inscription *Johan Uledinck hoer ic toe, M CCCC LXIX (I belong to Johan Uledinck 1469)* 16.5cm (6½in), *A 20 Oct,*
Dfl 27,600 (£8,518; $12,011)

11
An oval bronze pheasant pan, 17th/18th century, 24cm (9½in), *A 20 Oct,*
Dfl 3,105 (£958; $1,351)

12
An Italian bronze mortar, 16th century, red-brown patina, 15.5cm (6in), *L 11 Dec,*
£3,850 ($5,390)

1
A bronze nest of weights, Nuremberg, third quarter 17th century, by Christoph Weinmann, (Master 1657, d.1669), the lid stamped with maker's mark, some weights replaced, 21.5cm (8½in), *L 22 Apr,*
£2,860 ($4,490)

2
A bronze nest of weights, Nuremberg, 17th century, incomplete, 16.5cm (6½in), *A 20 Oct,*
Dfl 5,060 (£1,562; $2,202)

3
A bronze hand bell, 16th century, 20cm (8in), *A 20 Oct,*
Dfl1,437 (£443; $624)

4
A Flemish bronze hand bell, 17th century, 20cm (8in), *A 20 Oct,*
Dfl 2,070 (£639; $901)

5
An iron guild sign, Austrian, dated 1715, gilt and tin, the border pierced with hearts and chased with initials *A F.A W.I G M.* 25.5cm (10in), *NY 25 Nov,*
$990 (£707)

6
A pair of Italian wrought-iron doors, 17th/early 18th century, surmounted by flowering rose branches, with three panels *en suite*, 114cm (45in), *NY 25 Nov,*
$3,025 (£2,161)

7
A bronze nest of weights, Nuremberg, 18th century, by Joh. Conrad Schön, marked on the lid, 4cm (1½in), *A 20 Oct,*
Dfl 460 (£142; $200)

8
A pair of French wrought-iron doors, 17th century, traces of pigmentation and gilding, painted black, 79cm (31in), *NY 25 Nov,*
$2,750 (£1,964)

9
A cut steel lace shuttle, French, late 18th century, the two sides pierced with leafy scrollwork held together by a spool, 11.5cm (4½in), *L 22 Apr,*
£880 ($1,382)

10
An English log fork, early 18th century, with knotted ball handle and double-pronged baluster knotted stem, 117cm (46in); sold with another smaller fork, 81cm (31¾in), *S 12 Feb,*
£286 ($400)

11
A French iron candle snuffer, 18th century, with faceted mahogany pistol-type handle, 22cm (8½in), *L 22 Apr,*
£660 ($1,036)

12
An English steel snuffers stand with snuffers, mid 18th century, the snuffers signed *Dowler,* 19cm (7½in), *L 22 Apr,*
£1,815 ($2,850)

13
A French wool winder, 18th century, in gilt bronze and brass, 35cm (13¾in), *L 22 Apr,*
£1,265 ($1,986)

14
A French chased iron cane handle, mid 18th century, with gilt rococo decoration, 7.5cm (3in), *L 22 Apr,*
£308 ($484)

15
A North Italian arquebusier's brace, dated 1649, Brescia, a letter M and the date 1649, 28cm (11in), *L 22 Apr,*
£8,250 ($12,953)

16
A pair of steel scissors, mid 18th century, probably Spanish, 35cm (13¾in), *L 22 Apr,*
£495 ($777)

1

2

3

4

5

6

7

8

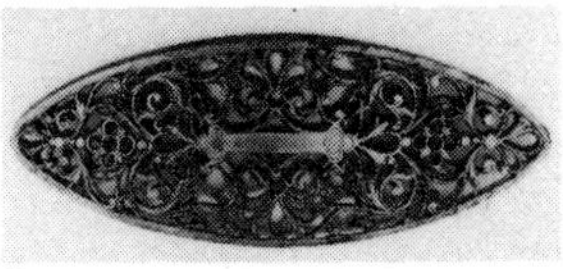
9

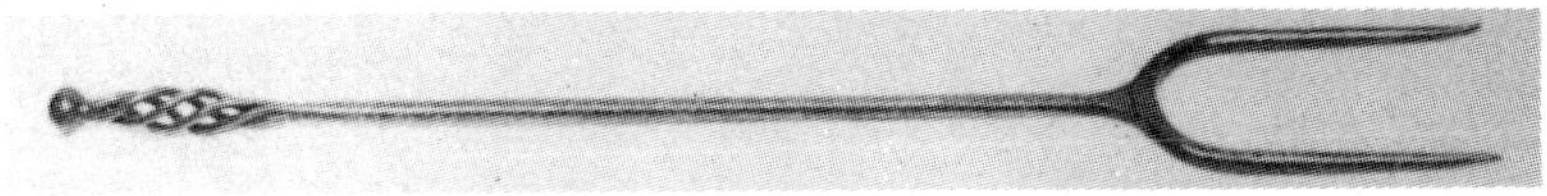
10

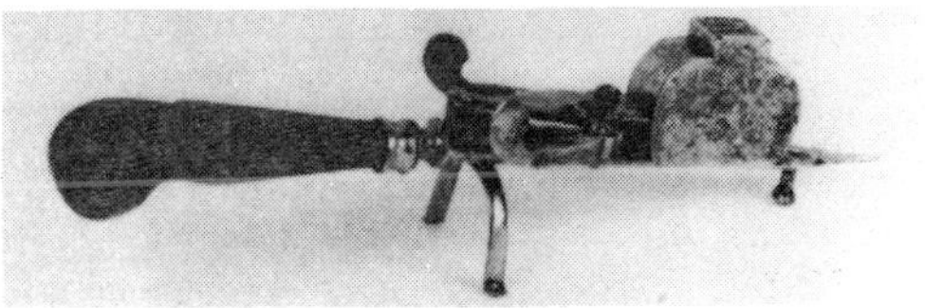
11

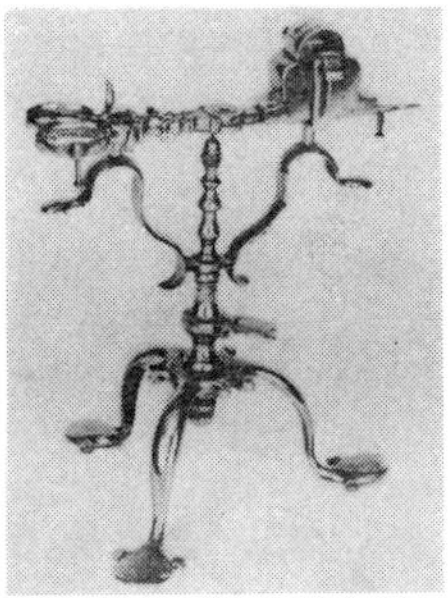
12

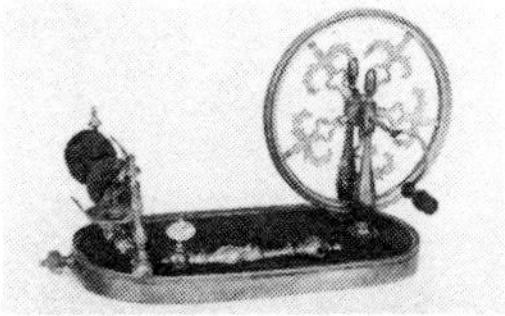
13

14

15

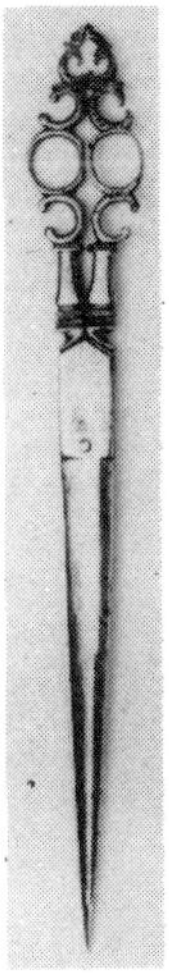
16

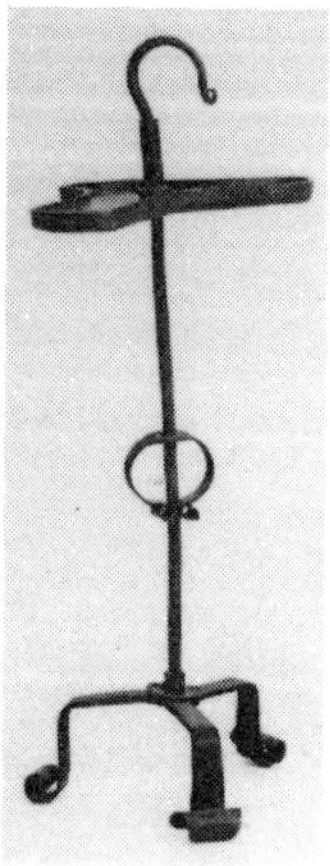
1

2

3

4

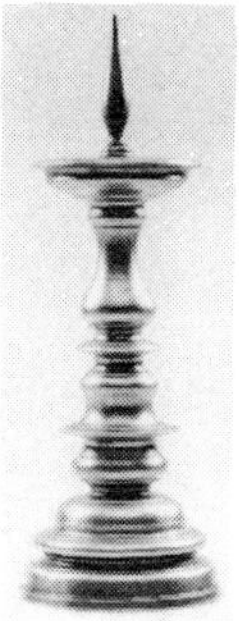
5

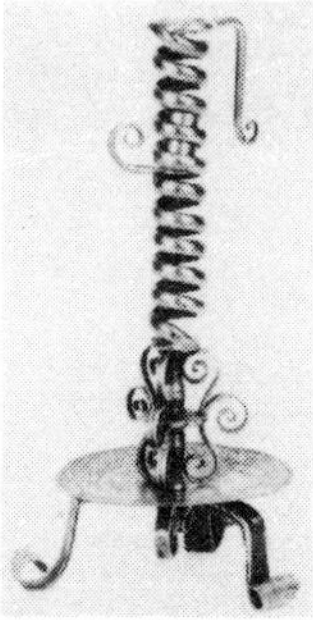
6

7

8

9

10

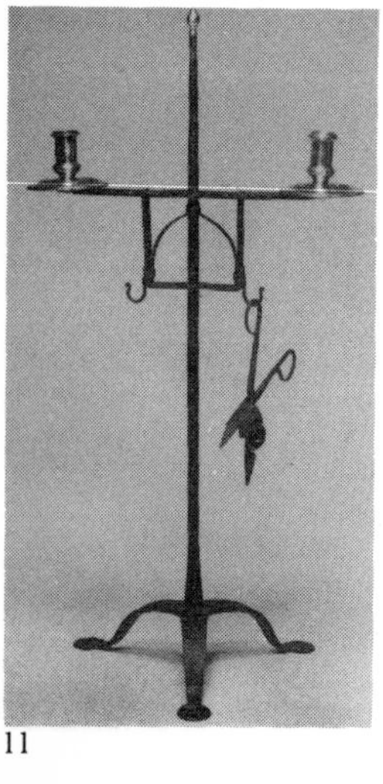
11

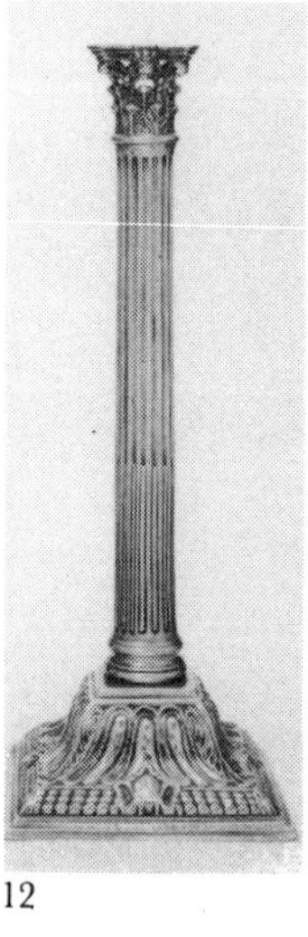
12

13

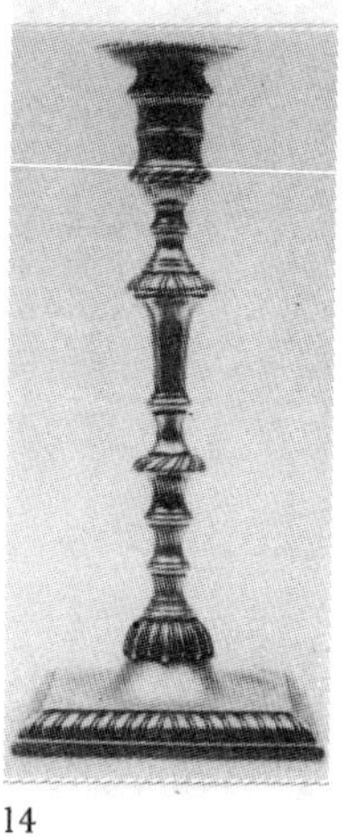
14

1
A wrought-iron pan light, 17th century, Swiss or German, 44cm (17¼in), *S 9 Dec,*
£319 ($446)

2
A Flemish brass Gothic candlestick, 15th century, with apertures for removing wax, 23cm (9in), *A 20 Oct,*
Dfl 5,520 (£1,703; $2,402)

3
A pair of brass altar pricket candlesticks, c.1600, Flemish or North German, 25cm (10in), *L 22 Apr,*
£880 ($1,382)

4
A Flemish brass candlestick, c.1500, 20.5cm (8in), *A 20 Oct,*
Dfl 2,070 (£639; $900)

5
A brass candlestick, 17th century, 39cm (15½in), *A 6 May,*
Dfl 2,990 (£906; $1,441)

6
A French iron candlestick, early 17th century, of the type called 'martinet', 30cm (12in), *L 22 Apr,*
£638 ($1,002)

7
A pair of brass table candlesticks, mid 18th century, push-up ejector bases, 23cm (9in), *C 16 Jan,*
£506 ($759)

8
A French adjustable iron candlestick, 17th century, stem secured by 'butterfly' nut beneath, 29cm (11½in), *L 22 Apr,*
£660 ($1,036)

9
A brass candlestick, 18th century, pierced socket cast with top girdle, 16cm (6¼in), *C 16 Jan,*
£154 ($231)

10
An Italian candle bracket, 18th century, in gilt iron and black sheet metal, 62cm (24½in), *L 22 Apr,*
£528 ($829)

11
A brass and wrought-iron adjustable candleholder, 18th century, sold with a wrought-iron snuffer, 54.5cm (21½in), *NY 1 Feb,*
$3,410 (£2,418)

12
A pair of paktong candlesticks, *(one illustrated),* c.1775, nozzles lacking, 33cm (13in), *L 3 July,*
£825 ($1,328)

13
A pair of bell-metal table candlesticks, *(one illustrated),* c.1780, push-up ejector, 28cm (11in), *C 17 Apr,*
£220 ($341)

14
A pair of paktong table candlesticks, *(one illustrated),* c.1770, 26cm (10¼in), *C 15 Apr,*
£2,200 ($3,410)

1
A pair of brass candle snuffers and stand, mid 18th century, 20cm (7¾in), *C 16 Jan,*
£396 ($593)

2
A pair of brass snuffers and stand, c.1740, the snuffers marked *I.S.,* 11cm (4½in), *S 18 Mar,*
£572 ($875)

3
A brass coffee pot, c.1730, the side with engraved coat of arms, 22cm (9in), *S 18 Mar,*
£1,210 ($1,851)

4
A brass castor, c.1740, 14cm (5½in), *C 16 Jan,*
£264 ($396)

5
A brass warming pan, late 17th century, with iron handle, engraved with Royal Arms, embossed *God Save King Charles Ye 2,* 114.5cm (45in), *L 3 July,*
£528 ($850)

6
An Iserlohn brass tobacco box, last half 18th century, by Johann Heinrich Giese, with portrait roundel of Frederick the Great, dated 1759, 16cm (6½in), *L 22 Apr,*
£462 ($725)

7
An Iserlohn brass tobacco box, last half 18th century, by Johann Adolph Keppelman, the lid embossed with *Die Edle Jägerrei,* copper sides, signed and dated 1762, 14.5cm (5¾in), *L 22 Apr,*
£550 ($864)

8
An Iserlohn copper and brass tobacco box, mid 18th century, embossed with the victory of Rheins, 1758, 16cm (6¼in), *S 18 Mar,*
£154 ($236)

9
A Dutch oval brass tobacco box, mid 18th century, engraved *Iohn Wetherell, Devizes, Wilts., Nov 30th 1749,* 13cm (5in), *S 18 Mar,*
£330 ($505)

10
A South German brass bowl, early 16th century, embossed with Joshua and Kaleb, with the combined initials, *CMDL,* 26.5cm (10½in), *NY 31 May,*
$3,190 (£2,170)

11
A South German brass bowl, c.1500, everted rim incised, broken in one place, 28.5cm (11¼in), *NY 31 May,*
$1,210 (£823)

12
A German brass alms dish, 16th century, with raised profile of Caesar, inscribed *MARCV.IVLIVS, CIC.PRO.CONS,* 30cm (11¾in), *S 9 Dec,*
£605 ($847)

13
A brass tobacco box, signed Frans Fransen, 1657, Stellingwerf, 8cm (3in), *A 6 May,*
Dfl 2,990 (£906; $1,441

14
An English brass honesty box, early 19th century, double hinged lid, coin and press-button operation, stamped *Rich's Patent,* key broken and defective, 23cm (9in), *S 20 May,*
£550 ($880)

1

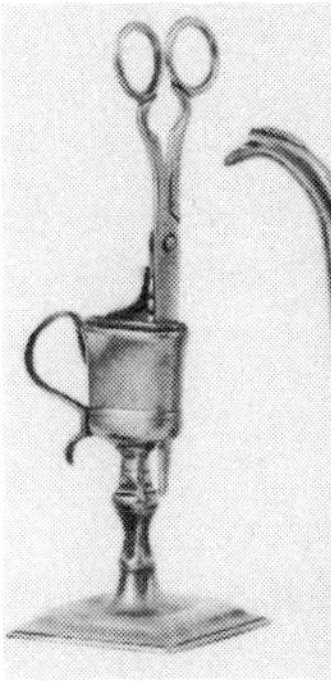
2

3

4

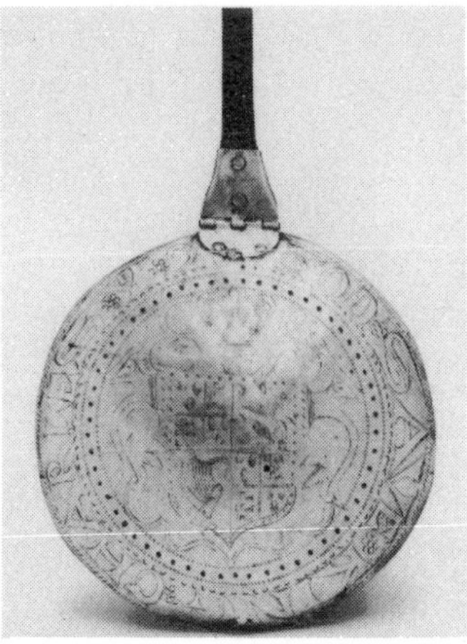
5

6 *(above)* 7 *(below)*

10

8 *(above)* 9 *(below)*

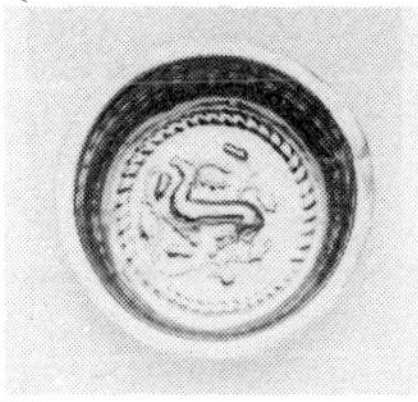
11

12

13

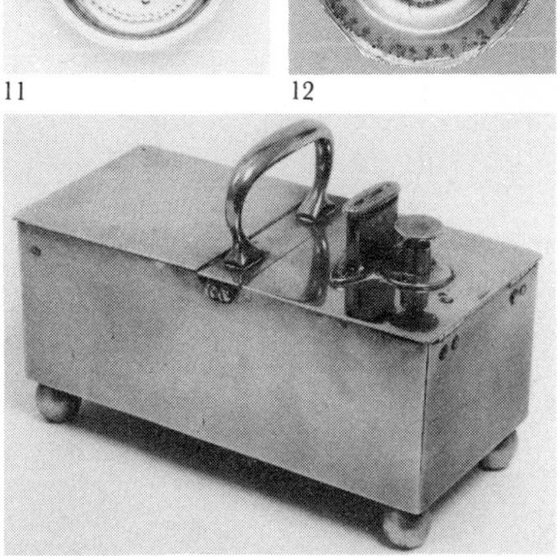
14

1

2

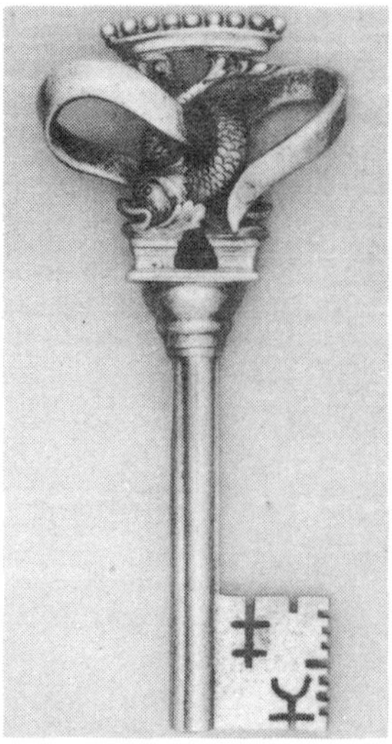
4

3

8

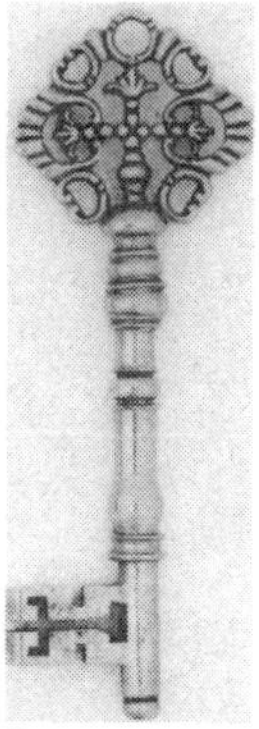
9

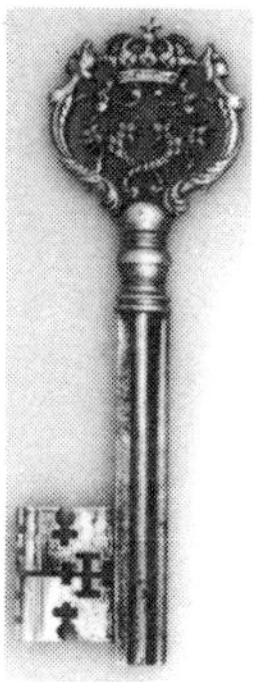
5

6

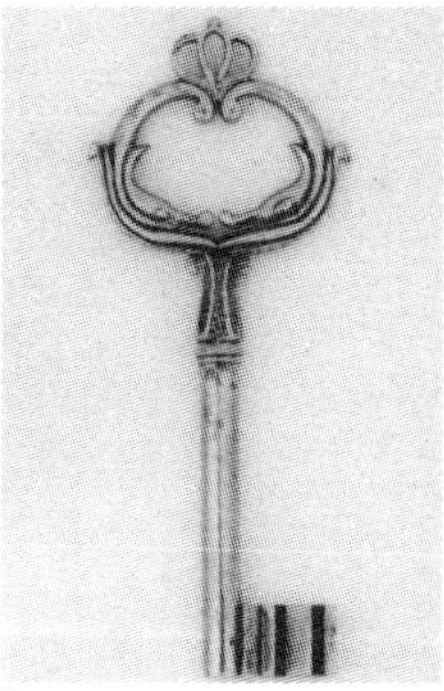
7

13

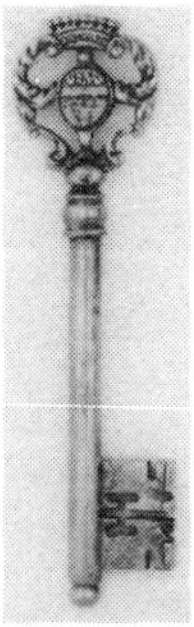
10

11

12

14

15

16

1
A French iron door knocker, late 17th century, 20.5cm (8in), *L 22 Apr,*
£990 ($1,554)

2
A French bronze knocker, 18th century, 28cm (11in), *L 22 Apr,*
£528 ($829)

3
A cast-iron boar's head door knocker, 18th century, 48.5cm (19in), *L 22 July,*
£462 ($725)

4
A French steel key, late 17th century, 16cm (6¾in), *L 22 Apr,*
£3,080 ($4,836)

5
A French steel key, early 18th century, 16cm (6¼in), *L 22 Apr,*
£2,090 ($3,281)

6
A French iron key, early 18th century, 18cm (7in), *L 22 Apr,*
£528 ($829)

7
An Italian steel key, 18th century, 11cm (4½in), *L 22 Apr,*
£308 ($484)

8
A German iron key, 18th century, 14.5cm (5½in), *L 22 Apr,*
£935 ($1,468)

9
An English steel key, 18th century, 10cm (4in), *L 22 Apr,*
£242 ($380)

10
A French iron key, mid 18th century, 12.5cm (5in), *L 22 Apr,*
£418 ($656)

11
An English steel key, early 18th century, with the crest of the Dukes of Somerset, 16cm (6¼in), *L 22 Apr,*
£1,540 ($2,418)

12
A German iron padlock and key, 16th century, 15.5cm (6in), *L 22 Apr,*
£825 ($1,295)

13
An English brass door lock, 18th century, *NY 25 Jan,*
$825 (£593)

14
An English brass and gilt-brass door lock, early 18th century, *NY 25 Jan,*
$2,200 (£1,583)

15
A German iron key, 18th century, 16cm (6½in), *L 22 Apr,*
£770 ($1,209)

16
A French steel masterpiece lock and key, early 18th century, with central 'secret' door, 19cm (7½in), *L 22 Apr,*
£7,920 ($12,434)

Russian Works of Art

See also:
Colour illustrations *p* 486

1613-1645	Michael I
1645-1676	Alexis I
1676-1682	Feodor II
1682-1725	Peter I
1725-1727	Catherine I
1727-1730	Peter II
1730-1740	Anna I
1740-1741	Ivan VI
1741-1762	Elizabeth
1762	Peter III
1762-1796	Catherine II
1796-1801	Paul I
1801-1825	Alexander I
1825-1855	Nicholas I
1855-1881	Alexander II
1881-1894	Alexander III
1894-1917	Nicholas II

1
An iron equestrian group, Kastinskoe foundry, 43cm (17in) long, *NY 12 Dec,*
$1,870 (£1,336)

2
Somonov. A bronze equestrian group, late 19th century, signed, with Woerffel foundry mark, St. Petersburg, 46cm (18in) high, *NY 12 June,*
$2,750 (£1,809)

3
C. Reca. A bronze equestrian group, 19th century, with the cypher of Alexander I, on a marble base, 72cm (28¼in) long, *NY 12 Dec,*
$3,630 (£2,593)

4
Evgenie Lanceray. A bronze group of a falconer, late 19th century, signed, 55cm (21½in) high, *NY 12 Dec,*
$5,225 (£3,732)

5
Evgenie Lanceray. A bronze group of a goatherd, late 19th century, signed, with Chopin foundry mark, 25.5cm (10in) long, *NY 12 Dec,*
$1,210 (£864)

6
Turatzky. A bronze group of Emperor Napoleon returning from Moscow, c.1880, foundry mark BS in a circle, 40cm (15¾in) long, *G 13 Nov,*
SF 5,500 (£2,292; $3,209)

1

2 3

4

5

6 7

8

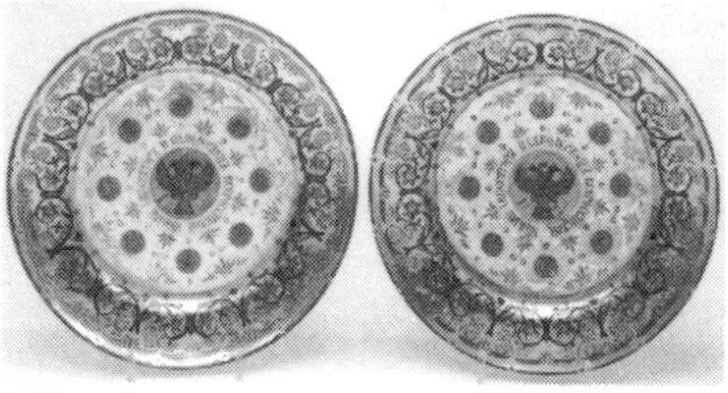
9

10

11

12

1
An Imperial porcelain tray, period of Catherine II, with a blue ribbon twist border, the centre painted *en grisaille*, marked with the underglaze-blue cypher of Catherine the Great, 24 by 35cm (9½ by 13¾in), *L 17 Oct,*
£1,430 ($2,002)

2
A porcelain figure, mid 19th century, Gardner factory, damaged, impressed factory mark, 17cm (6¾in), *L 13 Feb,*
£308 ($456)

3
A porcelain box, c.1880, possibly Gardner factory, with a girl in a blue, white and pink striped dress with a yellow apron, impressed mark and painted brown mark, slight damage, 16.5cm (6½in), *L 13 Feb,*
£330 ($448)

4
An Imperial porcelain soup tureen, cover and stand from the Cabinet Service, period of Paul, painted with views from the classical world, the border with pink roses, underglaze-blue cypher marks, stand 40.5cm (16in), *NY 12 Dec,*
$4,675 (£3,339)

5
An Imperial porcelain vase, period of Nicholas I, the plum coloured ground painted with an oriental scene, overglaze-blue cypher mark, hairline crack to rim, 20.5cm (8in), *L 17 Oct,*
£2,860 ($4,004)

6
A porcelain figure of the Avvocato, c.1850, Popov factory, impressed blue underglaze mark, some damage, 13.5cm (5¼in), *L 17 Oct,*
£715 ($1,001)

7
A porcelain group, late 19th century, Gardner factory, incised and stamped maker's marks, Moscow mark, 14.5cm (5¾in), *L 17 Oct,*
£495 ($693)

8
An Imperial porcelain shaped-oval tray, period of Alexander II, border in gilt and blue, painted *en grisaille* with the family of Darius before Alexander the Great, the base signed F. Morachkov, 1878, 26.5 by 31.5cm (10½ x 12½in), *L 17 Oct,*
£880 ($1,232)

9
A pair of Imperial porcelain dessert plates from the Kremlin Service, period of Nicholas II, in black, green and red, with blue cypher marks and Hermitage inventory marks, 22cm (8¾in), *NY 12 June,*
$2,420 (£1,592)

10
A pair of Imperial porcelain military plates, period of Alexander II, with blue and green cypher marks, 25cm (9¾in), *NY 12 June,*
$2,310 (£1,520)

11
An Imperial porcelain soup plate from the Raphael Service, period of Alexander III, dated 1893, the reverse painted with a large stylised monogram of Alexander III, 24cm (9½in), *NY 12 June,*
$1,540 (£1,013)

12
A set of four Imperial porcelain cups and saucers from the Kremlin Service, *(one illustrated)*, period of Nicholas II, dated 1899/1902, green cypher marks with dates, with Hermitage inventory numbers, saucers 14cm (5½in) diam., *NY 12 Dec,*
$4,125 (£2,946)

1
Three porcelain Easter eggs, late 19th century, painted with red, blue and purple, 10.5 and 8.5cm (4½ and 3½in), *L 13 Feb,*
£880 ($1,302)

2
A Soviet porcelain plate, dated 1921, the reverse with the cypher of Nicholas II cancelled and substituted with hammer and sickle of the State Porcelain Manufactory, 26.5cm (10½in), *L 13 Feb,*
£605 ($895)

3
A Soviet cup and saucer, State Porcelain Factory, dated 1921/2, painted with an urban landscape and a factory, the base with the cypher of Nicholas II, later applied with the hammer and sickle, signed M.K., 7.5cm (3in), *L 13 Feb,*
£275 ($407)

4
A Soviet porcelain teapot and cover, c.1920, by A. Vorobevsky, signed on base and dated 1927, 9cm (3½in) high, *L 13 Feb,*
£330 ($488)

5
A Suprematist saucer, dated 1923, the reverse with underglaze cypher of Nicholas II, later inscribed *Suprematism from the design by Chashnik,* (Ilya Gregorievich Chashnik 1902-29), 16cm (6¼in), *L 13 Feb,*
£2,200 ($3,256)

6
A Soviet porcelain teapot and cover, 1923, painted in the manner of Kliun, the base with hammer and sickle, 12.5cm (5in) high, *L 13 Feb,*
£1,265 ($1,872)

7
A papier-mâché and lacquer caddy, c.1860, decorated with views of Moscow, 12.5cm (5in), *NY 12 June,*
$1,320 (£868)

8
A lacquered papier-mâché cigar box, Vishniakov, late 19th century, maker's mark on interior of lid, slight wear, 13.5cm (5½in), *L 13 Feb,*
£176 ($260)

9
A papier-mâché snuff box, c.1850, the lid painted with the interior court of the Grand Kremlin Palace, maker's mark indistinct, 8.5cm (3¼in), *L 17 Oct,*
£605 ($847)

10
An hexagonal lacquered papier-mâché box, 19th century, painted *en grisaille* with the monument of Nicholas I, St. Petersburg, damaged, 14.5cm (5¾in), *L 17 Oct,*
£352 ($493)

11
A lacquered papier-mâché cigar case, Lukutin, 19th century, painted with a view across Red Square, maker's mark on interior of lid, 11cm (4¼in) high, *L 17 Oct,*
£572 ($801)

12
A lacquered papier-mâché box, Vishniakov, late 19th century, restored, maker's mark on interior of lid, 10cm (4in), *L 13 Feb,*
£176 ($260)

13
Three cut crystal glasses from the Alexandria Service, commissioned by Nicholas I Pavlovich for his summer residence at Peterhof, c.1830, fired with a midnight blue shield, with the gilt inscription *For faith, Tzar and Fatherland,* 10.5cm (4in), *L 17 Oct,*
£990 ($1,386)

14
A glass vodka set, c.1880, with tray, painted with orange, blue and white enamel decoration, carafe 15.5cm (6in) high, *L 13 Feb,*
£550 ($814)

1

2 3

4

5 6

7

8

9 10 11

12

13

14

1

2

3

4

5

6

7

8

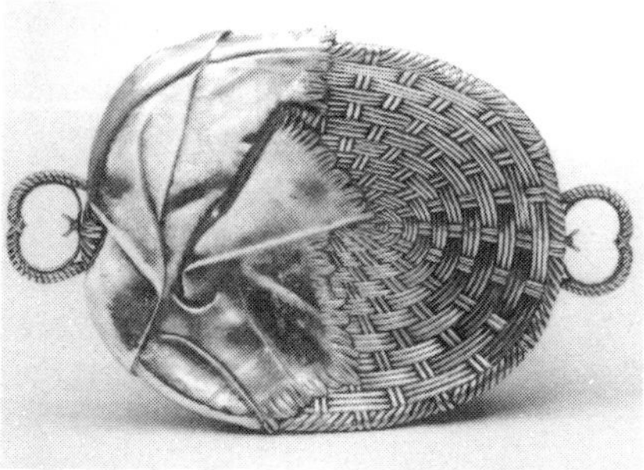
9

10

11

12

1
A silver beaker and cover, Timothy Silouyanov, Moscow, 1756, assay-master Michael Borovshikov, repoussé and chased with eagle and dolphin, gilt interior, 20.5cm (8in), *NY 12 Dec,*
$1,320 (£943)

2
A silver beaker, P. Möller, St. Petersburg, 1827, gilt interior, 12cm (4¾in), *G 13 Nov,*
SF 2,200 (£917; $1,284)

3
A trompe l'oeil silver cream jug *(illustrated)* **and sugar bowl,** late 19th century, St. Petersburg, engraved to simulate wickerwork, the cream jug with maker's mark V.I. 1894, the sugar bowl with maker's mark P.D., 9.5cm (3¾in), *G 13 Nov,*
SF 2,300, (£958; $1,341)

4
A trompe l'oeil silver miniature kvass jug, late 19th century, St. Petersburg, maker's mark I.I.N., 9.5cm (3¾in), *G 13 Nov,*
SF 1,500 (£625; $875)

5
A set of four trompe l'oeil silver salts and spoons, late 19th century, St. Petersburg, maker's mark N. D. Yanichkin, each modelled as a grain sack, 4.5cm (1¾in), *L 17 Oct,*
£2,530 ($3,542)

6
A silver tankard, Alexander Fuld, Moscow, 1891, engraved with strapwork, 21cm (8½in), *NY 12 Dec,*
$2,200 (£1,571)

7
A trompe l'oeil silver double vodka set, maker's mark G.A., St. Petersburg, 1888, hung with six cups, 21cm (8¼in), *G 13 Nov,*
SF 8,800 (£3,666; $5,133)

8
A silver barrel-form cigar box, Aron Lydikain, St. Petersburg, 1876, chased to simulate wood-grain, with slip-on cover, 17cm (6½in), *NY 12 June,*
$1,320 (£868)

9
A silver cake basket, Khlebnikov, Moscow, 1878, with a simulated overlaid napkin, 38cm (15in), *NY 12 June,*
$2,420 (£1,592)

10
A silver cigar box, c.1900, engraved with simulated tax bands, 16cm (6½in), *NY 12 Dec,*
$1,320 (£943)

11
A parcel-gilt silver cake basket, Moscow, 1886, simulated napkin engraved with flowers, 35cm (13¾in), *NY 12 June,*
$4,675 (£3,076)

12
A silver tea service, late 19th century, the teapot with maker's mark E.K., St. Petersburg, 1893, in fitted case with retailer's mark of Vladimir Morozov, teapot 15cm (6in), *L 17 Oct,*
£1,650 ($2,310)

1
A silver baluster-shaped samovar, P. Sazikov, Moscow, 1862, 42cm (16½in), *G 15 May,*
SF 7,700 (£2,593; $4,174)

2
A silver kovsh, Moscow, c.1900, set with red and blue stone cabochons, 17cm (6¾in), *NY 12 June,*
$1,430 (£941)

3
A silver four-piece teaset, Sazikov, St. Petersburg, 1880/82/84, monogrammed, with ivory insulator, gilt interiors, hot water pot 17cm (6¾in), *NY 12 June,*
$1,320 (£868)

4
A silver-gilt salt chair, P. Sazikov, St. Petersburg, 1874, the seat engraved wih interlaced initials, 13.5cm (5½in), *G 15 May,*
SF 4,400 (£1,481; $2,385)

5
A samorodok cigarette case, maker's mark A.B., St. Petersburg, 1908-17, cabochon sapphire thumbpiece, gold-coloured metal, 10cm (3½in), *L 13 Feb,*
£1,650 ($2,442)

6
A cigarette case, maker's mark D.B., St. Petersburg, 1908-17, cabochon sapphire thumbpiece, silver-coloured metal, 9.5cm (3½in), *L 13 Feb,*
£880 ($1,302)

7
A reeded gold cigarette case, maker's mark P.L., 1908-17, set with a cabochon sun stone, 9.5cm (3¾in), *G 15 May,*
SF 4,180 (£1,407; $2,266)

8
A reeded gold cigarette case, I. Marshak, Kiev, 1908-17, ruby cabochon clasp, 7.5cm (3in), *G 13 Nov,*
SF 4,500 (£1,875; $2,625)

9
A silver and cut glass centrepiece, Gratchev, St. Petersburg, 1899-1908, maker's mark, 43cm (17in), *G 13 Nov,*
SF 4,400 (£1,833; $2,567)

10
A silver sweetmeat dish, maker's mark of O. Kurliukov, Moscow, 1899-1908, 27cm (10½in), *L 13 Feb,*
£1,100 ($1,628)

11
A silver tea kettle on a stand, A. Mitin, St. Petersburg, 1886, 43cm (17in), *A 21 Apr*
Dfl 4,830; (£1,464; $2,298)

12
A frosted silver samovar with matching tray, Second Artel, Moscow, 1908-17, gilt interior, 45cm (17¾in), *G 15 May,*
SF 11,000 (£3,704; $5,963)

1

2

3

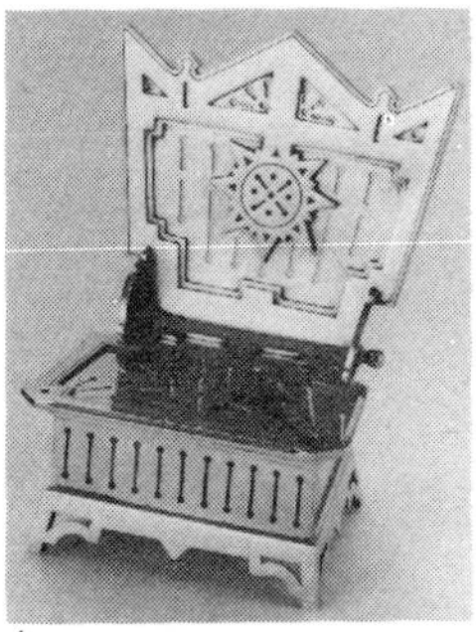
4

5

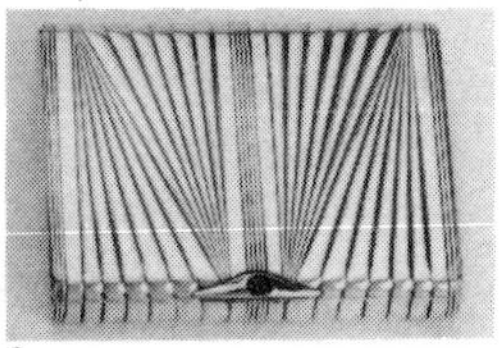
6

7

8

9

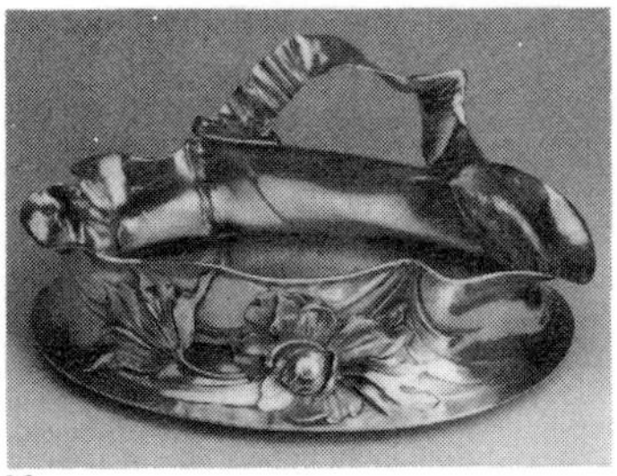
10

11

12

1

2

3

4

5

6

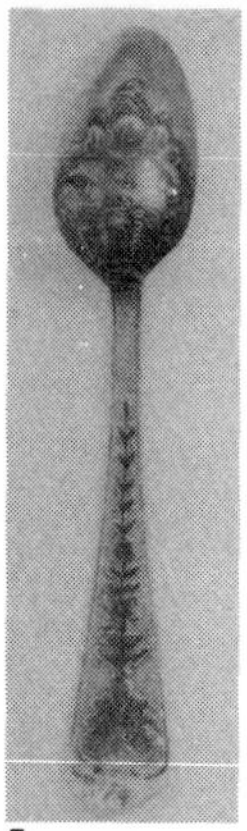
7

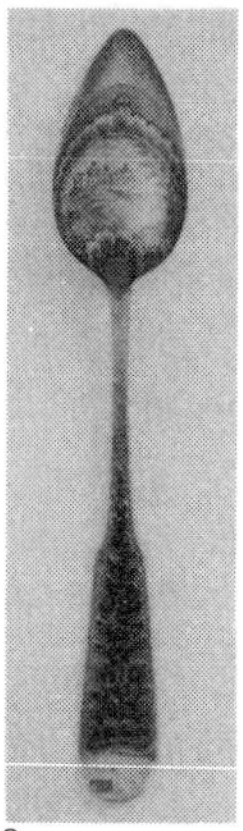
8

9

10

1
A silver-gilt and niello Imperial presentation kovsh, maker's mark A.V., Moscow, 1801, engraved with a portrait of Emperor Alexander I, the sides with inscribed panels, 26.5cm (10½in), *L 13 Feb,*
£5,720 ($8,466)

2
A parcel-gilt and niello snuff box, Paris, 1819-39, the lid decorated with Falconet's equestrian statue of Peter the Great in St. Petersburg, maker's mark A.W. in a lozenge, 8cm (3in), *L 13 Feb,*
£605 ($895)

3
A silver and niello snuff box, M. Karpinski, Moscow, 1819, the lid engraved with Emperor Alexander I and Empress Elizabeth, inscribed *Peace for Europe,* gilt interior, 9.5cm (3¾in), *G 15 May,*
SF 4,950 (£1,666; $2,683)

4
A silver and niello cigarette case, Gustave Klingert, Moscow, 1884, 9cm (3½in), *M 24 Feb,*
FF 4,440 (£429; $644)

5
A silver and enamel cigarette case, Gustave Klingert, Moscow, 1891, the back mounted with various gold monograms, with cabochon sapphire, 8.5cm (3¼in), *NY 12 Dec,*
$3,410 (£2,436)

6
A silver and champlevé enamel cup and saucer, Ovchinnikov, Moscow, 1879, in green and blue enamel, engraved with an interlaced monogram, maker's mark, sold with an enamelled teaspoon, 11.5cm (4½in), *L 13 Feb,*
£462 ($684)

7
A set of four silver and niello teaspoons, *(one illustrated),* Veliki Ustiug, 1804, maker's mark possibly of Ya Moiseev, one restored, 13.5cm (5in), *G 15 May,*
SF 1,540 (£518; $835)

8
A set of ten silver-gilt and niello dessert spoons, *(one illustrated),* A. Jhillin, Veliki Ustiug, 1823, 17cm (6¾in), *G 15 May,*
SF 2,640 (£889; $1,431)

9
A parcel-gilt silver and niello five-piece teaset, Cyrillic maker's mark F.Ya., Moscow, 1894, with troika scenes, the teapot and sugar bowl with ivory finials, 30.5cm (12in), *NY 12 June,*
$3,300 (£2,171)

10
A set of six silver-gilt and enamel sherbet cups, Antip Kuzmichev, Moscow, c.1900, decorated in multicoloured champlevé enamel, the interiors in sky blue, royal blue and purple, 17cm (6½in), *NY 12 June,*
$7,975 (£5,247)

1
A silver-gilt and shaded cloisonné enamel kovsh, Eleventh Artel, Moscow, 1908-17, 21.5cm (8½in), *G 13 Nov,*
SF 6,600 (£2,750; $3,805)

2
A silver and shaded enamel kovsh in the form of a duck, Fyodor Rückert, Moscow, c.1900, multicoloured, mounted with coloured stone cabochons, 27cm (10½in), *NY 12 June,*
$7,975 (£5,247)

3
A silver-gilt and shaded enamel bowl and spoon, Fyodor Rückert, Moscow, c.1900/1910, 8.5cm (3¼in), *NY 12 June,*
$3,025 (£1,990)

4
A silver-gilt and enamel sugar bowl, cream jug and sugar shovel, Antip Kuzmichev, Moscow, c.1885, borders of blue beads, bowl 17.5cm (7in) diam., *NY 12 Dec,*
$1,870 (£1,336)

5
A silver-gilt and shaded enamel tea glass holder, Nicholai Alexaev, Moscow, c,1900, on ground of brick red and cream, with a matching teaspoon, 9.5cm (3¾in), *NY 12 Dec,*
$2,640 (£1,886)

6
A silver-gilt and cloisonné enamel pen box, Gratchev, Moscow, 1899-1909, of typical Near Eastern form, maker's mark below Imperial warrant, 24.5cm (9¾in), *G 15 May,*
SF 7,700 (£2,593; $4,174)

7
A silver-gilt and shaded enamel tea caddy, Nicholai Alexaev, Moscow, c.1910, 10cm (4in), *NY 12 June,*
$1,980 (£1,303)

8
A silver, shaded enamel and plique-à-jour jewel box, Sixth Artel, Moscow, c.1910, multicoloured, set with four carnelian cabochons, 14cm (5½in), *NY 12 June,*
$3,575 (£2,352)

9
A silver-gilt and enamel Easter egg, Ivan Saltykov, Moscow, c.1900, the interior with fittings for conversion to egg cups, 9cm (3½in), *NY 12 June,*
$2,310 (£1,520)

10
A set of four silver-gilt and cloisonné enamel serving spoons, A. Lobavin, St. Petersburg, 1899-1908, with original case, 17cm (6¾in), *G 15 May,*
SF 2,420 (£815; $1,312))

11
A silver-gilt and cloisonné enamel serving spoon, Gustave Klingert, Moscow, 1893, 18cm (7in), *L 17 Oct,*
£308 ($431)

12
A silver-gilt and shaded enamel cream jug, late 19th century, maker's mark rubbed, the case with retailer's mark Morozov, St. Petersburg, 8cm (3¼in), *L 17 Oct,*
£880 ($1,232)

13
A silver-gilt and champlevé enamel chair salt, maker's mark Ivan Khlebnikov, Moscow, 1875, inscribed *Without bread and salt 'tis but half a meal,* maker's mark beneath Imperial warrant, 10cm (4in), *L 17 Oct,*
£1,485 ($2,079)

1

2

3

4

5

6

7

8

9

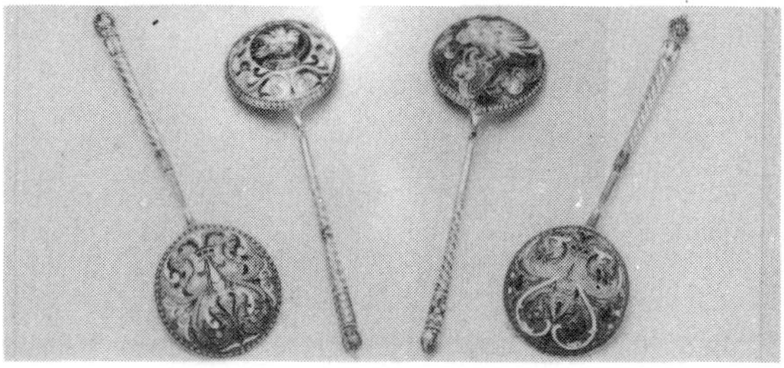
10

11 12 13

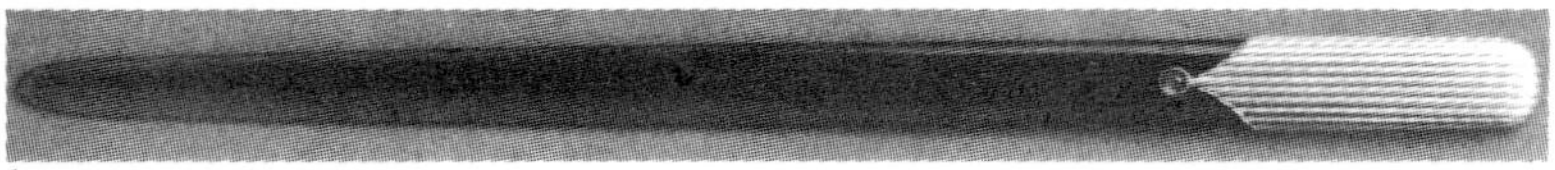
1

2

3

4

5

6

7

8

9

10

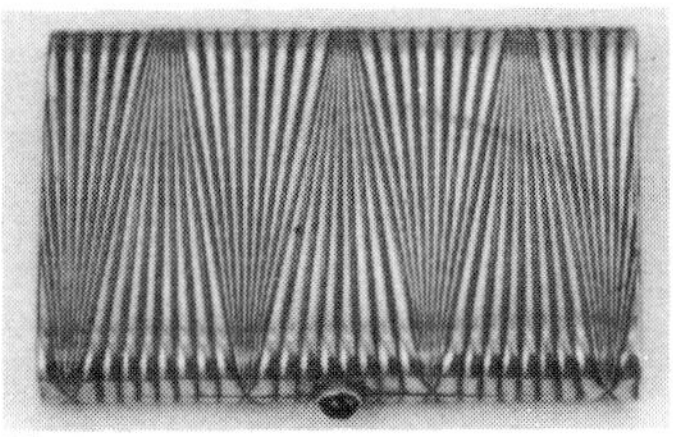
11

12

1
A Fabergé gold and nephrite letter opener, workmaster August Holström, St. Petersburg, c.1900, set with a cabochon red stone, 21cm (8¼in), *NY 12 Dec,*
$7,700 (£5,500)

2
A Fabergé carved bowenite miniature rhinoceros, St. Petersburg, c.1900, retailed by Wartski, London, 4cm (1½in), *NY 12 Dec,*
$19,800 (£14,143)

3
A Fabergé silver-mounted hardstone bowl, Moscow, late 19th century, maker's mark below the Imperial warrant, 22.5cm (9in), *G 13 Nov,*
SF 6,500 (£2,708; $3,791)

4
A Fabergé two-handled dish, workmaster Alexander Wäkevä, St. Petersburg, 1908-17, silver-coloured metal, maker's mark under Imperial warrant, 31cm (12¼in), *L 17 Oct,*
£2,090 ($2,926)

5
A Fabergé silver and cut glass hand mirror and a pair of toilet bottles, Moscow, c.1900, marked K. Fabergé in Cyrillic with Imperial warrant, mirror 30.5cm (12in) long, *NY 12 Dec,*
$2,475 (£1,768)

6
A Fabergé silver seven-piece tea and coffee set, Moscow, c.1900, repoussé and chased, marked K. Fabergé in Cyrillic with Imperial warrant, coffee pot 25cm (9¾in), *NY 12 Dec,*
$17,600 (£12,571)

7
A Fabergé silver and cut glass sweetmeat basket, Moscow, c.1900, gilt interior, marked K. Fabergé in Cyrillic, 14cm (5½in) diam., *NY 12 Dec,*
$3,850 (£2,750)

8
A Fabergé silver double cup, Moscow, c.1900, in late 17th century German style, repoussé and chased, monogramed and inscribed, marked K. Fabergé in Cyrillic with Imperial warrant, 9.5cm (3¾in), *NY 12 Dec,*
$4,400 (£3,143)

9
A pair of Fabergé silver-gilt and cut glass decanters, Moscow, 1899-1908, maker's mark below Imperial warrant, 25.5cm (10in), *G 13 Nov,*
SF 6,600 (£2,750; $3,850)

10
A Fabergé silver cup and saucer, Moscow, 1894, illustrating a Russian fairy tale, marked K.F. 84 standard, 12cm (4¾in), *NY 12 June,*
$2,420 (£1,592)

11
A Fabergé silver cigarette case, workmaster A. Hollming, St. Petersburg, 1899-1908, gilt interior, 10cm (4in), *G 15 May,*
SF 3,190 (£1,074; $1,729)

12
A Fabergé silver-gilt and shaded enamel table cigarette box, Moscow, c.1910, enamelled in blue and green on a brown ground, marked K. Fabergé in Cyrillic with Imperial warrant, 10cm (4in), *NY 12 Dec,*
$6,050 (£4,321)

1
A Fabergé gold, silver and enamel miniature frame, H. Armfeldt, St. Petersburg, 1899-1908, purple translucent enamel, chased gold borders, ivory back, *G 15 May,*
SF 20,900 (£7,037; $11,330)

2
A Fabergé silver, gold, enamel and jewelled buckle, workmaster Henrik Wigström, St. Petersburg, c.1900, set with seed pearls, 6.5cm (2½in), *NY 12 Dec,*
$3,080 (£2,200)

3
A Fabergé silver-gilt and mauve enamel photograph frame, workmaster A. Nevalainen, St. Petersburg, 1899-1908, 22cm (8¾in), *G 13 Nov,*
SF 26,000 (£10,833; $15,166)

4
A Fabergé silver, gold and enamel belt buckle, workmaster Michael Perchin, St. Petersburg, c.1890, enamelled translucent royal blue, 7cm (2¾in), *NY 12 June,*
$2,640 (£1,737)

5
A pair of Fabergé gold and enamel cufflinks, A. Höllming, St. Petersburg, late 19th century, enamelled in translucent red, set with diamonds, restored, 1.5cm (¾in), *G 13 Nov,*
SF 7,500 (£3,125; $4,375)

6
A Fabergé gold and translucent enamel miniature Easter egg pendant, workmaster Andrei Gorianov, St. Petersburg, c.1900, apple green over a guilloché ground, embellished with strawberry red cross, 1.5cm (¾in), *NY 12 June,*
$6,050 (£3,980)

7
A Fabergé bowenite, gold and enamel bell push, St. Petersburg, c.1890, enamelled translucent red over a guilloché ground, 6.5cm (2½in), *NY 12 Dec,*
$13,200 (£9,428)

8
A Fabergé globular enamelled and gold-mounted gum pot, late 19th century, maker's mark, 5cm (2in), *G 15 May,*
SF 9,350 (£3,148; $5,068)

9
A Fabergé silver-gilt and enamel beaker, workmaster A.P., St. Petersburg, c.1900, in rose pink over a guilloché ground, the base with a plique-à-jour green enamel flower head, 4.5cm (1¾in), *NY 12 Dec,*
$8,250 (£5,893)

10
A Fabergé cylindrical gold-mounted enamel scent bottle, workmaster H. Wigström, St. Petersburg, 1899-1908, mauve over a guilloché ground, chased two-colour gold borders, 5.5cm (2¼in), *G 15 May,*
SF 14,300 (£4,815; $7,752)

11
A Fabergé hardstone carving of a seated rabbit, c.1900, in Norwegian sunstone, gold-mounted ruby eyes, 8cm (3in), *G 13 Nov,*
SF 38,000 (£15,833; $22,166)

12
A Fabergé carved coral model of a Persian cat, St. Petersburg, 1905-10, the eyes set with cabochon red stones, 5cm (2in), *NY 12 June,*
$22,000 (£14,474)

13
A Fabergé silver and nephrite seal, workmaster August Höllming, St. Petersburg, c.1900, 5cm (2in), *NY 12 June,*
$1,045 (£688)

14
A Fabergé gold-mounted, enamel and hardstone knife handle, M. Perchin, late 19th century, in grey-blue chalcedony, the mount in shades of purple, red and yellow, chipped, 18cm (7in), *G 13 Nov,*
SF 21,000 (£8,750; $12,250)

1

3

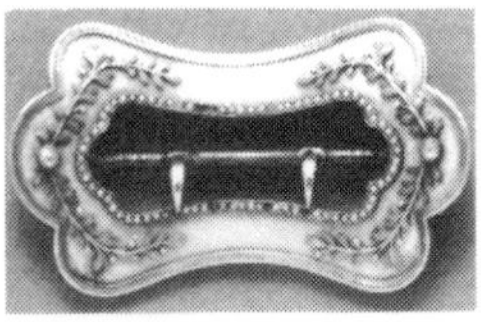
2

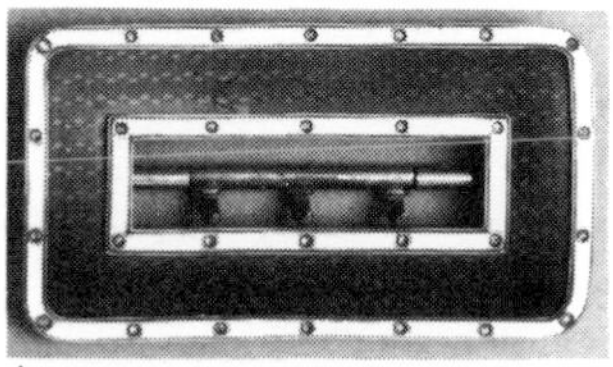
4

5

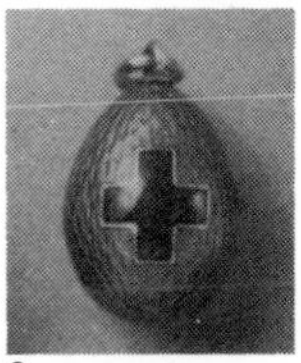
6

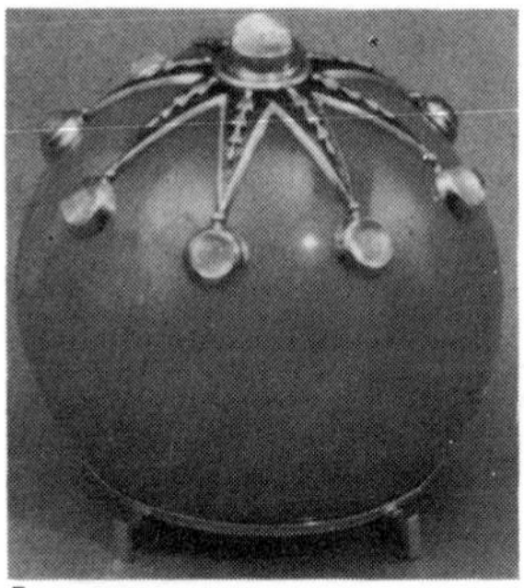
7

8

9

10

11

12

13

14

Silver

1

2

3

4

5

6

7

1
An Austrian silver-gilt tankard, Andre Kotzum, Vienna, c.1590, 17cm (6¾in), 19oz (592gr), *G 13 May,*
SF 35,200 (£11,891; $19,146)

2
A Transylvanian silver-gilt tankard, Gregorius Gunesch (Herrmannstadt, Sibiu), c.1590, 19cm (7½in), 22oz 18dwt (715gr), *G 13 May,*
SF 33,000 (£11,149; $17,949)

3
A German parcel-gilt tankard, Elias Geier, Leipzig, c.1610, 15cm (6in), 10oz 18dwt (339gr), *G 13 May,*
SF 18,700 (£6,318; $10,171)

4
A German silver-gilt tankard, Esaias zur Linden, Nuremberg, c.1620, with six shaped panels engraved with birds, fruit and foliage, 20cm (8in), 18oz 10dwt (577gr), *G 11 Nov,*
SF 20,900 (£8,636; $12,350)

5
A Russian silver-gilt tankard, Moscow, c.1790, with a sleeve and plaquette, late 17th century, probably German, the detachable sleeve depicting the Triumph of Silenius in the manner of Rubens, the cover with a plaquette chased with a scene probably from the life of Scipio, 25.5cm (10in), 84oz 16dwt (2640gr), *G 11 Nov,*
SF 13,200 (£5,455; $7,800)

6
A Norwegian peg tankard, Herman Fridrichsen, (Bergen), c.1700, maker's mark only, 23.5cm, (9¼in), 39oz 8dwt (1226gr), *G 13 May,*
SF 13,200 (£4,459; $7,180)

7
A German parcel-gilt tankard, Paul Solanier, Augsburg, c.1720, fitted with a sleeve depicting the Birth of Christ, the cover centred by a plaque embossed with a related scene, 20cm (8in), 45oz 2dwt (1405gr), *G 11 Nov,*
SF 9,900 (£4,091; $5,850)

1
A Swedish parcel-gilt tankard, Niclas Warneck, Karlstad, 1743, the hinged lid inset with a Frederick I thaler commemorating the bicentenary of the Reformation in Sweden, 20cm (8in), 42oz 6dwt (1315gr), *L 11 Feb,*
£2,860 ($4,204)

2
A William III tankard, John Porter, London, 1700, 20.5cm (8in), 30oz 4dwt (939gr), *L 16 Oct,*
£1,870 ($2,618)

3
A Queen Anne tankard, John Elston, Exeter, 1702, the reeded, hinged and stepped lid with denticulation at the front, Britannia Standard, 18.5cm (7¼in), 28oz 3dwt (880gr), *L 24 Apr,*
£3,850 ($6,160)

4
A George I tankard, Nathaniel Lock, London, 1714, 18.5cm (7¼in), 24oz 10dwt (761gr), *HS 24 Sept,*
IR£2,310 (£2,100; $3,045)

5
A George II tankard, Isaac Cookson, Newcastle, 1736, 16.5cm (6½in), 17oz 4dwt (534gr), *L 16 Oct,*
£1,430 ($2,002)

6
A George II baluster tankard, Gurney & Cooke, London, 1754, 20cm (8in), 30oz 1dwt (933gr), *C 15 April,*
£1,375 ($2,131)

7
An early George III tankard, London, 1766, maker's mark WF, 19cm (7½in), 22oz 8dwt (700gr), *S 23 Apr,*
£858 ($1,347)

8
A George II tankard, Thomas Whipham, London, 1755, the body engraved at a slightly later date with armorials, 20cm (8in), 26oz 7dwt (819gr), *L 20 Nov,*
£2,420 ($3,388)

9
A large German tankard, L. Neresheimer & Co., Hanau, c.1897, imported by B. Muller & Son, the barrel cast with a hunting scene, the cover surmounted by a figure of Diana, 49cm (19¼in), 98oz 12dwt (3066gr), *L 20 Mar,*
£2,750 ($4,317)

10
A George III tankard, William & James Priest, London, 1764, 20.5cm (8in), 28oz 10dwt (886gr), *NY 12 June,*
$1,650 (£1,086)

11
A George III tankard, Barek Mewburn, London, 1784, 17.5cm (7in), 24oz 10dwt (761gr), *NY 12 June,*
$2,200 (£1,447)

12
A George III tankard, Septimus & James Crespell, London, 1768, with later crest and monogram, 12.5cm (5in), 16oz (497gr), *NY 12 June,*
$660 (£434)

13
A George III tankard, Thomas Robins, London, 1810, applied with a band of oak leaves and acorns, 21cm (8¼in), 39oz 10dwt (1228gr), *NY 12 June,*
$1,760 (£1,158)

14
A large German tankard, c.1890, inset with semi-precious stones and coloured pastes, inscribed in French and with a frieze depicting the death of the Chevalier Bayard after the Battle of Rebec in 1524, the lid surmounted by a figure of a warrior, gilt interior, 51cm (20in), 83oz 16dwt (2601gr), *L 6 Nov,*
£3,960 ($5,623)

1

2

3

4

5

6

9

7

8

10

11

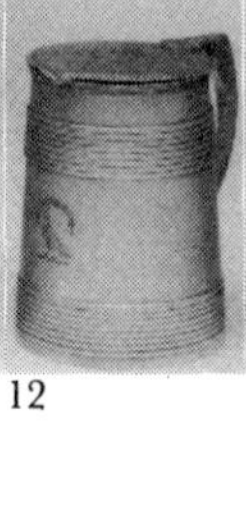
12

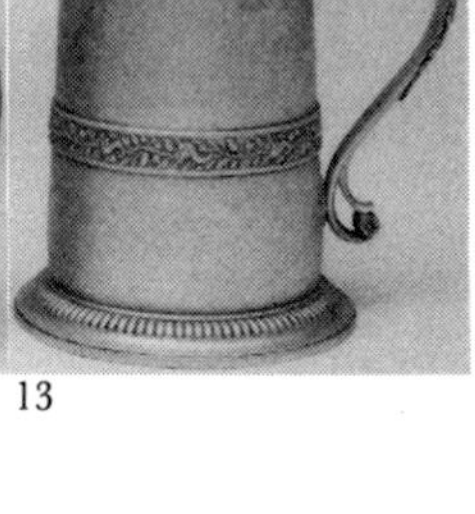
13

14

1

2

3

4

5

6

7

8

9

10

11

12

16

17

13
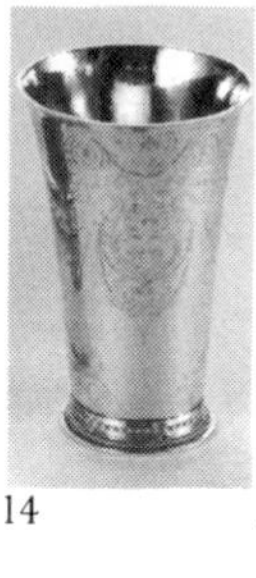
14

15

18

1
A Queen Anne mug, John Read, London, 1704, 11.5cm (4½in), 11oz (342gr), *S 20 June,*
£880 ($1,390)

2
A George III mug, Hester Bateman, London, 1780, 12.5cm (5in), 11oz (342gr), *NY 5 Nov,*
$770 (£542)

3
An Elizabeth I chalice, maker's mark a pair of bellows, London, 1570, 15.5cm (6¼in), 5oz (155gr), *L 17 July,*
£2,750 ($4,318)

4
A George III double beaker, Peter & Ann Bateman, London, 1794, 14.5cm (5¾in), 7oz 15dwt (241gr), *L 17 July,*
£990 ($1,554)

5
A pair of George III wine cups, *(one illustrated),* Hester Bateman, London, 1783, 16cm (6¼in), 14oz 14dwt (457gr), *L 20 Nov,*
£1,210 ($1,694)

6
A pair of Victorian goblets, Elkington & Co., Birmingham, 1876, engraved with classical maidens, 19cm (7½in), 19oz 18dwt (618gr), *C 25 June,*
£605 ($944)

7
A German silver-gilt beaker, maker's mark three stars above a bar in an oval surround, Nuremberg, c.1608, 7.5cm (3in), 6oz 8dwt (200gr), *G 11 Nov,*
SF 30,800 (£12,727; $18,200)

8
A German parcel-gilt rummer-shaped beaker, maker's mark P. in a shield, Frankenthal, c.1600, 8.5cm (3¼in), 2oz 10dwt (86gr), *L 8 July,*
£3,960 ($6,376)

9
A German parcel-gilt setzbecher, Hieronymus Bang, Nuremberg, c.1600, 9cm (3½in), 3oz 18dwt (115gr), *L 8 July,*
£6,820 ($10,980)

10
A German silver-gilt wager cup, Meinrad Bauch the Elder, Nuremberg, c.1610, 22.5cm (8¾in), 13oz 10dwt (421gr), *G 13 May,*
SF 148,500 (£50,169; $80,772)

11
A German silver-gilt beaker, c.1623, unmarked, inset with a Saxe-Altenburg thaler, 7.5cm (3in), 4oz (125gr), *L 11 Feb,*
£2,310 ($3,396)

12
A German silver-gilt beaker, maker's mark R.R. within a rectangle, Nuremberg, early 17th century, 9cm (3½in), 3oz 4dwt (100gr), *L 8 July,*
£1,705 ($2,745)

13
A Dutch beaker, probably Harlingen, mid 17th century, 11.5cm (4½in), 3oz 15dwt (116gr), *NY 12 June,*
$1,760 (£1,158)

14
A Dutch beaker, Eelke Wyntjes, (Leeuwarden), c.1632, 15.5cm (6¼in), 7oz 14dwt (241gr), *G 13 May,*
SF 13,200 (£4,459; $7,180)

15
A German parcel-gilt standing cup and cover, Marx Merzenbach, Augsburg, c.1670, in the form of a pear, 14cm (5½in), 3oz (95gr), *G 11 Nov,*
SF 17,600 (£7,273; $10,400)

16
A German parcel-gilt beaker and cover, Ulrich Schnell, Augsburg, c.1670, 17.5cm (6½in), 12oz 3dwt (379gr), *L 8 July,*
£2,860 ($4,605)

17
A German silver-gilt beaker and cover, Hans Scholler, Leipzig, c.1680, later flower finial, 24.5cm (9¾in), 22oz 16dwt (711gr), *L 8 July,*
£2,860 ($4,605)

18
An Hungarian silver-gilt marriage beaker, c.1696, unmarked, 11.5cm (4½in), 6oz 12dwt (207gr), *L 8 July,*
£2,090 ($3,365)

1
A Swiss parcel-gilt beaker, maker's mark H.I.B. conjoined, Basel, late 17th century, 8cm (3¼in), 4oz (124gr), *NY 8 Apr,*
$2,750 (£1,897)

2
A pair of German silver-gilt beakers, *(one illustrated),* Johann Baptist Ernst I, Augsburg, c.1690, 9cm (3½in), 10oz 14dwt (334gr), *G 13 May,*
SF 9,350 (£3,159; $5,086)

3
A German beaker, Philipp Stenglin, Augsburg, 1696-1700, traces of gilding, 9cm (3½in), 4oz 12dwt (146gr), *A 21 Apr,*
Dfl 2,530 (£767; $1,204)

4
A German gilt-metal beaker, second half 17th century, embossed with biblical scenes, 13cm (5in), *L 8 July,*
£528 ($850)

5
A German silver-gilt beaker, Johann Christoph Treffler II, Augsburg, 1705, 9.5cm (3¾in), 4oz 8dwt (138gr), *G 11 Nov,*
SF 8,800 (£3,636; $5,199)

6
A French silver-gilt beaker, Simon Boulanger, Paris, 1694, 7.5cm (3in), 3oz 12dwt (115gr), *G 11 Nov,*
SF 12,100 (£5,000; $7,150)

7
A German parcel-gilt beaker, maker's mark HH conjoined, Nuremberg, c.1720, chased with bands of Régence ornament, 8.5cm (3¼in), 3oz (94gr), *G 11 Nov,*
SF 2,640 (£1,091; $1,560)

8
A German parcel-gilt beaker, Johann Mittnacht III, Augsburg, 1736-37, flat-chased with Régence ornament, 9cm (3½in), 2oz 14dwt (86gr), *G 11 Nov,*
SF 5,500 (£2,273; $3,250)

9
Two similar parcel-gilt German beakers, *(one illustrated),* Johann Mittnacht III, Augsburg, 1751-53, 9cm (3½in), 6oz 2dwt (190gr), *G 11 Nov,*
SF 12,100 (£5,000; $7,150)

10
A pair of German silver-gilt beakers, *(one illustrated),* Matthaüs Baur II, Augsburg, 1731-33, engraved with bands of Régence strapwork, 6cm (2½in), 7oz 14dwt (240gr), *G 13 May,*
SF 9,350 (£3,159; $5,086)

11
A German beaker, Berlin, c.1750, 12cm (4¾in), 5oz 8dwt (170gr), *A 21 Apr,*
Dfl 1,150 (£348; $547)

12
A French beaker, apparently Nicolas Linguet, Paris, 1722, 9.5cm (3¾in), 9oz 8dwt (295gr), *M 24 June,*
FF 44,400 (£3,961; $6,179)

13
A French silver-gilt beaker, Tobias Krug, Strasbourg, c.1730, engraved with a band of Régence ornament, 8.5cm (3¼in), 3oz 10dwt (111gr), *G 11 Nov,*
SF 9,350 (£3,864; $5,525)

14
An American standing cup, A. Rasch & Co., Philadelphia, c.1818, 14.5cm (5¾in), 8oz 15dwt (272gr), *NY 31 Jan,*
$3,190 (£2,262)

15
A German silver-gilt covered beaker, Franz Christoph Saler, Augsburg, 1745-47, 14.5cm (5¾in), 5oz 15dwt (178gr), *NY 12 June,*
$1,430 (£941)

16
A Swedish parcel-gilt beaker, Johan Lund, Stockholm, 1711, 19.5cm (7¾in), 16oz 11dwt (515gr), *L 11 Feb,*
£2,200 ($3,234)

17
A Swedish parcel-gilt beaker, Berndt Johan Eschenburg, Enköping, 1769, 21cm (8¼in), 13oz 16dwt (429gr), *L 8 July,*
£660 ($1,063)

18
A Norwegian parcel-gilt beaker and cover, Andreas G. Svindland, (Stavanger), c.1815, 10.5cm (4in), 4oz (126gr), *L 11 Feb,*
£495 ($728)

1

2

3

4

5

6

7

8

9

10

11

12

13

14

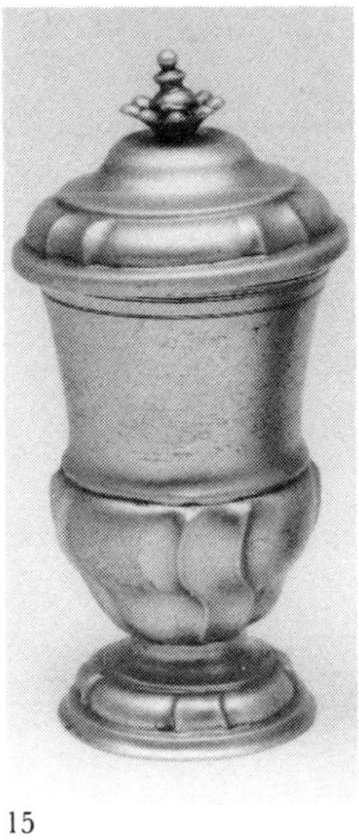
15

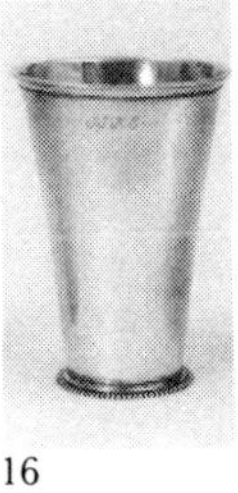
16

17

18

1

2

3

4

5

6

7

8

9

10

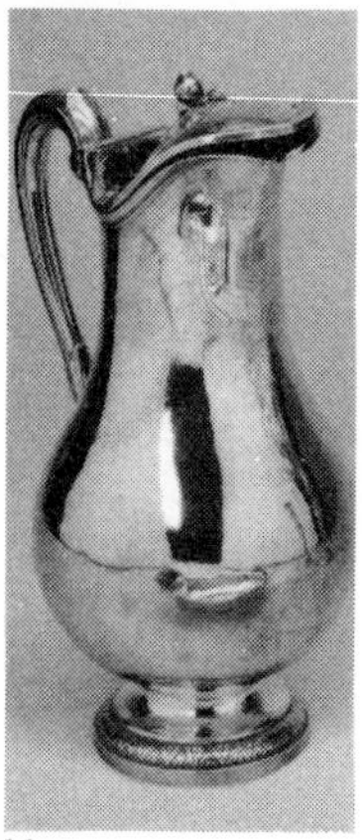
11

12

13

14

1
An Elizabeth I silver-mounted tigerware jug, William Cobbold, Norwich, 1571, 16.5cm (6½in), *L 17 July*,
£2,530 ($3,972)

2
An Elizabeth I jug, with German stoneware body and contemporary English silver-gilt mounts, late 16th century, apparently unmarked, 23.5cm (9¼in), *L 3 July*,
£5,280 ($8,500)

3
A George II beer jug, Phillips Garden, London, 1752, with later crests, 23cm (9in), 26oz 2dwt (811gr), *L 6 Feb*,
£2,640 ($3,854)

4
A George I shaving jug, William Fawdery, London, 1726, 18.5cm (7¼in), 20oz 15dwt (645gr), *L 19 June*,
£9,900 ($15,640)

5
A French ewer and basin, Pierre Belleville, Montpellier, 1754, basin 35cm (13¾in) wide, 71oz 14dwt (2230gr), *G 11 Nov*,
SF 44,000 (£18,182; $26,000)

6
A Maltese ewer, c.1730, assay master's mark only, with applied bearded mask spout, 28cm (11in), 37oz 2dwt (1156gr), *G 13 May*,
SF 17,600 (£5,960; $9,573)

7
A French ewer, Jean-Pierre Charpenat, Paris, 1784, flat-chased with matted strapwork, 31.5cm (12½in), 36oz 7dwt (1132gr), *L 8 July*,
£2,750 ($4,428)

8
Design for the basin illustrated as number 9, drawing in pen and ink by Jean-Guillaume Moitte, provenance Jean-Baptiste-Claude Odiot collection, 23 x 57cm (9 x 22½in), *M 22 Feb*,
FF 39,960 (£3,865; $5,798)

9
A French silver-gilt ewer and basin, to the designs of Jean-Guillaume Moitte, Henry Auguste, Paris, 1789, supplied to William Beckford of Fonthill Abbey in 1802, ewer 44cm (17¼in), 259oz (8055gr), *NY 8 Apr*,
$154,000 (£106,207)

The pair to this ewer and basin was sold in Monaco, 24 June 1986.

10
A French silver-gilt ewer, Jean-Baptiste-Claude Odiot, Paris, 1798-1809, the body applied with a winged classical figure, the handle in the form of a seahorse, 27cm (10½in), 26oz (808gr), *NY 5 Nov*,
$9,075 (£6,391)

11
A French ewer and basin, *(ewer illustrated)*, maker's mark M.P., Paris, 1785, both engraved with laurel wreaths, ewer 28cm (11in), 52oz (1620gr), *F 30 Sept*,
L 9,350,000 (£4,659; $6,523)

12
A French ewer, Jean-Baptiste-Claude Odiot, Paris, 1798-1809, applied with a winged classical figure, serpent handle, engraved with the arms of Borghese, 26.5cm (10½in), 19oz 10dwt (6064gr), *NY 8 Apr*,
$2,310 (£1,593)

13
A William IV silver-gilt claret jug, retailed by Rundell, Bridge & Co., London, 1835, maker's mark of John Tapley & Co., of *oinochoe* form, the polished trefoil cover with grape cluster finial, the scroll handle rising from a bearded mask and topped by a large eagle finial, 30cm (11¾in), 39oz 6dwt (1222gr), *NY 5 Nov*,
$8,325 (£5,863)

14
An American jug, Baldwin Gardiner, New York, c.1825, 31cm (12¼in), 46oz (1430gr), *NY 31 Jan*,
$2,640 (£1,872)

1
Two matching silver-mounted glass claret jugs, *(one illustrated)*, one Storr & Mortimer, London, 1836, maker's mark of Paul Storr, the other Hunt & Roskell, London, 1845, maker's mark of J. S. Hunt, each in the form of a Pompeian *acsos*, 22cm (8¾in) high, *L 20 Nov*,
£10,450 ($14,630)

2
A Victorian parcel-gilt ewer and a pair of goblets, Elkington & Co., Birmingham, 1873/74, all chased round the centre with classical friezes, ewer 23cm (9in) high and goblets 21cm (8¼in) high, 69oz 17dwt (2172gr), *C 15 Apr*,
£3,190 ($4,945)

3
A Victorian water jug, Stephen Smith & Son, London, 1876, engraved with humming birds and exotic flowers, 18.5cm (7¼in) high, 28oz 11dwt (887gr), *L 24 Apr*,
£605 ($968)

4
A Victorian mint julep jug and two beakers, Holland, Aldwinckle & Slater, London, 1882, engraved in Japanese taste, the jug with bamboo handle, 20 and 9.5cm (7¾ and 3¾in) high, 28oz 5dwt (878gr), *L 16 Oct*,
£1,155 ($1,617)

5
A pair of Victorian silver-gilt mounted cut glass claret jugs, *(one illustrated)*, Charles Edwards, London, 24cm (9½in) high, *L 20 Nov*,
£1,650 ($2,310)

6
A Victorian silver-mounted glass claret jug, W. & G. Sissons, Sheffield, 1879, the body engraved with sprays of ferns, 26cm (10¼in) high, *C 30 Apr*,
£638 ($1,034)

7
A Victorian silver-mounted cut glass claret jug, maker's mark FC over CH, Sheffield, 1855, 29cm (11½in) high, *C 14 May*,
£297 ($478)

8
A pair of Victorian presentation ewers, *(one illustrated)*, maker's mark AB, Sheffield, 1895/96, each hinged lid with 'automatic' opening device, 40cm (15¾in) high, 58oz 18dwt (1827gr), *L 20 Feb*,
£2,420 ($3,533)

9
A Victorian silver-mounted cut glass claret jug, Charles Edwards, London, 1883, the hinged cover showing traces of gilding, the body engraved with a butterfly, a stork and foliage, 29.5cm (11¾in) high, *L 19 June*,
£1,760 ($2,781)

10
A pair of glass claret jugs with French silver mounts, *(one illustrated)*, c.1880, stamped *L. Lapar Sr. De Beguin Paris* over the maker's mark E.T., 27.5cm (10¾in) high, *L 11 Feb*,
£2,200 ($3,234)

11
A pair of German silver and etched glass claret jugs, *(one illustrated)*, c.1900, the mounts stamped with pastoral scenes and trophies, flower finials, 32.5cm (12¾in) high, *NY 5 Nov*,
$3,575 (£2,518)

12
A pair of beer jugs, maker's mark BP LC L, London, 1939, in George I style, 23cm (9in) high, 71oz 2dwt (2211gr), *L 24 Apr*,
£1,760 ($2,816)

1

2

3

4

5

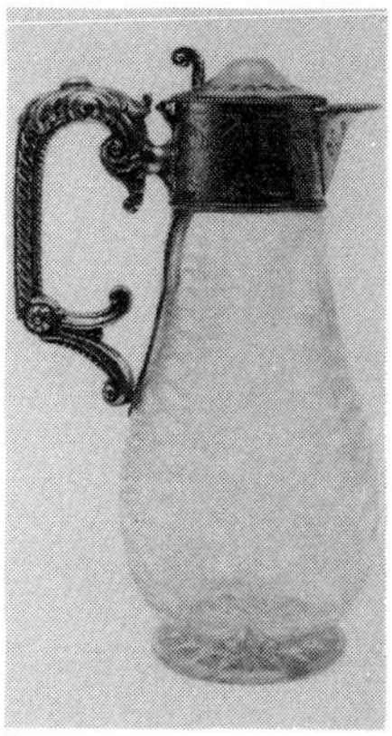
6

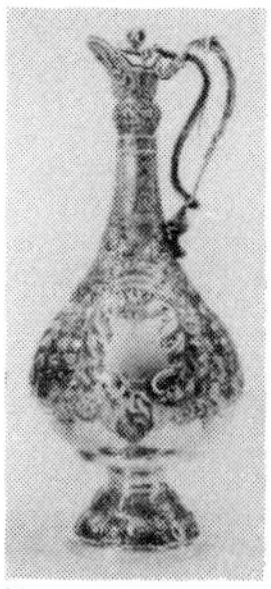
8

7

9

10

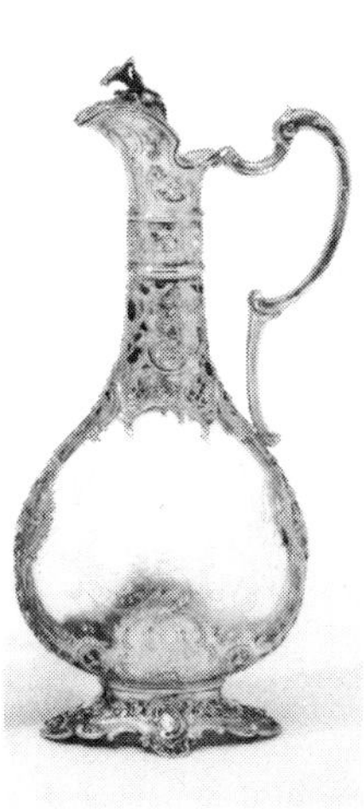
11

12

1

2

3

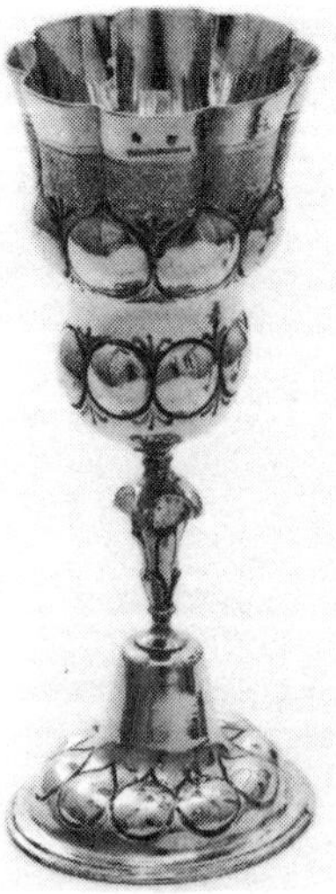
4

5

6

7

10

8

9

11

12

1
An Austrian silver-gilt standing cup and cover, maker's mark VL in monogram, Vienna, c.1610, the body embossed with three ovals enclosing animals and buildings, 27cm (10½in), 11oz (350gr), *G 11 Nov,*
SF 24,200 (£10,000; $14,300)

2
A German silver-gilt standing cup and cover, maker's mark a cleaver, Nuremberg, c.1620, embossed with pineapple lobes, engraved in Russian on the base *Sent to the Sovereign as a gift from Christian, King of Denmark,* 41cm (16in), 33oz (1030gr), *G 11 Nov,*
SF 26,400 (£10,909; $15,600)

3
A German silver-gilt cup and cover, Hans Weber, Nuremberg, c.1620, embossed with pineapple lobes, the rim with a Russian inscription dated 1712 recording the cup to be a gift from the Siberian government to the State Magistrate of Tumen in appreciation of their increased revenue from wine sales, 45cm (17¾in), 20oz (622gr), *NY 8 Apr,*
$3,520 (£2,428)

4
A German silver-gilt standing cup, Theodor or Tobias Riederer, Augsburg, c.1630, the bowl embossed with pineapple lobes, 18cm (7in), *G 11 Nov,*
SF 7,150 (£2,955; $4,225)

5
A George II cup and cover, Augustine Courtauld, London, 1728, 32cm (12½in), 80oz (2488gr), *HS 24 Sept,*
IR£4,510 (£4,100; $5,945)

6
A George III silver-gilt cup and cover, William Holmes, London, 1791, 46cm (18in), 83oz (2589gr), *L 19 June,*
£2,970 ($4,693)

7
A pair of German silver-gilt standing cups, *(one illustrated),* Melchior Burtenbach, Augsburg, c.1680, 19cm (7½in), 15oz 10dwt (483gr), *G 11 Nov,*
SF 17,600 (£7,273; $10,400)

8
A George III silver-gilt cup and cover, Peter & William Bateman, London, 1811, the body with two plaques depicting racing scenes, the cover with horse and jockey finial, 41.5cm (16¼in), 107oz (3327gr), *L 19 June,*
£4,620 ($7,300)

9
A George III silver-gilt cup and cover, Louisa Courtauld & George Cowles, London, 1772, 37cm (14½in), 70oz 14dwt (2192gr), *S 23 Apr,*
£5,280 ($8,290)

10
A Victorian cup and cover on plinth, Robert Hennell, London, 1864, with presentation inscription, 59cm (23¾in), 88oz (2736gr), *L 16 Oct,*
£1,760 ($2,464)

11
A George IV silver-gilt cup and cover, Fenton, Danby & Webster, Sheffield, 1825, the body chased on one side with a fighting cock and on the other with a wild boar, fighting cock finial, 45cm (17¾in), 81oz 14dwt (2522gr), *C 7 Oct,*
£990 ($1,386)

12
A Victorian parcel-gilt cup, Henry Bourne, Birmingham, 1881, after the Nuremberg Columbine cup, the body decorated with pineapple lobes, vignettes and various motifs, 21.5cm (8½in), 22oz (684gr), *L 24 Apr,*
£385 ($616)

1
A Louis XIV wine taster, maker's mark ?G, Bordeaux, 1696-99, 10cm (4in) diam., 2oz 8dwt (74gr), *NY 12 June,*
$3,080 (£2,026)

2
A set of four George III wine coasters, *(one illustrated)*, Hester Bateman, London, 1786, 12cm (4¾in) diam., *NY 12 June,*
$5,225 (£3,438)

3
A pair of George III wine coasters, *(one illustrated)*, William Elliott, London, 1816, 15cm (6in) diam., *L 16 Oct,*
£2,200 ($3,080)

4
A pair of George III wine coasters, John Roberts & Co., Sheffield, 1807, 14.5cm (5¾in) diam., *NY 25 Jan,*
$1,980 (£1,424)

5
A pair of George IV wine coasters, Waterhouse, Hodson & Co., Sheffield, 1824, 17.5cm (7in) diam., *NY 5 Nov,*
$990 (£697)

6
A pair of George III wine coasters, Emes & Barnard, London, 1809, 16cm (6¼in) diam., *C 15 Apr,*
£1,210 ($1,876)

7
A pair of George III wine coasters, W. & P. Cunningham, Edinburgh, 1790, 12.5cm (5in) diam., *NY 5 Nov,*
$2,090 (£1,472)

8
A pair of early Victorian wine coasters, *(one illustrated)*, Joseph and John Angell, London, 1837, 14cm (5½in) diam., *NY 5 Nov,*
$2,640 (£1,859)

9
A set of four George III silver-gilt wine coasters, *(two illustrated)*, Rundell, Bridge & Rundell, London, 1815, maker's mark of Paul Storr, engraved with the arms of Lascelles, 14.5cm (5¾in) diam., *L 19 June,*
£69,300 ($109,494)

10
A pair of George IV silver-gilt wine coasters, *(one illustrated)*, William Elliott, London, 1820, 15cm (6in) diam., *L 20 Nov,*
£9,900 ($13,860)

11
A pair of French wine coasters, *(one illustrated)*, A. Aucoc, Paris, mid 19th century, 19cm (7½in) diam., 18oz (559gr), *NY 14 Oct,*
$1,210 (£840)

12
A William IV brandy waggon, John Tapley, probably for Rundell, Bridge & Co., London, 1837, the oak and split cane cask on a silver trolley, 25cm (9¾in) long, *HS 24 Sept,*
IR£4,730 (£4,300; $6,235)

13
An American parcel-gilt two bottle decanter stand, John C. Moore for Tiffany & Co., New York, 1854-70, 32cm (12½in), 43oz (1337gr), *NY 26 June,*
$1,430 (£947)

14
A pair of George III wine glass coolers, *(one illustrated)*, Benjamin Smith II, London, 1807, 12cm (4¾in) high, 29oz (901gr), *NY 8 Apr,*
$12,100 (£8,345)

15
An Empire wine cooler, Jean-Baptiste-Claude Odiot, Paris, 1809-19, with the arms of François-Xavier Branicki and his wife Alexandra Engelhardt (accepted as the daughter of Catherine the Great and Potemkin), 33.5cm (13in) high, 128oz (3980gr), *NY 5 Nov,*
$27,500 (£19,366)

16
Two Victorian wine coolers, *(one illustrated)*, Hunt & Roskell, London, 1862-71, 32cm (12½in) high, 247oz 15dwt (7705gr), *L 20 Nov,*
£11,000 ($15,400)

17
A pair of Victorian wine coolers, *(one illustrated)*, Elkington & Co. Ltd., London, 1897, 26cm (10¼in) high, 165oz (5130gr), *HS 24 Sept,*
IR£5,720 (£5,200; $7,540)

1

2

3

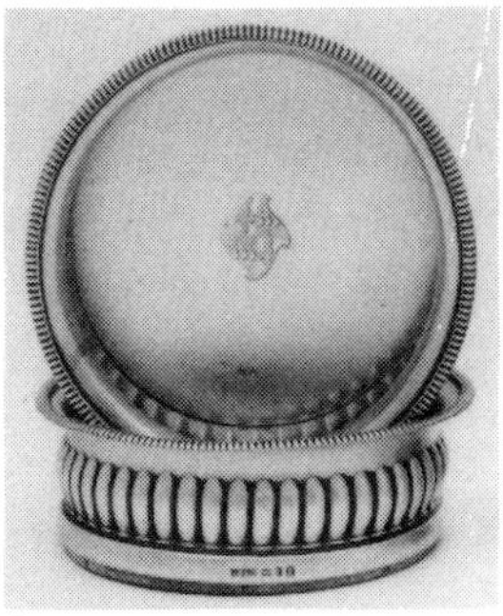
4

5

6

9

7

8

10

11

12

13

14

15

16

17

1

2

3

4

5

6

7

8

9

10

11

12

13

14

15

16

17

1
A Queen Anne coffee pot, maker's mark T.E. crowned, Exeter, 1710, ivory handle, 24.5cm (9¾in), 25oz 5dwt (785gr), *L 6 Feb,*
£3,520 ($5,139)

2
A George II coffee pot, Richard Bayley, London, 1735, 21.5cm (8½in), 21oz 13dwt (673gr), *L 17 July,*
£1,100 ($1,727)

3
A German chocolate pot, Lewin Dedeke, Celle, c.1725, applied with cut-card work, 27cm (10½in), 36oz 12dwt (1139gr), *G 13 May,*
SF 36,300 (£12,264; $19,744)

4
A George II coffee pot, Richard Bayley, London, 1737, with later armorials, 26cm (10¼in), 36oz 7dwt (1130gr), *L 16 Oct,*
£3,520 ($4,928)

5
An Italian coffee pot, mid 18th century, probably Rome, apparently unmarked, the spout rising from a satyr mask and moulded with a female head, 27cm (10½in), 25oz 10dwt (793gr), *NY 8 Apr,*
$3,080 (£2,124)

6
A Belgian coffee pot, maker's mark two flaming hearts, c.1740, 30cm (11¾in), 30oz 6dwt (944gr), *G 13 May,*
SF 8,800 (£2,973; $4,786)

7
An Italian coffee pot, maker's mark apparently D.V., a bell below, c.1760, with a monster mask spout, 30cm (11¾in), 33oz 14dwt (1050gr), *G 11 Nov,*
SF 9,900 (£4,091; $5,850)

8
A Belgian coffee pot, maker's mark B.F. crowned, Namur, 1751, 33.5cm (13¼in), 34oz 2dwt (1062gr), *G 13 May,*
SF 9,900 (£3,345; $5,385)

9
A George II coffee pot, Aymé Videau, London, 1743, 25cm (9¾in), 28oz 14dwt (892gr), *S 23 Apr,*
£2,310 ($3,627)

10
A George II coffee pot, Humphrey Payne, London, 1748, with later armorials and crest, 26.5cm (10½in), 29oz 16dwt (926gr), *L 16 Oct,*
£1,760 ($2,464)

11
A George II coffee pot, Thomas Whipham, London, 1751, 23.5cm (9¼in), 25oz 8dwt (789gr), *S 20 June,*
£1,012 ($1,599)

12
A George III hot water jug, maker's mark TI (Grimwade, no.3841), London, 1769, wicker covered handle, 23.5cm (9¼in), 15oz 18dwt (478gr), *C 7 Oct,*
£858 ($1,201)

13
A Belgian coffee pot, Rémy-Joseph Renier, Liège, 1768, with dolphin's head spout, later wood handle, 32cm (12½in), 51oz 8dwt (1600gr), *G 11 Nov,*
SF 39,600 (£16,364; $23,400)

14
A George III hot water jug, ?David Whyte (Grimwade, no.3625), London, 1768, wicker covered handle, 27.5cm (10¾in), 22oz (684gr), *NY 12 June,*
$605 (£398)

15
A French coffee pot, Jean-Baptiste Leroux, Lille, c.1775, 31cm (12¼in), 44oz (1370gr), *M 24 June,*
FF 33,300 (£2,971; $4,634)

16
A German coffee pot, Wilhelm Jakob Kolb, Augsburg, 1777-79, 22.5cm (8¾in), 14oz 2dwt (439gr), *L 11 Feb,*
£1,430 ($2,102)

17
A German coffee pot, Christian Gottlieb Schu(h)mann II, Augsburg, 1785-87, 17.5cm (7in), 7oz 18dwt (245gr), *L 11 Feb,*
£825 ($1,213)

1
A French teapot, maker's mark P.D. with crown, Bordeaux, c.1775, 20cm (8in), 24oz 14dwt (770gr), *M 24 June,*
FF 38,850 (£3,466; $5,406)

2
A French coffee pot, René-Pierre Ferrier, Paris, 1787, 26cm (10¼in), 28oz 4dwt (880gr), *M 24 June,*
FF 16,650 (£1,485; $2,317)

3
A French chocolate pot, Jacques-Pierre Marteau, Paris, 1776, 14cm (5½in), 8oz 16dwt (275gr), *M 24 June,*
FF 8,880 (£792; $1,236)

4
A Sicilian coffee pot, Catania, 1812, maker's mark rubbed, 16cm (7½in), 11oz 7dwt (355gr), *L 11 Feb,*
£1,760 ($2,587)

5
A George III coffee jug, Andrew Fogelberg, London, 1777, applied with two cherub medallions, 32cm (12½in), 27oz 8dwt (852gr), *L 16 Oct,*
£2,750 ($3,850)

6
A George III covered jug, John Denziloe, London, 1779, 31.5cm (12½in), 25oz 3dwt (782gr), *L 19 June,*
£1,045 ($1,651)

7
A George III coffee pot, Charles Hougham, London, 1790, richly bright-cut, 31.5cm (12½in), 24oz 4dwt (752gr), *L 16 Oct,*
£1,540 ($2,156)

8
A George III coffee pot, John Robins, London, 1794, 30.5cm (12in), 29oz 2dwt (905gr), *C 29 Jan,*
£770 ($1,132)

9
A George III coffee pot, Hester Bateman, London, 1780, engraved with later armorials, 31cm (12¼in), 29oz 10dwt (917gr), *NY 12 June,*
$3,575 (£2,352)

10
A George III coffee biggin on lampstand, Richard Cooke, London, 1803, with detachable cover, the stand with detachable burner, 31oz 7dwt (974gr), *Glen 25 Aug,*
£935 ($1,468)

11
A French coffee pot, Paris, 1819-38, 19.5cm (7¾in), 14oz (435gr), *NY 12 June,*
$825 (£543)

12
An American coffee pot, Browne & Seal, Philadelphia, c.1810, 27.5cm (10¾in), 32oz 12dwt (1013gr), *NY 31 Jan,*
$2,200 (£1,560)

13
A German coffee pot, Gustav Friedrich Gerich, Augsburg, 1807, the body chased with band of foliage incorporating monsters on a matted ground, 20cm (8in), 14oz 16dwt (464gr), *L 8 July,*
£880 ($1,417)

1

2 3

4

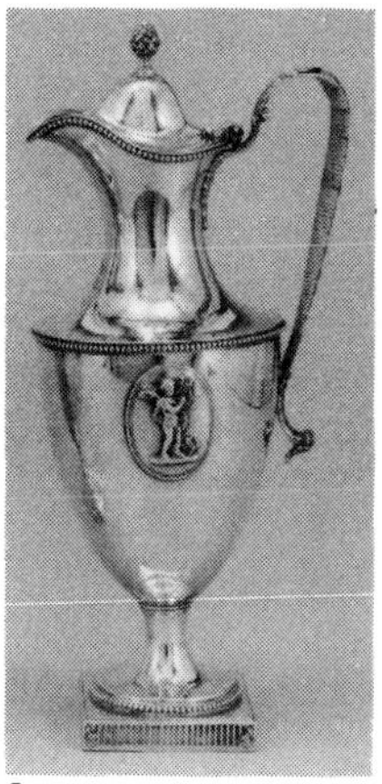
5

6

7

8

9

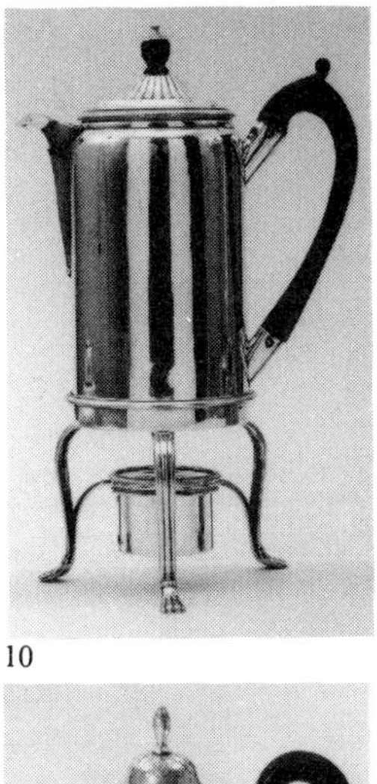
10

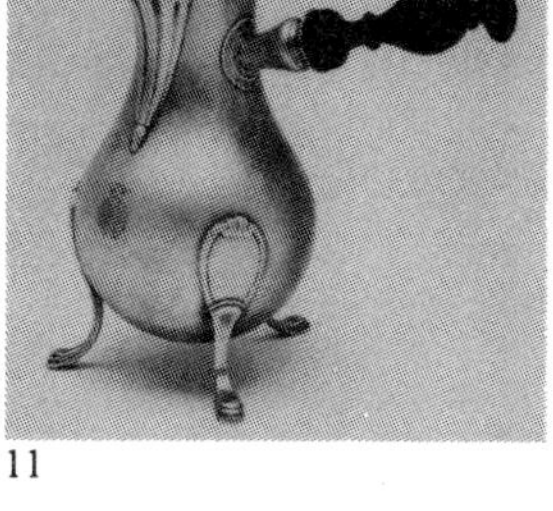
11

12

13

1

2

3

4

5

6

7

10

8

9

11

12

1
A Maltese coffee pot, maker's mark A.P., first half 19th century, with Régence ornament, 24cm (9½in), 21oz 3dwt (658gr), *L 11 Feb,*
£3,080 ($4,528)

2
An Italian coffee pot, Angelo Gianotti, Rome, c.1825, with griffin's head spout, 35.5cm (14in), 33oz 18dwt (1056gr), *F 30 Sept,*
L 3,850,000 (£1,918; $2,686)

3
A Belgian coffee pot, maker's mark B, crowned, Mons, c.1780, 26.5cm (10½in), 15oz 2dwt (470gr), *M 24 June,*
FF 21,090 (£1,881; $2,935)

4
A French coffee pot and milk jug, Jean-Pierre Bibron, Paris, c.1810, the coffee pot with a horse's head spout, 28.5cm (11¼in), 29oz 18dwt (930gr), *M 24 June,*
FF 13,320 (£1,188; $1,854)

5
A Swedish coffee pot, Bengt Walquist, Jönköping, c.1820, 22.5cm (9in), 25oz 18dwt (807gr), *L 11 Feb,*
£990 ($1,455)

6
A George III coffee jug and stand with burner, Rundell, Bridge & Rundell, London, 1814, maker's mark of Paul Storr for Storr & Co., the stand stamped 163/5, 28.5cm (11in), 59oz 9dwt (1849gr), *L 6 Feb,*
£2,970 ($4,336)

7
A George III hot water jug, Joseph Cradock & William Reid, London, 1814, ivory handle, 20cm (8in), 18oz 12dwt (580gr), *JHB 19 Mar,*
R 3,200 (£1,000; $1,530)

8
A Victorian coffee pot, Edward Barnard & Co. London, 1844, on four supports, 27cm (10½in), 28oz 4dwt (877gr), *C 6 Aug,*
£451 ($699)

9
A Victorian coffee pot, maker's mark FB, London, 1863, handle repaired, 23cm (9in), 21oz 4dwt (659gr), *C 26 Mar,*
£462 ($707)

10
A Victorian coffee pot, E. Barnard & Sons, London, 1870, 23.5cm (9¼in), 24oz 2dwt (750gr), *JHB 19 Mar,*
R 2,300 (£719; $1,099)

11
A coffee pot and hot water jug, Mappin & Webb, Sheffield, 1953, 24cm (9½in), 49oz 4dwt (1530gr), *C 7 Oct,*
£572 ($801)

12
A French silver-gilt coffee pot and milk jug, Puiforcat, Paris, early 20th century, in Régence style, the spouts formed as bearded masks, 24cm (9½in), 27oz (839gr), *NY 14 Oct,*
$522 (£363)

1
A George I teapot, Thomas Mason, London, 1718, 18cm (7¼in), 23oz (715gr), *HS 24 Sept,*
IR£6,930 (£6,300; $9,135)

2
A George I teapot, Paul Crespin, London, 1721, 12cm (4¾in), 15oz 10dwt (482gr), *L 6 Feb,*
£2,640 ($3,854)

3
A George II teapot, Benjamin Godfrey, London, 1735, flat-chased with diaper, shells and foliate motifs, scratch weight '16-16', 13cm (5in), 17oz (528gr), *L 16 Oct,*
£825 ($1,155)

4
A German teapot, Johann Samuel Beckensteiner, Nuremberg, c.1750, ivory handle, 9cm (3½in), 4oz 8dwt (138gr), *L 11 Feb,*
£682 ($1,003)

5
A German teapot, Jacob Bartels, Hamburg, c.1748, 12cm (4½in), 11oz 2dwt (345gr), *L 11 Feb,*
£1,760 ($2,587)

6
A Dutch teapot, François van Stapele, 's Gravenhage, 1740, later bone finial, 10.5cm (4in), 10oz 2dwt (316gr), *A 21 Apr,*
Dfl 3,910 (£1,185; $1,860)

7
A Dutch teapot, probably Bartholomeus Vos, Amsterdam, 1742, 17cm (6¾in), 8oz 9dwt (260gr), *L 11 Feb,*
£715 ($1,051)

8
A French teapot, maker's mark P.I.M. Lille, 1763, facetted with gadroon borders and griffin's head spout, 17cm (6¾in), 18oz (560gr), *M 24 June,*
FF 72,150 (£6,436; $10,040)

9
A George III teapot, Robert Hennell, London, 1789, bright-cut engraved, 16.5cm (6½in), 14oz 10dwt (450gr), *NY 12 Dec,*
$715 (£511)

10
A George III teapot and stand, Robert Hennell, London, 1787, teapot 15cm (6in), 17oz 8dwt (541gr), *NY 12 June,*
$1,210 (£796)

11
A George III teapot, Hester Bateman, London, 1784, bright-cut engraved, 13cm (5in), 13oz (404gr), *L 16 Oct,*
£1,265 ($1,771)

12
A George IV teapot, Rundell, Bridge & Rundell, London, 1820, maker's mark of Philip Rundell, 13.5cm (5½in), 30oz (933gr), *NY 5 Nov,*
$1,210 (£852)

13
An American teapot, S. Kirk, Baltimore, c.1830-46, chased with chinoiserie buildings and figures, 21.5cm (8½in), 40oz 10dwt (1259gr), *NY 26 June,*
$1,540 (£1,020)

1

2

3

4 5

6

7

8

9

10

11

12

13

1

2

3

4

5

6

7

8

9

10

1
A George II tea kettle on lampstand, Peter Archambo, London, 1735, 34.5cm (13½in), 69oz 7dwt (2156gr), *L 19 June,*
£4,620 ($7,300)

2
A George II tea kettle on lampstand, John Swift, London, 1741, 35cm (13¾in), 77oz (2394gr), *HS 24 Sept,*
IR£2,640 (£2,400; $3,480)

3
A George III tea urn, Francis Butty and Nicolas Dumee, London, 1767, 57cm (22¼in), 92oz (2861gr), *NY 25 Jan,*
$5,225 (£3,759)

4
A George III hot water urn on stand, John Emes, London, 1797, 48.5cm (19in), 123oz 10dwt (3840gr), *NY 12 June,*
$2,200 (£1,447)

5
A George III silver-gilt tea urn, Digby Scott and Benjamin Smith II, London, 1805, 38cm (15in), 212oz (6593gr), *NY 8 Apr,*
$99,000 (£68,276)

6
A George IV silver-gilt tea urn on lampstand, Benjamin Smith, London, 1826, 40cm (15¾in), 150oz 2dwt (4668gr), *L 16 Oct,*
£6,820 ($9,548)

7
A William IV tea urn, Battie, Howard & Hawksworth, Sheffield, 1836, 39.5cm (15½in), 147oz (4571gr), *NY 8 Apr,*
$3,960 (£2,731)

8
A George IV tea kettle on stand, Joseph Craddock, London, 1826, 34cm (13¼in), 84oz 5dwt (2620gr), *C 7 Oct,*
£2,200 ($3,080)

9
A Victorian tea kettle on lampstand, R. & S. Garrard & Co., 40cm (15¾in), 113oz 10dwt (3529gr), *L 24 Apr,*
£2,420 ($3,872)

10
A tea kettle on lampstand Sheffield, 1899, 32cm (12½in), 35oz 5dwt (1096gr), *C 26 Mar,*
£407 ($623)

1
A George III three-piece teaset and teapot stand, Urquhart & Hart, London, 1802/03, 31oz 19dwt (988gr), *C 14 Jan,*
£1,155 ($1,733)

2
A Portuguese five-piece tea and coffee service, Oporto, c.1820, coffee pot 31cm (12in), 107oz 17dwt (3355gr), *L 11 Feb,*
£3,740 ($5,498)

3
A George IV four-piece tea and coffee set and lampstand with burner, John Houle, London, 1821, 117oz 4dwt (3645gr), *L 19 June,*
£2,860 ($4,519)

4
A Dutch five-piece tea and coffee set, A. Homan, Amsterdam 1824/25, 18cm (7in), 74oz 8dwt (2314gr), *A 21 Apr,*
Dfl 7,130 (£2,161; $3,392)

5
A William IV three-piece teaset, William Bateman, London, 1830, 44oz 12dwt (1387gr), *S 20 June,*
£594 ($938)

6
A William IV four-piece tea and coffee set, Joseph & John Angell, London, 1834, 67oz 14dwt (2105gr), *S 23 Apr,*
£1,320 ($2,072)

7
An American matching three-piece teaset, New York, c.1830, comprising a teapot by Frederick Marquand and a covered sugar bowl and creamer by John Crawford, teapot 26cm (10¼in), 64oz 10dwt (2005gr), *NY 31 Jan,*
$1,430 (£1,014)

8
A French five-piece tea and coffee set with tray, Odiot, Paris, c.1840-50, kettle on stand 42.5cm (16¾in), 374oz 10dwt (11646gr), *NY 8 Apr,*
$10,450 (£7,207)

9
A Victorian five-piece tea and coffee set, Hunt & Roskell, London, 1848/57, maker's mark John S. Hunt, kettle on stand 42.5cm (16¾in), 179oz 10dwt (5582gr), *NY 12 June,*
$5,500 ($3,618)

1

2

3

4

5

6

7

8

9

1

2

3

4

5

6

7

8

1
A Victorian four-piece teaset, London, 1852, maker's mark GR, 86oz 18dwt (2702gr), *C 25 June,*
£1,430 ($2,231)

2
A Victorian three-piece teaset, J. C. Edington, London, 1858/61, 63oz (1959gr), *L 6 Feb,*
£935 ($1,365)

3
An American seven-piece assembled tea and coffee service with tray, Gorham Mfg. Co., c.1865-71, retailed by T. Kirkpatrick, New York, tea urn 44.5cm (17½in) high, 426oz (13248gr), *NY 31 Jan,*
$9,350 (£6,631)

4
An American six-piece tea and coffee set with tray, Gorham Mfg. Co., 1876, tray 61.5cm (24¼in), 266oz (8272gr), *NY 26 June,*
$6,050 (£4,007)

5
A Victorian four-piece tea and coffee set, maker's mark FE overstriking that of another, London, 1873, coffee pot 23cm (9in), 71oz (2210gr), *JHB 18 June,*
R 4,180 (£1,306; $1,829)

6
A Victorian four-piece tea and coffee set and matching electroplate tea kettle, W. & G. Sissons, London, 1867 and circa, 67oz 18dwt (2111gr), *L 16 Oct,*
£1,925 ($2,695)

7
A French tea and coffee service, Odiot, Paris, c.1880, kettle 42cm (16½in), 184oz 8dwt (5735gr), *M 24 June,*
FF 33,300 (£2,971; $4,634)

8
A four-piece Regency style tea and coffee set, E. Barnard & Sons, London, 1898/99, coffee pot 22cm (8¾in), 82oz 12dwt (2570gr), *JHB 18 June,*
R 6,050 (£1,891; $2,647)

1
An Edwardian five-piece matching tea and coffee set with tea tray, London, 1901/7/8, in Regency style, coffee pot 21cm (8¼in), 367oz 10dwt (11429gr), *NY 8 Apr,*
$10,450 (£7,207)

2
An American six-piece tea and coffee set with matching tea tray, Gorham Mfg. Co., 1904, tray 79cm (31in), 334oz 10dwt (10402gr), *NY 25 Jan,*
$6,875 (£4,946)

3
A five-piece tea set, Edward Barnard & Sons, London, 1904, 164oz 3dwt (5106gr), *L 20 Feb,*
£2,310 ($3,373)

4
A three-piece tea set, Nathan & Hayes, Chester, 1906, 38oz 2dwt (1184gr), *C 3 Dec,*
£385 ($539)

5
A four-piece tea set, W. & G. Sissons, London, 1909/10, 66oz 17dwt (2079gr), *C 7 Oct,*
£902 ($1,263)

6
A three-piece tea set, Daniel & Arter, Birmingham, 1914, 39oz 7dwt (1223gr), *C 14 Jan,*
£506 ($759)

7
A five-piece tea set, Elkington & Co. Ltd., Birmingham, 1921-22, the tea kettle with wicker-covered handles and ivory buttons, 108oz 5dwt (3366gr), *L 19 June,*
£1,650 ($2,607)

8
An American five-piece tea and coffee set, S. Kirk & Son Co. Inc., Baltimore, c.1930, all embossed and chased with flowers, coffee pot 26.5cm (10½in), 117oz (3638gr), *NY 31 Jan,*
$2,860 (£2,028)

9
A four-piece teaset, Birmingham, 1941, with green fan-shaped finials, 66oz 6dwt (2061gr), *C 23 July,*
£858 ($1,347)

1

2

3

4

5

6

7

8

9

1

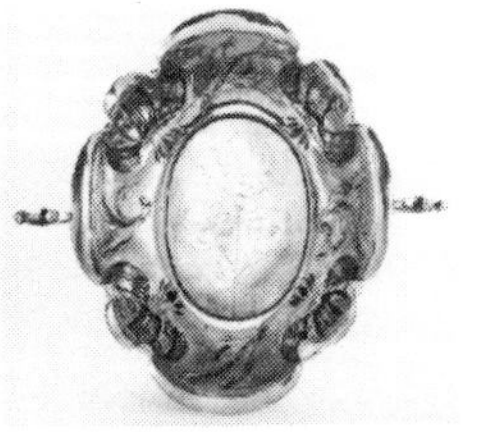
2

3

4

5

6

7

8

9

10

11

12

13

1
A German parcel-gilt sweetmeat dish, Balthasar Haydt, Augsburg, c.1670, the centre embossed with an anemone, 13cm (5in), 2oz 10dwt (79gr),
G 13 May,
SF 2,860 (£966; $1,556)

2
A German parcel-gilt sweetmeat dish, possibly a member of the Ferrn family, Nuremberg, c.1680, centred by stippled engraved carnations, the sides with embossed lilies, 19cm (7½in), 7oz 14dwt (240gr), *G 11 Nov,*
SF 18,700 (£7,727; $11,050)

3
A German silver-gilt sweetmeat dish, Balthasar Haydt, Augsburg, c.1665, the centre embossed with a bunch of fruit, 15.5cm (6¼in), 4oz 2dwt (129gr),
G 13 May,
SF 5,500 (£1,858; $2,992)

4
A German sweetmeat dish, maker's mark IMH in monogram, Augsburg, 1705, with three shell-shaped divisions, the centre embossed with a flowerhead, 13cm (5in), 2oz 16dwt (89gr),
G 13 May,
SF 7,700 (£2,601; $4,188)

5
A Swiss sweetmeat dish, Samuel Bonvèpre, Neuchâtel, c.1760, on ball and claw supports, 17cm (6¾in), sold with another, smaller, modern, 12oz 4dwt (380gr), *G 11 Nov,*
SF 5,280 (£2,182; $3,120)

6
A George I bowl and cover, William Fleming, London, 1724, 10cm (4in) diam., 7oz (218gr),
L 6 Feb,
£2,145 ($3,132)

7
A Victorian sweetmeat basket, W. R. Smiley, London, 1849, with ruby glass liner, 14cm (5½in), 8oz 12dwt (267gr),
C 12 Feb,
£308 ($459)

8
A George II sugar bowl, James Shruder, London, 1738, the body applied with festoons of spume, shells and other marine motifs, 12cm (4¾in) diam., 11oz 7dwt (352gr),
L 24 Apr,
£3,520 ($5,632)

9
A pair of Swedish sugar vases and covers, *(one illustrated)*, maker's mark A.K., Gothenburg, 1790, the bodies applied with medallions depicting the muses of Song and Tragedy, 25cm (10in), 37oz 10dwt (1125gr),
L 11 Feb,
£2,970 ($4,366)

10
A Cape covered sugar box, Daniel Heinrich Schmidt, late 18th century, on four shell feet, the cover with detachable flower finial,, 10cm (4in) wide, 7oz 4dwt (225gr),
JHB 18 June,
R 8,250 (£2,578; $3,609)

11
A silver-gilt sugar box, probably Swedish, c.1780, of oval form, marks obliterated, with eagle thumbpiece and bracket supports, 15cm (6in) wide, 12oz 5dwt (372gr),
L 11 Feb,
£770 ($1,132)

12
A Dutch sugar basket, Pieter van der Toorn, Amsterdam, 1791, with blue glass liner, 17cm (6¾in) wide, 7oz 14dwt (241gr), *A 21 Apr,*
Dfl 1,725 (£523; $821)

13
A George III sugar basket, Robert Hennell, London, 1792, 15cm (6in) wide, 6oz 14dwt (208gr),
L 16 Oct,
£572 ($801)

1
A George III cream pail, apparently unmarked, c.1770, with clear glass liner, 7cm (2¾in), sold with a cream ladle en suite, 2oz 16dwt (90gr), *JHB 19 Mar,*
R 650 (£203; $311)

2
A George III sugar basket, William Plummer, London, 1770, clear glass liner, foot rim split, 9cm (3½in), 4oz 6dwt (135gr), *JHB 19 Mar,*
R 950 (£296; $454)

3
A pair of George III sugar vases, *(one illustrated)*, Robert Hennell, London, 1784, 15.5cm (6in), 11oz 10dwt (357gr), *L 17 July,*
£660 ($1,036)

4
A George III sugar basket, Hester Bateman, London, 1777, lacking glass liner, 12.5cm (5in), 10oz 14dwt (180gr), *JHB 18 June,*
R 2,750 (£859; $1,203)

5
A George III sugar basket, Hester Bateman, London, 1789, 16.5cm (6½in), 7oz 2dwt (221gr), *C 14 Jan,*
£385 ($578)

6
A French sugar vase with cover, Paris, c.1825, apparently without maker's mark, the sides chased with neoclassical figures, 23cm (9in), 21oz 10dwt (670gr), *M 24 June,*
FF 6,660 (£594; $927)

7
An Italian sugar bowl with cover, Tommaso Panizza, Milan, mid 19th century, with triton finial, 20cm (8in), 11oz 10dwt (360gr), *F 14 Apr,*
L 3,000,000 (£1,229; $1,904)

8
A George II caddy set, John Payne, London, 1752, comprising a pair of caddies and a sugar bowl and cover, the finials formed as birds perched on leafy branches, sugar bowl 13.5cm (5¼in) high, 27oz 10dwt (855gr), *NY 25 Jan,*
$2,200 (£1,583)

9
A George II tea caddy, Peze Pilleau, London, 1746, with shell finial, 13cm (5¼in), 7oz 14dwt (239gr), *Glen 25 Aug,*
£935 ($1,468)

10
A George III tea caddy, Emes & Barnard, London, 1815, the sides incised with vertical lines and Chinese characters, and with flower finial, 9.5cm (3¾in), 16oz 12dwt (516gr), *S 23 Apr,*
£2,530 ($3,972)

11
A Dutch tea caddy, François Marcus Simons, The Hague, 1807, 9.5cm (3¾in), 12oz 8dwt (387gr), *A 21 Apr,*
Dfl 5,750 (£1,742; $2,736)

12
A George III tea caddy, Walter Tweedie, London, 1784, of oval form, bright cut with bands of foliage and star motifs, with pineapple finial, 14cm (5½in), 11oz 2dwt (345gr), *C 7 Oct,*
£1,012 ($1,417)

1 2

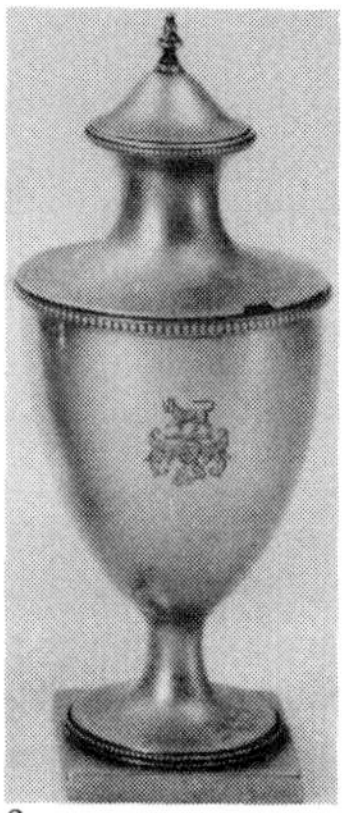
3

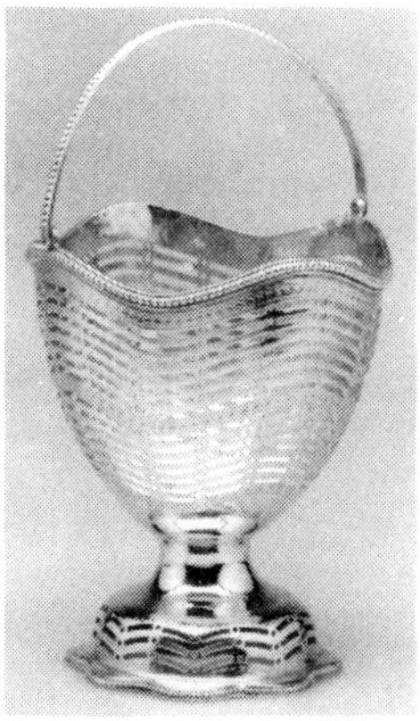
4

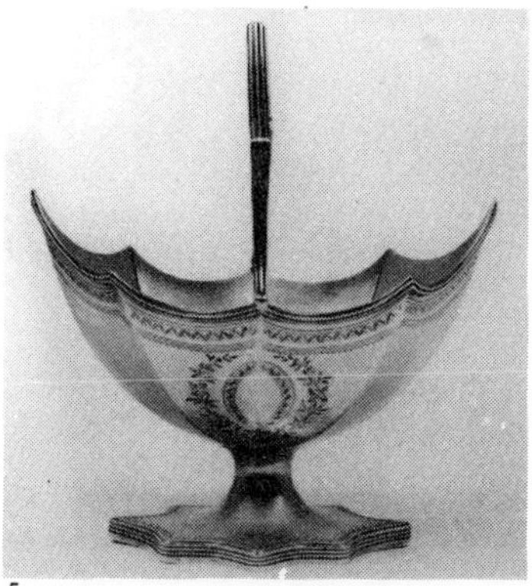
5

6

7

8

9

10

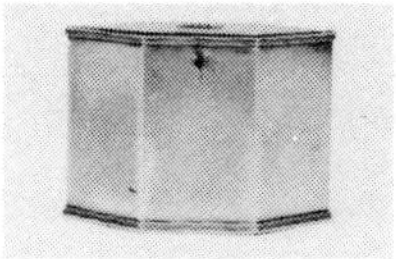
11

12

1

2

3

4

5

6

7

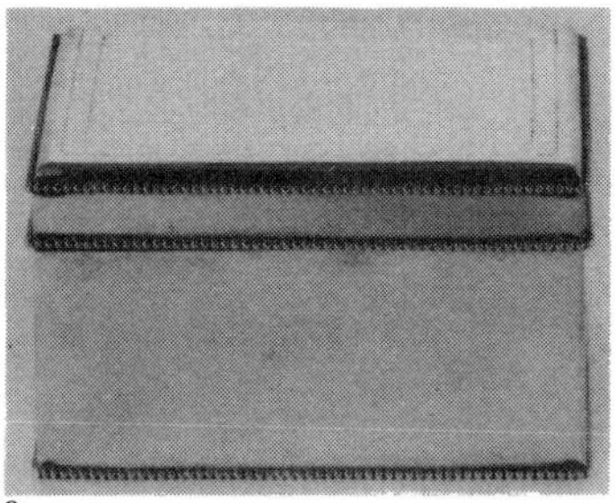
8

9

10

11

12

13

14

1
A set of three George III tea caddies, Samuel Taylor, London, 1763, the sides of each embossed with quaint chinoiserie figures, vases of flowers or rococo cartouches, each detachable brickwork cover topped by a pagoda roof hung with bells, 16.5 and 15cm (6½ and 6in), 36oz 4dwt (1125gr), *L 17 July,*
£10,120 ($15,888)

2
A Victorian tea caddy, Hunt & Roskell, London, 1850, maker's mark of John Samuel Hunt, flat-chased with panels of diaper and strapwork, 15.5cm (6in) high, 12oz (373gr), *HS 24 Sept,*
IR£462 (£420; $609)

3
A set of three George III tea caddies, *(one illustrated),* Edward Aldridge, London, 1766, detachable lids with bud finials, in fitted case, 14cm (5½in), 31oz 10dwt (979gr), *L 24 Apr,*
£3,080 ($4,928)

4
A Dutch tobacco box, possibly Albertus van Dosen, Utrecht, 1767, of circular form, with flame finial, on an openwork foot, 19cm (7½in), 26oz 12dwt (830gr), *G 11 Nov,*
SF 10,450 (£4,318; $6,175)

5
A Dutch tobacco box, Jan Buysen, Amsterdam, 1778, of circular form, with cone finial, on three leaf and scroll supports, 15.5cm (6in), 20oz 2dwt (625gr), *L 8 July,*
£2,860 ($4,605)

6
A George II cream jug, London, 1728, 8cm (3in) high, 2oz 18dwt (92gr), *M 24 June,*
FF 5,328 (£475; $741)

7
A George II cream jug, John Eckfourd, London, 1729, with three hoof feet, 10.5cm (4in) high, 5oz 12dwt (174gr), *L 19 June,*
£1,705 ($2,694)

8
A Dutch biscuit box, Jan Ensinck, Amsterdam, 1791, 14.5cm (5¾in), 20oz 2dwt (627gr), *G 13 May,*
SF 3,520 (£1,189; $1,915)

9
A German hot milk jug, Leonhard Tobias Drescher, Augsburg, 1769-71, with a fruit finial, 20.5cm (8½in), 9oz 10dwt (296gr), *G 13 May,*
SF 3,740 (£1,264; $2,034)

10
A George I hot milk jug, unmarked, c.1720, wood finial and handle, 11.5cm (4½in) high, 8oz 5dwt (256gr), *L 24 Apr,*
£1,210 ($1,936)

11
A Swiss coffee pot, Thomas Dautun, Geneva, 1760, the body of ovoid form, on three hoof feet, 12.5cm (5in), 16oz 16dwt (525gr), *G 11 Nov,*
SF 7,700 (£3,182; $4,550)

12
A George I hot milk jug, David Willaume, London, 1717, the ovoid body initialled below a ducal coronet, detachable cover with ball finial, on three hoof feet, 10.5cm (4in), 8oz 10dwt (246gr), *L 20 Nov,*
£6,270 ($8,778)

13
A George II cow creame
John Schuppe, London, 1758, with hinged flower and bee lid, 15cm (6in) long, 5oz (155gr), *L 16 Oct,*
£3,850 ($5,390)

14
A George III cream jug, Rundell, Bridge & Rundell, maker's mark of Paul Storr, London, 1816, the circular body with alternating shell and palm motifs, 17cm (6¾in) wide, 16oz 3dwt (502gr), *C 15 Apr,*
£1,210 ($1,876)

1
A Danish lighthouse caster, Agatius Louman, (Viborg), c.1715, maker's mark only, 17.5cm (6¾in), 7oz 4dwt (225gr), *L 11 Feb,*
£2,090 ($3,072)

2
A Queen Anne caster, London, c.1710, marks rubbed, 15cm (6in), 5oz (155gr), *Mel 24 June,*
Aus$660 (£287; $448)

3
A George I caster, Glover Johnson, London, 1719, 17.5cm (6¾in), 8oz (248gr), *NY 12 June,*
$990 (£651)

4
A French sugar caster, maker's mark I.?, a goblet between, Bordeaux, c.1710, 23cm (9in), 14oz 10dwt (451gr), *G 13 May,*
SF 14,300 (£4,831; $7,778)

5
A George II kitchen pepper, Dublin, c.1735, 7.5cm (3in), 2oz 3dwt (66gr), *L 16 Oct,*
£638 ($893)

6
A Flemish sugar caster, Gilles Berryer, Liège, apparently 1723-25, 15cm (6in), 5oz 12dwt (177gr), *G 11 Nov,*
SF 10,450 (£4,318; $6,175)

7
A George I caster, Thomas Bamford, London, 1722, 12.5cm (4¾in), 3oz 10dwt (110gr), *L 16 Oct,*
£605 ($847)

8
A George I caster, Charles Adam, London, 1714, 20.5cm (8in), 11oz 5dwt (349gr), *L 17 July,*
£1,870 ($2,936)

9
A German sugar caster, Lorentz Johann Röper, Rostock, c.1740, 19.5cm (7¾in), 11oz 4dwt (350gr), *G 11 Nov,*
SF 4,950 (£2,045; $2,925)

10
A George II caster, Samuel Wood, London, 1733, 18.5cm (7¼in), 9oz 1dwt (281gr), *L 16 Oct,*
£880 ($1,232)

11
A French sugar caster, David André, Paris, 1714, 22.5cm (8¾in), 16oz (500gr), *G 13 May,*
SF 57,200 (£19,324; $31,112)

12
A pair of late Victorian casters, *(one illustrated),* maker's mark E.W., Chester, 1895, 21cm (8¼in), 13oz 18dwt (432gr), *C 22 Oct,*
£407 ($570)

13
A pair of French casters, c.1900, in Régence style, 17cm (6½in), 21oz (653gr), *NY 14 Oct,*
$660 (£458)

14
A Victorian owl sugar caster, Richards & Brown, London, 1866, detachable head, 12.5cm (5in), 5oz 3dwt (157gr), *Glen 25 Aug,*
£715 ($1,123)

15
A Victorian cat caster, maker's mark ESB, London, 1893, 6cm (2½in), 3oz 7dwt (104gr), *C 5 Nov,*
£275 ($388)

16
A Victorian terrier caster, maker's mark WH, London, 1899, 7.5cm (3in), 4oz 10dwt (139gr), *C 5 Nov,*
£231 ($326)

17
A fox's head pepper caster, London, 1961, 4oz 15dwt (147gr), *C 14 May,*
£99 ($159)

1

2

3

4

5

6

7

8

9

10

11

12

13

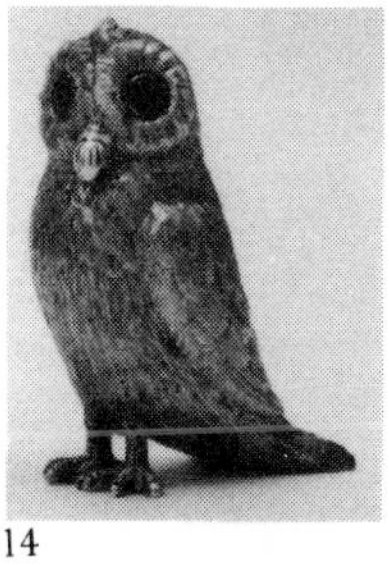
14

15 16

17

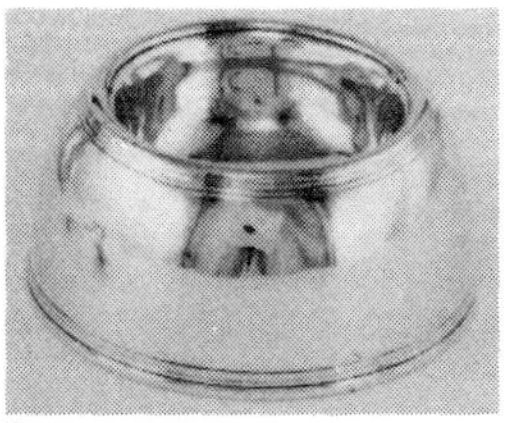
1

2

3

4

5 6

7

8

9 *(above)* 10 *(below)*

11

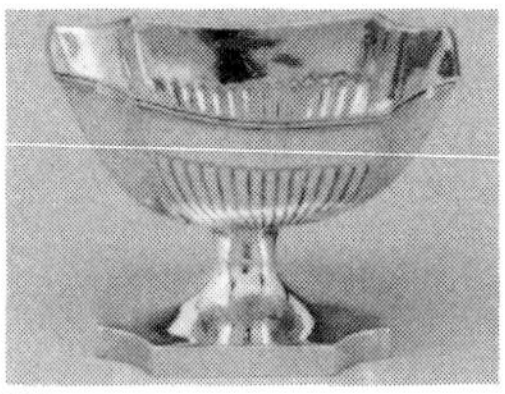
12

13

14

15

16

17

1
A pair of Queen Anne trencher salts, *(one illustrated)*, James Goodwin, London, 1713, 7cm (2¾in) diam., sold with a pair of salt spoons, London, c.1750, 3oz 8dwt (105gr), *L 16 Oct,*
£550 ($770)

2
A pair of George II salt cellars, *(one illustrated)*, Edward Wood, London, 1732, 7cm (2in) wide, 3oz 6dwt (104gr), *M 24 June,*
FF 13,320 (£1,188; $1,854)

3
A set of four George II salt cellars, *(two illustrated)*, Peter Archambo, London, 1731, 8.5cm (3¼in) diam., 25oz 17dwt (803gr), *L 19 June,*
£1,980 ($3,128)

4
A set of six George II salt cellars, *(one illustrated)*, Edward Wakelin, London, 1759, 12.5cm (5in) wide, 39oz 7dwt (1223gr), *L 16 Oct,*
£4,840 ($6,776)

5
A pair of George III double salts, Frederick Kandler, London, 1771, in early George II style, 13.5cm (5¼in) wide, sold with four George III silver-gilt salt shovels, 23oz 16dwt (740gr), *NY 12 Dec,*
$6,325 (£4,518)

6
A pair of George III double salts, T. & J. Guest and Joseph Cradock, London, 1806, matching no.5 above, 13.5cm (5¼in) wide, sold with four silver-gilt salt shovels, 30oz 8dwt (945gr), *NY 12 Dec,*
$6,325 (£4,518)

7
A pair of Dutch salt cellars, *(one illustrated)*, Hendrik Fortman, Leiden, 1766, 6.5cm (2½in) diam., 3oz 18dwt (123gr), *A 21 Apr,*
Dfl 2,530 (£767; $1,204)

8
A French covered salt, Simon-Thadée Puchberger, Aix, 1769, 8.5cm (3¼in) wide, 4oz 19dwt (150gr), *G 11 Nov,*
SF 2,420 (£1,000; $1,430)

9
A pair of French parcel-gilt double salt cellars, Paris, c.1805, 15cm (6in), 20oz 14dwt (645gr), *M 24 June,*
FF 16,650 (£1,485; $2,317)

10
A pair of French parcel-gilt double salt cellars, Henry Auguste, Paris, c.1810, 15.5cm (6in) wide, with two spoons, 25oz 12dwt (798gr), *M 24 June,*
FF 26,640 (£2,376; $3,707)

11
A pair of Dutch salt cellars, *(one illustrated)*, Ste. van Gaasbergh, Zwolle, 1782, 5.5cm (2¼in), 6oz 8dwt (202gr), *A 21 Apr,*
Dfl 5,750 (£1,742; $2,736)

12
A set of four George III salt cellars, *(one illustrated)*, John Robins, London, 1798, 9.5cm (3¾in) wide, 9oz 5dwt (287gr), *L 16 Oct,*
£550 ($770)

13
A pair of Victorian figure salt cellars, Edward Barnard & Sons, London, 1863, lightly gilt, 19.5cm (7¾in), 34oz 12dwt (1076gr), *L 20 Nov,*
£5,500 ($7,700)

14
A Dutch mustard pot, Roemond, c.1770, 16.5cm (6½in), 6oz 18dwt (216gr), *G 13 May,*
SF 5,500 (£1,858; $2,992)

15
A set of four William IV salt cellars and spoons, *(one illustrated)*, Rundell, Bridge & Co., London, 1834, maker's mark of William Bateman, 9.5cm (3¾in) diam., 17oz 14dwt (550gr), *L 6 Feb,*
£1,265 ($1,847)

16
A pair of Victorian salt cellars, *(one illustrated)*, Henry Wilkinson & Co., Sheffield, 1844, 6.5cm (2¾in) diam., 4oz 10dwt (139gr), *C 7 Oct,*
£187 ($262)

17
A pair of French silver-gilt mustard pots, *(one illustrated)*, Martin-Guillaume Biennais, Paris, c.1810, 10cm (4in), 18oz 4dwt (569gr), *G 13 May,*
SF 15,400 (£5,203; $8,376)

1
A set of six salt cellars and one mustard pot, *(mustard illustrated)*, probably William Bell, London, 1816, each with four animal paw feet and original glass liners, 10cm (4in), 3oz 10dwt (108gr), *Mel 24 June,*
Aus$1,540 (£669; $1,044)

2
A Victorian mustard pot and spoon, C. T. & G. Fox, London, 1855, the body in the form of a drum, the spoon with Union Jack terminal, 7cm (2¾in) diam., 7oz 19dwt (247gr), *L 16 Oct,*
£1,155 ($1,617)

3
A Victorian mustard pot, C. T. & G. Fox, London, 1866, in the form of a penguin, 14cm (5½in), 6oz (186gr), *NY 12 Dec,*
$935 (£668)

4
A George III cruet frame, Robert Peaston, London, 1767, 27.5cm (10¾in), and five silver-mounted glass bottles, *L 16 Oct,*
£572 ($801)

5
A George II Warwick cruet, Samuel Wood, London, 1743-44, fitted with three casters and two silver-mounted glass bottles, 21cm (8¼in), 33oz 14dwt (1050gr), *JHB 18 June,*
R 9,350 (£2,922; $4,091)

6
A George III cruet set, John Delmester, London, 1763, fitted with three casters and two silver-mounted glass bottles, 29cm (11½in), 66oz (2052gr), *NY 25 Jan,*
$3,850 (£2,770)

7
A pair of Dutch salt cellars *(one illustrated)* **with matching mustard pot,** Hendrik Smits, Amsterdam, 1801, 12cm (4¾in) long, 7oz 6dwt (229gr), *A 21 Apr,*
Dfl 2,415 (£732; $1,149)

8
A French two-bottle cruet frame, Philippe Lamotte, Dunkirk, 1768, 28cm (11in), 19oz 17dwt (619gr), *L 11 Feb,*
£825 ($1,213)

9
A Belgian cruet frame, Ath, 1764, 23cm (9in), 17oz 4dwt (538gr), *F 14 Apr,*
L 2,400,000 (£983; $1,523)

10
A Flemish cruet frame, *(illustrated)*, **and two matching salt cellars,** Antwerp 1789-95, the central column chased with portrait medallions, 27.5cm (10¾in), *A 21 Apr,*
Dfl 2,530 (£767; $1,204)

11
A Swedish cruet frame, Johan Malmstedt, Gothenburg, 1824, with four bottles, 39.5cm (15½in), 42oz 2dwt (1107gr), *L 11 Feb,*
£748 ($1,100)

12
A George III cruet frame, Rundell, Bridge & Rundell, London, 1806-07, with six silver-mounted glass bottles, all maker's mark of Paul Storr for Storr & Co., 28.5cm (11¼in), 32oz 10dwt (1010gr), *L 19 June,*
£3,960 ($6,257)

13
A Victorian cruet frame, Martin Hall & Co., London, 1875, the oval stand on four panel feet, with detachable handle and seven associated cut glass bottles, 31cm (12in), *Ct 27 Oct,*
R 858 (£268; $375)

1

2

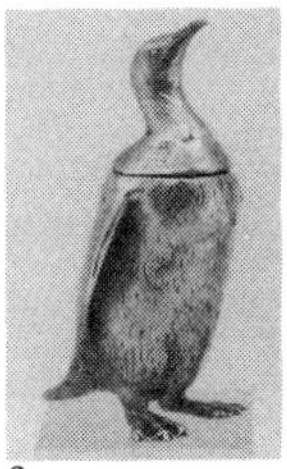
3

4

5

6

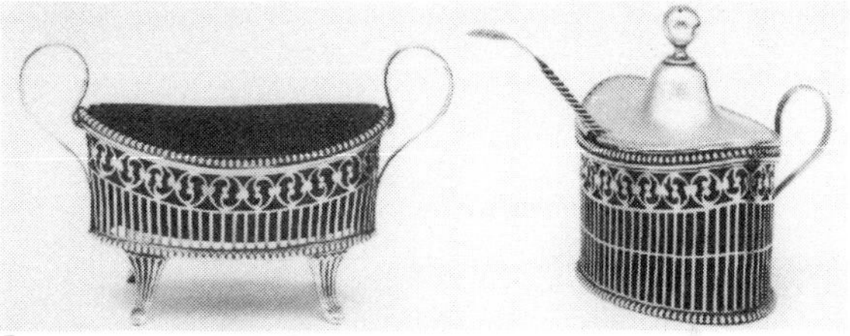
7

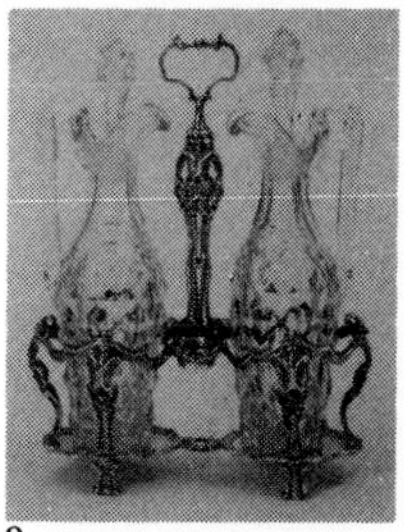
8

9

10

11

12

13

1

2

3

4

5

6

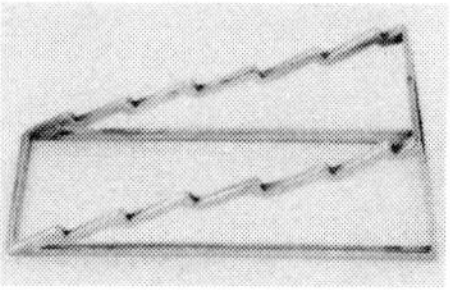
7

8

9

10

11

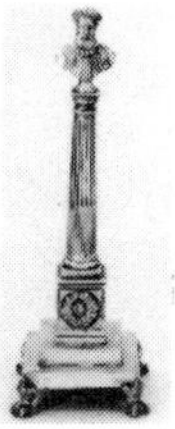
12

13

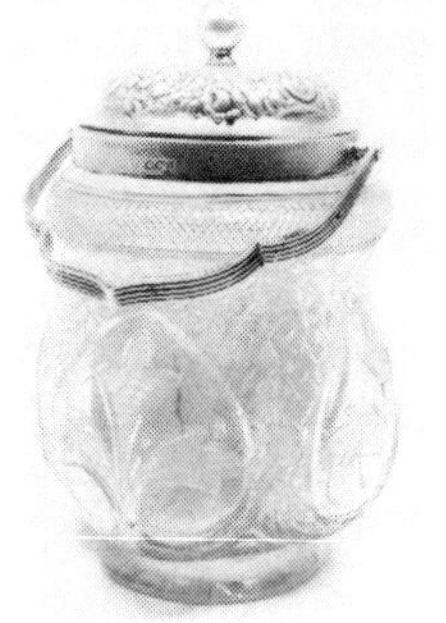
14

15

16

17

1
A lemon strainer, London, c.1725, 15cm (6in) wide, 2oz 8dwt (77gr), *M 24 June,* **FF 4,440 (£396; $618)**

2
A George II lemon strainer, Joseph Johns, Limerick, c.1750, 28.5cm (11¼in) wide, 5oz 17dwt (182gr), *NY 5 Nov,* **$4,400 (£3,099)**

3
A George III silver-gilt brandy saucepan, Thomas Heming, London, 1762, 24.5cm (9¾in) long, 10oz 9dwt (324gr), *L 16 Oct,* **£2,200 ($3,080)**

4
A George III saucepan, Hester Bateman, London, 1781, 10.5cm (4in) diam. at rim, 15oz (466gr), *NY 8 Apr,* **$2,530 (£1,745)**

5
An American saucepan, Joseph Lownes, Philadelphia, c.1810, 11cm (4¼in) diam., 6oz 10dwt (202gr), *NY 31 Jan,* **$3,080 (£2,184)**

6
A George II dish cross, Samuel Herbert & Co., London, 1759, with lamp and detachable cover, 33.5cm (13¼in) long, 24oz 10dwt (762gr), *NY 25 Jan,* **$1,650 (£1,187)**

7
A pair of George III dish wedges, *(one illustrated),* Peter & Ann Bateman, London, 1796, 15.5cm (6in) long, 7oz 12dwt (236gr), *L 20 Nov,* **£825 ($1,155)**

8
A George III dish ring, James Graham, Dublin, c.1770, 21.5cm (8¼in) diam., *HS 24 Sept,* **IR£1,540 (£1,400; $2,030)**

9
A George III double spirit barrel with candle branches, Phipps & Robinson, London, c.1800, the branches and sconces with maker's mark C.A., mounted on tilting stem, 37.5cm (14¾in) high, *NY 19 Sept,* **$7,425 (£5,017)**

10
A George IV honey pot, Rebecca Emes and Edward Barnard, London, 1822, detachable cover, 11.5cm (4½in) high, 8oz (249gr), *NY 5 Nov,* **$6,600 (£4,648)**

11
A George III honey pot, cover and stand, Paul Storr, London, 1797, 11.5cm (4½in) high, 14oz 7dwt (446gr), *L 17 July,* **£12,650 ($19,860)**

12
A Portuguese toothpick holder, maker's mark apparently A.B.B., Oporto, c.1860, in the form of a Doric column supporting a bust of a Roman emperor, 30cm (11½in), 15oz 12dwt (490gr), *L 8 July,* **£990 ($1,594)**

13
An Italian cup and saucer, Milan, c.1830, saucer 15cm (6in) diam., 5oz 8dwt (168gr), *F 14 Apr,* **L 1,000,000 (£410; $636)**

14
A Victorian silver-mounted glass biscuit jar, Sheffield, 1895, small chip, 19.5cm (7¾in), *C 17 Dec,* **£242 ($339)**

15
A French silver-gilt perfume burner, Jean-Baptiste-Claude Odiot, Paris, c.1800, in the form of an urn on a stand, 16.5cm (6¾in), 12oz 14dwt (395gr), *G 13 May,* **SF 9,350 (£3,159; $5,086)**

16
A set of four George III butter shells, *(one illustrated),* William Plummer, London, 1763, each on two conch shell feet, sold with another similar, by Edward Aldridge, London, 1749, 14cm (5½in), 13oz 10dwt (420gr), *NY 12 Dec,* **$1,650 (£1,179)**

17
A George III silver-gilt butter dish and cover, Rebecca and William Emes, London, 1808, of oval form, 18cm (7in) long, 23oz (727gr), *L 19 June,* **£1,155 ($1,825)**

1
An American covered pap boat, Anthony Rasch, Philadelphia, c.1810-20, 17cm (6¾in) long, 3oz (93gr), *NY 31 Jan,*
$715 (£507)

2
An American knife tray, William Adams, New York, c.1830-40, 41cm (16¼in), 24oz (746gr), *NY 26 June,*
$5,500 (£3,643)

3
A pair of George III snuffer's trays, Rundell, Bridge & Rundell, London, 1809, maker's mark of Paul Storr for Storr & Co., 27.5cm (10¼in), and two pairs of snuffers, James Scott, Dublin, 1810, 29oz 12dwt (920gr), *L 24 Apr,*
£2,420 ($3,872)

4
A George II snuffer's tray, Robert Calderwood, Dublin, c.1750, on four scroll and hoof feet, 22cm (8½in), 12oz 12dwt (392gr), *NY 25 Jan,*
$770 (£554)

5
A Dutch table bell, Willem Pont, Amsterdam, 1791, 14cm (5½in), 11oz 10dwt (356gr), *L 8 July,*
£2,090 ($3,365)

6
A Dutch table bell, first half 18th century, 15cm (6in), *A 21 Apr,*
Dfl 4,640 (£1,406; $2,208)

7
A Roman four-light oil lamp, Giuseppe Bartolotti, c.1770, 80cm (31½in), *F 14 Apr,*
L 8,000,000 (£3,276; $5,078)

8
A Roman oil lamp, Angelo Giannotti, c.1830, the lamp upheld by a figure of Mercury, 63cm (24¾in), *F 30 Sept,*
L 6,600,000 (£3,288; $4,604)

9
A set of four parcel-gilt menu holders, *(one illustrated)*, London, 1905, each applied with the head of a foxhound with red glass eyes, 2.5.cm (1in), 6oz 15dwt (210gr), *C 23 July,*
£407 ($638)

10
A German menu holder, J. H. Werner, Berlin, c.1901, in the form of a stag's skull in a leafy setting, silver-coloured metal, 26cm (19in), 21oz 15dwt (675gr), *L 11 Feb,*
£330 ($485)

11
A pair of Victorian silver-mounted champagne bottles, *(one illustrated)*, John Grinsell & Sons, London, 1893, one of cranberry and the other of dark green glass, with ground glass stoppers, 32cm (12½in), *L 24 Apr,*
£880 ($1,408)

12
A William III silver-gilt clothes whisk, Pierre Harache, London, 1695, engraved with a monogram below a French marquess's coronet, (provenance: Marquess of Exeter, Burghley House, sold 1888), 15cm (6in), *L 19 June,*
£14,300 ($22,594)

13
A silver-mounted mirror frame, William Comyns, London, 1892, 28cm (11in), *C 26 Mar,*
£418 ($640)

14
A silver-mounted ram's head snuff mull, apparently unmarked, Scottish, c.1846, set with one snuff box before and one behind the horns, centred with an ivory hammer, a rabbit-paw brush, a probe, a snuff spoon and a rake, on three castors, 43cm (17in) long, *Glen 25 Aug,*
£2,200 ($3,454)

1

2

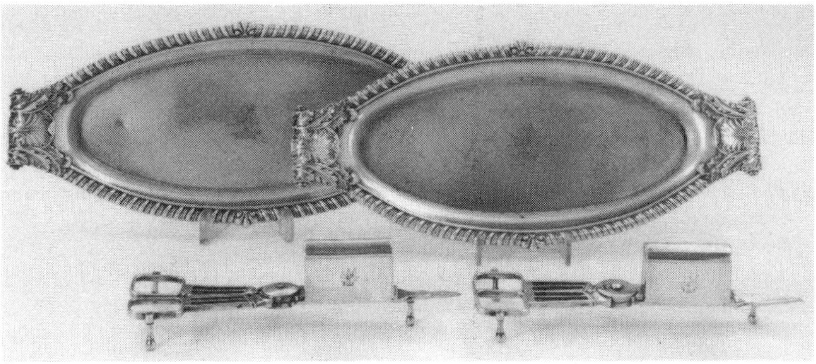
3

4

5

6

7

8

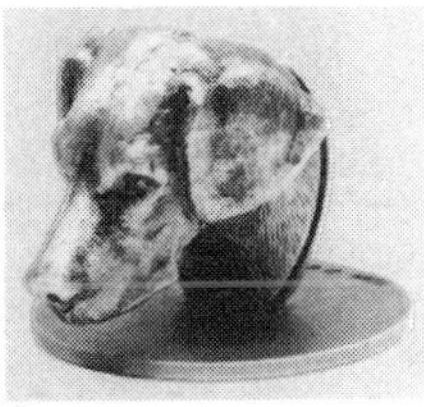
9

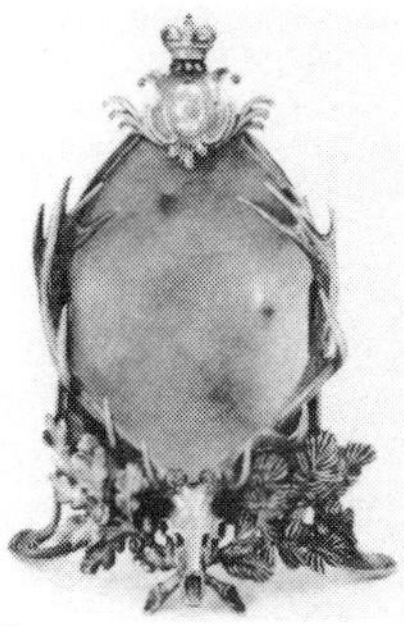
10

11

12

13

14

Later-Decorated Silver

JOHN WEBSTER

One category of silver that will not normally be found within this publication is that of later-chased and engraved silver, by which is meant articles chased or embossed in relief, or engraved, at a date later than their manufacture. Such pieces have long been regarded as the bastards of the silver market, their integrity and appeal undermined for collector, academic and auctioneer alike, because of the presence of decorative work of a later period.

Traditionally such pieces attracted little attention and normally sold for prices which reflected their intrinsic bullion value. However in the last decade, with the enormous growth in the silver market and particularly the emergence of Victorian silver as a strong and more fully appreciated part of that market, later-decorated silver has become received with more interest, is fetching higher prices and is no longer being consigned to the melt-pot.

On the whole, prior to the 19th century silver was not later-worked for decorative reasons but for personalisation. A large proportion of silver has for centuries been engraved with arms, crests, monograms and initials, and prior to our own times any such personalised pieces changing hands would have the former arms etc. removed and those of the new owner re-engraved. This habit is largely separate to the present subject but serves to illustrate that later decoration executed until the last decades of the 18th century was limited to such work.

The salver of 1727 (fig.1) has engraved armorials of some twenty years later, whereas the salver (fig.2) also 1727, has later

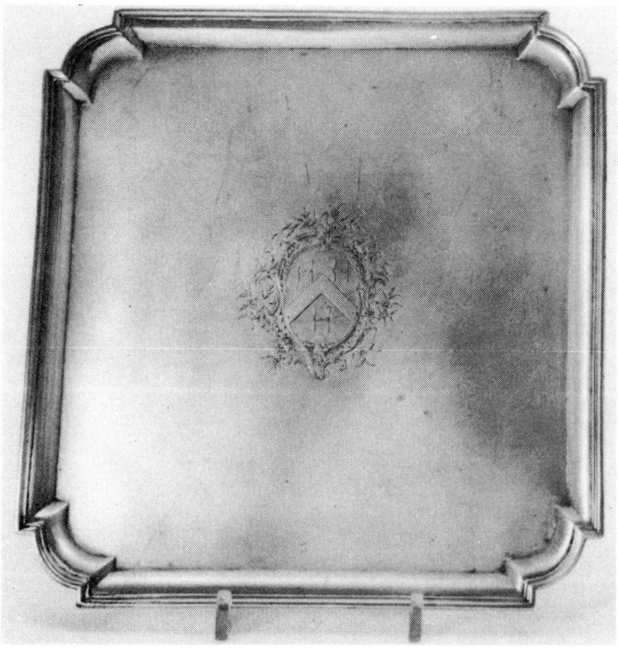

1

2

1
A George II salver, Edward Cornock, London, 1727, the arms engraved about twenty years later, 25cm (10in), 24oz 12dwt (765gr), *L 24 Oct 1985,* **£3,960 ($5,068)**

2
A George II salver, Edward Cornock, London, 1727, later engraved with the arms of William Thackeray (1811-63) within a border of masks and interlaced strapwork, 33cm (13in), 44oz 16dwt (1,393gr), *L 24 Apr,* **£9,020 ($14,432)**

3
A George III tankard, Francis Crump, London, 1763, 19.5cm (7¾in), 25oz 6dwt (786gr), *S 30 Jan,* **£1,485 ($2,183)**

4
A George II tankard, Richard Bayley, London, 1738, chased in the 19th century, 19.5cm (7¾in), 29oz 14dwt (923gr), *S 30 Jan,* **£1,012 ($1,488)**

5
A Queen Anne coffee pot, London, 1705, later chased in the 19th century

6
A George II soup tureen, perhaps Frederick Kandler, London, 1741, with 19th century chasing, 39cm (15½in), 113oz 6dwt (3,523gr),

7
A George II chocolate pot, Pentecost Symonds, Exeter, 1736, 24.5cm (9½in), 30oz 8dwt (945gr), *L 24 Oct 1985,* **£1,980 ($2,534)**

8
A George II coffee pot, John Jacobs, London, 1742, with contemporary decoration of engraved armorials within flat-chased scrolls and foliage, 24cm (9½in), 27oz 2dwt (842gr), *L 6 Feb,* **£1,595 ($2,233)**

arms within a band of later strapwork and masks engraved for the author William Makepeace Thackeray in the mid 19th century. The work on the Thackeray salver is of a stylistically accurate nature for the decorative band is based on the contemporary engraving of the famous Walpole salver by de Lamerie of 1728 (now in the Victoria & Albert Museum). Such precise imitations are not typical of Victorian later decoration.

The soup tureen, tankard and coffee pot (figs 6, 4 & 5) are more usual examples of the 18th century. These pieces all have a similar characteristic, namely that they were originally Georgian hollow-ware with no decorative features other than cast bases, supports, girdles and thumbpieces, such as the plain tankard (fig.3) and chocolate pot (fig.7). These illustrations give a clear 'before and after' indication of this type of later-chasing: fussy, without reference to a specific style, purely decorative and mostly executed in the middle years of the 19th century.

Such examples are the commonest form of later decoration to be encountered, but they stem from rather more purposeful antecedents to be found in the Regency period. The beer jugs of 1705 by Harache (fig.10) and charger of 1727 by de Lamerie (fig.9), were later chased by Edward Farrell in 1822 and William Pitts in 1809 respectively. These two silversmiths are to date the only individuals to whom later chasing can be specifically attributed and accurately dated. Both worked for important retail goldsmiths holding Royal warrants to the Prince Regent (Rundell, Bridge and Rundell) and his brother the Duke of York (Kensington Lewis).

The work of Pitts and Farrell stands apart from the majority of later-chased silver, for their products are of excellent quality, have been properly designed and possess all the traits of important presentation and Royal silver. In this respect the craftsmanship of Pitts and Farrell is an uncharacteristic haven in a sea of mediocrity. Many of their pieces were Royal commissions and although the loosely neoclassical taste of Pitts' work is very different to the enigmatic and highly individual work of Farrell (which is inspired by 18th century rococo and 17th century Dutch taste in the style of Teniers — see page 340), nonetheless both fit comfortably into the archaelogising Regency period and their virtuoso products can be attributed to the direct patronage of the Prince Regent and the influential retailers who supplied him.

Determining the origins of later decoration prior to the 19th century is not an easy task and one which would benefit from

3

4

5

6

7

8

extensive stylistic analysis of the earlier periods.

Later-chasing was less prevalent in the last quarter of the 18th century than it was post 1800. This seems illogical for the earlier period, too, was an age of dilettanti looking to the ancient world for inspiration. One would think that the profusion of neo-classical and other revival styles, together with the surviving chinoiserie and rococo tastes, would have been the ideal setting for later decoration. That it was not so can only be attributed to the habits and mentality of both patrons and smiths alike. In this period it seems more likely that silver was melted and fashioned anew when a fresh style was desired. Hence we do not see what one would expect: an early or mid 18th century coffee pot chased in the late 18th century in neoclassical or other current taste. This state of affairs would seem to be confirmed by the few pieces of this period which on cursory inspection appear to have later-chased characteristics, for example 1780s mugs and tankards chased with broad bands of slender vertical pales — a decorative motif taken from the 17th century — but when found at this date most usually purpose made with contemporary chasing albeit in an earlier style (figs 11 & 12).

In conclusion it may be as well to consider later-decorated silver in relation to the collector. The instance of later-engraved armorials presents many pitfalls. Prior to electroplating, unwanted arms were normally scraped off the surface resulting in a thinness in the body which can be felt and even flexed or, on a thick gauge of metal, causing a depression which can be seen. Later-engraving under these circumstances can be readily detected. Similarly, given the great stylistic changes that occur in the engraving of armorials and their associated cartouches between the 17th and 18th centuries, obvious differences between the date of an object and stylistic date of the engraved arms on it can again be easily spotted. However, should there be no evident erasure or stylistic imbalance, or when the arms have been re-engraved after only twenty or thirty years (as is the case with the salver illustrated (fig.1)), the resulting subtlety of stylistic differences makes detection less simple. Further difficulties arise when arms are engraved with erudition and care and in keeping with the object date. This may occur in the 19th century for laudable antiquarian reasons (as fig.2), but the incentive for such work to be carried out today is great (fig.13), given the enhancement of value that contemporary armorials usually have on a piece of period silver. Add to this situation the benefits of

9
A George II sideboard dish, Paul de Lamerie, London, 1727, later chased c.1809 probably under the direction of William Pitts for Rundell, Bridge & Rundell, 52cm (20½in), 135oz 10 dwt (4,214gr),

10
A pair of Queen Anne beer jugs, Peter Harache, London, 1705, chased and with later additions, Edward Farrell, London, 1822, 27.5cm (10¾in), 95oz (2,971gr), *L 6 Feb,* **£4,400 ($6,424)**

11
A George III tankard, Whipham and Wright, London, 1763, with contemporary decoration, 24cm (9½in), 42oz 9dwt (1,320gr), *L 19 Dec 1974,* **£715 ($1,644)**

flooding rather than erasing defunct armorials, then electroplating the restored surface prior to further engraving, or even the possibility that the piece was never engraved in the first place, it can be appreciated that later-engraving presents serious problems. The collector can only learn to detect such work by handling many pieces and comparing 'right' with 'wrong'.

With later-chasing the problems are more straightforward, for such work is normally self-evident, with the possible exception of confusion arising between the common mid 19th century floral decoration (figs 4-6) and that of a similar nature which occurs in the mid 18th century (fig.8 and p.394 figs 9-11). To differentiate briefly: 19th century chasing may be seen to occupy the whole or greater part of the available body surface and to be of a dense, laboured and intricate nature, whilst 18th century chasing is loose, with areas of the body evident within the chasing and is executed with a sympathy for the body shape and with a flowing simplicity and economy of hammer. The chasing talents of the silversmiths of the 17th to 19th centuries are largely lost today and the scope for modern deception is on the whole limited to work associated with repair or restoration, which normally involves the alteration of a piece. Although this indeed proposes difficulties for the collector, it is beyond the scope of this essay.

Finally, as evidence of the increasing regard in which later-decorated silver is currently held, one has only to reflect that the later-chased tankard (fig.4) is worth more than half the value of the unaltered example illustrated with it (fig.3).

Further reading:

Michael Clayton, *The Collectors Dictionary of the Silver and Gold of Britain and North America,* 1971
John Culme, *Nineteenth Century Silver,* 1977
Philippa Glanville, *Silver in England,* 1987
Peter Waldron, *The Price Guide to Antique Silver,* 1982

11

12

13

14

12
A George III mug, James Stamp or John Swift, London, 1727 with contemporary decoration.

13
A set of three George I salvers, Edward Feline, London, 1723, with later engraved armorials, 30cm (11¾in) and 13cm (5in), 69oz 8dwt (2,158gr), *L 19 June,*
£15,400 ($24,332)

14
A George III vase-shaped ewer, W & P Cunningham, Edinburgh, 1798, later engraved and with later handle, 41cm (16in), 47oz (1,474gr), *F 14 Apr,*
L 3,500,000 (£1,433; $2,222)

1

2

3

4

5

6

7

8

9

10

11

12

1
A Charles II porringer, maker's mark P.R. in script monogram, London, 1670, 8.5cm (3¼in) high, 7oz (217gr), *HS 24 Sept,*
IR£1,155 (£1,050; $1,522)

2
A Charles II porringer, maker's mark TC below a fish, London, 1667 or 1668, 9.5cm (3¾in) high, 7oz 16dwt (242gr), *L 16 Oct,*
£1,980 ($2,772)

3
A Charles II porringer, London, 1664, maker's mark HB conjoined, mullet below, 5.5cm (2¼in) wide, 1oz 14dwt (47gr), *C 14 Jan,*
£407 ($611)

4
A German silver-gilt bowl and cover, Daniel Schäffler I, Augsburg, 1719-20, with nine sides, 21cm (8½in) wide, 16oz (505gr), *G 11 Nov,*
SF 21,450 (£8,864; $12,675)

5
A French écuelle and cover, Louis Dulaurier II, Toulouse, 1784, with cabbage finial, 31cm (12in) wide, 34oz (1050gr), *M 24 June,*
FF 44,400 (£3,961; $6,179)

6
A North German parcel-gilt bowl, maker's mark PE in a shield, c.1600, of oval form, 30.5cm (12in) wide, 16oz (500gr), *G 11 Nov,*
SF 82,500 (£34,091; $48,750)

7
A French silver-gilt écuelle and cover on stand, maker's mark ?P.C., Paris, 1798-1809, stand 15cm (6in) diam., 17oz (528gr), *NY 5 Nov,*
$1,320 (£930)

8
A George I monteith bowl, John East, London, 1718, with detachable rim, 25.5cm (10in) diam., 52oz 4dwt (1623gr), *L 19 June,*
£7,480 ($11,818)

9
A James II chinoiserie monteith bowl, George Garthorne, London, 1685, with eight panels of chased figures, birds and flowers and leaves, 28cm (11in) diam., 36oz 8dwt (1132gr), *L 19 June,*
£33,000 ($52,140)

10
A Queen Anne monteith bowl, Edmund Pearce, London, 1707, detachable rim, engraved with the arms of Sir Walter Long Bt. (1626-1710) and a contemporary inscription, 27cm (10½in) diam., 71oz 14dwt (2230gr), *L 20 Nov,*
£15,400 ($21,560)

11
A silver-gilt monteith bowl, London, 1894, maker's mark WC over JL, 25cm (9¾in) diam., 40oz (1244gr), *C 25 June,*
£682 ($1,064)

12
A rose bowl, London, 1901, chased with blooms and scrolls, 28cm (11in) diam., 30oz 8dwt (949gr), *C 14 May,*
£495 ($797)

1
A pair of George II sauce-boats, *(one illustrated)*, John Le Sage, London, 1732, 19cm (7½in), 35oz 6dwt (1097gr), *L 17 July,*
£10,780 ($16,925)

2
A pair of German sauce-boats, *(one illustrated)*, Johann Jakob Bruglocher II, Augsburg, 1749-51, 19cm (7½in), 19oz (592gr), *G 13 May,*
SF 11,550 (£3,902; $6,282)

3
A pair of George III sauceboats, *(one illustrated)*, Parker & Wakelin, London, 1763, 21.5cm (8½in), 29oz 4dwt (908gr), *L 20 Nov,*
£3,080 ($4,312)

4
A pair of George II sauce-boats, *(one illustrated)*, Edward Wakelin, London, 1757, 23.5cm (9¼in), with a pair of sauce ladles en suite, 51oz 7dwt (1597gr), *L 24 Apr,*
£7,700 ($12,320)

5
A pair of George III sauceboats, *(one illustrated)*, William & James Priest, London, 1770-71, later crests, 13cm (5¼in), 20oz 18dwt (650gr), *L 6 Feb,*
£1,650 ($2,409)

6
A pair of George III sauceboats, *(one illustrated)*, Sebastian & James Crespell, London, 1762, engraved with the arms of Sir Brownlow Cust, later Baron Brownlow of Belton (1744-1807), 19.5cm (7¾in), 29oz 19dwt (931gr), *L 6 Feb,*
£1,155 ($1,686)

7
A pair of George III Irish sauceboats, Matthew West, Dublin, c.1775, 23cm (9in), 25oz 10dwt (793gr), *NY 12 June,*
$1,100 (£724)

8
A pair of George III sauceboats, *(one illustrated)*, John Carter, London, 1773, engraved with the arms of Williams-Wynn. Now in the Victoria & Albert Museum. 22cm (8½in), 43oz 6dwt (1346gr), *L 20 Nov,*
£7,150 ($10,010)

9
A pair of French sauce-boats, *(one illustrated)*, probably Nicolas Martin, Paris, c.1800, 29.5cm (11½in), 67oz 4dwt (2090gr), *M 24 June,*
FF 24,420 (£2,178; $3,398)

10
An American sauceboat, Baldwin Gardiner, New York, c.1830, 27.5cm (10¾in), 22oz (684gr), *NY 26 June,*
$1,870 (£1,238)

11
A pair of French sauce-boats, *(one illustrated)*, Bointaburet, Paris, early 20th century, 21.5cm (8½in), 32oz (995gr), *NY 14 Oct,*
$1,100 (£764)

1

2

4

3

6

5

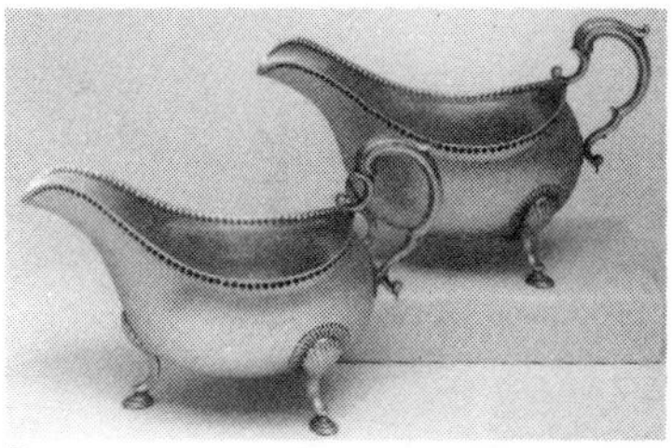
7

8

9

10

11

1

2

3

4

5

6

7

8

9

1
A pair of George III sauc tureens and covers, Carter, Smith & Sharp, London, 1784, 24.5cm (9¾in) wide, 44oz 10dwt (1384gr), *NY 12 June,*
$2,750 (£1,809)

2
A pair of George III sauc tureens and covers, *(one illustrated)*, Thomas Robins, London, 1807, 18cm (7in) long, 39oz 19dwt (1242gr), *L 24 Apr,*
£1,320 ($2,112)

3
A pair of George III sauc tureens and covers, *(one illustrated)*, John Romer, London, 1784, 18.5cm (7¼in) wide, 30oz (933gr), *HS 24 Sept,*
IR£1,815 (£1,650; $2,392

4
Two George III sauce tureens and covers, Paul Storr, 1802, and Burwash & Sibley, 1811, London, 27cm (10½in) wide, 63oz 10dwt (1974gr), *L 24 Apr,*
£4,730 ($7,568)

5
A pair of George III sauc tureens and covers, *(one illustrated)*, William Fountain, London, 1813, 24cm (9¼in) wide, 73oz 18dwt (2298gr), *L 24 Apr,*
£3,190 ($5,104)

6
A German oval soup tureen and cover, Müllers Berlin, c.1765, 45cm (17¾in) wide, 70oz 8dwt (2192gr), *G 13 May,*
SF 14,300 (£4,831; $7,778

7
A North German soup tureen and cover, August Ludwig Konow, Schwerin, c.1758, 35cm (13¾in) wide, 55oz (1710gr), *NY 8 Apr,*
$6,050 (£4,172)

8
A George II soup tureen and cover, John Letablere, Dublin, c.1750, 38cm (15in) wide, 139oz 15dwt (4346gr), *L 6 Feb,*
£4,400 ($6,424)

9
A Swiss soup tureen, cover and ladle, Wilhelm Brenner, Lausanne, c.1780, 41cm (16in) wide, 128oz 12dwt (4000gr), *G 11 Nov,*
SF 32,000 (£13,223; $18,909)

. George III oval soup ıreen and cover, Peter ıd Ann Bateman, 1798, ,ondon, 44cm (17½in), 8oz (2736gr), *NY 19 Sept,* **8,250 (£5,574)**

. George III soup tureen, over, stand and liner, .ndrew Fogelberg and tephen Gilbert, London, 788, 55.5cm (22in), 92oz 15dwt (5994gr), *IY 12 June,* **15,400 (£10,132)**

A Directoire soup tureen, over, liner and stand, ean-Baptiste-Claude)diot, Paris, 1798-1809, vith the monogram of Robert Smith of Baltimore (1757-1842), 5cm (17¾in), 225oz 0dwt (7013gr), *NY 8 Apr,* **23,100 (£15,931)**

4
A William IV soup ureen, cover and liner, torr & Mortimer, ,ondon, 1835, maker's nark Paul Storr, 37cm 14½in), 141oz 10dwt 4400gr), *L 20 Nov,* **£11,000 ($15,400)**

5
A Victorian soup tureen, cover and liner, Hunt & Roskell, London, 1845, maker's mark J. S. Hunt, 37cm (14½in), 152oz 10dwt (4743gr), *L 19 June,* **£4,070 ($6,431)**

6
A Danish soup tureen, Michelsen, Copenhagen, 1923, with the monogram of Christian X, 41cm (16in), 88oz (2736gr), *NY 14 Oct,* **$5,060 (£3,514)**

7
A French silver-gilt soup tureen, cover and stand, Puiforcat, Paris, 20th century, in Empire style, stand 30cm (11¾in) diam., 105oz 10dwt (3281gr), *NY 12 June,* **$1,760 (£1,158)**

8
An American soup tureen and cover, Wood & Hughes, New York, c.1845, 36cm (14in) wide, 46oz 18dwt (1460gr), *G 11 Nov,* **SF 4,950 (£2,045; $2,925)**

1

2

3

4

5

6

7

8

1

2

3

4

5

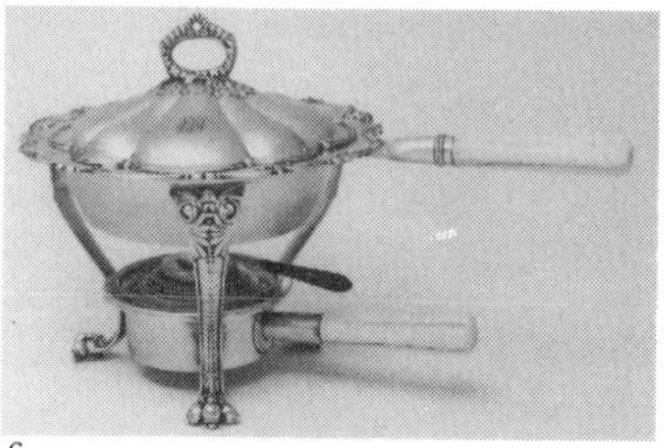
6

7

8

9

10

11

12

1
A George III entrée dish and cover, Edward Jay, London, 1792, 30.5cm (12in), 41oz (1276gr), *M 24 June,*
FF 7,770 (£693; $1,081)

2
A George III vegetable dish and cover, Thomas Robins, London, 1807, of oval form, 40cm (15¾in), 141oz 12dwt (4405gr), *M 24 June,*
FF 21,090 (£1,881; $2,935)

3
A pair of George IV entrée dishes and covers, *(one illustrated)*, Edward Barnard & Sons, London, 1829, detachable handles, 30.5cm (12in), 144oz 7dwt (4489gr), *L 16 Oct,*
£3,190 ($4,466)

4
A pair of William IV entrée dishes and covers, *(one illustrated)*, Edward Barnard & Sons, London, 1834, 30cm (11¾in) wide, 123oz 12dwt (3843gr), *S 20 June,*
£2,035 ($3,215)

5
A French vegetable dish and cover on stand, Marc-Augustin Lebrun, Paris, c.1840, stand 30.5cm (12in) diam., 77oz 19dwt (2425gr), *L 8 July,*
£2,310 ($3,719)

6
An American chafing dish, cover and hot water liner on lampstand, Gorham Mfg. Co., Providence, R.I., 1893, the dish and burner with silver and ivory handles, 27.5cm (10¾in) high, 121oz (3763gr), *NY 12 Dec,*
$1,650 (£1,179)

7
A George II bread basket, William Cripps, London, 1746, on four shell and scroll supports, 37.5cm (15in) wide, 64oz 12dwt (2010gr), *L 16 Oct,*
£4,620 ($6,468)

8
A George III cake basket, maker's mark W. T., London, 1768, of oval form, 36cm (14¼in), 28oz (870gr), *NY 12 June,*
$1,430 (£941)

9
A George III cake basket William Plummer, London, 1777, 37.5cm (14¾in) long, 44oz (1368gr), *HS 24 Sept,*
IR£2,530 (£2,300; $3,33

10
A George III cake basket Robert Hennell, London, 1783, of oval form, 36cm (14¼in) wide, 23oz (715gr), *NY 5 Nov,*
$3,575 (£2,518)

11
A George III bread basket, Benjamin Smith II, London, 1808, of circular form, 31cm (12¼in) diam., 46oz (1430gr), *NY 5 Nov,*
$4,950 (£3,486)

12
A George III cake basket J. W. Story & William Elliott, London, 1811, 33.5cm (13¼in), 39oz 15dwt (1236gr), *NY 12 June,*
$880 (£579)

1
A Victorian cake basket, Henry Wilkinson & Son, Sheffield, 1845, 32.5cm (12¾in) diam., 29oz 8dwt (914gr), *S 20 June,*
£594 ($938)

2
A cake basket, Goldsmiths & Silversmiths Co. Ltd., London, 1905, on three fish supports, 34cm (13¼in) wide, 75oz 14dwt (2354gr), *L 6 Feb,*
£3,080 ($4,497)

3
Two Victorian sweetmeat stands, *(one illustrated)*, C. T. & G. Fox, London, 1860/63, the stems cast as cherubs, 23cm (9in) high, 49oz 16dwt (1548gr), *L 20 Nov,*
£1,540 ($2,156)

4
A dessert basket, maker's mark JR, Sheffield, 1903, 42cm (16½in) wide, 40oz (1245gr), *JHB 18 June,*
R 2,970 (£928; $1,299)

5
A dessert basket, C. S. Harris, London, 1895, of oval form, 29cm (11¼in), 23oz 6dwt (724gr), *C 28 May,*
£528 ($834)

6
A French double dessert stand, C. Aucoc (Ainé), Paris, mid 19th century, with coronet finial, 37cm (14½in), 87oz (2705gr), *NY 12 Dec,*
$2,750 (£1,964)

7
A pair of dessert dishes, *(one illustrated)*, one C. S. Harris, the other Goldsmiths & Silversmiths Co. Ltd., both London, 1902, of oval form, 30.5cm (12in), 42oz 6dwt (1315gr), *C 10 Sept,*
£858 ($1,287)

8
A dessert basket, imported London, 1891, of oval form, dolphin handles, 37cm (14½in), 21oz 16dwt (677gr), *C 14 May,*
£341 ($549)

9
A pair of German dishes, *(one illustrated)*, late 19th century, both formed as shells, one capped by a cherub playing a violin, the other by a cherub playing a trumpet, each raised on four shell feet, 23.5cm (9¼in), 29oz (901gr), *NY 5 Nov,*
$1,980 (£1,394)

10
A French table garniture, Christofle, Paris, c.1900, comprising a centrepiece and two dishes in enamelled crystal, centrepiece 45cm (17¾in) wide overall, 219oz 18dwt (6840gr), *M 24 June,*
FF 74,370 (£6,634; $10,349)

11
A pair of dessert stands, *(one illustrated)*, William Comyns, London, 1912, pierced and engraved with trailing foliage and vines, 22.5cm (8¾in) diam., 37oz 18dwt (1178gr), *C 7 Oct,*
£792 ($1,109)

12
A Dutch bread basket, 1969, 33cm (13in), 26oz 16dwt (836gr), *A 13 Mar,*
Dfl 1,380 (£418; $644)

1

2

3

4

5

7

6

8

9

10

11

12

1

2

3

4

5

6

9

7

8

10

1
A George III epergne, Francis Butty & Nicholas Dumee, London, 1768-69, 58.5cm (23in) high, 175oz (5442gr), *NY 8 Apr,*
$8,800 (£6,069)

2
A George III epergne, Henry Chawner, London, 1791, 50.5cm (19¾in) high, 105oz (3265gr), *NY 8 Apr,*
$11,000 (£7,586)

3
A William IV silver-gilt centrepiece, Paul Storr, London, 1836, 65cm (25½in) high, 510oz (15861gr), *NY 12 Dec,*
$60,500 (£43,214)

4
A French jardinière, Fray Fils, Paris, late 19th century, 63cm (26¾in) wide, 197oz 10dwt (6140gr), *L 11 Feb,*
£4,180 ($6,145)

5
A French jardinière, Charles-Nicolas Odiot, Paris, c.1850, 66cm (26in), 189oz (5879gr), *G 11 Nov,*
SF 20,900 (£8,636; $12,350)

6
A German jardinière, D. Vollgold & Söhn, Berlin, c.1895, 52cm (20½in) wide, 7oz 10dwt (2205gr), *L 20 Mar,*
£2,090 ($3,281)

7
A German centrepiece, J. C. Schlund, Frankfurt, c.1890, 58cm (22¾in) high, 190oz 6dwt (5918gr), *L 11 Feb,*
£3,740 ($5,498)

8
A Victorian table centrepiece-cum-candelabrum, Edward Barnard & Sons, London, 1853, 71.5cm (28¼in) high, 180oz 12dwt (5616gr), *C 15 Apr,*
£3,630 ($5,627)

9
A German jardinière, c.1901, 33.5cm (11½in) wide, 49oz 16dwt (1548gr), *L 12 June,*
£1,320 ($2,112)

10
A swan jardinière, C. J. Vander, London, 1975, 34.5cm (13½in) wide, 132oz 12dwt (4123gr), *C 14 Jan,*
£1,705 ($2,558)

German dish, Evert
ierdes, Aurich, c.1680,
9cm (11½in) diam., 12oz
2dwt (392gr), *G 13 May,*
F 10,450 (£3,530; $5,684)

**set of four George II
lishes,** *(two illustrated),*
Charles Kandler, London,
731, in Régence style,
1cm (21¼in) long, 76oz
7dwt (2390gr), *L 20 Nov,*
11,000 ($15,400)

German dish, Daniel
Michael, Augsburg,
.1680, of oval form, em-
ossed with a mythologi-
al scene, 31cm (12¼in),
oz 10dwt (298gr),
11 Feb,
935 ($1,374)

**German parcel-gilt
lish,** Johann Pepfen-
auser II, Augsburg,
708-10, 52cm (20½in),
4oz 10dwt (1075gr),
8 July,
2,420 ($3,896)

5
**Twelve George III dinner
plates,** John Wakelin &
Robert Garrard, London,
1792, 25cm (9¾in), 199oz
10dwt (6204gr), *NY 12 Dec,*
$10,450 (£7,464)

6
**Twelve George II dinner
plates,** Eliza Godfrey,
London, 1750-51, 25cm
(10in), 210oz 6dwt
(6541gr), *L 6 Feb,*
£9,680 ($14,133)

7
**Twelve George II dinner
plates,** Eliza Godfrey,
London, 1750-51, 25cm
(10in), 213oz 9dwt
(6638gr), *L 6 Feb,*
£9,680 ($14,133)

8
**Twelve Victorian soup
plates,** Hunt & Roskell,
London, 1896, 25cm
(10in), 249oz 2dwt
(7747gr), *L 6 Feb,*
£2,970 ($4,336)

9
**Two George III meat
dishes,** James Young,
London, 1785, 59cm
(23¼in) wide, 202oz
18dwt (6310gr), *L 6 Feb,*
£6,380 ($9,315)

Captions continued on
p.422.

1

2

3

4

5

6-11

12

13

14

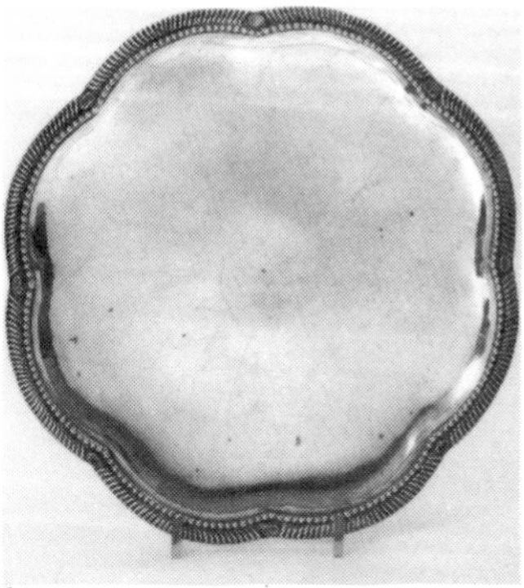
1

2

3

4

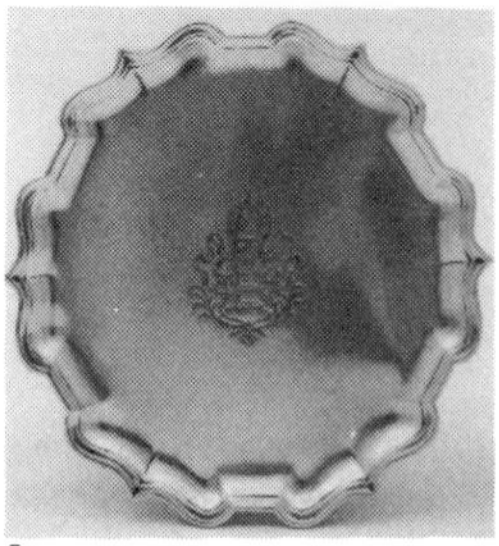
5

6

7

8

9

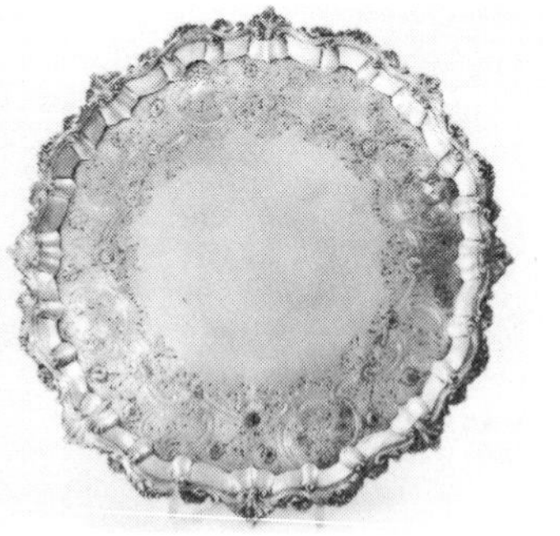
10

11

12

Captions continued from p.421.

10
Two George II meat dishes, Eliza Godfrey, London, 1751, 40cm (15¾in) wide, 69oz 17dwt (2172gr), *L 6 Feb,*
£3,190 ($4,657)

11
Four small George II meat dishes, Eliza Godfrey, London, 1751, 32cm (12¾in) wide, 93oz 8dwt (2905gr), *L 6 Feb,*
£2,860 ($4,176)

12
A set of twelve German silver-gilt dinner plates, Johann Alois Seethaler, Augsburg, 1819, 25cm (10in), 228oz (7090gr), *NY 12 June,*
$5,060 (£3,329)

13
A set of twelve Austrian dinner plates, *(one illustrated),* Stephan Mayerhofer, Vienna, 1824-27, 24cm (9½in), 142oz 14dwt (4440gr), *M 24 June,*
FF 11,100 (£990; $1,545)

14
An Indian colonial sideboard dish, Cooke & Kelvey, Calcutta, c.1870, 78cm (30½in), 357oz (11102gr), *NY 5 Nov,*
$3,575 (£2,518)

1
A German salver on foot, Bernhard Wendels, Cologne, c.1700, 30cm (11¾in) diam., 21oz 10dwt (668gr), *L 8 July,*
£1,540 ($2,479)

2
A pair of George I tazzas, Paul de Lamerie, London, 1720, engraved with the arms of the Rt. Hon George Treby, 16cm (6¼in) diam., 25oz 5dwt (785gr), *L 17 July,*
£16,500 ($25,905)

3
A pair of George I salvers on foot, *(one illustrated),* Dublin, 1719, 16.5cm (6½in) diam., 17oz 16dwt (553gr), *L 16 Oct,*
£1,760 ($2,464)

4
A pair of George I salvers *(one illustrated),* David Tanqueray of London, c.1725, maker's mark only, 15.5cm (6in), 21oz 4dwt (674gr), *L 16 Oct,*
£4,620 ($6,468)

5
A George II salver, Edward Cornock, London, 1730, 17cm (6¾in), 9oz 15dwt (303gr), *L 20 Nov,*
£1,320 ($1,848)

6
A George II salver, Francis Nelme, London, 1731, 32.5cm (12¾in), 39oz 10dwt (1228gr), *L 16 Oct,*
£4,950 ($6,930)

7
A George II salver, Francis Pages, London, 1733, 20cm (8in) diam., 13oz (404gr), *NY 14 Oct,*
$1,760 (£1,222)

8
A George II salver, Robert Abercromby, London, 1741, engraved with contemporary armorials within a chased border, 54.5cm (21½in) diam., 131oz (4074gr), *NY 12 June,*
$4,675 (£3,076)

9
A George II waiter, Abraham Portal, London, 1749, 15cm (6in) diam., 5½oz (158gr), *Syd 12 Nov,*
Aus$825 (£375; $525)

10
A George II salver, Robert & William Peaston, London, 1758, flat-chased with flowers, fruit and foliage, 36cm (14in) diam., 42oz 14dwt (1328gr), *L 17 July,*
£1,100 ($1,727)

11
A set of three George III salvers, John Carter, London, 1771, in two sizes, 35.5 and 23cm (14 and 9in) diam., 68oz 10dwt (2130gr), *NY 25 Jan,*
$4,400 (£3,165)

12
A Dutch salver, Reynier Brandt, Amsterdam, 1763, on bracket supports, 35.5cm (14in) square, 28oz 15dwt (895gr), *L 8 July,*
£1,925 ($3,099)

1
A Dutch salver, Barend Swierink, Amsterdam, 1774, on bracket supports, 30.5cm (13¾in) wide, 24oz 8dwt (760gr), *G 11 Nov,*
SF 7,150 (£2,955; $4,225)

2
A George III salver, Robert Jones, London, 1774, four claw and ball feet, engraved with the arms of Sir William Smyth, 6th Bt. (d.1777), 36cm (14¼in) diam., 39oz 15dwt (1236gr), *L 24 Apr,*
£1,430 ($2,288)

3
A George III salver, Rundell, Bridge & Rundell, maker's mark of Paul Storr, London, 1814, on four panel supports, engraved with the arms of Clifton, 31cm (12¼in) diam., 36oz 12dwt (1138gr), *NY 5 Nov,*
$6,600 (£4,648)

4
A George IV salver, John Mewburn, London, 1819, in mid 18th century style, shell and honeysuckle pattern panel supports, engraved with the arms of Boyle, Earls of Glasgow, 56.5cm (22¼in) diam., 139oz 11dwt (4340gr), *L 19 June,*
£2,970 ($4,693)

5
A George III tea tray, Crouch and Hannam, London, 1783, four panel feet, 58cm (23¾in) wide, 65oz (2021gr), *NY 19 Sept,*
$5,775 (£3,902)

6
A pair of Dutch coffee trays, Diederik Willem Rethmeyer, Amsterdam, 1806, of navette outline, 39cm (15¼in) wide, 38oz 3dwt (1185gr), *L 11 Feb,*
£2,420 ($3,357)

7
A Dutch tea tray, Diederik Willem Rethmeyer, Amsterdam, 1806, of navette outline, 67cm (26¼in) wide, 87oz 10dwt (2720gr), *L 11 Feb,*
£1,980 ($2,911)

8
A William IV salver, E. Crofton, Dublin, 1831, chased with shamrocks, flowers and leaves, on four lion mask feet, 52.5cm (20¾in) diam., 156oz 8dwt (4864gr), *L 6 Feb,*
£2,035 ($2,971)

9
A French tea tray, Charles-Nicolas Odiot, Paris, 1819-38, on four panel supports, 63.5cm (25in) wide, 106oz (3296gr), *NY 5 Nov,*
$3,575 (£2,518)

10
A William IV tea tray, William Ker Reid, London, 1834, engraved with the arms of Lovett impaling Henniker Major, 73cm (28¾in) wide, 155oz 12dwt (4839gr), *L 17 July,*
£3,850 ($6,045)

11
A Victorian tea tray, Elkington, Mason & Co., Birmingham, 1855, with later presentation inscription, 75.5cm (29¾in) wide, 177oz 13dwt (5525gr), *L 16 Oct,*
£3,520 ($4,928)

12
A Victorian tea tray, Hunt & Roskell, maker's mark of John Samuel Hunt, London, 1850, in late 18th century style, engraved with the crest and coronet of the Earls of Glasgow, 87.5cm (34½in) wide, 215oz 15dwt (6710gr), *L 19 June,*
£4,620 ($7,300)

1

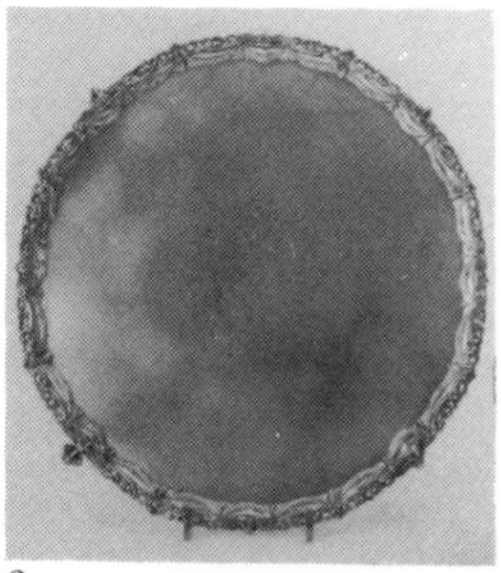
2

3

4

5

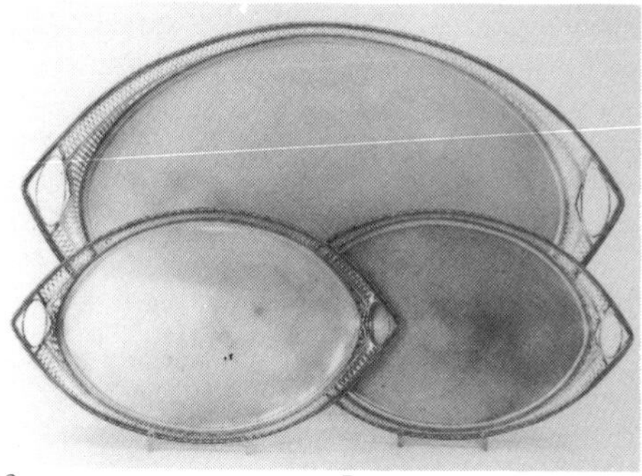
6 7

8

9

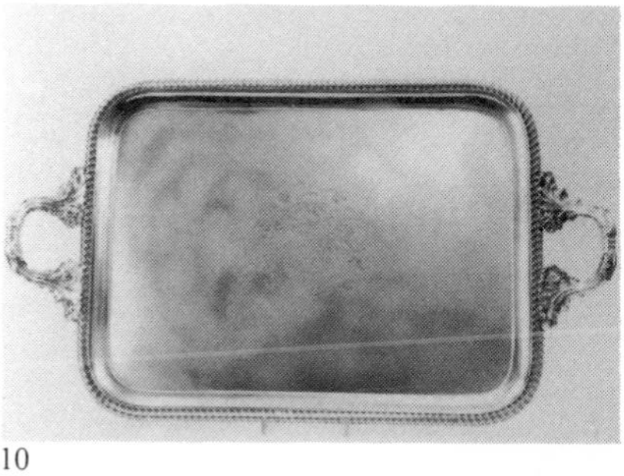
10

11

12

American Silver Before 1800

KEVIN TIERNEY

The main centres of silver-making in North America were Boston, New York and Philadelphia. A certain amount was also made at Newport, Rhode Island, Albany and, at the end of the 18th century, in Baltimore. The output of other cities such as Charleston, South Carolina, or Alexandria, Virginia, was small and silversmiths listed there seem often to have been retailers rather than makers. Pieces made in these cities are therefore scarce and appeal particularly to local collectors.

The early settlers brought their European traditions and tastes with them and these can be seen in the new pieces they made in America, which, however, have their own separate character. The silver was the product of an emergent, hard working, essentially merchant community, among whom there was little place for luxurious silver-gilt or the grand display items of an aristocracy. The choice was for simple forms, which were practical and of good proportions, but the patrons were not blind to the latest fashions from Europe and silver was for them, as well, a mark of status; it was also an inheritance for later generations and a reserve fund in time of need. The primary range of objects made was small and comprises, approximately in order of frequency seen today: spoons, sugar tongs, canns (or mugs) (figs 13, 18 & 24), porringers of the flat single-handled variety (figs 15 & 16), creamers (cream jugs) (fig.9), sugar nips (fig.21) or tongs (fig.11), soup and toddy ladles, bowls of different sizes, teapots, tankards, beakers, coffee pots, pepper boxes and casters, salts, sauce boats, snuff boxes (fig.26), small salvers, flagons and lemon strainers (fig.22). Two-handled cups, spout cups, inkstands, tea caddies and candlesticks are rarer. By the end of the 18th century tea sets and water pitchers appear, as does an occasional two-handled tray and a number of peace medals and swords. Small items of jewellery were made continually but often do not have a maker's mark.

The earliest New York items, from the late 17th century, show Dutch as well as English influence. A few existing tall beakers recall a standard article in Holland (see page 388, figs 13 & 14). The Dutch brandy bowl, used for passing brandied fruits, has a New York relative in bowls made by such craftsmen as Benjamin Wynkoop (1675-1728) (fig.1), Bartholomew le Roux the elder (1687-1713?), Gerrit Onckelbag (1691-1732) or Cornelius Kierstede (1675-1757). These are often embossed with flowers in the Dutch tradition and were sometimes large enough to be called punch bowls. At this time the New York or Albany tankard can reach a surprising level of elaborate decoration. The form is essentially English of the late 17th century. The new makers added a serrated leaf-tip band above the base moulding, apparently borrowed from Dutch beakers. They also applied decoration to the handle in the form of a lion passant or swag of fruit at the top and a mask at the tip, and sometimes a circle of engraved foliage on the cover to surround an interlaced cypher or inset coin (fig.2). This decoration recalls Scandinavian tankards of this date. In this, its most decorated form, the American tankard is one of the high points of American decorative arts.

The silver of Boston and Newport stayed closer to England in style. The late 17th and early 18th century makers such as Jeremiah Dummer (1645-1718), John Coney (1655-1722) and Edward Winslow (1669-1753) produced high-quality baroque silver, including rare items such as chafing dishes, plates, sugar boxes, chocolate pots and even monteith bowls. Coney's monteith (now in the Garvan Collection, Yale University Art Gallery), may rank as the finest known piece of American silver. New England tankards show local characteristics. By the second quarter of the 18th century they have domed covers in keeping with English custom (New York persisted with flat covers) and have, in

1

1
A two-handled bowl,
Benjamin Wynkoop, New York, c.1707, 15oz 12dwt (485gr), 28cm (11in) diam.,
NY 17 Nov 1981,
$121,000 (£67,598)

addition, a finial of urn or bell form. Armorials occasionally appear, sometimes finely engraved in a rococo cartouche, as by the silversmith and engraver Nathaniel Hurd (1729-77). However, most owners were content to have their initials engraved either on the base or on the top of the handle, arranged in a triangle, with the initial of the family name above those of the first names of husband and wife (as commonly found in Europe) (fig.14).

A pleasing form derived from England and Holland is the New York pear-shaped teapot, in fashion between 1720 and 1750. Myer Myers has interpreted this form well (fig.4), with an unusually high baluster finial and an elongated octagonal swan-neck spout. The form was also used by Peter van Dyck (1684-1750), in one case octagonally panelled, a Huguenot fashion which appears only rarely in American silver. A number of octagonal pepper boxes exist (fig.25). Joseph Richardson of Philadelphia (1711-84) made an octagonal covered sugar bowl in 1736 (fig.5). Described as a sugar dish in Richardson's account book, it cost £5.3.0d. for the silver and £2.5.0d. for making. By 1760 the pear-shaped teapot becomes inverted as in the example by Samuel Casey (1726-80) (fig.6). Such a teapot is shown in the hands of Paul Revere in the famous painting by Copley in the Boston Museum of Fine Arts. This shape was replaced towards the end of the century by the drum-shaped and oval teapot, which were both more in keeping with the neoclassical taste and simpler to make, usually being made of sheet silver with a vertical seam, a quicker process than raising from the flat (fig.17).

Tea sets became current in England about 1770; America followed the fashion with, as usual, a small time lag. It was Philadelphia that excelled in these, producing tea sets of large size and great elegance. They could comprise two teapots (for black and green tea), cream jug, sugar bowl, coffee pot and waste bowl,

2
A tankard, Henricus Boelen II, New York, c.1720, engraved with the interlaced cypher C.W.T.D., the cover inset with a Louis XIV coin, 38oz 12dwt (1,200gr), 18.5cm (7¼in), *NY 31 Jan,*
$51,700 (£35,957)

3
A teapot, Christian Wiltberger, Philadelphia, c.1790, with contemporary monogram T.E.P., marked foot C. Wiltberger, 25oz 15dwt (800gr), 28cm (11in) high, *NY 31 Jan,*
$6,050 (£4,291)

4
A teapot, Myer Myers, New York, c.1750-60, marked MM in shaped cartouche, 21oz 10dwt (668gr), 18.5cm (7¼in), *NY 27 Jan 1982,*
$63,250 (£35,335)

5
An octagonal sugar bowl and cover, Joseph Richardson, Philadelphia, 1736, maker's mark IR in oval struck twice, 11oz 5dwt (349gr), 11.5cm (4½in) wide, *NY 19 Nov 1980,*
$37,400 (£15,915)

2

3

4

5

6

7

8

9

10

6
A teapot, Samuel Casey, Exeter and South Kingston, R.I., c.1765, marked S:Casey in rectangle, 20oz 8dwt (634gr), 17.5cm (7in) high, *NY 31 Jan,*
$30,800 (£21,843)

7
A water pitcher, Ebenezer Moulton, Boston and Newburyport, Mass., c.1800-10, engraved with monogram E.M.H., marked on base MOULTON, 25oz 16dwt (802gr), 21.5cm (8½in) high, *NY 31 Jan,*
$13,200 (£9,361)

8
A seven piece tea and coffee set, Joseph Lownes, Philadelphia, c.1795, each engraved with contemporary monogram M.H., marked on bases of teapot, tea caddy and on sugar tongs, 122oz, 10dwt (3,809gr), coffee pot, 37cm (14½in) high, *NY 31 Jan,*
$41,800 (£29,645)

9
A creamer, John Tanner, Newport, R.I., c.1750-60, engraved with foliate monogram A.L., the base initialled E*B, marked IT in rounded rectangle, 4oz (124gr), 10cm (4in) high, *NY 31 Jan,*
$4,070 (£2,886)

10
A presentation punch bowl, Hugh Wishart, New York, c.1799, one side engraved with armorials in a shield and a crest above, the other with presentation inscription, signed by engraver 'Rollinson Sculp', marked Wishart in rectangle on base, 94oz 15dwt (2,946gr), 34.5cm (13½in) diam., *NY 23 June 1979,*
$115,500 (£56,341)

11
A pair of sugar tongs, Paul Revere Jr., Boston, c.1780, monogrammed S.P.B., marked Revere in rectangle, 1oz 4dwt (37 gr), 14.5cm (5¾in) long, *NY 31 Jan,*
$4,675 (£3,315)

a quantity of objects per set which overshadows any English counterpart (fig.8). The makers understood the neoclassical idiom: the vessels were of vase shape with urn-shaped finials and narrow beaded borders, the rims were sometimes fitted with pierced galleries (not current in England), and bright-cut engraved, (fig.20).

At about the same time (the 1780s and 1790s), the water pitcher was introduced. Boston produced a plain barrel-shaped pitcher based upon a Liverpool pottery prototype (fig.7), a form which seems to be confined to New England. In the 19th century the water pitcher developed as an object considered suitable for presentation pieces and therefore became more elaborate.

Bowls existed throughout the century in various forms and were also thought suitable for presentation; such is the bowl by Hugh Wishart of New York (1784-1825). Of pleasing form and raised on a tall moulded foot, this is finely engraved with ships in battle as well as armorials and presentation inscription (fig.10). Unusually, the decoration is signed by the engraver William Rollinson (1762-1842), who is known for copper-plate engraving of portraits and banknotes.

The makers who are especially sought after by collectors are those of the earliest date and those whose work is of the highest quality, such as John Coney, Joseph Richardson, Simeon Soumaine (1685-1750) (fig.24), and Charles le Roux (1689-1745). Extraneous factors also influence the choice of collectors today. Myer Myers was a high-quality New York maker of the mid 18th century, but part of his popularity today lies in his Jewish background. This would have been a burden in Europe where he might have been excluded from the guilds; in America, in a tolerant religious climate, he could work freely and be patronized by Jews and gentiles alike. Samuel Casey of Rhode Island, whose work is highly competent has the flavour of the popular anti-hero; arrested for counterfeiting coins, he was sprung from jail by supporters, went into hiding and was finally pardoned through the entreaties of his wife. Philip Syng Jr of Philadelphia (1703-89) made the inkstand used in the signing of the Declaration of Independence, and thereby holds an historic position. Paul Revere Jr, 'The Patriot' (1735-1818) still ranks as the most sought-after of all American makers. Even a pair of sugar tongs by him will cause lively competition and reach a price at least fifty times that of its London counterpart (fig.11). An enterprising man, engraver, political pamphleteer, bell-maker and prolific silversmith, he is a reminder of the relatively prominent social position occupied by the 18th century silversmith in America;

12
A lemon strainer, Thomas Arnold, Newport, R.I., c.1760-70, one handle initialled S.B., some repairs, marked T.A. in rectangle, 2oz 8dwt (74gr), 27.5cm (10¾in) long, *NY 31 Jan,* **$3,850 (£2,730)**

13
A cann, Samuel Edwards, Boston, c.1730-40, engraved with a foliate interlaced cypher G.M.B., marked S.E. crowned above a star, 8oz 12dwt (267gr), 9.5cm (3¼in) high, *NY 31 Jan,* **$22,000 (£15,602)**

14
A tankard, William Simpkins, Boston, c.1750-70, handle engraved TCE, marked Simpkins in rectangle, 32oz 8dwt (1,007gr), 23cm (9in) high, *NY 31 Jan,* **$9,900 (£7,021)**

15
A porringer, Samuel Edwards, Boston, c.1740, handle engraved with initials SES, centre marked S.E. crowned, 7oz 15dwt (241gr), 13cm (5in) diam., *NY 31 Jan,*

16
A porringer, John Potwine, Boston, c.1730-40, engraved with later initials A.C. above traces of original initials I.I.R., maker's mark I.P., 8oz (248 gr), 13.5cm (5¼in) diam., *NY 31 Jan,* **$4,070 (£2,769)**

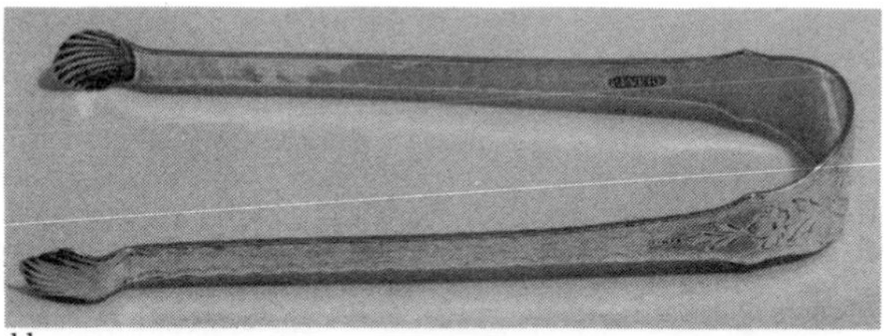

11

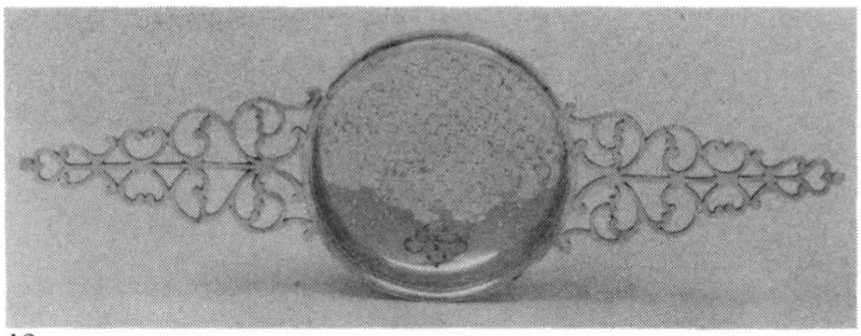

12

13

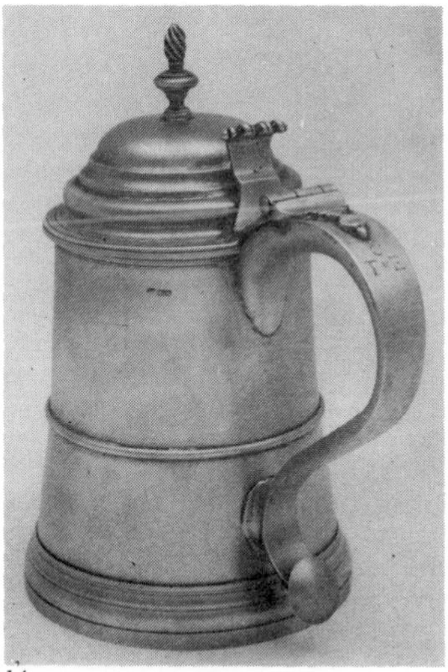

14

15

16

17
A teapot, Joseph Richardson Jr., Philadelphia, c.1800, engraved F.R. to H.P. & C.R., marked J.R. in rectangle twice, 19oz 8dwt (603gr), 16cm (6¼in) high, *NY 26 June,*
$2,640 (£1,748)

18
A cann, William Homes, Boston, c.1770, engraved with the monogram J.A.D., marked on base WHomes in rectangle, 11oz (342gr), 14cm (5½in) high, *NY 31 Jan,*
$1,650 (£1,170)

19
A waste bowl, Joseph Richardson Jr., Philadelphia, c.1790, engraved with a contemporary monogram R.M.T., marked JR in rectangle, 16oz 4dwt (503gr), 16.5cm (6½in) diam., *NY 31 Jan,*
$3,630 (£2,574)

20
An oval covered sugar bowl, Joseph Lownes, Philadelphia, c.1800, marked J. Lownes, in italics, 19oz 12dwt (609gr), 18cm (7in) long, *NY 31 Jan,*
$2,640 (£1,872)

21
A pair of sugar nips, Thomas Edwards, Boston, c.1750, engraved BSR, marked TE in rectangle, 1oz (31gr), 13cm (5½in) long, *NY 31 Jan,*
$1,320 (£936)

17

18

19

20

21

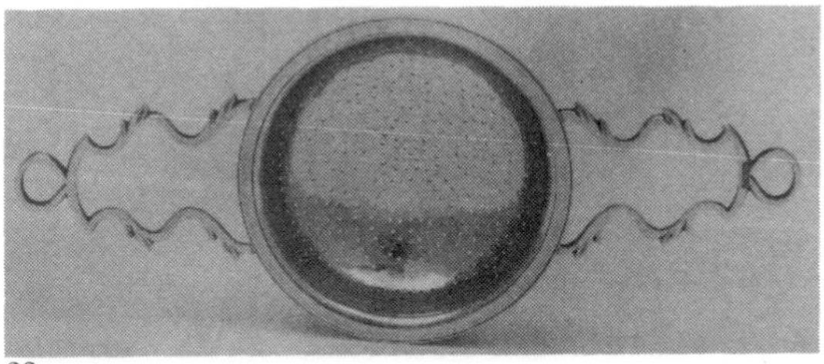
22

23

24

25

22
A lemon strainer, Benjamin Burt, Boston, c.1750-60, initialled on back GAP, marked B.Burt in rectangle, 4oz 12dwt (143gr), 28.5cm (11¼in) long, *NY 31 Jan,*
$4,125 (£2,925)

23
A sugar vase and cover, Joseph Lownes, Philadelphia, c.1780, initialled LW, maker's mark struck four times on base, 11oz 16dwt (369 gr), 23.5cm (9¼in) high, *G 13 May,*
SF 3,960 (£1,338; $2,154)

24
A cann, Simeon Soumaine, New York, c.1740, engraved with initials TEM, marked SS in square punch, 11oz (342gr), 11cm (4½in) high, *NY 31 Jan,*
$6,050 (£4,290)

25
An octagonal pepper, Andrew Oliver, Boston, c.1740, marked A.Oliver in rectangle, 3oz 10dwt (108gr), 11cm (4½in), *NY 31 Jan,*
$7,150 (£5,070)

many held civic or military rank.

Silversmiths served a seven-year apprenticeship but unlike European craftsmen they did not have the benefit of the protective and helpful environment of the guild system. Nor could they order parts, such as sheet metal, handles, spouts, mouldings etc., from a specialist. Instead they probably had to start a piece by melting coins or older silver. Their achievement in making fine silver is therefore remarkable. Remarkable, too, is the fact that no assay office forced them to keep their silver up to sterling standard (Baltimore was the only city to introduce a short-lived assay office in the early 19th century). Trust among the early population was such that the maker's mark was sufficient. The marks change gradually from the initials of the maker in a shaped shield, sometimes crowned and with pellets or other devices (figs A-E), to simpler punches containing initials or full name in capitals or italics (figs F-I). In the mid 18th century the mark may be in a scrolled ribbon-form punch or cartouche, befitting the rococo period (figs J-L). The mark could be struck more than once: in Philadelphia it was commonly struck four times. By the end of the century it might be accompanied by pseudo-hallmarks including an eagle. Baltimore pieces made before the assay office period are occasionally marked 'Sterling' as well. (The universal stamp 'Sterling' became current about 1865.)

Collectors will pay extra for pieces with proven historic ownership; they look for a known family history even if not historic. Special attention is paid to condition: a good 'skin', clear mark, absence of splits or repairs and presence of original engraving are important. Such factors can change the price of an early tankard, salver or coffee pot from $3,000 (£1,875) to $30,000 (£18,750) or more. But even the finest piece of American silver, in choicest condition, seems inexpensive compared to prices realised today for the furniture on which it once stood.

Further reading:

Louise Conway Belden, *The Marks of American Silversmiths in the Ineson-Bissell Collection*, 1980
Kathryn C. Buhler, *American Silver 1655-1823 in the Museum of Fine Arts, Boston*, 2 vols, 1972
Kathryn C. Buhler and Graham Hood, *American Silver: Garvan and Other Collections in the Yale University Art Gallery*, 2 vols, 1970
Martha Gandy Fales, *Early American Silver*, 1970
Robert Alan Green, *Marks of American Silversmiths*, 1977
Graham Hood, *American Silver: A History of Style 1650-1800*, 1971

26
A snuff box, Samuel Vernon, Newport, R.I., c.1710-30, the base engraved Lydia Rhodes, marked inside base and cover SV in heart, 16dwt (24gr), 5cm (2in) long, *NY 31 Jan*, **$2,970 (£2,106)**

27
A sauce boat, Daniel Henchman, Boston, c.1750, marked Henchman in rectangle, 11oz 12dwt (360gr), 18.5cm (7½in) long, *NY 31 Jan*, **$5,500 (£3,900)**

A
Henricus Boelen II
New York
1697-1755

B
John Coney
Boston, Mass.
1655-1722

C
John Tanner
Newport, R.I.
1713-85

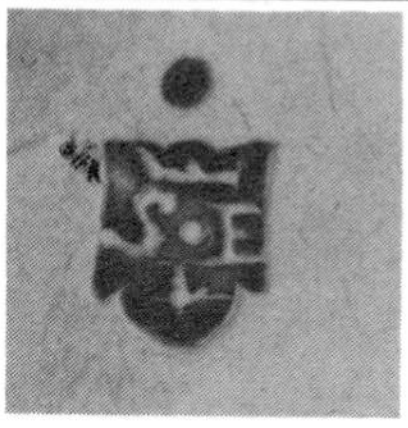

D
Samuel Edwards
Boston, Mass.
1705-62

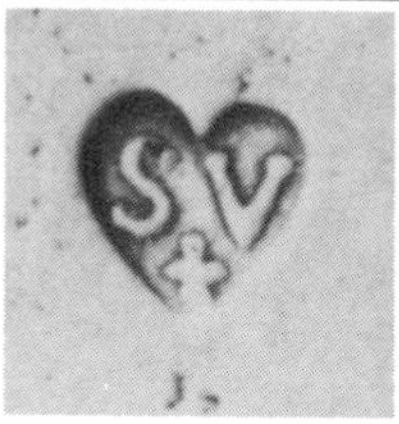

E
Samuel Vernon
Newport, R.I.
1683-1737

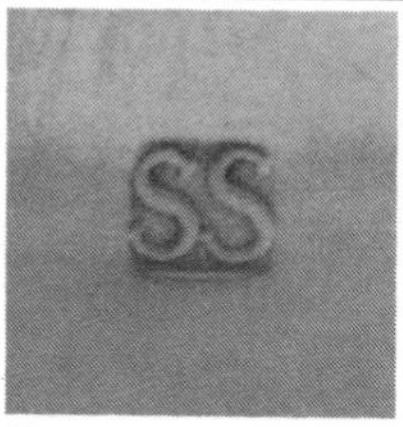

F
Simeon Soumaine
New York
1685-1750

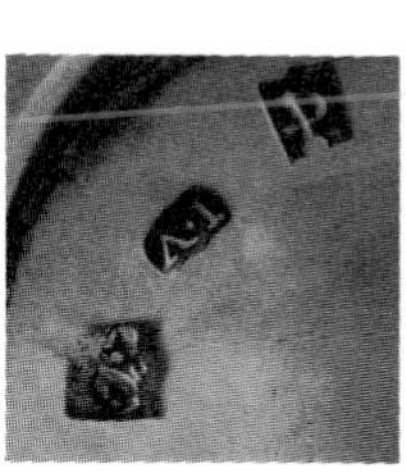

G
John Vernon
(with two pseudo-marks)
New York
from 1787

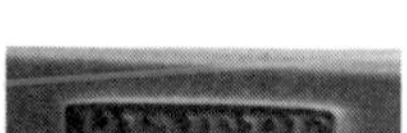

H
Paul Revere Jr
Boston, Mass.
1735-1818

I
Samuel Casey
Exeter & South Kingston, R.I.
1726-80

J
Zachariah Brigden
Boston, Mass.
1734-87

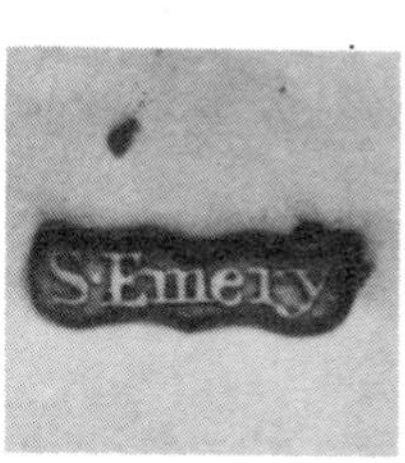

K
Stephen Emery
Boston, Mass.
1752-1801

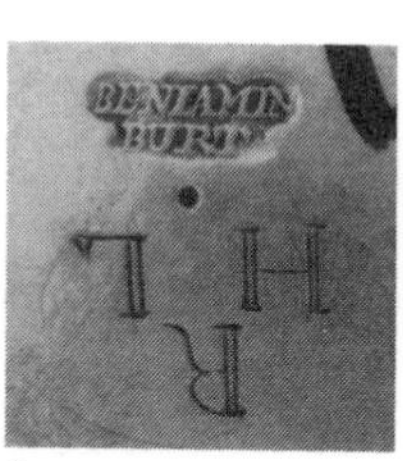

L
Benjamin Burt
Boston, Mass.
1729-1805

M
Ebenezer Moulton
Boston, Mass.
1768-1824

1

2

3

4

5

6

7

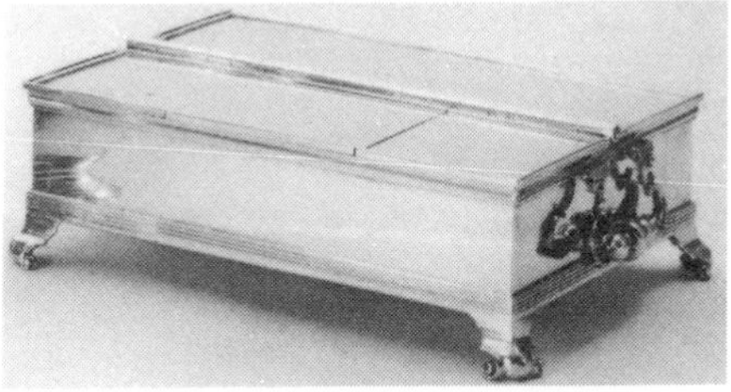
8

9

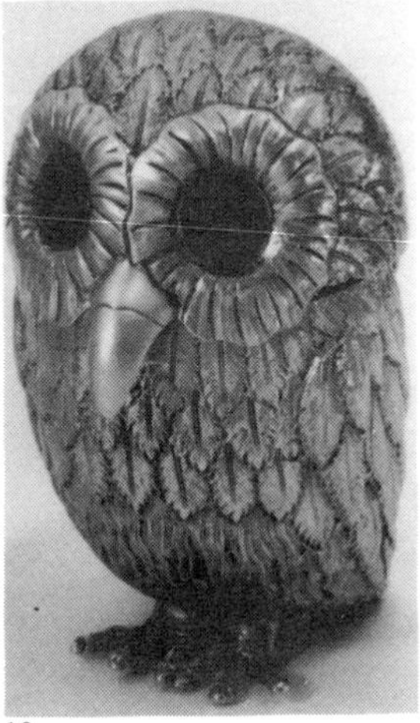
10

1
A George III inkstand, William Plummer, London, 1780, complete with silver-mounted cut glass inkwell, quill holder and caster, with pierced panel supports, 27cm (10½in) long, 22oz 4dwt (690gr), *L 24 Apr,*
£1,210 ($1,936)

2
A George III inkstand, William Elliott, London, 1818, on four winged paw feet, fitted with cut glass seal box, inkwell and sander with silver mounts, 28cm (11in) long, 31oz (964gr), *NY 25 Jan,*
$3,410 (£2,453)

3
A Portuguese inkstand, Joaquim Prudêncio Vital Dinis, Lisbon, c.1830, fitted with two quill holders, inkwell and pounce pot, on claw and ball supports, 18cm (7in) wide, 18oz 7dwt (572gr), *L 8 July,*
£715 ($1,151)

4
A Victorian inkstand, William Ker Reid, London, 1846, on three panel feet, the scroll handle emerging from a mask, complete with two silver-mounted cut glass bottles with detachable covers in the form of a marquess's coronet, 29cm (11½in), 29oz 13dwt (922gr), *L 20 Nov,*
£2,200 ($3,080)

5
A Victorian silver-gilt inkstand, Messrs Barnard, London, 1843, on four Dutch style supports, fitted with two inkwells with Dutch style leafy covers, the back mounted with a pen rest of leafy scrolls and buds, 37.5cm (14½in) long, 47oz 10dwt (1477gr), sold with a silver-gilt letter opener and pen, *NY 5 Nov,*
$11,000 (£7,746)

6
A Spanish inkstand, Royal silver factory, Madrid, c.1800, designed as an Empire sofa, the inkpot and pounce pot shaped as cushions, 23.5cm (9in) long, 17oz 4dwt (536gr), *A 21 Apr,*
Dfl 5,980 (£1,812; $2,845)

7
An early Victorian inkstand, Henry Wilkinson & Co., Sheffield, 1837, the central seal box with detachable taperstick, flanked by two silver-topped cut glass bottles, 29cm (11½in) long, 26oz (808gr), *NY 8 Apr,*
$1,760 (£1,214)

8
A Treasury inkstand, Carrington & Co., London, 1910, with scrolled panel supports, drop handles and centrally hinged lids, gilt interiors, bottles missing, 32cm (12½in) wide, 112oz 2dwt (3486gr), *L 24 Apr,*
£1,540 ($2,464)

9
An Australian silver and gold inkstand, William Edwards, Melbourne, c.1865, retailed by Kilpatrick & Co., the cover of the central seal box with a gold scene of two kangaroos below spreading ferns, and the covers of the two containers formed as emus, inscribed *Presented to John Todd Esquire of Manchester by Thomas Bibby Guest as a token of gratitude for the liberal assistance and continued confidence so generously accorded him, whereby he has been enabled to establish himself in a profitable business in Australia Melbourne Victoria March 1865,* 30.5cm (12in) wide, 53oz 8dwt (1660gr), *NY 5 Nov,*
$36,300 (£25,563)

10
A Victorian novelty inkstand, G. J. Richards, London, 1851, cast and chased in the form of an owl, the head forming a hinged lid with gilt interior, 10cm (4in) high, 4oz 12dwt (143gr), *L 17 July,*
£605 ($950)

1
A model of a donkey, Berthold Müller, London import mark, 1900, 28cm (11in), 32oz (995gr), *HS 24 Sept,*
IR£1,870 (£1,700; $2,465)

2
A model of an Irish setter, Berthold Müller, London import mark, 1900, with detachable head, 32cm (12½in), 20oz (622gr), *HS 24 Sept,*
IR£1,100 (£1,000; $1,450)

3
A model of an ostrich, sponsor's mark of John Smith for J. G. Smith & Co., proprietors of the Continental Daily Parcels Express, London import mark, 1899, detachable back, 41.5cm (16½in), 58oz (1803gr), *HS 24 Sept,*
IR£3,630 (£3,300; $4,785)

4
A model of a cockerel, Berthold Müller, Chester import mark, 1898, the detachable head with wattle and comb cold-enamelled in red, 49.5cm (19½in), 80oz (2488gr), *HS 24 Sept,*
IR£3,190 (£2,900; $4,205)

5
A model of a stork, Berthold Müller, Chester import mark, 1901, detachable head, 44.5cm (17½in), 48oz (1502gr), *HS 24 Sept,*
IR£2,970 (£2,700; $3,915)

6
A model of a stag, Berthold Müller, Chester import mark, 1898, detachable head, 54cm (21¼in), 72oz (2239gr), *HS 24 Sept,*
IR£6,600 (£6,000; $8,700)

7
A model of a kangaroo on marble base, early 20th century, 9cm (3½in), *C 3 Dec,*
£352 ($493)

8
A pair of parcel-gilt figures of a knight and his lady, Neresheimer of Hanau, c.1911-12, importer's mark of B. Muller, London, both with detachable carved ivory heads, 21.5cm (8½in), 28oz 4dwt (877gr), *L 12 June,*
£990 ($1,584)

9
A German model of a monkey, import mark Berthold Müller, London, 1905, 16.5cm (6½in), 14oz 5dwt (443gr), *C 15 Apr,*
£935 ($1,449)

10
Four parcel-gilt wager cups or models, Berthold Müller, Chester import mark, 1898, two as bearded men, two as maidens, the former with detachable stands in the form of their legs on grassy base, 35 and 38cm (13¾ and 15in), 103oz (3203gr), *HS 24 Sept,*
IR£4,730 (£4,300; $6,235)

11
A model of an elephant, sponsor's mark of S. B. Landeck, London import mark, 1900, with detachable head, 28cm (11in) long, 39oz (1212gr), *HS 24 Sept,*
IR£3,190 (£2,900; $4,205)

12
A German parcel-gilt figure of a knight on horseback, c.1900, his armour set with cabochon stones, 41oz (1275gr), 24cm (9½in), *NY 14 Oct,*
$2,310 (£1,604)

13
A pair of German parcel-gilt figures of a knight and a lady, 20th century, the bases set with cabochon stones, both with carved ivory heads, the lady with ivory hands, 23.5 and 25cm (9¼ and 9in), 35oz (1089gr), *NY 14 Oct,*
$2,200 (£1,528)

14
A German nef, late 19th century, the deck applied with numerous armed sailors and cannon, on four sea horse supports with casters, 58cm (22¾in), 75oz (2333gr), *NY 5 Nov,*
$3,575 (£2,518)

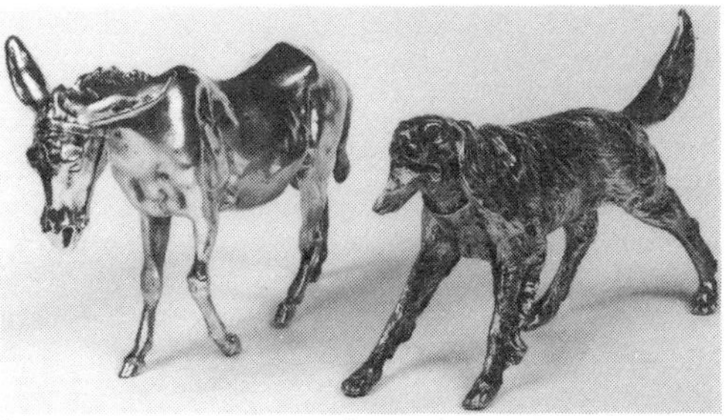

1 2

6

3 4 5

9

7

8

10

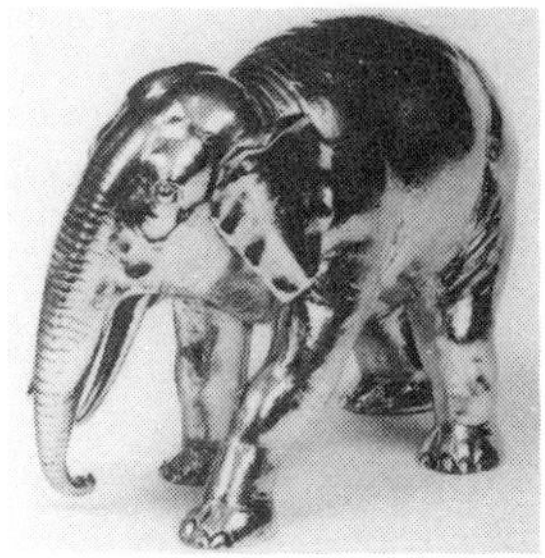

11

12 13

14

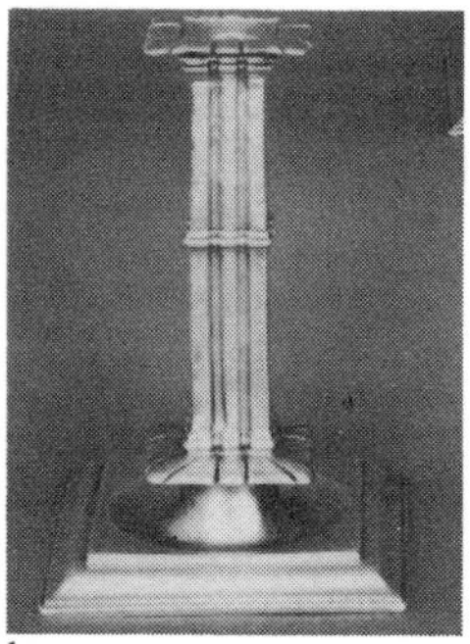
1

2

3

4

5

6

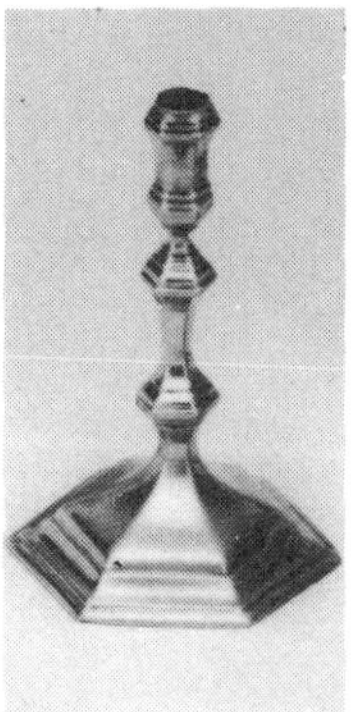
7

8 9

10

11

12

13

1
A pair of French table candlesticks, *(one illustrated)*, maker's mark L.M. with a star and a moon, Orléans, c.1680, detachable nozzles, 19cm (7½in), 33oz 14dwt (1050gr), *M 24 June,*
FF 388,500 (£34,657; $54,064)

2
A pair of William III table candlesticks, Richard Syng, London, 1699, the bases with later crest, 25.5cm (10in), 30oz (933gr), *HS 24 Sept,*
IR£3,080 (£2,800; $4,060)

3
A pair of French table candlesticks, *(one illustrated)*, probably by Pierre Merlin, Paris, 1686, 18cm (7in), 27oz 8dwt (855gr), *M 24 June,*
FF 222,000 (£19,804; $30,894)

4
A pair of German table candlesticks, *(one illustrated)*, Johann Pepfenhauser II (Seling, no.1919), Augsburg, 1708-10, 19.5cm (7¾in), 27oz 6dwt (849gr), *NY 5 Nov,*
$8,800 (£6,197)

5
A set of four George I table candlesticks, Augustin Courtauld, 1719, 15cm (6in), 53oz (1648gr), *NY 5 Nov,*
$25,300 (£17,817)

6
A pair of George I table candlesticks, *(one illustrated)*, Jacob Margas, London, 1719, 16cm (6½in), 26oz 4dwt (817gr), *NY 12 June,*
$3,960 (£2,605)

7
A George I taperstick, London, 1713, maker's mark rubbed, 11cm (4¼in), 2oz 14dwt (87gr), *M 24 June,*
FF 3,330 (£297; $463)

8
A George I taperstick, James Gould, London, 1724, 10.5cm (4¼in), 3oz 10dwt (108gr), *L 19 June,*
£990 ($1,564)

9
A George I taperstick, William Darker, London, 1725, 11cm (4¼in), 3oz 10dwt (108gr), *L 19 June,*
£1,210 ($1,912)

10
A pair of French table candlesticks, *(one illustrated)*, Gilles Gouel, Paris, 1713, engraved with armorials, probably of the Neys of Lorraine family, detachable nozzles, 23cm (9in), 41oz 2dwt (1280gr), *M 24 June,*
FF 122,100 (£10,892; $16,992)

11
A pair of Swiss table candlesticks, *(one illustrated)*, Jérôme-Paul Lenoir, Geneva, c.1730, 21.5cm (8½in), 28oz 4dwt (880gr), *G 11 Nov,*
SF 19,800 (£8,182; $11,700)

12
A pair of George II table candlesticks, *(one illustrated)*, John Luff, London, 1739, 18cm (7in), 31oz 16dwt (989gr), *L 17 July,*
£3,740 ($5,872)

13
A pair of George II table candlesticks, *(one illustrated)*, Dublin, c.1745, detachable nozzles, 20cm (8in), 30oz 17dwt (943gr), *L 16 Oct,*
£1,760 ($2,464)

1
A pair of German table candlesticks, *(one illustrated)*, Antoni Grill II, Augsburg, 1732-33, 16.5cm (6½in), 16oz 10dwt (513gr), *NY 8 Apr,*
$3,575 (£2,466)

2
A pair of Italian table candlesticks, *(one illustrated)*, Naples, 1746, 17.5cm (6¾in), 14oz 4dwt (444gr), *F 14 Apr,*
L 4,200,000 (£1,720; $2,666)

3
A pair of French table candlesticks, *(one illustrated)*, maker's mark A.B., Lille, 1779, 26cm (10¼in), 25oz 3dwt (774gr), *L 11 Feb,*
£2,530 ($3,719)

4
A pair of German table candlesticks, *(one illustrated)*, Wilhelm Heinrich Gerhard Dautzenberg, Aachen, c.1760, 20cm (8in), 20oz 6dwt (632gr), *G 13 May,*
SF 18,700 (£6,318; $10,171)

5
Four Dutch table candlesticks, three maker's mark Willem Brandenburg, 1763-64, the fourth Beniamgen Overdorp, 1728, all Deventer, 20cm (8in), 58oz (1806gr), *G 11 Nov,*
SF 29,700 (£12,273; $17,550)

6
A pair of German table candlesticks, *(one illustrated)*, Johann Jakob Baur V, Augsburg, 1777-79, 21.5cm (8½in), 18oz 15dwt (582gr), *L 11 Feb,*
£2,310 ($3,396)

7
A pair of German table candlesticks, *(one illustrated)*, Johann Georg Eckhardt, Hannover-Neustadt, c.1770, 21cm (8¼in), 33oz 2dwt (1030gr), *G 11 Nov,*
SF 17,600 (£7,273; $10,400)

8
A pair of French provincial table candlesticks, *(one illustrated)*, maker's mark M.O.J., Béthune, 18th century, 22cm (8½in), 29oz 10dwt (920gr), *G 11 Nov,*
SF 12,100 (£5,000; $7,150)

9
A pair of French table candlesticks, *(one illustrated)*, Orléans, 1780-82, 20.5cm (8in), 21oz 16dwt (680gr), *M 24 Feb,*
FF 16,650 (£1,610; $2,415)

10
A pair of George II table candlesticks, *(one illustrated)*, Ebenezer Coker, London, 1769, detachable nozzles, 25.5cm (10in), 36oz 13dwt (1139gr), *C 7 Oct,*
£1,760 ($2,464)

11
A set of four George II table candlesticks, John Cafe, London, 1752, detachable nozzles, 21cm (8¼in), 66oz 16dwt (2076gr), *L 6 Feb,*
£3,850 ($5,621)

12
A set of four George III table candlesticks, William Cripps, London, 1768, detachable nozzles, 31.5cm (12¼in), loaded, *L 20 Nov,*
£2,640 ($3,696)

13
A set of four George III table candlesticks, *(two illustrated)*, George Ashforth & Co., Sheffield, 1781, detachable nozzles, 30cm (11¾in), loaded, *S 19 Sept,*
£4,070 ($5,698)

1

2

3

4

5

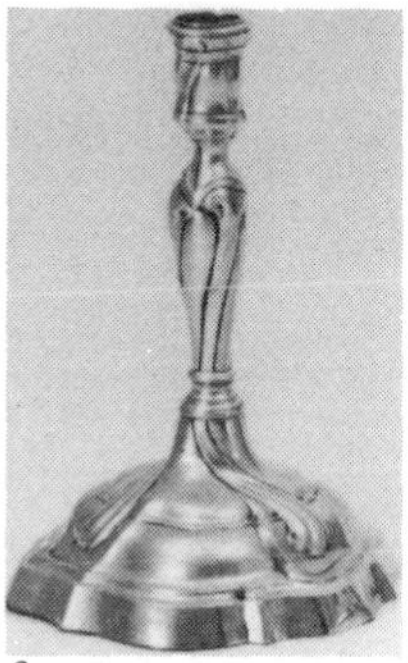
6

7

8

9

10

11

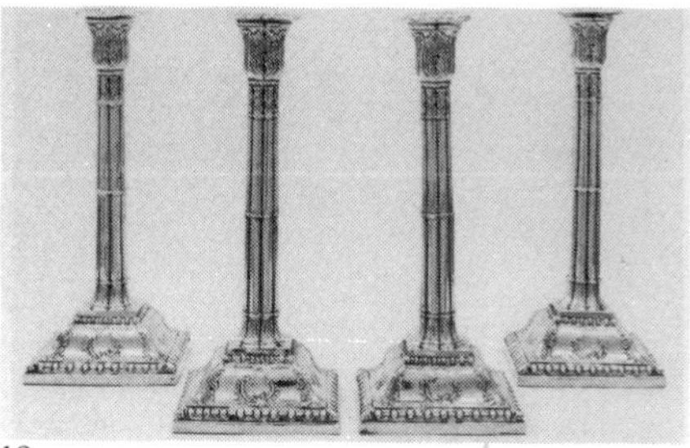
12

13

1

2

3

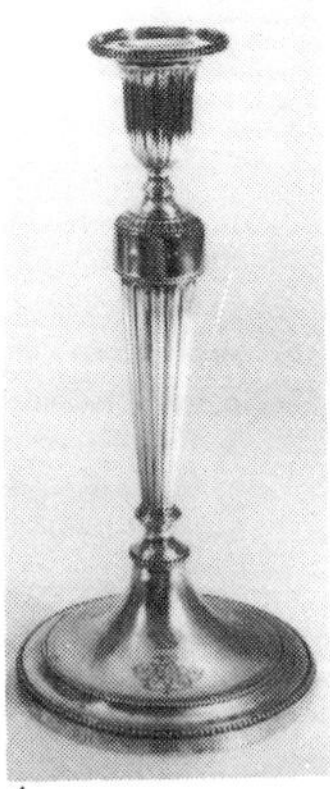
4

5

6

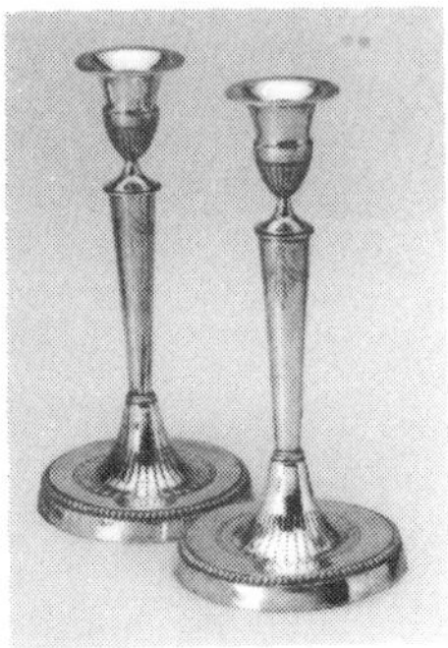
7

8

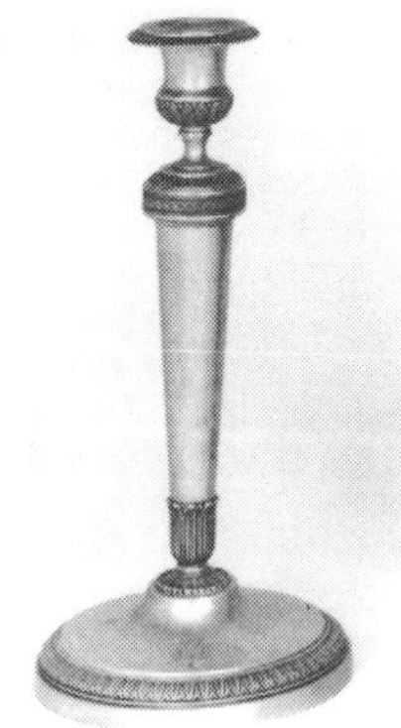
9

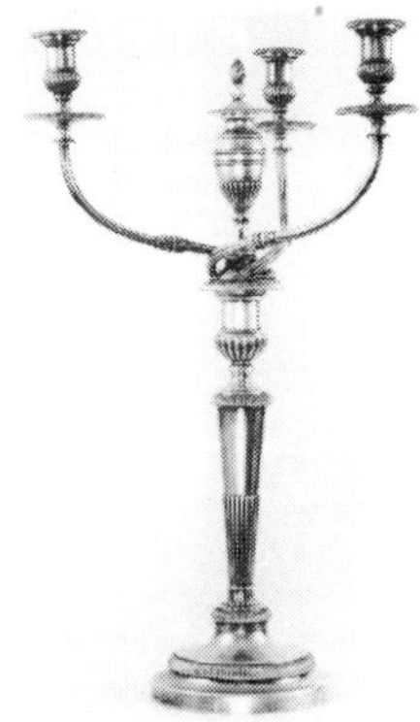
10

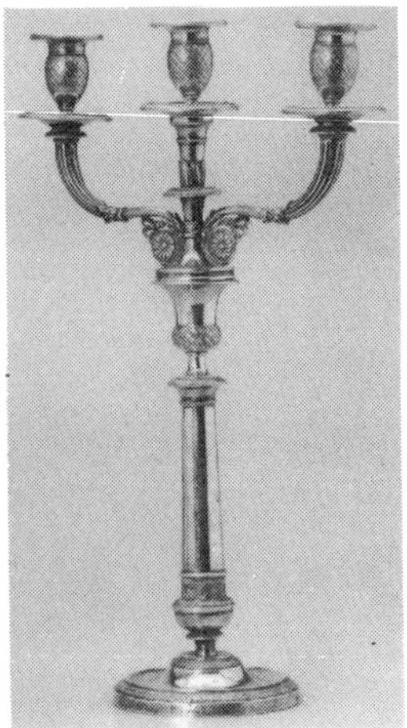
11

12

13

1
A pair of George III table candlesticks, *(one illustrated)*, William Cafe, London, 1761, 27cm (10½in), 50oz (1555gr), *NY 12 June*,
$4,180 (£2,750)

2
A pair of Flemish table candlesticks, *(one illustrated)*, maker's mark H in a rectangle, Malines, 1795, detachable nozzles, 28.5cm (11¼in), 27oz (840gr), *G 11 Nov*,
SF 4,400 (£1,818; $2,600)

3
A pair of George III silver-gilt table candlesticks, *(one illustrated)*, Benjamin Smith II and III, London, 1817, in late 18th century style, from the collection of William Beckford of Fonthill Abbey, detachable nozzles, 19cm (7½in), 40oz (1244gr), *NY 12 Dec*,
$13,750 (£9,821)

4
A pair of George III table candlesticks, *(one illustrated)*, John Scofield, London, 1799, detachable nozzles, 28.5cm (11¼in), 29oz 11dwt (919gr), *L 19 June*,
£2,640 ($4,171)

5
A set of six George III table candlesticks *(two illustrated)* **with two two-light candelabra branches,** John Green & Co., Sheffield, 1794/95, 50.5cm (20in), loaded, *NY 19 Sept*,
$16,500 (£11,149)

6
Four George IV table candlesticks, *(one illustrated)*, S. C. Younge & Co., Sheffield, 1822, detachable nozzles, 29cm (11¼in), *L 16 Oct*,
£1,980 ($2,772)

7
A pair of Italian table candlesticks, Rome, Antonio Cappelletti, c.1815, 24.5cm (10in), 9oz 2dwt (284gr), *F 30 Sept*,
L 1,540,000 (£767; $1,074)

8
A pair of Dutch table candlesticks, Rudolph Sondag, Rotterdam, late 18th century, detachable nozzles, 28cm (11in), 36oz (1120gr), *A 12 June*,
Dfl 5,405 (£1,618; $2,589)

9
A pair of French table candlesticks, *(one illustrated)*, Jacques-Gabriel-André Bompart, Paris, c.1825, detachable nozzles, 26.5cm (10¼in), 33oz 2dwt (1030gr), *M 24 June*,
FF 6,660 (£594; $927)

10
A George III four-light candelabrum, Matthew Boulton, Birmingham, 1804, detachable nozzles, 66cm (26in), 140oz 12dwt (4373gr), *S 23 Apr*,
£2,310 ($3,627)

11
A pair of Italian three-light candelabra, *(one illustrated)*, Emanuele Caber, Milan, c.1830, 40cm (15¾in), 54oz 2dwt (1685gr), *F 30 Sept*,
L 6,050,000 (£3,014; $4,220)

12
A pair of William IV table candlesticks, *(one illustrated)*, Storr & Mortimer, London, 1836, maker's mark of Paul Storr, after a design used by Paul Crespin based upon a Régence original, with the crest of the Earls of Ashburnham, 25.5cm (10in), 47oz (1461gr), *NY 5 Nov*,
$18,150 (£12,782)

13
A pair of Victorian seven-light candelabra, *(one illustrated)*, R. & S. Garrard & Co., London, 1875/79, detachable nozzles, 69.5cm (27¼in), 447oz 15dwt (13926gr), *L 6 Feb*,
£16,500 ($24,090)

1
A pair of Victorian five-light candelabra, *(one illustrated)*, West & Son of Dublin, London, 1897, 59cm (23¼in), *L 16 Oct,*
£4,400 ($6,160)

2
A pair of American table candlesticks, *(one illustrated)*, William Meyers, Newark, N.J., 20th century, detachable nozzles, 31.5cm (12½in), 34oz (1057gr), *NY 26 June,*
$825 (£546)

3
A set of four American table candlesticks, *(two illustrated)*, early 20th century, retailed by Tiffany & Co., detachable nozzles, 23.5cm (9¼in), 85oz (2643gr), *NY 14 Oct,*
$2,310 (£1,604)

4
A pair of four-light candelabra and two pairs of candlesticks en suite, *(one candelabra and one pair candlesticks illustrated)*, Hawksworth, Eyre & Co., Sheffield, 1894-95, in early 18th century style, 38.5 and 25.5cm (15¼ and 10in), loaded, *C 14 Jan,*
£2,640 ($3,960)

5
A pair of table candlesticks, *(one illustrated)*, maker's mark WL & S., Sheffield, 1907, detachable nozzles, 25.5cm (10in), loaded, *C 17 Dec,*
£484 ($678)

6
A pair of Adam-style table candlesticks, *(one illustrated)*, Sheffield, 1908, 30cm (11¾in), loaded, *C 23 July,*
£506 ($794)

7
A pair of three-light candelabra, *(one illustrated)*, Adie Bros., Birmingham, 1934, 29cm (11½in), 36oz 2dwt (1122gr), *C 6 Aug,*
£726 ($1,125)

8
A Swiss chamber candlestick, maker's mark R.H., Schaffhausen, c.1750, 10cm (4in) square, 4oz (125gr), *L 11 Feb,*
£1,650 ($2,426)

9
A George II chamber candlestick, Edward Wakelin, London, 1748, 14cm (5½in) diam., 10oz 17dwt (337gr), *L 16 Oct,*
£1,870 ($2,618)

10
A George III chamber candlestick, Nathan Smith & Co., Sheffield, 1806, detachable nozzle, 10.5cm (4in) wide, 10oz 12dwt (330gr), *JHB 11 Nov,*
R 2,600 (£813; $1,138)

11
A pair of chamber candlesticks, *(one illustrated)*, Garrard & Co. Ltd. of London, Birmingham, 1979, detachable nozzles and extinguishers, 10cm (4in), 27oz 10dwt (855gr), *L 14 July,*
£418 ($652)

12
A pair of William IV chamber candlesticks, Edward Barnard & Sons, London, 1830, detachable nozzles and extinguishers, 14.5cm (5½in) diam., 24oz 8dwt (758gr), *L 16 Oct,*
£1,760 ($2,464)

13
A George III wax jack, Burrage Davenport, London, 1776, 13.5cm (5¼in), 5oz (155gr), *NY 25 Jan,*
$1,210 (£870)

1

2

3

4

5

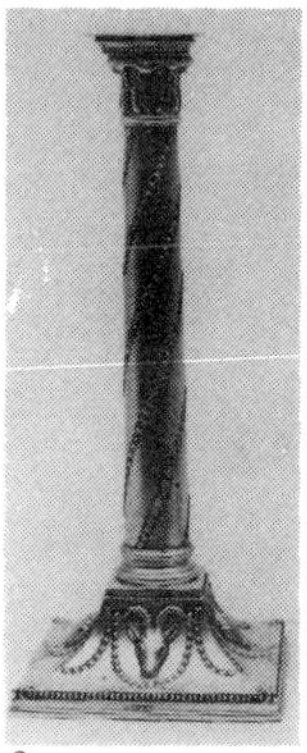
6

8

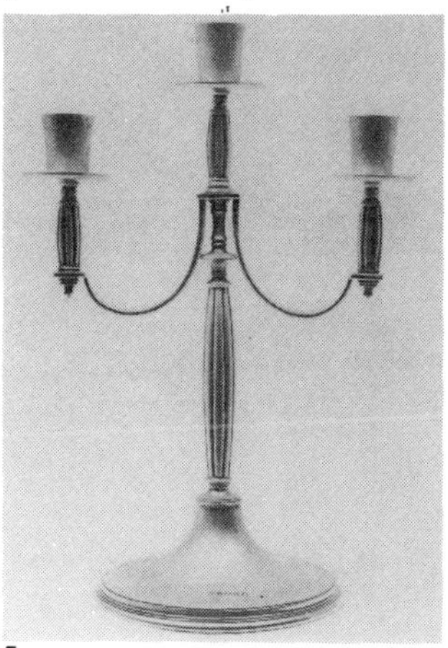
7

9

10

11

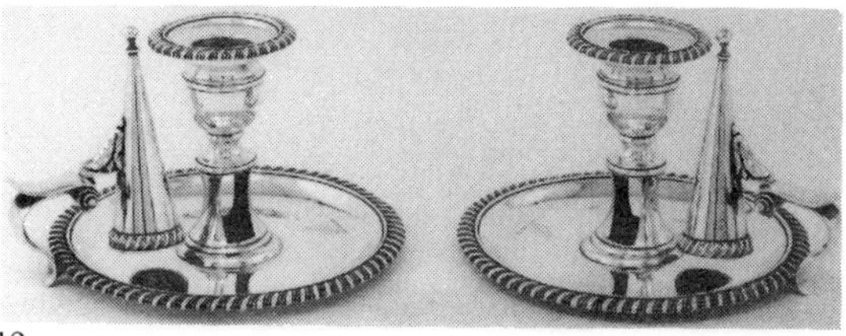
12

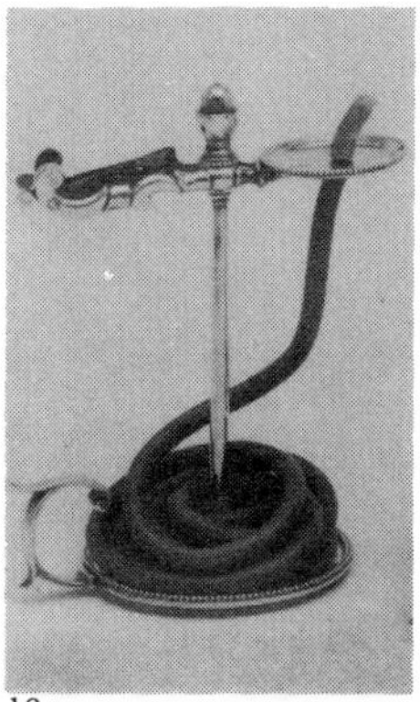
13

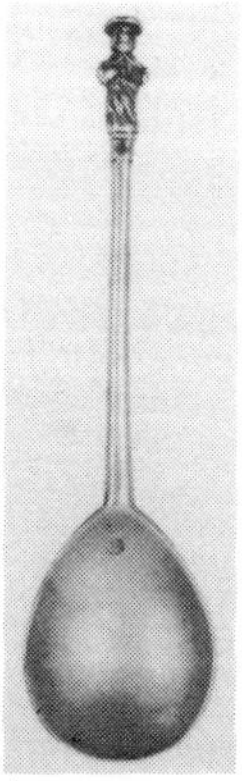
1

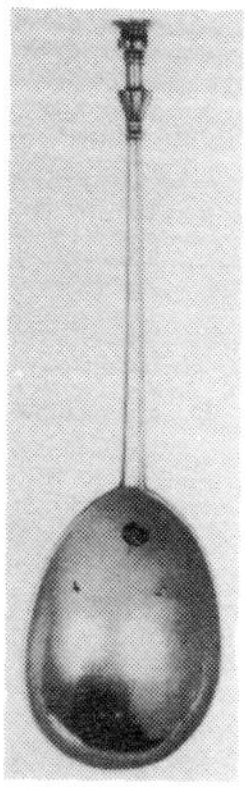
2

3

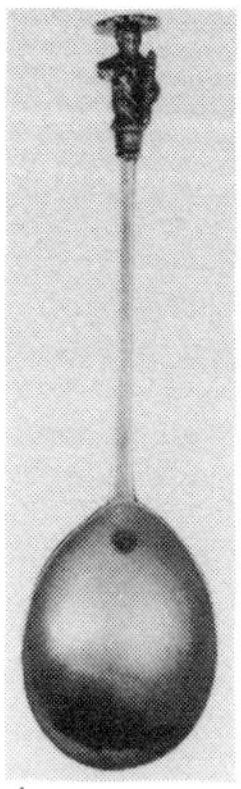
4

5

6

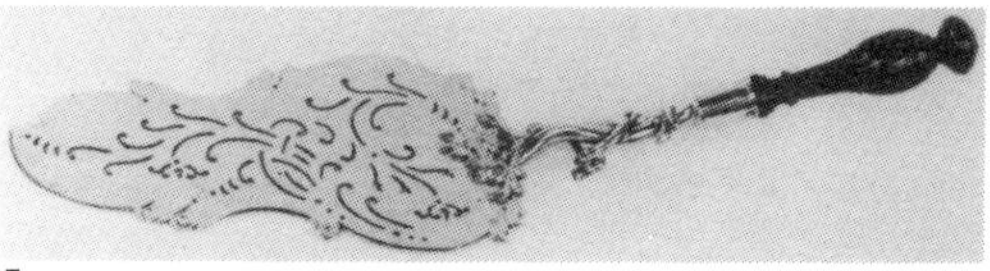
7

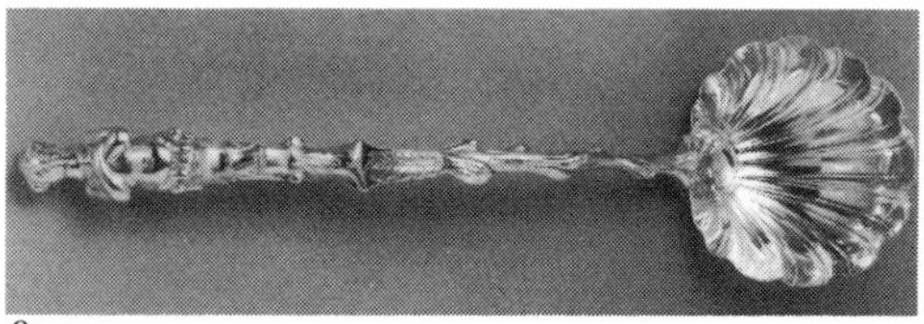
8

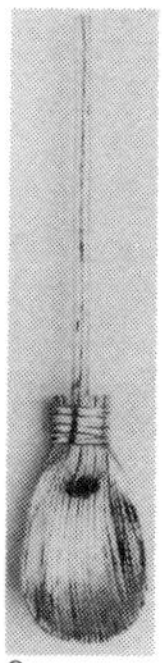
9

10

11

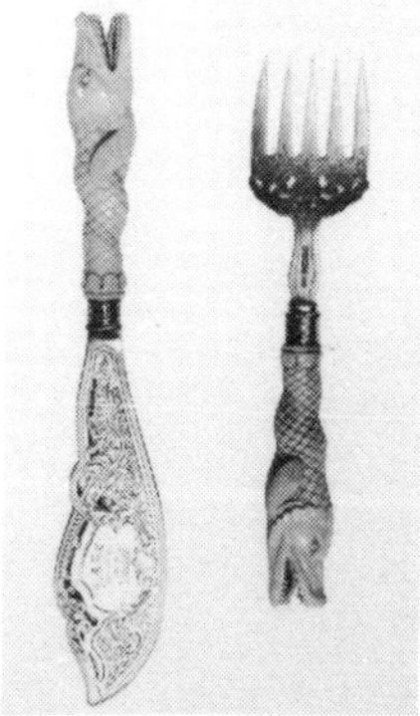
12

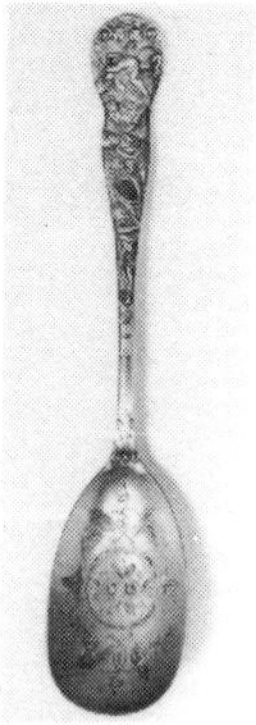
13

14

15

1
A Henry VIII apostle spoon, William Simpson, London, 1535, possibly St. Matthew, 1oz 11dwt (48gr), *L 24 Apr,*
£1,155 ($1,848)

2
A seal top spoon, Truro, c.1600, the terminal pricked with the date 1611 over earlier date, 18cm (7in), *L 24 Apr,*
£352 ($563)

3
A James I provincial seal top spoon, Christopher Harrington, York, 1608, 16cm (6½in), 1oz 14dwt (52gr), *C 7 Oct,*
£506 ($708)

4
An apostle spoon, Truro, c.1650, St. James the Less, 1oz 10dwt (46gr), *L 24 Apr,*
£715 ($1,144)

5
An apostle spoon, Edward Anthony, Exeter, c.1650, emblem missing, 18.5cm (7¼in), *L 24 Apr,*
£550 ($880)

6
A William III marrow spoon, maker's mark T.T. crowned, London, 1696, 18cm (7in), 16dwt (24gr), *NY 12 June,*
$1,100 (£724)

7
A German cake slice, apparently Johann Hues, Hamburg, c.1775, *M 24 June,*
FF 17,760 (£1,584; $2,472)

8
A William IV soup ladle, Edward Farrell, London, 1831, the handle cast with a female demi-figure, 38.5cm (15¼in), 15oz 10dwt (482gr), *NY 12 June,*
$1,870 (£1,230)

9
A Victorian parcel-gilt sugar spoon, C. T. & G. Fox, London, 1861, in the form of a rustic broom, 16.5cm (6¾in), 1oz 11dwt (48gr), *L 16 Oct,*
£396 ($554)

10
A Victorian silver-gilt three-piece christening set, Mortimer & Hunt, London, 1840, the gift of Queen Victoria and each piece engraved on one side with her cypher, 18-23cm (7-9in), 10oz (311gr), *L 17 July,*
£1,320 ($2,072)

11
Fiddle-thread and shell pattern table silver, *(part illustrated),* the majority William Traies, London 1828-46, comprising 107 pieces, 323oz (10045gr), *L 6 Feb,*
£5,720 ($8,351)

12
A pair of Victorian fish servers, Harrison Bros. & Howson, Sheffield, 1868, the ivory handles carved as sea serpents, *C 7 Oct,*
£462 ($647)

13
A Victorian parcel-gilt Bacchanalian pattern dessert set, *(one illustrated),* H. & H. Lias, London, 1870, comprising six serving spoons and a sifter ladle, 20oz 22dwt (625gr), *C 7 Oct,*
£594 ($832)

14
A Victorian silver-gilt dessert set, *(part illustrated),* Francis Higgins, London, 1851, in a chased and pierced vine pattern, comprising twelve knives, twelve forks and twelve spoons, 49oz (1523gr), *NY 12 Dec,*
$2,420 (£1,729)

15
Georgian and later Kings pattern silver-gilt table silver, *(part illustrated),* London, 1819-65, fish knives and forks and cheese knives, 1951, 328oz (10200gr) of weighable silver, *NY 12 June,*
$8,800 (£5,789)

1
Victorian table silver, *(part illustrated)*, George Adams, London, 1875-77, fiddle and thread pattern, comprising 134 pieces, 233oz (7246gr), with modern knives, *NY 5 Nov,*
$8,525 (£6,004)

2
A set of twelve American dinner forks, *(part illustrated)*, Tiffany & Co., c.1880, in the lap-over-edge pattern, the handles engraved with flowers, foliage, birds, insects, a seahorse or fish, 30oz (933gr), *NY 14 Oct,*
$1,210 (£840)

3
A set of German table silver, *(part illustrated)*, Koch & Bergfeld, Bremen, 1895, comprising 153 pieces, 136oz 12dwt (4249gr), *F 14 Apr,*
L 7,500,000 (£3,071; $4,760)

4
An American silver-gilt and parcel-gilt dessert set, *(part illustrated)*, designed by Charles T. Grosjean for W. K. Vanderbilt, Tiffany & Co., New York, 1884, comprising 12 forks, 12 spoons, 12 knives and 12 small forks, all decorated with hunting and mythological subjects, 86oz 10dwt (2690gr), *NY 26 June,*
$9,075 (£6,010)

5
A set of French table silver, *(part illustrated)*, Odiot, Paris, third quarter 19th century, fiddle pattern, comprising 236 pieces in fitted box, 419oz (13030gr), *NY 8 Apr,*
$10,450 (£7,207)

6
A set of American table silver, *(part illustrated)*, Gorham Mfg. Co., 20th century, comprising 176 pieces, 210oz (6531gr), *NY 14 Oct,*
$4,400 (£3,056)

7
American table silver, *(part illustrated)*, Gorham & Co., Providence, R.I., c.1897, comprising 182 pieces including 24 table forks and dessert spoons, 241oz 10dwt (7500gr), *L 11 Feb,*
£2,090 ($3,072)

8
A set of French table silver, *(part illustrated)*, Cardeilhac, Paris, c.1920, comprising 353 pieces in fitted box, 500oz (15550gr) of weighable silver, *NY 12 Dec,*
$23,100 (£16,500)

9
A set of American table silver, *(part illustrated)*, Tiffany & Co., New York, c.1925, St. Dunstan pattern, comprising 361 pieces, 428oz (13310gr), of weighable silver, in fitted box, *NY 26 June,*
$15,950 (£10,563)

1

2

3

4

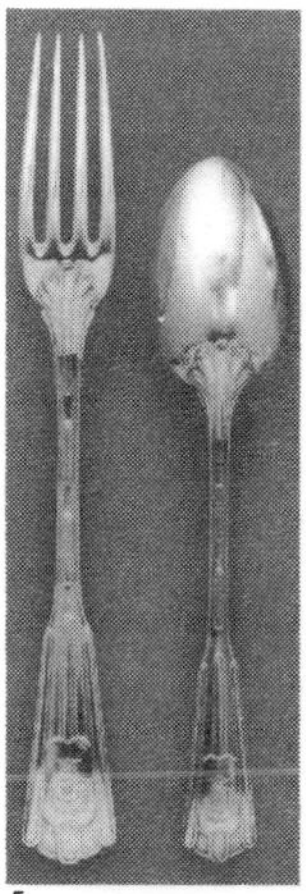
5

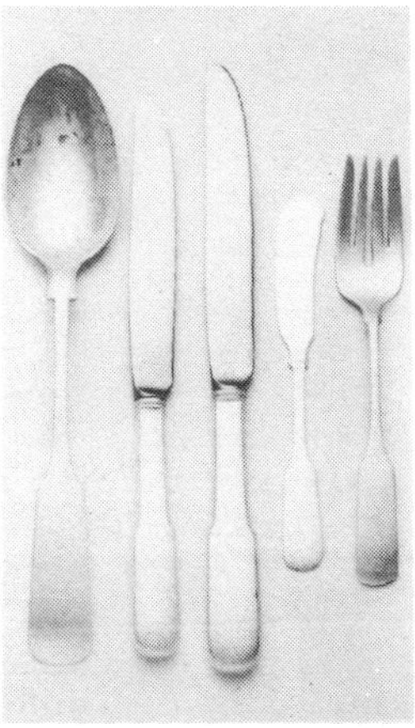
6

7

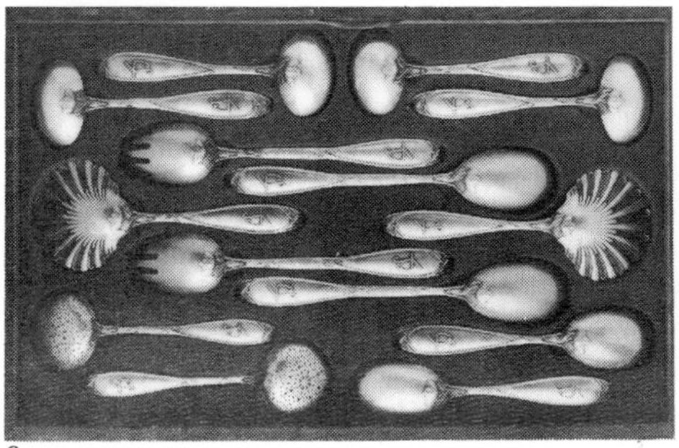
8

9

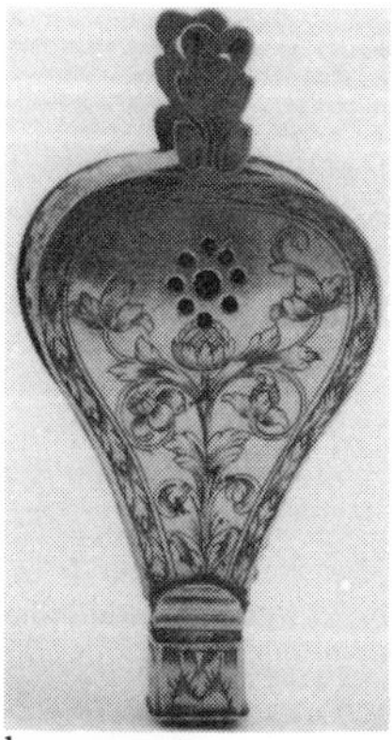
1

2

3

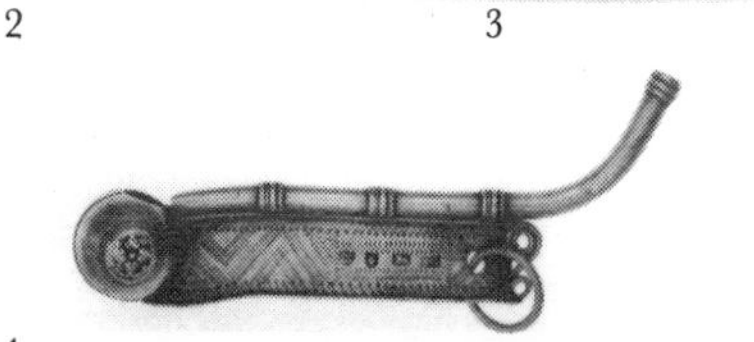
4

5

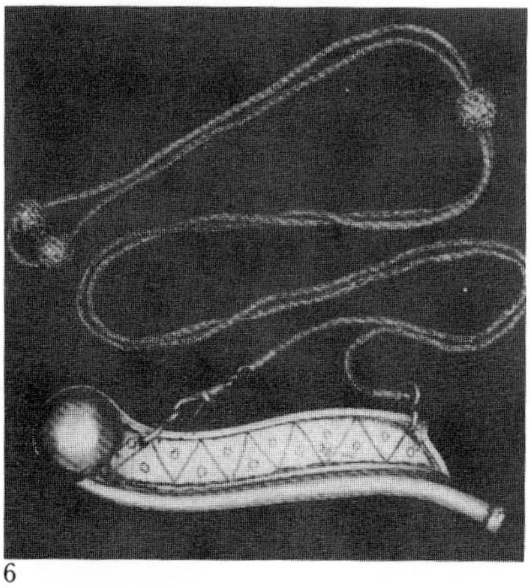
6

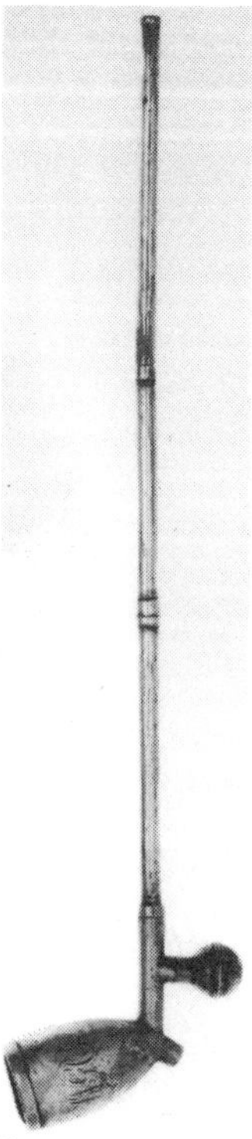
7

8

9

10

11

12

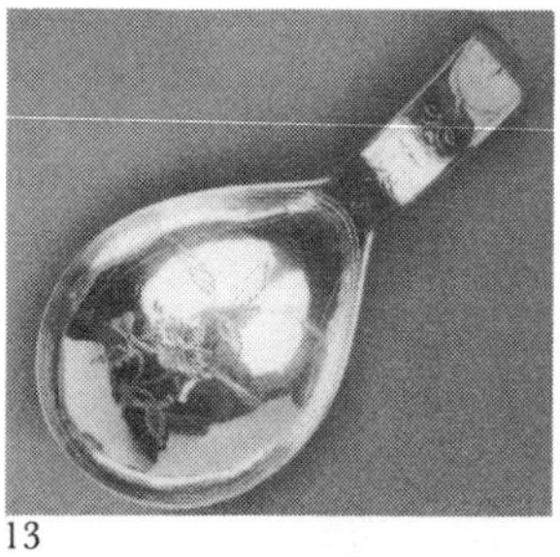
13

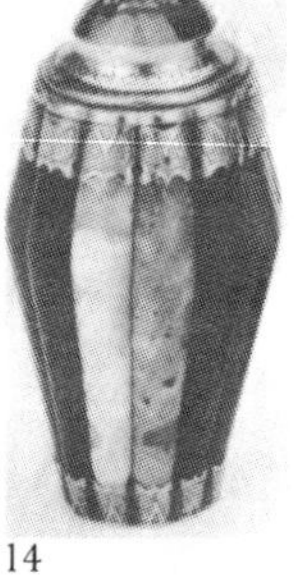
14

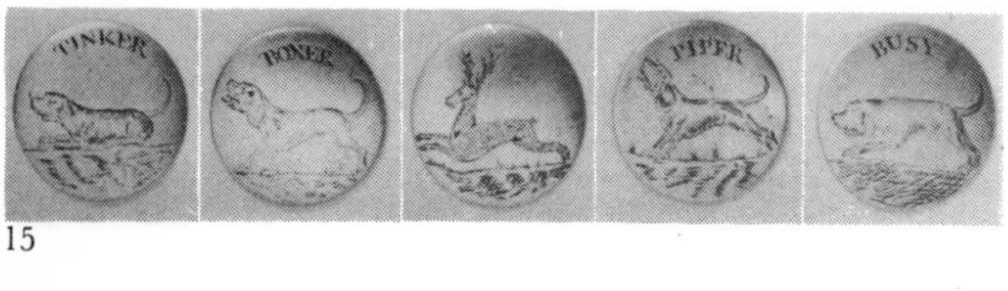

15

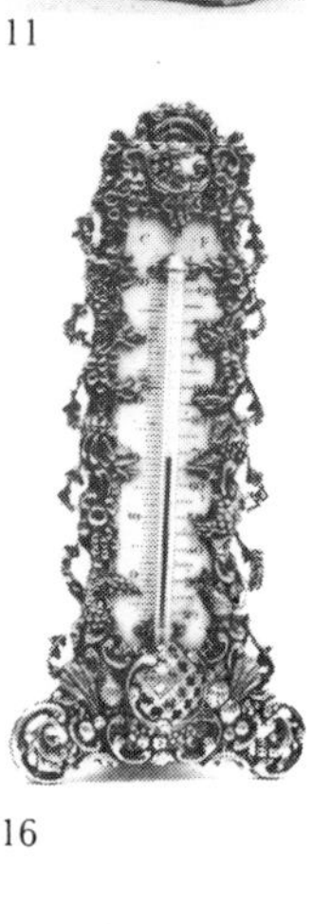
16

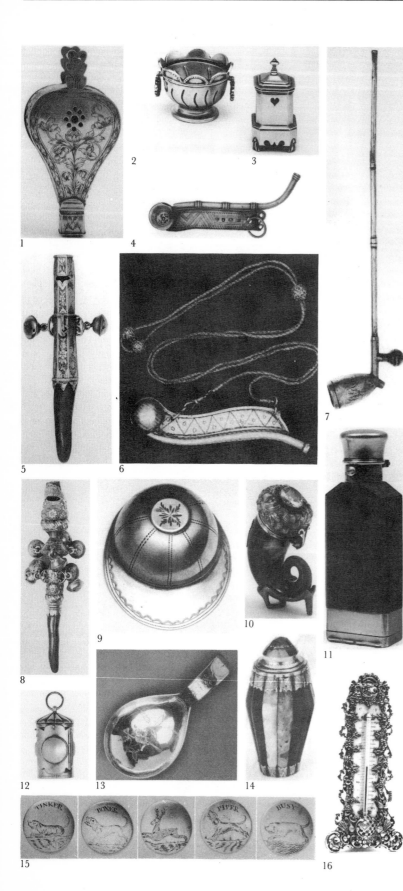

1
A miniature pair of silver-gilt bellows, probably Dutch, late 17th century, with detachable cap and leather windbag showing traces of silk covering, 8cm (3in), *G 11 Nov,*
SF 2,090 (£864; $1,235)

2
A Dutch miniature wine cooler, 18th century, 7cm (2¾in) diam., 2oz 8dwt (75gr), *A 21 Apr,*
Dfl 2,415 (£732; $1,149)

3
A Dutch miniature brazier with cover, Arnoldus van Geffen, Amsterdam, 1751, 7cm (2¾in) high, 2oz 14dwt (84gr), *A 21 Apr,*
Dfl 4,830 (£1,464; $2,298)

4
A George II bosun's whistle, maker's mark IR (perhaps John Raymond), London, 1757, 14cm (5½in) long, 1oz 5dwt (38gr), *L 24 Apr,*
£792 ($1,267)

5
A George II gold child's rattle, mid 18th century, apparently unmarked, fitted at one end with a coral teether and at the other with a whistle, also fitted with scroll mounts supporting three bells (one missing), 13.5cm (5¼in) long, *C 25 June,*
£990 ($1,544)

6
A large George III bosun's whistle, dated 1789, on silver neck chain, 16cm (6¼in), *L 3 June,*
£1,265 ($1,960)

7
A tobacco pipe, c.1800, of contemporary clay pipe form, with detachable residue collector and three-part stem, 26cm (10¼in), *L 24 Apr,*
£385 ($616)

8
A George III child's rattle, Richard May of London, c.1765, maker's mark only, hung with eight bells in tiers, coral teether, 16cm (6¼in), *C 7 Oct,*
£330 ($462)

9
A George III jockey cap caddy spoon, Joseph Taylor, Birmingham, 1798, 5cm (2in) wide, *S 19 Feb,*
£286 ($435)

10
A Victorian snuff mull, unmarked, c.1880, with horn body, 12cm (4¾in), *HH 29 Apr,*
£352 ($570)

11
A Victorian scent-bottle-cum-vinaigrette, London, 1865, with silver-gilt mounts, the body of blue glass, 9.5cm (3¾in) high, *C 14 May,*
£165 ($266)

12
A Victorian silver-gilt Vesta case/fusee/cigar cutter, H. W. & L. Dee, London, 1869, in the form of a railway lantern, the glass front concealing the fusee wheel and vesta striker, the base fitted with a sliding steel cigar cutter, 4.5cm (2in) high excluding ring, *L 6 Feb,*
£682 ($997)

13
A George III caddy spoon, Birmingham, late 18th century, perhaps by Samuel Pemberton, wriggleworked and punched with leaves and flowers, 8cm (3in) long, 5oz (155gr), *Mel 24 June,*
Aus$72 (£31; $49)

14
A scent-bottle, Scottish, c.1840-60, maker's mark M.C. & Co., composed of various hardstones, with gold mounts, the cover inset with a citrine, 7.5cm (3in) high, *M 1 Dec,*
FF 18,700 (£2,033; $2,907)

15
A set of thirteen stag hunt buttons, *(five illustrated),* eight Thomas Tearle, c.1740, the other five William Dean or William Downes, c.1770, 3.5cm (1¼in) diam., 3oz 4dwt (99.5gr), *S 19 Sept,*
£1,540 ($2,156)

16
A silver-mounted thermometer, William Comyns, London, 1896, 20cm (8in), *C 29 Jan,*
£319 ($469)

1
A William and Mary nutmeg grater, maker's mark T.K. (?Thomas Kedder), c.1690-1700, 5.5cm (2¼in), *NY 8 Apr,*
$550 (£379)

2
An early 18th century English snuff box, marks rubbed, 7cm (2¾in), 2oz 5dwt (70gr), *Mel 24 June,*
Aus$330 (£143; $224)

3
A snuff box, probably English, late 17th century, mark obscured, 7.5cm (3in), *S 12 Nov,*
£352 ($493)

4
A Queen Anne tobacco box, Edward Cornock, London, 1713, 9.5cm (3¾in), 3oz 17dwt (119gr), *L 16 Oct,*
£1,100 ($1,540)

5
A German box and cover, David Baumann, Augsburg, c.1690, the cover engraved with an old man in a landscape, 8cm (3in), 2oz 2dwt (66gr), *G 11 Nov,*
SF 3,300 (£1,364; $1,950)

6
A Queen Anne patch box, Thomas Kedder, London, c.1710, stamped with the monarch's head and the letters *Q* and *A*, 2.5cm (1in) diam., *Syd 12 Nov,*
Aus$264 (£120; $168)

7
A Dutch silver-gilt marriage casket, c.1680, maker's mark indistinct, later fitted with two mounted green cut glass scent bottles, 7cm (2¾in) wide, *L 8 July,*
£2,860 ($4,605)

8
A Dutch tobacco box, probably Johannes Henricus Bing, Amsterdam, 1805, stamped with three scenes of the parable of The Prodigal Son, 16.5cm (6½in), 6oz 7dwt (198gr), *L 11 Feb,*
£440 ($647)

9
A George III nutmeg grater, Thomas Hyde, London, 1789, 4.5cm (1¾in), *L 16 Oct,*
£440 ($616)

10
A George IV nutmeg grater, Thomas Shaw, Birmingham, 1829, 5cm (2in), *Mel 24 June,*
Aus$396 (£172; $269)

11
A George III nutmeg grater, Samuel Massey, London, c.1790, of egg-shaped form, 5cm (2in), *Syd 12 Nov,*
Aus$352 (£160; $224)

12
A William IV cigar case, Henry Wilkinson & Co., Sheffield, 1832, engraved on one side with a man holding two hounds in the grounds of a Palladian mansion, and on the other with the dogs chasing a hare, 13.5cm (5¼in), *HH 29 Apr,*
£770 ($1,247)

13
A Victorian vesta case, Thomas Johnson, London, 1882, in the form of a fisherman's basket, the lid opening to reveal a panel inset with a crystal intaglio of a pair of trout on a straw bed, 5.5cm (2in), *L 17 July,*
£3,190 ($5,008)

14
A pill box, import mark London, 1893, the lid stamped with a cherub gardening, 4cm (1½in), *Mel 24 June,*
Aus$121 (£53; $82)

15
A Victorian silver and enamel cheroot case, Thomas Johnson, London, 1887, painted with a scene depicting two anglers netting a salmon, 8cm (3in), *S 19 Feb,*
£308 ($468)

16
A German box, import mark Chester, 1909, pierced and engraved with three couples in mid 17th century dress, 11cm (4¼in), 6oz 10dwt (202gr), *C 6 Aug,*
£220 ($341)

1

2

3

4

5

6

7

8

9

10

11

13
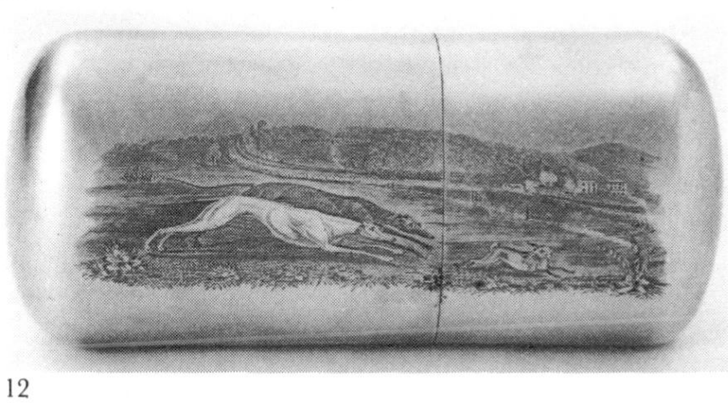
12

14

15

16

1

2

3

4

5

6

7

8

9

10

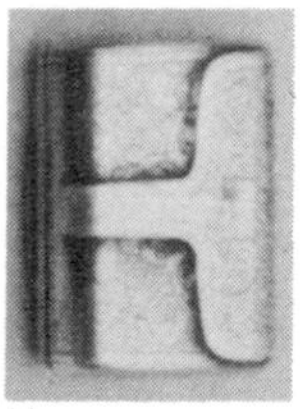
11

12

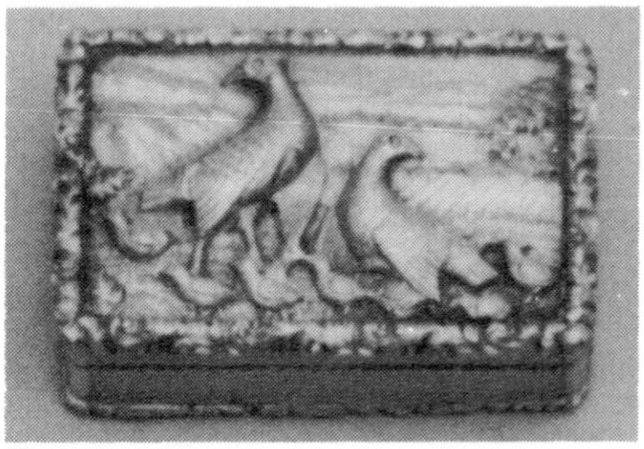
13

14

15

16

17

18

1
A George III purse-shaped vinaigrette, John Thompson, London, c.1790, 2cm (¾in), *Syd 12 Nov,*
Aus$407 (£185; $259)

2
A George III silver-gilt vinaigrette, Matthew Linwood, Birmingham, 1808, 4.5cm (1¾in), *L 16 Oct,*
£495 ($693)

3
A George III fish vinaigrette, Lea & Clark, Birmingham, 1818, 8cm (3in), *L 16 Oct,*
£638 ($893)

4
A George III purse-shaped vinaigrette, Joseph Taylor, London, 1818, 2.5cm (1in), *Syd 12 Nov,*
Aus$374 (£170; $238)

5
A George III vinaigrette, Simpson & Son, Birmingham, 1817, 2.5cm (1in), 10dwt (15gr), *Syd 12 Nov,*
Aus$220 (£100; $140)

6
A George III Nelson memorial vinaigrette, Matthew Linwood, Birmingham, 1805, of purse form, the grille pierced and cast with the *Victory* above the words *Trafr. Octr 21 1805,* 4.5cm (1¾in), *NY 8 Apr,*
$1,650 (£1,138)

7
A George III vinaigrette, Birmingham, 1807, maker's mark I.M., 2.5cm (1in), *Mel 24 June,*
Aus$165 (£72; $112)

8
A George IV vinaigrette, Birmingham, 1824, maker's mark TF, 3.5cm (1¼in), 15dwt (23gr), *Mel 24 June,*
Aus$264 (£115; $179)

9
A George III silver-gilt snuff box, maker's mark WP (?William Parker), London, 1800, engraved all over with a trellis and chequer pattern, 6.5cm (2½in), *L 16 Oct,*
£528 ($739)

10
A George IV silver-gilt vinaigrette, Birmingham, 1822, maker's mark TN, 3.5cm (1¼in), *Mel 24 June,*
Aus$220 (£96; $149)

11
A William IV purse-shaped vinaigrette, Thomas Shaw, Birmingham, 1832, 2.5cm (1in), *S 17 Sept,*
£154 ($216)

12
An early Victorian 18ct gold snuff box, Charles Rawlings & William Summers, London, 1839, 7cm (2¾in), 2oz 8dwt (77gr), *JHB 18 June,*
R 5,720 (£1,788; $2,503)

13
A William IV silver-gilt vinaigrette, Thomas Shaw, Birmingham, 1830, cast and chased with a pair of game birds in a heathery landscape, 5cm (2in), *S 17 Sept,*
£792 ($1,109)

14
A George III snuff box, Samuel Pemberton, Birmingham, 1814, 6.5cm (2½in), *S 12 Nov,*
£220 ($308)

15
A Victorian vinaigrette, Nathaniel Mills, Birmingham, 1840, chased with a view of Westminster Abbey, 4.5cm (2in), *L 17 July,*
£660 ($1,036)

16
A Victorian silver-gilt vinaigrette, Nathaniel Mills, Birmingham, 1837, die-stamped with a view of Abbotsford, the home of Sir Walter Scott, 4cm (1½in), *L 17 July,*
£484 ($760)

17
A William IV silver-gilt vinaigrette, Taylor & Perry, Birmingham, 1835, chased with a view of Abbotsford, 4.5cm (1¾in), *S 17 Sept,*
£715 ($1,001)

18
A George IV vinaigrette, Nathaniel Mills, Birmingham, 1827, cast and chased with a view of Warwick Castle, 4.5cm (1¾in), *S 17 Sept,*
£792 ($1,109)

1
A Victorian vinaigrette, Nathaniel Mills, Birmingham, 1843, cast and chased with a view of the Scott memorial, 5cm (2in), *S 17 Sept,*
£572 ($801)

2
A Victorian silver-gilt vinaigrette, Nathaniel Mills, Birmingham, 1837, cast and chased with a view of Windsor Castle, 4cm (1½in), *S 17 Sept,*
£418 ($585)

3
A Victorian vinaigrette, Edward Smith, Birmingham, 1848, engraved with a view of Westminster Abbey, 4cm (1½in), *S 17 Sept,*
£154 ($216)

4
A Victorian snuff box, Thomas Eley, London, 1839, cast and chased with a peddler with tavern in the background, 9cm (3½in), 6oz 10dwt (202gr), *NY 5 Nov,*
$1,980 (£1,394)

5
A Victorian vinaigrette, Nathaniel Mills, Birmingham, 1845, engraved with a view of Lincoln Cathedral, 4.5cm (1¾in), *S 17 Sept,*
£330 ($462)

6
A William IV silver-gilt vinaigrette, Thomas Shaw, Birmingham, c.1835, cast and chased with rampant foliage, 5cm (2in), *S 17 Sept,*
£374 ($524)

7
A Victorian vinaigrette, S. Mordan & Co., London, 1870, in the form of a hunting horn, the screw-on mouthpiece concealing a scent flask, 10.5cm (4in), *S 19 Feb,*
£187 ($284)

8
A William IV vinaigrette, Taylor & Perry, Birmingham, 1835, chased with a view of Newstead Abbey, 4.5cm (1¾in), *L 17 July,*
£484 ($760)

9
A George IV vinaigrette, Nathaniel Mills, Birmingham, 1825, 4.5cm (1¾in), *S 17 Sept,*
£198 ($277)

10
A George III vinaigrette, Samuel Pemberton, Birmingham, 1812, engraved with amatory trophies and flowers, 5cm (2in), *S 17 Sept,*
£220 ($308)

11
A Victorian snuff box, John Linnit, London, 1837, engraved all over with scrolled foliage, 7.5cm (3in), *L 16 Oct,*
£352 ($493)

12
A Victorian snuff box, Edward Edwards, London, 1844, applied with a chased scene of a lion and stallion after Stubbs, 8cm (3in), *L 16 Oct,*
£572 ($801)

13
A George III 18ct gold snuff box, A. J. Strachan, London, 1817, the lid with an applied border in three-colour gold of roses and foliage, 8.5cm (3¼in), 4oz (124gr), *L 24 Apr,*
£1,650 ($2,640)

14
A Victorian snuff box, Nathaniel Mills, Birmingham, 1844, 10cm (4in), *L 16 Oct,*
£440 ($616)

1

2

3

4

5

6

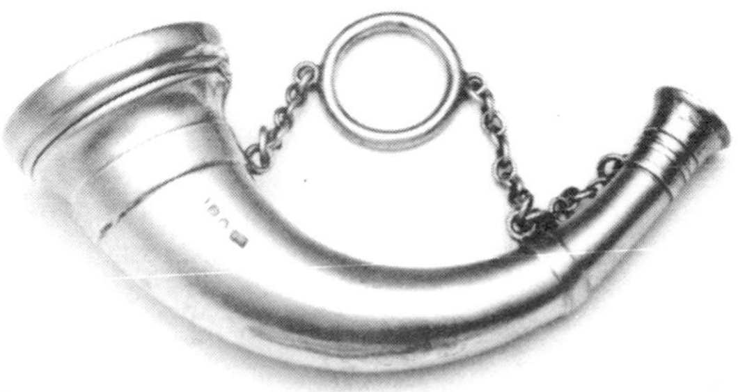
7

8

9

10

11

12

13

14

1

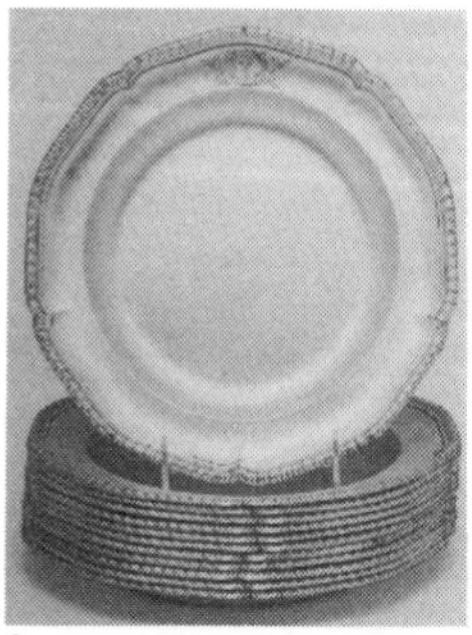
2

3

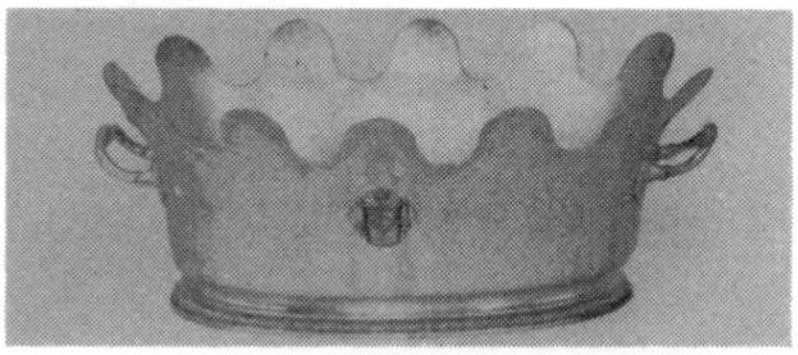
4

5

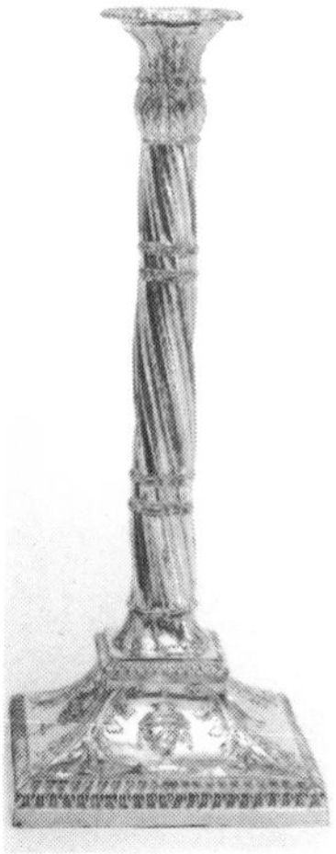
6

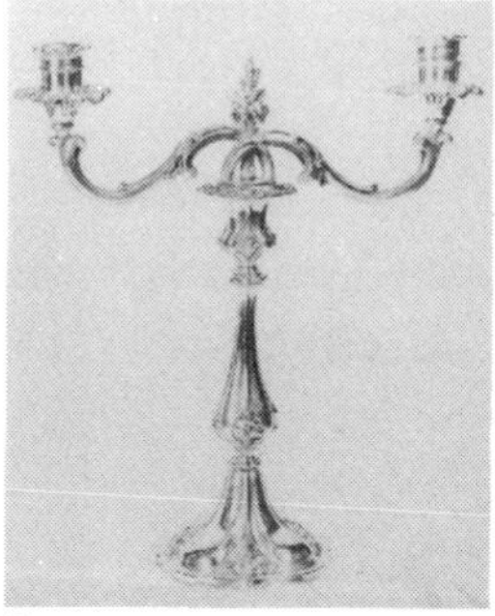
7

8

9

10

11

12

1
A pair of Sheffield plate telescopic two-light candelabra, A. Goodman & Co., c.1805, detachable nozzles, 48cm (19in), *C 15 Apr,*
£1,045 ($1,620)

2
A set of twelve Sheffield plate soup plates, c.1765, 24.5cm (9½in), *NY 5 Nov,*
$1,430 (£1,007)

3
A Sheffield plate globe inkwell, c.1800, 22.5cm (9in), *C 15 Apr,*
£462 ($716)

4
A pair of French verrières *(one illustrated),* early 19th century, of oval form, with the arms of Talleyrand, 35cm (13¾in) wide, *M 24 June,*
FF 44,400 (£3,961; $6,179)

5
A pair of Sheffield plate double wine coaster trolleys, c.1790, the stands of boat form, each mounted with two coasters, 40cm (15¾in), *NY 19 Sept,*
$2,970 (£2,007)

6
A pair of Sheffield plate table candlesticks, *(one illustrated),* c.1780, with twisted bamboo column stems, detachable nozzles, later gilt, 32cm (12½in), *NY 5 Nov,*
$1,210 (£852)

7
A pair of two-light candelabra, *(one illustrated),* English, late 19th century, the detachable branches centred by a bunch of flowers, 36cm (14in), *JHB 11 Nov,*
R 900 (£281; $394)

8
A pair of Sheffield plate wine coolers, *(one illustrated),* c.1800, detachable rims and liners, 19.5cm (7¾in), *NY 12 June,*
$2,640 (£1,737)

9
A pair of Sheffield plate wine coolers, c.1810, detachable liners, 23.5cm (9¼in), *L 20 Nov,*
£2,860 ($4,004)

10
A pair of Sheffield plate wine coolers, *(one illustrated),* c.1820, detachable rims and liners, 19cm (7½in), *NY 12 Dec,*
$3,850 (£2,750)

11
A pair of Sheffield plate wine coolers, *(one illustrated),* c.1815, detachable rims and liners, 23cm (9in), *C 15 Apr,*
£1,430 ($2,217)

12
A pair of wine coolers, c.1820, detachable liners and rims with flower borders, 29cm (11½in), *S 23 Apr,*
£1,540 ($2,418)

1
A pair of Sheffield plate entrée dishes and covers with silver finials, *(one illustrated)*, c.1800, the finials in the form of demi-lions rampant, by Thomas Robins, c.1800, 29.5cm (11½in) long, *NY 12 June,*
$1,760 (£1,158)

2
A pair of Sheffield plate soup tureens, covers and stands, *(one illustrated)*, c.1820, apparently a variation of a design attributed to Edward Hodges Baily of Rundell, Bridge & Rundell, the stands of oval form with raised centres, stands 48.5cm (19in) long over handles, *NY 8 Apr,*
$10,120 (£6,979)

3
A set of four Sheffield plate entrée dishes and covers on hot water bases, *(one illustrated)*, c.1830, of oval form, 38cm (15in) long over handles, *NY 5 Nov,*
$3,300 (£2,324)

4
A soup tureen, c.1845, of oval form, with detachable oak tree crest finial, PODR mark for 20 June 1845, 42cm (16½in) over handles, *S 23 Apr,*
£902 ($1,416)

5
A Sheffield plate epergne, c.1840, with four detachable branches and central stem, and five cut glass bowls, 25.5cm (10in) high, *L 20 Nov,*
£1,100 ($1,540)

6
A decanter wagon, 19th century, the circular coaster with wood base, the detachable base with cast and pierced handle, 35cm (13¾in), *JHB 11 Nov,*
R 480 (£150; $210)

7
A Sheffield plate decanter wagon, c.1820, with a pair of coasters and a pair of contemporary cut glass decanters with labels, 40cm (15¾in) long, *C 15 Apr,*
£770 ($1,194)

8
A three-piece teaset, c.1870, engraved with strapwork arches containing blooms, *C 12 Mar,*
£165 ($249)

9
A four-piece tea and coffee set, each piece decorated with blooms and scrolls and on four supports, *C 28 May,*
£440 ($695)

10
A trefoil decanter stand, c.1880, fitted with three tapering blue, green or red overlay glass decanters, 46cm (18in), *C 25 Jan,*
£297 ($463)

11
An electroplate novelty cocktail shaker, Asprey & Co. Ltd., c.1930, in the form of a fire extinguisher, the applied shield stamped 'The Thirst Extinguisher, Instructions for filling', the revolving base with cocktail recipes, 37cm (14½in), *L 3 Feb,*
£495 ($727)

12
A tea kettle on stand, c.1900, 39cm (15¼in), *C 22 Oct,*
£242 ($339)

13
A French coffee percolator, early 19th century, the detachable top fitted with mesh strainer, tamper and top strainer, 26.5cm (10½in), *C 15 Apr,*
£187 ($290)

1

2

3

4

5

6

8

7

9

10

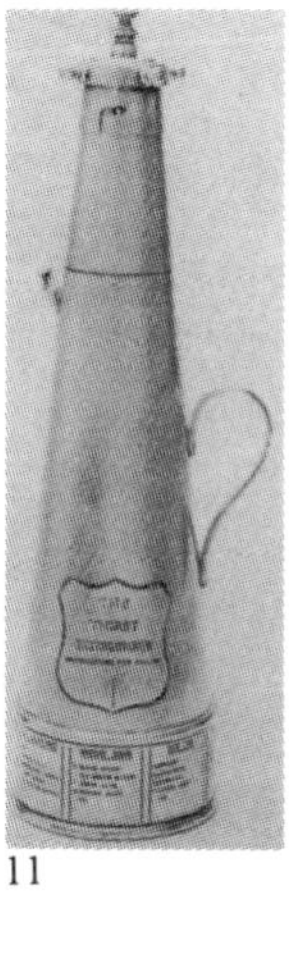
11

12

13

Objects of Vertu

Article:
Roman mosaics of the 18th and 19th centuries *pp* 452-455
See also:
Colour illustrations *p* 484   European works of art *pp* 362-363   Silver *pp* 438-441

1

2

3

4

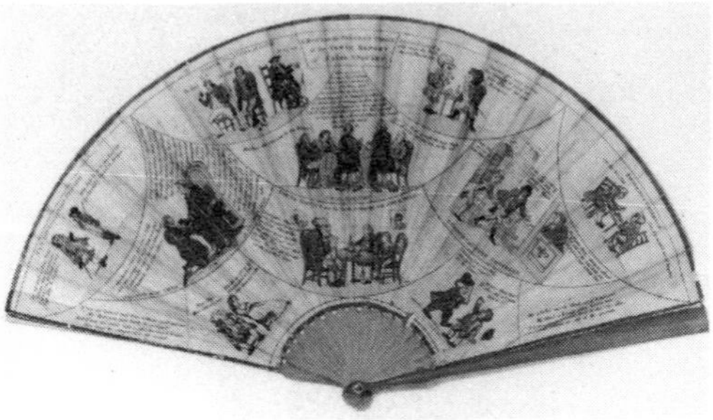
5

6

7

8

9

1
A lacquered ivory and mother-of-pearl fan, North European, c.1735, some wear, 28.5cm (11¼in), *S 19 Feb,*
£660 ($1,003)

2
A pierced ivory fan, French, c.1750, painted with architectural vignettes and a chinoiserie scene, leaf torn, 27cm (10½in), sold with a bone fan and fan case, *S 19 Feb,*
£143 ($217)

3
An ivory fan, French, mid 18th century, painted with chinoiserie scenes, 27cm (10½in), *S 12 Nov,*
£418 ($585)

4
A mother-of-pearl fan, French, c.1760, painted with pastoral and mythological scenes, repaired, 27.5cm (10¾in), *S 19 Feb,*
£253 ($385)

5
A rare printed fan, English, c.1805, entitled *A Hint on the Present Times; or the Tenth Report of Naval Enquiry*, the leaf with ten satirical vignettes after Williams and Cruikshank, 19.5cm (7¾in), *S 18 June,*
£1,155 ($1,825)

6
A 'Mandarin' fan, Chinese, c.1860, 29cm (11½in), with original case, *S 17 Sept,*
£1,815 ($2,541)

7
A silver and enamel fan, Chinese, mid 19th century, 20.5cm (8in), with case, *S 19 Feb,*
£682 ($1,037)

8
An ivory fan mounted with silver and jewels, Continental, third quarter 19th century, painted with mythological scenes and flowers, 21.5cm (8½in), *NY 12 Dec,*
$880 (£628)

9
A gold and jewelled fan, German, c.1900, painted with Mars and Venus, the guards jewelled, 27cm (10½in), *G 13 Nov,*
SF 12,100 (£5,042; $7,058)

1
An ivory piqué malacca walking cane, English, c.1695, silver-mount damaged, 90cm (35½in), *S 19 Feb,*
£264 ($401)

2
An ivory and malacca walking cane, South German, c.1860, the handle carved with a general, some wear, 102cm (40in), *S 12 Nov,*
£770 ($1,078)

3
A whalebone and ivory walking stick, late 19th century, 89cm (35in), *L 3 June,*
£330 ($511)

4
A whalebone and ivory walking stick, late 19th century, 84cm (33in), *L 3 June,*
£330 ($511)

5
An ivory and wood walking cane, Austrian or German, c.1918, gold mounts, 92.5cm (36½in), *S 19 Feb,*
£220 ($334)

6
An ivory and wood walking cane, English, late 17th century, decorated in silver piqué, silver mounts, 89cm (35in), *S 19 Feb,*
£308 ($468)

7
An ivory and narwhal horn walking cane, English, c.1880, the ivory handle carved as a bust of Disraeli, 92cm (36¼in), *S 19 Feb,*
£1,430 ($2,174)

8
An ivory and wood walking cane, probably Bavarian, c.1880-90, the ivory top carved as a young couple in early 19th century dress, 95.5cm (37½in), *S 19 Feb,*
£396 ($602)

9
A damascened steel and malacca walking cane, Spanish, late 19th century, 94cm (37in), *S 19 Feb,*
£418 ($635)

10
A tortoiseshell piqué walking cane, Neapolitan, c.1745, later tortoiseshell shaft, gold mounts, chips, 95.5cm (37½in), *S 19 Feb,*
£1,485 ($2,257)

11
A tortoiseshell walking cane, probably Spanish, c.1825, gold mounts, 93.5cm (36¾in), *S 19 Feb,*
£748 ($1,137)

12
A gold-topped malacca walking cane, Chinese, in European taste, c.1770, some wear, 92.5cm (36½in), *S 19 Feb,*
£715 ($1,087)

13
An ivory and malacca walking cane, Bavarian, c.1860, the handle carved with a huntsman, restored, 88cm (34½in), *S 19 Feb,*
£770 ($1,170)

14
An articulated novelty walking cane, c.1880, the ivory grip carved as a negro's head, 91cm (35¾in), *S 12 May,*
£858 ($1,201)

15
A rolled gold walking cane handle, American, c.1875, on ebony shaft, 89cm (35in) overall, *S 12 Nov,*
£231 ($323)

16
A silver and malacca walking cane, Charles Dumesnil, London, 1890, 95cm (37¼in), *S 19 Feb,*
£440 ($669)

17
An ivory piqué and malacca walking cane, English, c.1700, silver mount, 93cm (36½in), *S 19 Feb,*
£132 ($201)

18
An ivory and wood walking stick, English, c.1880, the handle carved as a skull, silver mounts, 71cm (28in), *S 18 June,*
£418 ($660)

19
An ivory walking stick, c.1800, gilt-metal mounts, some wear, 92cm (36¼in), *S 18 June,*
£220 ($347)

1

2

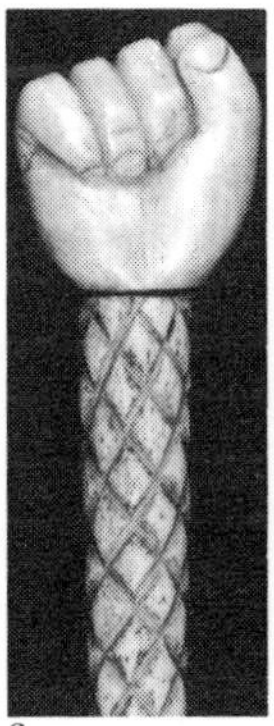
3

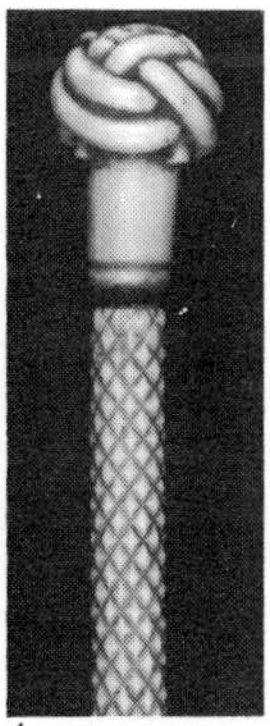
4

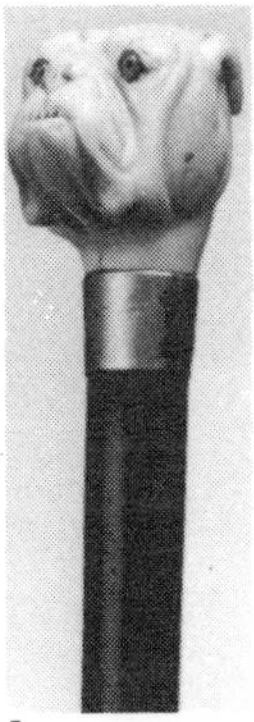
5

6

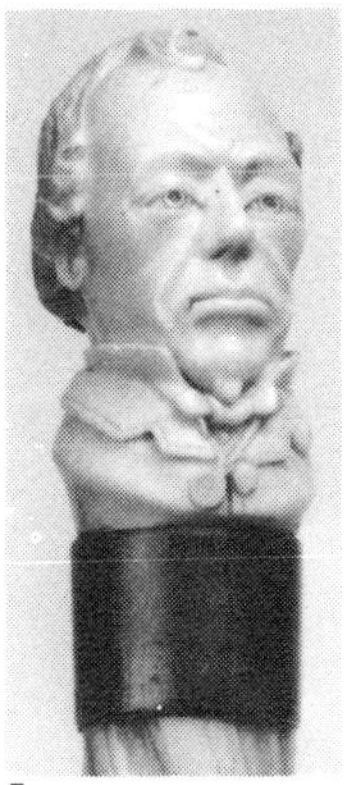
7

8

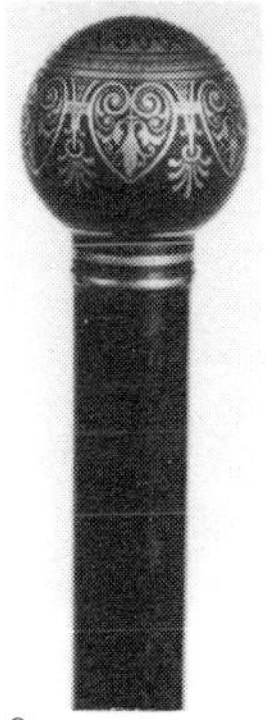
9

10

11

12

13

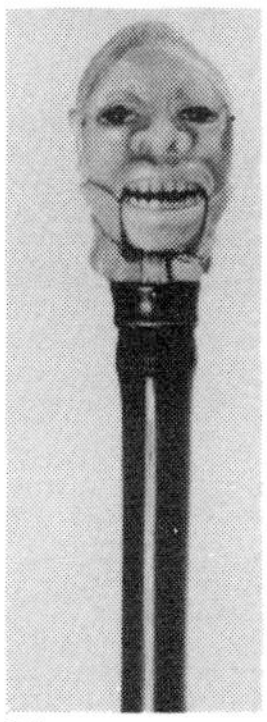
14

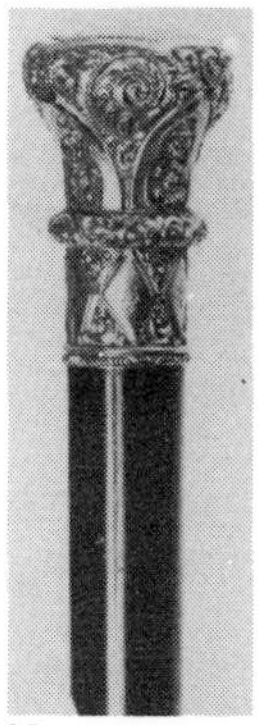
15

16

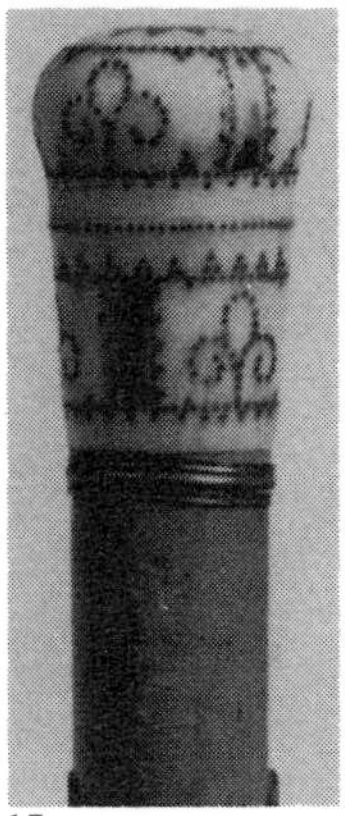
17

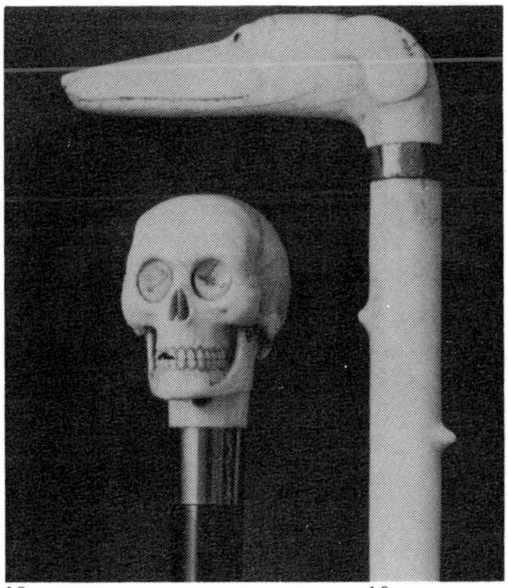
18 19

1

2

3

4

5

6

7

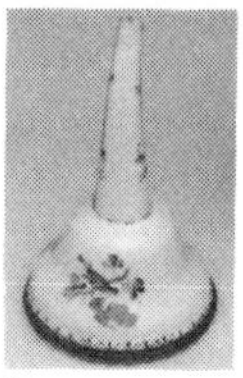
8

9

10

11

12

13

14

15

16

1
A pair of Birmingham chamber candlesticks, *(one illustrated)*, c.1765-70, detachable nozzle, damage and restoration, 18cm (7in) diam., *L 7 July,*
£2,145 ($3,475)

2
A Staffordshire patch box, late 18th century, the lid painted with *The Grecian Daughter*, slight damage, 5.5cm (2¼in), *L 21 Oct,*
£396 ($554)

3
A Staffordshire patch box, c.1785, with a view entitled *Buxton Crescent* and further inscribed *A Trifle from Buxton*, slight damage, 4cm (1½in), *L 21 Oct,*
£220 ($308)

4
A Staffordshire enamel taper pot, c.1765-70, decorated with sprays of brightly coloured flowers, gilt-metal mounts, 6cm (2¼in) high, *L 7 July,*
£495 ($802)

5
A Staffordshire ink standish, c.1765, painted in greens, blues and browns with herding scenes, cracks, 20cm (8in), *L 7 July,*
£1,485 ($2,406)

6
A Staffordshire snuff box, c.1775-80, the lid with raised fruit on a pink ground patched with simulated tortoiseshell, 6cm (2½in), *L 21 Oct,*
£264 ($370)

7
A Staffordshire patch box, c.1800, with a view entitled *Chapel Wells*, restored, 4.5cm (1¾in), *L 21 Oct,*
£198 ($277)

8
A Staffordshire wine funnel, late 18th century, painted in crimson with a bird pecking grapes, gilt-metal mounts, 11.5cm (4½in) high, *L 7 July,*
£902 ($1,461)

9
A Staffordshire patch box, c.1825, painted with an early steamship and inscribed *A Present from Chepstow*, 4cm (1½in), *L 21 Oct,*
£330 ($462)

10
A hunting knife in enam sheath, c.1765, the knife decorated in the manner of James Cox with agate handle carved to simulate horn, the sheath painted with small pastoral scenes, gilt mounts, 20cm (8in), *L 7 July,*
£5,500 ($8,910)

11
An enamel snuff box, German, c.1755, the lid painted in enamels with giant plants and a retriever chasing wild duck, French silver-gilt mounts (re-gilt), 7.5cm (3in), *L 7 Oct,*
£1,595 ($2,233)

12
An enamel snuff box, German, c.1756, decorated overall with *papiers trouvés* including maps of Silesia and Bohemia and a description of battles between the Prussian and the Austrian armies in 1756, some wear, 8cm (3¾in), *L 17 June,*
£1,012 ($1,599)

13
A Meissen snuff box, mid 18th century, decorated on the exterior with flower sprays and on the interior with a bird on a basket of flowers, gilt-metal mounts, 9cm (3½in), *L 7 Oct,*
£1,100 ($1,540)

14
An enamel pug dog bonbonnière, German, c.1765, the lid painted with country promenaders, gilt-metal mounts, some wear, 7.5cm (3in), *G 15 May,*
SF 660 (£222; $358)

15
An enamel box, Paris, 1750, decorated in raised gilding with red, blue, turquoise and green enamels, silver mounts with maker's mark of Jean-Jacques Charbonné, 8cm (3¼in), *L 17 June,*
£1,100 ($1,738)

16
An enamel snuff box, Paris, 1739, decorated in gold, green and blue, silver-gilt mounts, 9.5cm (3¾in), *L 17 June,*
£3,080 ($4,866)

1
A printed and coloured Battersea plaque, 1753-55, with the arms of the Anti-Gallican Society (founded c.1745 to 'oppose the insidious Arts of the French Nation'), in original gilt-metal frame, chipped, 10.5cm (4¼in), *L 7 July,*
£1,045 ($1,693)

2
A Battersea portrait plaque, c.1753-55, transfer-printed and over-painted in sepia with a portrait of a gentleman, in original gilt-metal frame, 10.5cm (4in), *L 21 Oct,*
£660 ($924)

3
A Battersea portrait plaque, c.1753-55, printed and overpainted in sepia with Elizabeth Gunning, afterwards Duchess of Hamilton and later Duchess of Argyll, some restoration, original gilt-metal frame, 8.5cm (3¼in), *L 7 July,*
£495 ($802)

4
A Bilston soap box, c.1765-70, gilt-metal mounts, 6.5cm (2½in), *L 7 July,*
£935 ($1,515)

5
A Bilston necessaire, c.1765, painted with small landscape views, gilt-metal mounts, lacking fittings, 7cm (2¾in), *L 7 July,*
£638 ($1,034)

6
A Bilston spaniel patch box, c.1780, the brown and white dog on a pink ground, restored, 4.5cm (1¾in) diam., *L 25 Feb,*
£1,540 ($2,310)

7
A Bilston hot water jug, c.1770, painted with a river scene and pastoral vignettes, gilt-metal mounts, 24cm (9½in), *L 7 July,*
£2,640 ($4,277)

8
A Bilston bullock's head bonbonnière, c.1775, the lid painted with flowers, some damage and restoration, 5cm (2in), *L 21 Oct,*
£1,980 ($2,772)

9
A Bilston bird bonbonnière, c.1780, the bird painted in green, red, yellow and grey, metal mounts, chip, 4.5cm (1¾in) wide, *L 25 Feb,*
£770 ($1,155)

10
A Bilston goldfinch bonbonnière, c.1775-80, the bird painted in black, pink, yellow and crimson, metal mounts, chips, 6cm (2¼in) wide, *L 25 Feb,*
£935 ($1,402)

11
A Birmingham canary bonbonnière, c.1765-70, the bird with yellow plumage and grey-tipped wings, metal mounts, slight wear, 6.5cm (2½in) wide, *L 25 Feb,*
£990 ($1,485)

12
A yellow-ground snuff box, London or Birmingham, c.1760, gilt-metal mounts, some damage, 5.5cm (2½in), *L 25 Feb,*
£495 ($742)

13
An early Birmingham snuff box, c.1745-50, the lid painted in the typical subdued palette, gilt-metal mounts, 7cm (2¾in) diam., *L 25 Feb,*
£506 ($759)

14
A Birmingham snuff box, c.1750-55, printed in dark brown and coloured with *Autumn* and Italianate scenes, cracks and chip, 7cm (2¾in), *L 7 July,*
£880 ($1,426)

15
A Birmingham snuff box, c.1760, printed overall in grey/black, the lid with *Parrot and Fruit,* chips, 8cm (3in), *L 7 July,*
£990 ($1,604)

16
A Birmingham plaque, c.1750-55, painted with Orpheus playing to the three-headed dragon guardian of the Golden Fleece, 8cm (3in) diam., *L 7 July,*
£286 ($463)

1

2

3

4

7

5

6

9

8

10

11

12

13

14

15

16

1

2

3

4

5

6

7

8

11

9

10

12

13

1
A tortoiseshell box, Naples, 18th century, decorated in mother-of-pearl and gold piqué with cherubs and mythological scenes, 24cm (9½in) wide, *M 30 Nov,*
FF 104,500 (£11,359; $15,902)

2
A small tortoiseshell box, Naples, 18th century, decorated in mother-of-pearl and copper piqué, 13cm (5in) wide, *M 30 Nov,*
FF 17,600 (£1,913; $2,678)

3
A tortoiseshell snuff box, Naples, c.1760, decorated in gold piqué with aquatic scenes, gold shell thumb-piece, some damage, 8cm (3in) wide, *G 13 Nov,*
SF 2,200 (£917; $1,283)

4
A tortoiseshell toilet box, probably Neapolitan, c.1730, decorated in mother-of-pearl and silver piqué, silver thumbpiece, 13.5cm (5¼in) wide, *G 13 Nov,*
SF 8,250 (£3,438; $4,813)

5
A tortoiseshell snuff box, English or Italian, early 18th century, decorated with mother-of-pearl and silver piqué, some piqué lacking, 7cm (2¾in) wide, *S 18 June,*
£198 ($313)

6
A silver and tortoiseshell snuff box, A.J. Strachan, London, 1827, the lid applied with a tortoise-shell panel inset in hard-stones with a parrot, damaged, 7.5cm (3in) wide, *S 19 Feb,*
£374 ($568)

7
A silver and tortoiseshell snuff box, John Salkeld, London, 1810, the lid inset with an earlier piqué panel, 7cm (2¾in) wide, *Mel 24 June,*
Aus$352 (£153; $239)

8
A tortoiseshell snuff box, possibly German, early 18th century, decorated in piqué and mother-of-pearl, later gold mounts, damaged, 8cm (3in) wide, *S 17 Sept,*
£792 ($1,109)

9
A tortoiseshell snuff box, English, early 19th century, inlaid with a bust of George III and decorated with brass piqué, gilt-metal mounts, *S 18 June,*
£275 ($434)

10
A tortoiseshell snuff box, probably German, c.1735, decorated in silver with a figure of Venus, 7cm (2¾in) wide, *S 18 June,*
£187 ($295)

11
A stained horn snuff box, French, c.1760, the red ground decorated with piqué stars and inlaid in metal and mother-of-pearl, some wear, 7.5cm (3in) diam., *S 18 June,*
£176 ($278)

12
A silver and mother-of-pearl snuff box, Dutch, Johannes Paschalis Jonckbloet, Den Bosch, c.1765, the shell lid carved with two portraits, 12cm (4¾in) wide, *S 19 Feb,*
£550 ($836)

13
A silver and tortoiseshell snuff box, c.1710, decorated in mother-of-pearl and engraved metal with a figure of Polcinello, 8cm (3in) long, *S 18 June,*
£253 ($399)

1
A blonde tortoiseshell snuff box, French, c.1780, the lid with an allegory of Age blessing Youth, gold mounts, some wear, 6.5cm (2½in) diam., *S 12 Nov,*
£440 ($616)

2
An ivory patch box, probably French, c.1790, the lid with a pastoral scene, gold mounts, 9cm (3½in) wide, *S 19 Feb,*
£209 ($318)

3
A tortoiseshell boîte à miniature , French, early 19th century, the lid inset with a miniature of the Tuileries Gardens by *** Sebelle, within a gold frame, 9cm (3½in) wide, *L 9 June,*
£3,520 ($5,562)

4
A poudre d'écaille snuff box, French, c.1820, the lid inset with a miniature of a young man, gilt-metal mounts, chipped. 6.5cm (2½in) diam., *S 19 Feb,*
£308 ($468)

5
A tortoiseshell snuff box, Paris, 1798-1809, the lid inset with a miniature on vellum of a village fête by Edmé-Charles de Lioux de Savignac, signed and dated 1772, 9cm (3½in) wide, *L 9 June,*
£9,900 ($15,642)

6
A gold and ivory tooth-pick case, English, c.1790, applied with glass paste classical profiles, 9.5cm (3¾in) wide, *S 19 Feb,*
£495 ($752)

7
A lacquered papier-mâché snuff box, English, c.1832, the lid painted with a political satire on the passing of the Electoral Reform Bill, some wear, 10cm (4in) wide, *S 18 June,*
£286 ($452)

8
A lacquered papier-mâché snuff box, Stobwasser, Brunswick, late 18th century, the lid painted with a nymph and inscribed inside *L'attente du plaiser d'après A. Carrache,* 9.5cm (3¾in) diam., *S 12 Nov,*
£1,210 ($1,694)

9
A lacquered papier-mâché cheroot case, Stobwasser, Brunswick, early 19th century, painted with a Compostela pilgrim and inscribed *Heloise* on the base, *S 12 Nov,*
£605 ($847)

10
A lacquered papier-mâché snuff box, Stobwasser, Brunswick, c.1815, painted with a miniature of Lord Byron after a painting by Richard Westall, some wear, 9.5cm (3¾in) diam., *S 19 Feb,*
£440 ($669)

11
A lacquered papier-mâché snuff box, Stobwasser, Brunswick, c.1830, the lid with a scene entitled *Elle attend!*, slight cracks, 9cm (3½in) wide, *S 18 June,*
£352 ($556)

12
A papier-mâché snuff box, German, probably Stobwasser, c.1820, the lid painted with a tavern scene after Ostade, crack and chips, 9.5cm (3¾in) wide, *S 18 June,*
£440 ($695)

13
An ivory snuff box, North European, early 18th century, the lid carved with Zephyr and Flora, silver mounts, some restoration, 8.5cm (3¼in) wide, *S 18 June,*
£341 ($539)

14
An ivory bodkin case, possibly South German, c.1735, carved with flowers and fruits and a seated musician, gold mounts, containing six ivory implements, 11.5cm (4½in), *S 18 June,*
£198 ($312)

1

2

3

4

5

6

7

8

9

10

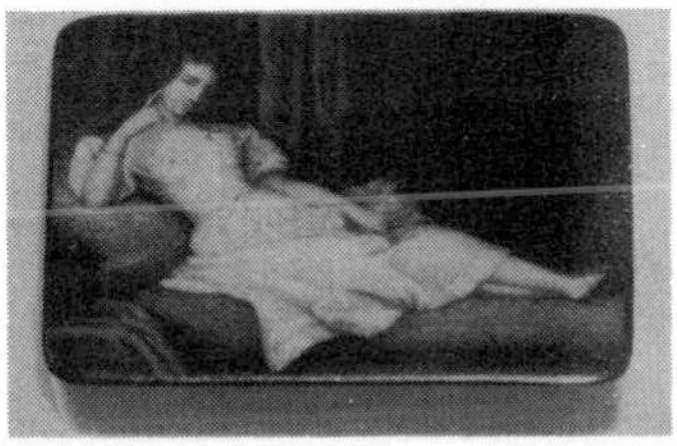
11

12

13

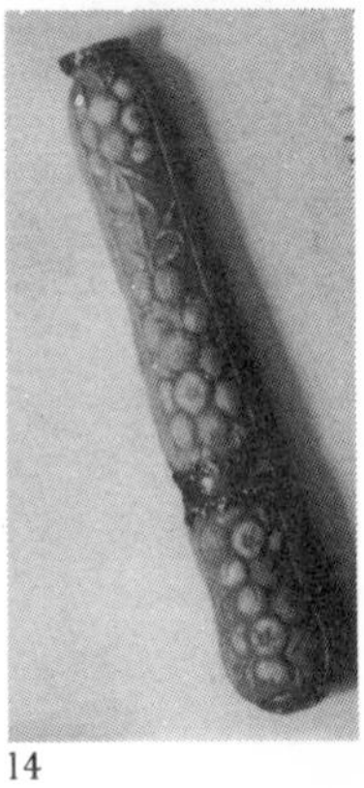
14

1

2

3

4

5

6

7

8

9

10

11

12

13

14

15

1
A gold snuff box, English, c.1745-50, chased with an allegorical scene of Rinaldo and Armida, 6cm (2½in), *NY 12 June,*
$6,600 (£4,342)

2
A gold and hardstone snuff box, German, c.1760, the lid and base of petrified wood, the wide gold mounts chased with putti, 9cm (3½in), *L 9 June,*
£990 ($1,564)

3
A three-colour gold and enamel snuff box, Paris, 1764, set with enamel medallions painted *en grisaille* with figures of the Arts and Sciences, the ground and border enamelled in translucent blue, 9cm (3½in), *G 13 Nov,*
SF 35,200 (£14,667; $20,533)

4
A parcel-gilt portrait snuff box, Paris, 1773, the lid inset with a gold-mounted enamel miniature of Catherine the Great, attributed to Hurter, 8cm (3in), *L 9 June,*
£605 ($956)

5
A gold and enamel snuff box with miniatures, Adrien-Jean-Maximilien Vachette, Paris, 1782, the top, base and sides mounted with miniatures *en grisaille* of neo-classical Bacchic friezes by Jacques-Joseph de Gault, 8.5cm (3¼in), *NY 12 Dec,*
$8,250 (£5,893)

6
A gold and enamel snuff box, Swiss, c.1775, enamelled *en plein* in sepia and *en grisaille* with pastoral vignettes, 7.5cm (3in), *G 15 May,*
SF 18,700 (£6,296; $10,137)

7
A gold snuff box, Jean-George Rémond & Co, Geneva, late 18th century, the cover chased with a love trophy, 6cm (2½in), *NY 12 June,*
$2,640 (£1,737)

8
A gold and cameo vinaigrette, English, late 18th century, the lid inset with a stone cameo carved with the chariot of Bacchus, 4cm (1½in), *G 13 Nov,*
SF 3,520 (£1,466; $2,053)

9
A gold and enamel vinaigrette, Swiss, c.1790, inscribed in gold *AMITIE* on a white ground, the surround enamelled in dark blue, 2cm (¾in), *S 17 Sept,*
£407 ($570)

10
A gold and enamel vinaigrette, Swiss, early 19th century, the dark blue translucent enamel lid painted in bright colours, 3cm (1¼in), *S 17 Sept,*
£1,320 ($1,848)

11
A gold and enamel portrait snuff box, Etienne-Lucien Blerzy, Paris, c.1804-9, the lid inset with a miniature of the Empress Josephine by Daniel Saint, rose diamond frame, 9cm (3½in), *L 9 June,*
£7,700 ($12,166)

12
A gold and enamel case, Swiss, c.1800, royal blue ground, painted with pastoral scenes within borders of pearls, 9cm (3½in) high, *NY 12 Dec,*
$6,050 (£4,321)

13
A gold snuff box, Simon-Achille Leger, Paris, 1809-19, 7.5cm (3in), *S 17 Sept,*
£1,430 ($2,002)

14
A gold snuff box, Moulinié, Bautte & Cie., Geneva, 1807-14, the lid inset with a hairwork allegorical scene of *Constance,* 7cm (2¾in), *S 17 Sept,*
£1,265 ($1,771)

15
A gold and citrine vinaigrette, English or Scottish, c.1835, with a pierced gold grille engraved with an exotic bird, turquoise thumbpiece, some damage, 4.5cm (1¾in), *S 17 Sept,*
£792 ($1,109)

1
A gold and cameo snuff box, Paris, 1819-38, the lid with a cameo carved with a Bacchanalian scene, *L 9 June,*
£1,045 ($1,651)

2
A gold and enamel snuff box, Swiss, c.1800, the cover enamelled with three young girls playing with chicks in a garden, 7cm (2¾in), *NY 12 June,*
$5,225 (£3,437)

3
A four-colour gold vinaigrette, English, early 19th century, turquoise-set thumbpiece, 4cm (1½in), *S 17 Sept,*
£1,320 ($1,848)

4
A gold vinaigrette, Swiss, early 19th century, maker's mark M.B., 3.5cm (1¼in), *G 15 May,*
SF 1,430 (£481; $775)

5
A gold vinaigrette, Swiss, early 19th century, 3cm (1¼in), *S 17 Sept,*
£1,375 ($1,925)

6
A two-colour gold and enamel snuff box, Swiss, early 19th century, the lid inset with an enamel plaque, 8.5cm (3¼in), *G 15 May,*
SF 7,700 (£2,593; $4,174)

7
A gold and enamel snuff box, Swiss, c.1820, the cover enamelled with a mythological scene, 9cm (3½in), *NY 12 June,*
$6,600 (£4,342)

8
A gold and hardstone vinaigrette, London, 1812, the lid set with a cameo carved with Pan and Syrinx, 2.5cm (1in), *S 17 Sept,*
£550 ($770)

9
A gold and enamel vinaigrette, Swiss, early 19th century, the dark blue enamel lid painted with a basket of pink and white roses, maker's mark G.R. I.C., 4cm (1½in), *S 17 Sept,*
£825 ($1,155)

10
A silver-gilt and citrine vinaigrette, English, c.1830, the pierced grille engraved with music trophies, 3cm (1¼in), *S 17 Sept,*
£528 ($739)

11
A jewelled three-colour gold and enamel snuff box, Swiss, c.1820-40, the lid inset with a blue enamel panel applied in rose diamonds with a vase of flowers, further applied with rose diamond clusters, maker's mark CCS, 9cm (3½in), *L 9 June,*
£3,300 ($5,214)

12
A gold and enamel snuff box, Paris, 1819-38, decorated overall in the manner of Turin in dark blue *taille d'épargne* enamelling, 7.5cm (3in), *G 13 Nov,*
SF 6,050 (£2,521; $3,529)

13
A gold snuff box, Reily and Storer, London, 1831, the lid engraved with a crest, 7cm (2¾in), *S 17 Sept,*
£880 ($1,232)

14
A vari-coloured gold snuff box, Swiss, c.1815, with a reserve chased with two hounds, 8.5cm (3¼in), *NY 12 Dec,*
$1,540 (£1,100)

1

2

3

4

5

6

7

8

9

10

11

12

13

14

Roman Mosaics of the 18th and 19th Centuries

JULIA CLARKE

The Vatican Mosaic Workshop in Rome was founded by Pope Gregory XIII in 1576 and, under Urban VIII, it was pledged to replace the deteriorating paintings of St. Peter's Basilica with mosaic copies — an undertaking only nearing completion late in the 18th century. An English visitor, Lady Shelley, wrote in 1816 '...in the interior of St. Peter's we saw paintings in mosaic which imitate paintings so well that I was completely satisfied to look at a copy of the Transfiguration, and to believe it to be the original...'.[1] An earlier traveller, John Moore, wrote in 1781 of '...the astonishing improvements which have of late been made in the art of copying pictures in mosaic. Some of the artists here have already made copies with a degree of accuracy, which nobody could believe who had not seen the performances'.[2]

It was inevitable that craftsmen who could draw such praise should wish to profit from their skill, especially since the Vatican workers could see the end of their official function in sight and were also, apparently, extremely illpaid. Both they and independent mosaicists had been experimenting with the glass pastes *(smalti)* used for the tesserae of the large mosaics. This resulted in the creation of *smalti filati* — an invention attributed to Giacomo Rafaelli who exhibited works in the technique in 1775. Small lumps of the paste, which could be coloured into innumerable shades, were melted and stretched into slender rods, then split to create the minute segments, 'scarcely larger than pins' heads',[3] used for a micro-mosaic. These tiny lengths were then sunk in soft mastic but would still bristle unevenly — like a

1 *(top left)* 2 *(bottom left)* 3 *(top right)* 4 *(bottom right)* 5

1
A Roman mosaic plaque, early 19th century, showing a view of the Italian countryside, leaf-chased gold frame, 8.5cm (3¼in), *G 13 Nov,*
SF 3,080 (£1,283; $1,797)

2
A Roman mosaic and marble paperweight, mid 19th century, with orange marble base, 11cm (4½in), *G 13 Nov,*
SF 1,540 (£642; $898)

3
A Roman mosaic plaque, Vincenzo Verdejo and Nicola Zeloni, Rome, early 19th century, paper label on reverse inscribed 'Etude de Mosaique/des Mrs Verdajo et Zeloni/associes a la Rue Condotti/No.34', in original tooled leather case, 7.5cm (3in), *G 13 Nov,*
SF 3,850 (£1,604; $2,246)

4
A Roman mosaic plaque, early 19th century, of a spaniel and a cat, based on a painting by Wenceslaus Peter, silver frame, 7cm (2¾in), *G 13 Nov,*
SF 5,830 (£2,429; $3,401)

5
A micro-mosaic marble top centre table, c.1870, raised on a carved giltwood base, 87cm (34¼in) diam., *NY 13 Sept,*
$35,200 (£23,946)

hedgehog's spines. Wax was poured in between and coloured with ground *smalto* powder. The rough surface was polished first with lead and then a soft cloth. The backing could be either a shallow copper tray forming a plaque (fig.3), or more commonly later, a type of marble known as 'Belgian black' for large tabletops (figs 5 & 6) or paperweights (fig.7) or black glass for very tiny items, particularly jewellery (fig.9).

Once the means existed to shrink large-scale mosaicwork into small, subtly-coloured 'paintings', the demand for the work was not slow to follow. Plaques which could be purchased by tourists or retailers and incorporated into snuff boxes, vinaigrettes, paperweights and jewellery either locally or at home, made ideal souvenirs. Because of its religious, artistic and classical associations Rome had long been the ultimate goal of Northern European (and later American) travellers. In the 18th century, tourists would have their portrait painted by Battoni or buy 'antique' statues or the sombre prints of Piranesi, to remind them of their trip.[4] 19th century visitors, according to the early guidebooks, were tempted by cameos, Roman pearls, striped silks, and of course, mosaics.[5]

The subjects most popular in the 19th century were not necessarily those which are prized by collectors today. Both for plaques and jewellery, it is evident that the most common subjects were views of local classical ruins based on prints (figs 3 & 18), 'Italianate' landscapes of the Roman Campagna (fig.1 & colour illustration p.484, fig.6), animals (particularly dogs — figs 8, 10 & 11) and, increasingly, later in the 19th century, flowers (fig.2), peasants (fig.12) and views of St. Peter's Square (fig.13). 'Archaeological' jewels based on Etruscan, early Christian (fig.14) and Egyptian (fig.15) motifs were popularised by Castellani and other Roman jewellers.

In fact, the subject most copied and included in the repertoire of all the leading mosaicists is one that finds little favour with modern collectors precisely because it is seen so often. This was the famed, so-called 'Capitoline Doves of Pliny'. In the appendix to his *Natural History*, the elder Pliny describes the work of Sosos, the celebrated Greek worker in mosaic 'who laid the floors of a house at Pergamon, known as the...Unswept House, because he represented in small bits of many-coloured mosaic the scraps from the table and everything which is usually swept away as if they had been left lying on the floor. Among these mosaics is a marvellous dove drinking and casting the shadow of its head on

6

8

11

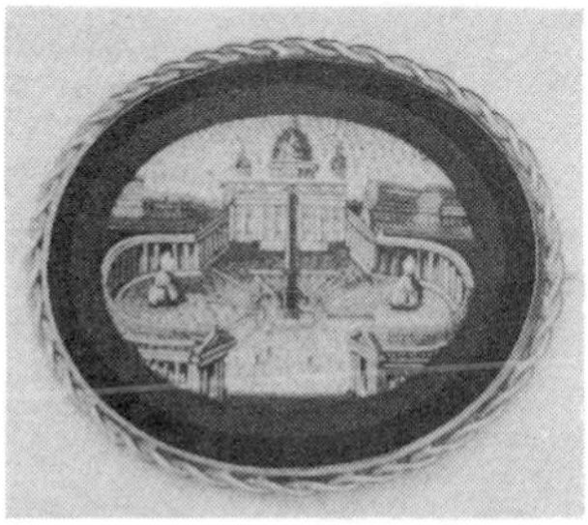
9

7

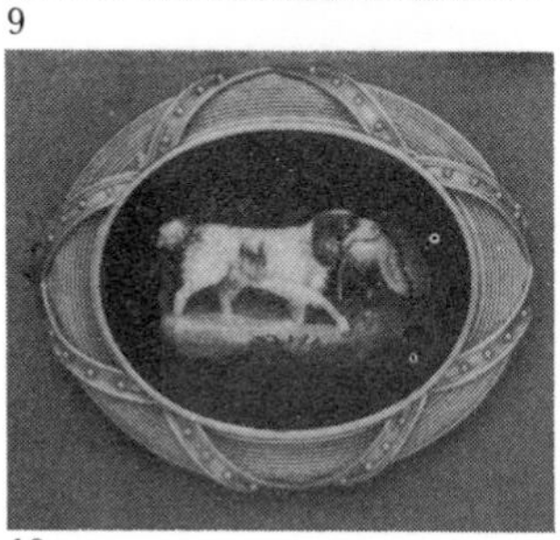
10

6
A micro-mosaic and walnut table, third quarter 19th century, depicting scenes of Rome, surrounded by specimen marbles, 56cm (22in) diam., *NY 26 Apr,*
$3,025 (£1,964)

7
A Roman micro-mosaic plaque, c.1860, set against a black marble ground, several chips along the edges, 21cm (8¼in), *S 18 June,*
£1,067 ($1,686)

8
A Roman micro-mosaic plaque, in a silver-gilt frame, maker's mark T.D., probably Thomas William Dee, London, 1855, plaque 7.5cm (3in), *G 15 May,*
SF 6,820 (£2,296; $3,697)

9
A Roman oval brooch, late 19th century, decorated with a view of St. Peter's, set into blue glass, back chipped, 5.5cm (2¼in), *S 19 Feb,*
£154 ($234)

10
A gold and Roman mosaic brooch, c.1870, depicting a spaniel retrieving a duck, *L 8 May,*
£1,210 ($1,960)

11
A Russian micro-mosaic plaque, by George Wekler, St. Petersburg, inscribed on the reverse 'D'après l'original de Paul Potter par George Wekler membre de l'Académie Impériale à St. Petersburg 1834', slight damage, 7.5cm (3in), *S 12 Nov,*
£2,090 ($2,926)

the water. Other doves are pluming their feathers in the sun on the lip of a goblet'.[6] Although one would have been fascinated to see the first mosaics mentioned, it was a copy of the second, made for Emperor Hadrian, which was found by Cardinal Furietti in 1737, in the course of excavations at the Villa Adriana in Tivoli. On the Cardinal's death in 1764, the mosaic was purchased by Pope Clement XIII for the Capitoline Museum. 19th century copies vary from vague approximations (figs 16 & 17) to exact copies including the original mosaic frame (colour illustration p.484, fig.8). This large plaque is a perfect example of a Roman souvenir, signed and dated by Agostino Francescangeli in 1837 — family tradition held that it was purchased by Sir Francis Darwin on a visit to Rome in 1871. Its Roman tortoiseshell, ebony and ivory frame is dated 1871 and decorated with antique masks, views of the Temple of Vesta, the Campidoglio and the Colosseum and is inscribed in Latin with Pliny's description. Apparently because of the banality of the subject and not for any lack of quality, this fine plaque fetched less than a plaque (fig.18) of similar size showing the Roman forum.

The average small ruin plaque, set into an Italian hardstone snuff box or mounted elsewhere in Europe now brings a figure between £1,000 and £2,000 ($1,600 and $3,200), (colour illustrations p.484, figs 4 & 5). It is the animals which are currently the most expensive subjects; perhaps a reflection of their universal appeal or a modern wish for naturalism even in this most formal of media. A tiny oval plaque, measuring a mere 3.5cm (1¼in), showing a dewy-eyed spaniel (fig.20) — a subject originally attributed to Antonio Aguatti (died c.1846) who continued Raffaelli's experiments in the colouring of *smalti filati* — fetched £825 ($1,304) recently. A more unusual scrawny tabby cat mounted in a gold vinaigrette (fig.19) brought £2,530 ($3,542). Two versions of the same scene of a dog scrapping with a cat, after a painting by the Bohemian artist Wenceslaus Peter (1742-1829) who worked in Rome from 1774 and specialised in portraying battling fauna, fetched £2,429 ($3,401) as a plaque (fig.4) and £4,400 ($6,160) mounted in a Paris gold box of 1809-19 (fig.21).

Two major factors have stimulated a sharp rise in mosaic prices over the last few years. First was the influence of Rosalinde and Arthur Gilbert, whose superb mosaic collection, started in the 1960s and now housed in the Los Angeles County Museum of Art, rivals the comprehensive but comparatively unavailable

12

13

14

15

16

12
A gold and Roman mosaic bracelet, c.1820, depicting figures in folk costume, imperfect, *L 9 Oct,*
£1,210 ($1,694)

13
A hardstone and Roman mosaic snuff box with silver mounts, Giovanni Andrea Mascelli, c.1830, depicting St. Peter's Square, 8cm (3in), in original leather case, *L 9 June,*
£880 ($1,390)

14
A gold and Roman micro-mosaic cross pendant, with a cherub at the centre, slight damage, *C 8 July,*
£550 ($858)

15
A gold and mosaic pendant, c.1865, with the head of a pharaoh, the reverse with miniature compartment, slightly imperfect, *L 19 June,*
£880 ($1,390)

16
A horn, piqué and micro-mosaic snuff box, the box late 18th century, the Roman mosaic early 19th century, minor repairs to horn, 6.5cm (2½in), *G 1 May,*
SF 4,180 (£1,407; $2,266)

17
A gilt-bronze and mosaic casket, mid 19th century, probably Italian, lid with a panel of Roman doves within malachite crossbanding, 20cm (8in), *L 21 Mar,*
£1,870 ($2,917)

18
A Roman micro-mosaic plaque, third quarter 19th century, against a black marble ground, set within a wooden box frame, 96.5cm (38in), *NY 13 Sept,*
$20,900 (£14,218)

collection of the Hermitage in Leningrad. Secondly, the publication in Italy in 1981 of Petochi's excellently illustrated book (see below) has encouraged a growing number of enthusiastic Italian collectors.

Collecting mosaics has certain advantages for amateurs. To start with, the colours are still as fresh as the day they were made and often respond magically to a polish. Furthermore, condition is immediately obvious — once one tessera has fallen, the rest will follow very quickly. Finally, even the untutored eye can recognise that the smallest tesserae produce the finest and most detailed mosaics.

References

1. Ed. Richard Edgcumbe, *The Diary of Frances, Lady Shelley*, London, 1912
2. John Moore, *A View of Society and Manners in Italy*, London, 1781
3. Mariana Starke, *Letters from Italy*, 2nd edition, London, 1815
4. Lady Methuen, *Letters from Italy*, 2nd edition, London 1777
5. Francis Coghlan *Handbook for Italy*, London, 1845
6. Trans. K.Jex-Blake, *The Elder Pliny's Chapters on the History of Art*, London, 1896

Further reading:

Alvar Gonzalez-Palacios, *The Art of Mosaics, selections from the Gilbert Collection*, 1977
Domenico Petochi, *I Mosaici Minuti Romani*, 1981 (English summary available)
Ed.Hugh Tait, *The Art of the Jeweller, a Catalogue of the Hull Grundy Gift to the British Museum*, 1984
Alfieri Branchetti Cornini, *Mosaici Minuti Romani*, catalogue of Vatican exhibition, 1986

17

18

19
An oval two-colour gold and Roman micro-mosaic vinaigrette, early 19th century, depicting a tabby cat, 3.5cm (1½in), *S 17 Sept,*
£2,530 ($3,542)

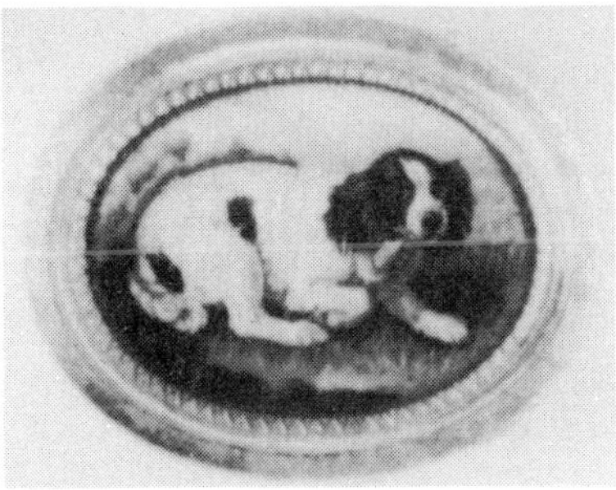

20
A miniature Roman micro-mosaic plaque, early 19th century, depicting a spaniel, gold and silver-gilt mount, 3.5cm (1½in), *L 9 June,*
£825 ($1,304)

21
A French gold and mosaic snuff box, Paris, 1809-19, makers' marks NL and LAB in vertical lozenges, set with a Roman micro-mosaic, enamel chipped, 8cm (3in), *S 17 Sept,*
£4,400 ($6,160)

1

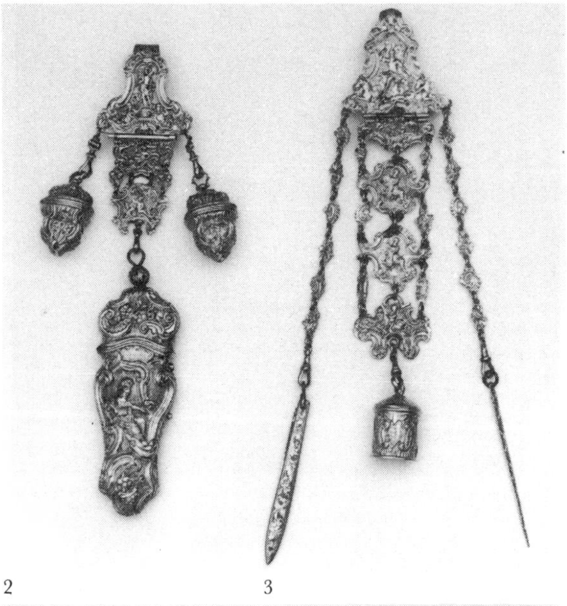

2 3

4

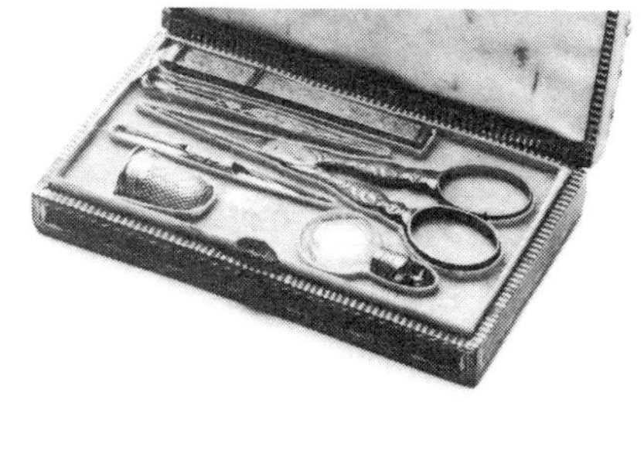

5

6

7

8

9

1
A set of four counter boxes, *(two illustrated)*, Mariaval le Jeune, Paris, c.1730, of stained and natural ivory, containing counters and discs inscribed with mottos, 8.5cm (3¼in), *S 19 Feb,*
£880 ($1,338)

2
A gilt-metal chatelaine, English, mid 18th century, cast with the figures of Mars and Minerva, later pendant ball and loop, 21cm (8¼in), *S 19 Feb,*
£286 ($435)

3
A gilt-metal chatelaine, Birmingham, c.1755, decorated with mythological subjects including Neptune, 26cm (10¼in), *S 19 Feb,*
£209 ($318)

4
A shagreen and gold necessaire, possibly Dutch or German, Koper, c.1760, 5.5cm (2¼in), *L 9 June,*
£2,640 ($4,171)

5
A necessaire, early 19th century, red morocco case, 11.5cm (4½in) wide, *M 24 Feb,*
FF 8,880 (£862; $1,257)

6
A gold-mounted ivory souvenir, French, c.1780, the lid applied in gold *SOUVENIR D'AMITIE,* lid cracked, 8.5cm (3¼in), *S 19 Feb,*
£253 ($385)

7
A gold-mounted ivory souvenir, French, c.1785, the lid applied in gold *SOUVENIR D'AMITIE,* damaged, 9cm (3½in), *S 19 Feb,*
£462 ($702)

8
A gilt-metal and mother-of-pearl etui, English or German, c.1740, lacking fitments, 10cm (4in), *S 19 Feb,*
£286 ($435)

9
A gilt-metal etui, English, probably Birmingham, mid 18th century, damaged, 9cm (3½in), *S 19 Feb,*
£198 ($301)

1
A crystal perfume flask, Continental, late 19th century, with gold mounts, the cover set with a red stone bordered by diamonds, 9cm (3½in), *NY 12 June,*
$2,420 (£1,592)

2
A gold perfume flask, Maison Janisset, Paris, c.1875, each side with an Egyptian-style mask and a baroque-style cartouche, set with rubies, emeralds, pearls and diamonds, the cover with a cabochon sapphire, 7cm (2¾in), *NY 12 June,*
$6,325 (£4,161)

3
A gold and enamel vinaigrette, Swiss, c.1830, in the form of an acorn, enamelled green and mounted with garnets and pearls, 4cm (1½in), *NY 12 June,*
$2,310 (£1,520)

4
An opaline glass scent bottle, c.1840, with gold mounts, 6.5cm (2½in), *S 18 June,*
£253 ($399)

5
A glass scent flask, Jules Wiese, Paris, c.1860, the silver mounts set with garnets, 9cm (3½in), *S 19 Feb,*
£440 ($669)

6
A glass scent bottle, French, c.1870, with gold mounts and cover (slightly damaged), 9cm (3½in), *S 19 Feb,*
£209 ($318)

7
A gold and glass combination scent flask and pill box, Continental, late 19th century, with enamelled borders and set with diamonds, the base opening to reveal a pill box, 11cm (4¼in), *NY 12 Dec,*
$2,530 (£1,807)

8
A glass scent bottle, English, c.1835, the gold mounts and stopper decorated in enamels, damaged, 10.5cm (4in), *S 12 Nov,*
£286 ($400)

9
A pair of enamel and ivory opera glasses, French, c.1860, 10.5cm (4in), *S 19 Feb,*
£264 ($401)

10
A gold and enamel posy holder, Swiss, second quarter 19th century, of shuttlecock form, 13cm (5in), *G 15 May,*
SF 3,740 (£1,259; $2,027)

11
A gilt-metal and enamel bonbonnière, probably German, c.1755, in the form of a pug dog, 8cm (3in), *G 15 May,*
SF 6,050 (£2,037; $3,280)

12
A gold telephone dialling stick, Petochi, Rome, c.1950, the handle set with a diamond trefoil, 12.5cm (5in), *G 15 May,*
SF 1,210 (£407; $656)

13
A gold telephone dialling stick, Petochi, Rome, c.1950, surmounted by a terrier's head with cabochon sapphire eyes and nose, 11cm (4¼in), *G 15 May,*
SF 1,320 (£444; $716)

14
A jewelled gold magnifying glass, French, c.1930, the butterfly handle set with cabochon emeralds and with ruby eyes, 9.5cm (3¾in), *G 15 May,*
SF 3,190 (£1,074; $1,729)

15
A gold lorgnette, 19th century, 8-carat gold, *A 21 Apr,*
Dfl 2,300 (£697; $1,094)

1 2 3

4

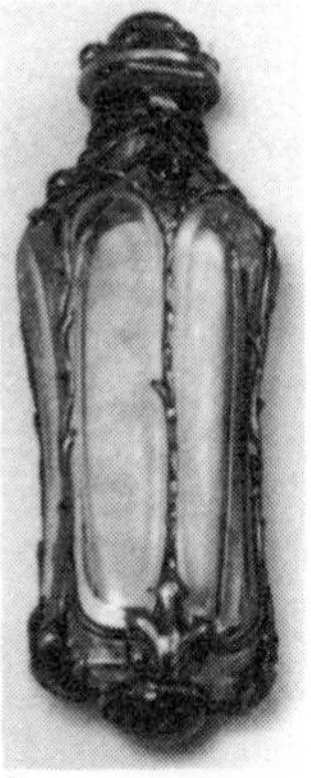
5

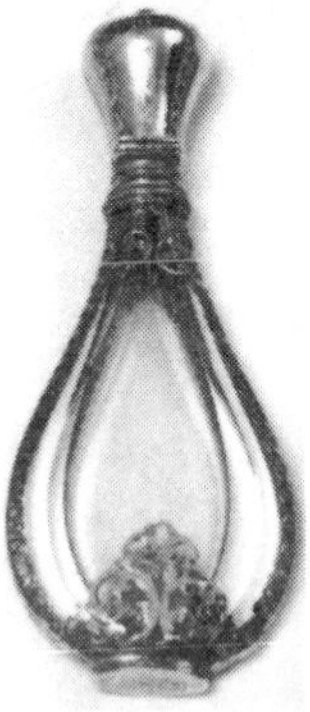
6

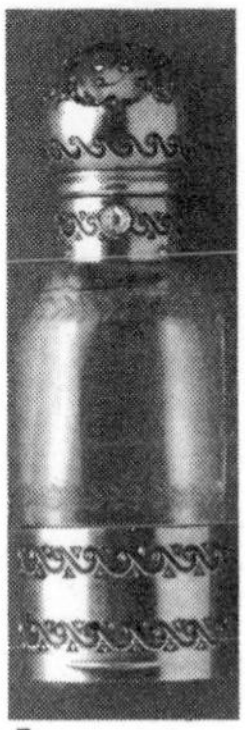
7

8

9

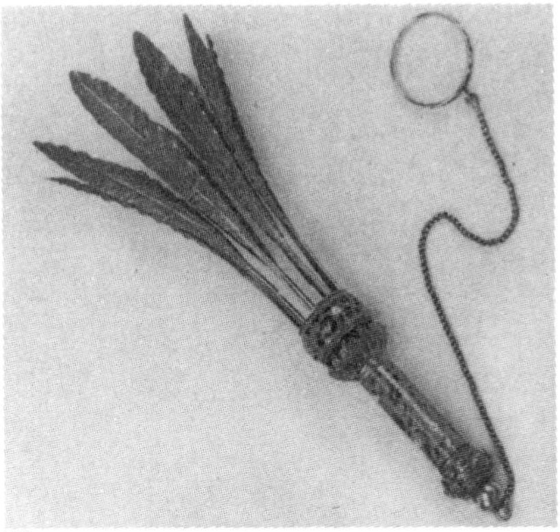
10

11

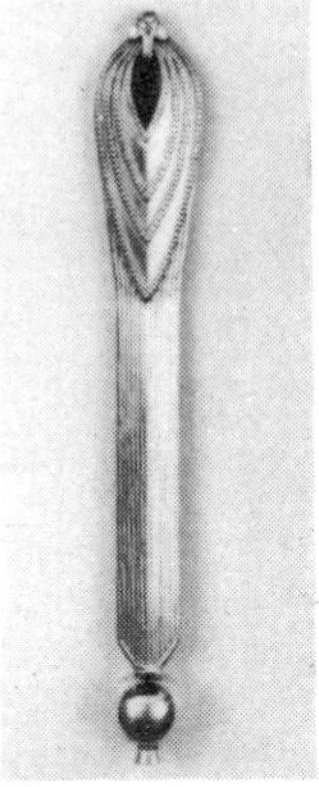
12

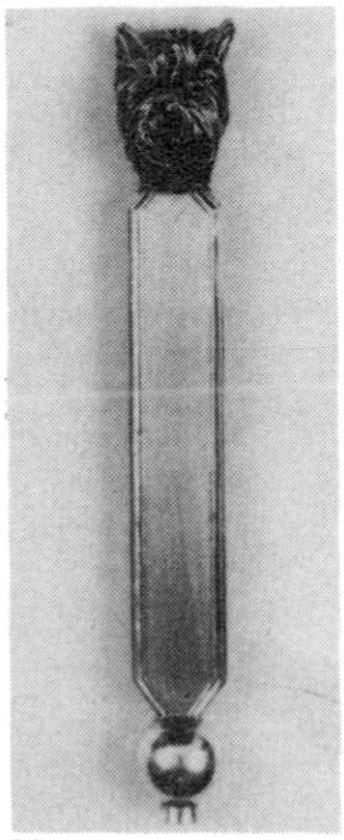
13

14

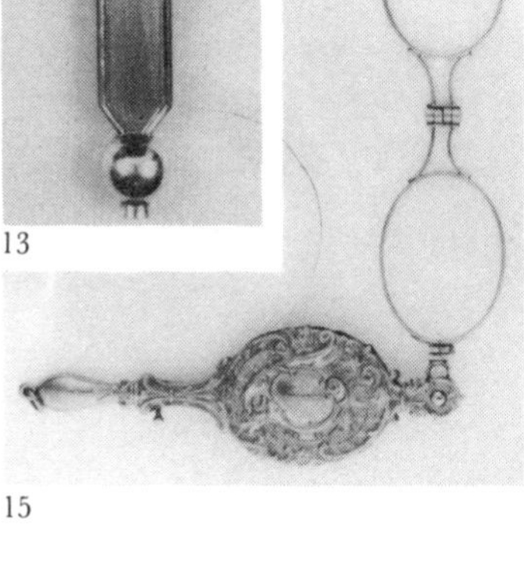
15

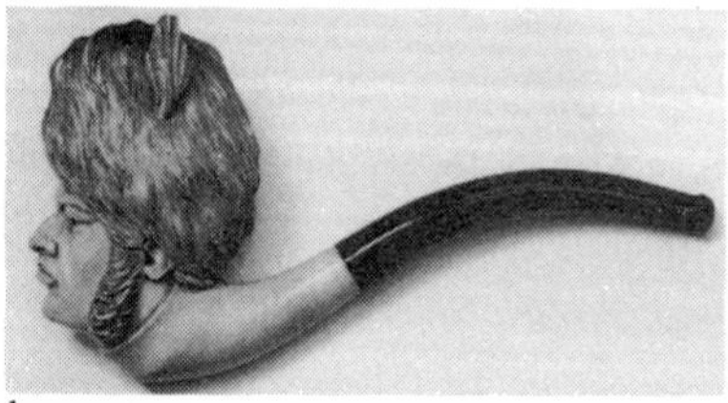
1

2

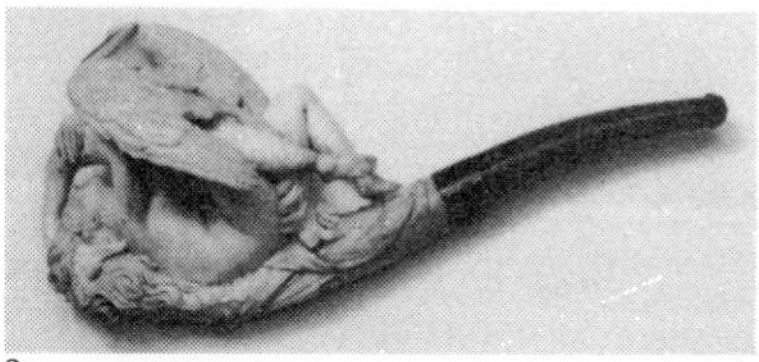
3

4

5

6

7

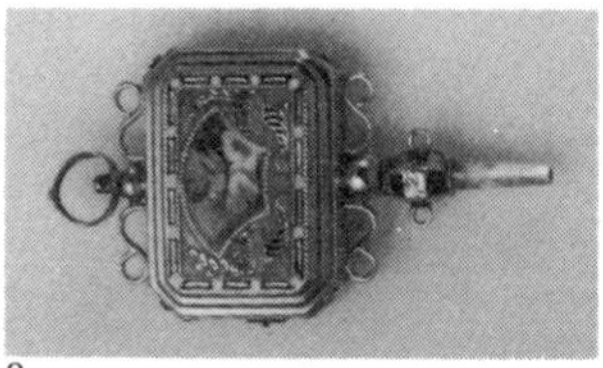
8

9

10 11

12

13

14

15

1
A meerschaum pipe, Austrian, late 19th century, in the form of a guardsman's head with bearskin, amber mouthpiece, 20cm (8in), *S 12 Nov,*
£286 ($400)

2
A meerschaum pipe, French, late 19th century, in the form of an eagle attacking a kid, case stamped *G.B.D.* (Ganneval, Bondier, Donniger), amber mouthpiece, 24.5cm (9¾in), *S 12 Nov,*
£462 ($647)

3
A meerschaum cheroot holder, German, late 19th century, in the form of Leda and the swan, silver-mounted amber mouthpiece, 18cm (7in), *S 12 Nov,*
£528 ($739)

4
A meerschaum pipe, Vienna, late 19th century, the bowl in the form of an eagle's claw with animals between the talons, silver mounts, amber mouthpiece, 19cm (7½in), *S 18 June,*
£385 ($608)

5
A meerschaum pipe, late 19th century, the bowl in the form of the bust of a Victorian lady, the stem carved with her four children, 35cm (13¾in), *C 29 Jan,*
£352 ($517)

6
A meerschaum cheroot holder, German, dated 1905, the stem carved with four portrait busts of a German family, amber mouthpiece, 25cm (10in), *S 12 Nov,*
£374 ($524)

7
A meerschaum cheroot holder, Austrian, late 19th century, in the form of a cheroot-smoking grisette, silver-mounted amber mouthpiece, 20cm (8in), *S 12 Nov,*
£242 ($339)

8
A gold and enamel musical watch key, Swiss, c.1825, 6cm (2½in), *NY 12 June,*
$4,675 (£3,076)

9
A gold and enamel musical fob seal, Swiss, c.1835, the winding stem set with four red stones, 4cm (1½in), *NY 12 Dec,*
$1,100 (£786)

10
A silver-gilt and enamel miniature birdcage, Vienna, late 19th century, containing an enamelled silver peacock set with rubies and sapphires, 17.5cm (7in), *NY 12 Dec,*
$2,420 (£1,728)

11
A silver and enamel miniature birdcage, Vienna, c.1885, containing a bird with jewelled wings, 13cm (5in), *NY 12 Dec,*
$1,100 (£786)

12
A silver-gilt and enamel singing bird box, Swiss, c.1860, the lid enamelled with an alpine scene, 9.5cm (3¾in), *S 12 Nov,*
£3,080 ($4,312)

13
A tortoiseshell and gilt-metal singing bird box, Finnigans, London, 20th century, 10cm (4in) wide, *S 12 Nov,*
£495 ($693)

14
A Palais Royal gilt-metal and mother-of-pearl musical necessaire, c.1820, in the form of a piano, the lid lifting to reveal a tray containing sewing accessories, 23cm (9in) long, *S 19 Feb,*
£1,650 ($2,508)

15
A silver-gilt and enamel musical necessaire, Vienna, late 19th century, maker's mark K.B., in the form of a piano, the 'keyboard' containing two inkwells and a watch, the 'soundboard' containing a mirror, key and miniature brush and comb, 18.5cm (7¼in), *NY 12 Dec,*
$6,600 (£4,714)

Portrait Miniatures

Measurements are those of the miniature excluding the frame.

1
School of Jean Baptiste Jacques Augustin, The Marquise de Segonzac at a Harpsichord, signed and dated 1796, set within the lid of a tortoiseshell box, 8cm (3in) diam., *L 17 Mar,*
£1,540 ($2,356)

2
Jean Baptiste Jacques Augustin, A Young Lady, c.1805, gilt-metal frame, 13cm (5in), *L 17 Mar,*
£2,090 ($3,197)

3
Charles Boit, A Gentleman, signed, c.1695, enamel, gold frame, 3.5cm (1½in), *L 17 Mar,*
£1,012 ($1,548)

4
Henry Bone, The Prince Regent, signed and dated 1818, wearing the insignia of the Order of the Fleece and the breast star of the Order of the Garter, enamel, gilt-metal frame, 3.5cm (1½in), *L 17 Mar,*
£660 ($1,009)

5
Henry Bone, Mary Jane Burdett, signed, inscribed and dated 1803, enamel, gilt-metal frame, 7cm (2¾in), *L 9 June,*
£935 ($1,477)

6
Joseph Marie Bouton, Two Children of the Polignac Family, signed, c.1790, gilt-metal mount, 8cm (3in), *L 17 Mar,*
£6,050 ($9,256)

7
Robert Bowyer after John Smart, Mrs Robert Frith, c.1800, gilt-metal mount, 5.5cm (2¼in), *S 18 June,*
£374 ($591)

8
Ignazio Pio Vittoriano Campana, The Milkmaid, c.1780, gilt-metal frame, 7cm (2¾in), *L 9 June,*
£4,620 ($7,299)

9
Ignazio Pio Vittoriano Campana, A Young Lady, c.1780, gold mount, set within a box, 5.5cm (2¼in), *L 9 June,*
£880 ($1,390)

10
Marie Gabrielle Capet, A Cartographer, c.1795, ormolu frame, 9cm (3½in), *L 17 Mar,*
£50,600 ($77,418)

11
Marie Gabrielle Capet, A Gentleman, possibly Etienne Pallière, signed and dated 1802, gilt-metal frame, 6.5cm (2½in), *L 17 Mar,*
£3,520 ($5,385)

12
Richard Collins, A Gentleman, c.1780, gold slide frame, 4cm (1½in), *S 18 June,*
£143 ($226)

Augustin, Jean Baptiste Jacques, d.Paris 1832, fl.Paris.

Boit, Charles, 1662-1727, fl.Holland, Germany and Vienna.

Bone, Henry, 1755-1834, fl.London.

Bouton, Joseph Marie, 1768-1823, fl.Paris and London.

Bowyer, Robert, c.1758-1834. Pupil of John Smart.

Boy, Peter the Younger, 1681-1742, fl.Frankfurt.

Campana, Ignazio Pio Vittoriano, 1744-86, fl.Turin and Paris.

Capet, Mlle Marie Gabrielle, 1761-1818, fl. Paris after 1791.

Collins, Richard, 1755-1831. Pupil of Plott; worked on ivory and enamel.

Cosway, Richard, 1742-1821, fl.London.

Daffinger, Michael Moritz, 1790-1849, fl.Vienna.

Daniel, Joseph, 1760-1803, fl.Bristol, Bath and London.

Dawe, Elizabeth, fl. London, early 19th century.

Deranton, Joseph, 1756-1832, fl.Paris.

See also: Colour illustrations *p* 485

1

2

3

4

5

6

7

8

9

10

11

12

1

2

3

4

5

6

7

8

9

10

11

12

1
Richard Cosway, A Lady, signed and dated 1787, gold frame, 7cm (2¾in), *L 9 June,*
£990 ($1,564)

2
Richard Cosway, A Gentleman, c.1790, gold frame, 6cm (2½in), *L 9 June,*
£770 ($1,216)

3
Moritz Michael Daffinger, A pair of Miniatures of Heinrich Graf Bellegarde and Paula Gräfin Wolkenstein, the former signed, c.1830, (*one illustrated*), he wearing the badge of the Order of St. George of the Reunion, gold frames, 8.5cm (3¼in), *L 9 June,*
£8,800 ($13,904)

4
Joseph Daniel, Captain William Cox, 5th Regiment, c.1790, gold frame, 5cm (2in), *L 9 June,*
£1,760 ($2,781)

5
Elizabeth Dawe, A Lady, signed and dated 1825, gilt-metal frame, 7cm (2¾in), *L 17 Mar,*
£418 ($639)

6
Joseph Deranton, A Young Gentleman, signed and reputedly dated 1785, gold frame, 6cm (2¼in), *L 17 Mar,*
£10,120 ($15,483)

7
Joseph Deranton, A Lady, c.1785, three-colour gold mount within a gilt-metal frame, 5.5cm (2¼in), *L 17 Mar,*
£1,980 ($3,029)

8
Charles G. Dillon, A Gentleman, c.1810, gold frame, 5.5cm (2¼in), *S 18 June,*
£154 ($243)

9
Frédéric Dubois, A Lady, signed, c.1805, gilt-metal mount, 7.5cm (3in), *L 17 Mar,*
£1,650 ($2,524)

10
A Lady, bearing signature *Dumont*, c.1780, gilt-metal mount, 6.5cm (2½in), *S 19 Feb,*
£187 ($284)

11
François Dumont, A Lady, signed, c.1795, gold and silver frame, 6cm (2½in), *L 9 June,*
£8,250 ($13,035)

12
Attributed to Henry Edridge, An Officer, English School, c.1810, silver-gilt frame, 8.5cm (3¼in), *S 18 June,*
£418 ($660)

Dillon, Charles G., fl.1810-30, Plymouth.

Dubois, Frédéric, fl.London and St. Petersburg 1804-18.

Dumont, François, 1751-1831, fl.Paris.

Edridge, Henry, 1768-1821, fl.London.

Engleheart, George, 1750-1829, fl. London. Pupil of Sir Joshua Reynolds.

Engleheart, John Cox Dillman, 1782-1862, fl.London.

Füger, Heinrich Friedrich. 1751-1818, fl.Vienna.

Gibson, Richard, 1615-1690, fl.London and Holland.

Graff, Anton, 1736-1813, fl.Regensburg, Winterthur and Zurich.

Guérard, E.Bernard, Chevalier de, d.Naples 1836, fl.Vienna.

Hall, Pierre Adolphe, 1739-93, fl.Stockholm and Paris.

Hargreaves, Thomas, 1774-1846, Liverpool, assistant to Sir Thomas Lawrence.

Hénard, Charles, b.1757, fl.France and England.

Hone, Nathaniel, 1718-74, fl.London.

Hue de Bréval, Mlle Virginie, Mme Rousseau, fl.Paris 1810-22. Pupil of Augustin.

1
Henry Edridge, Anna Maria Blunt, née Gatehouse, c.1795, gold frame, 7cm (2¾in), *L 9 June,*
£418 ($660)

2
George Engleheart, A Gentleman, c.1810, gold frame, 8.5cm (3¼in), *S 18 June,*
£924 ($1,460)

3
George Engleheart, A Young Gentleman, c.1815, signed, 8.5cm (3½in), *L 9 June,*
£880 ($1,390)

4
George Engleheart, A Lady, c.1785, gold frame, the border set with diamonds, the reverse with seed pearl monogram, 4cm (1½in), *L 9 June,*
£4,620 ($7,300)

5
John Cox Dillman Engleheart, A Gentleman, signed and dated 1825, 9cm (3½in), *S 18 June,*
£495 ($782)

6
Perhaps by Guglielmo Faya, A Young Girl called Ellen Cooper, seated beside a black and tan King Charles spaniel, gilt and ebonised wood frame, 9.5cm (3¾in), *S 17 Sept,*
£352 ($493)

7
Heinrich Friedrich Füger, Prinz Friedrich Wilhelm Hohenlohe-Kirchberg, c.1794, unfinished, mounted on card, 7cm (2¾in). The sitter (1732-96) was an Austrian general; the miniature is based on a life-sized painting in Schloss Kirchberg, Wurtemberg, dated 1794. *G 15 May,*
SF 13,200 (£4,444; $7,156)

8
Heinrich Friedrich Füger, Prinz Friedrich Wilhelm Hohenlohe-Kirchberg, c.1794, unfinished, gilt-metal frame, 17cm (6¾in). See note above. *L 17 Mar,*
£8,250 ($12,622)

9
Heinrich Friedrich Füger, A Gentleman, c.1790, gilt-metal frame, 6.5cm (2½in), *L 17 Mar,*
£10,450 ($15,988)

10
Heinrich Friedrich Füger, Doctor Stoll, signed, c.1795, the sitter holding an old master drawing, gilt-metal frame, 12.5cm (5in), *L 17 Mar,*
£9,900 ($15,147)

11
Anton Graff, A Lady, c.1805, gilt-metal frame, 6cm (2¼in), *L 17 Mar,*
£1,155 ($1,767)

12
Ascribed to E* Bernard, Chevalier de Guérard,** Maria Isabella, Queen of Naples, (1785-1848, d. of Charles IV of Spain), signed and dated 1833, background with a view of Vesuvius, gold frame set with garnets, 6.5cm (2½in), *L 17 Mar,*
£2,090 ($3,197)

13
E* Bernard, Chevalier de Guérard,** A Young Lady, signed and dated Vienna 1817, gilt-metal frame, 6.5cm (2½in), *L 9 June,*
£1,320 ($2,085)

14
E* Bernard, Chevalier de Guérard,** Maria Ludovica, Archduchess of Austria-Este, (1787-1816), signed, c.1805, gilt-metal mount, 7cm (2¾in), *L 17 Mar,*
£3,300 ($5,049)

15
Pierre Adolphe Hall, A Young Lady, c.1785, enamel, gold mount, 5cm (2in), *L 17 Mar,*
£2,090 ($3,197)

Hurter, Johann Heinrich von, 1734-99, fl.Paris, The Hague and Berne. Enamellist.

Isabey, Jean Baptiste, 1767-1855, fl.London, Paris and Vienna.

Jacques, Nicolas, 1780-1844, fl. Paris. Pupil of Isabey.

1

2

3

4

5

6

7

8

9

10

11

12

13

14

15

1

2

3

4

5

6

7

8

9

10

11

12

13

14

15

1
Pierre Adolphe Hall, A Lady, signed, c.1784, mounted within the lid of a tortoiseshell box, 7.5cm (3in), *L 17 Mar,*
£6,050 ($9,256)

2
Pierre Adolphe Hall, Louise Félicité Victoire d'Aumont, Princesse de Monaco, signed, c.1782, four-colour gold frame, 8cm (3in), *L 17 Mar,*
£46,200 ($70,686)

3
In the manner of Pierre Adolphe Hall, A Young Girl, c.1780, gilt-metal mount, 5.5cm (2¼in), *L 10 Nov,*
£792 ($1,133)

4
Thomas Hargreaves, A Lady, signed and dated 1829, gilt-metal mount, 9cm (3½in), *S 17 Sept,*
£484 ($678)

5
Charles Hénard, A Young Lady, reputedly signed and dated 1795, gilt-metal frame, 8cm (3in), *L 17 Mar,*
£4,620 ($7,068)

6
Nathaniel Hone, A Gentleman, signed with monogram and dated 1751, enamel, silver-gilt frame, 4cm (1½in), *L 9 June,*
£990 ($1,564)

7
Johann Heinrich von Hurter, after Nathaniel Dance, Rear Admiral Sir Richard Edwards, inscribed and dated 1784, enamel, gilt-metal frame, 5.5cm (2¼in). Detail of a portrait by Dance dated 1780. *L 9 June,*
£1,375, $2,172)

8
Johann Heinrich von Hurter, Queen Charlotte, consort of King George III, signed and dated 1782, enamel, gilt-metal bezel, 5.5cm (2¼in), *L 17 Mar,*
£3,960 ($6,058)

9
Jean Baptiste Isabey, Marquis de Gouy d'Arcy, signed and dated 1842, wearing the badges of the Légion d'Honneur, the Order of St. Louis and the Swedish Order of the Sword, on paper, gilt-metal mount, 13cm (5¼in), *L 9 June,*
£9,020 ($14,251)

10
After Jean Baptiste Isabey, The Empress Josephine, c.1810, enamel, gold frame with blue enamel border, 5cm (2in), *L 10 Nov,*
£3,300 ($4,719)

11
Follower of Jean Baptiste Isabey, A Young Boy, c.1825, gilt-metal frame, 7cm (2¾in), *L 17 Mar,*
£1,210 ($1,851)

12
Nicolas Jacques, Madame Récamier, from an original painting by Baron von Gérard given to the sitter by Prince August of Prussia, signed, gilt-metal mount, 8.5cm (3¼in), *L 9 June,*
£968 ($1,529)

13
Louis Ami Arlaud-Jurine, A Gentleman, c.1790, signed, gold frame with blue enamel border, 6cm (2½in), *L 9 June,*
£1,045 ($1,651)

14
Louis Ami Arlaud-Jurine, A Young Lady, c.1795, signed, gold frame, 5cm (2in), *L 9 June,*
£1,430 ($2,259)

15
Carl Christian Kanz, Tête d'Expression, c.1800, enamel, gilt-metal frame, 11.5cm (4½in), *L 10 Nov,*
£4,180 ($5,977)

Arlaud-Jurine, Louis Ami, 1751-1829, fl.London, Paris and Switzerland. Studied with Liotard.

Kanz, Carl Christian, 1758-1818, fl.Paris.

Klingstedt, Carl Gustav, 1657-1734, fl.Sweden and Paris.

1
Carl Christian Kanz, A Young Lady, signed, c.1800, enamel, gilt-metal mount, 6.5cm (2½in), *G 15 May,*
SF 6,160 (£2,074; $3,339)

2
Carl Gustav Klingstedt, A Young Gallant with a Kitchen Maid, c.1720, grisaille heightened with red, on paper, wood frame, 5cm (2in), *L 9 June,*
£1,375 ($2,172)

3
Carl Gustav Klingstedt, Gallant Lovers, c.1720, on paper, wood frame, 5.5cm (2¼in), *L 9 June,*
£902 ($1,425)

4
Nicolas Lafrensen, A Lady, signed and dated 1790, ormolu easel frame, 4.5cm (1¾in), *L 10 Nov,*
£770 ($1,101)

5
Attributed to Jean Baptiste Lampi, Major General Basil Stepanovitch Popov, c.1785, wearing the Order of Saint Alexander-Nevsky. The sitter (1743-1822) was President of the Russian Council of State and friend of Tzars Paul I and Alexander I. Gilt-metal frame, 6cm (2½in), *L 10 Nov,*
£2,200 ($3,146)

6
In the manner of Jean Etienne Liotard, A Young Lady in Turkish Style Costume, c.1770, gilt-metal frame, 8cm (3in), *L 9 June,*
£2,200 ($3,476)

7
Circle of Jean Etienne Liotard, A Gentleman, c.1750, gilt-metal frame, 4.5cm (1¾in), *L 9 June,*
£603 ($953)

8
François Meuret, Robert Arthur des Acres, Marquis de l'Aigle, signed and dated 1858, gilt-metal mount within giltwood frame, 10cm (4in), *G 15 May,*
SF 8,800 (£2,963; $4,770)

9
François Meuret, Comtesse de Clermont-Tonnerre, signed and dated 1861, ormolu easel frame signed by Alphonse Giroux, Paris, 10cm (4in), *L 9 June,*
£7,700 ($12,166)

10
Mme Lizinska Aimée Zoé de Mirbel, née Rue, Edouard, Duc de Fitz-James (1776-1838), signed and dated 1828, gilt-metal mount within wood frame, 10cm (4in), *L 9 June,*
£1,980 ($3,128)

11
Sir William John Newton, A Lady, signed with initials and dated 1812, ormolu frame, 9cm (3½in), *L 9 June,*
£638 ($1,008)

12
Emanuel Peter, Frau von Kraynay, c.1830, gilt-metal mount, 7.5cm (3in), *L 9 June,*
£2,035 ($3,215)

13
Andrew Plimer, A Lady, signed and dated 1785, gilt-metal frame, 4cm (1½in), *L 9 June,*
£506 ($799)

14
Augustin Ritt, A Lady, signed, c.1795, gold frame, 7cm (2¾in), *L 10 Nov,*
£880 ($1,258)

15
Attributed to John Plott, A Young Gentleman, c.1780, gold frame, 5cm (2in), *S 17 Sept*
£176 ($246)

Lafrensen, Nicolas, 1737-1807, fl. Stockholm and Paris.

Lampi, Jean Baptiste, 1751-1830, fl.Austria, Poland and Russia.

Laurent, Jean-Antoine, 1763-1832, fl.Paris and Epinal.

Liotard, Jean Etienne, 1701-89, fl.Italy, Vienna, Paris and London.

Meuret, François, 1800-87, fl.Paris.

1

2

3

4

5

6

7

8

9

10

11

12

13

14

15

1

2

3

4

5

6

7

8

9

10

11

12

13

14

15

1
Augustin Ritt, An Officer, signed, c.1792, gilt-metal frame, 8cm (3in), *L 10 Nov,*
£5,280 ($7,550)

2
Manner of Augustin Ritt, A Gentleman, c.1795, gilt-metal mount, 7.5cm (3in), *L 10 Nov,*
£440 ($629)

3
Daniel Saint, A Young Gentleman, signed, c.1815, gilt-metal mount, 8cm (3in), *G 15 May,*
SF 13,750 (£4,630; $7,454)

4
Samuel Shelley, A Lady, c.1795, later gilt-metal frame, 4cm (1½in), *S 19 Feb,*
£440 ($669)

5
Samuel Shelley, A Young Cadet, c.1795, gold frame, 6.5cm (2½in), *L 9 June,*
£1,980 ($3,128)

6
Charles Shirreff, A Lady, signed and dated 1799, gold frame, 6cm (2½in), *L 9 June,*
£418 ($660)

7
Louis Marie Sicardi, Madame d'Alembert, signed and dated 1800, gilt-metal frame, 7cm (2¾in), *L 9 June,*
£6,380 ($10,080)

8
Jean Baptiste Singry, A Lady, signed and dated 1816, ormolu easel frame, 15cm (5¾in), *L 10 Nov,*
£2,970 ($4,247)

9
Jean Baptiste Singry, A Self Portrait, signed and dated 1817, gilt-metal frame, 12.5cm (5in), *L 9 June,*
£25,300 ($39,974)

10
John Smart, Miss Fisher, c.1775, on paper, gilt-metal frame, 6cm (2½in), *L 9 June,*
£770 ($1,217)

11
Franciszek Smiadecki, A Gentleman, signed with initials, c.1650, oil on copper, gilt-metal frame, 6.5cm (2½in), *L 9 June,*
£1,375 ($2,173)

12
Antoine Vestier, An Elderly Lady, c.1780, gold mount, 4cm (1½in), *L 10 Nov,*
£880 ($1,258)

13
Antoine Vestier, A Lady, signed and dated 1781, 19th century silver frame set with rose cut diamonds, 5cm (2in), *L 10 Nov,*
£3,300 ($4,719)

14
Jean Baptiste Weyler, A Lady, signed and dated 1789, set within the lid of a tortoiseshell box, base missing, 7cm (2¾in), *L 10 Nov,*
£10,780 ($15,415)

15
Jean Baptiste Weyler, A Lady, c.1785, enamel, set in the lid of a lacquer box with gold mounts, maker's mark of Claude Brisson, 8cm (3in), *L 10 Nov,*
£3,850 ($5,506)

Mirbel, Mme Aimée Zoé Lizinska de, née Rue, 1796-1849, fl.Paris. Studied under Augustin.

Muss (Musso), Charles, 1785-1824. Enamellist, fl.London..

Newton, Sir William John, 1758-1869, fl.London.

Peter, Emanuel Thomas, 1799-1873, fl.Vienna. Pupil of Daffinger.

Plimer, Andrew, 1764-1837, fl.West Country, London and Scotland.

Plott, John, 1732-1803, assistant to Nathaniel Hone. Worked on ivory and enamel.

Ritt, Augustin, 1765-99, fl.Paris and St. Petersburg.

Saint, Daniel, 1778-1847, fl.Paris. Pupil of Isabey.

Shelley, Samuel, 1750-1806, fl.London.

Shirreff, Charles, b.Scotland 1750.

1
Jean Baptiste Weyler, A Gentleman, said to be Charles Claude La Billarderie, Comte d'Angiviller, signed, c.1780, gilt-metal mount, 6cm (2½in), *L 9 June,*
£1,375 ($2,192)

2
Christian Frederick Zincke, Harrington Gibbs, signed and dated 1717, enamel, gold frame, 4.5cm (1¾in), *L 9 June,*
£1,210 ($1,912)

3
Christian Frederick Zincke, A Lady, signed and dated 1716, enamel, gilt-metal mount, 6cm (2½in), *L 10 Nov,*
£1,155 ($1,652)

4
French School, A Gentleman, c.1720, on vellum, mounted in a silver locket, 6cm (2½in), *L 17 Mar,*
£1,375 ($2,103)

5
French School, A Young Girl, c.1760, enamel, gilt-metal mount, 3cm (1¼in), *L 17 Mar,*
£154 ($235)

6
French School, late 18th century, Jean Baptiste Lully (1632-87), musician and composer at the court of Louis XIV, enamel, engraved gold mount, 5cm (2in), *L 10 Nov,*
£715 ($1,022)

7
French School, A Gentleman, c.1795, giltwood frame, 7cm (2¾in), *L 17 Mar,*
£528 ($807)

8
French School, A Lady, 18th century, on ivory, 6.5cm (2½in), *A 6 May,*
Dfl 1,437 (£435; $692)

9
French School, A Lady, 18th century, on ivory, 6cm (2½in), *A 6 May,*
Dfl 805 (£244; $388)

10
French School, A Young Boy with a Kite, c.1800, gilt-metal frame, 7.5cm (3in), *L 17 Mar,*
£1,155 ($1,767)

11
French School, A Gentleman, c.1800, gold frame, 5cm (2in), *S 19 Feb,*
£176 ($268)

12
Dutch School, A Gentleman, 18th century, oil on copper, gilt frame, 9cm (3½in), *A 6 May,*
Dfl 1,725 (£523; $832)

13
Franco-Swiss School, A Gentleman, c.1800, enamel, gilt-metal mount, 11cm (4¼in), *L 10 Nov,*
£1,210 ($1,730)

14
English School, A Lady, c.1740, enamel, gold mount with gilt-metal reverse, 4.5cm (1¾in), *L 10 Nov,*
£495 ($708)

15
English School, A Gentleman, c.1780, 3.5cm (1¼in), *S 19 Feb,*
£132 ($201)

Sicardi, Louis Marie, 1746-1825, fl.Paris.

Singry, Jean Baptiste, 1782-1824, fl.Paris. Pupil of Isabey.

Salbreux, Louis Lié Périn, 1753-1817, fl.Paris. Studied under Sicardi.

Smart, John, 1742-1811, fl.India and London.

Smiadecki, Franciszek, mid 17th century, fl.Poland and Russia.

Soret, Nicolas, 1759-1830, fl.London, Geneva and St. Petersburg. Enamellist.

Vestier, Antoine, 1740-1824, fl.Holland, London and Paris.

Huet-Villiers, Jean François Marie, 1772-1813, fl.Paris and London.

Weyler, Jean Baptiste, 1747-91, fl.Paris.

Zincke, Christian Friedrich, 1683-1767, fl.Germany and England.

1

2

3

4

5

6

7

8

9

10

11

12

13

14

15

Instruments of Science and Technology

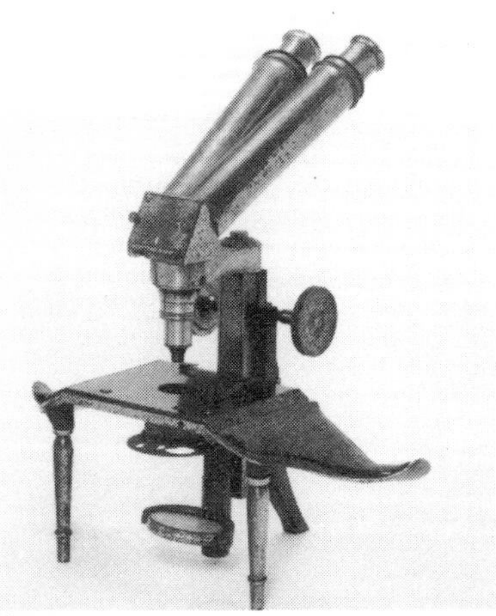
1

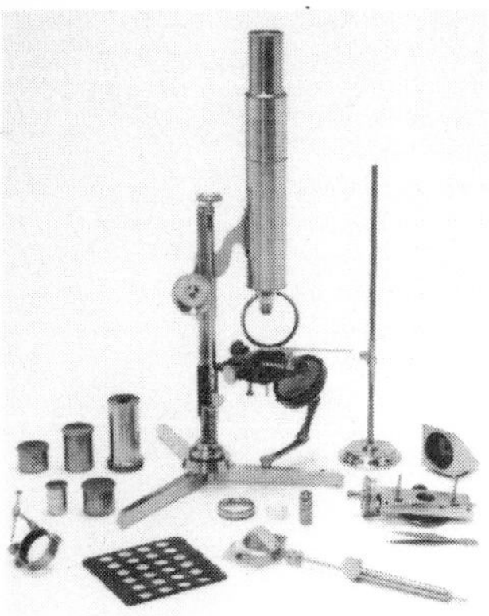
2

3

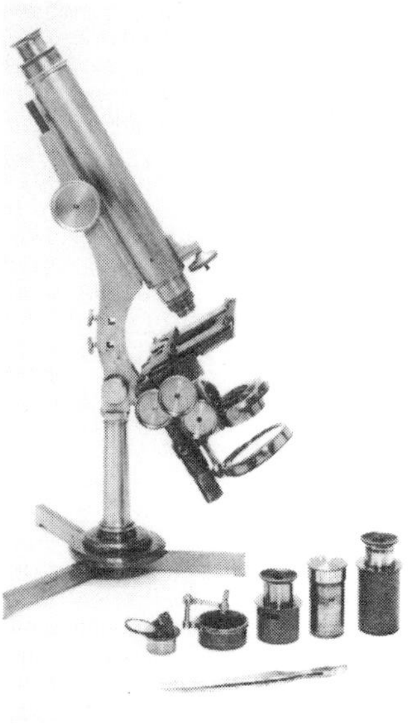
4

5

6

7

8

9

1
A Swift & Son brass compound binocular dissecting microscope, English, c.1880, 34cm (13½in) high, *L 25 Mar,* **£605 ($944)**

2
A Simon Plossl brass compound monocular microscope, Austrian, mid 19th century, 43cm (17in) high, *L 25 Feb,* **£4,950 ($7,425)**

3
A Dollond brass binocular microscope, English, c.1880, 43cm (17in) high, *L 18 June,* **£715 ($1,130)**

4
A Smith & Beck brass monocular microscope, English, mid 19th century, 41cm (16in) high, *L 25 Feb,* **£352 ($528)**

5
A fruitwood tripod microscope, South German, early 19th century, 33cm (13in) high, *L 25 Mar,* **£770 ($1,201)**

6
A Powell & Lealand brass compound monocular microscope, English, dated 1851, 41cm (16in) high, *L 18 June,* **£1,100 ($1,738)**

7
An R. & J. Beck brass compound binocular microscope, English, c.1880, 41cm (16in) high, *C 4 June,* **£462 ($716)**

8
A McArthur inverted prismatic compound microscope, English, c.1950, 12cm (4¾in) long. Dr Jon McArthur began production of this type of microscope in the early 1950s; Cooke Troughton & Simms of York took over manufacture in 1959. *L 25 Mar,* **£440 ($686)**

9
A Powell & Lealand brass compound binocular microscope, English, dated 1876, Model No. 1, 48cm (19in) high, *L 18 June* **£2,200 ($3,476)**

1
A Martin 'Universal' type compound monocular microscope, English, mid 18th century, 28cm (11in) high, with accessories, *L 28 Oct,*
£1,045 ($1,463)

2
A John Bleuler brass Culpeper-type microscope, English, c.1800, with accessories, in mahogany pillar case, 37cm (14½in) high, *L 28 Oct,*
£1,210 ($1,694)

3
A Gilbert & Co. brass opaque solar microscope, English, c.1780, with accessories, 33cm (13in) wide, *L 25 Mar,*
£1,650 ($2,574)

4
A brass simple botanical microscope, English, c.1800, with accessories, 10cm (4in) high, *L 25 Mar,*
£330 ($515)

5
A Scarlett-form Culpeper microscope, English, c.1730, with accessories, in original pillar oak case, 39cm (15½in) high, *L 25 Mar,*
£10,450 ($16,302)

6
A brass Culpeper-pattern compound monocular microscope, English, mid 18th century, on mahogany base, with accessories, 38cm (15in) high, *L 25 Mar,*
£1,815 ($2,831)

7
A Dellebarre brass compound monocular microscope, Dutch, c.1770, 42cm (16½in) high, *L 25 Feb,*
£1,980 ($2,970)

8
An ivory compound monocular microscope, probably Dutch, early 18th century, on mahogany base, mirror cracked, 34cm (13½in) high, *L 25 Feb,*
£3,190 ($4,785)

9
A Wilson-type screw barrel pocket microscope, English, early 18th century, the microscope unsigned but with instruction booklet by Ralph Sterrop, with accessories, 13cm (5¼in) long, *L 25 Feb,*
£748 ($1,122)

10
A John Bleuler ivory spy glass, English, late 18th century, extended length 8cm (3in), *L 25 Mar,*
£275 ($429)

11
A Thomas Rubergall 1½-inch gilt-brass spy glass, English, c.1830, decorated in guilloche, 12cm (4¾in) long, *L 25 Mar,*
£352 ($549)

12
A Moschino 1¼-inch ivory spy glass, Italian, early 19th century, extended length 11cm (4¼in), *L 25 Mar,*
£418 ($652)

Microscope an optical instrument consisting of a lens (simple microscope) or series of lenses (compound microscope) for viewing small objects.

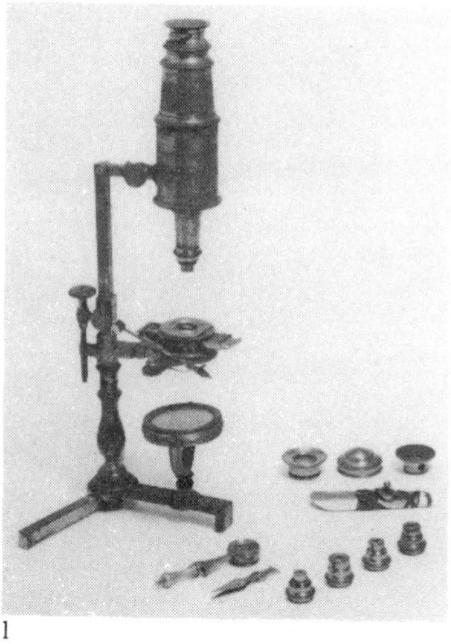
1

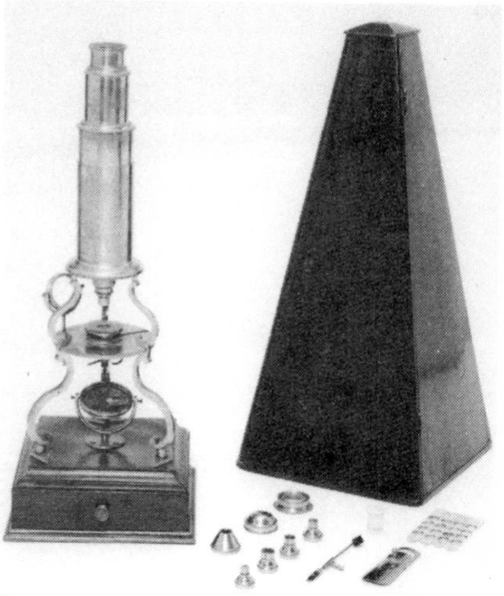
2

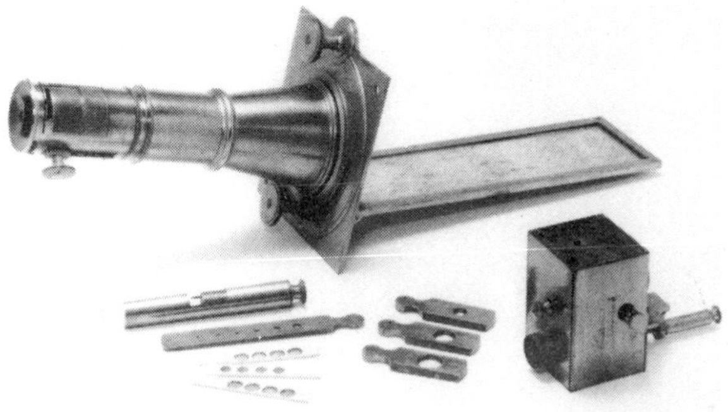
3

4

5

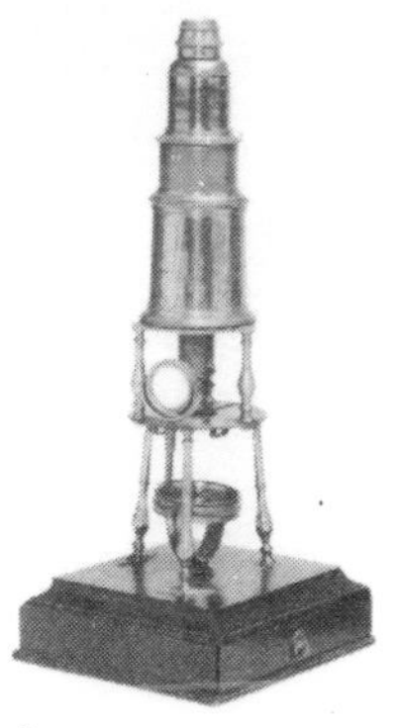
6

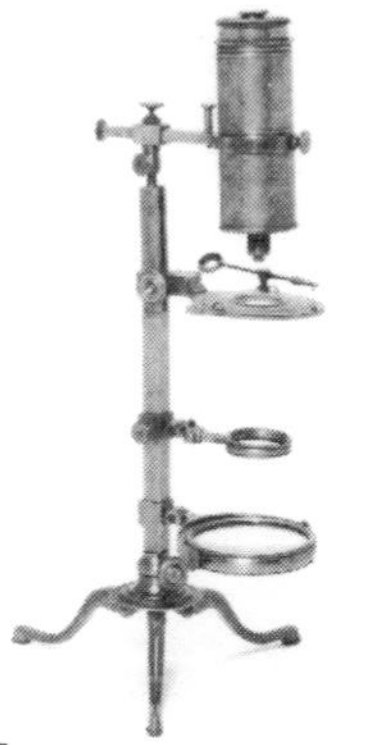
7

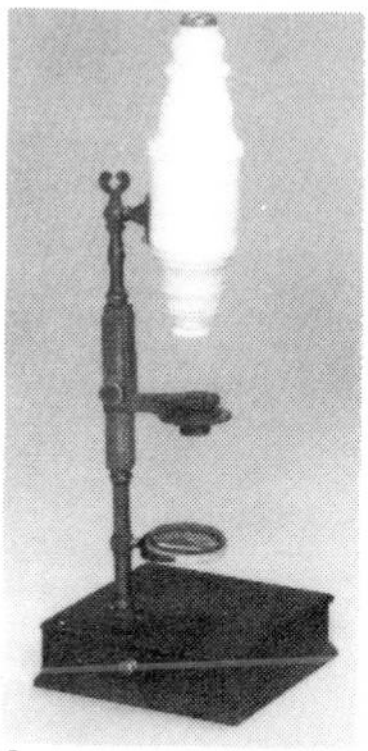
8

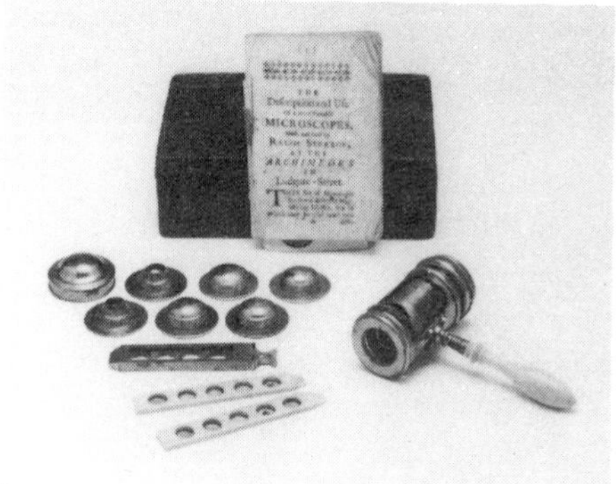
9

10

11

12

1

2

3

4

5

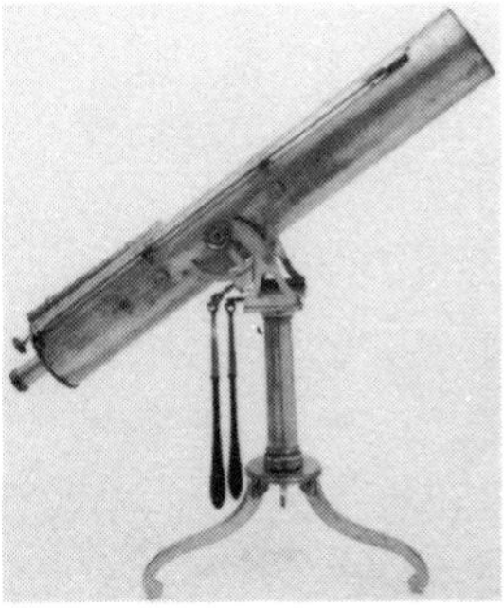
6

7

8

9

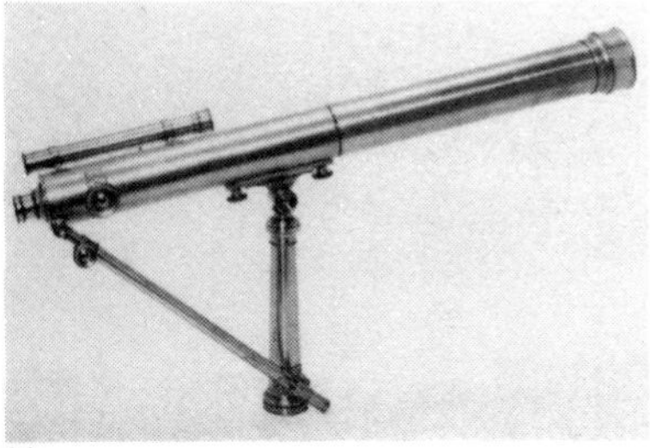
10

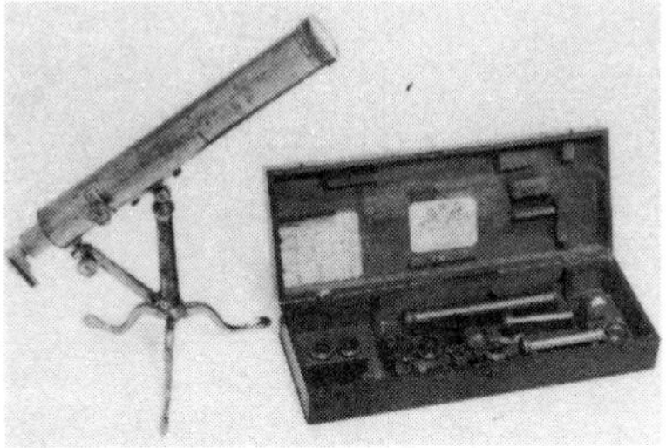
11

1
A 1-inch Angelo Deregni pasteboard and horn refracting telescope, Italian, 18th century, with three drawers and tube stamped with maker's name and floral swag decoration, 78cm (30¾in) extended length, *L 28 Oct,*
£418 ($585)

2
A quarter plate telescope camera, English, early 20th century, the teak body with ground glass screen and focal plane shutter with speeds from 1/1000th of a second, 32cm (12½in) long, *L 25 Feb,*
£176 ($264)

3
A Cuff 2½-inch brass Gregorian reflecting telescope on stand, English, mid 18th century, on baluster column with vertical and horizontal slow adjustments, tube 36cm (14in) long, *L 25 Feb,*
£528 ($792)

4
A brass transit instrument, French, late 19th century, the telescope mounted with engraved 360° silver scale, telescope 35.5cm (14in) long, *L 28 Oct,*
£440 ($616)

5
A 2¾-inch Troughton & Simms transit instrument, English, mid 19th century, signed *Troughton & Simms London 1854*, the tube mounted with two circles of degrees, modern stand, 122cm (48in) long, *L 25 Mar,*
£1,320 ($2,059)

6
An Edward Nairne 5-inch brass Gregorian reflecting telescope on stand, English, c.1760, star finder and tripod of later date, tube 89cm (35in) long, *L 2 Mar,*
£2,420 ($3,775)

7
A George Adams 4½-inch Gregorian brass telescope, English, late 18th century, lacking sighting tube and front lens, 80cm (31¼in) long, *NY 15 Feb,*
$1,100 (£759)

8
A 3¾-inch Steinheil refracting telescope on stand, German, mid 19th century, on beechwood stand in the Biedermeier style, tube 132cm (52in) long, *L 18 June,*
£3,630 ($5,735)

9
A Troughton & Simms 3¼-inch brass refracting telescope on stand, English, mid 19th century, the tube with rack and pinion focusing and sighting telescope mounted in parallel, tube 110cm (43in) long, *L 25 Mar,*
£1,650 ($2,574)

10
A Cary 3-inch brass refracting telescope on stand, English, late 19th century, tube 92cm (36in) long, *L 25 Mar,*
£990 ($1,544)

11
A William Harris & Co. 2-inch brass refracting telescope on stand, English, c.1820-30, tube 43cm (17in) long, *L 28 Oct,*
£1,870 ($2,618)

Telescope optical instrument which, by a combination of lenses (refracting telescope) or mirrors (reflecting telescope) makes distant objects appear closer.

1
A Watkins & Hill ebony octant, English, early 19th century, 24cm (9½in) radius, *L 28 Oct,*
£264 ($370)

2
A Charles Jones ebony octant, English, c.1830, 30.5cm (12in) radius, *L 18 June,*
£484 ($764)

3
A John Uring mahogany Hadley's quadrant, English, c.1760, 46cm (18in) radius, *L 25 Mar,*
£3,080 ($4,805)

4
A Thomas Hemsley & Son compass corrector, English, early 20th century, 25.5cm (10in) diam., *L 3 June,*
£352 ($545)

5
A McGregor's patent polar compass, late 19th century, the 9½-inch diameter suspended paper compass card pivotted in brass case, *L 28 Oct,*
£638 ($893)

6
A brass tell-tale compass, English, mid 19th century, the 5-inch diameter printed compass card by W. Hooper of Portsmouth, gimbal mounts, 23cm (9in) wide, *L 25 Feb,*
£858 ($1,287)

7
A Thomas Parnell tell-tale compass, English, c.1800, in brass drum mounting with gimbal mounts, bezel 12.5cm (5in) diam., *L 3 June,*
£605 ($938)

8
A Cary silver pocket compass, London, 1840, 5cm (2in) diam., *S 18 Sept,*
£231 ($323)

9
A brass anchor, English, late 19th century, patent model, 30.5cm (12in), *L 3 June,*
£242 ($375)

10
A brass ship's bell on stand, English, dated 1852, 86cm (34in) high, *L 28 Oct,*
£715 ($1,001)

11
A brass ship's bell, German, mid 19th century, the bell lettered *Aline Woermann Hamburg,* 58cm (23in) high, *L 28 Oct,*
£682 ($955)

12
A Siebe Gorman & Co. brass and copper diver's helmet, English, early 20th century, 51cm (20in) high, *L 25 Feb,*
£825 ($1,238)

13
A brass ship's bell, German, late 19th century, engraved *Kammerun Hamburg,* 42cm (16½in), *L 3 June,*
£770 ($1,193)

14
A Chadburns ship's telegraph, English, early 20th century, 117cm (46in) high, *L 28 Oct,*
£418 ($585)

15
A walnut and brass ship's wheel, late 19th century, 136cm (53½in) diam., *C 18 Mar,*
£187 ($286)

16
A mahogany and brass ship's wheel, English, late 19th century, 122cm (48in) diam., *L 25 Feb,*
£374 ($561)

Compass indicates directions on the earth's surface by means of a magnetic needle.

Octant so named as the arc occupies an eighth of a circle but can measure angles up to 90 degrees; superceded by the sextant.

Quadrant shaped as a quarter of a circle and used to measure the altitude of stars.

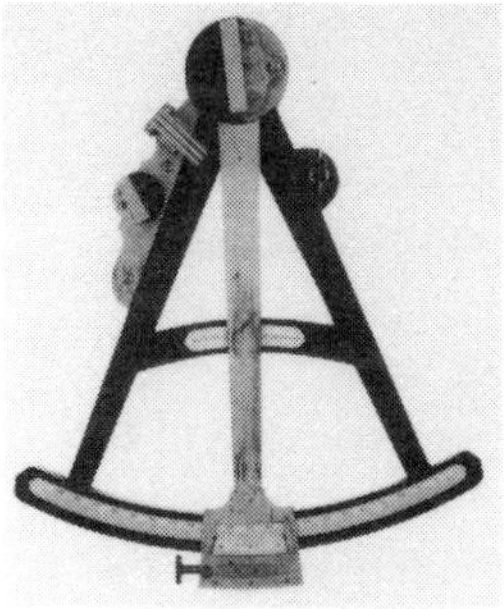
1

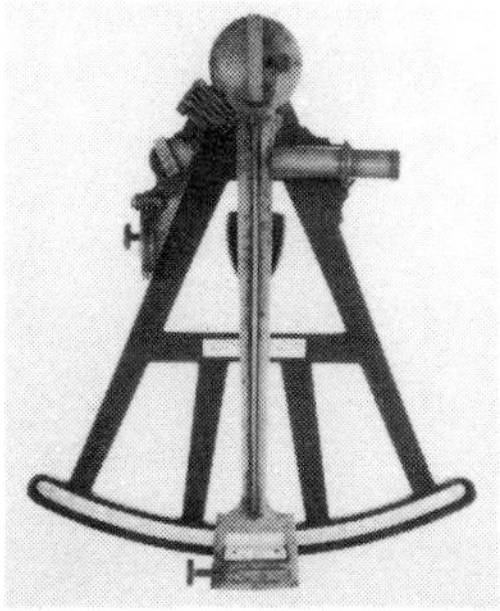
2

3

4

5

6

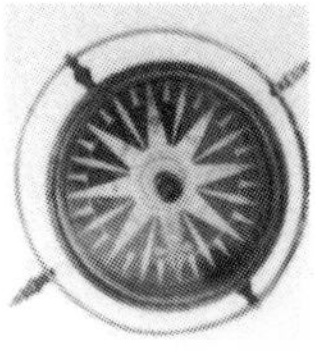
7

8

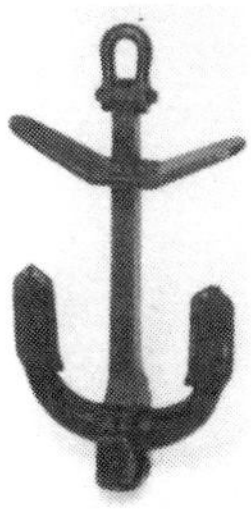
9

10 11

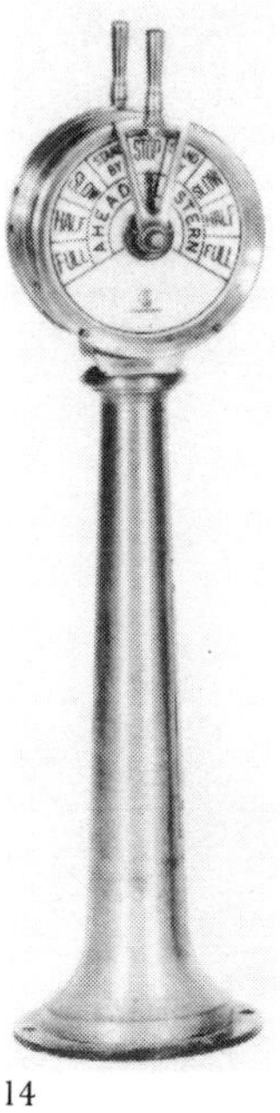
14

12

13

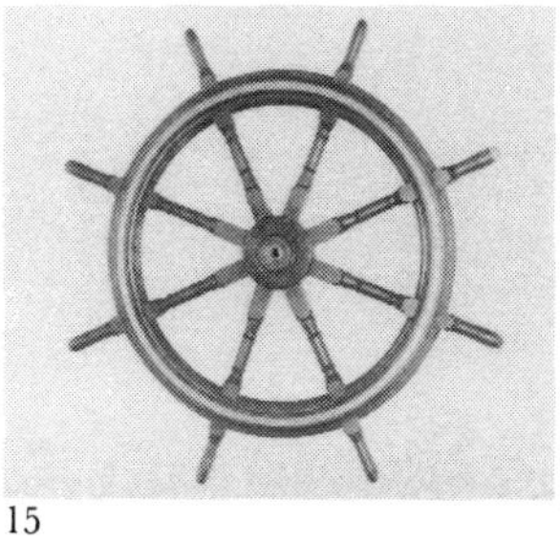
15

16

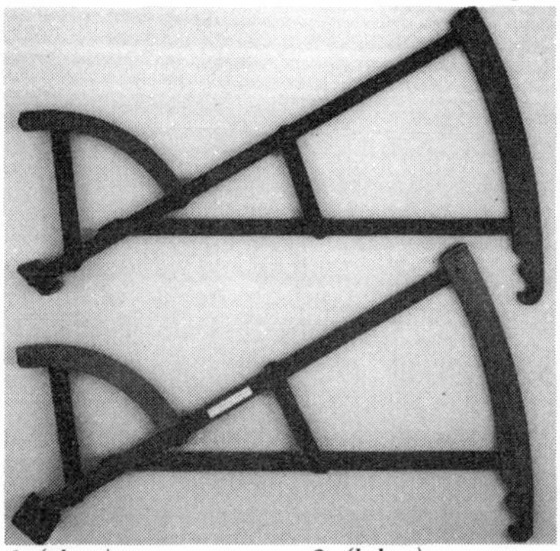

1 *(above)* 2 *(below)*

3

4

5

6

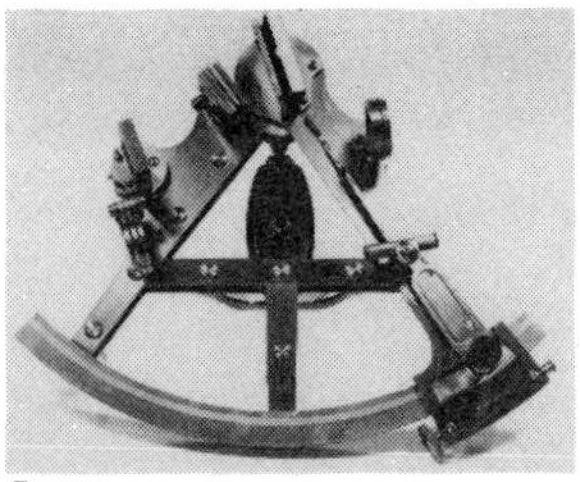

7

8

9

10

11

12

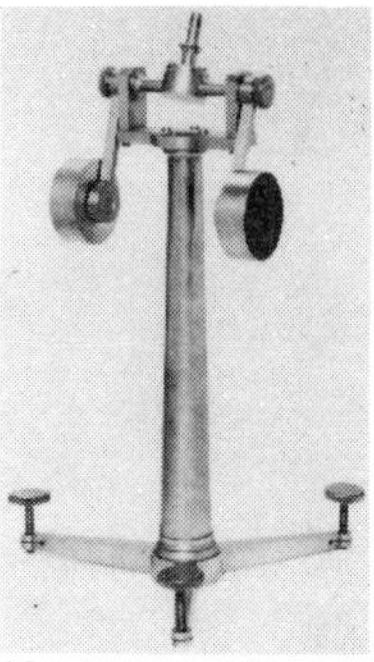

13

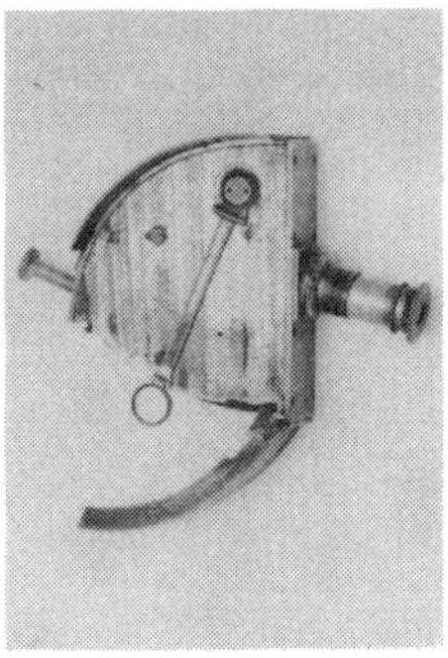

14

1
A Henry Gregory mahogany and boxwood backstaff, English, mid 18th century, 64cm (25in) long, *L 25 Mar,*
£3,520 ($5,490)

2
A Thomas Greenough mahogany and boxwood backstaff, American, dated 1753, 63.5cm (25in) long, *L 25 Mar,*
£3,850 ($6,006)

3
A very rare gilt-brass mariner's astrolabe, probably Portuguese, early 17th century, stamped *R 1602*, 17.5cm (7in) diam., *L 28 Oct,*
£27,500 ($38,500)

4
An Edward Troughton brass reflecting circle, English, c.1800, 29cm (11½in) diam., *L 25 Mar,*
£1,320 ($2,059)

5
A Troughton & Simms brass reflecting and repeating circle, English, mid 19th century, 32cm (12½in) diam., *L 25 Feb,*
£3,520 ($5,280)

6
An Edward Troughton small brass sextant, English, early 19th century, 10cm (4in) radius, *L 18 June,*
£1,155 ($1,825)

7
A Troughton & Simms brass double frame sextant, English, early 20th century, 20cm (8in) radius, *C 4 June,*
£462 ($716)

8
A Cary brass pillar sextant, English, c.1820, 18cm (7in) radius, *L 25 Mar,*
£682 ($1,064)

9
A Dollond brass sextant, English, early 19th century, 19cm (7½in) radius, *L 25 Mar,*
£660 ($1,030)

10
A Thomas Jones brass bridge-framed sextant, English, early 19th century, 19cm (7½in) radius, *L 28 Oct,*
£990 ($1,386)

11
An unusual brass double sextant, English, mid 19th century, 13cm (5in) diam., *L 25 Mar,*
£968 ($1,510)

12
A Cary brass sextant, English, early 19th century, lacking one telescope, 22.5cm (8½in) radius, *L 25 Feb,*
£550 ($825)

13
A brass sextant pillar, English, mid 19th century, 38cm (15in) high, *L 25 Mar,*
£495 ($725)

14
A Jesse Ramsden brass pocket sextant, English, c.1800, 5.5cm (2¼in) radius, *L 28 Oct,*
£4,290 ($6,006)

Astrolabe for measuring the altitudes of heavenly bodies; it embodies a stereographic projection of the globe and of the hemisphere of the heavens.

Backstaff for measuring the altitudes of heavenly bodies.

Reflecting circle used by navigators to find longitudes by the method of lunar distances.

Sextant so named as the arc occupies a sixth of a circle; used to measure angular distances between objects.

Double sextant fitted with two mirrors to allow two bearings to be obtained at the same time.

1
A set of Thomas Wright drawing instruments, English, c.1730, comprising protractor, sector, dividers, compasses and pencils, 17cm (6¾in), *L 25 Feb,*
£825 ($1,238)

2
A pocket set of drawing instruments, late 18th century, the shagreen and silver-coloured metal case containing a part set of instruments, 9cm (3½in) long, *S 18 Sept,*
£176 ($246)

3
A Soleil brass graphometer, French, late 18th century, 25.5cm (18in) wide, *L 25 Feb,*
£825 ($1,238)

4
A T. Blunt cased set of drawing instruments, late 18th century, the shagreen-covered case with silver mounts containing sector, protracting rule, parallel rule, compass etc., 17.5cm (7in) long, *S 13 Nov,*
£363 ($508)

5
A pair of gilt brass gunner's dividers, German, stamped *BLEY STEIN EISEN*, dated 1659, 17cm (6¾in) radius, *L 28 Oct,*
£1,012 ($1,417)

6
An Edward Spicer brass miner's dial, Irish, late 18th century, the compass rose inscribed *Edwd Spicer Dublin Fecit*, some wear, 44cm (17½in) long, *L 18 June,*
£264 ($417)

7
A Sisson waywiser or hodometer, English, mid 18th century, the 81cm (32in) diameter oak wheel connected to a geared mechanism, *L 18 June,*
£1,430 ($2,259)

8
A Troughton & Simms brass circumferentor, English, late 19th century, sighting telescope 21cm (8¼in), *C 4 June,*
£286 ($443)

9
A W. & T. Gilbert brass theodolite, English, mid 19th century, tube 35cm (13¾in) long, *C 4 June,*
£418 ($648)

10
A Rothwell brass level, English, mid 19th century, 39.5cm (15½in) long, *L 25 Mar,*
£418 ($652)

11
A Morin brass theodolite, French, mid 19th century, 19cm (7½in) high, *L 18 June,*
£385 ($608)

12
A Troughton & Simms brass transit theodolite, English, late 19th century, tube 26cm (10¼in) long, *C 4 June,*
£308 ($477)

13
A Cary brass transit theodolite, English, c.1910, the 2-inch refracting telescope with prism and trunnion eyepiece, 44cm (17½in) high, *L 25 Mar,*
£792 ($1,236)

14
A Baker brass transit theodolite, English, c.1870, 34cm (13½in) high, *L 18 June,*
£462 ($730)

Circumferentor for measuring vertical and horizontal angles.

Graphometer for measuring the angles between two points in either the horizontal or vertical planes.

Level used to find a horizontal.

Theodolite for measuring at the same time the horizontal and vertical angles between two points.

Waywiser/Hodometer a hand-held wheel used to measure distances.

1

2

3

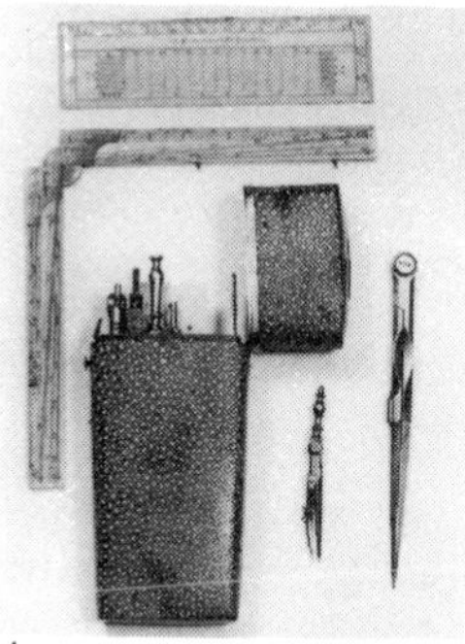
4

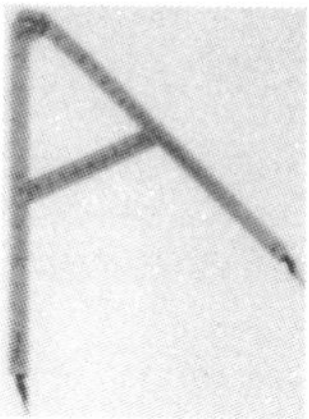
5

6

7

8

9

10

11

12

13

14

Pocket Sundials

JON BADDELEY

Broadcasters on the radio and television today are constantly bombarding us with 'time checks'. In the 17th and 18th centuries the only way the accuracy of a pocket watch could be checked was by using either a garden or pocket sundial. In addition, a pocket watch would have to be adjusted as the owner moved about the country since every locality had its own time prior to standard time being made uniform throughout the country. For example, the local time at Oxford was five minutes slower than Greenwich since it lies 1¼ degrees west of Greenwich in longitude. A pocket sundial provided a quick and convenient method of giving the time — always assuming that the sun shone.

The majority of sundials function by casting a shadow formed by a gnomon (in the form of a string, shaped piece of metal or rod), on to an hour scale. One of the most popular pocket sundials was named after an Englishman, Michael Butterfield (1635-1724), who worked in Paris at the end of the 17th century. Made from either silver or brass, the octagonal base is inset with a magnetic compass and marked with four rings showing the hours for four different latitudes. The plate is mounted with a gnomon shaped in the form of a bird and the underside engraved with a list of European towns together with their corresponding latitudes. Butterfield dials of similar style were made by a number of French and English makers including Le Maire, Macquart, Cadot, Culpeper and Bion. Their value today varies according to quality and condition from as little as £200 ($320) to £1,000 ($1,600); (figs 1, 2 & 3).

A diptych dial (figs 4, 7 & 8) is one that has two plates hinged together which in use are opened to form a right angle. A string gnomon is then drawn tight and the shadow falls on to a vertical and a horizontal dial. Made from either ivory or wood the dials have engraved or punched scales and often incorporate smaller dials to determine Italian and Babylonian hours together with a lunar disc and windrose mounted on the outer faces. Nuremberg was the centre of production for such dials in the late 16th and early 17th centuries. Elaborate examples made by a respected maker can fetch several thousand pounds today. Wooden versions with printed paper scales were made in Germany in the early 19th century; these are much more readily available to the collector, with prices ranging from £100 ($160) to £300 ($480).

An equitorial or equinoctial dial (figs 5-6, 9-12 & 14) is constructed with the hour scale parallel to the Equator. Usually made of brass the base is inset with a magnetic compass and is

1

1
A Macquart silver Butterfield-style dial, French, early 18th century, signed *Macquart a Paris,* in original velvet-lined leather case, 7cm (2¾in), *L 18 June,*
£770 ($1,217)

3
A Butterfield silver horizontal dial, French, early 18th century, signed *Butterfield a Paris,* engraved with hour scales for latitudes 43, 46, 49 and 52, the reverse with latitudes of European cities, 6.5cm (2½in), *L 28 Oct,*
£880 ($1,232)

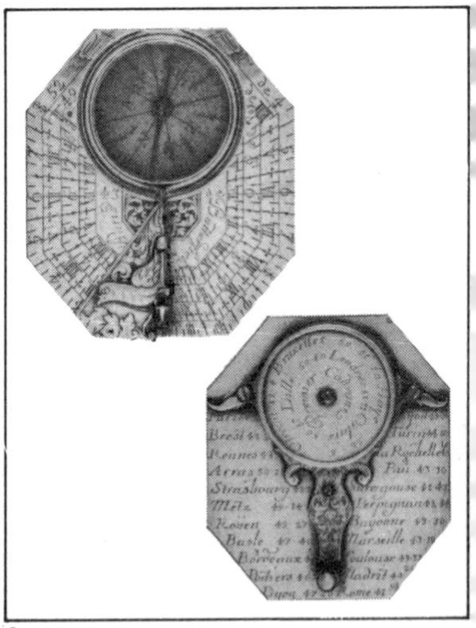
3

2

2
A Butterfield silver dial, French, early 18th century, signed *Butterfield A Paris,* the reverse with the names and latitudes of 29 European towns, in original case, 6cm (2¼in), *L 25 Feb,*
£660 ($990)

4
A Jacques Senecal ivory Bloud-type diptych dial, late 17th century, signed *Jacques Senecal Dieppe fecit,* the lower limb with compass applied with list of French towns and their latitudes, 7cm (2¾in), *L 11 June 1985,*
£1,155 ($1,478)

4

Altitude The angle of elevation of a heavenly body above the horizon.

Azimuth The horizontal angle of a heavenly body east or west of the meridian.

Babylonian hours A system of hour reckoning in which the twenty-four hour period is equally divided with zero at sunrise.

Equinoctial The great circle on the heavens, or on a celestial globe, in the plane of the earth's equator. It passes through the equinoxes.

Equinox Time or date at which sun crosses equator and day and night are equal.

Gregorian calendar A calendar proposed by Pope Gregory XIII in 1582 in which the equinoxes were restored to their original dates, adopted in most Catholic countries.

Italian hours A system of hour-reckoning in which the whole day and night period is divided into twenty-four equal hours with zero half-an-hour after sunset.

Julian calendar A calendar originally proposed by Julius Caesar and generally adopted in Europe in a modified form, following the Council of Nicaea in 325AD, modified later by Pope Gregory (see Gregorian calendar).

Meridian The great circle passing through the celestial poles and the zenith at a specific place for the armillary sphere; the great circle passing through the poles and the place in question for a terrestrial sphere.

Volvelle A simple calculating device including a rotating disc.

Wegweiser A ring of compass points with a rotating index mounted above.

Windrose A ring of compass points, named usually by their directions and sometimes with the Italian names of the corresponding winds.

Zodiac The circular band in the heavens in which the sun, moon and major planets have their orbits. It is divided into twelve equal parts.

5
An Andreas Vogler gilt-brass universal equinoctial dial, Augsburg, c.1785, signed *And. Vogler,* in original case, 7.5cm (3in), *L 25 Mar,*
£715 ($1,115)

6
A Johann Schretteggar brass universal equinoctial dial, Augsburg, c.1800, signed *Johan Scretteggar in Augsburg,* in original case, 6.5cm (2½in), *L 25 Mar,*
£352 ($549)

7
Ivory diptych dial, South German, early 17th century, 6.5cm (2½in), *L 25 Mar,*
£418 ($652)

mounted on the south side with a plumb-bob in a frame. The hour scale is mounted with a gnomon and is adjustable over the hinged arc which is engraved with a degree of latitudes. A variation of the equitorial dial is called a 'crescent dial' due to its distinctive shape. The hour circle is divided into two and inverted, making a double crescent. The gnomon is also in the form of a crescent with tips casting the shadow. These dials were predominently made in Augsburg in the late 17th century often of gilt brass or silver. The Hahn-type dial, illustrated as fig.11, would not, of course, have been suitable for pocket use.

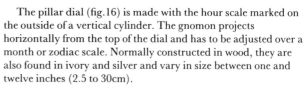

One of the most attractive types of all sundials is the universal ring dial (figs 13 and 15). Its three main constituents are an outer meridian ring, an inner hour ring and central bar with cursor and pinhole moving over a zodiac and calendar scale. The dial is suspended from a loop and is turned until the spot of sunlight from the pinhole hits the hour ring; the time can then be read, having made adjustments for latitude and date. They measure from as little as two inches in diameter to twelve inches (5 to 30cm) and in value vary between £300 ($480) and £2,000 ($3,200).

The simplest type of dial is called the ring or poke dial. It is still used today in some of the remoter parts of South America. It consists of a metal ring inset with a sliding collar with a pinhole to let a spot of sunlight fall on the graduated hour scale which is stamped on the inner surface. This inexpensive and innacurate dial was popular in the 18th and 19th centuries among country people. Examples can be bought today at between £100 ($160) and £300 ($480).

The pillar dial (fig.16) is made with the hour scale marked on the outside of a vertical cylinder. The gnomon projects horizontally from the top of the dial and has to be adjusted over a month or zodiac scale. Normally constructed in wood, they are also found in ivory and silver and vary in size between one and twelve inches (2.5 to 30cm).

One of the most accurate dials is the dipleidoscope (fig.17). In March 1848 Edward Dent, the English chronometer maker, patented a device for noting the meridian passage of the sun with great accuracy. The invention consisted of a hollow right-angled prism with two sides silvered and one of glass. When correctly levelled and orientated the two images of the sun coincided exactly at noon.

It was not until the development of the railway system, which required a standard time to be used throughout the network, that the pocket sundial became redundant; in Great Britain this happened by the 1850s. The electric telegraph that was introduced in 1837 ensured that all railway clocks showed Greenwich time. Similarly the National Telegraph Company had offices in all the major towns and the populace was able to check their watches against the town clock. Greenwich Mean Time was universally adopted in 1884.

Pocket sundials are eagerly sought by collectors. Many are wonderfully engraved in great detail and are constructed from fine materials such as silver, ivory and gilt metal. Prices for dials still have a long way to catch up with other works of art of the same period.

8
A Hans Troschel ivory diptych dial, Nuremburg, dated 1611, upper face showing planetary hours, the lower face with pin gnomon dial showing Babylonian and Italian hours, 9cm (3½in), *L 18 June,*
£1,650 ($2,607)

8

9
A Dudley Adams brass universal equinoctial dial, English, early 19th century, signed *D. Adams, London,* in fishskin case, 13.5cm (5¼in), *L 25 Mar,*
£935 ($1,459)

10
A brass universal equinoctial dial, English, late 19th century, the brass chapter ring stamped *Inner Circle of Letters & Figures Used in South Latitudes,* with retailer's signature *Schwalb Hermanos,* 10cm (4in), *L 25 Feb,*
£330 ($495)

11
A Hahn-type mechanical equinoctial ring dial, German, c.1770, the 8¾in diameter brass meridian ring engraved with 0-90 degree scale, 38cm (15in) high, *L 11 June 1985,*
£4,620 ($5,914)

10

9

11

12

12
An E. Hunter brass universal mechanical equinoctial dial, probably Irish, c.1800, signed, *Edn. Hunter Fecit,* in case with retailer's label, 8.5cm (3¼in), *L 25 Feb,*
£1,870 ($2,805)

13
A brass universal ring dial, Continental, early 18th century, 9cm (3½in), *L 25 Mar,*
£638 ($995)

14
An Adie brass universal equinoctial dial, Scottish, mid 19th century, 11cm (4½in), *L 25 Mar,*
£440 ($686)

15
A brass universal ring dial, Continental, early 18th century, 8.5cm (3¼in), *L 25 Mar,*
£682 ($1,064)

16
A silver pillar dial, English, 18th century, stamped with hour, calendar and zodiac scales, 4.5cm (1¾in), *L 11 June 1985,*
£462 ($591)

17
A Dent brass dipleidoscope, English, c.1870, in original mahogany case, *L 11 June 1985,*
£1,045 ($1,338)

Further reading:

Maurice Daumas, *Les Instruments Scientifique aux xvii et xviii siècles,* 1972
René R.J.Rohr, *Die Sonnenuhr,* 1982
Gerard L'E Turner, *Antique Scientific Instruments,* 1980
Harriet Wynter and Anthony Turner, *Scientific Instruments,* 1975

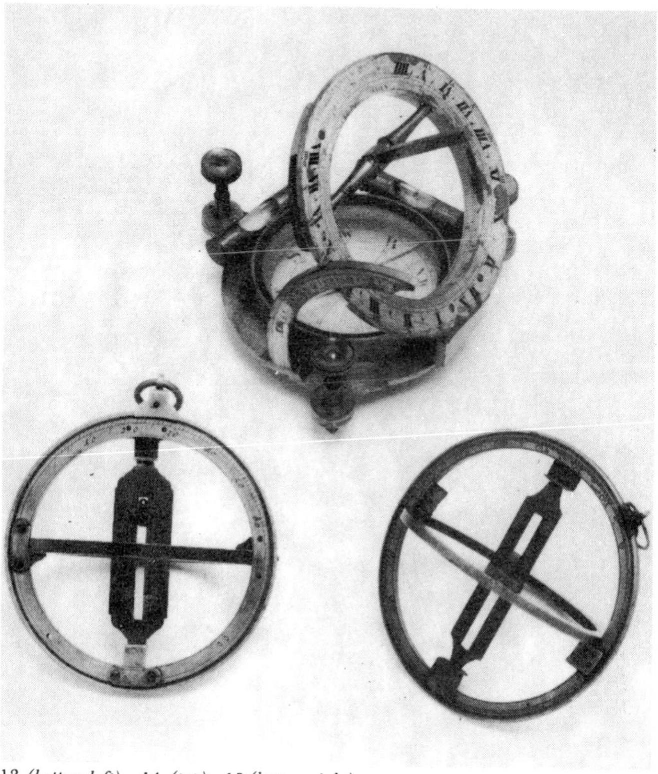
13 *(bottom left)* 14 *(top)* 15 *(bottom right)*

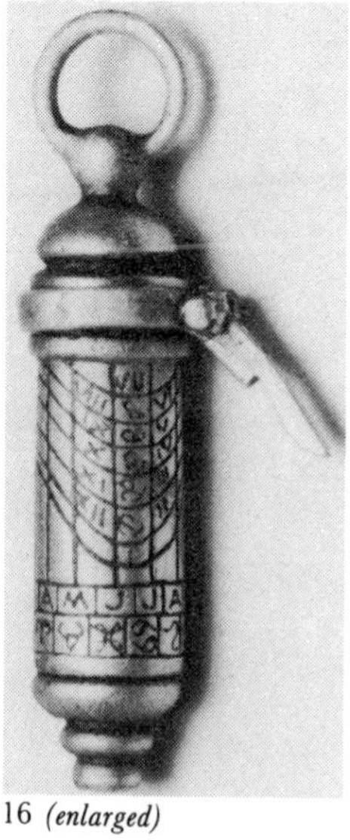
16 *(enlarged)*

17

1

2

3

4

5

6

7

8

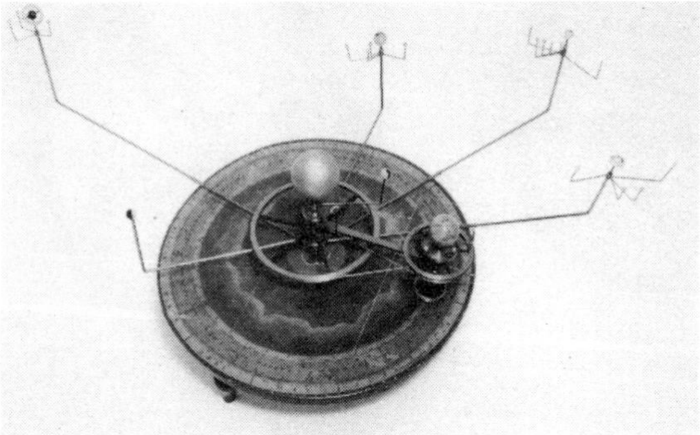
9

10

11

12

1
A Dudley Adams 3-inch pocket terrestrial globe, English, early 19th century, the plaster sphere applied with coloured gores, slight damage, *L 25 Mar,*
£418 ($652)

2
A 2½-inch Nathaniel Hill pocket terrestrial globe, English, mid 18th century, *L 28 Oct,*
£2,200 ($3,080)

3
A 3-inch J. & W. Cary pocket celestial globe, English, mid 19th century, the sphere applied with coloured and printed gores of the heavens, *L 28 Oct,*
£990 ($1,386)

4
A 12-inch Cary terrestrial globe, English, c.1827, *S 21 Feb,*
£572 ($869)

5
A Wylde's 12-inch terrestrial table globe, dated 1847 and signed *James Wylde,* 43cm (17in) overall, *C 17 Apr,*
£594 ($921)

6
A pair of 12-inch Cary terrestrial and celestial globes, *(one illustrated),* English, c.1842, both restored, 43cm (17in) high, *L 28 Oct,*
£1,595 ($2,233)

7
A 2-inch Malby & Co. terrestrial globe, English, mid 19th century, 7.5cm (3in) high, *L 25 Feb,*
£572 ($858)

8
A W. & S. Jones 'New Portable Orrery', English, c.1794, the wooden base applied with engraved paper scales, including the months, signs of the zodiac, solar system and tables of distances, mounted with models of the earth and brass planets, operated by gears and winding handle to one side, 33cm (13in) diam., together with a subsidiary base, similarly mounted, 20.5cm (8in) diam., *L 18 June,*
£4,180 ($6,604)

9
A Newton & Son orrery, English, mid 19th century, the wooden table applied with print of calendar and zodiac scales and mounted with a model of the sun, the earth and planets, base 43cm (17in) diam., *L 28 Oct,*
£4,620 ($6,468)

10
A Finger orrery and armillary sphere, French, early 19th century, with central model of the sun surrounded by ten ivory model planets within meridian rings and horizontal ring stamped with zodiac and calendar scales, ebonised base, 46cm (18in) high, *L 28 Oct,*
£660 ($924)

11
A C. Smith & Son armillary sphere, English, late 19th century, 40cm (16in) high, *L 25 Mar,*
£880 ($1,373)

12
An armillary sphere, probably French, early 19th century, models of the sun, earth and moon mounted within bands representing the zodiac tropics and equator, base inset with compass, 54cm (21¼in) high, *L 25 Feb,*
£1,430 ($2,145)

Armillary sphere an astronomical model composed of rings representing the circles of the celestial sphere.

Orrery a moving model of the solar system.

1
A Hammond No. 1 typewriter, American, c.1890, the swinging sector type mechanism with two-row curved keyboard and ebony keys, *C 28 Oct,*
£770 ($1,078)

2
A Salter Standard No. 10 typewriter, English, c.1892, with down-stroke mechanism and three-row keyboard, *L 25 Feb,*
£275 ($413)

3
A James Watt & Co. patent copying machine, English, late 18th century, the mahogany case opening to hinged writing surface, platten with brass roller and mahogany handle, the drawer in the base containing a damping tray and original horsehair brush, 29cm (11½in), *L 18 June,*
£682 ($1,077)

4
A Johannes Schmidt pocket wind vane, German, early 19th century, 6.5cm (2½in), sold with a Negretti & Zambra pocket barometer, *S 18 Sept,*
£935 ($1,309)

5
A set of Holzapffel ornamental turning hand tools, English, mid 19th century, with silvered mounts and ivory handles, in later japanned case, case 50cm (19½in) wide, *L 28 Oct,*
£6,600 ($9,240)

6
A Gramont brass table telephone, French, c.1910, 34cm (13½in) high, *C 18 Mar,*
£220 ($337)

7
A Lambert typewriter, American, c.1900, *No.1695,* the spherical index machine in cast-iron frame and original oak case, *C 12 Nov,*
£374 ($535)

8
An Elliott Brothers brass gyroscope, English, late 19th century, 25.5cm (10in) high, *L 18 June,*
£462 ($729)

9
A Thomas de Colmar-type arithmometer, c.1860-80, in ebony and brass-lined case, 59cm (23in), *S 18 Sept*
£1,078 ($1,509)

10
A Thomas de Colmar calculating machine, French, c.1860, with turned ivory grips to the handles, in oak case, 59cm (23¼in) long, *L 18 June,*
£1,430 ($2,259)

11
A painted and ebonised wall thermometer, 19th century, inscribed *Joseph Franks ... Manchester,* 101.5cm (40in) long, *C 10 July,*
£484 ($779)

12
A combined weather station and timepiece, English, c.1880, the oak stand mounted with mercury thermometer, Thornhill & Co. timepiece and aneroid barometer, and surmounted by 'In' and 'Out' signals, 81cm (32in) high, *L 28 Oct,*
£528 ($739)

13
A J. Brown barograph, c.1900, with nine vacuum discs, turned tapered pillars supporting the movement and mercury thermometer, 48cm (19in) long, *S 24 Apr,*
£462 ($725)

14
A Thomas Armstrong brass barograph, English, late 19th century, 43cm (17in) long, *L 18 June,*
£385 ($608)

Arithmometer type of calculating machine introduced by Thomas of Colmar in 1820, the mechanism being based on the Leibnitz stepped wheel.

Barograph for recording the changes in atmospheric pressure.

Gyroscope a mounted spinning wheel which demonstrates the dynamics of rotating objects.

1

2

3

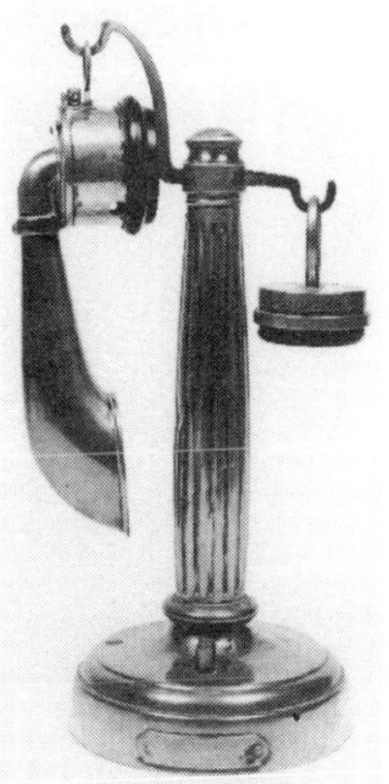
6

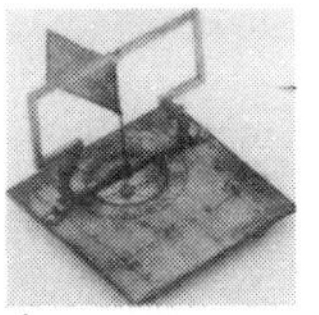
4

5

7

8

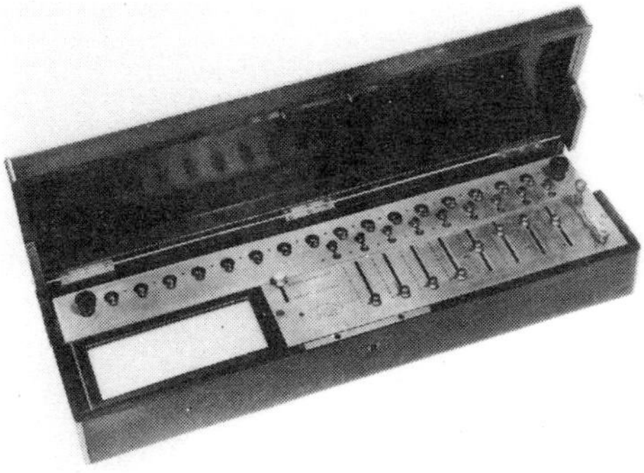
9

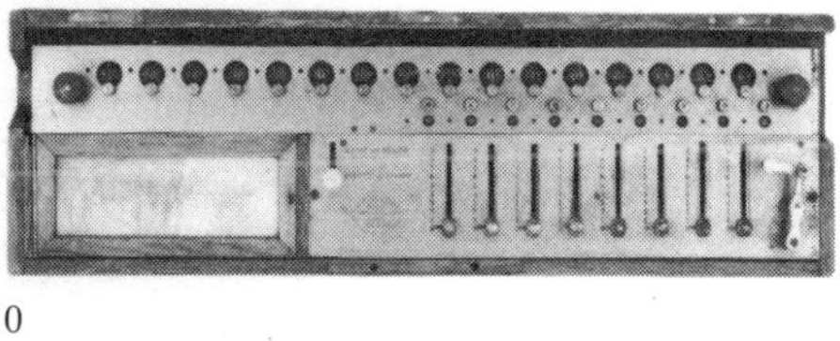
10

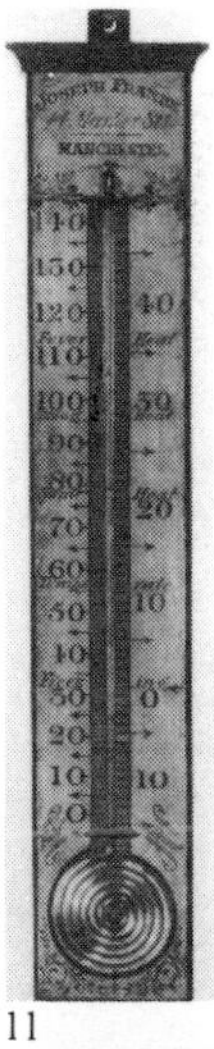
11

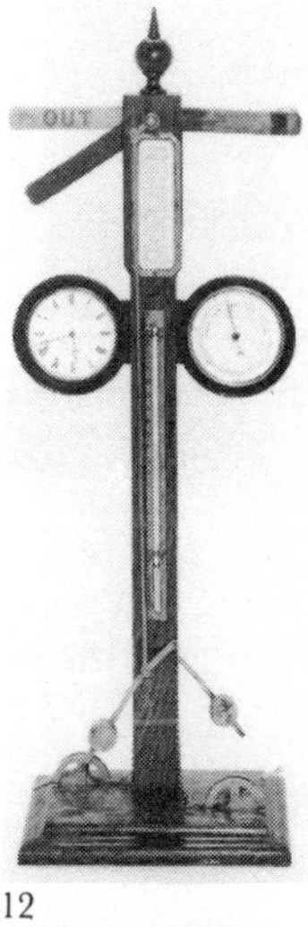

12

13

14

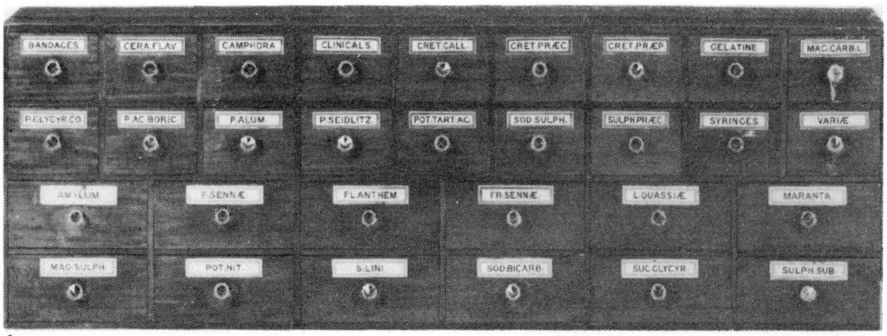

1

2

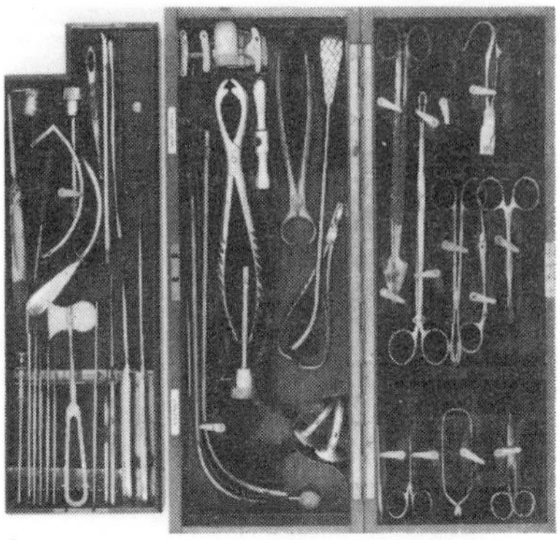
3

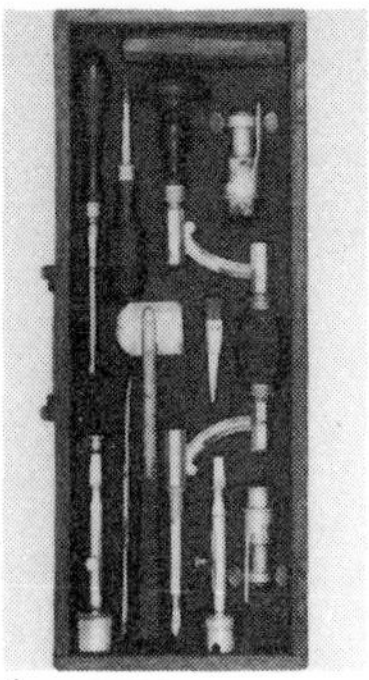
4

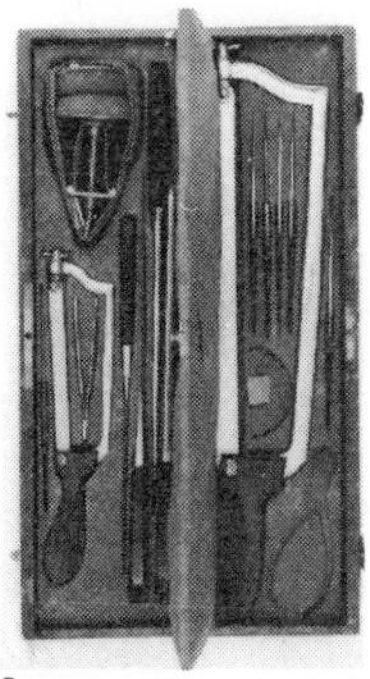
5

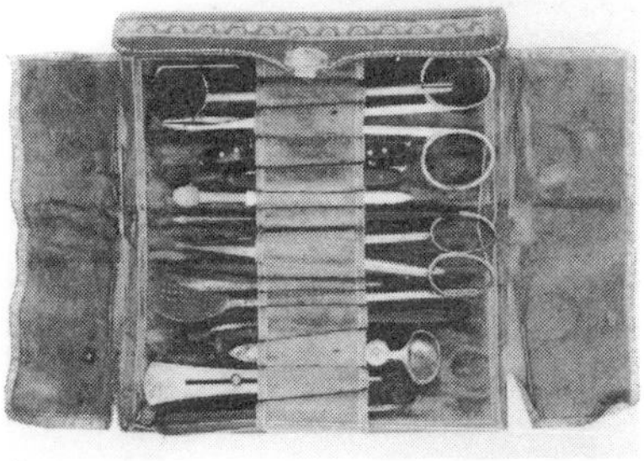
6

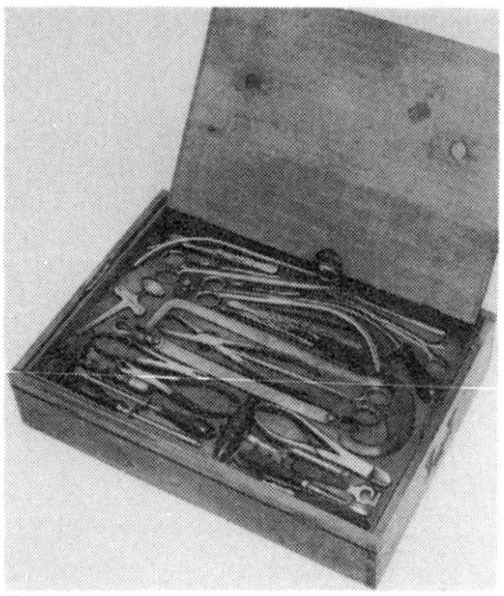
7

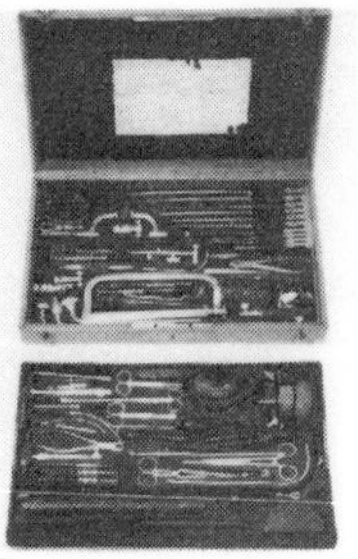
8

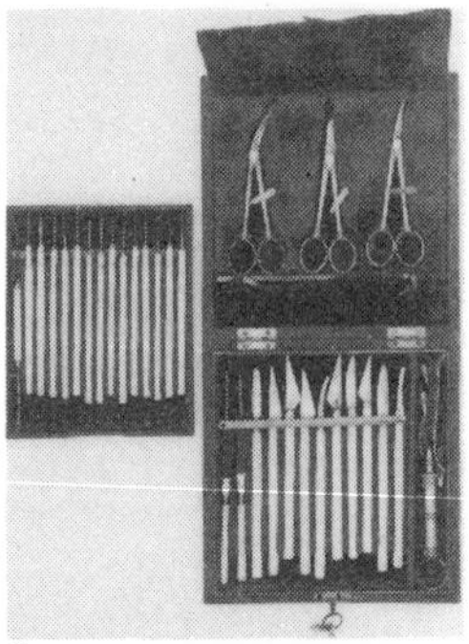
9

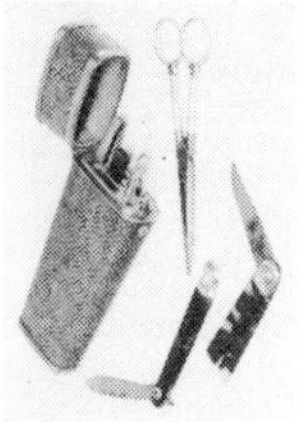
10

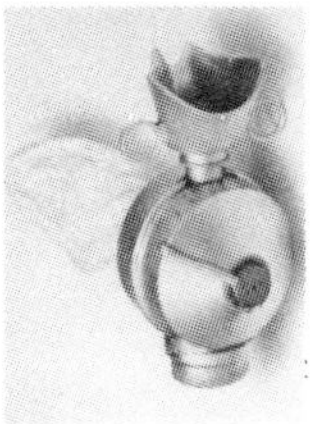
11

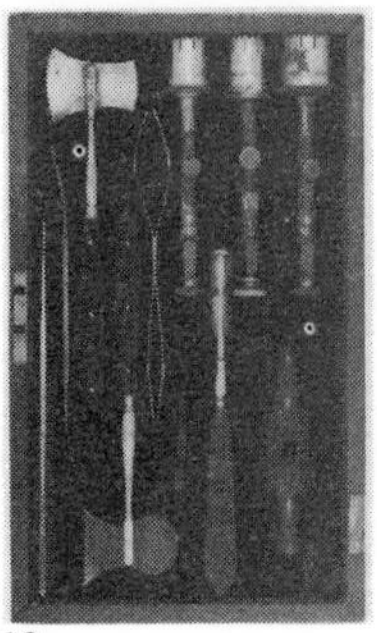
12

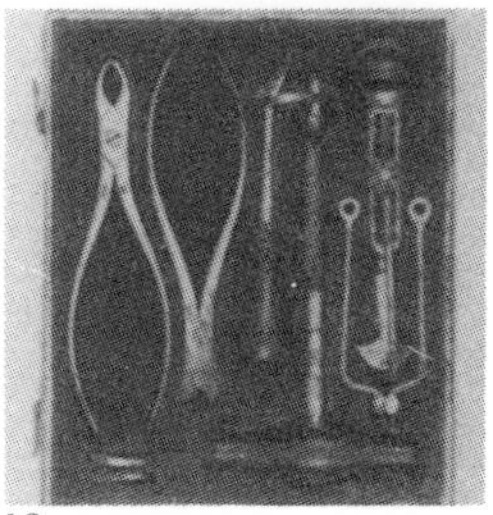
13

1
A pine drug run, English, mid 19th century, the 30 drawers each with glass handle and compound name, 183cm (72in) long, *L 25 Feb,*
£286 ($429)

2
A chemist's shop drug run, late 19th century, the 21 drawers each with glass handle and compound name, 140cm (55in) wide, *C 12 Nov,*
£462 ($661)

3
A Down Brothers surgical instrument set, English, third quarter 19th century, the mahogany and brass-bound case containing various instruments including large bone saws, Hey's saw and crows bill forceps, case 40cm (15¾in) long, *L 18 June,*
£308 ($486)

4
A cased set of trepanning instruments, English, mid 19th century, the brass-bound mahogany case containing various instruments including three trephines with common ebony handle, case 27.5cm (10¾in) long, *L 18 June,*
£660 ($1,042)

5
A set of Charrière amputation instruments, French, mid 19th century, the leather-covered wooden case containing various instruments including large and small amputation saws, tweezers and large tourniquet, 46cm (18in) wide, *L 28 Oct,*
£550 ($770)

6
A set of surgeon's pocket instruments, French, early 19th century, stamped *Grangeret, Coutelier a Paris,* the red morocco case containing 17 assorted small instruments in silver, steel, ivory, ebony and tortoiseshell, *L 28 Oct,*
£264 ($370)

7
A cased set of surgical instruments, mostly Savigny & Co., London, c.1840, the brass-bound mahogany case containing various instruments, most with chequered ebony handles, *S 18 Sept,*
£528 ($739)

8
A large chest of Charrièr and Collin ship's surgeon's instruments, French, late 19th century, the brass-bound walnut case with two layers of instruments, case 58.5cm (23in) wide, *L 18 June,*
£1,540 ($2,433)

9
A set of Weiss opthalmic instruments, English, mic 19th century, the brass-bound rosewood case containing 27 faceted ivory-handled instruments and associated items, case 17cm (6¾in) wide, *L 28 Oct,*
£352 ($493)

10
A medical etui, late 18th century, the white metal mounted ray skin case opening to reveal various instruments, 16cm (6¼in) high, *C 12 Nov,*
£880 ($1,258)

11
A brass ether apparatus, French, late 19th century, *L 25 Feb,*
£220 ($330)

12
A set of Charrière trepanning instruments, French, mid 19th century, the walnut case containing various instruments including a signed ebony-handled steel brace, case 37cm (14½in) long, *L 18 June,*
£880 ($1,390)

13
A cased set of dental instruments, probably French, late 18th century, the leather-covered case containing various instruments including a fine pelican with turned ebony handle, case 20cm (8in) wide, *L 28 Oct,*
£1,760 ($2,464)

n anatomical model of e human foot, mid 19th entury, with two movable sections on the rch, 38cm (15in) high, *18 Sept,*
385 ($539)

plaster model of the uman heart, English, mid 9th century, the painted odel with three hinged ctions opening to reveal e inner arteries, 33cm 3in) high, *L 25 Feb,*
550 ($825)

pair of silver-coloured etal 'anatomical' earing aids, Continental, te 19th century, 6cm 2½in) long, *L 25 Feb,*
264 ($396)

hand-blown glass roscopy flask, probably Continental, mid 18th entury, 14cm (5½in) igh, *L 18 June,*
440 ($695)

n anatomical model of he human brain, robably English, early 0th century, 15cm (6in) ong, *L 28 Oct,*
352 ($493)

n anatomical model of he eye, English, dated 779, the rosewood case nscrewing to a model of he eye with eight onstituent parts made in lass, horn, lignum vitae nd ivory, 18cm (7in) igh, *L 25 Feb,*
3,080 ($4,620)

cupping and bleeding et, English, mid 19th entury, with six-bladed carifier signed *S Maw ... ondon,* case 26cm (10¼in) vide, *L25 Feb,*
660 ($990)

John Weiss & Son upping and bleeding set, nglish, mid 19th century, ase 21cm (8¼in) wide, *28 Oct,*
396 ($554)

9
An F. C. Rein & Son silver-plated hearing aid, c.1865, lacking ivory earpiece, 9cm (3½in) long, *S 13 Nov,*
£231 ($323)

10
An apothecary chest, mid 19th century, the mahogany case opening to reveal various bottles, pan balance, irons, beaker, glass mortar and pestle, and with concealed sliding panel to rear containing four additional bottles, 27cm (10½in) high, *C 12 Nov,*
£484 ($692)

11
A myophone, French, late 19th century, stamped *Chas. Verdin Paris,* 25.5cm (10in) long, *L 18 June,*
£330 ($521)

12
An L. N. Fowler porcelain phrenology head, English, late 19th century, 28cm (11in) high, *L 28 Oct,*
£572 ($801)

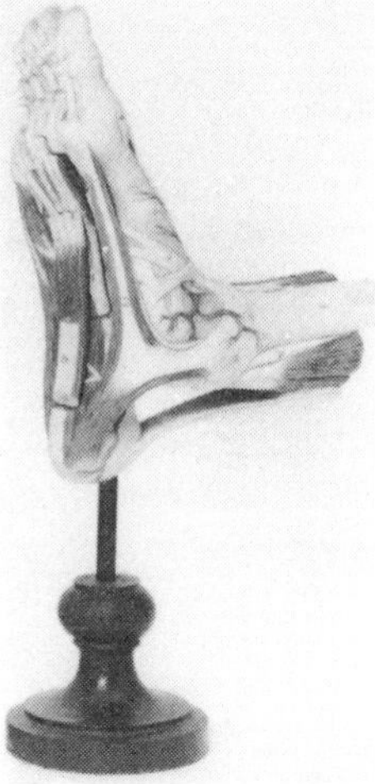
1

2

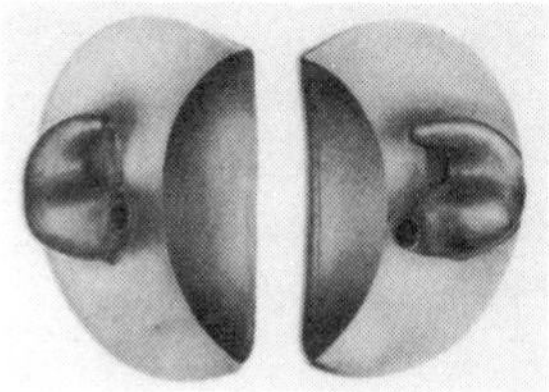
3

4

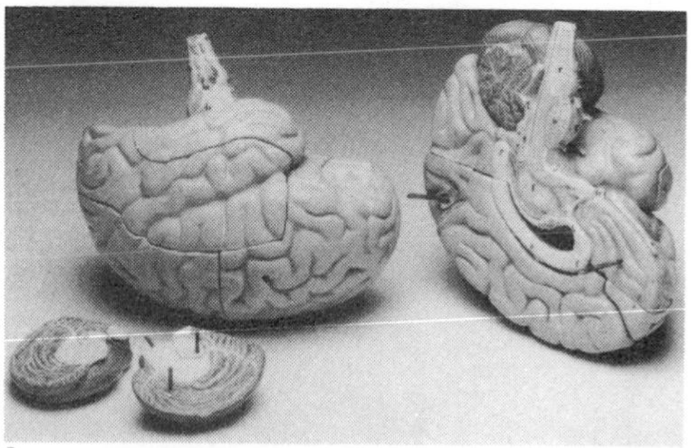
5

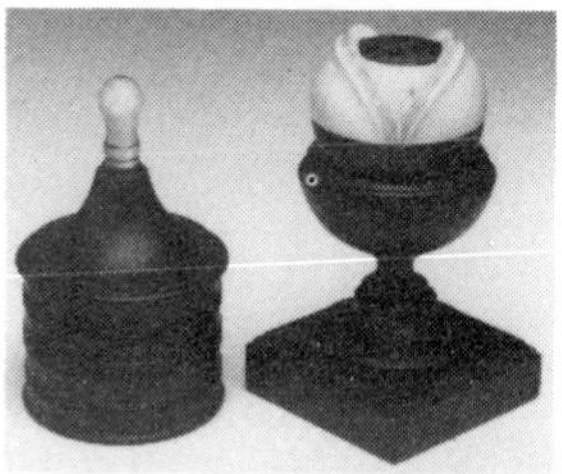
6

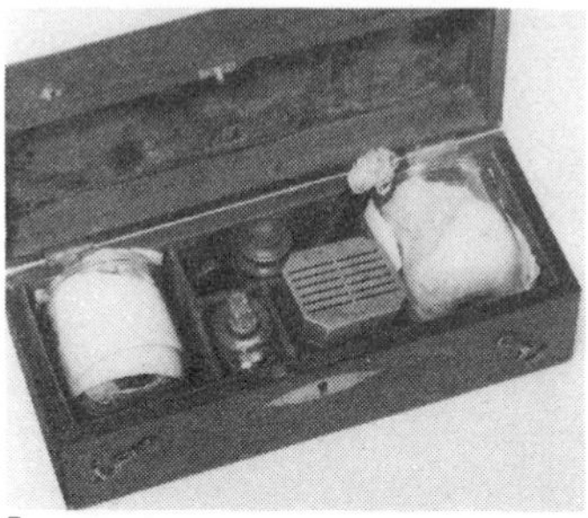
7

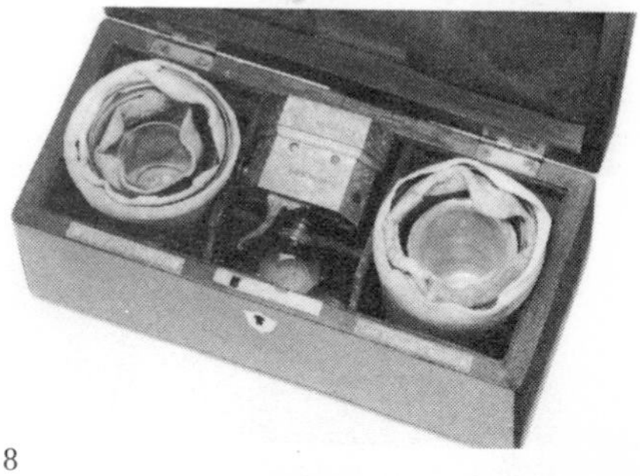
8

9

10

11

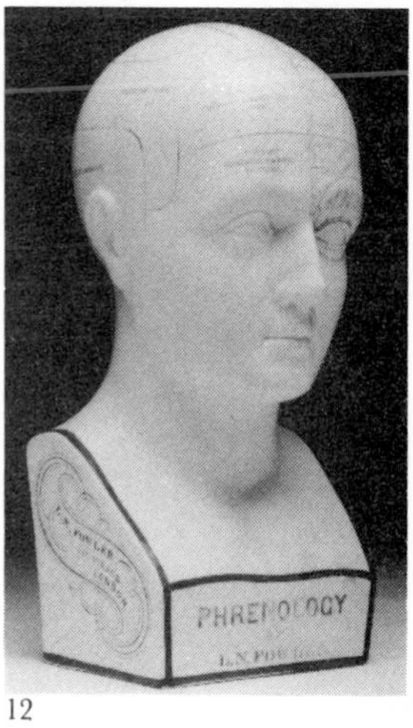

12

1

2

3

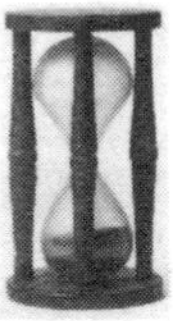
4

5

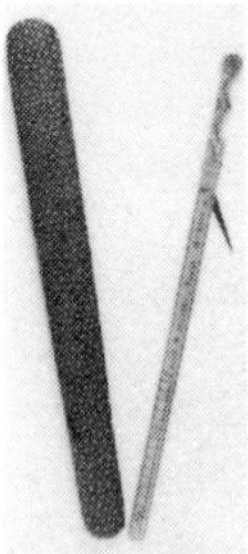
6

7

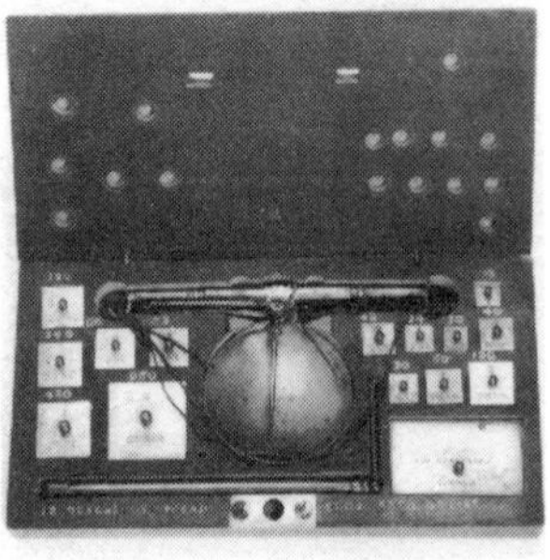
8

9

10 11

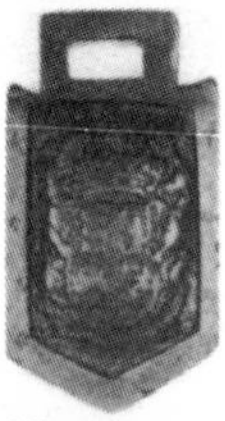
12

13

14

15

16

1
A 15-minute sand glass, 18th century, with brass mounts, 27cm (10½in) high, *M 25 Feb,*
FF 14,430 (£1,396; $2,093)

2
A large hour glass, 18th century, wooden, some wear, 61cm (24in) high, *M 25 Feb,*
FF 3,885 (£376; $564)

3
A half-hour sand glass, American, late 18th century, mahogany mount, 20cm (8in) high, *L 3 June,*
£440 ($682)

4
An unusual 14-second sand glass, American, early 19th century, of turned deal. A 14-second hour glass was used in conjunction with a ship's log to determine the speed of a vessel, 12cm (4¾in) high, *L 3 June,*
£220 ($341)

5
A 7lb beam scale, English, late 19th century, with cast iron base, brass hanging pan and ceramic weighing plate, 81cm (32in) high, with part set of brass weights, *L 25 Feb,*
£275 ($413)

6
A Benjamin Martin ivory and silver money steelyard, English, c.1780, used for weighing gold coins from 4s.6d. to 72s., some parts missing, 16cm (6¼in) long, *L 25 Feb,*
£682 ($1,023)

7
A steelyard letter scale, French, first half 19th century, with turned ivory column supporting brass arm, inscribed with 1.2oz, 1oz and 2oz scale, gilding worn, 14cm (5½in) high, *L 28 Oct,*
£506 ($708)

8
An A. W. Herberts brass gold scale, English, mid 18th century, the wooden case opening to reveal the steel beam scale and assorted weights, 18cm (7in) long, *L 28 Oct,*
£572 ($801)

9
A W. T. Avery jockey scale, London, c.1880, the oak frame with stuffed leather seat, brass side rails and steelyard to 19 stone on one side and 14oz on the other, 64.5cm (25½in) long, *JHB 27 Feb,*
R 935 (£292; $453)

10
A Young's jockey scale, English, late 19th century, the oak frame with upholstered seat, brass scales and brass weights from 1 to 8 stone, 92cm (36in) wide, *C 12 Nov,*
£1,210 ($1,694)

11
An Avery height and weight scale, late 19th century, of oak and brass construction, the base with needleworked pad, with set of weights from 1 to 16 stone, height bar replaced, 140cm (55in), *C 12 Nov,*
£484 ($678)

12
A cast brass wool weight, English, early 18th century, cast with the royal coat of arms and stamped with master signs, 18.5cm (7¼in) long, *L 25 Feb,*
£550 ($825)

13
A set of nine brass imperial measures, English, dated 1890, and ranging from 4 gallons to ½ a gill, largest 41cm (16in) high, *L 25 Feb,*
£1,100 ($1,650)

14
A set of six Gaskell & Chambers 'Chekpump' brass and copper petrol measures, *(five illustrated),* Birmingham, 20th century, ranging from 5 gallons to ½ gallon, largest 43cm (17in) high, *C 12 Nov,*
£660 ($924)

15
A set of fifteen brass imperial weights, English, 1884, ranging from 56lb to ½ a dram, *JHB 25 Mar,*
R 2,200 (£687; $1,072)

16
A set of nine Avery bronze cylindrical imperial weights, English, c.1894, ranging from 56lb to 4oz, largest 28cm (11in) high, *L 25 Feb,*
£1,760 ($2,640)

. William Storer 1½-inch ›rass refracting telescope, ;nglish, c.1780, 19cm 7½in) long, *L 25 Mar,* **:2,530 ($3,947)**

:
\ large and rare Henricus ›neewins brass sector,)utch, c.1650, the arc ngraved with 180 degree cale, the two limbs ngraved with geometric ymbols, names of various netals and elements, unctions and scales, 33cm 13in) radius, *L 18 June,* **:7,150 ($11,297)**

\ Culpeper pattern :ompound monocular nicroscope, English, mid 8th century, of Mathew ,oft design, the mahoany base with drawer :ontaining various ccessories, in oak pillar ase, 42cm (16½in) high, *: 25 Feb,* **:4,400 ($6,600)**

\ steel surgical brace or repan, 18th century, 'rench, signed *ichtenberger,* with reeded otating nut at mid-point, urned ebony handle, 30cm (11¾in) long, *: 22 Apr,* **:660 ($1,036)**

5
\ rare 16-inch Mercator elestial globe on stand, nid 16th century, the phere applied with handoloured gores printed vith named constellations ind their symbols, two :artouches with inscripions, one forbidding mitation within the Empire for a ten year)eriod, the other with a ledication to Prince George of Austria, son of he Emperor Maximilian, ind signed *Gerardus Mercator Rupelmondanus,* with ater brass meridian, the base inset with magnetic compass, needle and glass missing, restored overall, Gerhard Mercator (1512-94), one of the finest cartographers of the 16th century, published his terrestrial globe in 1541 and his celestial one in 1551, *L 18 June,* **£19,800 ($31,284)**

1

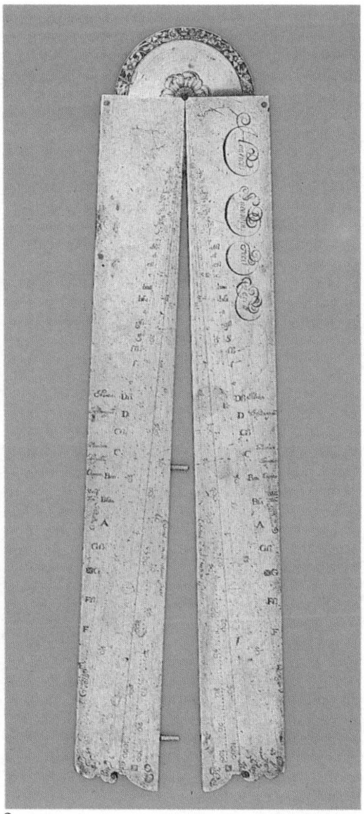
2

3

4

5

1

2

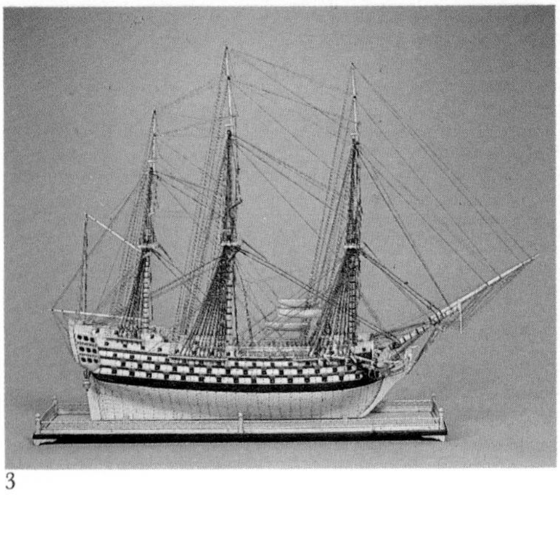

3

4

1
A rare ivory and ebony sea horse jagging wheel, c.1870, with a band of ebony at the centre, the horn a three-pronged pickle fork, the eyes and nostrils inlaid with small pieces of ebony, the forelegs grasping the crenellated wheel held in place with small silver pins, 20cm (8in) long, *NY 1 Feb,* **$18,700 (£13,262)**

2
A moulded and gilded copper stag weathervane, American, 19th century, the flattened figure in the full round with applied sheet copper rack of antlers and ears, the body covered in gilding with details picked out in black paint, on a rod, 77cm (31in) high, *NY 1 Feb,* **$6,875 (£4,876)**

3
A large prisoner-of-war bone model of a 120-gun ship-of-the-line, French, c.1810, the stern with two-tier gallery and carved balustrading with carved panel above decorated with flowers and classical figures, the deck mounted with skylights, belaying rails, companionways, water barrels, hammock netting, ship's bell, capstan and two stove pipes, with bone and baleen base raised on four bracket feet, some restoration and replacement, 63.5 x 86cm (25 x 34in), *L 3 June,* **£12,100 ($18,755)**

4
A pair of painted and decorated maple rush-seat chairs, *(one illustrated),* Pennsylvania, c.1835, the backs painted with apple and cherry motifs, *NY 25 Oct,* **$5,775 (£4,096)**

1
Louis-Ernest Barrias, a gilt-bronze and marble figure of Nature unveiling herself before Science, c.1895, foundry mark enclosing *Susse Frères Editeurs Paris*, one finger missing, (the original model shown in the 1893 Salon), on an onyx base, 73.5cm (29in), *NY 13 Sept,*
$14,300 (£9,728)

2
Leopoldo Ansiglioni, a marble figure of Venus, c.1864, 183cm (72in), on a rotating base, *L 6 Nov,*
£19,800 ($28,116)

3
Frederic, Lord Leighton, a bronze figure entitled *The Sluggard*, (the life size bronze was exhibited at the Royal Academy in 1886), founded by *J. W. Singer & Sons, Frome, Somerset*, rich dark brown patination, 52cm (20½in), *L 26 Nov,*
£6,050 ($8,470)

4
Auguste Moreau, a bronze group entitled *Naissance de Venus* ('Birth of Venus'), c.1880, the goddess riding on a chariot supported by clouds, rich brown, light brown and gilt patination, foundry mark *A. B. Paris*, marble plinth, 92cm (36in), *L 6 Nov,*
£6,380 ($9,060)

1

2

3

4

1

2

3

4

5

6

7

8

1
A tortoiseshell piqué casket, Neapolitan, c.1730, decorated with Pluto seizing Persephone, some wear, 15.5cm (6in) wide, *G 13 Nov,*
SF 12,100 (£5,042; $7,058)

2
A two-colour gold and enamel boite à mouches, probably French, c.1770, set with miniatures of putti playing, gold mounts, marks rubbed, 6cm (2½in), *G 15 May,*
SF 17,600 (£5,926; $9,541)

3
A hardstone and mosaic snuff box, Giovanni Andrea Mascelli, Rome, c.1830, the black onyx body with a view of St. Peter's Square, silver mounts, maker's mark, 8cm (3in), *L 9 June,*
£880 ($1,390)

4
A hardstone and mosaic stuff box, Camillo Picconi, Rome, c.1815-25, with micro-mosaic panel of the tomb of Cecilia Metella, gold mounts, maker's mark, 10cm (4in), *L 9 June,*
£1,100 ($1,738)

5
A hardstone and mosaic snuff box, Giovanni Andrea Mascelli, Rome, c.1840, with micro-mosaic panel of the temple of Hercules at Cora, silver mounts and frame, maker's mark, chip, 8.5cm (3¼in), *L 9 June,*
£1,595 ($2,520)

6
A micro-mosaic plaque, Roman, early 19th century, inlaid with an Italianate landscape in the manner of Claude Lorrain, gilt-metal mount, 7cm (2¾in), *L 9 June,*
£1,870 ($2,955)

7
A gold and hardstone desk seal, British, c.1825, engraved with the arms of Hay, Earls of Kinnoull, 9cm (3½in), *L 9 June,*
£3,740 ($5,909)

8
A mosaic panel, Agostino Francescangeli, Rome, 1837, depicting the Capitoline Doves of Pliny, 38cm (15in), later frame, *G 13 Nov,*
SF 31,900 (£13,292; ($18,608)

1
Jean Baptiste Jacques Augustin, A Young Lady, signed, c.1800, 7cm (2¾in), mounted within the lid of a tortoiseshell box, *L 17 Mar,*
£6,050 ($9,256)

2
Mlle Virginie Hue de Bréval, Queen Julie, wife of Joseph Bonaparte, King of Naples and Sicily, later King of Spain, signed and dated 1813, 7cm (2¾in), set within the lid of a tortoiseshell box, *L 9 June,*
£6,600 ($10,428)

3
Charles Boit, Henrietta, Lady Godolphin (1681-1733), afterwards Duchess of Marlborough, signed, c.1700, 5.5cm (2¼in), gilt-metal frame, *L 17 Mar,*
£2,640 ($4,039)

4
Richard Gibson, Sir Thomas Wolryche, 3rd Bt. of Dudmaston, Shropshire (1672-1701), on vellum, 7.5cm (3in), gold frame, *L 9 June,*
£10,450 ($16,511)

5
Charles Muss, probably after John Smart, A Lady, signed and dated 1818, 12.5cm (5in), gold bezel, *L 10 Nov,*
£2,640 ($3,775)

6
Louis Lié Périn Salbreux, A Young Lady, signed, c.1800, 7cm (2¾in), silver-gilt mount, *L 10 Nov,*
£20,900 ($29,887)

7
Nicolas Soret, A Northern Patron of the Arts, signed, inscribed and dated 1793, enamel, 6.5cm (2½in), gold bezel, *L 10 Nov,*
£5,500 ($7,865)

8
Peter Boy the Younger, A Bavarian Prince, signed and dated 1708, enamel, 4cm (1½in), pierced foliate gold frame, *L 17 Mar,*
£5,720 ($8,751)

9
French School, A Family Group, c.1780, 7cm (2¾in), gilt-metal mount, *L 17 Mar,*
£2,200 ($3,366)

1

2

3

4

5

6

7

8

9

1

2

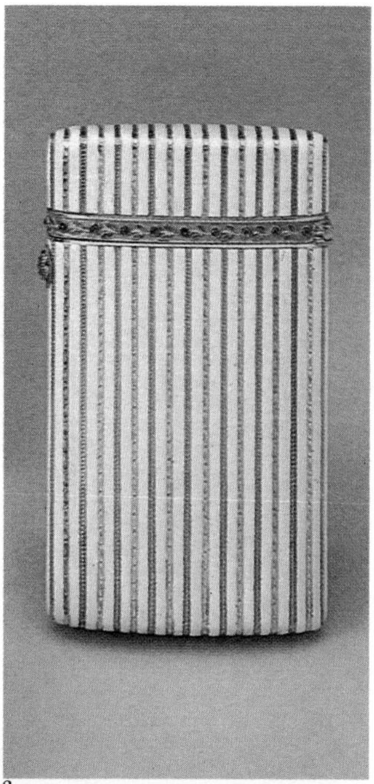
3

4

5

1
A Fabergé carved agate cat, St. Petersburg, c.1900, 5.5cm (2¼in), *NY 12 Dec,*
$33,000 (£23,571)

2
A Fabergé gold and nephrite fruit-shaped gum pot, Henrik Wigström, late 19th century, the brush with gold stem set with a ruby, workmaster's mark, 6cm (2¼in) high, *G 15 May,*
SF 18,700 (£6,296; $10,137)

3
A Fabergé two-colour gold, jewelled and enamelled cigarette case, H. Wigström, St. Petersburg, 1899-1908, with green and yellow bands, the lid set with cabochon rubies, diamond thumbpiece, the original case inscribed *Fabergé/St.Petersburg, Moscow, Odessa,* 9cm (3½in), *G 13 Nov,*
SF 38,000 (£15,833; $22,166)

4
A Fabergé two-colour gold and yellow enamel hat pin, A. Hollming, St. Petersburg, late 19th century, surmounted with a cabochon moonstone, maker's and workmaster's marks, 22.5cm (9in), *G 13 Nov,*
SF 9,500 (£3,958; $5,541)

5
A silver-gilt and shaded enamel eight-piece tea and coffee set, Gratchev Brothers, St. Petersburg, c.1900, with mother-of-pearl finials, in original fitted oak chest, tray 39.5cm (15½in), *NY 12 Dec,*
$19,800 (£14,143)

1
A Franco-German parcel-gilt silver Torah shield, Daniel Hammerer, Strasbourg, c.1660, the reverse later engraved c.1840, includes original suspension chain, height overall 43cm (17in), *NY 18 Dec,*
$34,100 (£23,846)

2
An Italian silver spice tower, maker and assay master marks CL and FB, Venice or Padua, late 17th/early 18th century, fully marked, 27cm (10¾in), *NY 28 May,*
$19,800 (£13,200)

3
A Polish parcel-gilt silver Torah shield, late 18th century, maker's mark AI, quality mark 12, Hebrew silversmith signature for Yosef ben Yisrael Tsorif, probably Warsaw, later suspension chain, 33cm (13in), *NY 18 Dec,*
$22,000 (£15,384)

4
A Dutch silver Sabbath lamp, Joseph Sliepers, Amsterdam, 1786, fully marked, 98cm (38½in), *NY 28 May,*
$71,500 (£47,667)

1

2

3

4

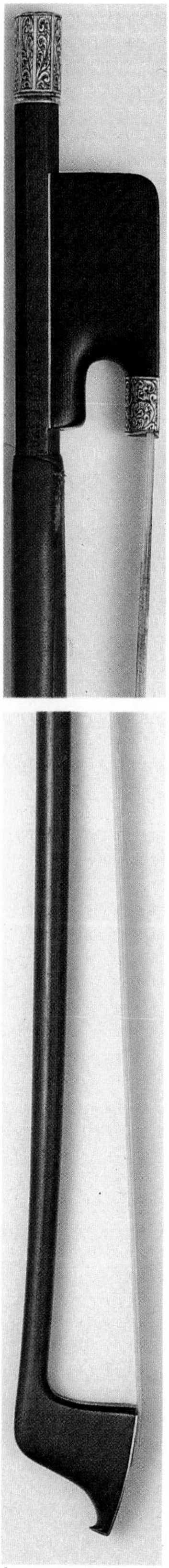

1

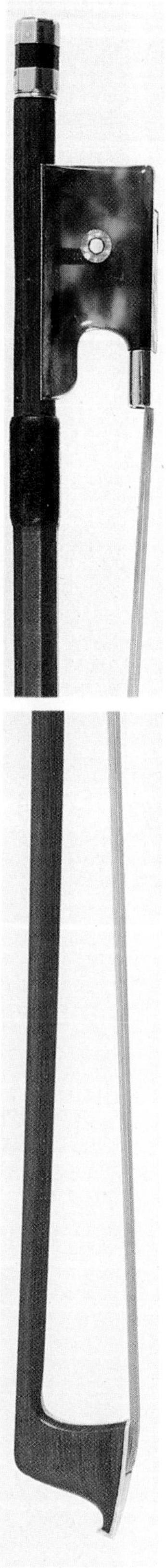

2

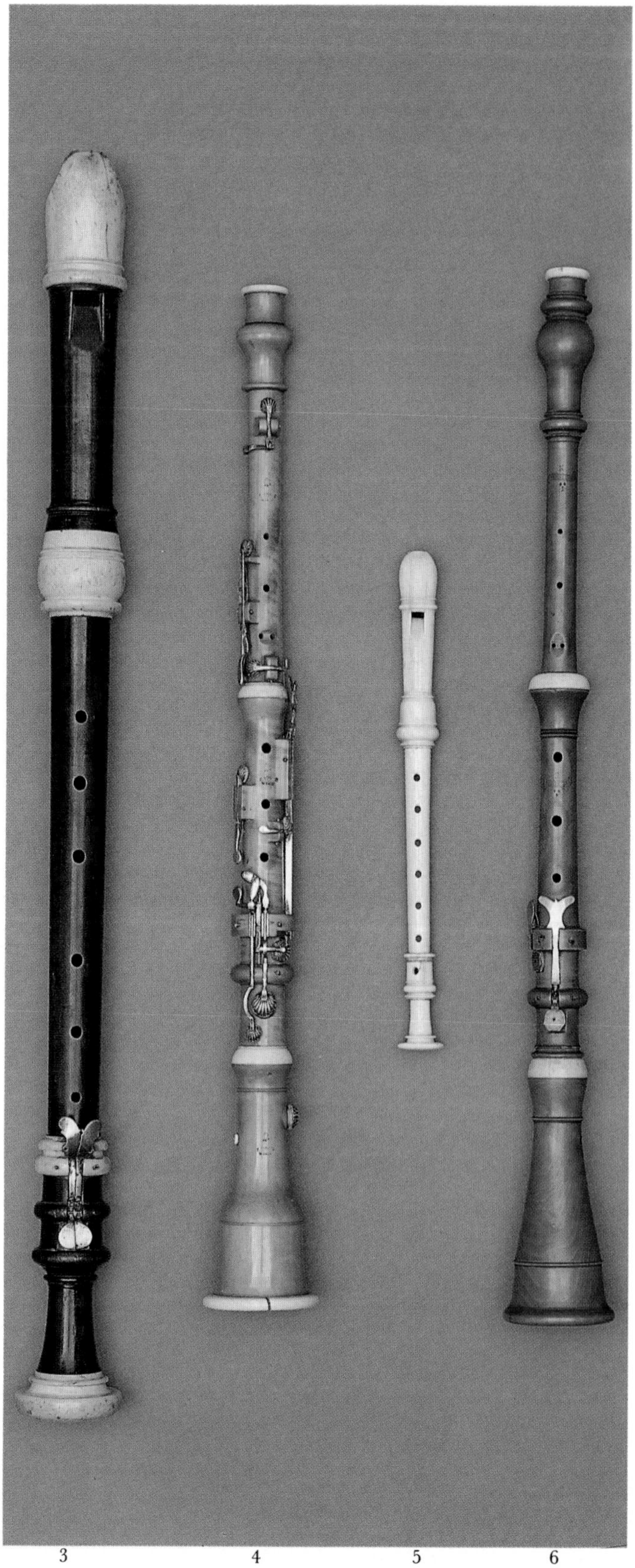

3 4 5 6

1
James Tubbs, London, a chased gold-mounted violin bow, 61 grams, *L 22 May,*
£3,740 ($5,947)

2
Nicolas François Vuillaume, Paris, a gold and tortoiseshell-mounted violin bow, 60 grams, *L 19 Mar,*
£5,720 ($8,752)

3
Peter Bressan, London, first quarter 18th century, a tenor recorder, 68.5cm (27in), *L 12 Nov,*
£24,200 ($34,606)

4
Stephan Koch, Vienna. c.1825, a ten-keyed boxwood 'Sellner system' oboe, 55.5cm (22in), *L 12 Nov,*
£5,280 ($7,550)

5
An ivory sopranino recorder, probably German, early 18th century, 27.5cm (10¾in), *L 12 Nov,*
£4,620 ($6,607)

6
Johann Friedrich Engelhard, Nuremberg, c.1770, a two-keyed oboe, later bell joint by another maker, 57.5cm (22½in), *L 12 Nov,*
£2,860 ($4,090)

:arlo Ferdinando .andolfi, Milan, c.1775, a violin, 35.5cm (14in), *. 22 May,* **:20,900 ($33,231)**

'rancesco Emiliani, Rome, c.1725, a violin, 35.5cm (14in), *L 12 Nov,* **19,800 ($28,314)**

Nicolas Gagliano, Naples, .772, a violin, 35.5cm 14in), *L 22 May,* **:15,950 ($25,360)**

:amillus Camilli, Mantua, c.1745, a violin, 35.5cm (14in), *L 12 Nov,* **:28,600 ($40,898)**

1

2

3

4

1 2 3 4 5

6

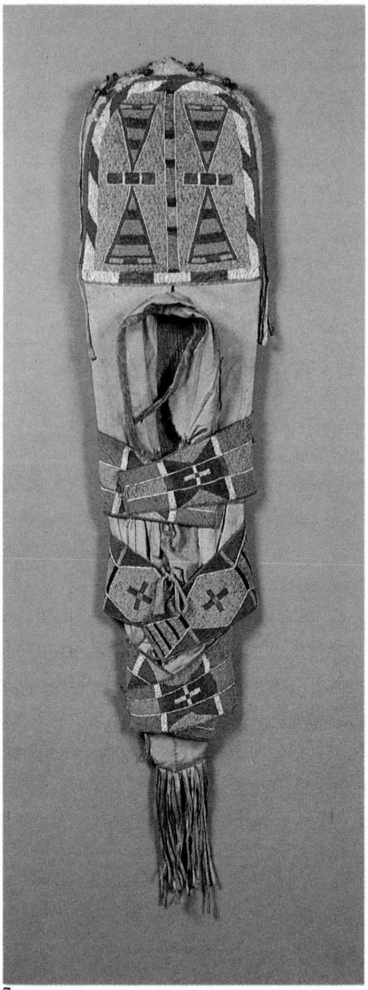

7

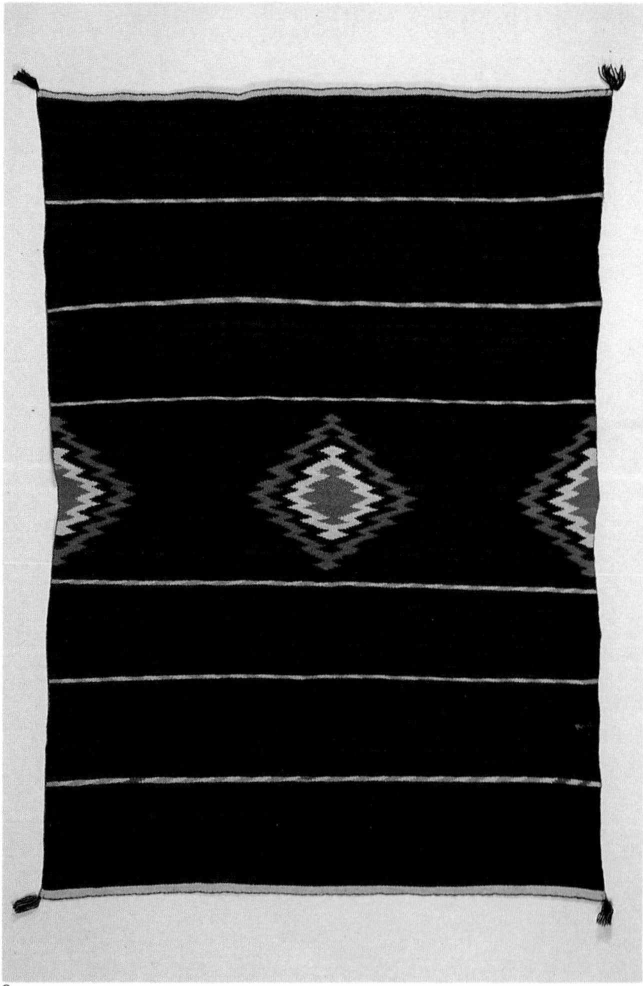

8

1
A Yokuts polychrome coiled gambling tray, woven on a saw grass ground in black bracken-fern root and redbud, 35cm (13¾in), *NY 30 May,*
$5,610 (£3,816)

2
An Attu twined and lidded cylindrical basket, woven in rye grass, embroidered in violet, red and blue commercial silk thread, 10.5cm (4in), *NY 30 May,*
$1,760 (£1,197)

3
An Attu twined and lidded cylindrical basket, woven in rye grass, chain motifs on the handle, 10cm (4in), *NY 30 May,*
$1,760 (£1,197)

4
An Attu twined basketry bottle, woven in rye grass over a faceted glass jar, 11cm (4¼in), *NY 30 May,*
$1,870 (£1,272)

5
An Attu twined and lidded cylindrical basket, woven in rye grass, embroidered in lavender, red and blue commercial silk thread, 9cm (3½in), *NY 30 May,*
$2,200 (£1,497)

6
A Crow beaded and fringed hide shirt, decorated with hide, strips strung with white ermine pelts and human hair, bound with red trade cloth and short strands of blue glass beads, 155cm (61in), *NY 3 Dec,*
$60,500 (£42,307)

7
A Crow beaded hide cradleboard, wood panel overlaid with softly tanned hide, the hood of trade cloth, 103cm (40½in), *NY 3 Dec,*
$20,900 (£14,615)

8
A Classic Navajo man's wearing blanket, *serape,* 189cm (74½in) long, *NY 30 May,*
$8,250 (£5,612)

1
A Cypriot pottery amphora, c.700-600 BC, decorated between the handles with bands of rosettes, guilloche and lotus motifs, 90.5cm (35½in), *L 14 July,*
£17,050 ($26,598)

2
A glass jug, Cologne, 1st/2nd century AD, on an everted foot, traces of weathering, 23.5cm (9¼in), *L 14 July,*
£9,020 ($14,071)

3
A Hellenistic cast single-handled flask, c.1st century BC, lathe-cut and polished, with carinated body, the ground rim with a single wheel-cut groove within, some weathering, minor repair, 10cm (4in), *L 14 July,*
£13,200 ($20,592)

4
An Egyptian bronze figure of a cat, Late Period, c.712-30 BC, 12.5cm (5in), *L 14 July,*
£11,000 ($17,160)

5
A Hellenistic terracotta figure of a young woman, c.3rd century BC, a rolled fillet and vine leaves in her hair, 35cm (13¾in), *L 8 Dec,*
£2,090 ($2,926)

6
A Hellenistic terracotta female figure, c.3rd century BC, vine leaves and bosses in her hair, carrying a bird on her left arm and a large ball in her left hand, her right hand on her hip, a diminutive female figure to either side, 30cm (11¾in), *L 8 Dec,*
£1,320 ($1,848)

7
A Hellenistic terracotta figure of Eros, 3rd/2nd century BC, the winged figure posed in flight, wearing a torque, a rolled fillet with vine leaves attached around his head, 27.5cm (10¾in), *L 8 Dec,*
£6,050 ($8,470)

1

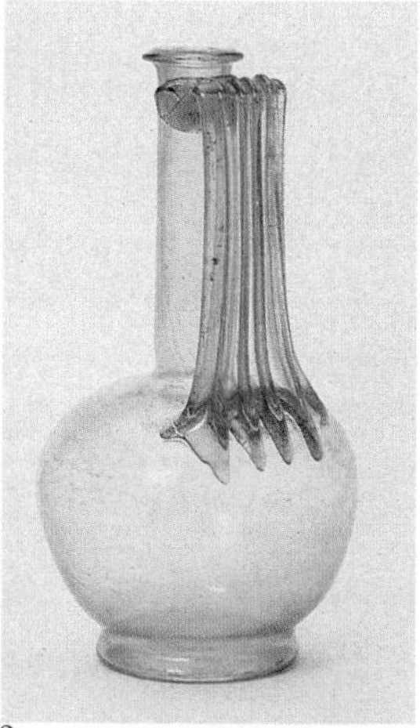
2

3

4

5 6 7

1

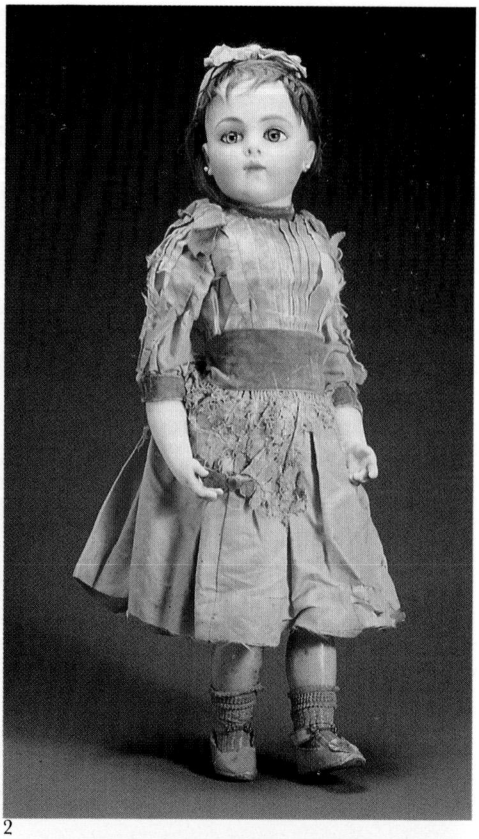
2

3

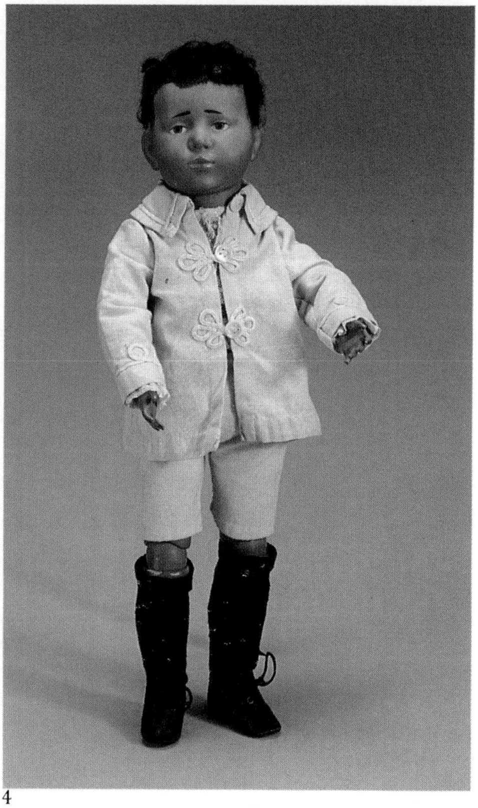
4

1
A J.D. Kestner bisque oriental doll, German, c.1914, impressed *F10 243 J.D.K.*, weighted glass eyes, real hair wig, composition body, in original outfit slightly fraying on front, 33cm (13in), *L 5 Feb,*
£2,310 ($3,326)

2
A Casimir Bru bisque doll, French, c.1875, impressed *BRU Jne.9,* fixed eyes, sparse mohair wig over cork pate, leather body, bearing label *Bebe BRU Bte.S.G.D.G.*, original dress badly torn, 62cm (24½in), *L 5 Feb,*
£11,000 ($15,840)

3
A Kammer and Reinhardt bisque character doll, German, c.1909, impressed *112 46,* painted eyes, real hair, jointed wood and composition body, label *BEBE JUMEAU Diplome d'Honneur,* paint flaked, 46cm (18in), *L 23 Sept,*
£4,950 ($6,930)

4
A Kammer and Reinhardt bisque mulatto doll, German, 1909, impressed *101 39,* painted brown eyes, sparse mohair wig, ball-jointed wood and composition body, 39cm (15¼in), *L 23 Sept,*
£2,970 ($4,158)

1
A French clockwork automaton of a Spaniard shooting, c.1880, possibly Theroude or Vichy, with bisque head, glass eyes, moulded moustache and goatee beard, 33cm (13in), *NY 28 June,*
$3,575 (£2,337)

2
A French musical automaton of a photographer, c.1870, possibly Decamps, the figure sways and lowers her head and arms, the dog wags its tail and a bird pops out of the lens, 66cm (26in) high, *NY 28 June,*
$17,050 (£11,144)

3
A tinplate steam car, c.1898, probably Carette, German, with sprung suspension and spirit-fired steam mechanism driving rear axle, some wear to paint, lacking driver, 23cm (9in) long, *L 20 May,*
£13,750 ($22,000)

4
A Bing fire engine, German c.1900, spirit-fired with brass boiler dome, some heat damage to paintwork, front of driver's cab loose, 23cm (9in) long, *L 23 Sept,*
£6,600 ($9,240)

5
A Marklin warehouse, German, 1902, catalogue no. 1045, hand painted, 41cm (16in) long, *L 23 Sept,*
£638 ($893)

1

2

3

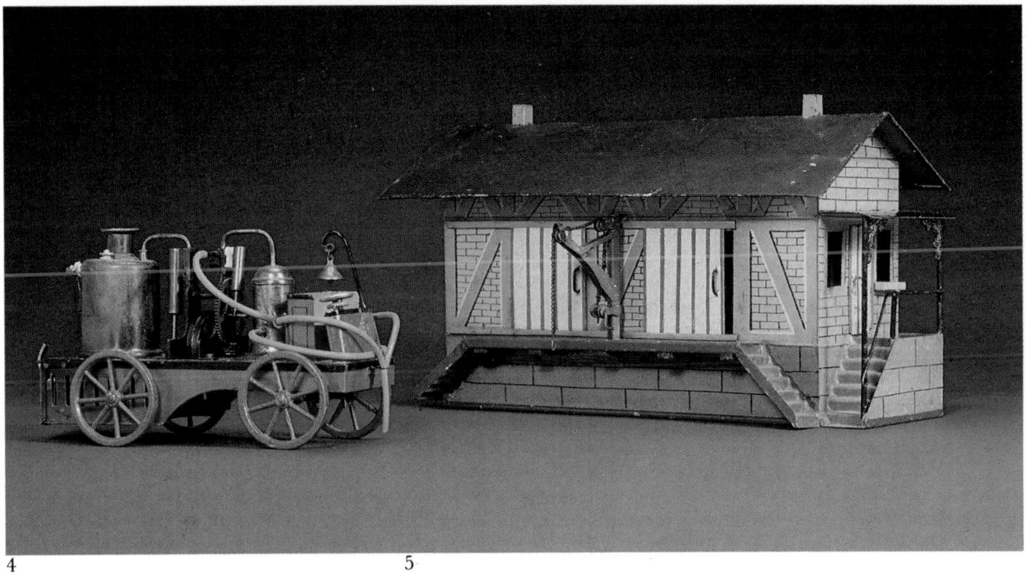
4 5

1

2

3

1
A 1900 Cudell de Dion Bouton 3½ h.p. Vis-à-vis, built under licence in Aachen, Germany,
L 23 June,
£12,650 ($19,734)

2
A Delage D8N 29.5 h.p. Sedanca de Ville, coachwork by Fernandez,
L 1 Dec,
£38,500 ($55,055)

3
A Lincoln V8 39.2 h.p. Dual Cowl Phaeton, 1928, National First Prize winner at the Hershey Concours d'Elégance in Pennsylvania in 1970,
M 25 May,
FF 748,000 (£66,430; $104,295)

1
James Bond 007's Aston Martin from the film 'Goldfinger', 1963, painted silver with extras such as machine guns concealed behind parking lights, a tack spreader from the left rear light, a rotating licence plate and radar screen on the dash-board. After the film, the James Bond gadgets were removed and replace-ments fitted, *NY 28 June,* **$275,000 (£179,739)**

2
A pair of bronze urns, *(one illustrated)*, c.1860, cast with a border of foliage, Greek key and vines, the sides with wild boar masks, 89cm (35in), *S 28 May,* **£26,400 ($41,712)**

3
Francis Cucchiari. A Carrara white marble group of a bitch and puppy, c.1840, signed, puppy's tail missing, on associated plinth, 99cm (39in), *S 28 May,* **£8,250 ($13,035)**

1

2

3

1

2

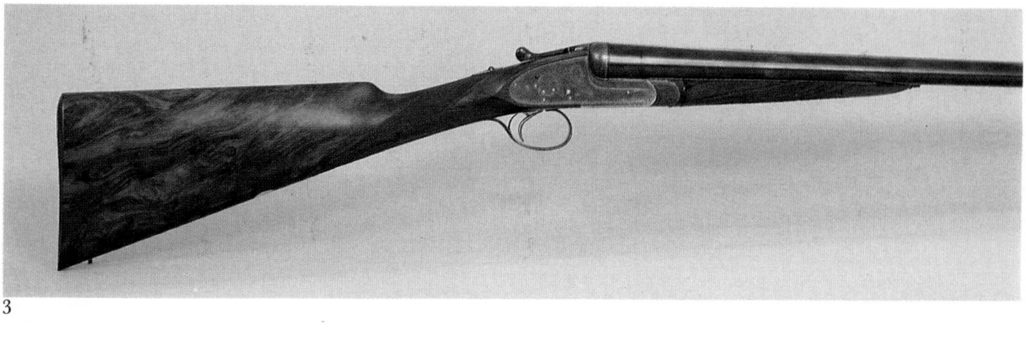

3

1
A 3-inch scale model live steam coal-fired compound showman's road locomotive 'Ivanhoe', built by R. Anderson & Sons, Buckhaven, 128.5cm (50½in), *C 30 Apr,*
£5,500 ($8,910)

2
A 5-inch gauge live steam 4-2-2 locomotive, largely based on a Stirling 'single', 142.5cm (56in), *C 30 Apr,*
£3,520 ($5,702)

3
Boss & Co. A 12-bore single-trigger assisted-opening sidelock ejector gun, built in 1911, 30-inch chopper lump barrels, *Glen 25 Aug,*
£7,700 ($12,089)

See also:
Islamic works of art *pp* 622-624
Japanese works of art *pp* 684-685
Sporting guns *pp* 521-524

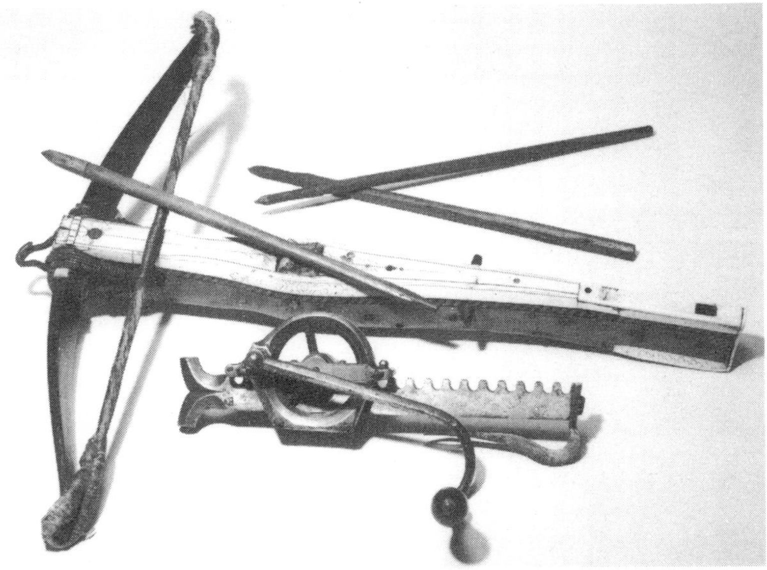

1 2

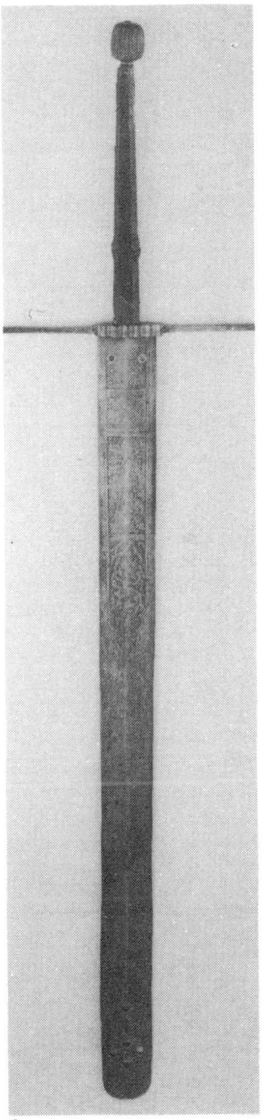

9

3

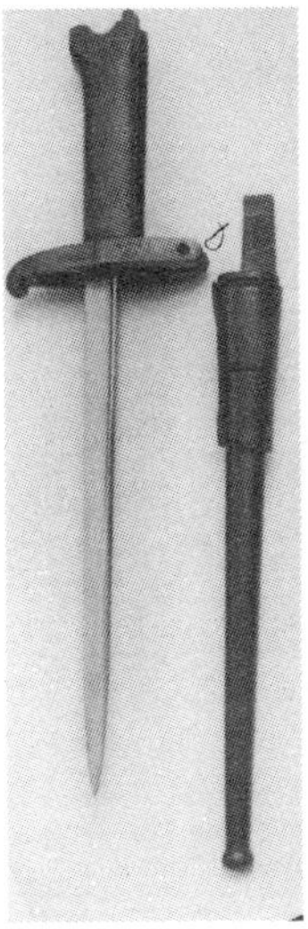

6

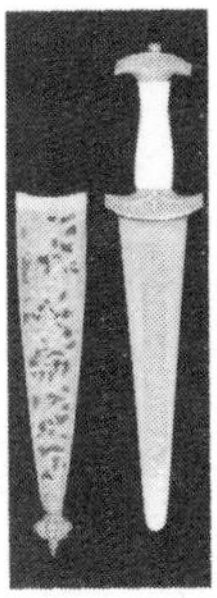

4

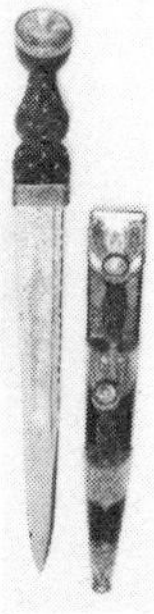

5

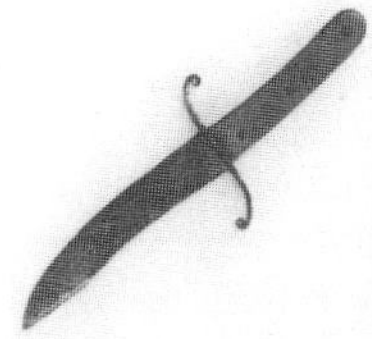

7

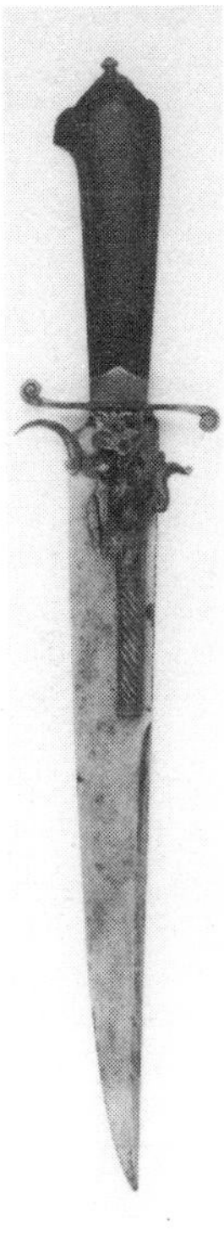

8

10

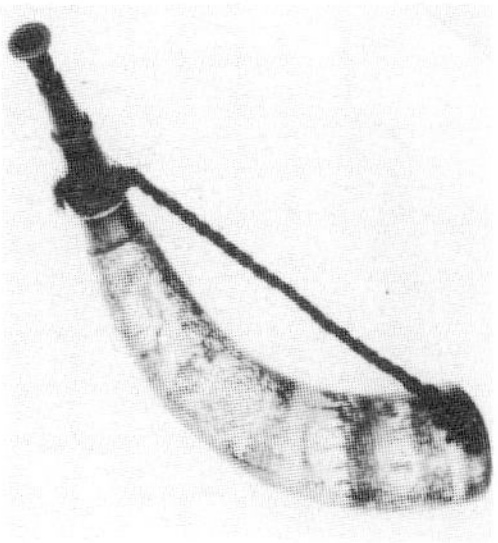

11

German crossbow, first uarter 17th century, ntler inlaid, Christ risen n the underside, struck vith makers mark, some osses and repair; together vith three bolts of oak, etaining iron heads, 66 nd 42.5cm (26 and 17in), *YY 31 May,*
4,400 (£2,993)

2
A German steel and iron ranequin, 17th century, truck with mark, brass nlay, 35cm (14in), *VY 31 May,*
$1,045 (£711),

3
A central European owder horn, 17th entury, probably Swiss, rass furniture, 18cm 7in), *NY 31 May,*
$440 (£299)

4
A Swiss commemorative dagger, dated 1901, etched *Basler Bundesfeier 1901,* commissioned by the Council of Basel to commemorate the 400th anniversary of the town's entry into the Swiss Confederacy, 36.5cm (14½in), *L 15 May,*
£1,430 ($2,302)

5
A Victorian Highlander's regimental dirk of the 42nd (Black Watch), etched with crowned *V.R.*, gilt-metal mounts, in matching leather sheath with knife and fork, spring catch missing from knife, 28cm (11in), *S 6 Oct,*
£660 ($924)

6
A Pritchard Greener bayonet for the Webly Mk.VI service revolver, engraved *Patent no.17143116* and *W.W.G.*, stamped *45,* in steel sheath with leather frog, blade 20.5cm (8¼in), *S 7 July,*
£726 ($1,176)

7
An American steel knife, mid 19th century, struck *Walter H. Tyler*, ochre coloured hard rubber grip, 29cm (11½in), *NY 25 Nov,*
$220 (£157)

8
A Spanish Miquelet-lock percussion knife pistol, c.1840, inscribed *Galbasoro en eybar*, small brass pommel, lock faulty, slight wear and rust stains, 52cm (20½in), *L 15 May,*
£462 ($744)

9
A German executioner's sword, probably 16th century, inscribed *V. Vespein Wachrichter(?) zu Frankfurt am Main, anno 1563,* signed, leather covered grip. 124.5cm (49in), *NY 25 Nov,*
$3,080 (£2,200)

10
An ivory powder horn, dated 1665, the body of engraved hollowed tusk, mounts of engraved brass, inscribed *W.K. 1665,* nozzle loose, 18.5cm (7¼in), *L 5 Nov,*
£330 ($462)

11
An American horn, dated 1761, engraved with the British Royal arms, inscribed *To George Boone, 1761,* detailed views of New York and topography of North America and Canada, some staining, fitted with brass mouthpiece 18/19th century, 46cm (18in), *L 5 Nov,*
£2,970 ($4,158)

1

2

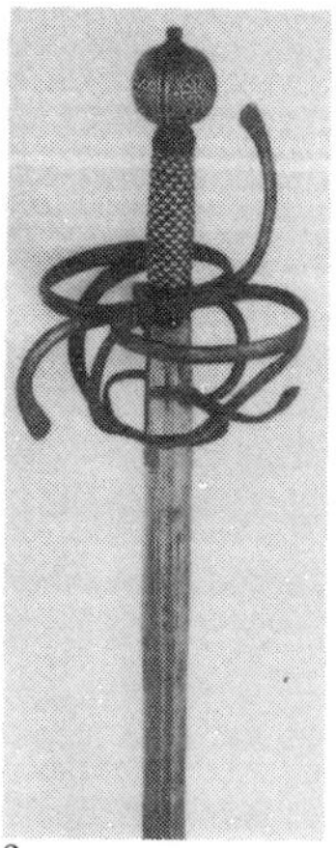
3

4

5

6

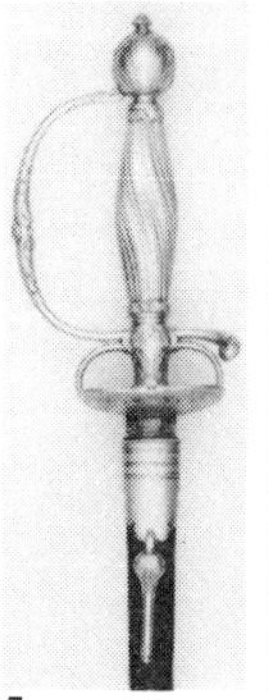
7

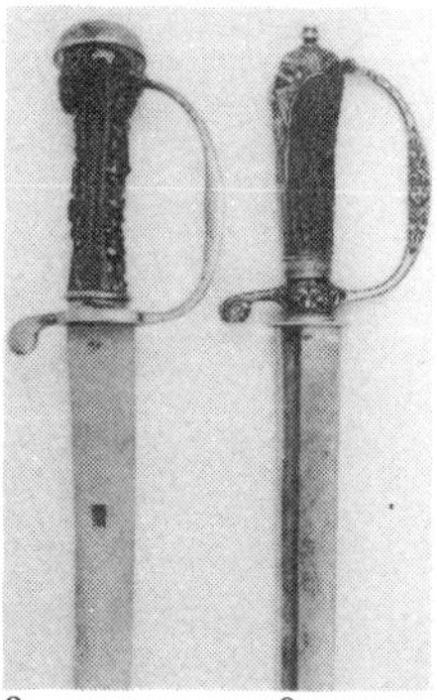
8 9

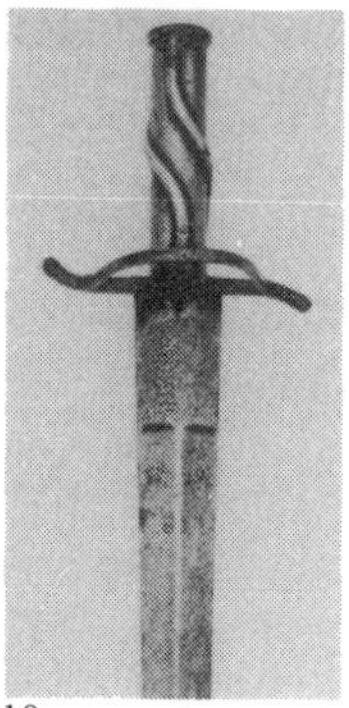
10

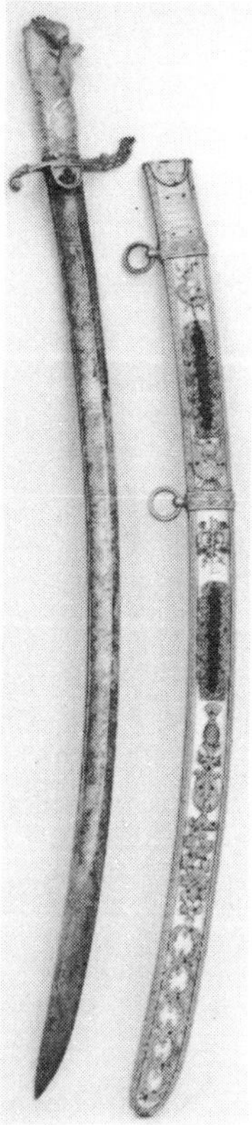
14

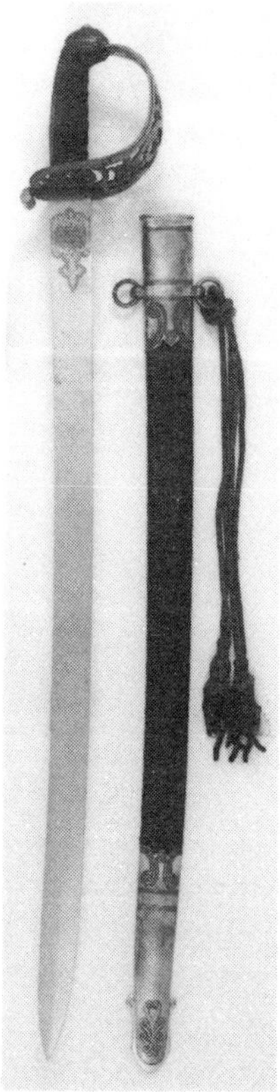
15

11 12 13

16 17

1
A German two-handed fighting sword, c.1540, maker's mark of fleur-de-lis, grip worn, engraving later, 133.5cm (52½in), *L 15 May,*
£1,980 ($3,188)

2
An Austro-Hungarian basket-hilt sabre, 17th century, maker's mark, wood grip bound with string, sold with another similar, 87 and 89cm (34¼ and 35in), *NY 31 May,*
$1,650 (£1,122)

3
A swept-hilt rapier, late 16/17th century, possibly South German, inscribed *Iohanni Picinni*, maker's mark, encrusted with silver over original etching, 107cm (42¼in), *NY 31 May,*
$1,760 (£1,197)

4
A German beheading sword, dated 1737, the crossguard and pommel of gilt brass and facetted, etched inscription and figures, 110.5cm (43½in), *NY 31 May,*
$2,640 (£1,796)

5
A French silver-hilted court sword, Paris 1781-89, marked, 96.5cm (38in), *NY 31 May,*
$825 (£561)

6
A German broadsword, mid 17th century, cutler's mark, grip replaced, 107.5cm (42¼in), *L 5 Nov,*
£462 ($647)

7
A French gold-hilted smallsword, c.1740, maker's mark BC, the mouthpiece inscribed *Collomb A Paris*, minor rust patches, 85.5cm (33¾in), *L 5 Nov,*
£5,280 ($7,392)

8
A silver-hilted hunting hanger, c.1700, struck cutler's mark, rough buckhorn grip, blade bright, 61.5cm (24¼in), *L 5 Nov,*
£220 ($308)

9
A silver-hilted hunting hanger, early 18th century, Solingen mark, staghorn grip, blade slightly stained, 81.5cm (32in), *L 5 Nov,*
£352 ($493)

10
A Continental socket sword bayonet, mid 18th century, inscribed 1769 (?), patination and staining, 85.5cm (33¾in), *L 5 Nov,*
£572 ($801)

11
A silver-hilted hunting hanger, mid 18th century, ivory grip, black leather scabbard with silver mounts, mouthpiece inscribed *Cullum Charing Cross*, 76cm (30in), *L 5 Nov*
£374 ($524)

12
A silver hilted hunting hanger, early 18th century, mark of Johannes Wundes, buckhorn grip, blade stained and slightly pitted, pommel repaired, 64cm (25in), *L 5 Nov,*
£264 ($370)

13
A silver-hilted hunting hanger, c.1730, Solingen cutler's mark, London hallmarks for 1730-31, blade and grip worn, 58cm (23in), *L 5 Nov,*
£253 ($354)

14
A Georgian presentation sword, c.1809, etched with the motto *Always ready*, section of knucklebow missing, 76cm (30in), *S 7 July,*
£2,145 ($3,475)

15
A naval officer's sword with cutlass blade, mid 19th century, some wear, 88.5cm (35in), *L 5 Nov,*
£825 ($1,155)

16
A George V Scottish officer's broadsword, by Henry Wilkinson, plated basket hilt, 83cm (32¾in), *S 6 Oct,*
£242 ($339)

17
A Georgian Scottish broadsword, steel half-basket hilt, defective, 80cm (31¾in), *S 6 Oct,*
£154 ($216)

1
A Brescian wheel-lock pistol, c.1630, wear commensurate with age and use, 39.5cm (15½in), *L 15 May,*
£1,430 ($2,302)

2
A Liègois flintlock over-and-under single trigger holster pistol, late 17th century, inscribed *Desellier,* wear commensurate with age and use, 39.5cm (15½in), *L 5 Nov,*
£1,100 ($1,540)

3
A gold damascened flintlock, third quarter 18th century, 14.5cm (5½in) length of plate, *NY 25 Nov,*
$1,210 (£864)

4
A Brescian snaphaunce lock, dated 1786, some screws replaced, 15.5cm (6in) length of plate, *NY 25 Nov,*
$1,320 (£943)

5
A flintlock double-barrelled travelling pistol, late 18th century, inscribed *D Egg London,* one mainspring broken, ramrod missing, patinated overall, 19.5cm (7¾in), *L 15 May,*
£770 ($1,240)

6
A silver-mounted flintlock belt pistol, mid 18th century, approx 22 bore, some repairs and replacements, cleaned bright, 32cm (12½in), *L 5 Nov,*
£484 ($678)

7
A flintlock tap-action double-barrelled boxlock travelling pistol, c.1800, Bird & Ashmore, London, 20cm (8in), *C 30 Jan,*
£242 ($356)

8
A four-barrelled flintlock revolver, c.1800, by Mossocke, sold with an antler mounted wheel-lock pistol, 19th century, 29cm (11½in) and 40cm (15¾in), *NY 25 Nov,*
$1,980 (£1,414)

9
A pair of double-barrelled flintlock boxlock tap-action pocket pistols, c.1800, inscribed *Spencer, London,* slight wear, 19.5cm (7½in), *L 15 May,*
£660 ($1,063)

10
A pair of silver-mounted and plated flintlock over-and-under tap-action travelling pistols, early 19th century, inscribed *J & W Richards London,* 21cm (8¼in), *L 5 Nov,*
£1,045 ($1,463)

11
A 20 bore cannon-barrelled flintlock pistol, early 18th century, by Joyner, Holborn, London, *S 6 Oct,*
£495 ($693)

12
A pair of flintlock saw-handled duelling pistols, c.1820, approx 38 bore, inscribed *E. Bond,* one top jaw and screw replaced, in brass-bound case, 41cm (16in), *L 15 May,*
£1,760 ($2,834)

13
A flintlock holster pistol, early 19th century, maker's mark *Collins Vigo Lane,* cock replaced, barrel refinished, 36.5cm (14½in), *L 5 Nov,*
£528 ($739)

14
A 54 bore six-shot percussion open-frame hammerless double-action revolver, signed *Wood Howden,* defective action, grip cracked, rammer missing, *S 7 July,*
£462 ($748)

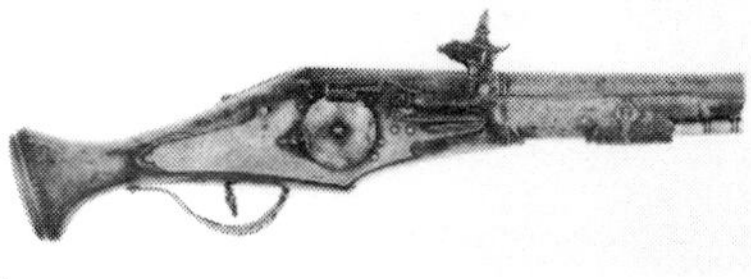
1

2

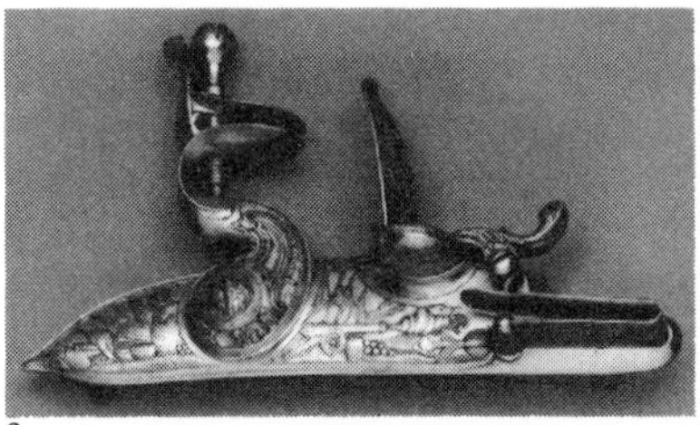
3

4

5

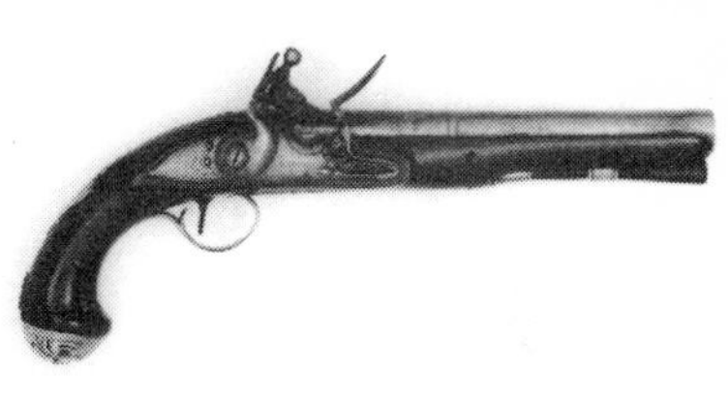
6

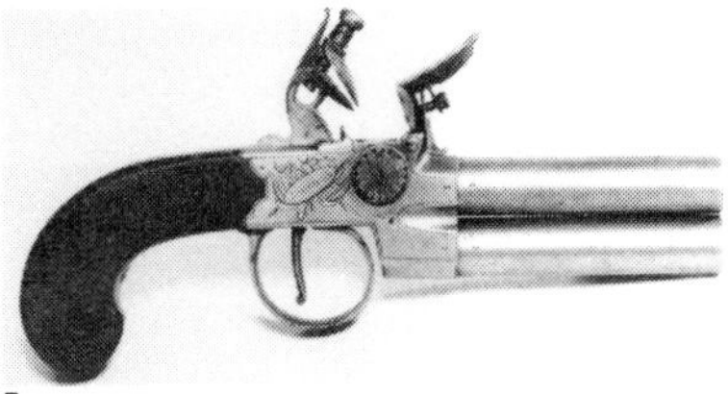
7

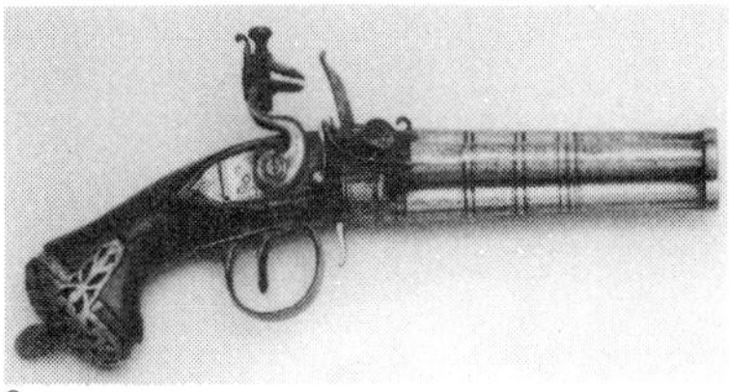
8

9

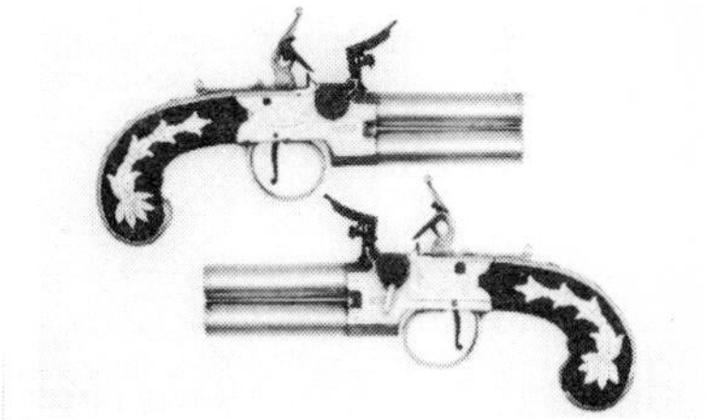
10

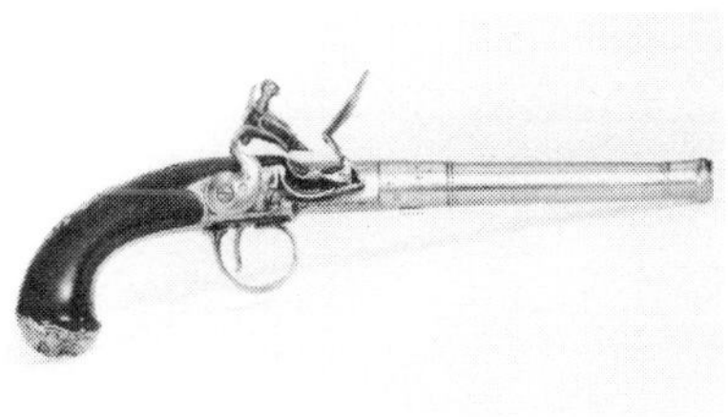
11

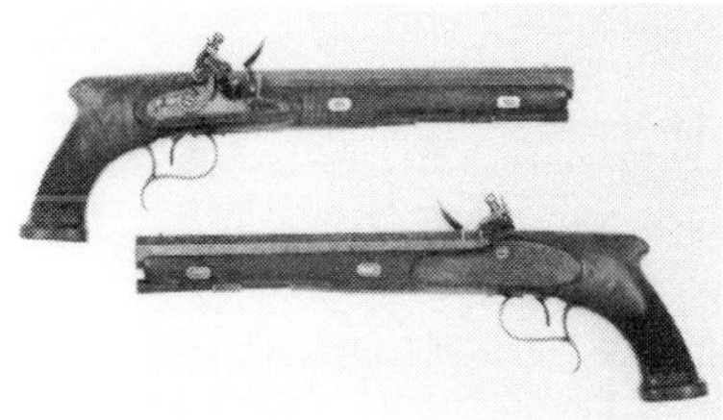
12

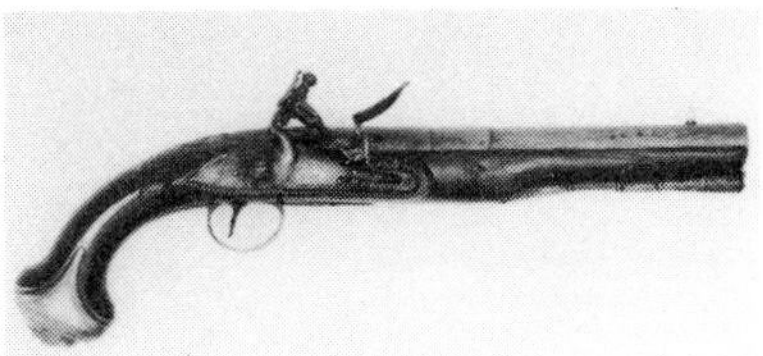
13

14

1

2

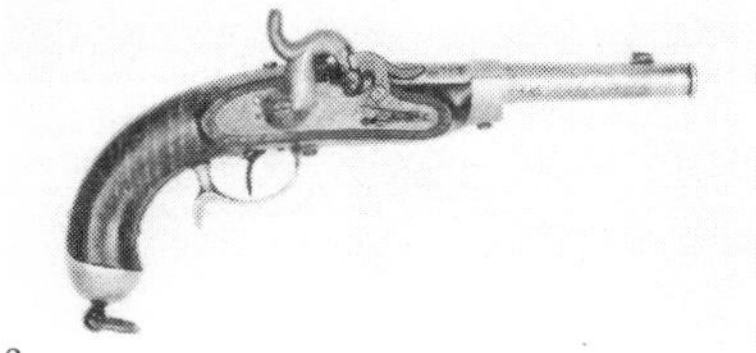
3

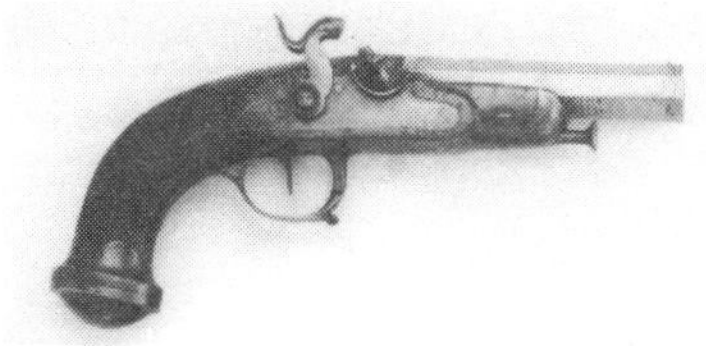
4

5

6

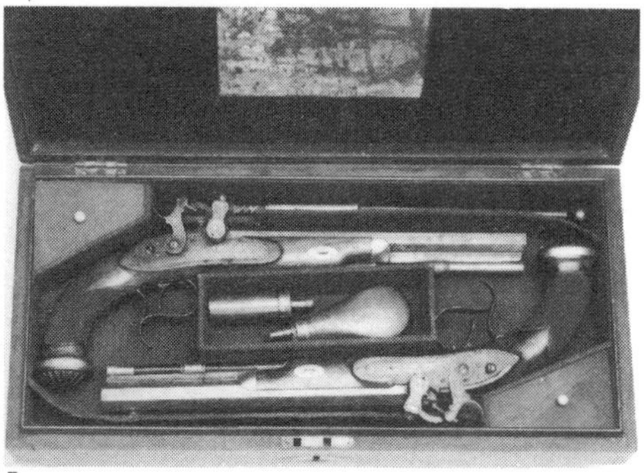
7

8

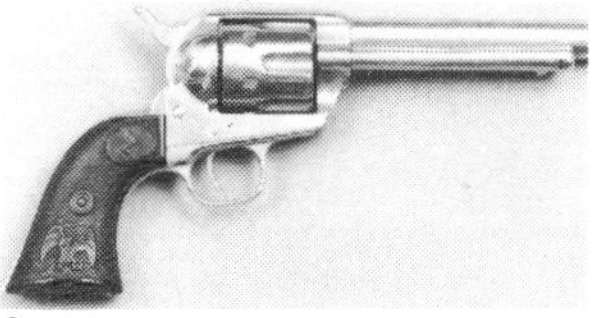
9

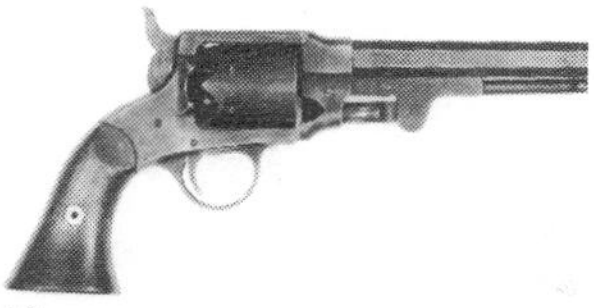
10

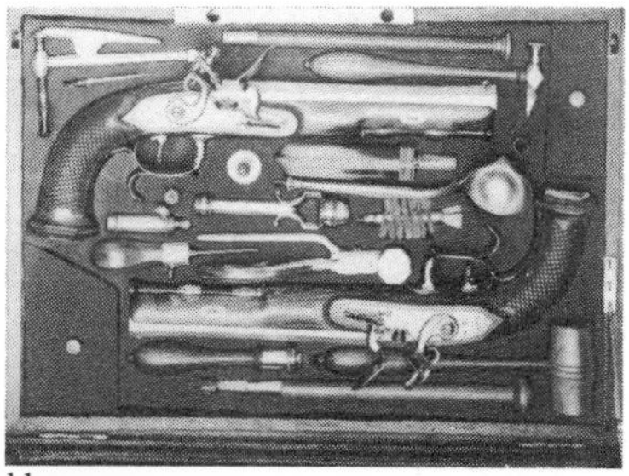
11

12

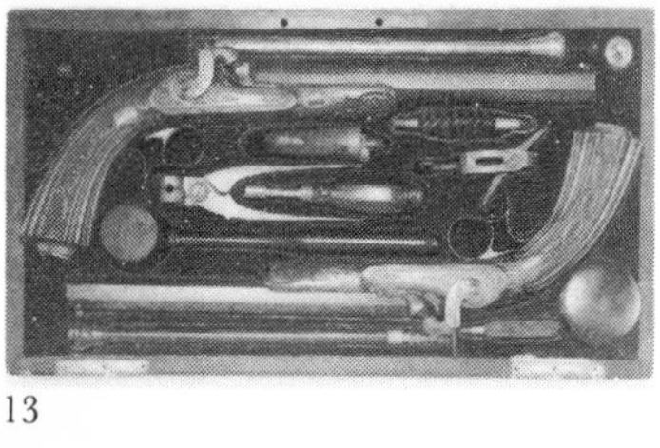
13

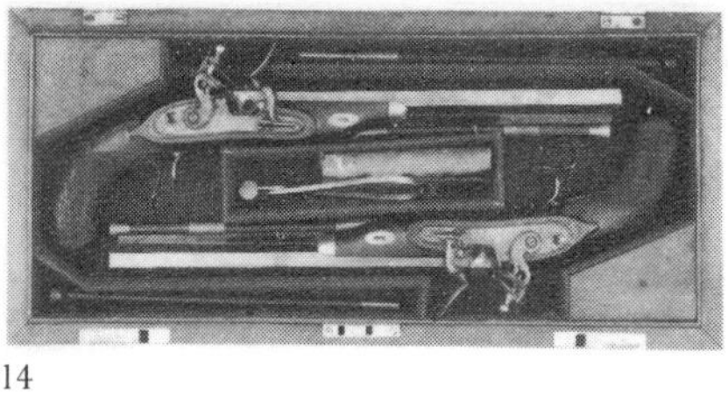
14

1
A pair of flintlock pocket pistols, *(one illustrated)*, c.1815, with spring bayonets, locks inscribed *Clark London*, slight wear, 19cm (7½in), *L 15 May,*
£440 ($708)

2
A Deane-Harding second model percussion revolver, c.1860, London proof marks, some light rusting and staining, 33cm (13in), *L 15 May,*
£462 ($744)

3
A Prussian cavalry percussion pistol, c.1850, calibre 15.6mm, inscribed *Potsdam*, barrel cleaned bright, 38cm (15in), *L 15 May,*
£396 ($637)

4
A pair of French percussion pistols, *(one illustrated)*, c.1830s, by Pirmet, Paris, one ramrod replaced, 29.5cm (11½in), *NY 25 Nov,*
$880 (£628)

5
A .36-cal Colt navy six-shot percussion revolver, one-piece walnut grip stamped *Enfield, London,* retaining some original finish, action defective, *S 7 July,*
£814 ($1,319)

6
A Colt 1851 London navy model percussion revolver, late 1853, some original colour, 33cm (13in), *L 5 Nov,*
£2,860 ($4,004)

7
A pair of English cased pill-box lock pistols, c.1821-32, by Ann Patrick, Liverpool, two powder flasks and a cleaning rod, 40.5cm (16in), *NY 25 Nov,*
$5,500 (£3,928)

8
An Adams model 1851 54 bore percussion revolver, c.1854, with original mould for conical and spherical bullets, embossed flask, nipple wrench with pricker, cleaning rod, wallet with nipples, and soft leather cap bag, 28.5cm (11¼in), *L 5 Nov,*
£528 ($739)

9
A Colt nickel-plated 'Peacemaker'.45 single-action army revolver, c.1881, proof certificate in lieu of marks, 33cm (13in), *S 7 July,*
£770 ($1,247)

10
A Rogers and Spencer percussion army revolver, c.1864, .44in calibre, some original finish, patinated overall, 34cm (13½in), *L 15 May,*
£484 ($779)

11
A pair of French cased flintlock pistols, first quarter 19th century, by Jean Lepage, lined walnut case retaining all accessories, lacquered with brass mounts, 37cm (14½in), *NY 25 Nov,*
$13,200 (£9,428)

12
A cased percussion pepperbox revolver, c.1850, approx 58 bore, frame inscribed *Tipping & Lawden*, traces of original finish , 23cm (9in), *L 15 May,*
£528 ($850)

13
A cased pair of percussion pistols, 19th century, probably French, retaining most original accessories, 40cm (16in), *NY 31 May,*
$2,310 (£1,571)

14
A cased pair of flintlock duelling pistols, c.1815, approx 22 bore, bolted locks inscribed *W Ketland and Co.*, barrels and some components refinished, 42cm (16½in), *L 15 May,*
£2,750 ($4,427)

1
A bench rest percussion rifle, third quarter 19th century, by C. Siebert Columbus, Ohio, barrel 77.5cm (30½in) long, *NY 25 Nov,*
$550 (£393)

2
A percussion bench rest rifle, third quarter 19th century, by Joseph Tonks, Boston, barrel 64cm (25¼in) long, *NY 25 Nov,*
$1,100 (£786)

3
A Brunswick flintlock gilt-mounted sporting gun, c.1750, by Johann Ulrich Mäntz, Brunswick, some wear, 142cm (56in), *L 15 May,*
£1,980 ($3,188)

4
A Swiss percussion target rifle, mid 19th century, slight wear and staining, 89cm (35in), *L 5 Nov,*
£2,310 ($3,234)

5
A German wheel-lock gun, 17th century, the walnut shaft inlaid with ivory and antler's horn, some replacements and repair, 166cm (65¼in), *NY 25 Nov,*
$10,450 (£7,464)

6
A North German flintlock hunting rifle, first third 18th century, by Johann Bernhard Fischer, Hanover, damascened in gold with a hunting scene, gilt brass mounts, 108cm (42½in), *NY 25 Nov,*
$11,550 (£8,250)

7
A German wheel-lock hunting rifle, last quarter 17th century, the walnut stock inlaid in antler's horn and ivory with hunting scenes, 97cm (38¼in), *NY 25 Nov,*
$5,500 (£3,928)

8
A flintlock sporting rifle, mid 18th century, inscribed *Johann Lippert Culmbac,* brass furniture, inlaid with horn stars, some wear, 105.5cm (41½in), *L 5 Nov,*
£935 ($1,309)

9
A percussion rifle, Pennsylvania, mid 19th century, inscribed *Whitmore & Wolff, Pittsburg,* brass furniture, some wear, 134.5cm (53in), *L 5 Nov,*
£297 ($416)

10
A Winchester model 1873, .32 centrefire rifle, c.1890, iron frame and furniture, some wear, 108.5cm (42¾in), *L 5 Nov,*
£451 ($631)

11
A Winchester model 1866 .44 rimfire rifle, c.1872, brass frame and furniture, some wear, 110.5cm (43½in), *L 5 Nov,*
£1,650 ($2,310)

12
A German flintlock sporting rifle, dated 1787, inscribed *Ioh Andre Kuchenreiter Regenspurg,* decorated with inlaid silver scrolls, brass furniture, traces of original finish, some wear, 109cm (43in), *L 5 Nov,*
£1,760 ($2,464)

13
A light sporting air-gun, early 19th century, engraved iron furniture, some wear, 129cm (50¾in), *L 5 Nov,*
£506 ($708)

14
A pattern 1853 second model percussion rifle-musket for volunteers, c.1860, inscribed *Greener,* little evidence of use, 140cm (55in), *L 15 May,*
£550 ($885)

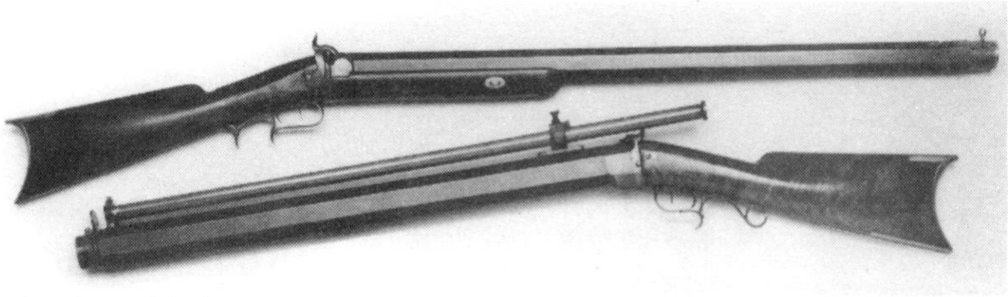
1 *(above)* 2 *(below)*

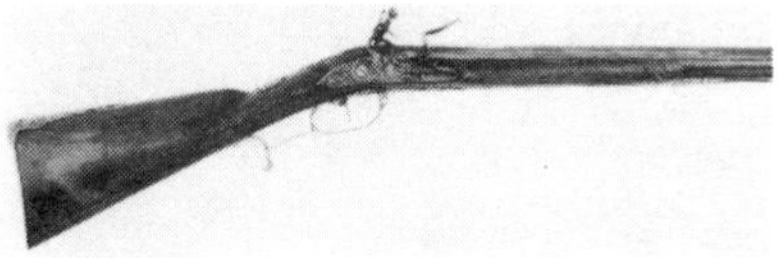
3

4

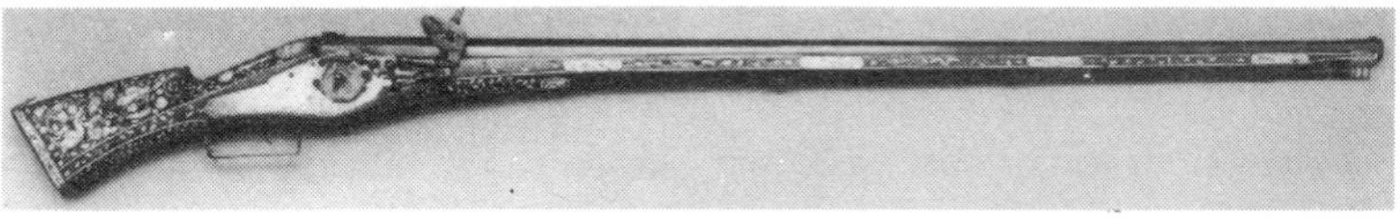
5

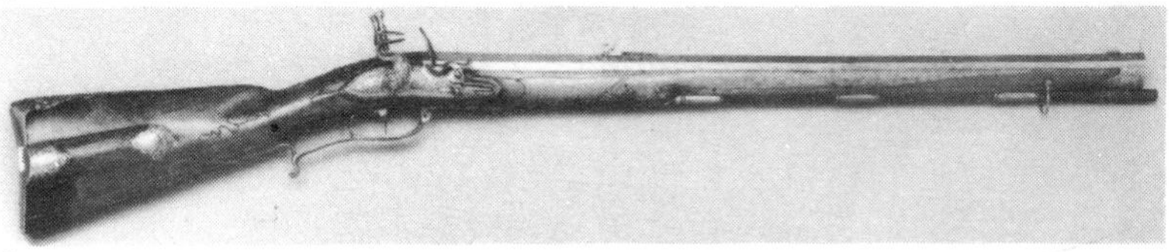
6

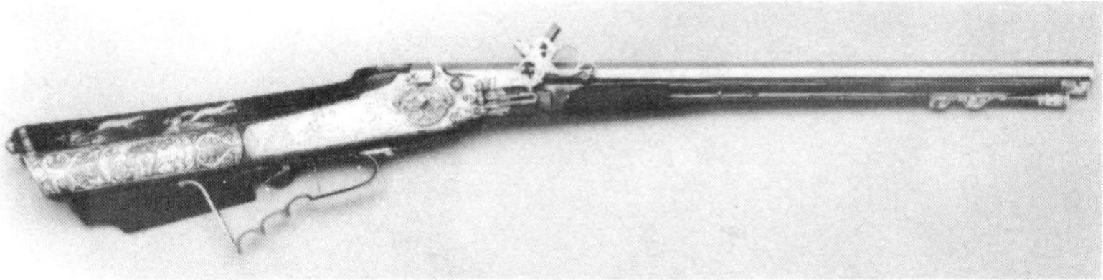
7

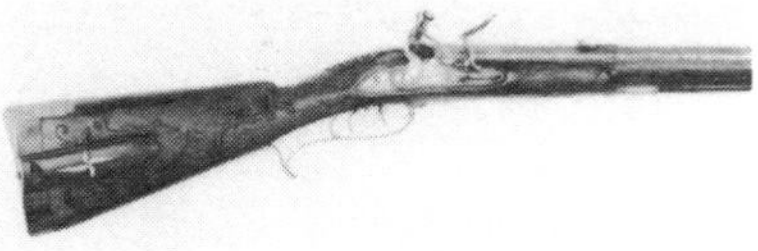
8

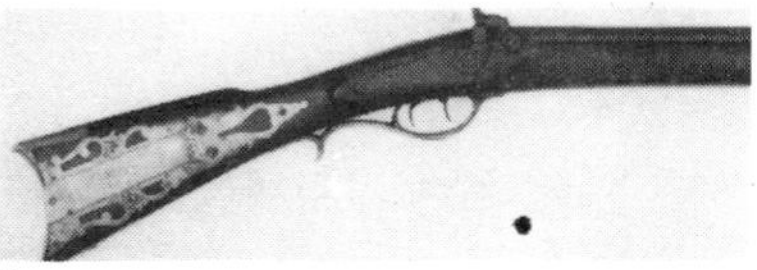
9

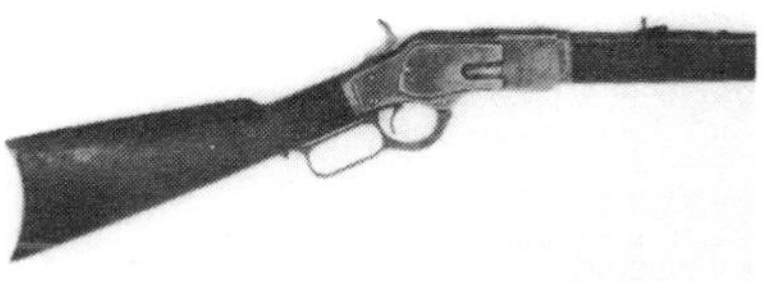
10

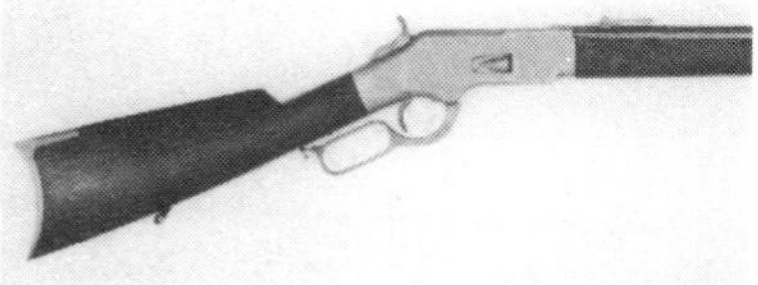
11

12

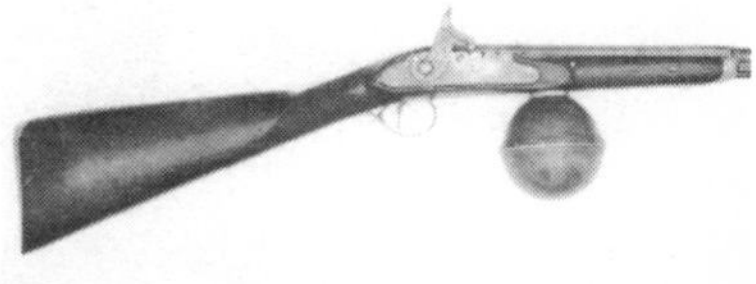
13

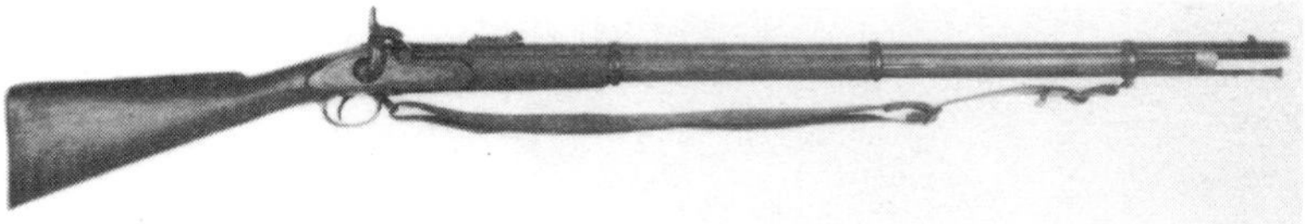
14

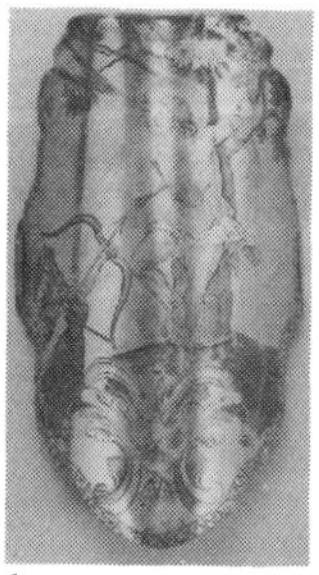
1

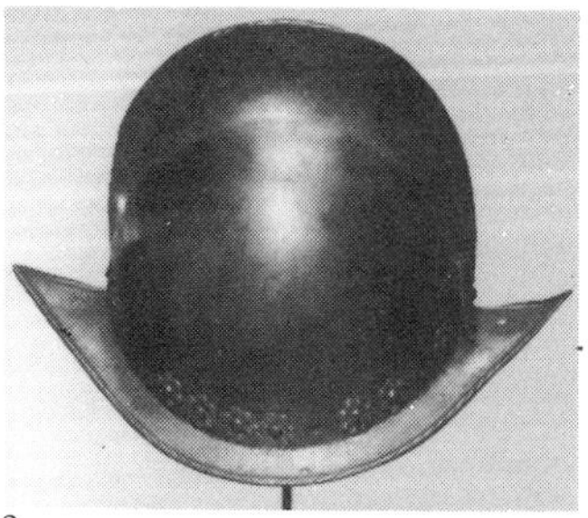
2

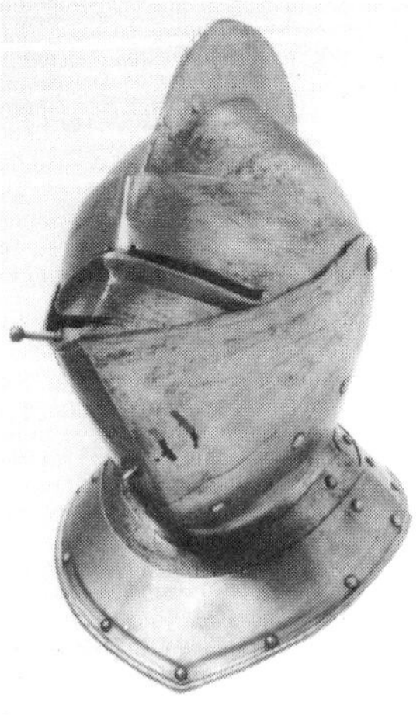
3

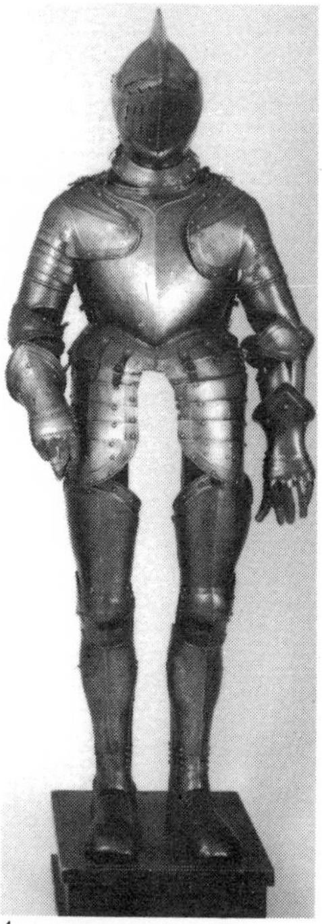
4

5

6

7

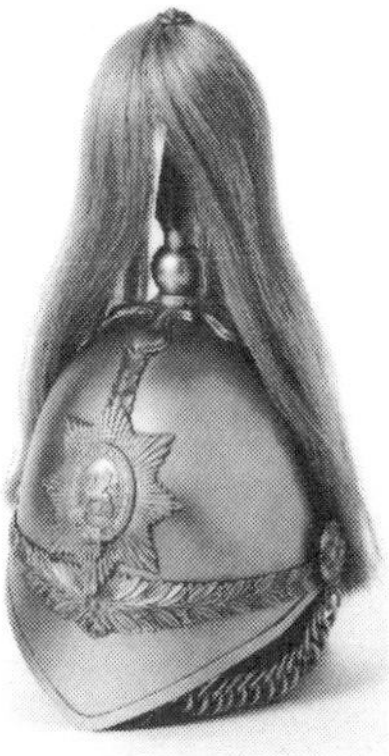
8

9

10

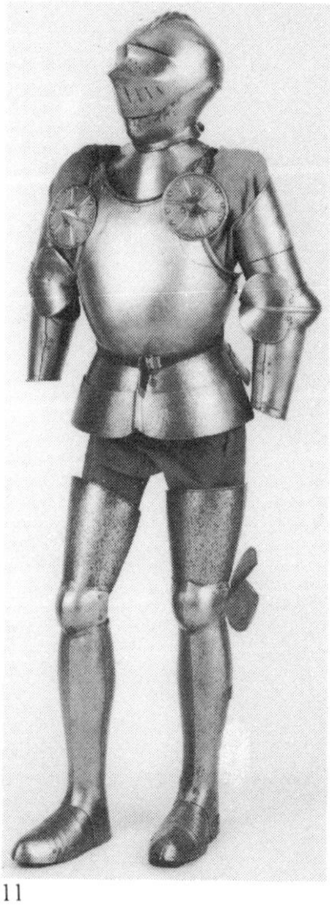
11

1
A French brass archer's arm guard, dated 1752, engraved with St. Sebastian, inscribed around the border *Ioseph de Somme. 1752*; sold with a Flemish ivory figure, 17th century, the guard 16cm (6¼in), *NY 25 Nov,*
$2,860 (£2,043)

2
A crested morion, late 16th century, probably South German, the brass rosettes mostly replaced, 24cm (9½in) high, *NY 31 May,*
$770 (£523)

3
An English or Flemish close helmet, late 16th century, brass rivets, three gorget plates replaced, several repairs, 30.5cm (12in) high, *L 15 May,*
£1,320 ($2,125)

4
A composite Italian armour, late 16th century, breastplate with panels of etched and engraved decoration, helmet possibly German, some elements replaced and decorated in the 19th century, 203cm (80in), *L 5 Nov,*
£3,520 ($4,928)

5
A 16th century style armour, 19th century, with a circular spiked shield and associated schiavona, some damage to rivets and leathers, 213.5cm (84in), *L 5 Nov,*
£3,080 ($4,312)

6
A composed North Italian half armour, late 16th century, partly decorated in so-called Pisan manner, rear gorgets replaced, fastenings modern, *L 15 May,*
£5,720 ($9,209)

7
A set of gilt brass parade armour, last quarter 16th century, repoussé and chased with figures of legendary warriors, 19th century lining and rivets, 46cm (18in), *NY 25 Nov,*
$9,350 (£6,678)

8
A helmet for other ranks Montgomeryshire Imperial Yeomanry, c.1900, original leather lining inscribed in ink *G H Owen and W Ward*, white plume, little used, 43cm (17in), *L 5 Nov,*
£605 ($847)

9
A pair of Royal Sussex Light Infantry officer's epaulettes, c.1840, by Hamburger Rogers & Co., London, *S 7 July,*
£297 ($481)

10
An officer's lance cap of the 12th (Prince of Wales's Royal) Lancers, late 19th century, top of scarlet, with Royal cypher *VR* on blue velvet and plume socket, original lining with label *Hawkes & Co.*, in original japanned tin case, slight wear and moth, case 26cm (10¼in), *L 5 Nov,*
£1,210 ($1,694)

11
A full length suit of armour, in late Gothic style, lacking gauntlets, mounted on wooden dummy, 182cm (71½in), *NY 25 Nov,*
$3,300 (£2,357)

Musical Instruments

See also:
Colour illustrations *pp* 488-489
Furniture *p* 105
Mechanical musical instruments and musical boxes *pp* 526-528
Rock 'n Roll *p* 536

1
Peter Bressan, London, first quarter 18th century, a bass recorder, later brass crook, 108cm (42½in), *L 12 Nov,*
£31,900 ($45,617)

2
Proff, Tours, first quarter 19th century, a seven-keyed pearwood bassoon, 125cm (49in), *L 12 Nov,*
£3,080 ($4,404)

3
William Henry Potter, London, late 18th century, a six-keyed boxwood flute, sounding length 60cm (23¾in), *L 22 May,*
£3,410 ($5,422)

4
A rare ivory flageolet, probably English, early 18th century, 13.5cm (5½in), *L 12 Nov,*
£7,150 ($10,225)

5
Robert Wolf & Co., London, first half 19th century, a two-keyed boxwood oboe, 56.5cm (22¼in), *L 22 May,*
£2,860 ($4,547)

6
Rudall & Rose, London, c.1852, a cocuswood 'Carte's 1851 Patent' flute, sounding length 58cm (23in), *L 12 Nov,*
£462 ($661)

7
Thomas Cahusac the elder, London, third quarter 18th century, a one-keyed ivory flute, sounding length 53.5cm (21in), *L 12 Nov,*
£3,080 ($4,404)

8
Urquhart, London, early 18th century, a stained boxwood treble (alto) recorder, 50.5cm (20in), *L 22 May,*
£9,350 ($14,867)

9
William Milhouse, London, first quarter 19th century, a seven-keyed boxwood flute, longest sounding length 59.5cm (23½in), *L 12 Nov,*
£5,500 ($7,865)

10
John Broadwood & Sons, London, 1826, an English grand pianoforte, 249cm (8ft 2in) long, *L 22 May,*
£3,630 ($5,772)

Bressan, Peter, 1663-1731, fl.London.

Cahusac, Thomas, the elder, fl.London from 1755, d.1798.

Koch, Stephan, 1772-1828, fl.Vienna.

Milhouse, William, b.1761, fl.London until 1834.

Potter, William Henry, 1760-1848, fl.London.

Rudall & Rose, Partnership of George Rudall and J. M. Rose, founded c.1820.

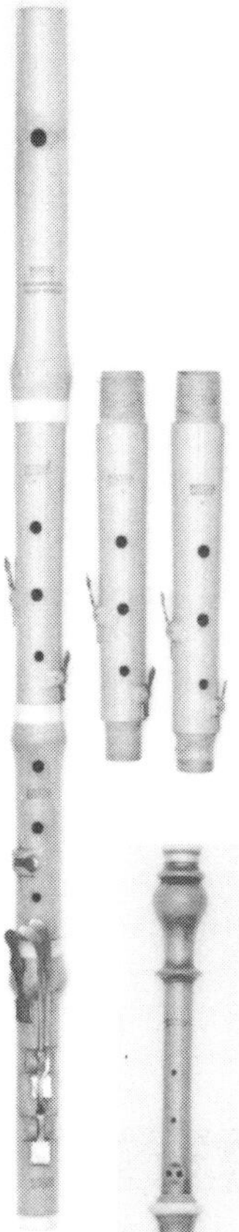
3

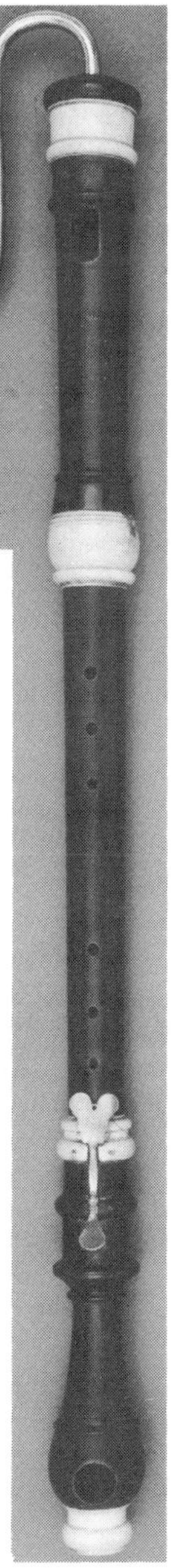
1

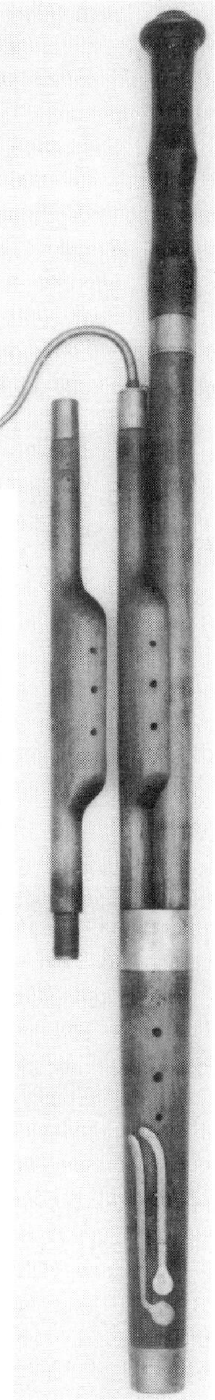
2

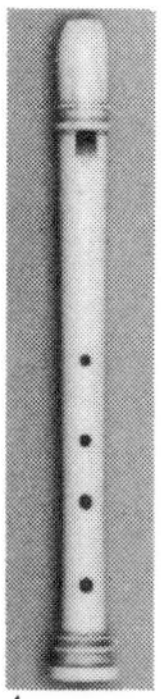
4

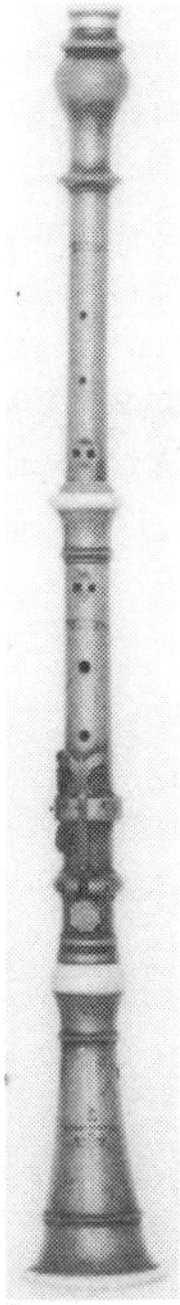
5

6

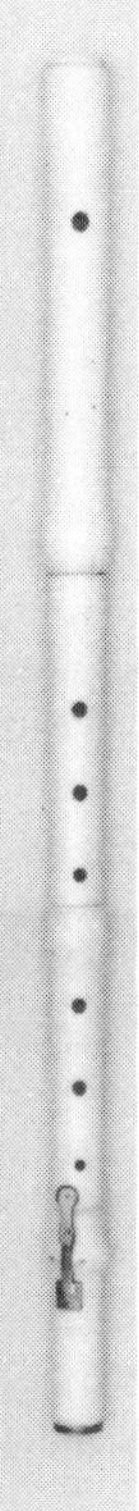
7

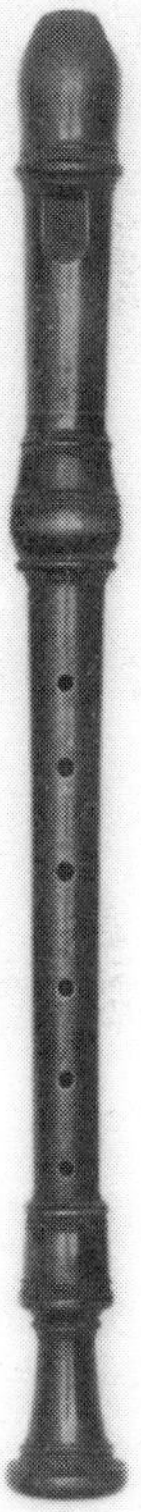
8

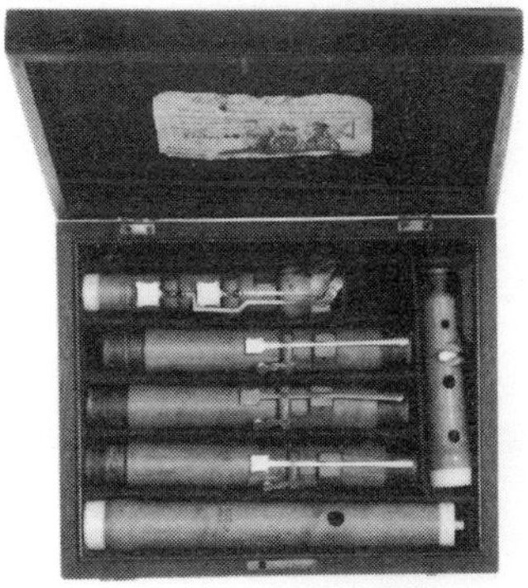
9

10

1

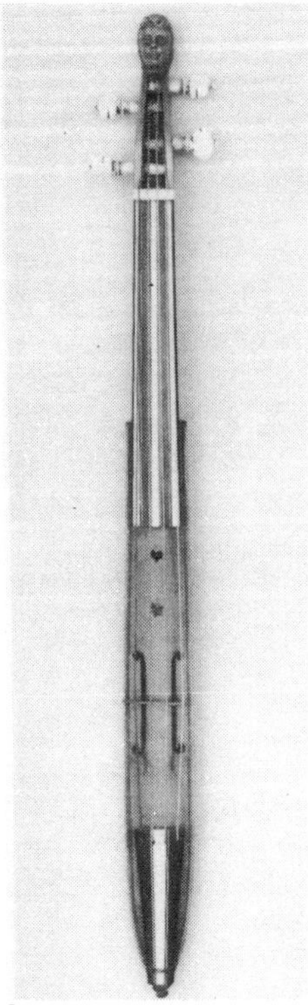
2

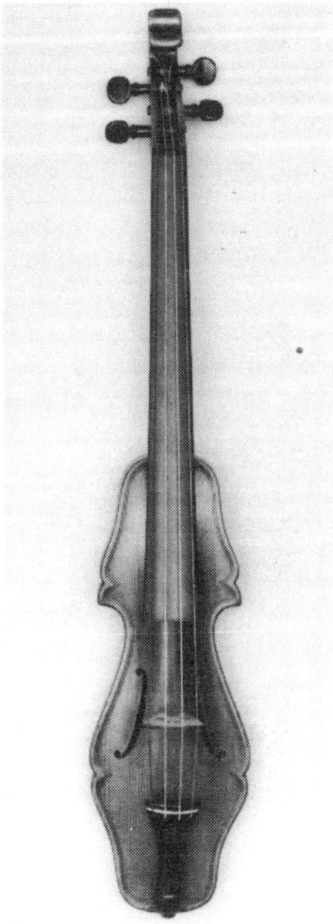
3

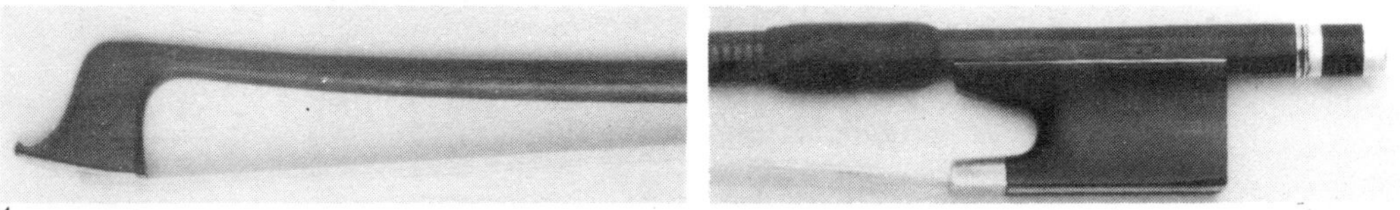
4

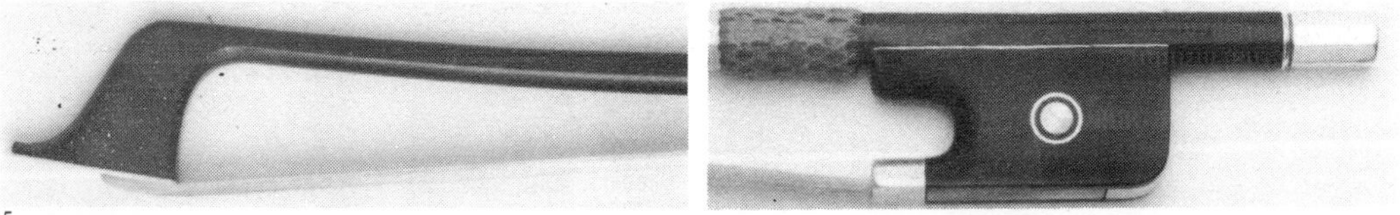
5

6

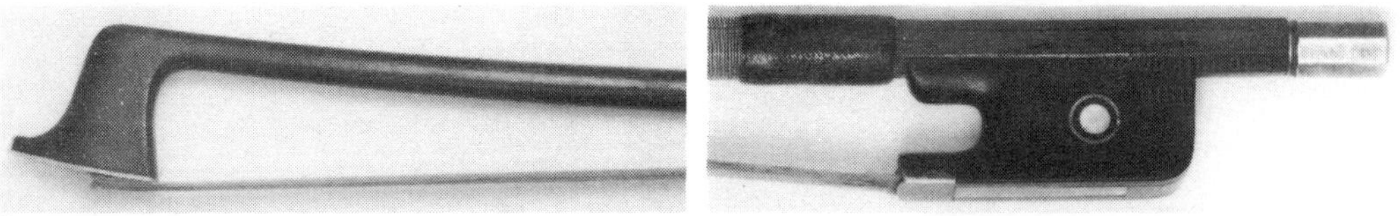
7

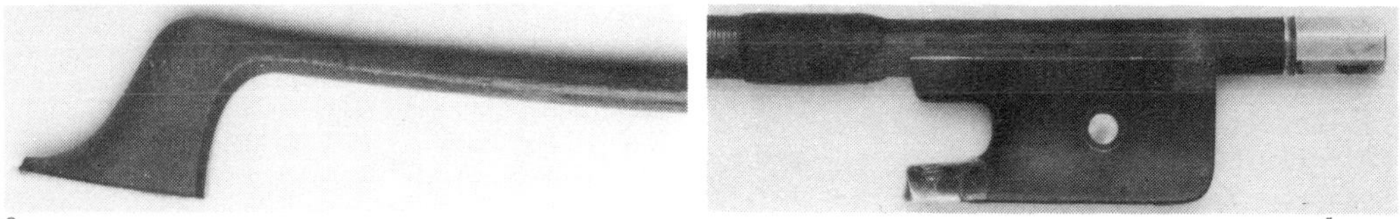
8

1
A rare Irish harp, Dublin or Wicklow, c.1720, the backing board probably later, 119cm (47in), *L 22 May,*
£3,520 ($5,597)

2
Mathias Wörle, Augsburg, 1670, a Tyrolese pochette, 44.5cm (17½in), *L 12 Nov,*
£3,960 ($5,663)

3
Gaspar Borbon, Brussels, c.1690, a dancing master's kit, 48.5cm (19in), *L 12 Nov,*
£3,080 ($4,404)

4
Alfred Lamy, Paris, a violin bow, 61 grams, *L 12 Nov,*
£2,420 ($3,461)

5
Eugène Sartory, Paris, a silver-mounted violoncello bow, 77 grams, *L 12 Nov,*
£2,970 ($4,247)

6
Victor Fétique, Paris, a silver-mounted violin bow, 57 grams, *L 19 Mar,*
£1,980 ($3,029)

7
Victor Fétique, Paris, a silver-mounted viola bow, 68 grams, *L 22 May,*
£2,970 ($3,291)

8
André Vigneron, Paris, a silver-mounted violoncello bow, 66 grams, *L 12 Nov,*
£1,430 ($2,045)

1
Eugène Sartory, Paris, a silver-mounted violin bow, 64 grams, *L 12 Nov,*
£3,080 ($4,404)

2
André Vigneron, Paris, a silver-mounted violin bow, 56 grams, *L 12 Nov,*
£2,090 ($2,989)

3
Albert Nürnberger, Markneukirchen, a silver-mounted violin bow, 60 grams, *L 19 Mar,*
£682 ($1,043)

4
W. E. Hill & Sons, London, a silver and tortoiseshell-mounted violin bow, 56 grams, *L 19 Mar,*
£1,540 ($2,356)

5
W. E. Hill & Sons, London, a gold and tortoiseshell-mounted violin bow, 61 grams, *L 12 Nov,*
£2,860 ($4,090)

6
Garner Wilson, Bury St. Edmunds, a gold and tortoiseshell-mounted violin bow, 62 grams, *L 12 Nov,*
£825 ($1,180)

7
Arthur Bultitude, Hawkhurst, a gold and tortoiseshell-mounted violin bow, 59 grams, *L 22 May,*
£880 ($1,399)

8
James Tubbs, London, a silver-mounted violin bow, 61 grams, *L 19 Mar,*
£2,750 ($4,208)

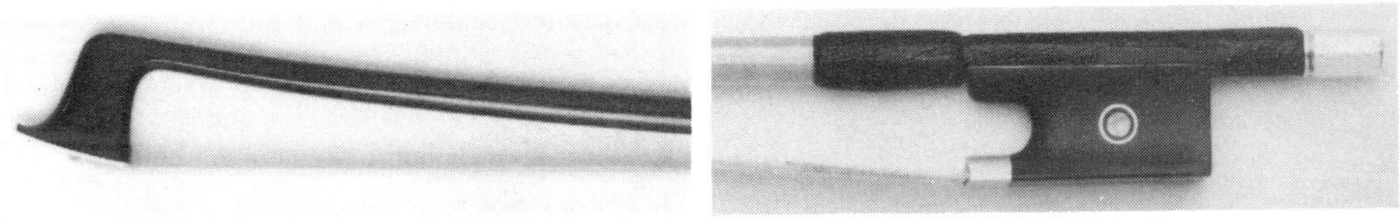
1

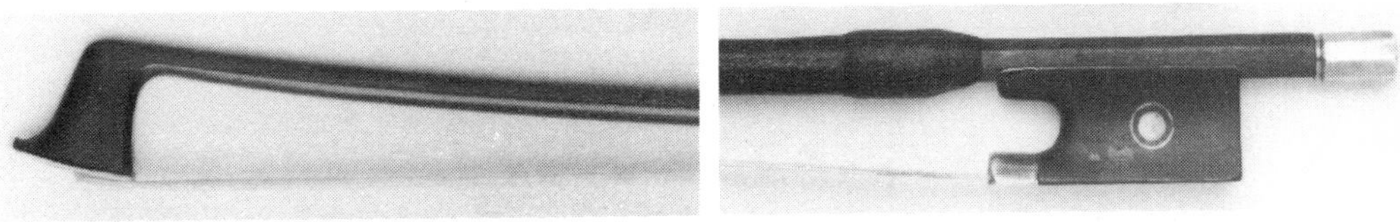
2

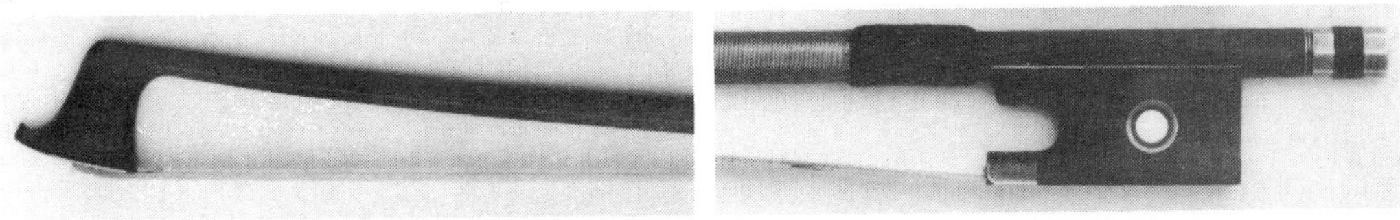
3

4

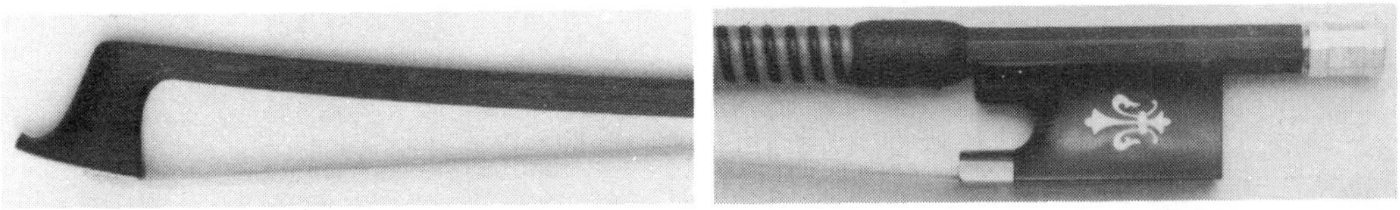
5

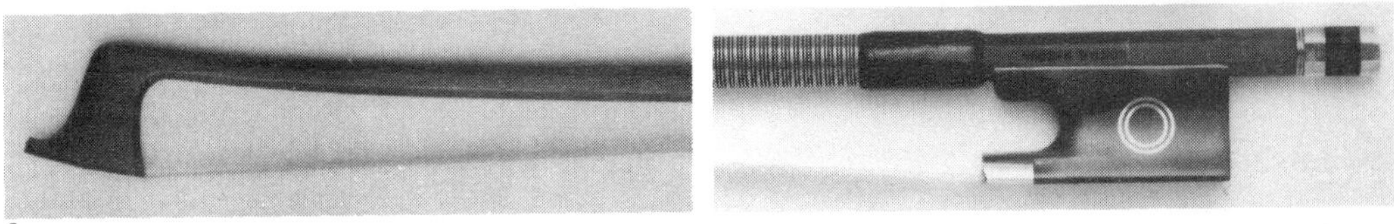
6

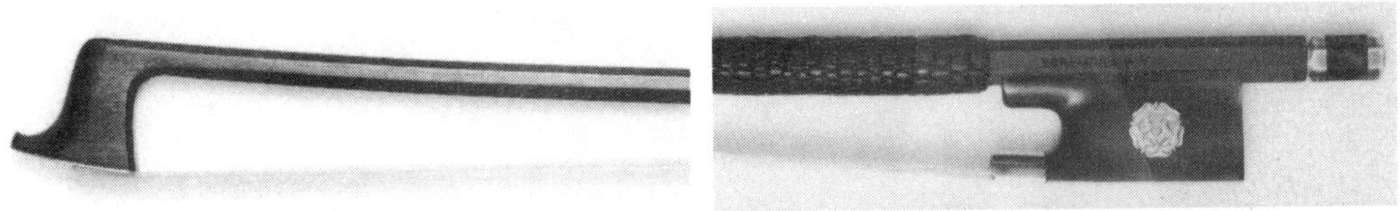
7

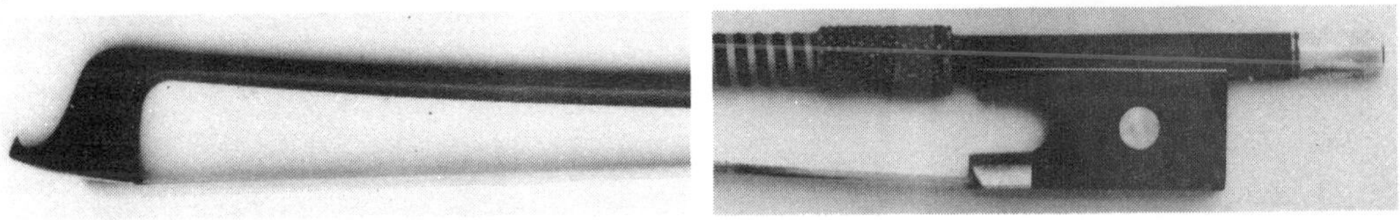
8

Bultitude, Arthur, b.1908, fl.London.

Fétique, Victor, 1872-1933, fl.Paris.

Nürnberger, Albert, 1854-1931.

Lamy, Alfred, 1850-1919, fl.Paris and Château Thierry.

Sartory, Eugène, 1871-1946, fl.Paris. Worked for Lamy until 1893.

Tubbs, James, 1835-1919, fl.London.

Vigneron, André, 1882-1924.

1

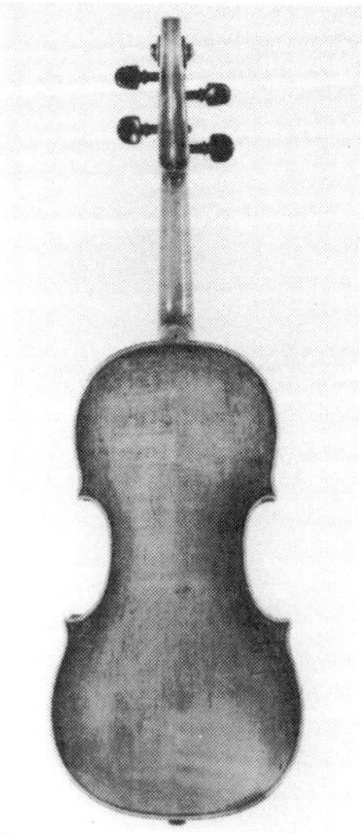
2

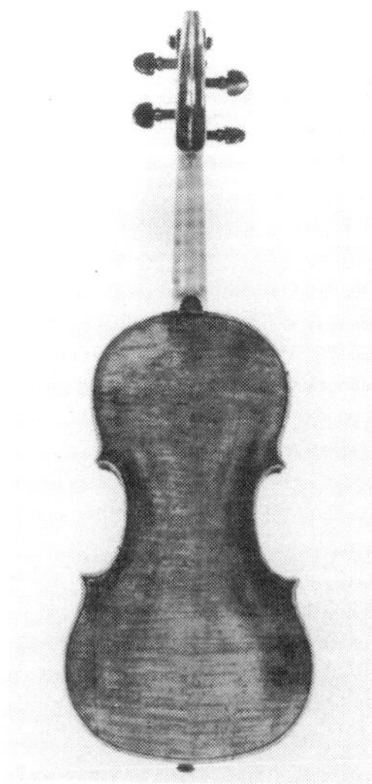
3

4

5

6

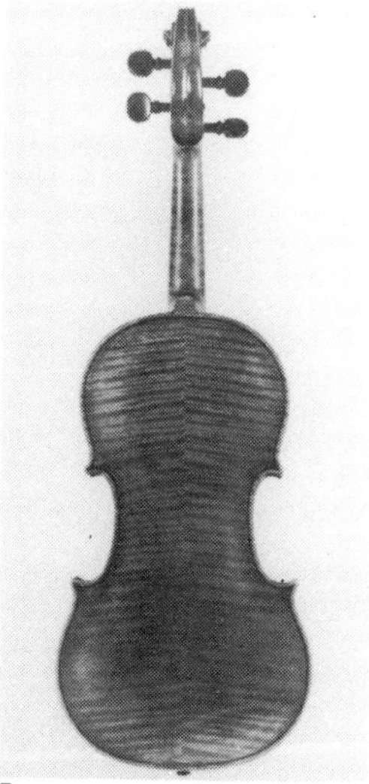
7

8

9

10

11

12

1
Joseph Kloz, Mittenwald, a Bavarian violin, 35.5cm (14in), with bow, *L 12 Nov,* **£2,750 ($3,932)**

2
Aegidius Kloz, Mittenwald, 1777, a Bavarian violin, 35.5cm (14in), *L 12 Nov,* **£2,310 ($3,303)**

3
Joseph Laske, Prague, 1799, a Bohemian violin, 35.5cm (14in), *L 12 Nov,* **£660 ($944)**

4
Wilhelm Ruprecht, Vienna, mid 19th century, an Austrian violin in the manner of Joseph Guarneri del Gesù, 35.5cm (14in), *L 12 Nov,* **£3,300 ($4,719)**

5
Hendrik Jacobs, Amsterdam, c.1690, a violin, 35.5cm (14in), *L 19 Mar,* **£4,620 ($7,069)**

6
Matthys Hofmans, Antwerp, c.1720, a violin, 35.5cm (14in), with two bows, *L 12 Nov,* **£8,250 ($11,798)**

7
James W. Briggs, Glasgow, a violin, 35.5cm (14in), *L 22 May,* **£1,650 ($2,624)**

8
W. E. Hill & Sons, London, 1903, a violin after the 'Tuscan' Stradivari of 1690, 35.5cm (14in), with bow, *L 22 May,* **£5,720 ($9,095)**

9
Benjamin Banks, Salisbury, 1764, a violin, 35.5cm (14in), *L 25 Sept,* **£1,760 ($2,464)**

10
Georges Chanot, Manchester, 1895, a violin, 36cm (14in), *L 12 Nov,* **£4,620 ($6,607)**

11
George Darbey, Bristol, 1916, a violin, 35.5cm (14in), *L 19 Mar,* **£2,530 ($3,871)**

12
George Craske, Stockport, a violin, 35.5cm (14in), *L 25 Sept,* **£1,320 ($1,848)**

1
Jean Baptiste Vuillaume, Paris 1855, a violin, St. Cecilia model, 36cm (14in), *L 12 Nov,*
£8,800 ($12,584)

2
Auguste Sébastian Philippe Bernardel, Paris, 1850, a violin, 36.5cm (14¼in), *L 22 May,*
£5,500 ($8,745)

3
Nicolas Vuillaume, c.1840, a violin, 36.5cm (14¼in), *L 22 May,*
£3,300 ($5,247)

4
Caressa & Français, Paris, 1912, a violin, 36cm (14in), *L 12 Nov,*
£4,840 ($6,921)

5
Albert Blanchi, Nice, 1907, a violin, 36cm (14in), *L 12 Nov,*
£3,520 ($5,034)

6
Charles Jean Baptiste Collin-Mézin, Paris, 1887, a violin, 35.5cm (14in), *L 19 Mar,*
£1,760 ($2,693)

7
Honoré Derazey, Mirecourt, a violin, 36cm (14in), with two bows, *L 12 Nov,*
£2,090 ($2,989)

8
Justin Derazey, Mirecourt, 1861, a violin in the manner of Caspar Duiffoprucar, 36cm (14in), *L 12 Nov,*
£2,090 ($2,989)

9
Paul Kaul, Paris, 1940, a violin, 36cm, *L 12 Nov,*
£1,760 ($2,517)

10
Joseph Aubry, Le Havre, 1928, a violin, 36cm (14in), *L 12 Nov,*
£1,320 ($1,888)

11
Dominique Didelot, Paris, a violin, 36.5cm (142in), *L 19 Mar,*
£770 ($1,178)

12
Charles Jean Baptiste Collin-Mézin, Paris, 1883, a violin, 35.5cm (14in), *L 19 Mar,*
£1,100 ($1,683)

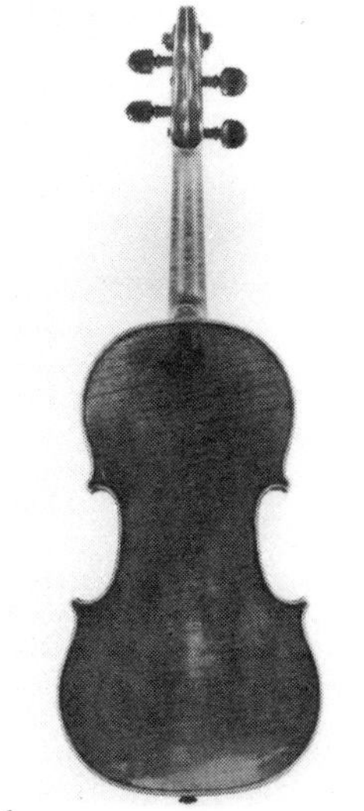
1

2

3

4

5

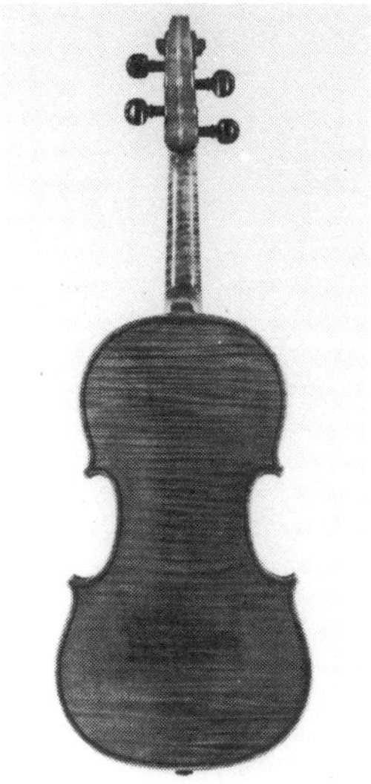
6

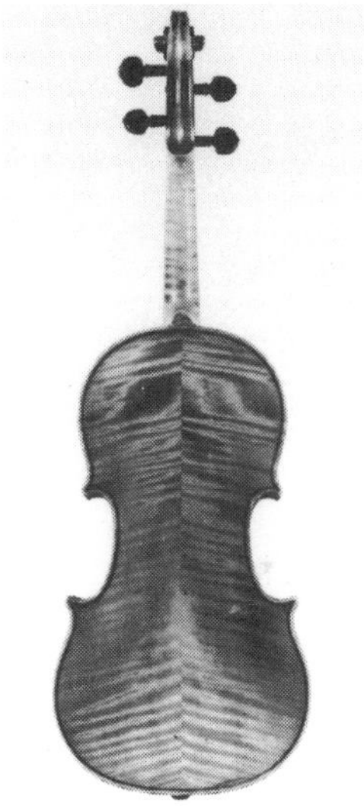
7

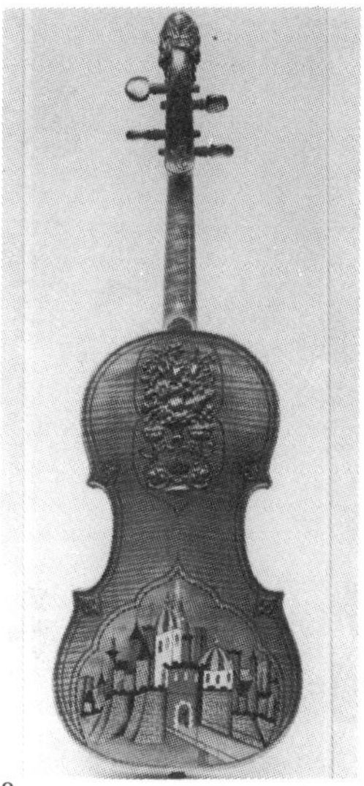
8

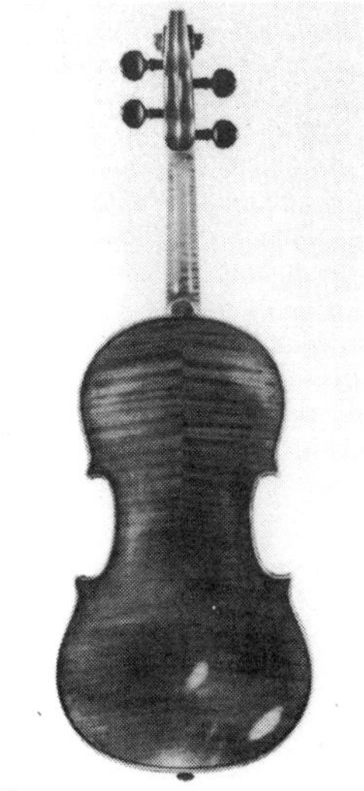
9

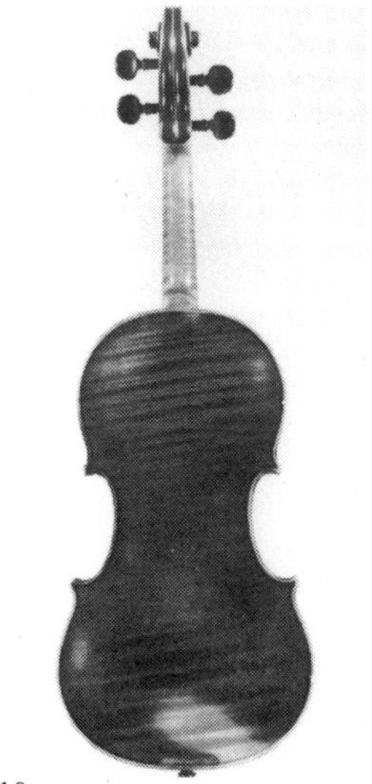
10

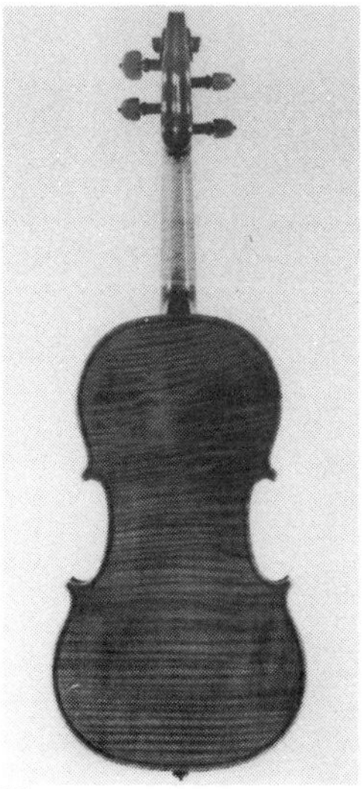
11

12

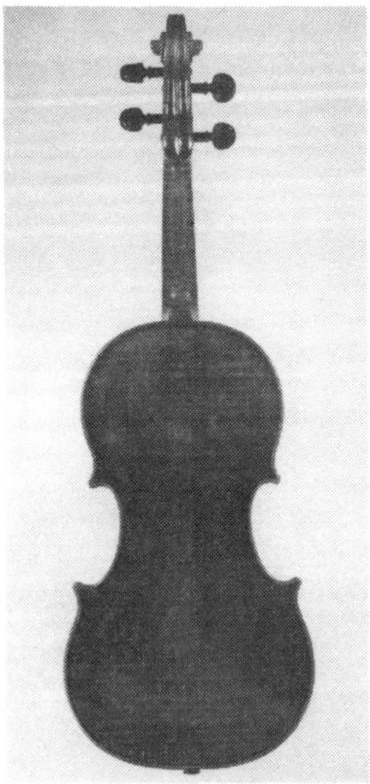
1

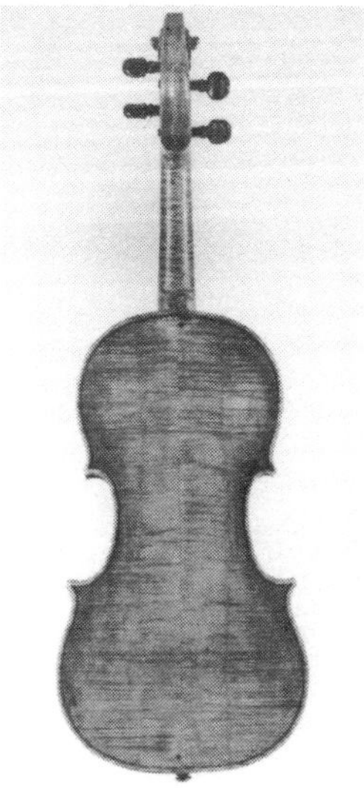
2

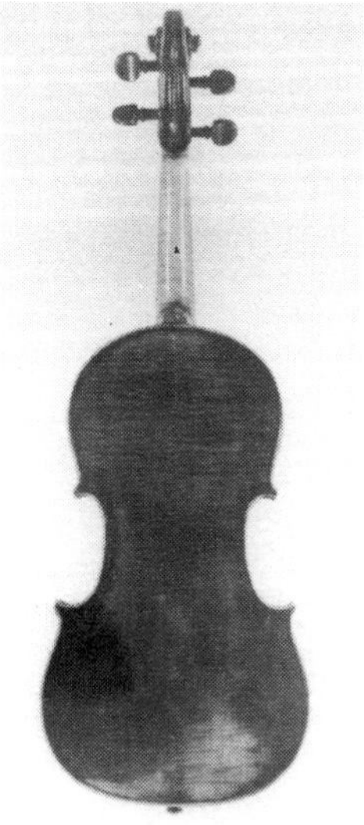
3

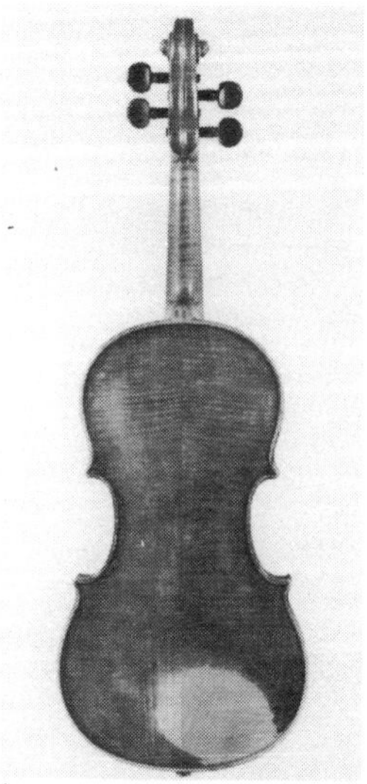
4

5

6

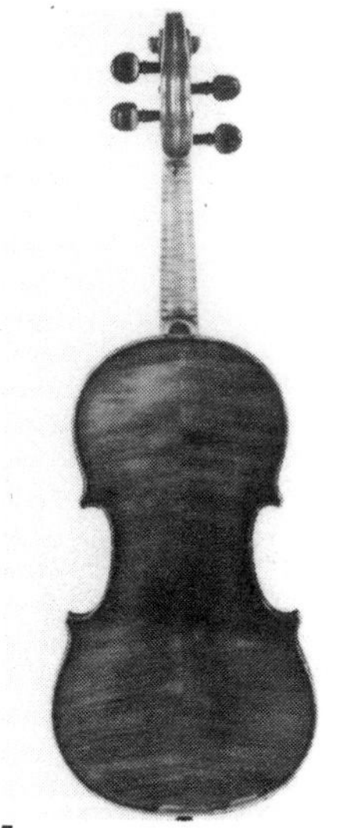
7

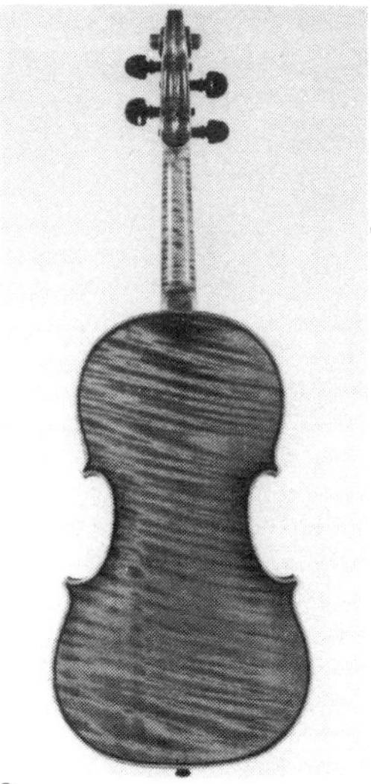
8

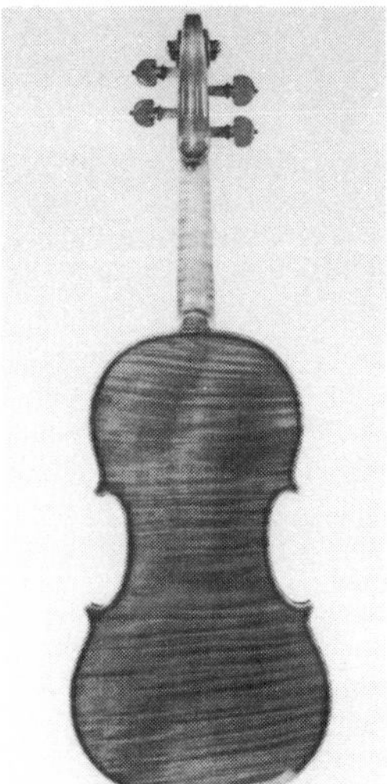
9

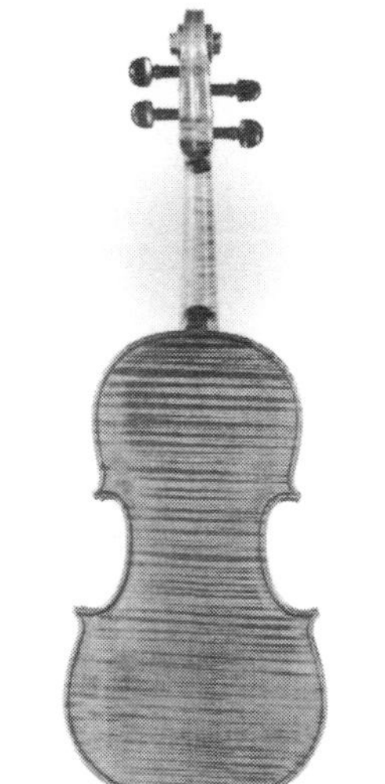
10

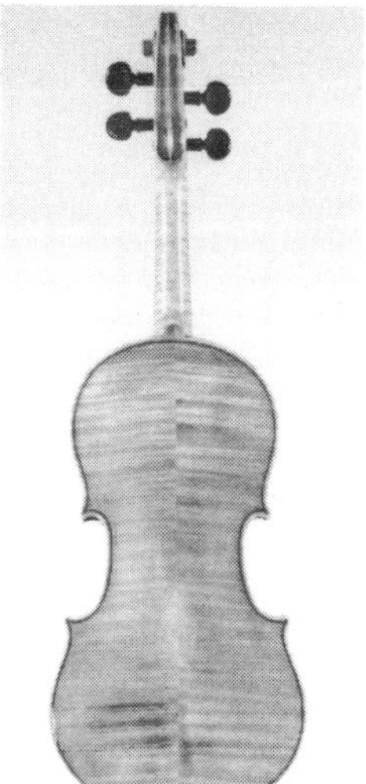
11

12

1
Giovanni Maria del Bussetto, Cremona, 1675, an important violin, 35.5cm (14in), *L 12 Nov,*
£50,600 ($70,840)

2
Carlo Antonio Testore, Milan, 1734, a violin, 36cm (14in), *L 22 May,*
£9,350 ($14,867)

3
Francesco Guadagnini, Turin, c.1890, a violin, 35.5cm (14in), *L 22 May,*
£8,250 ($13,118)

4
Lapo di Serafino Casini, Florence, early 20th century, a violin, 35.5cm (14in), *L 12 Nov,*
£3,960 ($5,663)

5
Giovanni Maria Ceruti, Cremona, 1923, a violin, 36cm (14in), *L 25 Sept,*
£1,155 ($1,617)

6
Giuseppe Pedrazzini, Milan, 1926, a violin, 35.5cm (14in), *L 22 May,*
£8,800 ($13,992)

7
Andreas Renisto, 1927, an Italian violin, 36cm (14in), *L 25 Sept,*
£2,090 ($2,926)

8
Marino Capicchioni, Rimini, 1966, an Italian violin in the manner of Guarneri del Gesù, 35.5cm (14in), *L 22 May,*
£3,960 ($6,296)

9
Mario Gadda, Mantua, 1976, a violin, 35.5cm (14in), *L 12 Nov,*
£2,200 ($3,146)

10
Enzo Barbieri, Mantua, 1985, a violin, 35.5cm (14in), *L 12 Nov,*
£1,210 ($1,730)

11
Georges Chanot, London, 1878, a child's violin, 32.5cm (13in), *L 19 Mar,*
£1,430 ($2,190)

12
Jean Baptiste Vuillaume, Paris, 1892, a child's violoncello, St. Cecilia model, 60.5cm (23¾in), *L 22 May*
£5,500 ($8,745)

1
Ferdinando Gagliano, Naples, 1783, a viola, 38cm (15in), with bow, *L 12 Nov,*
£12,650 ($18,090)

2
Giovanni Schwarz, Venice, 1913, a viola, 41cm (16in), *L 12 Nov,*
£5,720 ($8,180)

3
A French viola, Château-Thierry, 1907, labelled *François Barzoni,* 40cm (16in), *L 12 Nov,*
£1,980 ($2,831)

4
Gustave Bernardel, Paris, 1900, a viola, 40.5cm (16in), *L 22 May,*
£4,620 ($7,346)

5
Alexander McDonnell, Dublin, 1770, a viola, 38.5cm (15in), *L 22 May,*
£990 ($1,574)

6
Barak Norman, London, a violoncello, 71.5cm (28¼in), *L 22 May*
£8,800 ($13,992)

7
Edward Heesom, London, mid 18th century, a violoncello, 74.5cm (29¼in), with bow, *L 25 Sept,*
£1,980 ($2,772)

8
Kurt Schuster, Leipzig, 1945, a violoncello, 75cm (29½in), *L 12 Nov,*
£1,320 ($1,888)

9
Johann Kriner, Mittenwald, 1827, a Bavarian violoncello, 74.5cm (29¼in), *L 19 Mar,*
£2,750 ($4,208)

10
Gaetano Pareschi, Ferrara, 1949, a violoncello, 73.5cm (29in), *L 12 Nov,*
£6,600 ($9,438)

11
Jean Baptiste Deshayes Salomon, Paris, 1754, a violoncello, 75.5cm (29½in), *L 12 Nov,*
£6,600 ($9,438)

12
School of Bertrand, first quarter of 18th century, a French bass viola da gamba, 75.5cm (29¾in), with bow, *L 12 Nov,*
£8,250 ($11,797)

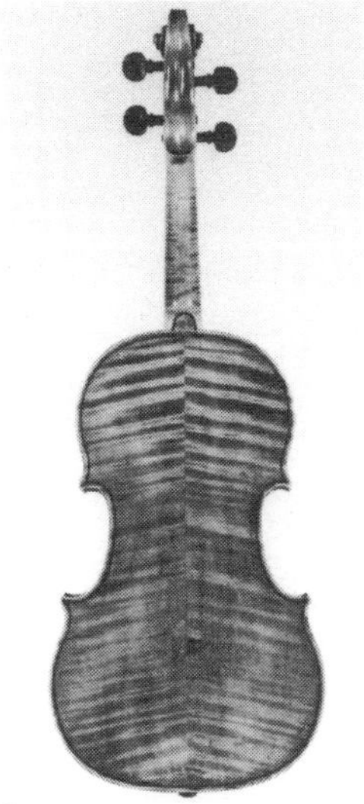
1

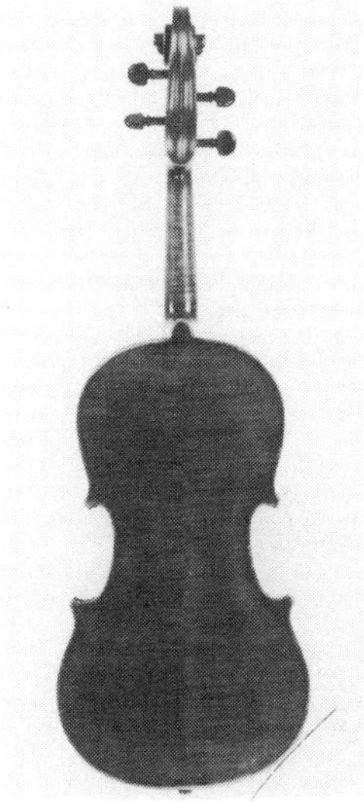
2

3

4

5

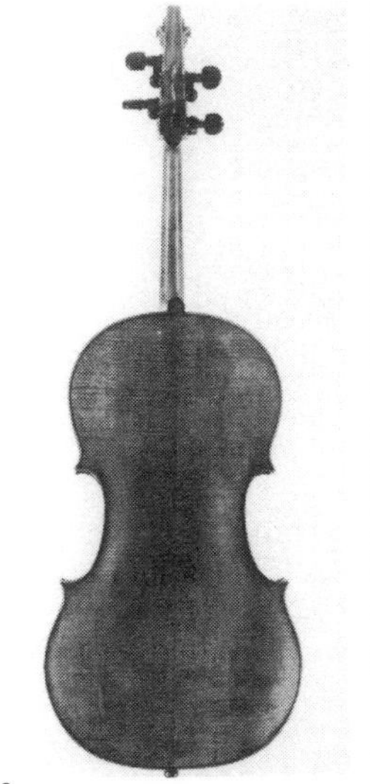
6

7

8

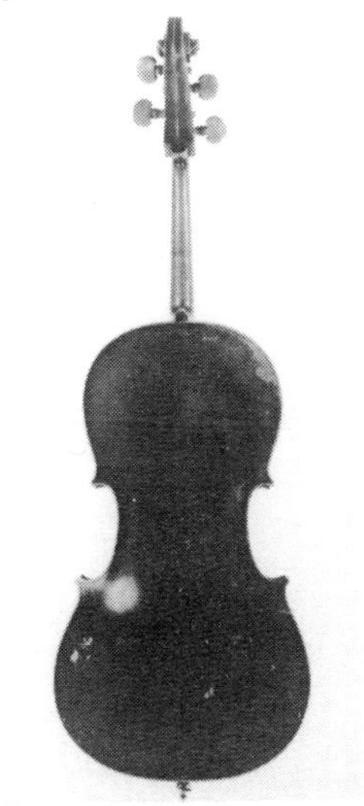
9

10

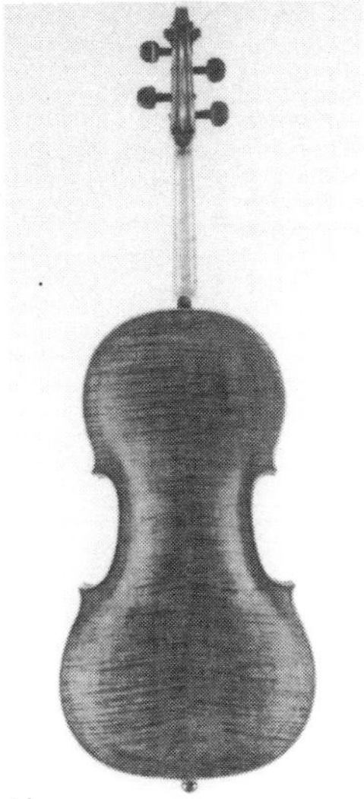
11

12

1

2

3

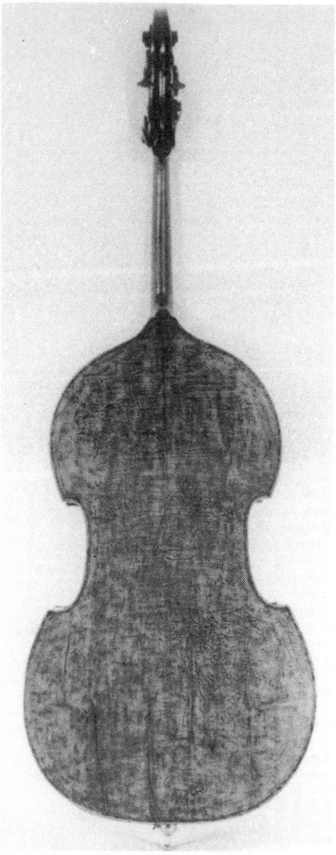

4

1
Johannes Cuypers, The Hague, 1766, a violoncello, 71.5cm (28¼in), *L 22 May,*
£8,250 ($13,118)

2
August Gemunder & Sons, New York, 1898, a violoncello, 75cm (29½in), *L 12 Nov,*
£1,870 ($2,674)

3
Justin Derazey, Mirecourt, 1848, a double bass, string length 103.5cm (41in), *L 19 Mar,*
£3,080 ($4,712)

4
An English double bass, string length 104cm (41in), *L 12 Nov,*
£1,540 ($2,202)

Banks, Benjamin, b.?Salisbury 1727, d.1795.

Briggs, James, b.Wakefield 1885, fl.Leeds and Glasgow.

Craske, George, b.Bury St. Edmunds 1795, d.Bath 1888.

Cuypers, Johannes Theodorus, b.Dornick 1724, d.The Hague 1808.

Darbey, George, b.Taunton 1849, fl.Bristol 1882-1920.

Gemunder, August Martin, b.New York 1862, d.1928.

Heesom, Edward, fl.London 1745-53.

Hill & Sons, W. E., established in London 1887.

Hofmans, Matthys (the Younger?). fl.Antwerp c.1700-45.

Jacobs, Hendrik, b.Amsterdam 1630, d.1699.

Kloz, Aegidius, b.Mittenwald, Bavaria, 1733, d.1808.

Kloz, Joseph, b.Mittenwald 1743.

Kriner, Johann (Joseph), b.Mittenwald 1788, d.1835.

Laske, Joseph Anton, b.Bohemia 1738, d.1805, fl.Prague.

Norman, Barak, c.1670-1740, fl.London.

Ruprecht, Wilhelm, 1837-62, fl.Vienna.

Schuster, Kurt, b.Markneukirchen 1878, fl.Leipzig.

Italian Violin Makers

Bussetto, Giovanni Maria del, fl.c.1670-80, probably in Cremona and Brescia.

Camilli, Camillus, c.1704-54, fl.Mantua.

Capicchioni, Marino, b.1895, fl.Northern Italy.

Casini, Lapo di Serafino, fl.Florence from 1899.

Ceruti, Giovanni Maria, 20th century, fl.Cremona.

Gagliano, Ferdinando, son of Nicolas, fl.Naples c.1770-95.

Gagliano, Nicolas, fl.Naples c.1740-80.

Guadagnini, Francesco, fl.Turin 1889-1935.

Guarneri, Giuseppe (del Gesù), 1698-1744, fl.Cremona.

Landolfi, Carlo Ferdinando, fl.Milan 1750-75.

Pareschi, Gaetano, b.1900, fl.Ferrara.

Pedrazzini, Giuseppe, b.Nr.Cremona 1879, d.1958.

Schwarz, Giovanni, d.Venice 1952.

Testore, Carlo Antonio, fl.Milan 1720-60.

French Violin Makers

Aubry, Joseph, b.Mirecourt 1873, fl.Le Havre from 1927.

Bernardel, Auguste Sebastian Philippe, b.Mirecourt 1798, d.Bougival 1870, fl.Paris; see Caressa; worked with Jean Baptiste Vuillaume.

Bertrand, Nicolas, fl.Paris c.1687-1725.

Blanchi, Albert, b.1871, fl.Nice.

Bourgard, Jean, b.Prague, fl.Nancy 1775-92.

Caressa & Français, Caressa 1866-1930, Français b.1861. Successors to Gustave Bernardel in 1901.

Collin-Mézin, Charles Jean Baptiste, b.Mirecourt 1841, d.Paris 1923, fl.Paris.

Chanot, Georges (the Younger), b.Paris 1831, d.London 1893, fl.London from 1851.

Château Thierry violins bearing Barzoni's label are of good quality commercial manufacture, generally imported into England.

Derazey, Honoré, b.Darney 1794, d.Mirecourt 1883. Worked at Vuillaume workshop in Paris.

Derazey, Justin Amadée, 1839-83 Mirecourt.

Didelot, Dominique, fl.Mirecourt 1816-30.

Kaul, Paul, b.Mirecourt 1870, fl.Paris.

Salomon, Jean Baptiste Deshayes, fl.Paris c.1740-72.

Vuillaume, Jean Baptiste, b.Mirecourt 1798, d.Paris 1875, fl.Paris. Workshop continued after his death.

Vuillaume, Nicolas, 1802-76. Brother of Jean Baptiste, fl.Brussels.

Sports

Article:
Early and classic motor cars *pp* 513-517

See also:
Colour illustrations *pp* 494 & 496

Main sub-sections:
Automobilia and travel *pp* 518-520
Cricket, golf and tennis *pp* 511-512
Fishing tackle *p* 524
Sporting guns *pp* 521-524

1
An H. Philp long-nosed scared-head baffing spoon, St. Andrews, c.1835, the apple head on hickory shaft, *L 21 July,*
£2,530 ($3,972)

2
An H. Philp long-nosed putter, St. Andrews, c.1840, on hickory shaft, some damage, *L 21 July,*
£990 ($1,554)

3
A McEwan long-nosed driving putter, Musselburgh, c.1870, beech head with hickory shaft (slightly shortened), *L 21 July,*
£495 ($777)

4
A Tom Hood long-nosed long spoon, Musselburgh, c.1870, the head probably holly, stamped with a monogram, hickory shaft, *L 21 July,*
£1,320 ($2,072)

5
A rut iron, c.1860, hickory shaft, *L 21 July,*
£385 ($604)

6
An Urquhart patent adjustable iron, Edinburgh, c.1900, the variable pitch iron on original hickory shaft, *L 21 July,*
£528 ($829)

7
A D.M. Patrick wooden niblick, Scottish, c.1920, beech scared head with hickory shaft, *L 21 July,*
£286 ($449)

8
A J. Gourlay feathery ball, Scottish, c.1840, of stitched leather, stamped *J. Gourlay*, 4cm (1in), *L 21 July,*
£1,760 ($2,763)

9
A W. Gourlay feathery golf ball, c.1840s, stitched leather, stamped with maker's name, 4cm (1in), *L 21 July,*
£1,870 ($2,936)

10
A presentation silver golfing vesta case, Birmingham, 1907, with golfing scene on one side, presented to *J.S.McDonald, July 1913*, 4cm (1in), *L 21 July,*
£385 ($604)

11
A cast-iron golf ball press and mould, mid 19th century, cast *R Con*ie St Andrews*, 33cm (13in), *L 21 July,*
£660 ($1,036)

12
A golfing medal, Edinburgh, 1902, for Inverleith Golf Club, engraved with winners' names, 8.5cm (3¼in), *L 21 July,*
£264 ($414)

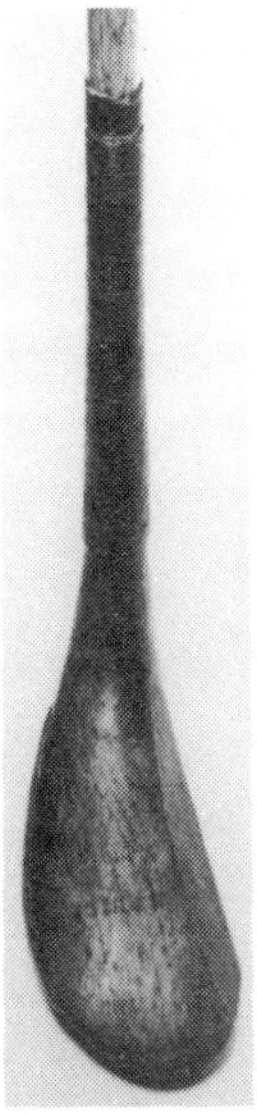
1

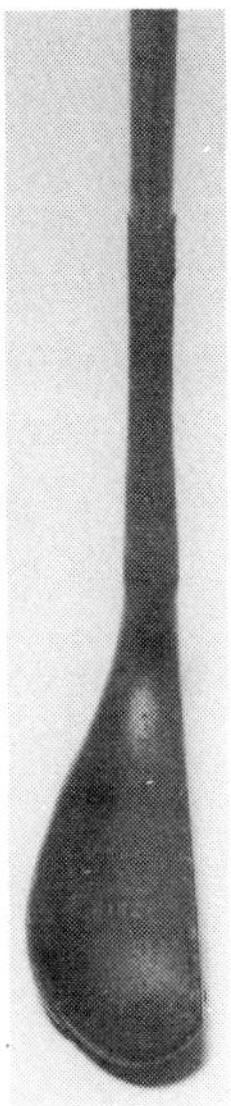
2

3

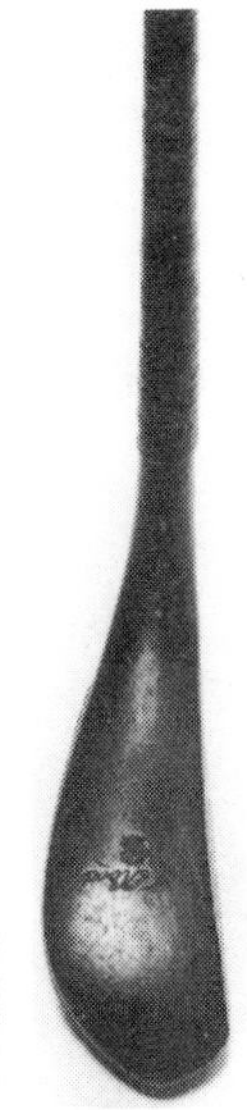
4

8

9

10

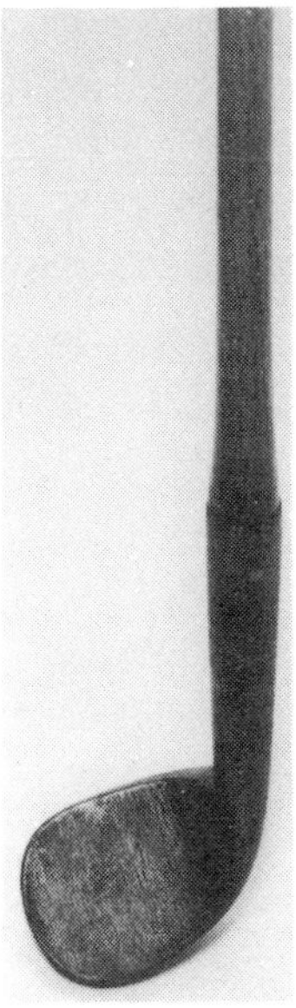
5

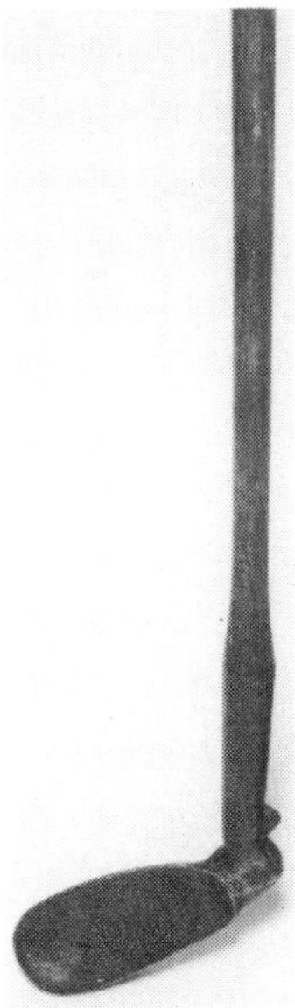
6

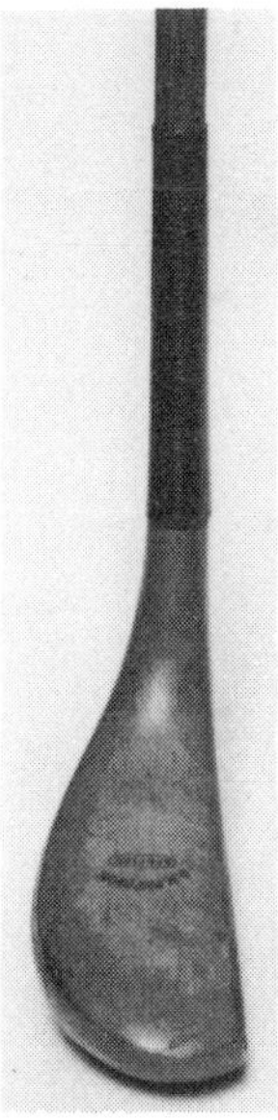
7

11

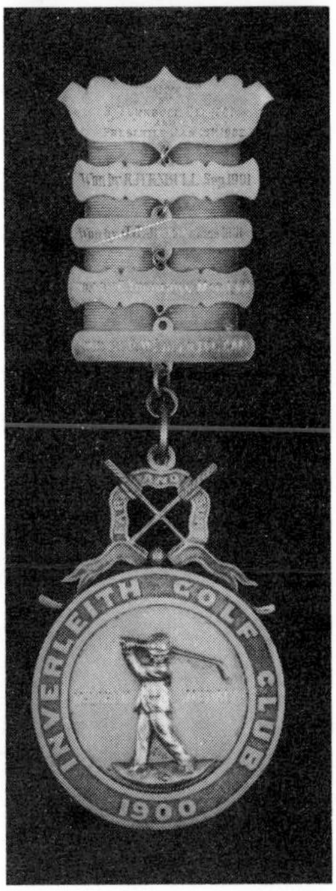

12

1

2

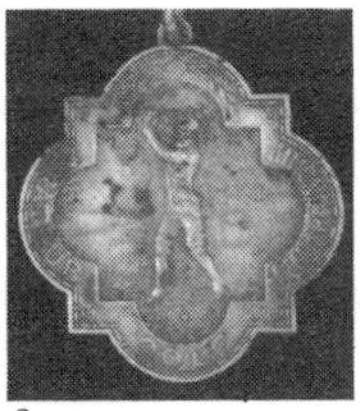
3

4

5

6

7

8

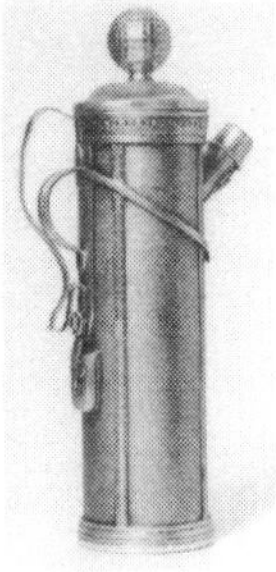
9

10

11

12

13

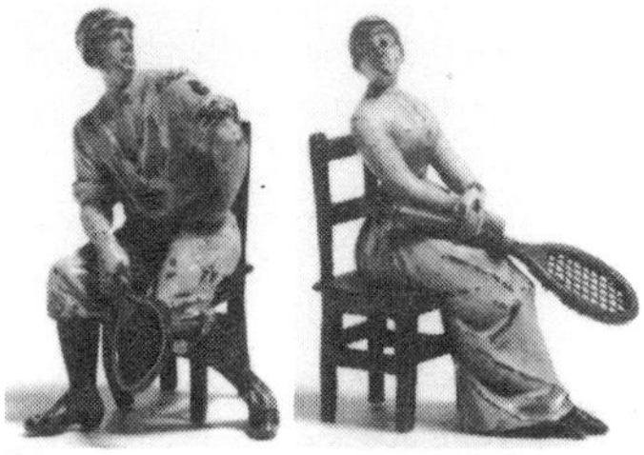
14

15

16

17

18

19

1
A silver golfing medal, Birmingham, 1893, 5.5cm (2in), *L 21 July,*
£352 ($553)

2
An early golfing medal, dated 1827, for Bruntesfield Links Golfing Society, silver-coloured metal, 4.5cm (1¾in), *L 21 July,*
£1,265 ($1,986)

3
A golfing medal, dated 1889, for the Amateur Golf Championship, silver-coloured metal, 4.5cm (1¾in), *L 21 July,*
£572 ($898)

4
A silver golfing trophy, Edinburgh, 1902, 19cm (7½in), *L 21 July,*
£880 ($1,382)

5
A Royal Doulton ceramic jardinière, English, c.1915, transfer-printed with Charles Crombie-style golfing figures, 25cm (9¾in) diam., *L 21 July,*
£605 ($950)

6
A Royal Doulton glazed ceramic plate 'The Nineteenth Hole', c.1920, transfer-printed and hand painted 26.5cm (10½in), *L 21 July,*
£440 ($691)

7
A Royal Doulton stoneware golfing tankard, English, c.1903, the rim with a silver band, 15cm (6in) high, *L 21 July,*
£880 ($1,382)

8
A Doulton Lambeth stoneware golfing jug, English, c.1900, applied with three raised groups of golfers, 23cm (9in), *L 21 July,*
£825 ($1,295)

9
A golf bag cocktail shaker, chrome-plated, in the form of a canvas bag, 32cm (12½in), *L 21 July,*
£770 ($1,209)

10
A Jacques ash and elm croquet set, on a brass-mounted frame, *C 27 Feb,*
£352 ($528)

11
A W.G. Grace cast-iron pub table, late 19th century, with mahogany top, each leg cast with a bust of the great man, 74cm (29in) high, *C 11 June,*
£198 ($311)

12
A Doulton Lambeth salt-glazed stoneware 'Cricketer' mug, Sheffield, 1899, with silver rim, 15cm (6in) high, *Ct 27 Oct,*
R 1,045 (£327; $457)

13
A Doulton Lambeth stoneware cricketing jug, English, c.1910, with three raised panels depicting cricketers in action, 21cm (8¼in), *L 21 July,*
£385 ($604)

14
A pair of Viennese painted bronze tennis players, Austrian, c.1895, one racquet replaced, 7.5cm (3in), *L 21 July,*
£407 ($639)

15
An electroplated tennis racquet cruet set, late 19th century, 19cm (7½in), *L 21 July,*
£165 ($259)

16
Four chromolithographs of tennis-playing cats, German, c.1890, each framed and glazed, image size 10 x14.5cm (4 x 5¾in), *L 21 July,*
£242 ($380)

17
A gold and rose-diamond tennis racquet brooch, late 19th century, with 23 rose diamonds mounted in white gold, 5.5cm (2in), *L 21 July,*
£825 ($1,295)

18
A pair of porcelain tennis figures, German, c.1895, 33cm (13in), *L 21 July,*
£418 ($656)

19
A silver lawn tennis belt buckle, London, 1897, stamped *Rd No 317307,* 14cm (5½in), *L 21 July,*
£715 ($1,123)

Early and Classic Motor Cars

STEWART SKILBECK

As the motor car enters its second century of development, man's love affair with the internal combustion engine is showing no signs of waning. Karl Benz and Gottlieb Daimler, pioneers of the motor car as we know it, would perhaps view with some amusement the fact that their earliest products are now highly prized by collectors. As one generation of motorists follows another, so interest moves into different eras of the motor car's development and cars pass from being of nostalgic interest to being of historic interest. Headlines are made by Grand Prix Bugattis, Type 55s or 57s (figs 22 & 23) from the same stable, the Rolls-Royce Silver Ghost or the Alfa Romeo 8C. However the market is equally interesting at a lower price level, with cars to suit every pocket.

Although Great Britain is considered to be the breeding ground of the hobby of car collecting (The Veteran Car Club of Great Britain was founded in 1930 and The Vintage Sports Car Club in 1934), the market is now truly international. There is

1
A 1931 Morris Minor 8 h.p. folding-head saloon, *CS 26 Apr,* **£1,980 ($3,168)**

2
A 1936 Austin 7 h.p. Ruby four-seat tourer, *CS 26 Apr,* **£2,970 ($4,752)**

3
A 1926 Morris Cowley 11.9 h.p. two-seater, with dickey, *L 23 June,* **£5,665 ($8,837)**

4

5

4
A 1938 Morris Eight series II four-seater open tourer, *L 1 Dec,* **£5,775 ($8,258)**

5
A 1934 Riley 9 h.p. Lynx four-seater tourer, *L 1 Dec,* **£10,780 ($15,415)**

6
A 1936 Riley Sprite 1½ litre two-seater sports, *L 1 Dec,* **£19,800 ($28,314)**

7
A 1934 British Salmson S4C 12/70 four-seat tourer, *S 25 Oct,* **£8,965 ($12,551)**

6

7

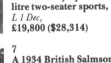

particularly strong interest in the more exotic, for example Alfa Romeo, Bugatti and Hispano-Suiza. Collectors come from Japan, Australia and the U.S.A. and recent years have also seen keen interest in classic sports cars of the 1950s from the Italians, with typical patriotic loyalty to products of their own country.

Before entering this market the enthusiast should budget carefully, setting aside a contingency fund, as, no matter how well restored or how superbly maintained a car might be, there will inevitably be costs to face when the car is used. A car which has been in the hands of one owner for many years may be less than sympathetic to its inexperienced new owner and mechanical failure or metal fatigue may take its expensive toll. The numerous clubs catering for collectors' cars are a useful source of information, advice and, of course, spare parts. The novice would be well-advised to avoid a rare car as one would be unlikely to find, for example, an active and supportive Horstman Owners' Club, although an Austin or Morris of the same era would be well catered for by The Vintage Austin Register or The Bullnose Morris Club.

The humble Austin 7 is an ideal starting point for the novice; spare parts are readily available, either original or re-manufactured and the clubs catering for the marque are numerous. Expect to pay more for a pre-1931 Austin 7 as these robust and versatile little cars are eligible for and widely used in Vintage Sports Car Club competitions. A post-1930 Austin 7 saloon, as with its contemporary Morris Minor, can be acquired for as little as £2,000 ($3,200) — fig.1. As a general rule, an open tourer will command a price almost double that of its saloon equivalent, (fig.2). Light Edwardian cars and family cars of the 1920s represent good value for money, the prices in this sector of the market having been stable for a number of years. The 'evergreen' Bullnose Morris with its Hotchkiss engine can still be

8
A 1939 Bentley 4¼ litre MX sports saloon,
CS 26 Apr,
£12,540 ($20,064)

9
A 1968 Daimler Sovereign 4.2 litre saloon,
S 25 Oct,
£1,045 ($1,463)

10
A 1933 Rolls-Royce Phantom II 40/50 h.p. close coupled sports limousine, *L 23 June,*
£35,200 ($54,912)

11
A 1957 Daimler 3½ litre sportsman 'Empress' saloon, *S 25 Oct,*
£5,170 ($7,238)

12
A 1964 Bristol 408 sports saloon, *S 25 Oct,*
£6,380 ($8,932)

13
A 1959 Lister Jaguar sports/racing two-seater,
L 1 Dec,
£95,700 ($136,851)

14
A 1953 Bentley 'R' type sports saloon, *L 1 Dec,*
£7,700 ($11,011)

15
A 1953 Austin-Healey 100/4 BN1 two-seater sports, *L 1 Dec,*
£4,950 ($7,079)

8

9

10

11

12

13

14

15

bought for around £6,000 ($9,600) — fig.3. Cars made before 1905 are eligible for the famous annual run from London to Brighton which takes place in November. A Brighton Run car will cost about £9,000 ($14,500) for two seats if you are prepared to pedal-assist your journey, £12,000 ($19,200) for two seats and relative comfort, or £20,000 ($32,000) and upwards for four seats and a modicum of speed.

Strong upward movement is evident amongst cars of the 1930s, open cars being once again at the forefront. A Morris 8 Tourer realised £5,775 ($8,258) in London in December 1986 (fig.4). The octagonal badge of the M.G. marque will command high prices on either side of the Atlantic: the M.G.J2, a boy racer in its day, with exceptional good looks but only modest performance, will now command a five figure sum (fig.29). The Riley marque, with its arguably superior engineering, is now fast catching up with the M.G.: a handsome and well-restored Riley 9 h.p. Lynx realised £10,780 ($15,415) in December 1986 (fig.5), and an unrestored but very rare Sprite made £19,800 ($28,314) at the same sale (fig.6). Even the relatively unknown British Salmson has now come in from the cold, the open tourer configuration and a well detailed restoration once again influencing a resounding £8,965 ($12,551) — fig.7. The pre-war Bentley, made in Derby, represents good value for money (fig.8), whereas its Rolls-Royce counterpart will command higher prices for examples with more sporting coachwork (fig.10). An interesting aspect of the Rolls-Royce market is that the formal black limousines of the 1930s, so popular with undertakers in the 1950s, are now donning ivory livery and are keenly sought-after by present-day wedding fleet operators.

In the post-World War II era interest is varied, with Daimler (figs 9 & 11), Armstrong-Siddeley and Lanchester a little unloved, despite the quality of manufacture, while the Bentley Mark VI

16
A 1959 Jaguar Mk IX saloon, *L 23 June,*
£5,060 ($7,894)

17
A 1954 Aston Martin DB2/4 Mk I, *L 23 June,*
£9,900 ($15,444)

18
A 1954 Aston Martin DB2/4 2+2 sports saloon, *L 1 Dec,*
£11,000 ($15,730)

19
A 1924 Austin 20 h.p. chassis and running gear, *CS 26 Apr,*
£2,310 ($3,696)

20
A 1967 Morris Mini Moke, *CS 5 July,*
£2,530 ($4,073)

21
A 1971 Volvo 1800 ES estate car, *L 1 Dec,*
£2,365 ($3,382)

16

17

18

19

20

21

and R-Type (fig.14) and Bristol (fig.12) cars appear to be an area with strong growth potential. Open and closed sports cars are enjoying popularity, Jaguar (fig.16), Aston Martin (figs 17 & 18) and Austin-Healey (fig.15) being the favourites, and a car with a good works competition history will command a premium. With increasing activity in the historic sports and racing car scene this sector of the market has moved strongly ahead, consistent race winners amongst Ferraris, Maseratis, Jaguars and Lister Jaguars being highly prized (fig.13).

A question frequently asked is: should one buy an unrestored or restored car? Unless a well-equipped workshop and considerable skills are at the disposal of the collector, restoration projects, or barn discoveries, are well avoided. Professional restoration costs bear no relation to the restored value of a car and only where a car has great sentimental value, or where it is the only way of acquiring that particular model, should the novice commit himself to a professional restoration. There is no doubt that a professionally restored car will give great satisfaction to its owner, but the restoration bill should be regarded as an investment in future enjoyment and not a contributing factor in the value of the motor car. Many car enthusiasts, however, derive pleasure and recreation from amateur restoration, part of the fun being in scouring Auto jumble stalls for the elusive missing parts. The 1924 Austin 20 chassis and running gear illustrated as fig.19 is soon to emerge restored to its former glory as a magnificent five seat open tourer. Despite all the impending headaches and heartaches, restoration projects are a bouyant sector of the market and it is not unknown for a semi-derelict car to command a price equivalent to or higher than its restored counterpart. Time spent in research before embarking on a restoration is always well rewarded. Standards of judging in *Concours d'Elégance* events have risen markedly in recent years, as have standards of

22

23

24

25

26

27

restoration. Wherever possible the original should be retained. However, where paint, upholstery or mechanical components have suffered irretrievably through neglect or wear, great care should be taken to replace them exactly to original specification. The one-make clubs or the reference library at The National Motor Museum at Beaulieu in England, will help and advise.

With newly restored cars continually emerging and with a seemingly endless supply of 'new' discoveries, future market trends are difficult to predict. There are no immediate signs of the market reaching saturation point. If entering the collectors' car market for the first time, don't buy because a car looks quaint or sporty. Always try to find an opportunity to drive a similar example and be sure that you are comfortable in it and that it will cover the ground at a pace which will satisfy you. Don't forget the passengers: they will not have the thrill of driving, so they too must be considered. Do make sure that your first car is well catered for by an active owners' club with events and facilities in your area.

What will be tomorrow's collectors cars? The Ferrari 288GTO, produced in limited numbers and only two years old, is already in this field; the ill-fated De Lorean may be one day; and which brave auctioneer will be first to offer a Nissan under the hammer?

Further reading:

G.N. Georgano, *The Complete Encyclopaedia of Motor Cars*, 1968
R.C. Wheatley and B. Morgan, *The Restoration of Vintage and Thoroughbred Cars*, 1957

28

29

22
A 1939 Bugatti type 57 Galibier four-door saloon, *M 25 May,*
FF 418,000 (£37,123; $58,282)

23
A 1938 Bugatti type 57 'C' supercharged Atalante coupé, *M 25 May,*
FF 1,842,500 (£163,632; $256,903)

24
A 1959 B.M.W. model 503 two-door coupé, *L 23 June,*
£7,920 ($12,355)

25
A 1930 Austin 7 h.p. Swallow two-seater open sports, *L 23 June,*
£6,050 ($9,438)

26
A 1939 Lagonda V12 41.85 h.p. drophead coupé, *M 25 May,*
FF 275,000 (£24,423; $38,344)

27
A 1934 Delage D8-15 pillarless saloon, *M 25 May,*
FF 143,000 (£12,700; $19,939)

28
A 1939 Alvis 12/70 sports saloon, *L 1 Dec,*
£4,400 ($6,292)

29
A 1933 M.G.J2 two-seater sports tourer, *S 25 Oct,*
£10,670 ($14,938)

1

2

3

4

5

6

7

8

9

10

11

12

13

14

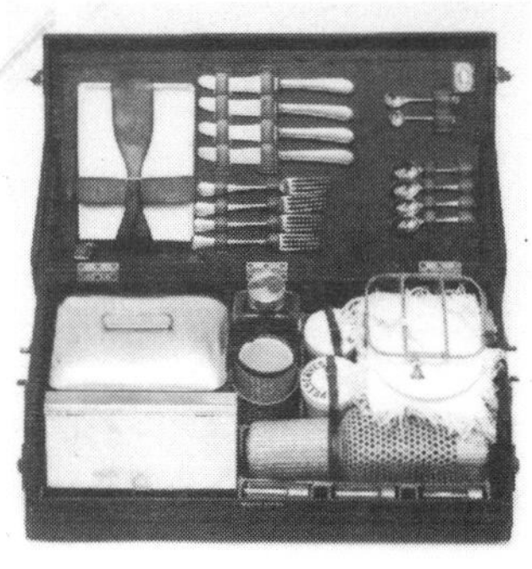
15

16

1
A Great Western Railway ticket numbering machine, early 20th century, of brass with cast-iron stand, 35cm (15in), *C 30 Apr,*
£231 ($374)

2
A wooden sleigh, Austrian, 18th century, painted and gilt with figures, animals, flowers and shells, 90cm (35½in) high, *M 24 Feb,*
FF 13,320 (£1,288; $1,932)

3
A child's sleigh, probably Scandinavian, late 19th century, with stencil decoration, finished in scarlet and black, 107cm (42in) high, *L 22 July,*
£715 ($1,123)

4
A locomotive nameplate 'Berkeley Castle', raised brass lettering, 173cm (68in), *CS 5 July,*
£2,640 ($4,250)

5
A carved and polychrome painted wooden sledge, dated 1732, 97cm (38in) long, *A 14 Oct,*
Dfl 6,210 (£1,941; $2,911)

6
A Louis XV leather-covered sedan chair, mid 18th century, with glazed sides and Régence-style giltwood mouldings, 170cm (67in) high, *L 28 Nov,*
£1,980 ($2,772)

7
A 24-inch child's Ordinary or 'Penny Farthing' bicycle, English, late 19th century, replaced pedals and cranks, *L 23 June,*
£605 ($944)

8
A 52-inch Ordinary or 'Penny Farthing' bicycle, English, c.1880, cranks and pedals replaced, *CS 26 Apr,*
£825 ($1,320)

9
A Michaux velocipede, French, c.1865, *the 'Parisienne', made by Maison Michaux & Cie, Paris,* with iron backbone and tyres and wooden spoked wheels, *CS 26 Apr,*
£748 ($1,197)

10
A Cheylesmore tricycle, English, c.1880, made by the Coventry Machinist Company, *CS 26 Apr,*
£3,410 ($5,456)

11
A Quadrant tricycle, English, c.1885, with tubular frame, *CS 26 Apr,*
£3,300 ($5,280)

12
A lady's solid-tyred bicycle, c.1891, *L 23 June,*
£770 ($1,201)

13
A contemporary photograph of a Napier, c.1905, signed on the print *Clerk and Hoyde, photographers, London,* 73 x 122cm (29 x 48in), *L 23 June,*
£550 ($858)

14
A Griffon motorcycle chromolithographic poster, French, c.1904, signed *J. Hugo D'Alesi,* published by Du Griffon, Paris, laid down on linen, 195 x 128cm (77 x 50in), *L 23 June,*
£462 ($721)

15
A Mawson, Swan and Morgan combined picnic set and footrest, English, c.1905, green leather covered case, fitted interior, 56cm (22in) wide, *CS 26 Apr,*
£550 ($880)

16
A Rolls-Royce radiator, suitable for Rolls-Royce 25/30 hp, 84cm (33in) high, *L 23 June,*
£1,485 ($2,317)

. pair of Lucas 10-inch '80 'bullseye' headlamps, .nglish, c.1930, with hrome metal bodies, . *23 June,* **990 ($1,544)**

. pair of Lucas 10-inch '80S headlamps, English, .1928-39, with chrome ıetal bodies, *L 23 June,* **286 ($446)**

. Bugatti radiator cap, 'rench, c.1935, stamped vith the Bugatti E.B. nonogram, 8cm (3¼in) liam., *L 23 June,* **83 ($129)**

. Bosch tail lamp, suit- .ble for a Mercedes SSK, ılly restored, 18cm (7in) vide, *L 23 June,* **:935 ($1,459)**

. pair of Scintilla tail amps, Swiss, 1930s, each ılly restored, 20cm (8in) ong, *L 23 June,* **:385 ($601)**

. Tapley & Company radient meter, English, :.1912, the dial graduated rom plus 1-in-4 to minus -in-4, 7.5cm (3in) diam., *: 23 June,* **.176 ($275)**

7
. Charles Frodsham & :o. dashboard timepiece, he keyless movement in orass case, 8cm (3in) liam., *L 23 June,* **:66 ($103)**

8
. Bentley Speed six dash- ooard timepiece, made in Switzerland and retailed oy S. Smith & Sons, in nahogany frame, bezel 9cm (3½in) diam., *L 23 June,* **£462 ($721)**

9
An Automobile Associ- ation member's badge, in nickel, 16.5cm (6½in) high, *L 23 June,* **£66 ($103)**

10
A Royal Automobile Club life member's badge, stamped *Elkington & Co. Ltd.*, 17cm (6¾in) high, *L 23 June,* **£715 ($1,115)**

11
A Motor Union brass badge, c.1905, 21cm (8¼in), sold with an AA key, *L 1 Dec,* **£572 ($818)**

12
A Farman nickelled-brass mascot, French, 1920-30, signed *Colin George* and stamped with founder's mark, wingspan 19cm (7½in), *L 1 Dec,* **£935 ($1,337)**

13
A Lalique archer glass mascot, French, 1920s, signed *R Lalique, France,* on metal mount, 15.5cm (6¼in) high, *M 25 May,* **FF 28,000 (£2,487; $3,904)**

14
An F. Bazin Duesberg mascot, French, c.1930, the chromed bronze Pegasus on radiator cap mount, 14cm (5in) high, *L 23 June,* **£242 ($378)**

15
A Charles Sykes Rolls-Royce 'Spirit of Ecstasy' mascot, English, c.1920s, signed, in solid nickel, 17cm (6¾in) high, *M 25 May,* **FF 5,280 (£469; $736)**

16
A Rolls-Royce 'Kneeling Lady' mascot trophy, English, c.1947, the chromed metal figure on weighted base, 10cm (4in) high, *CS 26 Apr,* **£121 ($194)**

17
A Bentley 'B' mascot, on radiator cap, 10cm (4in) long, *S 25 Oct,* **£110 ($154)**

18
A Lincoln greyhound mascot, in chromed metal, stamped on the base *Lincoln Motor Company*, on brass stand, 22cm (8½in) long, *L 23 June,* **£110 ($172)**

19
A Buick mascot, American, mid 1920s, mounted on radiator cap, 11.5cm (4½in) long, *CS 26 Apr,* **£126 ($202)**

1

2

3

4

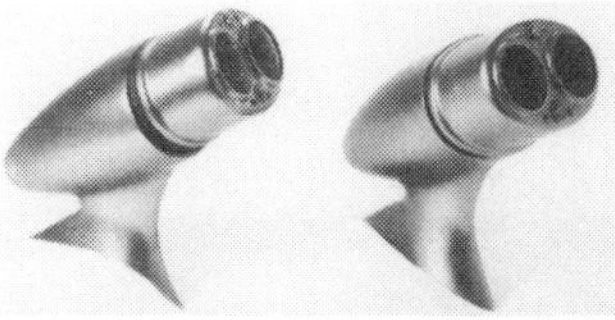
5

6

7

8

9

10

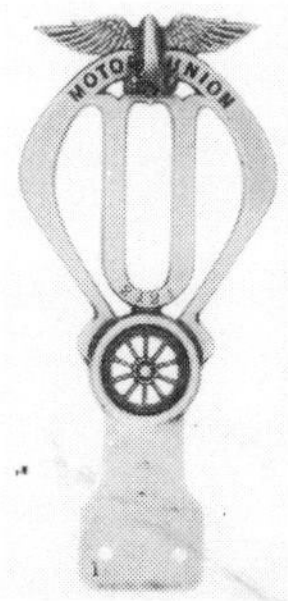

11

12

13

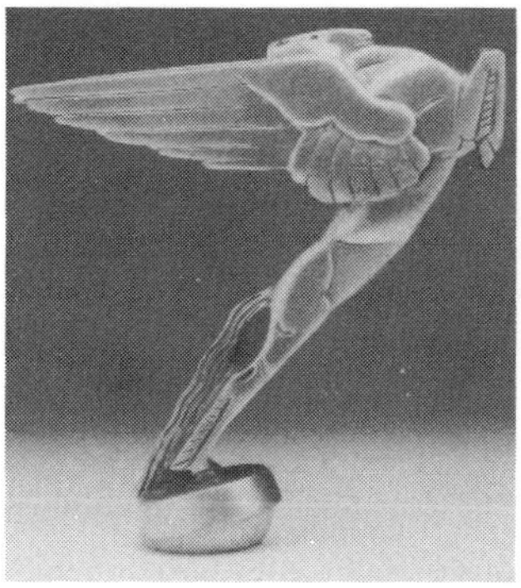
14

15

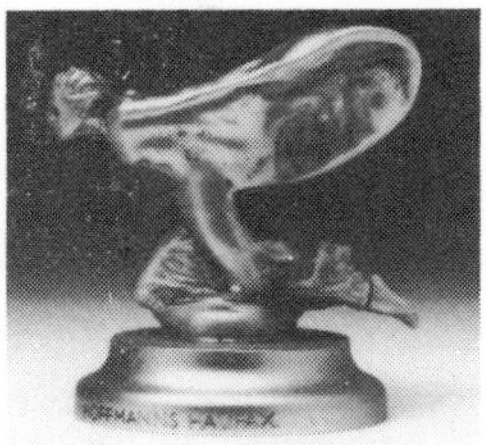
16

17

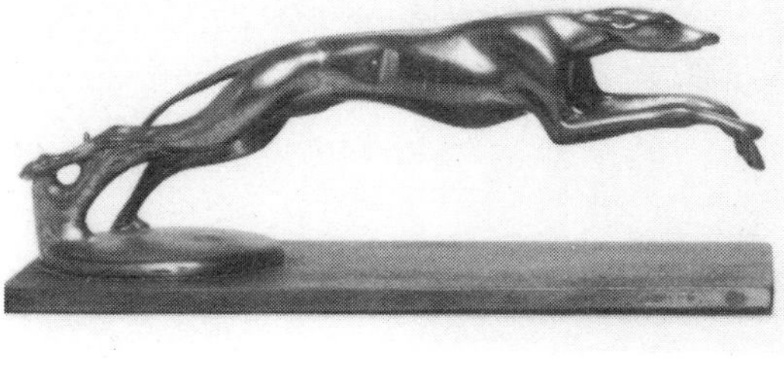
18

19

1

2

3

4

5

6

7

8

9

10

1
A 1912 Vindec Special 770 c.c. solo motorcycle, made in Germany, JAP engine, *L 23 June,*
£2,860 ($4,462)

2
A 1928 Matchless V/2 4.95 h.p. Super Sports solo motorcycle, *CS 5 Oct,*
£2,035 ($2,849)

3
A c.1935 Ravat 98 c.c. lightweight solo motor-cycle, made in France, *CS 5 Oct,*
£242 ($339)

4
A c.1936 Cyc-Auto Model A 98 c.c., *CS 26 Apr,*
£352 ($563)

5
A c.1946 Royal Enfield 125 c.c. solo motorcycle, *CS 5 Oct,*
£132 ($185)

6
A 1948 Vincent HRD Rapide Series B, *L 1 Dec,*
£5,280 ($7,550)

7
A 1949 B.S.A. A10 Golden Flash 650 c.c. with Hedingham S/S sidecar, *CS 5 Oct,*
£1,100 ($1,540)

8
A 1951 Cymota cycle-motor fitted to B.S.A. Streamlight bicycle, *CS 5 Oct,*
£473 ($662)

9
A 1952 Norton International 490 c.c. solo motorcycle, *CS 26 Apr,*
£1,760 ($2,816)

10
A 1971 B.S.A. Bantam Super 175 c.c. solo motor cycle, *CS 26 Apr,*
£187 ($299)

1
A Bacon patent bolt-action D.B. 12-bore sporting gun, 32½in damascus barrels, half-length stock, 6lb 12oz., rebrowned and reblacked, *S 12 Mar,*
£935 ($1,440)

2
Boss & Co. A 12-bore sidelock ejector gun, 28in chopper lump barrels, 6lb 8oz, nitro proof, in leather case, *S 12 Mar,*
£9,020 ($13,891)

3
Boss & Co. A composed pair of 12-bore round-bodied assisted-opening single-trigger sidelock ejector guns, *(one illustrated)*, 29in chopper lump barrels, 6lb 7oz, nitro proof, restocked, *S 12 Mar,*
£12,650 ($19,481)

4
Boss & Co. A pair of 12-bore self-opening round-bodied sidelock ejector guns, *(one illustrated)*, 28in chopper lump barrels, 6lb 8oz, nitro proof, *S 12 Mar,*
£3,410 ($5,251)

5
Boss & Co. A pair of lightweight 12-bore single-trigger assisted-opening sidelock ejector guns, *(one illustrated)*, 28in barrels, 6lb 3oz and 6lb 5oz respectively, nitro proof, *Glen 25 Aug,*
£13,750 ($21,313)

6
Boss & Co. A 12-bore round-bodied single-trigger assisted-opening sidelock ejector gun, 29in barrels, 6lb 8oz, nitro proof, *S 12 Mar,*
£4,730 ($7,284)

7
Cogswell & Harrison Ltd. A 12-bore single-trigger sidelock ejector gun, 27½in Argus steel barrels, 6lb 8oz, nitro proof, *L 16 Dec,*
£1,485 ($2,124)

8
Boss & Co. A 12-bore single-trigger assisted-opening sidelock ejector gun, 30in chopper lump barrels, 6lb 8oz, nitro proof, *Glen 25 Aug,*
£7,700 ($11,935)

9
John Dickson & Son. A 12-bore assisted-opening round-action ejector gun, 29in chopper lump barrels, 6lb 10oz, nitro proof, *S 12 Mar,*
£2,420 ($3,727)

10
William Evans. A 12-bore sidelock ejector gun, 26¾in barrels, 6lb 6oz, nitro proof, bores marked and dented, *L 16 Dec,*
£3,190 ($4,562)

11
Holland & Holland. A pair of 12-bore 'Royal' self-opening detachable sidelock ejector guns, *(one illustrated)*, 28in chopper lump barrels, 6lb 6oz, nitro proof, no.1 bores worn, *Glen 25 Aug,*
£9,900 ($15,345)

12
Alexander Henry. Patent .360 express falling block take down sporting rifle, 27in round barrel, black powder proof, with accessories, *L 16 Dec,*
£1,540 ($2,202)

13
E.J. Churchill. A lightweight 12-bore 'Premiere XXV' sidelock ejector gun, 25in chopper lump barrels, 6lb 4oz, *Glen 25 Aug,*
£4,620 ($7,161)

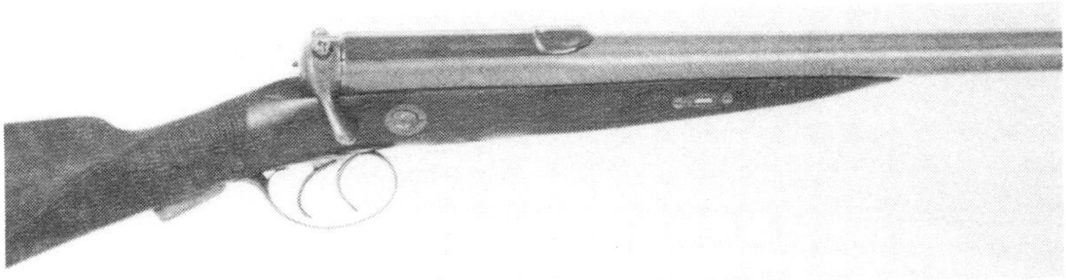
1

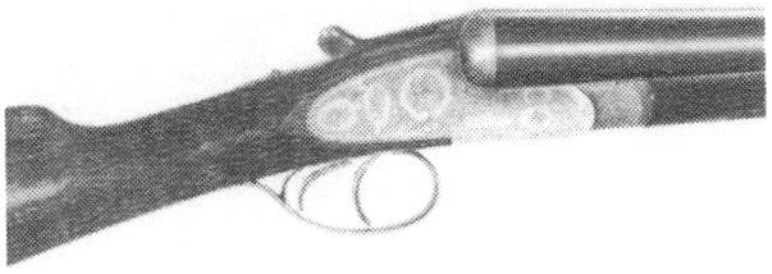
2

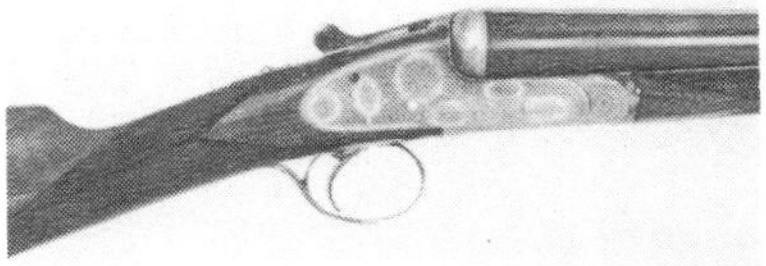
3

4

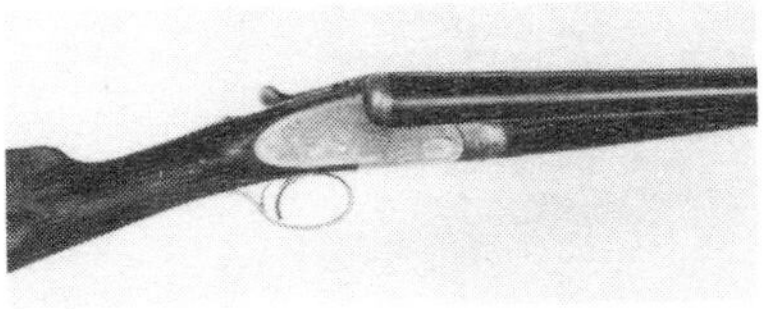
5

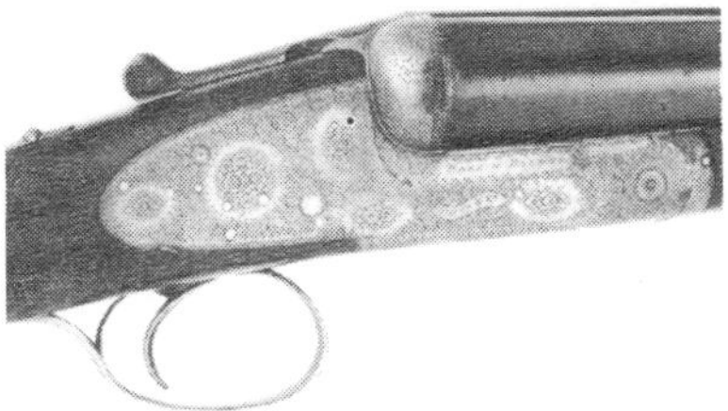
6

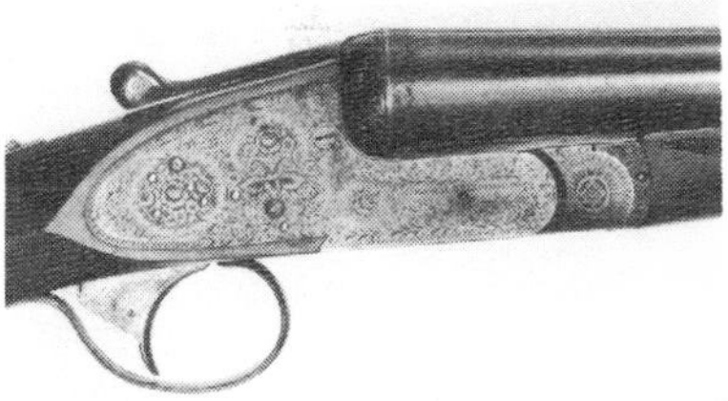
7

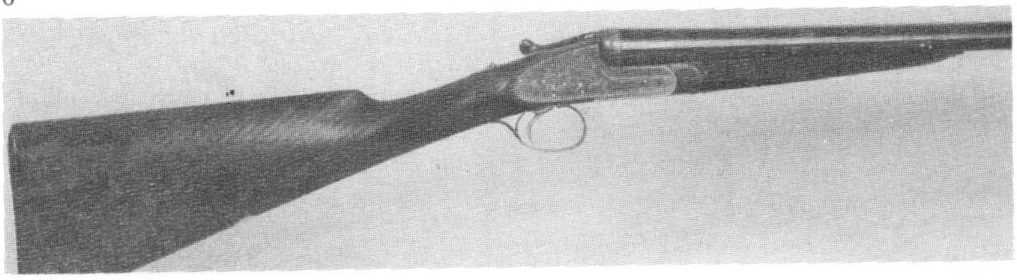
8

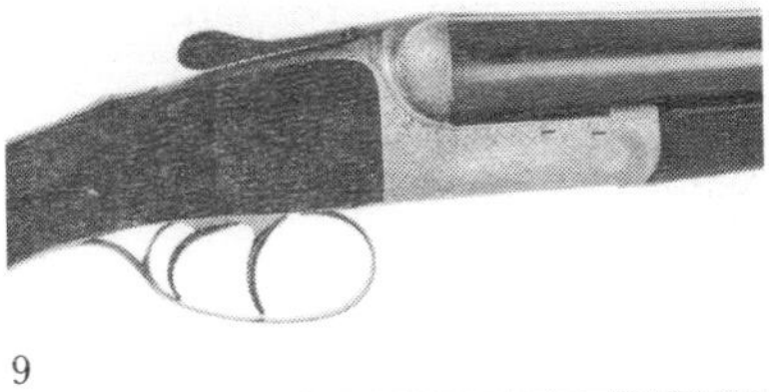
9

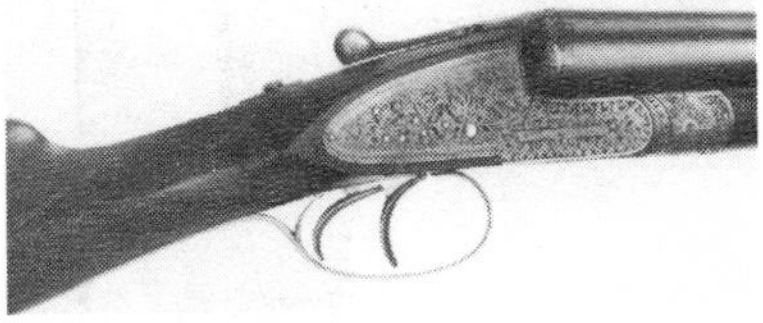
10

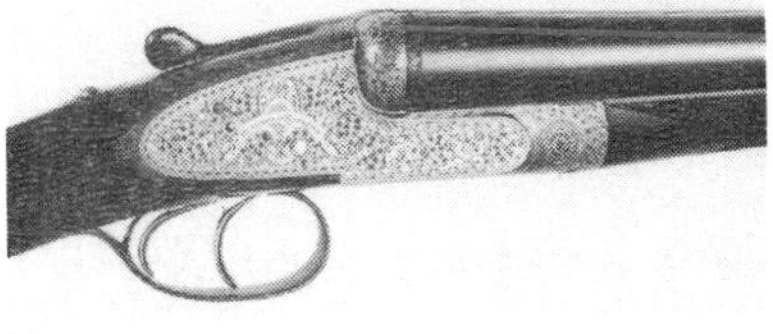
11

12

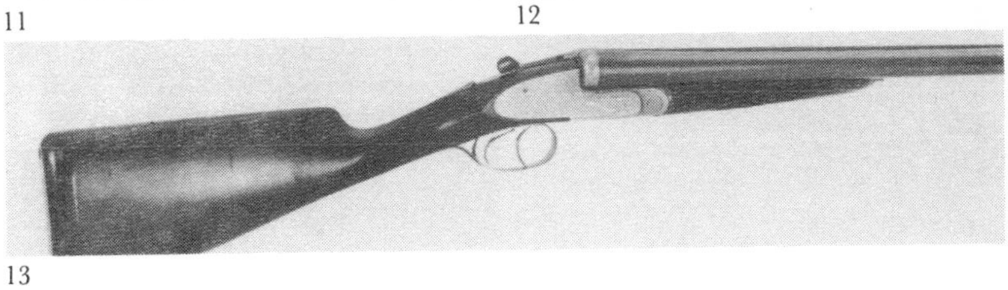
13

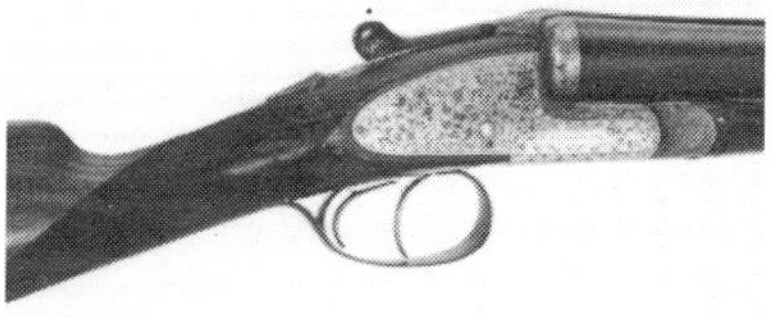
1

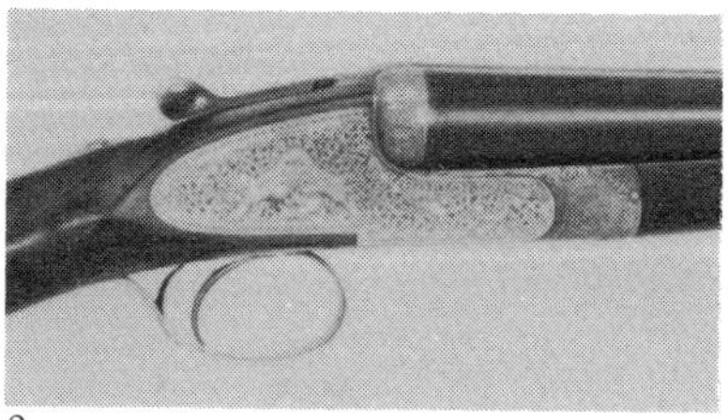
2

3

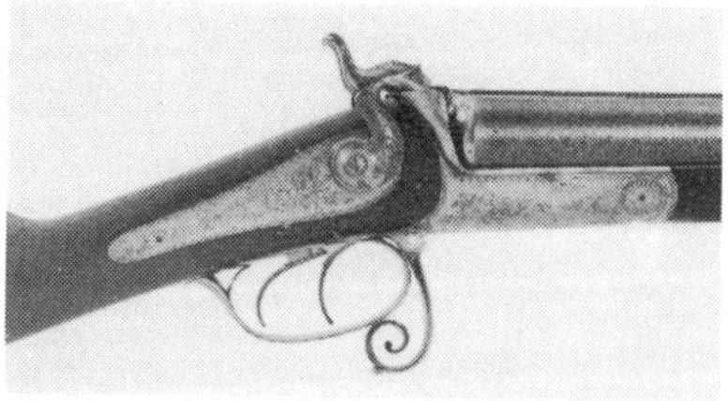
4

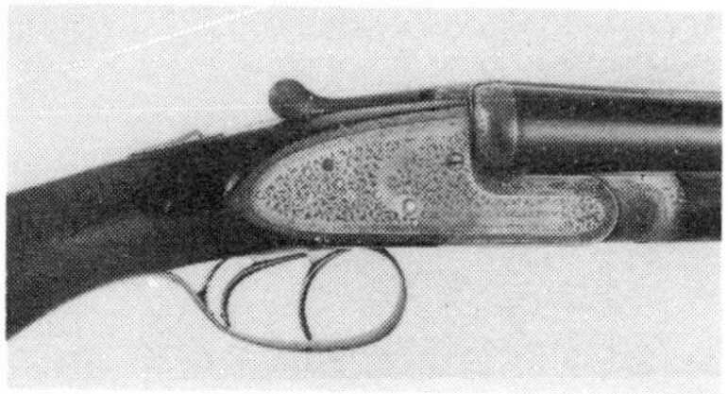
5

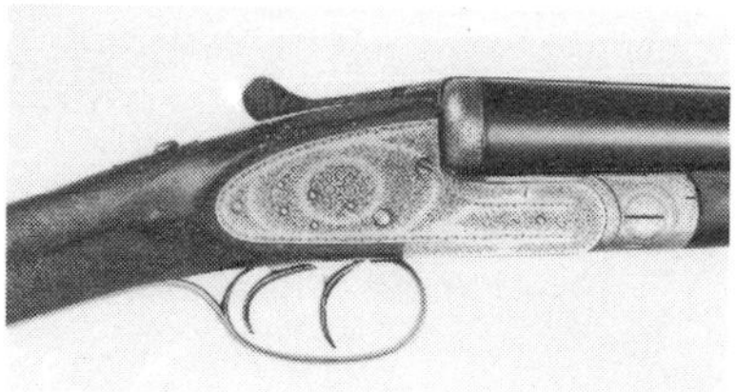
6

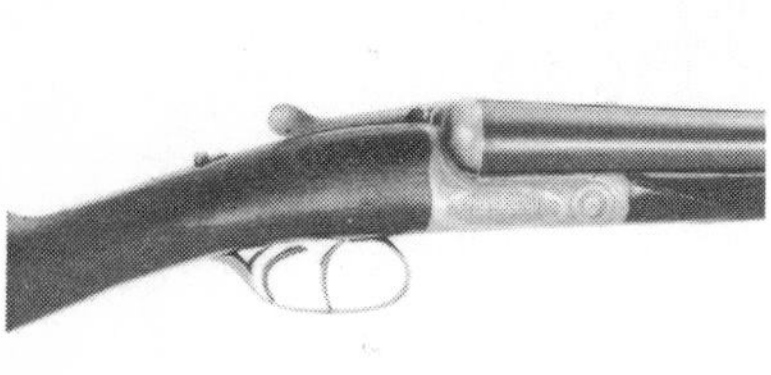
7

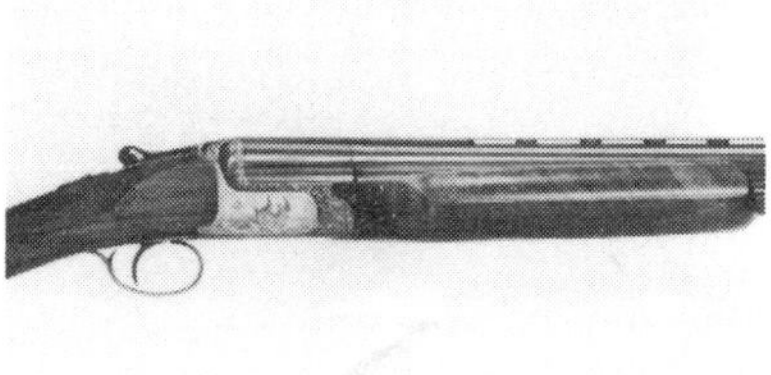
8

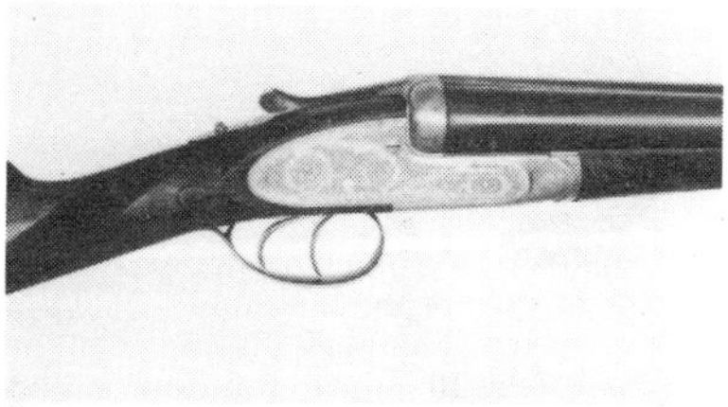
9

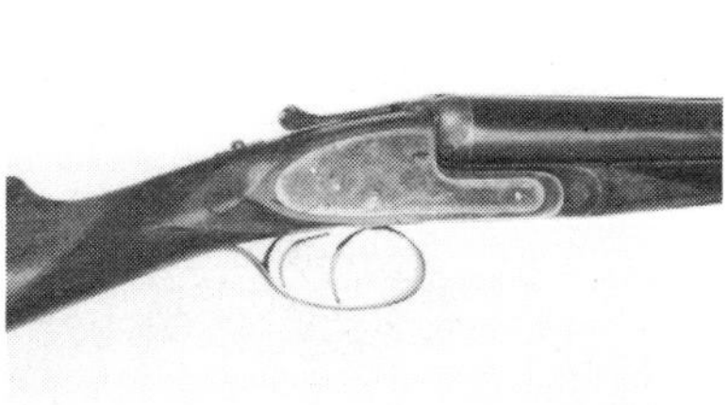
10

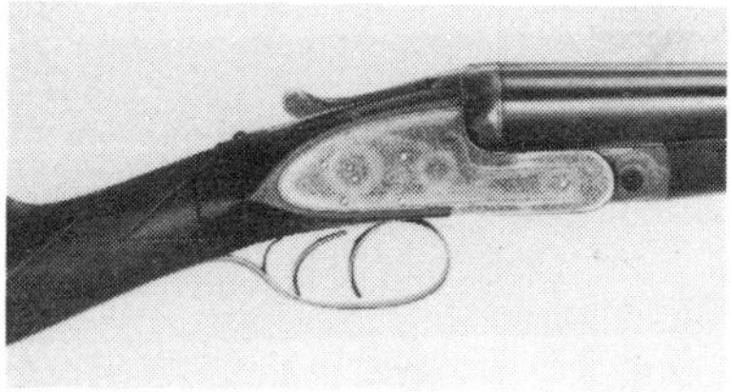
11

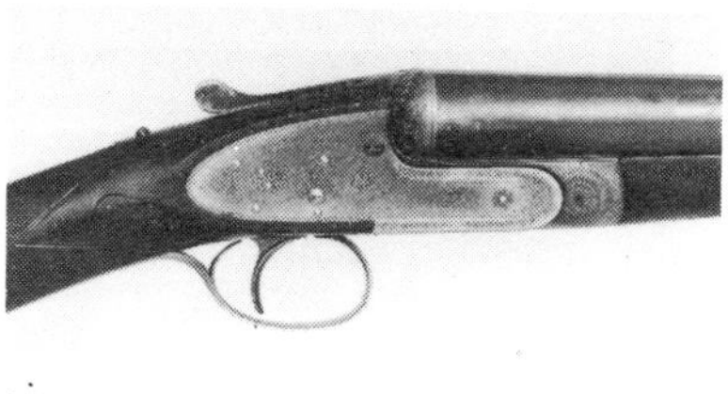
12

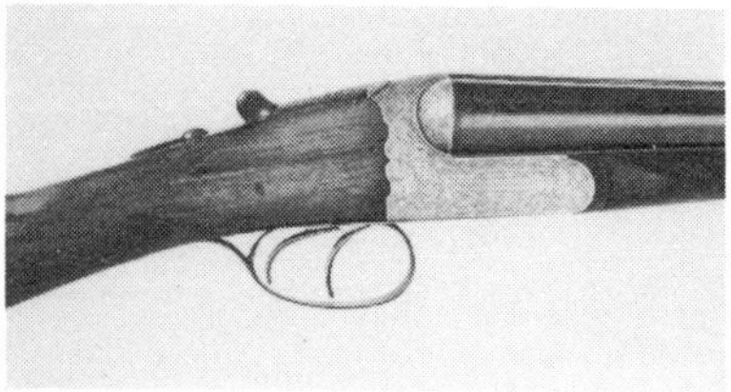
13

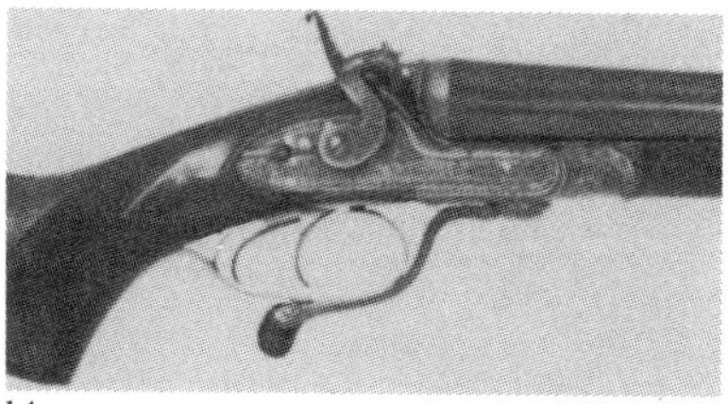
14

1
E.J. Churchill (Gunmakers Ltd.) A crown grade 12-bore 'XXV' sidelock ejector gun, 25in chopper lump barrels, 6lb 3oz, nitro proof, *Glen 25 Aug,*
£2,750 ($4,262)

2
Holland & Holland. A pair of 12-bore 'Royal' self-opening single-trigger detachable sidelock ejector guns, *(one illustrated)*, 26½in chopper lump barrels, 6lb 5oz and 6lb 7oz, some damage to bores, no.2 restocked, in oak and leather case, *Glen 25 Aug,*
£11,550 ($29,453)

3
Lefaucheux. A Lefaucheux-system 12-bore pinfire gun, dated 1861, 29in damascus barrels struck below, *Albert Bernard Çanonnier à Paris,* proof exemption, *L 16 Dec,*
£352 ($503)

4
Fauré LePage. A French 12-bore Schneider patent snap-action hammer non-ejector gun, 29¾in damascus barrels struck below *Leopold Bernard Cannonier A Paris,* proof exemption, *Glen 25 Aug,*
£770 ($1,194)

5
Charles Lancaster. A Grade 'B' 20-bore sidelock ejector gun, 28in barrels, nitro proof, bores with slight marks, *S 12 Mar,*
£3,300 ($5,082)

6
Charles Lancaster. A lightweight 12-bore assisted-opening boxlock ejector gun, with dummy sidelocks, 28in chopper lump barrels, 6lb, nitro proof, bores dented, *Glen 25 Aug,*
£2,640 ($4,092)

7
MacNaughton & Sons. A 12-bore round action ejector gun, 28in barrels, 6lb 14oz, nitro proof, *Glen 25 Aug,*
£1,870 ($2,899)

8
Perazzi. A Galeazzi engraved 12-bore grade Map Sco single-trigger detachable lock over/under gun, 7lb 6oz, Italian nitro proof, *L 16 Dec,*
£3,080 ($4,404)

9
J. Purdey & Sons. A 12-bore self-opening sidelock ejector gun, 28in chopper lump barrels, 6lb 11oz, nitro proof, *S 12 Mar,*
£7,920 ($12,197)

10
J. Purdey & Sons. A pair of 12-bore self-opening sidelock ejector guns, *(one illustrated)*, 29in Whitworth steel chopper lump barrels, 6lb 8oz, nitro proof, in case with accessories, *Glen 25 Aug,*
£15,950 ($24,723)

11
J. Purdey & Sons. A pair of 12-bore self-opening sidelock ejector guns, *(one illustrated)*, 28in chopper lump barrels, 6lb 13oz, nitro proof, bores marked, case, *L 16 Dec,*
£7,480 ($10,696)

12
J. Purdey & Sons. A 12-bore self-opening single-trigger sidelock ejector gun, 29in Whitworth steel chopper lump barrels, 6lb 8oz, nitro proof, bores pitted, *L 16 Dec,*
£6,050 ($8,652)

13
Westley Richards & Co. A 12-bore boxlock ejector gun, 28in barrels, 6lb 8oz, nitro proof, barrels probably shortened, *S 12 Mar,*
£1,430 ($2,202)

14
Jno. Rigby & Co. A 12-bore hammer non-ejector gun, 30in barrels, 7lb 15oz, black powder proof, bores pitted, *S 12 Mar,*
£770 ($1,186)

1
Orvil M. Robinson. A tube loading rifle, model 1872, manufactured by Adirondack Firearms Co, Plattsburgh, New York, 23½in barrel, lacquered walnut butt, brass butt plate, *NY 25 Nov,*
$2,640 (£1,886)

2
A Spencer repeating sporting rifle, probably model 1867, apparently unfired, 26½in barrel, case hardened lock and cock, walnut forestock silver tipped, walnut butt, *NY 25 Nov,*
$1,760 (£1,257)

3
Frank Wesson. A two-trigger carbine, c.1863, apparently unused, 24in barrel, maker's mark and also Kittredge mark, the walnut butt with suspension ring, *NY 25 Nov,*
$880 (£628)

4
A Whitney Phoenix breech loading sporting rifle, c.1867-75, apparently unused, 28¾in barrel, lacquered walnut stock with metal tipped fore-end, spring action faulty, *NY 25 Nov,*
$1,320 (£943)

5
A Winchester .45-90 W.C.F. lever action rifle, model 1886, 26in barrel with open sights, shotgun butt-plate, *L 16 Dec,*
£1,540 ($2,202)

6
J. Woodward & Sons. A pair of 12-bore sidelock ejector guns, *(one illustrated),* 28in Whitworth steel chopper lump barrels, 6lb 7oz and 6lb 9oz respectively, nitro proof, some damage, no.1 restocked by Purdeys, *L 16 Dec,*
£9,680 ($13,842)

7
W.W. Greener. A Greener harpoon gun, 20in barrel chambered for Greener's special cartridges, cased with accessories, *L 16 Dec,*
£495 ($708)

8
Darne. A French 37mm punt gun, 8ft 6in overall, St. Etienne proof, *L 16 Dec,*
£1,430 ($2,045)

9
A double-barrelled 3-bore punt gun, maker unknown, 59¼in choked ribless barrels, in wooden crate with accessories, *S 12 Mar,*
£3,850 ($5,929)

10
A Wilkinson double-barrelled .500 hammer howdah pistol, 6½in barrels, frame engraved *Wilkinson's no.420 patent 1882,* 13in, some colour hardening, black powder proof, *S 12 Mar,*
£990 ($1,525)

11
Mauser Oberndorf. A 7.63mm M96 self-loading carbine, c.1905, 15¾in barrel, detachable polished walnut stock, minor scratches, in fitted case, *L 16 Dec,*
£7,480 ($10,696)

12
Mauser Oberndorf. A 7.63mm 'broomhandle' self-loading pistol, 5½in barrel, ribbed walnut grips, matching walnut stock, minor light rust patches, *S 12 Mar,*
£1,100 ($1,694)

13
A French 20-bore lever-cocking trigger-plate action hammer gun, c.1860, 30in twist barrels with sling loop, proof exemption, *Glen 25 Aug,*
£880 ($1,364)

14
A French 16-bore dual system pinfire/centrefire rifle, 23½in blued damascus barrels, *L 16 Dec,*
£770 ($1,101)

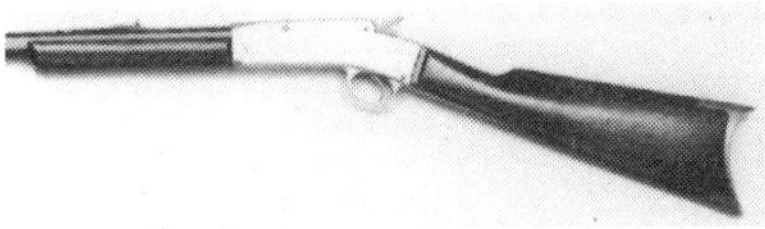
1

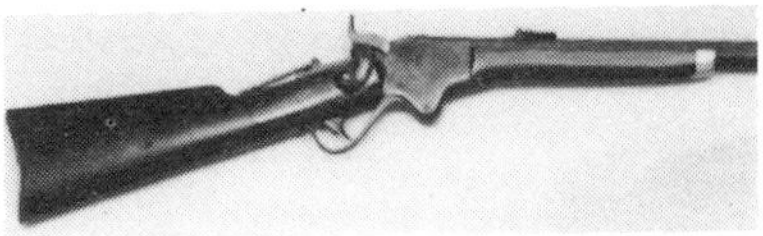
2

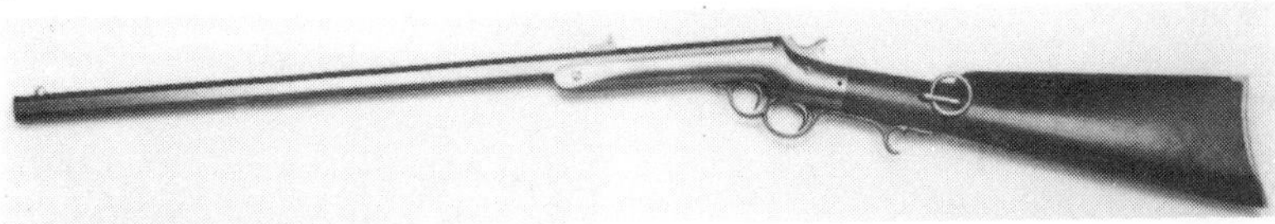
3

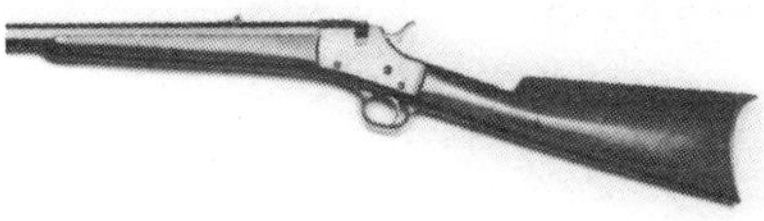
4

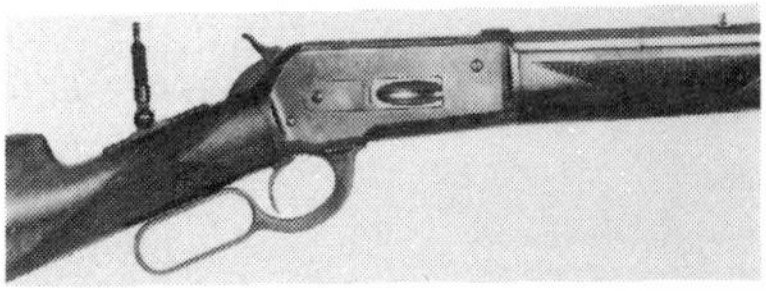
5

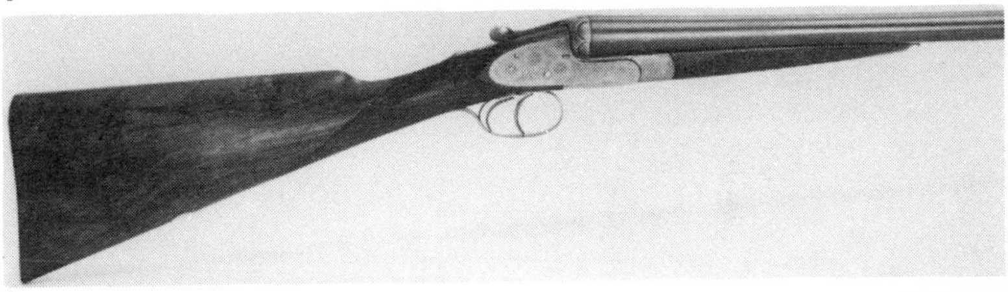
6

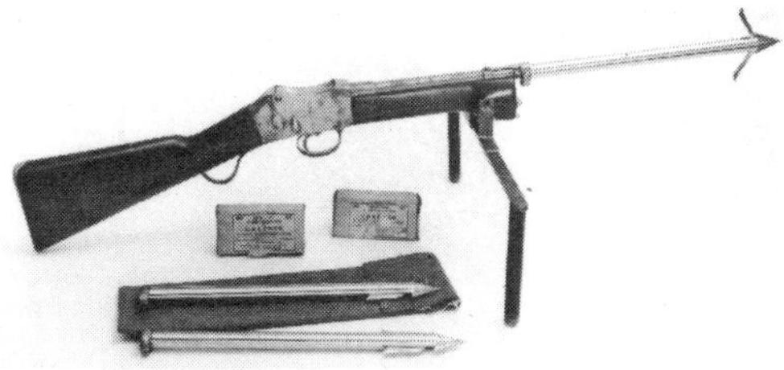
7

8

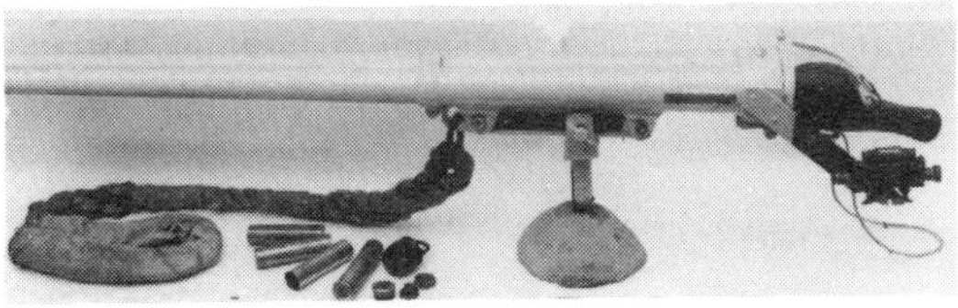
9

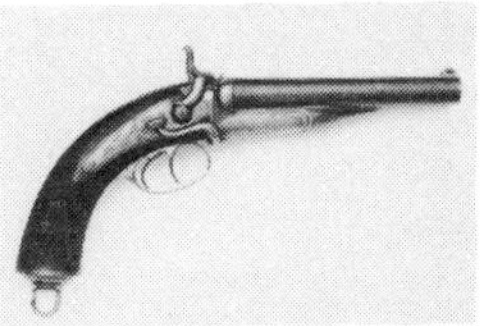
10

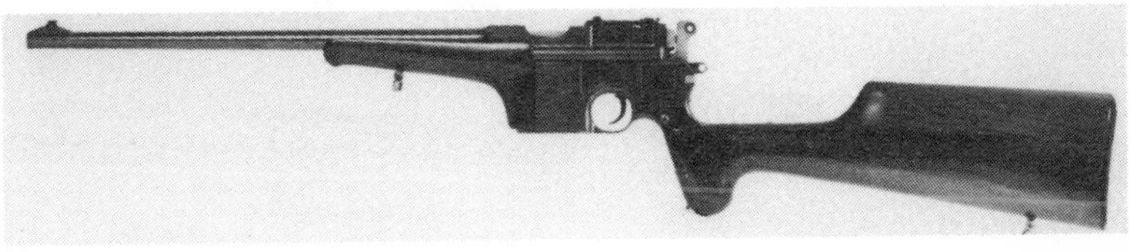
11

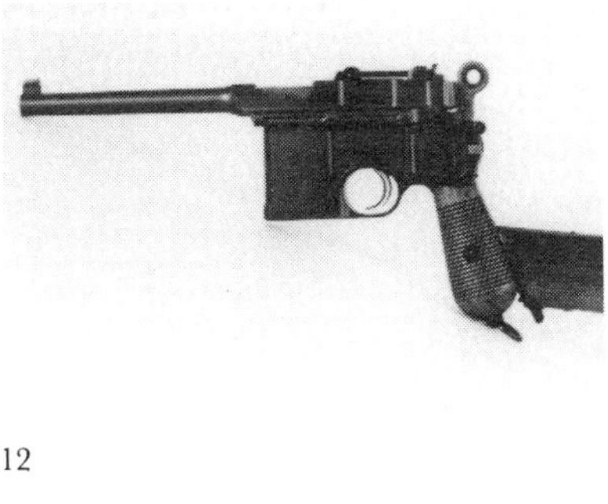
12

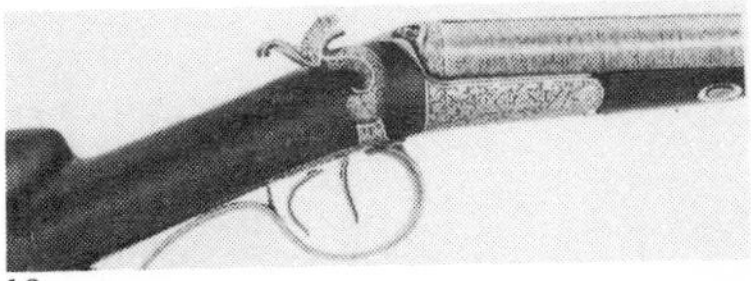
13

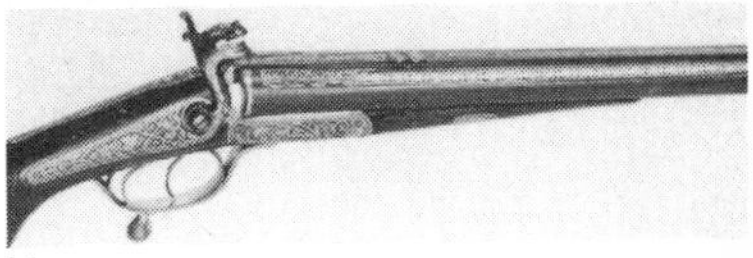
14

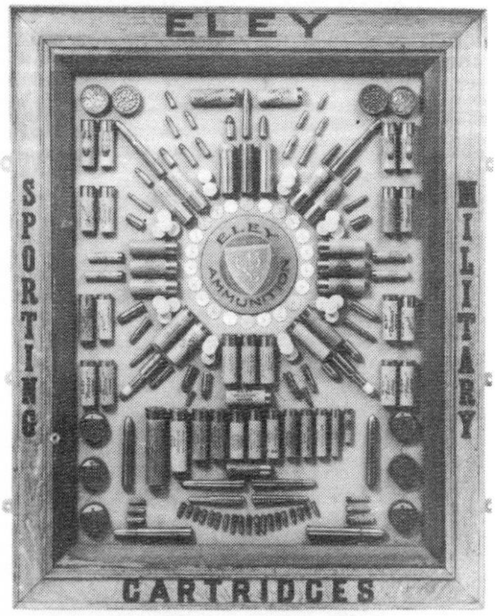

1

2

3

4

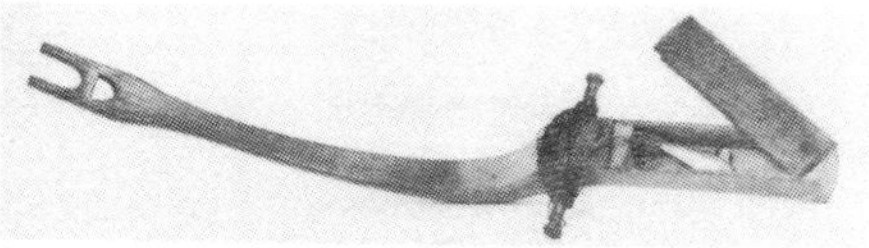
5

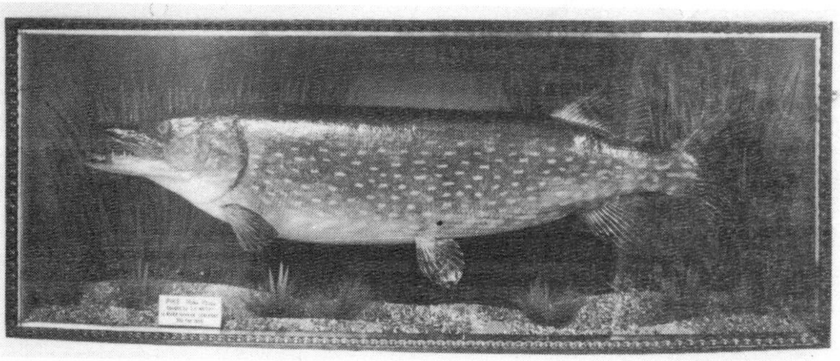
6

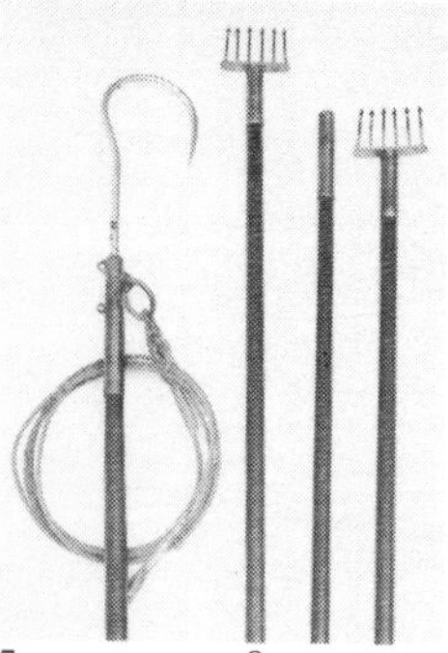
7 8

9

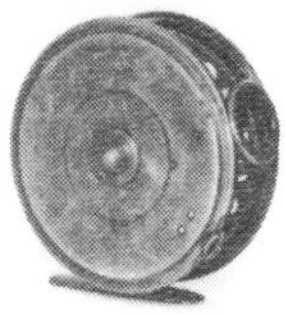
10

11

1
Eley. A 'Sporting and Military Cartridge' display board, in glazed oak frame, 78.5 x 65cm (31 x 25½in), *Glen 25 Aug,* **£2,860 ($4,433)**

2
A decorative cartridge display board, symmetrically arranged, framed and glazed with W. Darlow label on back, 61 x 48cm (24 x 19in), *L 16 Dec,* **£990 ($1,416)**

3
R. Nicholson, Castleford. An Eley 'Sporting and Military Cartridge' display board, 80 x 65cm (31½ x 25½in), *L 16 Dec,* **£2,200 ($3,146)**

4
A Bogardus-type glass ball target launcher, c.1850, the pinewood base mounted with decoratively forged iron fittings, 68.5cm (27in) long, *S 14 Apr,* **£264 ($409)**

5
An ice fishing rig, the curved wooden shank with forked tip, hollowed butt with swivel lid and turned cross-pieces for line storage, 48cm (19in), *S 6 May,* **£176 ($280)**

6
A stuffed pike, the well coloured 16lb 10oz, 37in fish caught by G.H. Wright in the River Severn, Coalport, 5th Feb. 1939, mounted against reeds and grasses in bow-fronted case with gilt and beaded edges, 112cm (44in) long, *S 6 May,* **£253 ($402)**

7
Hardy's. A big game gaff, the crook-shaped head mounted in quick-detachable socket with steel hawser and swivel, mounted on 96in dark wood shaft with brass ends and centre joint, *S 6 May,* **£104 ($166)**

8
Hardy's. Two eeling forks, nos. 3 and 4, each with three-piece greenheart shafts with bronzed brass screw-socket ferrules, in a mahogany rod box, each approx. 376cm (12ft 4in), *S 6 May,* **£231 ($367)**

9
A variation 'perfect' fly reel, the plate with oval logo and rod-in-hand mark, ivorine handle, regulator with brass guard, surface with light overall pitting, *S 6 May,* **£638 ($1,014)**

10
A 1911 model 'St. George' fly reel, unnamed and without patent marks, with filed toe, re-bronzed or replaced, *S 6 May,* **£396 ($630)**

11
A 3½-inch special 'perfect' fly reel, one bronzed roller pillar, ivorine handle on raised front plate, retaining most leaded and bright finish, in leather case, *S 6 May,* **£374 ($595)**

Hobbies and Pastimes

1
A mahogany, rosewood and parquetry 'campaign' chess table, late 19th century, 75cm (29½in), sold with a Staunton chess set *(part illustrated)*, by J. Jaques & Son, *S 16 Sept,*
£286 ($400)

2
An Indian ivory chess set, *(part illustrated)*, natural and brown-stained, slight damage, the kings 11cm (4¼in), *S 16 Sept,*
£330 ($462)

3
The Jaques & Son Ltd. 'In Statu Quo' chessboard and set, the pieces ivory and red-stained, in original leather case with *Jaques* brass label, *S 16 Sept,*
£209 ($293)

4
An ivory chess set, Western European, 19th century, the king and queen carved as portraits, the pieces stained green on one side and black on the other, largest 7cm (2¾in), *L 20 May,*
£275 ($440)

5
A coromandel and brass-bound games compendium, English, c.1870, containing ivory chess pieces, draughts, dominoes, accessories, cards and totopoly, 32cm (12½in) wide, *S 22 Apr,*
£715 ($1,122)

6
A Chinese ivory chess set, late 19th century, with rooks as castellated elephants and pawns as infantry, largest piece 13cm (5¼in), in a lacquered box with backgammon board within and chess squares on the exterior, *L 23 Sept,*
£385 ($539)

7
A games compendium, late 19th century, the oak case containing a set of Staunton bone chess pieces and various other games, 34cm (13½in) wide, *L 14 July,*
£242 ($378)

8
An Asprey & Son coromandel games compendium, English, c.1900, containing a Staunton pattern ivory chess set and various other games, 33cm (13in) wide, *L 14 July,*
£374 ($583)

9
An Asprey galuchat and ivory games set, English, 1930s, comprising a box covered in sharkskin edged with ivory, original playing cards and bridge scoring pads, and a tray of counters, box 23cm (9in) wide, *L 16 May,*
£858 ($1,364)

1 2 3

4

5

6

7

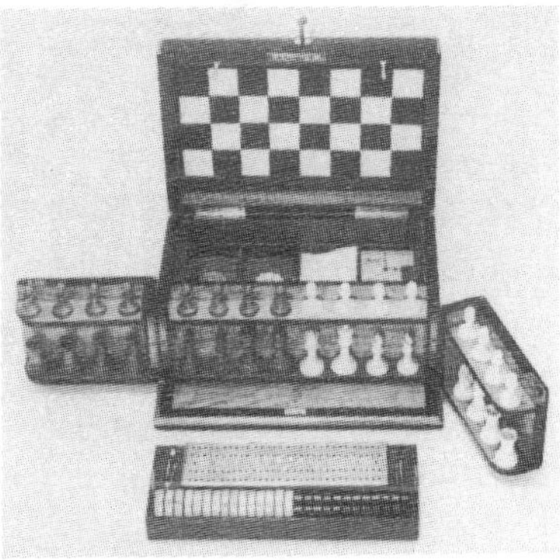

8

9

1

2

3

4

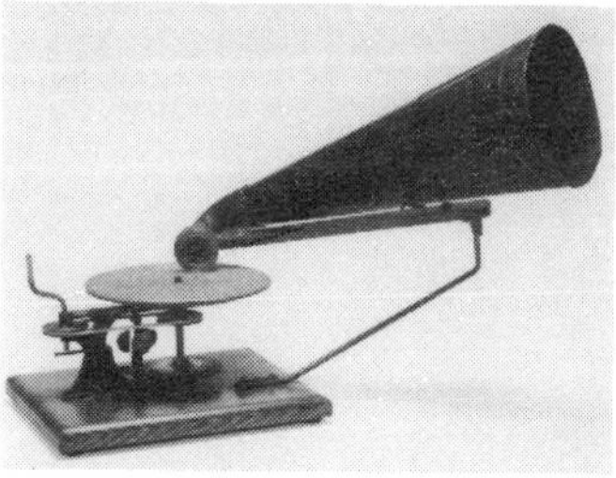
5

6

7

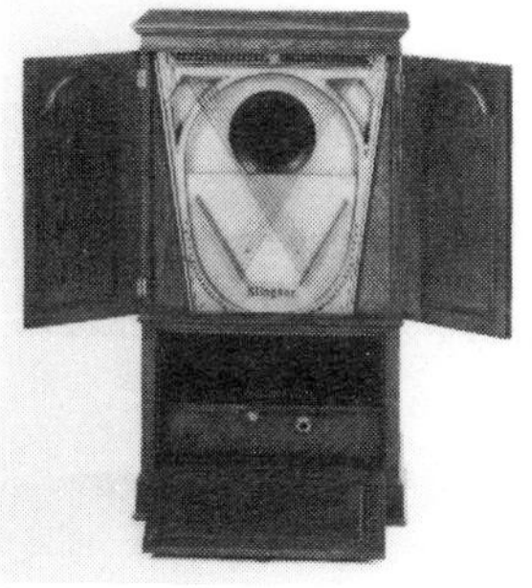
8

9

10

11

12

13

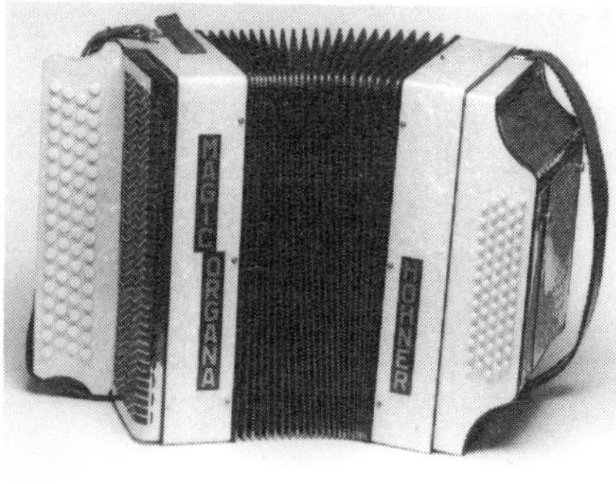

14

15

1
A Klingsor gramophone, German, c.1910, with 10-inch turntable, winding handle and speed control, 89cm (35in) high, *L 20 May,*
£550 ($880)

2
An Edison diamond disc phonograph, American, c.1920, with 12-inch turntable, contained in mahogany case, together with a collection of discs, 114cm (45in) high, *L 20 May,*
£308 ($493)

3
An Aeolian vocalion cabinet gramophone, 1930s, with 12-inch turntable, *volunome graduola* adjustments, gold painted oriental fretwork, the body lacquered red, gold and black, 122cm (48in) high, *C 18 Mar,*
£308 ($471)

4
A Gramophone and Typewriter Co. Monarch Junior gramophone, c.1902, with 10-inch turntable, tapering brass horn, oak case, containing a selection of records, together with an Amplion Loudspeaker, 81cm (32in) high, *C 12 Nov,*
£506 ($724)

5
A Gramophone Company hand-cranked gramophone, English, c.1900, with 7-inch turntable, black painted metal horn, oak base, trade transfer, *L 5 Feb,*
£1,100 ($1,584)

6
An Edison 'Red' gem, American, c.1909, model D, bentwood case, with collection of approximately 50 cylinders, *L 5 Feb,*
£484 ($697)

7
An E.M.G. Mark XB horn gramophone, English, c.1935, converted to electric power, papier-mâché horn, together with a number of accessories, *L 22 Sept,*
£715 ($1,001)

8
A Klingsor gramophon
German, c.1912, front opening to horn aperture with piano wire grill, 109cm (43in), *L 22 Sept,*
£715 ($1,001)

9
An Operaphone gramophone, English, 1920s, contained in miniature mahogany piano case, 56cm (22in) wide, *L 22 Sep*
£880 ($1,232)

10
An Alexander Debain antiphonel mechanical piano, French, mid 19th century, 129.5cm (51in) wide, *NY 16 Dec,*
$5,500 (£3,846)

11
An H.M.V. Monarch gramophone, English, c.1905, laminated oak horn, applied with trade transfer, *L 20 May,*
£880 ($1,408)

12
A Pathé gramophone, French, c.1910, bearing Pathé Disc thrower transfer, enamelled green flower petal horn, together with 26 discs, *L 5 Feb,*
£462 ($665)

13
A National musical cabinetto organette, English, late 19th century, in gilt stencilled wooden case, Hermann Loog retailer's label, 45cm (17½in) wide, *C 4 June,*
£418 ($648)

14
A Hohner 44-key 'Magic Organa' automatic accor- dion, probably German, 1920s, complete with foot pump, paper rolls, *L 20 May,*
£2,970 ($4,752)

15
An Ariston organette, German, late 19th century, 19-key movement, in ebonised case, together with floor support and six cardboard discs, 35cm (14in) wide, *L 22 Sept,*
£418 ($585)

1
A portable dulcimer, English, mid 19th century, with 32cm pinned wooden barrel operating 24 hammers, with fruitwood inlay, restored, 95cm (37½in) high, *L 20 May,* **£880 ($1,408)**

2
A chamber barrel organ, English, early 19th century, 14-key movement, playing from 35cm pinned wooden barrel ten popular airs, 160cm (63in) high, *L 22 Sept,* **£748 ($1,047)**

3
A 22½-inch polyphon bell box, German, late 19th century, the periphery drive upright movement playing on two combs and sixteen saucer bells, coin-operated motor, together with six metal discs, 147cm (58in) high, *L 20 May,* **£6,380 ($10,208)**

4
A 13½-inch symphonion longcase clock, German, c.1900, centre drive movement with *Sublime Harmonie* comb arrangement, together with eight metal discs, 125cm (49in), *L 5 Feb,* **£3,520 ($5,069)**

5
A 19½-inch polyphon disc musical box, German, c.1900, periphery driven movement playing on two combs, the base with coin drawer, together with 47 discs, 220cm (7ft 3in) high, *L 22 Sept,* **£2,200 ($3,080)**

6
A 19½-inch polyphon autochange disc musical box on stand, German, c.1900, periphery drive playing on two combs, together with 60 discs, 229cm (7ft 6in) high, *L 22 Sept,* **£12,100 ($16,940)**

7
A Lochmann 24¾-inch disc musical box on stand, German, c.1905, coin-operated with peripheral driven movement, with trade motifs, together with eight discs, 233.5cm (7ft 8in) high, *NY 16 Dec,* **$7,425 (£5,192)**

8
A symphonion 12-inch disc musical box, German, c.1900, centre driven movement, with ten discs, 48cm (19in) wide, *NY 28 June,* **$1,210 (£791)**

9
A 27-inch Regina Sublima disc musical box, American, c.1900, periphery driven disc playing on two combs, together with 28 metal discs, 86cm (34in) wide, *L 22 Sept,* **£5,500 ($7,700)**

10
A 4½-inch symphonion disc mantel clock, German, c.1905, centre drive movement playing on single comb, 44cm (17¼in) high, *L 5 Feb,* **£880 ($1,267)**

1

2

3

4

5

6

7

8

9

10

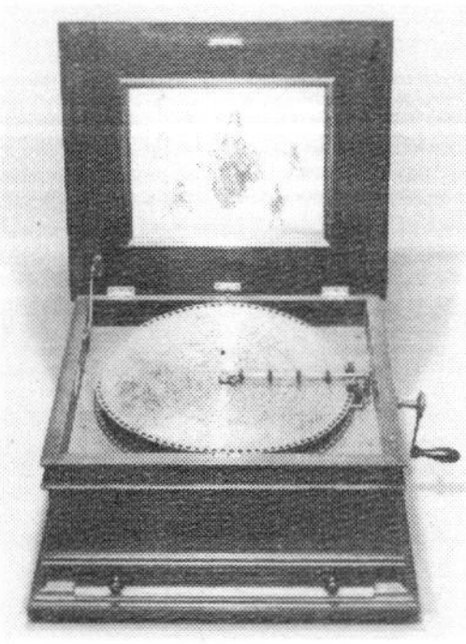
1

2

3

4

5

6

7

8

9

10

11

12

1
A Regina 15-inch disc musical box, American, c.1895, peripheral driven movement with a single comb, with 54 metal discs, 53cm (21in) wide, *NY 16 Dec,*
$1,980 (£1,385)

2
A 12-inch Mira disc musical box, Swiss, c.1905, centre drive with top wind motor and single comb, with trade transfer, together with 13 discs, 42cm (16½in) wide, *L 20 May,*
£462 ($739)

3
A 9-inch Kalliope disc musical box, German, c.1900, single comb with centre drive, with 16 metal discs, 29cm (11½in) wide, *C 4 June,*
£330 ($512)

4
A 15½-inch polyphon disc musical box, German, c.1900, the table model with periphery drive and single comb, together with 67 discs, 53cm (21in) wide, *L 22 Sept,*
£1,650 ($2,310)

5
A Regina 'Sublima'-style 25 20-inch disc musical box, American, c.1900, coin operated with peripheral drive movement, double comb, with eleven discs, 118cm (70in) high, *NY 28 June,*
$6,600 (£4,314)

6
A polyphon 19-inch coin-operated disc musical box, German c.1900, peripheral driven movement with double combs, with ten discs, 96.5cm (38in) high, *NY 28 June,*
$1,760 (£1,150)

7
A mandolin cylinder musical box, Swiss, c.1870, 33cm cylinder playing eight popular airs, rosewood case inlaid with tulipwood banding, 58.5cm (23in) wide, *L 20 May,*
£495 ($792)

8
A buffet-style sublime harmony musical box, Swiss, late 19th century, with 28cm cylinder playing eight airs, on two combs, top mounted with engraved plaque dated 1889, 54cm (21in) wide, *L 22 Sept,*
£1,430 ($2,002)

9
An orchestral cylinder musical box, Swiss, late 19th century, 33cm cylinder playing twelve airs, accompanied by five saucer bells with coloured butterfly strikers, snare drum and castanets, 66cm (26in) wide, *L 5 Feb,*
£1,320 ($1,901)

10
A Charles Paillard grand format mandolin interchangeable cylinder musical box, Swiss, c.1880, each of the five 47cm cylinders playing six airs, sides with ornate cast gilt metal handles, 107 x 165 x 74cm (42 x 65 x 29in), *L 20 May,*
£4,180 ($6,688)

11
A Nicole Frères piano forte overture cylinder musical box, Swiss, c.1870, 33cm cylinder playing four overtures, walnut veneered case, inlaid with boxwood and coloured enamels, 60cm (23in) wide, *L 22 Sept,*
£5,280 ($7,392)

12
A Nicole Frères overture interchangeable musical box, Swiss, late 19th century, each of the twelve 41cm cylinders playing 48 overtures, stamped *Nicole Frères, Geneve,* case inlaid with mother-of-pearl flowers, 117cm (46in) wide, *NY 28 June,*
$13,200 (£8,627)

Amusement Machines

ALISON KURKE

The auction market for amusement devices has been growing steadily over the past few years both in the United States and in Europe. The first serious auction in England was held by Sotheby's in 1975. The machines have proved to have an international appeal which defies even the physical limitations of the size and weight of the objects. In general terms, virtually any amusement device made between 1890 and 1950 will find a ready market, though prices will vary widely within these chronological limits.

Many of the machines purchased at auction are destined for private collections, deluxe games rooms, museums devoted to the history of the beloved traditional pier and to modern theme parks displaying vintage machines beside their modern equivalents.

It is interesting to note that until the late 1970s in the United States it was illegal to own, sell or buy amusement machines or to transport them across State lines. There is much to be said for the stimulating effect such prohibition had on early trading and illicit collecting. Despite the fact that the machines are obviously collected for historical and mechanical interest rather than as gambling devices, confiscation often resulted in their destruction, further reducing the already limited number of machines to have survived. Companies also had a policy of destroying or remodelling outdated machines. Both juke boxes and amusement

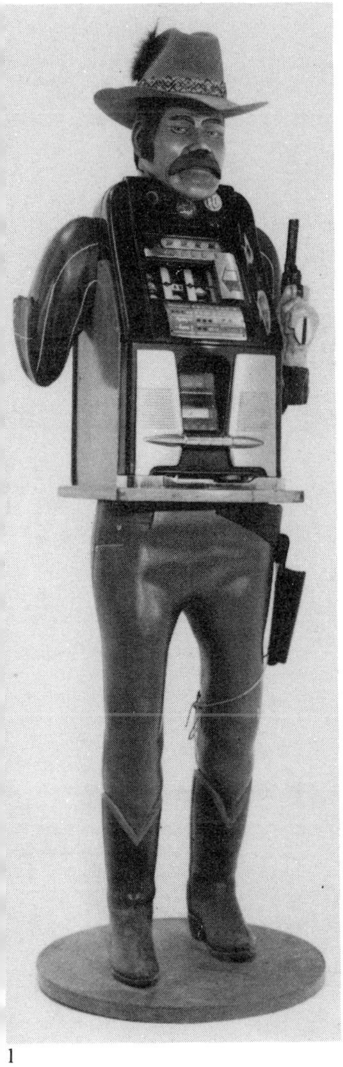

1

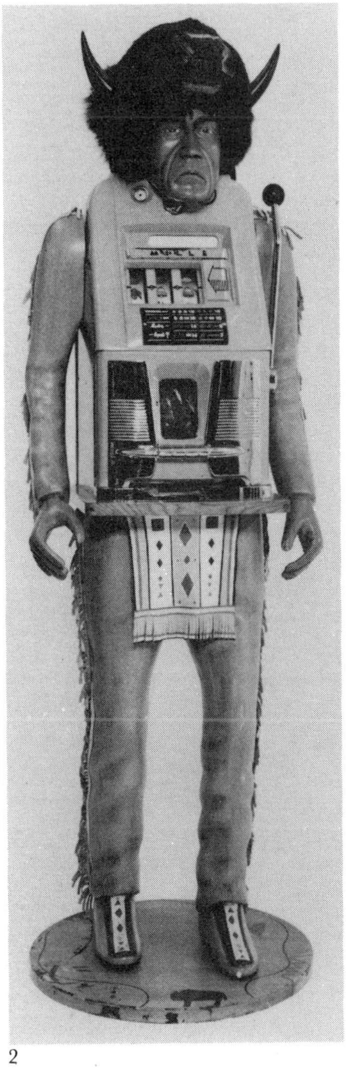

2

3

4

1
A Mills 'Cowboy' fruit machine, the figure lifesize with painted wooden head, 183cm (72in), *C 4 June,*
£1,760 ($2,728)

2
A Mills three-reel fruit machine, modern, the figure made of wood, 183cm (72in), *C 12 Nov,*
£2,200 ($3,146)

3
A Jennings counter top 'Little Duke' amusement machine, c.1932, decoratively cast front with red, yellow and green highlights, 58cm (23in), *C 4 June,*
£825 ($1,278)

4
A mutoscope 'Lady Windermere's Fan' by International Mutoscope Reel Co., 188cm (74in), *C 4 June,*
£506 ($784)

machines attract fanatical collectors now for much the same reasons that contemporary players were attracted to them. For auction purposes collectors are seeking good, early, rare and well-preserved machines.

The majority of the early machines and those of the 1920s and 1930s are undeniably decorative objects in their own right. In the arcades and piers decoratively cast metal fronts, full-sized cowboys, Indians, pirates (figs 1 & 2) and automated scenes jostled for the attention and the limited coins of prospective players. The often magnetic visual appeal of a gaming machine was coupled with the charm or novelty of the mechanism which provided entertainment and the temptation of a possible reward for a small outlay.

Machines such as the Jennings 'Little Duke' (fig.3) was considered an inexpensive machine at the time it was produced in 1932, but its unusual use of spinning wheels in place of the standard reels and its stunningly cast front have made it a highly desirable item today. Early and large floorstanding wheel of fortune machines (now often referred to generically as 'Cailles' after the most prolific manufacturer of the type) rarely appear; they change hands for thousands of dollars among devotees and seldom reach the auction market. Although these early beauties are universally covetted by collectors, they are rare finds and out of the reach of the collector of modest means.

Perennial and more affordable favourites at auction are the mutoscopes or peep shows, which allow the viewer to see a private moving picture show (figs 4-6). These machines originated in the United States in the 1890s and are most individual's idea of what an amusement machine should be. The view delivered is hardly ever as titillating as the title flashes promise, but the cases are more decorative than the stereoscopic views of Victorian times, from which the form developed. Working models or automated pieces had their origins in the expensive clockwork automata which enlivened the parlours of the well-to-do (see page 555). In England, Dennison, Bolland and Ahrens were mesmerising the public with moving scenes of executions, haunted houses, Egyptian tombs, and torture, from the 1890s through to the 1930s. Fortune telling machines in various forms, either dispensing cards or revealing the future through a crystal ball, are also popular now (fig.8).

5

6

5
A mutoscope, American, c.1910, entitled 'The Naked Truth', sold with one reel, 188cm (74in), *L 18 June,*
£792 ($1,251)

6
A 'What the Butler Saw' mutoscope, in metallic blue repainted octagonal cast drum body, side door replaced, 109cm (43in), *C 12 Nov,*
£385 ($550)

7

7
A 'Secrets of Egypt' working model, the scen of the inside of an ancient Egyptian tomb, 185cm (73in), *C 12 Nov,*
£605 ($865)

8
A 'Chinese Crystal Gaze amusement machine, c.1935, with the Chinese characters for Health, Happiness and Love , silv painted cast Buddah at to beckons player to insert 1(to look at his crystal ball, paintwork renewed, 146cn (57½in), *C 18 Mar,*
£440 ($673)

9
A Caille 'Ben Hur' counter top gaming machine, c.1920, in oak case, 58cm (22½in), *C 4 June,*
£396 ($614)

10
A cast-iron 'La Comete' Caille-type trade stimulator, c.1910, repainted blue, gold and orange, 53cm (21in), *C 18 Mar,*
£660 ($1,010)

11
A Jennings 'Peacock' fru machine, c.1933, with thre reels, cast case painted yellow, blue and red, 69cm (27in), *C 18 Mar,*
£440 ($673)

Fruit machines, or one-armed bandits, have been in roduction in the United States since the turn of the century and ne American firms of Mills Novelty, Jennings, Caille and Pace ave been responsible for issuing myriad forms of the familiar ype with refinements in payout, mechanisms, front decoration nd amount of skill required for a win. Prices for fruit machines oday vary widely, as some models have rarity value which makes nem desirable, or simply an unflagging visual appeal (figs 9-15).

Laws in England made the manufacture of gambling machines legal until 1960 so American models were imported and either isguised or adapted into legally acceptable forms. Trade timulators, which paid the winner in sweets or tokens, and games f skill, were however considered innocent fun. It has always been he case that gambling machines are more lucrative for manufacurers than skill games, and accounts for their prevalence on the narket in all forms.

Games with a sporting theme, especially football and golf, ould accommodate two or more players and have retained their ppeal to modern collectors; though the pace of such games of kill cannot match that of computer-aided models, the sporting theme guarantees collectability (fig.16).

British and European manufacturers excelled in other fields before the legalisation of gambling machine production, most notably in ingenious wall-mounted machines which are an almost exclusively European form (figs 17-18, 21-22). The sturdy and reliable machines invented by William Bryan of Derby, for example, are still affordable for the collector of limited means. Bryan's catalogue included more than thirty models, all of which are now finding willing purchasers in Europe (fig.20).

Juke boxes are the direct descendants of coin-operated phonographs and disc musical boxes which once graced public houses and bars, and their present market value has surpassed all but the grandest examples of these two earlier forms. Prospective purchasers fall victim to the sensuous, gaudy, sentimental and glowing charms of the juke boxes produced by the Wurlitzer, Seeburg, Rockola, AMI and Mills companies in the 1930s and 1940s — the golden age of the juke box. Fierce rivalry amongst these companies resulted in the production of the extraordinary constructions in moulded and marbled plastic, incandescent tubes and mirrors, which now fetch substantial sums at auction.

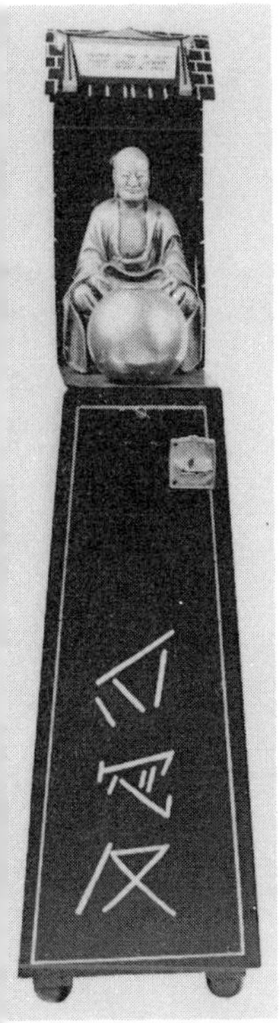
8

9

10

11

12

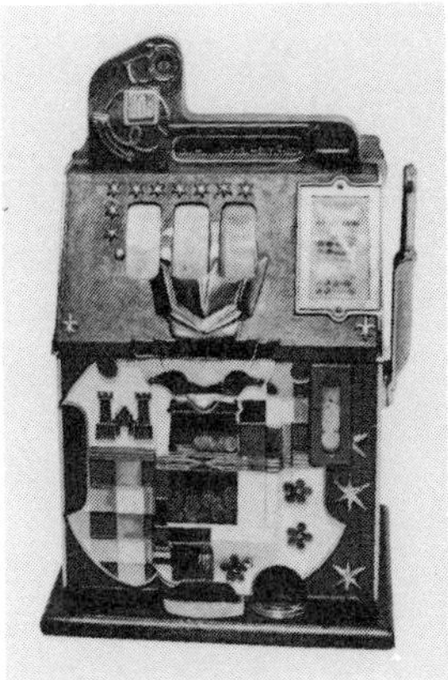
13

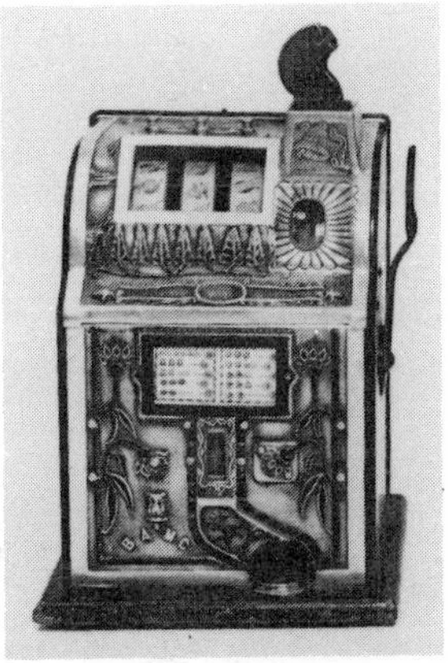
14

15

16

12
A Caille four-reel fruit machine, double jackpots, in wood and metal case, 62cm (24½in), *C 18 Mar,* **£880 ($1,346)**

13
A Mills Mystery Bell Castle Front three-reel fruit machine, early 1930s, restored, 86cm (34in), *C 12 Nov,* **£682 ($975)**

14
A Mills Poinsettia three-reel gaming machine, c.1928, restored, 66cm (26in), *C 4 June,* **£352 ($546)**

15
A Mills 'Extraordinary' Century Console amusement machine, c.1938, in deco-style metal case within an oak case, 153cm (60in), *C 4 June,* **£616 ($955)**

16
A Football penny-in-the-slot amusement game, c.1950, electrically powered, contains 22 articulated players in knitted jerseys, restored, 157cm (62in), *C 18 Mar,* **£528 ($808)**

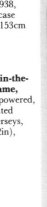

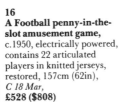

Although Wurlitzer, in its most productive year (1938) sold 45,000 machines, old models and unfashionably styled machines were unceremoniously scrapped on a regular basis, so few of these striking machines have survived. Even juke boxes in less than perfect condition are irresistible to serious collectors eager to renovate them (figs 23-27).

While it is true that any machine in good original working order has added appeal to a collector, familiarity with the mechanics of the game motivates many purchasers to restore them to their former glory inside and out. Condition is always a determining factor in the auction price achieved. Often in the United States a machine in superb restored condition can fetch a price well in excess of the same machine in its original though somewhat time-served state.

There may be some scepticism in more conservative circles that amusement devices have the intrinsic value of some objects traditionally bought and sold at auction, but as the value of these items continues to increase, their presence as a valid collecting field cannot be denied. For the true enthusiast, the choice between the older machine and a computer-generated or operated game is simple. The modern game lacks the element of cajoling the player into the often false belief that he has some chance of victory, and rewards only superior co-ordination. There is no way to deny that high fidelity sound is not the preoccupation of the keen juke box collector, but these classic machines succeed in conjuring up the simple delights of the time which created them. No doubt in the distant future a market for vintage computer-aided amusement games will develop.

Further reading:
Ken Rubin, *Drop Coin Here*, 1978
Jerry Ayliffe, *Juke Boxes and Slot Machines*, 1985
Vincent Lynch and Bill Henkin, *Jukeboxes, The Golden Age*, 1981

17

18

19

20

21

22

17
A Domino wall-mounted gambling machine, German, c.1920, bartender shakes the dice, winning numbers cause drinkers to lift glass, 63cm (25in), *C 12 Nov,*
£836 ($1,195)

18
A Bussoz 'The Clown' amusement machine, French, c.1920, player attempts to catch a ball in the clown's hat, 61cm (24in), *C 4 June,*
£396 ($614)

19
An Olwin 'Treble Pools' wall-mounted amusement machine, 63.5cm (25in), *C 12 Nov,*
£297 ($425)

20
A Bryan's clock amusement machine, pale oak case with cast metal title, 81cm (32in), *C 12 Nov,*
£286 ($409)

21
An early Fortuna Automatic Bagatelle wall gaming machine, 1890s, 89.5cm (35¼in), *C 12 Nov,*
£418 ($598)

22
The 'Wizard' wall-mounted skill game, back replaced, 70cm (27½in), *C 12 Nov,*
£308 ($440)

23
A Wurlitzer 700 78-RPM juke box, American, c.1940, with 24 disc selection, poor condition, 142cm (56in), *C 12 Nov,*
£1,595 ($2,281)

23

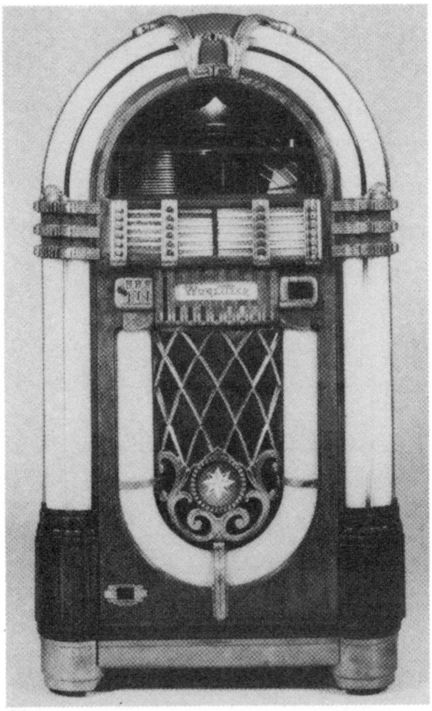

24

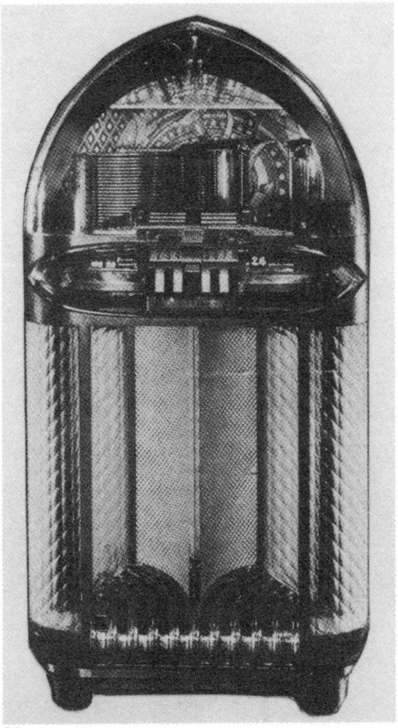

25

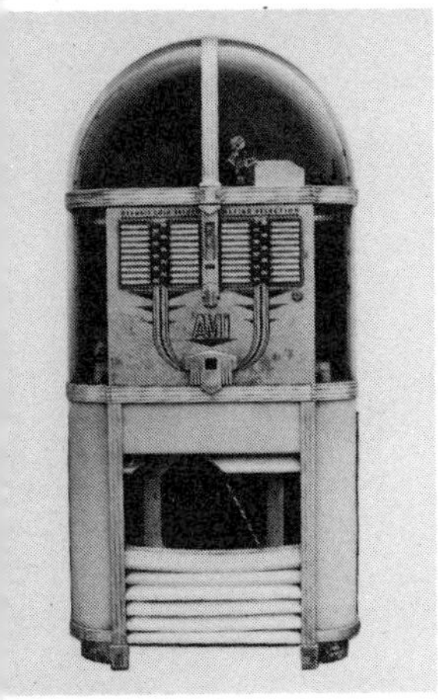

26

27

28

29

24
A Wurlitzer model 1015 juke box, c.1946, case restored, 152cm (60in), *NY 28 June,*
$10,450 (£6,830)

25
A Wurlitzer model 1100 juke box, c.1948, with 24 selections with 45-RPM records, case restored, 144.5cm (57in), *NY 28 June,*
$4,400 (£2,876)

26
An Ami model 500 juke box, 1960s, speaker damaged, 170cm (67in), *C 12 Nov,*
£440 ($629)

27
A Wurlitzer 'Lyric' juke box, with 56 selections, 127cm (50in), *C 12 Nov,*
£286 ($409)

28
An Ahren's Rifleman amusement skill machine, 1920s, 188cm (74in), *C 4 June,*
£792 ($1,228)

29
A Shefras 'Test Your Strength' machine, the oak body with hanging leather punch bag, 200cm (78½in), *C 4 June,*
£330 ($512)

1

2

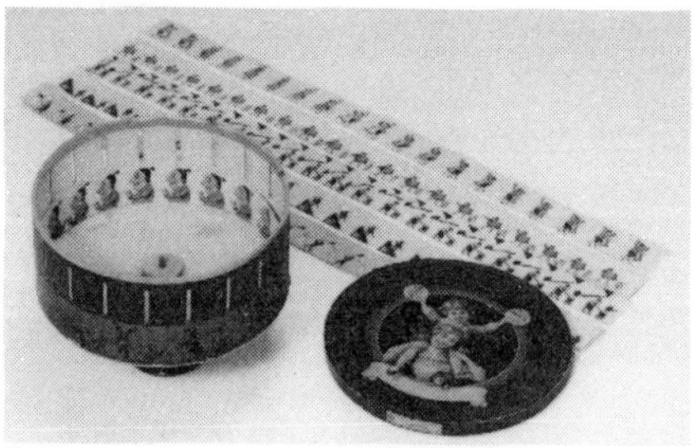
3

4 5

6

7

8

9

10

11

1
An Ives Patent 'Kromskop' viewer, c.1890, with hinged mahogany body and adjustable mirror, together with six boxes of Kromograms, 23cm (9in) long, *L 18 June,*
£550 ($869)

2
A Kinora viewer, English, c.1920, with japanned metal eyepiece and hand-cranked mechanism, oak platform and base, 28cm (11in) long, *L 28 Oct,*
£308 ($431)

3
A printed cardboard zoetrope, German, c.1905, with a coloured lithographic lid, pierced card drum, turned wood stand and six cartons, 28cm (11in) diam., *L 28 Oct,*
£572 ($801)

4
A Perkensson & Rayment optimus detective camera, c.1890, with brass-bound mahogany body, key lacking, *C 12 Nov,*
£330 ($472)

5
An Andre Debrie 'Le Parvo' motion picture camera, French, c.1920, model L, for 35mm film, wear to case, *C 12 Nov,*
£220 ($315)

6
A tripod camera, Compur, in a mahogany case, height overall 131cm (51½in), *A 29 Jan,*
Dfl 747 (£226; $333)

7
An Andre Debrie 25mm 'Parvo' tropical cine camera, French, c.1910, the teak body with brass fittings and with Tessar 50mm f/3.5 lens, in leather case with complete set of accessories, *L 18 June,*
£1,430 ($2,260)

8
A Marion & Co. Ltd. tropical reflex camera, early 20th century, the teak body with brass reinforcements, and with Dallmayer 6in f/3.5 lens, 9 x 13cm (3½ x 5in), *L 25 Feb,*
£660 ($990)

9
A tailboard portrait camera, late 19th century, the mahogany body with black canvas bellow, Hermagis lens on mahogany and cast-iron adjustable studio stand, lacking focusing screen, 24cm (9½in), *C 18 Mar,*
£308 ($471)

10
A Watson & Sons bi-unia lantern, English, late 19th century, the mahogany body with brass mounts, black painted metal chimney, 69cm (27in) high, *L 25 Feb,*
£495 ($742)

11
A Hirst & Wood patent 'The Natural Stereoscop viewer, English, c.1865, veneered in burr walnut and supported by adjustable column, some wear, 58cm (23in) high, sold with 42 stereographs of scenic and architectural content, *L 18 June,*
£7,700 ($12,166)

1
Julie Andrews, two-piece grey outfit from 'The Sound of Music', 20th Century Fox, 1965, costume designer Dorothy Jeakins, *NY 28 June,*
$2,530 (£1,654)

2
Mae West, evening gown from 'Myra Brecken-ridge', 20th Century Fox, 1970, costume designer Edith Head, label with star's name, *NY 28 June,*
$2,310 (£1,510)

3
Judy Garland, dancing costume from 'Easter Parade', MGM, 1948, costume designer Irene, *NY 28 June,*
$1,320 (£863)

4
Jane Russell, black leotard from 'The French Line', RKO, 1953, costume designer Jane Russell and Howard Greer, *NY 28 June,*
$3,190 (£2,085)

5
Betty Grable, dancing brief from 'Mother Wore Tights', 1947 sold with a dress from 'How to Marry a Millionaire', 1953, 20th Century Fox, *NY 28 June,*
$1,870 (£1,222)

6
Marilyn Monroe, silk pyjamas from 'The Seven Year Itch', 20th Century Fox, 1955, costume designer Travilla, *NY 28 June,*
$2,640 (£1,725)

7
Judy Garland, cotton blue and white dress from 'The Wizard of Oz', MGM, 1939, costume designer Adrian, *NY 28 June,*
$22,000 (£14,379)

8
Vivien Leigh, two-piece cotton day dress from 'Gone with the Wind', MGM, 1939, costume designer Walter Plunkett, labelled Scarlett, *NY 28 June,*
$16,500 (£10,784)

9
Marilyn Monroe, pink cotton dress from 'Niagara', 20th Century Fox, 1952, *NY 28 June,*
$2,860 (£1,869)

10
Burt Ward, Robin's costume from 'Batman', 20th Century Fox, 1966, *NY 16 Dec,*
$7,425 (£5,192)

11
Adam West, Batman's costume, 20th Century Fox, 1966, *NY 16 Dec,*
$8,525 (£5,962)

12
Robert Taylor, wool and chain mail costume from 'Ivanhoe', MGM, 1952, costume designer Roger Furse, *NY 16 Dec,*
$2,750 (£1,923)

1

2

3

4

5

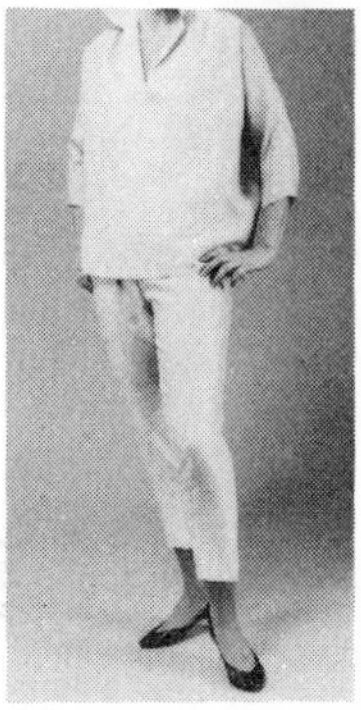
6

7

8

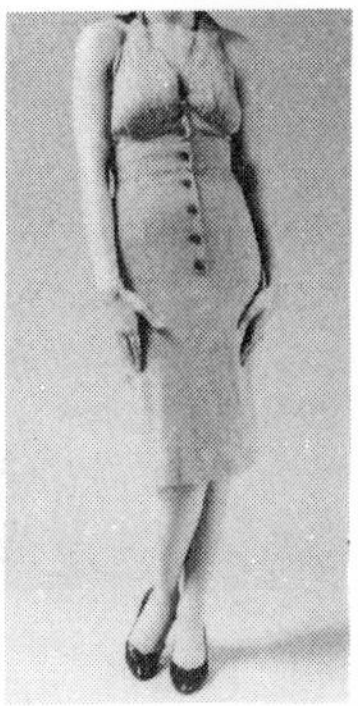
9

10 11

12

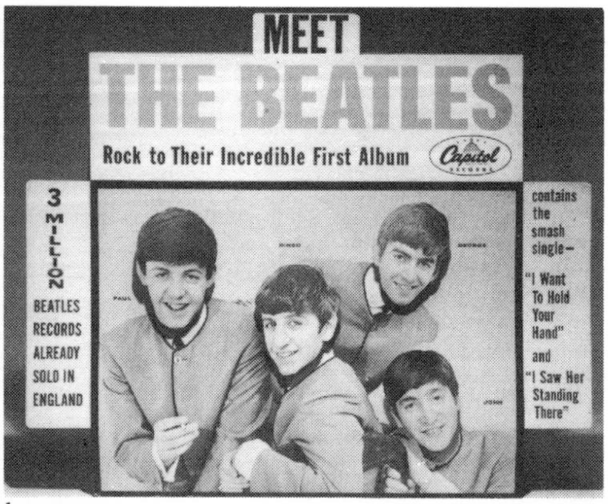

1

2

3

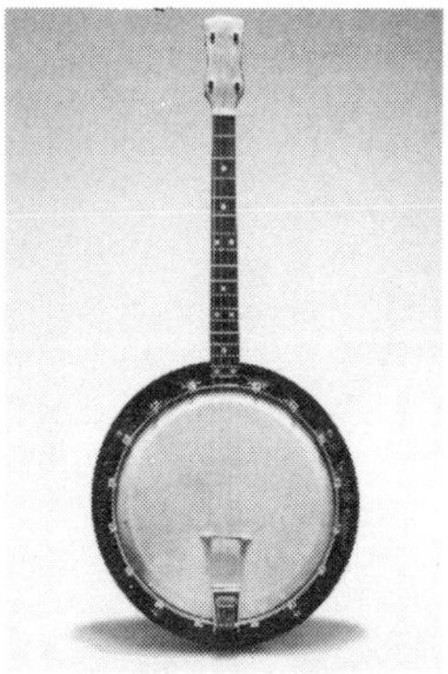

4

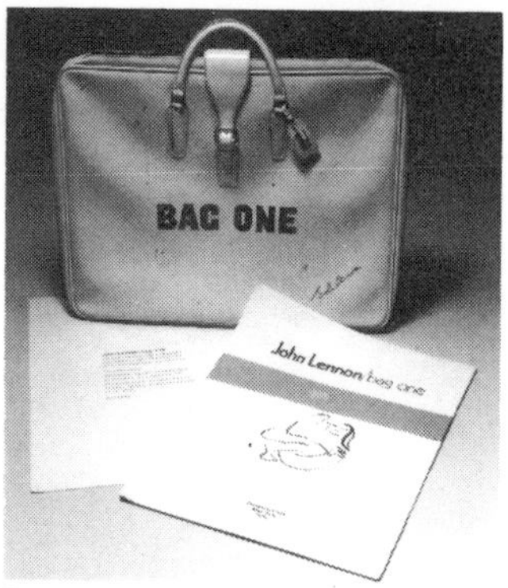

5

6

7

1
An animated 'Meet the Beatles' promotional display, Capital Records, 71cm (28in) wide, *NY 28 June,* **$2,200 (£1,438)**

2
Two printed cotton Beatles dresses, c.1964, sold with a Beatles elasticated garter and a brooch watch, *L 28 Aug,* **£990 ($1,535)**

3
An early Beatles concert handbill, for the Heswall Jazz Club, 1962, sold with a Daily Mirror headline poster for 'The Big Beat Craze' by Donald Zec, *L 28 Aug,* **£528 ($818)**

4
A George Harrison banjo, indistinctly marked on the headpiece, *NY 28 June,* **$2,420 (£1,582)**

5
A John Lennon 'Bag One', 1969, limited edition, artist proof numbered 26/300, fourteen narrative and erotic lithographs of the Ono-Lennon marriage, 76cm (30in), *NY 28 June,* **$7,700 (£5,033)**

6
Goldfinger's Rolls-Royce Phantom III from the film 'Goldfinger', 1937, custom body by Parker & Co Ltd., 7.4f litre engine, finished in yellow and black, *NY 28 June,* **$121,000 (£79,085)**

7
A Chad Valley Snow White and the Seven Dwarfs, English, c.1935, Snow White with her original paper label and with original 'Happy' box, *L 23 Sept,* **£385 ($539)**

\n acetate record of Cliff ₹ichard's first recording, .1958, inscribed *Cliff ₹ichard and The Drifters, ₹reathless/Lawdy Miss Glawdy* old with another Cliff ₹ichard record, *L 28 Aug,* **,1,155 ($1,790)**

:
\ poster for The Who at The Marquee', November .964, framed, slight tears, '8cm (30¾in), *L 28 Aug,* **,2,097 ($3,250)**

3rian Epstein's presen- ation 'Gold' album for 'A Iard Day's Night' by the 3eatles, 1964, framed, ›1cm (20in), *L 28 Aug,* **:5,500 ($8,525)**

\ 'Gold' record for 'A Iard Day's Night', RIAA :ertified album, framed, ›4.5cm (21½in), *VY 28 June,* **$8,800 (£5,752)**

An autographed 'Help!' ₹oyal world premiere programme, c.1965, signed on the back outside :over, 46cm (18¼in), *VY 28 June,* **$1,870 (£1,222)**

An original celluloid of ohn Lennon from the :artoon 'Yellow Submarine', mounted and glazed, 41cm (16in), *L 28 Aug,* **£385 ($597)**

7
A group of early editions of Mersey Beat and other pop magazines, *(part illus- trated),* dating from 1961, including the edition announcing 'Beatles Sign Recording Contract!', 21 items, *L 28 Aug,* **£385 ($597)**

8
Three early Beatles concert handbills, 1961, the largest 20.5cm (8in), *L 28 Aug,* **£418 ($648)**

9
An early photograph of John Lennon, George Harrison and Stuart Sutcliffe on a truck hood, by Astrid Kirchherr, signed by the photogra- pher, 60cm (23½in), *L 28 Aug,* **£572 ($887)**

10
A photographic portrait of John Lennon, by Astrid Kirchherr, signed by the photographer, mounted, 27cm (10¾in), *L 28 Aug,* **£462 ($716)**

11
A set of Beatles pro- motional nodding head dolls, 1964, Car Mascots Inc., with facsimile signatures, 38cm (15in), sold with another set, 20.5cm (8in), *NY 28 June,* **$3,300 (£2,157)**

12
A boxed set of 'Bobb'n Head Beatles', American, 1964, by Car Mascots Inc., in original cardboard box, 19cm (7½in), *L 28 Aug,* **$330 ($512)**

13
An Apple promotional wristwatch, inscribed in the back Old England, sold with a design of the Apple logo, *NY 28 June,* **$935 (£611)**

14
A group of Apple mer- chandise, dating from c.1968, comprising a wrist- watch designed by Richard Loftus, two money clips and Apple Records book matches, *L 28 Aug,* **£605 ($938)**

1

2

3

4

5

6

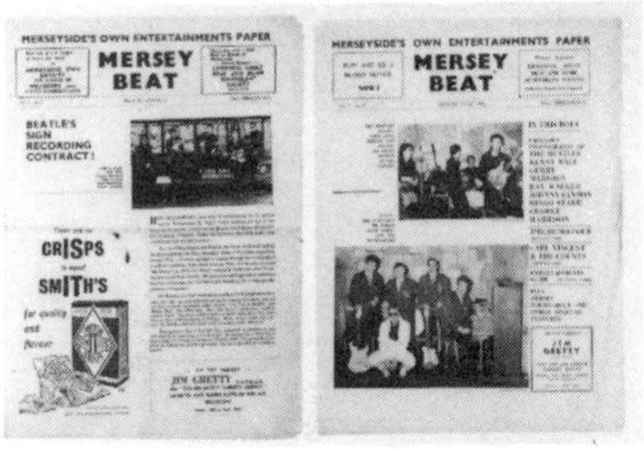

7

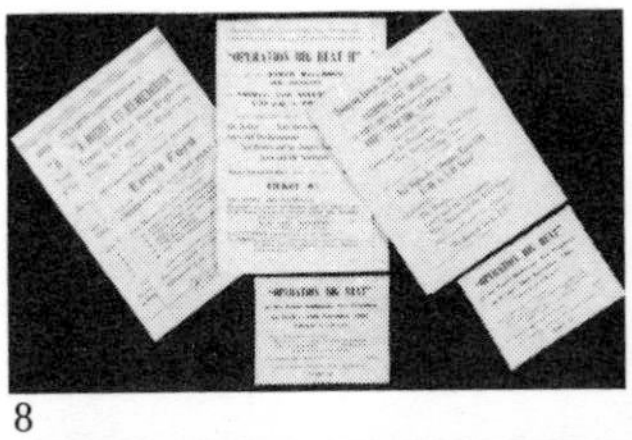
8

9

10

11

12

13

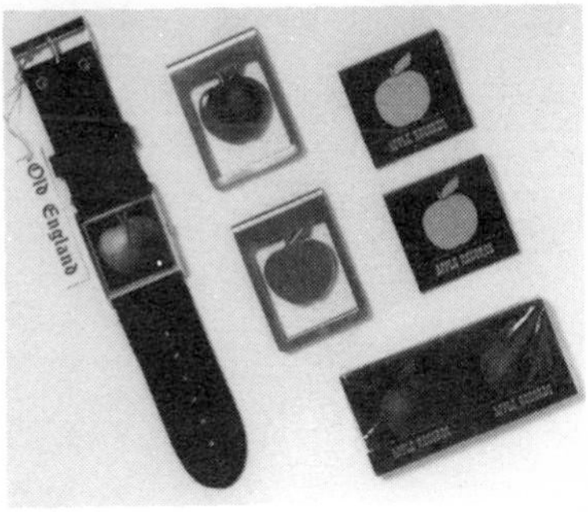

14

The Magic of Disney

DANA HAWKES

Ask any child to describe Dopey and he might say, 'big eared, with drooping clothes — cute, gentle, stumbling and tripping'. This image has little to do with the original Dopey in Grimm's fairytale, *Snow White*, written between 1812 and 1822. It is instead Walt Disney's unforgettable characterisation of Dopey in his most successful animated feature film, *Snow White and the Seven Dwarfs*, made in 1937, that has lived on in the imagination of children during the last fifty years.

Today there is an active market for Disneyana. Collectors are able to participate in this magical world through buying the celluloids from which the films were made. Other Disneyana which appears in the saleroom (see p.536, also vol.1 p.211 and vol.2 pp.324 & 560) is manufactured under licence and is not a direct product of the Disney Studio. Characters such as Mickey Mouse and Donald Duck became a multi-million dollar enterprise, with Walt Disney licences for chinaware, belts, Lionel electric toys, Ingersoll watches, and Dennison paper goods. However, it is on the creation of the film, through the medium of celluloid, that this article concentrates.

Walt Disney was born on 5 December 1901 in Chicago, Illinois, and grew up in Marceline, Missouri, on a 48-acre farm. After the war, in 1919, determined to pursue art as a career, he started working for Kansas City Film Ad, a company which made crude animated films for commercials in local movie theatres. Here he learned the basics of animated art and met Ib Iwerk, who eventually became one of his major animators and draftsmen. Before long, Disney and Iwerk started their own film company called Laugh-o-grams. The young and ambitious Disney started on a series of short cartoons of fairy tales, such as *Jack and the Beanstalk, Little Red Riding Hood,* and *Puss in Boots,* but soon realised that in order to succeed he would have to come up with an innovative idea. In 1923, Disney made *Alice's Wonderland,* where Alice, played by a real person, becomes part of the cartoon and finds herself involved with a variety of animals. By filming Alice separately against a white background and then combining this image with the animation, Disney created a new dimension in animated motion pictures. A series of Alice cartoons lasted for sixty episodes until, by 1927, the theme was exhausted.

After a series called *Oswald the Lucky Rabbit*, which failed because of legal problems, Disney was forced to look for a new concept.

1

2

3

4

5

1
A Walt Disney pencil and watercolour drawing of 'Snow White and the Seven Dwarfs', 1938, with studio signature Walt Disney, 30.5 × 37cm (12 × 14½in), *NY 16 Dec,*
$4,675 (£3,269)

2
A Walt Disney celluloid of Dopey from 'Snow White and the Seven Dwarfs', 1938, mounted with WDE copyright, 18 × 20cm, (7 × 8in), *L 23 Sept,*
£1,100 ($1,540)

3
A Walt Disney celluloid from 'Pinocchio', 1939, depicting Jiminy Cricket taking off his hat to Pinocchio, inscribed 'Hi Pinoki', 19 × 24cm (7½ × 9½in), *NY 28 June,*
$3,850 (£2,516)

4
A Walt Disney celluloid from 'Pinocchio', 1939, applied to an airbrushed background, Courvoisier Galleries label, 16 × 21.5cm (6¼ × 8½in), *NY 16 Dec,*
$4,675 (£3,269)

5
A Walt Disney watercolour background from 'Pinocchio', 1939, depicting Geppetto's workshop, 27.5 × 37cm (10¾ × 14½in), *NY 16 Dec,*
$18,700 (£13,077)

The collaborative efforts of Ib Iwerk and Walt Disney this time gave birth to a legendary figure: Mickey Mouse. Mickey's physical characteristics were based on Oswald's, using a series of circles for head, body and ears with tubular limbs. The secret of Mickey's success was that he was a recognisable character with a personality created by Walt Disney to which the audience could relate. It was always Walt Disney's philosophy that a cartoon character should think for itself.

On 23 October 1927 Warner Brothers released the sound movie *The Jazz Singer*, and Walt Disney determined to produce a talking cartoon with Mickey Mouse as the star. Just a year later, on 8 November 1928, *Steamboat Willie* was premiered at Manhattan's Colony Theater, the first animation film with music, sound effects and action all synchronised. The cartoon was not only a success, but also a major breakthrough for the animation industry. In 1929, Walt Disney recruited Carl Silling to compose music for his cartoons. These *Silly Symphonies*, as they were called, were highly successful between 1929 and 1935.

During these years there were several breakthroughs in the animation industry. In 1931, Webb Smith came up with the story board idea. Previously, several cartoons had been drawn on one sheet of paper annotated with notes. Now each drawing was on a separate sheet of paper and pinned to a board in sequential order, which made it much easier to see the plot and action at a glance. Then in 1932, Technicolor introduced a three-colour system (as opposed to a two-colour), making the colours more accurate. Walt Disney immediately put this to use in the cartoon *Flowers and Trees*. By 1933, Mickey Mouse and Donald Duck, a character drafted by Dick Lundy and Fred Spencer, had become as famous as Gary Cooper, Cary Grant and Clark Gable.

By 1935, Walt Disney decided to make an aggressive move and produce a full-length feature animated film that could compete with the live-action film. He chose the German fairy tale *Snow White and the Seven Dwarfs*. Three hundred newly-employed artists had to attend the Disney Art School for six to eight weeks to give them guidelines for drawing Mickey Mouse, Donald Duck and Goofy as training. Each animator was then given a character — just like casting parts for a live-action movie — and each dwarf's personality was painstakingly created through dozens of drawings. Disney established a bonus system whereby anyone inventing a gag would receive $5 and anyone submitting an idea to enhance the entire cartoon would get $100. A number of technical problems confronted Walt Disney and his staff. To produce the numerous scenes with the seven dwarfs and Snow White, the figures had to be drawn on a minute scale. This required creating a new field and readjusting all the cell boards, checking boards, painting boards and animation cameras. For the first time the artists had to animate a human being; live models were brought in for study in order to examine their movements. Depth and realism was another problem for animation: when a camera closes in on a close-up shot, there is no difference between the foreground and the background. To overcome this Disney created the multiplane camera. The animators would draw each sequence; the sketch would be traced onto the celluloid, hand painted and then sent to the camera department along with the backgrounds, which were painted in toned-down colours to give

6

7

8

6
A Walt Disney celluloid from 'Pinocchio', 1939, Courvoisier Galleries label, inscribed in pencil 'From Pinocchio', 19.5cm (7¾in) diam., *NY 28 June,*
$2,970 (£1,941)

7
A Walt Disney celluloid from 'Dumbo', 1941, *(illustrated)*, 18 × 21.5cm (7 × 8½in), sold with an original story sketch from 'Dumbo', 1941 depicting a group of elephants under a tent, *NY 16 Dec,*
$2,200 (£1,538)

9

10

them a sense of age and to set off the characters distinctly. Only a handful of backgrounds were needed for each scene, compared with the hundreds, if not thousands, of celluloids placed in front of them before the camera. It is these celluloids that appear in the salerooms today.

After more than five million drawings and sketches, *Snow White* premiered in 1937 at the Cathay Circle Theater in Hollywood, ultimately winning an Academy Award. This was only the beginning for Walt Disney, who went on to produce other feature films such as *Pinocchio* (1939), *Fantasia* (1940), *Dumbo* (1941), *Bambi* (1942), *Cinderella* (1950), *Peter Pan* (1953), and *Sleeping Beauty* (1959). By 1961, with the film *One Hundred and One Dalmations*, the studio used a Xerox camera to transfer the animators' drawings directly onto the celluloids, thus saving time and money.

At intervals since the late 1930s the Walt Disney Studio has put celluloids onto the market — initially to raise funds. Drawings and black-and-white celluloids from the late 1920s to the early 1930s have not come up for auction. The most famous scenes were selected for sale from the millions of drawings made. Most celluloids do not have their original watercolour backgrounds and are placed against an airbrushed or wooden background, the work of Courvoisier Galleries, who distributed celluloids for the Walt Disney Studio. The original watercolour backgrounds (against which, of course, many celluloids were placed), can fetch as much as $30,000 (£18,750). Although millions of drawings were made, most have been destroyed. Celluloid is a highly flammable material and many were simply thrown away. The condition of a celluloid is an important factor for determining value, because many have buckled or have suffered heavy paint loss. Celluloids from the early feature films such as *Snow White* (fig.2), *Pinocchio* (figs 3-6), *Dumbo* (figs 7 and 8), *and Brave Little Taylo* (fig.10) can fetch anywhere between $600 (£375) and $5,000 (£3,100), depending on the condition and the rarity of the frame from the film. In the last three years, the Walt Disney celluloids from these films have doubled in value and many new collectors have entered the market.

8
A Walt Disney celluloid from 'Dumbo', 1940, 17 x 23cm (6¾ x 9in), sold with a pastel drawing also from *Dumbo*, both stamped WDP, Courvoisier Galleries, *NY 16 Dec,*
$2,750 (£1,964)

9
A Walt Disney watercolour of Mickey Mouse from 'Fantasia', 1941, Walt Disney studio signature, 20 x 25.5cm (8 x 10in), *NY 16 Dec,*
$2,090 (£1,461)

10
A Walt Disney celluloid from 'Brave Little Taylor', 1938, stamped on lower left WDP, Courvoisier Galleries label, 16.5 × 18cm (6½ × 7in), *NY 28 June,*
$5,225 (£3,415)

Illustrations for figs 8-10 are on page 539.

Further reading:

Adrian Bailey, *Walt Disney's World of Fantasy*, 1984
Marcia Blitz, *Donald Duck,* 1979
John Culhane, *Walt Disney's Fantasia,* 1983
Christopher Finch, *The Art of Walt Disney from Mickey Mouse to the Magic Kingdom,* 1983
Leonard Maltin, *Of Mice and Magic, a History of American Animated Cartoons,* 1980

11
A Walt Disney celluloid from 'Der Fuehrer's Face, 1943, stamped WDP, 19 × 23cm (7½ × 9in), *NY 28 June,*
$2,090 (£1,366)

12
A Walt Disney celluloid from 'Little Hiawatha', 1937, Courvoisier Galleries label, 20.5cm (8in) sq., *NY 16 Dec,*
$1,100 (£769)

13
A Walt Disney celluloid from 'Peter and the Wolf', 1946, lower left signed by Walt Disney, stamped WDP, 19 × 23.5cm (7½ × 9½in), *NY 16 Dec,*
$1,210 (£846)

14
A Walt Disney celluloid from 'Wynken, Blynken and Nod', 1938, the wooden shoe sailboat passing starfish, 24 × 28cm (9½ × 11in), *NY 16 Dec,*
$5,500 (£3,846)

11

13

12

14

One card only illustrated from each set.

1
Wills Our Gallant Grenadiers, 1902, the complete set of 20 cards, *C 25 July,*
£187 ($294)

2
Wills Seaside Resorts, 1899, the complete set of 50 cards, *C 25 July,*
£165 ($259)

3
Wills Seaside Resorts, 1899, mixed backs, (50), *S 7 July,*
£132 ($214)

4
Footballers, two early sets by Wills, 1902, set of 66, and Churchman 1914, set of 50, *C 25 July,*
£143 ($225)

5
Gallaher's The Great War Series, 1915, first and second series, both complete, (100), *C 19 Nov,*
£121 ($169)

6
Wills Soldiers of the World, 1895, the complete set of 100 cards, *C 19 Nov,*
£242 ($339)

7
Marsuma Co. Famous Golfers and their strokes, 1914, the complete set of 50, *C 25 July,*
£209 ($328)

8
Player's Famous Authors and Poets, 1903, narrow card, complete set of 20, *C 25 July,*
£132 ($207)

9
Wills Vanity Fair, 1902, un-numbered, first and second series, (three sets, 150 cards), *C 25 July,*
£209 ($328)

10
Ogden's Advertising cards, early 20th century, 13 cards, sold with 12 similar cards, *C 25 July,*
£3,520 ($5,526)

11
Wills Sports of all Nations, 1901, mixed backs, (50), *S 7 July,*
£165 ($267)

12
Wills Double Meaning, 1898, 50 cards, *S 7 July,*
£132 ($214)

13
Taddy & Co. British Medals and Ribbons, 1912, 50 cards, *S 5 Mar,*
£165 ($247)

14
Taddy & Co. British Medals and Decorations, second series 1912, (50), *S 5 Mar,*
£165 ($247)

15
Taddy & Co. Orders of Chivalry, 1911, 25 cards, *S 5 Mar,*
£132 ($198)

16
Wills Cricketers, 1901, odds, 20 cards, *S 5 Mar,*
£187 ($280)

1

2

3

4

5

6

7

8

9

10

11

12

13

14

15

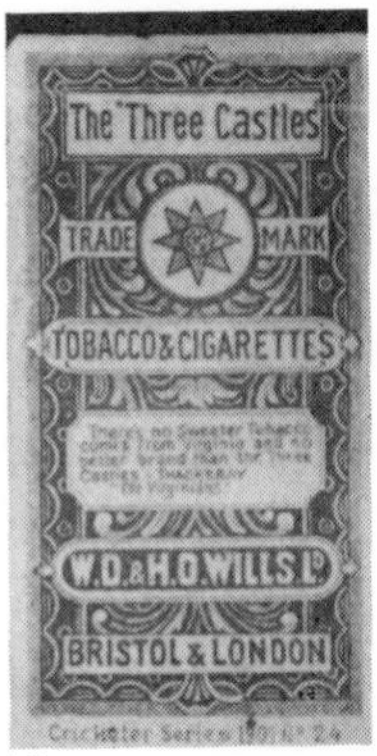

16

1

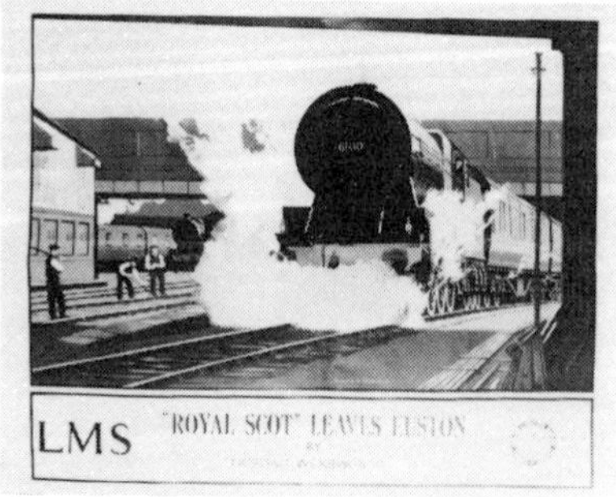

2

3

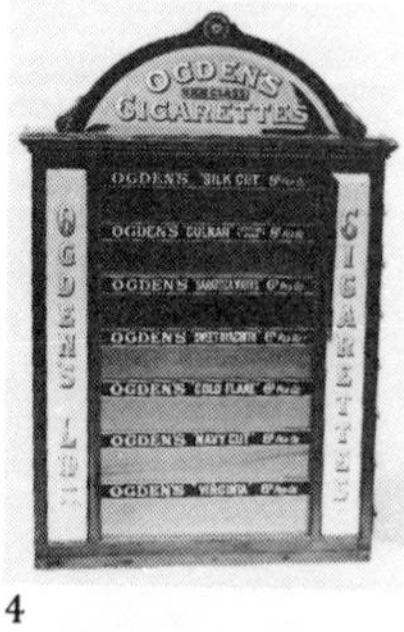

4

5

6

7

8

9

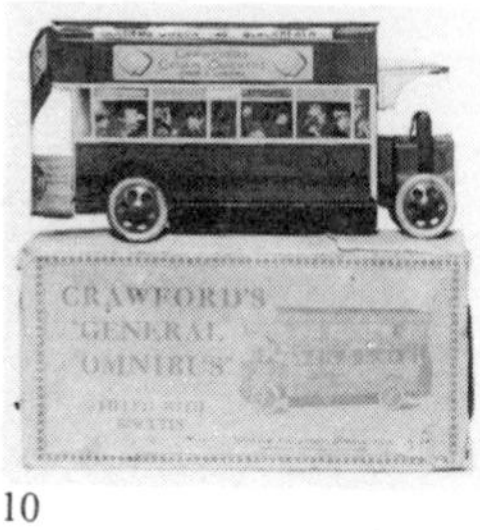

10

11

1
Norman Wilkinson. A colour lithographed poster, 'Salmon Fishing on the LMS', in white, brown, beige, green and blue, 126 x 120cm (49½ x 40in), sold with another by Norman Wilkinson, 'Royal Highlander Approaches Aberdeen', *C 30 Apr,*
£440 ($713)

2
Norman Wilkinson. A colour lithographed poster, 'LMS "Royal Scot" Leaves Euston', in red, grey, black and white, 127 x 102cm (50 x 40in), *C 30 Apr,*
£374 ($606)

3
A W. Crawford & Sons 'Meteor' racing car biscuit tin, English, 1920s, lithographed in scarlet and silver stripes, 46cm (18in) long, *L 23 Sept,*
£660 ($924)

4
An Ogden's cigarette display/dispenser, early 20th century, of stained oak, flanked by two mirrored panels and with arched mirror panel above, one side with seven drawers with brass handles, 96cm (58in) high, *C 18 Mar,*
£660 ($1,010)

5
A Jacob's biscuit display cabinet, early 20th century, of mahogany with black glass flash to top, four tilted bins, brass fittings and handles, 204cm (6ft 8½in) wide, *C 4 June,*
£352 ($546)

6
A Crawford's Atlantic Liner tinplate biscuit tin, English, c.1920, lithographed in red, black, yellow and cream, and named *Berengaria*, in original box, 38cm (15in), *L 20 May,*
£528 ($845)

7
A Huntley & Palmer 'Reading' steam launch biscuit tin, English, 1920s, the hull lithographed pink below cream, lacking flag, some rust, 43cm (17in) long, sold with a tinplate gunboat, *L 23 Sept,*
£220 ($308)

8
A Harper Automatics 'Day and Night' cigarette service machine, English, 1930s, 172cm (67¾in) high, *C 4 June,*
£187 ($290)

9
A pressed metal advertising sign, English, c.1905, 49 x 34cm (19½ x 13½in), *L 23 June,*
£264 ($412)

10
A Crawford's 'General Omnibus' biscuit tin, English, c.1920, displaying advertising for 'Bonnie Mary Shortbread' and 'Cream Crackers', the hinged lid lithographed with seats, 27cm (10½in), *L 5 Feb,*
£1,540 ($2,218)

11
A Carlton ware 'Toucan' lamp, 1950-55, modelled with a toucan standing beside a glass of Guinness, brightly coloured in orange, red and green and with advertising inscription, 24cm (9½in), *C 28 Jan,*
£198 ($291)

1
A lead cistern, English, dated *1687*, with panelled front and sides, 84cm (33in) high, *S 28 May,*
£4,620 ($7,300)

2
A lead cistern, the front and sides decorated with shaped panels centred with urns and flowers and dated *1766*, top removed, 157cm (62in), *S 28 May,*
£2,860 ($4,519)

3
A circular lead cistern, dated 1757 and cast with a galleon, 51cm (20in) diam., *C 8 Oct,*
£396 ($554)

4
A gardener's elm cart, English, early 19th century, 102cm (40in) long, *L 22 July,*
£682 ($1,071)

5
A pair of cast-iron plant stands, *(one illustrated),* English, c.1860, each with five circular dishes on three tiers, 112cm (44in), *S 28 May,*
£1,320 ($2,086)

6
A cast-iron plant stand, c.1870, with eleven moveable plant holders, 130cm (51in) high, *NY 26 Apr,*
$1,980 (£1,286)

7
A Coalbrookdale cast-iron garden seat, c.1870, fern and blackberry pattern, replaced slatted seat, 150cm (59in) wide, *C 16 Jan,*
£528 ($792)

8
A pair of Coalbrookdale cast-iron garden chairs, *(one illustrated),* c.1870, fern and blackberry pattern, slatted seats, 66cm (26in) wide, *S 28 May,*
£1,925 ($3,040)

9
A pair of cast-iron garden chairs, *(one illustrated),* c.1860, the seats and backs pierced with classical maidens, flowers and crestings, *S 28 May,*
£1,980 ($3,128)

10
A Coalbrookdale cast-iron garden seat, designed by Christopher Dresser, 1881, the back cast with typically formalised foliate design, cast mark and PODR mark, 143cm (56¼in) wide, *L 19 Dec,*
£2,970 ($4,158)

11
A wrought-iron garden seat, early 19th century, with segmented back and slatted seat, 112cm (44in) wide, *S 28 May,*
£1,320 ($2,086)

12
A wrought-iron garden seat, early 19th century, of semi-circular form, the raised back with reeded cross supports, 140cm (55in) wide, *S 28 May,*
£1,870 ($2,955)

13
A wrought-iron garden seat, early 19th century, with trellis back and wooden slatted seat, 124cm (49in) wide, *S 28 May,*
£825 ($1,303)

1

2

3

4

5

6

7

8

9

10

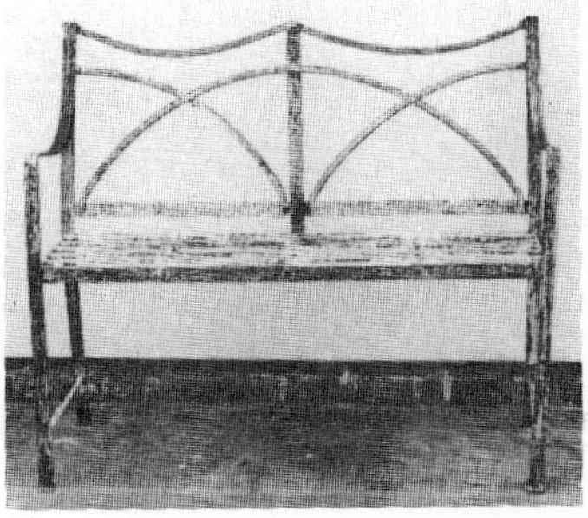
11

12

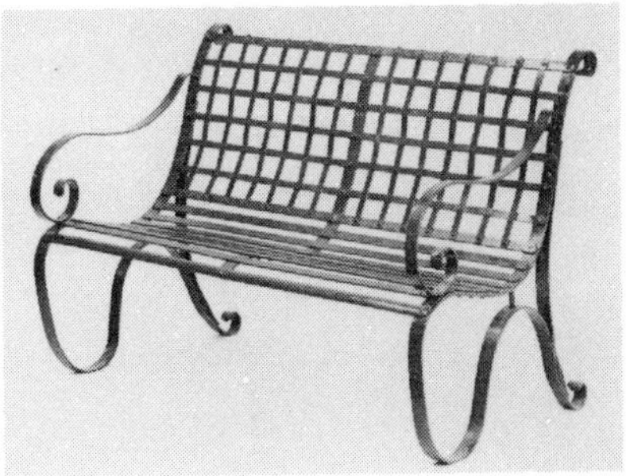
13

1

2

3

4

5

6 7

8

9

10

11

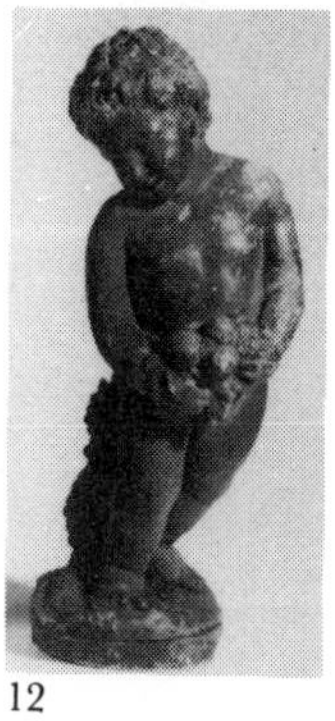
12

13

14

15

16

1
A graduated set of three terracotta jardinières, *(one illustrated),* decorated with swags and flowerheads, 48 to 69cm (19 to 27in), *S 28 May,*
£572 ($904)

2
A Doulton salt-glazed stoneware jar, c.1880, stamped *Doulton & Co. Limited, Lambeth,* 89cm (35in) high, *S 28 May,*
£440 ($695)

3
A set of six lead garden urns, *(one illustrated),* late 17th century, probably English, with scrolled eagle's head handles, the bowls with cherubs' heads, 34.5cm (13½in) high, *L 3 July,*
£7,150 ($11,512)

4
A pair of salt-glazed garden urns, *(one illustrated),* mid 19th century, mounted with mask handles, scrolls and a leaf-decorated foot, 74cm (29¼in) high, *NY 7 June,*
$6,600 (£4,429)

5
An Italian Travertine marble basin, Florence, 17th century, 109cm (43in) high, *M 23 June,*
FF 72,150 (£6,436; $10,040)

6
A set of four carved stone baskets, *(one illustrated),* 19th century, each filled with fruit, 40cm (16in) high, *S 28 May,*
£2,860 ($4,519)

7
A pair of carved stone urns, *(one illustrated),* each of semi-lobed campana form and filled with fruit and flowers, 61cm (24in) high, *S 28 May,*
£2,860 ($4,519)

8
A pair of cast-iron garden urns, *(one illustrated),* 19th century, of fluted campana form, *C 27 Mar,*
£297 ($454)

9
A pair of cast-iron garden urns, *(one illustrated),* mid 19th century, each with a tongue-cast border above a continuous band, 63.5cm (25in), *C 13 Mar,*
£462 ($698)

10
A cast-iron garden urn, c.1840, of shallow form, 48cm (19in) high, on a moulded plinth, *S 28 May,*
£605 ($956)

11
A pair of cast-iron garden urns, *(one illustrated),* mid 19th century, each of campana form, 71cm (28in) high, *S 28 May,*
£1,155 ($1,830)

12
A lead figure of a young faun, 19th century, holding a garland of fruit, 74cm (29in) high, *S 28 May,*
£308 ($487)

13
A lead fountain in the form of a young boy, 19th century, seated naked on a rock pouring water from a pitcher, 124cm (49in) high, *S 28 May,*
£3,850 ($6,083)

14
A lead figure of a Neapolitan fisher-boy, 19th century, about to throw a stone, 71cm (28in) high, *S 28 May,*
£528 ($834)

15
A pair of figural bronze garden fountains, early 20th century, after Henri Crenier, one of a young boy holding a goose, the other of a young girl holding a turtle, each animal set with fountain attachment, weathered green patina, inscribed *H. Crenier,* 72.5cm (28½in) high, *NY 26 Apr,*
$14,300 (£9,286)

16
A pair of lead dolphins, *(one illustrated),* 18th century, probably from fountains, tails repaired, 96.5cm (38in) high, *L 3 July,*
£3,520 ($5,567)

1
A French lead fountain group, 18th century, of a cherub embracing a writhing dolphin, 132cm (52in) long, *L 3 July,*
£26,400 ($42,504)

2
A pair of composition stone gate pier capitals, *(one illustrated)*, in the form of eagles, 104cm (41in) high, *S 28 May,*
£968 ($1,529)

3
An Italian carved marble fountain, 19th century, in the form of a boy astride a dolphin, 71cm (28in) high, *S 28 May,*
£1,408 ($2,225)

4
A pair of composition stone lions, *(one illustrated)*, 74cm (19in) long, *S 28 May,*
£858 ($1,356)

5
A pair of carved marble lions, *(one illustrated)*, 19th century, 86cm (34in) high, *S 28 May,*
£2,970 ($4,693)

6
A stone figure of a Muse, late 18th century, in the manner of Canova, 168cm (66in) high, *L 3 July,*
£2,530 ($4,073)

7
An Italian marble figure of Bacchus, 19th century, his raised right arm holding a bunch of grapes, 145cm (57in) high, *S 28 May,*
£1,760 ($2,781)

8
An Italian marble group of a water nymph and cupid, 19th century, the maiden seated on an upturned pitcher of water teasing cupid with a quiver of arrows, 109cm (43in), *S 28 May,*
£4,290 ($6,778)

1

2

3

4

5

6

7

8

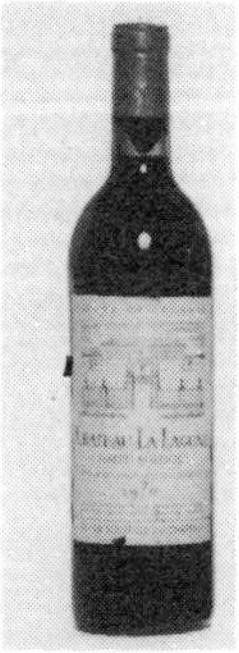

1

2

3

4

5

6

7

8

9

10

11

12

13

14

15

1
Claret. Château La Lagune 1970 CB, Ludon, 12 bottles, *L 15 Oct,*
£242 ($363)

2
Claret. Château Cheval Blanc 1955 CB, St. Emilion, 6 bottles, *L 30 July,*
£308 ($484)

3
Claret. Château Mouton Rothschild 1953 CB, 3 bottles, *T 26 Nov,*
Yen 170,000 (£739; $1,035)

4
Claret. Château Ducru Beaucaillou 1978 CB, St. Julien, 12 bottles, *L 19 Nov,*
£220 ($312)

5
Claret. Château Lynch Bages 1978 CB, Pauillac, 12 bottles, *L 19 Nov,*
£143 ($203)

6
Claret. Château Beychevelle 1967 CB, St. Julien, 12 bottles, *L 19 Nov,*
£110 ($156)

7
Claret. Château Margaux 1959 CB, Margaux, 2 magnums, *L 24 Sept,*
£462 ($702)

8
Claret. Château Lanessan 1900 CB, Cussac (Haut-Médoc), 1 magnum, *L 28 May,*
£320 ($480)

9
Claret. Château Mouton Rothschild 1946 CB, 1 bottle, *G 12 May,*
SF 6,820 (£2,304; $3,710)

10
Burgundy. Musigny, Vieilles Vignes 1969 DB, Comte Georges de Vogüé, Côte de Nuits, 6 bottles, *L 30 July,*
£297 ($466)

11
Claret. Château Latour 1959 CB, Pauillac, 1 double magnum, *L 24 Sept,*
£715 ($1,087)

12
Claret. Château Latour 1970 CB, Pauillac, 1 imperial, *L 3 Dec,*
£770 ($1,078)

13
Burgundy. Vougeot 'Le Prieuré' 1961 OB Pierre Ponnelle, Côte de Nuits, 1 double magnum, *L 24 Sept,*
£209 ($318)

14
Claret. Château Mouton Rothschild 1960 CB (*illustrated*); Château Latour 1958 CB, 2 magnums, *L 24 Sept,*
£160 ($242)

15
Claret. Château Margaux 1908 CB, Margaux, in original wooden case, 1 jeroboam, *L 3 Dec,*
£1,375 ($1,925)

1
Spanish. Gran Coronas, Gran Reserva 1964 OB Miguel Torres, 12 bottles, *L 3 Dec,*
£220 ($308)

2
Rhône. Hermitage, La Chapelle 1978 OB Paul Jaboulet Aîné, 6 bottles, *L 3 Dec,*
£242 ($339)

3
Hungarian Tokay. Tokaji Borvidék Eszenzia 1888 OB Baro Waldbott-Bassenheim, 1 bottle, *L 28 May,*
£176 ($276)

4
White Burgundy. Bâtard Montrachet 1978 DB Latour, 12 bottles, *L 19 Nov,*
£396 ($562)

5
White Burgundy. Clos du Château, Bourgogne Chardonnay 1981 DB, Domaine du Château de Meursault, 12 bottles, *L 30 July,*
£79 ($139)

6
White Bordeaux. Château d'Yquem 1949 CB, Sauternes, 2 bottles, *L 3 Dec,*
£407 ($570)

7
White Bordeaux. Château d'Yquem 1937 CB, Sauternes, 2 bottles, *L 26 Mar,*
£440 ($673)

8
White Bordeaux. Château d'Yquem 1921 CB, Sauternes, 1 bottle, *L 26 Mar,*
£242 ($370)

9
White Bordeaux. Château Montbrun, Goutte d'Or, Vin Blanc Sec, Cantenac (Margaux), 12 bottles, *L 24 Sept,*
£154 ($234)

10
Hock. Wallhäuser Mühlenberg Riesling 1982, 60 bottles, *L 2 June,*
£154 ($237)

11
Hock. Dürkheimer Hochmess Scheurebe Spätlese 1959 (UK) Arthur Hallgarten Gmbh, Rheinpfalz, 12 bottles, *L 24 Sept,*
£66 ($100)

12
Champagne. Dom Pérignon 1964 OB; Louis Roederer Cristal Brut 1966 OB, 2 bottles, *L 30 July,*
£68 ($107)

13
Green Chartreuse. Grande Chartreuse OB 1901-21, 1 bottle, *L 26 Mar,*
£115 ($177)

14
Absinthe. Pernod Extrait d'Absinthe OB, 1 bottle, *L 26 Mar,*
£198 ($303)

1

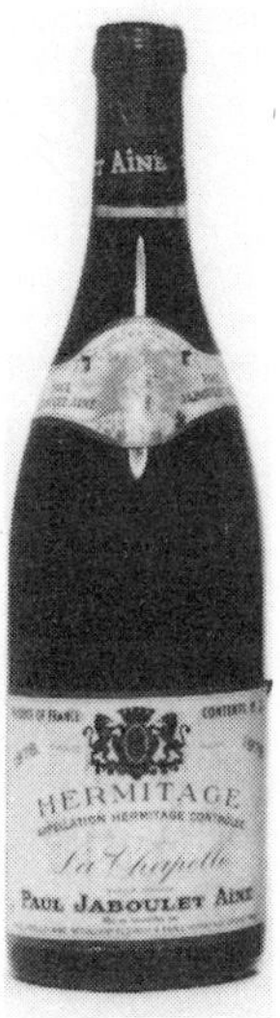

2

3

4

5

6

7

8

9

10

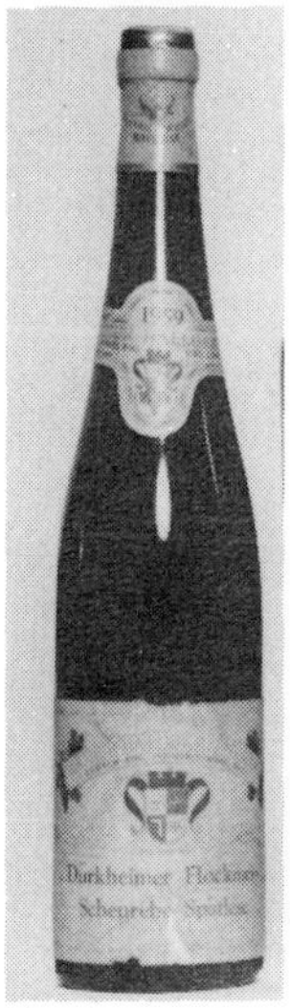
11

12

13

14

1

2

3

4

5

6

7

8

9

10

11

12

13 14 15

1
Port. Taylor 1945 OB, 12 bottles, *L 8 Oct,*
£1,430 ($2,145)

2
Port. Croft 1955 UK, 12 bottles, *L 8 Oct,*
£418 ($627)

3
Port. Quinta do Noval, Nacional 1960 OB, 3 bottles, *L 3 Dec,*
£264 ($370)

4
Port. Croft 1963 UK, 12 bottles, *L 3 Dec,*
£374 ($524)

5
Port. Graham 1963 UK, 1 bottle, *L 30 July,*
£28 ($43)

6
Port. Dow 1970 UK, 12 bottles, *L 3 Dec,*
£198 ($277)

7
Madeira. Bual vintage 1907 OB Blandy, 3 bottles, *L 26 Mar,*
£86 ($132)

8
Brandy. Cognac Napoléon, Grande Fine Champagne, Réserve 1811 OB, 1 bottle, *L 3 Dec,*
£220 ($308)

9
Brandy. Cognac Bisquit Dubouché, Grande Fine Champagne 1870 OB, 1 bottle, *L 24 Sept,*
£148 ($226)

10
Brandy. Cognac Bisquit Dubouché, Grande Fine Champagne, Extra Vieille 1838 OB, 3 bottles, *L 24 Sept,*
£308 ($468)

11
Brandy. Cognac Bisquit Dubouché, Grande Champagne 1850 OB, 1 bottle, *L 24 Sept,*
£110 ($167)

12
Brandy. Cognac Rémy Martin, Grande Champagne, Louis Treize OB, 1 bottle in presentation box, *L 3 Dec,*
£198 ($277)

13
Brandy. Cognac 1865, 2 bottles, *L 26 Mar,*
£110 ($168)

14
Brandy. Cognac Hine, Grande Champagne 1955 UK bottled 1982, 6 bottles, *L 26 Mar,*
£176 ($269)

15
Brandy. Cognac Chateau de Lafot, Fine Champagne 1865 OB, 2 bottles, *L 26 Mar,*
£154 ($236)

1
A green metal shaft and globe bottle, c.1670, 20cm (8in), *L 24 Sept,*
£550 ($836)

See also p.257 for wine bottles.

2
A Whelan's patent corkscrew, 1881, *L 28 May,*
£720 ($1,080)

3
A Charles Hull 1864 patent Royal Club corkscrew, all-metal construction, *L 28 May,*
£620 ($979)

4
A G. W. Lewis & Co. silver salmon handle corkscrew, 1933, metal shank and helix, *L 28 May,*
£260 ($410)

5
A John Loach 1844 patent corkscrew, with bone handle and outer brass barrel, *L 28 May,*
£750 ($1,185)

6
A James Heeley 1890 patent double lever Empire corkscrew, *L 26 Mar,*
£180 ($275)

7
A Lund steel London Rack, *L 24 Sept,*
£240 ($365)

8
A steel T.F. corkscrew, c.1887, advertising Thomas Foster & Co. Wine & Spirit Merchants, *L 24 Sept,*
£125 ($190)

9
An English steel and brass corkscrew, 19th century, the brass shank in the form of a hand, *L 24 Sept,*
£100 ($152)

10
A Robert Jones & Son corkscrew, 1840, with brass barrel and wooden handle, *L 24 Sept,*
£420 ($638)

11
A 'Bonsa' type corkscrew, probably English, 10cm (4in), *L 24 Sept,*
£240 ($365)

12
A silver-plated decanting cradle, late 19th century, French decorative style, *L 28 May,*
£980 ($1,548)

13
An iron bottle cradle, the carriage of looped and twisted wire, *L 26 Mar,*
£120 ($183)

14
A silver-plated decanting cradle, the uprights, spindle supports and handle in the form of vine stems, *L 26 Mar,*
£600 ($918)

15
An iron decanting cradle, the uprights in the form of vine stems, *L 26 Mar,*
£200 ($306)

See pp.393, 442-443 for wine accessories in silver and silver-plate, and p.257 for wine bottles.

1

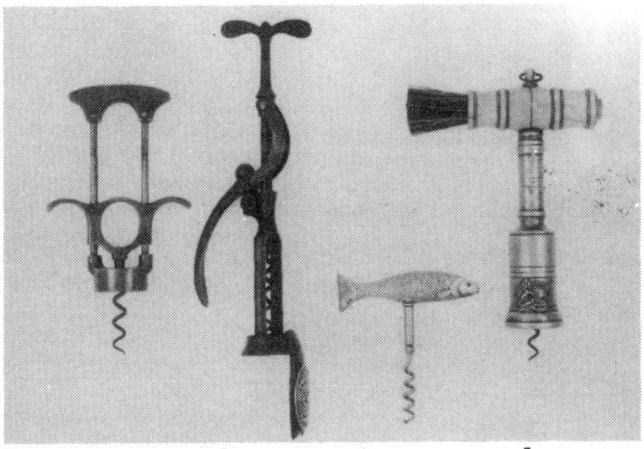

2 3 4 5

6

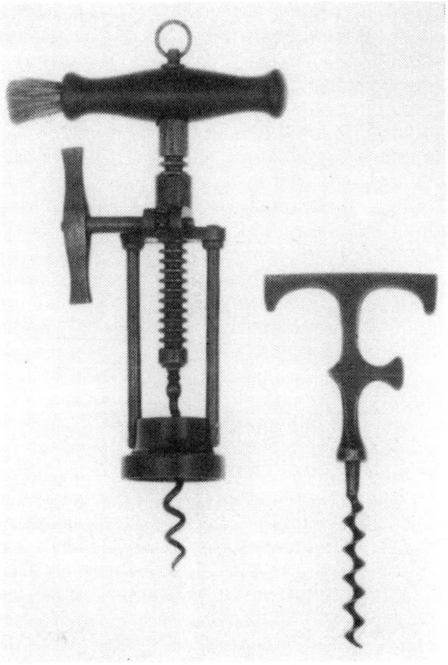

7 8

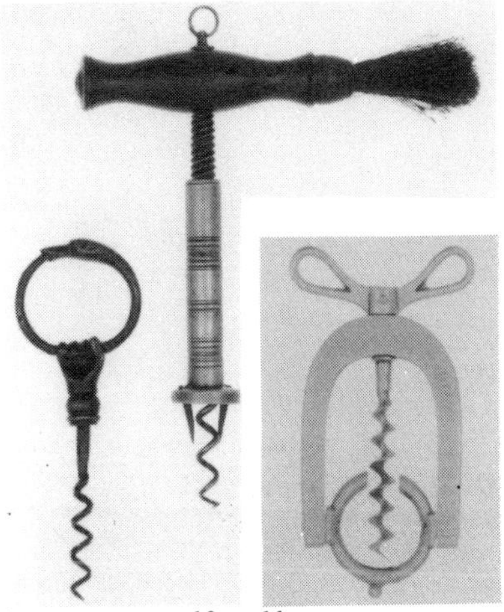

9 10 11

12

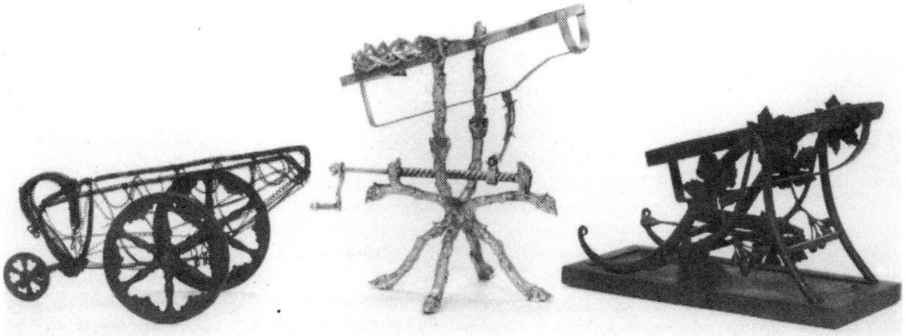

13 14 15

Toys and Dolls

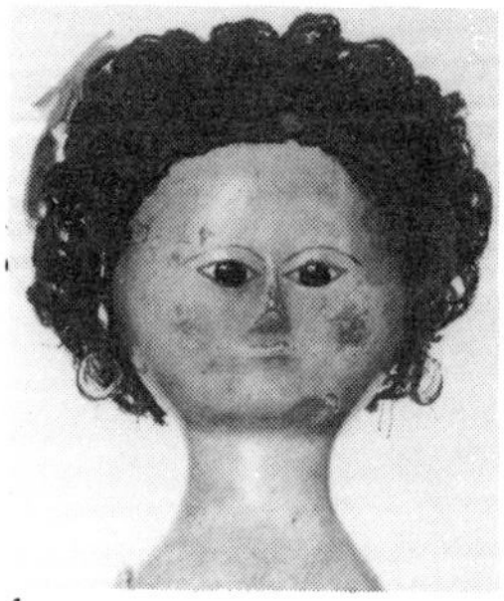
1

2

3

4

5

6

7

8

9

10

11

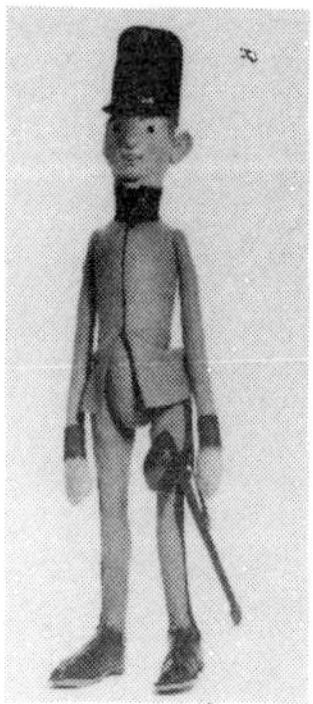
12

13

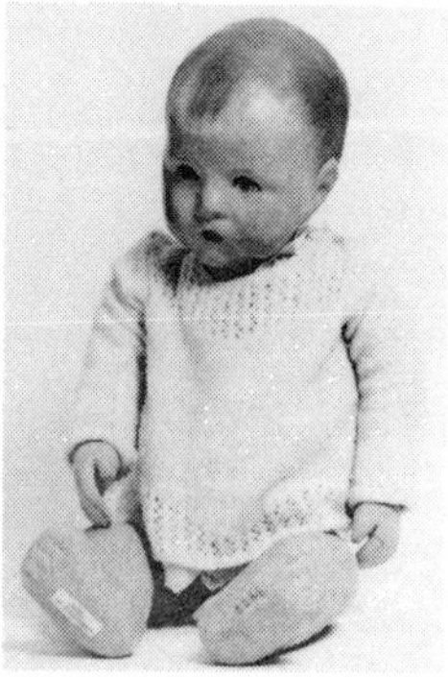
14

15 16

17 18

19

See also:
Colour illustrations *pp* 492-493

1
A wooden doll, English, c.1790, now with cloth arms, both legs missing, 35cm (13¾in), *L 5 Feb,*
£495 ($713)

2
A papier-mâché shoulder-head doll, German, c.1825, unclothed, minor damage, 36cm (14½in), *L 20 May,*
£935 ($1,496)

3
A china shoulder-head, German, c.1870, 20cm (8in), *L 5 Feb,*
£286 ($412)

4
A papier-mâché shoulder-head doll, German head on French body, c.1850, cracking on shoulder, 52cm (20½in), *L 23 Sept,*
£440 ($616)

5
A wooden doll, German, c.1770, two thumbs and one finger missing, paint rubbed, 49cm (19¼in), *L 20 May,*
£6,380 ($10,208)

6
A poured-wax shoulder-doll, English, c.1880, cloth body with poured-wax lower limbs, one little finger missing, 52cm (20½in), *L 23 Sept,*
£770 ($1,078)

7
A china shoulder-doll, German, c.1870, in pink and white patterned dress, 71cm (28in), *L 23 Sept,*
£638 ($893)

8
A parian shoulder-doll, German, c.1880, with kid body and limbs, 61cm (24in), *L 5 Feb,*
£550 ($792)

9
A china half-doll, German, early 20th century, holding a pink rose, 9cm (3½in), *S 3 Nov,*
£99 ($139)

10
A Dressel & Kister chin bathing belle, German, c.1930, with blue factory mark on base, thumb on left hand missing, 13cm (5in), *S 3 Nov,*
£341 ($477)

11
A papier-mâché shoulde doll, German, c.1835, stuffed body with separately stitched fingers cracked on head, 48cm (19in), *L 5 Feb,*
£682 ($982)

12
A Steiff felt soldier doll, German, c.1908, with Steiff button in left ear, minor damage, 47cm (18½in), *L 23 Sept,*
£1,595 ($2,233)

13
A Mabel Lucie Attwell/ Chad Valley doll, Englis c.1924, with felt head and velvet body, 45cm (17¾in), *S 10 Feb,*
£220 ($308)

14
A Kathe Kruse sand bab cloth doll, German, c.1925, with original box, 48cm (19in), *S 3 Nov,*
£2,860 ($4,004)

15
A Lenci glass-eyed felt doll, c.1930, 51cm (20in), *NY 28 June,*
$2,750 (£1,797)

16
A Lenci felt doll, c.1925, in a Lenci box, 43cm (17in), *NY 28 June,*
$550 (£359)

17
A Lenci felt doll, model 110/57, c.1930, holding a doll, 43cm (17in), *NY 28 June,*
$990 (£647)

18
A Lenci felt doll, model 109, c.1925, wearing an Art Deco design dress, Lenci label, 56cm (22in), *NY 28 June,*
$825 (£539)

19
A Lenci felt doll, model 187, c.1925, wearing Russian costume, 99cm (39in), *NY 28 June,*
$1,045 (£683)

1
A bisque character doll, German, c.1910, impressed *Germany 6*, two fingers repaired, 61cm (24in), *L 20 May,*
£462 ($739)

2
A J.D. Kestner bisque googly-eyed doll, German, c.1913, impressed *C.7.J.D.K. Ges.gesch*, one leg loose, 30cm (11¾in), *L 23 Sept,*
£2,200 ($3,080)

3
A Gebruder Heubach bisque character boy doll, German c.1912, impressed *7603 5*, stringing loose, paint cracking on legs, 36cm (14in), *L 23 Sept,*
£2,090 ($2,926)

4
A Kammer & Reinhardt/ Simon & Halbig bisque character doll, German, c.1911, impressed *116/A28*, stringing loose, 38cm (15in), *L 5 Feb,*
£1,320 ($1,901)

5
A Gebruder Heubach bisque character doll's head, German, c.1914, impressed *3 square Heubach mark 9141,* firing flaws, 9cm (3½in), *L 23 Sept,*
£1,760 ($2,464)

6
A bisque googly-eyed doll, German, c.1911, impressed *241 0*, minor chips, 24cm (9½in), *L 23 Sept,*
£1,100 ($1,540)

7
A Gebruder Heubach bisque character girl doll, German, c.1912, impressed *13 square Heubach mark 2*, 61cm (24in), *L 20 May,*
£7,700 ($12,320)

8
A Kammer & Reinhardt mulatto bisque character doll, German, c.1909, impressed *101 46*, stringing loose, 46cm (18in), *L 5 Feb,*
£4,620 ($6,653)

9
A Bähr & Pröschild bisque character doll, German c.1912, impressed *2025 BSW in a heart 529,* stringing loose, 48cm (19in), *L 23 Sept,*
£3,080 ($4,312)

10
A bisque shoulder-doll, French c.1875, unmarked, body patched, unclothed, 46cm (18in), *L 20 May,*
£770 ($1,232)

11
A Simon & Halbig bisque shoulder-head, German, c.1889, impressed *SH 1010-14 DEP*, 20cm (8in), *L 5 Feb,*
£352 ($507)

12
A French bisque-head smiling portrait bébé, Bru, incised on head *Depose L* with paper label on body, a replica of the Duchess of Marlborough and commissioned by her, the dress with Rouf-Paris label, 56cm (22in), *NY 16 Dec,*
$23,100 (£16,154)

13
A Swaine & Co 'Lori' bisque doll, German, c.1910, impressed *Lori 2*, some damage, unclothed and unstrung, 48cm (19in), *L 5 Feb,*
£1,155 ($1,663)

14
A Jumeau black bisque doll, French, c.1885, impressed *7*, eyes loose, unclothed and unstrung, 47cm (18½in), *L 5 Feb,*
£1,012 ($1,457)

15
A Simon & Halbig bisque lady doll, German, c.1894, impressed *DEP 1159 9½*, 61cm (24in), *L 5 Feb,*
£1,980 ($2,851)

16
A bisque swivel-head doll, French, c.1875, impressed on each shoulder *11*, 86cm (34in), *L 20 May,*
£4,180 ($6,688)

17
A J.D. Kestner four-headed bisque doll, German c.1909, in original box with sixteen pieces of clothing, stringing perished, 37cm (14½in), *L 20 May,*
£6,600 ($10,560)

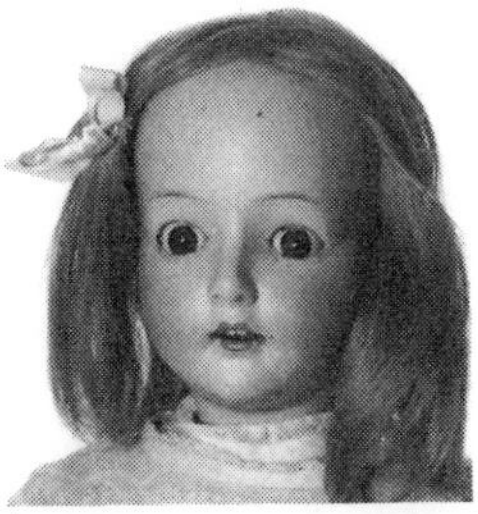
1

2

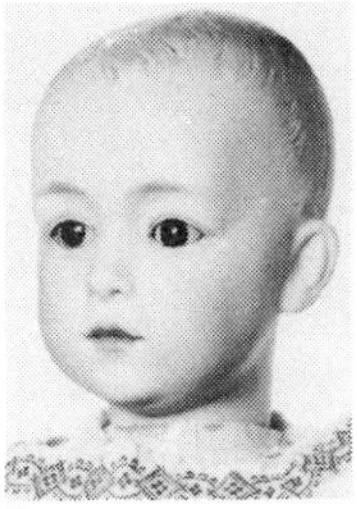
3

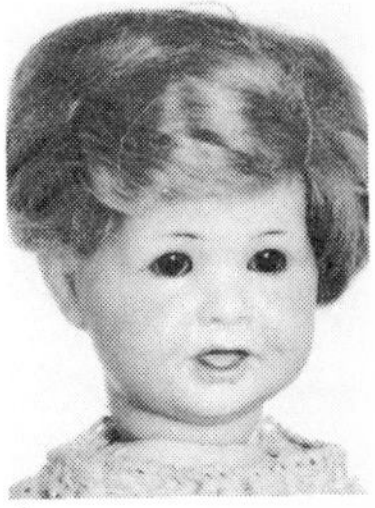
4

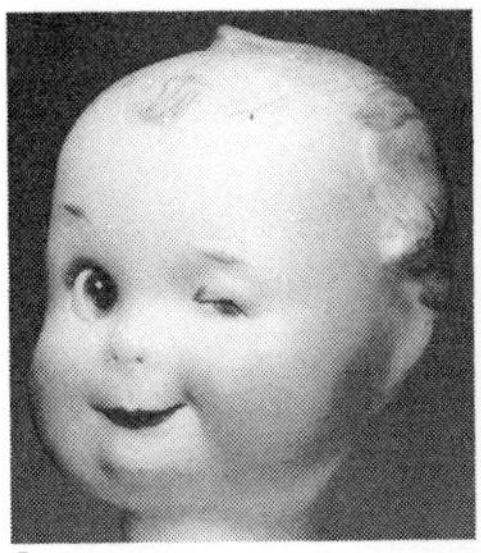
5

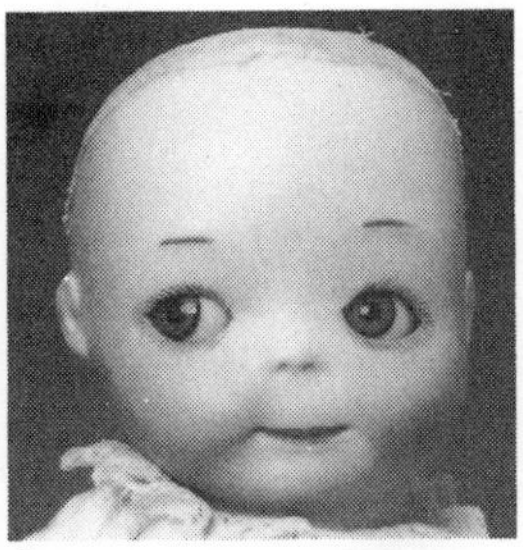
6

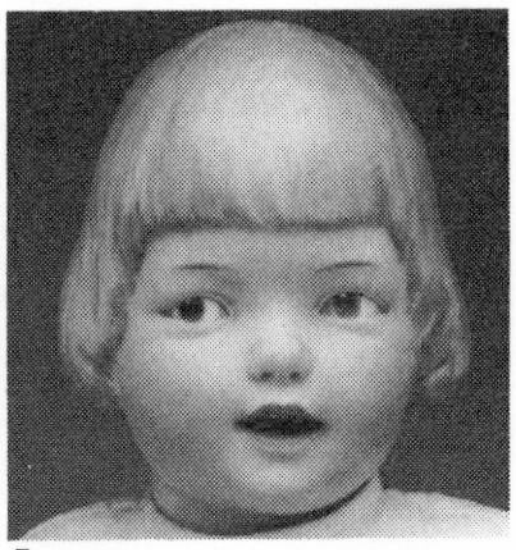
7

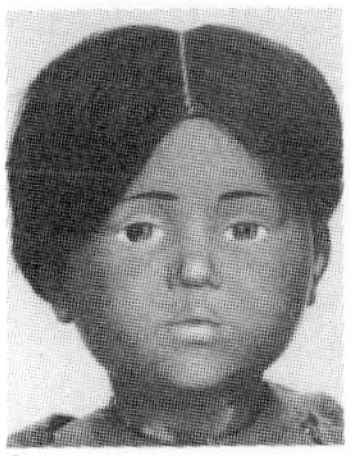
8

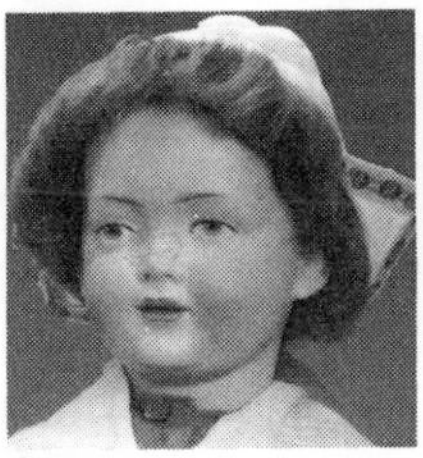
9

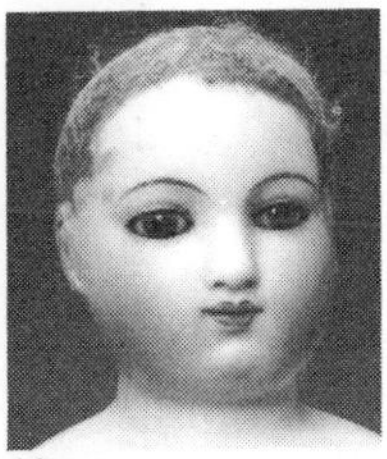
10

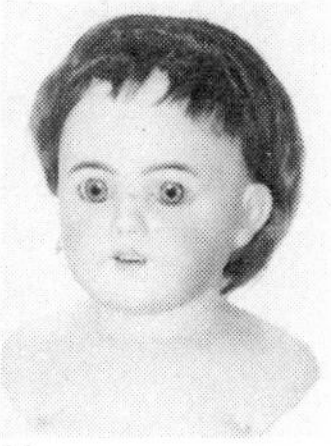
11

12

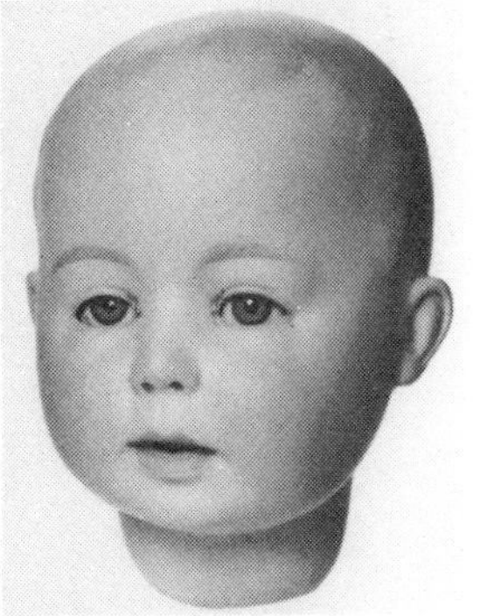
13

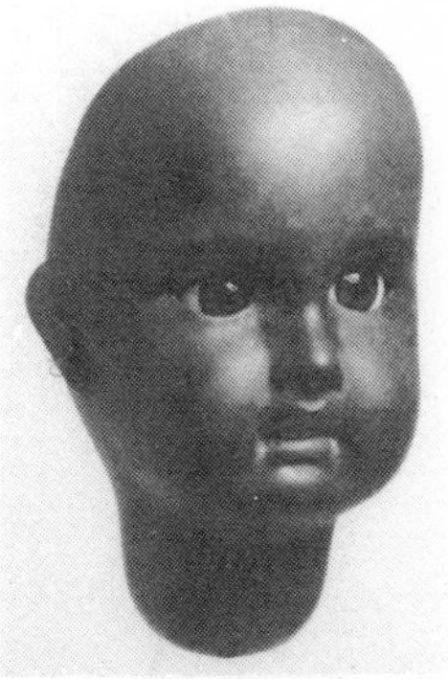
14

15

16

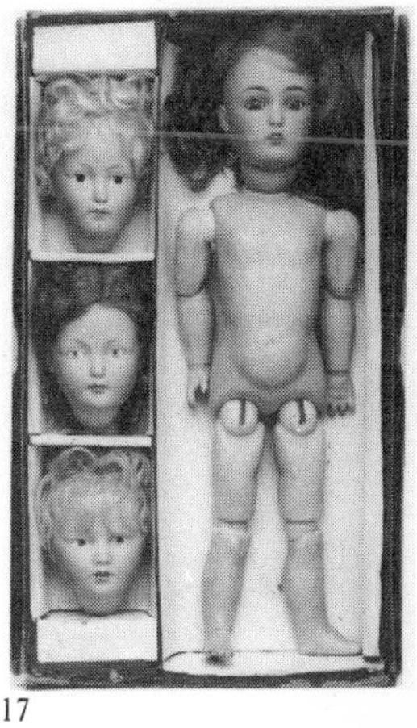
17

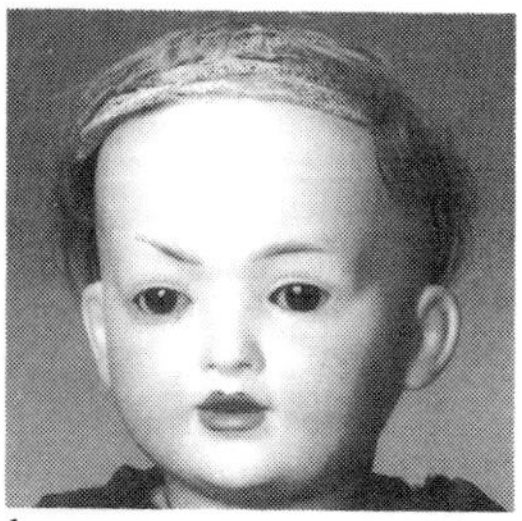
1

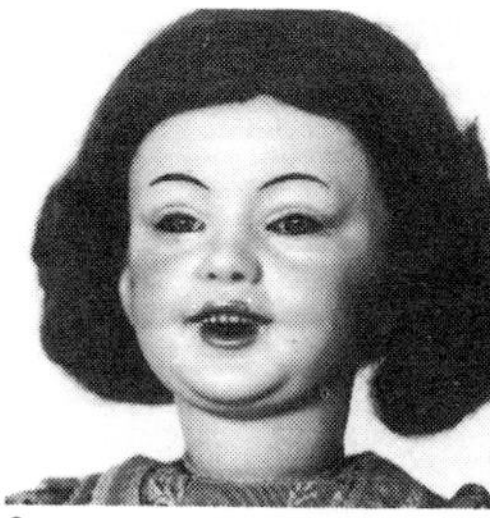
2

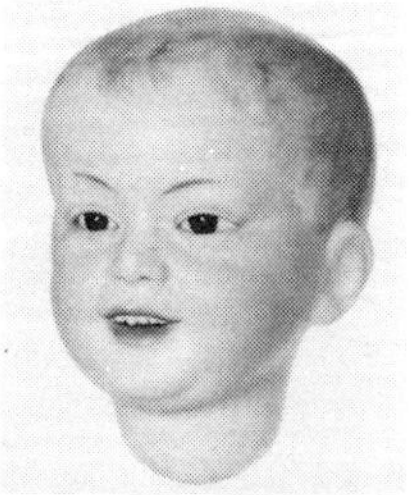
3

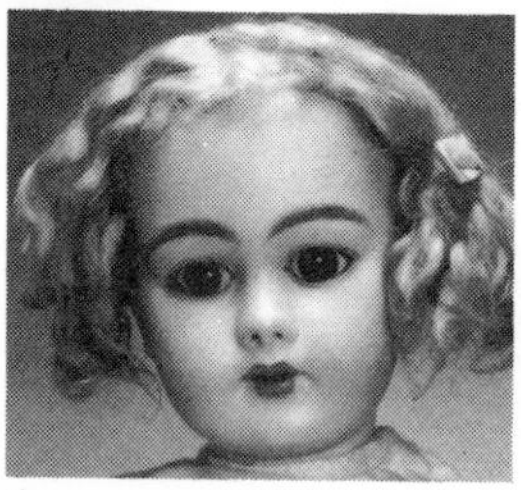
4

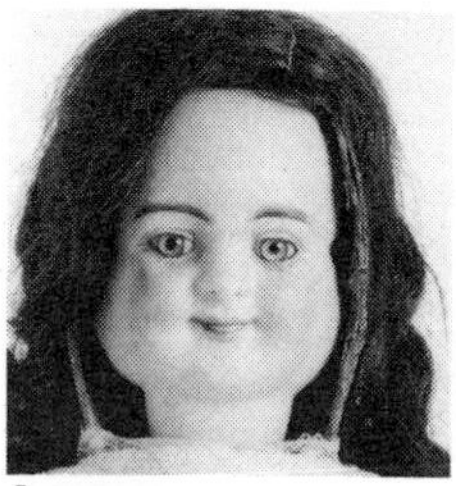
5

6

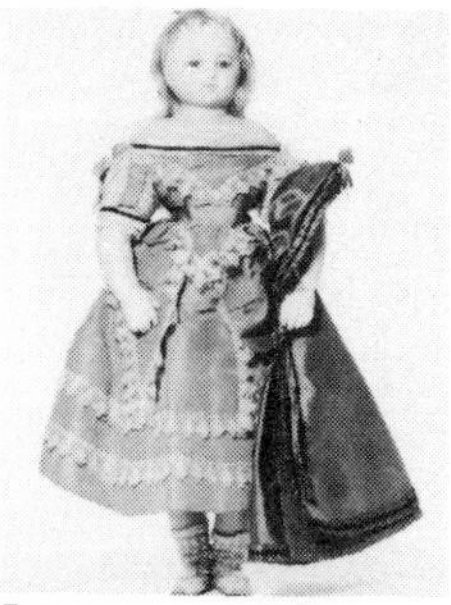
7

8

9

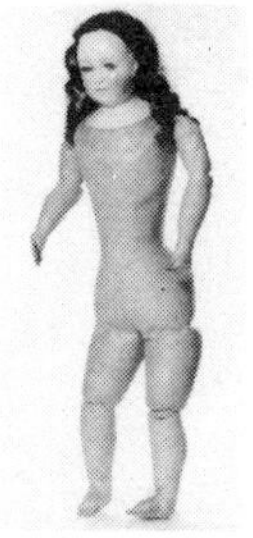
10

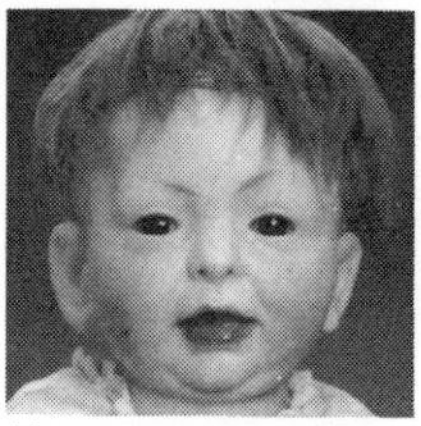
11

12

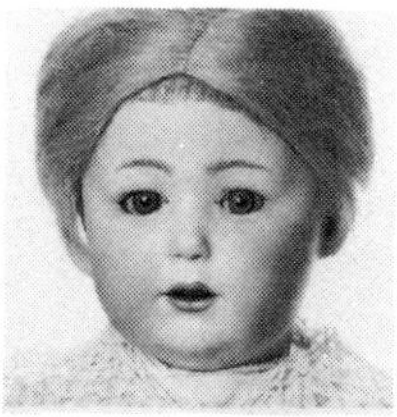
13

14

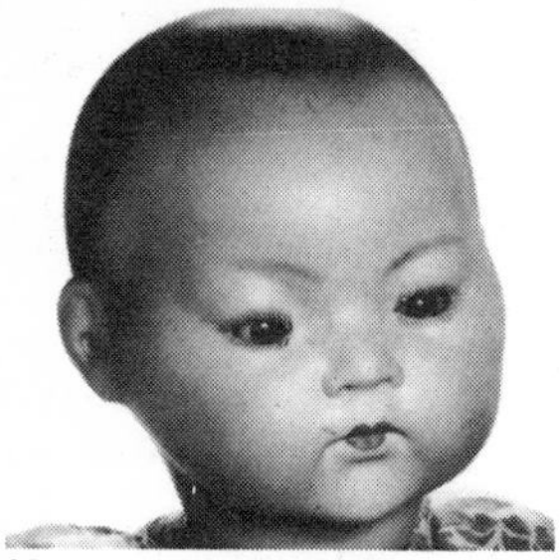
15

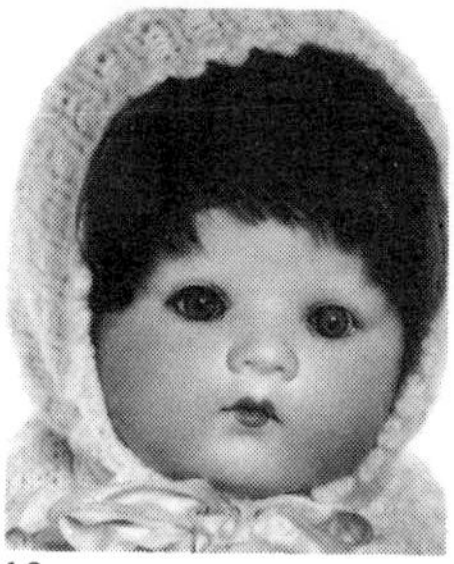
16

17

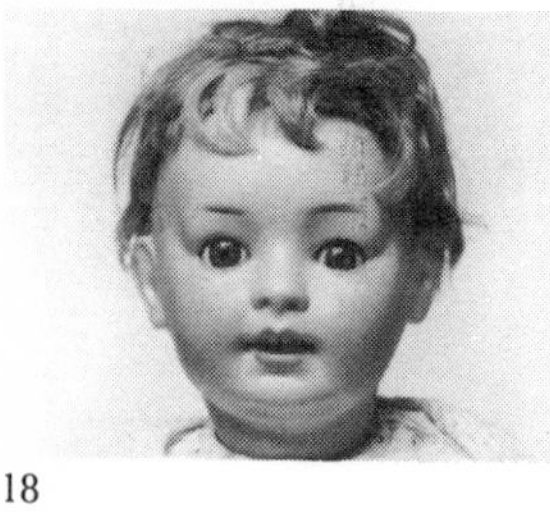
18

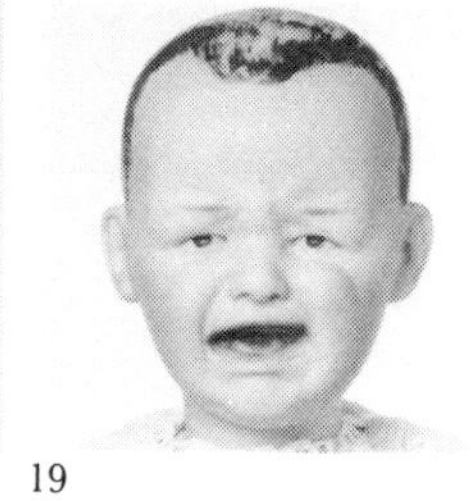
19

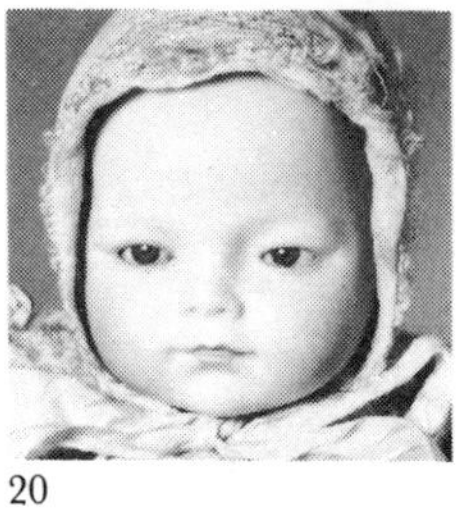
20

1
A Hertel Schwab & Co bisque character doll, German, c.1912, impressed *141 5*, 34cm (13½in), *L 23 Sept,*
£880 ($1,232)

2
A S.F.B.J. bisque laughing character doll, French, c.1910, impressed *229/4*, 36.5cm (14¼in), *C 4 June,*
£605 ($938)

3
An S.F.B.J. bisque character boy doll, French, c.1910, impressed *227 8*, unclothed and unstrung, 50cm (19¾in), *L 5 Feb,*
£550 ($792)

4
A Simon & Halbig bisque character doll, German c.1888, impressed *S15H939*, some cracking, 61cm (24in), *L 5 Feb,*
£715 ($1,030)

5
A bisque three-faced doll, German, c.1895, probably by Carl Bergner, originally with pull-string mechanism, 32cm (12½in), *L 5 Feb,*
£660 ($950)

6
A Kammer & Reinhardt bisque character doll, German, c.1909, impressed *Kstar R 101 43*, lower legs replaced, 43cm (17in), *L 23 Sept,*
£1,595 ($2,233)

7
A Cremer poured-wax shoulder-doll, English, c.1885, stamped *Cremer,* 58cm (23in), *L 5 Feb,*
£2,200 ($3,168)

8
A Bähr & Pröschild or Bruno Schmidt bisque character doll, German, c.1912, impressed *2033 BSW in a heart 537*, 29cm (11½in), *L 23 Sept,*
£2,970 ($4,158)

9
A Simon & Halbig bisque lady doll, German, c.1915, impressed *1468, S & H 2½*, 38cm (15in), *S 3 Nov,*
£1,705 ($2,387)

10
A china shoulder-doll, French, c.1850, with kid body, minor damage, 65cm (25½in), *L 20 May,*
£1,870 ($2,992)

11
A Kammer & Reinhardt Kaiser baby bisque doll, German, c.1909, impressed *28*, 28cm (11in), *L 23 Sept,*
£638 ($893)

12
A Jumeau bisque doll, French c.1880, stamped in red *Depose tete Jumeau Bte S.G.D.G. 8*, *L 23 Sept,*
£1,980 ($2,772)

13
A Gebruder Heubach bisque character doll, German, c.1920, impressed *10532 6*, paint worn, 36cm (15in), *L 20 May,*
£528 ($845)

14
A Bähr & Pröschild bisque character doll, German, c.1912, impressed *531 6*, knee ball missing, 48cm (19in), *L 23 Sept,*
£770 ($1,078)

15
An Armand Marseille Oriental bisque 'My Dream Baby' doll, German, c.1926, impressed *353/3K*, 32cm (12½in), *L 5 Feb,*
£550 ($792)

16
An Armand Marseille bisque doll, German, c.1926, impressed *355/4K*, 38cm (15in), *L 5 Feb,*
£550 ($792)

17
A J.D. Kestner character doll, German, c.1910, impressed *JDK/6*, 29cm (11¼in), *C 4 June,*
£275 ($426)

18
A Gebruder Ohlaver bisque character doll, German, c.1920, impressed *Revalo 22-12*, firing flaw, 55cm (21½in), *C 12 Nov,*
£308 ($440)

19
A character bisque boy doll, German, c.1912, probably Gebruder Heubach, impressed *6*, 38cm (15in), *L 5 Feb,*
£770 ($1,109)

20
A Schoenau & Hoffmeister 'My Dream Baby' bisque doll, German, c.1926, impressed *NOB*, 25.5cm (10in), *L 5 Feb,*
£352 ($507)

1
A painted wood doll's house, English, c.1900, the hinged façade revealing four furnished rooms, 19th/20th century furnishings, 99cm (39in), *NY 28 June,*
$1,870 (£1,222)

2
A lithographed paper-on-wood doll's house, American, Bliss, c.1895, 50.5cm (20in), *NY 28 June,*
$1,430 (£935)

3
A lithographed paper-on-wood National Guard Building, American, c.1910, opening to reveal four rooms, 53cm (21in), *NY 28 June,*
$1,650 (£1,078)

4
A painted wood doll's house, English, mid 19th century, opening to reveal four rooms, a garden concealed in a drawer at the base of the house, with a quantity of furniture, 100cm (39½in), *S 3 Nov,*
£770 ($1,078)

5
A painted wood doll's house, English, c.1790, some damage, 133cm (52½in), *L 20 May,*
£7,700 ($12,320)

6
A painted wood 'Tramp Art' doll's house, American, c.1900, opening to reveal four rooms, 71cm (28in), *NY 28 June,*
$3,520 (£2,301)

7
A milliner's shop, German, c.1890, with a bisque and a china doll, the shop 34cm (13½in) high, *L 23 Sept,*
£1,265 ($1,771)

8
A child's miniature open kitchen, French, c.1880, one corner piece missing, 30cm (11¾in) high, *L 23 Sept,*
£462 ($647)

9
A rattan and leather three-piece doll's furniture suite, English, c.1860, 38cm (15in), *NY 14 Oct,*
$605 (£420)

10
A group of eight miniature hanging and standard lamps, mainly German, c.1860-80, the tallest 8.5cm (3¼in), the shortest 2.5cm (1in), *L 23 Sept,*
£1,540 ($2,156)

11
A Duncan Phyfe doll's bookcase, German, late 19th century, one knob missing, 21cm (8¼in), *L 23 Sept,*
£1,045 ($1,463)

12
A set of Duncan Phyfe 'Boulle' furniture, late 19th century, *L 5 Feb,*
£1,870 ($2,693)

13
A set of gilt-metal doll's house furniture, French, 19th century, upholstered in painted silk depicting Napoleonic figures, *L 5 Feb,*
£3,520 ($5,069)

1

2 3

4

5

6

7

8

9

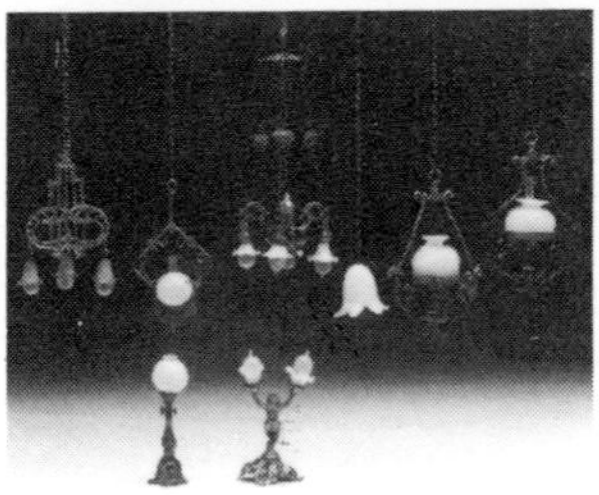
10

11

12

13

1

2

3

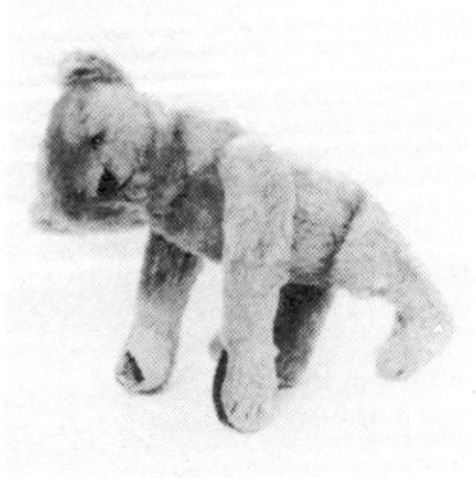
4

5

6

7

8

9

10

11

12

13

1
A collection of nine wooden hand puppets, German, c.1880, including Punch and Judy, some with slight damage, *L 20 May,*
£660 ($1,056)

2
A Punch and Judy set, by T.W. Coombs, c.1955, all with carved and painted heads, includes accessories, red and white striped tent, wooden storage box and canvas bag, *S 10 Feb,*
£594 ($832)

3
A Schoenhut/Delvan Humpty Dumpty circus set, American, c.1952, comprising thirteen pieces, *NY 16 Dec,*
$605 (£423)

4
A Steiff blonde plush tumbling teddy bear, early 20th century, wear to pads, mechanism inoperative, 33cm (13in), *C 12 Nov,*
£264 ($378)

5
A Steiff blonde mechanical bear, German, c.1908, with metal disc in ear, the left arm winding to operate the clockwork mechanism causing the bear to somersault, pads worn, 33cm (13in), *L 20 May,*
£550 ($880)

6
A Steiff blonde plush teddy bear, German, c.1913, with metal disc in ear, named Arthur, 42cm (16½in), *L 5 Feb,*
£935 ($1,346)

7
A Steiff blonde plush teddy bear, German, c.1920, with Steiff metal button in ear, named Brumm, some fraying, 59cm (23in), *L 23 Sept,*
£1,650 ($2,310)

8
A Steiff blonde plush teddy bear, German, c.1905, with Steiff metal disc in ear, some wear and repairs, 74cm (29in), *L 5 Feb,*
£1,210 ($1,742)

9
A Steiff beige plush tedd bear, German, c.1904, with metal disc in ear, original price tag on right paw, in excellent condition, 75cm (29½in), *C 4 June,*
£5,280 ($8,184)

10
A Steiff white plush tedd bear, German, c.1904, with Steiff metal button in ear, with growler, excellent condition, 42cm (16½in), *L 23 Sept,*
£2,200 ($3,080)

11
A teddy/doll, German, c.1912, probably by Simon & Halbig, his head swivelling to reveal a bisque character doll's face, 42cm (16½in), *L 5 Feb,*
£1,320 ($1,901)

12
A Steiff blonde plush teddy bear, German, c.1902, with small disc in left ear, called Johnny, some wear and pads renewed, 76cm (30in), *L 5 Feb,*
£2,750 ($3,960)

13
A Steiff brown plush teddy bear, German, c.1905, with metal disc in ear, slight damage, 71cm (28in), *L 20 May,*
£2,640 ($4,224)

1
A Schuco electrically-operated bear and monkey automaton, German, c.1935, stamped *Schuco TRICKY patent Ang.*, the animals seated on a platform attached to a small motor, 39cm (15½in) high, *L 23 Sept,*
£1,650 ($2,310)

2
A jumping tiger automaton, probably French, early 20th century, tail frail, 36.5cm (14¼in), *C 12 Nov,*
£396 ($566)

3
A musical automaton kitten in a churn, French, c.1912, the kitten popping his head out of a milk churn and sticking out his metal tongue, 24cm (9½in), *L 20 May,*
£550 ($880)

4
An automaton of a conjuror, c.1900, with papier-mâché head, the figure alternately lifting a pointed cone in one hand, a baton in the other, revealing various objects while turning his head, 71cm (28in), *L 20 May,*
£2,750 ($4,400)

5
A Leopold Lambert musical automaton of a pierrot playing a violin, French, late 19th century, the figure turning and nodding his head, the bow arm moving across the violin, in red, cream and green silk outfit, 63.5cm (25in), *NY 28 June,*
$3,575 (£2,337)

6
A Vichy musical automaton of a peasant and a pig, French, c.1870, the man feeding the pig with a bottle, minor repairs, 76cm (30in), *NY 28 June,*
$25,300 (£16,536)

7
A Leopold Lambert musical automaton of a lady playing a tambourine, French, late 19th century, her right hand 'shaking' the tambourine, her left hand bringing a mask up to her face, 43cm (17in), *NY 28 June,*
$3,575 (£2,337)

8
A Decamps musical automaton of Puss-in-Boots, French, c.1890, the cat in faded yellow and blue satin coat and the movement causing him to pirouette, some wear, 48cm (19in), *L 23 Sept,*
£1,100 ($1,540)

9
A Leopold Lambert musical automaton of a tea pourer, French, c.1880, impressed *No.3 and with red check mark,* in original navy, gold and blue brocaded robe over a gold skirt, some wear, 46cm (18in), *L 20 May,*
£2,310 ($3,696)

10
A Leopold Lambert musical automaton of a lady with a fan and lorgnettes, French, c.1880, the head stamped *Depose Tete Jumeau Bte. S.G.D.G. 1,* in original crimson silk dress and satin and lace underskirt, some wear, 42cm (16½in), *L 20 May,*
£2,200 ($3,520)

11
A musical automaton of a monkey marksman, possibly by Blaise Bontems, French, c.1860, the papier-mâché headed monkey holding a rifle and aiming at a bull's-eye on a stand, with French clock, the base with pull-string musical movement, under glass dome, 60cm (23½in) high, *L 23 Sept,*
£4,950 ($6,930)

12
A J. Phalibois automaton of a monkey artist, French, c.1880, stamped *Phalibois*, the animal nodding and turning his head while his right hand waves a brush over a canvas, dressed in navy velvet suit edged in gold and cream silk bows, some wear, *L 20 May,*
£2,200 ($3,520)

13
A monkey chef automaton, French, c.1885, probably by Phalibois, the monkey stirring liquid in a saucepan while a chicken rotates below, some wear, 67.5cm (26½in) high, *L 5 Feb,*
£2,200 ($3,168)

1

2

3

4

5

6

7

8

9

10

11

12

13

1 *(above)* 2 *(below)*

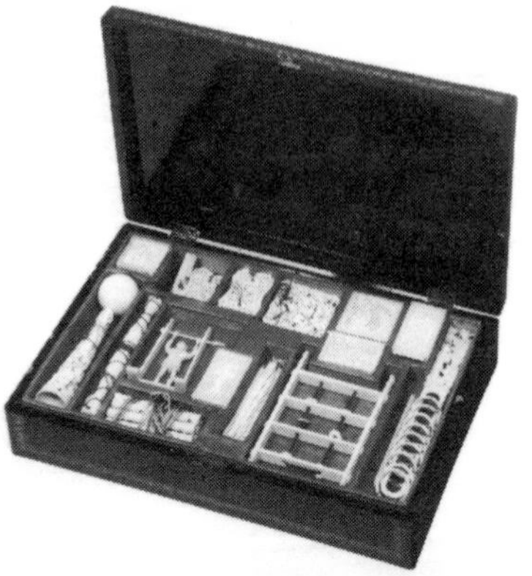
3

4

5

6

7

8

9

10

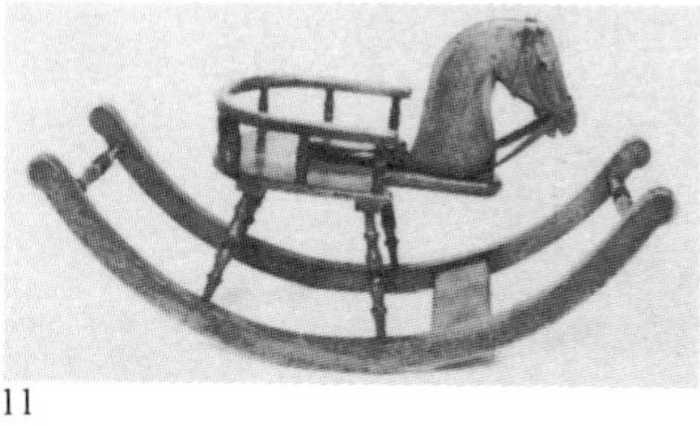
11

12

1
A Bassett-Lowke motor lifeboat, c.1935, access to electric motor through removable hatch, space for battery, operating rudder, on mahogany stand, 60cm (23¾in), *S 3 Nov,*
£572 ($801)

2
A Bassett-Lowke clockwork tug, *Edith,* London, c.1935, good superstructure detail, on mahogany stand, 59cm (23in), *S 3 Nov,*
£385 ($539)

3
A lacquer box of ivory puzzles, Chinese, late 19th century, comprising fifteen carved ivory games, puzzles, and amusements, 42.5cm (16¾in), *L 5 Feb,*
£2,200 ($3,168)

4
A Chad Valley 'Edition de Luxe' blow football game, English, c.1910-20, in original box, 43cm (17in), *L 21 July,*
£110 ($173)

5
A Schuco Ingenico 5300 MK de Luxe car construction set, German, c.1950, in original box, incomplete, *L 23 Sept,*
£275 ($385)

6
A Noah's Ark, German, mid 19th century, containing approx 240 pieces, including elephants, giraffes, grasshoppers and beetles, with five human figures, mainly good condition, ark 58.5cm (23in) long, *L 22 July,*
£1,430 ($2,245)

7
A Noah's Ark, German, mid 19th century, containing approx 190 pieces, all brightly painted, some damaged, the ark painted cream, blue and pink, 61cm (24in), *L 20 May,*
£770 ($1,232)

8
An Austin J40 child's pedal car, English, c.1950, finished in original scarlet, with hinged bonnet opening to simulated engine, 150cm (59in), *L 1 Dec,*
£572 ($818)

9
A child's pedal car, English, c.1950, repainted apple green, 122cm (48in), *L 1 Dec,*
£253 ($362)

10
A child's galloper tricycle, English, c.1900, the wooden horse body painted dapple grey, leather saddle and bridle, 81cm (32in) long, *L 20 May,*
£495 ($792)

11
A child's rocking horse chair, English, c.1900, the chair in turned and shaped pine, 107cm (42in), *L 2 June,*
£341 ($525)

12
A rocking horse, English, c.1900, the hide-covered horse with horsehair mane and tail, mounted on pine trestle, restored overall, 153cm (60in), *L 3 Feb,*
£880 ($1,285)

1
An F. Martin mechanical 'L'Hercule Populaire' strong man, French, c.1905, worn overall, 19cm (7½in), *L 20 May,*
£385 ($616)

2
A clockwork toy in the form of an old woman, probably Gunthermann, c.1905, hand-painted, the mechanism causing her to move forwards, 17.5cm (7in), *L 23 Sept,*
£264 ($370)

3
A tinplate clown musician, probably by Gunthermann, German, c.1900, 17.5cm (6¾in), *L 23 Sept,*
£220 ($308)

4
A set of eight hollow-cast fusiliers, c.1905, one base and three rifle arms missing, *S 3 Nov,*
£93 ($131)

5
A tumbling Chinaman toy, mid 19th century, 31cm (12¼in), *L 23 Sept,*
£682 ($955)

6
A tinplate bagatelle player, German, c.1910, 15cm (5in), *C 18 Mar,*
£242 ($370)

7
A Tipp tinplate group of petrol pumps, German, c.1925, with printed moulded-glass finials, some wear, 23.5cm (9¾in), *L 20 May,*
£286 ($458)

8
A tinplate carousel, German, c.1910, accompanied by a four-note tune, worn, 33cm (13in), *C 18 Mar,*
£220 ($337)

9
A lead elephant hunting scene, early 20th century, possibly Heyde, comprising 24 pieces, *C 4 June,*
£462 ($716)

10
A Britain's 18in. heavy howitzer No.211, English, c.1905, with original box, some wear, 43cm (17in), *L 20 May,*
£880 ($1,408)

11
An Ives 'General Butler' mechanical walking figure, American, c.1880, slight wear, 24cm (9½in), *L 20 May,*
£1,100 ($1,760)

12
A tin rowing boat, German, c.1925, probably by Kellermann, some wear, 74cm (29in), *A 24 Apr,*
Dfl 1,725 (£522; $819)

13
A group of Imperial Russian Guard lead soldiers, German, c.1900, probably by Heyde, comprising 68 pieces, *L 23 Sept,*
£330 ($462)

14
A Marklin tinplate Graf-Zeppelin, German, late 1930s, lithographed silver, numbered *D-LZ130*, 62cm (24¼in), *L 5 Feb,*
£715 ($1,030)

15
A Gebruder Bing clockwork tinplate gunboat, German, c.1912, repainted, losses, 63.5cm (25in), *L 20 May,*
£660 ($1,056)

1

2 3

4

5

6

7

8

9

10

11 12

13

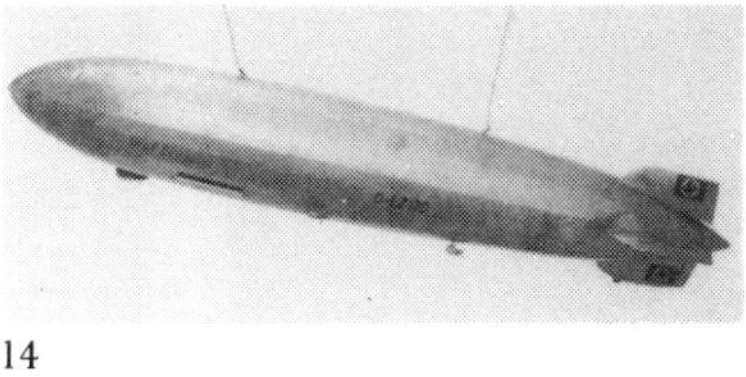
14

15

1

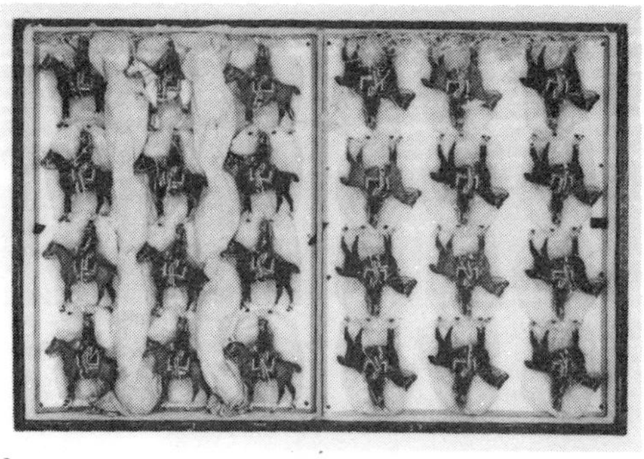
2

3

4

5

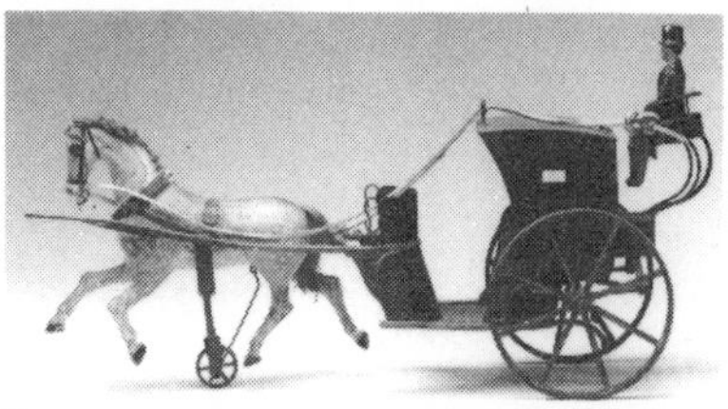
6

7

8

9

10

11

12

13

14

1
A Britains' No.433 monoplane, with pilot, in original hangar box, minor damage, *S 3 Nov,*
£1,650 ($2,310)

2
A box of 24 large-scale Heyde Belgian cavalry, German, c.1900, the figures still stitched to the base of the box, 82.5cm (32½in), *L 5 Feb,*
£1,155 ($1,663)

3
A Britains' George VI Coronation display set, No.1477, English, c.1936, in original cardboard box, *L 5 Feb,*
£440 ($634)

4
A Carette tinplate two-seat open tourer, German, c.1908, lacking driver, some wear, 26cm (10¼in), *L 20 May,*
£1,870 ($2,992)

5
A Bub tinplate two-seat runabout, German, c.1908, some wear, 21.5cm (8½in), *L 20 May,*
£1,760 ($2,816)

6
A tinplate hansom cab, probably Lutz, German, late 19th century, some wear, reins replaced, 37cm (14½in), *L 23 Sept,*
£1,870 ($2,618)

7
A Lehmann lithographed tin clockwork autobus, German, c.1910, inoperative, 20cm (8in), *NY 16 Dec,*
$770 (£538)

8
Thirty-two die cast Citroën toys, *(one illustrated),* four boxed, mixed condition, *L 23 Sept,*
£242 ($339)

9
Twenty-two die cast Chrysler, Dodge, Hudson, Panhard and De Soto cars, *(one illustrated),* four boxed, mixed condition, *L 23 Sept,*
£275 ($385)

10
Twenty die cast Studebaker, Pontiac and Oldsmobile cars, *(one illustrated),* one boxed, mixed condition, *L 23 Sept,*
£220 ($308)

11
Twenty-two die cast Cadillac, Buick and Corvette cars, *(one illustrated),* one boxed, mixed condition, *L 23 Sept,*
£264 ($370)

12
Twenty die cast Lincoln and Chevrolet vehicles, *(one illustrated),* one boxed, mixed condition, *L 23 Sept,*
£308 ($431)

13
A tinplate Tipp limousine, German, c.1920s, with clockwork mechanism, some losses, 39cm (15½in), *L 23 Sept,*
£935 ($1,309)

14
A Lehmann 'Berolina' tinplate motor car, EPL No.686, German, c.1918, with clockwork mechanism, lacking windshield and flag, 16.5cm (6½in), *L 23 Sept,*
£550 ($770)

1
A Lehmann 'Panne' tinplate touring car, EPL No.687, German, c.1925, with clockwork mechanism, 17cm (6¾in), *L 20 May,*
£462 ($739)

2
A Lehmann Li-La tinplate toy, German, c.1910, EPL 520, with clockwork mechanism, 14cm (5½in), *L 20 May,*
£572 ($915)

3
A Gunthermann tinplate and clockwork 'General' double-deck bus, c.1936, battery-operated lights, 33cm (13in), *S 10 Feb,*
£418 ($585)

4
A Burnett tinplate limousine, English, c.1915, some wear, 35cm (13¼in), *C 4 June,*
£308 ($477)

5
A George Mangold tinplate Cadillac, German, c.1955, model Gama 300, 32cm (12½in), *C 18 Mar,*
£385 ($589)

6
A Tri-Ang tinplate and clockwork M.G. Midget record car, repainted green, original driver, 40cm (15¾in), *S 10 Feb,*
£187 ($262)

7
A Britains' No.1656 Railton record car, detachable 'teardrop' body, in original box (damaged), *S 3 Nov,*
£187 ($262)

8
A Gunthermann tinplate 'Napier Campbell' 'Bluebird III' record car, German, c.1931, clockwork mechanism, 51cm (20in), *L 23 Sept,*
£605 ($847)

9
A Märklin Standard petrol tanker, German, 42cm (16½in), *A 24 Apr,*
Dfl 4,140 (£1,254; $1,968)

10
A Dinky toys 28/2 series 2nd type delivery vans, set of six, in original box, some fatigue, *S 3 Nov,*
£1,430 ($2,002)

11
An A.J. & E. Stevens cast-iron mechanical 'Dentist' bank, American, late 19th century, 24cm (9½in), *L 5 Feb,*
£935 ($1,346)

12
A William Tell cast-iron mechanical bank, probably American, 20th century, base stamped *Pat Apld For*, 26.5cm (10½in), *L 23 Sept,*
£330 ($462)

13
A tinplate frog and snake mechanical money box, German, c.1925, some wear, 13cm (5¼in), *L 20 May,*
£2,530 ($4,048)

14
A Kyser & Rex cast-iron 'Lion and Monkeys' money box, American, c.1883, base inscribed *Pat. July 17.83*, overcleaned, 24cm (9½in), *C 4 June,*
£253 ($392)

1

2

3

4

5

6

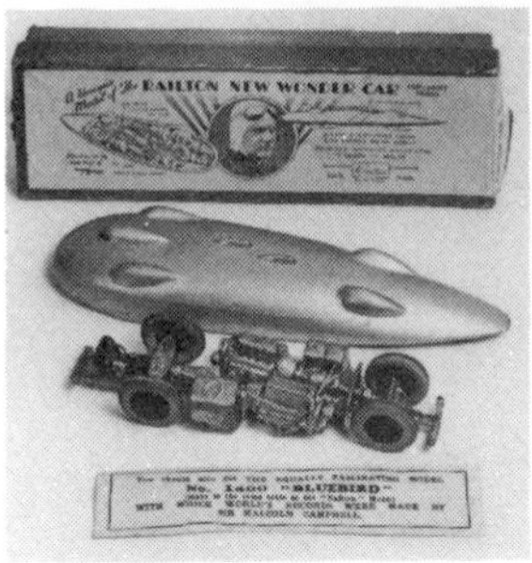

7

8

9

10

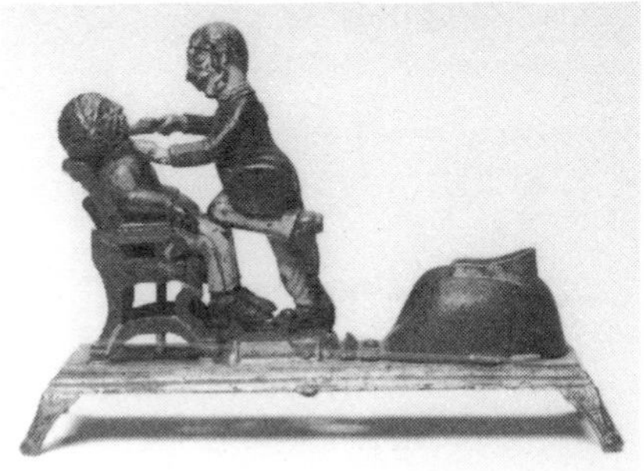
11

12

13

14

1

2

3

4

5

6

7

8

9

10

11 12

13

14

15

16

17

18

19

20

21

1
A Bassett-Lowke gauge '3' 4-4-0 spirit-fired tank engine 'The Brighton', *CS 5 July,*
£429 ($691)

2
A Bing for Bassett-Lowke 0-4-0 clockwork Peckett Pannier locomotive, No.1017, *CS 5 July,*
£418 ($673)

3
A Bassett-Lowke gauge '0' clockwork 0-6-0 tank locomotive, *S 14 May,*
£88 ($140)

4
A Hornby gauge '0' No.2 special clockwork Bramham Moor locomotive, No.201, with matching tender, *S 14 May,*
£198 ($315)

5
A gauge '0' clockwork 2-6-4 tank locomotive, No.21, with maker's plate *Built 1972, Preston, S 14 May,*
£132 ($210)

6
A Märklin tin gauge '1' locomotive, c.1905, 23.5cm (9¼in), *A 24 Apr,*
Dfl 391 (£118; $186)

7
A Merkelbach metal and brass steam locomotive, c.1900, stamped *VULKAN,* 26cm (10¼in), *A 24 Apr,*
Dfl 2,760 (£836; $1,313)

8
A Bing spirit-fired gauge II 2-2-0 locomotive, German, c.1898, unpainted, 23cm (9in), *L 5 Feb,*
£198 ($285)

9
A Marklin gauge '1' live steam spirit-fired 4-6-2 locomotive 'Great Bear', German, c.1925, repairs, *L 23 Sept,*
£715 ($1,001)

10
A Marklin gauge '0' fitted bogie coach and passengers, German, c.1905, sold with a workman's hut and a guard's hut, *L 20 May,*
£935 ($1,496)

11
A hand-painted and lithographed tinplate gauge '1' station building, c.1910, possibly Marklin, 85cm (33½in), *C 4 June,*
£1,210 ($1,876)

12
A Bing gauge '1' 4-4-0 clockwork tinplate locomotive, German, c.1904, No.7096, of Adams Flyer type, lacking front lamps, *C 4 June,*
£682 ($1,057)

13
A gauge '1' Bassett-Lowk London & North Wester Railway 4-6-0 locomotiv c.1927, with four sections of track, *L 23 Sept,*
£2,200 ($3,080)

14
An Ives gauge '1' 'President Washington' electri locomotive, 33cm (13in), *NY 16 Dec,*
$605 (£423)

15
A Lionel Hudson type super detail scale model No.700E locomotive, wit a 'New York Central' tender, 61cm (24in), *NY 16 Dec,*
$2,750 (£1,923)

16
A Knapp standard gauge cast-iron electric locomotive and tender, c.1905, 34cm (13½in), *NY 16 Dec,*
$1,760 (£1,231)

17
A Bassett-Lowke gauge ' 4-6-0 clockwork 'Royal Scot' locomotive, No.6100, *CS 5 July,*
£396 ($638)

18
A Lionel standard gauge painted metal No.300 'Hell Gate' bridge, Ameri can, with various accessories, *NY 16 Dec,*
$1,100 (£769)

19
A Lionel gauge '0' twin-motored 0-4-0 electric locomotive, American, 1930s, No.254E, lacking electric lamps, *C 18 Mar,*
£143 ($219)

20
A tinplate gauge '0' Rock & Graner station, German, c.1895, some chips, 27cm (10½in) wide, *L 23 Sept,*
£550 ($770)

21
A Marklin painted tin warehouse, German, 1902, No.1045, 39.5cm (15½in), *NY 16 Dec,*
$935 (£654)

\ Mughal marble plant ot, c.18th century, buff-oloured, standing on ight bracket feet, the des carved with large onds, 86cm (34in) diam., *24 Nov,*
7,700 ($10,934)

Tibetan copper inlaid rass figure of a Iahasiddha, 15th/16th entury, with brownish atina, sealed, 10cm (4in), *10 Mar,*
770 ($1,170)

\ Tibetan bronze figure of 'ajradhara, 17th century r earlier, Pala style, traces f cold-gilding, unsealed, 6cm (6¼in), *L 10 Mar,*
880 ($1,338)

\n Indian brass figure of he Bodhisattva Padma-ani, Pala, c.12th century, nsealed, 7cm (2¾in), *10 Mar,*
902 ($1,371)

\ Western Indian white narble stele depicting a emale musician, 8th/19th century, olding a drum, 119cm 43in), *L 11 Mar,*
2,750 ($4,152)

\ Western Indian white narble stele depicting a emale musician, 8th/19th century, olding a child in one rm, a lotus in the other, 18cm (42½in), *L 11 Mar,*
2,750 ($4,152)

\ Western Indian white narble stele depicting a emale musician, 8th/19th century, olding a *vina,* 118cm 42½in), *L 11 Mar,*
2,750 ($4,152)

\ Western Indian white narble stele depicting a emale musician, 8th/19th century, olding a horn, 117.5cm 42¼in), *L 11 Mar,*
2,750 ($4,152)

These four sculptures probably served as ceiling or eave brackets within a emple.

1

2

3

4

5 6 7 8

1

2

3

4

1
A Chinesco male figure, Protoclassic, c.100 BC-250 AD, painted overall in reddish-brown, with a necklace of buff-painted beads and finely incised hair falling down his back, 56cm (22in), *NY 24 Nov,*
$24,200 (£17,042)

2
An Olmec blackware duck, Las Bocas, Middle Preclassic, c.1150-550 BC, an opening at the top of the head, 20.5cm (8in), *NY 20 May,*
$24,200 (£16,026)

3
An early Huari shell pendant, Central coast, c.800-1000 AD, the spondylus shell inlaid with an Huari dignitary, his limbs of translucent olive green stone, the facial plane of salmon-coloured spondylus, applied mother-of-pearl and jet eyes, the shirt of mother-of-pearl, green stone, spondylus and mussel shell, 13.5cm (5¼in), *NY 20 May,*
$19,800 (£13,113)

4
A Jalisco wrestler, Protoclassic, c.100 BC-250 AD, his body painted overall in reddish-brown, his face in cream with remains of black facial decoration along the chin and mouth, 45.5cm (18in), *NY 20 May,*
$20,900 (£13,841)

Yoruba head-dress, *Ere lede,* the female head with zenge scarification on ch cheek, her tall iffure bound in a wide oth criss-crossing at the ont, traces of red earth gment and indigo in the es and ears, 28cm (11in), *Y 18 Nov,*
11,000 (£7,857)

Kota wood and etalwork reliquary ardian figure, bamba/Mindumu area, *bulu ngulu,* decorated with oss-hatched copper eets on the collar and iffure, the crescent ove with stippled brass eeting, 46.5cm (18¼in), *Y 18 Nov,*
11,000 (£7,857)

Fijian wood figure, the rface worn through ear, very fine dark own patina with black crustations, 19cm ½in), *L 24 Mar,*
33,000 ($51,810)

Yaure wood face mask, ith very fine patina. The aure people are a small opulation who live in the aule country, west of uafflé, the most impor- nt centre in the Guro rea. 39cm (15½in), *24 Mar,*
4,950 ($7,772)

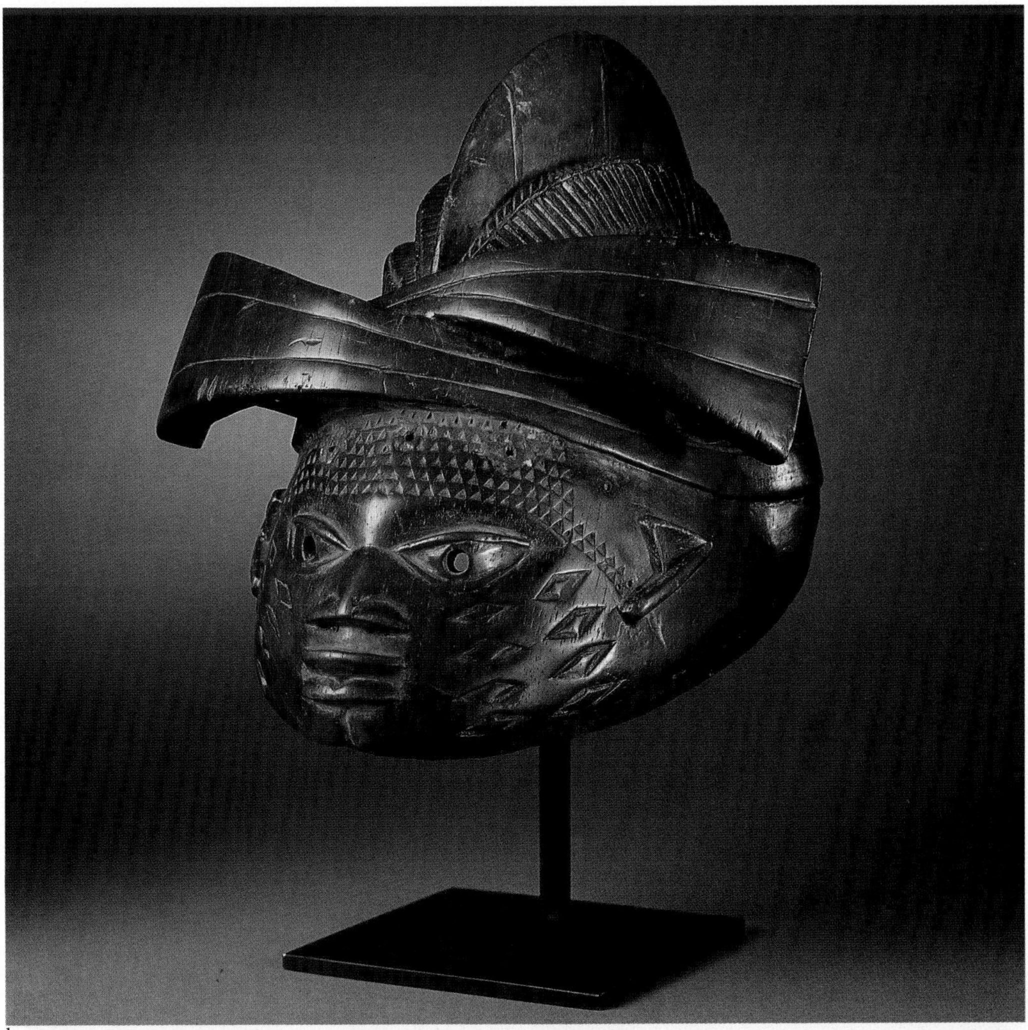
1

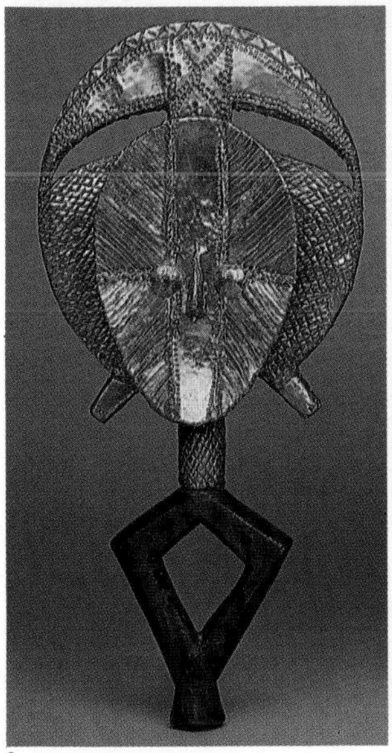
2

3

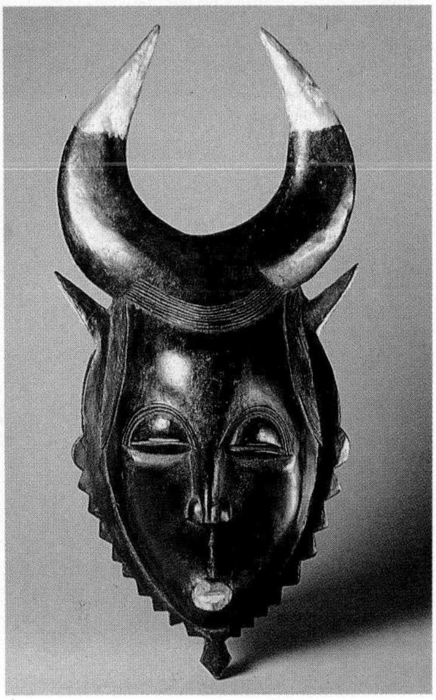
4

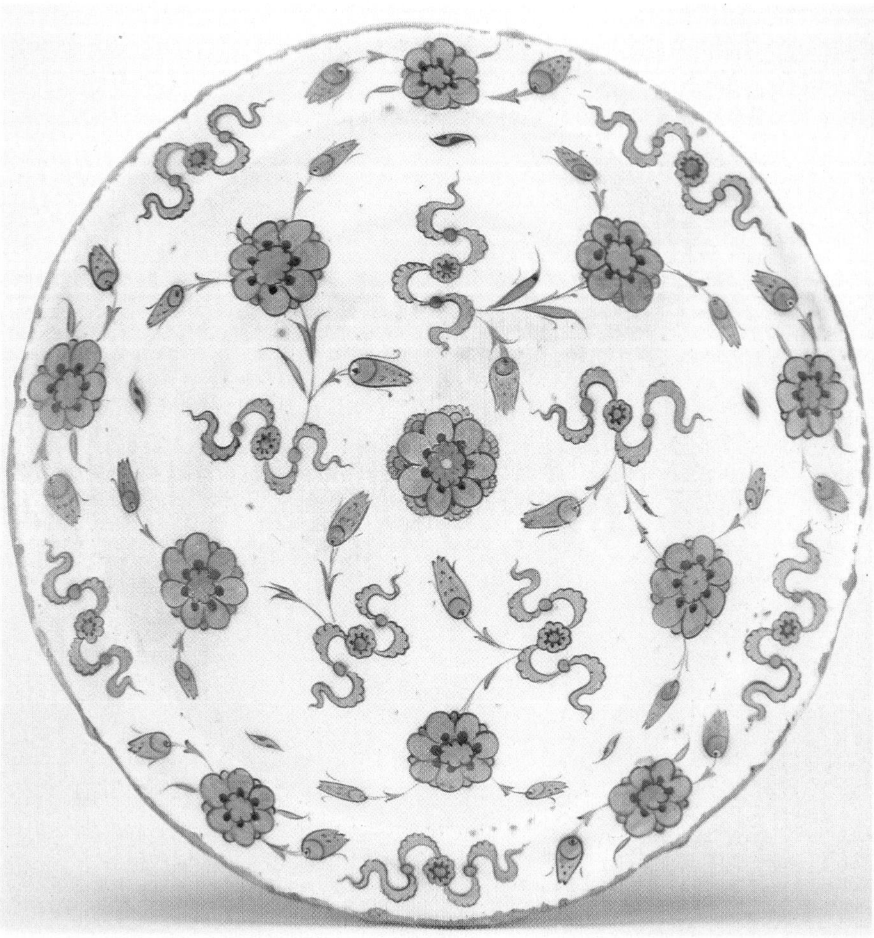
1

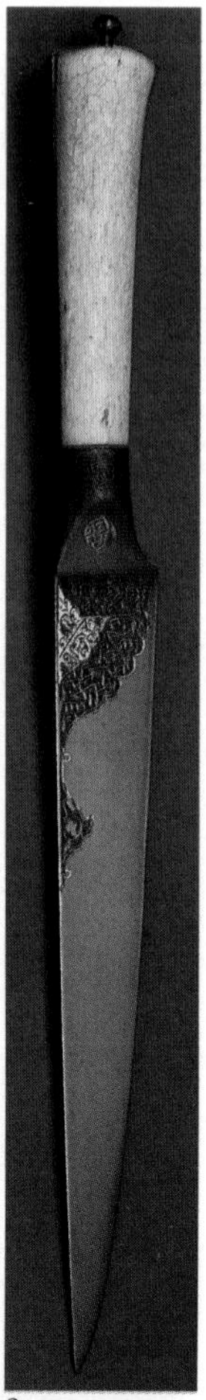
2

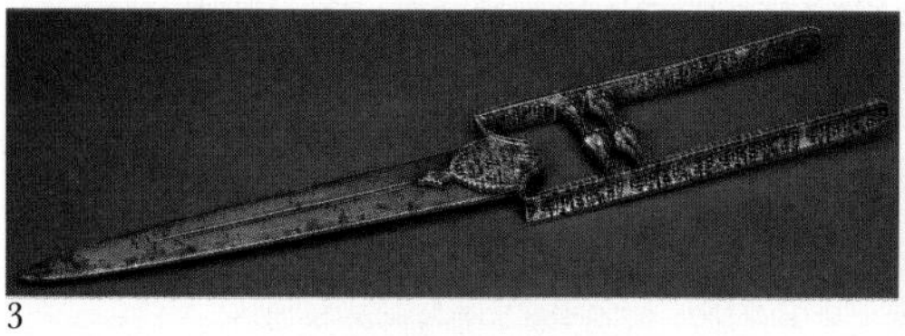
3

4

5

1
An Isnik 'Damascus' pottery dish, c.1530-50, with sloping bracketed rim, decorated with a design of cloudbands and tulip sprays forming a five-pointed star centred on a rosette, the rim with cloudbands alternating with rosettes and tulip sprays, the exterior with floral sprays, 36.5cm (14¼in) diam., *L 15 Oct,*
£18,150 ($25,410)

2
A Persian dagger *(kard)*, dated 1240 AH (1824-25 AD), the grips of walrus ivory, the watered steel blade and straps with chiselled cartouches of Koranic verse, the spine with an urn containing a flowering plant, some areas of gold damascening, 36.5cm (14½in), *L 15 Oct,*
£1,573 ($2,202)

3
An Indian dagger *(katar)*, Lucknow, 19th century, the hilt and forte decorated with silver enamel with panels containing flowering plants, all in shades of blue, green, red and yellow, the double-edged steel blade with single fuller, 48.5cm (19in), *L 15 Oct,*
£1,210 ($1,694)

4
A Persian underglaze-painted pottery bowl, la 13th/14th century, standing on a ring foot, decorated with panels of stripes, dots and scrolls radiating from a central roundel, the exterior with paired vertical stripes and a herring-bone band below the rim, 15.5cm (6in) diam., *L 15 Oct,*
£1,573 ($2,202)

5
A Safavid blue-and-whi dish, Meshed, 17th century, the central medallion painted with a stag leaping in a foliage landscape, quatrefoils flanked by trefoils on the exterior, a pseudo-Chinese mark underneath, 40cm (15¾in) diam., *NY 30 May,*
$15,400 (£10,476)

ın Ottoman parcel-gilt ravelling scribe set, 8th/19th century, comprising an inkpot and encase, maker's mark, 7.5cm (11in) long, *15 Oct,* **1,331 ($1,863)**

ın Ottoman silver ravelling scribe set, eriod of Abdülmecid, 839-61, comprising an ıkpot and pencase, with races of gilding, marked vith the *tughra* of Abdülıecid and the maker's ıark of Wasi?, 25.5cm 10in), *L 15 Oct,* **2,178 ($3,049)**

ın Ottoman parcel-gilt ravelling scribe set, eriod of Mahmud I, 730-54, the inkpot set vith a cabochon ruby and narked with the *tughra* of Aahmud I, 23.5cm 9¼in), *L 15 Oct,* **3,630 ($5,082)**

ın Ottoman silver ewer, tand and basin, late 19th entury, fully marked with *tughra*, ewer 31.5cm 12½in) high, *L 15 Oct,* **9,680 ($13,552)**

Safavid open-work steel laque, mid 16th century, vith a central inscription artouche reading *Blessings f God be upon him and his amily*, 14.5cm (5¾in) liam., *L 16 Apr,* **4,400 ($6,820)**

Safavid open-work steel laque, mid 16th century, rom a group of eight laques each containing a erse from an Arabic oem referring to the 'ourteen Innocent Ones, 8.5cm (15in) long, *16 Apr,* **19,800 ($30,690)**

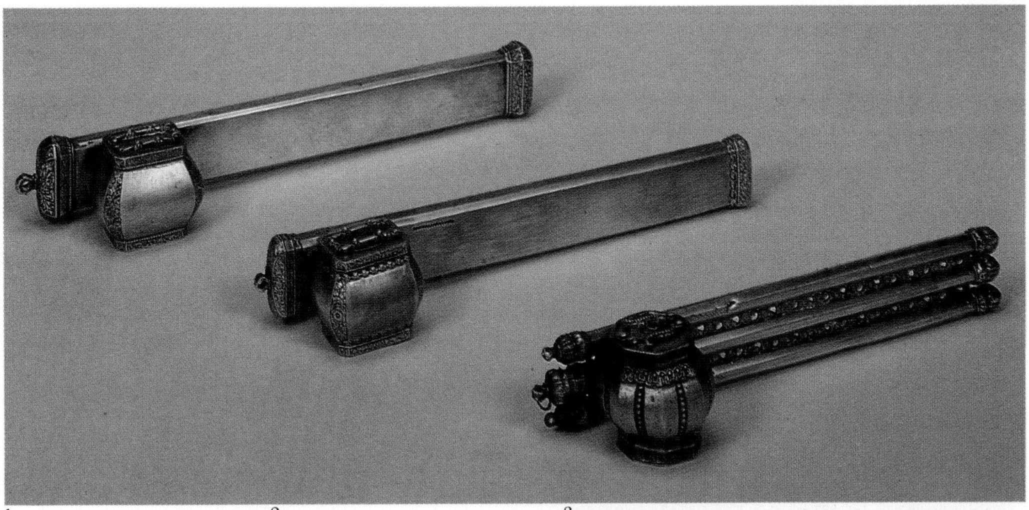

1 2 3

4

5

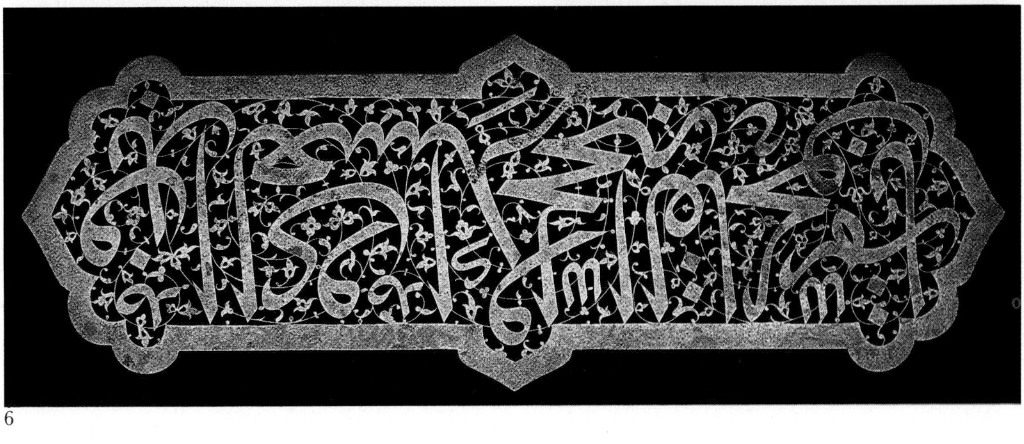

6

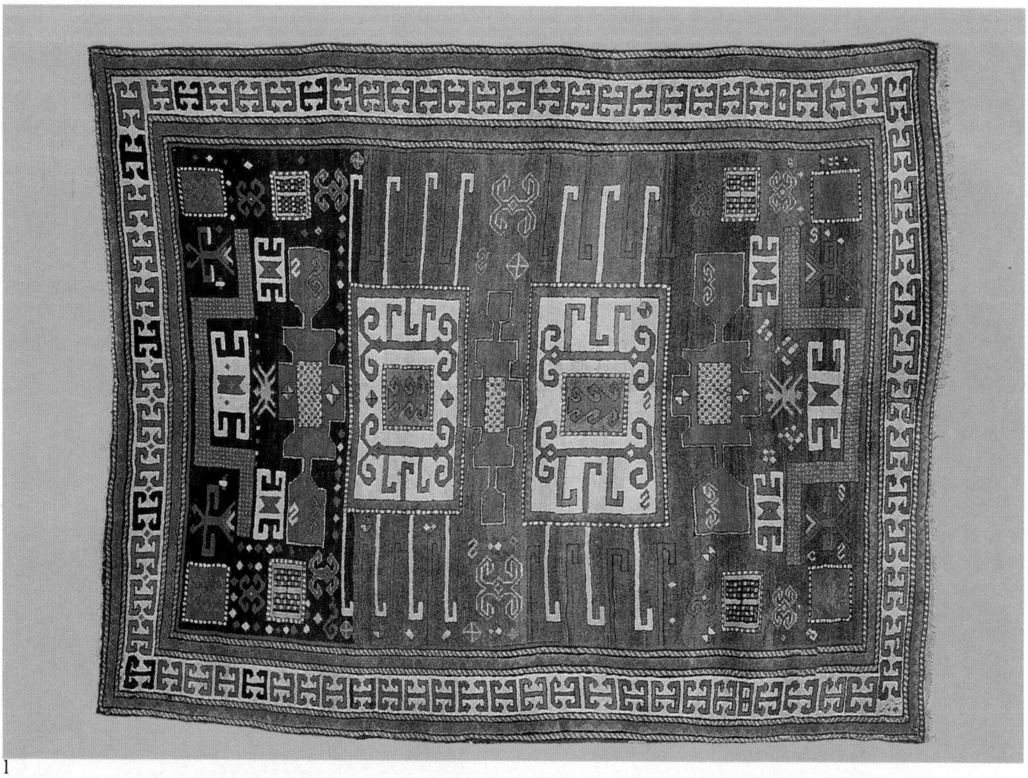

1

2

1
A Kazakh rug, late 19th century, 224 x 173cm (7ft 4in x 5ft 8in), *NY 31 May,* **$19,800 (£13,469)**

2
A Kazakh rug, late 19th century, 196 x 158cm (6ft 5in x 5ft 2in), *NY 13 Dec,* **$8,250 (£5,893)**

1
A Soumakh carpet, the madder field with three indigo medallions and saffron *guls*, 277 x 216cm (9ft 1in x 7ft 1in),
L 16 Apr,
£4,180 ($6,479)

2
An East Caucasian carpet, late 19th century, 559 x 295cm (18ft 4in x 9ft 8in),
NY 31 May,
$23,100 (£15,714)

3
A Shirvan carpet, the indigo field with twin pole medallion, within ivory love bird border, 280 x 191cm (9ft 2in x 6ft 3in),
L 16 Apr,
£1,870 ($2,899)

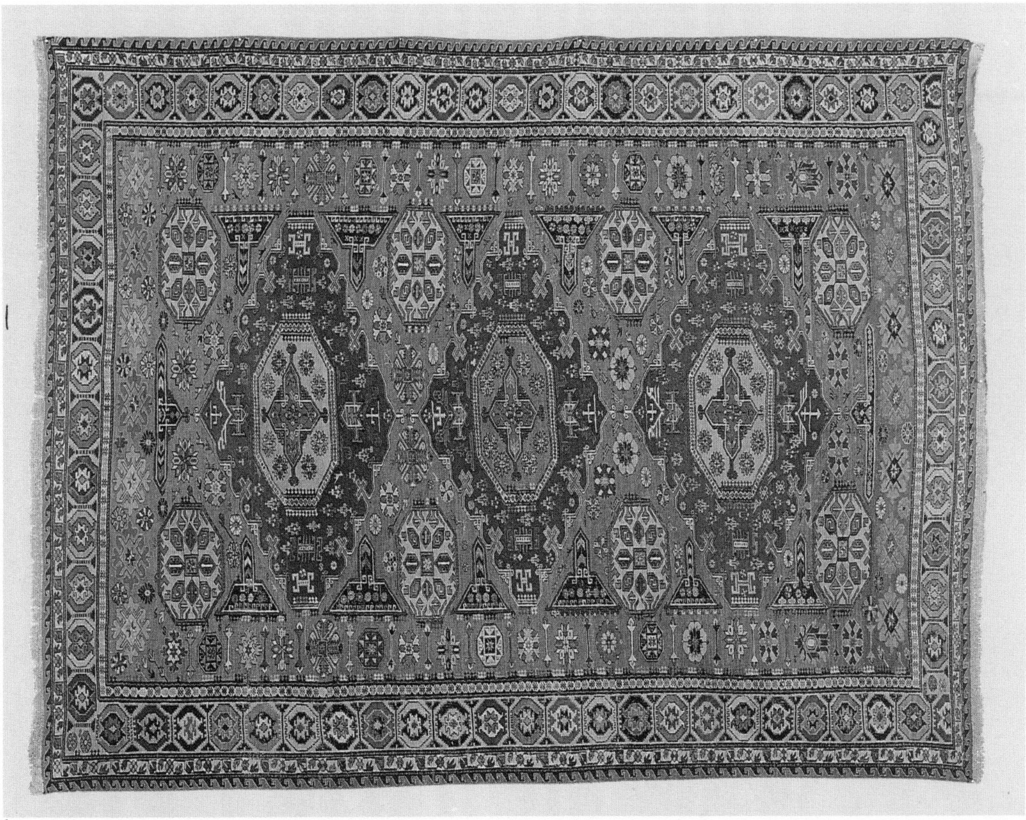
1

2

3

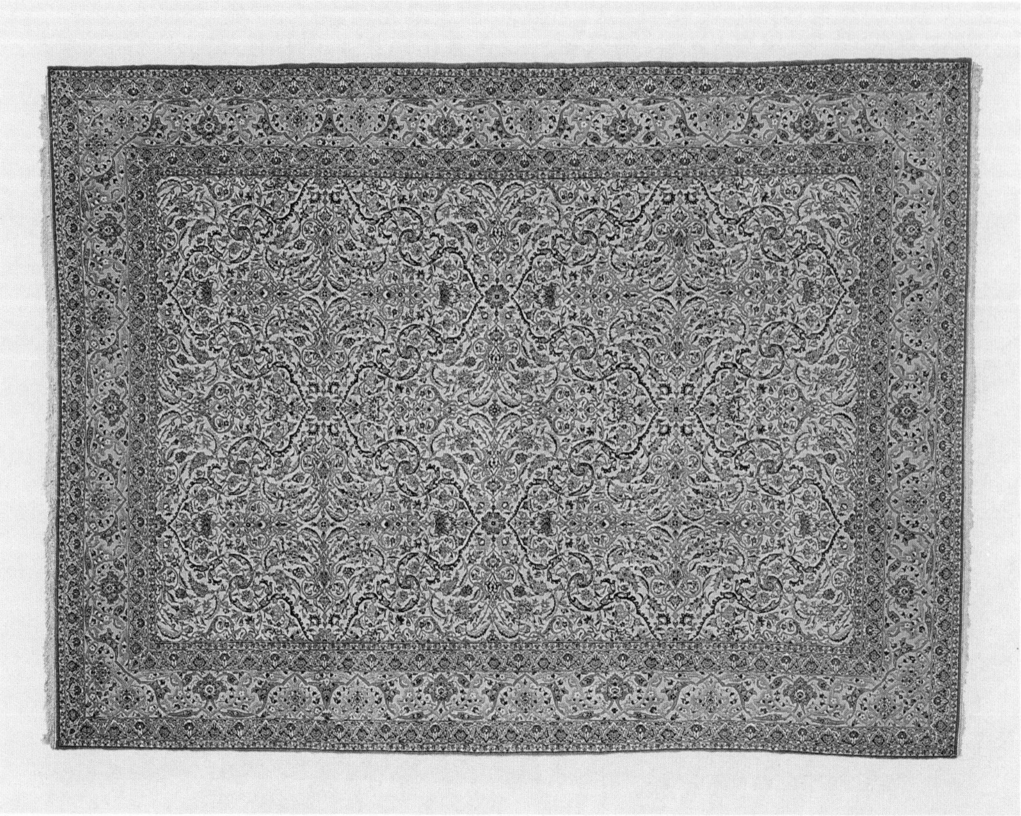

1

2

3

1
A Nain carpet, 20th century, 445 x 328cm (14ft 7in x 10ft 9in), *NY 31 May,*
$19,800 (£13,469)

2
A Heriz carpet, the indigo field with saffron, madder and pale indigo pole medallion and spandrels, 459 x 349cm (15ft 1in x 11ft 5in), *L 12 Feb,*
£3,190 ($4,753)

3
A Khamseh rug, c.1900, 297 x 152cm (9ft 9in x 5ft), *NY 13 Dec,*
$6,600 (£4,714)

1
A Bidjar silk rug, the plain camel field with madder medallion, pale indigo *botehs*, vine and leaf border, 180 x 143cm (5ft 11in x 4ft 8in), *L 15 Oct,*
£20,570 ($28,798)

2
A Kashan Kurk rug, the ivory field with indigo and ivory medallion, with overall design of vines, flowerheads and leaves, 185 x 132cm (6ft 1in x 4ft 4in), *L 15 Oct,*
£4,840 ($6,776)

3
A Kazakh Karatchop rug, the indigo field with ivory and madder hooked medallion, within a saffron *gul* and double E border, 215 x 158cm (7ft 1in x 5ft 2in), *L 15 Oct,*
£5,324 ($7,454)

1

2

3

1

2 3 2

1
A deep purple silk informal robe, c.1900, satin stitched with butterflies amid peonies and narcissus, 145cm (57in), *NY 25 Sept,*
$5,775 (£3,850)

2
A pair of cloisonné enamel beaker vases, Qianlong, the neck and foot with upright and pendent archaistic cicada blades and four *shou* medallions amongst stylised flowers, 32cm (12½in), *L 9 May,*
£3,520 ($5,667)

3
A cloisonné enamel censer and cover, Qianlong, of archaic inspiration, of rectangular *ding* form, with dissolved *taotie* masks divided and interspersed by notched vertical flanges, surmounted by a gilt bronze Buddhist lion, 39.5cm (15½in), *L 9 May,*
£3,080 ($4,959)

1
A ge-type vase, seal mark and period of Qianlong, ash-grey glaze suffused with dark crackle, footrim covered in purple wash, 23cm (9in), *L 10 June,*
£3,960 ($6,217)

2
A pale grey jade flower-form vase, 18th century, a branch of *lingzhi* fungus forming the base, 13cm (5in), *NY 26 Sept,*
$2,310 (£1,540)

3
A pair of dragon and phoenix bowls, *(one illustrated)* seal marks and period of Qianlong, the exterior decorated in 'famille-verte' enamels with details in underglaze-blue, 15.5cm (6in), *L 10 June,*
£4,400 ($6,908)

4
A splashed Junyao bowl, Song Dynasty, covered with a bubble-suffused glaze of greyish-blue, 11cm (4¼in), *HK 20 May,*
HK$93,500 (£8,274; $13,239)

5
A Ming-style bowl, seal mark and period of Jiaqing, decorated in *rouge-de-fer*, green enamel and underglaze-blue, 10cm (4in), *L 9 Dec,*
£924 ($1,294)

6
A 'famille-rose' bowl, seal mark and period of Qianlong, decorated with a flowering gourd vine, 11cm (4¾in), *L 9 Dec,*
£3,080 ($4,312)

7
A glass overlay snuff bottle, 1820-80, decorated with a lotus on a spray of red millet, *NY 27 June,*
$1,265 (£827)

8
An ivory snuff bottle, resting on a neatly finished footrim, *L 6 May,*
£660 ($1,049)

9
A Peking glass snuff bottle, 1750-1850, with tortoiseshell-like pattern of crimson and yellow patches, imitating realgar, *NY 27 June,*
$605 (£395)

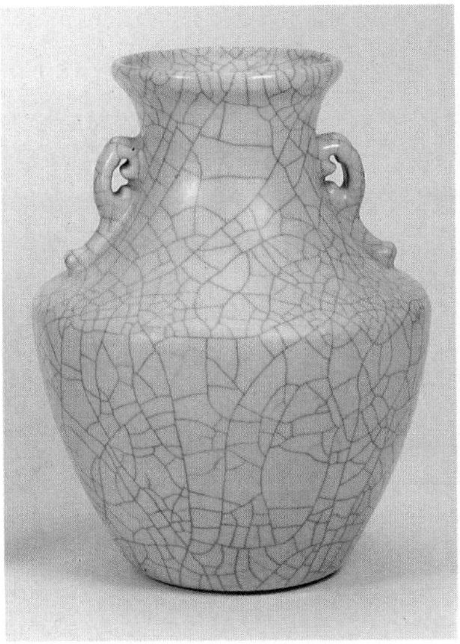
1

2

3

4

5 6

7

8

9

1 2

3 4

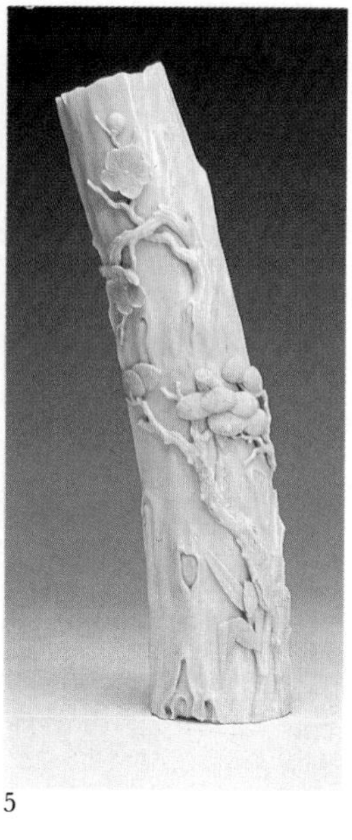

5

1
A marbled pottery wine cup, Tang Dynasty, covered inside and out in a translucent glaze of amber tint, 7.5cm (3in), *NY 3 Dec,*
$7,150 (£5,000)

2
A marbled pottery bottle vase, Tang Dynasty, the red and white marbled ware covered with a thin pale yellow glaze, 18cm (7in), *NY 3 Dec,*
$12,100 (£8,461)

3
An ivory figure of a lady, 17th century, a hare resting within her folded arms, the ivory of a rich honey tone, smooth patina, 22cm (8¾in), *HK 20 May,*
HK$ 17,600 (£1,558; $2,492)

4
An ivory tree boat, 18th century, carved as a prunus trunk, 19cm (7½in) high, *HK 20 May,*
HK$ 39,600 (£3,504; $5,607)

5
An ivory wrist rest, 19th century, carved as a section of prunus trunk, enveloped on the exterior by a branch in blossom, a pine tree and a spray of bamboo to form the 'Three Friends', 27cm (10½in), *HK 19 Nov,*
HK$ 55,000 (£4,955; $6,937)

1
A huanghuali side table, *(bienan)*, Ming Dynasty, 83cm (32¾in), *NY 11 Apr*, **$8,250 (£5,612)**

2
A pair of Zitan armchairs and a matching tea table, 17th century, the seats with extensive lacquer underneath, the table 77cm (30¼in) high, *NY 26 Sept*, **$11,000 (£7,333)**

1

2

1

2

3

See facing page for captions to illustrations.

TYPES OF DECORATION

Aogai blue/green mother-of-pearl shell inlay.

Cloisonné enamelware in which the design is delineated by wires.

E-nashiji nashiji forming design rather than background.

Fundame dull or matt gold or silver lacquer.

Guribori carved lacquer in layers of alternating colour.

Hiramakie flat lacquer decoration.

Hirame small metal flakes.

Iroe-takazogan relief inlay of coloured metals.

Ishime roughened surface technique.

Kinji bright gold lacquer.

Kirigane minute squares of gold foil applied to lacquer.

Mokko four-lobed, of cross section.

Mura-nashiji clouds of nashiji.

Nanako lit. 'fish-skin', punching technique, giving a pebbled appearance to metal.

Nashiji lit. 'pear-skin', powdered metals, usually gold, under a transparent lacquer forming a dense ground.

Nunome thin gold/silver sheet fastened to a cross-hatched ground.

Okibirame setting of dull gold flakes larger than fundame in lacquer.

Plique-à-jour enamelware in which the metal body is removed.

Raden white shell used for inlay.

Roiro polished black lacquer.

Sentoku an alloy of brass and copper.

Shakudo alloy of gold, silver and copper, black in colour.

Shibayama technique of inlaying minute pieces of various materials into ivory and lacquer; name of family that developed technique.

Shibuichi metal alloy of gold, silver and copper, dull grey in appearance.

Shippo enamels used in cloisonné work.

Takamakie relief design in lacquer.

Togidashi burnished lacquer design flush with surface.

ʌ Kakiemon dish, late 7th century, decorated vith a dragon descending rom clouds above bamboo and prunus before a ger, firing crack, 18cm 7¼in), *L 13 June,* **4,840 ($7,744)**

ʌ Kakiemon dish, first alf 18th century, decorated with a circular panel howing Moso tending amboo shoots, bordered y panels of pine, prunus nd bamboo, Fuku mark, 3cm (9in), *L 13 June,* **6,600 ($10,560)**

ʌ Nabeshima dish, early 8th century, raised on a all foot, decorated with a pray of peonies and inks, the reverse with hree groups of tasselled ash, hair crack, 19.5cm 7¾in) diam., *L 13 Mar,* **£7,700 ($11,858)**

aptions to illustrations n p.574:-

ʌ set of three vases and overs, late 17th century, ach of octagonal ovoid orm, decorated with haped panels showing ases of peonies and birds above prunus, reserved on *kiku* and peonies, the houlders with panels of irds and flowers, the overs (restored) with *hishi* knops, 62.5cm (24½in), *L 13 June,* **£6,270 ($10,032)**

2
naba Nanaho (attributed to), a pair of cloisonné vases, Meiji period, each body worked in varying thicknesses of silver wire with butterflies in flight against a midnight blue ground, unsigned, 31.5cm (12½in), *L 14 Nov,* **£10,450 ($14,630)**

3
A pair of inlaid Shakudo vases, Meiji period, each with a *shakudo ishime* body decorated in relief with swallows flying beneath trailing wistaria, worked in *shakudo, shibuichi,* patinated bronze, silver and gilt, slight dent, 24cm (9½in), *L 14 Nov,* **£3,850 ($5,390)**

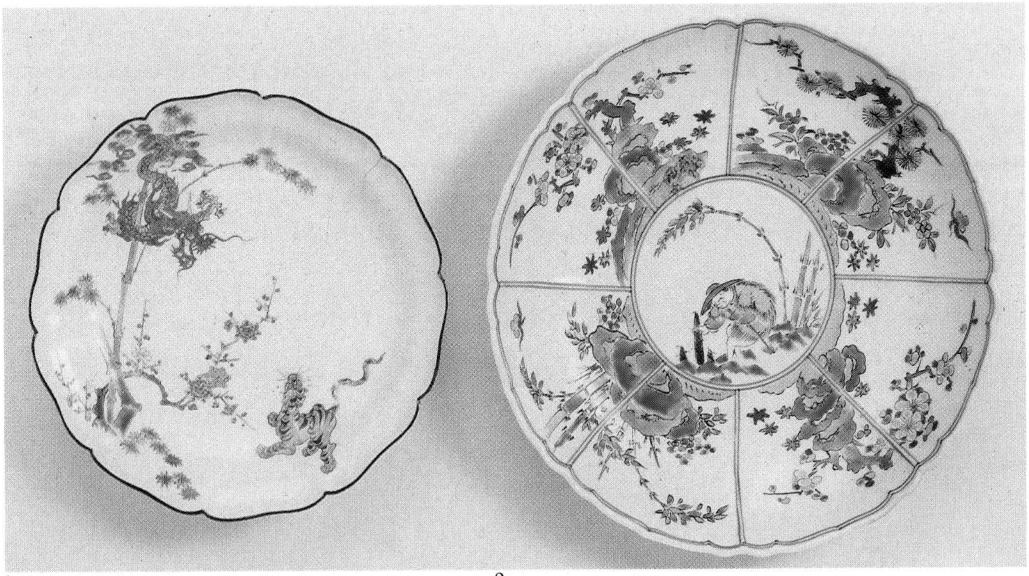

1 2

3

1

2 *(above)* 3 *(below)*

4

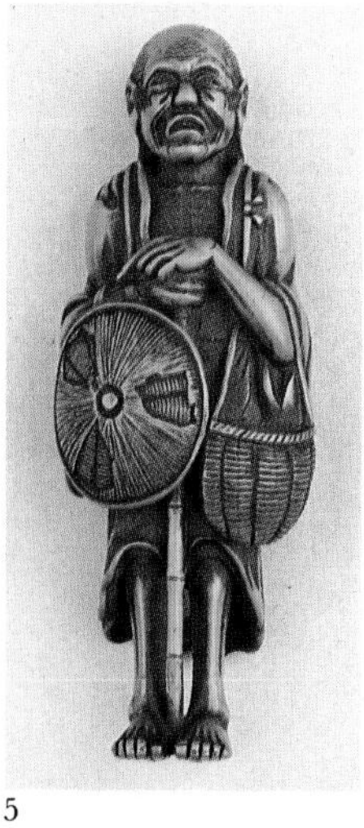
5

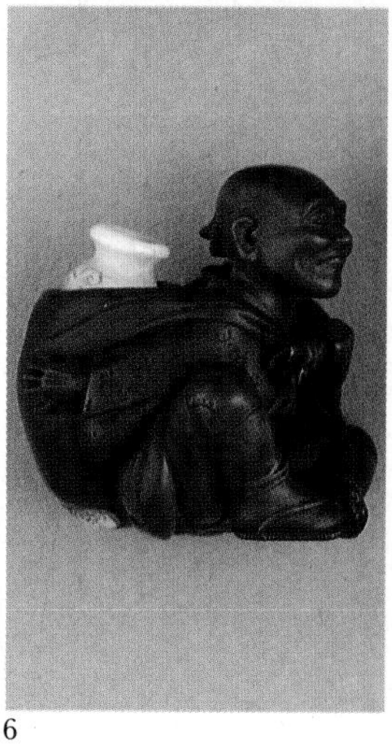
6

7

1
A lacquer travelling storage trunk, early 19th century, decorated in gold and silver *hiramakie* and *takamakie* with leafy bamboo, on a *nashiji* ground, engraved copper mounts, one hinge missing, supported on six legs, 104cm (41in) wide, *NY 10 Apr,*
$12,100 (£8,231)

2
Goto School: a shakudo kozuka, 19th century, applied in *iroe-takazogan* on the fine *nanako* ground, unsigned, *L 13 Nov,*
£770 ($1,078)

3
Nomura Masanao: a silve kozuka, 19th century, carved in relief with flowering peonies, signed *Nomura Masanao at the age of 70, L 13 Nov,*
£880 ($1,232)

4
A gold lacquer and Shibayama inro, 19th century, of four cases, decorated with several demons trying on costumes from a large clothes basket, in gold *takamakie* with inlay of mother-of-pearl, horn and coloured ivory, with an ivory ojime and kagamibuta, *L 13 Nov,*
£2,200 ($3,080)

5
A boxwood study of Ono no Komachi as an old woman, late 18th century, the wood slightly worn and with a good patina, toes restored, unsigned, 9cm (3½in), *L 12 June,*
£2,530 ($4,048)

6
Gyokuso: a wood figure o a man, Meiji period, holding a sack containing an ivory vase and other objects and wearing a coat with an applied ebony inro and an agate netsuke, 3.5cm (1¼in), *L 12 June,*
£1,320 ($2,112)

7
Hamano Motohira: a copper tsuba, dated 1867, applied in *iroe-takazogan* on the *ishime* ground with a Oni rising from behind a fence, pulling a grotesque face, 8cm (3in), *L 13 Mar,*
£3,190 ($4,913)

Judaica

See also:
Colour illustrations *p* 487

1
A Dutch pewter Sabbath lamp, 18th century, 91.5cm (36in), *NY 18 Dec,*
$4,675 (£3,269)

2
An Italian cast brass hanging Sabbath lamp, 18th century, 56cm (22in), *NY 28 May,*
$2,090 (£1,393)

3
An Italian brass hanging Sabbath lamp, Coneliano, 18th century, 50.5cm (20in), *NY 28 May,*
$4,675 (£3,117)

4
An Italian bookbinding, maker's mark a tree (Bulgari no.1182), Rome, c.1800, *L 13 Feb,*
£5,500 ($8,140)

5
A German silver covered prayerbook, maker's mark FS in a cartouche, Halberstadt, mid 18th century, with inscriptions recording bridal presentation, 19 x 14cm (7½ x 5in), *NY 18 Dec,*
$12,100 (£8,461)

6
An Italian silver amulet case, Venice, 18th century, the hinged lid engraved in Hebrew *Shadai*, 7.5cm (3in), *NY 28 May,*
$2,640 (£1,760)

7
A French silver amulet, P. Frères, Paris, mid 19th century, 9cm (3½in), *NY 18 Dec,*
$2,750 (£1,923)

8
An Austro-Hungarian tefellin case, maker's mark M.T., c.1870, the underside engraved in Hebrew *26 Tevet 1870*, 8.2cm (3¾in), *L 13 Feb,*
£770 ($1,140)

9
A pair of Polish silver Sabbath candlesticks, probably Warsaw, mid 19th century, maker's mark a deer, 33cm (13in), *NY 18 Dec,*
$1,980 (£1,385)

10
A German silver Sabbath plate, late 19th century, 38cm (15in), *NY 28 May,*
$2,530 (£1,687)

11
A Russian silver beaker, Moscow, 1774, engraved c.1840 with owner's monogram and Hebrew Sabbath blessing, 7.5cm (3in), *NY 28 May,*
$2,530 (£1,687)

12
A pair of Polish silver tefillin cases, quality mark 12, early 19th century, interiors velvet lined, 5.5cm (2¼in), *NY 28 May,*
$7,700 (£5,133)

13
An American silver and mahogany Sabbath wall plaque, Ilya Schor, probably 1960s, signed in English and Hebrew and with bird symbol, inscribed in Hebrew *Remember the Sabbath Day to keep it Holy,* 30.5cm (12in), *NY 18 Dec,*
$17,600 (£12,307)

14
A pair of English table candlesticks, *(one illustrated),* Abraham Frackman, London, 1892, in Polish style, 37.5cm (14¾in), *L 13 Feb,*
£550 ($814)

1

2

3

4

5

6

7

8

9

10

11

12

13

14

1

2

3

4

5

6

7

8

9

10

11

12

13

14

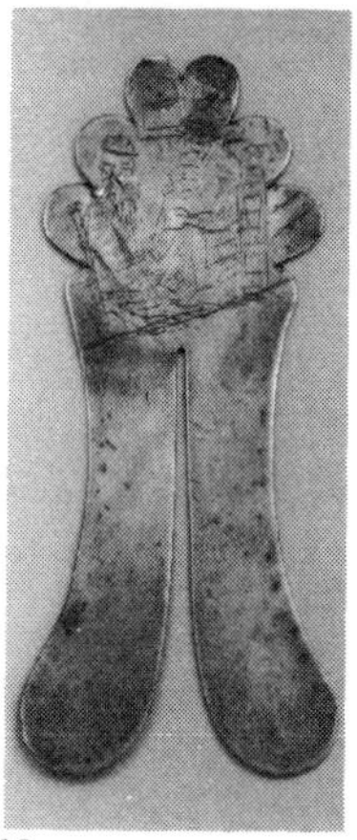

15

16

1
An Austro-Hungarian silver synagogue charity box, 1850, maker's mark rubbed, town mark unidentified, 12cm (4¾in), *L 13 Feb,*
£3,850 ($5,698)

2
An Austrian silver charity box, Vienna probably 1853, 9cm (3½in), *NY 18 Dec,*
$1,100 (£769)

3
An Austrian silver charity box, Vienna, 1838, 10cm (4in), *NY 28 May,*
$2,310 (£1,540)

4
An Austro-Hungarian silver burial society comb and nail implement, Vienna, 1867, 13.5cm (5¼in), *NY 28 May,*
$8,525 (£5,683)

5
A Royal Copenhagen porcelain cup and saucer, mid 19th century, Hebrew inscription, dated 1859, underglaze-blue factory mark, height of cup 10cm (4in), *NY 18 Dec,*
$440 (£308)

6
A German silver beaker, possibly Esaias Busch I, Augsburg, apparently 1670, with a later dedication in rhyming Hebrew, 8.5cm (3¼in), *L 13 Feb,*
£1,925 ($2,849)

7
A Central European pewter plate, probably Prague, late 18th century, 34cm (13½in), *NY 18 Dec,*
$1,320 (£923)

8
A German parcel-gilt silver dish, late 19th century, with embossed Hebrew inscription, 27cm (10¾in), *NY 28 May,*
$1,540 (£1,027)

9
A Hebrew-inscribed Hanau faience 'Enghals-krug', dated 5th November 1685, with pewter cover, chipped, 26.5cm (10½in), *L 4 Mar,*
£10,120 ($15,180)

10
An American gold hunt cased pocket watch with Hebrew numerals, Elgin Watch Co., c.1900, 4.5cm (2in), *NY 28 May,*
$2,530 (£1,687)

11
A Continental pocket watch, late 19th century, case in silver decorated on the reverse with Moses and the Decalogue, 5cm (2in), *NY 28 May,*
$1,430 (£953)

12
A Continental silver-plated brass burial socie charity container, probably Hungarian, late 19th century, inscribed in Hebrew *In memory of the souls,* some damage, 17.5cm (7in), *NY 18 Dec,*
$990 (£692)

13
An Austro-Hungarian silver presentation goble late 19th century, 20cm (8in), *NY 28 May,*
$825 (£550)

14
A Russian painted bisqu statuette of a Jewish man Alexander Gardiner, Moscow, 1880-90, printed factory mark in red with Imperial Eagle and impressed numeral 147, 21.5cm (8½in), *NY 28 May,*
$1,540 (£1,027)

15
A Continental silver circumcision shield, 19th century, 6.5cm (2½in), *NY 18 Dec,*
$715 (£500)

16
A German cup, Johann Friedrich Wilhelm Borcke, Berlin, c.1825, 15cm (6in), *L 13 Feb,*
£880 ($1,302)

. **Continental silver**
assover platter, probably
erman, late 19th
ntury, the central
edallion embossed in
lebrew with the order of
assover, 45.5cm (18in),
Y 28 May,
2,750 (£1,833)

. **German silver Passover**
late, late 19th century,
7cm (18½in), *NY 18 Dec,*
2,310 (£1,615)

. **French pewter Passover**
late, I.F. Bost, Stras-
ourg, late 18th century,
ngraved with the order
f Passover, reverse with
ouchmarks, 33.5cm
13¼in), *NY 18 Dec,*
715 (£500)

faience Passover plate,
robably German, early
9th century, centred by
he Hebrew word *Pesach,*
ninor rim chips, 23cm
9in), *L 13 Feb,*
242 ($358)

Continental faience
assover dish, 20th
entury, decorated in
nanganese, yellow and
reen, 37cm (12in),
13 Feb,
330 ($488)

Bohemian silver spice
ontainer, Czecho-
lovakia, late 19th century,
n the form of an apple,
1.5cm (4½in), *NY 28 May,*
$1,650 (£1,100)

7
A Polish silver spice tower, A. Riedel, Warsaw, 1871, fully marked, some damage to base, 26.5cm (10½in), *NY 18 Dec,*
$1,320 (£923)

8
An English silver spice tower and cup combination, Aaron Katz, London, 1893, hung with bells, some lacking, 36cm (14¼in), *NY 28 May,*
$2,860 (£1,907)

9
A Polish spice tower, 18th century, low grade silver, unmarked, 23cm (9in), *L 13 Feb,*
£7,150 ($10,582)

10
A filigree spice tower, German or Polish, c.1840, 23.5cm (9¼in), *L 13 Feb,*
£2,090 ($3,093)

11
A German square spice box, maker's mark L.H., probably Frankfurt a.M., c.1780, 6cm (2¼in), *L 13 Feb,*
£1,210 ($1,791)

12
A Bohemian flashed ruby glass Passover beaker, mid 19th century, a central cartouche inscribed in Hebrew 'Pesach', 7.5cm (3in), *NY 28 May,*
$1,045 (£697)

13
A German silver spice tower, Berlin, late 18th century, maker's mark rubbed, later pennant, 22cm (8¾in), *NY 18 Dec,*
$2,750 (£1,923)

14
A German parcel-gilt silver spice casket, c.1700, apparently unmarked, 6.4cm (2½in), *NY 18 Dec,*
$1,430 (£1,000)

15
A Ukrainian silver fruit-form spice container, Zhitomir, apparently 1856, 16cm (6¼in), *NY 18 Dec,*
$3,300 (£2,307)

Etrog A citrus fruit used on Sukkoth.

Havdalah The ceremony concluding the Sabbath on Saturday evening.

Kiddush The prayer recited over wine on Sabbaths and festivals.

Megillah Manuscript Book of Esther recited on Purim.

Mezuzah Small scroll containing a prayer fixed to the right door-post of each door.

Purim Festival commemorating the events in the Book of Esther.

Seder The ritual meal held at home on Passover eve.

Sukkoth The autumn festival of the Tabernacles.

1

2

3

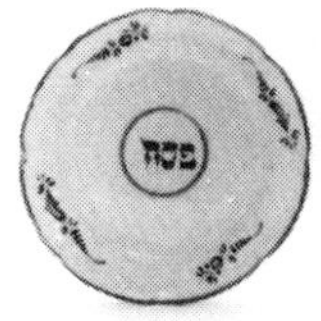

4

5

6

7

8

9

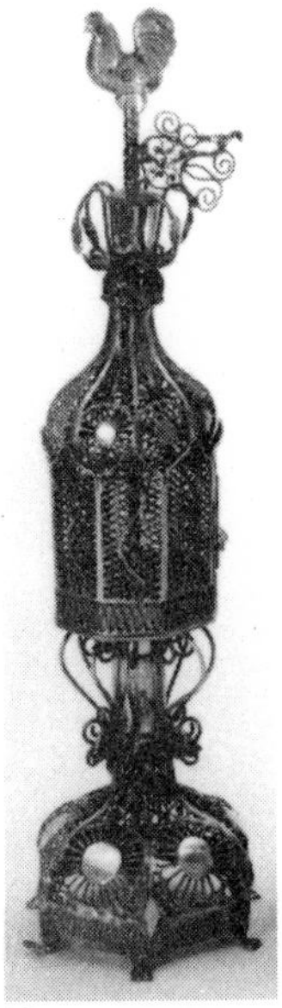
10

11

12

13

14

15

1

2

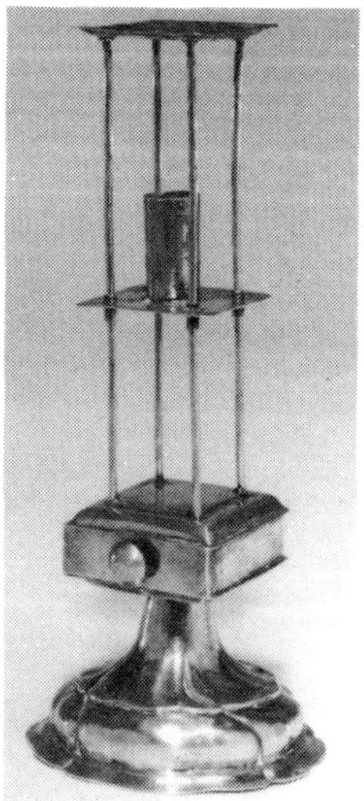
3

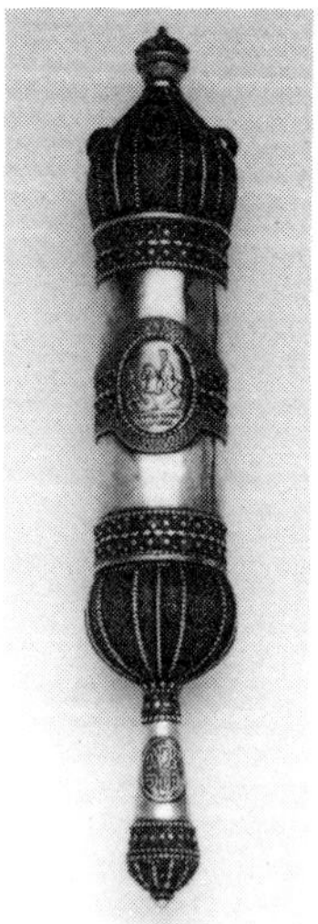
4

5

6

7

8

9 10 11

12

13

14

15

1
A German silver Havdalah compendium, apparently unmarked, early 19th century, 25cm (10in), *NY 18 Dec,*
$3,850 (£2,692)

2
A Continental carved wood Havdalah candle-holder, 17th/18th century, minor damages and repairs, 28cm (11in), *NY 18 Dec,*
$4,675 (£3,269)

3
A German silver Havdalah spice and candle compendium, maker's mark poorly struck, Nuremberg, c.1760, 22cm (8¾in), *NY 28 May,*
$7,700 (£5,133)

4
A Palestinian silver and stone-set silver Esther scroll case, 1930s, the central roundel depicting Mordecai riding in triumph, 22.5cm (9in), *NY 28 May,*
$1,870 (£1,246)

5
An Austrian silver Kiddush goblet, Lintz, dated 1858, some damage to foot, 11cm (4½in), *NY 28 May,*
$1,320 (£880)

6
A German silver-gilt Kiddush goblet, Konstanz, c.1600, with two Hebrew inscriptions, one dated 1764 the other 1866, 24cm (9½in), *NY 28 May,*
$22,000 (£14,667)

7
A German silver-gilt Sabbath Kiddush cup, Johann Friedrich Ehe, Nuremberg, 1780s, later gilding, 13.5cm (5½in), *NY 18 Dec,*
$5,775 (£4,038)

8
A silver Safed type Kiddush beaker, c.1870, 7.5cm (3in), *NY 28 May,*
$3,575 (£2,383)

9
A German silver etrog container, late 19th century, the interior gilt, 17.5cm (7in), *NY 18 Dec,*
$1,760 (£1,231)

10
A Polish silver etrog container, Lange, Danzig, c.1760, repair to hinge, 12.5cm (5in), *NY 18 Dec,*
$2,310 (£1,615)

11
A Dutch silver etrog container, late 19th century, with hollow interior, 16cm (6¼in), *NY 18 Dec,*
$2,750 (£1,923)

12
A German silver Passove Kiddush goblet, maker's mark poorly struck, Augsburg, 1763-65, marked on foot rim, some old repair, 11.5cm (4½in), *NY 28 May,*
$8,800 (£5,867)

13
A Polish silver Kiddush goblet, mid 19th century, struck twice with 12 standard mark, with Hebrew inscription dated 1855, 13cm (5in), *NY 18 Dec,*
$2,640 (£1,846)

14
An Austrian silver Kiddush cup, Vienna, 1840, engraved in Hebrew and German recording the birth of a child in 1840, 9.5cm (3¾in), *NY 18 Dec,*
$2,860 (£2,000)

15
An Italian silver-cased illuminated parchment Esther scroll, late 18th century, text with some wear, height of case overall 17cm (6¾in), *NY 28 May,*
$3,575 (£2,383)

. Dutch cast brass
lanukah lamp, 18th/19th
entury, 23cm (9¼in),
Y 28 May,
1,760 (£1,173)

. Polish brass Hanukah
amp, 18th century,
hamash lacking, 13cm
5in), *L 13 Feb,*
264 ($391)

. Polish brass Hanukah
amp, c.1800, 17.5cm
7in), *NY 28 May,*
990 (£660)

. German silver travel-
ing Hanukah lamp, late
9th century, maker's
nark obliterated, 10cm
4in), *L 13 Feb,*
660 ($977)

**n Italian bronze
lanukah lamp,** 17th
entury, later servant
ght, 19cm (7½in),
VY 18 Dec,
1,430 (£1,000)

**n Italian brass Hanukah
amp,** 17th century, old
epairs, height excluding
uspension ring 28.5cm
11¼in), *NY 18 Dec,*
1,980 (£1,385)

**German silver
Hanukah lamp,** Rötger
Herfurth, Frankfurt a.M.,
.1760, fully marked,
20cm (7¾in), *L 13 Feb,*
7,480 ($11,070)

8
**A Polish silver Hanukah
lamp,** Pogorzelski,
Warsaw, 1882, servant
light now lacking, 21.5cm
(8½in), *NY 28 May,*
$4,675 (£3,117)

9
**A coloured lead-glazed
redware Hanukah lamp,**
probably Southern
Germany, c.1800, servant
light lacking, cracks on
backplate and one side,
18cm (7½in), *NY 18 Dec,*
$8,250 (£5,769)

10
**A Central European
pewter Hanukah lamp,**
c.1800, several minor
repairs, struck with two
touchmarks, 25.5cm
(10in), *NY 18 Dec,*
$5,775 (£4,038)

11
**A German silver
Hanukah lamp,** early 20th
century, 24cm (9½in),
NY 28 May,
$770 (£513)

12
**A Polish brass synagogue
Hanukah lamp,** late 19th
century, 83.5cm (33in),
NY 18 Dec,
$3,575 (£2,500)

13
**A Polish silver Hanukah
lamp,** c.1925, some
repairs, 68.5cm (27in),
NY 18 Dec,
$1,430 (£1,000)

14
**An Austro-Hungarian
silver Hanukah lamp,**
c.1900, 38cm (15in),
NY 28 May,
$1,650 (£1,100)

Hanukah The mid-winter (December) festival of lights.

Menorah Hebrew for candelabrum. Now commonly the eight-branched Hanukah lamp lit on each day of the festival.

1

2

3

4

5

6

7

8

9

10

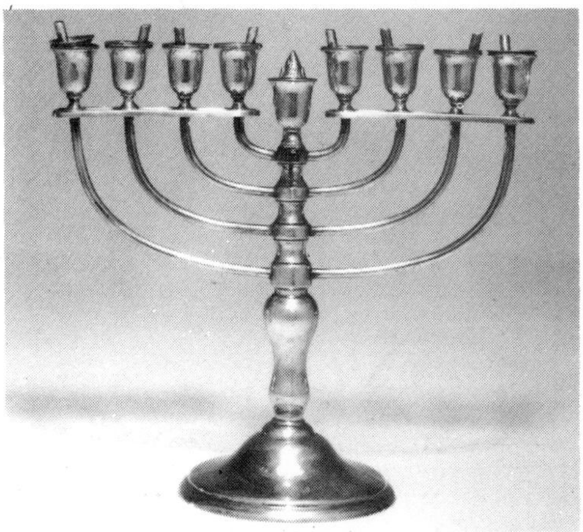
11

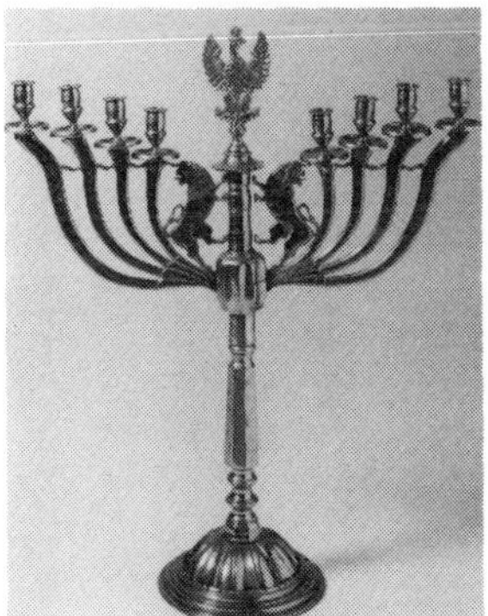
12

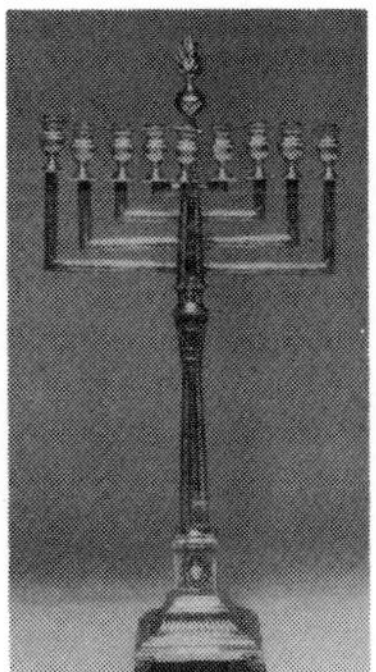
13

14

1

2

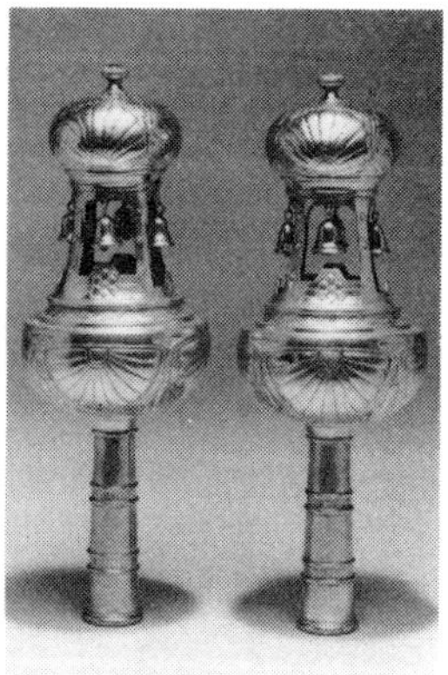
3

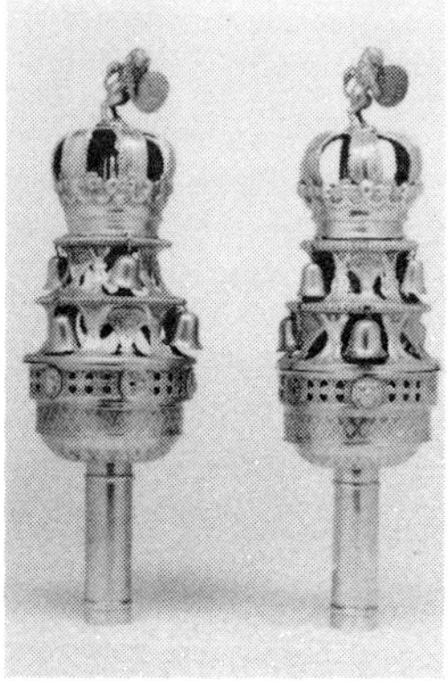
4

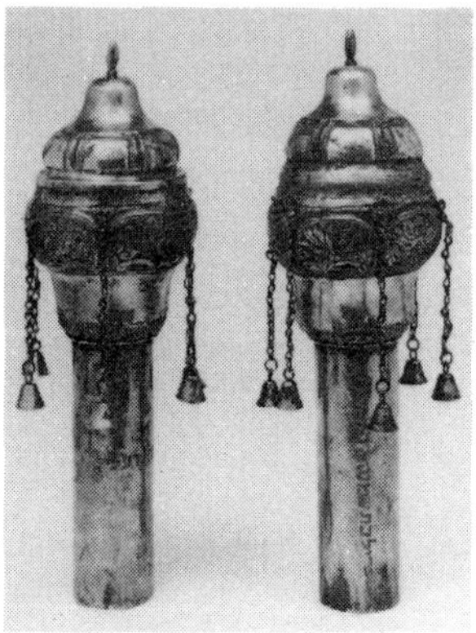
5

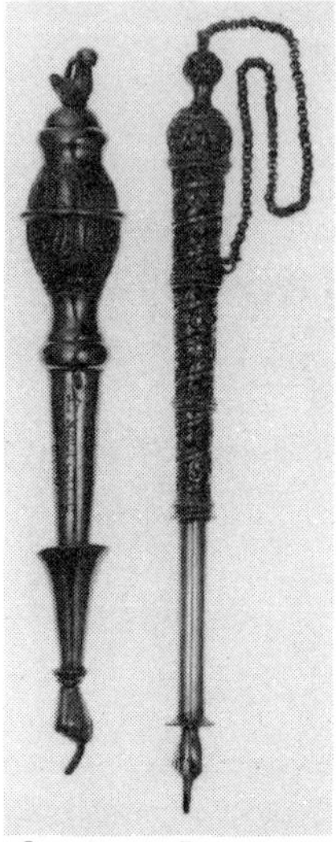
6 7

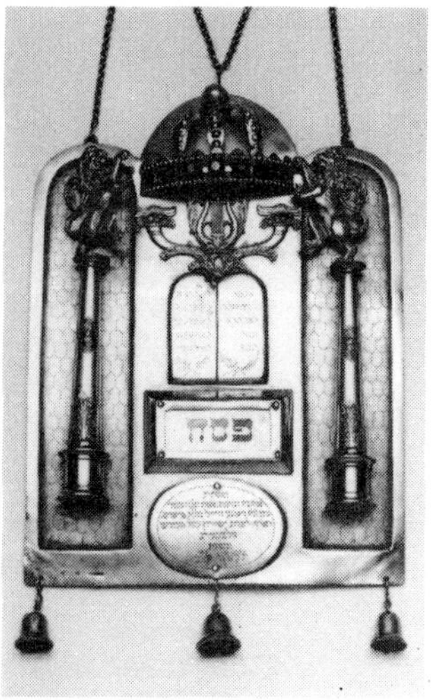

8

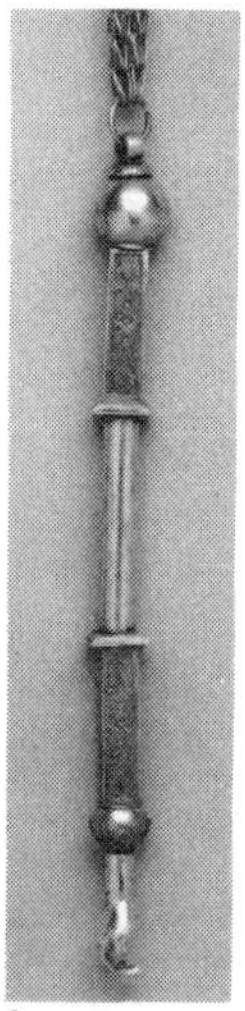
9

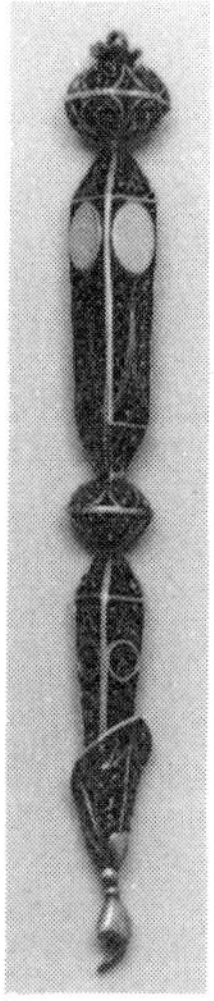
10

11

12

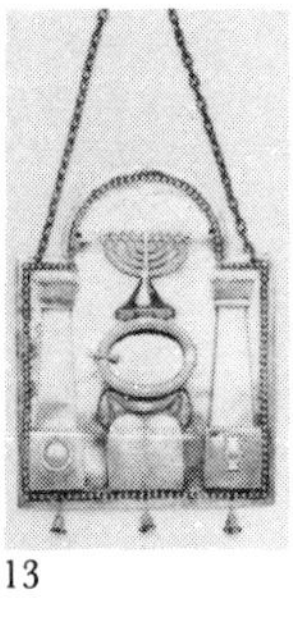
13

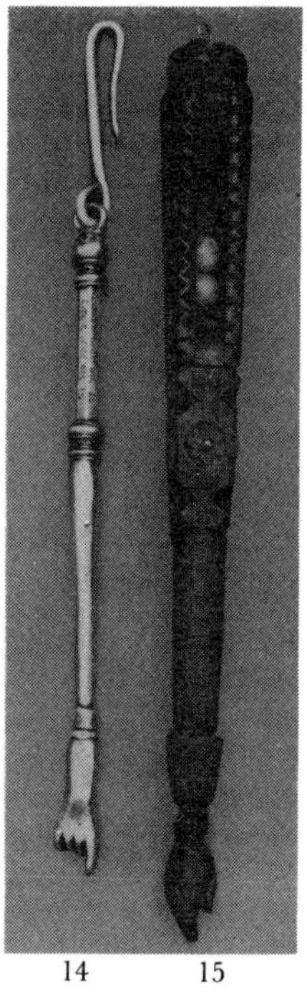
14 15

1
A pair of German silver Torah finials, maker IMS in a rectangle, probably Frankfurt, early 19th century, some bells replaced, old repairs, 34cm (13½in), *NY 28 May,*
$5,775 (£3,850)

2
A pair of German silver Torah finials, Berlin, c.1820-30, some bells replaced others lacking, some repairs, 34cm (13½in), *NY 28 May,*
$3,850 (£2,567)

3
A pair of German silver Torah finials, Horovitz, c.1910, some bells replaced, 30.5cm (12in), *NY 18 Dec,*
$1,650 (£1,154)

4
A pair of German silver-gilt Torah finials, Johann Aloiss Siffer, Augsburg, 1816, some bells replaced, later gilding, 34cm (13½in), *NY 18 Dec,*
$12,100 (£8,462)

5
A pair of Near Eastern parcel-gilt silver Torah finials, late 18th century, the stave engraved with a woman's name, 32cm (12½in), *NY 18 Dec,*
$2,860 (£2,000)

6
A Russian Torah pointer, maker's mark M.P., St. Petersburg, c.1905, silver-coloured metal, 22cm (8¾in), *L 13 Feb,*
£374 ($554)

7
A Near Eastern silver Torah pointer, c.1880, unmarked, 24cm (9½in), *L 13 Feb,*
£275 ($407)

8
A German parcel-gilt silver Torah shield, maker's mark JK (?) in script monogram, Nuremberg, c.1825, 31cm (12¼in), *NY 18 Dec,*
$7,150 (£5,000)

9
An Austrian parcel-gilt silver Torah pointer, marks unclear, c.1810, 28cm (11in), *NY 18 Dec,*
$2,750 (£1,923)

10
An English silver filigre Torah pointer, maker's mark unclear, London, 1897, 25.5cm (10in), *NY 18 Dec,*
$1,320 (£923)

11
An Austro-Hungarian silver Torah shield, apparently unmarked, late 19th century, lacks suspension chain, 37cm (14½in), *NY 18 Dec,*
$1,650 (£1,154)

12
A Polish parcel-gilt Tora crown, early 19th century, some repairs and restorations, 35.5cm (14in), *NY 28 May,*
$5,500 (£3,667)

13
A German or Polish parcel-gilt silver Torah shield, early 19th century, stamped with maker's mark TB in script and quality mark 12, bells replaced, *NY 28 May,*
$1,980 (£1,320)

14
A Dutch silver Torah pointer, maker's name Jan Haye, Amsterdam, 1790, 24cm (9½in), *NY 28 May,*
$8,800 (£5,867)

15
A Polish carved wood Torah pointer, 19th century, 25.5cm (10in), *NY 28 May,*
$1,650 (£1,100)

Torah Hebrew for law. Specifically the five books of Moses written on a parchment scroll that forms the focus of synagogue liturgy and is kept in the Aron Hakodesh.

Ornaments include:

Torah finials and *Rimmonim.*

Torah shield or breast plate (*Tas*), hung on the front of the Torah scroll.

Torah pointer (*Yad*).

Torah crown (*Keter*) usually to fit over the Torah when it is not in use.

Aron Hakodesh Commonly named the *Ark.* The cupboard containing the Torah scrolls in the synagogue.

Coins and Banknotes

Article:

Banknotes and paper money *pp* 586-589

The value of coins primarily depends on their condition, which is described by the following key:

F	=	**fine**
GF	=	**good/fine**
AVF	=	**almost very fine**
VF	=	**very fine**
GVF	=	**good/very fine**
AEF	=	**almost extremely fine**
EF	=	**extremely fine**

1
Julius Caesar, aureus, 46 BC, *GVF, Z 28 Nov,*
SF 3,850 (£1,638; $2,294)

2
Augustus, 27 BC-14 AD, denarius, *VF, L 4 Dec,*
£418 ($585)

3
Agrippa, died 12 BC, as, struck by Caligula, *EF, L 4 Dec,*
£770 ($1,078)

4
Augustus, 27 BC-14 AD, aureus of Pergamum, *GF, Z 28 Nov,*
SF 4,620 (£1,966; $2,752)

5
Augustus, 27 BC-14 AD, denarius of Einerita, *GVF, L 4 Dec,*
£605 ($847)

6
Julia Paula, wife of Elagabalus, 218-223, as, *VF, L 4 Dec,*
£462 ($647)

7
Vespasian, 69-79, aureus, reverse, Judaea type, *AVF, Z 28 Nov,*
SF 11,000 (£4,681; $6,553)

8
Nero, 54-68, sestertius, *AEF, L 4 Dec,*
£935 ($1,309)

9
Vitellius, 69, sestertius, *GVF, L 4 Dec,*
£1,870 ($2,618)

10
Trajan, 98-117, aureus, reverse, Trajan's column, *AVF, Z 28 Nov,*
SF 4,620 (£1,966; $2,752)

11
Trajan, 98-117, aureus, *VF, L 20 May,*
£935 ($1,496)

12
Hadrian, 117-138, silver-plated cistophorus, (a contemporary forgery), *VF, L 4 Dec,*
£154 ($216)

13
Aelius, Caesar, 136-138, sestertius, *VF, L 20 May,*
£275 ($440)

All coins are shown actual size.

1

2

3

4

5

6

7

8

9

10

11

12

13

1

2

3

4

5

6

7

8

9

10

11

1
Antoninus Pius, 138-161, sestertius, *EF, L 2 Oct,*
£990 ($1,386)

2
Lucius Verus, 161-169, dupondius, *EF, L 4 Dec,*
£462 ($647)

3
Ostrogothic, Theodoric, 493-526, solidus, *EF, Z 28 Nov,*
SF 1,540 (£655; $917)

4
Anastasius II, 713-715, solidus, *AEF, L 2 Oct,*
£990 ($1,386)

5
Basil II and Constantine VIII, 976-1025, miliaresion, *VF, L 20 May,*
£253 ($405)

6
Leo III, 717-741, solidus, *GVF, L 20 May,*
£242 ($387)

7
Theodora, 1055-56, tetarteron, *EF, Z 28 Nov,*
SF 3,300 (£1,404; $1,966)

8
Macedon, Philip II, 359-336 BC, tetradrachm of Amphipolis, *VF, L 20 May,*
£506 ($810)

9
Macedon, Acanthus, tetradrachm, c.500 BC, *GVF, L 2 Oct,*
£2,420 ($3,388)

10
Macedon, Alexander III, 336-323 BC, gold stater of Amphipolis, *VF, L 20 May,*
£638 ($1,021)

11
Parthia, Artabanus III, c.80-81 AD, tetradrachm, *VF, L 20 May,*
£506 ($810)

lacedon, Antigonus onatas, 277-239 BC, tradrachm, *GVF, 20 May,* **140 ($704)**

aly, Lucania, Heraclea, idrachm, 4th century BC, *F, L 2 Oct,* **682 ($955)**

asanian, Ardashir I, 24-241, hemidrachm, npublished variety, *F, 2 Oct,* **286 ($400)**

esbos, Mytilene, lectrum hecte, c.330 BC, *EF, Z 28 Nov,* **F 1,650 (£702; $983)**

yria, Seleucus I, 312-280 c, tetradrachm, *GVF, 20 May,* **660 ($1,056)**

icily, Syracuse, Hieron I, 275-215 BC, gold rachm, *AEF, Z 28 Nov,* **F 5,500 (£2,340; $3,277)**

icily, Syracuse, electrum 0 litrai, after c.310 BC, *VF, L 20 May,* **605 ($968)**

hrace, Lysimachus, 323-81 BC, drachm of phesus, *AEF, L 2 Oct,* **374 ($524)**

yria, Cleopatra and ntiochus VIII, 125-121 c, tetradrachm, *VF, 20 May,* **506 ($810)**

0
ings of Egypt, Ptolemy I, 285-246 BC, gold ctadrachm, *Z 28 Nov,* **F 8,800 (£3,745; $5,243)**

1
hrace, Abdera, drachm, .350 BC, *GVF, L 20 May,* **220 ($352)**

2
hrace, Lysimachus, 323-81 BC, tetradrachm of arium, *GVF, L 2 Oct,* **528 ($739)**

13
Bithynia, Nicodemia, Valerian I, Gallienus and Valerian II, Æ 25 mm, mid 3rd century AD, *AEF, L 2 Oct,* **£374 ($524)**

14
Thrace, Istrus, drachm, 4th century BC, *EF, L 2 Oct,* **£451 ($631)**

15
Thessaly, Larissa, drachm, c.340 BC, *GVF L 2 Oct,* **£242 ($339)**

16
Celtic, Gallo-Belgic, Ambiani, gold stater, 1st century BC, *VF, Z 28 Nov,* **SF 550 (£234; $328)**

Banknotes and Paper Money

JAMES MORTON

Whilst philately and numismatics have attracted avid collectors for decades, the field of banknotes and other financial documents has remained largely neglected until recent years. Fresh interest in the subject appears to stem from a developing market for ephemera of all kinds, combined with a generally growing enthusiasm for local and economic history. Much of the material now available offers excellent scope for research and good value for money in comparison to postage stamps or coins. In Great Britain an additional stimulus has been provided by the British Museum's acquisition of a large and important collection for the nation, a step which has helped considerably to enhance the status of 'notaphilists', as banknote collectors are sometimes (rather inelegantly) known.

Paper currency, or 'flying money' as it was first called, was invented by the Chinese as long ago as the 7th century AD and became known in Europe following the first expedition of Marco Polo. Notes of certain types issued under the Ming dynasty are surprisingly plentiful today and are thought to be made of paper manufactured from mulberry bark, a by-product of the silk industry (fig.1). By the time these were issued a sophisticated banking system had developed within China, in marked contrast to the West where the concept of an everyday paper currency evolved comparatively slowly. Right up to the 20th century nations and private citizens alike have tended to mistrust paper and prefer gold or silver, a reticence which is easily understandable in view of economic disasters of the past, throughout which the value of gold has tended to remain remarkably stable. Tangible evidence of famous crashes offers plenty of material for present-day collectors and is frequently inexpensive. Such items range from 1720s stock receipts in the

1
China, 1 kuan, 1368-99 period, block-printed on mulberry bark paper, *L 2 Oct,*
£220 ($308)

2
England, a provincial 50 guineas note of 1795, with typical bankruptcy endorsement attached to the reverse, *L 2 Oct,*
£242 ($339)

3
Printer's proof of a £10 for the Chepstow Bank, c.1804, *L 2 Oct,*
£176 ($246)

4
Isle of Man, token five shillings printed on card, 1812, *L 14 June 1978,*
£680 ($1,258)

5
Exchequer Bill, issued on behalf of the South Sea Company, 1720, signed by Lord Halifax, *L 21 Nov 1985,*
£660 ($845)

6
Bank of England, £100 released by the bank's Birmingham branch, 1894, *L 16 Apr 1985,*
£3,740 ($4,787)
Pre-1914 notes of this type are scarce, but 1930s-1950s 'white fivers' of similar design remain common.

7
Bank of England £50, 1780, believed to be the earliest surviving Bank of England note in private hands.

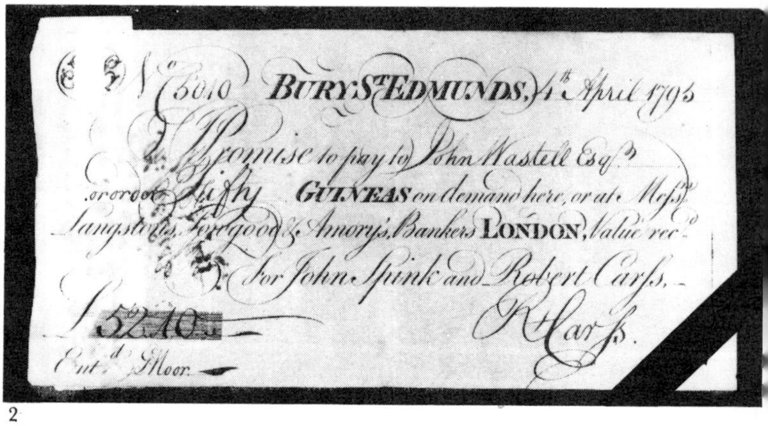

2

1

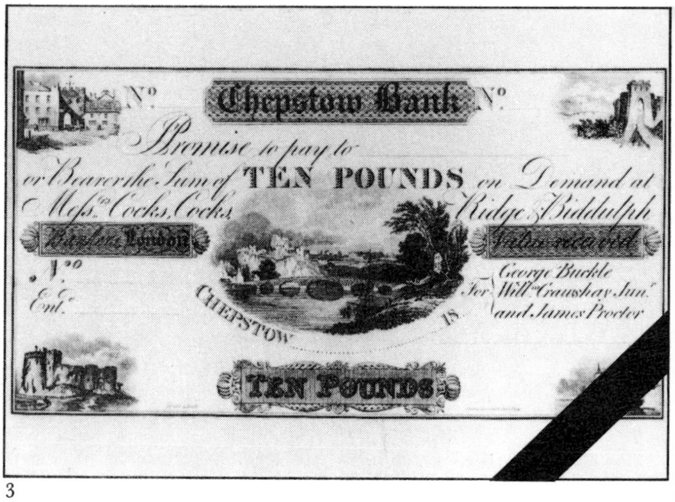

3

notorious 'South Sea Bubble' scandal in England (fig.5) to 1920s German inflationary banknotes, the highest denominations of which rose to the impressive but almost useless figure of 100 billion (or 100,000,000,000,000) reichsmarks.

In Britain, Exchequer bills, cheques and, in particular, goldsmiths' promissory notes began to acquire a degree of negotiability in the 17th century. Effectively the goldsmiths became individual bankers, whose activities were partly centralised in the 1690s with the establishment of the Bank of England. The Bank released the first 'true' banknotes in Britain in 1695, from which date all genuine issues remain redeemable at their face value. The idea of a national central bank was rapidly adopted elsewhere in Europe, notably in Scotland, Norway and France. In Sweden an emergency-induced paper currency had existed since the 1660s.

The often-cited strength of the Bank of England creates a problem for collectors in that the overwhelming majority of its early banknotes have been redeemed. With the exception of a series of emergency £1 and £2 which circulated between 1797 and 1826, uncancelled issues dating from before 1900 are now becoming scarce on the market (fig.6). On the other hand, provincial notes released by hundreds of private banks are easy to find in both issued and unissued form and are gaining in popularity; they relate to concerns which either failed or were absorbed by larger joint stock banks in the 19th century (figs 2-3). Frequently they are elaborately engraved for security purposes and carry attractive vignettes, though they betray their lack of credit-worthiness by the cancellations and bankruptcy stamps with which they are frequently endorsed.

In many parts of the world the advent of the Great War in 1914 and its economic repercussions led to a general suspension of the gold standard and more widespread use of paper currency than ever before. In Britain the Treasury was responsible for providing new £1 and ten shilling notes to replace gold sovereigns and half-sovereigns, a task which was achieved from scratch over the specially-extended August Bank Holiday of 1914 (fig.17). Really well-preserved examples of the earliest 'Bradbury's', as the new notes were soon nicknamed (after the Chief Cashier who signed them), are now hard to find. They were printed on reserve stocks of frail postage stamp paper, which was not designed to stand up to prolonged circulation in purses and pockets. Elsewhere, for example in Germany, Austria, Eastern Europe and South America, mass-production of paper money on a large scale contributed to the inflationary spiral and inevitable currency collapse, leaving a substantial legacy of unredeemable material. Sometimes, as in pre-Revolutionary Russia, the notes were of very high quality but the common varieties remain extremely plentiful and cheap. They can be purchased from dealers for only a few

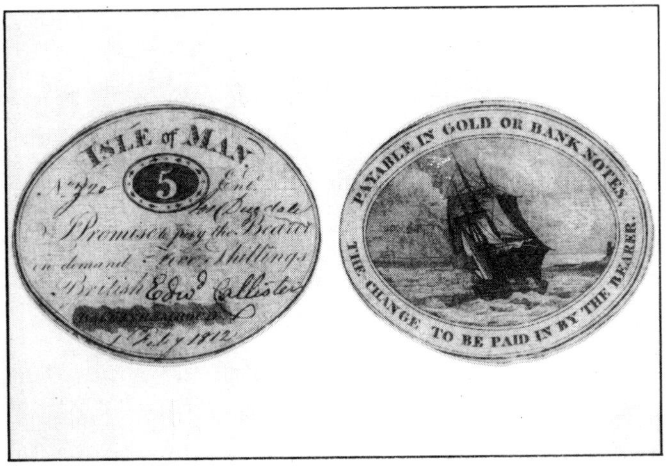

4

5

6

7

pence (or cents) each and are not saleable by auction.

Obsolete share certificates, bonds and cheques have much in common with banknotes and are now regularly included in sales of paper money. Some are beautifully engraved, often by the same security printers who prepared banknotes, and their elaborate designs were sometimes intended to tempt investors as well as to frustrate the efforts of forgers. Many bond issues have failed alongside the currencies of the authorities which issued them, the certificates of the Confederate States of America (1861-64), Imperial China and Tsarist Russia being notorious in this respect (although holders of the latter, after a seventy year interval, have recently been invited to apply for some degree of compensation). From a collector's point of view, items dating from before the mid-19th century attact most attention, especially those relating to well-known companies, famous industrialists, or now-familiar projects and inventions of the past.

The field of paper money offers numerous opportunities for specialisation and attracts a remarkably diverse group of collectors. Some are motivated by the historical appeal or research value of local, military, or emergency issues (fig.18), others by the more traditional desire to assemble a complete series of pieces from a particular country, individual bank, or specialist printer. Still more are attracted by the rarity value, excellent state of preservation or aesthetic quality of specific pieces, while specimen notes (never intended for circulation, fig.12), trial printings (figs 13-15), errors and even forgeries also have their followers.

Over the last ten years paper money has generally featured at auction as a section within coin and medal catalogues, but as the field continues to expand and further interest develops, it seems likely that regular, specialised auctions will be introduced in the future. Whereas the items illustrating this article are of relatively high value, the new collector should remember that a good proportion of every sale comprises multiple lots, sometimes containing over one hundred items while selling for well under £500 ($800) per lot, thus offering material at figures well within the means of the majority of collectors.

Further reading:

A. Pick, *Standard Catalog of World Paper Money,* 2 vols., 1986
C. Narbeth, *Collecting Paper Money,* 1986
V. Duggleby, *English Paper Money,* 1984

8

9

10

8
Great Britain, shilling banknote, 1919, prepared for issue in case the bullion value of silver coin were to rise too high, the notes were never used, *L 17 July,* **£1,870 ($2,936)**

9
Great Britain, serial Al no.1 of the 1917 £1 issue. Presented to Lloyd George in his capacity as First Lord of the Treasury, *L 19 July 1984,* **£2,970 ($4,128)**

10
Great Britain, a group of seven Treasury banknotes with matching serial nos Al/Bl 100, 1914-23, *L 21 July 1983,* **£2,200 ($3,058)**

11
Great Britain, Treasury 2nd issue £1, overprinted ir Arabic for use by British Expeditionary Forces in th Dardanelles, 1915, *L 2 Oct,* **£1,210 ($1,694)**

12
Bank of Scotland, specimen £1, 1885, sold wit a circulated example of the same note, *L 27 Mar 1987,* **£506 ($810)**

Specially designed to be 'forgery-proof', very competent copies appeared within only two years of the issue.

13
USA, a banknote trial featuring a vignette of President Andrew Jackson, c.1920, *L 27 Mar 1987,* **£165 ($264)**

14
Bank of England, trial £1, very rare, 1914, *L 22 June 19* **£1,700 ($2,890)**

15
Great Britain, trial design for a new £1, c.1916, by Bradbury, Wilkinson & Co. it was not adopted and only two or three specimens are believed to exist, *L 2 Oct,* **£4,070 ($5,698)**

16
Germany, a photograph of a printing plate used to forge Bank of England £10 notes during World War Two. The counterfeits were excellent and difficult to detect; any which survive remain liable to confiscation by the Bank of England.

17
Great Britain, an early trial printing of the first Treasury £1, August 1914, *L 22 Nov 1985,*
£1,650 ($2,112)

18
South Africa, Boer War, an emergency £5 issued during the siege of Koffyfontein, 1900. *L 17 July,*
£770 ($1,209)

Very rare. Banknotes were also issued at Mafeking and are comparatively easy to find.

11

12

13

14

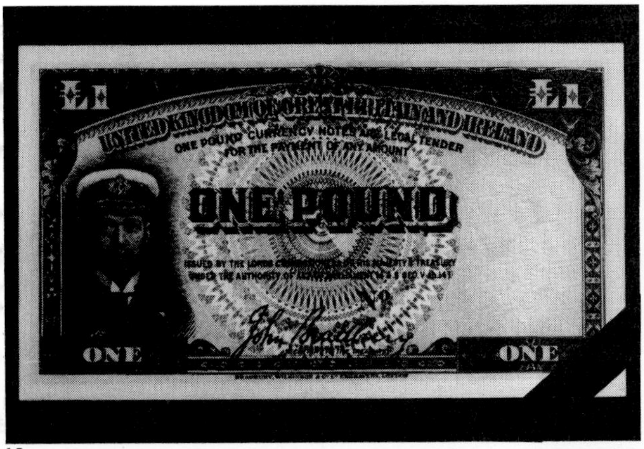

15

16

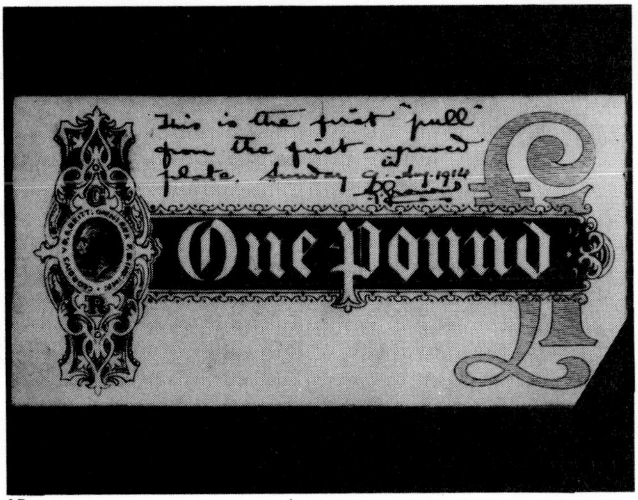

17

18

Antiquities

1 2 3

4

5

6

7

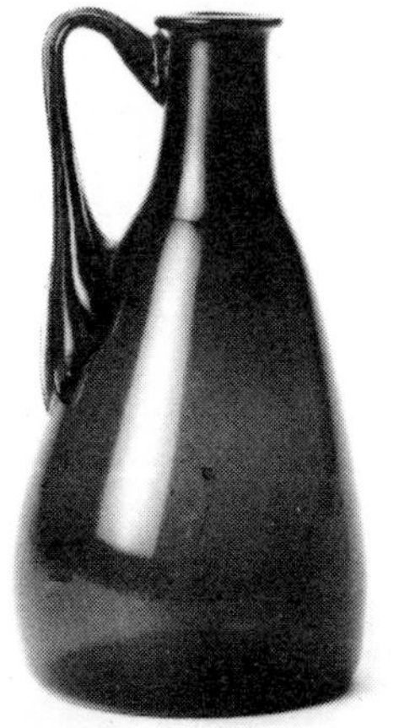

8

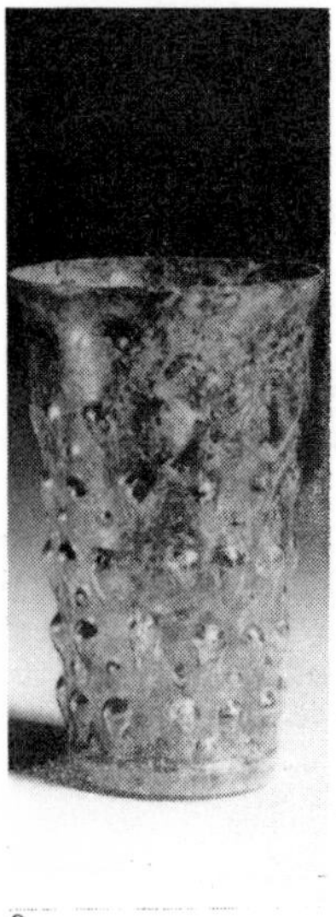

9

10

11

See also:
Colour illustrations *p* 491

Main sub-sections:
Egyptian *pp* 592-594
Glass *pp* 590-591
Greek, Roman and Etruscan *pp* 595-601

1
A dark blue sandcore glass amphoriskos, 6th-4th century BC, decorated with opaque yellow and turquoise spiral trailing, 8.5cm (3½in), *L 8 Dec,*
£858 ($1,201)

2
A dark blue sandcore glass amphoriskos, c.3rd century BC, decorated in yellow turquoise and white, foot reattached, slight repair and restoration, 8.5cm (3¼in), *L 8 Dec,*
£1,430 ($2,002)

3
A dark blue sandcore glass oinochoe, 6th-4th century BC, decorated in yellow, turquoise and white, foot restored, handle reattached, 7cm (2¾in), *L 8 Dec,*
£1,100 ($1,540)

4
A cobalt-blue core-formed albastron, c.4th century BC, decorated in opaque white and turquoise, 16.5cm (6½in), *NY 24 Nov,*
$18,700 (£13,169)

5
A Hellenistic dark manganese-purple glass cup, 1st century BC, some iridescence and encrustation, 8cm (3in), *L 8 Dec,*
£4,950 ($6,930)

6
A translucent manganese-purple mosaic glass patella cup, 1st century BC -1st century AD, opaque green and white canes set in manganese-purple matrix, repaired and restored, 9cm (3½in), *L 14 July,*
£4,400 ($6,864)

7
A greenish-blue glass flask, 1st-2nd century AD, Cologne, bands of wheel-engraving, 17cm (6¾in), *L 14 July,*
£3,080 ($4,804)

8
A manganese-purple glass jug, 1st century AD, 14cm (5½in), *L 19 May,*
£1,110 ($1,776)

9
A pale mould-blown glass 'lotus bud' beaker, c.1st century AD, iridescent, almost colourless, 10.5cm (4in), *L 14 July,*
£1,430 ($2,230)

10
An amber-coloured glass flask, 2nd-3rd century AD, wheel-engraved lines, some iridescence, 12.5cm (5in), *L 14 July,*
£605 ($943)

11
A blue-green bottle, c.2nd-3rd century AD, 30cm (11¾in), *NY 24 Nov,*
$2,090 (£1,472)

1
An olive-green bottle, 3rd-5th century AD, 27cm (10½in), *NY 24 Nov,*
$550 (£387)

2
A green mould-blown glass sprinkler flask, 3rd-4th century AD, some iridescence, 11cm (4½in), *L 19 May,*
£440 ($704)

3
An iridescent yellow glass jar, 3rd-4th century AD, the body with turquoise threads, fine iridescence, 9cm (3½in), *L 14 July,*
£550 ($858)

4
A green glass basket, c.3rd century AD, some iridescence, repaired, 12.5cm (5in), *L 8 Dec,*
£176 ($246)

5
A blue-green jug, c.4th-5th century AD, iridescence, 16cm (6¼in), *NY 24 Nov,*
$1,650 (£1,162)

6
An olive-green glass beaker, c.4th century AD, decorated with dark blue, some iridescence and encrustation, 10cm (4in), *L 19 May,*
£440 ($704)

7
A colourless glass jug, c.4th century AD, pale green glass handle, light encrustation, 27.5cm (11in), *L 14 July,*
£440 ($686)

8
An olive-green ewer, c.3rd-5th century AD, aquamarine thread at neck, 31.5cm (12½in), *NY 30 May,*
$1,100 (£748)

9
A yellow twin-handled glass flask, 3rd-4th century AD, fine iridescence, 16.5cm (6½in), *L 19 May,*
£385 ($616)

10
A Sassanian dark green glass jar, 5th-6th century AD, some iridescence and encrustation, 9cm (3½in), *L 14 July,*
£1,540 ($2,402)

11
A group of lapis lazuli and gold beads, early Dynastic-3rd Dynasty at Ur, c.3500-3000 BC, 40.5cm (16in), *NY 30 May,*
$2,090 (£1,421)

12
A group of folded glass beads, 1st Millennium BC, brightly coloured, 49.5cm (19½in), *NY 30 May,*
$1,760 (£1,197)

13
A group of Egyptian glass disk eye beads, 18th Dynasty, 1554-1305 BC, in blue, black, white and yellow, 61cm (24in), *NY 30 May,*
$1,430 (£972)

1

2

3

4

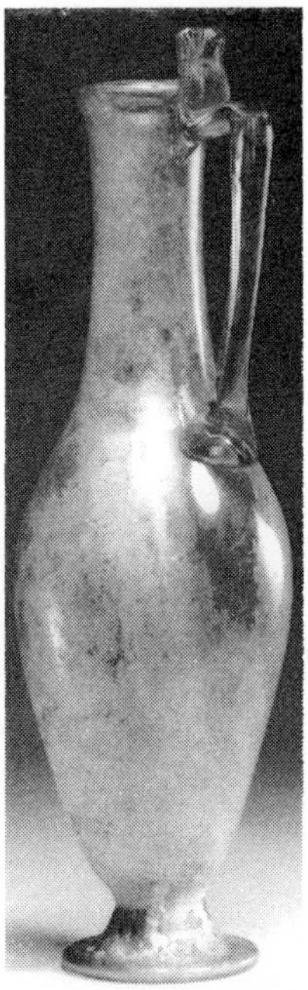
7

5

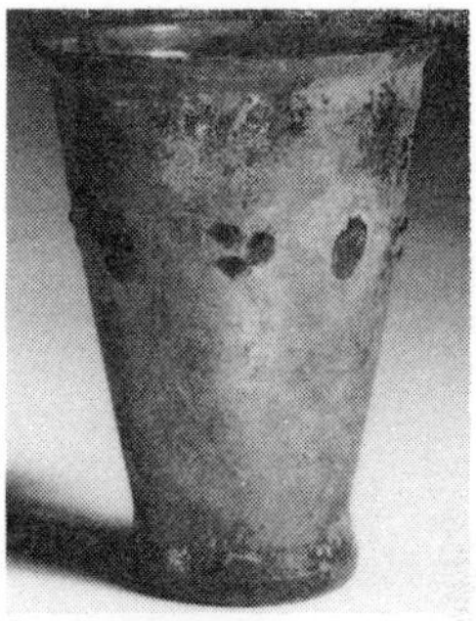
6

8

9

10

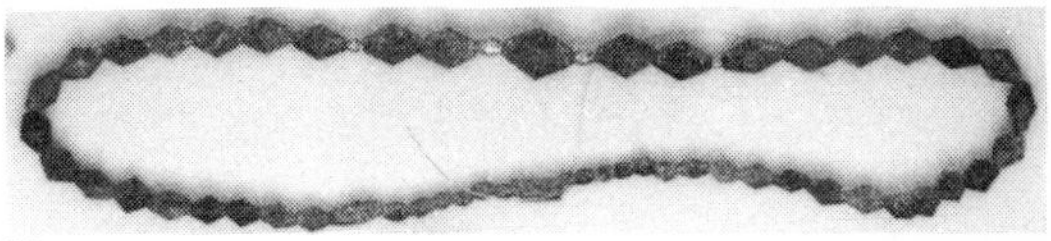
11

12

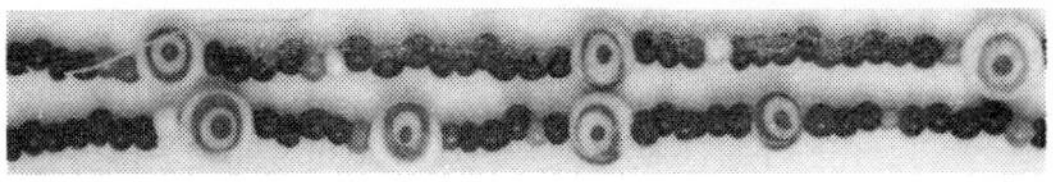
13

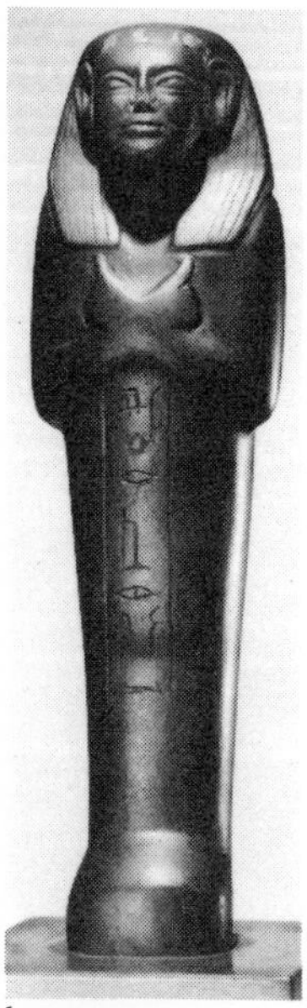
1

2

3

4

5

6

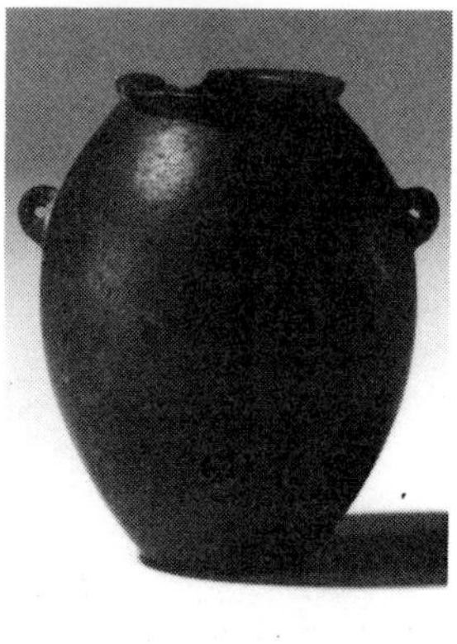
7

8

9

10

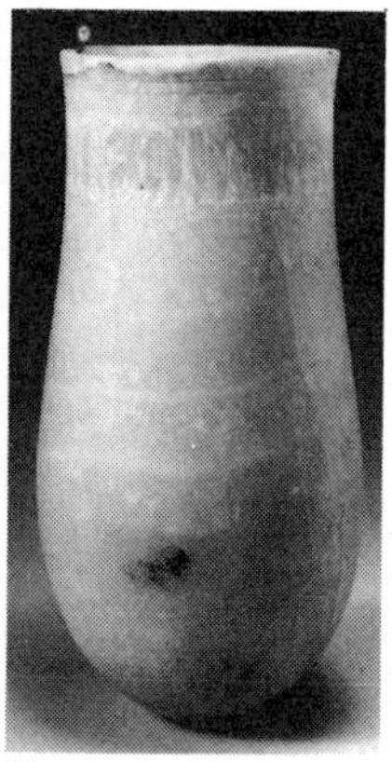
11

12

1
A schist ushabti of User, late 12th/early 13th Dynasty, c.1800-1750 BC, incised *Venerated before Osiris, User*, 23cm (9in), *NY 30 May,*
$4,675 (£3,180)

2
A brilliant blue faience ushabti, 21st Dynasty, 1080-946 BC, inscribed for Princess Nesi-ta-neb-asher, daughter of Pnodjem II and Nesi-Khonsu, with inscription from the sixth chapter of the Book of the Dead, 15cm (6in), *NY 24 Nov,*
$1,650 (£1,162)

3
A wood mummy mask, 19th/20th Dynasty, 1305-1080 BC, black-painted eyes and eyebrows and yellow perimeter, 26.5cm (10½in), *NY 30 May,*
$1,540 (£1,047)

4
A limestone round-topped stela, 19th/20th Dynasty, 1305-1080 BC, carved with a falcon-headed Ra, 'Lord of the Sky', 33.5cm (13in), *NY 24 Nov,*
$4,675 (£3,292)

5
An alabaster jar, 18th Dynasty, 1554-1305 BC, linen fragments inside, 7.5cm (3in), *NY 30 May,*
$990 (£673)

6
An Egyptian jasper ring, New Kingdom, c.1300-1100 BC, 2.5cm (1in), *L 14 July,*
£2,090 ($3,260)

7
A basalt vase, late Predynastic Period, c.3400-3200 BC, 8cm (3¼in), *NY 30 May,*
$1,430 (£972)

8
A pale blue faience amulet of Pataek, Late Period, 712-730 BC, a ribbed pendant loop behind the neck, 6.5cm (2½in), *NY 24 Nov,*
$1,430 (£1,007)

9
An Egyptian mottled hardstone vase, 1st-11th Dynasty, c.3000-1991 BC, 11.5cm (4½in), *L 19 May,*
£990 ($1,584)

10
A marble headrest, 5th/6th Dynasty, 2450-2155 BC, 20.5cm (8in), *NY 24 Nov,*
$4,675 (£3,292)

11
An Egyptian alabaster vase, late 18th Dynasty, c.1403-1336 BC, 29cm (11½in), *L 19 May,*
£3,300 ($5,280)

12
A bronze cat, 22nd-26th Dynasty, 946-525 BC, encrusted green and brown patina, missing ear, apparently an ancient restoration, 11cm (4¼in), *NY 24 Nov,*
$3,850 (£2,711)

1
An Egyptian bronze figure of a cat, Late Period, c.712-30 BC, 11cm (4¼in), *L 8 Dec,*
£3,080 ($4,312)

2
An Egyptian black stone figure of Osiris, Late Period, c.712-30 BC, of mummified form, holding the crook and flail, 19cm (7½in), *L 8 Dec,*
£1,540 ($2,156)

3
A sandstone relief fragment, 26th Dynasty, 664-525 BC, carved in sunk relief with falcon-headed Horus, the inscriptions referring to the city of Pe, and to Horus as city guardian, remains of pigment, 45cm (17½in), *NY 24 Nov,*
$1,540 (£1,085)

4
An Egyptian glazed faience Ushabti figure in duck egg blue, 26th Dynasty, 664-525 BC, with a nine-line hieroglyphic inscription identifying the owner as a Priest of Wadjet, Anemheres, son of (?) Kahtyt, 21cm (8¼in), *L 8 Dec,*
£1,870 ($2,618)

5
A bronze figure of Osiris, 26th Dynasty, 664-525 BC, the base with a dedicatory inscription, holding the crook and the flail, wearing the *atef*-crown with uraeus and ram's horns, brown and green patina, 20.5cm (8in), *NY 24 Nov,*
$3,850 (£2,711)

6
A bronze figure of the Hathor Cow, 26th Dynasty, 664-525 BC, wearing the disk with ureaus, remains of triangular electrum inlay on the forehead, brownish-black patina, 10cm (4in), *NY 30 May,*
$2,420 (£1,646)

7
An Egyptian bronze figure of Nehebka, Saite Period, c.664-525 BC, the snake-headed god wearing a kilt, 15.5cm (6in), *L 8 Dec,*
£3,520 ($4,928)

8
An Egyptian bronze group of Isis and Horus, 26th Dynasty, c.664-525 BC, the goddess seated with the infant Horus on her lap, wearing a vulture head-dress surmounted by a diadem of uraei and horned solar disc, 27cm (10in), *L 8 Dec,*
£2,090 ($2,926)

9
The upper half of the cover of an Egyptian wood anthropoid sarcophagus, c.600 BC, decorated in polychrome with a deep jewelled collar, the bearded face green and with turquoise and yellow striped wig, 71cm (28in), *L 19 May,*
£3,080 ($4,928)

10
An Egyptian bronze figure of a cat, 26th Dynasty, c.664-525 BC, with an asymmetrical inscribed base naming the donor as the man Pen-Pa-Sesu, 16.5cm (6½in), *L 8 Dec,*
£8,800 ($12,320)

11
A bronze figure of a king, 26th Dynasty, 664-525 BC, kneeling with his hands extended to hold an offering, wearing striped *nemes*-headcloth with uraeus and queue, deep brown patina with reddish areas, 11.5cm (4½in), *NY 24 Nov,*
$3,080 (£2,169)

12
A steatite osiphorus of Prince Pa-di-bastet, 26th Dynasty, period of Apries, 589-568 BC, son of Pa-sheri-mut, hereditary prince and overseer of prophets in the temples of Thinis and Karnak, holding before him an image of Osiris, with an inscription on the back pillar asking for offerings of bread, fowl, oxen and beer, 44.5cm (17½in), *NY 30 May,*
$18,700 (£12,721)

1

2

3

6

4

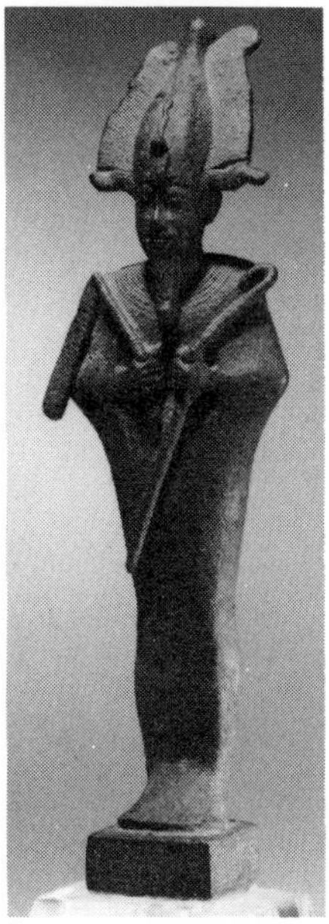
5

7

8

9

10

11

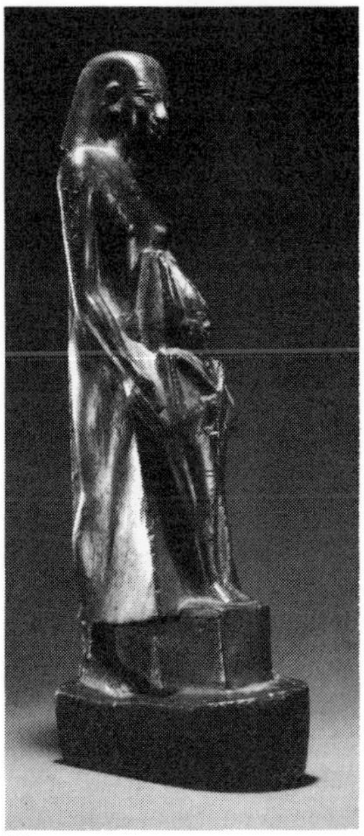
12

1

2

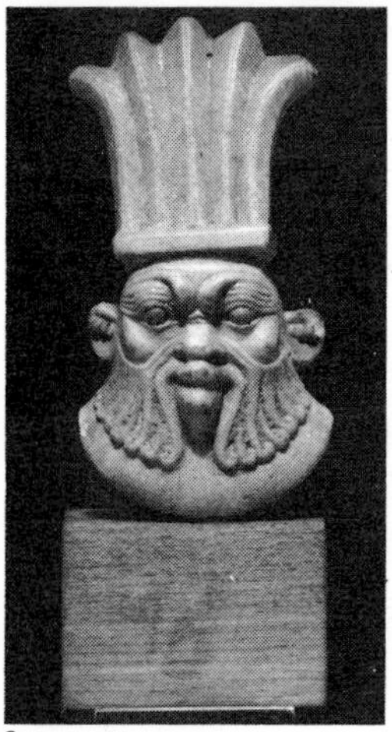
3

4

5

6

7

8

9

10

11

1
A limestone round-topped stela, 30th Dynasty, 380-342 BC, inscribed for the lady Teher, remains of pigment, 38.5cm (15in), *NY 24 Nov,*
$9,900 (£6,972)

2
A limestone stela, Ptolemaic Period, 330-305 BC, his feather head-dress with traces of painted detail, 26.5cm (10½in), *NY 24 Nov,*
$4,675 (£3,292)

3
A blue-green faience head of Bes amulet, Ptolemaic Period, 330-305 BC, 9cm (3½in), *NY 30 May,*
$2,640 (£1,795)

4
An Egyptian terracotta figure of a goddess, late Ptolemaic or Roman Period, c.100 BC-100 AD, with pink and black-painted decoration, 29cm (11¼in), *L 14 July,*
£1,430 ($2,230)

5
A Romano-Egyptian terracotta figure of a goddess, 1st century BC-1st century AD, traces of painted decoration, 41cm (16¼in), *L 8 Dec,*
£3,300 ($4,620)

6
A gilded Cartonnage mummy mask, Roman Period, 1st century AD, 25.5cm (10in), *NY 30 May,*
$1,210 (£823)

7
A Cartonnage mummy mask, Roman Period, 1st century AD, 32.5cm (12¾in), *NY 30 May,*
$2,750 (£1,870)

8
A stucco mummy portrait of a boy, c.1st century AD, eyes painted black and white behind glass, 20cm (8in), *NY 24 Nov,*
$2,860 (£2,014)

9
A Romano-Egyptian female plaster mummy portrait head, c.1st century AD, 28cm (11in), *L 14 July,*
£9,350 ($14,586)

10
A Romano-Egyptian male stucco mummy portrait head, c.3rd century AD, with inlaid eyes of glass, 23cm (9in), *L 14 July,*
£1,760 ($2,745)

11
A Romano-Egyptian plaster male mummy portrait head, c.3rd century AD, with inlaid glass eyes, 23cm (9in), *L 14 July,*
£1,760 ($2,745)

1
A bronze figure of Dionysus, c.2nd century AD, a mortise for attachment between the shoulder blades, green patina, 15cm (6in), *NY 24 Nov,*
$2,420 (£1,704)

2
A Roman bronze figure of Aphrodite, c.1st/2nd century AD, 21cm (8¼in), *L 8 Dec,*
£6,820 ($9,548)

3
A Roman bronze figure of Athena, c.1st century BC/1st century AD, 31cm (12¼in), *L 19 May,*
£7,150 ($11,440)

4
A Roman bronze figure of Pan, c.2nd/3rd century AD, the back hollow, green and black patina, 19.5cm (7½in), *NY 24 Nov,*
$4,400 (£3,098)

5
A Roman bronze figure of a young woman, c.1st/2nd century AD, 14cm (5½in), *L 8 Dec,*
£2,860 ($4,004)

6
A Roman bronze figure of Athena, c.2nd century AD, 20cm (8in), *L 19 May,*
£3,850 ($6,160)

7
A Roman bronze figure of Ceres, c.1st/2nd century AD, 11cm (4¼in), *L 14 July,*
£880 ($1,372)

8
A South Italian Greek bronze patera handle, c.500 BC, 27.5cm (11in), *L 14 July,*
£4,180 ($6,520)

9
A bronze figure of Ares, c.1st century BC, probably a portrait of one of the Diadochi, a lance and tropaeum(?) missing from his hands, 8.5cm (3½in), *NY 30 May,*
$7,150 (£4,863)

10
A Roman bronze head of Dionysus, 3rd century AD, 7.5cm (3in), *L 14 July,*
£2,090 ($3,260)

11
A Roman bronze lamp, c.late 1st century BC-2nd century AD, 21cm (8¼in), *L 19 May,*
£880 ($1,408)

12
A Roman bronze support, c.1st century AD, greenish black patina, 10cm (4in), *NY 24 Nov,*
$2,860 (£2,014)

13
A Roman bronze balsamarium, 2nd century AD, in the form of a bust of Dionysus, suspension handle missing, 13.5cm (5¼in), *NY 30 May,*
$2,750 (£1,870)

14
A Roman bronze balsamarium, c.3rd century AD, in the form of a crouching bear, the swivel lid a later restoration, 14cm (5½in), *NY 30 May,*
$3,300 (£2,244)

1

2

3

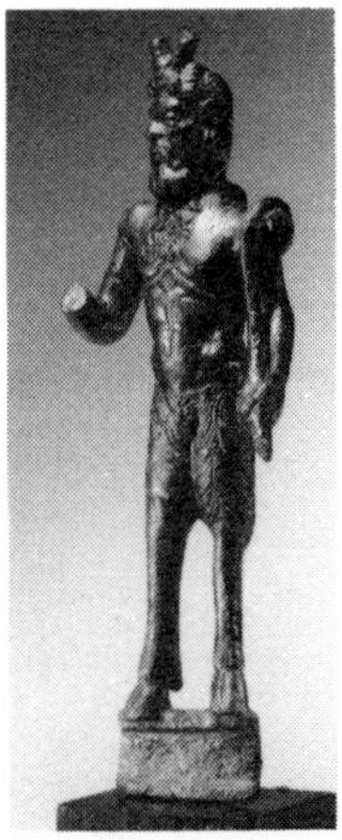
4

5

6

7

8

9

10

11

12

13

14

1

2

3

4

5

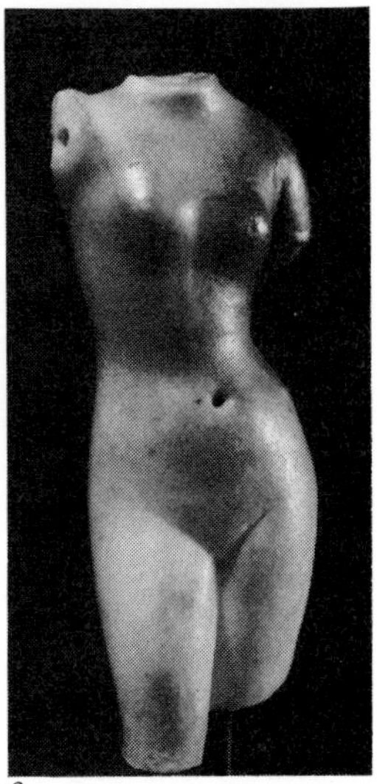
6

7

8

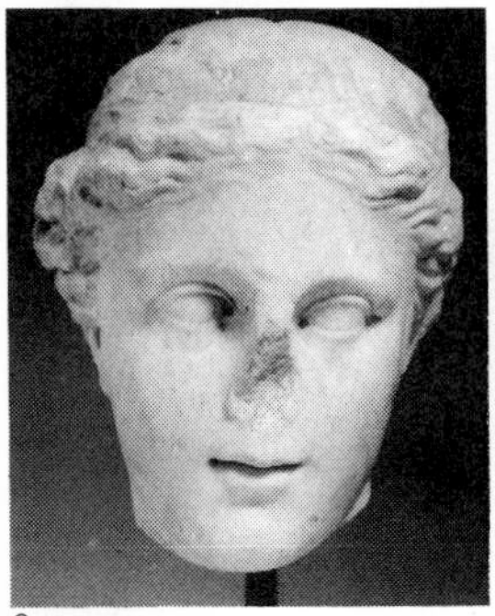
9

10

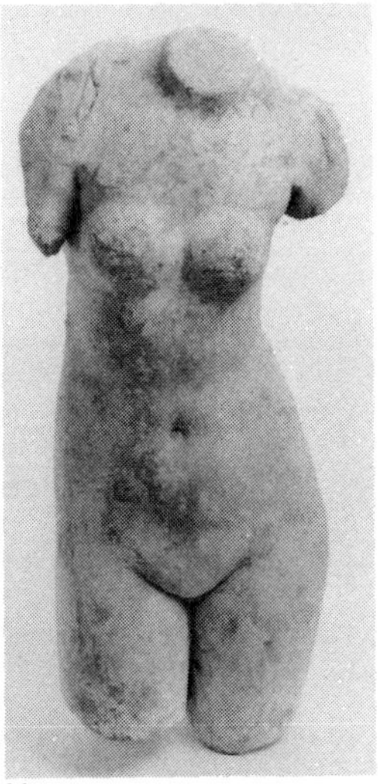
11

1
A marble figure of Athena Parthenos, c.1st century BC, 50cm (21in), *NY 30 May,*
$3,300 (£2,244)

2
A marble figure of a goddess, c.1st-2nd century AD, 50cm (16½in), *NY 24 Nov,*
$6,600 (£4,648)

3
A Roman marble figure of Athena, c.1st-2nd century AD, arms missing, 84cm (33in), *L 19 May,*
£4,950 ($7,920)

4
A fragmentary Roman grey stone male portrait head, c.1st-2nd century AD, 21cm (8¼in), *L 14 July,*
£2,860 ($4,461)

5
A Roman marble female head, c.1st-2nd century AD, 16.5cm (6½in), *L 19 May,*
£1,100 ($1,760)

6
A marble figure of Aphrodite Anadyomene, c.2nd-1st century BC, Alexandrian, remains of an ancient iron tenon in the left arm, 17cm (6¾in), *NY 24 Nov,*
$4,675 (£3,292)

7
A Roman marble female head, c.1st century AD, 37cm (14½in), *L 14 July,*
£4,180 ($6,520)

8
A Roman marble head of a satyr, c.1st-2nd century AD, 15cm (6in), *L 8 Dec,*
£2,420 ($3,388)

9
A Roman marble head of a young woman, c.1st-2nd century AD, 16.5cm (6½in), *L 14 July,*
£3,520 ($5,491)

10
A Roman marble female head, c.1st-2nd century AD, 43cm (17in), *L 14 July,*
£2,860 ($4,461)

11
A Roman marble torso of Aphrodite, c.1st century AD, traces of her long hair on her shoulders, 45.5cm (18in), *L 8 Dec,*
£13,200 ($18,480)

1
A marble figure of a Goddess, 2nd century AD, traces of red pigment, 86.5cm (34in), *NY 30 May,* **$15,950 (£10,858)**

2
A Roman marble fragment from a 'strigillated' sarcophagus, c.3rd century AD, 53.5cm (21in), *L 19 May,* **£1,320 ($2,112)**

3
A Roman marble female torso, c.1st/2nd century AD, 23.5cm (9¼in), *L 8 Dec,* **£1,980 ($2,772)**

4
A Roman marble column capital, c.3rd century AD, 76cm (30in), *L 8 Dec,* **£3,520 ($4,928)**

5
A marble torso of Aphrodite, c.early 2nd century AD, close to the Medici or Capitoline type, 14.5cm (5¾in), *NY 24 Nov,* **$1,430 (£1,007)**

6
A marble roundel bust of a Goddess, 3rd century AD, 44cm (17¼in), *NY 24 Nov,* **$5,500 (£3,873)**

7
A Roman marble sarcophagus fragment, c.last half 3rd century AD, 49.5cm (19½in), *NY 24 Nov,* **$13,200 (£9,296)**

8
A Roman marble season sarcophagus, 3rd/early 4th century AD, inscribed in Latin *the departed spirit of T. Claudio Pudentiano, who lived ten years...months, and 23 days...his dutiful mother Claudia Prisso set up this monument,* 123.5cm (48½in), *NY 24 Nov,* **$7,150 (£5,035)**

9
A Roman marble head of a man, c.2nd century AD, 28cm (11in), *L 19 May,* **£1,650 ($2,640)**

10
A Roman marble Silenus head, c.2nd century AD, 15.5cm (6in), *L 19 May,* **£2,420 ($3,872)**

11
A Roman marble figure of a woman, 2nd/3rd century AD, missing left arm, the head probably a 19th century restoration, 23.5cm (9¼in), *NY 30 May,* **$2,200 (£1,496)**

1

2

3

4

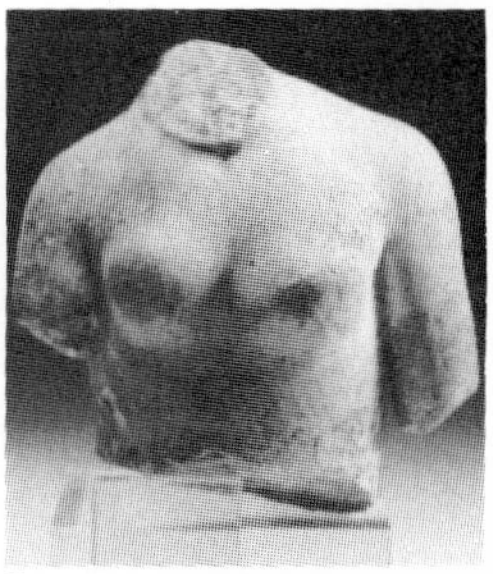
5

6

7

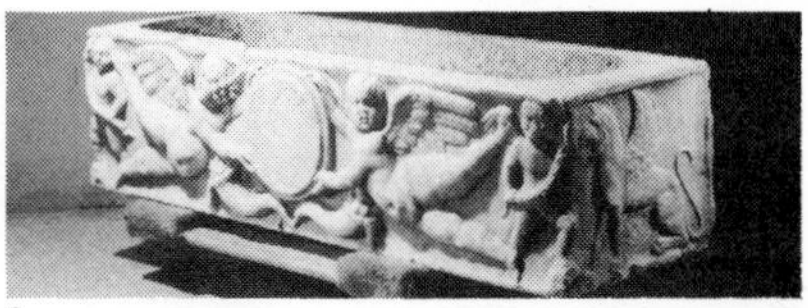
8

9

10

11

1

2

3

4

5

6

7

8

9

10

1
An Attic black-figure kylix, 6th century BC, the interior plain, the exterior decorated on both sides with the seated figure of Dionysus, the field with vine garlands, 37cm (14½in), *L 8 Dec,*
£1,650 ($2,310)

2
An Attic black-glazed pottery lekanis and cover, 5th century BC, 35.5cm (14in) diam., *L 8 Dec,*
£1,760 ($2,464)

3
An Attic black-figure lekythos, from the workshop of the Gela painter, c.520 BC, decorated with the figure of Athena in combat with two warriors, the decoration enriched with white and red paint, 31.5cm (12¼in), *L 14 July,*
£1,760 ($2,745)

4
An Attic red-figure kylix, c.450-430 BC, the central medallion depicting a bearded sage in conversation with a youth, the sides also decorated with figure paintings, 32.5cm (12¾in), *L 14 July,*
£1,100 ($1,716)

5
An Attic black-figure amphora, c.550-525 BC, decorated on both sides with a panel containing two warriors in combat, the decoration enriched with white and red paint, 34.5cm (13½in), *L 14 July,*
£5,500 ($8,580)

6
An Attic black-figure kylix, early 5th century BC, attributed to the Caylus painter, the exterior painted on each side with seated Dionysus and shield-bearing warriors, 21cm (8¼in) diam., *NY 30 May,*
$4,400 (£2,993)

7
A Paestan pottery trefoil-lipped oinochoe, 4th century BC, the front panel containing two confronted grotesque figures, the foot with a red-painted cruciform motif, 18cm (7in), *L 8 Dec,*
£4,070 ($5,698)

8
An Etruscan red-figure skyphos, late 4th century BC, attributed to the Clusium Group, painted on each side with a youth and a maiden confronted, both figures holding rhytons, 23.5cm (9¼in) diam., *NY 30 May,*
$1,760 (£1,197)

9
An Attic red-figure column krater, c.450-440 BC, painted on one side with a chiton-clad woman running to right, and on the other with two himation-clad youths facing a third, 22.5cm (9in), *NY 30 May,*
$2,310 (£1,571)

10
A Lucanian red-figure bell krater, c.400-375 BC, painted with a maenad in pursuit of a satyr, with himation-clad youths on the reverse, 26cm (10in) diam., *NY 30 May,*
$2,860 (£1,945)

1
An Apulian red-figure fragment, c.340-330 BC, from the tondo of a vessel decorated with Hermes and Artemis, 20.5cm (8in), *NY 30 May,*
$1,430 (£972)

2
An Apulian pottery incense stand, 4th century BC, in the form of a candlestick, the shaft decorated with the seated figure of a woman holding a mirror, the decoration with touches of white and yellow paint, 24cm (9½in), *L 14 July,*
£1,210 ($1,887)

3
A pair of Apulian red-figure epichyses, *(one illustrated),* c.330-320 BC, each body painted with a maenad and flying Eros, 20.5 and 21.5cm (8 and 8½in), *NY 30 May,*
$1,100 (£748)

4
An Apulian red-figure pelike, c.330-320 BC, painted with a maenad holding a tambourine and garland facing a seated youth, details in added white and yellow, 36.5cm (14¼in), *NY 30 May,*
$1,650 (£1,122)

5
An Apulian red-figure phiale, c.340-320 BC, painted with the profile head of a woman wearing a stephane, sakkos, pearl necklace and earrings, 17cm (6¾in), *NY 30 May,*
$825 (£561)

6
An Apulian pottery stamnos, c.350-330 BC, painted on one side with a female figure holding a casket, a draped youth and a funerary monument between; and on the other with a female figure holding a phiale and thyrsus, a nude youth and a figure of Eros above, 27cm (10½in), *L 8 Dec,*
£2,090 ($2,926)

7
An Apulian pottery kantharos, 4th century BC, with the seated figure of a Nike, the other side with Athena on horseback, *L 14 July,*
£3,300 ($5,148)

8
An Apulian pottery amphora, the Patera Painter, 4th century BC, decorated with the figure of a young woman holding a casket, the decoration enriched with white and yellow paint, 70cm (27½in), *L 19 May,*
£3,850 ($6,160)

9
An Apulian red-figure amphora, c.330-320 BC, 66.5cm (26in), *NY 24 Nov,*
$3,630 (£2,556)

10
An Apulian red-figure volute krater, c.330-320 BC, the details in yellow, white and purple, 74cm (29¼in), *NY 24 Nov,*
$11,550 (£8,134)

11
An Apulian pottery amphora, by the Haifa Painter, *(both sides illustrated),* 4th century BC, the decoration enriched with white and yellow paint, 73.5cm (29in), *L 8 Dec,*
£6,820 ($9,548)

12
An Apulian pottery volute krater, by the Patera Painter, 4th century BC, the decoration enriched with white and yellow paint, 64cm (25¼in), *L 19 May,*
£8,800 ($14,080)

1

2

3

4

5

6

7

8

9

10

11

12

1

2

3

4

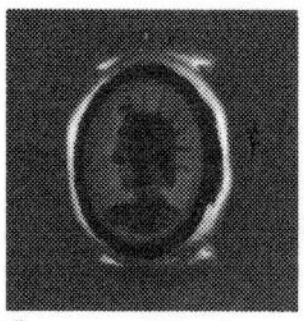
5

7

6

8

9

10

11

12

13

14

15

1
A Tarentine terracotta antefix in the form of a Gorgoneion mask, 6th century BC, 24cm (9½in), *L 14 July,*
£1,815 ($2,831)

2
A Hellenistic terracotta head of a goddess, late 4th/3rd century BC, Magna Graecia, 10.5cm (4in), *NY 30 May,*
$2,310 (£1,571)

3
An Etruscan terracotta male head, 4th/3rd century BC, 24cm (9½in), *L 8 Dec,*
£1,485 ($2,079)

4
An Apulian polychrome funerary vase, c.late 4th century BC, 38.5cm (15¼in), *NY 30 May,*
$880 (£598)

5
A Roman gold ring, c.3rd century AD, 2cm (¾in), *L 14 July,*
£1,430 ($2,230)

6
An Etruscan carnelian scarab, 4th/3rd century BC, 1.5cm (½in), *NY 24 Nov,*
$1,980 (£1,394)

7
A Roman gold ring, c.3rd century AD, 2.5cm (1in), *L 14 July,*
£5,500 ($8,580)

8
An Etruscan carnelian scarab, 4th century BC, one side of the scarab damaged in antiquity (?) and recarved. 1.5cm (½in), *NY 24 Nov,*
$990 (£697)

9
A pair of Canosan pottery funerary vases, c.3rd century BC, 47cm (18½in), *L 14 July*
£6,380 ($9,953)

10
A Hellenistic terracotta incense stand, 3rd/2nd century BC, Apulia, the hair with reddish painted decoration, the whole covered in a white slip, 19.5cm (7½in), *L 19 May,*
£660 ($1,056)

11
A Hellenistic terracotta figure of a young woman, c.3rd century BC, with some pink and blue-painted decoration, 28cm (11in), *L 8 Dec,*
£880 ($1,232)

12
A Hellenistic terracotta female figure, c.3rd century BC, the whole with traces of paint decoration, 29cm (11¼in), *L 19 May,*
£440 ($704)

13
A Hellenistic terracotta standing female figure, c.3rd/2nd century BC, with brilliant red, pink and white-painted decoration, 27cm (10¾in), *L 19 May,*
£660 ($1,056)

14
A Hellenistic terracotta female figure, c.3rd/2nd century BC, polychrome painted, 26.5cm (10½in), *L 19 May,*
£715 ($1,144)

15
A Canosan terracotta figure of a prancing unicorn, 3rd century BC, 24cm (9½in), and a Canosan terracotta figure of a rider, 19cm (7½in), *L 8 Dec,*
£8,580 ($12,012)

1
An Urartian bronze nose-let from a horse trapping, 8th-7th century BC, 16cm (6½in), *L 14 July,*
£2,530 ($3,946)

2
A Luristan bronze horse's bit, 8th-7th century BC, 18cm (7in), *L 14 July,*
£1,100 ($1,716)

3
A Daunian buffware double situla, 3rd century BC, decorated in black and red, 29cm (11½in), *NY 24 Nov,*
$1,980 (£1,394)

4
A Daunian buffware jar, 3rd century BC, with meander swastika incised on the base, 26cm (10in), *NY 24 Nov,*
$825 (£580)

5
A Daunian double-spouted askos, 3rd century BC, decorated in black, 17.5cm (7in), *NY 30 May,*
$550 (£374)

6
A Daunian pottery jar, c.late 4th century BC, brown and red over buff slip, 28.5cm (11¼in), *NY 24 Nov,*
$2,200 (£1,549)

7
A Celt-Iberian openwork pendant, c.3rd century BC, engraved 'S's on perimeter, 10cm (4in), *NY 24 Nov,*
$1,870 (£1,317)

8
A Luristan bronze 'Master of Animals' finial, 850-650 BC, 18cm (7in), *L 14 July,*
£550 ($858)

9
A Luristan bronze 'Master of Animals' finial, c.850-650 BC, 33.5cm (14in), *L 14 July,*
£715 ($1,115)

10
A Corinthian pottery skyphos, c.600 BC, red painted details, dark brown slip, 30cm (12in) diam., *L 8 Dec,*
£2,200 ($3,080)

11
A Corinthian pottery 'plastic vase' in the form of a squatting ram, c.600 BC, with brown-spotted decoration, 6cm (2¼in), *L 8 Dec,*
£935 ($1,309)

12
A Roman olive-green pottery beaker, c.1st century BC-1st century AD, 10cm (4in), *L 14 July,*
£440 ($686)

13
A Cycladic marble jar, early Cycladic I, 3200-2700 BC, with slender ribs pierced for suspension, fragmentary rim, 16cm (6½in), *NY 24 Nov,*
$12,100 (£8,521)

14
A Cycladic marble collared vase ('Kandela'), c.2500 BC, 16cm (6¼in), *L 8 Dec,*
£1,650 ($2,310)

15
A Cypriot pottery amphora, c.600 BC, in dark brown slip, 51.5cm (20¼in), *L 8 Dec,*
£770 ($1,078)

1

2

3

4

5

6

7

8

9

10

11

12

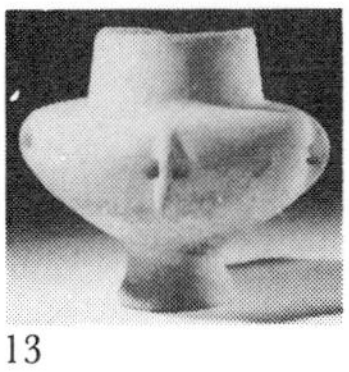
13

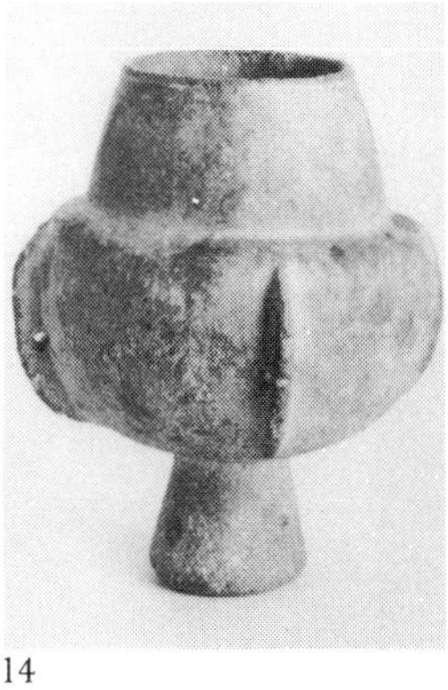
14

15

American Indian Art

1
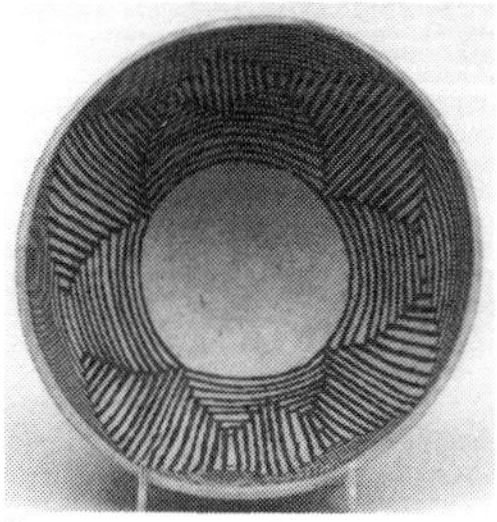
2

3

4

5

6

7

8

9

10

11

12

13 14

15

16

17

See also:
Colour illustrations *p* 490

1
A Mimbres black-on-white pottery bowl, c.1000-1100 AD, 29cm (11¼in), *NY 3 Dec,*
$1,760 (£1,230)

2
An Anasazi black-on-white bowl, possibly Taos, c.1250-1300 AD, 21.5cm (8¾in), *NY 3 Dec,*
$660 (£461)

3
A Mimbres black-on-white bowl, c.950-1150 AD, 24cm (9¼in), *NY 30 May,*
$1,980 (£1,347)

4
A Tonto polychrome pottery Olla, c.1250-1350 AD, 32.5cm (12¾in), *NY 3 Dec,*
$880 (£615)

5
An Anasazi black-on-white jar, possibly Tularosa, c.1000-1200 AD, 17.5cm (7in), *NY 30 May,*
$1,760 (£1,197)

6
A Zuni ceremonial polychrome jar, 37cm (14½in), *NY 3 Dec,*
$6,050 (£4,230)

7
A Casas Grandes polychrome jar, c.1160-1260 AD, painted over a deep cream slip in black and red, 21.5cm (8½in), *NY 30 May,*
$825 (£561)

8
A Cochiti polychrome pottery jar, painted over a cream slip in black and red, 20cm (8in), *NY 3 Dec,*
$550 (£384)

9
An Acoma polychrome jar, painted over a creamy slip in black, orange and deep red, 31.5cm (12½in), *NY 3 Dec,*
$3,850 (£2,692)

10
A Hopi polychrome seed jar, signed on the base *Fannie Nampeyo,* 28cm (11in), *NY 30 May,*
$2,640 (£1,796)

11
A Santo Domingo polychrome storage jar, nativ hide strip repair at the neck, 42cm (16½in), *NY 30 May,*
$3,300 (£2,245)

12
An Acoma polychrome pottery jar, 28.5cm (11¼in), *NY 3 Dec,*
$825 (£576)

13
A San Ildefonso blackware jar, incised on the base *Marie,* 19cm (7½in), *NY 30 May,*
$770 (£524)

14
A San Ildefonso blackware jar, incised on the base *Marie,* 20.5cm (8in), *NY 30 May,*
$1,760 (£1,197)

15
A Zuni polychrome pottery jar, signed on the indented base *Marie Qualo,* 25cm (9¾in), *NY 3 Dec,*
$605 (£423)

16
A Hopi (Hano) polychrome seed jar, in Sikyatki revival style, signed on the base *Fannie Nampeyo,* with corn symbol 20cm (8in), *NY 3 Dec,*
$1,650 (£1,153)

17
A San Ildefonso redware jar, signed on the underside *Marie,* 25cm (9¾in), *NY 3 Dec,*
$4,675 (£3,269)

n Apache coiled tray, 1.5cm (21¼in), *Y 30 May,* **1,430 (£973)**

Western Apache coiled ray, woven in willow and lack devil's claw, 62cm 24½in), *NY 3 Dec,* **6,600 (£4,615)**

Chemehueve poly-hrome coiled tray, oven in willow, black evil's claw and variegated ush, 35cm (13¾in), *Y 30 May,* **1,430 (£973)**

Pima coiled tray, 9.5cm (15½in), *Y 30 May,* **467 (£318)**

Pima coiled winnowing ray, woven in stylised lossom or meander attern, 46cm (18¼in), *Y 30 May,* **935 (£636)**

n Apache coiled olla, oven in a chequered attern, 46cm (18in), *Y 3 Dec,* **1,100 (£769)**

Maidu coiled utility asket, woven over a three od willow foundation in plit shoots of big leaf naple and redbud, 58cm 22¾in), *NY 3 Dec,* **5,500 (£3,846)**

Hopi coiled poly-hrome jar, woven with wo rows of steers' heads, 6cm (10¼in), *NY 30 May,* **440 (£299)**

Tlingit twined spruce oot basket, 31cm 12¼in), *NY 3 Dec,* **1,650 (£1,153)**

.0
n Achumawi twined urden basket, woven in umerous materials, with ear's foot motifs, 42.5cm 16¾in), *NY 30 May,* **1,100 (£748)**

11
A Yokuts polychrome coiled basket, woven in saw grass, brackenfern root and redbud, 25cm (10in), *NY 30 May,* **$1,650 (£1,122)**

12
A Karok twined fancy basket, 23cm (9in), *NY 3 Dec,* **$5,775 (£4,038)**

13
A Tubatulabul poly-chrome coiled bowl, 19.5cm (7¾in), *NY 3 Dec,* **$1,870 (£1,307)**

14
A Washo coiled bowl, 28.5cm (11¾in), *NY 3 Dec,* **$1,210 (£846)**

15
A Hupa twined utility basket, 28cm (11in), *NY 30 May,* **$1,430 (£973)**

16
A Tlingit twined and lidded spruce root basket, 15cm (6in), *NY 30 May,* **$990 (£673)**

1

2

3

4

5

6

7

8

9

10

11

12

13

14

15

16

1

2

3

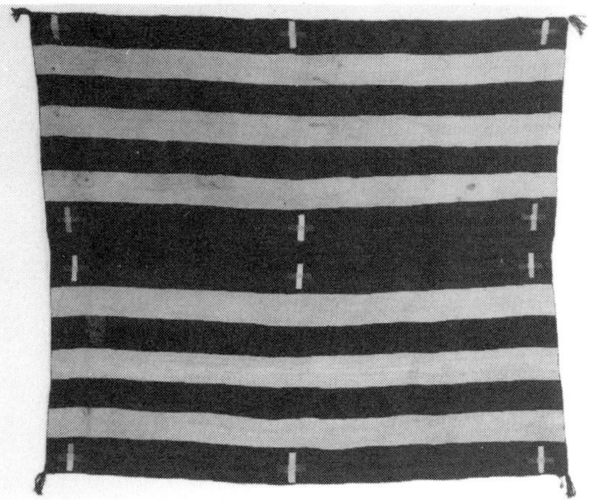
4

5

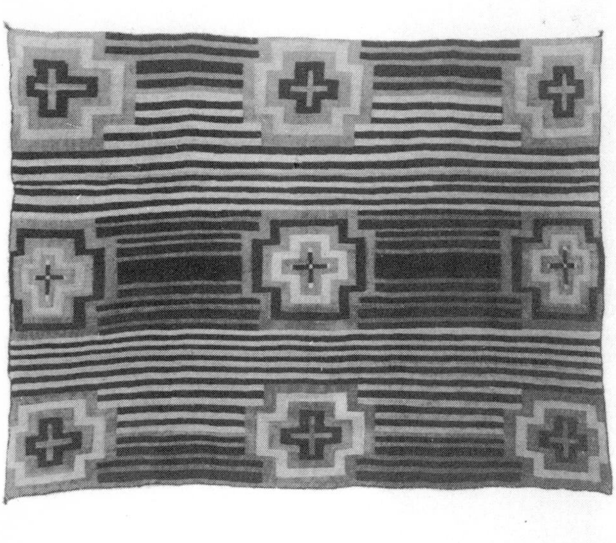
6

7

1
A Classic Navajo child's blanket, woven in ravelled, re-carded, commercial and handspun wool, in green, white, indigo and red on a grey ground, length 115cm (45¼in), *NY 3 Dec,*
$6,325 (£4,423)

2
A Navajo regional rug, woven in analine deep red and natural shades of grey, brown and white handspun, length 217cm (85½in), *NY 3 Dec,*
$1,320 (£923)

3
A Navajo Germantown blanket, woven on a red ground in ivory, black, red, green and grey, traces of a fringe, length 135cm (53½in), *NY 30 May,*
$1,760 (£1,197)

4
A Classic Navajo chief's blanket, woven with a second phase pattern in handspun and ravelled yarn in red, tan, green, indigo blue, ivory and brown, 173cm (68in), *NY 30 May,*
$35,200 (£22,945)

5
A Navajo Germantown blanket, woven in red and purple over a brownish black and white ground with a chief's style pattern, length 183cm (72in), *NY 30 May,*
$3,575 (£2,432)

6
A Classic Navajo woman's chief's blanket, woven in handspun wool with a third phase pattern in red, green and indigo blue over grey and brown stripes, length 132cm (52in), *NY 3 Dec,*
$8,800 (£6,153)

7
A Navajo Germantown rug, woven on a grey ground in white, black, brown, red and green commercial yarn, length 148.5cm (58½in), *NY 3 Dec,*
$1,760 (£1,230)

. **Navajo Germantown**
lanket, woven on a bright
·d ground in black,
hite, maroon, dark blue
nd bright green, 172 x
31cm (67¾ x 51¾in),
Y 3 Dec,
2,475 (£1,730)

. **Navajo Germantown**
lanket, woven with an
·yedazzler' pattern, black
nd white on a deep red
round, 209 x 148cm
32½ x 58½in), *NY 3 Dec,*
3,850 (£2,692)

. **Navajo regional rug,**
·oven on a natural
round in black, white and
amel, 285 x 177cm (112½
69¾in), *NY 30 May,*
1,980 (£1,347)

. **Transitional Navajo**
edgeweave blanket,
·oven in pale and deep
olours, 150 x 89cm (59 x
5in), *NY 30 May,*
1,980 (£1,347)

. **Transitional Navajo**
ug, woven on a rich red
round in black, white and
olden yellow, 205 x
27cm (81 x 50in),
IY 30 May,
1,100 (£748)

. **Transitional Navajo**
hief's blanket, woven in
andspun with a Third
hase nine-spot pattern,
77 x 145cm (69¾ x
7¼in), *NY 3 Dec,*
5,060 (£3,538)

. **Transitional Navajo**
ug, woven in red, brown
nd white, 182 x 123cm
71 x 49in), *NY 30 May,*
2,475 (£1,730)

. **Transitional Saltillo**
erape, woven in two
anels, in indigo-blue,
vory and deep red, 249 x
21cm (98 x 48in),
IY 30 May,
2,750 (£1,871)

1

2

3

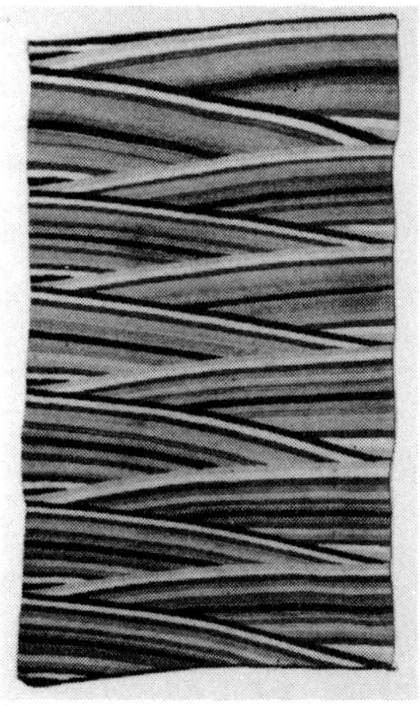
4

5

6

7

8

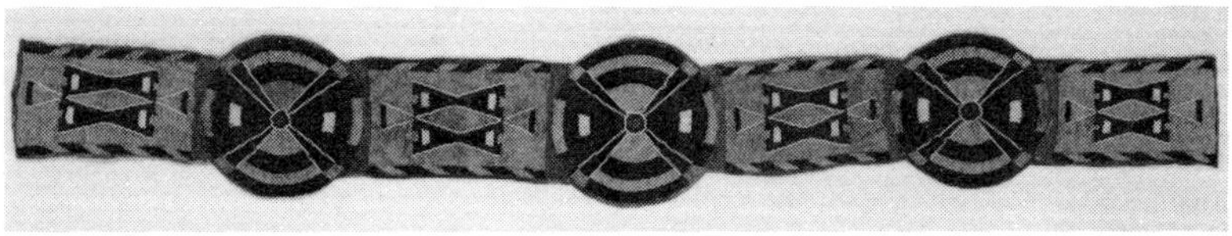
1

2

3

4 5

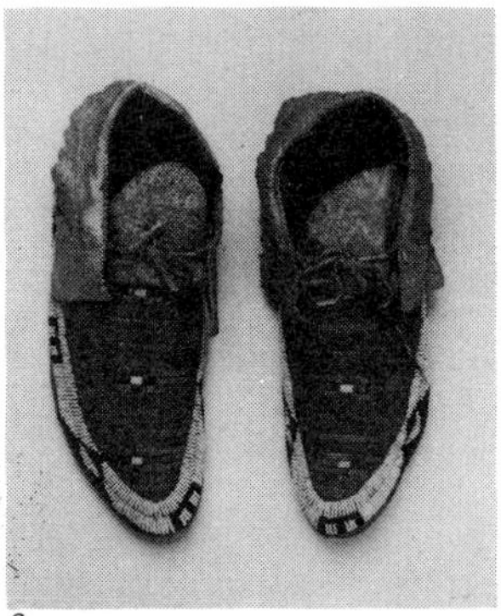
6

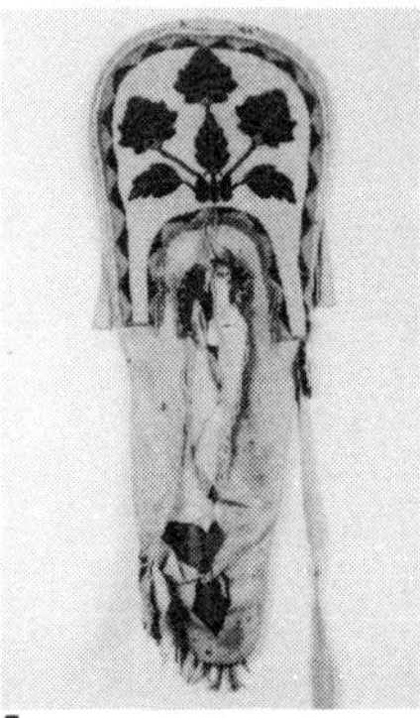
7

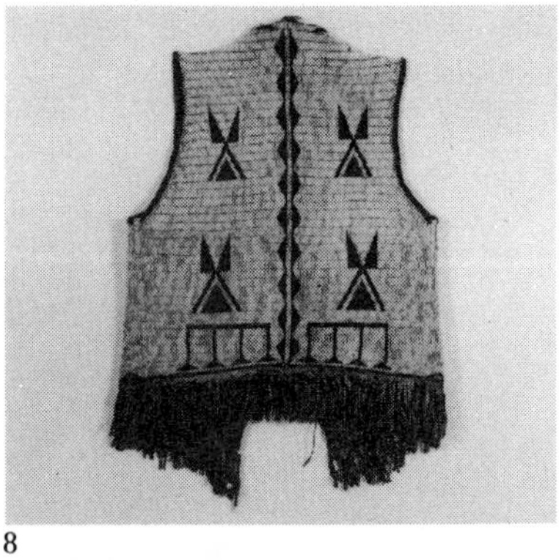
8

9

10

11

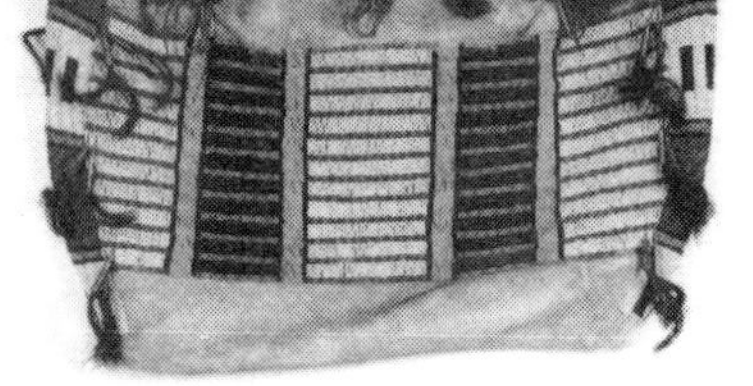
12

1
A Crow beaded hide blanket strip, stitched in pink, white, yellow and blue, translucent red and green glass bead work, red trade cloth trim possibly a later addition, 119.5cm (47in), *NY 3 Dec,*
$6,875 (£4,807)

2
A Lakota Sioux quilled and fringed hide man's jacket, remains of deep yellow pigment, stitched in yellow, red, purple and green-dyed porcupine quillwork, traces of ermine and red trade cloth suspensions, blue pigment on cuffs, lined with printed cotton trade cloth, 61cm (26in), *NY 3 Dec,*
$1,100 (£769)

3
A Blackfoot beaded hide knife sheath, enclosing steel bladed knife, wood haft bound with hide, 36.5cm (14½in), *NY 3 Dec,*
$1,320 (£923)

4
A Cree beaded and fringed hide pipe bag, stitched with yellow, red and blue, sold with a beaded leather belt, 102cm (40¼in), *L 1 Dec,*
£1,650 ($2,360)

5
An Eastern Great Lakes octopus bag, James Bay area, of pale buckskin, lined with cream chintz, embroidered in yellow, brown, cream, greens and blue, twisted pink and grey silk handle, 43.5cm (17in), *L 1 Dec,*
£1,100 ($1,573)

6
A pair of Sioux beaded and quilled hide man's moccasins, decorated in yellow, blue and pink-dyed porcupine quillwork, 25cm (9¾in), *NY 30 May*
$605 (£411)

7
A Nez Perce beaded and fringed hide cradleboard, bordered by triangles in opaque and translucent shades and metallic beads, a diamond umbilical fetish suspended below, 98.5cm (38¾in), *NY 3 Dec,*
$1,100 (£769)

8
A Sioux beaded and fringed hide man's vest, stitched in blue over a white beaded ground, 50.5cm (20in), *NY 30 May,*
$1,430 (£973)

9
A Northern Plains beaded and fringed hide pipe bag, stitched in opaque and translucent glass, and silver and brass facetted metal beads against a white ground, the hide strips below wrapped in red porcupine quills, 93.5cm (36¾in), *NY 30 May,*
$1,100 (£748)

10
A Great Lakes beaded cloth bandoleer, trimmed in multicoloured cotton hem tape, wool yarn tassels on the loom beaded flaps below, 74.5cm (29¼in), *NY 3 Dec,*
$1,760 (£1,230)

11
A Canadian Cree fringed moosehide sled bag, faceted metallic beads against the smoked hide ground, edged in red silk ribbon, 56cm (22in), *NY 30 May,*
$2,860 (£1,946)

12
A Sioux beaded hide 'possible' bag, tin cone and red horsehair suspensions, 49cm (19¼in), *NY 3 Dec,*
$1,320 (£923)

**\ Hopi wood wolf
Kachina doll,** possibly
Kweo, with brown body
.nd face mask, a wood
.nd feather suspension on
he crown, 25cm (10in),
VY 3 Dec,
1,320 (£923)

:
**\ Hopi wood Kachina
loll,** red painted body,
ainbow decoration on
acial perimeter, feather
ttachments, 20.5cm (8in),
VY 3 Dec,
660 (£461)

**\ Hopi wood Kachina
loll,** representing
Monogua, a guard for the
Third Mesa, a yellow
errace replacing the nose,
2cm (8½in), *NY 3 Dec,*
2,090 (£1,461)

**\ Kwakiutl model whale
rest/totem,** carrying a
eparately carved hawk on
ts back, with black, red
nd green painted details,
nsigned, but probably
he work of Charlie James,
1870-1938), 67.5cm
26½in), *NY 30 May,*
1,760 (£1,197)

\ Tlingit wood fish club,
profile of a bear's head
ncised and carved in
elief, 64cm (25¼in),
VY 3 Dec,
3,850 (£2,692)

**An Eskimo coiled whale
aleen basket,** carved in
igh relief with standing
olar bear, traces of
aleen inlays, 9.5cm
3½in) diam., *NY 30 May,*
1,540 (£1,048)

**\ Northwest Coast
eremonial wood rattle,**
n the form of a raven in
light, supporting a
haman reclining on its
ack, red, black and blue-
reen painted details,
33.5cm (13¼in), *NY 3 Dec,*
9,900 (£6,923)

8
A Tlingit mountain sheep and goat horn ladle, decorated with three copper plaques, facial and wing details incised and carved in low relief, 49cm (19in), *NY 3 Dec,*
$4,950 (£3,461)

9
A Northwest Coast wood face mask, possibly once overlaid with shell or copper, painted in black and red, faint traces of blue pigment on the eyes, pierced three times at the back, 26cm (10¼in), *NY 3 Dec,*
$3,190 (£2,230)

10
An Eskimo ivory female figure, fine old honeyed patina, 11cm (4¼in), *L 1 Dec,*
£1,100 ($1,573)

11
A Haida miniature wood bowl, carved in shallow relief with abstract totemic devices, once inlaid with shell or ivory, 12.5cm (5in), *NY 3 Dec,*
$1,210 (£846)

1 2 3

4

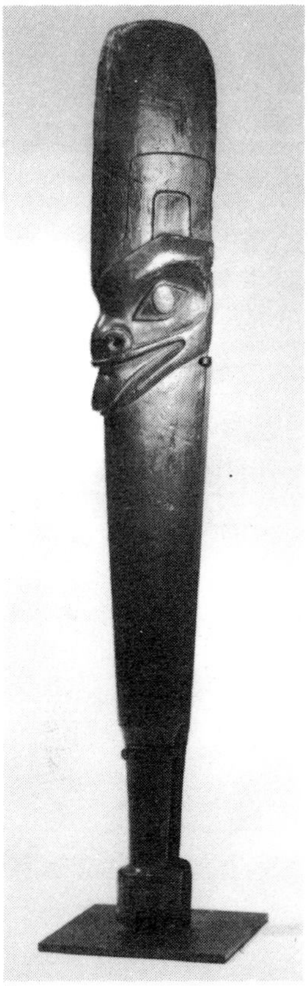
5

6

7

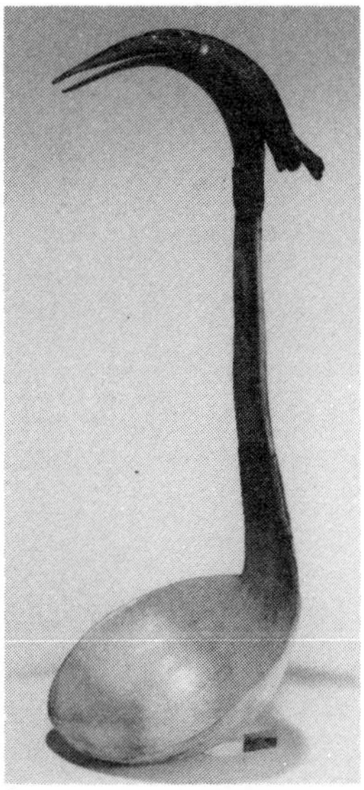
8

9

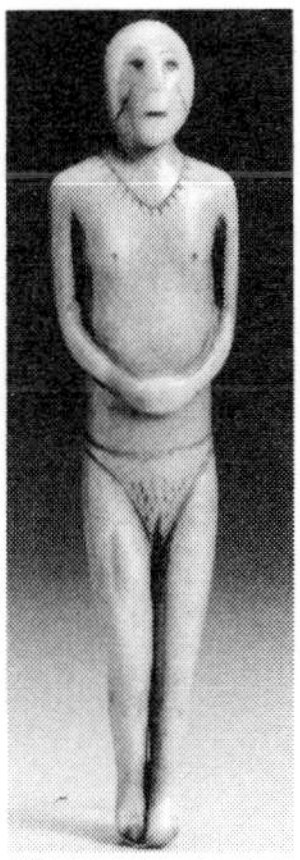
10

11

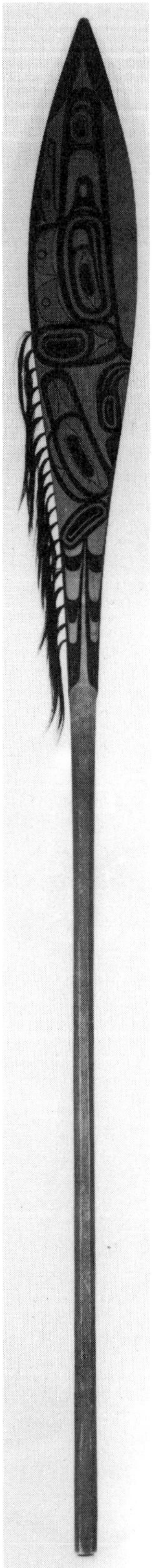

1

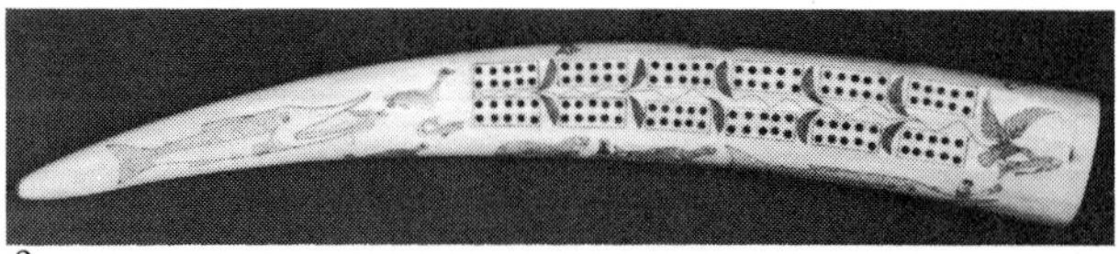

2

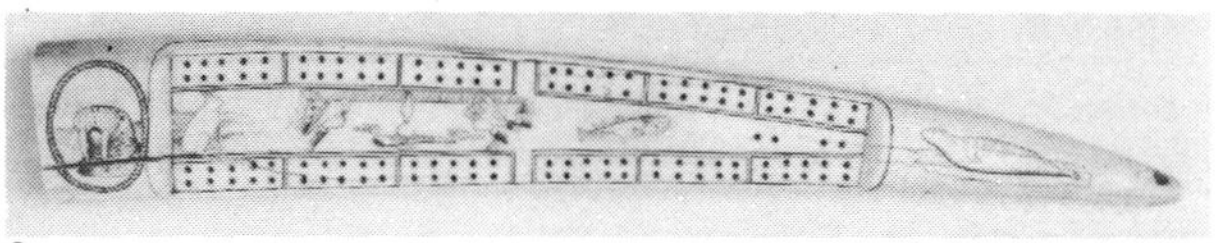

3

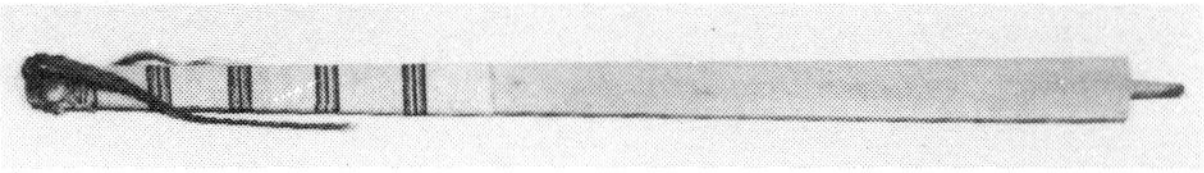

4

5

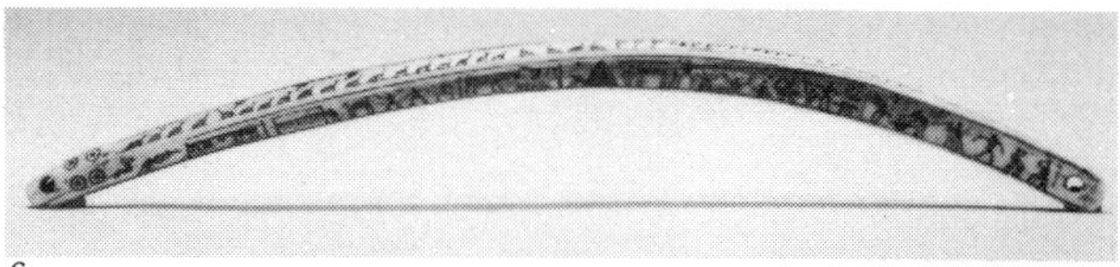

6

7

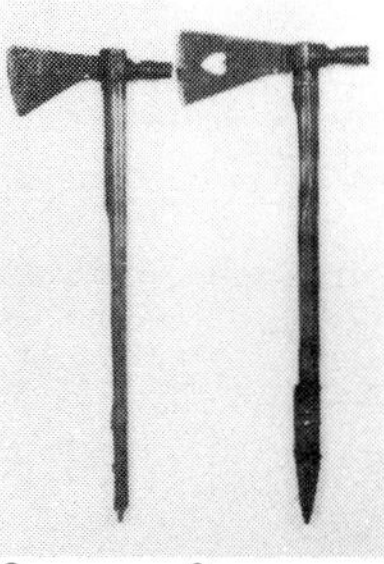

8 9

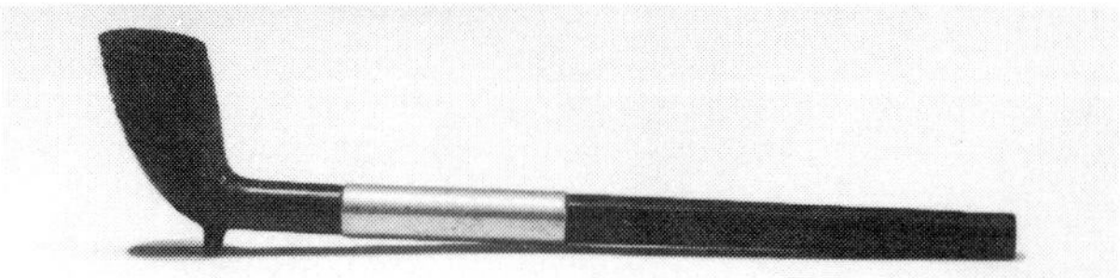

10

11

12

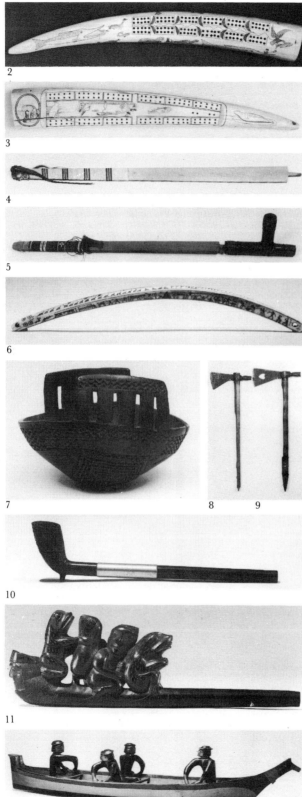

1
A Tlingit ceremonial dancing staff, decorated with a row of human hair suspensions inserted along one side, 268.5cm (105¾in), *NY 3 Dec,*
$7,700 (£5,384)

2
An Eskimo engraved ivory cribbage board, four game pieces remaining, 52cm (20½in), *NY 3 Dec,*
$1,320 (£923)

3
An Eskimo engraved ivory cribbage board, 43.5cm (17in), *NY 30 May,*
$605 (£412)

4
An Eastern Plains quilled wood pipe stem, a worn panel of bird's feathers and red horsehair bound to the mouthpiece with sinew, the pipe missing, 104.5cm (41in), *NY 3 Dec,*
$7,975 (£5,576)

5
A Sioux wood and stone pipe, 72.5cm (29in), *NY 3 Dec,*
$825 (£576)

6
An Eskimo engraved ivory drill bow, pierced through on each end, incised with birds and human figures, 33cm (13in), *NY 3 Dec,*
$1,760 (£1,230)

7
A Wasco bighorn sheep horn bowl, 19cm (7½in), *NY 3 Dec,*
$3,300 (£2,307)

8
An Eastern Plains pipe tomahawk, 54cm (21¼in), *NY 3 Dec,*
$1,980 (£1,384)

9
An Eastern Plains pipe tomahawk, with fire branding and brass tacks on the shaft, 54.5cm (21½in), *NY 3 Dec,*
$880 (£615)

10
A Haida argillite pipe, an abstract totemic band below the rim, 21cm (8¼in), *NY 3 Dec,*
$1,320 (£923)

11
A Haida argillite panel pipe, the bowl carved in the form of a European sailor's head, 30.5cm (12in), *NY 3 Dec,*
$1,980 (£1,384)

12
A Haida model canoe, r
and black painted details, 86cm (34in), *NY 30 May,*
$2,530 (£1,721)

Pre-Columbian Art

See also:
Colour illustrations *p* 562

 Costa Rican jade figure, 100-500 AD, in dark reen and white speckled one, 10cm (4in), *Y 20 May,* **1,870 (£1,238)**

 Costa Rican jade axe- od pendant, c.500-800 D, in greyish-green stone, ierced at the neck, 2.5cm (5in), *NY 24 Nov,* **1,100 (£775)**

 Costa Rican Metate, .800-1500 AD, curvilinear nd geometric motifs arved on the head, plat- orm and legs, 47cm 18½in), *NY 24 Nov,* **1,760 (£1,239)**

 Nicoya seated figure, Guanacaste, 800-1200 AD, ainted overall in cream, rown and orange with eometric designs indicat- ng clothing and tattooing, 8.5cm (7¼in), *NY 24 Nov,* **440 (£310)**

n early/middle Chavin reyware vessel, 1400- 00 BC, 22.5cm (8¾in), *Y 20 May,* **990 (£656)**

Chavin brownware essel, 700-400 BC, the umpkin-shaped body ivided into quadrants, ach finely incised with ows of zig-zag motifs, 5.5cm (10in), *NY 20 May,* **440 (£291)**

Chavin greyware essel, late Cupinisque, .500-300 BC, 25.5cm 10in), *NY 20 May,* **715 (£474)**

n early Mochica monkey essel, 300-100 BC, ainted in cream and eddish-brown, 14cm 5½in), *NY 20 May,* **$1,210 (£801)**

9
An early/middle Mochica copper mask, c.300 BC-300 AD, the eyes possibly once inlaid, the remains of suspension holes at sides, 23.5cm (9¼in), *NY 20 May,* **$1,650 (£1,093)**

10
An early Mochica warrior, c.400-100 BC, inlaid with mother-of-pearl, wearing a banded turban possibly once inlaid with turquoise, painted overall in brown, 14.5cm (5¾in), *NY 20 May,* **$1,760 (£1,166)**

11
A middle Mochica fox effigy vessel, c.100-500 AD, the tunic and skirt painted decoratively in cream and brown and covered overall in a brownish-orange slip, 42cm (16½in), *NY 24 Nov,* **$3,300 (£2,324)**

12
An Inca copper and silver ceremonial Tumi, possibly Southern Highlands, c.1400-1532 AD, 15.5cm (6in), *NY 20 May,* **$2,970 (£1,967)**

13
A middle Mochica figural vessel, 100-500 AD, the turban decorated with projecting feline heads, stylised maceheads and rectangular crest, painted overall in tan and brown, 24cm (9½in), *NY 20 May,* **$715 (£474)**

1

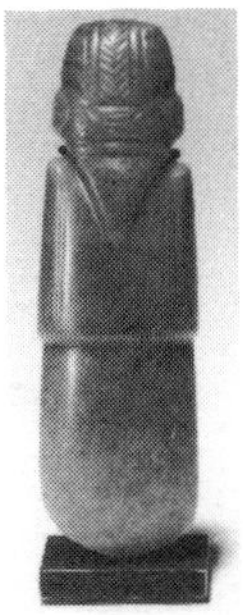
2

3

4

5

6

7

8

9

10

11

12

13

1

2

3

4

5

6

7

8

9

10

11

12

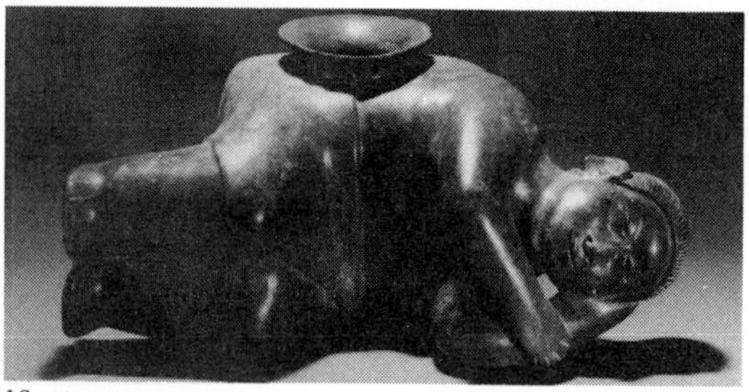
13

14

1
A Chinesco female figure, Protoclassic, c.100 BC-250 AD, her heart-shaped face painted in ochre, the rest painted in cream and reddish-brown, 28cm (11in), *NY 20 May,*
$2,970 (£1,967)

2
A Nayarit figure, Protoclassic, c.100 BC-250 AD, painted overall with brown, with red pigment on the head, 22cm (8¾in), *NY 20 May,*
$605 (£401)

3
A Colima gadrooned vessel, Protoclassic, c.100 BC-250 AD, painted overall in reddish-brown, 30.5cm (12in) diam., *NY 20 May,*
$1,870 (£1,238)

4
A Colima dog, Protoclassic, c.100 BC-250 AD, painted overall in deep reddish-brown, 40cm (15¾in), *NY 24 Nov,*
$2,530 (£1,782)

5
A Colima bird vessel, Protoclassic, c.100 BC-250 AD, the high upturned tail as spout, painted overall in brownish-red with areas of black, 18cm (7in), *NY 24 Nov,*
$3,300 (£2,324)

6
A Colima double duck vessel, Protoclassic, c.100 BC-250 AD, painted overall in reddish-tan, 21cm (8¼in), *NY 24 Nov,*
$1,210 (£852)

7
A Colima dancer, Protoclassic, c.100 BC-250 AD, painted overall in reddish-brown, with clothing and decorative elements in brown, 24cm (9in), *NY 20 May,*
$3,300 (£2,185)

8
A Colima warrior, Protoclassic, c.100 BC-250 AD, wearing a closely-fitted cap with a diminuitive shaman's horn, painted in reddish-brown and cream, 36.5cm (14¼in), *NY 24 Nov,*
$1,210 (£852)

9
A Colima parrot vessel, Protoclassic, c.100 BC-25 AD, the tail forming the spout, painted in reddish-brown with areas of brown, 27.5cm (10¾in), *NY 24 Nov,*
$6,875 (£4,842)

10
A Colima water carrier, Protoclassic, c.100 BC-25 AD, with faint remains of black patterning below th mouth, painted overall in brown with details in dee red, 35.5cm (14in), *NY 24 Nov,*
$7,700 (£5,422)

11
A Jalisco warrior, Amec region, Protoclassic, c.100 BC-250 AD, with details in reddish-brown, 40.5cm (16in), *NY 24 Nov,*
$7,425 (£5,229)

12
A Jalisco warrior, Amec region, Protoclassic, c.100 BC-250 AD, his armour probably made of animal skin stretched over a wooden frame, 44.5cm (17¼in), *NY 24 Nov,*
$4,400 (£3,099)

13
A Colima sleeping fema figure, Protoclassic, c.100 BC-250 AD, painted overal in rich reddish-brown, 46cm (18in), *NY 24 Nov,*
$11,550 (£8,134)

14
A Colima carrier, Protoclassic, c.100 BC-250 AD, the stacked branches on his back possibly that of maguey flowers, painted overall in brown, 24cm (9¼in), *NY 24 Nov,*
$3,850 (£2,711)

1
A Colima female figural vessel, Coahuayana style, Protoclassic, c.100 BC-250 AD, her long ears pierced with jade disc earrings added later, painted overall in reddish-brown, 36cm (14in), *NY 24 Nov,*
$1,320 (£929)

2
A Jalisco face mask, Protoclassic, c.100 BC-250 AD, wearing nose and earrings, with faint remains of white decorative details, pierced around the circumference for attachment, 15.5cm (6in), *NY 20 May,*
$770 (£510)

3
A Jalisco standing warrior, Protoclassic, c.100 BC-250 AD, wearing noseplug, earrings and headband, painted overall in reddish-brown, 35.5cm (14in), *NY 20 May,*
$880 (£583)

4
A Jalisco female figure, Protoclassic, c.100 BC-250 AD, painted in buff, black and reddish-brown, 54cm (21¼in), *NY 24 Nov,*
$3,080 (£2,169)

5
A Veracruz stone avial head Hacha, Classic, c.450-650 AD, in basalt with remains of cinnabar, 26.5cm (10¼in), *NY 24 Nov,*
$8,800 (£6,197)

6
A Veracruz head, Late Classic, c.550-950 AD, her ears pierced by large ear-spools, covered in a cream/orange slip, the hair in dark brown, 26.5cm (10½in), *NY 24 Nov,*
$3,300 (£2,324)

7
A Veracruz standing warrior, Late Classic, c.550-950 AD, the face with a hypnotic expression, 73cm (28¾in), *NY 24 Nov,*
$4,675 (£3,292)

8
A Veracruz seated priest, Classic, c.250-550 AD, painted extensively in black *chapapote,* 41.5cm (16¼in), *NY 24 Nov,*
$3,300 (£2,324)

9
A Zapotec Cocijo vessel, Monte Alban IIIB, Late Classic, c.550-950 AD, the head as spout, remains in red pigment overall, 13.5cm (5¼in), *NY 24 Nov,*
$660 (£465)

10
A Veracruz whistling jaguar toy, Classic, c.250-550 AD, wooden axles modern, 22.5cm (9in), *NY 20 May,*
$1,100 (£728)

11
An Aztec stone figure of Xochiquetzal, Tenochtitlan, c.1300-1521 AD, in grey basalt with remains of pigment, 32cm (12½in), *NY 24 Nov,*
$7,425 (£5,229)

12
An Aztec stone goddess, c.1300-1521 AD, with tasselled head-dress, in grey volcanic, tuffa-like stone, 41.5cm (16¼in), *NY 20 May,*
$4,675 (£3,096)

13
A Teotihuacan III stone head, Classic, c.250-550 AD, pierced at the fragmentary ears, in greyish-black stone, 18cm (7in), *NY 20 May,*
$2,860 (£1,894)

14
An Aztec stone mask, c.1370-1521 AD, in green speckled stone, 14.5cm (5¾in), *NY 20 May,*
$5,500 (£3,642)

1

2

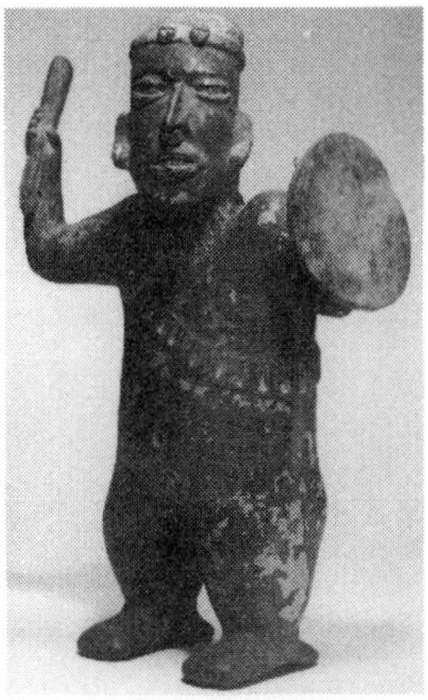
3

4

5

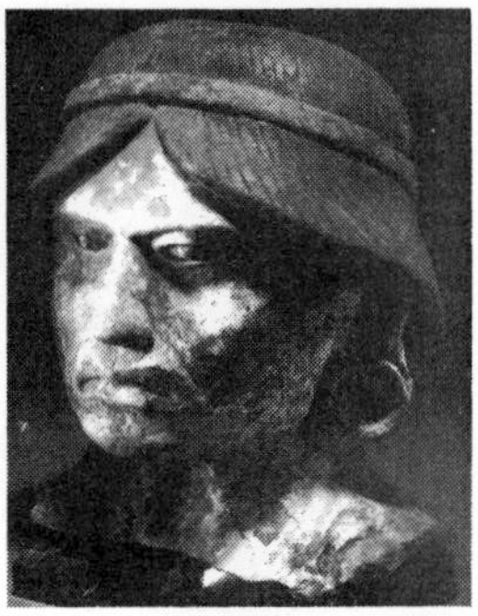
6

7

8

9

10

11

12

13

14

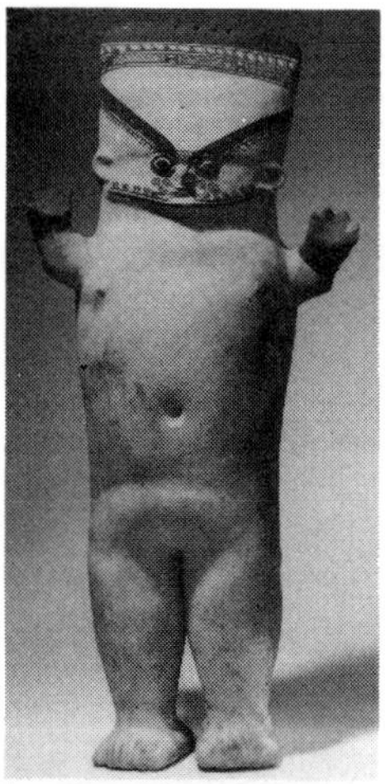
1

2

3

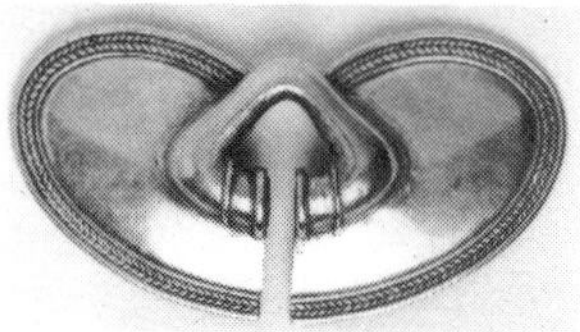
6

4

5

7

8

9

10

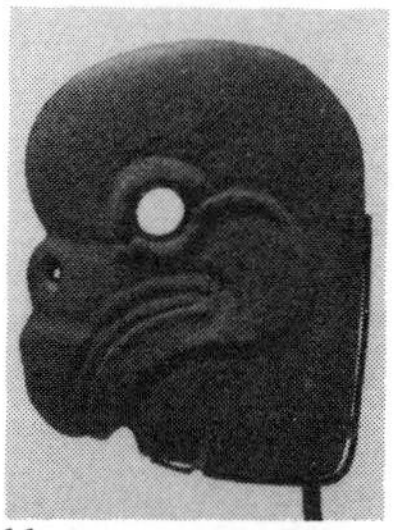
11

12

13

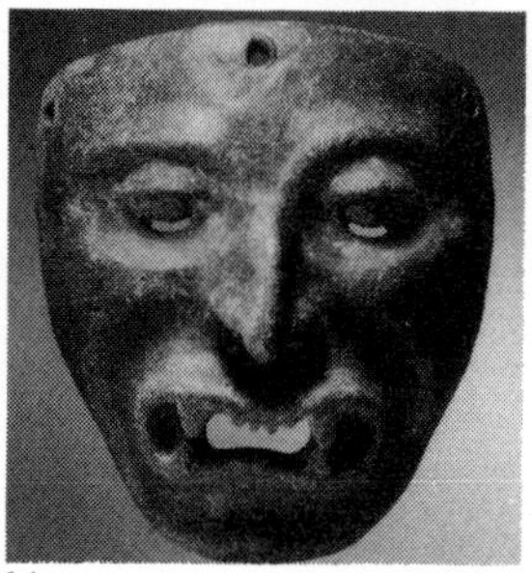
14

15

1
A Chancay figure, c.1100-1400 AD, painted overall in cream, 62cm (24½in), *NY 24 Nov,*
$1,430 (£1,007)

2
A Chancay wood mask, 1100-1500 AD, with recessed oval eyes once inlaid, wearing a head-band across the forehead woven in brown and black, 46cm (18¼in), *NY 20 May,*
$660 (£437)

3
A Chancay wood funerary mask, Central Coast, c.1440-1532 AD, the facial plane painted with deep red cinnabar, 26cm (10¼in), *NY 20 May,*
$1,100 (£728)

4
A Manabi female figure, Jama Coaque, c.500 BC-500 AD, some remains of white and turquoise pigment, 31cm (12½in), *NY 20 May,*
$935 (£619)

5
A Panamanian vessel, c.500-800 AD, the whole decorated with black linear bands against a tan ground, 24.5cm (9¾in), *NY 24 Nov,*
$2,420 (£1,704)

6
A Tairona gold nose ornament, c.1000-1500 AD, the curving form surrounded by a herring-bone pattern and with raised banded terminals at the aperture, 8cm (3¼in), *NY 24 Nov,*
$2,310 (£1,627)

7
A Tairona gold ornament, c.1000-1500 AD, hammered into two tightly spiralled portions, 7cm (2¾in), *NY 20 May,*
$1,045 (£692)

8
A Quimbaya gold figure of a Shaman, Cauca Valley region, c.500-1000 AD, the dancing priest engrossed in a ritual, a suspension loop at the back of the head, 9.5cm (3¾in), *NY 20 May,*
$40,700 (£26,954)

9
A Muisca gold warrior, c.1300-1500 AD, 13.5cm (5¼in), *NY 20 May,*
$4,675 (£3,096)

10
A Mayan brownware incised vessel, Pacific Slope region, Early Classic, 250-450 AD, boldl carved on both sides, 14.5cm (5¾in), *NY 20 May,*
$330 (£219)

11
A Mayan stone Hacha, Pacific Coast, Late Classi 550-950 AD, in grey-brow stone, 22 cm (8½in), *NY 24 Nov,*
$1,100 (£775)

12
A Mayan shell pendant, Campeche, Late Classic, c.550-950 AD, carved in th form of a glyph read as the numeral seven when seen horizontally and finely incised with the torso of the moon goddess, Ixchel, pierced at the top for suspension, 7cm (2¾in), *NY 24 Nov,*
$1,100 (£775)

13
A Mayan stone Hacha, Pacific Slope region, Late Classic, c.550-950 AD, curled ears pierced at the lobes, in grey volcanic stone, pierced at the top of the head, 25.5cm (10in), *NY 20 May,*
$4,400 (£2,914)

14
A Mayan terracotta mas Pacific Slope region, Late Classic, c.550-950 AD, painted overall in brown, 17cm (6¾in), *NY 20 May,*
$2,750 (£1,821)

15
A Mayan standing dignitary, Jaina, Late Classic, c.550-950 AD, wit remains of white pigment, 23.5cm (9¼in), *NY 20 Ma*
$6,600 (£4,371)

Mayan female figure ttle, Jaina, Late Classic, 550-950 AD, holding a etted, beaded satchel ith a container within, ith remains of bright lue and white pigment, 4cm (9½in), *NY 20 May,* **1,760 (£1,166)**

. Mayan seated noble- oman, Jaina, Late lassic, c.550-950 AD, emains of red pigment, 1.5cm (4½in), *NY 24 Nov,* **2,420 (£1,704)**

Mayan polychrome owl, Naranjo region, ate Classic, c.550-950 AD, ainted in black against an range ground, 14.5cm 5¾in), *NY 20 May,* **11,000 (£7,285)**

Mayan polychrome essel, Late Classic, c.550- 50 AD, painted in cream, eep orange, dark and ght brown on a pale range ground, 16cm 6½in), *NY 20 May,* **2,640 (£1,748)**

Mayan orangeware idded vessel, Peten egion, Late Classic, c.550- 50 AD, the domed lid with turkey, the wings incised ith abstract serpent's yes, 27.5cm (10¾in), *Y 20 May,* **3,025 (£2,003)**

Mayan blackware idded bowl, Peten region, ate Classic, c.550-950 AD, he domed lid with a urkey's head as handle, he large eyes, caruncle nd feathery crest finely ncised and filled with innabar, 38cm (15in), *VY 24 Nov,* **$4,400 (£3,099)**

Mayan carved orange- ware vessel, Lowlands, Late Classic, 550-950 AD, ne of the two swirling liagonal panels contain- ng a 'smoking *Xul*' glyph urrounded by curling notifs, 14cm (5½in), *NY 20 May,* **$3,575 (£2,368)**

8
A Mayan moulded orangeware vessel, El Salvador, Late Classic, c.550-950 AD, 20cm (8in), *NY 24 Nov,* **$2,750 (£1,937)**

9
A Mayan orangeware bowl, Northern Yucatan/Campeche region, Late Classic, c.550-950 AD, carved with boldly drawn Yucatec glyphs which include the owner's name, 20.5cm (8in), *NY 24 Nov,* **$2,310 (£1,627)**

10
A Mayan plumbate effigy vessel, Campeche, Post-classic, c.900-1100 AD, the lower jaw of the aged face forming a frog's head when reversed, 14.5cm (5¾in), *NY 24 Nov,* **$1,650 (£1,162)**

11
A Chupicuaro female figure, Late Preclassic, c.500-100 BC, painted overall in reddish-brown with geometric motifs in cream and black on the torso, head and back, 32cm (12½in), *NY 24 Nov,* **$4,400 (£3,099)**

12
An Olmec blackware duck, Las Bocas, Middle Preclassic, c.1150-550 BC, an opening at the top of the head, 15cm (6in), *NY 24 Nov,* **$6,600 (£4,648)**

13
A Guerrero stone head, Chontal region, Late Pre-classic, c.300-100 BC, in greyish-green speckled stone, 19cm (7½in), *NY 20 May,* **$1,100 (£728)**

14
A Guerrero stone mask, Chontal region, Late Pre-classic, c.300-100 BC, in mottled greyish-green stone pierced at the corners for suspension, 16.5cm (6½in), *NY 24 Nov,* **$7,975 (£5,616)**

1

2

3

6

4

5

9

7

8

12

10

11

14

13

Tribal Art

1

2

3

4

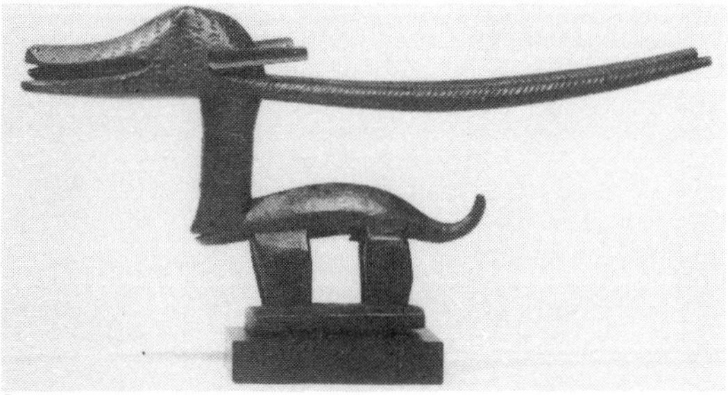
5

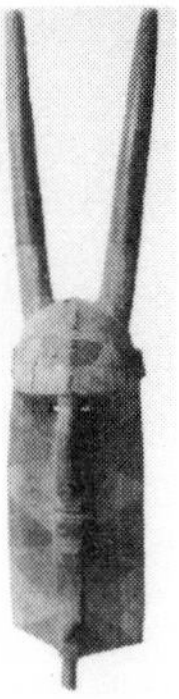
6

7

8

9

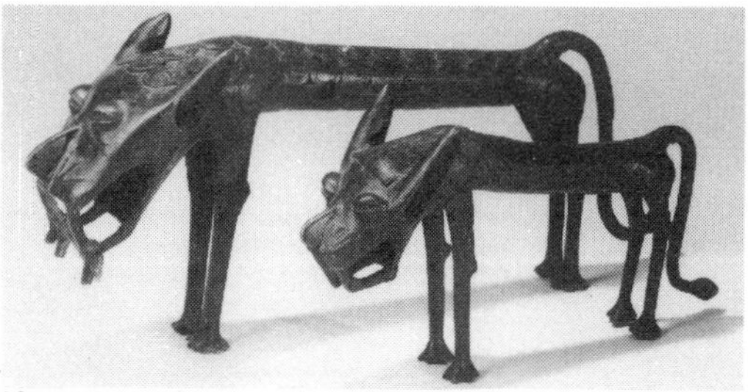
10

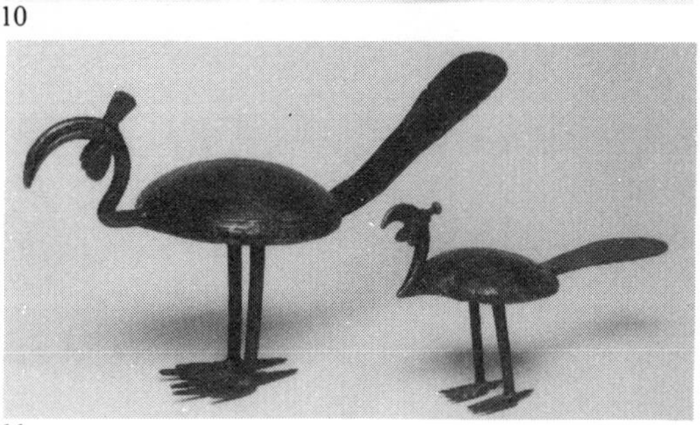
11

12

See also:
Colour illustrations *p* 563

A map showing locations of African tribes was included in last year's *Guide*, page 600.

1
A Bankoni terracotta equestrian group, the rider with scarification marks, one leg and both arms missing, 59cm (23¼in), *L 1 Dec,*
£1,650 ($2,360)

2
A Djenne terracotta figure, resting lowered head on folded knees, *L 23 June,*
£264 ($412)

3
A Mende Bundu helmet mask, *Sande Society*, typical compressed facial features, applied metal-work details, 39cm (15½in), *NY 18 Nov,*
$660 (£471)

4
A Dogon ceremonial stool, *imago mundi*, made for a *hogon*, natural weathering and erosion, encrusted ancient patinas, 31cm (12¼in), *NY 18 Nov,*
$3,300 (£2,357)

5
A pair of Bamana antelope headpieces, *(one illustrated)*, *tji wara*, wearing a metal collar, encrusted brown patina, 61 and 57cm (24 and 22½in), *NY 18 Nov,*
$3,740 (£2,671)

6
A Bobo wood mask, the whole painted in red, blue and white, 140cm (55in), *L 1 Dec,*
£770 ($1,101)

7
A Bobo wood helmet mask, with a tall crescent across the top, the whole with polychrome decoration, 48.5cm (19in), *L 23 June,*
£638 ($995)

8
A Gurunsi seat, in the form of an abstract animal, a splayed chameleon carved in high relief on the underside, brown patina with worn areas on seat, 119.5cm (47in), *NY 18 Nov,*
$3,300 (£2,357)

9
A Marka wood mask, a small antelope head projecting from the top, with painted decoration, 51.5cm (20¼in), *L 23 June,*
£1,100 ($1,716)

10
Two Mossi cast bronze figures, including a lion with an incised mane and leopard holding an antelope in its bared teeth 32.5 and 48.5cm (12¾ an 19in), *NY 18 Nov,*
$825 (£589)

11
Two Mossi cast bronze bird figures, 49.5 and 34cm (19½ and 13½in), *NY 18 Nov,*
$1,540 (£1,100)

12
A Senufo wood female figure, the face with classical features, 83cm (32½in), *S 20 June,*
£308 ($486)

Senufo wood firespitter
ıask, small head
rojecting from the top,
ıe whole with a fine dark
atina, 110cm (43¼in),
1 Dec,
308 ($440)

Senufo wood heddle
ulley, carved as a highly
ylised bird's head, the
hole with a fine dark
atina, 16.5cm (6½in),
1 Dec,
660 ($944)

Senufo wood kpelie
ıask, with raised
arification marks on the
rehead and cheeks,
ark, glossy patina, 42cm
16½in), *L 1 Dec,*
3,520 ($5,034)

Senufo firespitter
ıeadpiece, with
umanised nose, incised
carification, traces of
igment, 45.5cm (17½in),
Y 18 Nov,
1,100 (£786)

Senufo/Ligbe face
ıask, scarification
ıarkings on mouth
orners, the back
erimeter pierced for
ttachments, dark brown
atina with traces of
igment, 34.5cm (13½in),
VY 18 Nov,
1,650 (£1,179)

Dan face mask, inset
vith wood teeth, applied
ıative fibre coiffure, the
erimeter pierced for
ttachments, 20.5cm (8in),
VY 18 Nov,
1,100 (£786)

7
Dan bird mask, *geayagle,*
ısed in the bird
nasquerade, scarification
narkings, small spike inset
n the crown, back
erimeter pierced, rich
rown patina, encrusted
areas on the eye frames,
mounted on *inagaki* wood
base, 18.5cm (7¼in),
NY 18 Nov,
$31,900 (£22,786)

8
A Senufo maternity figure, beaded strands on the ankles and neck, incised scarification, surmounted by an avial head-dress, a beaded pendant suspended in her left ear, resinous deep brown patina, the front feet broken away, 37cm (14½in), *NY 18 Nov,*
$3,300 (£2,357)

9
A Dan wood mask, pierced around the sides for attachment, glossy black patina, 24.5cm (9¾in), *L 23 June,*
£1,980 ($3,089)

10
A Dan wood face mask, holes for attachment, black patina, 23cm (9in), *L 23 June,*
£1,100 ($1,716)

11
A Bassa wood passport mask, pierced at sides, 14.5cm (5¾in), *L 23 June,*
£605 ($944)

12
A Guro chair, incised details, 81cm (32in), *NY 18 Nov,*
$990 (£707)

13
A Guro wood heddle pulley, the finial in the form of an animal, fine black patina, 16cm (6¼in), *L 23 June,*
£1,925 ($3,003)

14
A Guro wood heddle pulley, with raised geometric decorations, the finial in the form of a human head, raised scarification marks, black patina, 17.5cm (6¾in), *L 23 June,*
£9,900 ($15,444)

1

2

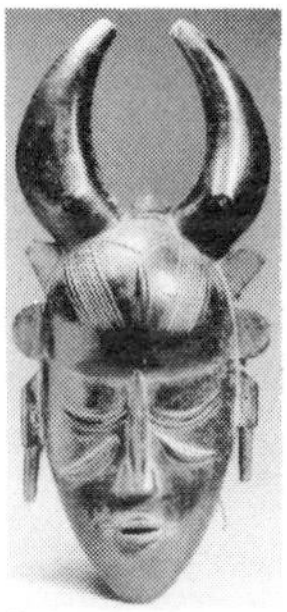
3

4

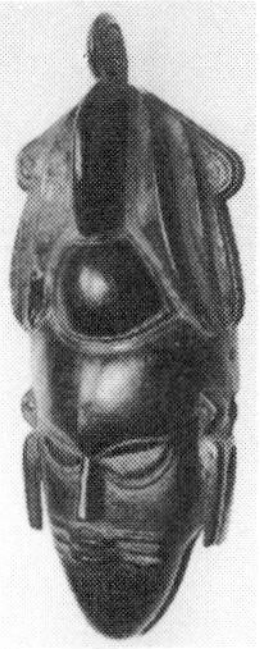
5

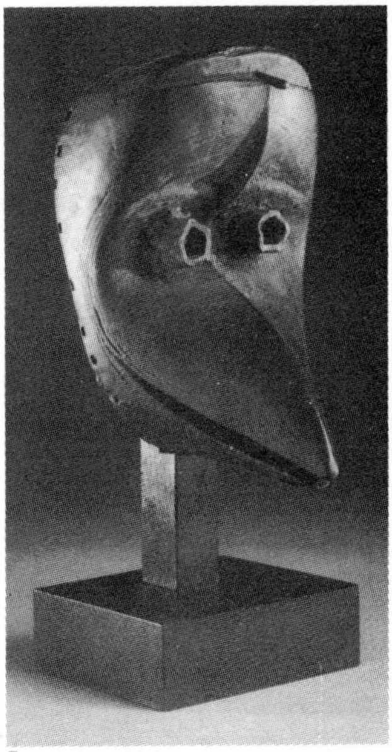
7

6

8

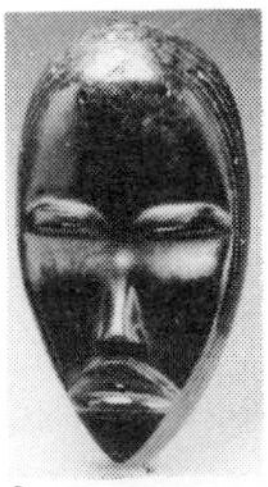
9

10

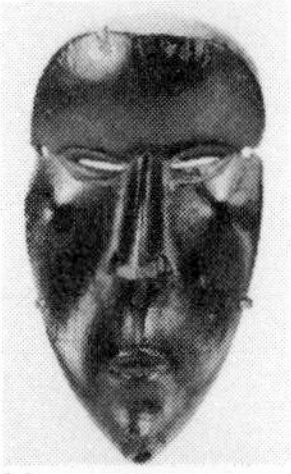
11

12

13 14

1

2

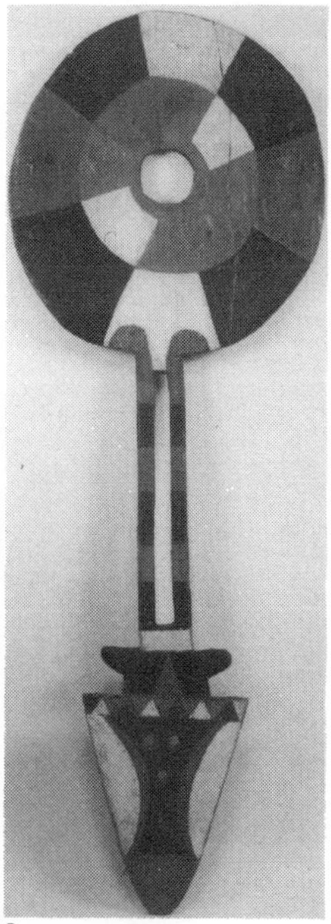
3

4

5

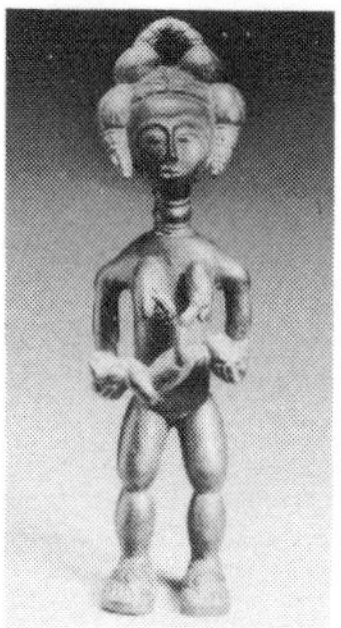
6

7

8

9

10

11

12

13

1
A Baule chief's throne, highly weathered, brown patina with areas of encrustation and traces of enamel pigment, 88cm (38½in), *NY 18 Nov,*
$4,950 (£3,536)

2
A Baule female figure, wearing beaded strands, scarification on the mouthcorners, temples and brow, plaited hair broken away, 36cm (14¼in), *NY 18 Nov,*
$770 (£550)

3
A Nafana masquerade mask, *bedu,* painted in red, black, white and blue, 225.5cm (7ft 4¾in), *NY 18 Nov,*
$7,700 (£5,500)

4
A Baule wood heddle pulley, one male face with projections partly missing, one female face with same scarification patterns, on an *inagaki* base, 21cm (8¼in), *L 23 June,*
£3,300 ($5,148)

5
An Asante stool, incised geometric devices simulating *kente* cloth patterns on centre of seat, 48cm (19in), *NY 18 Nov,*
$550 (£393)

6
An Akan wood maternity figure, scarification marks on back, elaborately arranged coiffure, black patina, 44cm (17¼in), *L 1 Dec,*
£660 ($944)

7
A Benin bronze plaque, the lower part missing, 29cm (11½in), *L 1 Dec,*
£5,500 ($7,865)

8
A Benin bronze belt mask, the head-dress with three rosettes of coral decoration, 18cm (7in), *L 1 Dec,*
£660 ($944)

9
A Yoruba wood mask, *Ere gelede,* coiffure and scarification marks with white kaolin decoration, 33cm (13in), *L 24 Mar,*
£550 ($864)

10
A Ngbaka face mask, the back perimeter pierced twice for attachment, rich dark patina with remains of pigment on face, 21cm (8¼in), *NY 18 Nov,*
$1,980 (£1,414)

11
A Thomas Ona model boat, a European gentleman seated in the bow, with carved parasol, pith helmet, paddles and pipes 34cm (30½in), *L 24 Mar,*
£990 ($1,554)

12
A pair of Yoruba female ibedj figures, *(one illustrated),* 28.5cm (11¼in), *A 13 June,*
Dfl 1,610 (£482; $771)

13
A pair of Yoruba wood figures, *(one illustrated), Igbomina,* incised scarification marks, domed coiffures with traces of blue decoration, wearing glass beads, dark patina, 28.5cm (11¼in), *L 1 Dec,*
£825 ($1,180)

'**hree Ibibio figures,** ecorated with black and 'hite pigment, sold with a hief's symbol of office, 31) 47cm (12 to 18½in), 24 Mar, **715 ($1,123)**

n Ibibio wood mask, the yelids indicated by hide, he whole with a crusty atina, 24cm (9½in), . 1 Dec, **462 ($661)**

n Ibibio face mask, *Idiok* *:kpo,* with deformed eatures, the worn erimeter pierced, 25.5cm 10in), *NY 18 Nov,* **1,430 (£1,021)**

n Ekoi wood head-dress, aised scarification marks, he whole covered with kin and tufts of human air attached to the top of he head, 22cm (8½in), *: 24 Mar,* **:550 ($864)**

Western Grasslands restige bowl, supported y a seated male figure, vith right foot broken way at the front, applied rass tacks in eyes, dark rown patina with traces f red pigment, 48cm 19in), *NY 18 Nov,* **$4,675 (£3,339)**

Zombo wood and fibre mask, covered with a fibre nd hessian super-structure, painted in white, red, blue and range, 50cm (19¾in), *S 20 June,* **£528 ($834)**

7
A Western Grasslands beaded ceremonial calabash, in numerous shades of translucent and paque glass, decorated with opposed buffalo masks, the base missing, 76cm (30in), *NY 18 Nov,* **$2,420 (£1,729)**

8
A Northern Suku wood helmet mask, the coiffure blackened, an antelope standing on the crown, the face painted white with red and black decoration, a fibre fringe around the bottom, 48cm (19in), *L 24 Mar,* **£550 ($864)**

9
A Bekom royal mask, with traces of red and white pigment, the left ear missing, patina encrusted in some areas, 47cm (18½in), *L 24 Mar,* **£1,100 ($1,727)**

10
A Bembe wood male figure, the eyes inset with bone, typical raised scarification marks on the abdomen, with light patina, 14.5cm (5¾in), *L 1 Dec,* **£440 ($629)**

11
A Bamileke wood mask, with traces of kaolin around the eyes and mouth, 30cm (11¾in), *L 1 Dec,* **£143 ($204)**

12
A Bamileke wood stool, supported by three standing human figures interspaced by the heads of a three-headed leopard, with a fine dark patina, 53cm (21in), *L 24 Mar,* **£660 ($1,036)**

13
A Yombe ivory cane finial, *ndumba mbenza,* wearing European costume, surmounted by a wide brimmed hat, restored at the front, deep brown patina, 14cm (5½in), *NY 18 Nov,* **$5,500 (£3,929)**

1

2

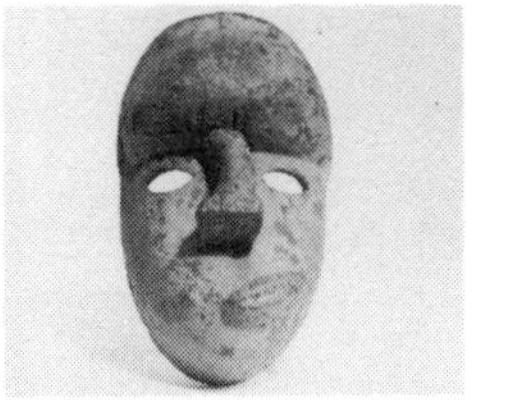
3

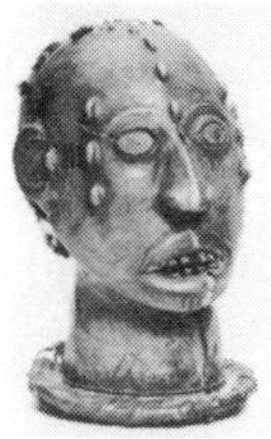
4

5

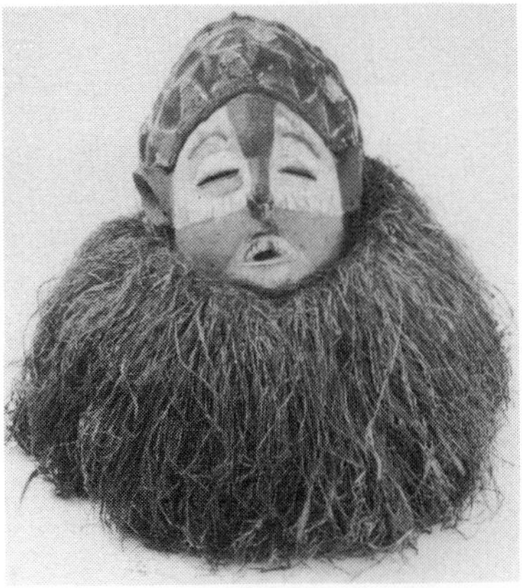
6

7

8

9

10

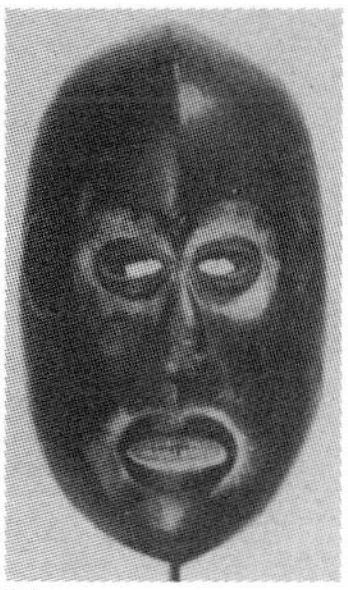
11

12

13

1

2

3

4

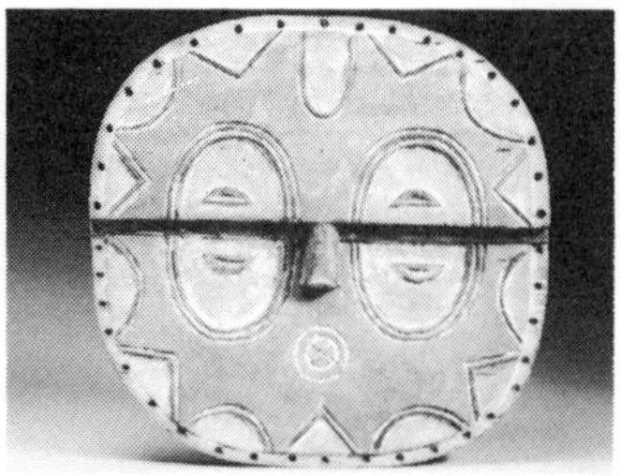
5

6

7

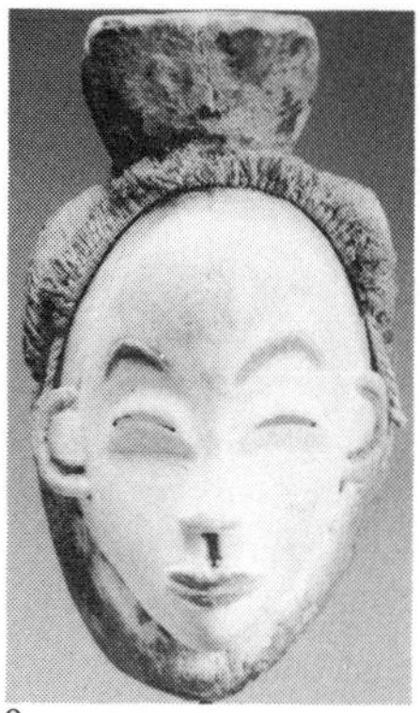
8

9

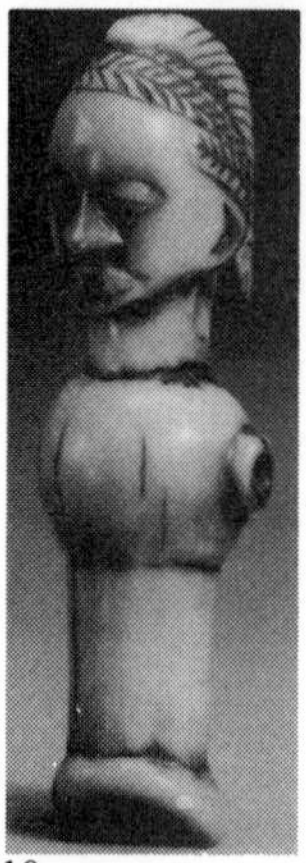
10

11

12

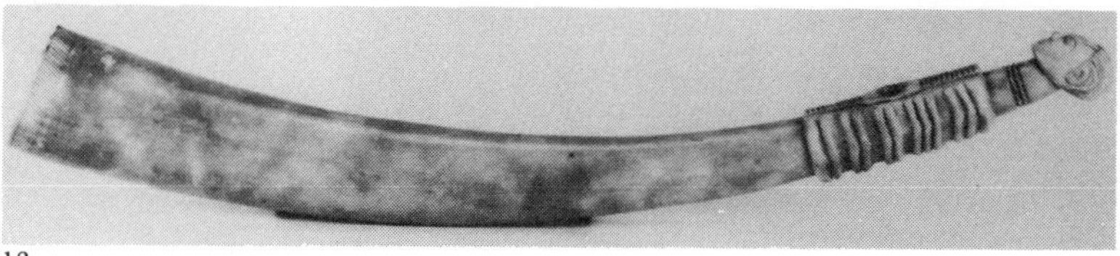
13

1
A Yombe ceremonial bell, *madibu*, surmounted by a kneeling female figure, mirrored glass set into the eyes, darkened eyebrows, brown patina, 27cm (10¾in), *NY 18 Nov,*
$11,000 (£7,857)

2
A Vili wood mask, with traces of black and red decoration, 25.5cm (10in), *L 23 June,*
£880 ($1,373)

3
A Kongo male fetish figure, seated in symbolic cross-legged position, mirrored glass eyes with painted pupils, mirrored glass affixed to abdomen replaced, 18cm (7in), *NY 18 Nov,*
$1,210 (£864)

4
A Kongo bronze Christ, taken from a crucifix, the surface very worn, with fine patina, 9cm (3½in), *L 1 Dec,*
£1,650 ($2,360)

5
A Teke wood mask, with traces of white kaolin, the central area painted red, 31.5cm (12½in), *L 1 Dec,*
£4,620 ($6,607)

6
A Punu wood mask, coiffure and brows blackened, forehead and lips painted red, with traces of kaolin, 37.5cm (14¾in), *L 23 June,*
£935 ($1,459)

7
A Punu wood white-faced mask, protruding reddened lips, incised reddened scarification marks, blackened coiffure, traces of kaolin, 26cm (10¼in), *S 20 June,*
£352 ($556)

8
A Punu wood white-faced mask, painted black coiffure with a band of woven raffia, worn back with holes for attachments, face painted white with kaolin, 30cm (11¾in), *L 1 Dec,*
£4,180 ($5,977)

9
A Kuba wood cosmetic box, a crack along the top edge, one side pierced to accommodate the hinge, 19.5cm (7½in), *L 23 June,*
£770 ($1,201)

10
A Kuba ivory whistle, carved as a highly stylised human bust, with a honeyed patina, 8cm (3¼in), *L 1 Dec,*
£2,420 ($3,461)

11
A Luba wood caryatid stool, supported by a female figure wearing a glass bead necklace, 36cm (14in), *L 24 Mar,*
£440 ($691)

12
A Hemba wood stool, supported by a female figure, a metal strip running down the forehead, the seat with native metal repair, 45.5cm (18in), *L 23 June,*
£352 ($549)

13
A Zande ivory oliphant, carved with raised ridges, the finial in the form of a human head, golden patina, 49.5cm (19½in), *L 1 Dec,*
£352 ($503)

1
A Hemba wood stool, on an eroded base, supported by a female figure, the swept back coiffure terminating at the back in a cruciform motif, brown patina, 53cm (21in), *L 23 June,*
£17,600 ($27,456)

2
A Pende wood mask, *kindombolo-mapombolo,* Kasai region, large oval face partly eroded, with black, white and red zig-zag decoration, 53cm (21in), *L 23 June,*
£4,400 ($6,864)

3
A Pende wood mask, painted red, white and black, 17.5cm (6¾in), *L 1 Dec,*
£770 ($1,101)

4
A Songe wood fetish figure, the legs, head and neck inset with small rounded seeds, coffee bean eyes, 22.5cm (9in), *L 23 June,*
£550 ($858)

5
A Holo wood comb, the finial carved with two figures carrying a stretcher with a body inside, 21cm (8¼in), *L 24 Mar,*
£220 ($345)

6
A Songe wood kifwebe mask, with incised and painted horizontal lines, 46cm (18in), *L 23 June,*
£5,500 ($8,580)

7
A Songe male fetish figure, Lusambo Province, cult statue, remains of fetish material in the drilled navel and cylindrical cavity on the crown, eyes inset with cowrie shells, brown patina with lighter areas, 129cm (50¾in), *NY 18 Nov,*
$4,125 (£2,946)

8
A Chokwe wood bowl, with geometric motifs and metal studs, supported by a figure wearing metal earrings, 26.5cm (10½in), *L 23 June,*
£550 ($858)

9
A Chokwe wood mask, pierced around the edge for attachment, 18cm (7in), *S 20 June,*
£330 ($521)

10
A Chokwe wood mask, the raffia coiffure overlaid with red clay, reddish patina, 23cm (9in), *L 1 Dec,*
£352 ($503)

11
A Chokwe wood chair, styled along European lines, upper panel with male mask wearing a *chihongo* head-dress, a carved animal on the lower stretcher, with hide seat, brass stud decoration and a dark glossy patina, 128cm (50½in), *L 23 June,*
£2,860 ($4,462)

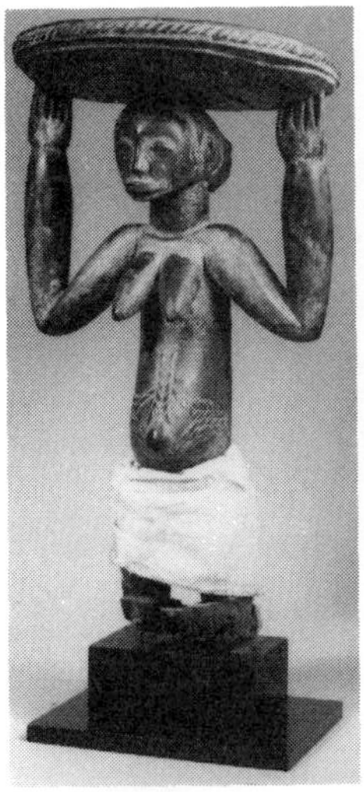
1

2

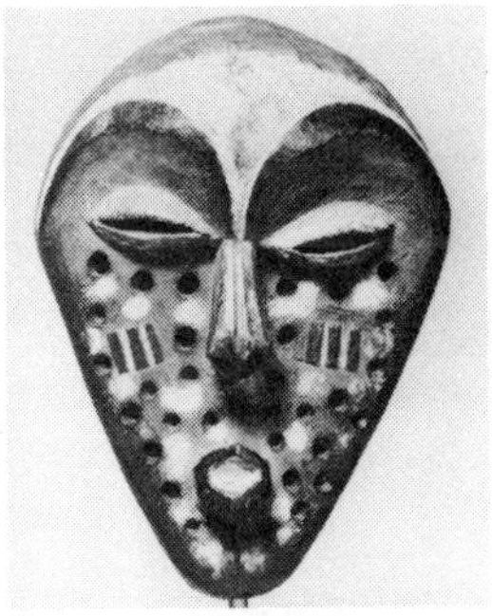
3

6

7

4

5

8

11

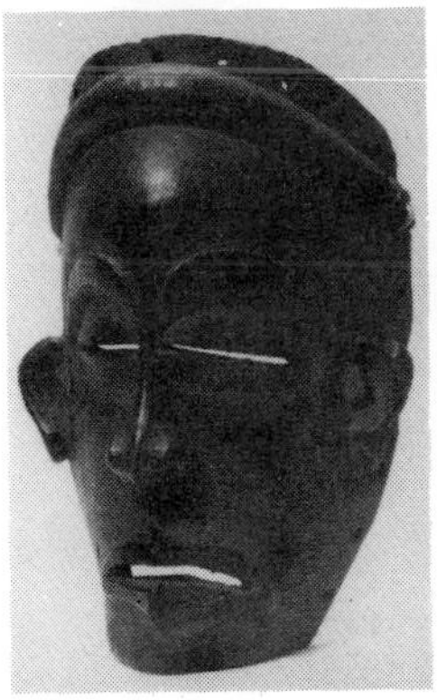
9

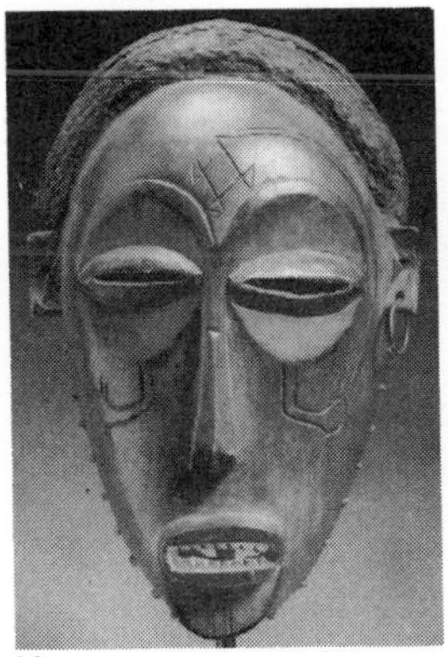
10

1

2

3

4

5

6

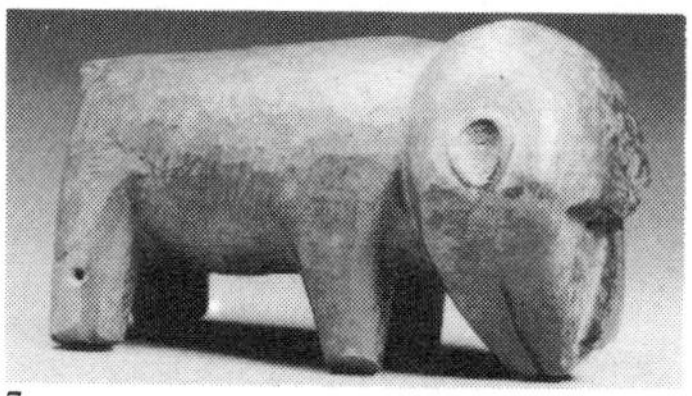
7

8

9

10

11

1
A Chokwe wood mask, with holes for attachments and a black patina, 28.5cm (11in), *L 1 Dec,*
£660 ($944)

2
A Chokwe face mask, *mwana pwo*, panels of notched *cicatrice* on the chin, cheeks and temples, the back perimeter pierced for attachments of the plaited and knotted wig, remains of red pigment, 18.5cm (7¼in), *NY 18 Nov,*
$1,650 (£1,178)

3
A Chokwe female caryatid stool, 30cm (11¾in), *NY 18 Nov,*
$1,100 (£786)

4
A Kamba stool, decorated with birds, animals, lizards and insects in multi-coloured beadwork, 61cm (24in), *NY 18 Nov,*
$990 (£707)

5
A Rotse wood stool, supported by a stylised horse, 36cm (14in), *S 20 June,*
£286 ($452)

6
A Zulu wood staff, feet, pupils and coiffure blackened, 106cm (41¾in), *S 20 June,*
£1,100 ($1,738)

7
A Zulu wood dog, of stylised form, with fine dark patina, 27cm (10½in), *L 1 Dec,*
£770 ($1,101)

8
A Zulu wood stool, supported by three figures, coiffures and decorated edge of seat blackened, fine brown patina, 43cm (17in), *L 1 Dec,*
£462 ($661)

9
A pair of Zulu colonial figures, clad in European attire, burnished details, 26.5 and 28.5cm (10½ and 11¼in), *NY 18 Nov,*
$1,430 (£1,021)

10
A South East African neckrest, carved as a torsoless creature, some blackened decoration, 14cm (8½in), *L 24 Mar,*
£935 ($1,468)

11
A Madagascar grave pos in the form of a female figure on a highly weathered block, 164cm (64½in), *NY 18 Nov,*
$1,650 (£1,179)

1
A Fijian Islands ceremonial club, *culacula*, carved of *nokonoko* wood, rich brown patina, 121.5cm (48in), *NY 18 Nov,*
$1,430 (£1,021)

2
A Fijian wood paddle club, ivory inlay on one side below the head, fine dark patina, 114cm (45in), *L 1 Dec,*
£352 ($503)

3
A Fijian wood oil dish, the whole with a fine glossy patina, lighter on the top, 12cm (4¾in), *L 1 Dec,*
£4,950 ($7,079)

4
A Hawaiian Islands poi bowl, *'umeke palapa'a*, carved of *kou*, honey brown patina, 25cm (9¾in), *NY 18 Dec,*
$2,310 (£1,615)

5
A Marquesas Island toa wood club, incised with geometrical figures and three small heads, *A 13 June,*
Dfl 2,760 (£826; $1,322)

6
A Tongan wood club, covered with decorations in relief, fine patina, 113cm (34½in), *L 1 Dec,*
£715 ($1,022)

7
A Cook Islands chief's seat, *no 'oanga*, carved from *tamanu* wood, brown patina, 49cm (19½in), *NY 18 Nov,*
$2,420 (£1,729)

8
A Maori greenstone pendant, *hei tiki*, worn surface, a hole drilled for suspension, 8cm (3¼in), *L 1 Dec,*
£1,100 ($1,573)

9
A Solomon Islands wood bowl, decorated with mother-of-pearl inlay, 53cm (21in), *S 20 June,*
£330 ($521)

10
A Maori nephrite pendant, *hei tiki*, worn facial features and applied *paua*-shell eye rims, pierced through the top for suspension, 11.5cm (4½in), *NY 18 Nov,*
$3,300 (£2,357)

11
A Maori whalebone hand club, *wahaika*, a *tiki* figure carved in relief at the base, aged yellowish-brown patina, 39.5cm (15½in), *NY 18 Nov,*
$2,310 (£1,650)

12
An Easter Islands stone head, resembling in a much smaller scale the larger heads, 31cm (12in), *S 20 June,*
£1,650 ($2,607)

13
A Sepik River wood mask, with red patina, 38cm (15in), *S 20 June,*
£176 ($278)

14
A Sepik River wood drum, with geometric decoration, the lower part of the handle carved as a bird's head, 61.5cm (24¼in), *L 1 Dec,*
£308 ($440)

15
A New Ireland wood Malanggan mask, Tatanua, the helmet-like coiffure of woven vegetable fibres, the whole with remains of white, red and black paints, 33cm (15in), *S 20 June*
£660 ($1,042)

16
A New Hebrides figure, comprised of bark and mud on a wood stave, with boar's tusks and feather decoration, painted cream, black and ochre, 109cm (43in), *L 1 Dec,*
£330 ($471)

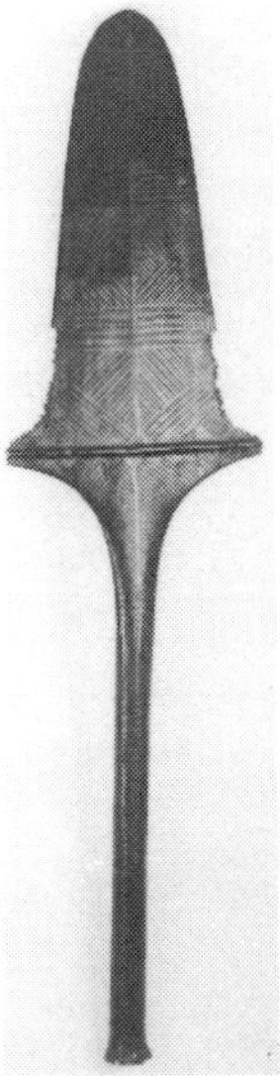
1

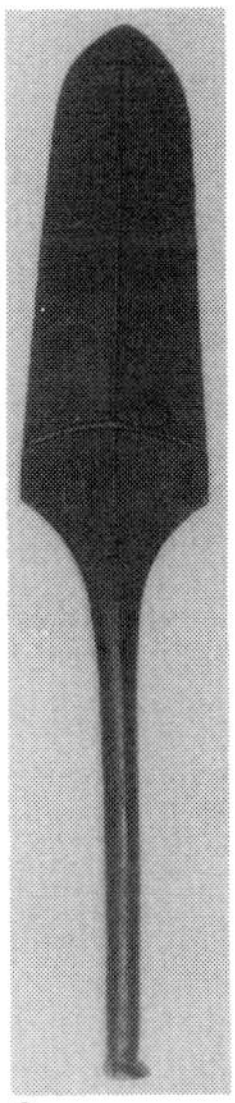
2

3

4

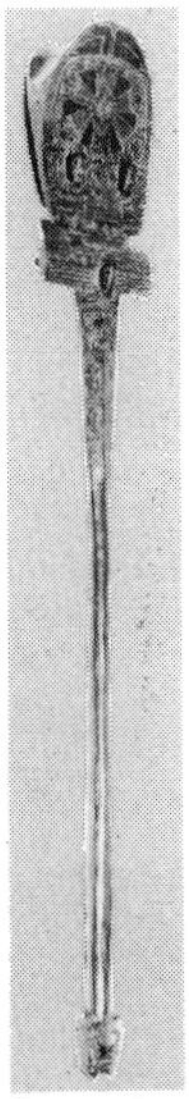
5

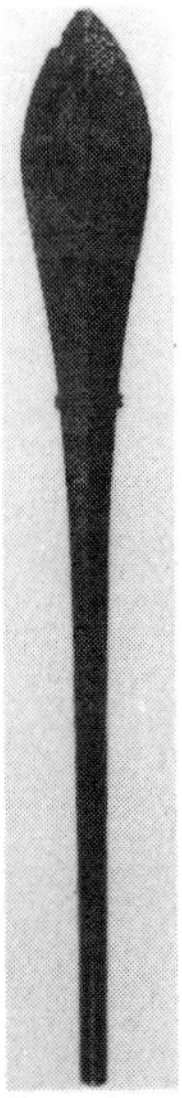
6

7

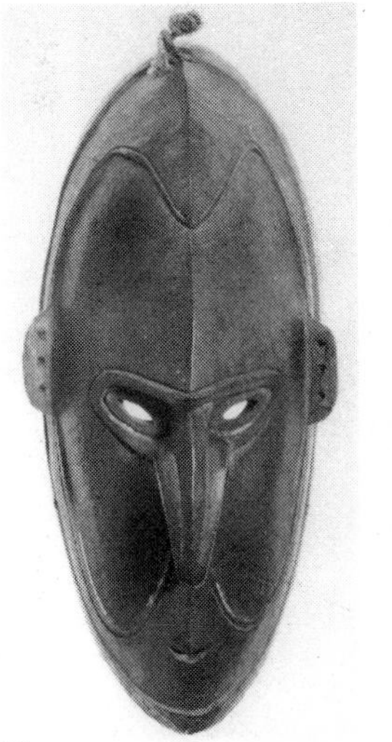
13

8

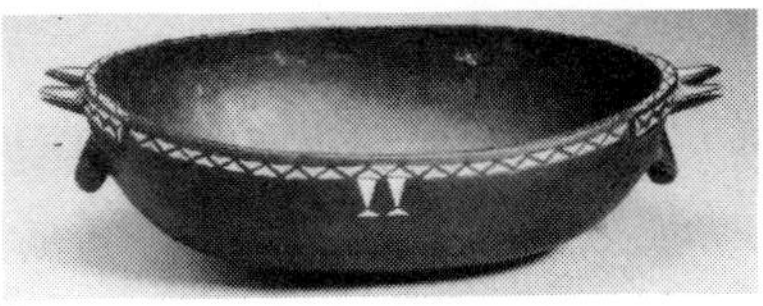
9

10

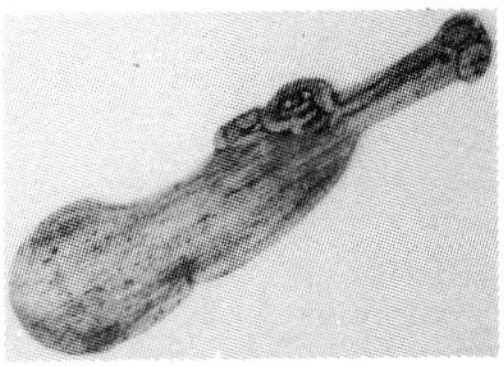
11

12

14

15

16

Islamic Works of Art

Major Islamic Dynasties

	AH*	AD		AH*	AD		AH*	AD
Umayyads	41-132	661-750	Seljuqs	429-590	1038-1194	Ottomans	680-1342	1281-1924
Abassids	132-656	749-1258	Seljuqs of Rum	470-707	1077-1307	Muzzaffarids	713-795	1314-1393
Samanids	204-395	819-1005	Ayyubids	567-648	1171-1250	Timurids	771-912	1370-1506
Fatimids	297-567	909-1171	Delhi Sultanate	602-962	1206-1555	Safavids	907-1145	1501-1732
Buyids	320-454	932-1062	Mamluks	648-922	1250-1517	Mughals	932-1274	1526-1858
Ghaznavids	366-582	971-1186	Il-Khanids	654-754	1256-1353	Qajars	1193-1342	1779-1924

*The Islamic era began in 622 AD which corresponds to AH1 (anno hijra=year of the flight of Muhammed to Medina) and is calculated in lunar years. Unless otherwise stated, dates in this book and Sotheby Islamic catalogues are in Christian years (AD).

See also: Colour illustrations *pp* 564-565

Main sub-sections:

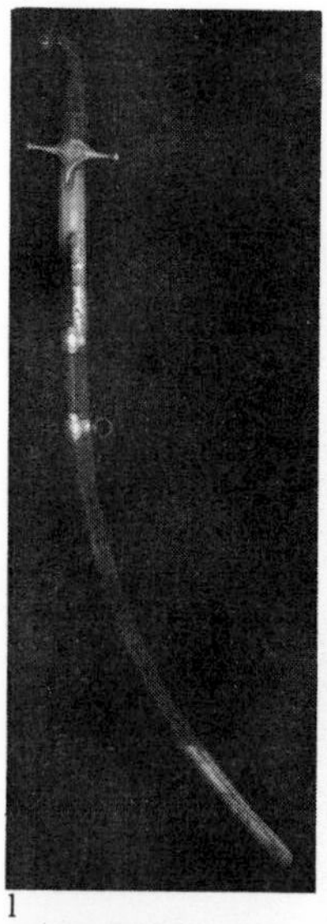

1

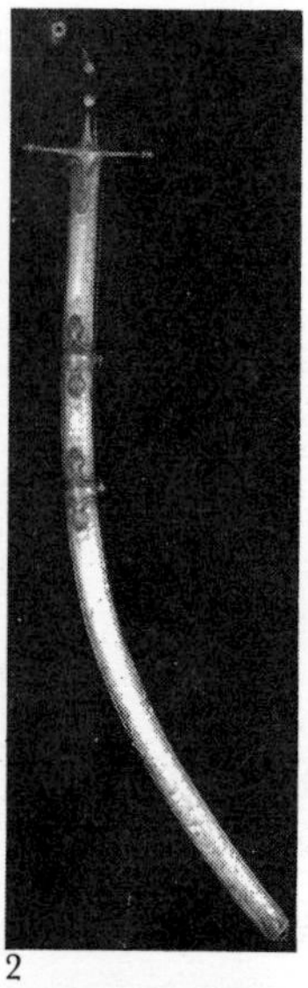

2

3

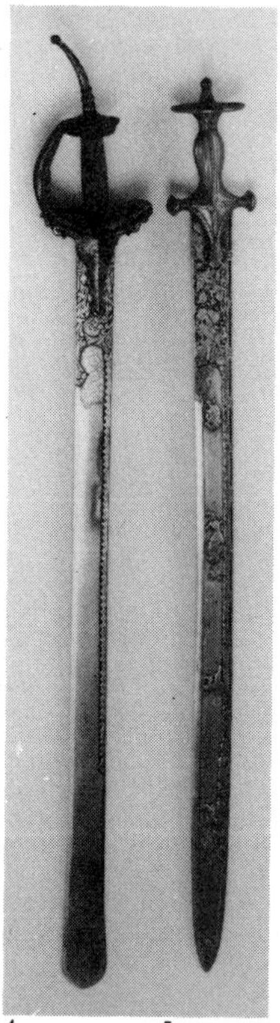

4 5

6

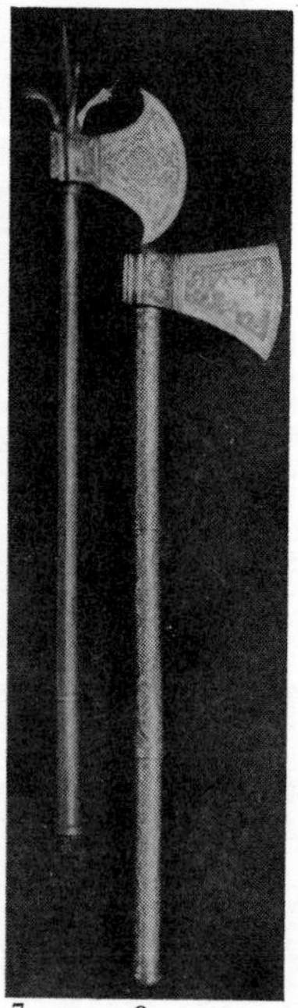

7 8

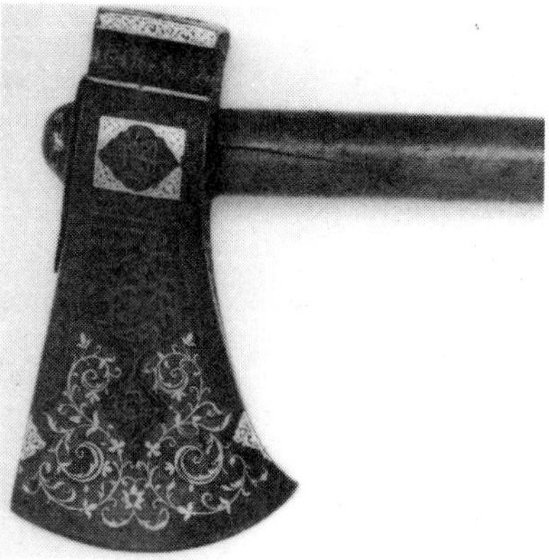

9

1
An Ottoman sword *(kilidj)*, 19th century, with silver mounts, 99cm (39in), *L 16 Apr,*
£495 ($767)

2
An Ottoman sword *(kilidj)*, 19th century, with silver scabbard, 102cm (40in), *L 16 Apr,*
£550 ($853)

3
An Indian sword *(tulwar)*, 19th century, 91.5cm (36in), *NY 25 Nov,*
$1,100 (£786)

4
An Indian sword *(tulwar)*, 19th century, sold with another, 86 and 89cm (34 and 35in), *NY 25 Nov,*
$880 (£628)

5
An Indian sword *(tulwar)*, 19th century, the blade chased with hunt and animal scenes, 81cm (32in), *NY 25 Nov,*
$440 (£314)

6
A Qajar processional axe, 19th century, the blades etched and gilded, the haft with a concealed dagger, 75cm (29½in), *L 16 Apr,*
£385 ($597)

7
A Persian steel axe *(tabarzin)*, first half 19th century, the head chiselled with animals and a Koranic inscription, decorated with turquoise, 69cm (27in), *L 16 Apr,*
£880 ($1,364)

8
A Qajar axe, early 19th century, the head chiselled with animals, buildings and flowers, within *koftgari* panels, 61cm (24in), *L 16 Apr,*
£605 ($938)

9
A Mughal axe, 19th century, the blade with gold damascening, 59cm (23¼in), *NY 31 May,*
$1,430 (£973)

1
An Indian dagger, *(katar)*, 18th century, the hilt of blued steel inlaid with gold and silver flowers, the blade with tree design in gold at the forte, 45cm (17¾in), *L 16 Apr,*
£1,320 ($2,046)

2
An Omani dagger, the silver hilt and scabbard with applied and repoussé floral decoration, with addorsed parrot motif, the lotus-bud chape with screw finial, with hooked steel blade, 31cm (12¼in), *L 15 Oct,*
£786 ($1,101)

3
An Omani silver powder-flask *(barutdan)*, the spine with a floral design on a punched ground, with brass stopper and spring, 23cm (9in), *L 15 Oct,*
£363 ($508)

4
An Omani dagger, the silver hilt and scabbard with incised floral decoration with addorsed parrot motif, lotus bud chape, 33cm (13in), *L 15 Oct,*
£385 ($539)

5
An Indian dagger *(katar)*, 19th century, the hilt damascened in silver, gold and copper with buildings and mosques, 36.5cm (14½in), *NY 25 Nov,*
$1,100 (£786)

6
An Indian dagger *(khanjar)*, 18th century, the rock crystal hilt carved as a vase containing pomegranates, silver sheet mount concealing the tang, scabbard with openwork silver mounts, 40cm (15¾in), *L 16 Apr,*
£1,188 ($1,841)

7
An Indian dagger *(katar)*, Jaipur, early 18th century, the grip and bars decorated in gold with floral sprays, set with rubies and diamonds on a green enamel ground, blade with damascening at the forte, later gold and enamel chape, 46cm (18in), *L 16 Apr,*
£3,960 ($6,138)

8
A Mughal jade-hilted dagger *(khanjar)*, 18th century, the pale green jade hilt carved with lotus flowers, later steel blade decorated with gold *koftgari*, later Chinese scabbard, 49cm (19¼in), *L 16 Apr,*
£1,265 ($1,961)

9
A Qajar dagger, dated 1213 AH (1798-99 AD) the ivory hilt carved with a Persian noble, a flowering plant and inscription cartouches including the maker's name, polychrome lacquer scabbard with ivory chape, 35.5cm (14in), *L 16 Apr,*
£1,650 ($2,558)

10
An Indian dagger *(katar)*, early 19th century, the hilt decorated with gold *koftgari* work, silver mounts, filigree bracelet, some wear, 33cm (13in), *L 15 May,*
£330 ($531)

11
A Turkish dagger, 19th century, the hilt and scabbard of silver-coloured metal set with corals and turquoise in a floral design, the blade with gold damascening, with Turkish inscription, 42cm (16½in), *L 15 Oct,*
£968 ($1,355)

12
A Turkish dagger, 19th century, with a silver-gilt effect, the hilt and scabbard in repoussé, the blade with gold damascening, with Turkish inscription, 43.5cm (17in), *L 15 Oct,*
£605 ($847)

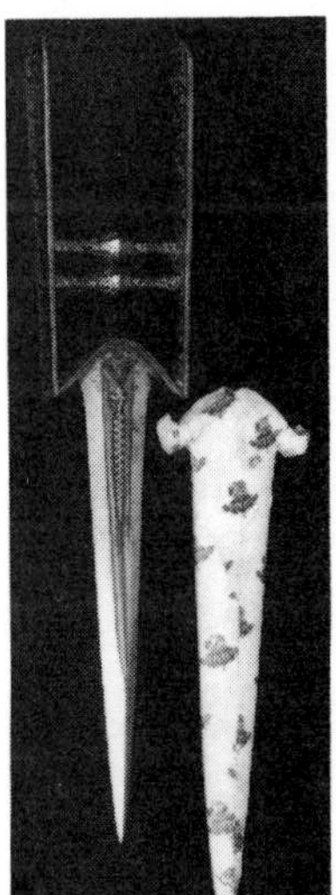
1

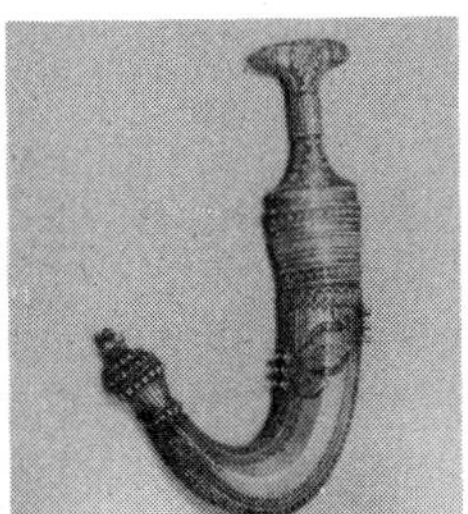
2

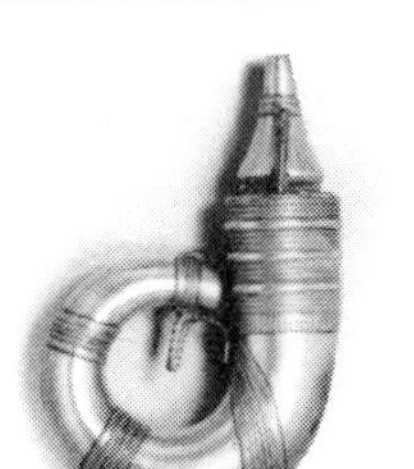
3

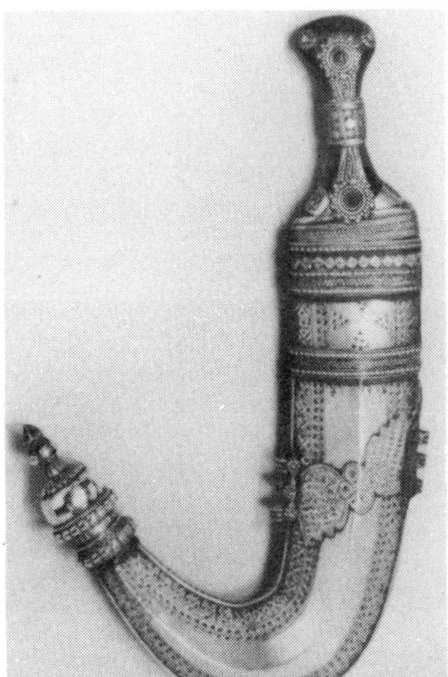
4

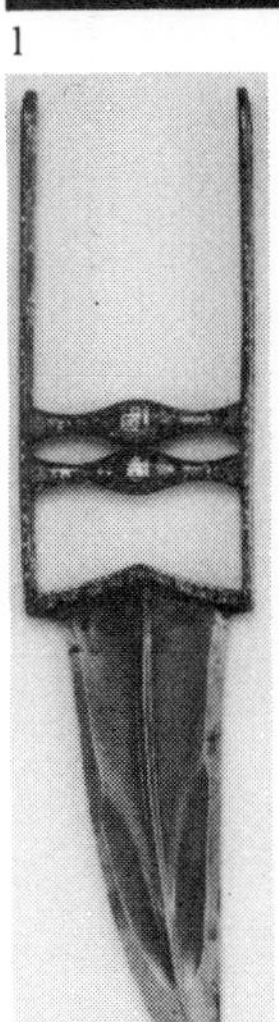
5

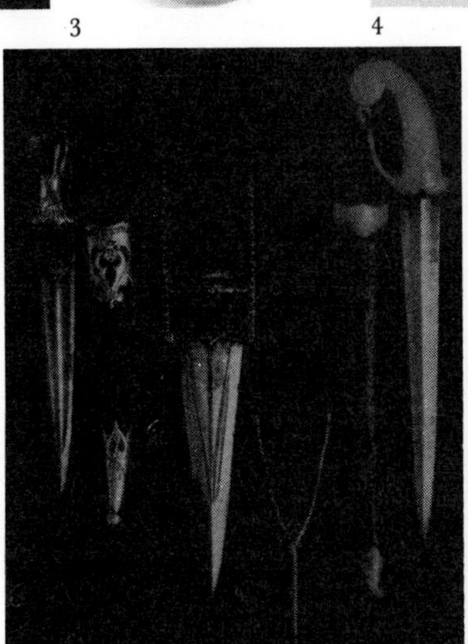
6 7 8

9

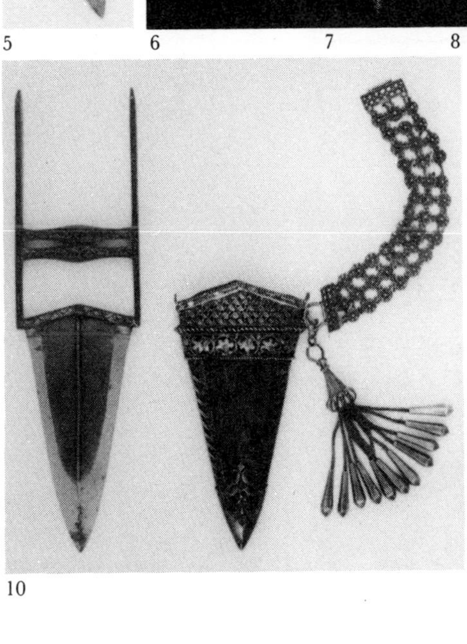
10

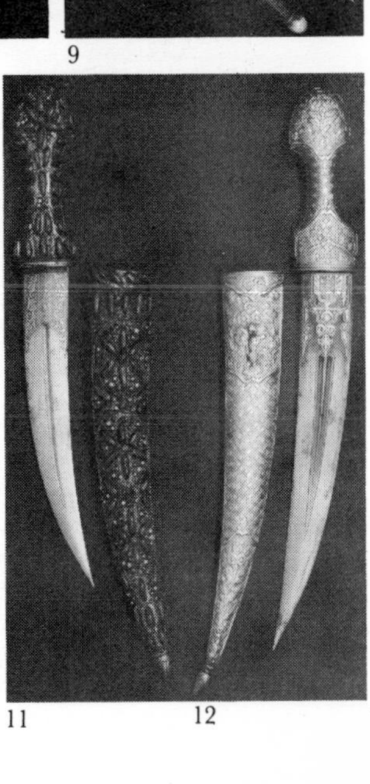
11 12

1

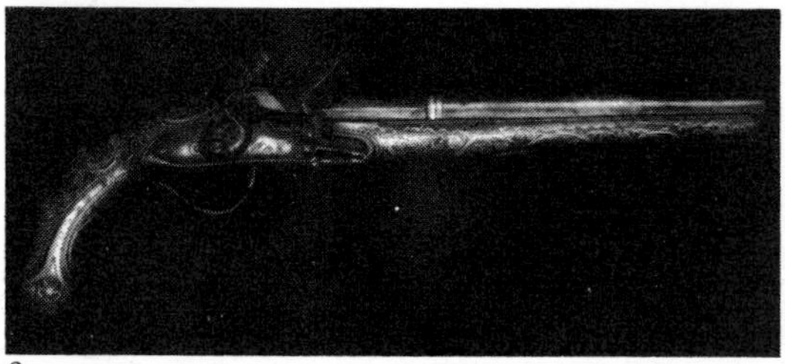
2

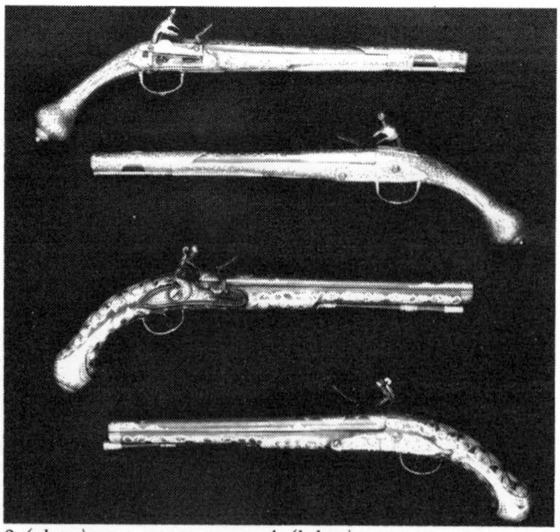
3 *(above)* 4 *(below)*

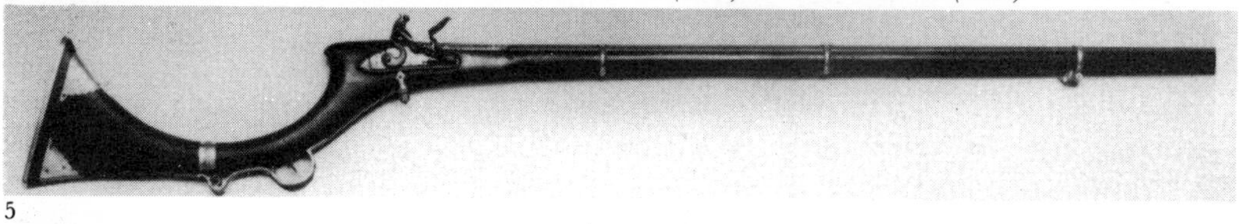
5

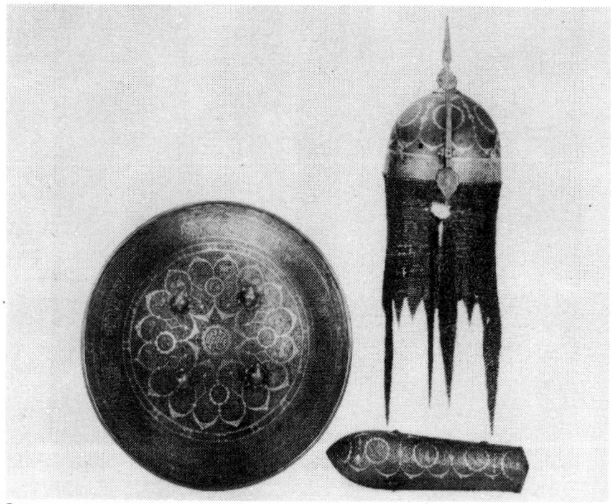
6

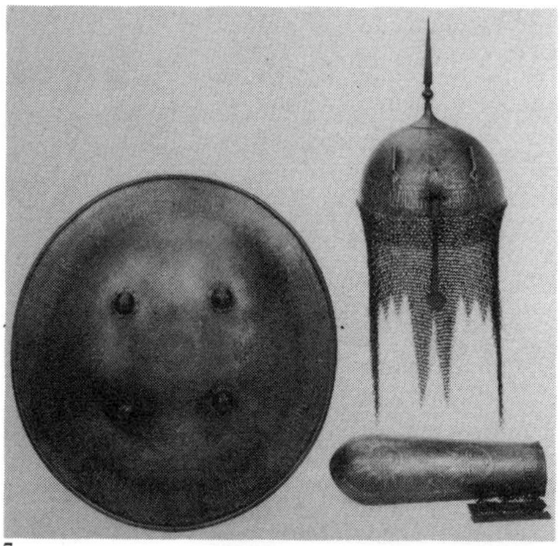
7

8

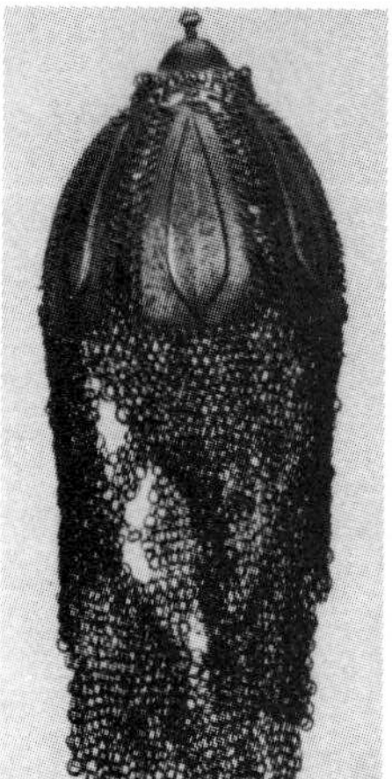
9

10

1
An Ottoman flintlock blunderbuss, early 19th century, the French export lock with pseudo maker's name, 63cm (25in), *L 16 Apr,*
£715 ($1,108)

2
An Ottoman flintlock pistol, early 19th century, the European export barrel and lock signed *Wilson* in gold, silver gilt furniture, 44.5cm (17½in), *L 16 Apr,*
£605 ($938)

3
A pair of Ottoman miquelet pistols, early 19th century, 49cm (19½in), *L 16 Apr,*
£2,420 ($3,751)

4
A pair of Algerian flint-lock pistols, late 18th century, 47cm (18½in), *L 16 Apr,*
£7,700 ($11,935)

5
A set of four Sindi flintlock rifles *(jezails) (one illustrated)*, early 19th century, of varying calibres, English locks, gilt brass mounts, 155cm (65in) average, *L 16 Apr,*
£5,500 ($8,230)

6
A Qajar steel shield, helmet and armguard, 19th century, with incised decoration of flowers, animals and roundels with gold damascening, shield 46.5cm (18¼in), *L 15 Oct,*
£2,178 ($3,049)

7
A Qajar steel helmet, armguard and shield, 19th century, decorated in filigree outlined with gold *koftgari*, *L 16 Apr,*
£880 ($1,364)

8
A Persian steel helmet, armguard and shield, 19th century, all damascened in gold, *NY 31 May,*
$2,420 (£1,646)

9
An Indian steel helmet, 17th/18th century, *L 30 July,*
£198 ($311)

10
A Safavid steel powder-flask, *(barutdan)*, 17th/18th century, 20cm (8in), *L 16 Apr,*
£4,180 ($6,479)

1
A Persian slip-painted pottery bowl, Nishapur, 9th/10th century, with flaring sides standing on a low splayed foot, decorated in deep brown on a cream ground with four *kufic* inscriptions and a pair of stylised fish, 20.5cm (8in) diam., *L 15 Oct,*
£935 ($1,309)

2
A Persian slip-painted pottery bowl, Nishapur, 9th/10th century, with convex sides and everted rim, standing on a low foot, decorated in shades of green on a cream ground, with central *kufic* inscription, 21cm (8¼in) diam., *L 16 Apr,*
£605 ($938)

3
A Persian slip-painted pottery bowl, Nishapur, 9th/10th century, with convex sides and standing on a low foot, decorated in brown and pale red on a cream ground with a line of pseudo-*kufic* inscription on one side and a winged palmette on the other, 18cm (7in) diam., *L 16 Apr,*
£220 ($341)

4
A Samanid clay incense vessel or lantern, probably Nishapur, 9th/10th century, with curled tripod feet, four sets of twin loop handles, the body encircled by bands of cut openwork decoration, 17cm (6¾in) rim diam., *NY 30 May,*
$357 (£242)

5
A Persian slip-painted pottery bowl, Nishapur, 9th/10th century, decorated in imitation of lustre in olive-green and terracotta with a central seated warrior, 36.5cm (14¼in) diam., *L 15 Oct,*
£4,840 ($6,776)

6
A Persian moulded pottery cup, 12th/13th century, decorated in relief with fluted ribs under a turquoise glaze, 10.5cm (4in) diam., *L 16 Apr,*
£462 ($716)

7
A Persian lustre star tile, dated 665 AH (1266-7 AD), decorated in brown lustre on a cream ground, the border with a Persian verse inscription, 19.5cm (7¾in) diam., *L 16 Apr,*
£715 ($1,108)

8
A Syrian Tel Minis pottery bowl, 11th/12th century, decorated with a turquoise glaze, with areas of iridescence, 20cm (8in) diam., *L 15 Oct,*
£3,388 ($4,743)

9
A Persian lustre pottery bottle, 1200-20, decorated in the Kashan style in brownish lustre on a cream ground, the body with a frieze of *naskhi* script and a band of *kufic* inscription, 14.5cm (5¾in) high, *L 16 Apr,*
£2,200 ($3,410)

10
A Seljuk whiteware cup, Kashan or Nishapur, 12th century, with crackled clear glaze, the handle and edges splashed with cobalt-blue, 13.5cm (5¼in) high, *NY 24 Nov,*
$38,500 (£27,113)

11
A Seljuk ewer, c.12th century, turquoise-glazed, 30cm (11¾in) high, *NY 24 Nov,*
$1,760 (£1,239)

1

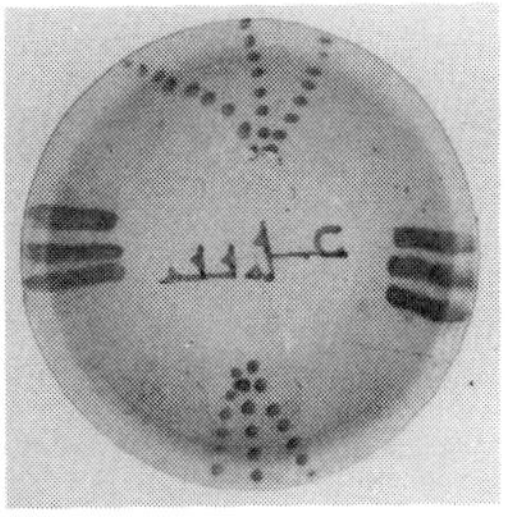
2

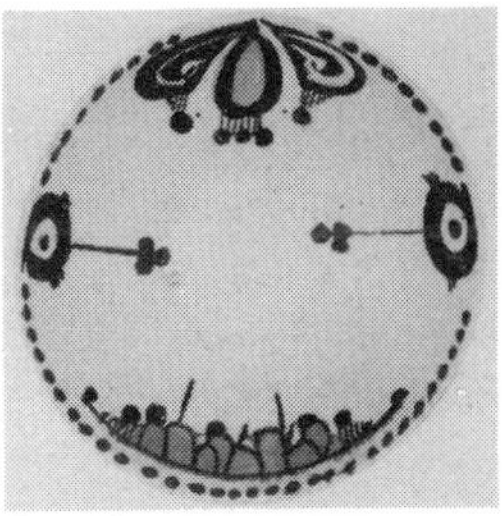
3

4

5

6

7

9

8

10

11

1

2

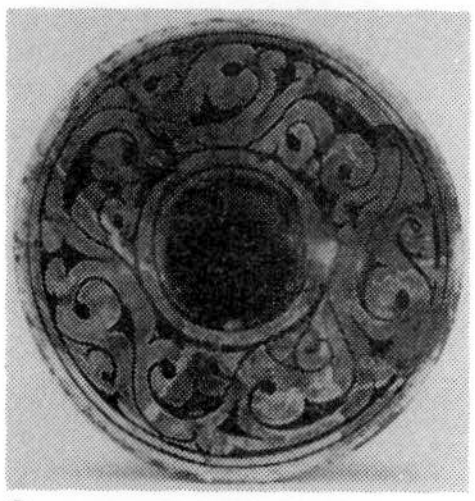
3

4

5

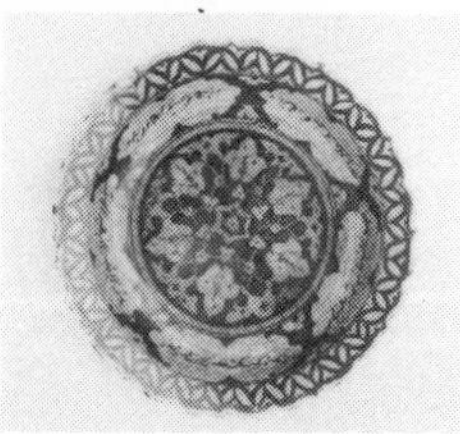
6

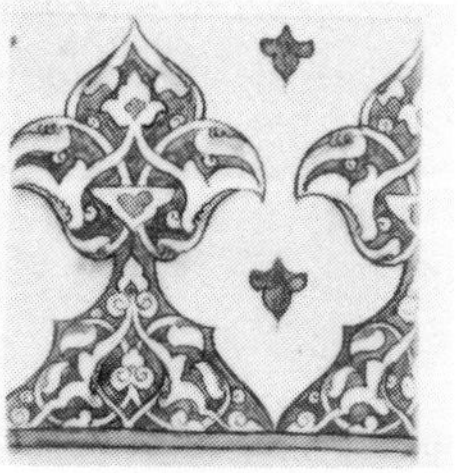
7

8

9

10

11

1
A Seljuk Minai beaker, early 13th century, painted with seven seated princely figures, six conversing and one playing the harp, a *kufic* inscription on a blue ground above, 11.5cm (4½in) high, *NY 24 Nov,*
$2,475 (£1,743)

2
A Seljuk Minai cup, early 13th century, painted with a frieze of striding sphinxes and a band of *kufic* inscription, 13.5cm (5¼in) high, *NY 24 Nov,*
$4,675 (£3,292)

3
A Garrus ware pottery bowl, 12th century, with convex flaring sides standing on a low splayed foot, the decoration carved through the slip under a green glaze with a frieze of vines, 13.5cm (5¼in) diam., *L 15 Oct,*
£387 ($542)

4
An Ilkhanid underglaze-painted bowl, Sultanabad, c.late 13th century, the interior painted in black beneath a dark turquoise glaze, 26cm (10½in) diam., *NY 30 May,*
$880 (£598)

5
A Safavid blue and white pottery dish, Kubachi, 16th century, with sloping rim, decorated in cobalt-blue and black, 33cm (13in) diam., *L 15 Oct,*
£1,210 ($1,694)

6
A Safavid dish, Kubachi, first half 16th century, the central medallion painted with fleurs-de-lis on a black ground, the whole with aquamarine glaze, 33cm (13in) diam., *NY 30 May,*
$935 (£636)

7
A Damascus 'crenellated' tile, late 16th century, decorated in cobalt-blue, turquoise and green with black outlines, 22cm (8½in) square, *L 16 Apr,*
£462 ($716)

8
A pair of Damascus tiles, *(one illustrated),* late 16th/17th century, decorated in cobalt-blue, turquoise, manganese and green, with black outlines, each 29.5cm (11½in) square, *L 16 Apr,*
£660 ($1,023)

9
A Safavid dish, Kubachi, early 17th century, the interior painted on the white ground in blue, yellow and red, with black outlines, 34.5cm (13½in) diam., *NY 30 May,*
$440 (£299)

10
A Safavid dish, Kubachi, 17th century, the interior painted on the white ground in blue, yellow and red, with black outlines, 34cm (13½in) diam., *NY 24 Nov,*
$440 (£310)

11
A Safavid blue and white pottery bowl, Kerman, 17th century, in the style of a Chinese 16th century original in shades of cobalt-blue, the base with four pseudo-Chinese marks, 50.5cm (20in) diam., *L 15 Oct,*
£1,452 ($2,033)

1
An Isnik blue and white pottery jar, 16th century, neck ground down, 21.5cm (8½in) high, *L 16 Apr,*
£3,300 ($5,115)

2
An Isnik tile and a fragmentary Isnik tile, late 16th century, mounted together and forming a rectangular panel, decorated in cobalt-blue, turquoise, green and raised red, 28 x 43cm (11 x 17in), *L 16 Apr,*
£1,430 ($2,224)

3
An Isnik pottery dish, late 16th century, decorated in cobalt-blue, green and raised red, 33.5cm (13¼in) diam., *L 15 Oct,*
£2,662 ($3,727)

4
An Isnik tankard, c.late 16th century, decorated in blue-green and cobalt-blue with a linked cloud pattern, red and white borders, 19cm (7½in), *NY 30 May,*
$3,960 (£2,693)

5
An Isnik dish, second half 16th century, decorated in blue-green, cobalt-blue and red, 37.5cm (14½in) diam., *NY 30 May,*
$5,500 (£3,741)

6
An Isnik dish, first half 17th century, decorated in white, green, red and cobalt-blue, 29.5cm (11½in) diam., *NY 30 May,*
$2,420 (£1,646)

7
An Isnik dish, c.late 16th century, decorated in white, green, cobalt-blue and red 31.5cm (12½in) diam., *NY 30 May,*
$6,875 (£4,677)

8
An Isnik tankard, 17th century, decorated in cobalt-blue, blue-green and salmon, traces of gilding, 20.5cm (8in) high, *NY 30 May,*
$2,750 (£1,871)

9
An Ottoman dish, c.18th century, decorated in blue-green, cobalt-blue, red and white, 30cm (11¾in) diam., *NY 30 May,*
$660 (£448)

10
An Ottoman dish, c.18th century, decorated in green, cobalt-blue and red, 28.5cm (11½in) diam., *NY 30 May,*
$1,210 (£823)

11
A large dish, North Africa, dated 1135 AH (c.1700 AD), painted in cobalt-blue, aubergine, red and black, 45.5cm (18in) diam., *NY 24 Nov,*
$440 (£310)

1

2

3

4

5

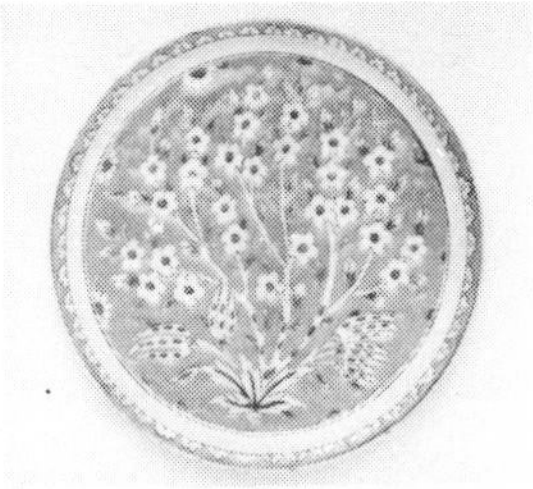
6

7

8

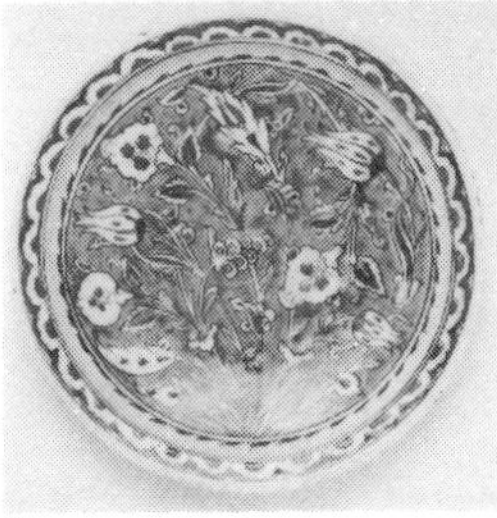
9

10

11

1

2

3

4

5

6

7

8

9

10

11

12

1
A Persian bronze ewer, Khorassan, 8th century, the body standing on a high splayed foot, the rim in the form of two stylised wings, 36.5cm (14½in) high, *L 16 Apr,*
£12,100 ($18,755)

2
A Persian bronze ewer (*aftabe*), Khorassan, 9th/10th century, standing on a splayed foot, the handle with stylised bird's head at the top and palmettes at the base, 29.5cm (11½in) high, *L 15 Oct,*
£605 ($847)

3
A Persian bronze bucket, 10th/11th century, the body incised with vines and a band of *kufic* inscription, 21cm (8¼in) diam., *L 16 Apr,*
£1,430 ($2,217)

4
A Persian bronze ewer (*aftabe*), 10th/12th century, the rim with stylised birds wings, replacement handle, base missing, 20.5cm (8in) high, *L 15 Oct,*
£605 ($847)

5
A Persian copper-inlaid bronze oil-lamp, (*cheragh*), Khorassan, 10th/12th century, with three spouts forming from the top of a stylised bird, lotus-bud shaped cover, ring handle surmounted by a harpie with five inlaid circles round the top, 16.5cm (6½in) high, *L 15 Oct,*
£1,331 ($1,863)

6
A brass cockerel, 11th/13th century, 6.5cm (2½in) high, *L 16 Apr,*
£440 ($682)

7
A spun brass bowl, Ghaznavid, Afghanistan, 11th century, the extérior decorated with gadrooning beneath a band of *kufic* inscription, the interior with central medallion containing the figure of a seated prince, 26.5cm (10½in) diam., *NY 30 May,*
$1,430 (£972)

8
A Seljuk bronze bird, 12t century, engraved with feathers and geometric motifs, green and brown patina, 18.5cm (7½in) high, *NY 24 Nov,*
$7,700 (£5,423)

9
A Mamluk gold and silver-inlaid brass bowl, first half 14th century, the decoration incised with much inlay remaining, the sides with a frieze of inscription alternating with lobed medallions, 30cm (11¾in) diam., *L 16 Apr,*
£2,200 ($3,410)

10
A Fars silver-inlaid brass bowl (*tas*), late 13th/14th century, the decoration incised with some inlay remaining, the sides with roundels of horsemen alternating with inscription cartouches, 28cm (11in) diam., *L 16 Apr,*
£1,540 ($2,387)

11
A Mamluk silver-inlaid brass bowl, mid 14th century, the decoration incised with much inlay remaining, the sides with bands of inscription alternating with roundels containing ducks in flight, 18cm (7in) diam., *L 16 Apr,*
£6,380 ($9,889)

12
A Mamluk tinned-copper tray, Syria or Egypt, 15th century, the rim with *thuluth* and inscriptions of Arabic verse with the owner's name, 45cm (21¼in) diam., *L 16 Apr,*
£1,155 ($1,790)

1
A Persian silver and copper inlaid bronze jug *(mashrabe)*, 12th/13th century, the incised decoration with much inlay remaining, the body with a row of rosettes within bands of *kufic* and *naskhi* inscription, 30cm (11¾in) high, *L 16 Apr,*
£8,800 ($13,640)

2
An Ottoman silver-gilt ewer, c.1500, decorated in relief with an overall design of curving vines and foliage, the neck, lid and foot with escutcheons, three retaining plaques enamelled in yellow, blue and green, 28cm (11in) high, *L 16 Apr,*
£24,200 ($37,510)

3
A Persian tinned-copper wine bowl *(badiye)*, 17th century, standing on a splayed foot, incised with medallions containing animals and seated figures alternating with inscription cartouches, 30.5cm (12in) diam., *L 16 Apr,*
£550 ($853)

4
An Ottoman parcel-gilt bowl, 16th century, chased in relief with gadrooning, 14.5cm (5¾in) diam., *L 16 Apr,*
£1,760 ($2,728)

5
An early Safavid silver and gold-inlaid brass jug *(mashrabe)* **and cover,** Khorassan, dated 918 AH (1512 AD), standing on a splayed foot, the body decorated with bands of rosettes with narrow vine borders, the base with a band of inscription giving the artist's name, 16.5cm (6½in) high, *L 15 Oct,*
£22,990 ($32,186)

6
An Ottoman copper ewer, 17th century, incised with an overall design of carnations against a stippled ground, later silvering, 34cm (13¼in) high, *L 16 Apr,*
£4,510 ($6,990)

7
A Safavid brass bath-pail (*satl*), c.1600, the decoration incised on a black composition-filled ground with friezes of palmettes containing floral motifs, alternating with inscription cartouches, 23.5cm (9¼in) diam., *L 15 Oct,*
£2,904 ($4,066)

8
A Safavid brass basin, c.1600, standing on a splayed foot, incised on a black composition-filled ground with a frieze of vines, arabesques and palmettes, 31cm (12¼in) diam., *L 15 Oct,*
£1,573 ($2,202)

9
A Safavid brass ewer (*aftabe*), c.1600, decorated with friezes of vines and palmettes and bands of inscriptions, the handle with opening and hinged cover at the top, the spout ending in a dragon's head, 28cm (11in) high, *L 15 Oct,*
£1,936 ($2,710)

10
A Safavid brass ewer (*aftabe*), c.1600, incised with a frieze of pendant trefoils alternating with palmettes, later foot, 26cm (10¼in) high, *L 16 Apr,*
£1,650 ($2,558)

11
A Safavid brass torch-stand (*mash'al*), late 16th century, decorated with gadrooned chevron bands enclosing arabesque panels, the neck and base with a *nastaliq* inscription, 29cm (11½in) high, *L 16 Apr,*
£935 ($1,449)

1

2

3

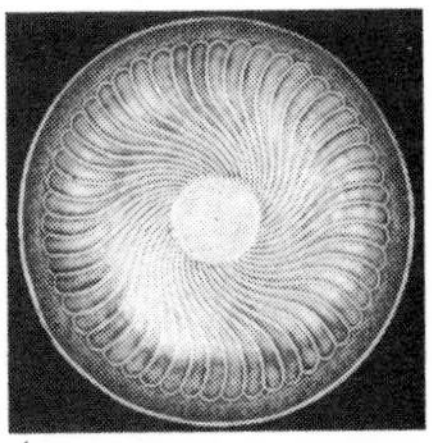
4

5

6

7

8

9

10

11

1

2

3

4

5

6

7 8 9

10

11

12

13

14

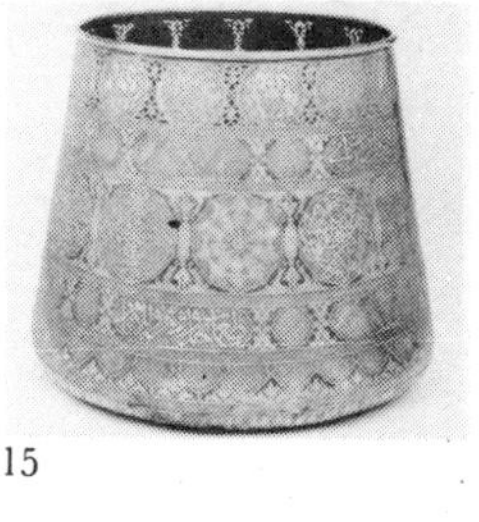
15

1
An Ottoman silver seal, dated 1290 AH (1873 AD), incised with the official stamp of the Governor of Mount Lebanon, *L 16 Apr,*
£528 ($818)

2
An Ottoman brass candlestick, early 16th century, the body incised with a foliate design, 21.5cm (8½in) high, *L 16 Apr,*
£1,650 ($2,558)

3
An Ottoman brass candlestick, 17th century, the shaft with a socket in the form of a tulip flower, 20.5cm (8in) high, *L 15 Oct,*
£1,573 ($2,202)

4
An Ottoman gilt-copper *(tombak)* **beaker and cover,** c.1800, with chased and engraved decoration of alternating *mehrab* panels and floral sprays, 10.5cm (4in) high, *L 15 Oct,*
£484 ($678)

5
An Ottoman bronze belt-buckle, 17th century, the hook with a stylised dragon's head at either end, 16cm (6½in) long, *L 15 Oct,*
£242 ($339)

6
An Ottoman silver jug, 1789-1807, incised with floral sprays, marked with the *tughra* of Selim III, 12.5cm (5in) high, *L 16 Apr,*
£1,540 ($2,387)

7
An Ottoman silver cup, cover and saucer, Egypt, late 19th century, decorated with floral sprays, the lid with a bird finial, 12.5cm (5in) high, *L 30 July,*
£275 ($432)

8
An Ottoman silver coffee-pot, late 19th century, decorated with birds against foliage and bands of inscription, bird finial, marked with a *tughra*, 20cm (8in) high, *L 30 July,*
£572 ($898)

9
An Ottoman silver cup and cover, late 19th century, decorated with a band of inscription, foliate finial, the interior gilded, marked with a *tughra*, 12.5cm (5in) high, *L 30 July,*
£275 ($432)

10
A silver-inlaid brass casket, Syria or Egypt, c.1900, decorated with inscription medallions and bands of fish and birds, 16.5cm (6½in) high, *L 30 July,*
£550 ($864)

11
A silver and copper-inlaid brass tray, c.1900, decorated with inscriptions and foliate arabesques with fish and bird terminals, 70.5cm (27¾in) diam., *L 16 Apr,*
£825 ($1,279)

12
An Ottoman silver beaker, late 19th century, marked with a *tughra*, 9.5cm (3¾in) high, *L 16 Apr,*
£462 ($716)

13
A set of four Ottoman silver covered dishes (*one illustrated*), late 19th century, on a splayed foot and with deer finial, marked with a *tughra*, 9.5cm (3¾in) high, *L 15 Oct,*
£4,598 ($6,437)

14
A pair of Ottoman silver beakers (*one illustrated*), marked with a *tughra*, 9cm (3½in) high, *L 16 Apr,*
£990 ($1,535)

15
A silver and copper-inlaid brass basin, c.1900, decorated with bands of polygons, inscriptions and guilloche cartouches, 39cm (15¼in) high, *L 16 Apr,*
£1,155 ($1,790)

1
A free-blown yellowish glass flask, Syrian, 7th/9th century, decorated with three applied pads drawn into six-pointed stars, some beige weathering, intact, 11cm (4¼in) high, *L 16 Apr,*
£352 ($546)

2
A Persian mould-blown aquamarine glass jug, 10th/12th century, with dimpled lower body, patchy silvery weathering, intact, 14.5cm (5¾in) high, *L 16 Apr,*
£352 ($546)

3
A pale-green mould-blown glass jug, probably Persian, 10th/12th century, the body decorated with a mould-blown design of flutes at the base and dimples above, patchy beige weathering, intact, 14cm (5½in) high, *L 16 Apr,*
£132 ($205)

4
A Persian free-blown green glass jug, 10th/11th century, some weathering, broken and repaired with some plastic insertions, 19.5cm (7¾in) high, *L 16 Apr,*
£385 ($597)

5
A bronze glass mould, possibly Mesopotamia, 9th/10th century, the interior with a honeycomb design in relief, the exterior incised with an inscription, 11cm (4¼in) high, *L 16 Apr,*
£2,310 ($3,580)

6
A wheel-cut colourless glass molar-tooth flask, probably Persian, 9th/10th century, standing on four flat feet (one missing), silvery weathering, 6cm (2½in) high, *L 16 Apr,*
£132 ($205)

7
An Ottoman embroidered hanging, 17th century, the natural linen ground with an overall design of vines and flowers, and with the *chintamani* pattern, in shades of madder, saffron, ivory, walnut, green and pale indigo silk, 211 x 138cm (6ft 11in x 4ft 6in), *L 15 Oct,*
£3,630 ($5,082)

8
A Mughal embroidered silk and metal thread prayer panel, the natural *mehrab* with a trellis of flowering plants, 110 x 73cm (3ft 7in x 2ft 5in), *L 16 Apr,*
£660 ($1,023)

9
A Bokhara Susani panel, the ivory panel with central flowerhead supported by floral sprays, 158 x 104cm (5ft 2in x 3ft 5in), *S 22 July,*
£1,045 ($1,641)

10
A Bokhara Susani, the natural linen ground with an overall design of meandering vines, 227 x 175cm (7ft 5in x 5ft 9in), *L 16 Apr,*
£660 ($1,023)

11
A Bokhara Susani, the natural linen ground with an overall design of stylised flowering plants, 243 x 164cm (8ft x 5ft 5in), *L 15 Oct,*
£1,694 ($2,372)

12
A Bokhara Susani, the natural linen ground decorated with flower-heads, 272 x 186cm (8ft 11in x 6ft 1in), *L 15 Oct,*
£2,541 ($3,557)

1

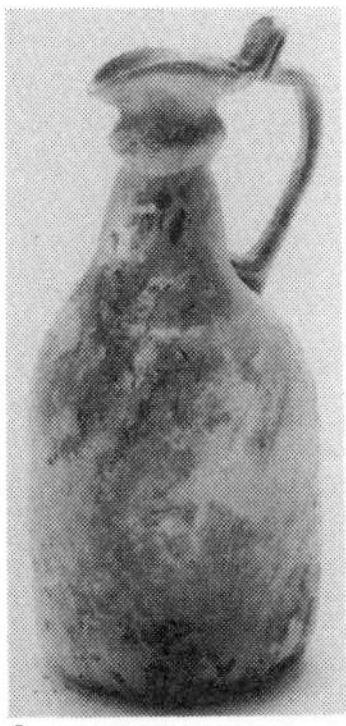
2

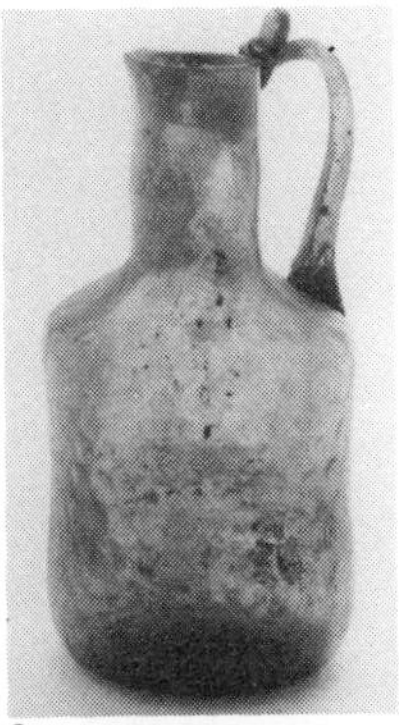
3

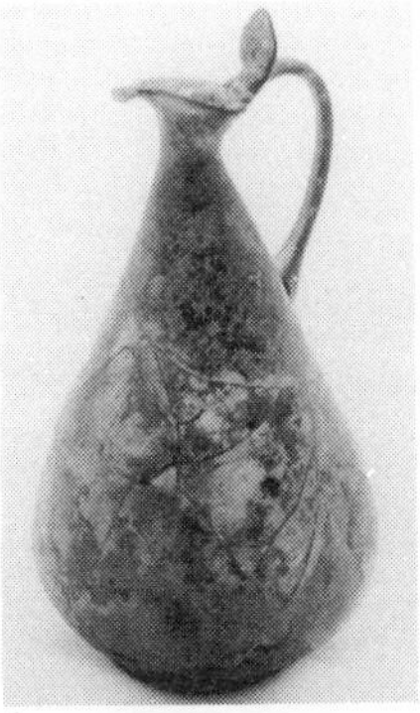
4

5

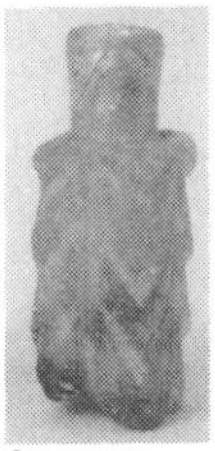
6

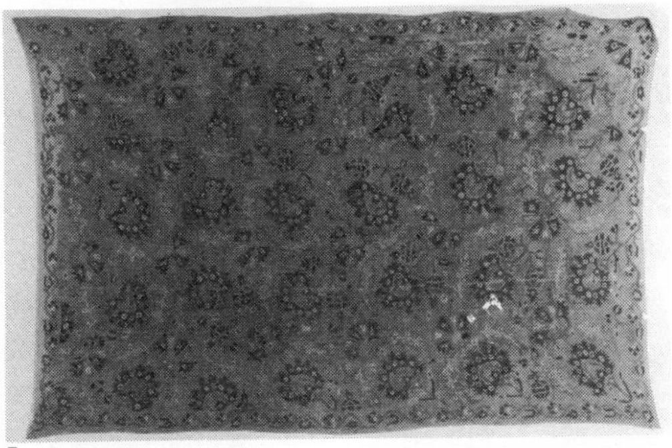
7

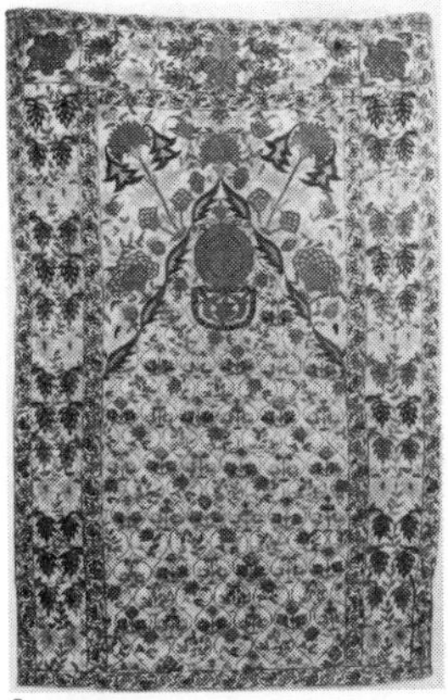
8

9

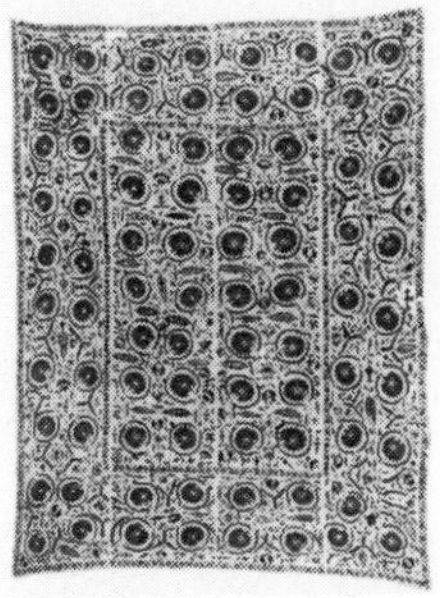
10

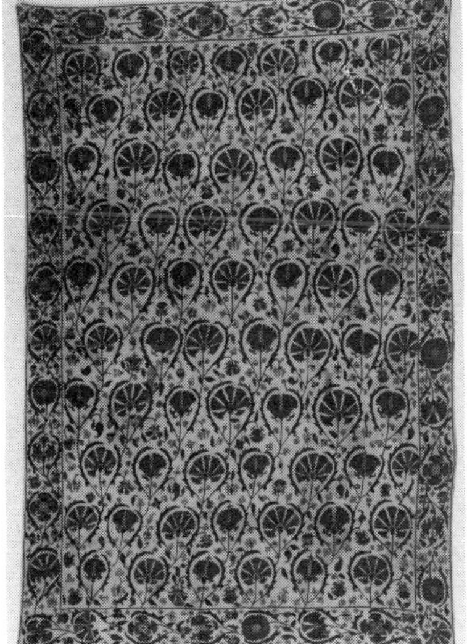
11

12

Oriental Rugs and Carpets

1

2

3

4

5

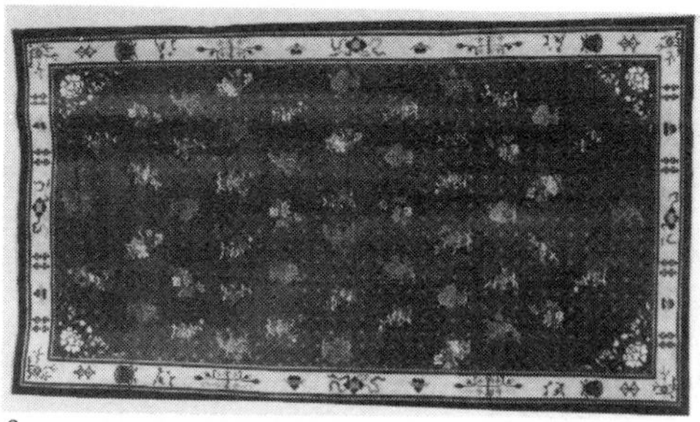
6

7

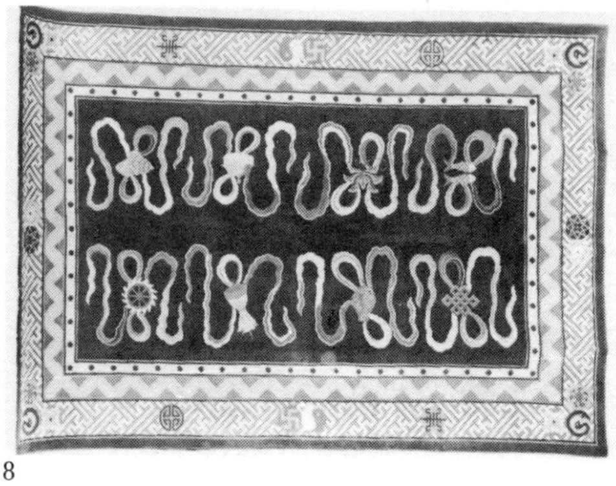
8

Article:
19th century Caucasian rugs *pp* 642-648

See also:
Colour illustrations *pp* 566-569

European rugs and carpets *pp* 186-188

1
A Chinese rug, 19th century, 192 x 104cm (6ft 4in x 3ft 5in), *L 9 May,*
£3,080 ($4,959)

2
A Chinese Imperial silk rug, 19th century, 247 x 157cm (8ft 1¼in x 5ft 1¾in), *L 9 May,*
£3,300 ($5,313)

3
A Ninghsia carpet, West China, early 19th century, the cream field with an overall blue peony and lotus vinery, 274 x 165cm (9ft x 5ft 5in), *NY 31 May,*
$2,090 (£1,422)

4
A Chinese Imperial silk rug, Guangxu, 244 x 156cm (8ft x 5ft 1in), *L 31 Oct,*
£2,970 ($4,158)

5
A Chinese carpet, c.1900, the sapphire blue field with cream and dark blue cartouches, 465 x 360cm (15ft 3in x 11ft 10in), *NY 31 May,*
$5,060 (£3,442)

6
A Chinese carpet, early 20th century, the royal blue field with dark blue trellis overlaid with floral sprays, 589 x 338cm (19ft 4in x 11ft 1in), *NY 31 May,*
$6,050 (£4,116)

7
An Amritsar carpet, 570 x 460cm (18ft 8in x 15ft 1in), *F 30 Sept,*
L 7,150,000 (£3,563; $4,988)

8
A Chinese carpet, the indigo field decorated with Buddhist symbols, 292 x 202cm (10ft 1½in x 6ft 7½in), *M 23 June,*
FF 11,100 (£990; $1,545)

PRINCIPAL WEAVING CENTRES

CAUCASIAN
43 AKSTAFA*
44 ARDEBIL
27 BAKU*
28 BIDJOV*
40 BORDJALOU*
32 CHAJLI*
41 CHELEBE*
24 CHICHI*
36 CHONDZORESK*
19 DERBEND
34 ERIVAN
38 FRACHLO*
21 GARAGASHLI*
25 GONAGHEND
31 GORADIS*
35 KARATCHOP*
30 KHILA*
23 KUBA
39 LAMBALO*
33 LENKORAN*
37 LORIPAMBAK*
29 MEREZE
22 PERIBEDIL*
20 SEYCHOUR*
42 SHULAVER*
26 SOUMAKH**

INDIAN
80 AGRA
79 AMRITZAR
88 DELHI
87 JAIPUR
78 LAHORE
81 SHRINIGAR

PERSIAN (IRAN)
67 ABADEH
50 BIDJAR
73 BIRJAND
72 DOROKSH
64 ESFAHAN
58 GHOM
46 HERIZ
52 HAMADAN
63 JOSHUGAN
45 KARAJAR
60 KASHAN
49 KAZVIN
69 KERMAN
55 KERMANSHAH
51 MAHAL
56 MALAYER
71 MASHHAD
61 MOSUL
65 NAIN
70 NERIZ
62 SARABAND
57 SAROUGH
51 SENNEH
48 SERAB
68 SHIRAZ
59 SULTANABAD
47 TABRIZ
53 TEHERAN
54 VERAMIN
66 YAZD
59 ZIEGLER (a manufactory in Sultanabad)

TURKISH
5 BERGAMA
4 BRUSSA
7 GHIORDES
2 HEREKE
13 KESHEHIR
17 KEYSERI
15 KONYA
9 KULA
1 KUM KAPI (atelier in Istanbul)
14 LADIK
12 MEGRI
11 MELAS
16 MUDJUR
3 PANDERMA
18 SIVAS
6 SMYRNA
10 SPARTA
8 USHAK

TURKMEN, AFGHAN AND EAST TURKESTAN
74 BOKHARA
86 BESHIR
77 HERAT
84 KASHGAR
82 KHOTAN
85 KIZILAYAK
76 PENDE
75 SAMARKAND
83 YARKAND

**more usually used to denote a particular design than to assign to a specific village or town*
***more usually used to denote a type of Caucasion flat-weave*

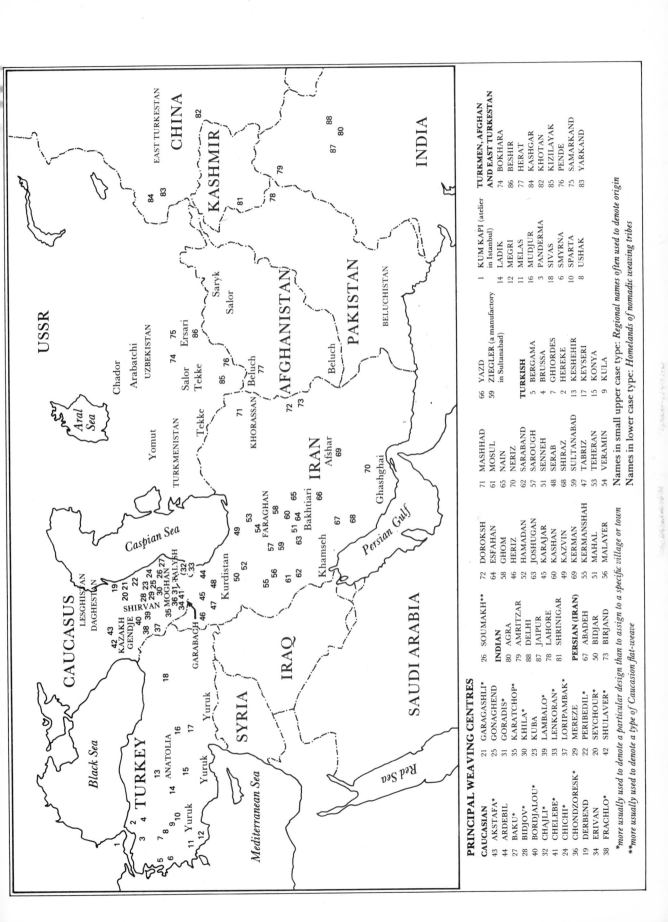

Names in small upper case type: *Regional names often used to denote origin*
Names in lower case type: *Homelands of nomadic weaving tribes*

1

2

3

4

5

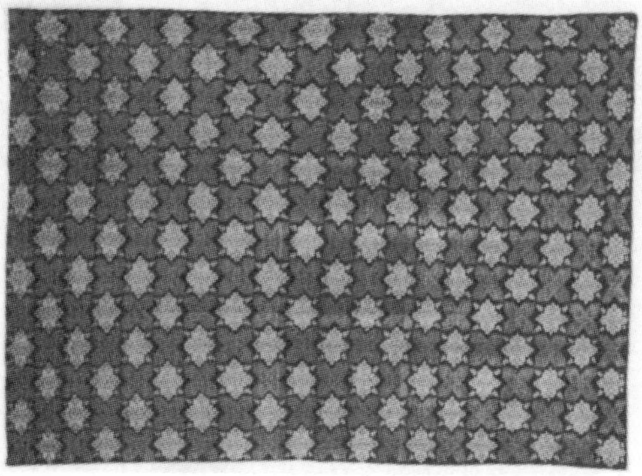
6

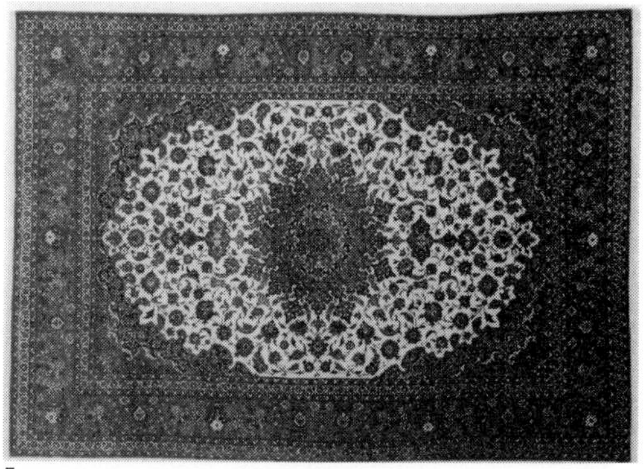
7

8

9

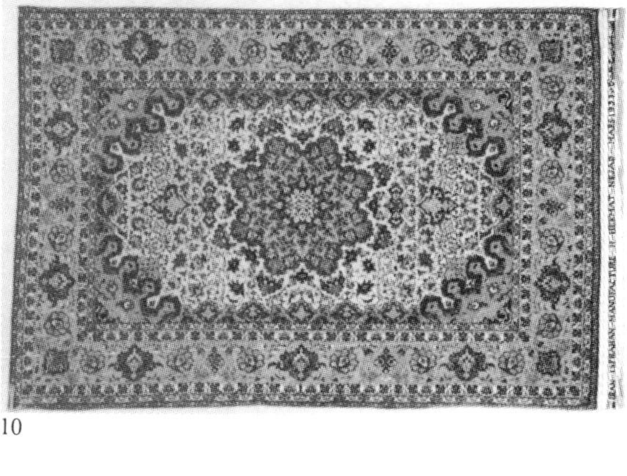
10

1
An Afshar rug, c.1900, the blue medallion flanked by saffron and blue palmettes, 183 x 142cm (6ft x 4ft 8in), *NY 13 Dec,*
$6,875 (£4,911)

2
A Bidjar carpet, late 19th century, the midnight blue field with scroll cartouches of European rose bouquets, 539 x 343cm (17ft 8in x 11ft 3in), *NY 31 May,*
$9,900 (£6,735)

3
A Bidjar carpet, the saffron field with a madder and indigo floral pole medallion, 567 x 360cm (18ft 7in x 11ft 10in), *L 16 Apr,*
£12,100 ($18,755)

4
A Bidjar carpet, late 19th century, 443 x 224cm (11ft 3in x 7ft 4in), *NY 13 Dec,*
$11,000 (£7,857)

5
A Bakhtiari rug, the floral indigo field with a madder pole medallion, 216 x 140cm (7ft 1in x 4ft 7in), *S 16 Dec,*
£990 ($1,386)

6
A Bakhtiari carpet, late 19th century, 490 x 350cm (16ft 1in x 11ft 6in), *NY 13 Dec,*
$15,400 (£11,000)

7
An Esfahan carpet, modern, 389 x 267cm (12ft 9in x 8ft 9in), *NY 13 Dec,*
$17,600 (£12,571)

8
An Esfahan rug, the pale indigo field with an indigo medallion and ivory spandrels, 180 x 107cm (5ft 11in x 3ft 6in), *L 2 June,*
£1,045 ($1,609)

9
An Esfahan rug, modern, the cream field with blue and crimson medallion, 226 x 150cm (7ft 5in x 4ft 11in), *NY 31 May,*
$6,325 (£4,303)

10
An Esfahan rug, modern, 218 x 150cm (7ft 2in x 4ft 11in), *NY 31 May,*
$11,000 (£7,483)

1
An Esfahan rug, the ivory field with flowering Trees of Life, 204 x 148cm (6ft 8in x 4ft 10in), *C 9 Oct,*
£418 ($585)

2
A Heriz rug, the indigo field with a design of stylised plants and birds, 236 x 127cm (7ft 9in x 4ft 2in), *C 18 Apr,*
£374 ($580)

3
A Ghashghai rug, the indigo field with ivory and madder medallions, 234 x 140cm (7ft 8in x 4ft 7in), *S 27 May,*
£1,540 ($2,464)

4
A Ghashghai rug, with indigo field within a saffron *boteh* border, 172 x 127cm (5ft 8in x 4ft 2in), *L 16 Apr,*
£1,760 ($2,728)

5
A Ghom silk rug, with indigo field and ivory medallions and spandrels, 199 x 138cm (6ft 6in x 4ft 6in), *L 12 Feb,*
£3,300 ($4,917)

6
A Ghom silk prayer rug, the ivory *mehrab* with a flowering tree filled with birds, 209 x 133cm (6ft 10in x 4ft 4½in), *S 27 May,*
£1,815 ($2,904)

7
A Hamadan rug, the indigo field with a design of hooked *guls*, 185 x 122cm (6ft 1in x 4ft), *C 18 Apr,*
£352 ($546)

8
A Heriz carpet, with indigo and madder medallion, 295 x 186cm (9ft 8in x 6ft 1in), *C 9 Oct,*
£902 ($1,263)

9
A Heriz rug, 19th century, the ivory field with a design of leaves, flowerheads and palmettes, 120 x 104cm (3ft 11in x 3ft 5in), *L 16 Apr,*
£2,530 ($3,922)

10
A Heriz silk rug, with central foliate tree, 192 x 122cm (6ft 4in x 4ft), *L 15 Oct,*
£2,420 ($3,388)

1

2

3

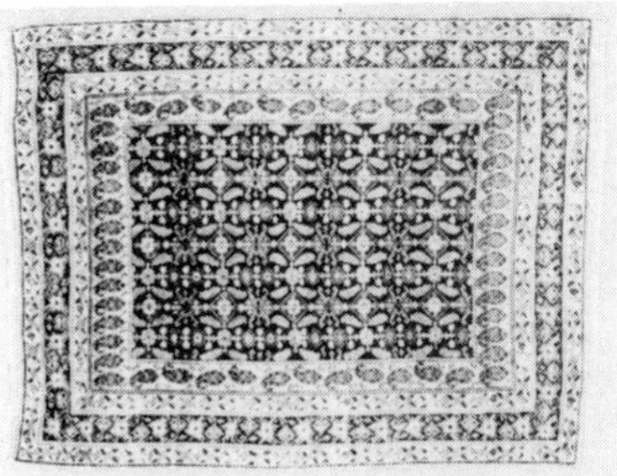
4

5

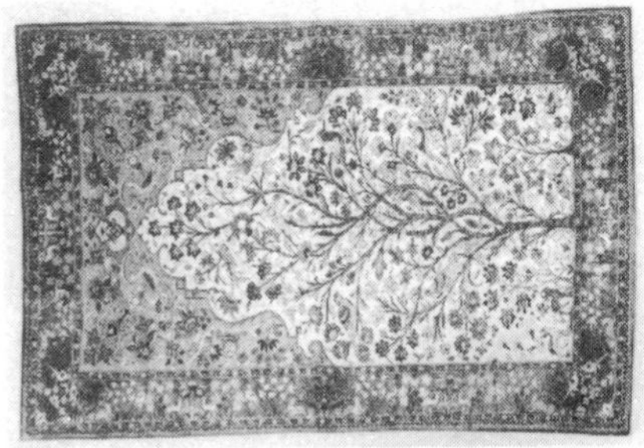
6

7

8

9

10

1

2

3

4

5

6

7

8

9

1
A Heriz carpet, late 19th century, 437 x 264cm (14ft 4in x 8ft 8in), *NY 31 May,* **$17,600 (£11,973)**

2
A Heriz carpet, late 19th century, 435 x 274cm (14ft 3in x 9ft), *NY 13 Dec,* **$22,000 (£15,714)**

3
A Heriz silk rug, the madder field with indigo medallion, ivory palmettes, 188 x 137cm (6ft 2in x 4ft 6in), *L 16 Apr,* **£15,400 ($23,870)**

4
A Heriz carpet, late 19th century, 381 x 274cm (12ft 6in x 9ft), *NY 13 Dec,* **$17,600 (£12,571)**

5
A Kashan carpet, the ivory field with vines, palmettes and birds, signed *Kashan,* 329 x 220cm (10ft 9½in x 7ft 3in), *L 30 July,* **£880 ($1,382)**

6
A Joshugan runner, c.1900, the blue field with ivory floral stripes, 594 x 112cm (19ft 6in x 3ft 8in), *NY 31 May,* **$6,050 (£4,116)**

7
A Kashan carpet, the madder field with camel medallion and surround, 456 x 310cm (15ft x 10ft 2in), *L 12 Feb,* **£990 ($1,475)**

8
A Kashan rug, the indigo field with a madder and ivory pole medallion, 198 x 131cm (6ft 6in x 4ft 3½in), *S 16 Dec,* **£1,078 ($1,509)**

9
A Kashan silk prayer rug, the ivory *mehrab* with a central vase of flowers, saffron floral spandrels, 201 x 130cm (6ft 7in x 4ft 3in), *L 30 July,* **£1,650 ($2,590)**

1
A Kashan silk carpet, the madder field with an indigo medallion and spandrels, 324 x 216cm (10ft 8in x 7ft 1in), *L 30 July,*
£3,300 ($5,181)

2
A Kashan rug, the indigo field with a madder pole medallion and ivory spandrels, 209 x 127cm (6ft 10in x 4ft 2in), *L 16 Apr,*
£5,060 ($7,843)

3
A Kashan Mohtasham carpet, late 19th century, 328 x 231cm (10ft 9in x 7ft 7in), *NY 13 Dec,*
$16,500 (£11,786)

4
A Khamseh carpet, 290 x 178cm (9ft 6in x 5ft 10in), *NY 14 Oct,*
$1,870 (£1,299)

5
A Khamseh rug, third quarter 19th century, the blue field with ivory and crimson medallions, 285 x 158cm (9ft 4in x 5ft 2in), *NY 31 May,*
$3,960 (£2,694)

6
A Kashan Mohtasham carpet, late 19th century, 521 x 379cm (17ft 1in x 12ft 5in), *NY 31 May,*
$29,700 (£20,204)

7
A Khamseh carpet, with saffron field, 247 x 100cm (8ft 1in x 3ft 3in), *L 16 Apr,*
£2,420 ($3,751)

8
A Khorassan rug, with ivory field and indigo palmette and floral spray border, 198 x 137cm (6ft 6in x 4ft 6in), *S 28 Jan,*
£495 ($743)

9
A Kurdish runner, the indigo field with polychrome medallions, 358 x 124cm (11ft 9in x 4ft 1in), *C 18 Apr,*
£374 ($580)

1

2

3

4

5

6

7

8

9

1

2

3

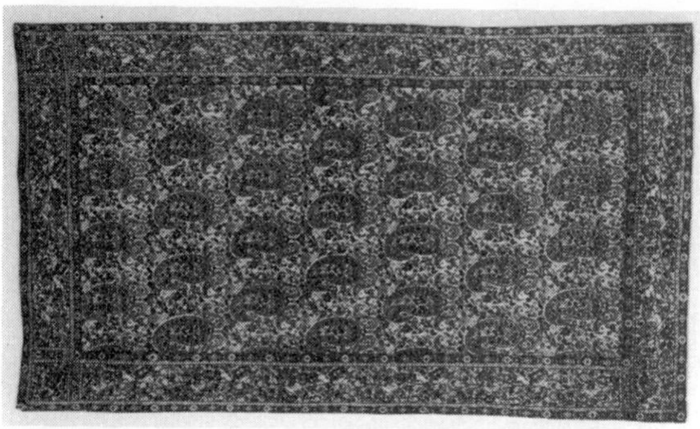
4

5

6

7

8

1
A Kerman pictorial rug, the madder field with an ivory cartouche depicting Kayumarth (a king in the *Shahnameh* of Firdawsi), 21 x 141cm (6ft 11in x 4ft 7½in), *L 30 July,*
£880 ($1,382)

2
A Kerman carpet, the indigo, madder and ivory field with tree and plant motifs, 510 x 327cm (16ft 9in x 10ft 9in), *L 12 Feb,*
£2,420 ($3,606)

3
A Kerman meditation carpet, early 20th century, 485 x 328cm (15ft 11in x 10ft 9in), *NY 31 May,*
$11,000 (£7,483)

4
A Kerman rug, the beige field with rows of plants with large *boteh* flower-heads, 240 x 137cm (7ft 10½in x 4ft 6in), *S 27 May,*
£660 ($1,056)

5
A Malayer rug, the dark indigo field with madder medallion, sprays and vines, 188 x 127cm (6ft 2in x 4ft 2in), *S 22 July,*
£572 ($898)

6
A Malayer rug, the ivory field with a madder pole medallion and indigo spandrels, 194 x 135cm (6ft 4½in x 4ft 5in), *S 25 Mar,*
£792 ($1,212)

7
A Malayer rug, the ivory field with indigo pole medallion and madder spandrels, 201 x 145cm (6ft 7in x 4ft 9in), *L 12 Feb,*
£5,060 ($7,539)

8
A Mashhad carpet, the ivory field with rows of polychrome *botehs* interspersed with birds and flowerheads, 362 x 264cm (11ft 10in x 8ft 8in), *L 12 Feb,*
£2,090 ($3,114)

1
A pair of Mashhad Tree of Life rugs, *(one illustrated)*, 180 x 140cm (5ft 11in x 4ft 7in), 183 x 132cm (6ft x 4ft 4in), *S 16 Dec,*
£770 ($1,078)

2
A Nain rug, the pale indigo field with beige medallion and spandrels, 298 x 184cm (9ft 9in x 6ft), *L 12 Feb,*
£1,540 ($2,295)

3
A Nain rug, with madder field and indigo border, 205 x 145cm (6ft 9in x 4ft 9in), *L 30 July,*
£2,200 ($3,454)

4
A pair of Nain prayer rugs, *(one illustrated)*, the ivory *mehrab* with central madder and indigo medallion, 207 x 156cm (6ft 9½in x 5ft 1½in), and 210 x 151cm (6ft 11in x 5ft), *L 16 Apr,*
£5,280 ($8,184)

5
A Nain carpet, modern, 411 x 315cm (13ft 6in x 10ft 4in), *NY 13 Dec,*
$17,600 (£12,571)

6
A Serapi runner, the camel field with ivory medallions, 312 x 118cm (10ft 1in x 3ft 10in), *F 14 Apr,*
L 1,200,000 (£491; $762)

7
A Sarough rug, the dark indigo field with madder pole medallion and ivory spandrels, 206 x 134cm (6ft 9in x 4ft 4½in), *S 28 Jan,*
£704 ($1,056)

8
A Sarough rug, the ivory field with an indigo medallion, 196 x 138cm (6ft 5in x 4ft 8in), *F 14 Apr,*
L 3,000,000 (£1,229; $1,904)

1

2

3

4

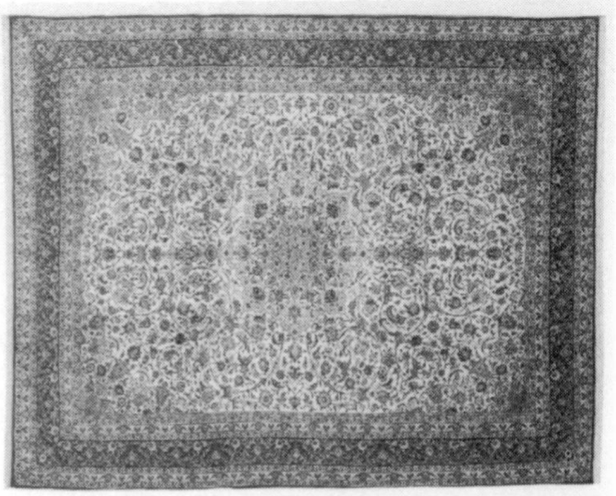
5

6

7

8

1

2

3

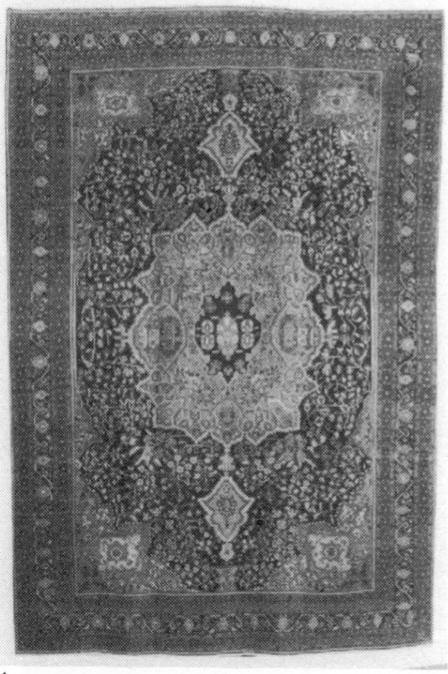
4

5

6

7

8

9

1
A Faraghan carpet, with ivory field and indigo medallion and border, 200 x 134cm (6ft 7in x 4ft 5in), *F 30 Sept,*
L 3,850,000 (£1,918; $2,686)

2
A Sarough rug, with indigo field and madder medallion and spandrels, 197 x 132cm (6ft 6in x 4ft 4in), *L 16 Apr,*
£4,180 ($6,479)

3
A Sarough Faraghan prayer rug, late 19th century, the cream *mehrab* with a flowering urn topped by an inscription cartouche, 203 x 130cm (6ft 8in x 4ft 3in), *NY 13 Dec,*
$4,180 (£2,986)

4
A Sarough Faraghan carpet, late 19th century, 511 x 366cm (16ft 9in x 12ft), *NY 31 May,*
$22,000 (£14,966)

5
A Sarough rug, with indigo field and madder border, 208 x 132cm (6ft 10in x 4ft 4in), *S 27 May,*
£880 ($1,408)

6
A Senneh gelim carpet, with black field, 190 x 120cm (6ft 3in x 3ft 11in), *M 23 June,*
FF 12,210 (£1,089; $1,699)

7
A Senneh rug, the saffron field with a design of floral *botehs*, 201 x 131cm (6ft 7in x 4ft 4in), *L 15 Oct,*
£3,872 ($5,421)

8
A Tabriz rug, the madder field with an indigo and madder lobed floral medallion and spandrels, 175 x 123cm (5ft 9in x 4ft 1in), *L 15 Oct,*
£2,783 ($3,896)

9
A Tabriz carpet, the madder field with an indigo diamond medallion, all with the *herati* pattern, 320 x 193cm (10ft 6in x 6ft 4in), *L 15 Oct,*
£6,050 ($8,470)

Tabriz carpet, 386 x
74cm (12ft 8in x 9ft),
Y 10 June,
5,720 (£3,643)

Tabriz carpet, with
nadder field and indigo
order, 598 x 378cm (19ft
½in x 12ft 5in), *L 16 Apr,*
3,190 ($4,945)

Tabriz rug, the ivory
eld with indigo diamond
nedallion, 186 x 141cm
6ft 1in x 4ft 7in),
15 Oct,
3,872 ($5,421)

4
A Tabriz carpet, the pale
ndigo field with a madder
and indigo medallion and
spandrels, 378 x 268cm
(12ft 5in x 8ft 9½in),
L 15 Oct,
£8,712 ($12,197)

5
A Tabriz carpet, late 19th
century, 411 x 310cm (13ft
5in x 10ft 2in), *NY 13 Dec,*
$17,600 (£12,571)

6
A Ziegler carpet, with a
Ghashghai design, the
field with bands of floral
botehs within a madder *gul*
border, 570 x 365cm (18ft
8in x 12ft), *L 30 July,*
£5,720 ($8,980)

7
A Tabriz garden carpet,
late 19th century, 360 x
274cm (11ft 10in x 9ft),
NY 13 Dec,
$16,500 (£11,786)

8
A Ziegler carpet, with
madder field and indigo
border, 559 x 415cm (18ft
4in x 13ft 7in), *L 30 July,*
£3,190 ($5,008)

1

2

3

4

5

6

7

8

19th Century Caucasian Rugs

MARY JO OTSEA

The abstract designs and sparkling colours of rugs woven in the Caucasus mountains and valleys, which stretch between the Caspian and Black Seas, appeal to collectors and amateurs alike. In the past year, many examples of Caucasian tribal and village weaving from the 19th century have come on the market and, as today's prices reflect, they find a strong buying audience. The highly stylised floral or purely abstract geometric motifs woven in primary colours, that predominate in Caucasian rug designs, make unrivalled graphic statements. This bold, straight-forward quality is easily appreciated by the Western eye. Further study of these rugs will clarify the sophisticated design balance and colour harmony, but there is an instant attraction to such rugs as the Kazakh (fig.2) that transcends historical and cultural differences.

The study of Oriental rugs is basically a 20th century development. Most rug scholarship is theoretical as the non-literate cultures producing carpets did not record why they made them, or where their design inspiration came from. At the beginning of this century, scholarship concentrated on 17th and 18th century Caucasian carpets which were probably manufactured in professional workshops for wealthy or noble people. Such workshops included a designer and a team of weavers to execute the carefully planned, sophisticated designs — a method similar to Ottoman and Safavid court workshops of the same period. It is now generally accepted that the workshops in the Caucasus manufacturing formal carpets were in the southern areas, such as Karabagh, where the influence of the Safavid reign extended. The 18th century was a time of political upheaval in the area and by the beginning of the 19th century the Caucasus were populated by diverse groups of people and nomadic tribes who did not enjoy court patronage and who produced weavings for their own use. These rugs, woven by women in domestic settings, have gained popularity over the years, and in the past two decades have earned the respect of rug scholars and collectors.

1

1
A Shirvan prayer rug, East Caucasus, late 19th century, the midnight blue *mehrab* with red, yellow and teal birds and a tomato red horse, within an ivory border, 140 × 114cm (4ft 7in × 3ft 9in), *NY 13 Dec,* **$6,600 (£4,714)**

2
A Karachopt Kazakh rug, Southwest Caucasus, last quarter 19th century, 206 × 173cm (6ft 9in × 5ft 8in), *NY 13 Dec,*
$28,600 (£20,428)

2

3
A Kazakh rug, Southwest Caucasus, third quarter 19th century, the cream field with tomato red octagons and ivory and blue borders, 254 × 203cm (8ft 4in × 6ft 8in), *NY 13 Dec,*
$8,250 (£5,892)

3

Within the Caucasus a variety of weaving traditions developed as a result of the diversity of the population. The place or tribe of origin can be established by examining the design, colour and structure of weavings. Kazakh rugs (such as colour illustrations p.566 fig.2 and p.569 fig.3) come from the south-west mountains and feature a thick, long pile and bold, abstract design in a primary colour palette. Two Shirvan rugs (fig.1 and colour illustration p.567 fig.3), feature the thin pile and more intricate design typical of rugs from the eastern plain near the Caspian Sea. The reasons for these differences are entirely speculative, perhaps in part due to climate as well as tradition.

In fig.4, another Kazakh rug, the plethora of latchhook motifs helps in attributing it more specifically to the Bordjalou group of Kazakh weavings. The delight in a variety of geometric patterns and decorations — abstract and removed from any realistic depiction — is a characteristic of many Kazakh weavings, as in figs 3 & 5. Occasionally, an animal or figure will be introduced along with the whimsical polygons and stars (fig.8).

4
A Kazakh bordjalou rug, with madder ground, 192 × 136cm (6ft 3in × 4ft 5½in), *C 9 Oct,*
£2,310 ($3,234)

5
A Kazakh runner, the indigo field with madder and ivory *guls*, 297 × 102cm (9ft 9in × 3ft 4in), *S 16 Dec,*
£1,100 ($1,540)

Soumac rug, 296 × 95cm (9ft 8½in × 6ft 4in),
30 Sept,
4,950,000 (£2,466; 3,453)

6

7
A pair of Soumac bags,
Caucasus, last quarter 19th century, the blue-black field with polychrome hexagons within an ivory border, 114 × 51cm (45 × 20in),
NY 13 Dec,
$4,730 (£3,378)

7

All rugs are woven on a grid foundation of vertical warps and horizontal wefts. Knots, which form the pile, are tied around the warps in rows which are then 'set' by the wefts. In the Caucasus the fabric of this structure, be it knot density or fibres used, will vary and there is a school of thought which bases attribution of rugs entirely on construction. Kazakh weaving employs a completely wool foundation and pile, while Kuba and Shirvan rugs often have cotton or even silk wefts, as in the silk-wefted Shirvan prayer rug (fig.10). The weaver of this Shirvan incorporated a fine foundation to enable her design to be intricate and delicate. The Kazakh weaver, employing fewer knots, creates a dramatic statement with a coarser weave. The selvage, or side binding of rugs, also differs from place to place. Shirvan rugs generally employ a white cotton selvage; Kubas often have a blue binding; Kazakhs, using wool, are often in madder red.

Two Shirvan rugs (figs 10 & 11), show stylised but recognisable floral motifs. Even in rugs of this area with purely geometric patterns, the designs tend to be very intricate (colour illustration p.567 fig.2). In comparing two Shirvan prayer rugs (figs 12 & 13), mid 19th century and c.1900 respectively, the evolution in design is evident. While the composition of the two rugs, a field densely filled with *boteh*, or paisley motifs, beneath a 'floating' prayer arch all with stylised floral borders, is very similar, the early rug (fig.12) sparkles with character and the presence of the weaver as she creates a prestigious tour de force. In fig.13, a later rug, the design seems a static format; commercialisation has set in and the weaver is simply supplying a market demand.

The dating of rugs is not exact, but by examining the evolution of design, colours and weaving techniques, and by comparison with rugs which are dated, a chronology can be established. Synthetic dyes were introduced into the rug-weaving world in the

8

8
A Kazakh rug, Southwest Caucasus, last quarter 19th century, the ivory field with midnight blue, madder and sea green within an ivory border, 188 × 142cm (6ft 2in × 4ft 8in), *NY 31 May*, **$4,675 (£3,180)**

9
A Shirvan runner, the sage field with ivory border, 305 × 108cm (10ft × 3ft 6½in), *S 28 Jan,*
£2,200 ($3,300)

10
A Shirvan Marasali prayer rug, East Caucasus, c.1850, the ivory *mehrab* with overall polychrome floral trellis, 137 × 102cm (4ft 6in × 3ft 4in), *NY 31 May,*
$14,850 (£10,102)

11
A Shirvan prayer rug, ivory trellis *mehrab* and indigo *mehrab* arch, 171 × 142cm (5ft 7in × 4ft 8in), *L 16 Apr,*
£1,265 ($1,961)

12
A Shirvan Marasali prayer rug, East Caucasus, mid 19th century, 112 × 91cm (3ft 8in × 3ft), *NY 13 Dec,*
$27,500 (£19,643)

13
A Shirvan prayer rug, East Caucasus, c.1900, pale mustard *mehrab*, deep blue prayer arch and ivory border, 158 × 96cm (5ft 2in × 3ft 5in), *NY 13 Dec,*
$4,510 (£3,221)

9

10

11

12

13

1850s. These dyes reached the more rural areas and tribal groups later than the urban centres, but by the last quarter of the 19th century they were widely used in the Caucasus. The bright tangerine oranges, pinks and purples that could be achieved with synthetic dyes are considered unpalettable by some contemporary collectors but were, in fact, pleasing to the weavers themselves. In the market today, the rugs which achieve the highest prices and which are coveted by collectors, are those which employ natural dyes and are therefore generally of greater age.

Other weaving techniques found in the Caucasus include kilims and soumac carpets. The soumac stitch, or weft brocading, was practised in the Eastern Caucasus as well as the Azerbaijan area of Northwest Persia. The patterns of these carpets (fig.6 and colour illustration p.567 fig.1) differ from pile weavings of the same areas. While they seem to have incorporated some of the minor motifs of pile rugs, their traditional design remained independent and was perhaps derived from their structure. It may be that soumacs were simply made for different uses than rugs, for example as table coverings or storage bags (fig.7).

Tracing the design origins of Caucasian rugs back to older weaving traditions can be difficult and problematic. There are elements of design where this tradition seems plausible, such as the 'kufesque' borders of figs 14 & 15 — an intricate pattern which is probably a legacy from the borders of 13th-17th century Anatolian carpets. Over time, designs migrate and are reinterpreted to such an extent that their origins become elusive. In these 19th century domestic rugs, the weaver works within a tradition, but it is her personal interpretation which makes a unique statement (colour illustration p.566 fig.1).

The rug market improved dramatically over the past year. Serious collectors generally purchase the more esoteric examples, but many Caucasian rugs are purchased for decoration: their abstract design and primary colour blending schemes suit current fashion for both floors and walls. Condition may affect the price of many rugs, but a worn, old and beautiful carpet will nonetheless find an appreciative buyer.

The cleaning and restoration of carpets, and textiles in general, is a subjective decision and should be undertaken with great care. Textiles of all sorts present some of the greatest challenges to conservators. The problems are such that it is usually advisable to consult professionals with regard to restoring or cleaning rugs.

The appreciation of Caucasian tribal, village and nomadic weaving of the 19th century has enjoyed a revival over the past twenty years. When the rugs first appeared on the market in the late 19th and early 20th century they were not seriously collected; however they were inexepensive and, therefore, popular. By the 1930s these rugs were being thrown out in favour of the new broadloom carpeting. Today, we have come full circle to admire these vibrant Caucasian rugs once more.

Further reading:

Ulrich Schurmann, *Caucasian Rugs,* 1964
Ian Bennett, *Oriental Rugs, volume I, Caucasian,* 1981
Raoul Tschebull, *Kazak,* 1971
Charles Grant Ellis, *Early Caucasian Rugs,* 1975
Serare Yetkin, *Early Caucasian Carpets in Turkey,* 1978, 2 volumes

14

15

14
A Perpedil prayer rug, South Caucasus, third quarter 19th century, ivory *mehrab* of polychrome motifs beneath a brick prayer arch within a deep blue border, 158 × 124cm (62 × 49in), *NY 13 Dec,*
$4,400 (£3,143)

15
A Kuba rug, the indigo field with ivory and madder medallions, 185 × 115cm (6ft 1in × 3ft 9in), *L 2 June,*
£968 ($1,491)

1
A Beluch prayer rug, the chequered *mehrab* filled with camel and walnut squares, 158 x 108cm (5ft 2in x 3ft 6½in), *S 25 Mar,* **£363 ($555)**

2
A Beluch pictorial rug, with animals on an ivory ground and ivory *gul* border, 190 x 107cm (6ft 3in x 3ft 6in), *L 12 Feb,* **£330 ($492)**

3
A Beluch prayer rug, with camel field, 178 x 90cm (5ft 10in x 3ft), *L 30 July,* **£990 ($1,554)**

4
A Beluch carpet, the indigo field with rows of madder and camel flower heads, madder *dyrnak* border, 267 x 157cm (8ft 9in x 6ft 2in), *S 22 July,* **£990 ($1,554)**

5
An East Turkestan silk and metal thread carpet, with saffron field, 352 x 278cm (11ft 6½in x 9ft 1½in), *L 15 Oct,* **£3,630 ($5,082)**

6
An East Turkestan carpet, 19th century, the saffron field with indigo trellis, 305 x 214cm (10ft x 7ft), *L 16 Apr,* **£5,500 ($8,525)**

7
A Beshir rug, the indigo field, with madder *guls* and *botehs*, 261 x 150cm (8ft 7in x 4ft 11in), *L 16 Apr,* **£4,950 ($7,673)**

8
A Khotan carpet, c.1800, moth damage, 352 x 152cm (11ft 7in x 5ft), *NY 31 May,.* **$24,200 (£16,462)**

9
A Tekke carpet, 290 x 200cm (9ft 4in x 6ft 7in), *F 30 Sept,* **L 4,950,000 (£2,466; $3,453)**

1

2

3

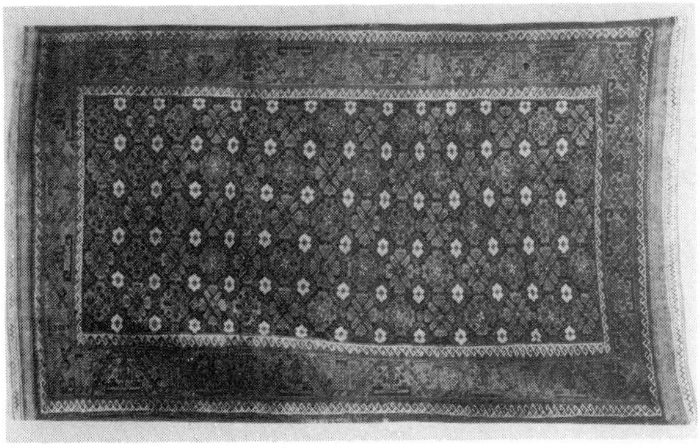
4

5

6

7

8

9

1

2

3

4

5

6

7

8

9

1
A Chador Bagface, late 19th century, reselvaged, 102 x 36cm (3ft 4in x 1ft 2in), *NY 13 Dec,*
$8,800 (£6,286)

2
A Chobash carpet, c.1800 the madder field with large *dyrnak* and *chobash guls* within ivory and vine border, 242 x 194cm (7ft 11in x 6ft 4in), *L 16 Apr,*
£2,310 ($3,580)

3
An Ersari juval, third quarter 19th century, with red, blue and ivory rhomboids framed by borders of yellow and red, reselvedged, 160 x 96cm (5ft 3in x 3ft 2in), *NY 13 Dec,*
$2,860 (£2,043)

4
A Yomut carpet, the madder field with rows of *tauk nuska guls*, interspersed with *dyrnak guls*, 267 x 147cm (8ft 9in x 4ft 10in), *L 15 Oct,*
£3,025 ($4,235)

5
A Bergama rug, the madder field with medallions, *guls*, and flowerheads, 183 x 175cm (6ft x 5ft 9in), *L 16 Apr,*
£3,850 ($5,968)

6
An Erzerum kilim prayer rug, late 19th century, the teal *mehrab* with polychrome honeycomb motifs, 193 x 122cm (6ft 4in x 4ft), *NY 13 Dec,*
$2,750 (£1,964)

7
A Bergama rug, late 19th century, the field woven with midnight blue and brick latchhooks, 239 x 178cm (7ft 10in x 5ft 10in), *NY 13 Dec,*
$4,400 (£3,143)

8
A Bergama rug, the madder field with *guls* in shades of ivory, madder and indigo, 108 x 103cm (3ft 6in x 3ft 5in), *L 12 Feb,*
£1,485 ($2,213)

9
A Bergama rug, late 19th century, with polychrome hexagons on a red surround, ivory border, 180 x 147cm (5ft 11in x 4ft 10in), *NY 13 Dec,*
$1,760 (£1,257)

1
A Ghiordes prayer rug, first half 19th century, 193 x 132cm (6ft 4in x 4ft 4in), *NY 31 May,*
$4,675 (£3,180)

2
A Ghiordes prayer rug, the ivory *mehrab* rising to an indigo vine arch, camel border, 160 x 132cm (5ft 3in x 4ft 4in), *S 16 Dec,*
£1,045 ($1,463)

3
A Kula prayer rug, c.1800, the cornflower blue *mehrab* of ivory and brown motifs, cream prayer arch topped by blue reserve of flower-heads, brick-speckled border, 175 x 135cm (5ft 9in x 4ft 5in), *NY 31 May,*
$6,270 (£4,265)

4
A Melas prayer rug, 147 x 106cm (4ft 10in x 3ft 6in), *NY 14 Oct,*
$2,860 (£1,986)

5
A Ladik prayer rug, first half 19th century, brick red *mehrab* beneath a cornflower blue arch, rust tulip and rosette border, 198 x 122cm (6ft 6in x 4ft), *NY 13 Dec,*
$3,300 (£2,357)

6
A white ground Ushak rug, 17th century, 188 x 122cm (6ft 2in x 4ft), *NY 31 May,*
$18,700 (£12,721)

7
An Ushak saph, late 17th/early 18th century, 447 x 297cm (14ft 8in x 9ft 9in), *NY 13 Dec,*
$16,500 (£11,786)

8
A Ladik prayer rug, early 19th century, 163 x 114cm (5ft 4in x 3ft 9in), *NY 31 May,*
$16,500 (£11,224)

1

2

3

4

5

6

7

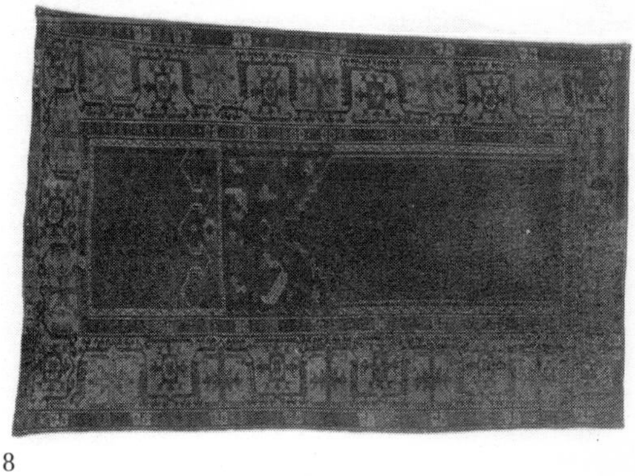
8

Indian, Himalayan and South-East Asian Art

1

2

3

4

5

6

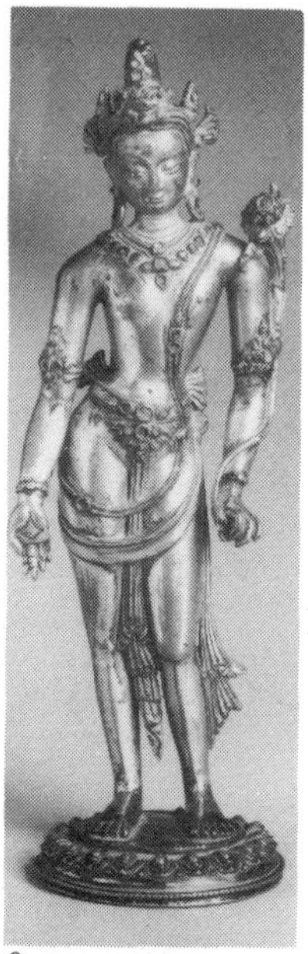
9

7

8

10

11

12

See also:
Colour illustrations *p* 561

1
A Sino-Tibetan gilt-bronze group of the Dharmapala Vajrabhairava in Yab-Yum with his Sakti, c.18th century, with 14 legs and 36 arms, his bull's head with the third eye and orange-pigmented hair and beard, with 8 further heads, resealed, 28cm (11in), *L 7 July,*
£2,530 ($4,099)

2
A Nepalese copper figure of Vasudhara, Goddess of Wealth, c.12th century, four of her six arms holding attributes, 13.5cm (5½in), *L 7 July,*
£1,210 ($1,960)

3
A Nepalese copper-gilt figure of Garuda, c.18th century, 11.5cm (4½in), *L 7 July,*
£1,760 ($2,851)

4
A Nepalese copper-gilt figure of the Saviouress Sitatara, the White Tara, c.18th century, with seven eyes, her chignon with traces of pigment, cast in two sections, unsealed, 20cm (8in), *L 10 Mar,*
£165 ($251)

5
A Nepalese bronze ritual dagger in the form of the God Phur-pa, 18th/19th century, with 30 arms and 36 heads, some animal-faced, arranged in 6 tiers, 39.5cm (15½in), *L 24 Nov,*
£715 ($1,015)

6
An Indian bronze figure of Virabhadra, 19th century, 39.5cm (15½in), *L 10 Mar,*
£220 ($334)

7
A South Indian bronze figure of Krishna, 16th/17th century, standing in a dancing position, 51cm (20in), *L 7 July,*
£6,820 ($11,048)

8
A South Indian brass figure of Durga slaying the buffalo-demon, c.18t century, the eight-armed goddess standing on top of the decapitated buffalo, 16.5cm (6½in), *L 7 July,*
£418 ($677)

9
A Nepalese copper-gilt figure of the Bodhisattva Padmapani, 13th/14th century, some semi-precious inlays remaining, unsealed, 31.5cm (12½in), *L 10 Mar,*
£9,900 ($15,048)

10
A South Indian bronze figure of Parvati, c.16th century, wearing a diaphanous floral robe, with greenish-brown patina, 62.5cm (24½in), *L 7 July,*
£14,850 ($24,057)

11
A Northern Indian bronz group depicting Lakshmi Narayana, c.15th century, with the seated figures of Vishnu and Lakshmi supported by a kneeling figure of Garuda on a lotus throne, 25.5cm (10in), *L 7 July,*
£572 ($927)

12
A South Indian bronze figure of Parvati, 12th/13th century, wearing extensive jewellery including a jewelled head-dress, with dark green patina, 57cm (22½in), *L 7 July,*
£6,820 ($11,048)

1
A Khmer bronze figure of Uma, Angkor Wat style, 12th/13th century, 20cm (8in), *L 7 July,*
£1,155 ($1,871)

2
A Thai bronze Buddha head, 15th/16th century, originally with inlaid eyes, with green patina and traces of gilding, 21cm (8¼in), *L 10 Mar,*
£605 ($920)

3
A Thai bronze figure of Buddha, Chen-Sen style, 15th/16th century, wearing a plain monastic robe, 22cm (8½in), *L 7 July,*
£1,210 ($1,960)

4
A Thai bronze figure of Buddha, Ayudhia style, c.17th century, the face originally with inlaid eyes, with dark greenish-brown patina, 35cm (13¾in), *L 10 Mar,*
£440 ($669)

5
A Tibetan copper-gilt figure of Buddha, 17th/18th century, the face with painted details, the base-plate with later incised inscription, 21cm (8¼in), *L 10 Mar,*
£660 ($1,003)

6
A Tibetan copper-gilt figure of Akshobya Buddha, 16th century, unsealed, 17cm (6¾in), *L 7 July,*
£440 ($713)

7
A Thai bronze figure of Buddha, Sukothai/Chen-Sen style, 15th/16th century, the whole with traces of gilding, the throne with traces of red paint, 72cm (28¼in), *L 24 Nov,*
£10,450 ($14,839)

8
A Sino-Tibetan gilt-bronze figure of Tsong-Kha-Pa, 1357-1419, 18th century, resealed, 25cm (10in), *L 10 Mar,*
£572 ($869)

9
A Sino-Tibetan gilt-bronze figure of the Saviouress Sitatara, the White Tara, 18th century, with some inset semi-precious jewels remaining, the face with three painted eyes, unsealed, 17cm (6¾in), *L 10 Mar,*
£770 ($1,170)

10
A Western Tibetan bronze figure of Vajradhara, 16th/17th century, the face with copper- and silver-inlaid eyes and copper-inlaid lips, 29cm (11½in), *L 24 Nov,*
£1,430 ($2,031)

11
A Western Tibetan bronze figure of Manjusri, 15th/16th century, the face and body with traces of cold-gilding, unsealed, 28.5cm (11¼in), *L 7 July,*
£1,540 ($2,495)

12
A Tibetan copper-gilt figure of a monk, c.18th century, with painted eyes, mouth and hair, sealed, 38.5cm (15in), *L 10 Mar,*
£3,300 ($5,016)

13
A Tibetan bronze figure of Buddha, 15th/16th century, with dark brown patina, resealed, 38cm (15in), *L 10 Mar,*
£1,980 ($3,010)

14
A Western Tibetan copper figure of Amitayus, 16th/17th century, unsealed, 14cm (5½in), *L 7 July,*
£352 ($570)

15
A Sino-Tibetan gilt-bronze figure of a Bodhisattva, 18th century, image and base separately cast, sealed, 18.5cm (7¼in), *L 24 Nov,*
£1,650 ($2,343)

16
A Sino-Tibetan figure of a warrior on horseback, 18th century, wearing elaborate armour, his hands poised to hold weapons, the face with painted details, sealed, 16.5cm (6½in), *L 24 Nov,*
£1,320 ($1,874)

1

2

3

4

5

6

7

8

9

10

11

12

13

14

15

16

1

2

3

4

5

9

7

6

8

10

11

12

1
A Gandhara grey schist figure of Buddha, 3rd/4th century, with areas of erosion, 38cm (15in), *L 10 Mar,*
£1,430 ($2,174)

2
A Gandhara grey schist figure of Maitreya Buddha, 3rd/4th century, flanked by two kneeling devotees, inscriptions on the halo, 51.5cm (20¼in), *L 7 July,*
£3,300 ($5,346)

3
A Gandhara grey schist figure of Buddha, 3rd/4th century, with light encrustation, 63.5cm (25in), *L 10 Mar,*
£3,300 ($5,016)

4
A Gandhara grey schist figure of a Bodhisattva, 3rd/4th century, flanked by a headless attendant, 23.5cm (9¼in), *L 7 July,*
£242 ($392)

5
A Gandhara grey schist figure of Buddha, Swat style, 3rd/4th century, 26.5cm (10½in), *L 7 July,*
£572 ($927)

6
A small Gandhara grey schist head of a Bodhisattva, 3rd/4th century, 11cm (4¼in), *L 10 Mar,*
£550 ($836)

7
A South Indian granite figure of Daksinamurti Siva, Chola, 12th/13th century, 72.5cm (28½in), *L 7 July,*
£16,500 ($26,730)

8
A South Indian black granite head of a Buddha, 12th/13th century, the tip of the nose damaged, 20cm (8in), *L 10 Mar,*
£1,320 ($2,006)

9
An Eastern Indian dark grey stone stele depicting Vishnu, Pala, 11th/12th century, the four-armed God standing on a lotus throne supported by a winged figure of Garuda, flanked by three devotees, 97.5cm (38½in), *L 7 July,*
£5,500 ($8,910)

10
A Western Indian pink sandstone figure of Krishna, 12th century, with four arms, holding the flute, 45cm (17¾in), *L 10 Mar,*
£935 ($1,421)

11
A Thai red sandstone Buddha head, 16th century, the chignon now defaced, 35.5cm (14in), *L 7 July,*
£374 ($606)

12
A Khmer buff sandstone figure of Buddha, Bayon style, 12th/13th century, 72.5cm (28½in), *L 7 July,*
£5,720 ($9,266)

1
A Mughal red sandstone arched Jali screen, Agra, c.17th century, with some whitish incrustation, 73.5cm (29in), *L 24 Nov,*
£990 ($1,406)

2
A Mughal red sandstone fragmentary Jali screen, 17th/18th century, originally forming an arch, 92.5cm (36½in), *L 7 July,*
£330 ($535)

3
A Mughal red sandstone panel, c.18th century, 45.5cm (18in), *L 7 July,*
£352 ($570)

4
A Mughal red sandstone elephant from a railing, 17th/18th century, with two headless *mahouts* on his back, 46cm (18¼in), *L 24 Nov,*
£1,012 ($1,437)

5
A Rajasthan polychrome-painted marble bench panel, 18th/19th century, 53.5cm (21in), *L 7 July,*
£352 ($570)

6
Two Indian white marble carpet-weights, 18th/19th century, a rosette carved in relief on the top, 23cm (9in) each, *L 11 Mar,*
£220 ($332)

7
An Indian white marble fountain, 19th century or later, 87cm (34¼in), *L 7 July,*
£385 ($624)

8
An Indian white marble bench, 122cm (48in) wide, *L 7 July,*
£2,860 ($4,633)

9
A Rajasthan white marble panel, 18th/19th century, with a central sunburst representing Surya the Sun-God, flanked by two female figures scattering lotus petals on his rays, 59cm (23¼in) wide, *L 11 Mar,*
£935 ($1,412)

10
An Indian white marble bench, 97.5cm (38½in) wide, *L 7 July,*
£990 ($1,604)

11
A Rajasthan white marble relief, Jaipur, 19th century, 69cm (27¼in), *L 11 Mar,*
£385 ($581)

12
A Western Indian marble figure of Ganesha, 19th century, 42.5cm (16¾in), *L 11 Mar,*
£550 ($830)

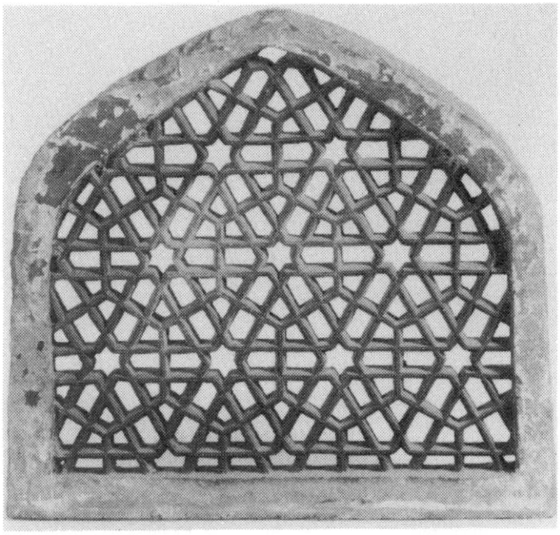
1

2

3

4

7

5

6

8

9

10

11

12

1

2

3

4

5

6

7

8

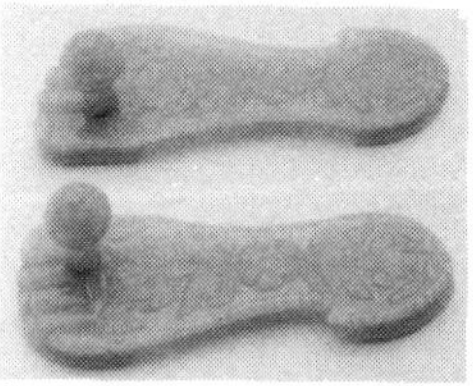
9

10

11

12

1
An Indian white marble figure of a deer, 19th century, 42.5cm (16¾in), *L 7 July,*
£550 ($891)

2
A pair of Indian painted wood horses, 18th/19th century, with traces of red and beige paint throughout, 63.5cm (25in), *L 7 July,*
£990 ($1,604)

3
An Indian wood figure of a lion, 19th century, with traces of original white and red paint, iron tail, 107cm (42in), *L 7 July,*
£1,155 ($1,871)

4
A pair of Gujarat painted wood elephants, wearing orange and green blankets, 52cm (20½in), *L 24 Nov,*
£770 ($1,093)

5
An Indian painted wood figure of a tiger, 19th century or later, painted to simulate its striped coat, 64cm (25in), *L 7 July,*
£825 ($1,337)

6
Two Rajasthan sheet-silver lions, 20th century, 39 and 33cm (15¼ and 13in), *L 24 Nov,*
£1,210 ($1,718)

7
An Indian sheet-silver figure of a guardian lion, 59.5cm (23½in), *L 7 July,*
£1,540 ($2,495)

8
An Indian brass figure of a Nandi bull, 18th/19th century, seated on a rectangular throne with lobed edge, a *lingam* beside his right foreleg, 15cm (6in), *L 10 Mar,*
£385 ($585)

9
A pair of miniature Indian jade sandals, 19th century, of pale green jade, each toe-grip in the form of a lotus bud, 12cm (4¾in), *L 11 Mar,*
£352 ($531)

10
A Mughal green jade bowl, late 18th/early 19th century, the boat-shaped body with duck's head finial with ruby and gold inlaid eyes at either end, 22cm (8½in) diam., *L 7 July,*
£5,500 ($8,910)

11
A pair of Rajasthan ivory figures, 18th/19th century, depicting a male and female figure, each wearing courtly robes and extensive jewellery, with traces of polychrome, 17 and 18cm (6¾ and 7in), *L 7 July,*
£770 ($1,247)

12
Two Indian ivory miniature groups depicting Europeans, probably Bengal, mid 19th century, the larger depicting a strolling lady and gentleman; the smaller on an oval base painted in blue and gold to resemble a carpet, carved with an Englishman seated on a Regency-style chair holding a coiled *huqqa*-snake in his hand, next to a servant carrying a bottle, 8 and 6.5cm (3 and 2½in), *L 24 Nov,*
£715 ($1,015)

1
A Mughal rock-crystal cup, 18th century, crack, 8cm (3in), *L 24 Nov,*
£1,760 ($2,499)

2
A South Indian bronze bowl, the ridged sides with two lizards and other decoration in relief, 94.5cm (37¼in) diam., *L 24 Nov,*
£770 ($1,093)

3
A South Indian gold bracelet, Toda, 7.5cm (3in) diam., *L 24 Nov,*
£1,650 ($2,343)

4
A Mughal gold-inlaid jade dagger-hilt, c.18th century, of pale grey colour, with lion's head pommel, set with stones including rubies and an aquamarine, slight damage, 12cm (4¾in), *L 24 Nov,*
£1,100 ($1,562)

5
A Mughal jade-hilted dagger, c.18th century, the pale green hilt with camel's head pommel, the eyes with gold inlay, 36cm (14in), *L 24 Nov,*
£440 ($625)

6
A pair of Indian silver-gilt rosewater sprinklers ***(one illustrated)*****,** late 19th century, decorated with filigree embellished with blue and green enamelled foliage, the sprinkler in the form of a bunch of flowers, 28cm (11in), *L 7 July,*
£605 ($980)

7
A Tibetan silver butter-lamp, 19th century, 25cm (9¾in), *L 7 July,*
£330 ($535)

8
An Indian silver parcel-gilt plate, 18th/19th century, 30cm (12in) diam., *L 11 Mar,*
£385 ($581)

9
An Indian silver begging-bowl, 19th century, 18cm (7in), *L 24 Nov,*
£440 ($625)

10
A set of 24 pieces of Indian silver, early 20th century, comprising 12 bowls and 12 plates, the body of each decorated with scrolling foliage, plates 18.5cm (7½in) diam., *L 11 Mar,*
£1,100 ($1,661)

11
An Indian silver huqqa, 19th century, the lower section in the form of a stylised bird, 41cm (16in), *L 11 Mar,*
£550 ($830)

12
An Indian painted marble huqqa-bottle, 19th century, painted with medallions, the body with a blue ground and the neck with a red ground, 15cm (6in), *L 11 Mar,*
£330 ($498)

13
An Indian Bidri huqqa-bottle, c.18th century, decorated with silver-inlaid flowering plants, 16cm (6¼in), *L 7 July,*
£605 ($980)

14
An Indian Bidri huqqa-bottle, late 18th century, decorated with silver inlaid trees, 17cm (6½in), *L 7 July,*
£330 ($535)

15
An Indian copper and silver-mounted huqqa base, 19th century, 20.5cm (8in), *L 11 Mar,*
£275 ($415)

16
A Mughal Bidri huqqa-bottle, c.18th century, decorated with silver inlaid fan-shaped plants, 18cm (7in), *L 7 July,*
£462 ($748)

17
An Indian woven ivory fan, 19th century, the handle with bud finials, the fan section of green and plain ivory banding interwoven with silver, 36.5cm (14½in), *L 24 Nov,*
£462 ($656)

1

2

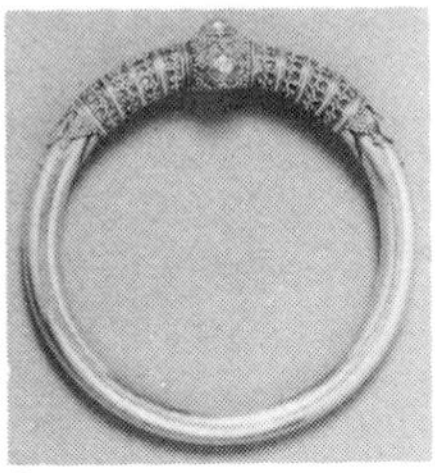
3

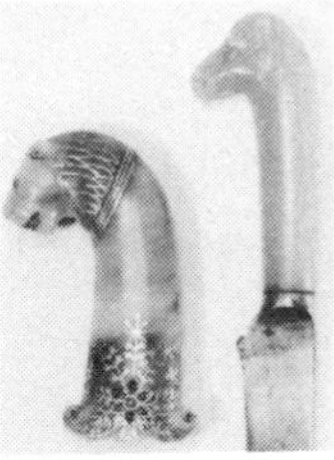
4 5

6

7

8

9

10

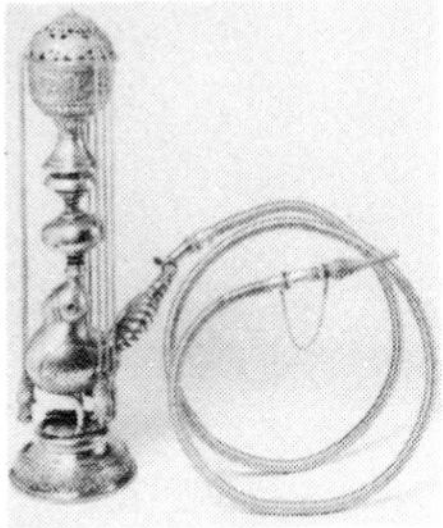
11

15

12

13

14

16

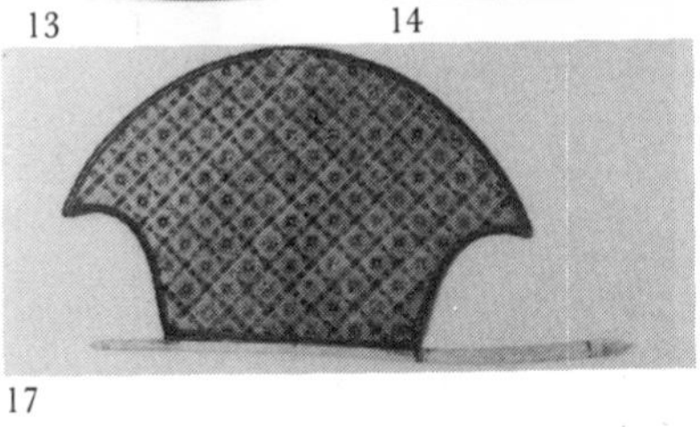
17

1

2

3

4

5

6

7

8

9

10

11

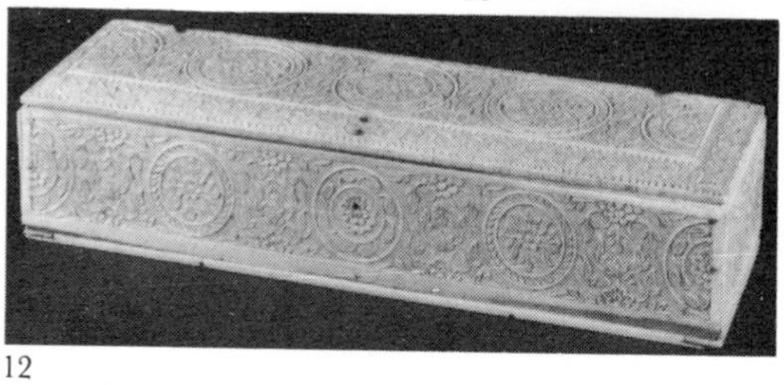
12

1
An Indian metal chest on wheels, decorated with small copper panels depicting stylised birds and animals alternating with cross-hatched panels, 112cm (44in) wide, *L 11 Mar,*
£660 ($997)

2
A Mughal ivory inlaid wood box, 18th century, copper-gilt mounts, 28.5cm (11¼in) wide, *L 7 July,*
£1,320 ($2,138)

3
An Indian ivory-inlaid wood box, the edges banded in brass, 46.5cm (18¼in) wide, *L 24 Nov,*
£462 ($656)

4
An Indian ivory-inlaid wood dressing-box, early 20th century, standing on four low feet, inlaid with two peacocks on the front, banded in brass at the corners, the interior with drawers and a mirror, 46cm (18in) wide, *L 11 Mar,*
£440 ($664)

5
A Kashmir polychrome-lacquered table, c.1900, the whole with a slightly raised decoration of flowering plants in pink, white, green, orange and blue, with black and gilt outlines, 72cm (28¼in) diam., *L 11 Mar,*
£660 ($997)

6
A South Indian sandal-wood casket, probably Mysore, 19th century, standing on four feet in the form of birds, the sides depicting tigers, deer, peacocks, leopards and snakes, the top with a male deity, 32cm (12½in), *L 11 Mar,*
£440 ($664)

7
An Indian sarcophagus-shaped casket, early 19th century, standing on four bracket feet, profusely decorated with 'koftgari' work, 13.5cm (5½in), *L 11 Mar,*
£154 ($232)

8
An Indian carved wood planter's chair, 19th century, the seat of matted cane, the arms with sliding extensions to support the feet, 91.5cm (36in), *L 11 Mar,*
£440 ($664)

9
An Indian ivory-inlaid wood letter-cabinet, the sides inlaid with hunting scenes, the front with floral inlaid roll-top, 45cm (17¾in), *L 24 Nov,*
£440 ($625)

10
An Indian ivory-inlaid folding wood chair, the arms with lion-head finials, the back in the form of two peacocks flanking a flowering plant, 95cm (37½in), *L 24 Nov,*
£330 ($469)

11
An Indian ivory and wood cabinet, c.1800, gilt-metal mounts, 30.5cm (12in) wide, *L 24 Nov,*
£440 ($625)

12
An Indian ivory pen-box, 18th/19th century, carved with floral medallions flanked by flowering plants, silver hinges, 24cm (9½in) long, *L 11 Mar,*
£220 ($332)

Japanese Works of Art

Article:
Netsuke *pp* 673-677
See also:
Colour illustrations *pp* 574-576

Early Muromachi	1331-1393
Middle Muromachi	1393-1467
Late Muromachi	1467-1573
Momoyama	1573-1615
Early Edo	1615-1688
Middle Edo	1688-1803
Late Edo	1803-1868
Meiji	1868-1912
Taisho	1912-1926
Showa	1926-

1
An Imari charger, late 17th century, decorated in underglaze-blue, iron-red and gilding, 54cm (21¼in), *L 13 Mar,*
£2,200 ($3,388)

2
An Imari dish, c.1700, 29cm (11½in), *C 29 Apr,*
£176 ($285)

3
An Imari barber's bowl, late 17th century, decorated in underglaze-blue, iron-red and gilding, the rim with roundels of buildings and landscape, 33.5cm (13in), *L 13 Mar,*
£660 ($1,016)

4
An Imari part-garniture, late 17th/early 18th century, comprising two jars and covers and a beaker vase, decorated in underglaze-blue, iron-red, enamels and gilding, some damage, 65.5cm (25¾in), *L 13 Mar,*
£3,080 ($4,743)

5
A pair of Imari covered vases, late 17th century, painted in typical palette with gilt highlights with plum branches, rocks and flowers, chip, 68.5cm (27in), *NY 24 Sept,*
$7,425 (£5,304)

6
A set of three Imari vases and covers, *(two illustrated),* late 17th/early 18th century, decorated in underglaze-blue, iron-red, enamels and gilding, with a continuous band of butterflies and *ho-o* among peonies, and with *shishi* knops, one restored, 49cm (19¼in), *L 14 Nov,*
£7,150 ($10,010)

7
An Imari bowl, early 18th century, painted in turquoise, iron-red, gilding, yellow and aubergine enamels over underglaze-blue, chip, 25cm (9¾in), *S 22 Jan,*
£380 ($570)

8
An Imari tokuri, early 18th century, decorated in underglaze-blue, iron-red, enamels and gilding with panels of cranes and *shishi*, 20cm (8in), *L 13 Mar,*
£990 ($1,525)

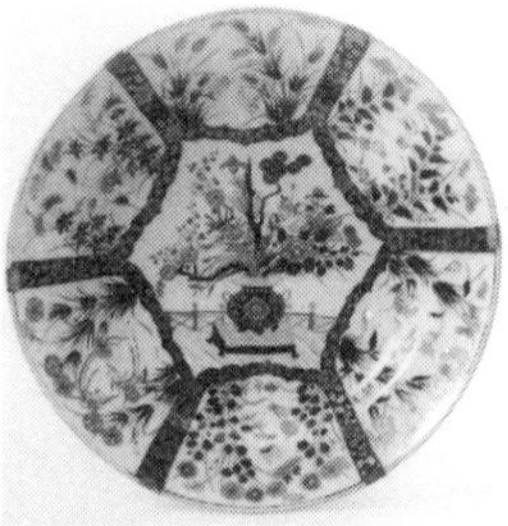
1

2

3

4

5

6

7

8

1

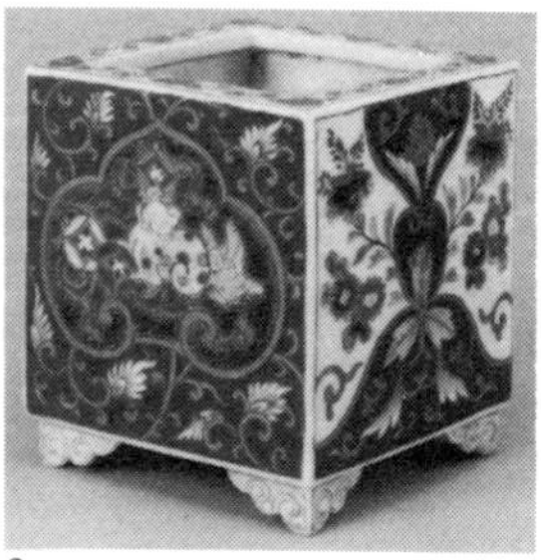
2

3

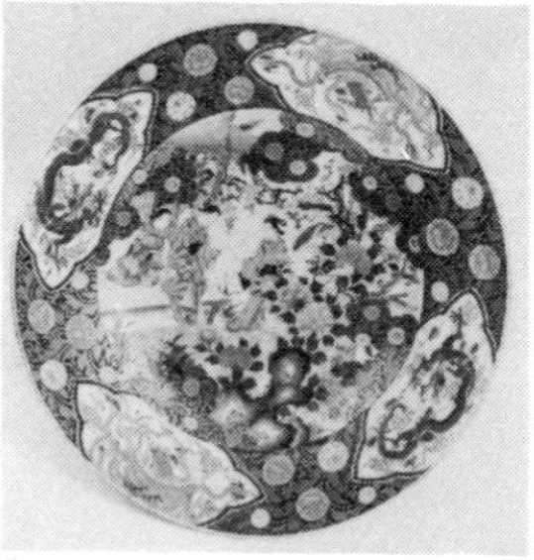
4

5

8

9

6

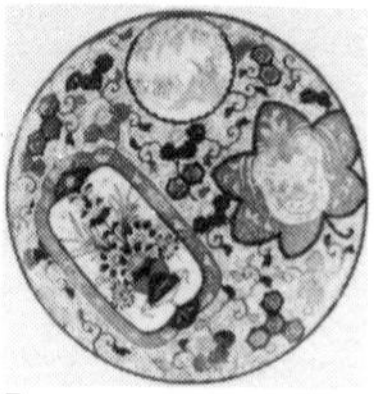
7

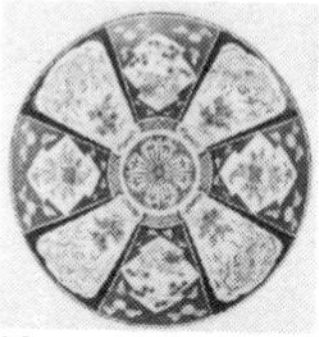
10

11

12

13

14

15

1
An Imari figure of a man, late 17th/early 18th century, enamelled in iron-red, aubergine, turquoise, and underglaze-blue, firing crack, 34.5cm (13½in), *S 22 Jan,*
£1,800 ($2,700)

2
An Arita censer, late 18th/early 19th century, decorated in iron-red, enamels and gilding with panels of *shishi* and floral designs, 8cm (3¼in), *L 13 Mar,*
£495 ($762)

3
An Imari dish, 19th century, of chrysanthemum form, painted *Fuku* mark, 31.5cm (12½in), *Mel 24 June,*
Aus$605 (£263; $410)

4
An Imari charger, Meiji period, painted in underglaze-blue, iron-red, yellow, green, aubergine, black and gilding with three maidens in front of a house, iris and chrysanthemum spray mark, 61.5cm (24¼in), *S 22 Jan,*
£1,700 ($2,550)

5
An Imari charger, Meiji period, decorated with *bijin* outside a pavilion, six character Chenghua mark, 51cm (20in), *C 16 Apr,*
£385 ($597)

6
An Imari dish, Meiji period, painted with panels of eagles superimposed by *mon* and gourds, 46cm (18in), *S 10 Apr,*
£121 ($188)

7
An Imari dish, Meiji period, the brocade ground with three panels of dragons, flowers and crane, 47cm (18½in), *S 10 Apr,*
£242 ($375)

8
An Imari vase, Meiji period, decorated in underglaze-blue, iron-red and gilt with panels of *ho-o* amongst flowering prunus, 107.5cm (42½in), *L 13 Mar,*
£4,180 ($6,437)

9
An Imari vase, Meiji period, the body with panels of birds, precious objects and flowers, 45.5cm (18in), *C 16 Apr,*
£418 ($648)

10
An Imari dish, Meiji period, with panels of *ho-o,* pine and pomegranate, 46.5cm (18¼in), *S 10 Apr,*
£121 ($188)

11
An Imari jardinière, late 19th century, painted with landscape reserves on a floral ground, 38cm (15in) diam., *NY 24 Sept,*
$1,650 (£1,179)

12
An Imari vase, cover and stand, Meiji period, decorated with foliage between ornamental borders, *shishi* finial, stand riveted, 59cm (23¼in), *S 21 May,*
£605 ($968)

13
An Imari vase, Meiji period, decorated with panels of shrubs on a diaper ground, rubbed, 68.5cm (23in), *C 16 Apr,*
£275 ($426)

14
An Imari jardinière, 20th century, decorated in underglaze-blue, iron-red, enamels and gilding with panels of dragons, *ho-o* and birds among flowers, 62cm (24½in), on a wood stand, *L 14 Nov,*
£2,090 ($2,926)

15
An Imari figure of a bijin, late 19th century, decorated in underglaze-blue, iron-red, enamels and gilding, 46.5cm (18½in), *L 13 Mar,*
£638 ($982)

1
An Arita V.O.C. dish, 1660-80, decorated in underglaze-blue, 38.5cm (15¼in), *A 12 May,*
Dfl 24,150 (£7,230; $11,713)

V.O.C. refers to Vereenigde Oostindische Companie (Dutch East India Company).

2
An Arita V.O.C. dish, second half 17th century, decorated in underglaze-blue. See note to no.1 above. 36cm (14in), *L 13 June,*
£4,400 ($7,040)

3
An Arita V.O.C. dish, 1660-80, painted in underglaze-blue. See note to no.1 above. 21.5cm (8½in), *NY 31 Jan,*
$2,640 (£1,872)

The difference in price between these three very similar dishes, all in good condition, is that no.1 is of good colour, no.2 is more greyish in colour, and no.3 is very much smaller.

4
An Arita blue and white apothecary's bottle, late 17th century, decorated with bands of scrolling flowers, 25cm (9¾in), *L 13 Mar,*
£1,980 ($3,049)

5
An Arita vase, third quarter 17th century, decorated in underglaze-blue with groups of three figures in a garden, 29cm (11½in), *L 13 June,*
£770 ($1,232)

6
An Arita apothecary's bottle, late 17th century, decorated in underglaze-blue with groups of peony, *kiku* and prunus, 34cm (11½in), *L 13 June,*
£4,180 ($6,688)

7
An Arita bowl, late 17th/early 18th century, decorated in underglaze-blue with a spray of peonies bordered by a band of *kiku*, six character mark *Jaiqing*, 28.5cm (11in), *L 13 June,*
£550 ($880)

8
An Arita dish, second half 17th century, decorated in underglaze-blue in *Wanli* style, 45.5cm (18in), *L 14 Nov,*
£990 ($1,386)

9
A set of three Arita vases and covers, *(two illustrated)*, late 17th/early 18th century, each decorated in underglaze-blue with a continuous band of figures in a landscape, two knops restored, minor chips, 48cm (19in), *L 13 Mar,*
£3,850 ($5,929)

10
A pair of Arita ewers, *(one illustrated)*, late 17th century, painted in underglaze-blue with panels of flowers, slight crack, 26.5cm (10½in), *C 15 Jan,*
£715 ($1,073)

11
An Arita vase and cover, late 17th century, painted in underglaze-blue with *ho-o* amongst peonies, chip, 50cm (19¾in), *C 15 Jan,*
£1,067 ($1,601)

12
An Arita jar, late 17th century, decorated in underglaze-blue with two panels of stylised *ho-o* separated by a formal bouquet of flowers, crack, 40cm (16in), *L 14 Nov,*
£1,870 ($2,618)

13
An Arita bowl and cover, late 17th century, decorated in underglaze-blue with a continuous band of plants among rocks, crack and chip, 32.5cm (12¾in), *L 13 June,*
£1,540 ($2,464)

14
An Arita vase, third quarter 17th century, decorated in underglaze-blue with figures in a garden, 21.5cm (8½in), *L 13 Mar,*
£935 ($1,440)

1

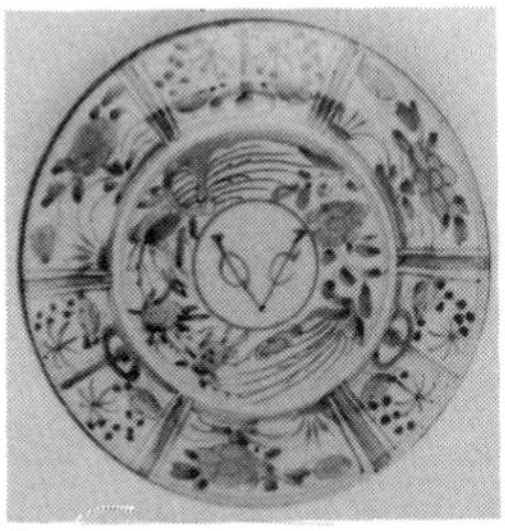
2

3

4

5 6

7

8

9

10

11

12

13

14

1

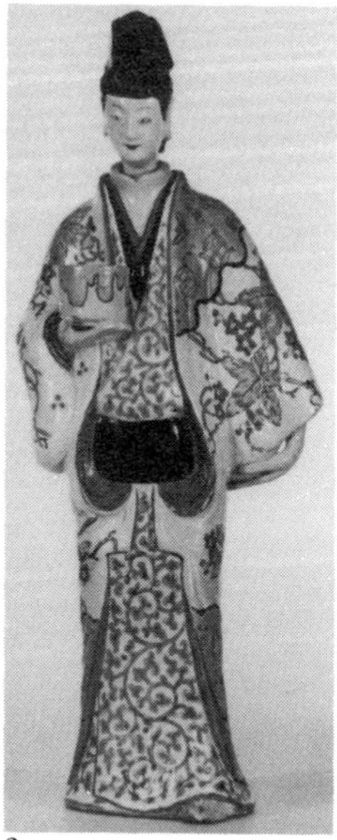
2

3

4

5

6

7

8

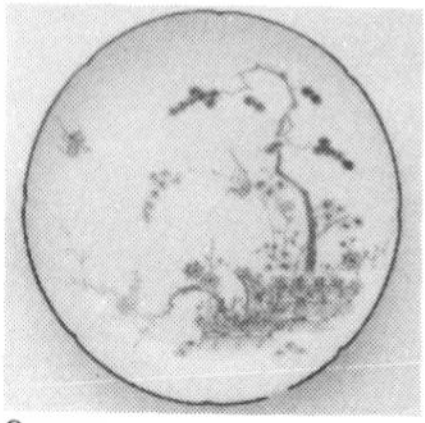
9

10

1
A Kakiemon figure of a bijin, late 17th century, her kimono decorated in iron-red, blue, green and yellow enamels, 39.5cm (15½in), *L 14 Nov,*
£26,400 ($36,960)

2
A Kakiemon figure of a bijin, late 17th century, with a bowl in her right hand, 43cm (17in), *A 12 May,*
Dfl 7,050 (£2,111; $3,419)

3
A Kakiemon jar, second half 17th century, decorated in iron-red and blue, green, brown and yellow enamels with various birds among flowering shrubs, the neck with jewels, crack, lacking cover, 27.5cm (10¾in), *L 13 Mar,*
£15,400 ($23,716)

4
A Kakiemon-style bottle, third quarter 17th century, decorated in iron-red and brilliant green, blue and yellow enamels with a band of continuous landscape, 24.5cm (9½in), *L 13 Mar,*
£14,300 ($22,022)

5
An Arita bottle, second half 17th century, painted in *Ko-Kutani* style in iron-red and blue, green, aubergine, yellow and black enamels with a pair of finches, some glaze cracks and rubbing, 27cm (10¾in), *L 13 Mar,*
£7,700 ($11,858)

6
A pair of Kakiemon vases, *(one illustrated),* third quarter 17th century, decorated in iron-red and blue, green and yellow enamels with a continuous band showing a *ho-o* on a branch of peony, both damaged, 28.5cm (11¼in), *L 13 Mar,*
£5,280 ($8,131)

7
A Kakiemon-style bowl, 18th century, of petal-lobed form, the exterior decorated in underglaze-blue, the interior painted in iron-red and yellow, green, blue and aubergine enamels with flowering shrubs, chips, 24cm (9½in), *L 14 Nov,*
£2,200 ($3,080)

8
A large Kakiemon-style dish, early 18th century, decorated in underglaze-blue, iron-red and blue, green, yellow and aubergine enamels with a flower cart on a *manji*-diaper ground, repaired, 53.5cm (21in), *L 13 June,*
£2,640 ($4,224)

9
A Kakiemon dish, late 17th century, decorated in iron-red, enamels and touches of gilding with two birds among pine, prunus and bamboo, 22cm (8½in), *L 13 June,*
£1,540 ($2,464)

10
A Kakiemon dish, second half 17th century, decorated in iron-red and brilliant green, blue and yellow enamels with a central panel depicting pavilions in a lakeside scene, 31.5cm (12½in), *L 13 June,*
£15,400 ($24,640)

Bijin beautiful girl.

Eboshi court hat.

Ho-o phoenix.

Hossu fly-switch

Oni demon.

Oshirorie Chinese or mandarin ducks.

Minogame 'hairy-tailed' turtle, symbol of long life.

Sarumawashi monkey trainer.

Shi-shi lion dog.

Takarabune treasure ship of the Seven Gods of Good Fortune.

1
A Kutani fish bowl, Meiji period, decorated in coloured enamels and gilding with panels of waterfowl, signed, 59.5cm (23½in), *C 15 Jan,*
£1,705 ($2,558)

2
Setsuzando: a pair of Kutani vases, Meiji period, each painted and gilt with numerous animals, with birds flying overhead, signed, 46cm (18in), *L 13 Mar,*
£1,650 ($2,541)

3
A Kutani dish, c.1880, each lobe with a brocade design in iron-red and gilding, and with *shishi* panel centre, 34.5cm (13½in), *S 22 Jan,*
£520 ($780)

4
A Kutani vase, c.1920s, decorated with a band of warriors brandishing spears on a gilt ground, 36.5cm (14¼in), *Mel 24 June,*
Aus$550 (£239; $373)

5
A Hirado bottle, first half 19th century, painted in underglaze-blue with three *karako* chasing butterflies, colour slightly smoked, 21.5cm (8½in), *L 13 June,*
£660 ($1,056)

6
A pair of Hirado beaker vases, *(one illustrated)*, Meiji period, decorated in underglaze-blue with boys pursuing butterflies beneath a pine tree, 23cm (9in), *L 14 Nov,*
£495 ($693)

7
A Hirado koro and cover, mid 19th century, decorated in underglaze-blue with *karako* among plants, 8cm (3in), *L 13 June,*
£440 ($704)

8
A porcelain vase, 19th century, probably Hirado, moulded with terrapins swimming through the eddies of a pond, washed in unglazed iron oxide, hair crack, 30.5cm (12in), *S 21 May,*
£220 ($352)

9
A polychrome vase, Meiji period, decorated on an iron-red ground with two pheasants among prunus and peonies, one crack, 92cm (36¼in), *L 13 Mar,*
£880 ($1,355)

10
A porcelain charger, Meiji period, painted in polychrome with a group of seven sages and a boy dressed in blue, green and pink robes, 77.5cm (33½in), *S 5 June,*
£1,210 ($1,875)

11
Makuzu Kozan: a porcelain vase, Meiji period, decorated in underglaze-green and mauve with wistaria, signed, 35cm (13¾in), *L 14 Nov,*
£1,650 ($2,310)

12
Makuzu Kozan: a porcelain vase, Meiji period, decorated in underglaze-blue, green, brown and red with two pigeons in flight beneath willow branches, slight glaze crack, signed, 36.5cm (14¼in), *L 13 Mar,*
£1,210 ($1,863)

13
A blue and white vase, Meiji period, painted with shaped reserves containing *shishi* playing with floral balls, 91.5cm (36in), *NY 24 Sept,*
$1,650 (£1,179)

1

2

3

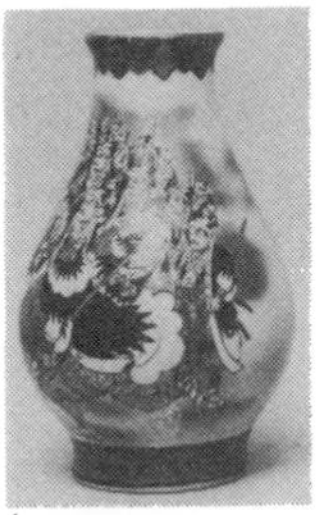
4

5

6

7

10

8

9

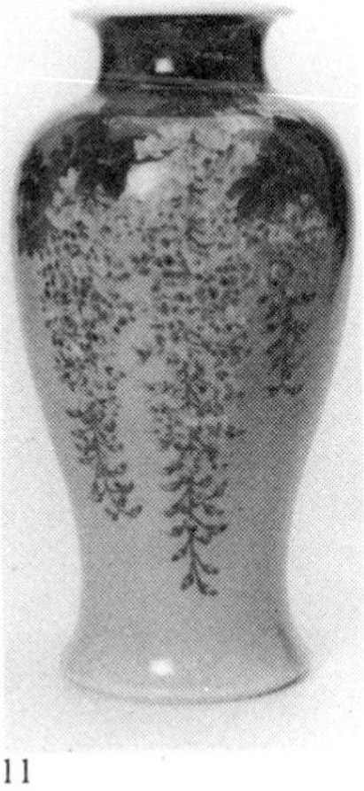
11

12

13

1

2

3

4

5

6

7

8

9

10

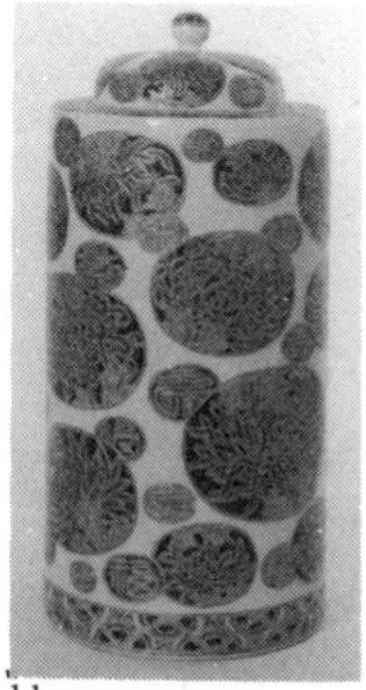
11

12

13

14

1
Meigado Kizan: a Satsuma jar and cover, late Edo period, enamelled and gilt with chrysanthemum, irises and flowering grasses, signed, 14cm (5½in), *L 13 Mar,*
£1,320 ($2,033)

2
A Satsuma tokuri, first half 19th century, decorated in iron-red, enamels and gilding with sprays of *kiku* on bands of diaper ground, 14cm (5½in), *L 13 June,*
£990 ($1,584)

3
A Satsuma teapot, mid 19th century, enamelled and gilt with chrysanthemum, with dragon-form spout and handle, signed, 16.5cm (6½in), *NY 24 Sept,*
$880 (£629)

4
A Satsuma earthenware koro, 19th century, decorated in enamels and gilding with panels showing a bird on a prunus branch, 9.5cm (3½in), *L 14 Nov,*
£1,100 ($1,540)

5
Meibido: a Satsuma earthenware koro and cover, Meiji period, painted with panels of deities with attendants and *ho-o,* signed, 12cm (4¾in), *L 13 Mar,*
£880 ($1,355)

6
Hododa: a pair of Satsuma earthenware vases and covers on stands, *(one illustrated),* mid 19th century, enamelled and gilt with flower arrangements, signed, 43cm (17in), *NY 24 Sept,*
$6,325 (£4,518)

7
Yasui: a pair of Satsuma earthenware vases, *(one illustrated),* Meiji period, painted and gilt with a carnival procession of figures, signed, 40.5cm (16in), *L 13 June,*
£1,100 ($1,760)

8
Kizan: a Satsuma earthe ware vase, Meiji period, painted with a procession of figures holding ropes attached to a large ceremonial carriage, signed, 19cm (7½in), *L 13 Mar,*
£770 ($1,186)

9
A Satsuma earthenware vase, Meiji period, painte with courtesans at leisure in a wooded landscape, signed, minor rubbing, 26cm (10¼in), *C 16 Apr,*
£440 ($682)

10
Shokuzan: a Satsuma earthenware bowl, Meiji period, decorated in thick blue enamel and gilt with roundels incorporating *kiku* and *kirimon,* signed, 22cm (8½in), *L 14 Nov,*
£880 ($1,232)

11
Tawara Koseki Toshimi su: a Satsuma earthenware jar and cover, Meij period, enamelled and gilt with roundels of *kiku* and calligraphy, hairline crack signed, 22.5cm (8¾in), *L 14 Nov,*
£1,045 ($1,463)

12
A Satsuma figure of Hotei, Meiji period, sligh repairs, 25cm (9¾in), *L 14 Nov,*
£660 ($924)

13
A Satsuma vase, Meiji period, intricately enamelled and gilt with a series of eight figure, bird and flower panels, 37cm (14½in), *S 21 May,*
£715 ($1,144)

14
Toyoyama: a Satsuma earthenware vase, Meiji period, decorated with morning glory and *kiku* entwined round a rush fence, crack, signed, 42.5cm (16¾in), *L 13 June,*
£715 ($1,144)

okozan: a Satsuma arthenware moon flask, leiji period, boldly ecorated in coloured namels and gilt, signed, 9cm (15¼in), *L 14 Nov,* **2,750 ($3,850)**

pair of Satsuma vases, *one illustrated),* painted with torks in flight on a blue round, the necks with ands of gilt and red, 0.5cm (12in), *C 11 Feb,* **275 ($410)**

Kinkozan: an earthenware ase, Meiji period, painted vith panels of two young vomen on a lake shore, ubbed signature, 24.5cm 9½in), *L 14 Nov,* **770 ($1,078)**

Kinkozan: an earthenware ase, Meiji period, each ide enamelled and gilded vith *bijin,* warriors and mmortals, some wear, igned, 24cm (9½in), *VY 24 Sept,* **$880 (£629)**

Kinkozan: an earthenware ase, Meiji period, painted vith panels of *bijin* and hildren, slight rubbing, igned, 20cm (8in), *C 9 July,* **£440 ($686)**

Kinkozan: an earthenware bottle, Meiji period, painted with a continuous scene of a rooster and hen among peonies and cherry trees, gilt borders, signed, 11.5cm (4½in), *NY 24 Sept,* **$1,045 (£746)**

7
Kinkozan: a vase, Meiji period, enamelled with a continuous scene of ladies in a garden, signed, 25.5cm (10in), *NY 24 Sept,* **$880 (£629)**

8
Kinkozan: an earthenware koro, Meiji period, painted with a procession of figures accompanying a nobleman on horseback, added silver cover, signed, 9.5cm (3¾in), *L 14 Nov,* **£1,320 ($1,848)**

9
Kinkozan: an earthenware koro and cover, Meiji period, painted with panels of figures picnicking, signed, 19cm (7½in), *L 13 Mar,* **£880 ($1,355)**

10
Kinkozan: an earthenware bottle, Meiji period, decorated with two fan-shaped panels, one showing a girl with chickens in a garden, drawn in coloured enamels and gilding, signed, 11.5cm (4½in), *L 13 June,* **£2,090 ($3,344)**

11
Kinkozan: an earthenware koro and cover, mid 19th century, enamelled and gilded with scholars and immortals, signed, 42cm (16½in), *NY 24 Sept,* **$2,200 (£1,571)**

12
Hankinzan: an earthenware bowl, Meiji period, decorated in coloured enamels and gilding with panels of figures at various domestic pursuits, signed, 12.5cm (5in), *L 13 Mar,* **£2,090 ($3,219)**

13
Kizan: an earthenware vase, Meiji period, painted and gilt with a travelling entertainer blowing up balloons for children, signed, 24.5cm (9½in), *L 13 Mar,* **£770 ($1,186)**

1

2

3

4

5

6

7

8

9

10

11

12

13

1

2

3

4

5

6

7

8

9

10

11

12

13

1
Kinkozan: an earthenware vase, Meiji period, enamelled and gilded with two heart-shaped reserves, one depicting *bijin* and children, the other *samurai*, signed, 40.5cm (16in), *NY 24 Sept,*
$5,500 (£3,929)

2
Meizan: a pair of earthenware vases, *(one illustrated)*, Meiji period, painted with bands of numerous figures, including immortals and attendants, signed, 12.5cm (5in), *L 13 June,*
£1,430 ($2,288)

3
Yabu Meizan: an earthenware koro, Meiji period, painted with chrysanthemum, silver cover, signed, 7cm (2¾in), *L 13 Mar,*
£495 ($762)

4
Ryozan: an earthenware beaker vase, Meiji period, painted and gilt with figures walking in a garden, signed, 15.5cm (6in), *L 13 Mar,*
£308 ($474)

5
Ryozan: a jar and cover, Meiji period, decorated in colours and gilding with panels of birds amongst flowers and figures in landscapes, signed, 15.5cm (6in), *C 16 Apr,*
£550 ($853)

6
Yabu Meizan: an earthenware dish, Meiji period, finely enamelled in gilt and colours with a large elephant, a multitude of boys on its back, at its feet and climbing up its sides, minor losses to gilt, signed, 37.5cm (14¾in) diam., *NY 24 Sept,*
$13,750 (£9,821)

7
Yabu Meizan: a jar and cover, Meiji period, enamelled and gilded with *chidori* amid wistaria, signed, 7cm (2¾in), *NY 24 Sept,*
$2,310 (£1,650)

8
A pair of Nanbu earthen ware vases, Meiji period, painted on one side with a mountainous landscape, and on the reverse with pheasants by a waterfall, reserved on a blue and gilt ground, signed, 24cm (9½in), *C 9 July,*
£660 ($1,030)

9
Ryozan: a vase, Meiji period, painted in coloured enamels and gilding with panels of diminutive figures and birds, signed, 14cm (5½in), *C 16 Apr,*
£682 ($1,057)

10
Watano: an earthenware koro and cover, Meiji period, painted on a gilt butterfly ground with *shikishi-e* depicting scenes from the *Genji Monogatari*, signed, 7cm (3in), *L 13 Mar,*
£385 ($593)

11
Yozan: an earthenware vase, Meiji period, paintec with panels of hunters in a landscape, signed, 30.5cm (12in), *L 14 Nov,*
£3,080 ($4,312)

12
Shozan: a pair of earthen ware studies of mandari ducks, late Meiji period, the plumage brightly enamelled and gilt, signed, 6.5 and 7.5cm (2½ and 3in), *L 13 Mar,*
£935 ($1,440)

13
Tomonobu: an earthenware vase, early/mid 19th century, each side enamelled and gilded with flowers and bamboo, signed, 30.5cm (12in), *NY 24 Sept,*
$715 (£511)

pair of cloisonné vases, *one illustrated),* Meiji
eriod, each worked in
ilver wire on a pale green
round, 24cm (9½in),
13 Mar,
715 ($1,101)

**pair of cloisonné
namel vases,** *(one illus-
rated),* Meiji period, 46cm
18in), *S 21 May,*
660 ($1,056)

pair of cloisonné vases,
one illustrated), inlaid with
ink and yellow daisies on
blue ground, 30.5cm
12in), *C 29 Apr,*
253 ($410)

pair of cloisonné vases,
one illustrated), Meiji
eriod, inlaid with birds
round a peony tree,
5cm (9¾in), *C 16 Apr,*
451 ($699)

**Namikawa Yasuyuki: a
loisonné vase,** Meiji
eriod, worked in varying
hicknesses of silver wire
with birds amongst cherry
ranches, signed, 18.5cm
7¼in), *L 13 Mar,*
£11,000 ($16,940)

A cloisonné vase, Meiji
eriod, decorated in
various thicknesses of
silver wire with two egrets
amongst irises, 46.5cm
(18¼in), *L 13 Mar,*
£1,320 ($2,033)

7
A pair of cloisonné vases,
(one illustrated), decorated
with a pair of doves and
flowers on a midnight
blue ground, minor
damage, 30.5cm (12in),
S 21 May,
£352 ($563)

8
**Namikawa Yasuyuki: a
cloisonné vase,** Meiji
period, inlaid with a bird
seated amongst pink,
green and mauve foliage
on a midnight blue
ground, signed, minor
wear, 23cm (9in), *C 16 Apr,*
£792 ($1,228)

9
A cloisonné vase, Meiji
period, decorated in silver
wire with pink and white
flowers, dark blue
ground, 18cm (7¼in),
L 14 Nov,
£715 ($1,001)

10
**Ando Jubei: a partial
plique-à-jour vase,** Meiji
period, worked in silver
wire with a bird on a
cherry branch, silver
mounts, cracked, signed,
21.5cm (8½in), *L 12 June,*
£935 ($1,496)

11
**Hayashi Kodenji: a
miniature cloisonné vase,**
Meiji period, worked in
gold and silver wire with a
butterfly and daisies, midnight blue ground, signed,
9.5cm (3¾in), *L 14 Nov,*
£660 ($924)

12
**Namikawa Sosuke: a
cloisonné tray,** Meiji
period, worked in silver
wire with white peonies on
a pale grey ground, some
wear, signed *Seitei* with
kakihan, 29.5cm (11½in),
L 14 Nov,
£1,870 ($2,618)

13
Ando: a cloisonné vase,
early Showa period, the
black body worked in
silver wire with cranes in
flight, silver mounts,
signed, 30.5cm (12in),
L 12 June,
£605 ($968)

14
**Ando Jubei: a cloisonné
vase,** Taisho period, the
body enamelled to simu-
late iron, decorated in
silver wire and coloured
enamels with egrets in
flight, silver mounts,
signed, 30.5cm (12in),
L 13 Mar,
£2,420 ($3,727)

See p.574 for glossary of types of decoration.

1

2

3

4

5

6

7

8

9

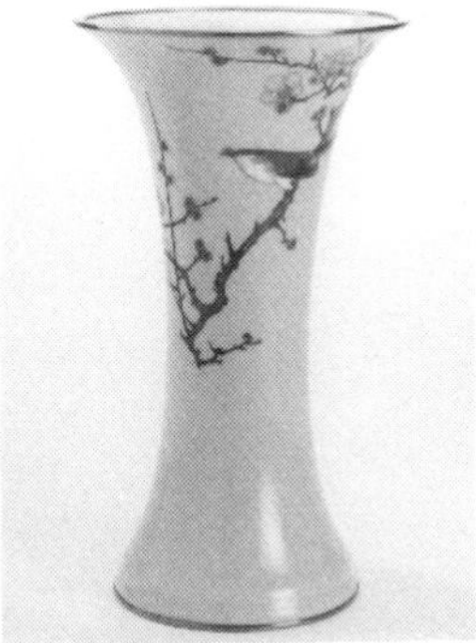
10

11

12

13

14

1

2

3

4

5

6

7

8

9

10

11

1
Hayashi Kodenji: a cloisonné vase and cover, Meiji period, worked with gold wire butterflies and silver wire leaves, midnight blue ground, silver mounts, signed, 12cm (4¾in), *L 12 June,*
£9,020 ($14,432)

2
Hayashi Kodenji: a cloisonné vase, Meiji period, worked in silver wire with stems of blue, white, violet and yellow hydrangea blossom, midnight blue ground, silver mounts, 9.5cm (3¾in), *L 12 June,*
£2,420 ($3,872)

3
Hayashi Kodenji: a cloisonné vase, Meiji period, worked with panels of flowers on grey and blue, midnight blue ground, silver mounts, signed, 24cm (9½in), *L 14 Nov,*
£6,600 ($9,240)

4
Ota Kichisaburo (attributed to): a cloisonné vase, Meiji period, worked in silver wire with panels of wistaria, hydrangea and iris, midnight blue ground, 15.5cm (6¼in), *L 12 June,*
£385 ($616)

5
Ota Tameshiro: a pair of cloisonné vases, Meiji period, worked with panels of birds and flowers on a midnight blue ground, slight cracks, 15.5cm (6¼in), *L 13 Mar,*
£825 ($1,270)

6
Tamura: a cloisonné vase, c.1930, worked in silver wire, *gin-bari* and enamel with pomegranates on branches, pale blue ground, chrome mounts, signed, 31cm (12¼in), *L 12 June,*
£660 ($1,056)

7
Style of Namikawa Yasuyuki: a cloisonné kodansu, Meiji period, th drawers and doors decorated *sans traverse* in silver wire with *kiku*, iris and funkia on a black ground, the sides, top, back and base with flecked green ground, 14.5cm (5¾in), *L 12 June,*
£5,280 ($8,448)

8
A cloisonné vase and cover, Meiji period, worked in silver wire with hanging blade panels of dragons and *ho-o*, 13.5cm (5¼in), *L 14 Nov,*
£1,100 ($1,540)

9
Bai-O: an enamelled silver koro and cover, Meiji period, applied in relief in *shakudo, shibuichi,* silver and gilt, and with enamelled silver peony and foliage, signed, 10.5cm (4in), *L 12 June,*
£3,080 ($4,928)

10
A plique-à-jour bowl, Meiji/Taisho period, enamelled with flowers on a pale green ground, silver mounts, cracks, 14cm (5½in), *L 12 June,*
£1,760 ($2,816)

11
A pair of cloisonné dishes, *(one illustrated)*, eac inlaid with a bird on a turquoise ground, 37cm (14½in), *C 11 Feb,*
£462 ($688)

Hiragana/Katakana forms of phonetic script.

Kakihan stylised script signature (written seal).

Kanemono horizontal scroll.

Kiku chrysanthemum, adopted as badge of Emperor.

Mon badge or crest.

Sagemono hanging scroll.

Saya Gata Testatire inscription on box.

Sosho (characters) 'grass writing'.

Tsukuru/Sei/Saku characters meaning 'made' (appears after signature).

Yaki character meaning 'fired', used on pottery after signature.

1
Masayuki: a pair of shibayama tusk vases, *(one illustrated)*, Meiji period, each inlaid in mother-of-pearl and stained in ivory with a pair of pheasants in a cherry tree, some inlay missing, signed, 34.5cm (13½in), *L 12 June,*
£715 ($1,144)

2
A pair of shibayama tusk vases, Meiji period, decorated in gold *hiramakie* and *takamakie* and inlaid in *aogai*, mother-of-pearl and coloured hardstones with peafowl amid shrubs, some inlay missing, unsigned, 47cm (18½in), *NY 24 Sept,*
$6,050 (£4,321)

3
A shibayama tusk vase, Meiji period, inlaid in mother-of-pearl, coloured ivory, coconut shell, horn and coral with a basket of flowers hanging from a prunus tree with birds, 36cm (14in), *L 14 Nov,*
£1,210 ($1,694)

4
An enamelled silver and shibayama tray, Meiji period, the central gold lacquer panel applied in coloured ivory, mother-of-pearl, horn and coconut shell with an egret perched on a stump, 33.5cm (13¼in), *L 12 June,*
£2,310 ($3,696)

5
A pair of shibayama vases, *(one illustrated)*, Meiji period, each decorated with ivory ground panels of birds and flower baskets, some inlay missing. 30.5cm (12in), *S 21 May,*
£935 ($1,496)

6
Shuko: a shibayama vase, Meiji period, inlaid with a cock and hen beneath ebony and prunus, signed, 23cm (9in), *L 12 June,*
£660 ($1,056)

7
A gold lacquer and shibayama vase, Meiji period, bearing a *kinji* ground and decorated with three dancing boys, chip, 12cm (4¾in), *L 12 June,*
£2,090 ($3,344)

8
A shibayama koro and cover, Meiji period, of ovoid form, on six scroll feet, decorated on one side with a painter recoiling as his work comes to life, the reserve with cranes by a stream, all in typical inlay, gold *takamakie, togidashi* and *kirigane*, silvered mounts, some wear, signed *Shibayama*, 16.5cm (6½in), *L 13 Mar,*
£3,300 ($5,082)

9
A shibayama five-case inro, Meiji period, decorated with three diminutive figures, some inlay missing, signed, *C 15 Jan,*
£242 ($363)

10
Nemoto: a shibayama tsuba, Meiji period, of *mokko* form, inlaid in ivory, mother-of-pearl, horn, coconut shell and *shibuichi* with an old man seated in a wooden tub drawn by attendants, the reverse with Yoshitsune chasing an *oni*, some missing inlay and cracking, signed, 11.5cm (4½in), *L 14 Nov,*
£1,980 ($2,772)

11
A gold lacquer and shibayama box and cover, Meiji period, in the form of two overlapping squares, the top decorated with a hanging curtain beneath a cherry tree, and a circular panel showing a flower cart, slight repairs, 11.5cm (4½in), *L 13 Mar,*
£1,980 ($3,049)

12
Masayuki: a shibayama kodansu, Meiji period, inlaid in mother-of-pearl, coconut shell, tortoiseshell and ivory with birds and butterflies amongst foliage, silver mounts, signed, 11cm (4¼in), *L 14 Nov,*
£1,100 ($1,540)

13
A silver and shibayama set of cutlery, 1884, comprising twelve knives and forks, the ivory handles decorated with mother-of-pearl inlay and gold, silver and sepia lacquer, silver mounts, hallmarks for Sheffield 1884, *C 16 Apr,*
£1,925 ($2,984)

1

2

3

4

5

6

7

8

9

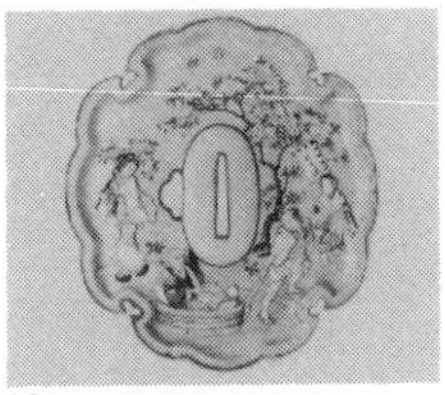
10

11

12

13

1

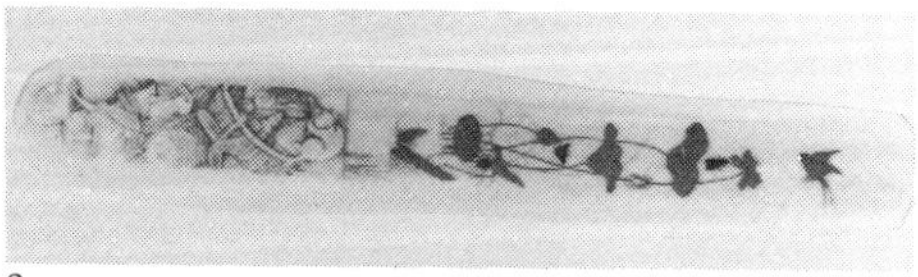
2

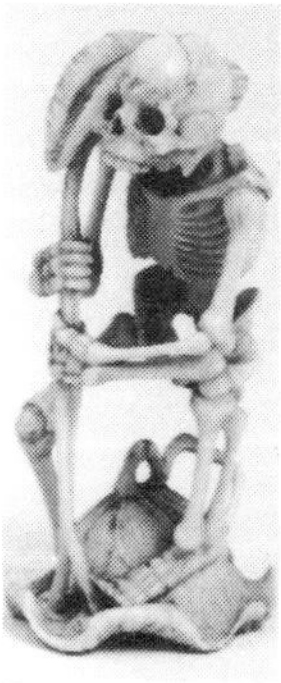
5

6

7

3 4

8

9

10

11

12

13

1
A silver-mounted inlaid ivory tankard, Meiji period, decorated in mother-of-pearl, coral, gold and coloured *hira-makie, takamakie* and *kirigane* with quail, sparrows and cranes, 21.5cm (8½in), *L 12 June,*
£935 ($1,496)

2
An ivory letter-opener, 19th century, the handle decorated with fish and mice, the blade with gold lacquer, 30cm (11¾in), *A 6 May,*
Dfl 1,035 (£314; $499)

3
An ivory okimono, Meiji period, of a farmer and three sons sheltering beneath a parasol, base cracked, signed, 22.5cm (8¾in), *C 15 Jan,*
£396 ($594)

4
An ivory okimono, Meiji period, depicting an entertainer, the man holding a puppet on a stick, signed, 22cm (8½in), *C 15 Jan,*
£187 ($281)

5
An ivory skeleton okimono, 19th century, clutching a lotus stem rising from a larger lotus leaf, 7cm (2¾in), *S 22 Jan,*
£300 ($450)

6
An ivory okimono, Meiji period, of a farmer holding a cockerel and a basket of grapes, engraved signature, 23cm (9in), *C 15 Jan,*
£385 ($578)

7
An ivory figure of a sage, Meiji period, the folds of his robe incised, stippled and stained, incised signature, 16cm (6¼in), *S 21 May,*
£253 ($405)

8
An ivory okimono of Shoki and Oni, Meiji period, Shoki holding a sword in front of a cauldron on a table, the Oni to the side, some cracks, 10.5cm (4¼in), *C 8 Oct,*
£286 ($400)

9
Shingyoku: an ivory figure of a bijin, Meiji period, holding the hem of her kimono in one hand, a tasselled *haka seko* in the other, slight repairs, signed, 28cm (11in), *L 12 June,*
£1,375 ($2,200)

10
An ivory figure of a bijin Meiji period, dressed in the manner of a Maiden Immortal, the details in stained ivory, some wear, 37cm (14½in), *L 13 Mar,*
£2,310 ($3,557)

11
An ivory figure of a female deity, c.1900, holding a fan-cum-flywhisk and a scroll, her diadem with a turquoise stud 16.5cm (6½in), *S 22 Jan,*
£400 ($600)

12
Toshichika: an ivory study of Benkei, Meiji period, carrying a *zushi* on his back, containing a figure of Fudo, sword replaced, signed, 16.5cm (6½in), *L 14 Nov,*
£1,210 ($1,694)

13
Ryushin: an ivory figure of Benten, Meiji period, carrying a ewer in one hand and a lotus stem in the other, an attendant at her feet, signed, 33.5cm (13in), *L 14 Nov,*
£660 ($924)

Okimono standing ornaments, figures, etc.

1
Gyokuzan: an ivory model of a boat, Meiji period, containing eight immortals, carved with dragons and roundels and with slight mother-of-pearl inlay, signed, 52cm (20½in), *L 13 Mar,*
£3,850 ($5,929)

2
An ivory group of a couple winnowing grain, Meiji period, the lady pounding the grain on a stone, the man folding a woven mat, a loom between them, a picnic box nearby, the details picked out in dark stain, signed illegibly, 11cm (4½in), *NY 24 Sept,*
$1,980 (£1,414)

3
Kozan: an ivory okimono, Meiji period, depicting nine small boys, three pulling and one pushing a cart containing five boy musicians, signed, 21.5cm (8½in), *L 13 Mar,*
£1,540 ($2,372)

4
Nobuyuki: an ivory group of a scholar and pupil, Meiji period, the scholar instructing the pupil in calligraphy, various writing implements stacked nearby, signed, 9.5cm (3¾in), *NY 24 Sept,*
$3,740 (£2,671)

5
Kamei: an ivory okimono of a fruit vendor, c.1900, smoking a pipe, his produce by his side, signed, 10cm (4in), *S 22 Jan,*
£460 ($690)

6
Shizuyuki: an ivory figure of a print maker and his apprentice, Meiji period, the man seated applying pressure to the wood-block, the boy with bowls of ink, books and paper, finger restored, signed with *kakihan*, 12.5cm (5in), *L 12 June,*
£1,320 ($2,112)

7
Ishikawa Komei: an ivory figure of a hunter, Meiji period, wearing a plain tunic and loose trousrs tucked into fur boots, a falcon on his left hand, his catch in a basket on his back, signed with *kakihan*, 38cm (15in), *L 13 Mar,*
£20,900 ($32,186)

8
An ivory figure of a rat-catcher, Meiji period, with his arms raised in alarm as rats run up his leg, 17.5cm (6¾in), *L 14 Nov,*
£418 ($585)

9
Tomomine: an ivory group of a fisherman and three karako, Meiji period, two children at his side while a third is tied to his back, signed, 34.5cm (13½in), *L 13 Mar,*
£1,760 ($2,710)

10
Munehide: an ivory figure of a scholar, Meiji period, wearing a *kimono* decorated with *tomoemon*, and holding an unrolled scroll, signed, 50cm (19¾in), *L 12 June,*
£2,200 ($3,520)

11
Masahide: an ivory figure of a basket seller, Meiji period, his wares hanging from a bamboo pole held over his shoulder, the details inlaid in coloured ivory, top of pole missing, signed, 15cm (6in), *L 12 June,*
£990 ($1,584)

12
Shomei (Masaaki): a Tokyo school ivory figure of a fisherman, Meiji period, holding a large basket of fish, a lobster on the top, a small boy standing on *geta* at his side, slight damage, signed with seal, 26.5cm (10½in), *L 13 Mar,*
£1,100 ($1,694)

13
Rishu: an ivory figure of a street vendor, Meiji period, seated over a portable *hibachi* grilling *dango* on skewers, a partly covered basket of wares at his side, signed, 7cm (2¾in), *L 14 Nov,*
£550 ($770)

1

2

3

4

7

5

6

8

9

10

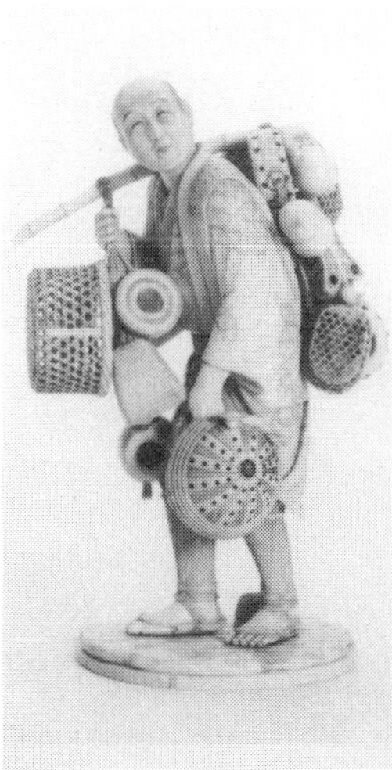
11

12

13

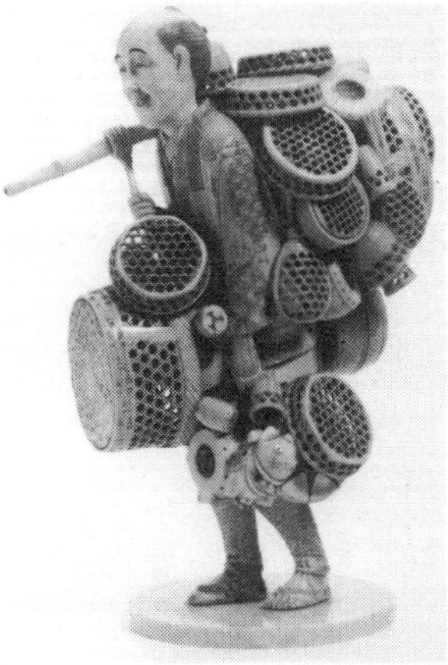

1

2

3

4

5

6

7

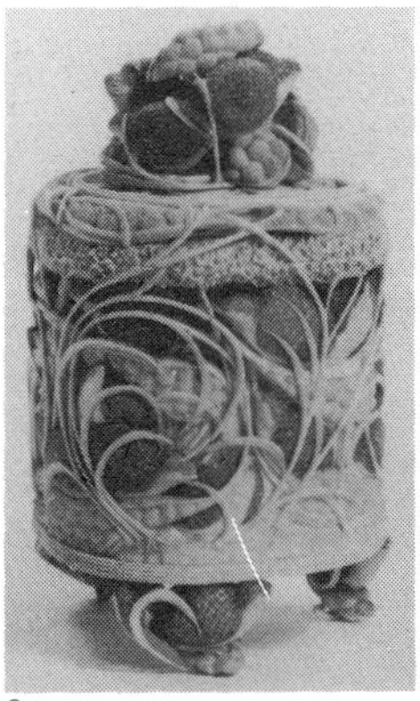

8

9

10

11

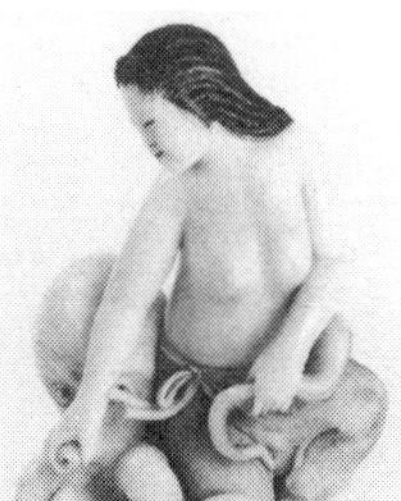

12

13

1
An ivory study of a basket seller, Meiji period, carrying a pole from which are suspended numerous baskets and drums, details of stained red and green ivory, and mother-of-pearl, some wear, indistinctly signed, 19.5cm (7¾in), *L 14 Nov,*
£1,100 ($1,540)

2
Ryuho: an ivory figure of a man, Meiji period, holding a net of fledglings in one hand whom he feeds from a short twig, signed, 21.5cm (8½in), *L 12 June,*
£824 ($1,318)

3
Seishu: an ivory figure of an archer, Meiji period, kneeling on a large bear-skin, and with a stand containing six arrows behind him, details in lightly stained ivory, signed, 12cm (4¾in), *L 13 Mar,*
£1,045 ($1,609)

4
Sei: an ivory okimono, Meiji period, of an elderly couple preparing their food around a *hibachi*, signed, 9cm (3½in), *L 14 Nov,*
£1,430 ($2,002)

5
Yoshida Homei: a Tokyo School ivory group of a father and son, Meiji period, the father holding a frog in his hands, the boy reaching up for it, signed, 33.5cm (13¼in), *L 14 Nov,*
£6,600 ($9,240)

6
A wood and ivory figure of a fisherman, Meiji period, carrying a basket in one hand and an oar in the other, 21cm (8¼in), *L 14 Nov,*
£550 ($770)

7
Muneyasu: a wood and ivory group of two Go players, Meiji period, one holding a fan, the other a pipe and tobaco pouch, their *kimonos* with gold lacquer detail, signed, 17cm (6¾in), *L 13 Mar,*
£1,210 ($1,863)

8
An ivory box and cover, Meiji period, carved with numerous quail amongst stems of millet, the feet and finial also carved with quail, chips, 18cm (7in), *L 14 Nov,*
£990 ($1,386)

9
Shizunaka (Seichu): a stagshorn model of a tea house, Meiji period, signed, 24cm (9½in), *L 13 Mar,*
£275 ($424)

10
An ivory tusk vase and cover, Meiji period, carved with a divinity and attendant figure enclosed by dragons and waves, fixed wood base on four scroll feet, some wear, signed, *C 16 Apr,*
£495 ($767)

11
Muneyoshi (Soju): an ivory jar and cover, Meiji period, carved with panels of immortals, the cover surmounted by an immortal at a low table, signed, 21cm (8¼in), *L 12 June,*
£1,045 ($1,672)

12
An ivory group of a fisherwoman and squid, c.1900, the semi-naked girl entangled in the tentacles of the mollusc and gripping its snout, unsigned, 10.5cm (4in), *S 22 Jan,*
£2,000 ($3,000)

13
An ivory okimono of a woman and child, c.1900, the former carrying a basket of vines and offering a cluster of grapes to the little boy, who is holding an axe, unsigned, 18cm (7in), *S 22 Jan,*
£360 ($540)

Netsuke

NEIL DAVEY

)ver the last few years, a large number of books and magazine rticles have been devoted to one of the world's smallest art orms, that of the netsuke.

The netsuke did not start its existence as a work of art, but ather as a utilitarian object, whose use was as a toggle incor-orating an attachment from which was suspended, by a slim ord, a small box or pouch from the wide belt or sash (*obi*) of the vearer. As such, in Japan, their country of origin, they were egarded as dress accessories of some beauty, rather as one would oday regard a designer purse or wristwatch.

It is believed that the netsuke were first made about 1600, round the same time as the inro, small boxes of between one and five closely fitting compartments, worn at the waist to contain medicines (see pp.678-679). Another school of thought is that they were produced in the middle of the 16th century, the period when the Portuguese first reached Japan and introduced tobacco and firearms. It became necessary to carry around the various smoking requirements such as the pipe and tobacco pouch, as well as powder flasks for the guns — the easiest method being to suspend them from the belt. The netsuke at this time would have been of a comparatively simple form, probably a node of bamboo, a knob of a gnarled tree root or a rough piece of wood, all bored with a suitable attachment for the cord. The netsuke remained in this simple form for some time, only gradually

1

2

3

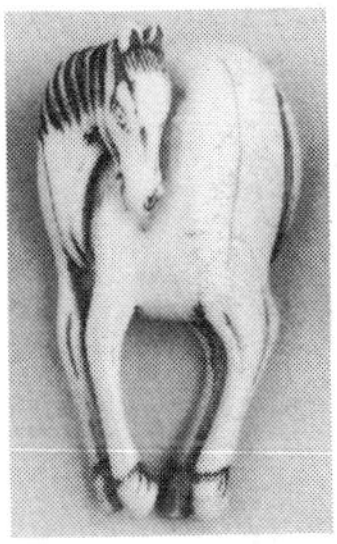
4

5

6

7

8

9

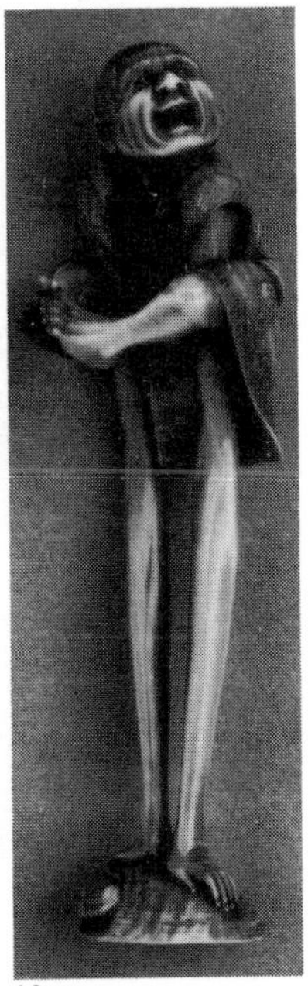
10

1
An ivory study of a dancer, 18th century, the eyes inlaid with dark horn, one chip, unsigned, *L 12 June,*
£1,650 ($2,640)

2
An ivory study of a Sennin, 18th century, carrying a *hossu* over his left shoulder, ivory slightly worn, unsigned, 6cm (2¼in), *L 12 June,*
£572 ($915)

3
An ivory group of a horse and monkey, late 18th century, detail slightly worn, one ear chipped, unsigned, 4.5cm (1¾in), *L 20 Feb,*
£308 ($468)

4
An ivory study of a grazing horse, 18th century, details slightly worn, later added signature Shunzan, *L 12 June,*
£880 ($1,408)

5
An ivory figure of Moso, 18th century, in a straw winter coat, unsigned, 5cm (2in), *L 20 Feb,*
£275 ($418)

6
An ivory figure of a Bugaku dancer, 18th century, holding a mask and a fan, unsigned, 7.5cm (3in), *L 20 Feb,*
£5,280 ($8,026)

7
An ivory figure of a boy with a drum, 19th century, inlaid eyes and detail, signed, 4cm (1½in), *S 21 May,*
£165 ($264)

8
An ivory figure of a Chinese nobleman, 18th century, slightly worn but well toned ivory, unsigned, 7cm (2¾in), *L 20 Feb,*
£4,400 ($6,688)

9
A manju, early 19th century, carved and pierced in Ryusa style with the 'Three Friends', unsigned, 5cm (2in), *L 12 June,*
£385 ($616)

10
Shigeyasu (?): a late Obi-hasami figure of Ashinaga, 19th century, holding an *awabi* shell, stained ivory, 9.5cm (3¾in), *L 13 Mar,*
£495 ($762)

becoming more sophisticated and carved to resemble recognisable forms: actual and mythical animals, traditional, legendary and religious figures and genre subjects.

The works we see that were made up to the middle of the 18th century are almost invariably unsigned and we know little about the makers. Towards the end of the 18th century, however, the formerly utilitarian object evolved into an art form, some of which were signed by the artist. Sculptors, whose output previously was of larger works, started to produce similar carvings in miniature. The earliest known record of netsuke carvers is in a seven-volume book published in 1781, called the *Soken Kisho*, by a native of Osaka, Inaba Tsuryu. The *Soken Kisho* was basically a guide to various art forms and the artists working at the time, including chapters on textiles, sword fittings, lacquer and netsuke. The latter section listed fifty-seven netsuke carvers who were known at the time. These were classified by the region they came from: twenty-two from Osaka, eleven from Kyoto, nine from Tokyo (Edo) and fifteen from various smaller centres. Each artist was listed with scant details of his work and a few line drawings. Regrettably, because the Japanese at that time did not regard the netsuke very highly, there is no other information regarding the 18th century carvers and so scholars today rely to a large extent on feel and supposition. In this respect the study of netsuke is at the same time highly rewarding, as we are forever learning new facts, but also frustrating, as there is so little source material from which to work.

By the beginning of the 19th century, a number of 'schools' of carvers had built up in various centres, though the system was probably more 'master and apprentice' than 'teacher and pupil'. The art became more and more sophisticated, the finest carvers producing magnificent netsuke which could stand comparison with any art form and which could be termed miniature sculpture. By this time, the Dutch had landed in Japan and they began trading, taking back to Europe many works of art, including netsuke; thus collections were formed in the West. This trait was much speeded up by the end of the 19th century, when Japan opened her doors to the outside world and Western merchants travelled in droves to trade and to take back to the West as much merchandise as they could carry. As more and more aliens entered Japan, it was found that the demand for netsuke was far

11

12

13

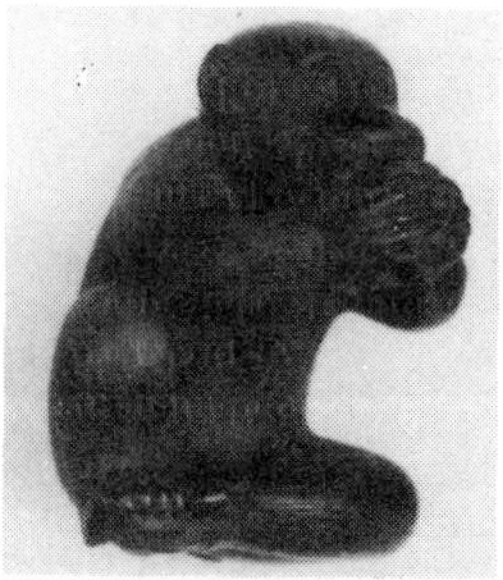
14

15

16

17

18

19

11
Kano Natsuo: a kagamibuta, 19th century, with a silver plate, signed Natsuo, 4cm (1½in), *L 13 Nov*,
£1,320 ($1,848)

12
An early wood figure of a Mongolian archer, 18th century, arrow shaft restored, unsigned, 8cm (3in), *L 12 June*,
£825 ($1,320)

13
A wood mask of Otobide 18th century, the eyes of horn and metal with glass, tied cords at the back, unsigned, 5cm (2in), *L 12 June*,
£638 ($1,021)

14
Ise, Yamada school: a wood study of a monkey, late 19th century, one leg forming the *himotoshi*, unsigned, 4.5cm (1¾in), *L 13 Mar*,
£308 ($474)

15
Chikuyu: a late figure of a Sarumawashi, late 19th century, one foot chipped, signed Chikuyu, 5cm (2in), *L 20 Feb*,
£264 ($401)

16
A Tsuishu lacquer manju, early 19th century, in two parts, unsigned, 4cm (1½in), *L 20 Feb*,
£396 ($602)

17
A lacquered wood study of a Shojo dancer, late 19th century, holding a *sake* cup, signed on an inlaid pearl tablet Tomin (?), 3.5cm (1½in), *L 20 Feb*,
£572 ($869)

18
Ikkan: a study of a performing monkey, Edo, 19th century, eyes in pale horn, signed in an oval reserve Ikkan, 4cm (1½in), *L 12 June*,
£8,580 ($13,728)

19
Miwa: an early figure of Jurojin, Edo, 18th century, slightly worn wood, signed Miwa with *kakihan*, 5cm (2in), *L 20 Feb*,
£1,045 ($1,588)

greater than the supply produced by the finest artists. Numerous copies were therefore made, some by apprentices but many by fringe carvers, making cheap imitations for unscrupulous dealers to sell to unwitting collectors. Small carvings for house decoration known as *okimono*, literally 'alcove ornaments' were bored with cord attachments and sold as netsuke.

The late 19th century was long considered to mark the end of the netsuke as an art form, though several good artists lived on into the 20th century. Subsequently, there has been a marked revival in the carving of netsuke, a number of Japanese artists finding that they have a great feeling for the miniature and in particular the netsuke. These carvers have recently been augmented by a small number of Western artists, particularly in England and America, who have turned their hands to the making of netsuke.

Around three to four thousand netsuke artists have been identified, producing a wide variety of styles and subject matter. Their choice of material has been dominated by accessibility and supply; thus we find that the artists living not too far distant from the coast of Japan favoured the use of ivory (imported from Africa and India), while those living inland utilised the abundant native woods. Subject matter is more individual, some artists preferred to produce naturalistic or stylised studies of animals while others chose real or imaginary figures, portrayed variously in a serious or comic manner. Thus we see the whole spectrum of Japanese life, over about two hundred years, reduced to a collection of sculptures ranging in size from one to six inches (2.5 to 15cm).

Serious netsuke collecting in the West began at the end of the last century, when Englishmen like Michael Tomkinson, Walter Lionel Behrens and Harry Seymour Trower amassed collections of several thousand netsuke, inro, sword fittings and other miniature Japanese works of art. In France, the names of Henri Joly (who moved to England), Louis Gonse, Gillot, Bing and others were foremost in their appreciation of this newly discovered art form, while in Germany, Albert Brockhaus formed a varied collection and produced a book on the subject which, for many years, was the standard work for other connoisseurs. These collections were mostly dispersed by auction in the early part of this century and fuelled the second generation collections. The collecting of netsuke then became a somewhat parochial

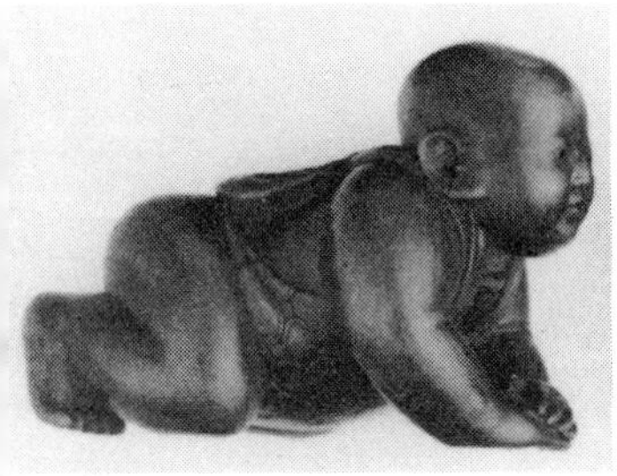
20

21

22

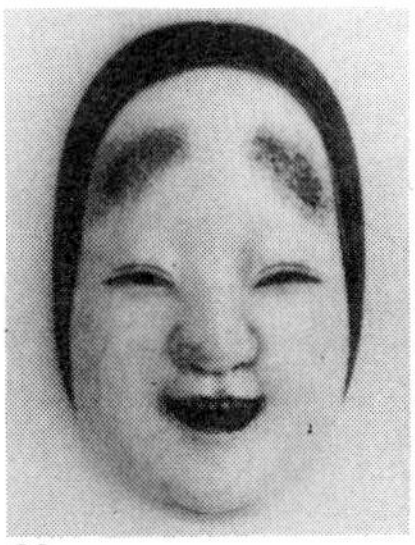
23

24

20
Masakatsu: a boxwood figure of a baby boy, Edo, 19th century, his crossed hands forming the *himotoshi*, slightly worn wood, signed Masakatsu, 5cm (2in), *L 12 June,*
£990 ($1,584)

21
Hosho (Yoshimasa): a wood study of a young boy, Edo, 19th century, signed Hosho (Yoshimasa), 3cm (1¼in), *L 13 Nov,*
£462 ($647)

22
Hojitsu: a wood figure of a nobleman, Edo, mid 19th century, signed, 7cm (2¾in), *L 12 June,*
£374 ($598)

23
An ivory mask of Mambi, Edo, 19th century, details etched in red and black, signed with an unidentified *kakihan*, 3.5cm (1½in), *L 12 June,*
£418 ($669)

24
Yasutaka (Hoko): an ivory figure of an actor, Edo, Meiji period, probably a member of the Danjuro family in the role of Soga no Goro, signed on inlaid pearl tablet Yasutaka (Hoko), 3.5cm (1¼in), *L 12 June,*
£2,860 ($4,576)

25

26

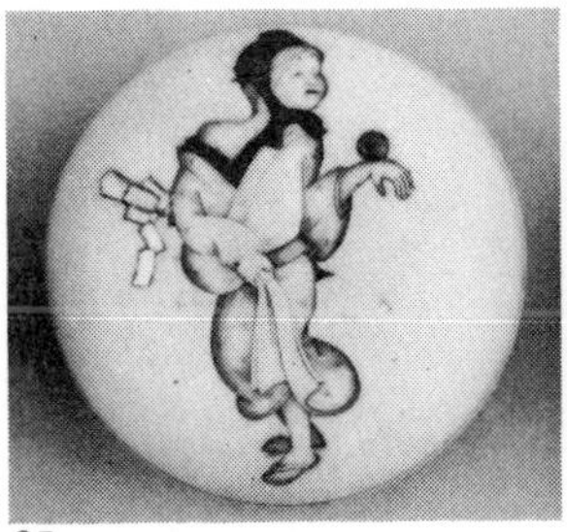
27

28

29

25
Shibayama family: an ivory study of Daikoku's sack, Edo, 19th century, inlaid with *takaramono* in various materials, cord holes ringed with horn and pearl, signed on a pearl tablet Shibayama, 3cm (1¼in), *L 12 June,*
£572 ($915)

26
Tomomasa: an ivory figure of Shoki, Edo, 19th century, slight damage, signed in a reserve Tomomasa, 6cm (2¼in), *L 20 Feb,*
£605 ($920)

27
Komin: an ivory manju, Edo, 19th century, carved in *shishiaibori*, details inlaid in mother-of-pearl and malachite, signed Komin with *kakihan*, with bead ojime, *L 12 June,*
£286 ($458)

28
Miyasaki Joso: an ivory figure of a cook, Edo, late 19th century, cutting open a gourd, signed Joso to, 3cm (1¼in), *L 20 Feb,*
£4,180 ($6,354)

29
Style of Shounsai Joryu: an ivory group of two egg-testers, Edo, 19th century, slightly worn and stained ivory, unsigned, 4.5cm (1¾in), *L 20 Feb,*
£374 ($568)

occupation, kept alive by comparatively few enthusiastic and extremely knowledgeable amateurs (pre-eminently W.W. (Billy) Winkworth and Mark Hindson), and a handful of dealers. Among the latter, Frederick Meinertzhagen stood out as not only selling some of the finest works for the enjoyment of collectors, but also by providing much study material, firstly in the pages of his book *The Art of the Netsuke Carver* but, more importantly, in his card index of over ten thousand recorded netsuke, now kept in the British Museum and recently published.

The sale at Sotheby's of the Mark Hindson collection from 1967 to 1969, formed a landmark in the manner of collecting netsuke. Aided by Hindson's own notes, largely written over a number of years in conjunction with Winkworth and Meinertzhagen, seven sale catalogues were compiled in such a way as to provide a new insight into this (at that time) somewhat neglected subject. The sale induced a number of collectors of other works of art to look at the netsuke with a new appreciation, thus stimulating the market and causing many new collections to be started. Today, the field of netsuke is truly international, collectors being located throughout the world. A flourishing collectors' society operates from America and conventions or symposiums for the study of netsuke are held in many different locations.

Given the wide variety of style and subject matter within the genre, there is still ample scope for collectors to find the new, the undiscovered and the relatively cheap, as well as work by the great masters. Each type can be found in proliferation at every auction sale.

Further reading:

Neil K. Davey, *Netsuke*, revised edition, 1982
Raymond Bushell, *Collectors' Netsuke*, 1971
Raymond Bushell, *Netsuke, Familiar and Unfamiliar*, 1975
Joe Earle, *An Introduction to Netsuke*, 1980

30

31

32

33

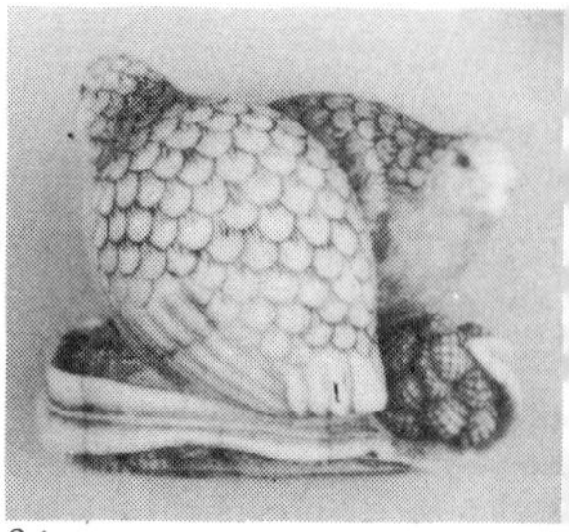
34

30
Bunzan: a lacquered ivory figure of a Hannya Dancer, Edo, late 19th century, signed in oval reserve Bunzan, 5cm (2in), *L 13 Nov,*
£352 ($493)

31
Gyokusho: an ivory study of a man, Edo, 20th century, seated before a *go* board, signed in red on an oval reserve Gyokusho, 4cm (1¾in), *L 20 Feb,*
£495 ($752)

32
Sosui: an ivory study of Yama Uba and Kintoki, Edo, early 20th century, lightly stained ivory, signed in an oval reserve Sosui, 4.5cm (1¾in), *L 20 Feb,*
£2,200 ($3,344)

33
An ivory study of a rat, Kyoto, 18th century, the tail forming the *himotoshi*, eyes inlaid with dark horn, unsigned, 5cm (2in), *L 12 June,*
£4,400 ($7,040)

34
Okatori: an ivory study of two quail, Kyoto, late 18th century, the eyes inlaid, signed Okatori, 3.5cm (1½in), *L 20 Feb,*
£1,650 ($2,508)

35

36

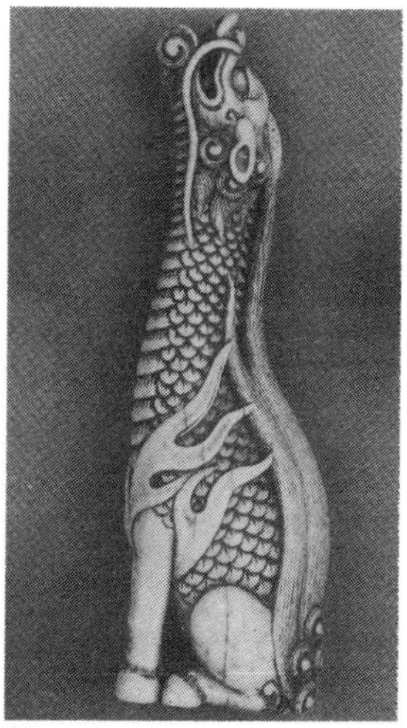
37

38

35
Okatomo: an ivory study of a rat, Kyoto, 18th century, eyes inlaid with dark horn, signed in a rectangular reserve Okatomo, 4.5cm (1¾in), *L 20 Feb,*
£8,250 ($12,540)

36
Tomotada (school): an ivory study of a recumbent ox, 18th century, eye pupils inlaid with dark horn, inscribed in a rectangular reserve Tomotada, 5.5cm (2¼in), *L 12 June,*
£715 ($1,144)

37
Tomotada: a study of a Kirin, Kyoto, 18th century, signed in a rectangular reserve Tomotada, 10.5cm (4¼in), *L 20 Feb,*
£19,800 ($30,096)

38
An ivory study of a monkey and its child, Kyoto, 18th century, eye pupils inlaid, unsigned, 4.5cm (1¾in), *L 20 Feb,*
£605 ($920)

39

40

41

42

43

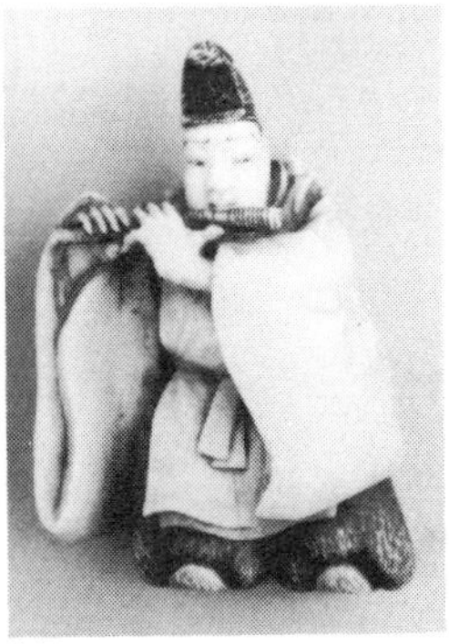
44

45

46

47

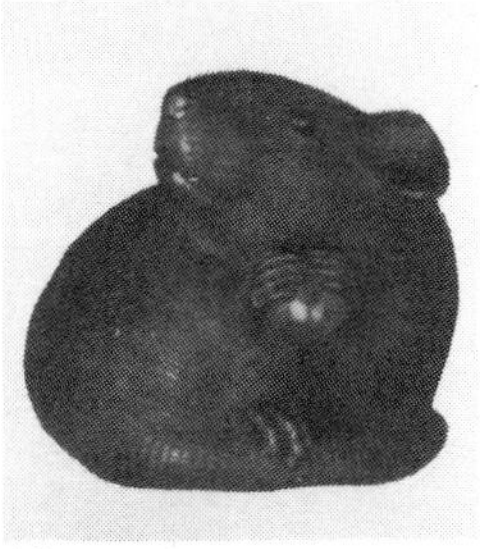
48

50 *(above)* 51 *(below)*

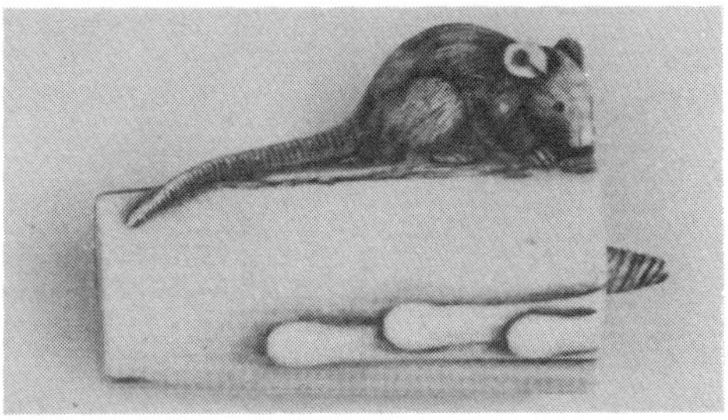
49

52

9
n ivory study of a hare,
Kyoto, early 19th century, he eyes inlaid, one ear hipped, unsigned, *. 12 June,*
880 ($1,408)

0
n ivory study of a uppy, Kyoto, 19th entury, eyes inlaid in dark orn, unsigned, 3.5cm 1½in), *L 12 June,*
605 ($968)

1
hara Mitsuhiro: an ivory igure of Hotei, Osaka, ated 1845, old crack, igned Mitsuhiro with *akihan* and dated Koka 2 to 1 tsuki koshi', 3.5cm (1¼in), *L 20 Feb,*
£4,180 ($6,354)

42
Okatori: an ivory figure of a Dutchman, Osaka, 18th century, signed in a rectangular reserve Okatori, 6cm (2¼in), *L 20 Feb,*
£1,980 ($3,010)

43
Style of Garaku: an ivory study of a pup, Osaka, late 18th century, eyes inlaid in dark horn, unsigned, 4.5cm (1¾in), *L 20 Feb,*
£1,430 ($2,174)

44
Kohosai: an ivory study of Yoshitsune, Osaka, 19th century, signed, 5cm (2in), *L 12 June,*
£770 ($1,232)

45
Ohara Mitsuhiro: an ivory model of two loquats, Osaka, 19th century, bearing old cracks, signed in an oval reserve Mitsuhiro, 5cm (2¼in), *L 12 June,*
£770 ($1,232)

46
An early ivory study of a Dutchman, Nagoya, 18th century, unsigned, 10cm (4in), *L 20 Feb,*
£1,540 ($2,341)

47
Ikkan: a wood study of a horse, Nagoya, 19th century, one leg forming the *himotoshi*, signed in an oval reserve Ikkan, 4cm (1½in), *L 20 Feb,*
£1,100 ($1,672)

48
Kano Tomokazu: a wood study of a rat, Nagoya, 19th century, eyes inlaid in dark horn, signed in an oval reserve Tomokazu, 3.5cm (1¼in), *L 20 Feb,*
£2,860 ($4,347)

49
An ivory study of a rat on a candle, 18th century, the candle with dripping wax and a later added wick, the details in slightly worn and patinated ivory, unsigned, 5.5cm (2¼in), *L 20 Feb,*
£550 ($836)

50
Tomochika: an ivory study of the legend of the Suikoden, 19th century, Edo, depicting Ka Osho Rochishin fighting the brigand Riu Shishin, the ivory lightly stained, 4cm (1½in), *L 12 June,*
£330 ($528)

51
Komin: an ivory figure of a young boy, 19th century, Edo, wearing a formal coat engraved with flowers and brocade designs, and holding an Okame mask, the details in lightly stained ivory, 3.5cm (1¼in), *L 12 June,*
£594 ($950)

52
Saneshige: a manju, 19th century, Edo, carved in *shishiaibori* with a woman beating cloth on a roller, the details stained, 5cm (2in), *L 12 June,*
£308 ($493)

1

2

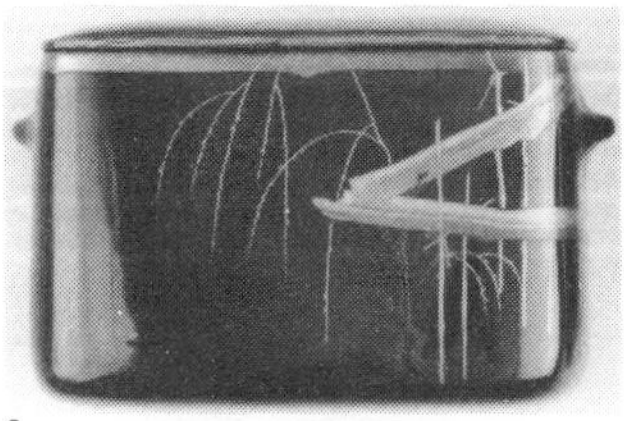
3

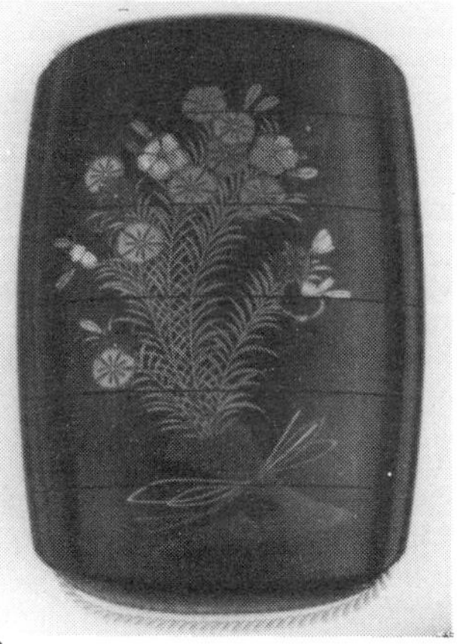
6

4

5

9

7

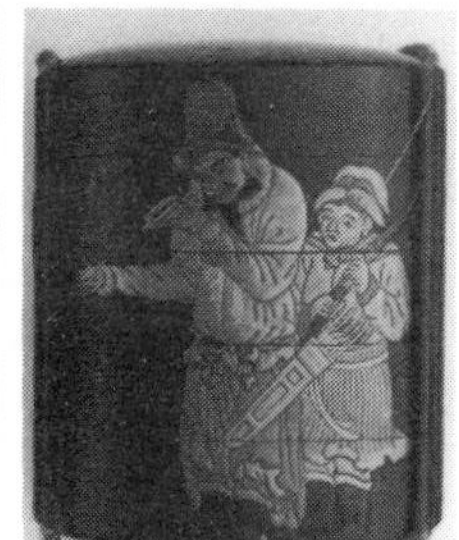
8

10

11

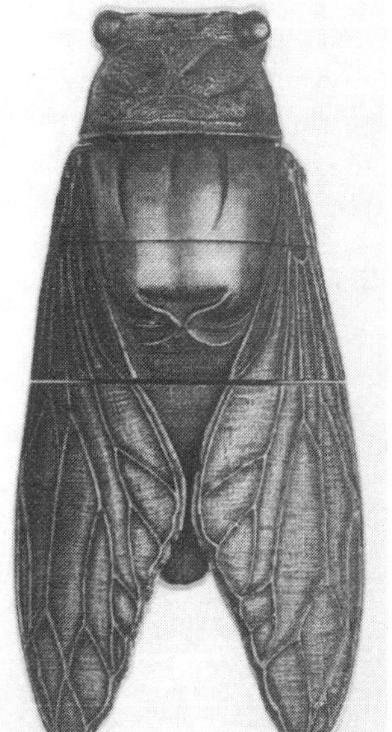
12

1
Shibata Zeshin: a woven rattan tabako-ire, 19th century, showing on one side a covered teapot, decorated in Mokubei style, and on the other two cups, all in gold, silver and black *takamakie*, signed, interior damaged, 8cm (3¼in), *L 13 Nov,*
£2,530 ($3,542)

2
Shibata Zeshin: a tabako-ire, in the form of a pottery chaire, 19th century, covered with a simulated glaze of dark brown lacquer, the rough red imitation biscuit paste showing beneath, ivory cover, slight dents, signed, 6.5cm (2½in), *L 13 Nov,*
£13,750 ($19,250)

3
Shibata Zeshin: a tabako-ire, 19th century, decorated in gold, silver and coloured *takamakie* with willow branches and a bird, signed, 7.5cm (3in), *L 13 Nov,*
£9,350 ($13,090)

4
Kakosai Shozan: a five-case inro, 19th century, decorated in gilt, copper, *shibuichi* and *shakudo* with the Emperor and an attendant seeking Taikobo, signed, 9.5cm (3¾in), sold with an ivory netsuke, 19th century, *L 13 Mar,*
£550 ($847)

5
Seifu: a gold lacquer and Shibayama sheath inro, 19th century, the *saya* decorated with chickens beside a peony, inlaid with pearl of various tones, coral, horn and coloured ivory, signed, 10cm (4in), *L 13 Mar,*
£2,860 ($4,404)

6
Kajikawa family: a five-case inro, 19th century, decorated in gold and coloured *takamakie*, slight chips and wear, signed *Kajikawa saku*, 8cm (3in), *L 12 June,*
£990 ($1,584)

7
A four-case inro, 17th century, decorated in gold and coloured *takamakie* with a monkey and a hare wrestling, some wear, 6cm (2½in), *L 12 June,*
£385 ($616)

8
Yamada Jokasai: a four-case inro, 18th century, decorated in gold and coloured *takamakie* with ar archer examining the flight of an arrow, 6.5cm (2½in), *L 12 June,*
£682 ($1,091)

9
Shiomi Masanari: a thre case inro, late 18th/early 19th century, decorated in gold and coloured *togidash* and *e-nashiji* with three actors, one cleaning the ear of another, slight wear, signed, 7.5cm (3in), *L 13 Nov,*
£1,045 ($1,463)

10
A four-case inro, 17th century, decorated in gold and coloured *takamakie* with moored boats beneath overhanging willow, slight wear, 6.5cm (2½in), *L 13 Mar,*
£352 ($542)

11
Shokasai and Shibayam a four-case gold lacquer inro, 19th century, decorated in gold and coloured *takamakie* with Ii no Hayat slaying the Nue, signed, 8cm (3in), *L 12 June,*
£1,430 ($2,288)

12
A wood inro in the form of a cicada, 19th century, unsigned, style of Harumitsu of Ise, Yamada, 13.5cm (5¼in), *L 20 Feb,*
£1,980 ($3,010)

Inro small set of infitting boxes for medicines, made usually of lacquer, hung at waist.

Netsuke toggle used to suspend pipe, inro etc. from waistband (obi).

Ojime small bead holding inro cords.

Manju netsuke of flattened bun form.

Kagamibuta netsuke with ivory bowl and infitting metal disc.

Tabako-ire tobacco pouch.

1
A miniature ivory two-case inro, early 19th century, the details carved in well patinated ivory, unsigned, 3.5cm (1¼in), and an ivory netsuke, 19th century, of Hotei, 3cm (1in), and an ivory ojime, *L 12 June,*
£715 ($1,144)

2
A gold lacquer two-case inro, 19th century, decorated wih a large *minogame*, applied in pewter, *aogai* and gold *takamakie*, slight inlay missing, 7.5cm (3in), *L 12 June,*
£660 ($1,056)

3
Kajikawa family: a four-case inro, 19th century, decorated in gold *takamakie* with Ono no Tofu beside a stream, slight chips and wear, signed *Kajikawa saku*, 8cm (3¼in), *L 12 June,*
£1,210 ($1,936)

4
Nakayama Komin: a four-case inro, 19th century, decorated in gold and coloured *takamakie* with the dream of Rosei, signed, 9.5cm (3¾in), *L 13 Nov,*
£2,860 ($4,004)

5
Kajikawa family, a four-case gold lacquer inro, 19th century, decorated in gold and silver *takamakie* with a flower arrangement beside a teapot and scissors, slight rubbing, signed *Kajikawa saku*, 8.5cm (3½in), *L 12 June,*
£880 ($1,408)

6
A three-case gold lacquer inro, 19th century, decorated in shibayama style with a branch of cherry blossom, slight wear and chips, 8.5cm (3½in), *L 13 Nov,*
£880 ($1,232)

7
Shokasai Masamitsu: a five-case gold lacquer inro, 19th century, decorated in gold and coloured *takamakie* with cranes, slight chips, signed with *kakihan*, 9cm (3½in), *L 13 Nov,*
£825 ($1,155)

8
Tokosai Setsuga: a metal sheath inro, 19th century, the inro contained within a *saya* in the form of a *sake* jar decorated with a dancing *shojo*, signed, 8cm (3in), with copper ojime, *L 12 June,*
£5,280 ($8,448)

9
Shokasai and Shibayama family: a four-case gold lacquer inro, 19th century, decorated with Chorio and Kosekiko, slightly worn, signed, 8.5cm (3¼in), *L 13 Nov,*
£990 ($1,386)

10
Yoju: a gold lacquer inro, 19th century, decorated in Shibayama style, signed, 8.5cm (3¼in), with a stag antler ojime, *L 12 June,*
£1,155 ($1,848)

11
Moei (Shigenaga): a two-case inro, 19th century, decorated in gold and coloured *togidashi* and *e-nashiji* with travellers struggling against a high wind, slight chips, signed, 6.5cm (2½in), *L 13 Nov,*
£880 ($1,232)

12
Hara Yoyusai: a four-case inro, 19th century, decorated in gold *takamakie* with a hen in a winnowing basket with three chicks, slight wear, signed, 8cm (3¼in), *L 12 June,*
£825 ($1,320)

13
Masanaga: a gold ojime, late 19th century, carved in relief with a singing bird on a flower stem, signed, 2cm (¾in), *L 20 Feb,*
£1,100 ($1,672)

14
Mitsunori: a gold ojime, late 19th century, carved in relief with a lily amongst grasses, signed, 2cm (¾in), *L 20 Feb,*
£605 ($920)

See p.574 for glossary of types of decoration.

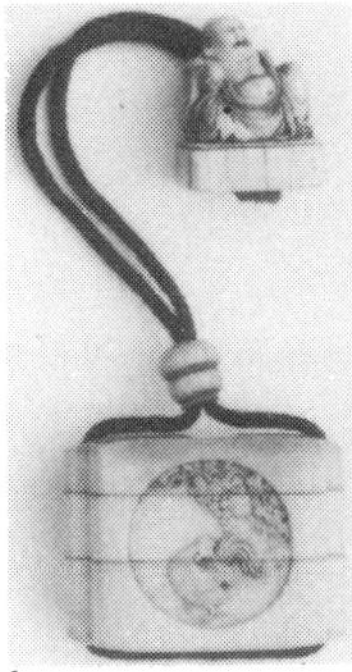
1

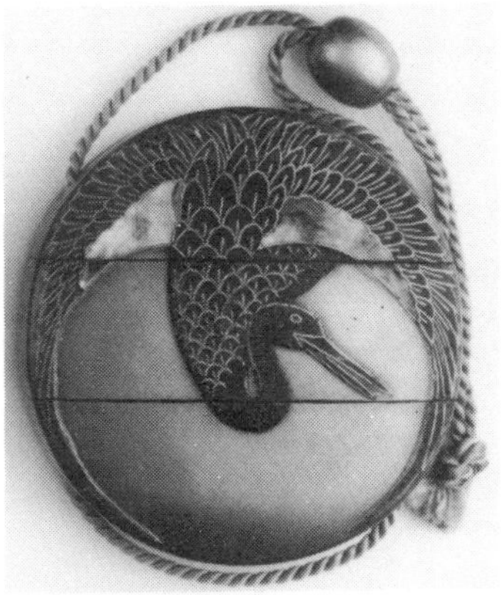
2

3

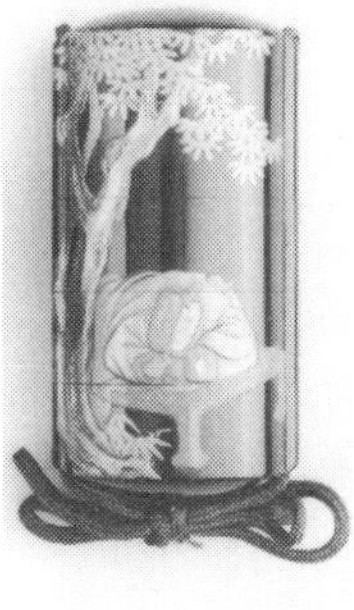
4

5

6

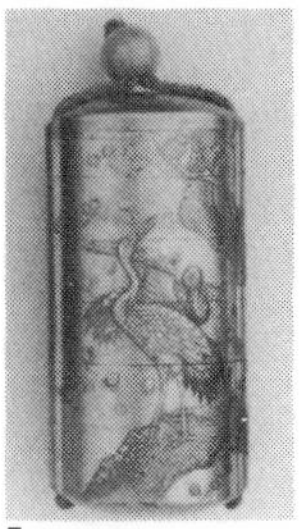
7

8

9

10

11

12

13

14

1

2

3

4

5

6

7

8

9

10

11

12

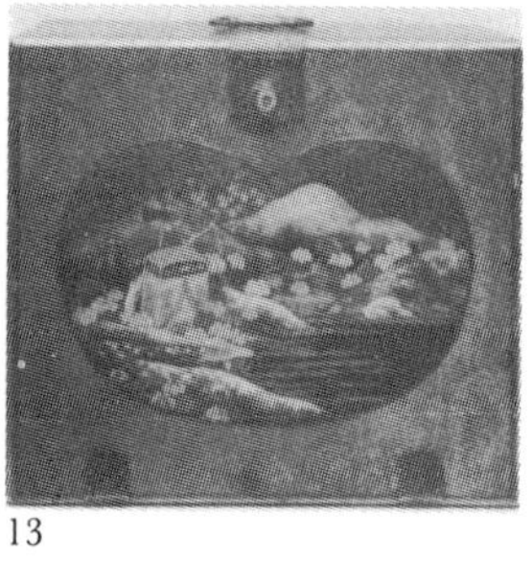
13

1
A tabako-bon, 19th century, decorated in gold *hiramakie* with sprays of bamboo, the copper fittings surmounted by *kiku*-form knops, 24.5cm (9½in) wide, *L 14 Nov,*
£715 ($1,001)

2
A lacquer kogo, late 19th century, decorated in gold *hiramakie* with *mon* scattered on an *aogai* ground, minor chips, 8.5cm (3¼in) wide, *NY 24 Sept,*
$660 (£471)

3
A lacquer two-tiered kogo, late 19th century, decorated in gold and *roiro hiramakie* with rows of stylised medallions, some wear and small chips, 14cm (5½in) wide, *NY 24 Sept,*
$1,045 (£746)

4
A lacquer document box, late 19th century, decorated in *kinji* and *fundame takamakie* with flowering cherry branches on a *roiro* ground, minor nicks, 40.5cm (16in) wide, *NY 24 Sept,*
$935 (£668)

5
Three sets of lacquer combs and hair pins, *(one illustrated),* late 19th century, lacquered with *aogai* flowers on a *roiro* ground, combs 9cm (3½in), *NY 24 Sept,*
$412 (£294)

6
A kogo, Meiji period, of circular form, decorated in bright *nashiji* with gold and silver florets in *takamakie*, the interior *nashiji*, 9.5cm (3¾in) diam., *NY 24 Sept,*
$1,870 (£1,336)

7
A pair of lacquer storage boxes, *(one illustrated),* Meiji period, of ovoid form, decorated in gold *hiramakie* and *mura-nashiji* with leafy vines on a *roiro* ground, both restored, 40.5cm (16in) diam., *NY 24 Sept,*
$1,650 (£1,179)

8
A lacquer kogo, Meiji period, decorated in gold and black *hiramakie* and *takamakie* with a cluster of *kiku*, with interior tray and silver mounts, minor wear, 8.5cm (3¼in) wide, *NY 10 Apr,*
$2,090 (£1,422)

9
Kaisuisai Shoga: a gold lacquer kogo, Meiji period, in the form of a *tama*, decorated in shades of gold and *hiramakie* with a flight of cranes above bamboo and *kiku*, details in red, signed, 6cm (2½in), *L 13 Mar,*
£968 ($1,491)

10
A gold lacquer ground shibayama box, cover and inner tray, c.1900, the top decorated with a peacock and hen on a perch, with iridescent mother-of-pearl plumage, the sides lacquered with flowers, the tray with ducks on a pond, 15cm (6in) wide, *S 22 Jan,*
£4,600 ($6,900)

11
A lacquer vase, Meiji period, the ground with brocade designs, decorated with several children in procession, with banners and musical instruments, in gold and coloured *takamakie*, details in ivory and mother-of-pearl, slight damage, signed *Shokasai*, 30cm (11¾in), *L 14 Nov,*
£6,050 ($8,470)

12
A natsume, 20th century, of typical form, decorated with dragonflies in gold and *takamakie*, the interior and base of *nashiji*, signed *Ko (Mitsu)*, 7cm (2¾in), *L 14 Nov,*
£660 ($924)

13
A lacquer storage box, Meiji period, with *nashiji* ground and fan-shaped panel containing a landscape in *hiramakie, takamakie, kirigane* and *mura-nashiji*, silver mounts, chips, signed *Jokasai* with *kakihan*, 35cm (13¾in) wide, *NY 10 Apr,*
$1,430 (£973)

1
Shibata Zeshin: a fan, 1879, of paper, painted in ink and colours on one side with swimming fish and on the other with plants, the struts of brown lacquer decorated with formal brocade designs in gold and coloured *takamakie*, signed, 24cm (9½in), *L 13 Nov,*
£2,860 ($4,004)

2
A black lacquer box, late Edo period, 82cm (32¼in) long, *M 30 Nov,*
FF 66,000 (£7,174; $10,259)

3
A lacquer karabitsu, late Edo period, decorated in gold *hiramakie* and *e-nashiji*, with the *mon* of the Doi of Koga, gilt copper mounts, 44cm (17in), *L 13 June,*
£1,210 ($1,936)

4
A lacquer storage chest, Edo period, decorated in red lacquer with Tokugawa *mon* on a *roiro* ground, gilt bronze mounts, some wear, 167.5cm (66in) long, *NY 24 Sept,*
$3,520 (£2,514)

5
A gold lacquer kodansu, 19th century, decorated in gold *takamakie* with temple buildings and streams in mountainous landscapes, silver mounts, unsigned, 17cm (6¾in) wide, *L 13 Nov,*
£27,500 ($38,500)

6
Taishin: a wood kobako, 19th century, decorated with a formalised swirling stream and grasses in black *ishime* lacquer and gold *takamakie*, signed, 11cm (4¼in), *L 14 Nov,*
£1,540 ($2,156)

7
A guri-lacquer box and cover, mid Edo period, deeply carved with scroll design, slight cracks, 11cm (4¼in), *L 13 June,*
£385 ($616)

8
A kobako, 19th century, in the form of an open fan, the cover of *fundame*, decorated with a bridge over a river, in gold and coloured *takamakie* with *e-nashiji* details, slight restoration, 13cm (5in), *L 13 June,*
£1,210 ($1,936)

9
A lacquer box and cover, mid 19th century, decorated on the *roiro* ground in gold *hiramakie*, gold, silver and coloured *togidashi*, *e-nashiji* and *aogai* with sprays of flowering grasses, 7cm (3in), *L 14 Nov,*
£3,960 ($5,544)

10
A kodansu, 19th century, decorated with salt-burner's huts beside a lake, all in gold *takamakie*, some wear, unsigned, 15cm (6in) wide, *L 13 June,*
£2,310 ($3,696)

11
A lacquered wood sword stand, 19th century, for a *daisho*, decorated in gold *takamakie* and *hiramakie* and gold and silver leaf, some cracks, 43.5cm (17¼in), *L 13 June,*
£2,860 ($4,576)

Bunko document box.

Hibachi portable brazier.

Jukobako tiered incense box.

Karabitsu large lacquered container.

Kendi ewer of Persian inspiration.

Kizeruzutsu pipe case.

Kobako incense box.

Kodansu perfume cabinet.

Kogo small incense box.

Koro incense burner on three legs.

Mizuire water dropper.

Natsume tea caddy.

Suzuri inkstone.

Suzuribako writing box.

Tabako-bon tobacco box.

1

2

3

4

5

6

7

8

9

10

11

1

2

3

4

5

6

7

8

9

10

11

12

13

1
A pair of silver presentation vases, *(one illustrated)*, cast with hawks on plum branches, the branches copper, the blossoms gilt, small dents, 35cm (13¾in), *NY 24 Sept,*
$4,070 (£2,907)

2
A silver lotus censer, 19th century, with fitted pierced cover in the form of a lotus root, 7cm (2¾in), *NY 24 Sept,*
$990 (£707)

3
A silver and enamel koro and cover, Meiji period, the sides modelled in relief with figures of Kannon amongst clouds, picked out with coloured enamels, some wear, 12.5cm (5in), *C 8 Oct,*
£880 ($1,232)

4
Eiichi: a bronze vase, Showa period, decorated with two bands of silvered chevrons beneath gilt bronze studs, signed, 18.5cm (7¼in), *L 12 June,*
£440 ($704)

5
An inlaid iron bottle vase, late 19th century, inlaid in silver and cloisonné with cranes in a marsh, rust patches, illegible signature, 28cm (11in), *NY 24 Sept,*
$2,200 (£1,571)

6
Miyabe Atsuyoshi: an inlaid bronze kodansu, Meiji period, the sides decorated with panels of birds, trees and foliage, worked in silver, gilt, *shakudo*, copper and bronze, repairs, signed, 20cm (8in), *L 12 June,*
£1,485 ($2,376)

7
Komai: a small metal cabinet, Meiji period, in the form of a shrine, decorated overall with exotic birds, flowers and landscapes, signed, 10cm (4in), *L 13 Mar,*
£660 ($1,016)

8
Inoue: a pair of inlaid iron spill vases, *(one illus trated)*, Meiji period, decorated in shades of gold *nunome* with pawloni among wild flowers, signed, 17cm (6¾in), *L 13 Mar,*
£1,320 ($2,033)

9
Komai: an inlaid iron cabinet, Meiji period, decorated in two shades o gold and silver, signed, 9cm (3½in), *L 14 Nov,*
£1,265 ($1,771)

10
An inlaid bronze koro a cover, Meiji period, inlai in gold, silver, *shakudo* and *sentoku*, supported by a seated *oni* worked in *sentok* and inlaid in gold, 30.5cm (12in), *NY 24 Sept,*
$16,500 (£11,786)

11
Iida: an inlaid bronze vase, Meiji period, inlaid in silver, *shakudo* and *shibuichi* with iris flowers and leaves, signed, 32.5cm (12¾in), *L 13 Mar,*
£1,375 ($2,118)

12
An inlaid bronze charge late 19th century, inlaid in gold, silver, and *sentoku* with a giant figure of Daruma leaning over the crest of Mt. Fuji, 46cm (18in) diam., *NY 10 Apr,*
$2,200 (£1,496)

13
A pair of inlaid bronze vases, Meiji period, inlaid in gold and silver with a woman by a waterfall and a fisherman, 35cm (13¾in), *NY 24 Sept,*
$1,650 (£1,179)

See p.574 for glossary of types of decoration.

1
A pair of inlaid bronze vases, *(one illustrated)*, Meiji period, inlaid on one side with a dragonfly among flowering shrubs, details silvered and gilt, 33.5cm (13in), *L 12 June,*
£935 ($1,496)

2
Toko: an inlaid bronze vase, Meiji period, applied in *shibuichi, shakudo, sentoku* and silver with wistaria silhouettetd against the moon, signed, 21.5cm (8½in), *L 12 June,*
£550 ($880)

3
A bronze inlaid vase, decorated in coloured metals with chrysanthemum and peony, wood stand, 15cm (6in), *C 29 Apr,*
£176 ($285)

4
A pair of bronze vases, *(one illustrated)*, Meiji period, modelled in relief with panels of birds amongst branches, dark brown patination, one with handles replaced, 49.5cm (19½in), *C 16 Apr,*
£605 ($938)

5
A small inlaid shakudo vase, Meiji period, decorated in *shibuichi, shakudo,* silver and gilt with three pigeons amongst grasses, 6cm (2½in), *L 12 June,*
£440 ($704)

6
Seiya: a bronze study of an owl, Meiji period, signed, 43cm (17in), *L 14 Nov,*
£1,870 ($2,618)

7
A bronze figure of a tiger, Meiji period, with finely stippled chocolate brown body, the stripes of a slightly paler tone, 78cm (30½in), *S 21 May,*
£2,420 ($3,872)

8
A bronze figure of a tiger, Meiji period, with cast mark *Jonan sei*, 49cm (19¼in), *NY 24 Sept,*
$1,210 (£864)

9
Teisui: a pair of bronze studies of carp, Meiji period, each naturalistically modelled swimming, rich brown patination, signed, 34cm (13½in), *L 12 June,*
£4,400 ($7,040)

10
A bronze figure of a boy with a dog, c.1900, greenish brown patina, unsigned, 56cm (22in), *NY 10 Apr,*
$2,970 (£2,020)

11
Miyao: a bronze figure of a courtier, Meiji period, holding a tray with two *tokuri* and a bell, unsigned, 24.5cm (9¾in), *L 14 Nov,*
£825 ($1,155)

12
Koichi: a bronze figure of a warrior, Meiji period, signed, 38cm (15in), *L 12 June,*
£1,210 ($1,936)

13
Genryusai Seiya: a bronze figure of a farmer, Meiji period, the old man with a sheaf of grain in one hand, the other hand holding a scythe behind his back, dark brown patination, signed, 46cm (18in), *NY 24 Sept,*
$880 (£629)

1

2

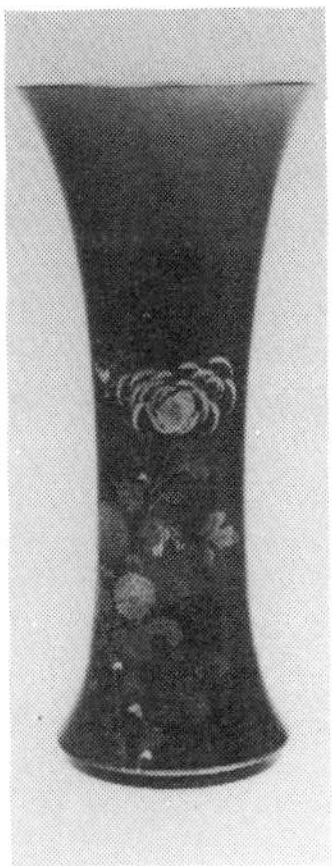
3

4

5

7

6

8

9

10

11

12

13

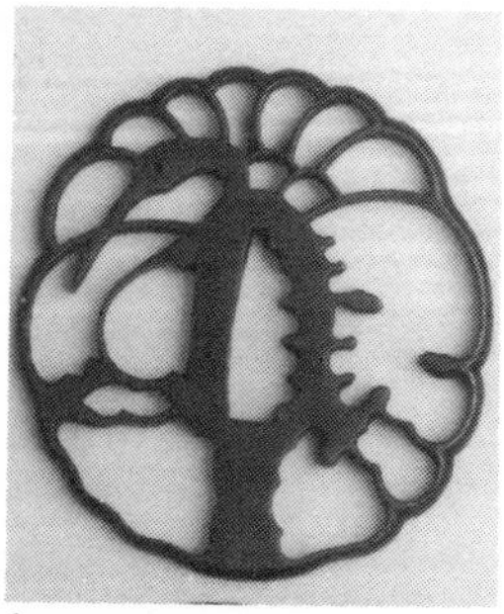
1

2

3

4

5

6

7

8

9

10

11

12

13

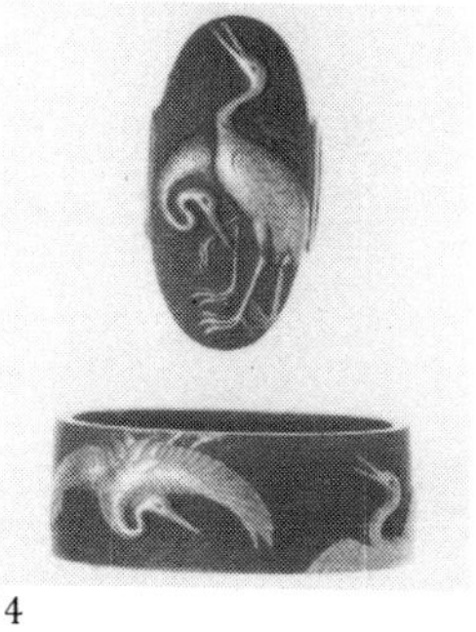
14

15

1
Nishigaki Kanshiro: a sukashi tsuba, 18th century, pierced with a crane with outstretched wings, unsigned, 8cm (3in), *L 13 Mar,*
£385 ($593)

2
Umetada Shigenari: an iron tsuba, the plate 18th century, pierced with *hitsu-ana* outlined in gold *nunome*, later decorated in Hirata-style enamels and gold wire, signed, 7cm (2¾in), *L 13 Mar,*
£462 ($711)

3
An Akasaka school tsuba, 18th century, pierced with a skein of wool and pine trees, unsigned, 8.5cm (3¼in), *L 13 Nov,*
£1,100 ($1,540)

4
Seppo Hidetomo: a sentoku tsuba, 19th century, fashioned as a coiled snake, details in gold *nunome*, signed, 8cm (3in), *L 13 Nov,*
£572 ($801)

5
Goto Tsunemasa: a tsuba, 19th century, pierced in *ito-sukashi* with branches of fruiting peach and *kiku* blossoms, signed, 8cm (3¼in), *L 13 Mar,*
£550 ($847)

6
Nagatsune (after): a tsuba, 19th century, applied with a sleeping *Oni* above whom appears a Hannya ghost, details in gilt, silver, gold *nunome* and *sentoku*, inscribed *Nagatsune*, 8cm (3in), *L 13 Mar,*
£935 ($1,440)

7
Takahashi Okitsugu: a shibuichi tsuba, late 18th century, decorated on both sides in *shakudo* and copper *guribori* with stylised reishi design, signed, 8cm (3in), *L 13 Mar,*
£605 ($932)

8
Tomotsune: a copper tsuba, 18th century, pierced with a *ho-o* above pawlonia, details in gold *nunome*, signed, 8cm (3in), *L 13 Mar,*
£3,080 ($4,743)

9
Soten school: an associated pair of tsuba, *(one illustrated)*, 19th century, for a *daisho*, each pierced and decorated with warriors battling in a landscape, details in silver, copper and gold *nunome*, each signed *Goshu Hikone ju Soheishi Nuido Soten sei*, 8 and 7.5cm (3in), *L 13 June,*
£1,210 ($1,936)

10
Yukitaka: a tsuba, late 18th/early 19th century, applied in gold wire, coloured enamels and soft metal with a *bugaku* dance hat and maple leaves, signed, 8cm (3in), *L 13 June,*
£638 ($1,021)

11
A pair of shibuichi tsuba, *(one illustrated)*, 19th century, for a *daisho*, of barbed *mokko* form, details in gilt and gold *nunome*, 7.5cm (3in), *L 13 June,*
£825 ($1,320)

12
A Kyo Sukashi tsuba, 17th century, pierced with dew upon iris, one *hitsu* plugged in *shakudo*, 8.5cm (3½in), *L 13 June,*
£308 ($493)

13
Sendai Zembei: a Sendai tsuba, 19th century, of *mokko* form, applied in two shades of gold *nunome* with *ho-o*, a snake and fox, signed with *kakihan*, 7cm (2¾in), *L 13 Nov,*
£528 ($739)

14
Sadayoshi: a shakudo nanako fuchi-kashira, 19th century, applied in silver and gold with three cranes in flight and two at rest, signed with *kakihan*, *L 13 Nov,*
£418 ($585)

15
Soten school: a shakudo nanako fuchi-kashira, 19th century, decorated in *iroe-takazogan* with Yoshitsune and Benkei battling on the Goto Bridge, details in gilt, copper, *shakudo*, *shibuichi* and silver, unsigned, *L 13 Mar,*
£374 ($576)

See p.574 for glossary of types of decoration.

1
Yasuchika: a copper kozuka, 19th century, incised and carved with Daruma wrapped in a robe, his eyes picked out in gold, the earring in silver, signed, *L 13 Nov,*
£198 ($277)

2
Tokimasa: a shibuichi kozuka, 19th century, carved in low relief with Daruma crossing the sea on a bamboo twig, details in gilt, signed, *L 13 Mar,*
£286 ($440)

3
A copper kozuka, 19th century, applied in *shakudo, shibuichi* and gold *nunome* with a *sake* bottle, the reverse with *katakiri* design and inscribed with a poem in praise of wine, *L 13 Nov,*
£374 ($524)

4
Yoshioka Yasutsugu: a shakudo nanako kozuka, 18th century, applied in silver, gold and *shakudo* with a banner tied to a pole, signed, *L 13 Nov,*
£330 ($462)

5
A Nara school sentoku kozuka, 18th century, applied with Rinnasei accompanied by the crane, details in silver, *shibuichi* and gilt, signed *Bosoken Yasuyuki* with seal, *L 13 Nov,*
£242 ($339)

6
Fukawa Kazunori: a shibuichi kozuka, 19th century, details in silver and gold, signed, *L 13 Nov,*
£506 ($708)

7
A suit of armour, Sabinuri Gomai Do Tosei Gusoku, mid Edo period, *L 13 Nov,*
£5,170 ($7,238)

8
A Kon-Ito-Odoshi Tachi Do Tosei Gusoku, helmet and mask c.1700, remainder c.1800, *L 13 June,*
£7,150 ($11,440)

9
A pair of iron abumi (stirrups), late 17th/early 18th century, each inlaid in silver with tied bundles of grasses above water, the interior of worn red lacquer, signed *Kanatsugu (Kinji) ju Nagatsugu,* some inlay missing, *L 13 June,*
£770 ($1,232)

10
Hizen Masahiro (ascribed to): a mounted o-tanto or wakizashi blade, 39.5cm (15½in), *L 13 June,*
£5,500 ($8,800)

11
A mounted daisho, shinto katana blade, 59.5cm (23½in), shinto wakizashi blade, 33cm (13in), *L 13 Nov,*
£4,400 ($6,160)

12
Izumi (no) Kami Kunisada (ascribed to): a mounted wakizashi blade, 50.5cm (20in), *L 13 June,*
£2,200 ($3,520)

13
A mounted wakizashi blade, 40.5cm (16in), *L 13 June,*
£1,870 ($2,992)

14
A silver-mounted itomaki-tachi blade ascribed to Gassan, 66.5cm (26in), *L 13 Nov,*
£8,800 ($12,320)

Aikuchi dagger.

Daisho pair of long and short swords.

Fuchi-kashira hilt end and band on sword handle.

Handachi long sword in court mount.

Katana sword blade mounted to hang edge upwards.

Koto old swords (14th to early 16th century).

Kozuka hilt of small knife accompanying sword in scabbard.

Shinto new swords (mid 16th to 18th century).

Tachi sword blade mounted to hang edge downwards, court mount.

Tanto dagger with tsuba.

Tsuba sword guard.

Wakizashi short sword.

1

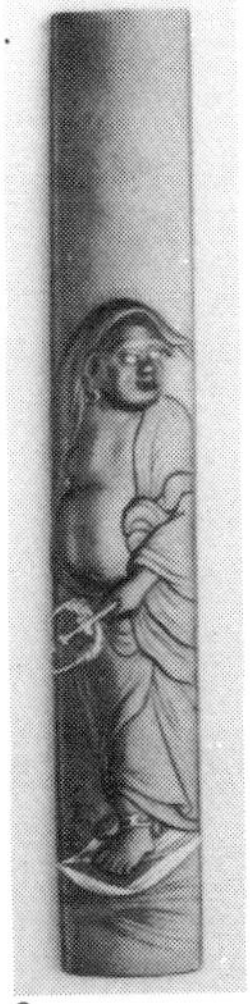
2

3

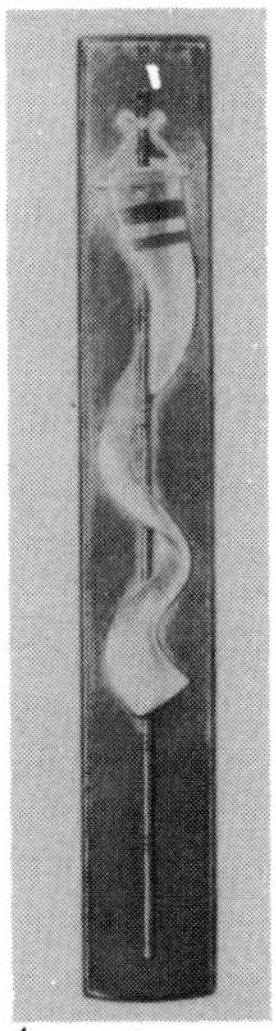
4

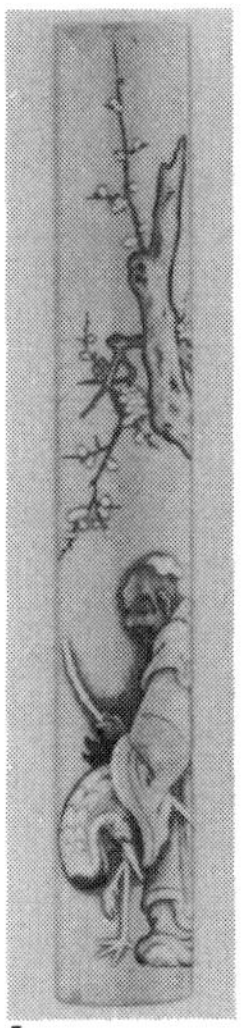
5

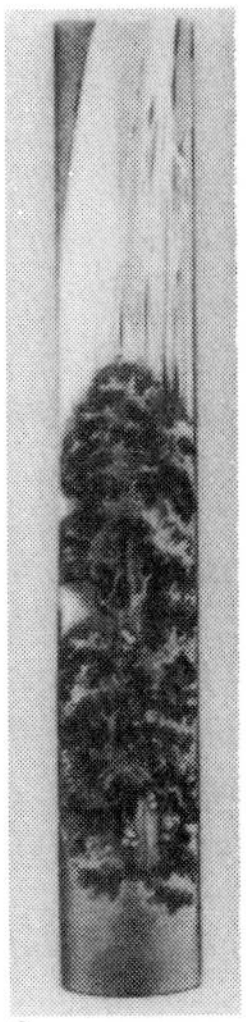
6

7

8

9

10

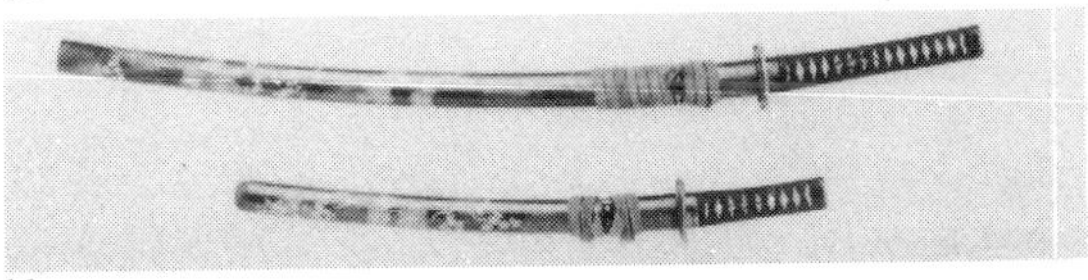
11

12

13

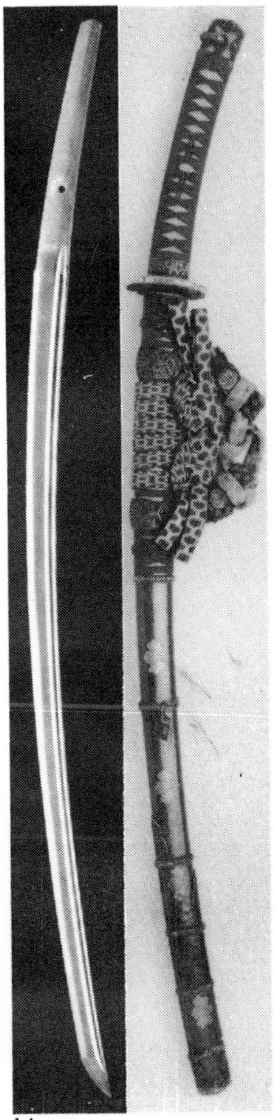
14

1

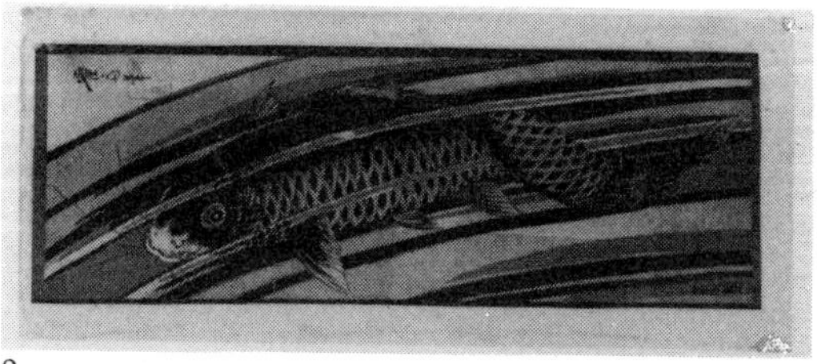
2

3

4

5

6

7

8

9

10

1
Buncho, *Hosoban*: the actor Iwai Hanshiro as the maidservant Osugi standing by a garden fence, seal Mori-uji, good impression, *L 18 Dec,*
£2,420 ($3,461)

2
Eisen, *Kakemono*: a giant carp leaping up a waterfall, signed *Keisai hitsu*, seal Eisen, publisher Kansen-do, good impression and colour, *L 13 June,*
£1,375 ($2,200)

3
Eishi, *Oban*: the courtesan Kisegawa of Matsuba-ya looking at the handscroll, from the series 'The Six Immortal Flowers (or Beautiful Poets) of the Green Houses', publisher Nishimura-ya Yohachi (Eijudo), good impression, *L 13 June,*
£2,200 ($3,520)

4
Eishi, *Oban*: a sheet from a triptych, a party in a teahouse in progress, with a seated *geisha*, publisher Izumiya Ichibei, good impression, *L 18 Dec,*
£770 ($1,101)

5
Hiroshige, *Oban*: the Evening Bell of the Mii Temple, from the set 'The Eight Views of Omi', a classic poem above, date seal, Year of the Snake (1857), publisher Shitaya Uoei, good impression and colour, *L 13 June,*
£935 ($1,496)

6
Gakutei, *Oban yoko-e*: Uji River and eight views of Shinzan, Osaka, signed *Gogaku*, seal Gogaku, very good impression and colour, *L 13 June,*
£1,760 ($2,816)

7
Hiroshige, *Oban yoko-e*: Hoeido Tokaido, no.46 from the series 'The Fifty-three Stations on the Tokaido Road', very good impression, *NY 24 Sept,*
$3,960 (£2,829)

8
Hiroshige, *Oban yoko-e:* View of Tenryu River, from the series 'The Fifty-three Stations on the Tokaido Road', publisher Hoeido, good, early impression and colour, *L 18 Dec,*
£1,100 ($1,573)

9
Hiroshige, *Oban yoko-e*: Mi River, from the Hoeido's Tokaido series, late but good impression and colour, *L 13 June,*
£1,760 ($2,816)

10
Hiroshige, *Oban yoko-e*: a snowy evening in a village, no.16 from Hoeido's Tokaido series, publisher Takeno-uchi, good impression, *L 13 June,*
£6,820 ($10,912)

1
Hiroshige, *Aiban yoko-e*: Ishiyakushi, from the *Gyosho Tokaido* series, good impression and state, *L 18 Dec,*
£1,210 ($1,730)

2
Hiroshige, *Oban yoko-e*: The Flight of Lady Tokiwa with three children, from the series 'Biography of Hero Yoshitusne', publisher Senkakudo, good impression and colour, *L 13 June,*
£385 ($616)

3
Hokusai, *Oban tate-e*: The Coast of Tago at Eijiri, from the series 'Thirty-six Views of Fuji', good impression and moderately good colour, large repaired area, *NY 24 Sept,*
$1,650 (£1,179)

4
Hokusai, *Oban yoko-e*: Sumida, one of the trilogy *Setsugekka*, 'Snow, Moon and Flowers', very good impression and colour, *L 18 Dec,*
£1,760 ($2,517)

5
Hokusai, *Oban yoko-e*: Fukui Bridge in Echizen Province, from the series 'Famous Bridges', publisher Eijudo, 1831-32, very good impression and colour, *NY 24 Sept,*
$3,850 (£2,750)

6
Hokusai, *Oban yoko-e*: butterfly and tree peonies from the 'Large Flower' set, 1830-31, publisher Eijudo, very good impression, good colour, *NY 24 Sept,*
$6,600 (£4,714)

7
Hiroshige, *Oban*: The Rapids in the Mountains of Izu, from the series 'Thirty-six views of Fuji', very good impression and colour, *L 13 June,*
£352 ($563)

8
Shun'ei, *Hosoban*: the actor Otani Oniji III, good impression and colour, *L 18 Dec,*
£770 ($1,101)

9
Toyokuni, Square *surimono*: the actor Ichikawa Danjuro seated beside a hearth with a kettle, a poem above by Rokugyokuen Tonomori, good impression, *L 13 June,*
£440 ($704)

10
Hasui, *Oban tate-e*: Shrine of Benten at Inokashira in Snow, publisher Watanabe-Shozaburo, very good impression, *NY 24 Sept,*
$1,320 (£943)

11
Toyokuni II, *Oban yoko-e*: Oshima Island seen from the Atami Beach, from the set 'The Eight Fine Views of Famous Places', publisher Iseya Rihei, good impression and colour, *L 13 June,*
£825 ($1,320)

1

2

3

4

5

6

7

8

9

10

11

1

2

3

4

5

6

7

8

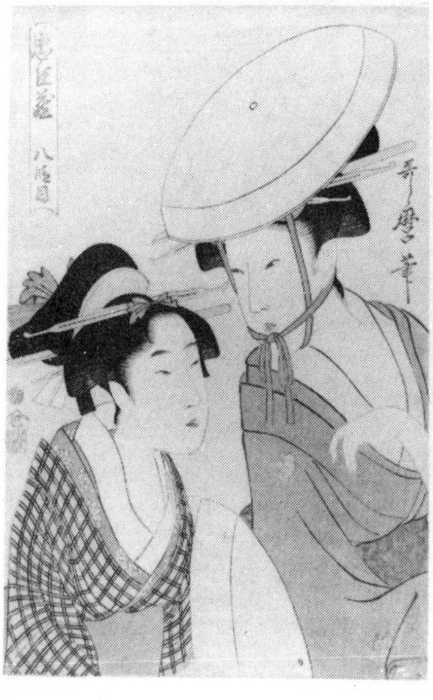
9

10

1
Kuniyoshi, *Oban tate-e*: the actor Ichikawa Kodanji as the ghost of Asakura Togo, in the play *Sakura-zoshi*, performed 1851, publisher Mera and Watanabe, engraver Take, very good impression and colour, *NY 24 Sept,*
$990 (£707)

2
Harunobu, *Chuban*: two *geishas*, each with a *samisen*, the *shoji* half opened to reveal a night view of Sumida River, from the set 'Journey from Kyoto', good impression, *L 13 June,*
£1,870 ($2,992)

3
Kunisada, *Oban*: a *geisha* seated pensively by a brazier, an inset picture of a pine tree and crane at top right corner, from the set 'A Collection of Fashionable Compatibles', publisher Ezaki-ya, very good impression and colour, *L 13 June,*
£880 ($1,408)

4
Kiyonaga, *Chuban*: a courtesan about to go to bed, talking to a passing maid, from the series 'Amorous Contest of Charming Women', good impression, *L 18 Dec,*
£1,650 ($2,360)

5
Shinsui, *Oban tate-e*: a young woman combing her hair against a background of sky, dated 1936, publisher Watanabe, very good impression and colour, *NY 24 Sept,*
$1,100 (£786)

6
Shunko, *Hosoban*: the actor Osagawa Tsuneyo II standing by a garden gate, good impression, *L 18 Dec,*
£660 ($944)

7
Shuncho, *Oban tate-e*: a *bijin* and three attendants, publisher Iseya Jisuke, good impression, moderately good colour, *NY 24 Sept,*
$770 (£550)

8
Koryusai, *Aiban*: Two *geisha* walking side-by-side 'talking about customers getting drunk' from the set 'Customs and Manners of Modern Geisha', with an inscription along the title 'when I heard he was tipsy, I felt reluctant ...', good impression and state, *L 18 Dec,*
£5,500 ($7,865)

9
Utamaro, *Oban*: The Bridal Journey, Act VIII of the drama *Chushingura*, two beauties portrayed as the characters of the drama, Tonase and her daughter Konami, on their way to Yamashina to find the latter's fiancé Rikiya, publisher Nishimuraya Yohachi, good impression and colour, *L 18 Dec,*
£10,450 ($14,944)

10
Utamaro, *Oban*: The courtesan Hanazuma of Hyogoya, wringing a letter in her hands, from the series 'A Comparison of the Outstanding Beauties of the Day', publisher Wakasaya Yoichi, very good impression and good colour, *L 13 June,*
£8,250 ($13,200)

Chinese Works of Art

Chinese Dynasties and Reign Titles

Shangyin	c.1600-c.1027 BC	Liao	916-1125
Zhou	1027-475	Song	560-1279
Qin	221-206	Jin	1115-1234
Han	206-220 AD	Yuan	1279-1368
Sui	581-618		
Tang	618-907		

MING			
Hongwu	1368-1398	Jiajing	1522-1566
Yongle	1403-1424	Longqing	1567-1572
Xuande	1426-1435	Wanli	1573-1619
Chenghua	1465-1487	Tianqi	1621-1627
Hongzhi	1488-1505	Chongzheng	1628-1643
Zhengde	1506-1521		

QING			
Shunzhi	1644-1661	Xianfeng	1851-1861
Kangxi	1662-1722	Tongzhi	1862-1873
Yongzheng	1723-1735	Guangxu	1874-1907
Qianlong	1736-1795	Xuantong	1908-1912
Jiaqing	1796-1820	Hongxian	1916
Daoguang	1821-1850		

Article:
Reign marks on Chinese porcelain *pp* 709-711

See also:
Colour illustrations *pp* 570-573

Main sub-sections:
Ceramics *pp* 703-728
Cloisonné enamels *pp* 698-699
Furniture *pp* 690-691
Ivories *p* 702
Jade *pp* 696-697
Lacquer, rhinoceros horn and wood *p* 695
Metalwork *pp* 700-701
Snuff bottles and glass *pp* 692-694
Textiles *p* 689

1
A couched gold blue silk dragon robe, Daoguang, in red, blue, grey and yellow satin stitch, 144.5cm (57in), *NY 10 Apr,*
$4,950 (£3,367)

2
An orange *kesi* dragon robe, 19th century, detailed with coral beads, 140cm (55in), *NY 10 Apr,*
$2,420 (£1,646)

3
A yellow silk embroidered jacket, late 19th century, satin-stitched with phoenix and peacock roundels, 79cm (31in), *NY 10 Apr,*
$2,310 (£1,571)

4
A pink quilted silk lady's robe, late 19th century, the borders embroidered with flowers, 142cm (56in), *NY 25 Sept,*
$990 (£660)

5
A blue wool felt jacket, 19th century, embroidered with the eight Immortals, 61cm (24in), *NY 10 Apr,*
$1,100 (£748)

6
A red gauze summer robe, late 19th century, 139.5cm (55in), *NY 25 Sept,*
$1,870 (£1,246)

7
A lady's informal robe, 19th century, the red ground embroidered in various stitches with a *lishui* border, *S 22 Jan,*
£240 ($360)

8
A dark blue silk lady's coat, 19th century, finely worked in Peking knot, 112cm (44in), *NY 25 Sept,*
$605 (£403)

1

2

3

4

5

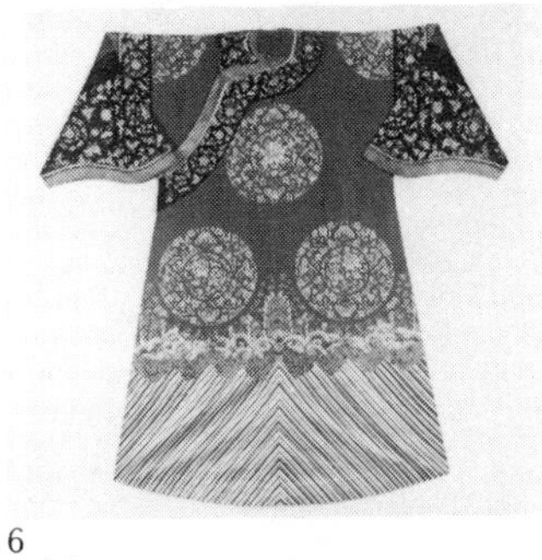
6

7

8

1

2

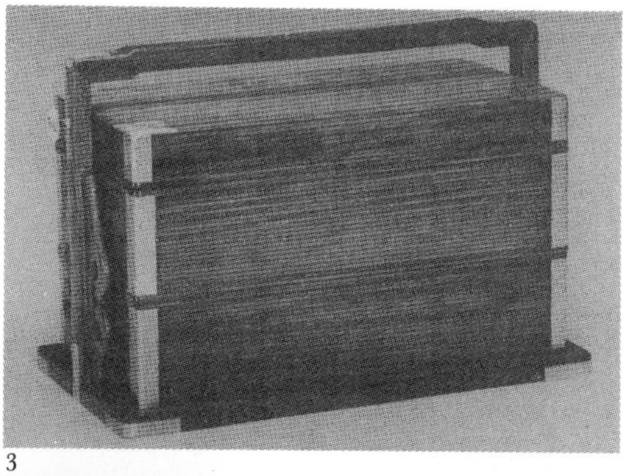
3

4

5

6

7

8

9

10

1
A huanghuali three-drawer altar coffer, (*jitaishichu*), 15th/16th century, 81.5cm (33¼in) high, *NY 11 Apr,*
$16,500 (£11,224)

2
A huanghuali seal chest, (*guanpixiang*), 17th century, 36.5cm (14½in) high, *NY 11 Apr,*
$3,300 (£2,245)

3
A bronze-mounted huanghuali travelling box, 17th century, 33.5cm (13in), *HK 22 May,*
HK$13,200 (£1,168; $1,857)

4
A pair of huanghuali tapered cupboards, (*gui*), 16th century, 111.5cm (44in), *NY 11 Apr,*
$20,900 (£14,218)

5
A huanghuali horseshoe-back armchair, (*jiaoyi*), 16th/17th century, extensive lacquer remaining, 101cm (39¾in), *NY 26 Sept,*
$12,100 (£8,066)

6
A huanghuali side table (*bienan*), 16th/17th century, 80cm (31½in), *NY 11 Apr,*
$13,200 (£8,979)

7
A huanghuali yokeback armchair (*guanmaoshi*), 17th century, 103cm (40½in), *NY 11 Apr,*
$4,675 (£3,180)

8
A huanghuali and Hongmu scroll chest, 17th century, 69cm (27in) wide, *NY 26 Sept,*
$1,540 (£1,026)

9
A huali low table, 17th century, 45cm (17¾in), *NY 26 Sept,*
$2,530 (£1,686)

10
A huanghuali clothes cupboard, (*gui*), 17th/18th century, 172.5cm (68in), *NY 26 Sept,*
$7,150 (£4,766)

1
A huanghuali side table, **(*bienan*),** 17th century, 134.5cm (53in), *NY 26 Sept,* **$13,750 (£9,166)**

2
A huanghuali horseshoe-back armchair, (*jiaoyi*), 17th century, 97.5cm (38½in), *NY 11 Apr,* **$6,600 (£4,490)**

3
A Tielimu side table, **(*bienan*),** 17th century, 83.5cm (33in), *NY 11 Apr,* **$3,300 (£2,245)**

4
A huali pedestal partners' desk (*shuzhuo*), 18th century, recessed brass pulls, 82cm (32¼in), *NY 11 Apr,* **$4,125 (£2,806)**

5
A pair of huanghuali square stools (*fangdeng*), 18th century, 46cm (18¼in), *NY 26 Sept,* **$2,475 (£1,650)**

6
A hongmu rectangular stool, 18th century, 52cm (20½in), *NY 11 Apr,* **$715 (£486)**

7
A hongmu and huamu spindleback armchair, 18th century, reduced in height, 77.5cm (30½in), *NY 11 Apr,* **$495 (£337)**

8
A huanghuali stand, 17th/18th century, with moveable columns set up to support a mirror or book, 41.5cm (16in), *HK 22 May,* **HK$7,150 (£633; $1,006)**

9
A nanmu low table, 18th century, of *kang* form, 90cm (35½in), *L 9 May,* **£2,090 ($3,365)**

10
A three-drawer huali desk, (*shuzhuo*), late 18th/early 19th century, 81cm (32in), *NY 11 Apr,* **$2,970 (£2,020)**

11
A hongmu stool, (*fang-deng*), late 18th/19th century, 52.5cm (20¾in), *NY 11 Apr,* **$385 (£262)**

12
A cinnabar lacquer cabinet, Qianlong, 62cm (24in), *HK 20 May,* **HK$26,400 (£2,336; $3,738)**

13
A pair of huali tall stands, 19th century, 86cm (34in), *NY 11 Apr,* **$1,320 (£898)**

14
A hardwood cabinet, late 18th/early 19th century, 183cm (72in), *L 31 Oct,* **£3,080 ($4,312)**

15
A set of three iron-wood tables, *(one illustrated),* early 19th century, 54cm (21¼in), *L 9 May,* **£2,255 ($3,630)**

16
A pair of hongmu side chairs, *(one illustrated),* 19th century, *NY 26 Sept,* **$2,530 (£1,686)**

17
A huali desk (*shuzhuo*), 19th century, 83cm (32¾in), *NY 26 Sept,* **$1,100 (£733)**

1

2

3

4

5

6

7

8

9

10

11

12

13

14

15

16

17

1

2

3

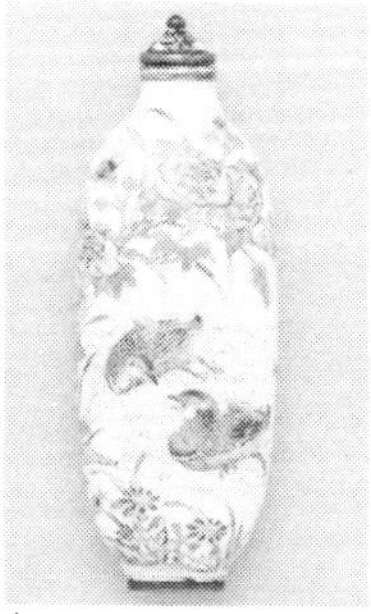
4

5

6

7

8

9

10

11

12

13

14

15

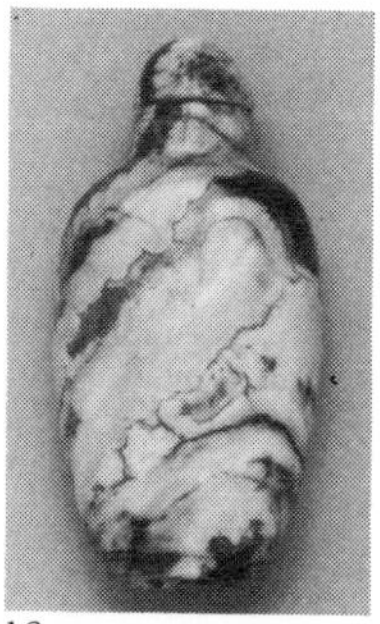
16

17

18

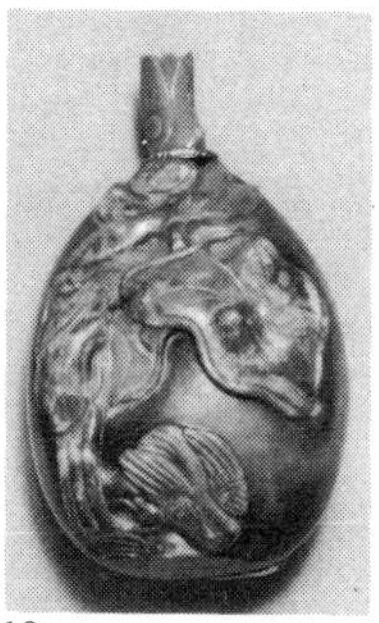
19

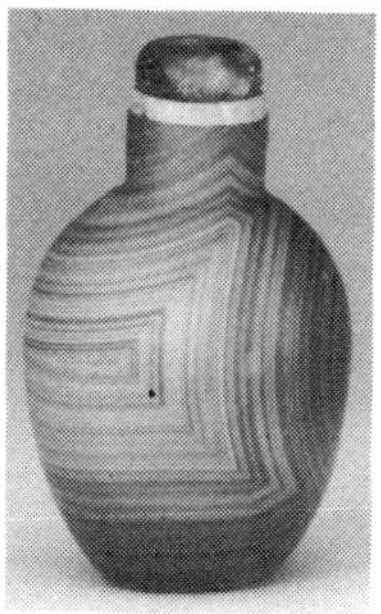
20

1
An enamelled glass snuff bottle, 1770-1820, *gu yuxuan* mark on the base, *NY 27 June,*
$7,975 (£5,212)

2
An enamelled glass snuff bottle, Ye Family Workshops, Peking, c.1933-43, painted in 'famille-rose' enamels, Qianlong mark on base, *L 6 May,*
£9,020 ($14,342)

3
A jadeite snuff bottle, 1800-60, the stone of moss-green tone with apple-green suffusions, *NY 27 June,*
$825 (£539)

4
A Canton enamel snuff bottle, Yongzheng/Qianlong, on one side a pair of mandarin ducks, the other an exotic bird, *NY 27 June,*
$5,500 (£3,595)

5
A cloisonné enamel snuff bottle, 1850-80, the black ground decorated with lotus spray, *NY 27 June,*
$275 (£180)

6
A Canton enamel snuff bottle, Qianlong, decorated with birds perched on peony sprigs, *L 6 May,*
£1,210 ($1,924)

7
A 'famille-rose' porcelain snuff bottle, Daoguang, *Yongle tang zhi* mark on base, *NY 27 June,*
$495 (£323)

8
A cinnabar lacquer snuff bottle, 1820-80, carved in relief, *NY 27 June,*
$550 (£359)

9
A reticulated porcelain snuff bottle, 1820-60, decorated with four bats enclosing a *shou* medallion, imitating jade, *NY 27 June,*
$440 (£287)

10
A moulded porcelain figural snuff bottle, depicting Liu Hai, *NY 27 June,*
$2,530 (£1,653)

11
A reticulated porcelain snuff bottle, 19th century, decorated with *shou* medallion encircled with *wu fu,* *L 6 May,*
£418 ($665)

12
A porcelain snuff bottle, moulded with quail amongst flowering shrubs, *C 29 Apr,*
£209 ($339)

13
A cinnabar lacquer snuff bottle, carved in deep relief, incised Qianlong mark, *L 6 May,*
£825 ($1,312)

14
A laque burgauté snuff bottle, inlaid with mother-of-pearl, *L 6 May,*
£638 ($1,014)

15
An ivory snuff bottle, carved with figures seated in a pavilion, *L 6 May,*
£374 ($595)

16
A mammoth tooth snuff bottle, of ivory tone with concentric darker bands, *NY 27 June,*
$412 (£269)

17
A faceted jasper snuff bottle, 1750-1820, the stone a rich moss-green, *NY 27 June,*
$6,050 (£3,954)

18
An amber snuff bottle, 1780-1860, of rich honey colour, well hollowed out, *NY 27 June,*
$1,045 (£683)

19
A chalcedony snuff bottle, 1820-80, of natural pebble form, *NY 27 June,*
$1,760 (£1,150)

20
A carnelian agate snuff bottle, 1800-80, the reddish stone suffused with a white thumb print pattern, *L 6 May,*
£682 ($1,084)

1
A glass inside-painted snuff bottle, by Sun Xingwu, signed and dated 1899, *L 6 May,*
£418 ($665)

2
A glass snuff bottle, 18th century, the metal suffused with 'tortoise-shell' pattern of yellow and red, *L 6 May,*
£165 ($262)

3
An inside-painted glass snuff bottle, signed by Ma Shao-hsuan, one side with a view of a sampan, the other with a long inscription, *L 6 May,*
£550 ($874)

4
An inside-painted rock crystal snuff bottle, signed Ye Zhongsan, dated 1922, *L 6 May,*
£440 ($700)

5
An interior painted snuff bottle, painted on one side with a rabbit, the other with a squirrel, *C 29 Apr,*
£110 ($178)

6
A Peking glass snuff bottle, 18th century, Peking Palace Workshops, the metal of rich ruby-red tone, *NY 27 June,*
$1,320 (£863)

7
A Yixing pottery snuff bottle, of ovoid fluted form, *NY 27 June,*
$1,320 (£863)

8
A glass overlay snuff bottle, 18th century, carved in red with a fruiting pomegranate, *L 6 May,*
£209 ($332)

9
A glass snuff bottle, 19th century, decorated with orange splashes in imitation of realgar, *L 6 May,*
£880 ($1,399)

10
A rock crystal snuff bottle, the stone with clusters of black needle-like inclusions, *C 29 Apr,*
£275 ($446)

11
A glass overlay snuff bottle, 18th century, decorated with 'the Three Abundances', *NY 27 June,*
$1,540 (£1,006)

12
A glass overlay snuff bottle, 1820-80, the milk-white ground decorated in green, *NY 27 June,*
$2,200 (£1,438)

13
A multi-coloured 'seal-type' glass overlay snuff bottle, Yangzhou School, decorated with ducks and lotus, *NY 27 June,*
$770 (£503)

14
A glass overlay snuff bottle, 18th century, decorated in red with a slender *chilong* in flight, *NY 27 June,*
$1,100 (£719)

15
A 'seal type' glass overlay snuff bottle, Yangzhou School, the white ground decorated in dark green, *L 6 May,*
£418 ($665)

16
A seven-colour overlay snuff bottle, 1820-80, decorated with flowering peonies, *L 6 May,*
£1,100 ($1,749)

17
A glass overlay snuff bottle, 1780-1820, decorated with peony spray, *L 6 May,*
£3,630 ($5,772)

18
A glass overlay snuff bottle, decorated in blue on each side with baskets of fruit and flowers, *L 6 May,*
£352 ($560)

19
A glass overlay snuff bottle, the snowflake ground decorated in red with a dragon and phoenix, *L 6 May,*
£275 ($437)

20
A red overlay snuff bottle, decorated with figures in a sampan, *C 29 Apr,*
£165 ($267)

1

2

3

4

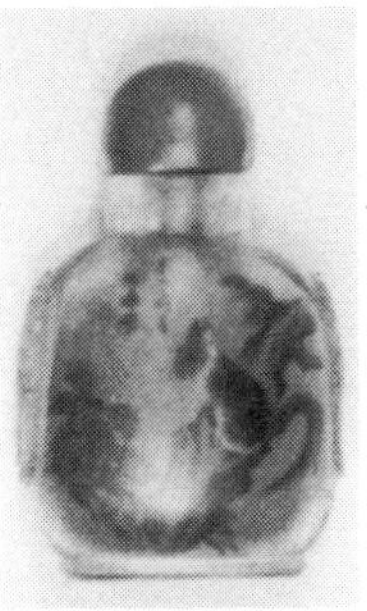
5

6

7

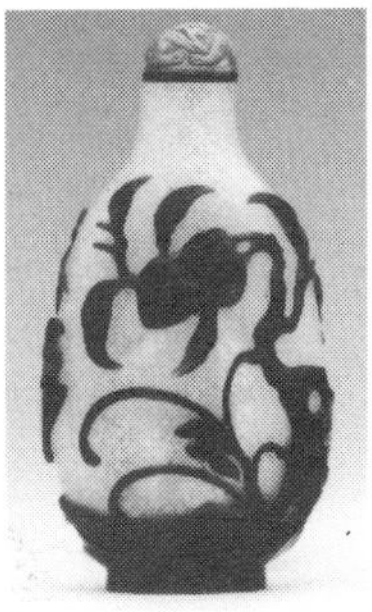
8

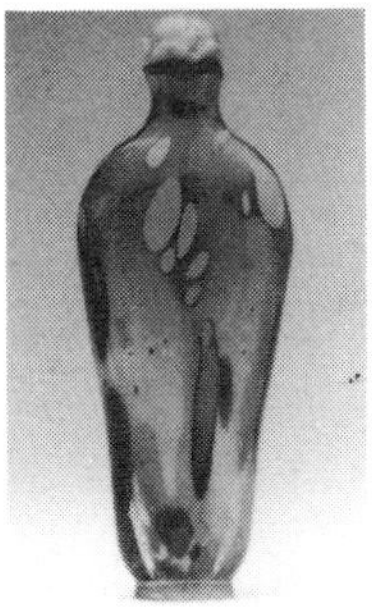
9

10

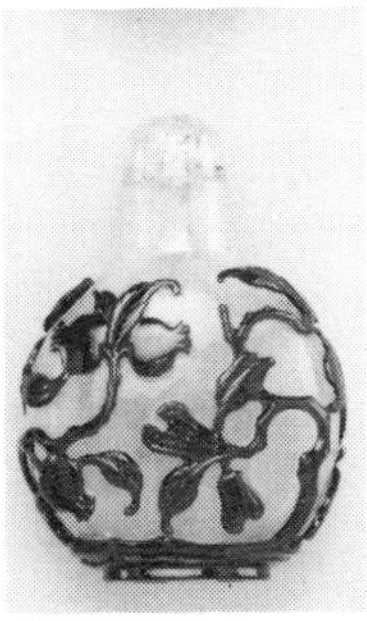
11

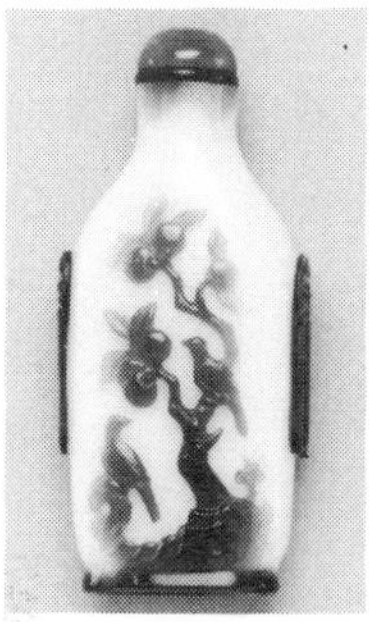
12

13

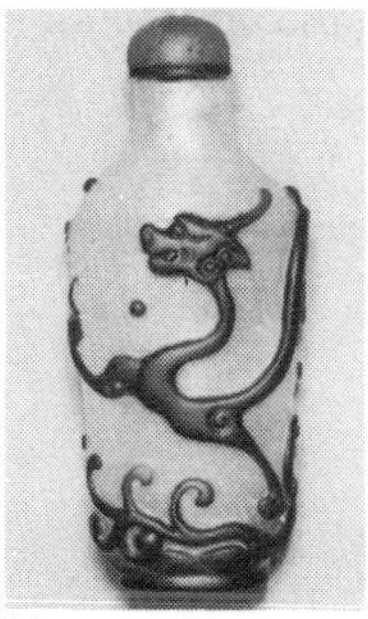
14

15

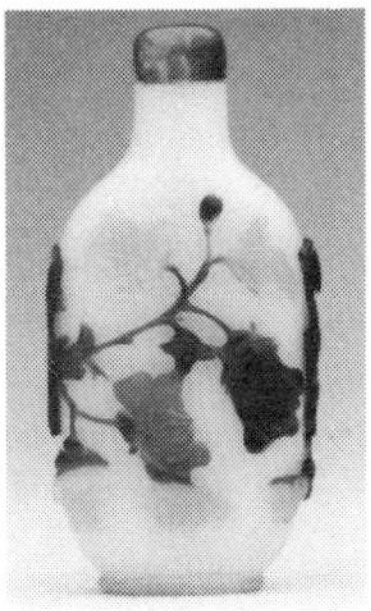
16

17

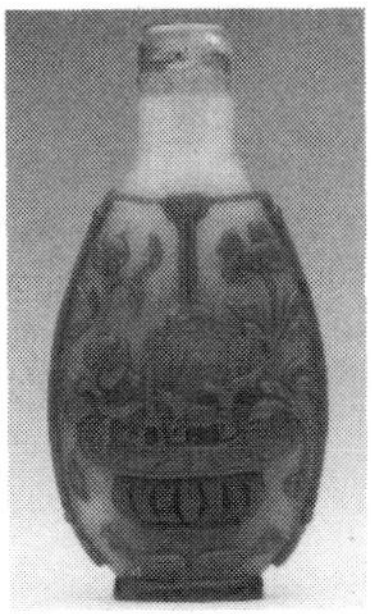
18

19

20

1

2

3

4

5
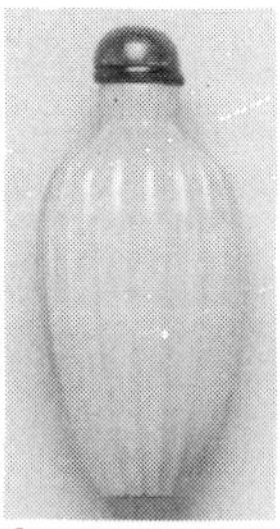
6
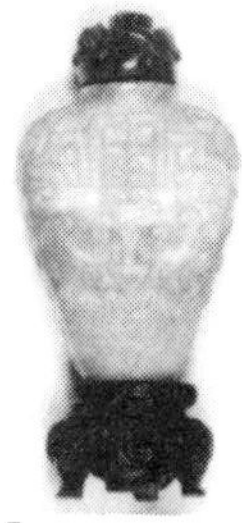
7

8

9

10

11

12

13

14

15 16

17
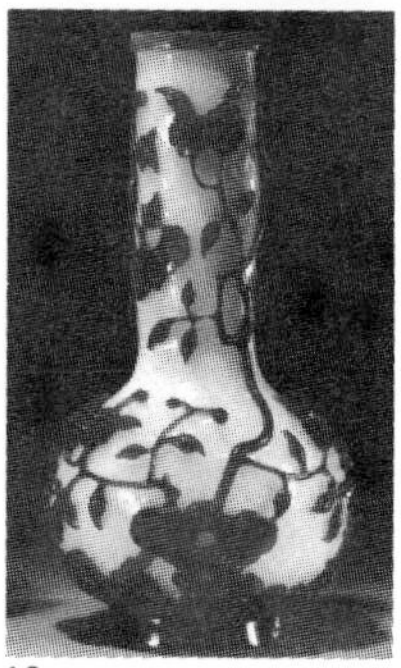
18
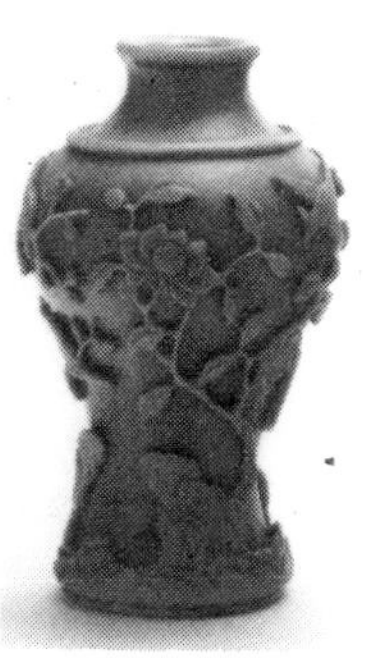
19

20

1
A moss agate snuff bottle, 1800-80, the stone suffused with russet, ochre and orange strands, *L 6 May,*
£396 ($630)

2
An amber snuff bottle, 1750-1850, the honey-coloured material suffused with crizzling, *L 6 May,*
£506 ($804)

3
A 'macaroni' agate snuff bottle, well hollowed out, *L 6 May,*
£396 ($630)

4
A jadeite snuff bottle, 1780-1880, the stone suffused with mottled emerald and darker green inclusions, *L 6 May,*
£770 ($1,224)

5
A white jadeite snuff bottle, 1750-1850, carved with wickerwork pattern, *NY 27 June,*
$825 (£539)

6
A yellow jade snuff bottle, 18th century, *NY 27 June,*
$2,750 (£1,797)

7
A nephrite jade snuff bottle and stopper, the whitish stone with emerald striations, *C 29 Apr,*
£110 ($178)

8
A Peking glass bowl and cover, mark and period of Qianlong, the metal of translucent blue tone, *L 31 Oct,*
£484 ($678)

9
A Peking glass vase, four-character mark and period of Qianlong, *L 31 Oct,*
£3,520 ($4,928)

10
An Imperial yellow Peking glass vase, four-character mark and period of Qianlong, of plain opaque metal, *L 9 May,*
£1,375 ($2,214)

11
A Peking glass vase, four-character mark and period of Qianlong, of ruby-red colour, *L 31 Oct,*
£1,980 ($2,772)

12
A pair of overlay Peking glass vases, *(one illustrated),* 19th century,, with ruby-red overlay, *L 9 May,*
£880 ($1,417)

13
A pair of glass overlay bottle vases *(one illustrated),* Jiaqing, *HK 19 Nov,*
HK$41,800 (£3,766; $5,272)

14
A red-overlay Peking glass jar, 19th century, the white body decorated in red relief, *L 9 May,*
£792 ($1,275)

15
A pair of green glass overlay vases *(one illustrated),* 19th century, *L 9 May,*
£462 ($744)

16
A pair of blue glass overlay vases, *(one illustrated),* 19th century, *L 9 May,*
£396 ($637)

17
A pair of blue overlay Peking vases *(one illustrated),* 19th century, *L 31 Oct,*
£880 ($1,232)

18
A red Peking glass overlay vase, 19th century, the pattern of prunus and roses growing from rockwork, *NY 26 Sept,*
$2,310 (£1,540)

19
A pair of overlay Peking glass vases, *(one illustrated),* 19th century, of vivid turquoise with yellow overlay, *L 9 May,*
£638 ($1,027)

20
A red Peking glass bottle-form vase, 19th century, with incised *yongzheng* mark, *NY 26 Sept,*
$660 (£440)

1
A jichimu scroll pot, 18th century, the base with recessed central medallion, the dark wood characteristically well-figured, 25.5cm (10in) high, *NY 11 Apr,*
$2,750 (£1,871)

2
A huanghuali brushpot, 17th century, with richly figured grain, the base with an inset plug, 20cm (8in) wide, *NY 26 Sept,*
$1,650 (£1,100)

3
A huanghuali brushpot, 17th/18th century, the wood of deep reddish-brown colour with 'eyes' and whorls, 19.5cm (7¾in), *HK 22 May,*
HK$6,050 (£535; $851)

4
A huanghuali brushpot, 17th century, carved in light reddish-brown wood to simulate a gnarled segment of tree trunk, 22.5cm (8¾in), *NY 11 Apr,*
$3,850 (£2,619)

5
A rhinoceros horn libation cup, 17th/18th century, carved with *chilong* clambering amid *lingzhi,* 9.5cm (3¾in), *NY 11 Apr,*
$4,125 (£2,806)

6
A rhinoceros horn libation cup, 17th century, carved with lotus pads amidst branches of lichee, the horn of golden colour and very smooth patina, 12.5cm (5in) wide, *NY 11 Apr,*
$1,100 (£748)

7
A rhinoceros horn libation cup, 17th century, carved as a cluster of lotus blossoms, leaves and waterweeds, a small crab and a snail nestled at the base, the horn of rich reddish-brown colour, 13.5cm (5½in) long, *NY 11 Apr,*
$5,225 (£3,554)

8
A rhinoceros horn libation cup, 17th century, carved on each side with a *taotie* mask, the handle formed from two *chilong,* 19cm (7½in) long, *HK 19 Nov,*
HK$55,000 (£4,955; $6,937)

9
A bronze-form rhinoceros horn libation cup, 18th century, carved with a band of *kui* dragons, 12.5cm (5in) high, *NY 11 Apr,*
$1,650 (£1,122)

10
A carved cinnabar lacquer box and cover, Qianlong, the cover with a medallion scene depicting a group of figures on a boat, 20cm (8in), *L 31 Oct,*
£990 ($1,386)

11
A rhinoceros horn libation cup, 19th century, the horn of rich chestnut tone and carved with birds flying among pine and prunus trees, 15.5cm (6in), *L 9 May,*
£1,210 ($1,948)

12
A laque-burgauté box and cover, 18th century, inlaid in mother-of-pearl, the top with a mythical animal, the front with two figures in a bamboo grove, 49cm (19¼in) wide, *L 31 Oct,*
£1,375 ($1,925)

13
A laque-burgauté four-tier box and cover, 18th century, the top inlaid with two peasants walking by a tree, the sides with figure and landscape vignettes, 14.5cm (5¾in), *L 31 Oct,*
£572 ($801)

1

2

3

4

5

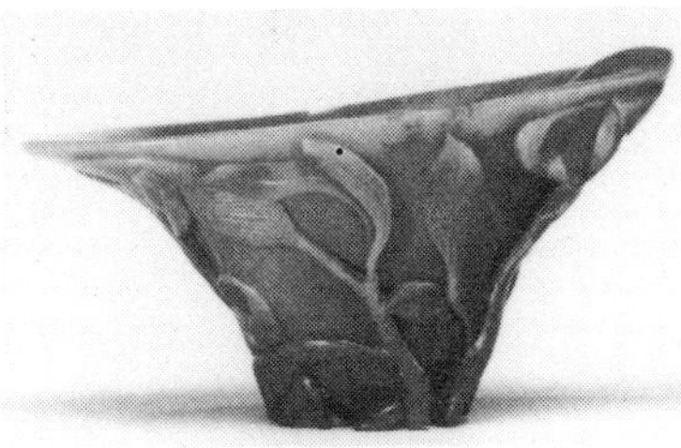
6

7

8

9

10

11

12

13

1

2

3

4

5

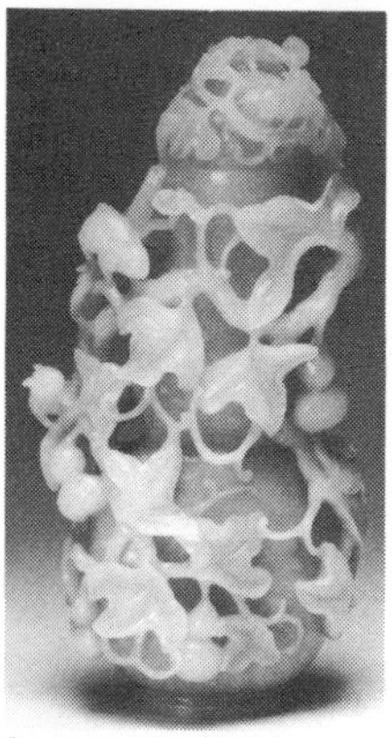
6

7

8

9

10

11

12

1
A dark green jade bowl, 18th century, thinly carved, 21cm (8¼in), *NY 26 Sept,*
$2,750 (£1,833)

2
A jade bowl, 18th/19th century, engraved on the exterior with rows of *shou* characters, 11.5cm (4½in), *NY 11 Apr,*
$990 (£673)

3
A pair of Mughal green jade chrysanthemum cups, *(one illustrated),* 18th/19th century, of apple green colour and translucent, 7cm (2¾in), *NY 26 Sept,*
$4,675 (£3,116)

4
A white jade joss-stick holder, 18th century, 8.5cm (3¼in), *L 9 May,*
£1,485 ($2,391)

5
A pair of jadeite bangles, *(one illustrated),* of pale green colour, 5.5cm (2in), *HK 19 Nov,*
HK$8,800 (£792; $1,110)

6
A greenish-white jade double-gourd vase and cover, 19th century, 22.5cm (8½in), *HK 19 Nov,*
HK$33,000 (£2,973; $4,162)

7
A spinach green jade vase, 19th century, of *hu*-form, the sides with elephant-head and loose ring handles, 24.5cm (9¾in), *NY 11 Apr,*
$3,575 (£2,432)

8
A white jade archaistic vase and cover, the stone of icy white with milky suffusions, 25cm (10in), *NY 26 Sept,*
$6,875 (£4,583)

9
A green jade figure of Guanyin, the stone with brown mottling, a dark green patch on the shoulder, 41cm (16¼in), *NY 26 Sept,*
$3,300 (£2,200)

10
A single-strand jadeite bead necklace, composed of 79 beads, of mottled apple and emerald-green colour, *HK 19 Nov,*
HK$60,500 (£5,450; $7,630)

11
A lavender and green jadeite koro and cover, 19th century, the cover with a *fu*-lion finial, 7cm (2½in), *NY 26 Sept,*
$3,850 (£2,566)

12
A spinach jade marriage bowl, 19th century, the interior incised with a pair of fish, 23.5cm (9¼in), *L 9 May,*
£1,320 ($2,125)

1
A white jade amulet, Song Dynasty, carved as a coiled serpent, 5cm (2in), *NY 3 Dec,*
$1,650 (£1,154)

2
A brown and white jade kylin, Yuan/Ming Dynasty, 6.5cm (2½in), *NY 3 Dec,*
$3,300 (£2,307)

3
A jade lotus leaf-form brushwasher, Ming Dynasty, 23.5cm (9¼in), *NY 11 Apr,*
$8,800 (£5,986)

4
A bronze-form brownish-white jade cup, Ming Dynasty, the side with a *chilong*-form handle, 12cm (4¾in), *NY 4 June,*
$3,850 (£2,601)

5
An Imperial Ming-style green jade vase, Qianlong mark and period, carved in *Wanli*-style, 26cm (10¼in), *NY 11 Apr,*
$17,600 (£11,972)

6
A jade brush holder, Qianlong, 26cm (10½in), *HK 19 Nov,*
HK$28,600 (£2,576; $3,607)

7
A pair of spinach green jade bowls, *(one illustrated)*, Qianlong mark and period, with characteristic black flecking, 19.5cm (7¾in), *NY 11 Apr,*
$19,800 (£13,469)

8
A jade group, carved as two carp rising from the waves, 27.5cm (10¾in), *L 31 Oct,*
£1,100 ($1,540)

9
A green jade brush-washer, Jiaqing, the exterior carved in relief with a Mughul-style feathery lotus scroll, the loop and ring handles rising to half-open blooms enclosed by leaves, 23cm (9in), *L 9 May,*
£3,300 ($5,313)

10
A spinach jade rhyton, Qianlong mark and period, the sides carved with nine *chilong*, 15.5cm (6in), *NY 11 Apr,*
$18,700 (£12,721)

11
A pale green jade bowl, Jiaqing, carved with archaistic *taotie* masks, 23.5cm (9¼in), *L 9 May,*
£1,705 ($2,745)

12
A white jade box and cover, Jiaqing, the cover carved in low relief to depict a phoenix confronted with a dragon, 5.5cm (2in), *HK 19 Nov,*
HK$35,200 (£3,171; $4,439)

1

2

3

4

5

6

7

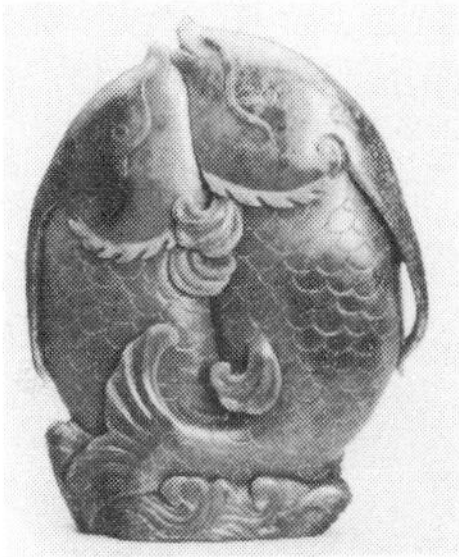
8

9

10

11

12

1

2

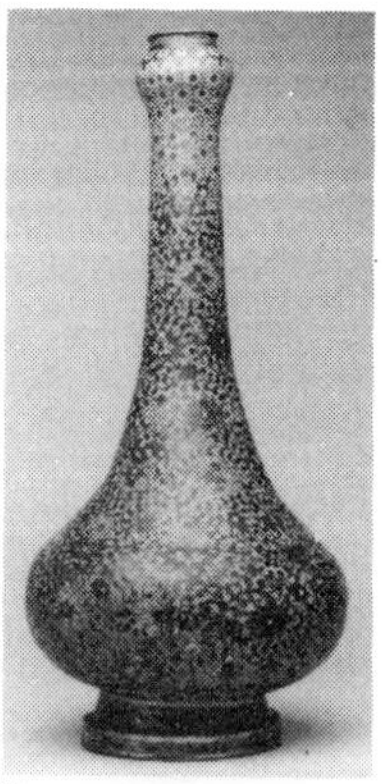
3

4

5

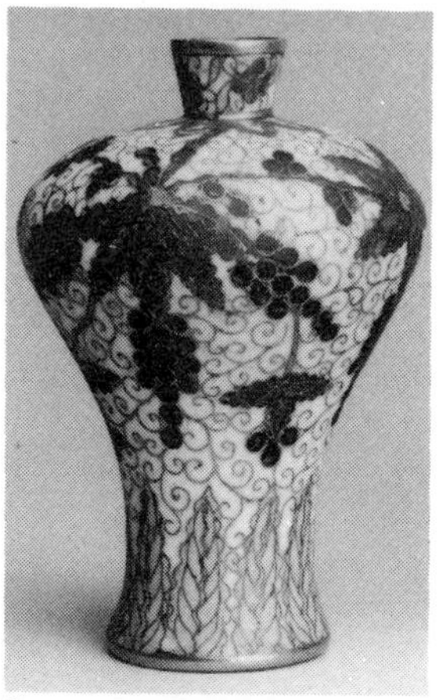
6

7

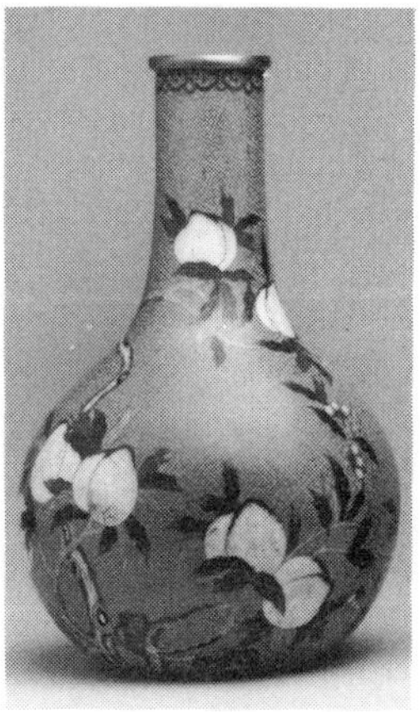
8

9

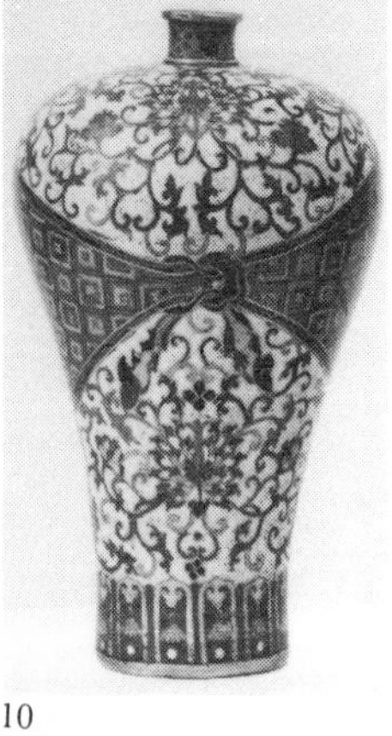
10

11

12

1
A cloisonné enamel cup stand, 16th century, the underside undecorated, 19cm (7½in), *L 10 June,*
£660 ($1,036)

2
A cloisonné enamel vase, 16th century, with projecting gilt-bronze elephant-head handles, 19cm (7½in), *L 31 Oct,*
£1,045 ($1,463)

3
A cloisonné enamel 'garlic' vase, 16th century, enamelled with Buddhist emblems, Jingtai mark, 42cm (16½in), *L 31 Oct,*
£2,970 ($4,158)

4
A Canton enamel ewer and cover, Qianlong, 12cm (4½in), *HK 20 May,*
HK$11,000 (£973; $1,558)

5
A cloisonné enamel meiping, 17th century, the turquoise ground decorated with lotus blooms in red, yellow, green, blue and white, 33cm (13in), *NY 26 Sept,*
$1,980 (£1,320)

6
A cloisonné enamel vase, Ming dynasty, 16th century, of *meiping* form, 18cm (7in), *L 31 Oct,*
£1,320 ($1,848)

7
A cloisonné enamel conjoined vase, 18th century, decorated with birds amongst branches, fitted wood stand, 15cm (5¾in), *C 8 Oct,*
£748 ($1,047)

8
A pair of cloisonné enamel yellow-ground vases, *(one illustrated)*, with Jing Yuan tang mark, 26.5cm (10½in), *L 31 Oct,*
£858 ($1,201)

9
A pair of cloisonné enamel vases *(one illustrated)*, Jiaqing, each side with a lapis-blue ground medallion enclosing a stylised tree, 25cm (10in), *L 31 Oct,*
£396 ($554)

10
A pair of cloisonné enamel meiping, *(one illustrated)*, Jiaqing, each decorated with formalised lotus flowers on a white ground on either side of a simulated brocade scarf, 28.5cm (11¼in), *S 21 May,*
£550 ($880)

11
A cloisonné enamel model of a stag, 19th century, the fur picked out in copper wire, 16cm (6¼in), *L 9 May,*
£572 ($921)

12
A pair of cloisonné enamel ducks, *(one illustrated)*, Qianlong, each decorated in red, green, blue, black and white on the blue ground, 13cm (5in), *L 9 May,*
£990 ($1,594)

1
A cloisonné enamel censer and cover, Jiaqing, 57.5cm (22¾in), *L 9 May,*
£902 ($1,452)

2
A cloisonné enamel incense burner and cover, Daoguang/Xiangfeng, 44cm (17½in), *S 21 May,*
£440 ($704)

3
A pair of cloisonné enamel elephant-shaped censers *(one illustrated),* 19th century, the backs with hinged covers, 13.5cm (5¼in), *L 31 Oct,*
£924 ($1,294)

4
A pair of blue-ground cloisonné enamel vases, *(one illustrated),* 19th century, 27cm (10¾in), *NY 11 Apr,*
$5,500 (£3,741)

5
A pair of reticulated cloisonné enamel vases and covers *(one illustrated),* 19th century, 49.5cm (19½in), *L 9 May,*
£2,200 ($3,542)

6
A pair of cloisonné enamel vases, *(one illustrated),* 19th century, 25cm (10in), *L 9 May,*
£418 ($673)

7
A pair of cloisonné enamel vases, *(one illustrated),* 19th century, each of archaistic *gu*-shaped form, 35cm (13¾in), *L 9 May,*
£1,210 ($1,948)

8
A pair of Canton enamel candlesticks *(one illustrated),* c.1800, 28.5cm (11¼in), *L 31 Oct,*
£2,090 ($2,926)

9
A Canton enamel vase, 18th century, of rectangular section, decorated with reserves of birds in a landscape, on a blue ground, 39cm (15in), *M 1 Dec,*
FF 22,000 (£2,376; $3,397)

10
A Canton enamel dish, 18th century, painted in bright enamels with a scene of a warrior returning home to his wife and child, 26.5cm (10½in), *L 9 May,*
£550 ($885)

11
A Canton enamel plate, Qianlong, decorated with a scene of European ladies and gentlemen seated in a garden, 39.5cm (15¾in), *L 9 May,*
£275 ($443)

1

2

3

4

5

6

7

8

9

10

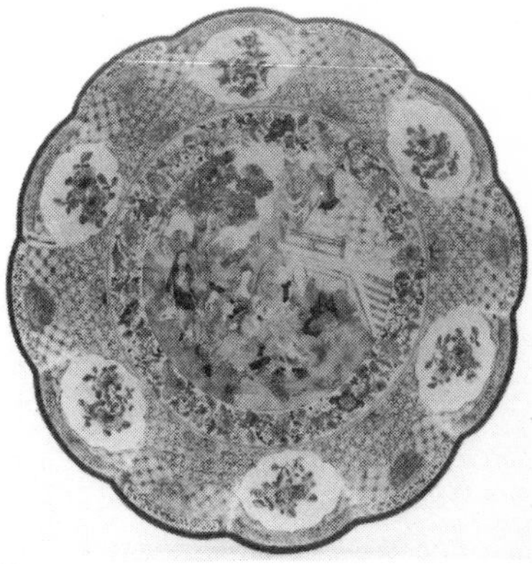
11

1

2

3

4

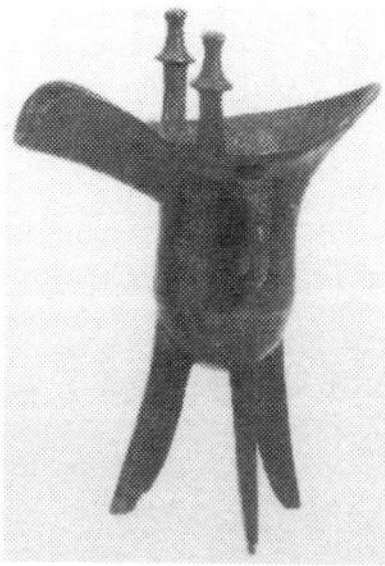
5

6

7

8

9

10

11

12

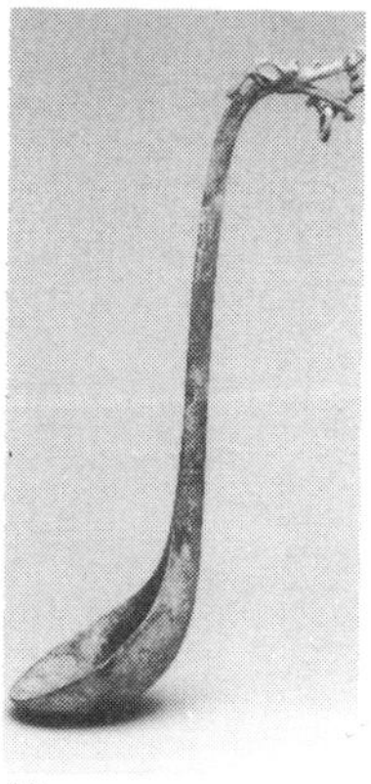
13

14

15

1
An Ordos bronze animal plaque, 4th/2nd century BC, smooth dark brown patina, 9cm (3½in), *NY 3 Dec,*
$2,750 (£1,923)

2
A bronze animal plaque, Warring States Period, 12.5cm (5in), *NY 3 Dec,*
$2,200 (£1,538)

3
A bronze kylin, Six Dynasties, cast with wings on the shoulders and feathers on the hind legs, 5cm (2in), *NY 4 June,*
$18,700 (£12,635)

4
An archaic bronze food vessel (gui), Shang Dynasty, the foot decorated with three pairs of *kui* dragons, 17.5cm (7in) high, *NY 3 Dec,*
$33,000 (£23,076)

5
An archaic bronze libation vessel (jue), Shang Dynasty, of conventional form, a pictogram beneath the handle and on finial, 22cm (8¾in), *L 10 June,*
£2,200 ($3,454)

6
An archaic bronze ritual beaker (gu), Shang Dynasty, the central area cast with *taotie* masks, 25cm (10in), *L 10 June,*
£2,200 ($3,454)

7
An archaic bronze food vessel (liding), Zhou Dynasty, green encrustation, 12cm (4¾in), *NY 4 June,*
$4,950 (£3,344)

8
An archaic bronze cauldron (ding), Western Zhou Dynasty, 23cm (9in), *L 9 Dec,*
£2,200 ($3,080)

9
A parcel-gilt bronze hu, Ming Dynasty, the surface inlaid with gold and silver, the neck interior with an inscription in seal script, 31.5cm (12½in), *NY 26 Sept,*
$2,475 (£1,650)

10
A gilt-bronze jardinière, 18th century, six character mark of Xuande on the base, 20.5cm (8in), *HK 19 Nov,*
HK$30,800 (£2,775; $3,885)

11
A parcel-gilt box and cover, 16th/17th century, decorated with characters from the Ming novel *Tales from the Water Margin,* 14.5cm (5¾in), *L 9 May,*
£1,760 ($2,834)

12
A parcel-gilt bronze censer, 17th century, by Hu Guangyu, of bombé form, 14.5cm (5¾in), *L 9 May,*
£990 ($1,594)

13
A bronze ladle, Han Dynasty, 35cm (13¾in), *L 9 Dec,*
£3,300 ($4,620)

14
A gilt-splashed bronze hu 18th/19th century, the base cast with Xuande seal mark, 36.5cm (14½in), *NY 26 Sept,*
$3,850 (£2,566)

15
A gold-splash double vase, 19th century, a simulated rope bound around their neck forming loop handles at the sides, 30.5cm (12in) wide, *L 9 May,*
£1,760 ($2,834)

1
An export silver coffee pot, 19th century, the base with a Lombardic H mark, for Hoaching, 18cm (7in), *L 9 May,*
£462 ($744)

2
An export silver teapot and cover, 19th century, repoussé with figures in combat, with an ivory-mounted handle, two character Chinese mark, 17cm (6¾in), *L 9 May,*
£572 ($921)

3
A silver claret jug, 19th century, with the mark L.W. and one Chinese character, 33cm (13in), *L 31 Oct,*
£3,520 ($4,928)

4
An assembled silver tea service, comprising ten pieces each repoussé with birds and prunus, *L 9 May,*
£858 ($1,381)

5
An export silver mug, 19th century, inscribed *A souvenir of the 'Mikado',* marked WL and two Chinese characters, 12cm (4¾in), *L 31 Oct,*
£638 ($893)

6
A silver ewer and basin, c.1860, both stamped with two-character Chinese mark and GW, ewer 36cm (14¼in) high, *NY 11 Apr,*
$6,600 (£4,490)

7
A set of four silver mugs, mid 19th century, from the Feng Xiang Workshop, 10.5cm (4in), *NY 26 Sept,*
$2,200 (£1,466)

8
A silver box and cover, 19th century, the base marked with the Chinese character Xie He 'harmony', 20.5cm (8in), *L 31 Oct,*
£990 ($1,386)

9
A bronze figure of Buddha, Ming Dynasty, seated in *dyanasana,* the flesh picked out in gilding, 39cm (15¼in), *L 9 May,*
£968 ($1,558)

10
A gilt-bronze figure of Maitreya, Ming Dynasty, wearing a crown surmounted with the Amitabha Buddha, details in red and blue, 18cm (7¼in), *NY 11 Apr,*
$1,210 (£823)

11
A gilt-bronze figure of a Guardian, Ming Dynasty, 23cm (9in), *L 31 Oct,*
£2,420 ($3,388)

12
A bronze jardinière, 19th century, each end supported by a slave, 35.5cm (14in), *L 31 Oct,*
£2,090 ($2,926)

13
A gilt-bronze figure, Jiajing, the reverse with a long inscription including the date Jiajing 13th year corresponding to 1534, 42cm (16½in), *NY 11 Apr,*
$3,025 (£2,058)

14
A gilt-bronze figure of Buddha, 19th century, hands held in *dhyana mudra,* 22cm (8½in), *L 10 June,*
£715 ($1,122)

1

2

3

4

5

6

7

8

9

10

11

12

13

14

1

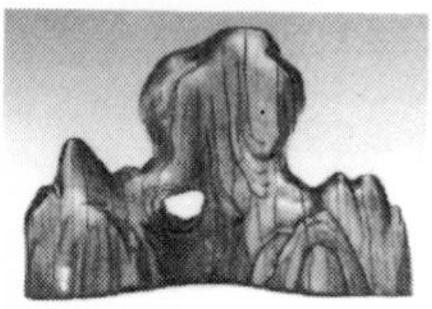
2

3

4

5

6

7 8

9

10

11 12

13

14

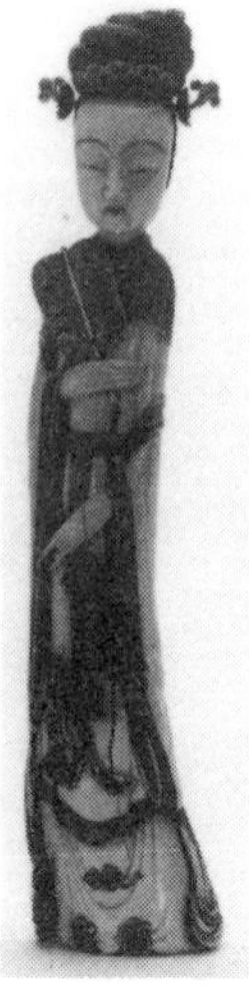
15

16

1
An ivory buckle, Ming Dynasty, carved as linked rings with a scrolling lotus vine, dark brown patina, 5cm (2in) long, *NY 3 Dec,*
$440 (£307)

2
A painted ivory brush-rest, 18th century, carved as a craggy outcrop of rocks, enamelled a deep green, 10cm (4in), *HK 20 May,*
HK$19,800 (£1,752; $2,804)

3
A Cantonese ivory casket, 19th century, the sides carved with figures in ornate gardens, the cover with flowers in bloom, 22.5cm (9in), *L 31 Oct,*
£682 ($955)

4
A Cantonese ivory chess set, *(part illustrated),* 19th century, in white and red-stained ivory, *L 31 Oct,*
£825 ($1,155)

5
An ivory brushpot, 18th century, carved with figures representing the four noble professions, including a fisherman, a farmer, a scholar and a figure on a water-buffalo, 10cm (4in), *HK 19 Nov,*
HK$19,800 (£1,784; $2,497)

6
An ivory brushpot, 18th century, decorated with the seven sages of the bamboo grove, picked out in mother-of-pearl, malachite, turquoise, agate, tortoiseshell and enamels, 12.5cm (5in), *HK 20 May,*
HK$16,500 (£1,460; $2,336)

7
An ivory figure of Shoulao, the God of Longevity, 17th century, 12cm (4¾in), *NY 11 Apr,*
$1,870 (£1,272)

8
An ivory figure of an Immortal, Ming Dynasty, holding a *lingzhi* stalk, 10.5cm (4in), *NY 11 Apr,*
$1,540 (£1,048)

9
An ivory wristrest, Guangxu, the upper surface carved with Liu Hai enticing the Three-Legged Toad from a pool, the underside with numerous figures outside a palace, 26cm (10¼in), *L 9 May,*
£550 ($885)

10
An ivory birdcage and fittings, the hook with dragon's head terminal, the fittings including an ivory bird, an ivory perch and two bird feeders, 38.5cm (15in), *L 9 May,*
£1,034 ($1,665)

11
An ivory carving of an Immortal, 24.5cm (9¾in), *C 29 Apr,*
£176 ($285)

12
An ivory carving of a woman, her robes engraved with flowers, 22.5cm (9in), *C 29 Apr,*
£132 ($214)

13
An ivory carving of Guanyin, Guangxu, the goddess with a child seated with a deer at her feet, 43cm (17in), *C 15 Jan,*
£286 ($429)

14
A pair of carved ivory figures, representing a court lady and gentleman, each wearing court robes, 42cm (15½in), *L 9 May,*
£1,375 ($2,214)

15
An ivory figure of a lady, painted in red, blue, green, gold and black, with her face, hands and most of the robe in natural ivory, 43.5cm (17¼in), *L 9 May,*
£682 ($1,098)

16
An ivory figure of Guanyin, standing on a lotus throne, her coiffure surmounted by a seated Buddha, two acolytes at her feet, 56cm (22in), *L 9 May,*
£660 ($1,063)

1
A Neolithic pottery mortuary jar, 3rd millenium BC, painted on the upper part in black and reddish brown, 35cm (13¾in), *L 10 June,*
£2,640 ($4,145)

2
A Neolithic pottery funerary urn, 3rd millenium BC 28.5cm (11¼in), *L 10 June,*
£5,500 ($8,635)

3
A Neolithic pottery mortuary urn, 3rd millenium BC, Banshan style, 35.5cm (14in), *L 10 June,*
£3,300 ($5,181)

4
A grey pottery figure of a horse, Han Dynasty, the head modelled separately, with traces of white slip, 37cm (14½in) long, *L 10 June,*
£4,180 ($6,563)

5
A grey pottery figure of a hen, Han Dynasty, with traces of red pigment, 14.5cm (5¾in) long, *NY 3 Dec,*
$1,980 (£1,384)

6
A grey pottery goose-head vessel, Han Dynasty, the top with a galleried aperture, 34cm (13½in) high, *NY 3 Dec,*
$4,620 (£3,230)

7
An unglazed figure of a camel, Tang Dynasty, extensive traces of red and ochre pigment, 40.5cm (16in), *L 10 June,*
£1,760 ($2,763)

8
A glazed pottery figure of a camel, Tang Dynasty, neck and humps splashed in cream the rest chestnut brown, 38cm (15in), *L 9 Dec,*
£7,150 ($10,010)

9
An unglazed pottery model of a horse, Tang Dynasty, with traces of red pigment, 28cm (11in), *L 9 Dec,*
£2,200 ($3,080)

10
A glazed pottery figure of a horse, Tang Dynasty, glazed in green, 59.5cm (23in), *L 9 Dec,*
£23,100 ($32,340)

11
A sancai pottery figure of a horse, Tang Dynasty, with a cream glaze, neck grooved for attachment of the mane, 52cm (20½in), *L 10 June,*
£15,400 ($24,178)

1 2 3

4

5

6

7

8

9

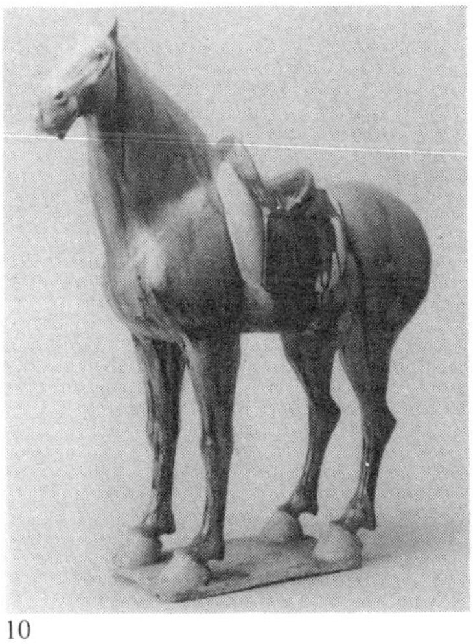
10

11

1

2

3

4

5

6

7

8 9

10

11

12

13

14

1
A straw-glazed pottery figure of a prancing horse, Tang Dynasty, with two silvered metal florets on the rump, 39cm (15¼in), *NY 4 June,*
$25,300 (£17,094)

2
A glazed pottery figure of a Zebu ox, Tang Dynasty, the head picked out in cream and the horns green, 16.5cm (6½in), *L 10 June,*
£3,300 ($5,181)

3
An unglazed pottery figure of an ox, Tang Dynasty, 20cm (8in), *L 9 Dec,*
£825 ($1,155)

4
A pair of unglazed pottery figures of dignitaries, *(one illustrated),* Tang Dynasty, the faces modelled with rounded Uighur Turkish features, traces of painted decoration, 69.5cm (27¼in), *L 9 Dec,*
£8,800 ($12,320)

5
A pair of unglazed pottery figures of officials, *(one illustrated),* Tang Dynasty, one with extensive decoration in red, black and green pigments, 56.5cm (22¼in), *NY 3 Dec,*
$2,310 (£1,615)

6
An unglazed pottery figure of a musician, Tang Dynasty, 18cm (7¾in), *L 9 Dec,*
£1,210 ($1,694)

7
A straw-glazed pottery figure of an officer, Tang Dynasty, traces of pigmentation, 24cm (9½in), *L 9 Dec,*
£385 ($539)

8
A green and yellow-glazed pottery figure of a soldier, Tang Dynasty, the glaze flaking, 28cm (11in), *NY 4 June,*
$990 (£669)

9
A sancai-glazed pottery figure of a lady, Tang Dynasty, wearing a cream-glazed shawl, 26cm (10¼in), *NY 4 June,*
$1,980 (£1,338)

10
A painted pottery figure of a court lady, Tang Dynasty, hair showing traces of black pigments, 40.5cm (16in), *NY 4 June,*
$35,200 (£23,784)

11
A glazed pottery equestrienne figure, Tang Dynasty, the rider unglazed, the horse with a pale green glaze, 34cm (13½in), *L 9 Dec,*
£2,640 ($3,696)

12
A glazed pottery figure of an Earth Spirit, Tang Dynasty, glazed in cream, green and chestnut brown, 37cm (14½in), *L 10 June,*
£1,980 ($3,109)

13
A glazed pottery jar, Tang Dynasty, splashed with straw glaze, 14cm (5½in), *L 9 Dec,*
£990 ($1,386)

14
A phosphatic-splashed stoneware jar, Tang Dynasty, of Huangdao type, 19.5cm (7¾in), *NY 4 June,*
$2,860 (£1,932)

1
A glazed Henan jar, Northern Song Dynasty, applied with lustrous black glaze, 19.5cm (7¾in), *NY 4 June,*
$4,125 (£2,787)

2
A splashed Henan jar, Song Dynasty, painted in russet black with sprays of foliage, with a knife-pared unglazed foot, 23cm (9in), *L 9 Dec,*
£2,420 ($3,388)

3
A painted Cizhou pillow, Jin Dynasty, painted with floral panels in chocolate brown slip on a cream ground, 43cm (17in), *NY 4 June,*
$3,850 (£2,601)

4
A painted Cizhou vase, Jin Dynasty, painted in brown on a white slip with foliate sprays, 42cm (16¾in), *L 9 Dec,*
£9,900 ($13,860)

5
A tiger-form Cizhou pillow, Jin Dynasty, 37cm (14½in), *NY 4 June,*
$1,430 (£966)

6
A carved Cizhou jar, Yuan Dynasty, the design picked out in brown, 18.5cm (7¼in), *L 10 June,*
£572 ($898)

7
A pair of yingqing covered jars *(one illustrated),* Yuan Dynasty, covered with thick bluish glaze, 16cm (6¼in), *L 9 Dec,*
£1,540 ($2,156)

8
A painted Cizhou jar, Yuan Dynasty, with bosses, ring handles and painted fish picked out in iron-brown on a cream ground, 10.5cm (4in), *L 10 June,*
£506 ($794)

9
A moulded yingqing vase, Yuan Dynasty, in translucent glaze of pale blue, 14cm (5½in), *L 9 Dec,*
£374 ($524)

10
A Yueyao waterpot, Six Dynasties, with light-green translucent glaze, 7cm (2¾in), *L 9 Dec,*
£242 ($339)

11
A Yueyao figure of a boy, Song Dynasty, aperture on top of the head, 7.5cm (3in), *NY 4 June,*
$2,090 (£1,412)

12
A Junyao jar, Yuan Dynasty, considerable kiln grit adhering, firing crack at the base, 28cm (11in), *NY 3 Dec,*
$4,620 (£3,230)

13
A yingqing ewer, Yuan Dynasty, covered in pale-blue glaze, 10.8cm (4¼in), *L 9 Dec,*
£308 ($431)

14
A Yueyao green-glazed vessel, Six Dynasties, in the form of a crouching Fabulous Animal, 13cm (5in), *L 9 Dec,*
£3,960 ($5,544)

1

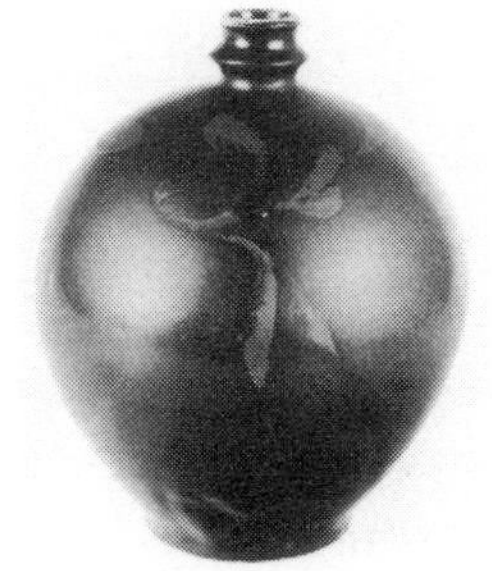
2

4

3

5

6

7

8

9

11

10

12

13

14

1

2

3

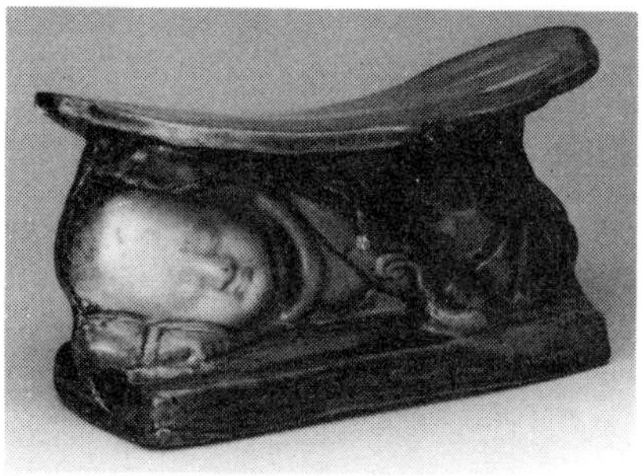
4

5

6

7

8

9

10

11

1
A white-glazed miniature ewer, Tang Dynasty, 7.5cm (3in), *L 9 Dec,*
£1,100 ($1,540)

2
A splash-glazed pottery jar, Tang Dynasty, splashed in green, cream and brown, 9cm (3½in), *L 10 June,*
£770 ($1,209)

3
A white-glazed pottery flask, Liao Dynasty, the form simulating a leather pouch, 33.5cm (13¼in), *NY 3 Dec,*
$11,000 (£7,692)

4
A lead-glazed pottery pillow, Song Dynasty, applied in green, cream and rich brown glazes, 20cm (8in), *L 9 Dec,*
£2,420 ($3,388)

5
A ribbed Henan jar, Song Dynasty, applied on the exterior in white slip with vertical ribs, rich brown glaze, 14.5cm (5¾in), *L 10 June,*
£902 ($1,416)

6
A ribbed Henan jar, Song Dynasty, applied in white slip with vertical ribs, 14cm (5½in), *NY 3 Dec,*
$2,970 (£2,076)

7
A yingqing bowl, Song Dynasty, covered in a pale blue glaze, 9.5cm (3¾in), *L 10 June,*
£396 ($622)

8
A yingqing jar and cover, Song Dynasty, the glaze of bluish tone, 7cm (2¾in), *L 10 June,*
£308 ($484)

9
A Junyao jar, Song/Yuan Dynasty, the interior with a bubbled blue glaze, 15cm (5¾in), *L 10 June,*
£440 ($691)

10
A Jianyao bowl, Song Dynasty, metal-bound around the rim, iridescent speckling revealing a purplish body, 12.5cm (4¾in), *L 10 June,*
£528 ($829)

11
A Henan bowl, Song Dynasty, the interior with thick black glaze, 13.5cm (5¼in), *L 9 Dec,*
£770 ($1,078)

1
A Northern celadon bowl, Northern Song Dynasty, the interior with fish swimming on a ground of waves, with pale olive-green glaze, 10cm (4in), *L 10 June,*
£935 ($1,468)

2
A Northern celadon bowl, Northern Song Dynasty, the exterior plain, the interior with an olive-green glaze, 13.5cm (5½in), *L 10 June,*
£1,210 ($1,900)

3
A Northern celadon bowl, Song Dynasty, the sides with a frieze of petal-shaped panels, with olive-green glaze, 13cm (5¼in), *HK 22 May,*
HK$8,800 (£779; $1,239)

4
A carved celadon lotus bowl, Song Dynasty, with a bluish-green glaze, 18.5cm (7½in), *NY 3 Dec,*
$1,430 (£1,000)

5
A Longquan celadon fluted bowl, Song Dynasty, with greyish-green glaze, 11cm (4¼in), *HK 22 May,*
HK$4,950 (£438; $776)

6
A Longquan celadon twin-fish dish, Song Dynasty, the reverse with a frieze of lotus petals, with minutely bubbled glaze, 20.5cm (8in), *L 9 Dec,*
£1,650 ($2,310)

7
A celadon lion censer, Ming Dynasty, with detachable lion's head cover, the grey-green glaze slightly crackled, 18cm (7in), *L 9 Dec,*
£1,045 ($1,463)

8
A Zhejiang celadon dish, Ming Dynasty, with fluted cavetto and central impressed floral sprig, 40.5cm (16in), *L 10 June,*
£935 ($1,468)

9
A Yixing 'monk's cap' teapot and cover, 17th century, in the style of Shin Dabin, the base incised *Da Bin*, 12.5cm (5in), *L 9 Dec,*
£1,210 ($1,694)

10
A Zhejiang celadon bulb bowl, Ming Dynasty, the sides with a floral frieze, on three mask bracket feet, crackled green glaze, 33.5cm (13¼in), *L 9 Dec,*
£572 ($801)

11
A celadon-glazed tazza, Qianlong seal mark and period, covered overall in a sea-green glaze draining to brown on the rim, 16cm (6¼in) wide, *HK 20 May,*
HK$11,000 (£973; $1,557)

12
An archaic bronze-form cup, Qianlong, moulded with a frieze of archaic zoomorphic scrolls, with pale celadon glaze, 7.5cm (3in) high, *HK 19 Nov,*
HK$19,800 (£1,784; $2,497)

13
An early Ming white-glazed bowl, mark and period of Xuande, the sides incised with a lotus petal frieze, the glaze of faint bluish tint, 21cm (8¼in), *L 9 Dec,*
£9,350 ($13,090)

14
A copper-red glazed vase, Yongzheng mark and period, the glaze suffused with minute speckling and draining to white at the rim, 20cm (8in), *HK 22 May,*
HK$12,100 (£1,071; $1,703)

15
A flambé-glazed meiping, 18th century, covered with a purple glaze streaked in blue at the top and in a reddish tone towards the base, 15cm (6in), *L 9 Dec,*
£682 ($955)

16
A turquoise-glazed vase, Jiaqing, applied on the biscuit with glaze of rich washed tones and minutely crackled overall, 41.5cm (16½in), *L 6 May,*
£539 ($857)

1

2

3

4

5

6

7

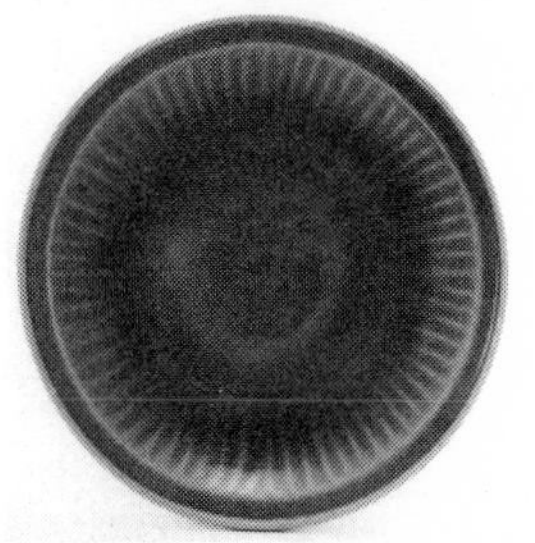
8

9

10

11

12

13

14

15

16

1

2

3

4

5

6

7

8

9

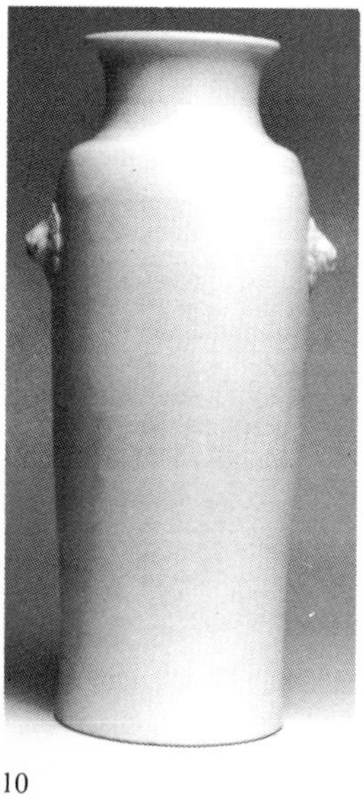
10

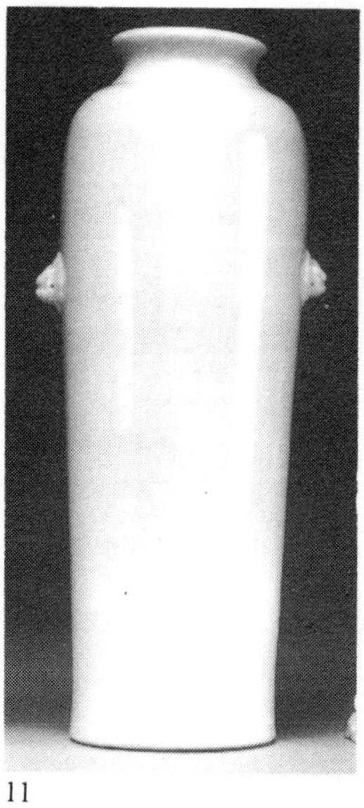
11

12

13

1
A pair of 'tea-dust' tazze, *(one illustrated)*, first half 19th century, the glaze of yellowish olive-green tone with minute speckling, 16cm (6¼in), *L 10 June,*
£935 ($1,468)

2
A pair of coffee-glazed ogee bowls, *(one illustrated)*, Qianlong seal marks and period, the interior glazed in white, 16cm (6¼in), *HK 20 May,*
HK$12,100 (£1,071; $1,713)

3
A robin's egg vase, Qianlong seal mark and period, with a turquoise glaze suffused with feathery yellow and pale blue droplets, 24cm (9¾in), *HK 20 May,*
HK$16,500 (£1,460; $2,336)

4
A peach-bloom beehive waterpot (taibo zun), mark and period of Kangxi, engraved with three medallions of stylised archaistic dragons, the glaze of liver-red tone with some darker red speckling, 12.5cm (5in), *L 10 June,*
£1,760 ($2,763)

5
A langyao zhadou, 18th century, the raspberry-red glaze thinning to a creamy tone on the rim, 8.5cm (3½in), *HK 19 Nov,*
HK$24,200 (£2,180; $3,052)

6
A 'blanc-de-Chine' figure of Guanyin, c.1700, the goddess holding a small boy in the crook of her left arm, 65cm (25½in), *L 6 May,*
£330 ($525)

7
A Fujian figure of Guanyin, Kangxi, a child in her lap and a book placed on a pinnacle at one side, 30cm (11¾in), *C 11 Feb,*
£253 ($380)

8
A 'blanc-de-Chine' figure of Guanyin, 18th century, holding a sceptre in her left hand, 61cm (24in), *NY 3 Dec,*
$8,250 (£5,769)

9
A 'blanc-de-Chine' figure of Guanyin, 19th century, holding a long-stemmed lotus leaf, her diadem set with a small Buddha, the white glaze of bluish tone, impressed marks, *Xuande Nian Zhi* and *De Hua*, 46cm (18¼in), *L 18 Nov,*
£660 ($937)

10
A 'blanc-de-Chine' vase, Kangxi, with mask handles, the glaze of ivory tone, 33cm (13in), *L 18 Nov,*
£1,210 ($1,718)

11
A white-glazed sleeve vase, 17th century, with lion-mask handles, the glaze of ivory tone, 29.5cm (11½in), *NY 10 Apr,*
$715 (£486)

12
A 'blanc-de-Chine' group Kangxi, depicting a dignitary wearing a court hat, with two acolytes, 22.5cm (8½in), *L 18 Nov,*
£990 ($1,406)

13
A 'blanc-de-Chine' wine-cup, Kangxi, on three short tripod feet, one side with an inscription, the glaze of ivory tone, 14cm (5½in), *L 18 Nov,*
£440 ($625)

Reign Marks on Chinese Porcelain

ROBERT KLEINER

Many Chinese ceramics possess marks of various types, usually on the base but on occasion in other areas such as the shoulders or neck. These marks may be divided into two main categories. The first category is that of reign marks, which denote a specific reign and period in which an item was made. The second category is a series of commendation or hall marks, which are not of such importance in helping to date any particular item. In this article only the first category will be discussed.

The earliest known reign mark on Chinese ceramics is that of the Yongle Emperor who reigned from 1403-24. These marks, however, are of extreme rarity and only a handful have been recorded. Reign marks generally were only applied to ceramics of the highest quality, intended for use in the Imperial households, and during the five hundred years following the Yongle period the majority of the reigns were represented by marked wares. The task of identifying these marks is not as difficult as might at first be feared.

Both in the Ming Dynasty (1368-1644) and the Qing Dynasty (1644-1911) reign marks were generally written using six characters, in the following order:

1.	The character *da*
2.	The dynastic name, *Ming* or *Qing*
3 & 4.	The actual Emperor's reign title
5 & 6.	The characters *nian* and *zhi* (period made) (fig. 1)

In every reign mark the only two characters which differed were numbers three and four, the actual reign names. The other four characters remain constant. The potters of the Ming Dynasty generally only used standard script (fig.1), whereas those of the Qing Dynasty used both standard script (fig.2) and seal script (fig.3). Finally, these marks were usually laid out vertically as follows:

4	1
5	2
6	3

or horizontally, as follows:

(a) 6 5 4 3 2 1 (fig.5)

(b) 5 3 1
6 4 2

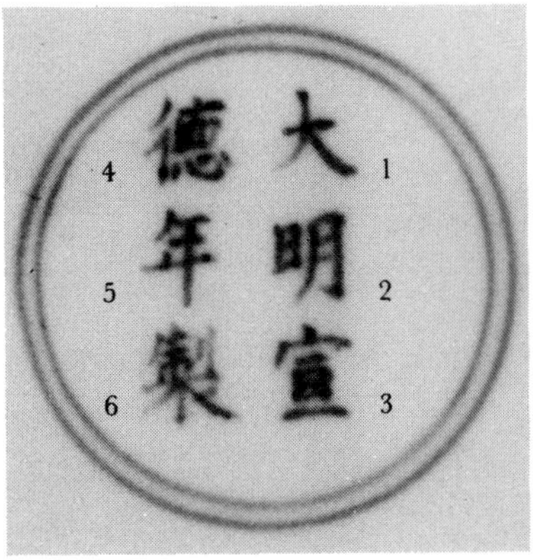

1
Xuande
(1426-35)

1

2
Yongzheng
(1723-35)

2

3
Yongzheng
(1723-35)

3

4
Chenghua
(1465-87)

4

The marks were generally enclosed by double circles or squares and occasionally only used four characters, with numbers 1 and 2 being omitted. The marks were usually painted on the base in underglaze-blue, but during the 18th century reign marks were, in addition, incised or impressed, and towards the end of that century and during the 19th century, iron-red was sometimes used.

Whilst the actual identification of the reign mark is not difficult, the Chinese did not always restrict their use of particular reign marks to the reign to which they belonged. Certain reigns produced porcelain which was particularly admired and these marks were often reproduced on later wares. The most often reproduced mark is that of the Chenghua Emperor (1465-87) — fig.4. The original, shown here, is always drawn with characteristic thick brushstrokes, whereas the later versions invariably have thin sloppy strokes (fig.6). The Kangxi Emperor's mark (1662-1722) — fig.7 — is often reproduced in the 19th century using only four characters, and the Qianlong Emperor's seal mark (1736-95) — fig.8 — is often incorrectly drawn with the 'S'-shaped part of character number three reversed and the left hand top part of the character number six having only three prongs instead of five.

For the unwary collector this proliferation of later reign marks is confusing and hazardous. The convention that Sotheby's use in their cataloguing is always to qualify the description of the reign

5

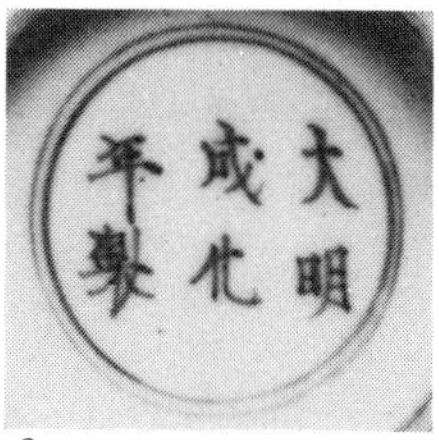

6

7

8

13

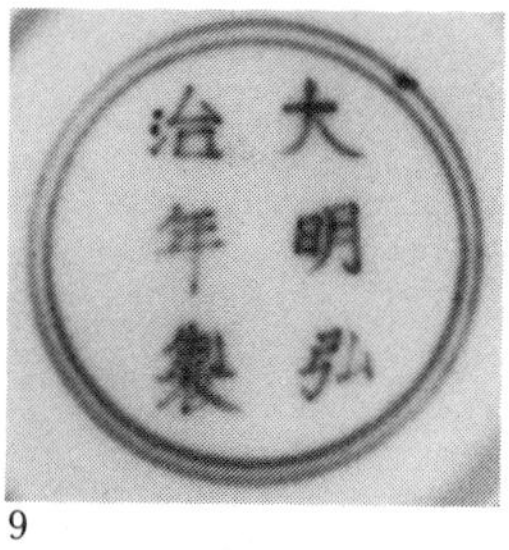

9

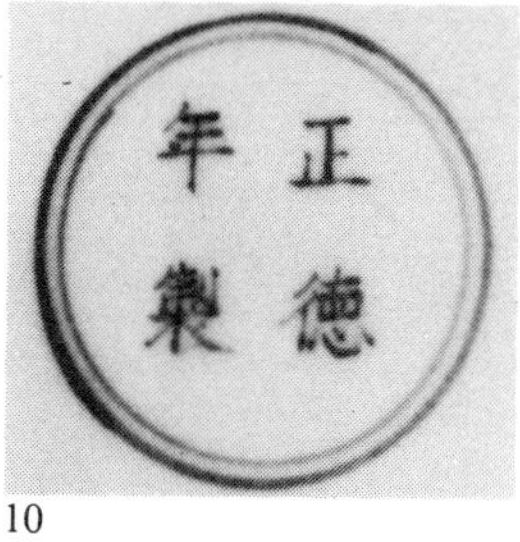

10

11

12

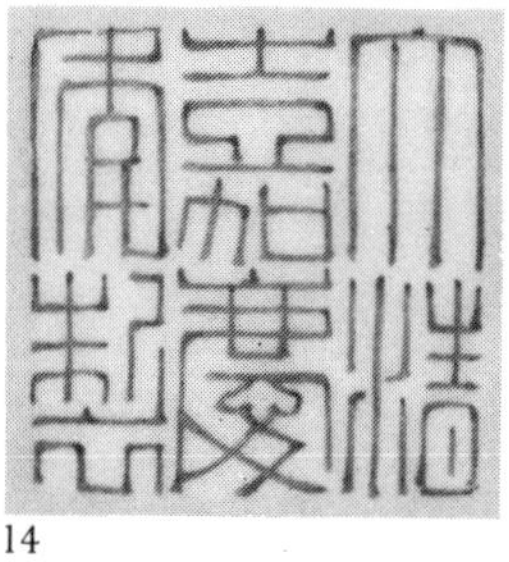
14

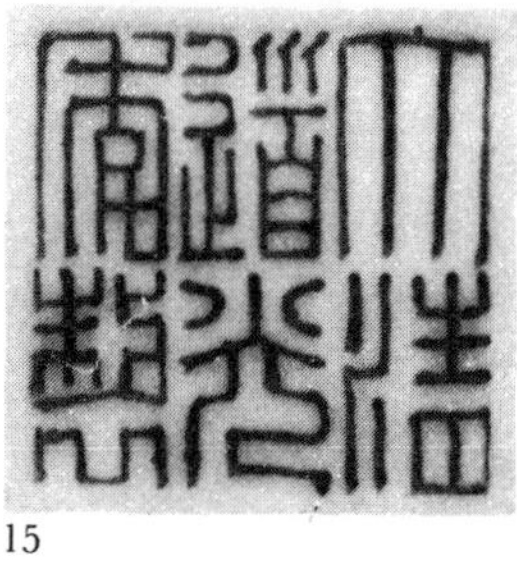
15

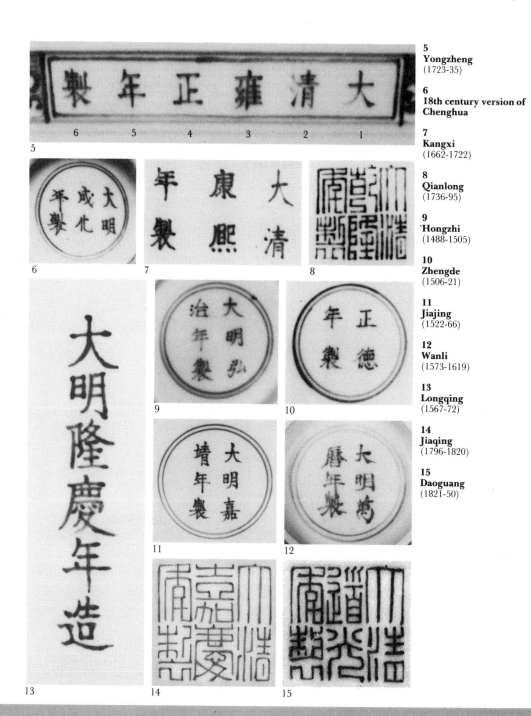

5
Yongzheng
(1723-35)

6
18th century version of Chenghua

7
Kangxi
(1662-1722)

8
Qianlong
(1736-95)

9
Hongzhi
(1488-1505)

10
Zhengde
(1506-21)

11
Jiajing
(1522-66)

12
Wanli
(1573-1619)

13
Longqing
(1567-72)

14
Jiaqing
(1796-1820)

15
Daoguang
(1821-50)

marks with the works 'of the period' if it is genuine, as say, 'A Ming blue and white bowl, mark and period of Wanli'. If these words do not appear, the mark and the piece are later than the mark suggests.

Genuine reign marks were supervised under close control in the Imperial porcelain factories in Jingdezhen and careful study of these soon reveals their particular characteristics.

Further reading:

Sotheby's, *Catalogue of the T.Y.Chao collection*, sold in Hong Kong, 18 November 1986 and 19 May 1987. These catalogues show one of the most comprehensive groups of Imperial reign mark illustrations (almost 200).

Sir Harry Garner, *Oriental Blue and White*, 1954

Margaret Medley, *The Chinese Potter*, 1976

16
A pair of ruby-ground medallion bowls, Daoguang seal marks and period, exterior decorated with gilt-edged medallions, interior in underglaze-blue, 15cm (6in), *HK 20 May*,
HK$35,200
(£3,115; $4,984)

17
A blue and white bowl, Transitional, interior painted in cobalt, 15.5cm (6in), *L 10 June*,
£1,980 ($3,109)

18
An early Ming blue and white fruit bowl, mark and period of Xuande, exterior in underglaze-blue, interior glazed in white, 29.5cm (11½in), *L 10 June*,
£71,500 ($112,255)

19
An early Ming blue and white fruit bowl, Xuande mark and period, exterior in underglaze-blue, interior glazed in white, 28.5cm (11¼in), *NY 4 June*,
$52,250 (£35,304)

20
A blue and white nine dragon vase, Yongzheng mark and period, 52cm (20½in), *HK 20 May*,
HK$770,000
(£68,142; $109,027)

16

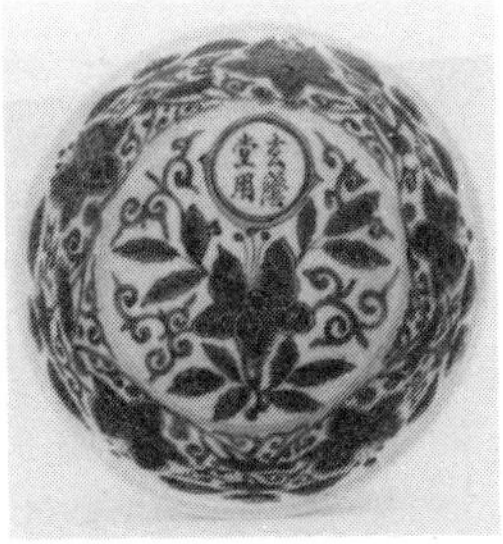
17

18

19

20

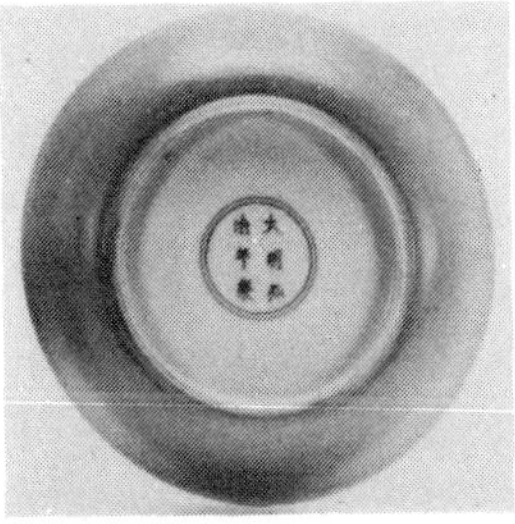
21

22

23

24

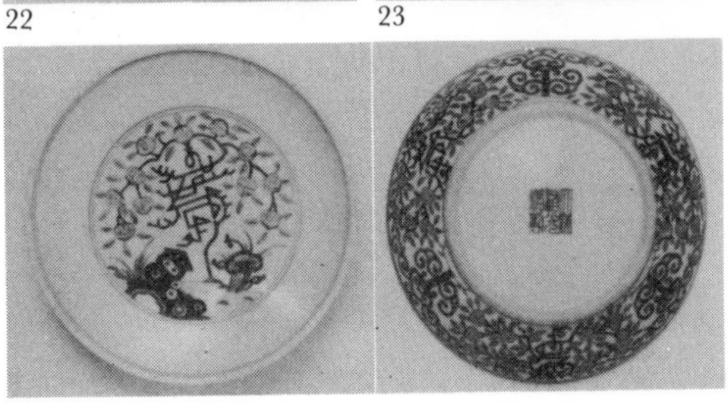
25

21
An Imperial yellow saucer dish, mark and period of Hongzhi, 17.5cm (7in), *L 10 June*,
£1,045 ($1,641)

22
A Ming white-glazed brushwasher, four-characte mark and period of Zhengde, 19.5cm (7½in), *L 9 Dec*,
£24,200 ($33,880)

23
A pair of copper-red saucer dishes, *(one illustrated)*, seal marks and period of Qianlong, 21.5cm (8in), *L 9 Dec*,
£572 ($801)

24
A blue and white small dish, Yongzheng, mark and period, painted in underglaze-blue, 9.5cm (3¾in), *HK 19 Nov*,
HK$55,000 (£4,954; $6,93

25
A pair of Doucai saucer dishes, Daoguang seal marks and period, 14.5cm (5½in), *NY 3 Dec*,
$3,850 (£2,692)

1

2

3

4

5

6

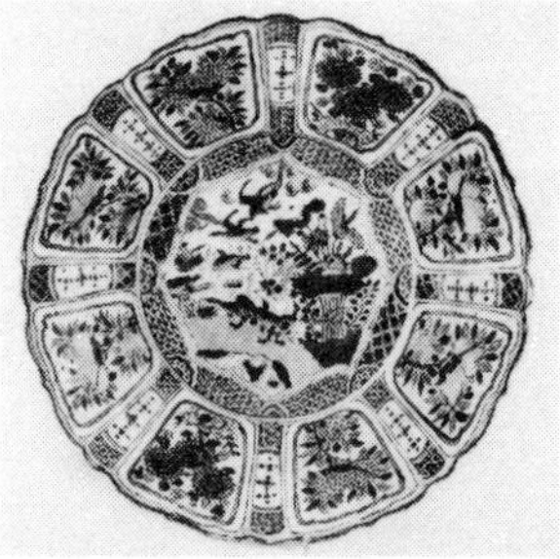
7

8

9

10

11 12

13

14

15

16

1
A Ming blue and white stembowl, 16th century, painted with a continuous scene of courtiers on a terrace, 15.5cm (6in), *L 10 June,*
£1,760 ($2,763)

2
A 'windswept' blue and white bowl, c.1500, painted with two scenes of figures at a pavilion, with characteristic billowing clouds, 30cm (11¾in), *L 10 June,*
£5,500 ($8,635)

3
A Ming blue and white dish, Jiajing mark and period, decorated with *ruyi*-shaped cloud motifs, the reverse with two phoenix, 19.5cm (7½in), *NY 4 June,*
$3,850 (£2,601)

4
A Ming blue and white jar, mark and period of Jiajing, decorated with peacocks, 12.5cm (5in), *L 9 Dec,*
£4,840 ($6,776)

5
A blue and white lobed jar, mark and period of Jiajing, painted with scenes of birds and water-fowl, 25.5cm (10in), *L 9 Dec,*
£1,155 ($1,617)

6
A Ming blue and white jar, mark and period of Jiajing, decorated with the Eight Immortals, 21cm (8¼in), *L 10 June,*
£2,090 ($3,281)

7
A blue and white charger, Wanli, the central medallion with birds and foliage, 47cm (18½in), *C 9 July,*
£682 ($1,064)

8
A blue and white vase, Wanli, painted with panels of shrubs, 23cm (9in), *C 8 Oct,*
£704 ($986)

9
A Ming blue and white bowl, mark and period of Wanli, painted with two dragons in a lotus frieze, 12.5cm (5in), *L 10 June,*
£5,500 ($8,635)

10
A Ming blue and white winecup, mark and period of Wanli, decorated with flowering peonies, and with dragon-form handles, 9.5cm (3¾in), *NY 4 June,*
$2,200 (£1,486)

11
A Ming blue and white box and cover, mark and period of Wanli, decorated by a frieze of dragons chasing 'flaming pearls' amongst flowers, the interior divided into six compartments, 21.5cm (8½in), *L 9 Dec,*
£3,300 ($4,620)

12
A blue and white jar, Wanli, decorated with birds in flight between the 'Three Friends', pine, prunus and bamboo, 16cm (6¼in), *L 9 Dec,*
£1,320 ($1,848)

13
A blue and white brush-rest, mark and period of Wanli, the three pinnacles each with a dragon in low relief above a band of rocks and crested waves, 18cm (7in), *NY 4 June,*
$5,225 (£3,530)

14
A blue and white pomegranate-shaped ewer, Wanli, painted with panels of flowers, 17.5cm (7in), *HK 20 May,*
HK$19,800 (£1,752; $2,804)

15
A blue and white jar, Wanli, decorated with a continuous frieze of pheasants with rockwork and peonies, the shoulders with four animal-mask boss handles, 40.5cm (16in), *L 10 June,*
£1,760 ($2,763)

16
A blue and white saucer dish, mark and period of Wanli, decorated with two fish amongst aquatic fronds, the exterior with a frieze of five fish, 18cm (7in), *HK 19 Nov,*
HK$44,000 (£3,963; $5,549)

1
A pair of late Ming blue and white vases, mark and period of Wanli, of *meiping* form, decorated with a bird in flight amongst flowering trees, 16cm (6¼in), *L 10 June,*
£880 ($1,382)

2
A late Ming blue and white vase, Wanli, decorated with flowering peonies, 16cm (6¼in), *L 6 May,*
£385 ($612)

3
A pair of blue and white double gourd vases, Wanli, decorated with panels of stylised flowers, 50cm (19½in), *A 12 May,*
Dfl 29,900 (£8,952; $14,502)

4
A blue and white bottle, Wanli, decorated with panels of birds and flowers, 28cm (11in), *A 12 May,*
Dfl 3,795 (£1,136; $1,841)

5
A 'kraak' bowl, Wanli, decorated with a gourd, a roll of inscriptions and *ruyi* motifs, 21.5cm (8½in), *A 12 May,*
Dfl 3,220 (£964; $1,562)

6
A pair of late Ming blue and white dishes, *(one illustrated),* Tianqi, painted with a view across a lake to mountains beyond, six-character marks of Chenghua, 14.5cm (5½in), *L 10 June,*
£308 ($484)

7
A pair of late Ming blue and white jars, *(one illustrated),* each decorated with a stylised chrysanthemum meander, 13.5cm (5½in), *L 6 May,*
£660 ($1,049)

8
A blue and white bottle, 17th century, painted with birds in flight and peonies, 26.5cm (10½in), *C 15 Jan,*
£682 ($1,023)

9
A Ming blue and white box and cover, the cover decorated with a crane, the sides with foliage sprigs, on four mask feet, 9.5cm (3¾in), *C 16 Apr,*
£418 ($648)

10
A Transitional blue and white brushpot, second quarter 17th century, painted with an episode from a romance: a woman fleeing from a soldier, 22cm (8¾in), *S 21 May,*
£528 ($845)

11
A Transitional blue and white brushpot, painted with *lingzhi* sprays, 21.5cm (8½in), *HK 19 Nov,*
HK$11,000 (£991; $1,387)

12
A Transitional blue and white brushpot, the sides painted with two maidens and a boy in a garden, 19cm (7½in), *L 9 Dec,*
£990 ($1,386)

13
A Transitional blue and white beaker vase, *(gu),* second quarter 17th century, decorated with prunus in a vase and descending stiff leaves, 29.5cm (11½in), *S 21 May,*
£286 ($458)

14
A Transitional blue and white jar, painted with a dragon writhing among clouds chasing a 'flaming pearl', 27cm (10½in), *L 6 May,*
£418 ($664)

15
A Transitional blue and white jar and cover, decorated with lotus flowers and pads growing from rockwork, 18.5cm (7¼in), *NY 4 June,*
$2,090 (£1,412)

16
A Transitional blue and white beaker vase, painted with a bird amongst flowering peonies, above scrolling lotus, 20cm (8in), *NY 10 Apr,*
$1,760 (£1,197)

1

2

3

4

5

6

7

8

9

10

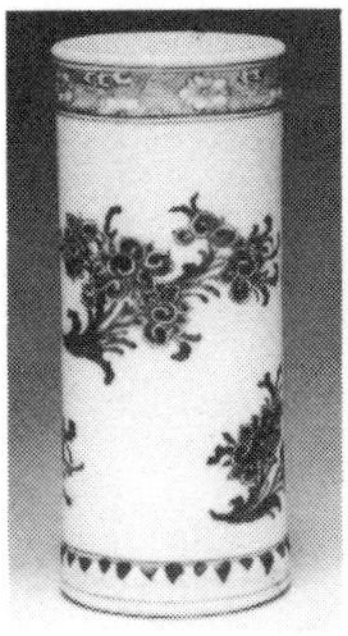
11

12

13

14

15

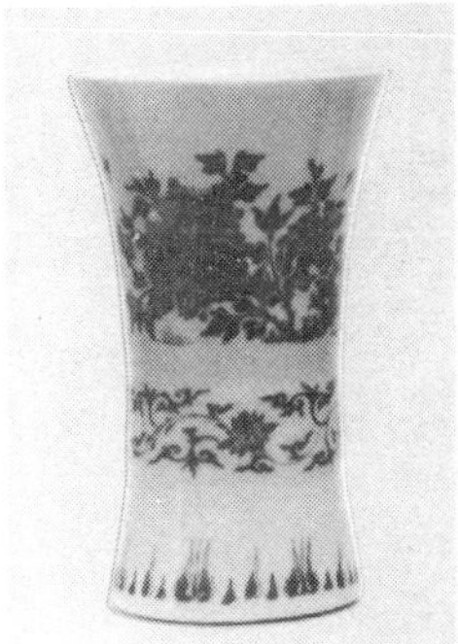
16

1

2

3

4

5

6

7

8

9

10

11

12

13

1
A blue and white bowl, mark and period of Kangxi, painted with a stylised peony scroll, 12cm (4½in), *L 9 Dec,*
£902 ($1,263)

2
A blue and white month cup, mark and period of Kangxi, painted with a pomegranate tree, emblematic of the eighth month, 6.5cm (2½in), *L 9 Dec,*
£3,410 ($4,774)

3
A blue and white bowl, mark and period of Kangxi, painted with a continuous scene of ladies in a garden, 20.5cm (8in), *L 18 Nov,*
£1,045 ($1,484)

4
A blue and white month cup, mark and period of Kangxi, decorated with clusters of orchids, emblematic of the eleventh month, 6.5cm (2½in), *HK 20 May,*
HK$19,800 (£1,752; $2,803)

5
A blue and white box and cover, Yongzheng mark and period, painted with flowering peony scrolls, 15.5cm (6¼in) wide, *NY 10 Apr,*
$770 (£524)

6
A blue and white faceted vase, Yongzheng mark and period, well painted in Ming style with *lingzhi* sprays, the underglaze-blue with simulated 'heaped and piled' effect, 10cm (4in), *HK 19 Nov,*
HK$79,200 (£7,135; $9,989)

7
A pair of blue and white stembowls, *(one illustrated),* seal marks and period of Qianlong, painted with the eight emblems of the *ba jixiang*, 18.5cm (7¼in), *L 10 June,*
£1,100 ($1,727)

8
A blue and white vase, mark and period of Kangxi, painted with landscapes with fishermen and scholars, 49.5cm (19½in), *L 10 June,*
£1,980 ($3,109)

9
A blue and white vase, Qianlong, decorated with a scaly dragon chasing a 'flaming pearl', 19.5cm (7¾in), *HK 20 May,*
HK$24,200 (£2,142; $3,427)

10
A blue and white vase, seal mark and period of Qianlong, in Ming style, painted with contrived 'heaping and piling', the sides with stylised stems and blooms, 45cm (17½in), *L 10 June,*
£3,740 ($5,872)

11
A blue and white bottle vase, Jiaqing seal mark and period, in Ming style, decorated with a composite floral scroll, the underglaze-blue with simulated 'heaped and piled' effect, 38cm (15in), *HK 20 May,*
HK$30,800 (£2,726; $4,362)

12
A pair of blue and white bottles, *(one illustrated),* seal marks and period of Daoguang, in Ming style, each painted with a frieze of bamboo and banana palms in a fenced garden, 28.5cm (11¼in), *L 9 Dec,*
£9,350 ($13,090)

13
A blue and white stem-cup, Daoguang seal mark and period, decorated with a frieze of Tibetan *lança* characters and lotus sprays, 8.5cm (3¼in), *HK 19 Nov,*
HK$12,100 (£1,090; $1,526)

1
A pair of baluster vases and covers, *(one illustrated)*, Kangxi, each decorated with a design of phoenix in flight amongst peonies, 42cm (16½in), *L 6 May,*
£1,155 ($1,836)

2
A blue and white beaker vase, Kangxi, painted with an overall scene of a pair of pheasants amongst flowering trees, 40.5cm (16in), *L 6 May,*
£330 ($525)

3
A pair of blue and white vases and covers, *(one illustrated)*, Kangxi, decorated with peony between leaf scrolling, 28cm (11in), *C 16 Apr,*
£275 ($426)

4
A blue and white vase, Kangxi, moulded with lotus lappets, each containing a landscape, flowers or auspicious animals, 34cm (13½in), *S 21 May,*
£308 ($493)

5
A blue and white bowl, Kangxi, decorated with three phoenix and lotus sprays, 19.5cm (7¾in) diam., *A 12 May,*
Dfl 977 (£293; $474)

6
A blue and white jardinière, Kangxi, decorated with a stylised floral design, 38cm (15in), *L 6 May,*
£1,320 ($2,099)

7
A blue and white ginger jar, Kangxi, painted with three medallions of the He He Twin Immortals, 20.5cm (8in), *L 6 May,*
£385 ($612)

8
A blue and white brush-pot, Kangxi, painted with a panel enclosing a bird on a plum branch, reserved on a ground of the 'Hundred Antiques', 15cm (6in), *HK 22 May,*
HK$7,700 (£681; $1,083)

9
A blue and white ginger jar and cover, Kangxi, painted with figures in a pavilion, 25.5cm (10in), *C 15 Jan,*
£462 ($693)

10
A blue and white jardinière, Kangxi, decorated with birds and butterflies amidst flowers, 19cm (7½in), *NY 26 Sept,*
$495 (£330)

11
A blue and white teapot and cover, Kangxi, painted with a maiden poling a ferry across a lake, three sages seated beneath the canopy, the reverse with an inscription from the 'Red Cliff' poem, 15cm (6in), *L 9 Dec,*
£1,375 ($1,925)

12
A blue and white box and cover, Kangxi, the exterior decorated with children at play, the interior with a recessed panel decorated with a carp leaping from crested waves, 24cm (9¼in), *HK 20 May,*
HK$15,400 (£1,363; $2,180)

13
A blue and white bowl, Kangxi, decorated with figures on a terrace, six-character mark of Cheng-hua, 21.5cm (8½in), *L 6 May,*
£462 ($734)

1 2

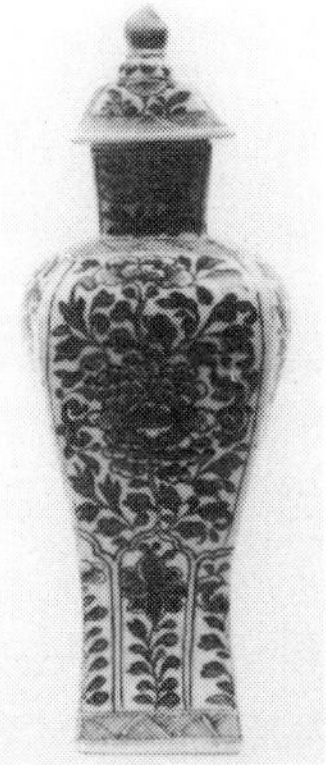
3

4

5

6

7

8

9

10

11

12

13

1

2

3

4

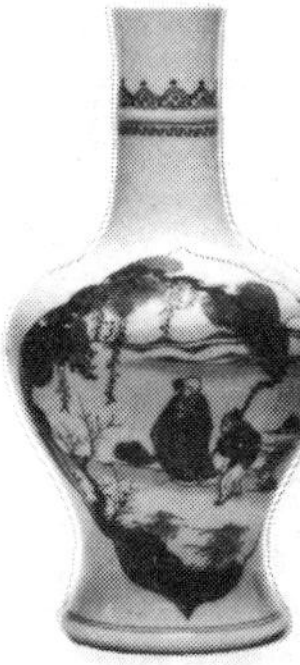
5

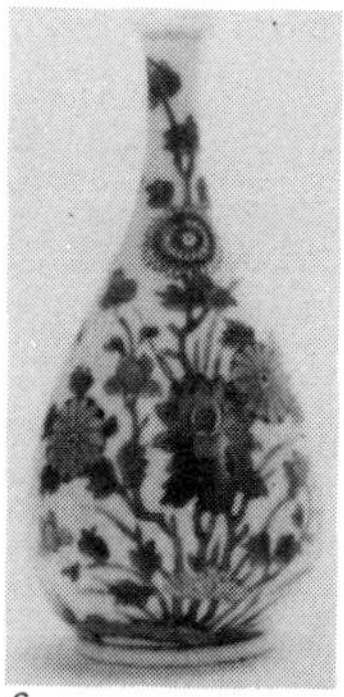
6

7

8

9

10

11

1
A pair of blue and white baluster jars and covers, *(one illustrated)*, Kangxi, each decorated with panels alternating with flowers and Antiques, 46cm (18in), *S 21 May,*
£1,100 ($1,760)

2
A blue and white rouleau vase, Kangxi, decorated with two maidens looking into a fish bowl, on the reverse two more maidens feeding a parrot, 47cm (18½in), *HK 20 May,*
HK$28,600 (£2,531; $4,050)

3
A blue and white bottle-vase, early Kangxi period, painted with an overall design of scrolling lotus, 48cm (19in), *NY 3 Dec,*
$5,500 (£3,846)

4
A blue and white jar and cover, Kangxi, painted with musicians in a garden playing to a lady and her attendants, 62.5cm (24½in), *L 6 May,*
£3,630 ($5,772)

5
A blue and white vase, Kangxi, decorated with two panels enclosing a scholar, an attendant and a fisherman on a river bank, 24cm (9½in), *NY 10 Apr,*
$2,750 (£1,871)

6
A pair of blue and white vases, *(one illustrated)*, Kangxi, decorated with flowering branches, 16.5 and 16cm (6½ and 6¼in), *L 6 May,*
£572 ($909)

7
A pair of blue and white vases, *(one illustrated)*, Kangxi, painted with flowers growing from rockwork, 19cm (7½in), *L 6 May,*
£396 ($630)

8
A Compagnie-des-Indes ewer, Qianlong, of European helmet form, the rim picked out with a broken brocade over *ruyi* borders, 24cm (9½in), *S 21 May,*
£572 ($915)

9
A Compagnie-des-Indes bowl, Qianlong, painted with a continuous lakeside scene, 40cm (15¾in), *S 21 May,*
£1,705 ($2,728)

10
A Compagnie-des-Indes vase, Qianlong, after a design by Cornelius Pronk, the body painted with four rococo cartouches each enclosing a chinoiserie figure of an archer, the whole in varying tones of blue, 40.5cm (16in), *L 6 May,*
£9,900 ($15,741)

11
A pair of blue Fitzhugh dishes, *(one illustrated)*, Qianlong, painted with a central medallion of pomegranates enclosed by dragon panels, surrounded by peony sprays enclosing Precious Objects, 44cm (17½in), *L 6 May,*
£748 ($1,189)

1
A pair of shell-shaped dishes, Qianlong, painted in the centre with peonies, 11cm (4¼in), *C 29 Apr,*
£198 ($321)

2
A blue and white tureen and cover, Qianlong, painted with buildings in a rocky river landscape, rabbit-head handles, 36cm (14in) diam., *C 29 Apr,*
£385 ($624)

3
A blue and white bowl, Qianlong, painted with flower sprays, 24cm (9½in), *C 29 Apr,*
£319 ($517)

4
A pair of export blue and white tureens, covers and stands, c.1785, each painted with a river landscape, 27.5 and 28.5cm (10¾ and 11¼in) long, *NY 31 Jan,*
$2,750 (£1,950)

5
A blue-ground slip-decorated vase, 18th century, the body with white sprigs and butterflies with incised details reserved on a blue ground, 25cm (10in), *HK 22 May,*
HK$6,160 (£545; $867)

6
A five-piece blue and white garniture, *(part illustrated)*, 18th century, comprising two beakers and three baluster bases with covers, all fluted and decorated with scrolling peonies, 30.5 and 26cm (12 and 10¼in), *NY 10 Apr,*
$2,200 (£1,496)

7
A blue and white jug, Qianlong, painted with branches of prunus, 15cm (6in), *C 29 Apr,*
£110 ($178)

8
A pair of blue and white chambersticks, c.1785, each with a scalloped dish painted with a river landscape, bamboo-moulded candlesticks and blue dragon-form handles, 11cm (4½in), *NY 24 Oct,*
$2,530 (£1,794)

9
A pair of blue and white jardinières, *(one illustrated)*, 19th century, decorated with prunus trees, 37cm (14½in), *L 18 Nov,*
£1,045 ($1,484)

10
A blue and white punch bowl, 18th/19th century, decorated with a flowering meandering vine, 53.5cm (21in), *NY 26 Sept,*
$1,760 (£1,173)

11
A blue and white platter, Guangxu, painted with flower sprays and sprigs, the border with *oeil-de-perdrix* ground, fitted with pierced draining-plate, 40cm (15¾in), *JHB 27 Feb,*
R 484 (£151; $234)

12
A blue and white vase, Guangxu, painted with a dragon disputing with a phoenix for the 'flaming pearl', pierced dragon handles, 71cm (28in), *S 21 May,*
£462 ($739)

1

2

3

4

5

6

7

8

9

10

11

12

1

2

3

4

5

6

7

8

9

10

11

12

1
A pair of doucai saucer dishes, *(one illustrated)*, Yongzheng marks and period, painted with a central *shou* medallion and *shou* characters, 11.5cm (4½in), *HK 19 Nov,*
HK$22,000 (£1,982; $2,775)

2
A pair of 'famille-rose' bowls, *(one illustrated)*, seal marks and period of Qianlong, decorated with prunus boughs and peony sprays, 12.5cm (5in), *L 9 Dec,*
£3,960 ($5,544)

3
A 'famille-verte' month cup, Kangxi mark and period, painted with orchids, emblematic of the eleventh month, 6.5cm (3¾in), *HK 19 Nov,*
HK$55,000 (£4,955; $6,937)

4
A 'famille-rose' jardinière, Qianlong seal mark and period, decorated with sprays of stylised Indian lotus, 26cm (10¼in), *HK 22 May,*
HK$13,200 (£1,168; $1,857)

5
A blue-ground vase, mark and period of Guangxu, decorated in gilding with an overall pattern of *mons*, 38.5cm (15in), *L 10 June,*
£935 ($1,468)

6
A 'famille-rose' vase, Qianlong seal mark and period, painted with a pair of quail enclosed by peony, chrysanthemum and coxcomb, 34cm (13½in), *HK 20 May,*
HK$187,000 (£16,549; $26,478)

7
A yellow-ground 'famille-rose' vase, Jiaqing seal mark and period, decorated with four raised panels alternately enclosing inscriptions and flower clusters, 27cm (10½in), *HK 19 Nov,*
HK$231,000 (£20,811; $29,135)

8
A copper-red decorated bowl, Daoguang seal mark and period, decorated with five phoenix medallions, 14cm (5½in), *HK 22 May,*
HK$7,700 (£681; $1,083)

9
A pair of iron-red-decorated wine cups, *(one illustrated)*, Daoguang seal mark and period, each decorated with two dragons leaping over cresting waves, 6cm (2½in), *NY 4 June,*
$3,575 (£2,415)

10
A 'famille-verte' month cup, Daoguang seal mark and period, decorated with a crab-apple, emblematic of the fifth month, 6.5cm (2½in), *HK 19 Nov,*
HK$14,300 (£1,288; $1,804)

11
A pair of coral-ground bowls, *(one illustrated)*, Daoguang seal marks and period, each decorated with bamboo sprays, 18cm (7in), *HK 20 May,*
HK$22,000 (£1,947; $3,115)

12
A pink-ground 'famille-rose' bowl, Daoguang mark and period, decorated with four panels enclosing chrysanthemum, coxcomb, berries and peony, 14.5cm (5¾in), *HK 19 Nov,*
HK$22,000 (£1,982; $2,775)

1
A Transitional polychrome jar and cover, painted in green, yellow and iron-red with a continuous scene of scholars playing *go*, 36.5cm (14½in), *L 18 Nov,*
£2,420 ($3,436)

2
A Transitional polychrome sleeve vase, decorated in underglaze-blue and enamels with a lady on a terrace watching over children at play, 23.5cm (9¼in), *L 10 June,*
£715 ($1,123)

3
A Transitional polychrome jar and cover, painted in underglaze-blue and enamels with groups of boys playing on a terrace, supervised by several ladies, 40.5cm (16in), *NY 26 Sept,*
$6,600 (£4,400)

4
A biscuit figure, 18th century, of a smiling bearded sage, his left hand holding a fungus sprig, his robe of a patchwork design, 24.5cm (9½in), *L 18 Nov,*
£825 ($1,172)

5
A pair of 'famille-verte' vases and covers, Kangxi, enamelled with landscape panels, 56cm (22in), *M 1 Dec,*
FF 176,000 (£19,130; $27,356)

6
A powder-blue guglet, c.1715, painted in 'famille-verte' palette with scholar's implements and flowering plants, 21.5cm (8½in), *NY 24 Oct,*
$770 (£546)

7
A 'famille-verte' bowl, Kangxi, painted with a continuous design of lotus, prunus and peony inhabited by birds, 30.5cm (12in), *S 10 Apr,*
£418 ($648)

8
A 'famille-verte' bowl, Kangxi, decorated with a frieze of barbed panels enclosing demi-florettes on an iron-red seeded ground, interspersed by sprays of Indian lotus, 18.5cm (7¼in), *HK 20 May,*
HK$13,200 (£1,168; $1,869)

9
A 'famille-verte' ginger jar, Kangxi, decorated with an overall scene depicting a child prince in the arms of a Maiden Immortal attended by a dignitary and his henchmen, 19cm (7½in), *L 18 Nov,*
£638 ($906)

10
A pair of 'famille-verte' tea caddies and cover, *(one illustrated)*, Kangxi, each painted with fighting cocks and foliage, 8.5cm (3¼in), *C 8 Oct,*
£748 ($1,047)

11
A pair of 'famille-verte' kylin censers, Kangxi, each body decorated with cloud-like motifs painted in *rouge-de-fer*, glazed in green and applied with curls, 21.5cm (8½in), *L 18 Nov,*
£2,750 ($3,905)

12
A pair of 'famille-verte' figures of boys, Kangxi, each clasping a lotus vase, their aprons in iron-red centred with a yellow peony, 28cm (11in), *L 6 May,*
£1,375 ($2,186)

1

2

3

4

5

6

7

8

9

10

11

12

1

2

3

4

5

6

7

8

9

10

11

12

13

1
A 'famille-verte' brush-pot, Kangxi, painted with a continuous scene of the inebriate poet Li Taibo leaning against a wine jar with his acolyte behind, 12cm (4¾in), *L 18 Nov,*
£550 ($781)

2
A 'famille-verte' deep bowl and cover, Kangxi, decorated with pairs of song birds in flight and perched amid rockwork and flowering branches, 23cm (9in), *NY 26 Sept,*
$2,310 (£1,540)

3
A 'famille-verte' ewer, 1710-20, of European silver shape, decorated with flower sprays, 28.5cm (11in), *NY 24 Oct,*
$2,200 (£1,560)

4
A 'famille-verte' ewer, Kangxi, with high scroll handle and mask spout, decorated with phoenix amongst scrolling flowers, 18.5cm (7½in), *C 8 Oct,*
£748 ($1,047)

5
A pair of 'famille-verte' small platters, *(one illustrated)*, c.1710, each painted with a pair of birds in flight above peonies, 31.5 and 31cm (12½ and 12¼in), *NY 31 Jan,*
$1,430 (£1,014)

6
A 'famille-verte' vase, Kangxi, decorated with a continuous riverscape, 56cm (22in), *NY 26 Sept,*
$2,475 (£1,650)

7
A pair of 'famille-verte' dishes, *(one illustrated)*, Kangxi, each finely painted with a single fruiting peach, 9.5cm (3¾in), *HK 19 Nov,*
HK$93,500 (£8,423; $11,792)

8
A 'famille-verte' fluted dish, Kangxi, decorated with an openwork basket with flowers, 24.5cm (9¾in), *A 12 May,*
Dfl 6,900 (£2,066; $3,347)

9
A 'famille-verte' dish, Kangxi, decorated with birds on bamboo reeds amongst chrysanthemums and pomegranate, 36cm (14¼in), *NY 26 Sept,*
$1,045 (£696)

10
A 'famille-verte' plate, Kangxi, decorated with two ladies in a garden, 24cm (9½in), *M 23 June,*
FF 4,440 (£396; $617)

11
A 'famille-verte' punch bowl, Kangxi, with central medallion enclosing a butterfly hovering over flowering lotus, 34.5cm (13½in), *L 6 May,*
£770 ($1,224)

12
A 'famille-verte' jardinière, late 19th century, enamelled with flower clusters and shaped reserves depicting birds and flowers, landscapes and fruit, 55cm (21½in), *NY 10 Apr,*
$2,970 (£2,020)

13
A 'famille-verte' jardinière, Guangxu, decorated with alternating rectangular and barbed quatrefoil panels, 33cm (13in), *L 18 Nov,*
£1,155 ($1,640)

1
A 'famille-rose' mug, Qianlong, with double strap handle, 15cm (6in), *C 24 June,*
£121 ($189)

2
A 'famille-rose' helmet-shaped jug, Qianlong, painted in pink, green and yellow, 12.5cm (5in), *C 11 Feb,*
£176 ($262)

3
A 'famille-rose' teapot and cover, Qianlong, the lid painted with furniture, 12.5cm (5in), *C 29 Apr,*
£88 ($143)

4
A 'famille-rose' teapot and cover, Qianlong, 11.5cm (4½in) high, *A 12 May,*
Dfl 1,207 (£361; $585)

5
A 'famille-rose' teapot and cover, Qianlong, 11cm (4¼in) high, *A 12 May,*
Dfl 2,760 (£826; $1,339)

6
A pair of 'famille-rose' hexagonal covered vases, *(one illustrated),* Qianlong, the covers with gilt Buddhistic lion finials, 49.5cm (19½in), *NY 10 June,*
$5,225 (£3,328)

7
A 'famille-rose' soup tureen, cover and stand, 1750-60, with a pomegranate sprig knop, 36cm (14in), *NY 31 Jan,*
$3,630 (£2,574)

8
A 'famille-rose' yellow-ground vase, Guangxu, decorated with panels of buildings and figures in a mountainous setting, 80.5cm (31¾in), *C 16 Apr,*
£550 ($853)

9
A circular soup tureen and cover, c.1760, painted in 'famille-rose' enamels, *grisaille* and gilding, 32cm (12¾in) wide, *NY 31 Jan,*
$1,320 (£936)

10
A Canton 'famille-rose' punch bowl, Daoguang, painted with panels of maidens and attendant figures on terraces, 39cm (15¼in), *C 15 Jan,*
£1,265 ($1,898)

11
A Canton 'famille-rose' celery pattern punch bowl, late 19th century, decorated overall with overlapping celery dotted with butterflies, floral borders, 40cm (15¾in), *S 5 June,*
£330 ($511)

12
A pair of figures of dogs, *(one illustrated),* 19th century, each animal washed in bright *rouge-de-fer* with fur-markings in gilding, its harness in blue, with a cloth over its back supporting a flared nozzle, 18cm (7in), *L 18 Nov,*
£3,080 ($4,374)

1

2

3

4 5

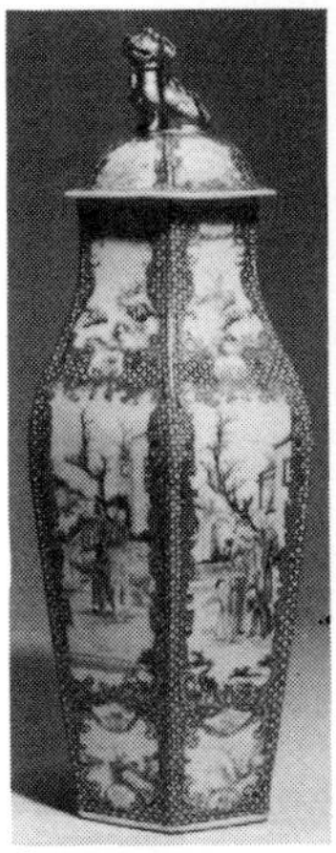
6

7

8

9

10

11

12

1

2

3

4

5

6

7

8

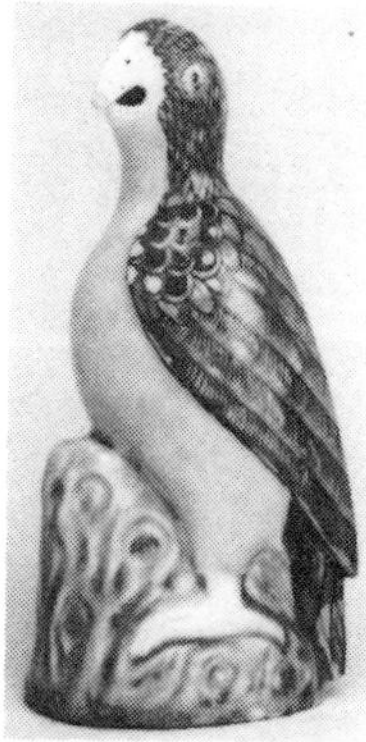
9

10

11

12

1
A 'famille-rose' dinner service, 18th century, comprising 46 pieces, *M 1 Dec,*
FF 71,500 (£7,772; $11,114)

2
A pair of 'famille-rose' plates, *(one illustrated),* c.1730, each painted in luminous enamels, 22cm (8¾in), *NY 31 Jan,*
$4,290 (£3,043)

3
A pair of 'famille-rose' plates *(one illustrated),* c.1735-40, 22cm (8¾in), *NY 31 Jan,*
$1,430 (£1,014)

4
A 'famille-rose' dish, Qianlong, 31cm (12in), *Mel 24 June,*
Aus$396 (£172; $269)

5
A 'famille-rose' plate, c.1745, sold with a pair of 'famille-rose' *gu*-form vases, 32cm (12½in), *NY 25 Jan,*
$467 (£336)

6
A 'famille-rose' plate, Qianlong, 31.5cm (12½in), *L 6 May,*
£462 ($734)

7
A 'famille-rose' figure of a dignitary, Qianlong, on a yellow base, 26.5cm (10½in), *L 6 May,*
£935 ($1,487)

8
A pair of 'famille-rose' figures, *(one illustrated),* Qianlong, each of a lady holding a lotus flower as a sconce, 28.5cm (11¼in), *L 6 May,*
£9,680 ($15,391)

9
A pair of figures of parrots, *(one illustrated),* 18th century, each with feather-markings in black on a green ground and with bright yellow breast, 19.5cm (7¾in), *L 18 Nov,*
£1,430 ($2,031)

10
A 'famille-rose' figure of an immortal, *(illustrated),* Qianlong, holding a *yenyen* vase, minor damage, sold with a similar figure, 42cm (16½in), *C 16 Apr,*
£5,280 ($8,184)

11
A 'famille-rose' group, Qianlong, of the He He Twins, the three-legged toad crawling up the rock between them, 20.5cm (8in), *L 6 May,*
£1,100 ($1,749)

12
A pair of Compagnie-des-Indes figures of monkeys, *(one illustrated),* Qianlong, each body with overall fur-markings pencilled in sepia, and holding a peach in one hand, 19cm (7½in), *L 6 May,*
£13,750 ($21,862)

1
An Imari mug, Kangxi, 15cm (6in), *S 22 Jan,*
£340 ($510)

2
An Imari chamber pot, c.1720, 22.5cm (8¾in), *NY 31 Jan,*
$1,210 (£858)

3
An Imari barber's bowl, 1710-25, painted with underglaze-blue butterflies amidst iron-red flowers, 26cm (10¼in), *NY 31 Jan,*
$1,540 (£1,092)

4
A three-colour vase, Kangxi, decorated in underglaze-blue, copper-red and celadon, with a scene of the eight horses of Mu Wang, 33cm (13in), *L 9 Dec,*
£3,300 ($4,620)

5
A doucai jar and cover, Yongzheng, 19.5cm (7¾in), *L 10 June,*
£880 ($1,382)

6
A pair of Compagnie-des-Indes vases and covers, *(one illustrated),* Qianlong, the knops modelled as 'dogs of Fo', 72cm (28¼in), *L 6 May,*
£1,540 ($2,449)

7
A set of four graduated Imari meat dishes, *(one illustrated),* Qianlong, 34 to 42cm (13¼ to 16½in), *S 21 May,*
£1,540 ($2,464)

8
A set of four Compagnie-des-Indes plates *(one illustrated),* Qianlong, painted in red, blue, green and gilt with lotus leaves between a flower and cloud border, 23cm (9in), *F 30 Sept,*
L 935,000 (£466; $652)

9
A chamfered rectangular soup tureen, cover and stand, c.1770, the knop with traces of gilding, 33cm (13in), *NY 31 Jan,*
$2,420 (£1,716)

10
A part dinner service, c.1775, comprising 74 pieces, painted in rose, purple, yellow, green, blue, iron-red and gold, the tureen 34.5cm (13½in) long, *NY 24 Oct,*
$20,350 (£14,432)

11
An export figure of a lady, c.1780, her white robe decorated with rose, brown and gold floral sprigs, 29cm (11¼in), *NY 24 Oct,*
$2,475 (£1,755)

12
An ice pail, Qianlong, picked out in brilliant *rouge-de-fer* enhanced in gilding, 28cm (11in), *L 18 Nov,*
£1,430 ($2,031)

13
An oval soup tureen and cover, c.1790, the cover with iron-red bud knop rising from leaves, 29.5cm (11½in), *NY 31 Jan,*
$1,100 (£780)

1

2 3

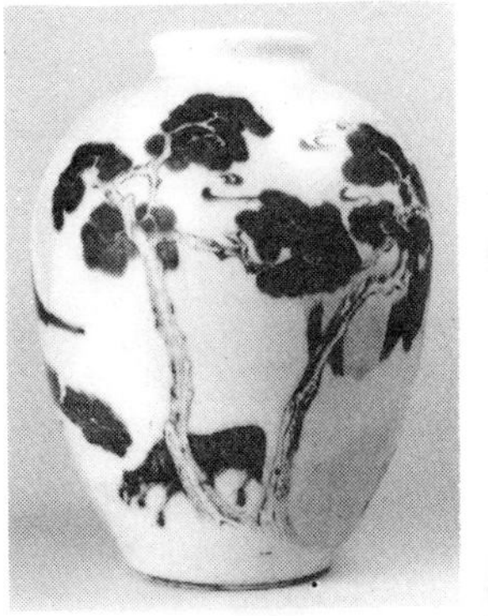
4

5

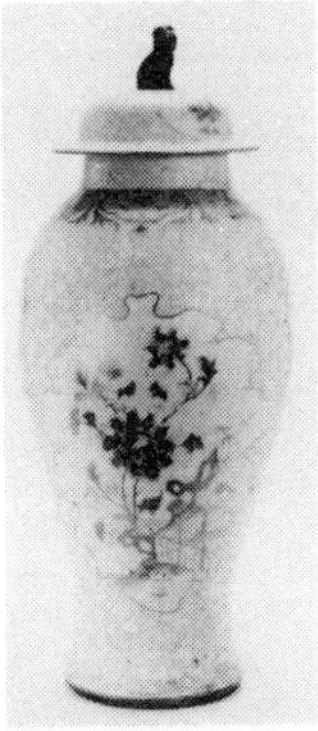
6

7

8

9

10

11

12

13

1

2

3

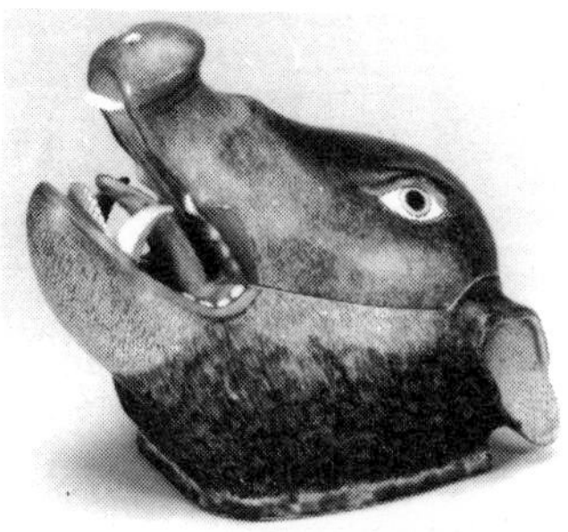
4

5

6

7

8

9

10

11

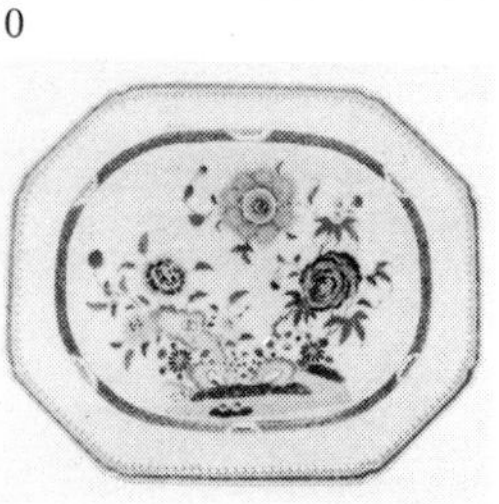
12

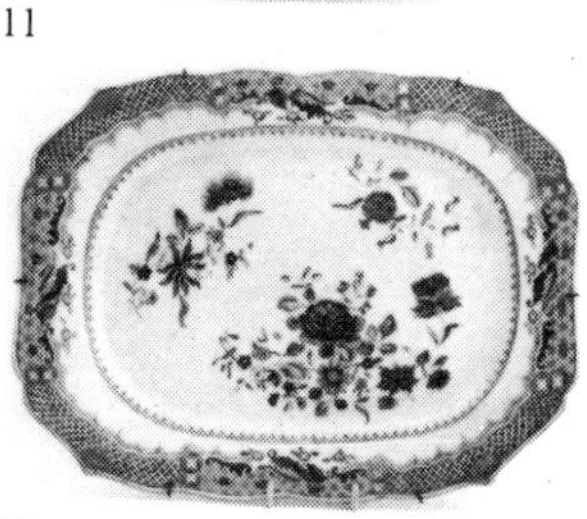
13

14

1
A pair of 'faux marbre' circular salt cellars, *(one illustrated)*, c.1760, after an English silver shape, painted in 'famille-rose' enamels, 7.5cm (3in), *NY 31 Jan,*
$1,100 (£780)

2
A punch bowl, c.1780, painted with Oriental ladies and children in a river landscape, 34cm (13½in), *NY 25 Jan,*
$990 (£712)

3
A jardinière, c.1785, divided into six panels painted with clusters of flowers, 40cm (15¾in), *NY 31 Jan,*
$3,960 (£2,809)

4
A boar's head tureen and cover, Qianlong, the form inspired by others made in European faience, 36cm (14in), *L 6 May,*
£6,160 ($9,794)

5
A set of thirteen enamelled plates, *(one illustrated)*, Qianlong, each painted *en grisaille* and *rouge-de-fer* with a partly unrolled landscape scroll, set among bowls of fruit and flowers, 23cm (9in), *L 6 May,*
£880 ($1,399)

6
A set of five plates, *(one illustrated)*, Yongzheng, each painted in 'famille-rose' enamels with a pair of ducks swimming amidst flowering lotus, 22.5cm (8¾in), *L 6 May,*
£616 ($979)

7
A 'famille-rose' dish, late Yongzheng, painted with a cockerel beside a peony, pink trellis border, 35.5cm (14in), *C 9 July,*
£330 ($515)

8
A reticulated dish, 1740-50, enamelled in 'famille-rose' colours with a seated lady, 28cm (11in), *NY 31 Jan,*
$1,980 (£1,404)

9
A pair of beaker vases, *(one illustrated)*, Qianlong, with a rich underglaze-blue ground, 61cm (24in), *L 18 Nov,*
£2,200 ($3,124)

10
A pair of 'tobacco-leaf' dishes *(one illustrated)*, Qianlong, 29.5cm (11¾in), *L 6 May,*
£2,420 ($3,848)

11
A pair of silver-shape dishes *(one illustrated)*, Qianlong, in 'famille-rose' enamels, sold with a larger dish, en suite, 34cm (13½in), *L 6 May,*
£1,210 ($1,924)

12
A pair of meat dishes, *(one illustrated)*, Qianlong, decorated in 'famille-rose' enamels, 45.5cm (18in), *L 6 May,*
£2,090 ($3,323)

13
A pair of 'famille-rose' dishes, *(one illustrated)*, Qianlong, 30cm (11¾in), *S 21 May,*
£990 ($1,584)

14
A pair of Compagnie-des-Indes figures of cranes, *(one illustrated)*, Qianlong, painted in red, brown, blue and green enamels, 43.5cm (17¼in), *L 18 Nov,*
£17,050 ($24,211)

1
A pair of export figures of kylins, *(one illustrated)*, 19th century, 11cm (4½in) long, *NY 31 Jan,*
$2,200 (£1,560)

2
A pair of jardinières, 19th century, 17.5cm (6¾in), *M 1 Dec,*
FF 14,300 (£1,554; $2,223)

3
A pair of Canton 'famille-rose' vases, *(one illustrated)*, painted with a scene of skirmishing warriors, 43cm (17in), *C 29 Apr,*
£264 ($428)

4
A Canton garden seat, Daoguang, 47cm (18½in), *C 9 July,*
£550 ($858)

5
A Canton 'famille-rose' pistol-handled urn and cover, mid 19th century, 37.5cm (14¾in), *NY 31 Jan,*
$1,210 (£858)

6
A pair of figures of cocks, *(one illustrated)*, 19th century, brightly coloured, 34cm (13½in), *L 6 May,*
£2,860 ($4,547)

7
A pair of Canton 'famille-rose' basins, *(one illustrated)*, 19th century, with a central panel of an audience scene, the sides with alternating figural and bird and flower panels, on a millefleur ground, 48cm (19in), *NY 10 Apr,*
$1,760 (£1,197)

8
A Canton 'famille-rose' punch bowl, mid 19th century, decorated with panels of Mandarin figures, 53cm (21in), *NY 31 Jan,*
$4,950 (£3,511)

9
A pair of 'famille-rose' fish bowls, *(one illustrated)*, 19th century, 51.5cm (20¼in), *L 6 May,*
£5,500 ($8,745)

10
A pair of 'famille-rose' jardinières *(one illustrated)*, 19th century, the interior with fish among waterweeds, 36cm (13¾in), *L 6 May,*
£1,045 ($1,661)

11
A pair of 'famille-rose' Samson vases and covers, *(one illustrated)*, 19th century, decorated with flowers and exotic birds, gilt lion finials, 154cm (60½in), *F 14 Apr,*
L 25,000,000 (£10,238; $15,868)

12
A pair of Samson 'famille-verte' style vases and covers, *(one illustrated)*, late 19th century, each decorated with panels of 'antiques' and shrubs reserved on a yellow ground, onion finials, 48cm (19in), *C 8 Oct,*
£1,430 ($2,002)

13
A Samson fish bowl, 19th century, decorated in 'famille-rose' colours, 59cm (23in), *A 6 May,*
Dfl 6,670 (£2,021; $3,214)

1

2

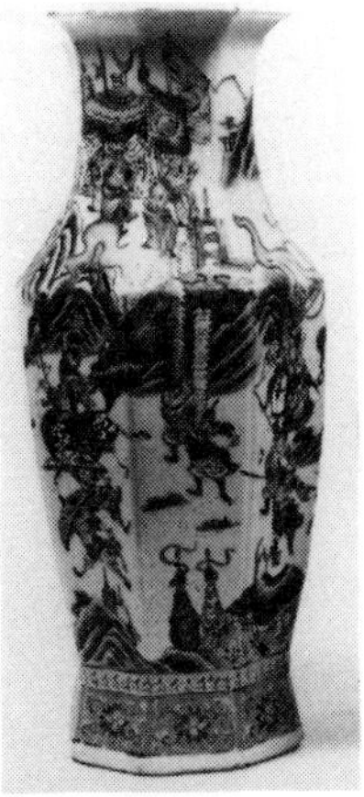
3

4

5

6

7

8

9

10

11

12

13

1

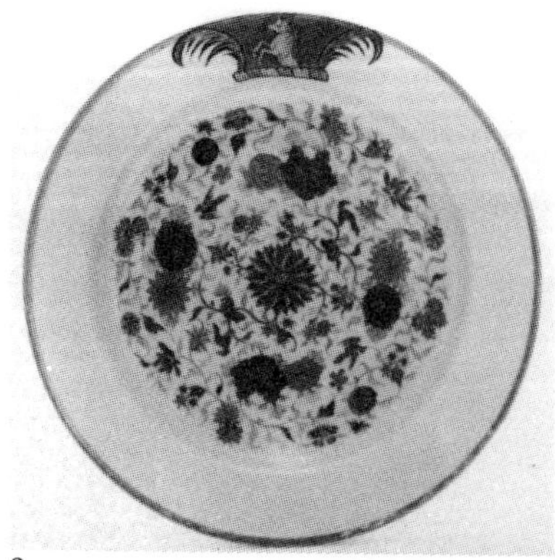
2

3

4

5

6

7

8 9

1
A Chinese armorial charger, 1690-1710, painted in underglaze-blue, the rim with the arms of Jacob Pelgrans, 39cm (15¼in), *NY 31 Jan,*
$2,420 (£1,716)

2
A pair of Chinese Imari dishes, *(one illustrated),* Kangxi, painted in underglaze-blue, iron-red and gilding, 47cm (18½in), *L 6 May,*
£9,900 ($15,741)

3
A Chinese punch bowl commemorative of John Wilkes, Qianlong, inscribed 'Always Ready in a Good Cause' 'Justice Sans Pitie', 26cm (10in), *C 15 Jan,*
£1,375 ($2,063)

4
A pair of Chinese export 'Rotterdam Riot' plates *(one illustrated),* 1691-95, the rioters attacking the house of Jacob van Zuylen van Nyevelt, 20cm (8in), *NY 31 Jan,*
$2,420 (£1,716)

5
A 'Sailor's Farewell' punch bowl, Qianlong, decorated in 'famille-rose' enamels, 26.5cm (10½in), *L 6 May,*
£2,200 ($3,498)

6
A shipping subject 'famille-rose' bowl, Qianlong, painted with a naval engagement, with a frigate flying British colours, the interior with festoons of flowers, 26cm (10¼in), *S 21 May,*
£1,650 ($2,640)

7
A 'famille-rose' chinoiserie 'Arbour' plate, early Qianlong, after a design by Cornelis Pronk, 26cm (10¼in), *M 23 June,*
FF 77,700 (£6,913; $10,812)

8
A pair of Chinese Imari plates with European figural decoration, *(one illustrated),* 1720-30, 23cm (9in), *NY 24 Oct,*
$2,970 (£2,106)

9
A pair of Chinese Imari plates with European figural decoration, *(one illustrated),* 1720-30, identical to the preceding pair, one with hair crack the other repaired, 23cm (9in), *NY 24 Oct,*
$770 (£546)

Note condition when comparing the prices of nos 8 and 9.

1
A set of three European-subject plates *(one illustrated)*, Qianlong, the centre of each enamelled in 'famille-rose' palette, depicting Venus in a chariot accompanied by Cupid aiming his bow at a sleeping figure, 23.5cm (9¼in), *L 6 May,*
£1,540 ($2,449)

2
A pair of 'Judgement of Paris' dishes, Qianlong, the centres painted in 'famille-rose' enamels, 39cm (15¼in), *M 23 June,*
FF 35,520 (£3,168; $4,943)

3
A European-subject plate, Qianlong, painted in 'famille-rose' enamels, 23cm (9in), *L 18 Nov,*
£2,145 ($3,046)

4
A set of fourteen Chinese export armorial octagonal plates, *(one illustrated)*, c.1755, each painted in the centre *en grisaille*, with gold, iron-red and turquoise with the arms of Hopper, 22cm (8¾in), *NY 31 Jan,*
$3,630 (£2,574)

5
A pair of octagonal armorial plates *(one illustrated)*, Qianlong, with the arms of Shard impaling Clarke, 21.5cm (8½in), *L 6 May,*
£1,155 ($1,836)

6
A 'Judgement of Paris' bowl, c.1745, 26cm (10¼in), *NY 31 Jan,*
$1,210 (£858)

7
A pair of armorial kidney-shaped dishes, *(one illustrated)*, 1798-1805, 27cm (10½in), *NY 31 Jan,*
$1,210 (£858)

8
An armorial fruit cooler, cover and liner, 1798-1805, modelled after a Derby porcelain original of c.1790-95, 27cm (10½in), *NY 31 Jan,*
$3,960 (£2,809)

9
An armorial dish, c.1780, painted in a 'Mandarin palette', with the arms of Anselmo José da Cruz Sobral, 29.5cm (11½in), *NY 31 Jan,*
$715 (£507)

10
An armorial plate, c.1743, painted in black, iron-red, white and gold with the arms of Okeover quarterly impaling Nichol, (one of twelve lots from this service included in the sale), 23cm (9in), *NY 31 Jan,*
$9,900 (£7,021)

11
A pair of Chinese export armorial shaped oval platters, c.1731, with the arms of Sir William Yonge, 4th Bt. of Colyton, Devon, 43cm (17in), *NY 31 Jan,*
$7,150 (£5,071)

1

2

3

4

5

6

7 8

9

10

11

1

2

3

4

5

6

7

8

9

10 11

12

13

1
A 'famille-rose' armorial plate, Qianlong, of barbed and lobed form, 23cm (9in), *L 6 May,*
£506 ($804)

2
An armorial dish, Qianlong, decorated in 'famille-rose' enamels, 47cm (18½in), *L 18 Nov,*
£1,870 ($2,655)

3
A pair of armorial tureen stands *(one illustrated),* dated 1767, decorated in 'famille-rose' enamels and with the arms of the Stones of Derby, 37.5cm (14¾in), *NY 31 Jan,*
$2,860 (£2,028)

4
An armorial oval platter, 1800-25, 46.5cm (18¼in), *NY 31 Jan,*
$715 (£507)

5
A crested well-and-tree platter, 1800-20, the centre painted with the crest of a recumbent stag, 44.5cm (17½in), *NY 31 Jan,*
$2,420 (£1,716)

6
A commemorative Canton 'famille-rose' dish, 19th century, painted with the American flag with fourteen stars crossed with another, 34cm (13½in), *L 18 Nov,*
£2,035 ($2,890)

7
A lighthouse coffee pot and cover 1805-15, for the American market, each side painted with an eagle in shades of brown heightened in gilding, 25cm (9¾in), *NY 24 Oct,*
$4,675 (£3,315)

8
An armorial ewer and cover, c.1760, painted with the arms of Legh, 40cm (15¾in), *NY 24 Oct,*
$880 (£624)

9
An armorial wine cooler, c.1770, painted in iron-red and gold with the arms possibly of Saint-Saens of Burgundy, 20cm (8in), *NY 31 Jan,*
$1,045 (£741)

10
An armorial teabowl and saucer, early Qianlong, decorated in 'famille-rose' enamels, *L 18 Nov,*
£1,980 ($2,812)

11
An armorial teabowl and saucer, Qianlong, of almost eggshell quality, *L 18 Nov,*
£935 ($1,328)

12
A pair of Canton 'famille rose' armorial oval dishes, *(one illustrated),* Jiaqing, with the arms of Chauncey of Northants, *A 12 May,*
Dfl 3,680 (£1,102; $1,785)

13
An armorial punch bowl, Qianlong, 29cm (11½in), *S 22 Jan,*
£1,100 ($1,650)

Concordance of Articles in previous Editions

AMERICAN INDIAN ART
An introduction (vol. 1)

ANTIQUITIES
Attic vases of the 6th and 5th centuries BC (vol. 1)

ARMS AND ARMOUR
A warning to owners (vol. 2)

ASIAN WORKS OF ART
Tibetan bronzes (vol. 2)

CHINESE WORKS OF ART
Export porcelain figures (vol. 1)
Ming blue and white porcelain (vol. 2)

CLOCKS AND WATCHES
Carriage clocks (vol. 1)
Wristwatches (vol. 2)

DECORATIVE ARTS FROM 1880
British art pottery and studio ceramics (vol. 1)
Georg Jensen silver (vol. 2)
Post-war decorative arts (vol. 2)

EUROPEAN CERAMICS
Commemorative wares (vol. 2)
Early 19th century English dinner services (vol. 2)
Italian maiolica (vol. 2)
Vincennes and Sèvres (vol. 1)

EUROPEAN WORKS OF ART
Iron (vol. 1)
Ivories (vol. 2)

FOLK ART
American folk art (vol. 1)

FURNITURE AND DECORATIONS
Altered and restored furniture (vol. 2)
American furniture (vol. 1)
Paris furniture of the 19th century (vol. 1)
Regional characteristics in 18th century American chairs (vol. 2)
Tunbridgeware (vol. 2)

GLASS
Biedermeier (vol. 1)

ISLAMIC WORKS OF ART
Persian metalwork (vol. 2)

JAPANESE WORKS OF ART
Prints (vol. 2)
Works of art of the Meiji period, 1868-1912 (vol. 1)

JEWELLERY
Edwardian diamond jewellery (vol. 1)
The Giuliano family (vol. 2)

MUSICAL INSTRUMENTS
Drawing room instruments (vol. 1)

OBJECTS OF VERTU
English enamels, 1745-1820 (vol. 1)

ORIENTAL RUGS AND CARPETS
Kum Kapour rugs (vol. 1)

PORTRAIT MINIATURES AND SILHOUETTES
Silhouettes (vol. 2)

RUSSIAN WORKS OF ART
Cloisonné enamel, 1880-1917 (vol. 2)

19TH AND 20TH CENTURY SCULPTURE
19th century marble sculpture (vol. 2)

SILVER
Electroplate (vol. 2)
Silversmiths' reproductions (vol. 1)

TEXTILES
Costume (vol. 2)

TOYS AND DOLLS
Toy cars (vol. 2)

TRIBAL ART
African furniture (vol. 2)

Volume 1: included objects sold in 1984 (1986 edition)
Volume 2: included objects sold in 1985 (1987 edition)

Index

A

B

C

D

N

O

P

Q

R

U

V

W

Y

Z